A richly historical land with some of the best cuisine you will ever taste, one of the world's greatest cities, and scenery from white-sand beaches to soaring mountains.

(left) Hot-air balloon above the fairy chimneys of Cappadocia (p447)
(below) Nargile cafe, İstanbul (p113)

subjects from kilims (flat-weave rugs) to the Aya Sofya's floating dome. Turkey's long history, coupled with its unique position at the meeting of Europe and Asia, has given it a profound depth of culture. Immersing yourself in that culture is as simple as soaking in a Seljuk or Ottoman hamam, eating a kebap and tasting influences brought along the Silk Road, or visiting the ancient ruins scattering the fields, bays and hills.

Landscapes & Activities

The greatest surprise for first-time visitors to Turkey, with its stereotypes of kebaps, carpets and moustachioed hustlers in the bazaar, is the sheer diversity found between its Aegean beaches and eastern mountains. In İstanbul, you can cruise – on the Bosphorus as well as through markets and nightclubs – in a Westernised metropolis offering equal parts romance and overcrowded insanity. In holiday spots such as Cappadocia and the southwestern coasts, mix trekking, horse riding and water sports with meze-savouring on a panoramic terrace. Then there are the less-frequented eastern quarters, where honey-coloured outposts overlook the plains of ancient Mesopotamia, and weather-beaten relics add lashings of lyricism to mountain ranges. It's hardly surprising Turkey has attracted so many folk over the centuries. Come and discover its legacy for yourself.

› Turkey

Gallipoli Peninsula
Now-tranquil site of
WWI battles (p146)

Edirne
Oil-drenched
wrestlers grapple (p136)

İstanbul
Historic sights; ferries
between Europe & Asia (p50)

Safranbolu
Storybook town of
Ottoman houses (p411)

BLACK SEA
(KARADENİZ)

ROMANIA

☆ Bucharest

BULGARIA

Burgas

GREECE

Kapıkule × Edirne Kırklareli
× Ipsala Tekirdağ Çorlu İstanbul
× Keşan
Gelibolu Darıca Kocaeli
Gallipoli Lapseki Yalova (İzmit)
Peninsula Çanakkale Bandırma Gemlik İznik Adapazarı
Troy Ayvacık Bursa Bolu
(Truva)
Assos Edremit Uludağ
Lesvos Ayvalık (2543m) Eskişehir
Bergama Pergamum Balıkesir
Chios Aliağa Kütahya
Yeni Manisa
Foça Sardis Afyon
Çeşme Uşak
İzmir Odemiş
Selçuk Aydın Pamukkale Akşehir
Kuşadası Nazilli Hierapolis
Priene Ephesus Lake
Samos Afrodisias Eğirdir Lake
Ikaria Didyma Milas Denizli Beyşehir
Güllük Yatağan Burdur Isparta
Bodrum Gökova Muğla Beyşehir Konya
Kos (Akyaka) Ortaca Çavdır Perge Aspendos
Marmaris Dalaman Termessos Akseki
Fethiye Antalya Side
Ölüdeniz Kemer Alanya
Kaş Olympos
Crete Finike Anamurium Anamur
Megiste
Lycian
Way

Sevastopol

Cide İnebolu Sinop
Amasra
Zonguldak Safranbolu Kastamonu
Karabük Tosya Osmancı
Gerede Kurşunlu Ilgaz
Çankırı Çorum
Gordion Sungurlu Hattu
Ankara
Kırıkkale Yoz
Polatlı
Kırşehir
Göreme
Nevşehir
Salt Lake Aksaray Derinkuyu
(Tuz Gölü) Cappadocia Yah
Niğ
Ereğli
Karaman
Lake
Suğla Ada
Kırobası Tarsus
Uzuncaburç Mer
Silifke Kızkalesi (İçe
Olukbaşı

The Bosphorus

The Dardanelles

Sea of
Marmara

Sakarya River

Ephesus
Best-preserved ruins in
the Mediterranean (p211)

Lycian Way
Walk past mountains,
villages and ruins (p35)

Lefkoşa/
Lefkosia
☆ (Nicosia)

Cyprus

Pamukkale
Calcite shelves and a
Roman pool (p295)

MEDITERRANEAN SEA
(AKDENİS)

Fethiye
Cruise on a *gület*
(wooden yacht) (p320)

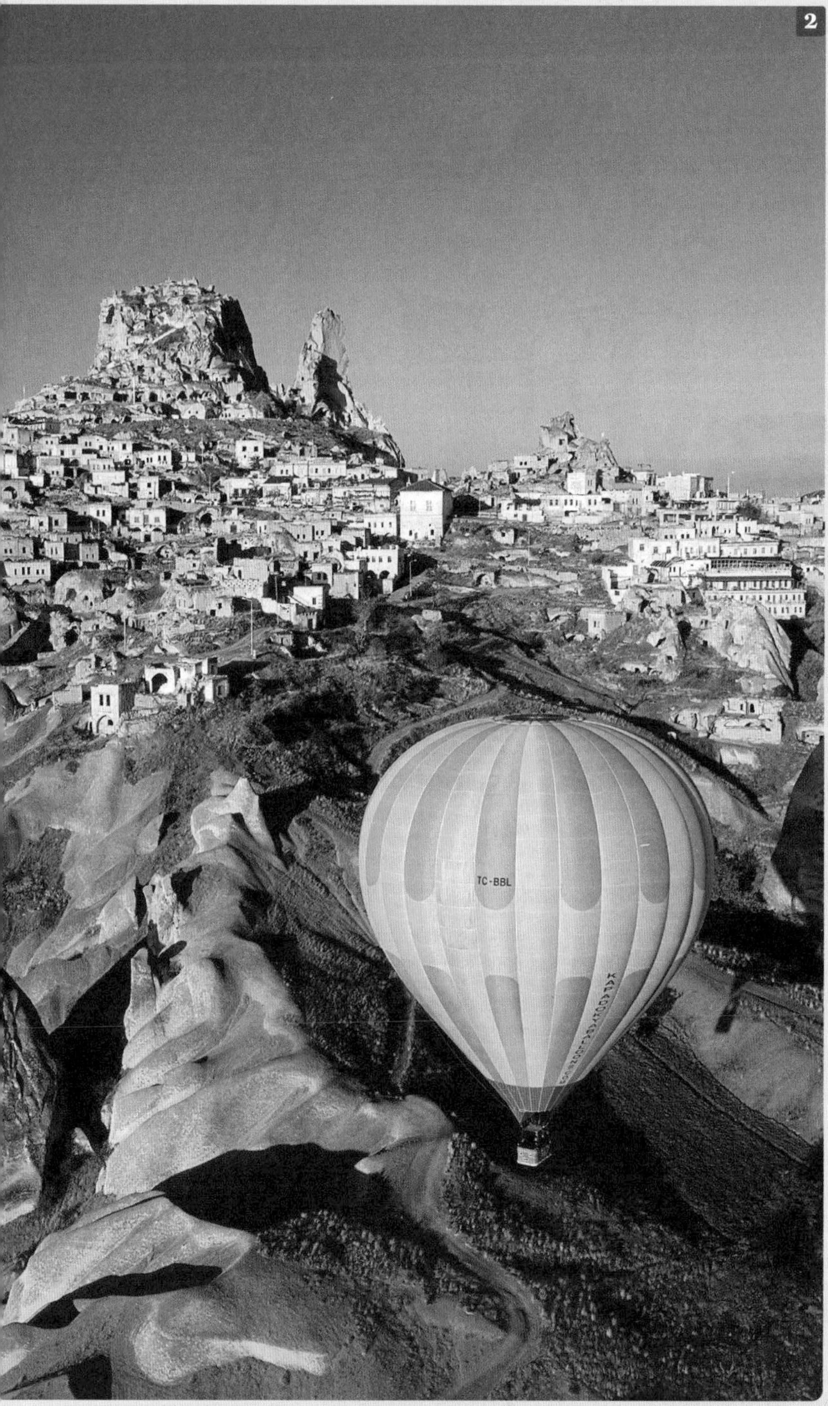

IZZET KERIBAR / GETTY IMAGES ©

Ephesus

3 Undoubtedly the most famous of Turkey's ancient sites, and considered the best-preserved ruins in the Mediterranean, Ephesus (p211) is a powerful tribute to Greek artistry and Roman architectural prowess. A stroll along the marble-coated Curetes Way (p215) provides myriad photo opportunities, but the true pièce de résistance is the Terraced Houses (p218) complex, offering incredible insight into the daily lives of the city's elite through vivid frescoes and sophisticated mosaics. Much of the city is yet to be unearthed. Temple of Hadrian (p218)

Aya Sofya

4 Even in mighty İstanbul, nothing beats the Church of the Divine Wisdom (p56), which was the greatest church in Christendom, until the Ottomans took Constantinople. Emperor Justinian had it built in the 6th century as part of his mission to restore the greatness of the Roman Empire. Gazing up at the floating dome, it's hard to believe this fresco-covered marvel didn't single-handedly revive Rome's fortunes. Entering the ancient interior, covered in mosaics and messages left by generations of rulers, leaves an impression that few buildings in the world can equal.

Hamams

5 At most of the traditional hamams in Turkey, plenty of extras are on offer: bath treatments, facials, pedicures and the like. However, we recommend you stick with the tried and true hamam experience – a soak and a scrub followed by a good (and optional) pummelling. The world (and your body) will never feel quite the same again. For a truly authentic and memorable experience, seek out a soak in a centuries-old hamam in Antalya's atmospheric old quarter or historic Sultanahmet, İstanbul. Men's baths at Cağaloğlu Hamamı (p96)

6

7

JEAN-BERNARD CARILLET / GETTY IMAGES ©

Sumela Monastery

6 The improbable cliff-face location of Sumela Monastery (p515) is more than matched by the surrounding verdant scenery. The gently winding roads to the Byzantine monastery twist past rustic riverside fish restaurants, and your journey from nearby Trabzon may be pleasantly hindered by a herd of fat-tailed sheep en route to fresh pastures. The last few kilometres afford tantalising glimpses across pine-covered valleys of Sumela's honey-coloured walls, and the final approach on foot leads up a forest path to the rock-cut retreat.

Meyhanes

7 Say *şerefe* (cheers) to Efes-drinking Turks in a *meyhane* (tavern). A raucous night mixing meze with rakı (aniseed brandy) and live music is a time-honoured Turkish activity. Melon, white cheese and fish go particularly well with the *aslan sütü* (lion's milk; the clear rakı turns white when added to water) and the soundtrack ranges from romantic ballads to *fasıl*, lively local gypsy music. A great place to sample Turkish nightlife is Beyoğlu, İstanbul, where the *meyhane* precincts around İstiklal Caddesi heave with people on Friday and Saturday nights. Beyoğlu nightlife

Beaches

8 Turkey's beaches are world-famous, offering a mix of sun, sand and azure waters. Heading the bucket list are Mediterranean and Aegean beauties such as Kaputaş, a tiny cove with dazzling shallows near Kalkan, and Patara, Turkey's longest beach. Many of the finest Mediterranean beaches are located on the ruin-dotted Teke peninsula and linked by the Lycian Way, while others are pleasingly remote. Quiet beaches on Gökçeada and Bozcaada islands offer activities ranging from windsurfing to trying the stringy local *dondurma* (ice cream). Kaputaş cove and beach

Lycian Way

9 Acclaimed as one of the top 10 long-distance walks in the world, the Lycian Way (p35) follows signposted paths for 500km between Fethiye and Antalya. This is the Teke peninsula, birthplace of the ancient and mysterious Lycian civilisation. The route leads through pine and cedar forests in the shadow of mountains rising almost 3000m, and past villages, stunning coastal views and an embarrassment of ruins at such ancient cities as Pınara, Xanthos, Letoön and Olympos. Walk it in sections (unless you have plenty of time and stamina). Hiker on the Lycian Way

Ani

10 Ani is a truly exceptional site. Historically intriguing, culturally compelling and scenically magical, this ghost city floating in a sea of grass looks like a movie set. Lying in blissful isolation right at the Armenian border, the site exudes an eerie ambience. Before it was deserted in 1239 after a Mongol invasion, Ani (p543) was a thriving city and a capital of both the Urartian and Armenian kingdoms. The ruins include several notable churches, as well as a cathedral built between 987 and 1010.

Pamukkale

11 Famed for its intricate series of travertines (calcite shelves) and crowned by the ruined Roman and Byzantine spa city of Hierapolis, the 'Cotton Castle' – a bleach-white mirage by day and alien ski slope by night – is one of the most unusual treasures in Turkey. Gingerly tiptoe through the crystal travertines and, when you reach the top, reward yourself with a refreshing dunk in Hierapolis' Antique Pool amid toppled marble columns and dramatic friezes. Antique Pool (p298) at Hierapolis

Mt Nemrut (Nemrut Dağı)

12 One man's megalomania echoes across the centuries atop the exposed and rugged summit of Nemrut Dağı (p572). A gently emerging sunrise coaxes stark shadows from the mountain's giant sculpted heads, and as dawn breaks, the finer details of the immense landscape below are gradually added. Huddling against the chill of a new morning, a warming glass of çay could not be more welcome. And when your time on the summit is complete, don't miss the graceful Roman bridge crossing the nearby Cendere River.

Gallipoli (Gelibolu) Peninsula

13 The narrow stretch of land guarding the entrance to the much-contested Dardanelles is a beautiful area, where pine trees roll across hills above Eceabat's backpacker hang-outs and Kilitbahir's castle. Touring the peaceful countryside is a poignant experience for many: memorials and cemeteries mark the spots where young men from far away fought and died in gruelling conditions. The passionate guides do a good job of evoking the futility and tragedy of the Gallipoli campaign, one of WWI's worst episodes. Lone Pine Cemetery (p151)

Kaçkar Mountains (Kaçkar Dağları)

14 Rippling along between the Black Sea coast and the Çoruh River, the Kaçkars (p526) rise to almost 4000m, affording superb hiking in summer. Spending a few days crossing the *yaylalar* (mountain pastures) between mountain hamlets such as Olgunlar and Ayder is one of Turkey's top trekking experiences, and the lower slopes offer cultural encounters. The local Hemşin people are a welcoming bunch, serving their beloved, fondue-like *muhlama* (cornmeal cooked in butter) in villages with Ottoman bridges and Georgian churches. Hikers in the Kaçkar Mountains

JEAN-PIERRE LESCOURRET / GETTY IMAGES ©

Whirling Dervishes

15 Over 700 years after the foundation of the Mevlevi brotherhood of whirling dervishes, you can still see *semas* (whirling dervish ceremonies) in places such as Konya, İstanbul and Cappadocia. *Semas* crackle with spiritual energy. The ceremony begins and ends with chanted passages from the Koran and is rich with symbolism; the dervishes' conical felt hats represent their tombstones, as the dance signifies relinquishing earthly life to be reborn in mystical union with God. Konya's turquoise-domed Mevlâna Museum (p434) gives further insight into the mystical brotherhood.

Bazaar Shopping

16 Turkey has a *çarşı* (market) for every mood – from İstanbul's famously clamorous Grand Bazaar to the donkeys winding through Mardin's hillside bazaar; and from the traditional shadow puppets in Bursa's *bedesten* (covered market) to the silk scarves in Şanlıurfa's ancient caravanserai. To take home the finest Turkish carpets you need a sultan's fortune, but don't be discouraged. Find something you like, drink some çay with the shopkeeper, and accept that you might not bag the world's best deal, but you'll hone your haggling skills.

Oil Wrestling

17 In late June or early July, the northern city of Edirne fills with beefy *pehlivan* (wrestlers) from across Turkey, along with crowds who come to watch this centuries-old sport. There's a festival atmosphere outside the riverside stadium, with families picnicking on the grass and stalls springing up. Inside, olive-oil-soaked hopefuls, from *baş* (first class) contestants to prepubescent whippersnappers, try to get a grip on their opponents' slippery sinews and topple them. Hands go down opponents' shorts, where it's easier to get a hold. Wrestlers at the annual Historic Kırkpınar Oil Wrestling Festival (p140), Edirne

Safranbolu

18 Listed for eternal preservation by Unesco in 1994, Safranbolu (p411) is Turkey's prime example of an Ottoman town brought back to life. Domestic tourists descend here full of sentiment in order to stay in half-timbered houses that seem torn from the pages of a children's storybook. And the magic doesn't end there. Sweets and saffron vendors line the cobblestone alleyways, and artisans and cobblers ply their centuries-old trades beneath medieval mosques. When the summer storms light up the night sky, the fantasy is complete.

Gület Cruising

19 Known locally as a blue voyage (*mavi yolculuk*), a cruise lasting four days and three nights on a *gület* (traditional wooden sailing boat) along the western Mediterranean's Turquoise Coast is the highlight of many a trip to Turkey. The cruises offer opportunities to explore isolated beaches, watch sunsets, and above all get away from it all, out at sea and (usually) away from the internet – a rare treat nowadays. The usual route is Fethiye–Olympos, but afficianados say Fethiye–Marmaris is even prettier.

need to know

Currency
» Türk Lirası
(Turkish lira; ₺)

Language
» Turkish and Kurdish

When to Go

İstanbul
GO Apr–May, Sep

Eastern Anatolia
GO May–Jun, Sep

Cappadocia
GO May, Sep–Oct

Aegean
GO May–Jun, Sep

Mediterranean
GO Apr, Sep–Oct

Desert, dry climate
Warm to hot summers, mild winters
Mild to hot summers, cold winters

High Season
(Jun–Aug)
» Prices and temperature highest
» Expect crowds, book ahead
» Turkish school holidays mid-June to mid-September
» İstanbul's high season April, May, September and October

Shoulder Season
(May & Sep)
» Fewer crowds
» Most businesses are open; prices are lower
» Warm temperatures
» İstanbul's shoulder season is June to August

Low Season
(Oct–Apr)
» October is autumn; spring starts in April
» Accommodations in tourist areas may close or offer discounts
» Kurban Bayramı holiday falls around October
» İstanbul's low season is November to March

Your Daily Budget

Budget less than
₺135
» Dorm bed: ₺20–45
» Rooms/dorms often include breakfast
» Take night buses and trains to skip accommodation costs
» Minimise your time in pricey İstanbul

Midrange
₺135–350
» Midrange hotel double room
» Eateries serving alcohol generally more expensive
» Buses and trains often cheaper than hire cars
» You can get flights for the same as, or less than, buses

Top end more than
₺350
» Top-end hotel double room from ₺170 (from ₺410 in İstanbul)
» Top-end restaurant main course: more than ₺17.50

Money

» ATMs are widely available. Credit and debit cards are accepted by most businesses in cities and tourist areas.

Visas

» To stay for up to 90 days, most Western nationalities either don't require a visa or can purchase one on arrival (from €15).

Mobile Phones

» SIM cards are cheap and widely available, although your phone must be unlocked. After as little as a week, the network will block your phone if you haven't registered it.

Transport

» Drive on the right; the steering wheel is on the left side of the car. Buses are fast and efficient; trains are generally slow.

Websites

» **Lonely Planet** (www.lonelyplanet.com) Info, bookings and forum.

» **Turkey Travel Planner** (www.turkeytravelplanner.com) Useful travel info.

» **Turkish Cultural Foundation** (www.turkishculture.org) Culture and heritage.

» **Go Turkey** (www.goturkey.com) Official tourism portal.

» **Hürriyet Daily News** (www.hurriyetdailynews.com) English-language website of the secularist daily newspaper.

» **All About Turkey** (www.allaboutturkey.com) Multilingual introduction.

Exchange Rates

Australia	A$1	₺1.87
Canada	C$1	₺1.85
Europe	€1	₺2.30
Japan	¥100	₺2.33
New Zealand	NZ$1	₺1.45
UK	£1	₺2.90
USA	US$1	₺1.82

For current exchange rates see www.xe.com.

Important Numbers

Local codes are listed under the names of locations.

Turkey country code	90
International access code from Turkey	00
Ambulance	112
Fire	110
Police	155

Arriving in Turkey

» **İstanbul Atatürk & Sabiha Gökçen International Airports**

Havataş (Havaş) Airport Bus – To Taksim Meydanı every 30 minutes (₺10 to ₺12)

Metro – From Atatürk to Zeytinburnu, then tram to centre (₺4)

Taxi – To Sultanahmet ₺40/120

Hotel Shuttle – Often free for longer stays

» **Big İstanbul Bus Station**

Metro – To Aksaray, and tram to centre (₺4)

Bus – One hour to Taksim Meydanı or Eminönü (₺2)

Taxi – 20 minutes to Sultanahmet (₺30)

Islam & Ramazan

On the whole, Islam is a moderate presence in Turkey. In İstanbul and the west there are as many bars as mosques and it is sometimes easy to forget you are in an Islamic country. The one time of year when Westerners do need to temper their behaviour is Ramazan, the holy month when Muslims fast between dawn and dusk. Ramazan currently falls in the summer.

» If you aren't a fasting Muslim, don't go to an *iftar* (evening meal to break fast) tent for a cheap feed.

» Don't eat, drink or smoke in public during the day.

» Cut the locals some slack; waiters and others might be grumpy if they are fasting in hot weather.

» Don't dress provocatively; Muslims have to give up sex for the month.

first time

Everyone needs a helping hand when they visit a country for the first time. There are phrases to learn, customs to get used to and etiquette to understand.

Language

English is widely spoken in İstanbul and touristy parts of western Turkey; less so in eastern and central Anatolia, where knowing a few Turkish phrases, covering relevant topics such as accommodation, is invaluable. Turkish is fun to learn as pronunciation is easy. Learning Turkish is more useful than Kurdish, as most Kurds speak Turkish (but not vice versa). Many Turks speak German.

Booking Ahead

In high season (see p16), reserving accommodation is recommended in popular areas such as İstanbul, Cappadocia, the Turquoise Coast and south Aegean. Off the tourist trail, it's possible to be spontaneous. During the winter, advance contact is helpful, as many accommodations close. Just turning up to restaurants is usually fine unless you want a slow-cooked dish or it's a popular restaurant. Around major Islamic holidays, purchase tickets for travel as early as possible.

Hello.	Merhaba.
I would like to book a room.	Biroda ayırtmak is tiyorum lütfen.
single/double room	tek/iki kişilikoda
My name is...	Benimadım ...
date	tarih
How much is it per ...?	... ne kadar?
night	Geceliği
person	Kişibaşına
Thank you (very much).	(Çok) Teşekkür ederim.

What to Wear

İstanbul and the Aegean and Mediterranean resort towns are used to Western dress. A bikini on the beach should not raise many eyebrows and short skirts abound in nightclubs. In eastern and central Anatolia, people are conservative; even men should stick to long trousers. In staunchly Islamic cities such as Erzurum, even T-shirts and sandals are inadvisable. Women do not need to cover their head unless they enter a mosque. Many Turkish men believe Western women are more 'available'; to avoid unwanted attention, dress on the conservative side.

What to Pack

» Passport
» Drivers licence/ permit
» Photocopies of above
» Credit and debit card
» Back-up cards
» Bank contact details
» Back-up euros/ dollars for visas
» Phrasebook
» Sun cream
» Insect repellent
» Oral rehydration salts
» Sunglasses
» Camera
» Swimwear
» T-shirts
» Long-sleeved tops
» Shorts
» Trousers/skirts
» Sandals
» Closed shoes
» Sunhat
» Headscarf (women)
» Medication
» Toilet roll
» Soap or handwash
» Chargers and adaptor
» Unlocked mobile phone

Checklist

» Check your passport will be valid for at least six months after entering Turkey.

» Check if you need a visa and how much it will cost.

» Inform your credit-card provider of your travel plans.

» Purchase travel insurance.

» Check that travel vaccinations are up to date.

» Organise airport transfer or onward connection.

» Book flights and hire car online.

» Book accommodation for popular areas.

» Check airline baggage restrictions.

Etiquette

» **Religion**
Dress modestly and be quiet and respectful around mosques.

» **Hospitality**
Generous Turks take it seriously; be prepared to receive a few offers.

» **Manners**
Turks value respect; greet or acknowledge people.

» **Alcohol**
Cut down; licensed restaurants are pricey and bars often attract sleazy characters.

» **Language**
Learn a few Turkish phrases; immeasurably helpful and appreciated by Turks.

» **Disputes**
Turks are generally honest; if you think you have been overcharged, keep cool.

» **Relationships**
Do not be overly tactile with your partner in public; beware miscommunications with locals.

» **Politics**
Be tactful; criticising Turkish nationalism can land you in prison.

» **Ramazan**
Do not eat, drink or smoke in public, and sympathise with fasting Muslims.

Tipping

» **When to Tip**
Tipping is customary in restaurants, hotels and taxis; optional elsewhere.

» **Restaurants**
A few coins in budget eateries; 10% to 15% of the bill in midrange and top-end establishments.

» **Hotel porter**
Give 3% of the room price in midrange and top-end hotels only.

» **Taxis**
Round up metered fares to the nearest 50 kuruş.

» **Hamam**
Masseur may appreciate 10% to 20%.

» **Dolmuş**
Not expected.

» **Special tour**
From a few lira to the custodian.

Money

Most businesses accept debit cards, but you usually require a credit card to hire a car. ATMs are readily available, as are exchange offices in cities and tourist areas. You can also get cash advances on credit cards. In addition to Turkish lira, euros and dollars are often accepted by hotels and restaurants in İstanbul and tourist spots. Visa and Master-Card are widely accepted by hotels, shops and restaurants, but often not by pensions and local restaurants outside main tourist areas. Amex is not widely accepted outside top-end businesses. Travellers cheques are not particularly useful, as changing them usually incurs high charges. Because hyperinflation led to Turkish lira having strings of zeros, many Turks still work in thousands and millions. Don't be alarmed if you're buying items worth, say, ₺6 and the shopkeeper asks for ₺6,000,000.

what's new

For this new edition of Turkey, our authors have hunted down the fresh, the transformed, the hot and the happening. These are some of our favourites. For up-to-the-minute recommendations, see lonelyplanet.com/turkey.

Historical Developments

1 Improvements at Turkey's historic sites include Boğazkale Museum's two Hittite sphinxes (p419), recently returned from Berlin and İstanbul, and the cable car to Pergamum acropolis (p186). Following a renovation, İstanbul's 15th-century Galata dervish lodge now houses a dervish museum (p86), and Seljuk's Byzantine-Ottoman Ayasuluk Fortress (p221) has opened after a 20-year excavation. Less positively, the honey-coloured rock-cut village of Hasankey is slated to vanish under dam water in 2015.

Aya Sofya

2 The 17-year restoration of the world's greatest Byzantine edifice, İstanbul's Aya Sofya (p56), has finished to rapturous applause, and the nearby Ayasofya Hürrem Sultan Hamamı (p96) has reopened after a US$13 million restoration.

Göbekli Tepe

3 Their fame was a long time coming (about 12,000 years), but Şanlıurfa's Neolithic megaliths (p563) featured on a *National Geographic* cover in 2011.

Culinary İstanbul

4 İstanbul has bolstered its gastronomic offering with culinary walks led by food bloggers, coffee workshops at the Museum of Turkish & Islamic Arts (p61), and new Ottoman restaurant Matbah (p106).

Gaziantep Zeugma Mosaic Museum

5 Opened in 2012, the museum (p556) showcases virtually complete floor mosaics from Roman villas, retrieved from Belkıs-Zeugma before dam waters closed in.

Kaçkar Mountains (Kaçkar Dağları)

6 On the range's southern side, day walks have been marked around the villages and a new package with East Turkey Expeditions (p527) makes summiting Mt Kaçkar affordable for independent travellers.

İstanbul

7 Exciting openings include writer Orhan Pamuk's whimsical Museum of Innocence (p88), SALT cultural centres (p86 and p88) and the new-look Pera Palace Hotel (p105), its opulent late-Ottoman interiors improved by a US$23 million renovation.

Troy Museum

8 A national archaeological and history museum (p166) is set to open near Troy in 2015, giving another reason to visit the site from nearby Çanakkale or the Gallipoli Peninsula.

Evliya Çelebi Way

9 Turkey's first long-distance walking and riding route (p35) follows the Ottoman traveller through Western Anatolia. Culture Routes in Turkey (p661) is developing several other trails.

if you like...

Bazaars

Centuries ago, Seljuk and Ottoman traders travelled the Silk Road, stopping at caravanserais to do business. The tradition is alive and so is haggling in Turkey's labyrinthine bazaars, where locals and tourists converge to buy gear ranging from carpets to mosque alarm clocks.

Grand Bazaar, İstanbul Hone your bargaining skills in the city's original and best shopping mall, with 64 winding lanes (p74)

Urfa Bazaar With its narrow alleyways, shady courtyards and proximity to Syria, Şanlıurfa's bazaar has a Middle Eastern flavour (p565)

Kapalı Çarşı, Bursa Explore the silk and shadow-puppet shops in this heritage labyrinth, far removed from more-touristy markets (p279)

Wait a minute, we're supposed to haggle! True to Monty Python's *Life of Brian*, bagging a carpet can be an entertaining, theatrical process, entailing repeat visits and gallons of çay (p656)

Spice Bazaar, İstanbul Jewel-like *lokum* (Turkish delight) and colourful pyramids of spices provide eye candy at the fragrant bazaar (p79)

Hamams

Hamams are also known as Turkish baths, a name coined by the Europeans who were introduced to their steamy pleasures by the Ottomans. With their domed roofs, they combine elements of Roman and Byzantine baths. Go for a massage or just soak in the calming atmosphere.

Sefa Hamamı, Antalya Retaining many of its Seljuk features, this restored 13th-century gem is found in Kaleiçi (Old Antalya) between Ottoman houses and the Roman harbour (p356)

Ayasofya Hürrem Sultan Hamamı, İstanbul Patrons have been getting soapy and steamy in Süleyman the Magnificent's luxurious hamam, near the Aya Sofya, since 1557 (p96)

Traditional Turkish contortionism You may feel truly pummelled if you've asked for 'the works', but many masseurs actually let foreigners off lightly; you might see towel-wrapped Turks getting literally walked over

Sokollu Mehmet Paşa Hamam, Edirne Mimar Sinan designed this 16th-century beauty, facing the famous three-balcony mosque (p138)

Beaches

Sun-seekers will find themselves swimming in options when deciding where to recline by the 'wine-dark sea' (in the words of Homer). Turkey is surrounded by the Mediterranean, the Aegean, the Black Sea and the Sea of Marmara. This being a country lathered in history, sunbathers can contemplate the Greek myths that took place on the Turkish coast.

Kaputaş The pale sandy cove and brilliant azure waters near Kalkan look brochure-perfect (p337)

Kabak Take a steep ride down to the Mediterranean beach community (p329)

Patara Visitors once came for the temple and oracle of Apollo, but today sun-seekers and sea turtles prefer the 18km of white sand (p335)

Aegean islands A Greek monastery overlooks Bozcaada's Ayazma beach (p169), and you might have Gökçeada's beaches (p162) to yourself

Lycian Way The 500km trail takes in Mediterranean beaches, ruins and soaring hinterland on the Teke peninsula (p35)

» Marina, old town and Roman walls, Antalya

Museums

In a country marked by great dynasties, from Hittite hill men to Ottoman sultans, museums are a regular sight. Every self-respecting town has a museum to preserve its local history, ranging from dusty collections of prehistoric fragments to innovative, interactive centres.

İstanbul Mix classics such as the Museum of Turkish & Islamic Arts (p61), its carpets fit for palaces, with Orhan Pamuk's new Museum of Innocence (p88)

Göreme Open-Air Museum Only in Cappadocia could a valley of rock-cut Byzantine churches be called a museum (p448)

Museum of Anatolian Civilisations, Ankara Sheds light on the ancient civilisations that warred and waned on the surrounding steppe (p399)

Museum of Health, Edirne The museum of Ottoman medicine occupies a mental hospital where patients were treated using music therapy (p139)

Gaziantep Zeugma Mosaic Museum Recently opened, it showcases virtually complete Roman floor mosaics, rescued from a dam site (p556)

Cities

Turks are a regionalist bunch; they will invariably tell you their town's *en çok güzel* (the most beautiful). In fact, with one notable exception, Turkey doesn't do cities as well as it does mountains and beaches, but there are some worthwhile places to experience urban Turkey.

İstanbul Today's megacity was once the capital of empires; you can't blame the İstanbullus for thinking their city is still the centre of the world (p50)

Antalya The gateway to the Turkish Riviera, and both classically beautiful and stylishly modern in its own right (p354)

İzmir The former city of Smyrna is right on the Aegean; ferries travel along the seafront, with its holiday atmosphere (p190)

Antakya (Hatay) The site of the biblical Antioch has a distinctively Arabic feel (p391)

Van Near the mountain-ringed lake of the same name, this relaxed oasis in southeastern Anatolia is fun from *kahvaltı* (breakfast) to meze o'clock (p598)

Boutique Hotels

From half-timbered Ottoman mansions to Greek stone houses, Turkey's architectural gems are increasingly being converted into small, one-off hotels. These distinctive properties offer a local experience with a stylish twist.

Cappadocia Take up residence in a fairy chimney and experience troglodyte living with luxurious features such as a cave hamam (p444)

Alaçatı More than 100 stone Greek houses in this Aegean village have been converted into boutique digs; options include a former olive warehouse and windmills (p204)

Ottoman Anatolia Safranbolu (p411) and Amasya (p424) – with rocky bluffs and, overlooking the latter, Pontic tombs – are idyllic settings for their many hotels in Ottoman piles

Kaleiçi A smattering of boutique hotels adds further charm to Antalya's Roman-Ottoman old quarter (p354)

Alanya Two recent openings in the Mediterranean city have transformed Ottoman houses below the Seljuk castle (p371)

If you like... James Bond
The spy's latest adventure, *Skyfall*, was filmed in screen-worthy spots including İstanbul's Grand Bazaar, Fethiye and Baba Dağ, Ölüdeniz's 1960m-high mountain

History

Turks are proud of their long, eventful history, and it's easy to share their enthusiasm at the country's mosques and palaces, ruins and museums. Just wander through a bazaar or eat a kebap and you'll get a sense of history; both contain influences introduced by Silk Road traders.

İstanbul Every acre of this former capital of empires exudes a sense of its historic significance, particularly in Sultanahmet at the Topkapı Palace (p50)

Dardanelles On one side is Troy (p164), with a replica Trojan Horse; on the other, the Gallipoli Peninsula (p146) saw a bloody WWI campaign

North Aegean There's living history in the communities descended from Turkmen nomads and from people displaced by the population exchange between Turkey and Greece (p167)

Christianity The Islamic country has a rich Christian past; check out Cappadocia's rock-cut Byzantine monasteries (p444), and the northeastern valleys' medieval Georgian churches (p534)

Ruins

On the list of what makes Turkey one of the world's greatest travelling destinations, its ruins compete with kebaps for first place. Whether in a city centre or atop a craggy cliff, the country's relics bring out the historical romantic in you.

Ephesus The best-preserved classical city in the eastern Mediterranean (p211)

Nemrut Dağı Atop Mt Nemrut are the remains of statues – mostly their heads – built by a megalomaniac pre-Roman king (p572)

Pergamum The Asclepion was ancient Rome's pre-eminent medical centre and the theatre is a vertigo-inducing marvel (p183)

Göbekli Tepi Predating Stonehenge by a cool 6500 years, Şanlıurfa's Neolithic site may be the world's first place of worship (p563)

Obscure sites Hiding in every corner of Turkey are seldom visited, overgrown ruins, where it might be just you, the wind and the caretaker

Armenian Eastern Anatolia's Armenian ruins include a 10th-century church on an island (p597) and Ani, a former capital (p543)

Activities

With its beautiful and diverse terrain, ranging from mountain ranges to beaches, Turkey is a prime spot for outdoor activities. Whether you try an extreme sport for the first time or just take a gentle stroll, be sure to reward yourself with some çay and baklava, or Efes beer and meze.

Walking Opportunities range from half-day wanders through Cappadocia's valleys to 500km Mediterranean trails (p34)

Diving Swim over ancient amphoras and, off the Gallipoli Peninsula, a WWI shipwreck (p36)

Water sports On the Aegean and Mediterranean coasts, windsurfing, kiteboarding, canoeing and waterskiing are among the fun on offer (p36)

Adventure sports Eastern Anatolia offers adrenaline-pumping activities including white-water rafting (p38) and mountain walking (p35)

Canyoning The 18km-long Saklıkent Gorge near Fethiye is Turkey's top spot for canyoning (p332)

Skiing Ski resorts across the country include Cappadocia's Erciyes Dağı (p490) and Bursa's Uludağ (p284)

If you like... obscure ancient civilisations
Seek out Hattuşa (p419) and the Phrygian Valley (p285)

Landscape

Apart from a toe sticking into Europe, Turkey is part of Asia, so it should come as no surprise that its landscapes are varied and stunning. With ancient ruins and bucolic villages dotting the rural areas, taking in the natural scenery couldn't be more pleasant.

Cappadocia The fairy chimneys and *tuff* valleys are best explored on foot or horseback (p444)

Northeastern Anatolia Mountains and rugged scenery including Turkey's highest peak, Mt Ararat (5137m) (p520)

Amasra to Sinop A great drive takes you past Black Sea beaches and green hills (p497)

Behramkale The hillside village has dreamy views of the Aegean coast (p172)

Lake Van A 3750-sq-km lake surrounded by snowcapped mountains (p597)

Datça and Bozburun Peninsulas Raw Mediterranean coast, riddled with coves and pine forests (p264)

Nemrut Dağı Mountain-top stone heads gaze at the Anti-Taurus Range (p572)

Ala Dağlar National Park Waterfalls crash down limestone cliffs in the Taurus Mountains (p481)

Food & Drink

Turkey has epicurean indulgence nailed, from street snacks to gourmet restaurants. Not only does every region offer local dishes, you can sample them in individualistic eateries; the culinary siblings of the country's boutique hotels.

Beyoğlu rooftop bars Toast İstanbul from above with breathtaking views across the Bosphorus and Golden Horn (p115)

Doyuranlar Gözleme On the Gallipoli Peninsula, a great example of the family-run eateries that offer fresh fare and a bucolic atmosphere (p154)

Köy Evi At the forefront of Cappadocia's back-to-basics culinary revolution, Göreme's Village House dishes up traditional soul food in a warren of cave rooms (p456)

İmam Çağdaş At this 125-year-old family firm, discover Gaziantep baklava, reputedly the planet's best, amid the epicurean city's storied streets (p560)

Antakya Evi Syrian and Arab culinary influences abound in Antakya's meze and salads, accompanied by live Turkish folk music at this old villa (p394)

Architecture

Turkey's legacy of mighty empires has left a bounty of imposing buildings: palaces, mosques, churches, monasteries and caravanserais are a few of the ancient structures evoking bygone eras. Touring historic sites, you will see Byzantine, Seljuk, Ottoman and other architectural styles.

İstanbul The city's glorious edifices include the Ottoman Topkapı and Dolmabahçe Palaces, contemporary Şakirin Mosque, and the stunning Aya Sofya, the world's greatest surviving Byzantine building with its seemingly floating dome (p50)

İshak Paşa Palace Perched on a plateau above the steppe, the restored 18th-century pile mixes Seljuk, Ottoman, Georgian, Persian and Armenian styles. (p548)

Ulu Camii & Darüşşifa, Divriği The remote Alevi village's Seljuk mosque and hospital complex have stone portal carvings so intricate that locals say they prove the existence of God (p435)

Boutique hotels From the Aegean's old Greek villages to Safranbolu and Amasya's Ottoman mansions, hoteliers have lovingly restored historic properties (p651)

month by month

Top Events

1 **Mountain Walking,** July

2 **Ski Season,** December

3 **Kafkasör Kültür ve Sanat Festivalı,** June

4 **Nevruz,** March

5 **Historic Kırkpınar Oil Wrestling Festival,** June

January

The dead of winter. Even İstanbul's streets are empty of crowds, local and foreign, and snow closes eastern Anatolia's mountain passes and delays buses.

New Year's Day
A surrogate Christmas takes place across the Islamic country, with the usual decorations, exchange of gifts and greeting cards. Christmas and New Year are an exception to the low season; prices rise and accommodation fills up. 1 January.

March

As in the preceding months, you might have sights to yourself outside the country's top destinations, and you can get discounts at the accommodation options that open their doors.

Nevruz
Kurds and Alevis celebrate the ancient Middle Eastern spring festival with much jumping over bonfires and general jollity. Banned until a few years ago, Nevruz is now an official holiday with huge parties, particularly in Diyarbakır, which last well into the morning. 21 March.

Çanakkale Deniz Zaferi
Turks descend on the Gallipoli (Gelibolu) Peninsula and the towns across the Dardanelles to celebrate what they call the Çanakkale Naval Victory – and commemorate the WWI campaign's 130,000 fatalities. The area, particularly the Turkish memorials in the southern peninsula, is busy with busloads of people. 18 March.

April

Spring. April and May are high season in İstanbul and shoulder season elsewhere. Not a great month to get a tan in northern Turkey, but you can enjoy balmy, breezy weather in the southwest.

Anzac Day, Gallipoli Peninsula
The WWI battles for the Dardanelles are commemorated again, this time with more emphasis on the Allied soldiers. Antipodean pilgrims sleep at Anzac Cove before the dawn services; another busy time on the peninsula. 25 April.

İstanbul Film Festival
For a filmic fortnight, the wonderful vintage cinemas on and around Beyoğlu's İstiklal Caddesi host a packed program of Turkish and international films and events, with cheap-as-çay tickets available. An excellent crash course in Turkish cinema, but book ahead. http://film.iksv.org/en.

İstanbul Tulip Festival
İstanbul's parks and gardens are resplendent with tulips, which originated in Turkey before being exported to the Netherlands during the Ottoman era. Multicoloured tulips are often planted to resemble the Turks' cherished 'evil eye'. Flowers bloom from late March or early April.

May

Another good month to visit. Shoulder season continues outside

İstanbul, with attendant savings, but spring is going strong and Aegean and Mediterranean beaches are heating up.

⭐ International Giresun Aksu Festival

The historical, hazelnut-producing Black Sea town hails fecundity and the new growing season with boat trips to Giresun Island, concerts, traditional dance performances and other open-air events. Four days in mid-May.

🏃 Windsurfing

In Turkey's windsurfing centre, Alaçatı, the season begins in mid-May. The protected Aegean bay hosts the Windsurf World Cup in August and the season winds down in early November, when many of the eight resident schools close. www.alacati.de.

👁 Ruins, Mosques, Palaces & Museums

This is your last chance until September to see the main attractions at famous Aegean and Mediterranean sights such as Ephesus (Efes) without major crowds, which can become almost unbearable at the height of summer.

June

Summer. Shoulder season in İstanbul and high season elsewhere until the end of August. Expect sizzling temperatures, inflexible hotel prices and crowds at sights – avoided by visiting early, late or at lunchtime.

⭐ Cherry Season

June is the best month to gobble Turkey's delicious cherries, which Giresun introduced to the rest of the world. On the Sea of Marmara, Tekirdağ's Kiraz Festivalı (Cherry Festival) in early June celebrates the juicy wonders.

⭐ Kafkasör Kültür ve Sanat Festivalı, Artvin

Join the crush at the *boğa güreşleri* (bloodless bull-wrestling matches) at Artvin's Caucasus Culture & Arts Festival, held in the Kafkasör Yaylası pasture, 7km southwest of the northeastern Anatolian mountain town. Late June or early July.

⭐ Historic Kırkpınar Oil Wrestling Festival, Edirne

In a sport dating back 650 years, brawny *pehlivan* (wrestlers) from across Turkey rub themselves from head to foot with olive oil and grapple. Late June or early July.

July

This month and August turn the Aegean and Mediterranean tourist heartlands into sun-and-fun machines, and temperatures peak across the country. The blue skies bring out the best in the hot-blooded Turkish personality.

🏃 Mountain Walking

Out in the northeastern Anatolian steppe, the snow clears from atop the Kaçkar

Mountains (Kaçkar Dağları) and Mt Ararat (Ağrı Dağı, 5137m), Turkey's highest peak, allowing multiday treks and sublime *yaylalar* (highland pastures) views in July and August. www .cultureroutesinturkey.com.

⭐ Kültür Sanat ve Turizm Festivalı, Doğubayazıt

The Kurdish town between Mt Ararat and the romantic İshak Paşa Palace hosts its Culture & Arts Festival, allowing you to immerse yourself in Kurdish heritage through music, dance and theatre performances. June or July.

⭐ Music Festivals

Turkey shows its European side at a string of summer music jamborees; including İstanbul, İzmir and Bursa's highbrow festivals, Aspendos Opera & Ballet Festival, plus multiple pop, rock, jazz and dance music events in İstanbul and other cities. June to July. http://muzik .iksv.org/en.

August

Even at night, the weather is hot and humid; pack sun cream and anti-mosquito spray. Walking and activities are best tackled early in the morning or at sunset.

⭐ Cappadocian Festivals

Two festivals take place in the land of fairy chimneys (rock formations). A summer series of chamber music concerts is held in the valleys and, for three days in mid-August, sleepy Hacıbektaş comes alive with the annual pilgrimage of Bektaşi dervishes. www .klasikkeyifler.org.

International Bodrum Ballet Festival

The 15th-century Castle of St Peter, as well as housing the Museum of Underwater Archaeology, is an atmospheric location for the fortnight-long festival, which features Turkish and international ballet and opera performances. www .bodrumballetfestival.gov.tr.

September

İstanbul's second high season begins; elsewhere, it's shoulder season – temperatures, crowds and prices lessen. Accommodation and activities, such as boat trips, begin winding down for the winter.

Diving

The water is warmest between May to October and you can expect water temperatures of 25°C in September. Turkey's scuba-diving centres are Kuşadası, Marmaris and Ayvalık on the Aegean, and Kaş on the Mediterranean.

İstanbul Biennial

The city's major visual-arts shindig, considered to be one of the world's most prestigious biennials, takes place from early September to early November in odd-numbered years. It typically features more than 100 projects by almost as many artists from dozens of countries. http://bienal.iksv.org /en.

October

Autumn is truly here; outside İstanbul, many accommodation options have shut for the winter. Good weather can't be guaranteed up north, but the Mediterranean and Aegean experience fresh, sunny days.

Walking

The weather in eastern Anatolia has already become challenging by this time of year, but in the southwest, autumn and spring are the best seasons to enjoy the scenery without too much sweat on your brow. www.trekkinginturkey .com.

Akbank Jazz Festival

From mid-September to early October, İstanbul celebrates its love of jazz with this eclectic line-up of local and international performers. The older sibling of July's İstanbul Jazz Festival, it celebrated its 21st in 2011, when performers included swing maestro Ray Gelato. www.akbanksanat.com.

Efes Pilsen Blues Festival

Between late September and late October, American blues twangers tour İstanbul and a varying selection of other Turkish cities. More than 20 years old, the festival's recent performers have included Mississippi axeman John Mooney. www.pozitif -ist.com.

November

Even on the coastlines, summer is a distant memory. Rain falls on İstanbul and the Black Sea, and eastern Anatolia is ensnarled in snow.

Karagöz Festival, Bursa

Five days of festivities and performances celebrate the city's Karagöz shadow-puppetry heritage, with local and international puppeteers and marionette performers. Originally a Central Asian Turkic tradition, the camel-hide puppet theatre developed in Bursa and spread through the Ottoman Empire.

December

Turks fortify themselves against the cold with hot çay and kebap-induced layers. Most of the country is chilly and wet or icy, although the western Mediterranean is milder and hill walking there is viable.

Ski Season

Hit the slopes: the Turkish ski season begins at half a dozen resorts across the country, including Cappadocia's Erciyes Dağı (Mt Erciyes), Uludağ (near Bursa), Palandöken (near Erzurum) and Sarıkamış, near Kars. Late November to April.

Snow in Anatolia

If you're really lucky, after skiing on Erciyes Dağı, you could head west and see central Cappadocia's fairy chimneys looking even more magical under a layer of snow. Eastern Anatolia is also covered in a white blanket, but temperatures get brutally low.

itineraries

Whether you've got six days or 60, these itineraries provide a starting point for the trip of a lifetime. Want more inspiration? Head online to lonelyplanet.com /thorntree to chat with other travellers.

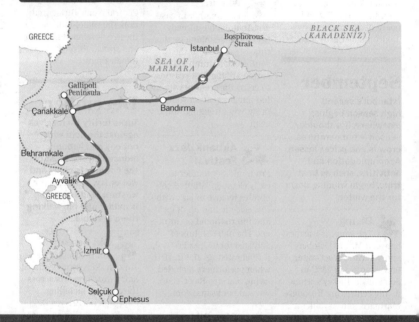

10 Days to Two Weeks
Classic Turkey

> Most first-time visitors to Turkey arrive with two ancient names on their lips: İstanbul and Ephesus. You'll need at least three days in **İstanbul** to even scrape the surface of its millennia of history. The top three sights are the Aya Sofya, Topkapı Palace and the Blue Mosque, but there's a sultan's treasury of other sights and activities, including a cruise up the Bosphorus to the Black Sea, nightlife around the heaving İstiklal Caddesi, and the Grand Bazaar's 2000-plus shops. From İstanbul you can head straight to **İzmir** – a laid-back coastal city near Ephesus with Aegean vistas and Levantine architecture. If you'd like to see a bit more on the way, take a bus from Bandırma to **Çanakkale**, a lively student town with sweeping views across the Dardanelles, and pay a visit to the **Gallipoli Peninsula**. An afternoon tour of the poignant battlefields is a memorable experience. From Çanakkale, it's a bus ride to tumbledown **Ayvalık**, and then a dolmuş from there to **Behramkale**, where you can climb to the Temple of Athena. Finish by taking a bus from Ayvalık to İzmir, and then on to Selçuk, where you can organise a taxi or tour to glorious **Ephesus**, the best-preserved classical city in the eastern Mediterranean.

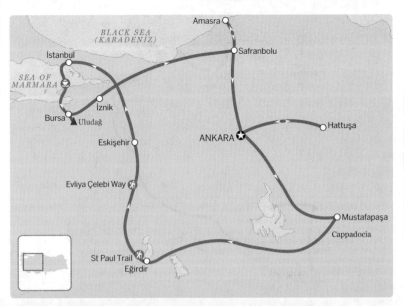

Three to Four Weeks
Cappadocia Express

> Travellers are often confronted with a tough choice when deciding where to go in Turkey after İstanbul: Cappadocia or the southwestern coast. If you feel drawn to the former's fairy-tale landscape, there are a few worthwhile stops en route across Anatolia. After following the **İstanbul** leg of the Classic Turkey itinerary, hop on a ferry across the Sea of Marmara to **Bursa**. The city does a good line in Ottoman mosques and mausoleums, İskender kebaps and Karagöz shadow puppets in the Kapalı Çarşı (Covered Market); and nearby, a cable car climbs to **Uludağ's** ski resort. Head north to **İznik**, where the city's proud Ottoman tile-making heritage is on display between its Roman-Byzantine walls.

Next, bus it to Ankara or, with more time, detour along the top of Turkey to **Safranbolu**. This Ottoman town, with half-timbered houses among rocky bluffs, is a wonderful introduction to rural Anatolian life. To have your kebap and eat it, you can see a little of the Turkish coast by taking a further 2½-hour detour to the Black Sea town of **Amasra**, with its castle and fish restaurants.

Ankara, the Turkish capital, is no match for that show-stealer on the Bosphorus, but two key sights here give an insight into Turkish history, ancient and modern: the Anıt Kabir, Atatürk's hilltop mausoleum, and the Museum of Anatolian Civilisations, a restored 15th-century *bedesten* (covered market) packed with finds from the surrounding steppe. Tying in with the latter, a detour east takes in the isolated, evocative ruins of **Hattuşa**, which was the Hittite capital in the late Bronze age.

Leave three days to explore **Cappadocia**, where there are valleys of fairy chimneys, rock-cut churches with Byzantine frescoes, underground cities and horse rides to occupy you. Schedule some time to just sit and appreciate the fantastical landscape in çay-drinking villages such as **Mustafapaşa**, with its stone-carved Greek houses and 18th-century church.

With time to spare on the return journey to İstanbul, stop in lakeside **Eğirdir**, with its crumbling old quarter ringed by beaches and mountains. In the region are the long-distance walking routes the **St Paul Trail** and **Evliya Çelebi Way**. **Eskişehir** is a worthy final stop, with river gondola rides, cultural events, a student-driven nightlife and picturesque old town.

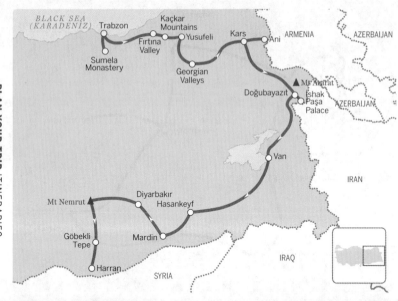

Four Weeks
Eastern Delights

Turkey's little-visited eastern reaches are sweeter than *bal* (honey) for adventurous travellers. Start with a couple of days in buzzing **Trabzon**, where sights include the 13th-century Aya Sofya, then move south to visit **Sumela Monastery**, peering down on a forested valley from its rockface. Head back to Trabzon, and then drive up **Fırtına Valley**, with its Ottoman humpback bridges. Circle the **Kaçkar Mountains** or tackle a multiday trek over the top to **Yusufeli**, where the Çoruh River white-water rafting is worth sampling before a dam floods the area. The drive from Yuufeli to Kars through the **Georgian Valleys** is one of Turkey's most scenic, heading over mountains, through gorges and past crumbling castles to medieval churches in hill villages.

Russian-influenced **Kars** is an intriguing city surrounded by the vast Anatolian steppe. The star attraction here is nearby **Ani**, once a thriving Armenian capital, and now a field strewn with magnificent ruins next to the border of modern Armenia. Aim to spend a couple of days in the area; longer if you'd like to find other weather-beaten ruins in the surrounding countryside. From Kars, head south past **Mt Ararat** (Ağrı Dağı, 5137m), Turkey's highest mountain, to **Doğubayazıt**. Perching above the predominantly Kurdish border town, the impossibly romantic **İshak Paşa Palace** – resembling a scene from *One Thousand and One Nights* – surveys the plains.

From Doğubayazıt, travel further south to **Van**, on the shore of a vast, mountain-ringed lake. Take a couple of days here to see the 10th-century Akdamar church, sole inhabitant of an island in Lake Van (Van Gölü), and Hoşap Castle, built by a 17th-century Kurdish chieftain, which has superb lion reliefs. Heading southwest from the church, don't miss **Hasankeyf**, a sort of Cappadocia in miniature, set to be submerged by a dam; and honey-coloured **Mardin**, with its minarets, churches and castle, overlooking the roasting Mesopotamian plains.

Turning northwest, enter the Byzantine city walls at Diyarbakır, the heartland of Kurdish culture, before climbing **Mt Nemrut** (Nemrut Dağı) to see the gigantic stone heads left by a megalomaniacal pre-Roman king – one of eastern Turkey's most famous sights. Head south to finish with a final hit of history at Şanlıurfa's Neolithic **Göbekli Tepe**, perhaps the world's first place of worship, and **Harran**, which hosted Abraham in 1900 BC and is one of the planet's oldest continuously inhabited spots.

» (above) Akdamar Kilisesi (Church of the Holy Cross; p597) on the shore of Lake Van
» (left) Interior of the Blue Mosque (p60), İstanbul

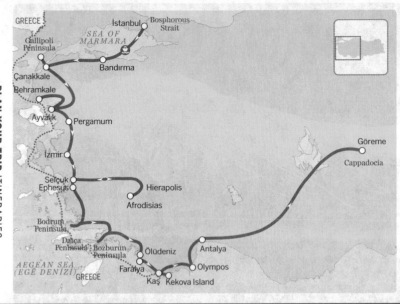

Three to Four Weeks
Palm Trees & Fairy Chimneys

If you have a kind boss, you don't have to choose between Cappadocia's wavy valleys and the coast's white-sand beaches – prepare to spend many hours on buses and check out both areas. Follow the Classic Turkey itinerary, with one extra stop in **Pergamum** (en route from Ayvalık to İzmir), where you can see some of Turkey's most awe-inspiring Roman ruins and climb the hill to the Acropolis.

After **Ephesus**, take a day trip from your base at Selçuk to the travertines and ruins of **Hierapolis** at Pamukkale. The brilliant white terraces can be dizzying in the midday sun, but swimming among submerged marble columns in the Antique Pool will restore your cool. Nearby **Afrodisias** is at least as impressive and less crowded – the only other people among the soaring colonnades might be archaeologists.

Returning to the coast, head along the chichi **Bodrum Peninsula** or the **Datça and Bozburun Peninsulas**, where the mountain towns and fishing villages are best explored by scooter. Continuing southeast, beautiful **Ölüdeniz** is the spot to paraglide over the Mediterranean or lie low on a beach towel. You're now within kicking distance of the 509km-long Lycian Way. Hike for a day through superb countryside to overnight in heavenly **Faralya**, overlooking Butterfly Valley; further inroads into the trail will definitely top your 'next time' list.

Continuing along the coast, have a pit stop at laid-back **Kaş**, its pretty harbourside square alive nightly with the hum of friendly folk enjoying the breeze, views, Mediterranean dishes and a beer or two. One of Turkey's most beguiling boat trips departs from here, taking in the sunken Byzantine city at **Kekova Island**. From Kaş, it's a couple of hours to **Olympos**, where you can spend a few days unwinding at the beach tree houses.

From Olympos, head onwards to **Antalya**. Its Roman-Ottoman quarter, Kaleiçi, is worth a wander, set against the backdrop of a jaw-dropping mountain range. Next, drag yourself away from the beach and catch the bus north to claim your cave in **Göreme**. This travellers' hang-out is the most popular base in Cappadocia, a surreal moonscape dotted with tuff cones, where you can easily spend three days or mroe. The famous formations line the roads to sights including the rock-cut frescoed churches of Göreme Open-Air Museum and the Byzantine underground cities at Kaymaklı and Derinkuyu.

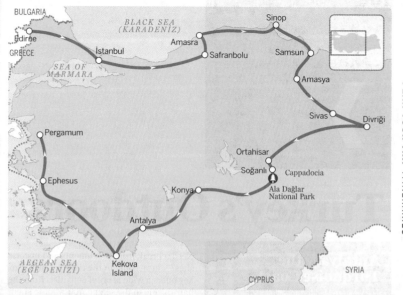

Four Weeks
Anatolian Circle

> This trip leaves out only eastern Anatolia, which is a mission in itself, and takes in obscure gems as well as prime sights. Begin in **Edirne**, home to the Selimiye Camii; the 16th-century mosque is the finest work of the great Mimar Sinan. After Edirne, spend a few days among more mosques, palaces and some 14 million folk in **İstanbul**, former capital of the Ottoman and Byzantine empires. Next, head east to **Safranbolu**, with its winding streets of Ottoman mansions, before turning north to **Amasra**, where Turkish holidaymakers wander the Byzantine castle and eat in fish restaurants on the two harbours. The Black Sea port town is the beginning of the drive through rugged hills to **Sinop**, birthplace of the Greek philosopher Diogenes the Cynic.

From Sinop, take a bus via Samsun to **Amasya** and spend a couple of days appreciating its Ottoman houses, Pontic tombs and castle. Heading further south through Sivas, detour up a mountain valley to **Divriği**, an Alevi town that offers a taste of eastern Anatolia. Here you'll find the 800-year-old Unesco-protected Ulu Camii and hospital complex, which has stone doorways with intricate carvings.

The next stop, **Cappadocia**, is wholeheartedly back on the beaten track. Spend about three days here and, instead of joining the rest on a tour bus or hot-air balloon, explore the fairy chimneys and cave churches by walking or horse riding. Göreme and Ürgüp are the usual bases, but you could stay in a less-touristy village such as **Ortahisar**, with its craggy castle.

South of central Cappadocia, see rock-cut churches without the crowds in **Soğanlı**, where Byzantine monastic settlements occupy two valleys. If you really want to get away from it all, head into the **Ala Dağlar National Park** for some of Turkey's most breathtaking scenery in the Taurus Mountains (Toros Dağları).

You're now fit for the journey across the hazy plains to **Konya**, a convenient stop en route to the Mediterranean and the birthplace of the Mevlâna (whirling dervish) order. The turquoise-domed Mevlâna Museum, containing the tomb of the order's 13th-century founder, is an enduring symbol of Turkey.

When you glimpse the glittering Med, follow the coastal part of the Palm Trees and Fairy Chimneys itinerary. You won't have time to stop everywhere if you want to sunbathe and hit the hamam – Seljuk Sefa Hamamı in **Antalya** is a good one – so pick some highlights, such as the ruins at **Kekova Island**, **Ephesus** and **Pergamum**.

Turkey's Outdoors

Antalya & the Turquoise Coast

The Western Mediterranean offers the widest array of activities, including sea-kayaking, boat trips, diving, two waymarked walking trails, canyoning, rafting and paragliding.

Cappadocia

Excellent for a half- or full-day hike, with a surreal landscape of curvy valleys and fairy chimneys. There are also mountain-walking opportunities, horse riding, and skiing on Erciyes Dağı (Mt Erciyes).

Eastern Anatolia

Head to the eastern wilds, especially the northern part, for serious adrenaline fixes – mountain walking, white-water rafting, skiing, snowboarding and snowshoeing.

South Aegean

Bring your swimming gear to the more-popular stretch of the Aegean, where operators in spots like Bodrum offer boat trips galore and water sports including diving and waterskiing.

Need a break from monuments and historic sites? You've come to the right country. Turkey offers a wide array of activities, from the hair-raising to the serene. You want to shoot down a river in a raft? Sail over archaeological remains? Tackle challenging summits? Explore the countryside on horseback? No problem, it's all here.

And Turkey's outdoor pursuits don't stop there. Active travellers from aspiring kayakers to dedicated skiers will find superb playgrounds. Good safety standards can be expected whatever activity you choose, provided you stick to reputable operators who employ qualified, English-speaking staff.

The good thing about Turkey is that epicurean indulgences are never far away. After all that exertion, few things could be better than gobbling up some baklava or relaxing in a hamam. The thrill of the outdoors, good food and well-being: what a great combination.

Walking & Hiking

Walking in Turkey is increasingly popular among both Turks and foreign travellers, and a growing number of local and foreign firms offer walking holidays here. The country is blessed with numerous mountains, from the Taurus Mountains in the southwest to the Kaçkars in the northeast, which all provide fabulous hiking opportunities. Hiking is also the best way to visit villages and sights rarely seen by holidaymakers, and it will give you a taste of life in rural Turkey.

Hiking options range from challenging multiday hikes, including Mt Ararat (Ağrı Dağı), Turkey's highest summit and a possible location of Noah's Ark, to gentle afternoon strolls, such as in Cappadocia.

More information on hiking in Turkey is available at www.trekkinginturkey.com and cultureroutesinturkey.com.

Safety Advice

Bar a few well-known and well-maintained trails, most are not signposted and it's recommended to hire a guide, or at least seek local advice before setting off.

Weather conditions can fluctuate quickly between extremes, so come prepared and check the local conditions.

Day Walks

For half- and full-day walks, Cappadocia is unbeatable, with a dozen valleys that are easily negotiated on foot, around Göreme and the Ihlara Valley. These walks, one to several hours in length with minor gradients, are perfectly suited to casual walkers and even families. The fairy chimneys are unforgettable, and walking is the best way to do the landscapes and sights justice – and discover areas that travellers usually don't reach. After all, there aren't many places in the world where you can walk along a string of ancient, rock-cut churches set in a lunar landscape.

Long-Distance Trails

Turkey has two iconic waymarked trails, the Lycian Way and St Paul Trail, plus several new long-distance routes in various stages of development, including the Evliya Çelebi Way through Western Anatolia. The routes are best tackled in spring or autumn and you don't have to walk them in their entirety; it's easy to bite off a small chunk. Consult the above-mentioned websites for information on the trails.

Lycian Way

Chosen by the *Sunday Times* as one of the world's 10 best walks, the Lycian Way is about 500km long and extends between Fethiye and Antalya, partly inland, partly along the coast of ancient Lycia, via Patara, Kalkan, Kaş, Finike, Olympos and Tekirova. Highlights include stunning coastal views, pine and cedar forests, laid-back villages, ruins of ancient cities, Mt Olympos and Baba

> **SADDLE UP!**
>
> Cappadocia is Turkey's top spot for horse riding, with numerous good riding tracks criss-crossing the marvellous landscapes. Outfits including Cappadocia's own horse whisperer are ready to take you on guided rides, ranging from one-hour jaunts to fully catered treks. The best thing about riding here is that you can access terrain you can't get to otherwise – a wise (and ecofriendly) way to escape the crowds.

Dağ. Kate Clow, who established the trail, describes it in detail in the walking guide *The Lycian Way*.

St Paul Trail

The St Paul Trail is also 500km long, from Perge, 10km east of Antalya, to Yalvaç, northeast of Eğirdir Gölü (Lake Eğirdir). Partly following the route walked by St Paul on his first missionary journey in Asia Minor, it's more challenging than the Lycian Way, with more ascents. Along the way you'll pass canyons, waterfalls, forests, a medieval paved road, Eğirdir Gölü, Roman baths and an aqueduct, and numerous quaint villages.

St Paul Trail, by Kate Clow and Terry Richardson, describes the trail in detail.

Mountain Walks

Turkey is home to some seriously good mountain walking.

Mt Ararat Turkey's highest mountain, the majestic and challenging 5137m Mt Ararat, near the Armenian border, is one of the region's top climbs and can be tackled in three days (but preferably four). You'll need to be cashed up and patient with all the bureaucracy (a permit is mandatory). To acclimatise, start with Turkey's second-highest mountain, Süphan Dağı (4053m), north of Lake Van.

Kaçkar Mountains In northeastern Anatolia, the Kaçkars are increasingly popular with Europeans. They offer lakes, forests and varied flora, at altitudes from about 2000m to 3937m. There are numerous possible routes, ranging from a few hours to several days, notably the multiday Trans-Kaçkar Trek.

Cappadocia Southern Cappadocia has a few good mountain walks, including 3268m Mt Hasan and the Taurus Mountains in Ala Dağlar National Park.

HIKER'S DILEMMA: ARARAT OR KAÇKARS?

Zafer Onay, a trekking guide based in Doğubayazıt, guides hikers on Mt Ararat and in the Kaçkars. 'Mt Ararat is a great climb, but landscapes in the Kaçkars are more scenic; they form a range, which means you can expect more diversity. It's more colourful, you can see wildflowers and, if you're lucky, you can spot bears and ibex. Bird-watching is also an option in the Kaçkars.'

Water Sports

Lounging on a white-sand beach is certainly tempting, but there are many opportunities to dip your toes in the sea.

Scuba Diving

OK, the Red Sea it ain't, but where else in the world can you swim over amphoras and broken pottery from ancient shipwrecks? Turkey also offers a wide choice of reefs, drop-offs and caves. The waters are generally calm, with no tides or currents, and visibility averages 20m (not too bad by Mediterranean standards). Pelagics are rare, but small reef species are prolific. Here you can mingle with groupers, dentex, moray eels, sea bream, octopus and parrot fish, as well as the occasional amberjack, barracuda and ray. You don't need to be a strong diver; there are sites for all levels of proficiency. For experienced divers, there are superb expanses of red coral to explore (usually under 30m of water).

The standard of diving facilities is high, and you'll find professional dive centres staffed with qualified, English-speaking instructors. Most centres are affiliated with internationally recognised dive organisations. Compared with other countries, diving in Turkey is pretty cheap, and it's also a great place to learn. Most dive companies offer introductory dives for beginners and reasonably priced open-water certification courses.

While it is possible to dive all year, the best time is May to October, when the water is warmest (you can expect up to 25°C in September).

Top Dive Spots

The following have a deserved reputation for fine scuba diving:

» Kuşadası, Bodrum and Marmaris (south Aegean)

» Kaş (western Mediterranean)

» Ayvalık (north Aegean)

Sea Kayaking & Canoeing

Look at the map of Turkey. See the tortuous coastline in the western Mediterranean area? So many secluded coves, deep blue bays, pine-clad mountains, islands shimmering in the distance, laid-back villages... Paddling is the best way to experience the breathtaking scenery of the aptly named Turquoise Coast, and to comfortably access pristine terrain.

Another draw is that you can disembark at places that are inaccessible by road – ideal for finding your own slice of paradise. Adding excitement to the journey, you might see flying fish and turtles, and if you're really lucky you might even come across frolicking dolphins.

Day trips are the norm, but longer tours can be organised with overnight camping under the stars on deserted beaches. They should include transfers, guides, gear and meals.

Top Paddling Spots

Kekova Sunken City This magical spot, with Lycian ruins partly submerged 6m below the sea, perfectly lends itself to a sea-kayaking tour from Kaş. This superb day excursion, suitable for all fitness levels, allows you to glide over underwater walls, foundations and staircases submerged during 2nd-century earthquakes, clearly visible through crystal-clear waters.

Patara Canoeing trips on the Xanthos River offer a unique opportunity to glide past jungle-like riverbanks and discover a rich ecosystem, with birds, crabs and turtles. Ending your journey on the splendid Patara beach adds to the appeal.

Canyoning

Canyoning is a mix of climbing, hiking, abseiling, swimming and some serious jumping or plunging – down waterfalls, river gorges, and water-polished chutes in natural pools. Experience is not usually necessary, but water confidence and reasonable fitness are advantageous. Expect adventure cen-

» (above) Hiking in the Kaçkar
Mountains (p526)
» (left) Kayaking over Kekova Sunken
City (p348)

tres offering canyoning to provide wetsuits, helmets and harnesses, and outings to be led by qualified instructors. The 18km-long Saklıkent Gorge (p332), southeast of Fethiye, features leaping into natural pools, swimming through narrow passages, scrambling over rocks and abseiling down waterfalls.

White-Water Rafting

It's important to choose an operator with the experience, skills and equipment to run a safe and exciting expedition. Stick to the more reputable operators. Your guide should give you a comprehensive safety talk and paddle training before you launch off downstream. Top rafting spots:

Çoruh River Come to Yusufeli from May to August for fantastic white-water rafting; and come as soon as possible, as the area is slated to be flooded by a dam. Thanks to rugged topography and an abundance of snowmelt, the iconic Çoruh River offers world-class runs with powerful Class II to V rapids to get the blood racing. An added thrill is the breathtaking scenery along the sheer walls of the Çoruh Gorge. Trips generally last three hours (p527).

İspir and Barhal Rivers Also near Yusufeli, the fainter of heart can take a mellower but equally scenic trip on these tributaries of the Çoruh (p528).

Çamlıhemşin On the other side of the Kaçkars, offering gentler rapids and impressive scenery (p528).

Köprülü Kanyon In the western Mediterranean region, near Antalya (p364).

Saklıkent Gorge An 18km-long gorge near Fethiye (p332).

Zamantı River In Cappadocia's Ala Dağlar National Park (p481).

Windsurfing & Kitesurfing

Professional Windsurfers Association World Cup competitions take place in Alaçatı, on the Çeşme Peninsula. With constant, strong breezes (around 16 to 17 knots) and a 2km-long beach with shallows and calm water conditions from mid-May to early November, Alaçatı is a world-class windsurfing destination. It's also an ideal place to learn, with a wide array of classes available. The area is a prime spot for kitesurfing, too. For more information check out www.alacati.de.

Winter Sports

Turkey is not just a summer destination. It's still little known outside Turkey that winter sports are widely available here, notably excellent skiing (*kayak* in Turkish).

Skiing

Don't get us wrong; it ain't the Alps, but powder junkies will be genuinely surprised at the quality of the infrastructure and the great snow conditions from December to April.

Whether you're a seasoned *kayakcı* (skier) or a novice standing in snow for the first time, there are options galore. Most ski resorts have been upgraded in recent years and now feature good facilities, including hotels equipped with saunas, hamams and even indoor pools. Best of all, prices are lower than at Western European resorts and the vibe is unpretentious and family-oriented.

Turks form a significant portion of the clientele, though Russians, Germans and vacationers from the Middle East account for a growing share of the crowd. Off the slopes there's a thriving nightlife. Ski resorts are some of Turkey's most liberal spots, with clubs and licensed bars (and steaming mulled wine!).

Most hotels offer daily and weekly packages including lift passes and full board. Rental of skis, boots and poles is available, as is tuition, though English-speaking instructors are hard to find.

DO YOU WANNA GÜLET?

For a boat trip along the Aegean or Mediterranean coast, there are endless possibilities, ranging from day trips – out of pretty much everywhere with a harbour, from Ayvalık in the north Aegean all the way around the coast to Alanya in the eastern Mediterranean – to chartering a graceful *gület* (traditional wooden yacht) for a four-day cruise around beaches and bays. The most popular *gület* route is between Demre (Kale; near Olympos) and Fethiye, although aficionados say the route between Marmaris and Fethiye is prettier.

PARAGLIDING

Picture yourself, comfortably seated, gracefully drifting over the velvety indigo of the sea, feeling the caress of the breeze... Paragliding from the slopes of Baba Dağ (1960m) in Ölüdeniz, which has consistently excellent uplifting thermals from late April to early November, is top notch. For beginners, local operators offer tandem flights, for which no training or experience is required. You just have to run a few steps and the rest is entirely controlled by the pilot, to whom you're attached with a harness. Parasailing is also available in Ölüdeniz, and Kaş is another popular destination for paragliding.

Resorts

Palandöken The biggest and most-renowned ski resort, on the outskirts of Erzurum (p525).

Sarıkamış The low-key resort near Kars is the most scenic of the lot, surrounded by vast expanses of pines. It's famous for its reliable snow pack and sunny skies. Snowboarders are also catered for (p547).

Uludağ Near Bursa, the 2543m-high 'Great Mountain' has chain hotels and a cable car from the city's outskirts. On winter weekends it's popular with İstanbullu snow bunnies, who come on the ferry across the Sea of Marmara (p284).

Davraz Dağı Also in western Anatolia, Mt Davraz (2635m) rises between three lakes near Eğirdir, offering Nordic and downhill skiing and snowboarding (p307).

Erciyes Dağı The resort on the northeast side of Mt Erciyes (3916m), above Kayseri in the Cappadocia region, offers empty pistes and a rugged ski experience (p490).

Nemrut Dağı Around Bitlis and Tatvan, a few small resorts make the most of 3050m-high Mt Nemrut (the one overlooking Lake Van; p596).

Other Sports

Cross-country skiing is possible in the Kaçkar Mountains and Sarıkamış, and snowshoeing in Cappadocia, Mt Ararat and Sarıkamış.

Travel with Children

Best Regions for Kids

Antalya & the Turquoise Coast

Water sports and activities from tandem paragliding to sea kayaking over submerged ruins. With younger children, holiday towns like Kaş offer picturesque lanes and sandy beaches.

Ephesus, Bodrum & the South Aegean

Ruins such as Ephesus for older children, plus beaches for kids of all ages. Holiday spots like Kuşadası, the Bodrum Peninsula and Pamucak offer plenty of sights, facilities and water sports, with less touristy coastline nearby.

Cappadocia

The fantastical landscape of fairy chimneys (rock formations) and underground cities will thrill older children, as will cave accommodation. A safe, relaxing rural area with activities including horse riding, hot-air ballooning and walking.

İzmir & the North Aegean

More Aegean beaches. İzmir's *kordon* (seafront) is a child-friendly promenade – spacious, flat and pretty and offering numerous eating options. Bozcaada island is easy to negotiate and enjoy, with safe swimming beaches and good cycling.

Turkey for Kids

Çocuklar (children) are the beloved centrepiece of family life in Turkey, and your children will be welcomed wherever they go. Your journey will be peppered with exclamations of *Maşallah* (glory be to God) and your children will be clutched into the adoring arms of strangers. Travelling in family-focused Turkey is a blessing with kids big and small – waiters play with babies, strangers entertain and indulge at every turn, and free or discounted entry to sights is common. On the downside, child-friendly facilities are often lacking and safety consciousness rarely meets Western norms.

Perhaps learn your child's age and sex in Turkish – *ay* (month), *yil* (year), *erkek* (boy) and *kız* (girl). To make polite inquiries about the other person's children: *Kaç tane çocuklariniz varmı?* (How many children do you have?).

See p96 for advice on İstanbul.

Children's Highlights
Accommodation

» Cappadocian cave hotels, Olympos tree houses and Kabak's beach retreats offer novel accommodation.

Activities

» In the western Mediterranean region, mix beach-based fun and water sports with activities such as tandem paragliding.

» The Aegean is good for a relaxed seaside holiday, with beaches, water sports and two major inhabited islands.

» Cappadocia offers activities including horse riding and hot-air ballooning.

» Teenagers will enjoy walking in Cappadocia or the Kaçkar Mountains.

» Cooking courses are available in locations such as İstanbul.

Historic Sites

» For older children and teenagers, Turkey offers numerous major sights, from Ephesus to Ani, Pergamum to Mt Nemrut (Nemrut Dağı).

» Ruins such as İstanbul's Hippodrome offer plenty of space for toddlers to expend energy.

» Children will love the creepy atmosphere of İstanbul's subterranean Basilica Cistern (Yerebatan Sarnıçı), with walkways suspended over the water.

» Exploring Cappadocia's fairy chimneys, caves and underground cities will prove memorable for kids.

» At Mediterranean spots such as Patara and Kekova, you can mix ruins with beach, boat trips and sea kayaking.

Museums

» The Rahmi M Koç Museums in İstanbul and Ankara are interactive museums with trains, planes, boats and automobiles on display.

» İstanbul Modern gallery has multimedia exhibits to amuse and engage, plus summer art workshops for children aged seven to 12.

» Children under 12 receive free or discounted entry to many museums and monuments.

Transport

» Ferries in İstanbul and İzmir are popular.

» İstanbul's antique tram and funicular railways are novelties.

» On the Black Sea coast, a cable car climbs to Ordu's hilltop park.

Treats

» Turkey does sweet treats as well as it does kebaps – including baklava, *dondurma* (ice cream) and *lokum* (Turkish delight).

Planning

Accommodation

» Many hotels in all price ranges have family suites, which usually accommodate up to five.

» Cots are increasingly common; most hotels will at least organise one with advance notice.

» Many hotels in tourist areas can arrange some sort of babysitting service, but kids' clubs and agencies are rare.

Eating

» Children's menus are uncommon, but hotels and restaurants will often prepare special dishes for children.

» High chairs are by no means common, but increasingly widespread in tourist areas (apart from İstanbul).

Facilities

» Public baby-changing facilities are rare, but found in branches of the *kebapçı* (kebap restaurant) chain Kırçiçeği.

» Many Turkish women breastfeed their babies in public; no one is likely to mind you doing the same – as long as you are discreet (ie don't show any flesh).

» Seaside towns and cities often have playgrounds, but check the equipment for safety.

Getting Around

» Buses often do not have functioning toilets, although they normally stop every few hours.

» Free travel on public transport within cities and discounted tickets for longer journeys are common.

» Most car-rental companies can provide child-safety seats for a small extra charge.

» Dangerous drivers and uneven surfaces make using strollers an extreme sport.

» A 'baby backpack' is useful for walking around sights.

Health

» Consider giving children the BCG tuberculosis vaccine if they haven't had it.

» In hot, moist climates, any wound or break in the skin may lead to infection. The area should be cleaned and then kept dry and clean.

» Encourage your child to avoid dogs and other

mammals because of the risk of rabies and other diseases.

» For children and pregnant or breastfeeding women, double-check drugs and dosages prescribed for travel by doctors and pharmacists, as they may be unsuitable. The same applies to practitioners in Turkey.

» Some information on the suitability of drugs and recommended dosage can be found on travel-health websites.

» See p677 for further information.

Products

» Double-check the suitability of prescriptions your children are given while in Turkey.

» Pasteurised UHT milk is sold in cartons everywhere, but fresh milk is harder to find.

» Consider bringing a supply of baby food – what little you find here, your baby will likely find inedible – or it will just be mashed banana.

» Migros supermarkets have the best range of baby food.

» Most supermarkets stock formula (although it is very expensive) and vitamin-fortified rice cereal.

» Disposable *bebek bezi* (nappies or diapers) are readily available.

» The best nappies are Prima and Huggies, sold in pharmacies and supermarkets; don't bother with cheaper local brands.

Resources

» If you will be looking for childcare in Turkey, the Australian organisation **Child Wise** (www .childwise.net) offers general advice.

» Lonely Planet's *Travel with Children* has practical information and advice on how to make travel with children as stress-free as possible.

Safety

» In hotels and other buildings, look out for open power points.

» Many taps are unmarked and reversed (cold on the left, hot on the right).

On the street, watch for these especially:

» Turkey's notorious drivers, particularly those on pavement-mounting mopeds.

» Crudely covered electric mains.

» Open stairwells.

» Serious potholes.

» Open drains.

» Carelessly secured building sites.

regions at a glance

İstanbul

History ✓✓✓
Nightlife ✓✓✓
Shopping ✓✓✓

History
The megacity formerly known as Constantinople and Byzantium was the capital of a series of empires, all of which left their mark. The Aya Sofya, a church-turned-mosque-turned-museum, is the most famous remnant of the Byzantine Empire, and Ottoman landmarks include the Blue Mosque and Topkapı Palace. Everywhere you look on the hilly streets, history looks back at you.

Nightlife
Beyoğlu is an exhilarating melting pot where anything goes after dark. Between the dusk and dawn calls to prayer, up-for-it crowds swirl through rooftop bars, pedestrian precincts and clubs on the Bosphorus. From Sultanahmet, wander over the Galata Bridge – where you don't have to be a troll to duck under the bridge for a sundowner – then grab a nargile (traditional waterpipe) or an Efes beer and join the party.

Shopping
The city's bazaars are justly famous: the Grand Bazaar, with more than 2000 shops; the arty Arasta Bazaar's carpet and ceramics stores; and the Spice Bazaar, for vividly coloured spices, Turkish delight and dried fruits. There are markets and malls galore, including Kadıköy's food market on the Asian side, and the Wednesday market in the streets around Fatıh Mosque. Central neighbourhoods range from bohemian Çukurcuma, which specialises in antiques and collectables, to Tünel/Galata for avant-garde fashion.

p50

Thrace & Marmara

History ✓✓✓
Battlefields ✓✓✓
Architecture ✓

History
Turkey's northwest corner is famous for the Gallipoli (Gelibolu) Peninsula, the site of WWI battles, and Troy. Further north is Edirne, once capital of the Ottoman empire, and Gökçeada island, with its Greek heritage and slow-paced Aegean lifestyle.

Battlefields
Over 100,000 soldiers died on the now-tranquil Gallipoli Peninsula, a pilgrimage site for Australians, New Zealanders and Turks. Touring the memorials, battlefields and trenches that dot the beaches and hills is simply heart-wrenching.

Architecture
Edirne's Ottoman gems include Selimiye Camii, one of the finest works of the great architect Mimar Sinan. Gökçeada's hilltop villages are time capsules, with their tumbledown Greek houses, while Çanakkale's Ottoman old town is dotted with mosques, hamams and an imposing 19th-century clock tower.

p135

İzmir & the North Aegean

History ✓✓
Village Life ✓✓
Food ✓✓

History
The hilltop ruins of Pergamum are renowned as some of Turkey's finest. There are also numerous, less-visited sites along the Biga Peninsula and echoes of the population exchange with Greece in Ayvalık and Bozcaada town's old Greek quarters, and in the Ayvacık area's descendents of Turkmen nomads.

Village Life
In laid-back spots such as Bozcaada island, the Biga Peninsula, Behramkale, Ayvalık and Bergama, life has an alluringly slow rural pace. Changing seasons and weekly markets are still the main events.

Food
This is the place to try Aegean *balık* (fish) and rakı (aniseed brandy) on a seafront terrace. There's even a saying about one town's pescetarian excellence: 'rakı, *balık,* Ayvalık'.

p167

Ephesus, Bodrum & the South Aegean

History ✓✓✓
Nightlife ✓✓✓
Sun & Surf ✓✓✓

History
Romans once bustled along the Curetes Way at Ephesus, Turkey's most visited ruins. Less-frequented sites include Didyma – the Temple of Apollo here was once the world's largest temple, after Selçuk's Temple of Artemis – and eerie Priene, a hilltop Ionian city.

Nightlife
The tourist machine humming between Bodrum's palm trees has created a mean nightlife, with waterfront bar-clubs making the most of the twin bays. Another sexy sundowner spot is Türkbükü, summer playground of İstanbul's jet set.

Sun & Surf
Smiles beam on the yachts cruising Turkey's Côte d'Azur. The beaches in and around Bodrum are excellent for sunning, swimming and water sports; and the Datça and Bozburun Peninsulas hide secluded coves and azure waters.

p209

Western Anatolia

History ✓✓✓
Ruins ✓✓✓
Crafts ✓✓

History
Bursa was the Ottoman capital before Constantinople, İznik's imposing gateways remain from the days of the Byzantines, and the Phrygian Valley's rock-hewn monuments survive from the distant Phrygian era. Meanwhile, Eskişehir mixes its pastel-painted Ottoman quarter with today's lively cultural scene and nightlife.

Ruins
At Hierapolis, you can bathe among fluted marble columns. Quieter alternatives include Sagalassos, a ruined Pisidian-Hellenistic-Roman city backed by sheer rock, and Afrodisias, overgrown but grand.

Crafts
İznik is famous for its tiles; the floral beauties, a trademark of Ottoman architecture, are still made here. Kütahya has been renowned for porcelain and tiles since the early 16th century, and in Bursa's markets you can buy Karagöz shadow puppets and Bursa silk.

p270

Antalya & the Turquoise Coast

History ✓✓✓
Beaches ✓✓✓
Ruins ✓✓✓

History

The coves and valleys along the Turqoise Coast are layered with history. Its two waymarked paths, the Lycian Way and St Paul Trail, name-check historical folk. The former meanders across the Teke peninsula, littered with sepulchres and sarcophagi left millennia ago by the Lycians.

Beaches

Patara, Turkey's longest beach, and İztuzu Beach near Dalyan both shelter Lycian ruins and nesting sea turtles. Olympos is famed for its 'tree house' accommodation and naturally occurring flames of Chimaera. For solitude, take a high-suspension vehicle down to Kabak's cliff-flanked beach.

Ruins

The trademark funerary monuments of the Lycian civilisation still nestle in spectacular spots such as Xanthos and Pınara. Other gems include Antalya's Roman-Ottoman antique quarter and the two Roman bridges spanning the Köprülü Canyon.

p311

Eastern Mediterranean

History ✓✓
Food ✓✓
Christian Sites ✓✓✓

History

Open-air museums are a Turkish speciality; the one in Karatepe-Aslantaş National Park features the ruins of a summer retreat for neo-Hittite kings. History has a fairy-tale quality here: Maiden's Castle seemingly floats offshore, and Zeus is said to have imprisoned hydra-headed Typhon in the Cave-Gorge of Hell.

Food

Seafront fish restaurants abound on this stretch of the Mediterranean coast, which leads east to the Turkish and Arab culinary melting pot of Antakya. Influences from nearby Syria include lemon wedges and mint, which accompany kebaps and local specialities.

Christian Sites

The early Christian and Old Testament sites in Tarsus include St Paul's ruined house, where pilgrims come to drink from the well. Paul and Peter both preached in Antakya (the biblical Antioch), and St Thecla, patron saint of teachers, fasted in the grotto near Silifke.

p366

Ankara & Central Anatolia

History ✓✓
Architecture ✓✓
Ruins ✓✓✓

History

This is where the whirling dervishes first whirled, Atatürk began his revolution, Alexander the Great cut the Gordion knot, King Midas turned everything to gold, and Julius Caesar uttered his famous line: '*Veni, vidi, vici*' ('I came, I saw, I conquered').

Architecture

Both Amasya and Safranbolu are in the grip of 'Ottomania', with boutique hotels occupying their half-timbered, black-and-white houses. Konya's turquoise-domed Mevlâna Museum is a Turkish icon, and magnificent Seljuk caravanserais dot the steppe.

Ruins

Sturdy Hattuşa was the Hittite capital more than 3000 years ago. There are Pontic tombs in the cliffs above Amasya, and Gordion's Phrygian tomb (c 700 BC) might be the world's oldest wooden structure.

p397

Cappadocia

History ✓✓
Hiking ✓✓
Caves ✓✓✓

History

Cappadocia was a refuge for Byzantine Christians, who carved monastic settlements into the rock, left frescoes on the cave walls and hid from Islamic armies in underground cities. You can see all these relics and relive the area's history on horseback.

Hiking

This is one of Turkey's best regions for going walkabout, with options ranging from gentle saunters through the dreamy valleys to serious missions. South of leafy Ihlara Valley, 3628m Mt Hasan and the Ala Dağlar National Park are both challenging.

Caves

Cappadocia's *tuff* cliff faces and surreal fairy chimneys (rock formations) are riddled with caves. Some are occupied by centuries-old churches, others by full-time cave-dwellers. Many are open for guests to sample the troglodyte lifestyle.

p444

Black Sea Coast

History ✓✓✓
Local Secrets ✓✓
Scenery ✓✓

History

Anatolia's north coast was once the Kingdom of Pontus, and Ottoman Greeks tried to create a post-WWI Pontic state here. Impressive ruins include Sumela, the Byzantine monastery clinging to a cliff face, and Trabzon's 13th-century Aya Sofya church.

Local Experiences

The Black Sea (Karadeniz) offers experiences unknown to non-Turkish holidaymakers, such as sipping çay in tea-producing Rize, wandering Amasra and Sinop's ancient fortifications, and staying in Ordu and Ünye's old Greek and Armenian quarters.

Scenery

The *yaylalar* (mountain pastures) above towns such as Giresun and Ordu offer rugged scenery, as does the coastline west of Sinop. The winding road from Amasra to Sinop is Turkey's answer to California's Hwy 1, and there are more coastal vistas around Cape Yason.

p493

Northeastern Anatolia

History ✓✓✓
Outdoor Activities ✓✓✓
Slow Travel ✓✓✓

History

Romantic relics are squirreled away here. Medieval Armenian and Georgian churches and castles can be found near the ruin-strewn steppe at Ani. Further south near the Iranian border, the mountainside İshak Paşa Palace is an impressive example of 18th-century Ottoman architecture.

Outdoor Activities

There's a raft of activities here: Yusufeli is a whitewater rafting and trekking centre; hikers can head to the Kaçkar Mountains and Mt Ararat; and snow bunnies to Palandöken and Sarıkamış.

Slow Travel

To enjoy mountainous countryside at a mellow pace, head up to the *yaylalar* in the Kaçkar Mountains or northeast of Artvin. Nestled in the landscape are villages, ruins, traditional wooden houses and the beginning of the Caucasus region, which stretches east to the Caspian Sea and north to Russia.

p520

Southeastern Anatolia

History ✓✓✓
Food ✓✓✓
Architecture ✓✓✓

History

The many remains of past civilisations in southeastern Anatolia include Lake Van's island church, built by an Armenian king, the statues atop Mt Nemrut, and Şanlıurfa's neolithic Göbekli Tepe. A dam will soon submerge the historic village of Hasankeyf.

Food

With Kurdish and Arabic influences, the area's cuisine is a knockout. Top places to try local dishes are Gaziantep, with the planet's tastiest pistachio baklava, and Şanlıurfa, home of Urfa kebaps.

Architecture

There are stunning buildings in the region, including the Morgabriel and Deyrul Zafaran monasteries, which rise mirage-like from their rocky surroundings. Mystery-shrouded Şanlıurfa, Mardin's gold-coloured labyrinth of lanes, and basalt-walled Diyarbakır are also worth a visit.

p553

Every listing is recommended by our authors, and their favourite places are listed first

Look out for these icons:

 Our author's top recommendation

 A green or sustainable option

 No payment required

On the Road

İstanbul

POP 14 MILLION

Best Places to Eat

» Asmalı Cavit (p109)

» Lokanta Maya (p109)

» Zübeyir Ocakbaşı (p110)

» Meze by Lemon Tree (p110)

» Fatih Damak Pide (p107)

Best Places to Stay

» Hotel Ibrahim Pasha (p101)

» Sirkeci Konak (p101)

» Beş Oda (p104)

» Witt Istanbul Hotel (p104)

» Marmara Guesthouse (p101)

Why Go?

Some ancient cities are the sum of their monuments. But others, such as İstanbul, factor a lot more into the equation. Here, you can visit Byzantine churches and Ottoman mosques in the morning, shop in chic boutiques during the afternoon and party at glamorous nightclubs through the night. In the space of a few minutes you can hear the evocative strains of the call to prayer issuing from the Old City's tapering minarets, the sonorous horn of a crowded commuter ferry crossing between Europe and Asia, and the strident cries of a street hawker selling fresh seasonal produce. Put simply, this marvellous metropolis is an exercise in sensory seduction like no other.

Ask locals to describe what they love about İstanbul and they'll shrug, give a small smile and say merely that there is no other place like it. Spend a few days here, and you'll know exactly what they mean.

When to Go
İstanbul

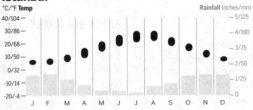

Apr Sunshine and balmy breezes usher in the colourful İstanbul Tulip Festival.

Jun & Jul Atmospheric venues around town host the high-profile Music and Jazz Festivals.

Sep Heat disperses and locals enjoy the season for *levrek* (bluefish), a favourite local fish.

History

BYZANTIUM

Legend tells us that the first historically significant settlement here was founded by Byzas, a colonist from Megara, a port city in Attica. Before leaving Greece, he asked the Delphic oracle where to locate his new colony and received the enigmatic answer: 'Opposite the blind'. When Byzas and his fellow colonists sailed up the Bosphorus in 657 BC, they noticed a small colony on the Asian shore at Chalcedon (modern-day Kadıköy). Looking left, they saw the superb natural harbour of the Golden Horn (Haliç) on the European shore. Thinking, 'Those people in Chalcedon must be blind', they settled on the opposite shore and named their new city Byzantium.

Byzantium submitted willingly to Rome and fought its battles for centuries. But it finally got caught out supporting the wrong side in a civil war. The winner, Septimius Severus, razed the city walls and took away its privileges in AD 196. When he relented and rebuilt the city, he named it Augusta Antonina.

CONSTANTINOPLE

Another struggle for control of the Roman Empire determined the city's fate for the next 1000 years. Emperor Constantine pursued his rival Licinius to Augusta Antonina, then across the Bosphorus to Chrysopolis (Üsküdar). Defeating his rival in 324, Constantine solidified his control and renamed Augusta Antonina 'New Rome'. He laid out a vast new city to serve as capital of his empire and inaugurated it with much pomp in 330.

Constantine died in 337, just seven years after the dedication of his new capital, but the city continued to grow under the rule of the emperors. Theodosius I ('the Great'; r 379–95) had a forum built on the present site of Beyazıt Meydanı (Beyazıt Square), while his son Theodosius II built his self-titled walls in 413 when the city was threatened by the marauding armies of Attila the Hun. Flattened by an earthquake in 447 and hastily rebuilt within two months, the Theodosian Walls still surround the Old City today.

Theodosius II died in 450 and was succeeded by a string of emperors, including the ambitious Justinian (r 527–65). Three years before taking the throne, Justinian had married Theodora, a strong-willed former courtesan. Together they further embellished Constantinople with great buildings, including the famous Aya Sofya, built in 537. Justinian's building projects and constant wars of reconquest exhausted his treasury and his empire. Following his reign, the Byzantine Empire would never again be as large, powerful or rich.

Much of ancient Constantinople's building stock remains, including churches, palaces, cisterns and the Hippodrome. In fact, there's more left than most people realise. Any excavation reveals ancient streets, mosaics, tunnels, water and sewage systems,

---

İSTANBUL IN...

Two Days

With only two days, you'll need to get cracking! On day one, visit the **Blue Mosque**, **Aya Sofya** and the **Basilica Cistern** in the morning and follow our walking tour of the **Grand Bazaar** in the afternoon. Enjoy dinner somewhere in Beyoğlu.

Day two should be devoted to **Topkapı Palace** and the Bosphorus. Spend the morning at the palace, then board one of the private excursion boats at Eminönü for a **Bosphorus cruise**. Afterwards, walk up through Galata to **İstiklal Caddesi**, have a drink at a **rooftop bar** and enjoy dinner at a **meyhane** (tavern).

Four Days

Follow the two-day itinerary, and on your third day visit the **İstanbul Archaeology Museums** or **Museum of Turkish & Islamic Arts** in the morning, and the **Süleymaniye Mosque** in the afternoon. For dinner, sample the succulent kebaps at **Hamdi** or **Zübeyir Ocakbaşı**. Day four should be devoted to a Golden Horn cruise; on your way back from Eyüp get off at Ayvansaray and walk uphill to visit the Byzantine mosaics and frescoes at the **Kariye Museum (Chora Church)**. Back in Sultanahmet, shop for souvenirs at the **Arasta Bazaar** before hitting the bar, restaurant and club scenes on the other side of Galata Bridge.

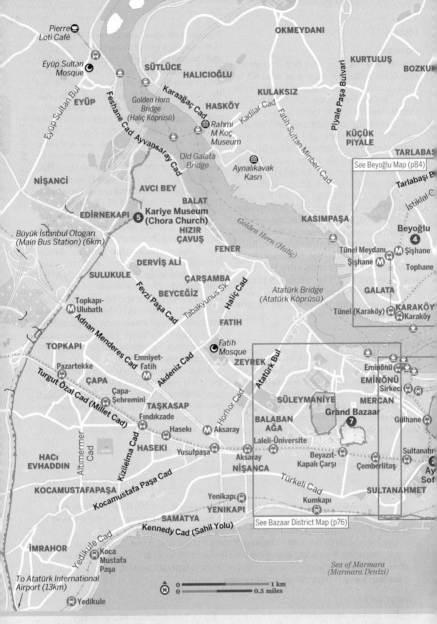

İstanbul Highlights

1 Uncover the secrets of the seraglio in opulent **Topkapı Palace** (p65)

2 Marvel at the interior of **Aya Sofya** (p56), one of the world's truly great buildings

3 Surrender to the steam in an Ottoman-era **hamam** (p95)

4 Head to **Beyoğlu** (p115) for drinks at a rooftop bar and dinner at a traditional *meyhane* (tavern)

5 Admire the extraordinary Byzantine mosaics at the **Kariye Museum** (Chora Church, p82)

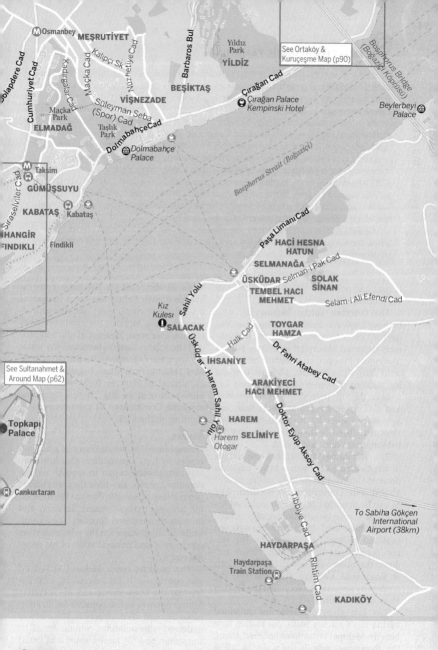

6 Take a **ferry trip** (p91) along the mighty Bosphorus, up the Golden Horn or to the Princes' Islands

7 Lose yourself in the hidden caravanserais and labyrinthine lanes of the **Grand Bazaar** (p74)

8 Contemplate the cutting edge at a **contemporary art gallery or cultural centre**

9 Kick back with the locals at a traditional **çay bahçesi** (tea garden)

ⓘ MUSEUM PASS İSTANBUL

Most visitors spend at least three days in İstanbul and cram as many museum visits as possible into their stay, so the recent introduction of this discount pass (www.muze.gov .tr/museum_pass) is most welcome. Valid for 72 hours from your first museum entry, it gives admission to Topkapı Palace and Harem, Aya Sofya, the Kariye Museum (Chora Church), the İstanbul Archaeology Museums, the Museum of Turkish and Islamic Arts and the Great Palace Mosaics Museum. Purchased individually, admission fees to these sights will cost ₺108, so the pass represents a saving of ₺36. Its biggest benefit is that it allows you to bypass ticket queues and make your way straight into the museums – something that is particularly useful when visiting ever-crowded Aya Sofya.

As well as giving entry to these government-operated museums, the pass also gives a 20% discount on entry to the privately run Rahmi M Koç Industrial Museum on the Golden Horn and a 30% discount on entry to the Sakıp Sabancı Museum on the Bosphorus, which is operated by the university of the same name.

The pass can be purchased from some hotels and also from the ticket offices at Aya Sofya, the Kariye Museum (Chora Church), Topkapı Palace and the İstanbul Archaeology Museums.

---

houses and public buildings buried beneath the modern city centre.

The Ottoman sultan Mehmet II, who became known as Fatih (meaning 'the Conqueror'), came to power in 1451 and immediately departed his capital in Edirne, aiming to conquer the once-great Byzantine city.

In four short months, Mehmet oversaw the building of Rumeli Hisarı (the great fortress on the European side of the Bosphorus) and also repaired Anadolu Hisarı, built half a century earlier by his great-grandfather Beyazıt I. Together these fortresses controlled the strait's narrowest point.

The Byzantines had closed the mouth of the Golden Horn with a heavy chain to prevent Ottoman boats from sailing in and attacking the city walls on the northern side. Not to be thwarted, Mehmet marshalled his boats at a cove (where Dolmabahçe Palace now stands) and had them transported overland by night on rollers, up the valley (present site of the Hilton Hotel) and down the other side into the Golden Horn at Kasımpaşa. Catching the Byzantine defenders by surprise, he soon had the Golden Horn under control.

The last great obstacle was provided by the city's mighty walls. No matter how heavily Mehmet's cannons battered them, the Byzantines rebuilt the walls by night and, come daybreak, the impetuous young sultan would find himself back where he'd started. Finally, he received a proposal from a Hungarian cannon founder called Urban who had come to help the Byzantine emperor defend Christendom against the in-fidels. Finding that the Byzantine emperor had no money, Urban was quick to discard his religious convictions and instead offered to make Mehmet the most enormous cannon ever seen. Mehmet gladly accepted and the mighty cannon breached the walls, allowing the Ottomans into the city. On 28 May 1453 the final attack began and by the evening of 29 May, the Turks were in complete control of the city. The last Byzantine emperor, Constantine XI Palaiologos, died fighting on the walls.

İSTANBUL

Seeing himself as the successor to great emperors such as Constantine and Justinian, Mehmet at once began to rebuild and repopulate the city. He chose the conspicuous promontory of Seraglio Point as the location for his ostentatious palace, Topkapı, and he also repaired and fortified Theodosius' walls. İstanbul was soon the administrative, commercial and cultural heart of his growing empire.

The building boom Mehmet kicked off was continued by his successors, with Süleyman the Magnificent and his architect Mimar Sinan being responsible for an enormous amount of construction. The city was endowed with buildings commissioned by the sultan and his family, court and grand viziers; these include the city's largest and grandest mosque, the Süleymaniye (1550). Later sultans also added mosques, and in the 19th century numerous palaces were built along the Bosphorus, among them Dolmabahçe.

As the Ottoman Empire grew to encompass the Middle East and North Africa as well as half of Eastern Europe, İstanbul became a fabulous melting pot of nationalities. On its streets people spoke Turkish, Greek, Armenian, Ladino, Russian, Arabic, Bulgarian, Romanian, Albanian, Italian, French, German, English and Maltese.

However, what had been the most civilised city on earth in the time of Süleyman eventually declined along with the Ottoman Empire, and by the 19th century İstanbul had lost much of its former glory. Nevertheless, it continued to be the 'Paris of the East' and, to affirm this, the first great international luxury express train, the famous *Orient Express,* connected İstanbul and the French capital in 1883.

After founding the Turkish Republic, Mustafa Kemal Atatürk decided to leave behind the imperial memories of İstanbul and set up his new government in Ankara, a city that could not be threatened by gunboats. Robbed of its status as the capital of a vast empire, İstanbul lost much of its wealth and atmosphere. The city's streets and neighbourhoods decayed, its infrastructure was neither maintained nor improved and virtually no economic development occurred.

The city stayed this way until the 1990s, when a renaissance took place. Since this time, public transport has been upgraded and continues to be improved, suburbs have been reinvigorated and parklands now line the waterways. When İstanbul won the right to become the European Capital of Culture in 2010, other ambitious projects were undertaken and many major buildings have benefited from painstaking restoration.

İstanbul's cultural transformation is just as marked. The seedy dives of Beyoğlu have been replaced by arty cafes, bars and boutiques, transforming the suburb into a bohemian hub. Galleries such as İstanbul Modern, ARTER, SALT and the Sakıp Sabancı Museum have opened, showcasing Turkey's contemporary art to the world. The live-music scene in the city has exploded, making İstanbul a buzzword for creative, energetic music with a unique East–West twist. And a new generation of artisans is refining and repositioning the city's traditional crafts industries – making for exciting and unexpected shopping experiences.

In short, İstanbul is a cosmopolitan and sophisticated megalopolis that has well and truly reclaimed its status as one of the world's truly great cities.

◉ Sights

The Bosphorus strait, between the Black and Marmara Seas, divides Europe from Asia and Anatolia. On its western shore, European İstanbul is further divided by the Golden Horn into the Old City (aka the Historical Peninsula) in the south and the New City in the north.

GREAT PALACE OF BYZANTIUM

Constantine the Great built this palace soon after he founded Constantinople in AD 324. Successive Byzantine leaders left their mark by adding to it, and the complex eventually consisted of hundreds of buildings enclosed by walls and set in terraced parklands stretching from the Hippodrome over to Aya Sofya and down the slope, ending at the sea walls and the Bucoleon Palace. The palace was finally abandoned after the Fourth Crusade sacked the city in 1204, and its ruins were pillaged and filled in after the Conquest, becoming mere foundations for much of Sultanahmet.

Various pieces of the Great Palace have been uncovered – many by budding hotelier 'archaeologists' – and an evocative stroll exploring the Byzantine substructure is a great way to spend an afternoon. The mosaics in the Great Palace Mosaic Museum (p60) once graced the floor of the complex and you can also walk past remnants of the **Bucoleon Palace** and **Magnaura Palace**.

Great Palace excavations at the **Sultanahmet Archaeological Park** (Map p62; Kabasakal Caddesi) southeast of Aya Sofya, have been ongoing since 1998 but had stalled due to controversy about some of the excavations being subsumed into a new extension of the neighbouring luxury Four Seasons Hotel.

For more information, check out www.byzantium1200.com, which has 3D images that bring ancient Byzantium to life, or purchase a copy of the lavishly illustrated guidebook, *Walking Through Byzantium: Great Palace Region,* which was also produced as part of the Byzantium 1200 project.

At the tip of the Historical Peninsula is Sultanahmet, the centre of İstanbul's Unesco-designated World Heritage Site. It's here that you'll find most of the city's famous monuments, including the Blue Mosque (Sultan Ahmet Camii), Aya Sofya and Topkapı Palace (Topkapı Sarayı). The adjoining area, with hotels to suit all budgets, is actually called Cankurtaran (*jan*-kur-tar-an), although if you say 'Sultanahmet' most people will understand where you mean.

Up the famous Divan Yolu boulevard from Sultanahmet you'll find the Grand Bazaar (Kapalı Çarşı). To its north is the Süleymaniye Mosque, which graces the top of one of the Old City's seven hills, and further on are the Western Districts. Downhill from the bazaar is the Golden Horn, home to the bustling transport hub of Eminönü.

Over Galata Bridge (Galata Köprüsü) from Eminönü is Beyoğlu, on the northern side of the Golden Horn. This is where you'll find some of the best restaurants, shops, bars and nightclubs in the city. It's also home to Taksim Meydanı, the heart of 'modern' İstanbul.

The city's glamour suburbs include Nişantaşı and Teşvikiye, north of Taksim Meydanı, and the suburbs lining the Bosphorus, especially those on the European side. However, many locals prefer to live on the Asian side. Üsküdar and Kadıköy are the two Asian hubs, reachable by a short ferry ride from Eminönü or a drive over Bosphorus Bridge.

SULTANAHMET & AROUND

It's not surprising that many visitors to İstanbul never make it out of Sultanahmet – after all, few cities have such a concentration of sights, shops, hotels and eateries within easy walking distance.

TOP CHOICE **Aya Sofya** MUSEUM

(Hagia Sophia; Map p62; www.ayasofyamuzesi.gov.tr; Aya Sofya Meydanı 1; adult/under 12yr ₺25/free; ☉9am-6pm Tue-Sun mid-Apr–Sep, to 4pm Oct–mid-Apr; ⛴Sultanahmet) There are many important monuments in İstanbul, but this venerable structure – commissioned by the great Byzantine emperor Justinian, consecrated as a church in 537, converted to a mosque by Mehmet the Conqueror in 1453 and declared a museum by Atatürk in 1935 – surpasses the rest due to its innovative architectural form, rich history, religious importance and extraordinary beauty.

Ground Floor

As you enter the building and walk into the inner narthex, look up to see a brilliant mosaic of *Christ as Pantocrator (Ruler of All)* above the third and largest door (the Imperial Door). Through this is the building's main space, famous for its dome, huge nave and gold mosaics.

The focal point at this level is the apse, with its magnificent 9th-century mosaic of

---

DON'T MISS

AYA SOFYA TOMBS

Part of the Aya Sofya complex but entered via Kabasakal Caddesi and thus often overlooked by tourists, these **tombs** (Aya Sofya Müzesi Padişah Türbeleri; Map p62; Kabasakal Caddesi; ☉9am-5pm; ⛴Sultanahmet) are the final resting places of five sultans – Mehmed III, Selim II, Murad III, İbrahim I and Mustafa I – most of whom are buried with members of their families. The ornate interior decoration in the tombs features the very best Ottoman tilework, calligraphy and decorative paintwork.

Mehmed's tomb dates from 1608 and Murad's tomb dates from 1599; both are adorned with particularly beautiful İznik tiles. Next to Murad's tomb is that of his five children; this was designed by Mimar Sinan and has simple but beautiful painted decoration.

Selim's tomb, which was designed by Sinan and built in 1577, is particularly poignant as it houses the graves of five of his sons, murdered on the same night in December 1574 to ensure the peaceful succession of the eldest, Murad III. It also houses the graves of 19 of Murad's sons, murdered in January 1595 to ensure Mehmet III's succession. They were the last of the royal princes to be murdered by their siblings – after this, the younger brothers of succeeding sultans were confined to the *kafes* (cage) in Topkapı Palace instead.

The fifth tomb is Aya Sofya's original baptistry, converted to a mausoleum for sultans İbrahim I and Mustafa I during the 17th century.

Aya Sofya

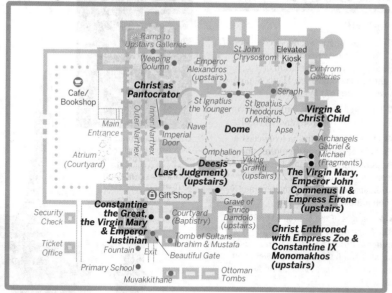

- Ramp to Upstairs Galleries
- Weeping Column
- Emperor Alexandros (upstairs)
- St John Chrysostom
- Elevated Kiosk
- Exit from Galleries
- Cafe/Bookshop
- **Christ as Pantocrator**
- Seraph
- St Ignatius the Younger
- St Ignatius Theodorus of Antioch
- **Virgin & Christ Child**
- Main Entrance
- Outer Narthex
- Inner Narthex
- Nave
- Imperial Door
- **Dome**
- Apse
- Archangels Gabriel & Michael (Fragments)
- Atrium (Courtyard)
- Omphalion
- Viking Graffiti (upstairs)
- **Deesis (Last Judgment) (upstairs)**
- **The Virgin Mary, Emperor John Comnenus II & Empress Eirene (upstairs)**
- Gift Shop
- Grave of Enrico Dandolo (upstairs)
- Security Check
- **Constantine the Great, the Virgin Mary & Emperor Justinian**
- Courtyard (Baptistry)
- **Christ Enthroned with Empress Zoe & Constantine IX Monomakhos (upstairs)**
- Ticket Office
- Tomb of Sultans İbrahim & Mustafa
- Fountain
- Exit
- Beautiful Gate
- Primary School
- Muvakkithane
- Ottoman Tombs

the *Virgin and Christ Child*. The mosaics above the apse once depicted the archangels Gabriel and Michael; today only fragments remain.

The Byzantine emperors were crowned while seated in a throne placed within the omphalion, the section of inlaid marble in the main floor.

Ottoman additions to the building include a *mimber* (pulpit) and *mihrab* (prayer niche indicating the direction of Mecca); large 19th-century medallions inscribed with gilt Arabic letters; a curious elevated kiosk known as the *hünkar mahfili*; and an ornate library behind the omphalion.

Looking up towards the northeast (to your left if you are facing the apse), you will see three mosaics at the base of the northern tympanum (semicircle) beneath the dome. These are 9th-century portraits of St Ignatius the Younger, St John Chrysostom and St Ignatius Theodorus of Antioch. To their right on one of the pendentives is a 14th-century mosaic of the face of a seraph (six-winged angel charged with the caretaking of God's throne).

In the side aisle to the northeast of the Imperial Door is a column with a worn copper facing pierced by a hole, known as the **Weeping Column**. Legend has it that the

pillar was blessed by St Gregory the Miracle Worker and that putting one's finger into the hole can lead to ailments being healed if the finger emerges moist.

Upstairs Galleries

To access the galleries, walk up the switch-back ramp at the northern end of the inner narthax. When you reach the top, you'll find a large circle of green marble marking the spot where the throne of the empress once stood.

In the south gallery (straight ahead and then left) are the remnants of a magnificent *Deesis (Last Judgment)*. This 13th-century mosaic depicts Christ with the Virgin Mary on his left and John the Baptist on his right.

Further on, at the eastern (apse) end of the gallery, is a 11th-century mosaic depicting *Christ Enthroned with Empress Zoe and Constantine IX Monomakhos*.

To the right of Zoe and Constantine is a 12th-century mosaic depicting *The Virgin Mary, Emperor John Comnenus II and Empress Eirene*. The emperor, who was known as 'John the Good', is on the Virgin's left and the empress, who was known for her charitable works, is to her right. Their son Alexius, who died soon after the portrait was made, is depicted next to Eirene.

Aya Sofya

TIMELINE

537 Emperor Justinian, depicted in one of the church's most famous mosaics **1** , presides over the consecration of Byzantium's new basilica, Hagia Sophia (Church of the Holy Wisdom).

557 The huge dome **2** , damaged during an earthquake, collapses and is rebuilt.

843 The second Byzantine Iconoclastic period ends and figurative mosaics begin to be added to the interior. These include a depiction of the Empress Zoe and her third husband, Emperor Constantine IX Monomakhos **3** .

1204 Soldiers of the Fourth Crusade led by the Doge of Venice, Enrico Dandolo, conquer and ransack Constantinople. Dandolo's tomb **4** is eventually erected in the church whose desecration he presided over.

1453 The city falls to the Ottomans; Mehmet II orders that Hagia Sophia be converted into a mosque and renamed Aya Sofya.

1577 Sultan Selim II is buried in a specially designed tomb, which sits alongside the tombs of four other Ottoman Sultans **5** in Aya Sofya's grounds.

1847–49 Sultan Abdül Mecit I orders that the building be restored and redecorated; the huge Ottoman Medallions **6** in the nave are added.

1935 The mosque is converted into a museum by order of Mustafa Kemal Atatürk, president of the new Turkish Republic.

2009 The face of one of the four seraphs **7** beneath the dome is uncovered during major restoration works in the nave.

2012 Restoration of the exterior walls and western upper gallery commences.

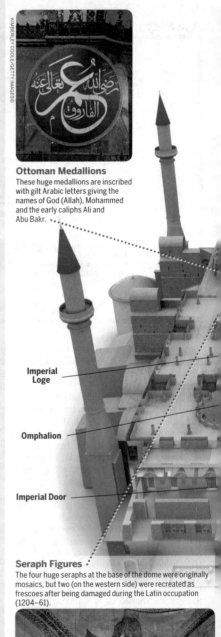

Ottoman Medallions
These huge medallions are inscribed with gilt Arabic letters giving the names of God (Allah), Mohammed and the early caliphs Ali and Abu Bakr.

Imperial Loge

Omphalion

Imperial Door

Seraph Figures
The four huge seraphs at the base of the dome were originally mosaics, but two (on the western side) were recreated as frescoes after being damaged during the Latin occupation (1204–61).

Dome

Soaring 56m from ground level, the dome was originally covered in gold mosaics but was decorated with calligraphy during the 1847–49 restoration works overseen by Swiss-born architects Gaspard and Giuseppe Fossati.

Christ Enthroned with Empress Zoe and Constantine IX Monomakhos

This mosaic portrait in the upper gallery depicts Zoe, one of only three Byzantine women to rule as empress in their own right.

Ottoman Tombs

The tombs of five Ottoman sultans and their families are located in Aya Sofya's southern corner and can be accessed via Kabasakal Caddesi. One of these occupies the church's original Baptistry.

Aya Sofya Tombs

Former Baptistry

Astronomer's House & Workshop

Grave of Enrico Dandolo

The Venetian doge died in 1205, only one year after he and his Crusaders had stormed the city. A 19th-century marker in the upper gallery indicates the probable location of his grave.

Exit

Ablutions Fountain

Primary School

Main Entrance

Constantine the Great, the Virgin Mary and the Emperor Justinian

This 11th-century mosaic shows Constantine (right) offering the Virgin Mary the city of Constantinople. Justinian (left) is offering her Hagia Sophia.

In the north gallery, look for the 10th-century mosaic portrait of the Emperor Alexandros.

Exiting the Building

Exit through the Beautiful Gate, a magnificent bronze gate dating from the 2nd century BC. As you leave the building, be sure to look back to admire the 10th-century mosaic of *Constantine the Great, the Virgin Mary and the Emperor Justinian* on the lunette of the inner doorway. Constantine (right) is offering the Virgin, who holds the Christ Child, the city of İstanbul; Justinian (left) is offering her Aya Sofya.

Just before you exit the building, there is a doorway on the left. This leads into a small courtyard that was once part of a 6th-century Baptistry. In the 17th century the Baptistry was converted into a tomb for Sultans Mustafa I and İbrahim I. The huge stone basin displayed in the courtyard is the original font.

On the opposite side of Aya Sofya Meydanı are the **Baths of Lady Hürrem** (Ayasofya Hürrem Sultan Hamamı), built between 1556 and 1557. Designed by Sinan, the hamam was commissioned by Süleyman the Magnificent in the name of his wife Hürrem Sultan, known to history as Roxelana.

Blue Mosque   MOSQUE

(Sultan Ahmet Camii; Map p62; Hippodrome; ⊙9am-12.15pm, 2-4.30pm & 5.30-6.30pm Sat-Thu, 9-11.15am, 2.30-4.30pm & 5.30-6.30pm Fri; ⊟Sultanahmet) İstanbul's most photogenic building was the grand project of Sultan Ahmet I (r 1603–17), whose **tomb** (Map p62; Kabasakal Caddesi; ⊙9.30am-4.30pm) is located on the north side of the site facing Sultanahmet Park. The mosque's wonderfully curvaceous exterior features a cascade of domes and six slender minarets. Blue İznik tiles adorn the interior and give the building its unofficial but commonly used name.

The mosque's architect, Sedefhar Mehmet Ağa, managed to orchestrate the sort of visual wham-bam effect with the mosque's exterior that Aya Sofya achieved with its interior. Its curves are voluptuous, it has six minarets and the courtyard is the biggest of all of the Ottoman mosques. The interior has a similarly grand scale: the İznik tiles number in the tens of thousands, there are 260 windows and the central prayer space is huge.

To best appreciate the mosque's design, enter the complex via the Hippodrome rather than from Sultanahmet Park. Once inside the courtyard, which is the same size as the mosque's interior, you'll appreciate the building's perfect proportions.

The mosque is such a popular attraction that admission is controlled so as to preserve its sacred atmosphere. Only worshippers are admitted through the main door; tourists must use the north door (follow the signs).

Great Palace Mosaic Museum   MUSEUM

(Map p73; Torun Sokak; admission ₺8; ⊙9am-6.30pm Tue-Sun Apr-Oct, to 4.30pm Nov-Mar; ⊟Sultanahmet) When archaeologists from the University of Ankara and the University of St Andrews (Scotland) excavated around the Arasta Bazaar at the rear of the Blue Mosque in the mid-1950s, they uncovered a stunning mosaic pavement featuring hunting and mythological scenes. Dating from early Byzantine times, it was restored from 1983 to 1997 and is now preserved in this museum.

Thought to have been added by Justinian to the Great Palace of Byzantium, the pavement is estimated to have measured from 3500 to 4000 sq metres in its original form. The 250-sq-metre section that is preserved here is the largest discovered remnant – the rest has been destroyed or remains buried underneath the Blue Mosque and surrounding shops and hotels.

The pavement is filled with bucolic imagery and has a gorgeous ribbon border with heart-shaped leaves. In the westernmost room is the most colourful and dramatic picture, that of two men in leggings carrying spears and holding off a raging tiger.

The museum has informative panels documenting the floor's rescue and renovation.

Hippodrome   PARK

(Atmeydanı; Map p62; ⊟Sultanahmet) The Byzantine Emperors loved nothing more than an afternoon at the chariot races, and this rectangular arena was their venue of choice. In its heyday, it was decorated by obelisks and statues, some of which remain in place today. Recently relandscaped, it is one of the city's most popular meeting places and promenades.

Originally the arena consisted of two levels of galleries, a central spine, starting boxes and the semicircular southern end known as the **Sphendone**, parts of which still stand. This, the only remaining built section of the Hippodrome, hints at how monumental the arena was. The level of galleries that once topped this section was damaged during the Fourth Crusade and totally dismantled in the Ottoman period – many of the original columns were used in construction of the Süleymaniye Mosque.

The Hippodrome was the centre of Byzantium's life for 1000 years and of Ottoman life for another 400 years and has been the scene of many popular uprisings. Despite this, emperors and sultans sought to outdo one another in beautifying it, adorning the centre with statues from the far reaches of their empire. Unfortunately, many priceless statues carved by ancient masters have disappeared from their original homes here. Chief among the villains responsible for such thefts were the soldiers of the Fourth Crusade, who invaded Constantinople, a Christian ally city, in 1204. After sacking Aya Sofya, they tore all the plates from the Rough-Stone Obelisk at the Hippodrome's southern end in the mistaken belief that they were solid gold (in fact, they were gold-covered bronze).

Near the northern end of the Hippodrome, the little gazebo in beautiful stonework is known as Kaiser Wilhelm's Fountain. The German emperor paid a state visit to Sultan Abdül Hamit II in 1901 and presented this fountain to the sultan and his people as a token of friendship.

The immaculately preserved pink granite Obelisk of Theodosius in the centre was carved in Egypt during the reign of Thutmose III (r 1549–1503 BC) and erected in the Amon-Re temple at Karnak. Theodosius the Great (r 379–95) had it brought from Egypt to Constantinople in AD 390. On the marble reliefs below the obelisk, look for the carvings of Theodosius, his wife, sons, state officials and bodyguards watching the chariot-race action from the *kathisma* (imperial box).

South of the obelisk is a strange column coming up out of a hole in the ground. Known as the Spiral Column, it was once much taller and was topped by three serpents' heads. Originally cast to commemorate a victory of the Hellenic confederation over the Persians in the battle of Plataea, it stood in front of the temple of Apollo at Delphi from 478 BC until Constantine the Great had it brought to his new capital city around AD 330. Though badly damaged in Byzantine times, the serpents' heads survived until the early 18th century. Now all that remains

of them is one upper jaw, housed in the İstanbul Archaeology Museums (p72).

TOP CHOICE **Museum of Turkish & Islamic Arts** MUSEUM

(Türk ve Islam Eserleri Müzesi; Map p62; www.tiem.gov.tr; Atmeydanı Caddesi 46; admission ₺10; ◷9am-6.30pm Tue-Sun Apr-Oct, to 4.30pm Nov-Mar; 🚇Sultanahmet) This Ottoman palace on the western edge of the Hippodrome was built in 1524 for İbrahim Paşa, childhood friend, brother-in-law and grand vizier of Süleyman the Magnificent. It's now home to a magnificent collection of artefacts, including exquisite examples of calligraphy and a collection of antique carpets that is generally held to be the best in the world.

Born in Greece, İbrahim Paşa was captured in that country as a child and sold as a slave into the imperial household in İstanbul. He worked as a page in Topkapı, where he became friendly with Süleyman, who was the same age. When his friend became sultan, İbrahim was made in turn chief falconer, chief of the royal bedchamber and grand vizier. This palace was bestowed on him by Süleyman the year before he was given the hand of Süleyman's sister, Hadice, in marriage. Alas, the fairy tale was not to last for poor İbrahim. His wealth, power and influence on the monarch became so great that others wishing to influence the sultan became envious, chief among them Süleyman's powerful wife, Haseki Hürrem Sultan (Roxelana). After a rival accused İbrahim of disloyalty, Roxelana convinced her husband that İbrahim was a threat and Süleyman had him strangled in 1536.

The museum's exhibits date from the 8th and 9th centuries up to the 19th century. Highlights include the superb calligraphy exhibits, with *müknames* (scrolls outlining an imperial decree) featuring the sultan's *tuğra* (monogram). Look out for the exquisite Iranian book binding from the Safavid period (1501–1786). And whatever you do, don't miss the extraordinary collection of carpets displayed in the *dîvânhane* (ceremonial hall) – it includes Holbein, Lotto, Konya, Uşhak, Iran and Caucasia examples. The lower floor of the museum houses ethnographic exhibits. Labels are in Turkish and English throughout.

While here, be sure to enjoy an expertly prepared Turkish coffee at Müzenin Kahvesi (p97) in the courtyard.

İSTANBUL

Sultanahmet & Around

Scale: 0 — 200 m / 0 — 0.1 miles

Bosphorus Excursion Ferry

Ferries to Üsküdar

Eminönü

9

EMİNÖNÜ

53

51

57

Şeyhülislam Hayri Efendi Cad

Yalı Köşkü Cad

Hamidiye Cad

Büyük Postane Cad

Ferries to Kadıköy

Car Ferry to Harem

SİRKECİ

Ankara Cad

Sirkeci

39

38

50

41

Hocapaşa Sk

Tourist Information Office (Sirkeci)

Sirkeci Train Station

İstasyon Arkası Sk

Nöbethane Cad

31

43

Ebussuud Cad

HOBYAR

Aşir Efendi Sk

Köprücü Sk

Cemal Nadir Sk

Ankara Cad

Hoca Han Sk

CAĞALOĞLU

Hükümet Konağı Sk

20

25

Cağaloğlu Yokuşu

Türkocağı Cad

Tasvir Sk

Şeref Efendi Sk

Mengene Sk

Hüdavendigar Cad

Taya Hatun Cad

33

Erdoğan Sk

Gülhane

15

1

6

9

5

Gülhane Park

Golden Horn (Haliç)

Kennedy Cad (Sahil Yolu)

Seraglio Point (Saray Burnu)

47

Topkapı Palace

Topkapı Palace Court of Janissaries (First Court)

İstanbul Archaeology Museums

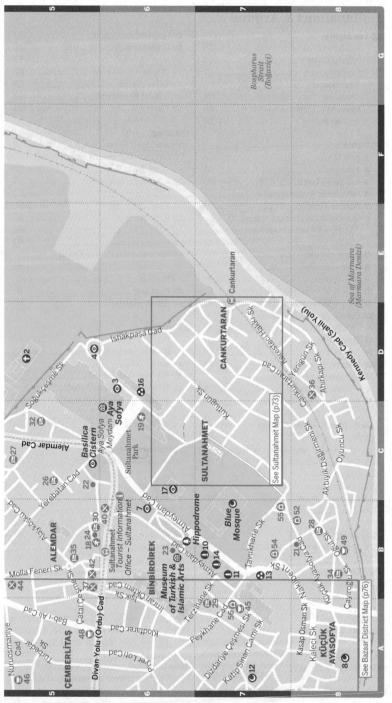

63

İSTANBUL

Bosphorus Strait (Boğaziçi)

Sea of Marmara (Marmara Denizi)

Kennedy Cad (Sahil Yolu)

Cankurtaran

CANKURTARAN

SULTANAHMET

See Sultanahmet Map (p73)

İshakpaşa Cad

Aya Sofya

Sultanahmet Park

Basilica Cistern

Meydanı Aya Sofya

Alemdar Cad

Yerebatan Cad

Soğukçeşme Sk

ÇEMBERLİTAŞ

ALEMDAR

BİNBİRDİREK

Museum of Turkish & Islamic Arts

Sultanahmet Tourist Information Office – Sultanahmet

Divan Yolu (Ordu) Cad

Nuruosmaniye Cad

Türbedar Sk

Çatal Çeşme Sk

Bab-ı Ali Cad

Işık Sk

İmran Öktem Cad

Klodfarer Cad

Piyer Loti Cad

Peykhane Cad

Dizdariye Çeşmesi Sk

Katip Sinan Cami Sk

Terzihane Sk

Atmeydanı Cad

Hippodrome

Blue Mosque

Tavukhane Sk

Nakilbent Sk

Küçük Ayasofya Cad

Kasap Osman Sk

Kaleci Sk

Çayıroğlu Sk

Oğul Sk

KÜÇÜK AYASOFYA

See Bazaar District Map (p76)

Akbıyık Değirmeni Sk

Oyuncu Sk

Ahırkapı Sk

İshakçeşme Hakkı Sk

Cankurtaran Cad

Küheylan Sk

Molla Feneri Sk

Kutlugün Sk

Sultanahmet & Around

Basilica Cistern   CISTERN

(Yerebatan Sarnıçı; Map p62; www.yerebatan.com; Yerebatan Caddesi 13; admission ₺10; ⊙9am-6.30pm; ⛿Sultanahmet) This subterranean structure was commissioned by Emperor Justinian and built in 532. The largest surviving Byzantine cistern in İstanbul, it was constructed using 336 columns, many of which were salvaged from ruined temples and feature fine carved capitals. Its symmetry and sheer grandeur of conception are quite breathtaking, and its cavernous depths make a great retreat on summer days.

Like most sites in İstanbul, the cistern has an unusual history. It was originally known as the Basilica Cistern because it lay underneath the Stoa Basilica, one of the great squares on the first hill. Designed to service the Great Palace and surrounding buildings, it was able to store up to 80,000 cu metres of water delivered via 20km of aqueducts from a reservoir near the Black Sea, but was closed when the Byzantine emperors relocated from the Great Palace. Forgotten by the city authorities some time before the Conquest, it wasn't rediscovered until 1545, when scholar Petrus Gyllius was researching Byzantine antiquities in the city and was told by local residents that they were able to miraculously obtain water by lowering buckets into a dark space below their basement floors. Some were even catching fish this way. Intrigued, Gyllius explored the neighbourhood and finally accessed the cistern through one of the basements. Even after his discovery, the Ottomans (who referred to the cistern as *Yerebatan Saray*) didn't treat the so-called Underground Palace with the respect it deserved – it became a dumping ground for all sorts of junk, as well as corpses.

The cistern was cleaned and renovated in 1985 by the İstanbul Metropolitan Municipality and opened to the public in 1987. It's now one of the city's most popular tourist attractions. Walking along its raised wooden platforms, you'll feel the water dripping from the vaulted ceiling and see schools of ghostly carp patrolling the water – it certainly has bucketloads (forgive the pun) of atmosphere.

TOP CHOICE **Topkapı Palace**　　　　PALACE

(Topkapı Sarayı; Map p62; www.topkapisarayi.gov.tr; Babıhümayun Caddesi; palace ₺25, Harem ₺15; ⊙9am-6pm Wed-Mon mid-Apr–Sep, to 4pm Oct–mid-Apr, Harem closes 4.30pm Apr-Oct, 3.30pm Nov-Mar; ⌐Sultanahmet) Topkapı is the subject of more colourful stories than most of the world's museums put together. Libidinous sultans, ambitious courtiers, beautiful concubines and scheming eunuchs lived and worked here between the 15th and 19th centuries when it was the court of the Ottoman empire. Visiting the palace's opulent pavilions, jewel-filled Treasury and sprawling Harem gives a fascinating glimpse into their lives.

Mehmet the Conqueror built the first stage of the palace shortly after the Conquest in 1453, and lived here until his death in 1481. Subsequent sultans lived in this rarefied environment until the 19th century, when they moved to the ostentatious European-style palaces they built on the shores of the Bosphorus.

Buy your tickets to the palace at the main ticket office just outside the gate to the Second Court. Guides to the palace congregate here, but charge a hefty €100 per small group for a one-hour tour, so many visitors instead choose to hire an audio guide with rudimentary commentary about the palace for ₺10. These are available at the audio booth just inside the turnstile entrance to the Second Court.

Before you enter the palace's Imperial Gate *(Bab-ı Hümayun)*, take a look at the ornate structure in the cobbled square just outside. This is the rococo-style **Fountain of Sultan Ahmet III**, built in 1728 by the sultan who so favoured tulips.

First Court

As you pass through the Imperial Gate, you enter the First Court, known as the Court of the Janissaries or the Parade Court. On your left is the Byzantine church of Hagia Eirene, more commonly known as **Aya İrini** (Church of the Divine Peace).

Second Court

The Middle Gate (*Ortakapı* or *Bab-üs Selâm*) led to the palace's Second Court, used for the business of running the empire. Only the sultan and the *valide sultan* (mother of the sultan) were allowed through the Middle Gate on horseback. Everyone else, including the grand vizier, had to dismount.

The Second Court has a beautiful parklike setting. Unlike typical European palaces, which feature one large building with outlying gardens, Topkapı is a series of pavilions, kitchens, barracks, audience chambers, kiosks and sleeping quarters built around a central enclosure.

The great **Palace Kitchens** on your right currently hold a small portion of Topkapı's vast collection of Chinese celadon porcelain, valued by the sultans for its beauty but also because it was reputed to change colour if touched by poisoned food.

On the left (west) side of the Second Court is the ornate **Imperial Council Chamber**. The imperial *dîvân* (council) met in the chamber to discuss matters of state while the sultan eavesdropped through a grille high on the wall.

Topkapı Palace (Topkapı Sarayı)

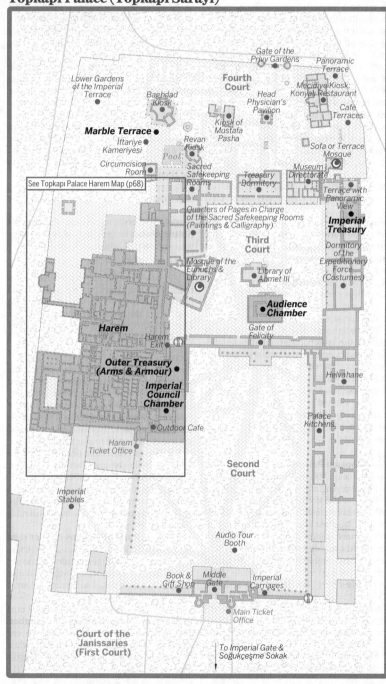

Gate of the
Privy Gardens

Panoramic
Terrace

Lower Gardens
of the Imperial
Terrace

**Fourth
Court**

Head
Physician's
Pavilion

Mecidiye Kiosk;
Konyalı Restaurant

Baghdad
Kiosk

Cafe
Terraces

Marble Terrace ●

Kiosk of
Mustafa
Pasha

İftariye ●
Kameriyesi

Revan
Kiosk

Sofa or Terrace
Mosque

Circumcision
Room

Pool

Sacred
Safekeeping
Rooms

Treasury
Dormitory

Museum
Directorate

Terrace with
Panoramic
View

See Topkapı Palace Harem Map (p68)

Quarters of Pages in Charge
of the Sacred Safekeeping Rooms
(Paintings & Calligraphy)

**Imperial
Treasury**

**Third
Court**

Dormitory
of the
Expeditionary
Force
(Costumes)

Mosque of the
Eunuchs &
Library

Library of
Ahmet III

Harem

**Audience
Chamber**

Harem ●
Exit

Gate of
Felicity

**Outer Treasury
(Arms & Armour)** ●

Helvahane

**Imperial
Council
Chamber** ●

● Outdoor Cafe

Palace
Kitchens

Harem
Ticket Office

**Second
Court**

Imperial
Stables

Audio Tour
Booth

Book &
Gift Shop

Middle
Gate

Imperial
Carriages

● Main Ticket
Office

**Court of the
Janissaries
(First Court)**

↓ To Imperial Gate &
Soğukçeşme Sokak

North of the Imperial Council Chamber is the **Outer Treasury**, where an impressive collection of Ottoman and European arms and armour is displayed.

Harem

The entrance to the Harem is beneath the Tower of Justice on the western side of the Second Court. If you decide to visit – and we highly recommend that you do – you'll need to buy a dedicated ticket from the Harem ticket office.

As popular belief would have it, the Harem was a place where the sultan could engage in debauchery at will (and Murat III did, after all, have 112 children!). In more prosaic reality, these were the imperial family quarters, and every detail of harem life was governed by tradition, obligation and ceremony. The word *'harem'* literally means 'private'.

The sultans supported as many as 300 concubines, although numbers were usually lower than this. Upon entering the harem, these girls would be schooled in Islam and in Turkish culture and language, as well as the arts of make-up, dress, comportment, music, reading, writing, embroidery and dancing. They then entered a meritocracy, first as ladies-in-waiting to the sultan's concubines and children, then to the *valide sultan* and finally – if they were particularly attractive and talented – to the sultan himself.

The sultan was allowed by Islamic law to have four legitimate wives, who received the title of *kadın* (wife). If a wife bore him a son she was called *haseki sultan*; *haseki kadın* if it was a daughter. The Ottoman dynasty did not observe primogeniture (the right of the first-born son to the throne), so in principle the throne was available to any imperial son. In the early years of the empire, this meant that death of a sultan regularly resulted in a fratricidal bloodbath as his sons – often from different mothers – battled it out among themselves for the throne. Later sultans imprisoned their brothers in the Harem, beginning the tradition of *kafes hayatı* (cage life).

The earliest of the 300-odd rooms in the Harem were constructed during the reign of Murat III (r 1574–95); the harems of previous sultans were at the Eski Saray (Old Palace), near current-day Beyazıt Meydanı.

The Harem complex has six floors, but only one of these can be visited. This is approached via the Carriage Gate. Inside the gate is the Dome with Cupboards. Beyond it is a room where the harem's eunuch guards were stationed. This is decorated with fine Kütahya tiles from the 17th century.

Beyond this room is the narrow Courtyard of the Black Eunuchs, also decorated with Kütahya tiles. Behind the marble colonnade on the left are the Black Eunuchs' Dormitories. In the early days white eunuchs were used, but black eunuchs sent as presents by the Ottoman governor of Egypt later took control. As many as 200 lived here, guarding the doors and waiting on the women of the harem.

At the far end of the courtyard is the Main Gate into the Harem, as well as a guard room featuring two gigantic gilded mirrors. From this, a corridor on the left leads to the Courtyard of the Women Servants and Consorts. This is surrounded by baths, a fountain, a laundry, dormitories and private apartments.

Further on is **Sultan Ahmet's Kiosk**, decorated with a tiled chimney, followed by the **Apartments of the Valide Sultan**, the centre of power in the Harem. From these ornate rooms the *valide sultan* oversaw and controlled her huge 'family'. Of particular note is the the **Salon of the Valide** with its lovely 19th-century murals featuring bucolic views of İstanbul.

Past the adjoining Courtyard of the Valide is a reception room with a large fireplace that leads to a vestibule covered in Kütahya and İznik tiles dating from the 17th century. This is where the princes, *valide sultans* and senior concubines waited before entering the handsome **Imperial Hall** for an audience with the sultan.

Nearby is the **Privy Chamber of Murat III**, one of the most sumptuous rooms in the palace. Dating from 1578, virtually all of its decoration is original. The three-tiered marble fountain was designed to give the sound of cascading water and to make it difficult to eavesdrop on the sultan's conversations. The gilded canopied seating areas are later 18th-century additions.

Take the left door in the Privy Chamber of Murat III to access the **Privy Chamber of Ahmed III** and an adjoining dining room built in 1705. This exquisite space is lined with wooden panels decorated with images of flowers and fruits painted in lacquer.

Northeast (through the door to the right) are two of the most beautiful rooms in the Harem – the **Twin Kiosk**. These two rooms date from around 1600 and were the

Topkapı Palace Harem

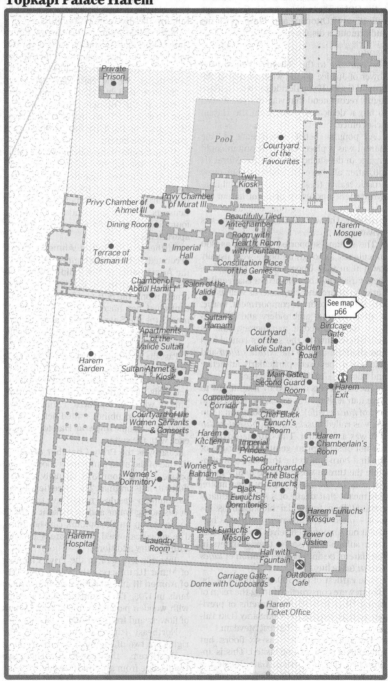

Private Prison

Pool

Courtyard of the Favourites

Twin Kiosk

Privy Chamber of Murat III

Privy Chamber of Ahmet III

Dining Room

Beautifully Tiled Antechamber

Room with Hearth; Room with Fountain

Harem Mosque

Imperial Hall

Terrace of Osman III

Consultation Place of the Genies

Chamber of Abdül Hamit

Salon of the Valide

See map p66

Sultan's Hamam

Apartments of the Valide Sultan

Courtyard of the Valide Sultan

Birdcage Gate

Golden Road

Harem Garden

Sultan Ahmet's Kiosk

Main Gate; Second Guard Room

Harem Exit

Concubines Corridor

Chief Black Eunuch's Room

Courtyard of the Women Servants & Consorts

Harem Kitchen

Imperial Princes School

Harem Chamberlain's Room

Women's Hamam

Courtyard of the Black Eunuchs

Women's Dormitory

Black Eunuchs Dormitories

Harem Eunuchs' Mosque

Harem Hospital

Laundry Room

Black Eunuchs' Mosque

Tower of Justice

Hall with Fountain

Carriage Gate; Dome with Cupboards

Outdoor Cafe

Harem Ticket Office

apartments of the crown prince; note the painted canvas dome in the first room and the fine İznik tile panels above the fireplace in the second.

On the other side of the Twin Kiosk is the **Courtyard of the Favourites**. Over the edge of the courtyard (really a terrace) you'll see a large pool. Just past the courtyard (but on the floor above) are the many small dark rooms that comprised the *kafes* where brothers or sons of the sultan were imprisoned.

From here, a corridor leads east to a passage known as the Golden Road and then out into the palace's Third Court.

Note that the visitor route through the Harem changes when rooms are closed for restoration or stabilisation, so some of the areas mentioned here may not be open during your visit.

Third Court

The Third Court is entered through the **Gate of Felicity**. The sultan's private domain, it was staffed and guarded by white eunuchs. Inside is the **Audience Chamber**, constructed in the 16th century but refurbished in the 18th century. Important officials and foreign ambassadors were brought to this little kiosk to conduct the high business of state. The sultan, seated on the divans whose cushions are embroidered with over 15,000 seed pearls, inspected the ambassadors' gifts and offerings as they were passed through the small doorway on the left.

Right behind the Audience Chamber is the pretty **Library of Ahmet III**, built in 1719.

On the eastern edge of the Third Court is the **Dormitory of the Expeditionary Force**, which now houses a rich collection of imperial robes, kaftans and uniforms worked in silver and gold thread. Also here is a fascinating collection of talismanic shirts, which were believed to protect the wearer from enemies and misfortunes of all kinds.

On the other side of the Third Court are the **Sacred Safekeeping Rooms**. These rooms, sumptuously decorated with İznik tiles, house many relics of the Prophet. When the sultans lived here, the rooms were opened only once a year so that the imperial family could pay homage to the memory of the Prophet on the 15th day of the holy month of Ramazan.

Next to the sacred Safekeeping Rooms is the **Dormitory of the Privy Chamber**, which houses an exhibit of portraits of 36 sultans. It includes a copy of Gentile Bellini's portrait of Mehmet the Conqueror (the original is in London's National Gallery) and a wonderful painting of the Enthronment Ceremony of Sultan Selim III (1789).

Treasury

Located on the eastern edge of the Third Court, Topkapı's Treasury features an incredible collection of objects made from or decorated with gold, silver, rubies, emeralds, jade, pearls and diamonds. The building itself was constructed during Mehmet the Conqueror's reign in 1460 and was used originally as reception rooms.

In the first room, look for the jewel-encrusted Sword of Süleyman the Magnificent and the Throne of Ahmed I, which is inlaid with mother-of-pearl and was designed by Sedefhar Mehmet Ağa, architect of the Blue Mosque. The Treasury's most famous exhibit, the Topkapı Dagger, is in the fourth room. The object of the criminal heist in Jules Dassin's 1963 film *Topkapi,* the dagger features three enormous emeralds on the hilt and a watch set into the pommel. Near it is the *Kaşıkçı* (Spoonmaker's) Diamond, a teardrop-shaped 86-carat rock surrounded by dozens of smaller stones. First worn by Mehmet IV at his accession to the throne in 1648, it's the world's fifth-largest diamond.

Before leaving the Treasury, be sure to admire the view of the Bosphorus from its terrace.

Fourth Court

Pleasure pavilions occupy the palace's Fourth Court. These include the **Mecidiye Köşkü**, which was built by Abdül Mecit (r 1839–61) according to 19th-century European models. Beneath this is the Konyalı restaurant, which serves cafeteria food at restaurant prices. West of the Mecidiye Köşkü is the Head Physician's Pavilion. Interestingly, the head physician was always one of the sultan's Jewish subjects. Nearby, you'll see the Kiosk of Mustafa Pasha, sometimes called the Sofa Köşkü. During the reign of Ahmet III, the Tulip Garden outside the kiosk was filled with the latest varieties of the flower.

Up the stairs at the end of the Tulip Garden is the **Marble Terrace**, a platform with a decorative pool, three pavilions and the whimsical İftariye Kameriyesi, a small structure commissioned by İbrahim the Crazy in 1640 as a picturesque place to break the fast of Ramazan.

Topkapı Palace

DAILY LIFE IN THE IMPERIAL COURT

A visit to this opulent palace compound, with its courtyards, harem and pavilions, offers a fascinating glimpse into the lives of the Ottoman sultans. During its heyday, royal wives and children, concubines, eunuchs and servants were among the 4000 people living within Topkapı's walls.

The sultans and their families rarely left the palace grounds, relying on courtiers and diplomats to bring them news of the outside world. Most visitors would go straight to the magnificent Imperial Council Chamber **1**, where the sultan's grand vizier and *dîvân* (council) regularly met to discuss affairs of state and receive foreign dignitaries. Many of these visitors brought lavish gifts and tributes to embellish the Imperial Treasury **2**.

After receiving any guests and meeting with the *dîvân*, the grand vizier would make his way through the ornate Gate of Felicity **3** into the Third Court, the palace's residential quarter. Here, he would brief the sultan on the deliberations and decisions of the *dîvân* in the ornate Audience Chamber **4**.

Meanwhile, day-to-day domestic chores and intrigues would be underway in the Harem **5** and servants would be preparing feasts in the massive Palace Kitchens **6**. Amid all this activity, the Marble Terrace **7** was a tranquil retreat where the sultan would come to relax, look out over the city and perhaps regret his sequestered lifestyle.

DON'T MISS

» There are spectacular views from the terrace behind the Imperial Treasury and from the Marble Terrace in the Fourth Court.

Harem
The sultan, his mother and the crown prince had sumptuously decorated private apartments in the harem. The most beautiful of these are the Twin Kiosks (pictured), which were used by the crown prince.

Harem Ticket Office

Middle Gate

Aya İrini

Imperial Gate

Imperial Council Chamber
This is where the Dîvân (Council) made laws, citizens presented petitions and foreign dignitaries were presented to the court. The sultan sometimes eavesdropped on proceedings through the window with the golden grill.

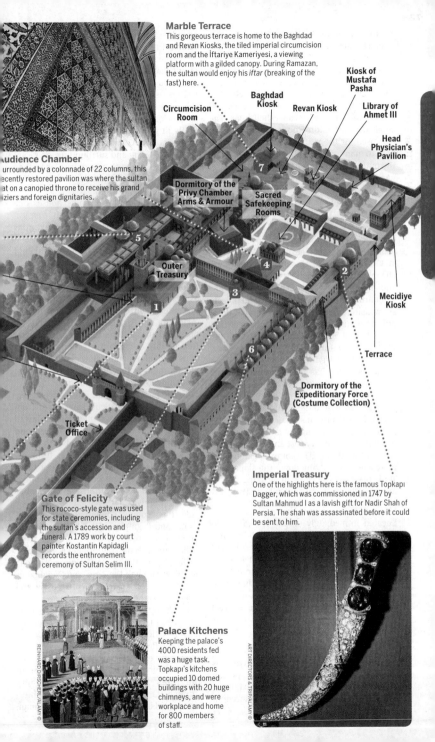

Marble Terrace
This gorgeous terrace is home to the Baghdad and Revan Kiosks, the tiled imperial circumcision room and the İftariye Kameriyesi, a viewing platform with a gilded canopy. During Ramazan, the sultan would enjoy his *iftar* (breaking of the fast) here.

Kiosk of Mustafa Pasha

Baghdad Kiosk

Revan Kiosk

Circumcision Room

Library of Ahmet III

Head Physician's Pavilion

Audience Chamber
Surrounded by a colonnade of 22 columns, this recently restored pavilion was where the sultan sat on a canopied throne to receive his grand viziers and foreign dignitaries.

Dormitory of the Privy Chamber Arms & Armour

Sacred Safekeeping Rooms

Outer Treasury

Mecidiye Kiosk

Ticket Office

Terrace

Dormitory of the Expeditionary Force (Costume Collection)

Gate of Felicity
This rococo-style gate was used for state ceremonies, including the sultan's accession and funeral. A 1789 work by court painter Kostantin Kapidagli records the enthronement ceremony of Sultan Selim III.

Imperial Treasury
One of the highlights here is the famous Topkapı Dagger, which was commissioned in 1747 by Sultan Mahmud I as a lavish gift for Nadir Shah of Persia. The shah was assassinated before it could be sent to him.

Palace Kitchens
Keeping the palace's 4000 residents fed was a huge task. Topkapı's kitchens occupied 10 domed buildings with 20 huge chimneys, and were workplace and home for 800 members of staff.

Murat IV built the **Revan Kiosk** in 1636 after reclaiming the city of Yerevan (now in Armenia) from Persia. In 1639 he constructed the **Baghdad Kiosk**, one of the last examples of classical palace architecture, to commemorate his victory over that city. Notice its superb İznik tiles, painted ceiling and mother-of-pearl and tortoiseshell inlay. The small **Circumcision Room** (Sünnet Odası) was used for the ritual that admits Muslim boys to manhood. Built by İbrahim I in 1640, the outer walls of the chamber are graced by particularly beautiful tile panels.

TOP CHOICE **İstanbul**

Archaeology Museums MUSEUM

(Map p62; www.istanbularkeoloji.gov.tr; Osman Hamdi Bey Yokuşu, Gülhane; admission ₺10; ⊗9am-6pm Tue-Sun mid-Apr–Sep, till 4pm Oct–mid-Apr; ⬚Gülhane) This superb museum houses archaeological and artistic treasures from the Topkapı collections. Its exhibits include ancient artefacts, classical statuary and objects showcasing Anatolian history. Though there are many highlights, history buffs will find the 'İstanbul Through the Ages' exhibition, which focuses on the city's Byzantine past, particularly satisfying.

The complex has three main parts: the Archaeology Museum (Arkeoloji Müzesi), the Museum of the Ancient Orient (Eski Şark Eserler Müzesi) and the Tiled Pavilion (Çinili Köşk). These museums house the palace collections formed during the late 19th century by museum director, artist and archaeologist Osman Hamdi Bey. The complex can be easily reached by walking down the slope from Topkapı's First Court, or by walking up the hill from the main gate of Gülhane Park.

Museum of the Ancient Orient

Located immediately on the left after you enter the complex, this 1883 building has a collection of pre-Islamic items collected from the expanse of the Ottoman Empire. Highlights include a series of large blue-and-yellow glazed-brick panels that once lined the processional street and the Ishtar gate of ancient Babylon. These depict real and mythical animals such as lions, dragons and bulls.

Archaeology Museum

On the opposite side of the courtyard is the heart of the complex, an imposing neoclassical building housing an extensive collection of classical statuary and sarcoph-agi plus a sprawling exhibit documenting İstanbul's history.

A Roman statue of Bes, an impish half-god of inexhaustible power and strength who was thought to protect against evil, greets visitors as they enter the main entrance of the museum. To its left, past the museum shop, cloakroom and small cafe, are two dimly lit rooms where the museum's major treasures – sarcophagi from the Royal Necropolis of Sidon and surrounding area – are displayed. These sarcophagi were unearthed in 1887 by Osman Hamdi Bey in Sidon (Side in modern-day Lebanon).

The second of these rooms houses one of the most accomplished of all classical artworks, the famous marble **Alexander Sarcophagus** – so named not because it belonged to the Macedonian general, but because it depicts him among his army battling the Persians, who were led by King Abdalonymos (whose sarcophagus it was). Truly exquisite, the sarcophagus is carved out of Pentelic marble and dates from the last quarter of the 4th century BC. Alexander, on horseback, has a lion's head as a headdress. Remarkably, the sculpture retains remnants of its original red-and-yellow paintwork. Also in this room is the stark and very moving **Mourning Women Sarcophagus**.

In the next room is an impressive collection of ancient grave-cult sarcophagi from Syria, Lebanon, Thessalonica and Ephesus. Beyond that is a room called the **Columned Sarcophagi of Anatolia**, filled with amazingly detailed sarcophagi dating from between AD 140 and AD 270. Many of these look like tiny temples or residential buildings; don't miss the **Sidamara Sarcophagus** from Konya.

Further rooms contain Lycian monuments and examples of Anatolian architecture from antiquity.

Back towards the statue of Bes is a staircase leading up to the underwhelming 'Anatolia and Troy Through the Ages' and 'Neighbouring Cultures of Anatolia, Cyprus, Syria and Palestine' exhibitions.

On the other side of Bes are the museum's famed Statuary Galleries, which were closed for renovation at the time of publication.

On the floor above the Statuary Galleries (accessed behind the cloakroom) is a fascinating exhibition called **İstanbul Through the Ages** that traces the city's history through its neighbourhoods during different periods: Archaic, Hellenistic, Roman,

Sultanahmet

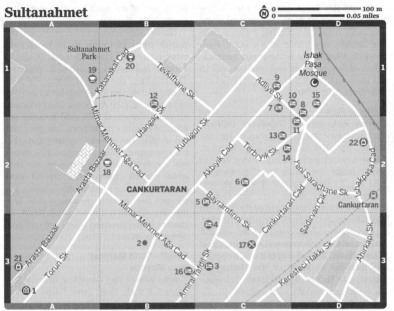

Sultanahmet

Byzantine and Ottoman. The exhibition continues downstairs, where there is an impressive gallery showcasing Byzantine artefacts.

Tiled Pavilion

The last of the complex's museum buildings is the Tiled Pavilion of Sultan Mehmet the Conqueror. Built in 1472 as an outer pavilion of Topkapı Palace, it was originally used for watching sporting events. The portico,

with its 14 marble columns, was constructed during the reign of Abdülhamid I (1774–89) after the original one burned down in 1737.

On display here is the best collection of Seljuk, Anatolian and Ottoman tiles and ceramics in the country; these date from the end of the 12th century to the beginning of the 20th century. The collection includes İznik tiles from the period between the mid-14th and 17th centuries when that city produced the finest coloured tiles in the world. When you enter the central room you can't miss the stunning *mihrab* from the İbrahim Bey İmâret in Karaman, built in 1432. Also of note is the pretty peacock-adorned fountain recessed into the wall in the room to the left at the back of the kiosk; this dates from 1590.

Gülhane Park
PARK

(Gülhane Parkı; Map p62; 🚇Gülhane) Gülhane Park was once the outer garden of Topkapı Palace, accessed only by the royal court. These days, crowds of locals come here to picnic under the many trees, promenade past the formally planted flowerbeds and enjoy wonderful views over the Golden Horn and Sea of Marmara from the Set Üstü Çay Bahçesi on the park's northeastern edge.

Recent beautification works have seen improvements to walkways and amenities, and have included the opening of a new museum, the **İstanbul Museum of the History of Science & Technology in Islam** (admission ₺5; ⏰9am-5pm Wed-Mon). Of interest to science buffs, the didactic exhibition argues that Islamic advances in science and technology preceded and greatly influenced those in Europe. Most of the exhibits are reconstructions of historical instruments and tools.

Next to the park's southern entrance is a bulbous little kiosk built into the park wall. Known as the **Alay Köşkü** (Parade Kiosk), this is where the sultan would sit and watch the periodic parades of troops and trade guilds that commemorated great holidays and military victories. It is now the İstanbul headquarters of the Ministry of Culture and Tourism.

Across the street and 100m northwest of the park's main gate is an outrageously curvaceous rococo gate leading into the precincts of what was once the grand vizierate, or Ottoman prime ministry, known in the West as the **Sublime Porte**. Today the buildings beyond the gate hold various offices of the İstanbul provincial government (the Vilayeti).

FREE Little Aya Sofya
MOSQUE

(Küçük Aya Sofya Camii, SS Sergius & Bacchus Church; Map p62; Küçük Ayasofya Caddesi; 🚇Sultanahmet or Çemberlitaş) Justinian and his wife Theodora built this little church sometime between AD 527 and 536, just before Justinian built Aya Sofya. You can still see their monogram worked into some of the frilly white capitals. Recently restored, the build-ing is one of the most beautiful Byzantine structures in the city.

Named after Sergius and Bacchus, the two patron saints of Christians in the Roman army, it has been known as Little (Küçük in Turkish) Aya Sofya for much of its existence. The building's dome is architecturally noteworthy and its plan – an irregular octagon – is quite unusual. Like Aya Sofya, its interior was originally decorated with gold mosaics and featured columns made from fine green and red marble. The mosaics are long gone, but the impressive columns remain. The church was converted into a mosque by the chief white eunuch Hüseyin Ağa around 1500; his tomb is to the north of the building. The minaret and *medrese* (seminary) date from this time. There's a tranquil *çay bahçesi* (tea garden) in the forecourt where you can relax over a glass of tea.

Sokollu Şehit Mehmet Paşa Mosque
MOSQUE

(Sokollu Mehmet Paşa Camii; Map p62; cnr Şehit Çeşmesi & Katip Sinan Camii Sokaks, Kadırga; 🚇Sultanahmet or Çemberlitaş) Sinan designed this mosque in 1571, at the height of his architectural career. Besides its architectural harmony, the mosque is unusual because the *medrese* is not a separate building but actually part of the mosque structure, built around the forecourt. The interior is decorated with spectacular red-and-blue İznik tiles – some of the best ever made.

BAZAAR DISTRICT

Crowned by the city's first and most evocative shopping mall – the famous Grand Bazaar – the bazaar district is also home to two of the grandest of all Ottoman buildings, the Süleymaniye and Beyazıt Mosques.

TOP CHOICE Grand Bazaar
MARKET

(Kapalı Çarşı, Covered Market; www.kapalicarsi.org.tr; ⏰9am-7pm Mon-Sat; 🚇Beyazıt-Kapalı Çarşı) This colourful and chaotic bazaar is the heart of the Old City and has been so for centuries. Starting as a small vaulted *bedesten* (warehouse) built by order of Mehmet the Conqueror in 1461, it grew to cover a vast area as laneways between the *bedesten*, neighbouring shops and *hans* (caravanserais) were roofed and the market assumed the sprawling, labyrinthine form that it retains today.

When here, be sure to peep through doorways to discover hidden *hans*, veer down narrow laneways to watch artisans at work and wander the main thoroughfares

THE GREAT SİNAN

Sultan Süleyman the Magnificent's reign is known as the golden age of the Ottoman Empire, in part due to his penchant for embellishing İstanbul with architectural wonders. Most of these monuments were designed by architect Mimar Sinan, who managed to perfect the design of the classic Ottoman mosque.

Born in 1497, Sinan was a recruit to the *devşirme,* the annual intake of Christian youths into the *janizaries* (Ottoman army). He became a Muslim (as all such recruits did) and eventually took up a post as a military engineer in the corps. Süleyman appointed him the chief of the imperial architects in 1538. Sinan designed a total of 321 buildings, 85 of which are still standing in İstanbul.

Most Sinan-designed mosques have a large forecourt with a central *şadırvan* (ablutions fountain) and domed arcades on three sides. On the fourth side stands the mosque, with a two-storey porch. The main prayer hall is covered by a large central dome rising much higher than the two-storey facade, and surrounded by smaller domes and semidomes.

İstanbul's superb Süleymaniye Mosque is the grandest and most visited work of Sinan's, so if you only have time to visit one of his masterpieces, make it this one. The Atik Valide Mosque (p90) in Üsküdar is similar to the Süleymaniye in many ways, most notably in the extent of its *külliye* (mosque outbuildings, often including hamam, *medrese*, hospital, cemetery and soup kitchen). The much smaller, tile-encrusted Rüstem Paşa Mosque (p78) is exquisite, well rewarding anyone who makes the effort to see it.

Sinan didn't only design and construct mosques. The Çemberlitaş Hamamı (p96) and Ayasofya Hürrem Sultan Hamamı (p96) are also his work, giving you a perfect excuse to blend your architectural studies with a pampering session.

Sınan's works survive in other towns of the Ottoman heartland, particularly Edirne, the one-time capital of the empire.

to differentiate treasures from tourist tack. It's obligatory to drink lots of tea, compare price after price and try your hand at the art of bargaining. Allow at least three hours for your visit; some travellers spend three days!

TOP CHOICE **Süleymaniye Mosque**　　　MOSQUE
(Map p76; Prof Sıddık Sami Onar Caddesi; ☒Beyazıt-Kapalı Çarşı) The Süleymaniye Mosque crowns one of İstanbul's seven hills, dominating the Golden Horn and providing a landmark for the entire city. Though it's not the largest of the Ottoman mosques, it is certainly one of the grandest and it is unusual in that many of its original *külliye* (mosque complex) buildings have been retained and sympathetically adapted for reuse.

Commissioned by Süleyman I, known as 'The Magnificent', the Süleymaniye was the fourth imperial mosque built in İstanbul and it certainly lives up to its patron's nickname. It and its surrounding buildings were designed by Mimar Sinan, the most famous and talented of all imperial architects. Sinan's *türbe* (tomb) is just outside the mosque's walled garden, next to a disused *medrese* building.

Mosque

The mosque was built between 1550 and 1557. Its setting and plan are particularly pleasing, featuring gardens and a three-sided forecourt with a central domed ablutions fountain. The four minarets with their 10 beautiful *şerefes* (balconies) are said to represent the fact that Süleyman was the fourth of the Osmanlı sultans to rule the city and the 10th sultan after the establishment of the empire.

In the garden behind the mosque is a terrace offering lovely views of the Golden Horn. The street underneath once housed the *külliye*'s *arasta* (street of shops), which was built into the retaining wall of the terrace. Close by was a five-level *mülazim* (preparatory school).

Inside, the building is breathtaking in its size and pleasing in its simplicity. Sinan incorporated the four buttresses into the walls of the building – the result is wonderfully 'transparent' (ie open and airy) and highly reminiscent of Aya Sofya, especially as the dome is nearly as large as the one that crowns the Byzantine basilica.

Bazaar District

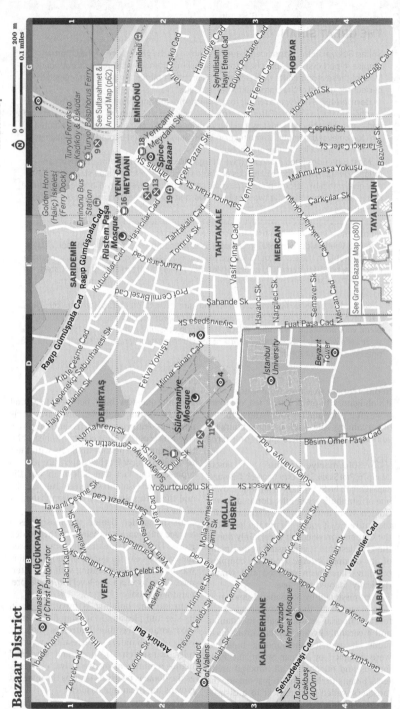

200 m
0.1 miles

See Sultanahmet &
Around Map (p62)

See Grand Bazaar Map (p80)

Golden Horn
(Haliç) İskelesi
(Ferry Dock)

Tünel Ferries to
Kadıköy & Üsküdar

Turyol Bosphorus Ferry

Turyol

Eminönü Bus
Station

SARIDEMIR

Rüstem Paşa
Mosque

Ragıp Gümüşpala Cad

YENİ CAMİİ
MEYDANI

Spice
Bazaar

EMİNÖNÜ

HOBYAR

Yeni Cami

Şeyhülislam
Hayri Efendi Cad

TAHTAKALE

MERCAN

TAYA HATUN

Süleymaniye
Mosque

İstanbul
University

Beyazıt
Tower

DEMİRTAŞ

VEFA

KÜÇÜKPAZAR

Monastery
of Christ Pantokrator

MOLLA
HÜSREV

KALENDERHANE

Şehzade
Mehmet Mosque

Aqueduct
of Valens

BALABAN AĞA

VEZNECILER

To Süt.
Ocakbaşı
(400m)

Şehzadebaşı Cad

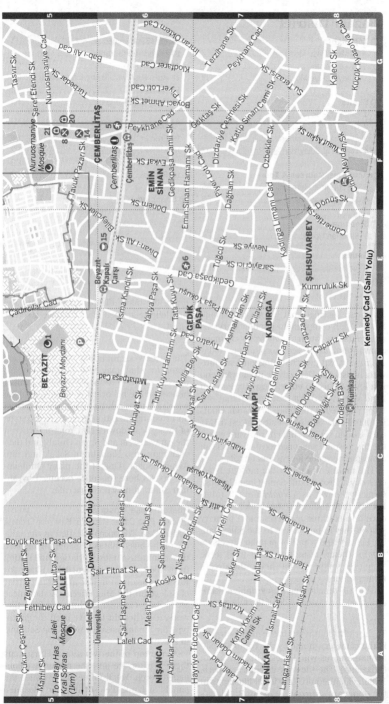

Bazaar District

Külliye

Süleyman specified that his mosque should have the full complement of public services: *imaret* (soup kitchen), *medreses*, hamam, caravanserai, *darüşşifa* (hospital) etc. Today the *imaret*, with its charming garden courtyard, houses the Dârüzziyafe Restaurant and is a lovely place to enjoy a çay. On its right hand side (north) is a caravanserai that was being restored at the time of research. On its left hand side (south) is Lale Bahçesi (p115), a tea garden set in a sunken courtyard where the the hospital was once located. This is an atmospheric venue for çay and nargile.

The main entrance to the mosque is accessed via Prof Sıddık Sami Onar Caddesi, formerly known as *Tiryaki Çarşışı* (Market of the Addicts). The buildings here once housed three *medreses* and a primary school; they're now home to the Süleymaniye Library and a raft of popular streetside *fasulye* (bean) restaurants that used to be teahouses selling opium (hence the street's former name).

The still-functioning **Süleymaniye Hamamı** is on the eastern side of the mosque.

Tombs

To the right (southeast) of the main entrance is the cemetery, home to the **tombs** of Süleyman and his wife Haseki Hürrem Sultan (Roxelana). The tilework in both is superb. In Süleyman's tomb, little jewel-like lights in the dome are surrogate stars. In Roxelana's tomb, the many tile panels of flowers and the delicate stained glass produce a serene effect.

Surrounding Area

The streets surrounding the mosque are home to what may well be the most extensive concentration of Ottoman timber houses on the historical peninsula, many of which are currently being restored as part of an urban regeneration project. To see some of these, head down Felva Yokuşu (between the caravanserai and Sinan's tomb) and then veer right into Namahrem Sokak and into Ayrancı Sokak. One of the many Ottoman-era houses here was once occupied by Mimar Sinan; it now houses a cafe.

Rüstem Paşa Mosque   MOSQUE
(Rüstem Paşa Camii; Map p76; Hasırcılar Caddesi, Rüstem Paşa; ⊞Eminönü) Nestled in the middle of the busy Tahtakale shopping district, this diminutive mosque is a gem. Dating from 1560, it was designed by Sinan for Rüstem Paşa, son-in-law and grand vizier of Süleyman the Magnificent. A showpiece of the best Ottoman architecture and tilework, it is thought to have been the prototype for Sinan's greatest work, the Selimiye in Edirne.

At the top of the two sets of entry steps there is a terrace and the mosque's colonnaded porch. You'll immediately notice the panels of İznik tiles set into the mosque's facade. The interior is covered in more tiles and features a lovely dome, supported by four tiled pillars.

The preponderance of tiles was Rüstem Paşa's way of signalling his wealth and influence – İznik tiles being particularly expensive and desirable. It may not have assisted his passage into the higher realm, though, because by all accounts he was a loathsome character. His contemporaries dubbed him *Kehle-i-Ikbal* (the Louse of Fortune) because he was found to be infected with lice on the eve of his marriage to Mihrimah, Süleyman's favourite daughter. He is best remembered for plotting with Roxelana to turn Süleyman against his favourite son, Mustafa. They were successful and Mustafa was strangled in 1553 on his father's orders.

The mosque is easy to miss because it's not at street level. There's a set of access stairs on Hasırcılar Caddesi and another on the small street that runs right (north) off Hasırcılar Caddesi towards the Golden Horn.

Spice Bazaar   MARKET

(Mısır Çarşısı, Egyptian Market; Map p76; ☉8am-6pm Mon-Sat, 9am-6pm Sun; 🚇Eminönü) Vividly coloured spices are displayed alongside jewel-like *lokum* (Turkish delight) at this Ottoman-era marketplace, providing eye candy for the thousands of tourists and locals who make their way here every day. As well as spices and *lokum*, stalls sell dried herbs, caviar, nuts, honey in the comb, dried fruits and *pestil* (fruit pressed into sheets and dried). The number of stalls selling tourist trinkets increases annually, yet this remains a great place to stock up on edible souvenirs, share a few jokes with the vendors and marvel at the well-preserved building. It's also home to one of the city's oldest restaurants, Pandeli (p115).

The market was constructed in the 1660s as part of the New Mosque; rent from the shops supported the upkeep of the mosque as well as its charitable activities, which included a school, hamam and hospital. The market's Turkish name, the Mısır Çarşısı (Egyptian Market), references the fact that the building was initially endowed with taxes levied on goods imported from Egypt. In its heyday, the bazaar was the last stop for the camel caravans that travelled the Silk Routes from China, India and Persia.

On the west side of the market there are outdoor produce stalls selling fresh foodstuff from all over Anatolia, including a wonderful selection of cheeses. Also here is the most famous coffee supplier in İstanbul, **Kurukahveci Mehmet Efendi** (Map p76; www.mehmetefendi.com/eng; cnr Tahmis Sokak & Hasırcılar Caddesi; ☉9am-6pm Mon-Sat; 🚇Eminönü), established over 100 years ago. This is located on the corner of Hasırcılar Caddesi, which is full of shops selling food and kitchenware.

New Mosque   MOSQUE

(Yeni Camii; Map p62; Yenicamii Meydanı Sokak, Eminönü; 🚇Eminönü) Only in İstanbul would a 400-year-old mosque be called 'New'. Dating from 1597, the design of this much-loved adornment to İstanbul's skyline references both the Blue Mosque and the Süleymaniye Mosque, with a large forecourt and a square sanctuary surmounted by a series of semidomes crowned by a grand dome. The interior is richly decorated with gold leaf, coloured İznik tiles and carved marble.

Galata Bridge   BRIDGE

(Galata Köprüsü; Map p76; 🚇Eminönü or Karaköy) To experience İstanbul at its most magical, walk across the Galata Bridge at sunset. At this time, the historic Galata Tower is surrounded by shrieking seagulls, the mosques atop the seven hills of the city are silhouetted against a soft red-pink sky and the evocative scent of apple tobacco wafts out of the nargile cafes under the bridge.

During the day, the bridge carries a constant flow of İstanbullus crossing between Beyoğlu and Eminönü. A handful or two of hopeful anglers trail their lines into the waters below, and a constantly changing procession of street vendors hawks everything from fresh-baked *simits* (sesame-encrusted bread rings) to Rolex rip-offs. Underneath, restaurants and cafes serve drinks and food all day and night. Come here to enjoy a beer and nargile while watching the ferries making their way to and from the Eminönü and Karaköy ferry docks.

Beyazıt Mosque   MOSQUE

(Beyazıt Camii, Mosque of Sultan Beyazıt II; Map p76; Beyazıt Meydanı, Beyazıt; 🚇Beyazıt-Kapalı Çarşı) The second imperial mosque built in İstanbul (after the Fatih Camii), Beyazıt Camii was built between 1501 and 1506 by order of Beyazıt II, son of Mehmet the Conqueror. Architecturally, it links Aya Sofya, which obviously inspired its design, with great mosques such as the Süleymaniye, which are realisations of Aya Sofya's design fully adapted to Muslim worship.

Grand Bazaar

Örücüler Hamamı Sk

Küçük Safran Han

Astarcı Han

Safran Han

Tığcılar Sk

SILVERWARE

Kızlar Ağası Hanı

İmameli Han

FABRIC Çukur Han

6 ⊗ **COPPERWARE**

İç Cebeci Han

Cebeci Hanı

Mercan Han

16

Zincirli Han

Ağa Hanı

14

Perdahçılar Sk

Acı Çeşme Sk

Yağlıkçılar Cad

⊗ 2

Takkeciler Sk

Sahaflar Bedesteni

CARPETS

Evliya Han

Kavaflar Sk

11

Halıcılar Çarşısı Sk

4

ANTIQUES & JEWELLERY

Yeşildirek Sk

8

9

7

Gani Çelebi Sk

5 ⊗

Ortakazalar Sk

Ressam Basmacılar Sk

CARPETS

Cevahir 15 (Jewellery) Bedesteni

Yorgancılar Cad

Takkeçiler Sk

Şerifağa Sk

Ali Paşa Hanı

Yarım Taş Han

13

12

Kesecıler Cad

Çadırcılar Cad

Bodrum Han

LEATHER

Feraceciler Sk

HANDBAGS, SUITCASES & BRIEFCASES

10

CARPETS

Divrikli Sk

Kolancılar Sk

Püskülcüler Sk

Kazaslar Sk

Koltuk Kazaslar Sk

LEATHER

Fesçiler Cad

Kalpakçılar Cad

Kebabçı Han

Kürkçüler Çarşısı

Serpuşcular Sokağı

Beyazıt Meydanı

GOLD

The mosque's exceptional use of fine stone is noteworthy, with marble, porphyry, verd antique and rare granite featuring. The *mihrab* is simple, except for the rich stone columns framing it. The courtyard features 24 small domes and a central ablutions fountain.

Of the original *külliye* buildings, the *imaret* has been turned into a library. Unfortunately, the once-splendid hamam has been

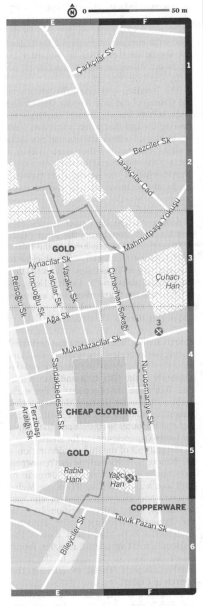

was once dotted with Byzantine churches and cisterns. While most of the churches have been converted to mosques and many of the cisterns have been demolished, a few hours' exploration will still evoke the ancient city.

Fatih Mosque   MOSQUE
(Fatih Camii, Mosque of the Conqueror; Fevzi Paşa Caddesi, Fatih; 🚌31E, 32, 336E, 36KE & 38E from Eminönü, 87 from Taksim) The Fatih was the first great imperial mosque built in İstanbul following the Conquest. For its location, Mehmet the Conqueror chose the hilltop site of the ruined Church of the Apostles, burial place of Constantine and other Byzantine emperors. Mehmet decided to be buried here as well – his tomb is behind the mosque and is inevitably filled with worshippers.

The original *külliye*, finished in 1470, was enormous. Set in extensive grounds, it included 15 charitable establishments such as *medreses*, a hospice for travellers and a caravanserai. Many of these still stand – the most interesting is the multidomed *tabhane* (dervish inn) to the southeast of the mosque. Its columns are said to have been originally used in the Church of the Apostles.

Unfortunately, the mosque you see today is not the one Mehmet built. The original stood for nearly 300 years before toppling in an earthquake in 1766. The current mosque was constructed between 1767 and 1771.

The front courtyard of the mosque is a favourite place for locals to congregate. On

closed for many years. Beyazıt's *türbe* is behind the mosque.

WESTERN DISTRICTS
Broadly described as the district between the Bazaar District and the city walls, this area

Wednesday the streets behind and to the north of the mosque host the **Çarşamba Pazarı**, a busy weekly market selling food, clothing and household goods.

Fethiye Museum

MUSEUM

(Fethiye Müzesi, Church of Pammakaristos; Fethiye Caddesi, Çarşamba; admission ₺5; ⊘9am-4.30pm Thu-Tue; ☐33ES, 90, 44B, 36C, 399B&C from Eminönü, 55T from Taksim) Not long after the Conquest, Mehmet the Conqueror visited this 13th-century church to discuss theological questions with the Patriarch of the Orthodox Church. They talked in the southern side chapel known as the parecclesion, which is now open as a small museum. The chapel was added to the church in the 14th century and is decorated with gold mosaics.

The most impressive of the mosaics are the *Pantokrator and 12 Prophets* adorning the dome, and the *Deesis (Christ with the Virgin and St John the Baptist)* in the apse.

The building itself was extended several times over the centuries before being converted to a mosque in 1573. It was named Fethiye (Conquest) to commemorate Sultan Murat III's victories in Georgia and Azerbaijan.

Mihrimah Sultan Mosque

MOSQUE

(Mihrimah Sultan Camii; Ali Kuşçu Sokak, Edirnekapı; ☐31E, 32, 36K & 38E from Eminönü, 87 from Taksim) The great Sinan put his stamp on the entire city, and this mosque, constructed in the 1560s next to the Edirnekapı section of the historic land walls, is one of his best works. Commissioned by Süleyman the Magnificent's favourite daughter, Mihrimah, it features a wonderfully light and airy interior with delicate stained-glass windows and an unusual 'birdcage' chandelier.

Occupying the highest point in the city, the mosque's dome and one slender minaret are major adornments to the city skyline; they are particularly prominent on the road from Edirne. Remnants of the *külliye* include a still-functioning **hamam** on the corner of Ali Kuşçu and Eroğlu Sokaks.

TOP CHOICE Kariye Museum

(Chora Church)

MUSEUM

(Kariye Müzesi; kariye.muze.gov.tr; Kariye Camii Sokak, Edirnekapı; admission ₺15; ⊘9am-7pm Thu-Tue Apr-Oct, to 4.30pm Nov-Mar; ☐31E, 32, 36K & 38E from Eminönü, 87 from Taksim) İstanbul has more than its fair share of Byzantine monuments, but few are as drop-dead gorgeous as this mosaic-laden church. Nestled in the shadow of Theodosius II's monumental land walls and now a museum overseen by the Aya Sofya curators, it receives a fraction of the visitor numbers that its big sister attracts but offers an equally fascinating insight into Byzantine art.

The building was originally known as the Church of the Holy Saviour Outside the Walls (Chora literally means 'country'), reflecting the fact that when it was first built it was located outside the original city walls built by Constantine the Great. Within a century the church and the monastery complex in which it was located were engulfed by Byzantine urban sprawl and enclosed within a new set of walls built by Emperor Theodosius II.

Around AD 500, the Emperor Anastasius and his court moved from the Great Palace of Byzantium in Sultanahmet to the Palace of Blachernae, a new complex built close to the point where Theodosius' land walls met the old sea walls on the Golden Horn. Its proximity to the Chora Monastery led to the monastery expanding and being rebuilt in 536 during the rule of Justinian.

What you see today isn't Justinian's church, though. That building was destroyed during the Iconoclastic period (711–843) and reconstructed at least five times, most significantly in the 11th, 12th and 14th centuries. Today, the Chora consists of five main architectural units: the nave, the two-storied structure (annex) added to the north, the inner and the outer narthexes and the chapel for tombs (parecclesion) to the south.

Virtually all of the interior decoration – the famous mosaics and the less renowned but equally striking frescoes – dates from 1312 and was funded by Theodore Metochites, a poet and man of letters who was *logothetes,* the official responsible for the Byzantine treasury, under Emperor Andronikos II (r 1282–1328). One of the museum's most wonderful mosaics, found above the door to the nave in the inner narthex, depicts Theodore offering the church to Christ.

Metochites also established a very large and rich library inside the monastery; unfortunately, no traces of this or the other monastery buildings have survived.

The structure and environs of the church weren't the only thing to change over the years – after centuries of use as a church the building became a mosque during the reign of Beyazıt II (1481–1512) and a museum in 1945.

Mosaics

Most of the interior is covered with mosaics depicting the lives of Christ and the Virgin Mary. Look out for the *Khalke Jesus*, which shows Christ and Mary with two donors – Prince Isaac Comnenos and Melane, daughter of Mikhael Palaiologos VIII. This is under the right dome in the inner narthex. On the dome itself is a stunning depiction of Jesus and his ancestors *(The Genealogy of Christ)*. On the narthex' left dome is a serenely beautiful mosaic of *Mary and the Baby Jesus Surrounded by Ancestors*.

In the nave are three mosaics: *Christ; Mary and the Baby Jesus;* and the *Dormition of the Blessed Virgin (Assumption)* – turn around to see this, as it's over the main door you just entered. The 'infant' being held by Jesus is actually Mary's soul.

Frescoes

To the right of the nave is the parecclesion, a side chapel built to hold the tombs of the church's founder and his relatives, close friends and associates. This is decorated with frescoes that deal with the themes of death and resurrection, depicting scenes taken from the Old Testament. The striking painting in the apse known as the *Anastasis* shows a powerful Christ raising Adam and Eve out of their sarcophagi, with saints and kings in attendance. The gates of Hell are shown under Christ's feet. Less majestic but no less beautiful are the frescoes adorning the dome, which show Mary and 12 attendant angels.

Though no one knows for certain, it is thought that the frescoes were painted by the same masters who created the mosaics. Theirs is an extraordinary accomplishment, as the paintings, with their sophisticated use of perspective and exquisitely portrayed facial expressions, are reminiscent of those painted by the Italian master Giotto, the painter who more than any other ushered in the Italian Renaissance.

Despite signs clearly prohibiting the use of camera flashes in the museum, many visitors wilfully ignore this rule, endangering these wonderful mosaics and frescoes. Please don't be one of them.

BEYOĞLU & AROUND

The suburb of Beyoğlu (*bay*-oh-loo) rises from the shoreline north of Galata Bridge and incorporates both Taksim Meydanı and the grand boulevard, İstiklal Caddesi. In the mid-19th century it was known as Pera and acknowledged as the 'European' quarter of town. Diplomats and international traders lived and worked here, and the streets were showcases for the latest European fashions and fads.

All this changed in the decades after the republic was formed. Embassies moved to Ankara, the glamorous shops and restaurants closed, the grand buildings crumbled and Beyoğlu took on a decidedly sleazy air. Fortunately the 1990s brought about a rebirth and Beyoğlu is once again the heart of modern İstanbul, full of galleries, cafes and boutiques. Here, hip new restaurants and bars open almost nightly, and the streets showcase cosmopolitan Turkey at its best. Put simply, if you miss Beyoğlu, you haven't seen İstanbul.

The best way to get a feel for this side of town is to spend an afternoon or day exploring by foot. If you're based in Sultanahmet, catch the tram to Kabataş and the connecting funicular up to Taksim Meydanı. Then work your way down İstiklal Caddesi, exploring its many side streets along the way. At the foot of the boulevard is Tünel Meydanı; follow Galipdede Caddesi downhill and you will be able to explore the historic neighbourhood of Galata before walking across Galata Bridge to Eminönü, from where you can catch a tram or walk back up to Sultanahmet. All up it's a walk of at least two hours from Taksim Meydanı – but dedicating a full day will be more rewarding.

İstanbul Modern   MUSEUM

(İstanbul Modern Sanat Müzesi; Map p84; www .istanbulmodern.org; Meclis-i Mebusan Caddesi, Tophane; adult/student/under 12yr ₺15/8/free; ⊙10am-6pm Tue, Wed & Fri-Sun, to 8pm Thu; 🚋Tophane) The İstanbul Modern is the big daddy of a slew of newish, privately funded art galleries in the city. Its stunning location on the shores of the Bosphorus and its extensive collection of Turkish 20th-century art make it well worth a visit. The icing on the cake is provided by a constantly changing and uniformly excellent program of exhibitions by local and international artists in the exhibition galleries in the basement.

There's also a well-stocked gift shop, a cinema that shows art-house films and a stylish cafe-restaurant with superb views of the Bosphorus.

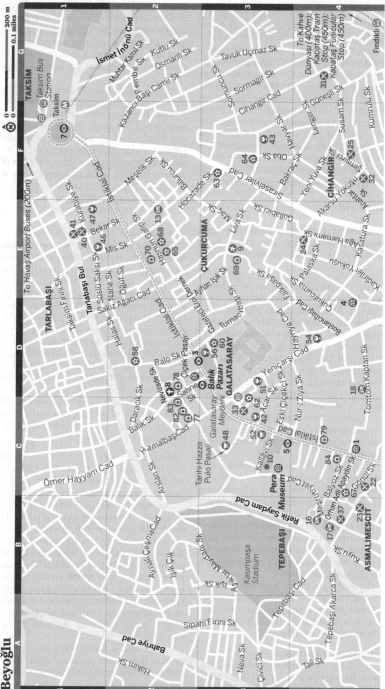

 İSTANBUL

Beyoğlu

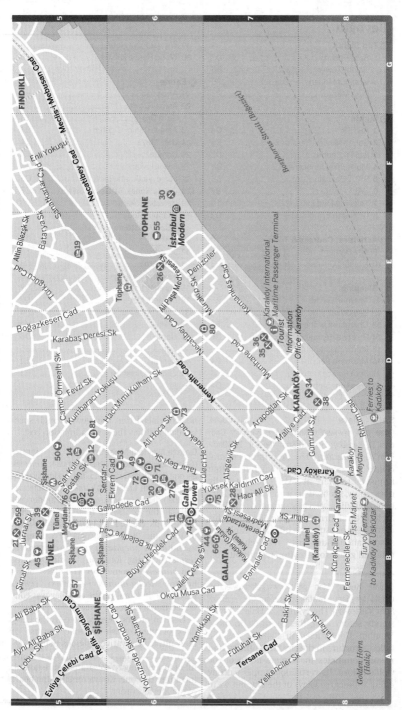

İSTANBUL SIGHTS

Beyoğlu

SALT Galata   CULTURAL CENTRE
(Map p84; www.saltonline.org/en; Bankalar Caddesi 11, Karaköy; ☺noon-8pm Tue-Sat, 10.30am-6pm Sun; ◉Karaköy) The descriptor 'cultural centre' is used a lot in İstanbul, but is often a misnomer. Here at SALT Galata it really does apply. Housed in a magnificent 1892 bank building cleverly adapted by local architectural firm Mimarlar Tasarım, this cutting-edge institution offers an exhibition space, auditorium, arts research library, cafe and glamorous rooftop restaurant.

Galata Tower   LANDMARK
(Galata Kulesi; Map p84; www.galatatower.net; Galata Meydanı, Galata; admission ₺12; ☺9am-8pm; ◉Karaköy) The cylindrical Galata Tower stands sentry over the approach to 'new' İstanbul. Constructed in 1348, it was the tallest structure in the city for centuries, and it still dominates the skyline north of the Golden Horn. Its vertiginous upper balcony offers 360-degree views of the city, but we're

not convinced that the view (though spectacular) justifies the steep admission cost.

Galata Mevlevi Museum   MUSEUM
(Galata Mevlevihanesi Müzesi; Map p84; www.mek der.org; Galipdede Caddesi 15, Tünel; admission ₺5; ☺9am-4.30pm Tue-Sun; ◉Karaköy, then funicular to Tünel) The *semahane* (whirling-dervish hall) at the centre of this *tekke* (dervish lodge) was erected in 1491 and renovated in 1608 and 2009. It is part of a complex including a *meydan-ı şerif* (courtyard), *çeşme* (drinking fountain), *türbesi* (tomb) and *hamuşan* (cemetery). The oldest of six historic *Mevlevihaneleri* (Mevlevi *tekkes*) remaining in İstanbul, the complex was converted into a museum in 1946.

Dervish orders were banned in the early days of the Turkish republic because of their ultraconservative religious politics. Although the ban has been lifted, only a handful of functioning *tekkes* remain in İstanbul, including this one. Konya remains the heart of the Mevlevi order.

Beneath the *semahane* is a fascinating exhibit that includes displays of Mevlevi clothing, turbans and accessories. The *mahfiller* (upstairs floor) houses the *tekke*'s collection of traditional musical instruments, calligraphy and ebru (marbling).

The *hamuşan* is full of stones with graceful Ottoman inscriptions, including the tomb of Galip Dede, the 17th-century Sufi poet whom the street is named after. The shapes atop the stones reflect the headgear of the deceased, each hat denoting a different religious rank.

See the boxed text p88 for details of the weekly *sema* (whirling-dervish ceremony) performed here.

İstiklal Caddesi STREET
(Independence Ave; Map p84) Once called the Grand Rue de Pera but renamed İstiklal (Independence) in the early years of the Republic, Beyoğlu's premier boulevard is a perfect metaphor for 21st-century Turkey. A long pedestrianised strip full of shops, cafes, cinemas and cultural centres, it showcases İstanbul's Januslike personality, embracing modernity one minute and happily bowing to tradition the next.

At its northern end is frantically busy Taksim Meydanı, the symbolic heart of the modern city. Here, a constant stream of locals arrive by car, bus, funicular and metro to shop, eat and be entertained. At its southern end is the relatively tranquil district of Galata, home to crooked cobblestone lanes and traces of a fortified settlement built by Genoese merchants in the 13th century.

Promenading along the length of İstiklal is the most popular activity in town, and huge crowds of İstanbullus head here in the early evening and at weekends to browse in boutiques and bookshops, see exhibitions at galleries, listen to the street buskers, drink coffee in chain cafes and party in *meyhanes* (taverns). We highly recommend that you join them.

ARTER GALLERY
(Map p84; www.arter.org.tr; İstiklal Caddesi 211; ⊙11am-7pm Tue-Thu, noon-8pm Fri-Sun; 🚇Karaköy, then funicular to Tünel) Funded by the Vehbi Koç Foundation, this four-floor contemporary

SEEING THE DERVISHES WHIRL

If you thought the Hare Krishnas or the Harlem congregations were the only religious orders to celebrate their faith through music and movement, think again. Those sultans of spiritual spin known as the whirling dervishes have been twirling their way to a higher plane ever since the 13th century and show no sign of slowing down soon.

There are a number of opportunities to see dervishes whirling in İstanbul. Probably the best of these is the weekly ceremony held in the *semahane* (whirling-dervish hall) in the Galata Mevlevi Museum (p121) in Tünel.

Another good option is to attend one of the *semas* held on most Monday nights at a *tekke* in Karagumruk in the Fatih District and on Thursday nights at a *tekke* in Silivrikapi, also in Fatih. These are the real deal, not performances put on for tourists. Note, though, that chanting – rather than whirling – is the main event. The easiest way to attend is to go with Les Arts Turcs (p97), a cultural tourism company that charges ₺60 per person to give you a briefing about the meaning of the ceremony, take you to the *tekkes* from its office near Aya Sofya and bring you back after the ceremony.

For a more touristy experience, the **Hocapaşa Cultural Centre** (Hocapaşa Hamamı Sokak 5), housed in a beautifully converted 15th-century hamam near Eminönü, presents whirling-dervish performances four evenings per week throughout the year.

Remember that the ceremony is a religious one – by whirling, the adherents believe that they are attaining a higher union with God – so don't talk, leave your seat or take flash photographs while the dervishes are spinning or chanting.

---

arts space has been neck-and-neck with the Garanti Bank's SALT cultural centres in the race for the accolade of most exciting new arts venue in the city. In our view, the result is tied.

SALT Beyoğlu CULTURAL CENTRE
(Map p84; www.saltonline.org/en; İstiklal Caddesi 136; ☺noon-8pm Tue-Sat, 10.30am-6pm Sun; ⓖKaraköy, then funicular to Tünel) Its three floors of exhibition space, bookshop, walk-in cinema and cafe make SALT Beyoğlu nearly as impressive as its Galata-based sibling. Occupying a former apartment building dating from the 1850s, it shows the work of both high-profile and emerging international and local artists.

Pera Museum MUSEUM
(Pera Müzesi; Map p84; www.peramuzesi.org.tr; Meşrutiyet Caddesi 65, Tepebaşı; adult/student/child under 12yr ₺10/7/free; ☺10am-7pm Tue-Sat, noon-6pm Sun; ⓖKaraköy, then funicular to Tünel) Head to this classy museum to admire works from Suna and İnan Kıraç's splendid collection of paintings featuring Turkish Orientalist themes. A changing program of thematic exhibitions provides fascinating glimpses into the Ottoman world from the 17th to the early 20th century. Some works are realistic, others highly romanticised – all are historically fascinating.

The most beloved painting in the Turkish canon – Osman Hamdi Bey's *The Tortoise Trainer* (1906) – is the standout work in the collection, but there's plenty more to see, including a permanent exhibit of Kütahya tiles and ceramics, and a somewhat esoteric collection of Anatolian weights and measures.

Museum of Innocence MUSEUM
(Map p84; www.masumiyetmuzesi.org; Dalgıç Çıkmazı 2, off Çukurcuma Caddesi, Çukurcuma; admission ₺25; ☺10am-6pm Tue-Sun, till 9pm Fri; ⓖTophane) His status as a Nobel laureate deserves respect, but we feel obliged to say that we think Orhan Pamuk is a bit cheeky to charge a whopping ₺25 for entrance to his new museum. That said, this long-anticipated museum and piece of conceptual art is worth a visit, particularly if you have read and admired the novel it celebrates.

The museum is set in a 19th-century house and seeks to evoke and recreate aspects of Pamuk's 1988 novel *The Museum of Innocence* by displaying found objects in traditional museum-style glass cases. It also includes strangely beautiful installations such as a wall dispaying the 4213 cigarette butts supposedly smoked by the book's heroine, Füsun. In all, the exhibits are successful in evoking what Pamuk has described as 'the melancholy of the period' in which he grew up and in which the novel is set.

Taksim Meydanı SQUARE
(Map p84; ⓖKabataş, then funicular to Taksim) Named after the 18th-century stone *taksim*

(water storage unit) on its western side, this busy square is the symbolic heart of modern İstanbul. Hardly a triumph of urban design, it is home to a chaotic bus terminus, a cultural centre, the upmarket Marmara Hotel and an often-overlooked monument to the founding of the Republic.

When this book went to print, İstanbul's newspapers were full of heated debate about the future of the square after the mayor of Beyoğlu, Ahmet Misbah Demircan, announced plans to redevelop the public park behind the bus terminal on the northeast side of the square as a shopping mall. Local activists cited it as one of many current instances of public space being sold off to private developers without proper public consultation or approval. The site, which has been a park since the early 1940s, was previousy occupied by an Ottoman military barracks.

Üç Horan Ermeni Kilisesi CHURCH

(Armenian Church of Three Altars; Map p84; Balık Pazarı, Sahne Sokak 24a, Galatasaray; 🚇Kabataş, then funicular to Taksim) The Üç Horan Ermeni Kilisesi dates from 1838. Look for the gigantic black doors to the courtyard – visitors can enter the church when the doors are open.

BEŞİKTAŞ, ORTAKÖY & KURUÇEŞME

Dolmabahçe Palace PALACE

(Dolmabahçe Sarayı; www.millisaraylar.gov.tr; Dolmabahçe Caddesi, Beşiktaş; Selâmlık ₺30, Harem ₺20, joint ticket ₺40; ⊙9am-6pm Tue, Wed & Fri-Sun Mar-Sep, till 4pm Oct-Feb; 🚇Kabataş) These days it's fashionable for architects and critics influenced by the less-is-more aesthetic of the Bauhaus masters to sneer at buildings such as Dolmabahçe. Enthusiasts of Ottoman architecture also decry this final flourish of the imperial dynasty, finding that it has more in common with the Paris Opera than with traditional pavilion-style buildings such as Topkapı. But whatever the critics might say, this 19th-century imperial residence with its opulent Selamlık (Ceremonial Suites) and slightly more restrained Harem is a clear crowd favourite.

Both the Selamlık and the Harem are visited on separate – and unfortunately rushed – guided tours. The Selamlık, with its huge chandeliers and crystal staircase made by Baccarat, is the most impressive of the two.

The tourist entrance to the palace is near the palace's ornate Clock Tower, built between 1890 and 1894. There's an **outdoor** cafe near here with premium Bosphorus views and cheap prices (yes, really).

At the end of your tour, make sure that you visit the **Crystal Kiosk**, with its fairy-tale-like conservatory featuring etched glass windows, a crystal fountain and myriad windows. There's even a crystal piano and chair. It's next to the aviary on the street side of the palace.

Note that visitor numbers in the palace are limited to 3000 per day and this ceiling is often reached on weekends and holidays – come midweek if possible, and even then be prepared to queue (often for a long period and in full sun).

ASIAN SHORE

Although most of İstanbul's noteworthy sights, shops, bars and eateries are on the European side of town, many locals prefer to live on the Asian (aka Anatolian) shore, citing cheaper rents and a better standard of living. For others, the best thing about living in or visiting this side of town is the scenic ferry ride between the continents.

ÜSKÜDAR

Üsküdar (*oo*-skoo-dar) was founded about two decades before Byzantium, and was originally called Chrysopolis. The Ottomans called it Scutari. Unwalled and therefore vulnerable, it became part of the Ottoman Empire at least 100 years before the Conquest.

Today Üsküdar is a bustling working-class suburb with a handful of important Ottoman mosques that attract visitors. If coming to Üsküdar from Sultanahmet, take the conventional passenger ferry from Eminönü. Dentur–Avrasya and Turyol ferry services also operate to/from Kabataş, Eminönü and Karaköy.

Judging that Scutari was the closest point in İstanbul to Mecca, many powerful Ottoman figures built mosques here to assist their passage to Paradise. Every year a big caravan set out from here, en route to Mecca and Medina for the Haj, further emphasising the suburb's reputation for piety.

As you leave Üsküdar dock, the main square, Demokrasi Meydanı (currently being redeveloped as part of the massive Marmaray transport project), is right in front of you. Its northeastern corner is dominated by the **Mihrimah Sultan Mosque** (Mihrimah Sultan Camii; Paşa Limanı Caddesi; 🚇Üsküdar), sometimes referred to as the İskele (ferry dock) Camii. This mosque was designed by Sinan

İSTANBUL SIGHTS

Ortaköy & Kuruçeşme

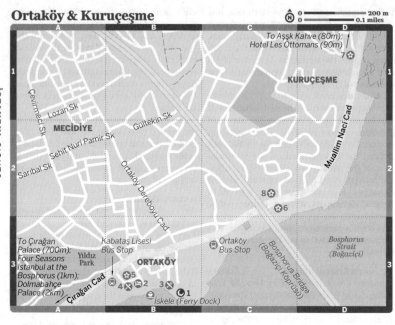

N 0 ⟶ 200 m
N 0 ⟶ 0.1 miles

To Aşşk Kahve (80m);
Hotel Les Ottomans (90m)

KURUÇEŞME

MECİDİYE

Bosphorus
Strait
(Boğaziçi)

Kabataş Lisesi
Bus Stop

To Çırağan
Palace (700m);
Four Seasons
Istanbul at the
Bosphorus (1km);
Dolmabahçe
Palace (2km)

Yıldız
Park

ORTAKÖY

Ortaköy
Bus Stop

Bosphorus Bridge
(Boğaziçi Köprüsü)

İskele (Ferry Dock)

Ortaköy & Kuruçeşme

for Süleyman the Magnificent's daughter and built between 1547 and 1548.

South of the square is the **Yeni Valide Mosque** (Yeni Valide Camii, New Queen Mother's Mosque; Demokrasi Meydanı; 🚢Üsküdar). Featuring a wrought-iron 'birdcage' tomb in its overgrown garden, it was built by Sultan Ahmet III from 1708 to 1710 for his mother, Gülnuş Emetullah.

West of the square, overlooking the harbour, is the charming **Şemsi Ahmed Paşa**

Mosque (Şemsi Paşa Camii, Kuskonmaz Camii; Paşa Limanı Caddesi; 🚢Üsküdar). Designed by Sinan and built in 1580 for Grand Vizier Şemsi Paşa, its modest size and decoration reflect the fact that its benefactor occupied the position of grand vizier for only a couple of months under Süleyman the Magnificent. Its *medrese* has been converted into a library and there's a popular *çay bahçesi* on its southern side.

The **Atik Valide Mosque** (Atik Valide Camii; Valide Imaret Sokak; 🚢Üsküdar) is another of Sinan's works, and is considered by many experts to be among his best designs. It was built for Valide Sultan Nurbanu, wife of Selim II (The Sot) and mother of Murat III, in 1583. Nurbanu was captured by Turks on the Aegean island of Paros when she was 12 years old, and went on to be a successful player in the Ottoman court. Murat adored his mother and on her death commissioned Sinan to build this monument to her on Üsküdar's highest hill.

The nearby **Çinili Mosque** (Çinili Camii, Tiled Mosque; Çinili Hamam Sokak; 🚢Üsküdar) is unprepossessing from the outside, but has an interior made brilliant with İznik tiles, the bequest of Mahpeyker Kösem (1640), wife of Sultan Ahmet I and mother of sultans Murat IV and İbrahim (r 1640–48).

To find the Atik Valide and Çinili Mosques, walk up Hakimiyet-i Milliye Caddesi until you get to the traffic circle. Continue up Dr Fahri Atabey Caddesi for about 1km until you get to little Sarı Mehmet Sokak, on your left. From here you'll spot the minarets of Atik Valide Mosque. To get to the Çinili Mosque from the Atik Valide Mosque, walk east along Çinili Camii Sokak for about 300m, after which it turns north and runs uphill. The Çinili Mosque is about 200m further on. All up it's about a 25-minute walk to the Çinili Mosque from the main square.

Behind the hill is the recently constructed **Şakirin Mosque** (cnr Huhkuyusu Caddesi & Dr Burhanettin Üstünel Sokak; 6, 9A, 11P, 11V, 12A, 12C), one of the city's most impressive examples of contemporary architecture. It's located opposite the Zeynep Kamil Hospital. To get here take a bus from the *iskele* and alight at the Zeynep Kamil stop, or continue walking up Dr Fahri Atabey Caddesi from the Atik Valide Mosque and turn right into Nuhkuyusu Caddesi.

KADIKÖY

If you've got a spare few hours, you may want to explore Kadıköy, the site of the city's first colony (originally called Chalcedon). Although there's nothing to show of its historic beginnings and there are no headline sights, Kadıköy is worth visiting for its fabulous fresh produce market, which is immediately south (ie in front) of the ferry dock. To get here, take a conventional passenger ferry from Eminönü, Karaköy or Beşiktaş.

Kadıköy and the affluent suburbs stretching southeast to Bostancı are the Asian side's entertainment hubs. For alternative culture, head to **Kadife Sokak** to check out its independent cinema, grunge boutiques, tattoo studios and hugely popular bars. And to see the wealthy at play, cruise down **Bağdat Caddesi** in neighbouring Moda, which is full of shops, restaurants and cafes.

To the north of Kadıköy is the neoclassical **Haydarpaşa Train Station**, resembling a German castle. In the early 20th century when Kaiser Wilhelm of Germany was trying to charm the sultan into economic and military cooperation, he presented the station as a small token of his respect. Now decommissioned, it recently suffered damage in a fire and has been placed on the World Monument Fund's list of the world's most endangered buildings.

Buses 12 and 12A link Kadıköy and Üsküdar.

🏃 Activities

Ferry Cruises

During the 18th and 19th centuries the Bosphorus and Golden Horn were alive with caiques (long, thin rowboats), their oars dipping rhythmically into the currents as they carried the sultan and his courtiers from palace to pavilion and from Europe to Asia. The caiques are long gone, but in their place are the sleek speedboats of the moneyed elite and the much-loved public ferries used by the rest of İstanbul's population. A trip on one of these ferries – whether it be the short return trip to Kadıköy or Üsküdar, on which you cross from Europe to Asia and back again, or one of the longer trips detailed below – is an essential activity while you are in İstanbul.

Bosphorus Ferry   FERRY
Divan Yolu and İstiklal Caddesi are always awash with people, but neither is the major thoroughfare in İstanbul. That honour goes to the mighty Bosphorus strait, which runs from the Sea of Marmara (Marmara Denizi) to the Black Sea (Karadeniz), located 32km north of the city centre. In modern Turkish, the strait is known as the Boğaziçi or İstanbul Boğazı (from *boğaz*, meaning throat or strait). On one side is Asia; on the other, Europe.

Departure Point: Eminönü
Hop onto a boat on the Eminönü quay. You can take the *Uzun Boğaz Turu* (Long Bosphorus Tour) operated by Istanbul Şehir Hatları (p128) (İstanbul City Routes) or you can opt for a shorter trip to Rumeli Hisarı and back on a private excursion boat.

It's always a good idea to arrive 30 minutes or so before the scheduled departure time and manoeuvre your way to the front of the queue that builds in front of the doors leading to the dock. When these open and the boat can be boarded, you'll need to move fast to score a good seat. The best spots are on the sides of the upper deck near the bow. The Asian shore is to the right side of the ferries as they make their way up the Bosphorus, Europe to the left.

As you start your trip, you'll see the small island and tower of **Kız Kulesı** on the Asian side near Üsküdar. This squat tower is one of the city's most distinctive landmarks. In ancient times, a predecessor of the current 18th-century structure functioned as a tollbooth and defence point; the Bosphorus could be closed off by means of a chain

İSTANBUL ACTIVITIES

stretching from here to Seraglio Point. More recently, the tower featured in the 1999 Bond film *The World is Not Enough*.

On the European shore, you'll pass grandiose Dolmabahçe Palace (p89). In his travelogue *Constantinople in 1890*, French writer Pierre Loti described this and the neighbouring Çırağan Palace as 'a line of palaces white as snow, placed at the edge of the sea on marble docks', a description that remains as accurate as it is evocative.

Beşiktaş to Kanlıca

After a brief stop at Beşiktaş, **Çırağan Palace** (www.ciragan-palace.com; Çırağan Caddesi 32, Ortaköy; Çırağan) looms up on the left. Next to it is the long yellow building occupied by the prestigious Galatasaray University. On the Asian shore is the **Fethi Ahmed Paşa Yalı**, a wide white building with a red-tiled roof that was built in the pretty suburb of Kuzguncuk in the late 18th century. The word *yalı* comes from the Greek word for 'coast', and describes the waterside wooden summer residences along the Bosphorus built by Ottoman aristocracy and foreign ambassadors in the 17th, 18th and 19th centuries, now all protected by the country's heritage laws. To your left a little further on is the pretty **Ortaköy Mosque** (Ortaköy Camii, Büyük Mecidiye Camii; Map p90; Ortaköy Meydanı, Ortaköy; Ortaköy), its dome and two minarets dwarfed by the adjacent Bosphorus Bridge, opened in 1973 on the 50th anniversary of the founding of the Turkish Republic.

Under the bridge on the European shore is the green-and-cream-coloured **Hatice Sultan Yalı**, once the home of Sultan Murad V's daughter, Hatice. On the Asian side is **Beylerbeyi Palace** (Beylerbeyi Sarayı; www.millisaraylar.gov.tr; Abdullah Ağa Caddesi, Beylerbeyi; admission ₺20; 8.30am-4.30pm Tue, Wed & Fri-Sun; Beylerbeyi Sarayı), a baroque-style building that was built for Sultan Abdül Aziz I (r 1861–76). Look for its whimsical marble bathing pavilions on the shore; one was for men, the other for the women of the harem.

Past the suburb of Çengelköy on the Asian side is the imposing **Kuleli Military School** (Çengelköy; Eminönü-Kavaklar tourist ferry), built in 1860 and immortalised in Irfan Orga's wonderful memoir, *Portrait of a Turkish Family*. Look for its two 'witch-hat' towers.

Almost opposite Kuleli on the European shore is **Arnavutköy** ('Albanian Village'), which boasts a number of gabled Ottoman-era wooden houses, On the hill above it are buildings formerly occupied by the American College for Girls. Its most famous alumni was Halide Edib Adıvar, who wrote about the years she spent here in her 1926 autobiographical work, *The Memoir of Halide Edib*.

Arnavutköy runs straight into the glamorous suburb of Bebek, famous for upmarket shopping and chic cafes. As the ferry passes, look out for the mansard roof of the **Egyptian consulate**, an art nouveau minipalace built for Emine Hanım, mother of the last khedive of Egypt, Abbas Hilmi II. It's just south of the waterside park. In the park itself is the Ottoman Revivalist–style **Bebek Mosque**.

Opposite Bebek is **Kandilli**, the 'Place of Lamps', named after the lamps that were lit here to warn ships of the particularly treacherous currents at the headland. Among the many *yalıs* here is the huge red **Kont Ostorog Yalı**, built in the 19th century by Count Leon Ostorog, a Polish adviser to the Ottoman court; Pierre Loti came here when he visited İstanbul in the 1890s. A bit further on, past Kandilli, is the long, white **Kıbrıslı** ('Cypriot') **Mustafa Emin Paşa Yalı**, which dates from 1760.

Next to the Kıbrıslı Yalı are the Büyük Göksu Deresi (Great Heavenly Stream) and Küçük Göksu Deresi (Small Heavenly Stream), two brooks that descend from the Asian hills into the Bosphorus. Between them is a grassy, shady delta, which the Ottoman elite thought just perfect for picnics. Foreign residents, who referred to the place as 'the sweet waters of Asia', would often join them. If the weather was good, the sultan joined the party – and did so in style. Sultan Abdül Mecit's version of a picnic blanket was the rococo **Küçüksu Kasrı** (216-332 3303; Küçüksu Caddesi, Beykoz; admission ₺5; 9.30am-4pm Tue, Wed & Fri-Sun; Küçüksu), constructed from 1856 to 1857. You'll see its ornate cast-iron fence, boat dock and wedding-cake exterior from the ferry.

Just before the Fatih Bridge, the majestic structure of **Rumeli Hisarı** (Fortress of Europe; 212-263 5305; Yahya Kemal Caddesi 42; admission ₺3; 9am-noon & 12.30-4.30pm Thu-Tue; Rumeli Hisarı) looms over a pretty village of the same name on the European shore. Mehmet the Conqueror had Rumeli Hisarı built in a mere four months during 1452 in preparation for his planned siege of Constantinople. For its location he chose the narrowest point of the Bosphorus, opposite Anadolu Hisarı (Fortress of Asia), which had been built by Sultan Beyazıt I in 1391. In doing so, Mehmet was able to control all traffic on the strait, thereby cutting off the city from resupply by sea. Just next to the fortress is a clutch of popular cafes and restaurants.

There are many architecturally and historically important *yalıs* in and around Anadolu Hisarı. These include the **Köprülü Amcazade Hüseyin Paşa Yalı** (Rumeli Hisarı; 🚢Eminönü-Kavaklar tourist ferry), built for one of Mustafa II's grand viziers in 1698 and the oldest *yalı* on the Bosphorus. Next door, the **Zarif Mustafa Paşa Yalı** was built in the early 19th century by the official coffee maker to Sultan Mahmud II. Look for its upstairs salon, which juts out over the water and is supported by unusual curved timber struts.

Almost directly under the Fatih Bridge on the European shore is the huge stone **Tophane Müşiri Zeki Paşa Yalı**, a mansion built in the early 20th century for a field marshall in the Ottoman army. Later, it was sold to Sabiha Sultan, daughter of Mehmet VI, the last of the Ottoman sultans, and her husband İmer Faruk Efendi, grandson of Sultan Abdül Aziz. When the sultanate was abolished in 1922, Mehmet walked from this palace onto a British warship, never to return to Turkey.

Past the bridge, still on the Asian side, is the charming suburb of **Kanlıca**, famous for its rich and delicious yoghurt, which can be sampled at the two cafes in front of the ferry stop or on the boat itself. This is the ferry's second stop and, if you so choose, you can stop and explore before reboarding the boat on its return trip or heading back to Üsküdar by bus. From here you can also catch a ferry across to Emirgan or Bebek on the European side and return to town by bus.

High on a promontory above Kanlıca is **Hıdiv Kasrı**, an art nouveau villa built by the last khedive of Egypt as a summer residence. Restored after decades of neglect, it now functions as a **restaurant** (mains ₺10-20.50) and **garden cafe** (tosts ₺4-4.50, cake ₺6). The villa is an architectural gem, and the extensive garden is superb, particularly during the İstanbul Tulip Festival in April. To get here from the ferry stop, turn left into Halide Edip Adivar Caddesi and then turn right into the second street (Kafadar Sokak). Turn left into Haci Muhittin Sokağı and walk up the hill until you come to a fork in the road. Take the left fork and follow the 'Hadiv Kasrí' signs to the villa's car park and garden.

Kanlıca to Sarıyer

Opposite Kanlıca on the European shore is the wealthy suburb of Emirgan. It's well worth coming here to visit the impressive **Sakıp Sabancı Museum** (Sakıp Sabancı Müsezi; 🖰212-277 2200; http://muze.sabanciuniv.edu; Sakıp Sabancı Caddesi 42; admission varies; ⏱10am-6pm Tue, Thu, Fri & Sun, to 10pm Wed & Sat; 🚌Emirgan), which hosts world-class travelling exhibitions. The museum is also home to one of the city's most glamorous eateries, Müzede Changa (p113), which has a terrace with sweeping Bosphorus views. If you're after a simpler snack, there's a branch of the popular chain eatery Sütiş (p113) opposite the ferry dock. It has outdoor seating and a delicious all-day breakfast menu.

On the hill above the museum is **Emirgan Woods**, a huge public reserve that is particularly beautiful in April, when it is carpeted with thousands of tulips.

North of Emirgan, there's a ferry dock near the small yacht-lined cove of İstinye. Nearby, on a point jutting out from the European shore, is the suburb of Yeniköy. This was a favourite summer resort for the Ottomans, as indicated by the cluster of lavish 18th- and 19th-century *yalıs* around the ferry dock. The most notable of these is the frilly white **Ahmed Afif Paşa Yalı**, designed by Alexandre Vallaury, architect of the Pera Palas Hotel in Beyoğlu, and built in the late 19th century. On the opposite shore is the suburb of Paşabahçe, famous for its glassware factory.

Originally called Therapeia for its healthy climate, the little cove of Tarabya to the north of Yeniköy on the European shore has been a favourite summer watering place for İstanbul's well-to-do for centuries, although modern development has sullied some of its charm. For an account of Therapeia in its heyday, read Harold Nicholson's 1921 novel, *Sweet Waters*.

North of the village are some of the old summer embassies of foreign powers. When the heat and fear of disease increased in the warm months, foreign ambassadors and their staff would retire to these palatial residences, complete with lush gardens. Such residences extended north to the village of Büyükdere, which is also notable for its churches and for the **Sadberk Hanım Müzesi** (☎212-242 3813; www.sadberkhanimmuzesi.org.tr; Piyasa Caddesi 27-29; adult ₺7, student ₺2; ◷10am-5pm Thu-Tue), named after the wife of the late Vehbi Koç, founder of Turkey's foremost commercial empire. There's an eclectic collection here, including beautiful İznik and Kütahya ceramics, Ottoman silk textiles, and Roman coins and jewellery. The museum is a 10-minute walk from the next ferry stop, at Sarıyer.

Sarıyer to Anadolu Kavağı

After stopping at Sarıyer, the ferry sails on to Rumeli Kavağı, known for its fish restaurants. After a short stop here it then crosses the strait to finish the journey at Anadolu Kavağı. Once a fishing village, its local economy now relies on the tourism trade and its main square is full of mediocre fish restaurants and their touts.

Perched above the village are the ruins of Anadolu Kavağı Kalesi (Yoros Kalesi), a medieval castle that originally had eight massive towers in its walls. First built by the Byzantines, it was restored and reinforced by the Genoese in 1350, and later by the Ottomans. Unfortunately, the castle is in such a serious state of disrepair that it has been fenced so that no one can enter and enjoy its spectacular Black Sea views. As a result, we suggest giving the steep 25-minute walk up here a miss.

❶ Getting There & Around

Most day trippers take the *Uzun Boğaz Turu* (Long Bosphorus Tour). This travels the entire length of the strait in a 90-minute one-way trip and departs from the Boğaz İskelesi at Eminönü daily at 10.35am. From April to October, there is usually an extra service at 1.35pm, and during summer there is an extra service at noon. A ticket costs ₺25 return (*çift*), ₺15 one way (*tek yön*). The ferry stops at Beşiktaş, Kanlıca, Sarıyer, Rumeli Kavağı and Anadolu Kavağı (the turnaround point). It is not possible to get on and off the ferry at stops along the way using the same ticket.

The ferry returns from Anadolu Kavağı at 3pm (plus 4.15pm from April to October).

From April to October, İstanbul Şehir Hatları also operates a two-hour *Kısa Boğaz Turu* (Short Bophorus Tour) cruise that leaves Eminönü daily at 2.30pm. It travels as far as the Fatih Bridge before returning to Eminönü. Tickets cost ₺10.

There are also occasional commuter ferries that cross the Bosphorus. Useful services include Kanlıca to Emirgan (1.05pm, 4.05pm, 5.20pm); Emirgan to Kanlıca and Bebek (4.15pm); and Anadolu Kavağı to Sarıyer (12 ferries per day from 7.15am to 11pm). Note that some of the services are more frequent on Sundays.

Check www.sehirhatlari.com.tr for timetable and fare updates for all services, as these often change.

Another option is to buy a ticket for a cruise on a private excursion boat. Although these only take you as far as Anadolu Hisarı and back (without stopping), the fact that the boats are smaller means that you travel closer to the shoreline and so are able to see a lot more. The entire trip takes about 90 minutes and tickets cost ₺10. Turyol boats leave from the dock on the western side of the Galata Bridge every hour from 11am to 6pm on weekdays and every 45 minutes or so from 11am to 7.15pm on weekends. Boats operated by other companies leave from near the Boğaz İskelesi.

From Sarıyer, bus lines 25E and 40 head south to Emirgan. From Emirgan, 22, 22RE and 25E head to Kabataş and 40, 40T and 42T go to Taksim. All travel via Rumeli Hisarı, Bebek, Ortaköy, Yıldız and Beşiktaş.

If you decide to catch the ferry to Anadolu Kavağı and make your way back to town along the Asian shore by bus, visiting sites along the way, catch no 15A, which leaves from a square straight ahead from the ferry terminal en route to Kavacık Aktarma. Get off at Kanlıca to visit Hıdiv Kasrı or to transfer to bus 15, 15F or 15P, which will take you south to Üsküdar via the Küçüksu stop (for Küçüksu Kasrı) and the Beylerbeyi stop (for Beylerbeyi Palace).

All bus tickets and commuter ferry trips cost ₺2 (₺1.75 with an İstanbulkart).

Golden Horn Ferry   FERRY

Most visitors to İstanbul know about the Bosphorus cruise, but not too many have heard about the *Haliç* (Golden Horn) trip. Until recently, this stretch of water to the north of Galata Bridge was heavily polluted and its suburbs offered little to tempt the traveller. All that's changing these days, though. The waters have been cleaned up, beautification works are underway along the shores, and the Haliç suburbs are being gentrified. Spending a day hopping on and off the ferry and exploring will give you an insight into a very different – and far less touristy – İstanbul.

Departure Point: Eminönü

These ferries start in Üsküdar on the Asian side before taking on most of their passengers at the Haliç İskelesi (Golden Horn Ferry Dock) on the western side of the Galata Bridge at Eminönü. The *iskelesi* is behind a car park next to the Storks building. The ferry then sails underneath the Atatürk Bridge and stops at Kasımpaşa on the opposite side of the Golden Horn. This area is where the Ottoman imperial naval yards were located, and some of the original building stock is still evident

Kasımpaşa to Hasköy

As the ferry makes its way to the next stop, Hasköy, you can see the fascinating Western District suburbs of Fener and Balat on the western (left) shore.

Fener is the traditional home of the city's Greek population and, although few Greeks are resident these days, a number of important Greek Orthodox sites remain. The prominent red-brick building on the hill is the Greek Lycée of the Fener (Megali School or Great School), the oldest house of learning in İstanbul. The school has been housed in Fener since before the Conquest – the present building dates from 1881. Sadly, it currently has a total enrolment of only 50 students.

The church building you can see in the waterside park is the Gothic Revival Church of St Stephen of the Bulgars.

The next suburb, Balat, was once home to a large proportion of İstanbul's Jewish population but is now crowded with migrants from the east of the country.

Passing the derelict remains of the original Galata Bridge on its way, the ferry then docks at Hasköy. In the Ottoman period, this part of the city was home to a naval shipyard and a sultan's hunting ground. Today, it has two sights of interest to visitors: the splendid **Rahmi M Koç Museum** (Rahmi M Koç Müzesi; www.rmk-museum.org .tr; Hasköy Caddesi 5, Hasköy; adult/child ₺6/3; ☉10am-5pm Mon-Fri, to 6pm/8pm Sat & Sun winter/summer; ☐47 from Eminönü, 54HT from Taksim, ⍾Hasköy), dedicated to the history of transport, industry and communications in Turkey; and **Aynalıkavak Kasrı**, an ornate 18th-century imperial hunting pavilion set in extensive grounds. The museum is located directly to the left of the ferry stop; to get to Aynalıkavak Kasrı, walk southeast (right) along Hasköy Caddesi, veer left into Aynalıkavak Caddesi and then right into Kasımpaşa-Hasköy Caddesi

Hasköy to Sütlüce

The ferry's next stop is at Ayvansaray on the opposite shore. From here, you can walk up the hill alongside Theodosius' monumental land walls to visit the Kariye Museum (Chora Church).

From Ayvansaray, the ferry crosses to Sütlüce and then returns to the western shore to terminate at Eyüp. This conservative suburb is built around the **Eyüp Sultan Mosque** (Eyüp Sultan Camii, Mosque of the Great Eyüp; Camii Kebir Sokak, Eyüp; ☉tomb 9.30am-4.30pm; ☐36CE, 44B or 99 from Eminönü, ⍾Eyüp), one of the most important religious sites in Turkey. After visiting the complex, many visitors head north up the hill to enjoy a glass of tea and the wonderful views on offer at the Pierre Loti Café (p117).

❶ Getting There & Around

Haliç ferries leave Eminönü every hour from 10.45am to 7.45pm; the last ferry returns to Eminönü from Eyüp at 7.45pm. The ferry trip takes 35 minutes and costs ₺2 per leg (₺1.75 if you use an İstanbulkart). Check www.sehirhatlari.com.tr for timetable and fare updates.

If you wish to return from Eyüp by bus rather than ferry, buses 36CE, 44B and 99 travel from outside the ferry stop at Eyüp to Eminönü via Balat and Fener. Bus 39 travels to Beyazıt via Edirnekapı, allowing you to stop and visit the Kariye Museum (Chora Church) on your way back.

To return to Taksim from Hasköy or Sütluce by bus, take bus 54HT. For Eminönü, take bus 47.

All bus tickets cost ₺2 (₺1.75 if you use an İstanbulkart).

Hamams

A visit to a hamam is a quintessential Turkish experience. We've listed six here – four tourist hamams in historic buildings on the historical peninsula, one historic hamam in Beyoğlu and one modern hamam that is known for its fantastic massages. The tourist hamams are pricey and their massages generally are short and not particularly good, but you'll be in gorgeous historic surrounds – weighing up these facts and deciding whether or not to go is up to the individual. For a total pampering experience, head to one of the luxe five-star hotel spas in the city – the Ritz Carlton, Hotel Les Ottomans and Four Seasons Istanbul at the Bosphorus all have excellent spas offering indulgent hamam treatments.

İSTANBUL FOR CHILDREN

Children of all ages will enjoy the Rahmi M Koç Müzesi (p95) in Hasköy, which offers loads of activities and gadgets. The spooky Basilica Cistern (p64), with its upside-down heads on columns, is also usually a hit. Older children will enjoy the ferry trip down the Bosphorus, particularly if it's combined with a visit to the fortress of Rumeli Hisarı (p92) – but beware of the steep stairs here, which have no barriers. On Büyükada (p131) and Heybeliada (p131), two of the Princes' Islands, you can hire bikes or circle the island in a *fayton* (horse-drawn carriage), which is lots of fun.

If you're staying in Sultanahmet, there are playgrounds in Kadırga Park, near Little Aya Sofya (p74), and in Gülhane Park (p74). If you're staying in Beyoğlu, there's one right at the water's edge, next to the Fındıklı tram stop and a *çay bahcesi* – very scenic, but be sure to watch your toddlers carefully!

If you need to resort to bribery to ensure good behaviour, look for the **Mado** (Map p90; ☎227 3876; İskele Square; ⏰7am-2am; 🚇Ortaköy) chain of ice-cream shops – there are branches on Divan Yolu in Sultanahmet, on İstiklal Caddesi in Beyoğlu and on Ortaköy Meydanı.

Ayasofya Hürrem Sultan Hamamı HAMAM
(Map p62; ☎212-517 3535; www.ayasofyahamami .com; Aya Sofya Meydanı ; bath treatments €70-165, massages €40-75; ⏰8am-11pm; 🚇Sultanahmet) Reopened in 2011 after a meticulous restoration, this twin hamam is now offering the most luxurious traditional bath experience in the Old City. Designed by Sinan between 1556 and 1557, it was built just across the road from Aya Sofya by order of Süleyman the Magnificent and named in honour of his wife Hürrem Sultan, commonly known as Roxelana.

Cağaloğlu Hamamı HAMAM
(Map p62; ☎212-522 2424; www.cagalogluhamami .com.tr; Yerebatan Caddesi 34; bath, scrub & massage packages €50-110; ⏰8am-10pm; 🚇Sultanahmet) This is undoubtedly the most atmospheric of the city's hamams. Built in 1741 by order of Sultan Mahmut I, it offers separate baths for men and women and a range of bath services that are – alas – overpriced considering how quick and rudimentary the wash, scrub and massage treatments are. Consider signing up for the self-service treatment (€30) only.

Çemberlitaş Hamamı HAMAM
(Map p76; ☎212-522 7974; Vezir Han Caddesi 8; bath, scrub & soap massage €29; ⏰6am-midnight; 🚇Çemberlitaş) There won't be too many times in your life when you'll get the opportunity to have a Turkish bath in a building dating back to 1584, so now might well be the time to do it – particularly as this twin hamam was designed by the great architect Sinan and is among the most beautiful in the city.

It costs an extra €20 to add an oil massage to the standard bath package, but all massages and treatments here are perfunctory so we'd suggest giving this a miss. Tips are meant to be covered in the treatment price and there's a 20% discount for ISIC student-card holders.

Ağa Hamamı HAMAM
(Map p84; ☎212-249 5027; www.agahamami .com; Turnacıbaşı Sokak 48b, Çukurcuma; bath ₺30, soap/oil massage ₺5/30, skin-peeling scrub ₺5; ⏰10am-10pm; 🚇Kabataş, then funicular to Taksim) Dating from 1562, this hamam has a low-key ambience and allows communal bathing for both genders, although scrubs and massages are conducted by same-sex masseurs in private spaces. Prices are surprisingly reasonable, particularly when compared with the historic hamams in the Old City, but standards of cleanliness could be higher.

Gedikpaşa Hamamı HAMAM
(Map p76; ☎212-517 8956; www.gedikpasahama mi.com; Emin Sinan Hamamı Sokak 61, Gedikpaşa; bath, scrub & soap massage ₺55; ⏰men 6am-midnight, women 9am-11pm; 🚇Çemberlitaş) This Ottoman-era hamam has been operating since 1475. Its interior isn't as beautiful as those at Cağaloğlu and Çemberlitaş, but services are slightly cheaper and there are separate hamams, small dipping pools and saunas for both sexes. The operators will sometimes transport guests to and from Sultanahmet hotels at no charge – ask your hotel to investigate this option.

ISTANBUL COURSES

Ambassador Spa HAMAM

(Map p62; ☑212-512 0002; www.istanbulambass adorhotel.com; Ticarethane Sokak 19; Turkish bath treatments €40-60, remedial & aromatherapy massage €25-90; ⏱9am-10pm; 🚇Sultanahmet) There's no Ottoman atmosphere on offer at the shabby spa centre of this hotel just off Divan Yolu, but all treatments are private, meaning that you get the small hamam all to yourself. Best of all is the fact that the signature 60- or 75-minute 'Oriental Massage' package includes both a hamam treatment and an expert 30-minute oil massage.

🎓 Courses

Note that prices for courses are often set in euros or US dollars rather than Turkish lira.

TOP CHOICE Cooking Alaturka COOKING

(Map p73; ☑0536 338 0896; www.cookingalaturka .com; Akbıyık Caddesi 72a, Cankurtaran; cooking class per person €60; 🚇Sultanahmet) Dutch-born Eveline Zoutendijk opened the first English-language Turkish cooking school in İstanbul in 2003 and since then has built a solid reputation for her hands-on classes, which offer a great introduction to Turkish cuisine and are suitable for both novices and experienced cooks. The delicious results are enjoyed over a five-course meal in the school's restaurant (p106).

Müzenin Kahvesi COFFEE

(Map p62; ☑212 517 4580; Museum of Turkish & Islamic Arts, Atmeydanı Caddesi 46; ⏱9am-6.30pm Tue-Sun Apr-Oct, to 4.30pm Nov-Mar; 🚇Sultanahmet) Head to the stylish cafe-laboratory in the courtyard of the Museum of Turkish & Islamic Arts for the best Turkish coffee on the Historic Peninsula. Afficionados can sign up for a 30-minute 'Treasures of Turkey' coffee experience (₺20) that demonstrates roasting, grinding, brewing and service techniques and includes, naturally, a cup of the stuff in question. Bookings are essential.

Turkish Flavours COOKING

(☑0532 218 0653; www.turkishflavours.com; Apartment 3, Vali Konağı Caddesi 14; per person tours US$100-145, cooking classes US$100) As well as running an excellent foodie tour of the Spice Bazaar and Kadıköy markets, which includes a huge lunch at award-winning Çiya Sofrası (p113), Selin Rozanes conducts small-group cooking classes in her elegant Nişantaşı home. The results of your labours are enjoyed over a four-course lunch with

drinks. If requested, the course can focus on a Sephardic menu.

👉 Tours

Note that most tour companies in İstanbul set their charges in euros or US$ rather than in Turkish lira.

TOP CHOICE İstanbul Walks WALKING & CULTURAL TOURS

(Map p62; ☑212-516 6300; www.istanbulwalks.net; 2nd fl, Şifa Hamamı Sokak 1; walking tours €25-75, child under 6yr free; 🚇Sultanahmet) Specialising in cultural tourism, this small company is run by a group of history buffs and offers a large range of guided walking tours conducted by knowledgeable English-speaking guides. Tours concentrate on İstanbul's various neighbourhoods, but there are also tours to major monuments including Topkapı Palace, the İstanbul Archaeology Museums and Dolmabahçe Palace. Student discounts are available.

TOP CHOICE Culinary Backstreets WALKING TOUR

(www.culinarybackstreets.com) Full-day walking tours of the Old City and Beyoğlu (with lunch) as well as an evening spent tasting regional dishes from southeastern Anatolia in a progression of eateries in Aksaray's 'Little Urfa' district. All are conducted by the dedicated foodies who produce the excellent blog of the same name.

Urban Adventures WALKING & CULTURAL TOURS

(Map p62; ☑212-512 7144; www.urbanadventures .com; 1st fl, Ticarethane Sokak 11; all tours ₺50; ⏱8.30am-5.30pm; 🚇Sultanahmet) The international tour company Intrepid offers a program of city tours including a popular four-hour guided walk around Sultanahmet and the Bazaar District. Also on offer is the 'Home Cooked İstanbul' tour, which includes a no-frills dinner with a local family in their home plus a visit to a neighbourhood teahouse for tea, a nargile and a game of backgammon.

Les Arts Turcs CULTURAL TOUR

(Map p62; ☑212-527 6859; www.lesartsturcs.com; 3rd fl, İncili Çavuş Sokak 19; workshops ₺100-150, tours from ₺150, dervish ceremony ₺60; 🚇Sultanahmet) This small cultural tourism company organises a range of tours and workshops, including visits to Sufi *tekke*s where the whirling-dervish ceremony is held, ebru and calligraphy workshops, belly-dancing lessons, tours of synagogues in the Western districts and photography tours.

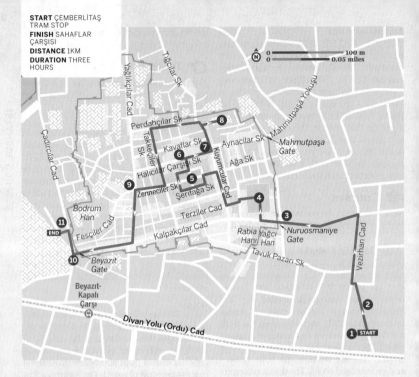

START ÇEMBERLİTAŞ
TRAM STOP
FINISH SAHAFLAR
ÇARŞISI
DISTANCE 1KM
DURATION THREE
HOURS

Walking Tour
Grand Bazaar

❯ Visitors are often overwhelmed by the bazaar's labyrinthine layout and vociferous touts, but if you follow this walking tour you should enjoy your visit.

Start at the tram stop next to the tall column known as ❶ **Çemberlitaş**, which was erected by order of Emperor Constantine to celebrate the dedication of Constantinople as capital of the Roman Empire in 330. From here, walk down Vezir Han Caddesi and you will soon come to the entrance to the ❷ **Vezir Han**, a *han* (caravanserai) built between 1659 and 1660 by the Köprülüs, one of the Ottoman Empire's most distinguished families. Five of its members served as grand vizier (*vezir*) to the sultan, hence its name. In Ottoman times, this *han* would have offered travelling merchants accommodation and a place to do business. Though gold manufacturers still work here, the *han* is in a sadly dilapidated state, as are the many (some experts say hundreds) of similar buildings dotted throughout the district. Look for the *tuğra* (crest) of the sultan over the main gateway.

Continue walking down Vezir Han Caddesi until you come to a cobbled pedestrianised street on your left. Walk along this until you come to the ❸ **Nuruosmaniye Mosque**, commissioned by Mahmut I in 1748. In front of you is one of the major entrances to the Grand Bazaar, the Nuruosmaniye Kapısı (Nuruosmaniye Gate, Gate 1), adorned by another sultan's seal.

The brightly lit street now in front of you is Kalpakçılarbası Caddesi, the busiest street in the bazaar. Originally named after the *kalpakçılars* (makers of fur hats) who had their stores here, it's now full of jewellers, who pay up to US$80,000 per year in rent for this high-profile location. Start walking down the street and then turn right and take the marble stairs down to the ❹ **Sandal Bedesteni**, a 17th-century stone warehouse featuring 20 small domes. This warehouse has always been used for the storage and sale of fabric, although the current range of cheap textiles on sale couldn't be more different to the fine *sandal* (fabric woven with silk) that was sold here in the past.

Exit the Sandal Bedestenı on its west side, turning right into Sandal Bedestenı Sokak and then left into Ağa Sokak, which takes you into the oldest part of the bazaar, the **5 Cevahir (Jewellery) Bedesten**, also known as the Eski (Old) Bedesten. This has always been an area where precious items are stored and sold, and these days it's where most of the bazaar's antique stores are located. Slave auctions were held here until the mid-19th century.

Exiting the *bedesten* from its south door, walk down to the first cross-street, Halıcılar Çarşışı Sokak, where popular shops including Abdulla Natural Products, Cocoon and Derviş are located. Also here is a good spot for a tea or coffee, **6 Ethem Tezçakar Kahveci**.

Walking east (right) you will come to a major cross-street, Kuyumcular Caddesi (Street of the Jewellers). Over the bazaar's history, most silversmiths working in the bazaar have been of Armenian descent and most goldsmiths have been of Arabic or Aramaic descent – this is still true to this day. Turn left and walk past the little kiosk in the middle of the street. Built in the 17th century and known as the **7 Oriental Kiosk**, it now houses a jewellery store but was once home to the most famous *muhallebici* (milk pudding shop) in the district. A little way further down, on the right-hand side of the street, is the entrance to the pretty **8 Zincirli (Chain) Han**, home to one of the bazaar's best-known carpet merchants. Returning to Kuyumcular Caddesi, turn sharp left into Perdahçılar Sokak (Street of the Polishers). Walk until you reach Takkeçiler Sokak, where you should turn left. This charming street is known for its marble *sebils* (public drinking fountains) and shops selling kilims (pileless woven rugs). Turn right into Zenneciler Sokak (Street of the Clothing Sellers) and you will soon come to a junction with another of the bazaar's major thoroughfares, Sipahi Sokak (Avenue of the Cavalry Soldiers). **9 Şark Kahvesi**, a traditional coffee house, is right on the corner. Sipahi Sokak becomes

Yağlıkçılar Caddesi to the north (right) and Feraceciler Sokak to the south (left).

Turn left into Sipahi Sokak and walk along this street and Feraceciler Sokak until you return to Kalpakçılarbası Caddesi, the street with all of the jewellery shops. Turn right and exit the bazaar from the **10 Beyazıt Kapısı** (Beyazıt Gate, Gate 7). Turn right again and walk past the market stalls to the first passage on the left, and you will find yourself in the **11 Sahaflar Çarşısı** (Old Book Bazaar), which has operated as a book and paper market since Byzantine times. At the centre of its shady courtyard is a bust of İbrahim Müteferrika (1674–1745), who printed the first book in Turkey in 1732. From here, you can exit to Beyazıt Meydanı and make your way down Divan Yolu Caddesi to Sultanahmet or continue walking north along the walls of İstanbul University to the Süleymaniye Mosque.

Many visitors choose to combine a visit to the Grand Bazaar with one to the Spice Bazaar at Eminönü. If you are keen to do this, backtrack through the bazaar to the Mahmutpaşa Kapısı (Mahmutpaşa Gate, Gate 18) and follow busy Mahmutpaşa Yokuşu all the way down the hill to the Spice Bazaar. Along the way you will pass one of the oldest hamams in the city, the Mahmutpaşa Hamamı (now converted into a shopping centre). If you veer left onto Tarakçılar Caddesi before coming to the hamam and walk all the way to Çakmakçılar Yokuşu you will see the historic Büyük Valide Han, a huge and sadly dilapidated caravanserai built by order of Murad IV's mother in 1651. It once accommodated up to 3000 travelling merchants and their animals every night.

This street and the streets to the west of the Spice Bazaar (collectively known as Tahtakale) are the busiest mercantile precincts in the Old City. This is where locals come to buy everything from wedding dresses to woollen socks and coffee cups to circumcision outfits – a wander around here (as opposed to the touristy streets around Sultanahmet) will give you a taste of the real İstanbul.

✷ Festivals & Events

During the warmer months İstanbul is buzzing with arts and music events, giving the visitor plenty of options when it comes to entertainment. Most of the big-name arts festivals are organised by the **İstanbul Foundation for Culture & Arts** (☎0212-334 0700; www.iksv.org/english; Sadi Konuralp Caddesi 5). Tickets to most events are available from **Biletix** (www.biletix.com).

April

İstanbul Film Festival　FILM
(http://film.iksv.org/en) Held early in the month in cinemas around town, this is a hugely popular festival. The program includes retrospectives and recent releases from Turkey and abroad.

İstanbul Tulip Festival　FLOWERS
The city's parks and gardens are planted with over 11 million tulips that come into bloom in late March or early April each year.

June

Efes Pilsen One Love　MUSIC
(www.pozitif-ist.com) This two-day music festival is held at one of İstanbul's hippest art venues, **Santralistanbul** (☎0212-311 7809; www.santralistanbul.org; Kazım Karabekir Caddesi 2/6; adult/over 65yr & under 13yr/student ₺7/5/3; ⊙10am-8pm Tue-Sun). International headline acts play everything from punk to pop, electronica to disco.

TOP CHOICE **İstanbul Music Festival**　MUSIC
(http://muzik.iksv.org/en) The city's premier arts festival includes performances of opera, dance, orchestral concerts and chamber recitals. Acts are often internationally renowned and the action takes place in atmosphere-laden venues including Aya İrini in Sultanahmet.

July

İstanbul Jazz Festival　MUSIC
(http://caz.iksv.org/en) This festival programs an exhilarating hybrid of conventional jazz, electronica, drum 'n' bass, world music and rock. Look out for **Tünel Feast**, its one-day 'festival within the festival', which stages free events around Tünel Meydanı.

September

TOP CHOICE **İstanbul Biennial**　ARTS
(http://bienal.iksv.org/en) The city's major visual-arts shindig takes place from early September to early November in odd-numbered years. An international curator or panel of curators nominates a theme and puts together a cutting-edge program that is then exhibited in a variety of venues around town.

October

İstanbul Design Biennial　DESIGN
(http://istanbuldesignbiennial.iksv.org/) A new addition to the İKSV's stellar calendar of festivals, this event sees the city's design community celebrating its profession and critically discussing its future. It's held in even-numbered years.

Akbank Jazz Festival　MUSIC
(www.akbanksanat.com) This older sister to the International İstanbul Jazz Festival is a boutique event, with a program featuring traditional and avant-garde jazz, as well as Middle Eastern fusions and a special program of young jazz. Venues are scattered around town.

November

Efes Pilsen Blues Festival　MUSIC
(www.pozitif-ist.com) This long-running event tours nationally, keeping blues fans smiling and leaving an echo of boogie-woogie, zydeco and 12-bar blues from Adana to Trabzon. It stops for a two-day program in İstanbul. The main venue is the Lütfi Kırdar Concert Hall.

🛏 Sleeping

Every accommodation style is available in İstanbul. You can live like a sultan in a world-class luxury hotel, doss in a friendly hostel dorm, or relax in a well-priced boutique establishment.

Hotels reviewed here have rooms with private bathroom and include breakfast in the room price. Exceptions are noted in the reviews. All prices given are for high season and include the KDV (*katma değer vergisi*; value-added tax). During low season (October to April, but not around Christmas or Easter) you should be able to negotiate a discount of at least 20% on the price. Before you confirm any booking, ask if the hotel will give you a discount for cash payment (usually 5% or 10%), whether a pick-up from the airport is included (it often is if you stay more than three nights) and whether there are discounts for extended stays. Book ahead from May to September and for the Christmas–New Year period.

Note that almost all hotels in İstanbul set their prices in euros, and we have listed them as such here.

SULTANAHMET & AROUND

The Blue Mosque (Sultan Ahmet Camii) gives its name to the quarter surrounding it. This is the heart of Old İstanbul and is the city's premier sightseeing area, so the hotels here and in the adjoining neighbourhoods to the east (Cankurtaran), south (Küçük Aya Sofya) and northwest (Binbirdirek, Çemberlitaş, Alemdar and Cağaloğlu) are supremely convenient. The area's only drawbacks are the number of carpet touts and the lack of decent bars and restaurants. Note, too, that some of the hotels in Cankurtaran can be noisy – late at night the culprits are the hostels and bars on Akbıyık Caddesi, which play loud music; early in the morning your sleep may be disturbed by the sound of the call to prayer issuing from the İşak Paşa Mosque behind Adliye Sokak.

Hotel Ibrahim Pasha TOP CHOICE BOUTIQUE HOTEL €€
(Map p62; ☏212-518 0394; www.ibrahimpasha. com; Terzihane Sokak 7; r standard €99-195, deluxe €139-265; ❄@🖥; ⓜSultanahmet) Located just off the Hippodrome, this exemplary designer hotel successfully combines Ottoman style with contemporary decor, and is notable for its high levels of service. All of the rooms are gorgeous but some are small – opt for a deluxe one if possible. We love the comfortable lounge and the terrace bar with its knockout views of the Blue Mosque.

Sirkeci Konak TOP CHOICE HOTEL €€
(Map p62; ☏212-528 4344; www.sirkecikonak.com; Taya Hatun Sokak 5, Sirkeci; d standard €155-185, superior & deluxe €170-270; ❄@🖥❄; ⓜGülhane) The owners of this terrific hotel overlooking Gülhane Park know what keeps guests happy – rooms are impeccably clean, well sized and loaded with amenities. There's a restaurant, a roof terrace, an indoor pool and a hamam. Top marks go to the incredibly helpful staff and the complimentary entertainment program, which includes cooking classes, walking tours and afternoon teas.

Marmara Guesthouse TOP CHOICE PENSION €
(Map p73; ☏212-638 3638; www.marmaraguesthouse.com; Terbıyık Sokak 15, Cankurtaran; s €30-65, d €40-70, f €60-100; ❄@; ⓜSultanahmet) There are plenty of family-run pensions in Sultanahmet, but few can claim the Marmara's levels of cleanliness and comfort. Manager Elif Aytekin and her family go out of their way to make guests feel welcome, offering plenty of advice and serving a delicious breakfast on the vine-covered, sea-facing roof terrace. Rooms have comfortable beds and double-glazed windows.

Hotel Empress Zoe BOUTIQUE HOTEL €€
(Map p73; ☏212-518 2504; www.emzoe.com; Akbiyik Caddesi 4, Cankurtaran; s €70-90, d €105-160, ste €135-300; ❄🖥; ⓜSultanahmet) Named after the feisty Byzantine Empress whose portrait is in Aya Sofya, this fabulous place is the prototype for most of Sultanahmet's boutique hotels but is unique in that it is constantly being changed and improved. Its garden suites are particularly enticing, overlooking a gorgeous flower-filled courtyard where breakfast is served in warm weather. The terrace bar has great views.

Sarı Konak Hotel BOUTIQUE HOTEL €€
(Map p73; ☏212-638 6258; www.istanbulhotelsarikonak.com; Mimar Mehmet Ağa Caddesi 42-46, Cankurtaran; r €69-179, ste €129-279; ❄🖥@🖥; ⓜSultanahmet) This is a truly classy joint. The deluxe rooms are spacious and beautifully decorated, the superior rooms are nearly as nice, and standard rooms, though small, are very attractive. Guests (mostly American) enjoy relaxing on the roof terrace with its Sea of Marmara and Blue Mosque views, but can also take advantage of the comfortable lounge and courtyard downstairs.

Saruhan Hotel HOTEL €
(Map p76; ☏212-458 7608; www.saruhanhotel.com; Cinci Meydanı Sokak 34, Kadırga; s €25-65, d €35-70, f €60-100; ❄🖥@🖥; ⓜÇemberlitaş) Hitherto bereft of hotels, the quiet residential pocket of Kadırga is inching its way into the limelight courtesy of impressive family-run operations like this one. The Saruhan offers 17 comfortable and well-equipped rooms and a lovely terrace with a sea view. It's a 20-minute walk to the sights in Sultanahmet and a shorter (but steep) walk to the Grand Bazaar.

Hanedan Hotel HOTEL €
(Map p73; ☏212-516 4869; www.hanedanhotel.com; Adliye Sokak 3, Cankurtaran; s €30-50, d €45-65, f €75-100; ❄@🖥; ⓜSultanahmet) The 11 rooms at this cheap, clean and comfortable choice feature lino floors, lace curtains and small white marble bathrooms. One large and two interconnected rooms are perfect for families, and the pleasant roof terrace overlooks the sea and Aya Sofya.

Hotel Alp
HOTEL €€

(Map p73; ☎212-517 7067; www.alpguesthouse.com; Adliye Sokak 4, Cankurtaran; s €35-60, d €55-80, f €80-110; ✿@☎; ☐Sultanahmet) The Alp lives up to its location in Sultanahmet's premier small-hotel enclave, offering a range of attractive, very well-priced rooms. Bathrooms are small but very clean, and there are plenty of amenities. The roof terrace is one of the best in this area, with great sea views and comfortable indoor and outdoor seating.

Hotel Peninsula
HOTEL €

(Map p73; ☎212-458 6850; www.hotelpeninsula.com; Adliye Sokak 6, Cankurtaran; s €30-50, d €40-65, f €90-120; ✿@☎; ☐Sultanahmet) Hallmarks here are friendly staff, comfortable rooms and bargain prices. There's a terrace with sea views and hammocks, and a breakfast room with outdoor tables. Basement rooms are dark, but have reduced prices. The same owners operate the slightly more expensive and comfortable Grand Peninsula (Map p73; ☎212-458 7710; www.grandpeninsula hotel.com; Cetinkaya Sokak 3, Cankurtaran; s €35-60, d €45-80; ✿@☎), a few streets away.

Hotel Şebnem
HOTEL €€

(Map p73; ☎212-517 6623; www.sebnemhotel.net; Adliye Sokak 1, Cankurtaran; s €40-70, d €50-100, f €70-120; ✿@☎; ☐Sultanahmet) Simplicity is the rule at the Şebnem, and it works a treat. Rooms have wooden floors, good bathrooms and comfortable beds with crisp white linen. The large terrace upstairs has views over the Sea of Marmara (as do the more expensive double rooms), and two downstairs rooms have a private courtyard garden.

Acra Hotel
HOTEL €€

(Map p73; ☎212-458 9410; www.acrahotel.com; Amiral Tafdil Sokak 15, Cankurtaran; s €60-145, d €70-160, f €115-250; ✿@☎; ☐Sultanahmet) Most of the small hotels in Sultanahmet fit the same pleasant if unexciting mould, but the Acra offers something different. Large, extremely attractive rooms with elegant Ottoman-influenced decor feature lovely marble bathrooms, spacious wardrobes and comfortable beds. There's no roof terrace, but the extraordinary breakfast-room-cum-Byzantine-archeological-site compensates, as does free afternoon tea in the foyer.

Neorion Hotel
HOTEL €€

(Map p62; ☎212-527 9090; www.neorionhotel.com; Orhaniye Caddesi 14, Sirkeci; d standard €155-185,

---

APARTMENT LIVING

We all daydream about packing our bags and escaping to live in another country at some stage in our lives. In İstanbul, it's easy to hire an apartment and do just that for a week or two.

There's a rapidly proliferating number of short-term apartment rentals on offer here, all of which are furnished and most of which come with amenities such as wi-fi, washing machines and weekly service. Many are located in historic apartment blocks and offer spectacular views – just remember that the usual trade-off for this is a steep flight of stairs.

The following companies are worth investigating; most have three- or four-day minimum rental periods:

1001 Nites (www.1001nites.com; Sultanahmet apt for 2 people per night €100, Çukurcuma apt for 4 people €120, 10% discount for weekly stays) Reasonably new outfit run by a charming American and her Turkish business partner. Locations in Sultanahmet, Gümüşsuyu, Çukurcuma and Cihangir.

Istanbul Apartments (☎0212-249 5065; www.istanbulapt.com; d €70-80, tr €85-95, q €110-120; ✿@) Run by an urbane Turkish couple, with properties in Cihangir, Tarlabası and off İstiklal.

İstanbul Holiday Apartments (☎212-251 8530; www.istanbulholidayapartments.com; apt per night €115-260, minimum stay 3 or 7 nights; ✿) Run by an American and with locations as diverse as Sultanahmet, Galata and Gümüşsuyu.

Manzara İstanbul (Map p84; ☎212-252 4660; www.manzara-istanbul.com/en; Serdar-ı Ekrem Sokak 14, Galata; per night €55-190; ✿☎) A huge operation run by a Turkish/German architect. Locations are mainly in Galata, Cihangir and Kabataş.

superior & deluxe €170-270; ✹@⛶≋; 🚇Sirkeci) This recent addition to the Sirkeci Group's hotel portfolio offers the comfortable, well-appointed rooms and high-level customer care that the group's properties are known for. The 'Modern Ottoman' decor here is attractive, the roof terrace has spectacular views, and there's a health club with small pool, jacuzzi, sauna and two hamams. Everyone loves the free early-evening meze buffet.

And Hotel
HOTEL €€

(Map p62; ☎212-512 0207; www.andhotel.com; Yerebatan Caddesi 36; ⊘s €79-99, d €99-109; ✹@⛶; 🚇Sultanahmet) We've included this resolutely old-fashioned place (imagine ivory wallpaper and floral carpets) for three reasons: it's wonderfully located opposite Aya Sofya; the Cihannüma (p106) restaurant on its top floor is one of the best in Sultanahmet; and its prices are remarkably reasonable. You could do a lot worse.

Cheers Hostel
HOSTEL €

(Map p62; ☎212-526 0200; www.cheershostel.com; Zeynep Sultan Camii Sokak 21; dm €15-20, d €60-75, tr €90-105; ✹@⛶; 🚇Gülhane) This friendly place has lovely dorms that are worlds away from the impersonal barracks-like spaces so often seen in hostels. Bright and airy, they feature wooden floorboards, rugs, lockers and comfortable beds; most have air-con. Bathrooms are clean and plentiful. It's a great choice in winter because the cosy rooftop bar has an open fire.

Metropolis Hostel
HOSTEL €

(Map p73; ☎212-518 1822; www.metropolishostel .com; Terbıyık Sokak 24, Cankurtaran; dm €13-18, s without bathroom €30-44, d €45-75, without bathroom €30-48; ✹@⛶; 🚇Sultanahmet) Located in a quiet street far enough away from noisy Akbıyık Caddesi that a good night's sleep is assured, this friendly place offers a mix of dorms and rooms – all with comfortable beds and private lockers. Showers and toilets are clean but in limited supply. Guests love the rooftop terrace with its sea views and enjoy the busy entertainment program.

Sultans Royal Hotel
HOTEL €€

(Map p62; ☎212-517 1307; www.sultansroyalhotel .com; Mustafa Paşa Sokak 29, Küçük Ayasofya; s €40-90, d €45-95, ste €65-140; ✹@⛶; 🚇Sultanahmet) Restrained but elegant decor and quietly efficient service are the hallmarks of this recently opened hotel in the peaceful Küçük Ayasofya neighbourhood. The 16 rooms feature wooden floorboards covered

by rugs, ceilings with hand-painted decoration, comfortable beds and plenty of amenities. Unfortunately, there's no roof terrace.

Hotel Uyan İstanbul
HOTEL €€

(Map p73; ☎212-518 9255; www.uyanhotel.com; Utangaç Sokak 25, Cankurtaran; s €50-60, d standard €79-99, deluxe €95-150; ✹@⛶) The Uyan's elegant decor nods towards the Ottoman style, but never goes over the top – everyone will feel comfortable here. The view from its spacious roof terrace is one of the best in the area, and the breakfast spread is generous. Rooms are comfortable and attractive, with a good range of amenities.

Tan Hotel
HOTEL €€

(Map p62; ☎212-520 9130; www.tanhotel.com; Dr Emin Paşa Sokak 20; s €65-115, d €70-125, ste €90-159; ✹@⛶; 🚇Sultanahmet) This well-run hotel off Divan Yolu is notable for its convenient location and excellent customer service. Rooms are large, with spacious bathrooms (all have tubs) and the lavish breakfast buffet includes freshly squeezed orange juice and eggs cooked to order. The roof terrace has views of the Blue Mosque and the Sea of Marmara.

Agora Life Hotel
HOTEL €€€

(Map p62; ☎212-526 1181; www.agoralifehotel.com; Cağoloğlu Hamamı Sokak 6, Cağoloğlu; s €69-129, d €79-209, ste €199-259; ✹@⛶) Opened in 2010, this hotel in a quiet cul-de-sac around the corner from the Cağaloğlu Hamamı isn't aiming for hip hotel credentials, instead focusing on service and quiet elegance as its signatures. There are plenty of amenities in the rooms, and the rooftop terrace has a simply extraordinary view. Opt for one of the deluxe or suite rooms if possible.

Emine Sultan Hotel
HOTEL €€

(Map p62; ☎212-458 4666; www.eminesultanhotel .com; Kapıağası Sokak 6, Cankurtaran; s €75-85, d €105-120; ✹@⛶; 🚇Sultanahmet) Solo female travellers and families will feel particularly at home here because manager Özen Dalgın is as friendly as she is efficient, and the rest of the staff follow her lead. Rooms have a pretty cream-and-pink decor and some have sea views. A delicious breakfast is served in the upstairs breakfast room, which overlooks the Sea of Marmara.

Hotel Nomade
BOUTIQUE HOTEL €€

(Map p62; ☎212-513 8172; www.hotelnomade. com; Ticarethane Sokak 15; s €85, d €100-120; ✹) Designer style and budget pricing don't often go together, but the Nomade bucks the trend. Just a few steps off busy Divan Yolu, it offers simple rooms that some guests find too small – book a superior version if possible. Everyone loves the roof-terrace bar (smack-bang in front of Aya Sofya) and the hip foyer.

Ottoman Hotel Imperial   HOTEL €€

(Map p62; ☎212-513 6150; www.ottomanhotelimperial.com; Caferiye Sokak 6; s €99-159, d standard €109-179, superior €139-259; ❄@❀; ☐Sultanahmet) This four-star hotel is in a wonderfully quiet location just outside the Topkapı Palace walls. Its large and comfortable rooms have plenty of amenities and are decorated with Ottoman-style objets d'art – opt for one with an Aya Sofya view or one in the rear annexe. No roof terrace, but the popular Matbah (p106) restaurant is based here.

Bahaus Hostel   HOSTEL €

(Map p73; ☎212-638 6534; www.bahaushostelistanbul.com; Bayram Fırını Sokak 11, Cankurtaran; dm €11-19, d €25-30, without bathroom €20-25; @❀; ☐Sultanahmet) There's no design-driven minimalism at this Bauhaus. A small and slightly chaotic operation, it stands in stark and welcome contrast to the huge institutional-style hostels found on nearby Akbıyık Caddesi. Dorms (some female-only with bathroom) have curtained bunks with good mattresses; those upstairs are nicest. Top marks go to the plentiful bathrooms, entertainment program and rooftop terrace bar.

Motif Apartments   APARTMENT €€

(Map p73; ☎212-458 7702; www.motifapart.com; Yeni Saraçhane Sokak 10, Cankurtaran; apt €60-150; ❄❀; ☐Sultanahmet) Apartments are relatively hard to find in Sultanahmet, so this recently opened place is most welcome. Three well-sized rooms (one on each floor) have a bed, sofa bed and kitchenette, making them a good choice for families of three or – at a pinch – four. The top-floor apartment has a sea view and there's a small communal roof terrace.

Agora Guesthouse & Hostel   HOSTEL €€

(Map p73; ☎212-458 5547; www.agoraguesthouse.com; Amiral Tafdil Sokak 6, Cankurtaran; dm €12-20, s €45-65, d €55-90; ❄@❀) Worth considering for its comfortable bunk beds (all with large lockers underneath), good roof terrace and clean, modern bathrooms. Drawbacks: an inadequate number of showers and toilets and a lack of natural light in the basement dorms.

BEYOĞLU & AROUND

Most visitors to İstanbul stay in Sultanahmet, but Beyoğlu is becoming a popular alternative. Stay here to avoid the touts in the Old City, and because buzzing, bohemian Beyoğlu has the best wining, dining and shopping in the city. It's also where most of the suite hotels and apartment rentals are located.

Getting to/from the historical sights of Old İstanbul from Beyoğlu is easy: you can either walk across Galata Bridge (approximately 45 minutes), or catch the Taksim Meydanı–Kabataş funicular and tram.

TOP CHOICE Beş Oda   BOUTIQUE HOTEL €€

(Map p84; ☎212-252 7501; www.5oda.com; Şahkulu Bostan Sokak 16, Galata; ste €85-150; ❄@❀; ☐Karaköy, then funicular to Tünel) The name means 'Five Rooms', and that's exactly what this stylish and friendly suite hotel in bohemian Galata is offering. A great deal of thought has gone into the design here – each suite has an equipped kitchenette, lounge area, custom-designed furniture, large bed with good reading lights, black-out curtains, and windows that open to let in fresh air.

TOP CHOICE Witt Istanbul Hotel   BOUTIQUE HOTEL €€€

(Map p84; ☎212-293 1500; www.wittistanbul.com; Defterdar Yokuşu 26; ste €160-390; ❄@❀; ☐Tophane) Showcasing nearly as many designer features as an issue of *Monacle* magazine, this stylish apartment hotel in the trendy suburb of Cihangir has 18 suites with fully equipped kitchenettes, seating areas, CD/DVD players, iPod docks, Nespresso machines, king-sized beds and huge bathrooms. Penthouse and Sea View suites have fabulous views. The hotel is conveniently located near the Tophane tram stop.

TomTom Suites   BOUTIQUE HOTEL €€€

(Map p84; ☎212-292 4949; www.tomtomsuites.com; Tomtom Kaptan Sokak 18; ste €185-720; ☐Karaköy, then funicular to Tünel) We're more than happy to beat the drum about this suite hotel occupying a former Franciscan nunnery off İstiklal. Its contemporary decor is understated but elegant, with particularly impressive bathrooms, and each suite is beautifully appointed. There's also a rooftop bar-restaurant with fantastic views

Anemon Galata   HOTEL €€

(Map p84; ☎212-293 2343; www.anemonhotels.com; cnr Galata Kulesi Sokak & Büyük Hendek Sokak, Galata; s US$140-210, d US$160-230, ste

US$225-270; ❉ @; 🚇Karaköy) Located on the attractive square surrounding Galata Tower, this wooden building dates from 1842 but has been completely rebuilt inside. Rooms are elegantly decorated and well equipped; some have water views (ask for room 405) There's a rooftop bar-restaurant with great views, and the atmospheric Sensus Wine Bar (p116) is in the basement.

Marmara Pera HOTEL €€€
(Map p84; ☎212-251 4646; www.themarmarahotels .com; Meşrutiyet Caddesi 1, Tepebaşı; r €107-269, ste €238-458; ❉@🛜🏊; 🚇Karaköy, then funicular to Tünel) A great location in the middle of Beyoğlu's major entertainment enclave makes this high-rise modern hotel an excellent choice. Added extras include a health-club, a tiny outdoor pool and the Mikla (p115) rooftop bar and restaurant. It's worth paying extra for a room with a sea view.

World House Hostel HOSTEL €
(Map p84; ☎212-293 5520; www.worldhouseistan bul.com; Galipdede Caddesi 85, Galata; dm €10-18, d €45-55; @🛜; 🚇Karaköy, then funicular to Tünel) Some hostels in İstanbul are impersonal hulks with junglelike atmospheres, but World House is reasonably small and very friendly. Best of all is its location, close to Beyoğlu's entertainment strips but not too far from the sights in Sultanahmet. There are large and small dorms (one shower for every six beds), but none are female-only. Internet costs ₺3 per hour.

Chambers of the Boheme HOSTEL €
(Map p84; ☎212-251 0931; www.hostelsistanbul .net; Küçük Parmak Kapı Sokak 13 , Taksim; dm €14-20, f €100; ❉@🛜; 🚇Kabataş, then funicular to Taksim) Despite its name, this popular hostel isn't a bit prententious. A friendly vibe prevails, but the location is very noisy – bring earplugs or prepare to party throughout the night.

Galateia Residence APARTMENT €€€
(Map p84; ☎212-245 3032; www.galateiaresi dence.com; Şahkulu Bostan Sokak 9, Galata; 2-/3-bed apt €140-270, 4-/5-bed apt €170-360; ❉🛜; 🚇Karaköy, then funicular to Tünel) Galateia's 13 attractive and extremely comfortable apartments opened in 2009 and are wearing well. Housed in two adjacent 19th-century buildings, they are perfect for families or for those on business. Good work desks, large beds, well-equipped kitchens, home-entertainment sytems and ample wardrobe space offer all of the comforts of home, sometimes with extraordinary views. A four-night minimum stay applies.

Pera Palace Hotel HISTORIC HOTEL €€€
(Map p84; ☎212-377 4000; www.perapalace.com; Meşrutiyet Caddesi 52, Tepebaşı; r €205-325, ste €350-2600; ❉@🛜; 🚇Karaköy, then funicular to Tünel) Rarely has a reopening engendered as much anticipation as this one. The hotel's €23-million restoration was completed in 2010 and locals have flocked here to see the result. Rooms have been given a luxurious facelift and, although most are cramped, the sumptuous breakfast buffet and extensive facilities (restaurants, spa, gym) compensate. Don't bother paying extra for a Golden Horn view.

BEŞİKTAŞ, ORTAKÖY & KURUÇEŞME

Four Seasons İstanbul at the Bosphorus LUXURY HOTEL €€€
(☎212-381 4000; www.fourseasons.com/bospho rus; Çırağan Caddesi 28; s €370-540, d €400-570, ste €600-18,000; ❉@🛜🏊; 🚇Bahçeşehir University or Çırağan) One of two Four Seasons choices in İstanbul, this hotel incorporates an Ottoman building known as the Atik Paşa Konak. Service here is exemplary, rooms are luxurious and the setting on the Bosphorus is truly magical. Add to this an excellent spa, restaurant, terrace bar-cafe and huge outdoor pool overlooking the Bosphorus and you are left with an unbeatable package.

House Hotel BOUTIQUE HOTEL €€€
(Map p90; ☎212-244 3400; www.thehousehotel .com; Salhane Sokak 1, Ortaköy; r €200-250, ste €260-820; ❉🛜; 🚇Kabataş Lisesi) This handsome 19th-century building presides over Ortaköy's main square and has balconies fronting the Bosphorus. Recently converted into a 26-room hotel by the people behind the wildly successful House Cafes (one of which is on the ground floor), the hotel offers fabulous suites and less-impressive (cramped) 'superior' rooms. All are noisy on weekends. There are other branches in Nişantaşı (great) and Galatasaray (so-so).

✖ Eating

İstanbul is a food-lover's paradise. Teeming with affordable fast-food joints, cafes and restaurants, it leaves visitors spoiled for choice when it comes to choosing a venue. Unfortunately, Sultanahmet has the least impressive range of eating options in the city. Rather than eating here at night, we recommend crossing Galata Bridge and joining the locals in Beyoğlu and the Bosphorus suburbs.

Note that, if we've included a telephone number in the review, it means you should book ahead.

For a good local foodie website, check Culinary Backstreets (p97).

SULTANAHMET & AROUND

TOP CHOICE **Ahırkapı Balıkçısı** SEAFOOD €€
(Map p62; ☎212-518 4988; Keresteci Hakkı Sokak 46, Cankurtaran; mezes ₺5-25, fish ₺15-70; ☺4-11pm; ⓜSultanahmet) For years we've been promising locals we won't list this neighbourhood fish restaurant in our book. We sympathised with their desire to retain the place's low profile, particularly as it's tiny and relatively cheap. However, the food here is so good and the eating alternatives in this area so bad that we've finally decided to share the secret. Book ahead.

TOP CHOICE **Hafız Mustafa** SWEETS €
(Map p62; www.hafizmustafa.com; Muradiye Caddesi 51, Sirkeci; börek ₺5, baklava ₺6-7.50, puddings ₺6; ☺7am-2am; ⓜSirkeci) Making locals happy since 1864, this *şekerlemeleri* (confectionery shop) sells delicious *lokum*, baklava, milk puddings, pastries and *börek* (filled pastries). Put your sweet tooth to good use in the upstairs cafe, or choose a selection of indulgences to take home. There's a second branch in the Kıraathanesi Foundation of Turkish Literature on **Divan Yolu** (Map p62; Divan Yolu Caddesi 14, Sultanahmet; ⓜSultanahmet) and a third on **Hamidiye Caddesi** (Map p62; ☎212-526 5627; Hamidiye Caddesi 84-86; ☺8am-8pm Mon-Sat, 9am-8pm Sun; ⓜEminönü) close to the Spice Bazaar.

TOP CHOICE **Cihannüma** TURKISH €€€
(Map p62; ☎212-520 7676; www.cihannumaistanbul.com; And Hotel, Yerebatan Caddesi 18; mezes ₺5-19, mains ₺27-47; ⓜSultanahmet) The view from the top-floor restaurant of this modest hotel is probably the best in the Old City. The Blue Mosque, Aya Sofya, Topkapı Palace, Galata Tower, Dolmabahçe Palace and the Bosphorus Bridge provide a stunning backdrop to a menu showcasing good kebaps (we recommend the the *kuzu şiş*), interesting Ottoman-influenced stews and a few vegetarian dishes.

Cooking Alaturka TURKISH €€
(Map p73; ☎212-458 5919; www.cookingalaturka.com; Akbıyık Caddesi 72a, Cankurtaran; set lunch or dinner ₺50; ☺lunch Mon-Sat & dinner by reservation Mon-Sat; ⓜSultanahmet) Dutch-born owner-chef Eveline Zoutendijk and her Turkish colleague Fehzi Yıldırım serve a set four-course menu of simple Anatolian dishes at this tranquil restaurant near the Blue Mosque. The menu makes the most of fresh seasonal produce, and can be tailored to suit vegetarians or those with food allergies (call ahead). No children under six at dinner and no credit cards.

Paşazade TURKISH €€
(Map p62; ☎212-513 3750; www.pasazade.com; İbn-i Kemal Caddesi 5a, Sirkeci; mezes ₺7-18, mains ₺18-28; ☺lunch & dinner; ⓜGülhane) Advertising itself as an *Osmanlı mutfağı* (Ottoman kitchen), Paşazade has long garnered rave reviews from tourists staying in the hotels around Sirkeci. Well-priced dishes are served in the streetside restaurant or on the rooftop terrace (summer only). Portions are large, the food is tasty and service is attentive. Top marks go to the traditional meze platter (₺17).

Matbah OTTOMAN €€€
(Map p62; ☎212-514 6151; www.matbahrestaurant.com; Ottoman Imperial Hotel, Caferiye Sokak 6/1; mezes ₺10-22, mains ₺28-48; ☺lunch & dinner; ⓜSultanahmet) This recent addition to the city's growing number of restaurants specialising in so-called 'Ottoman Palace Cuisine' is well worth a visit. The chef has sourced 375 recipes from the imperial archives and offers an array of dishes, some of which are more successful than others. The surrounds are attractive and live Ottoman music is performed on Friday and Saturday nights.

Balıkçı Sabahattin SEAFOOD €€€
(Map p73; ☎212-458 1824; www.balikcisabahattin.com; Seyit Hasan Koyu Sokak 1, Cankurtaran; mezes ₺10-30, fish ₺30-60; ☺noon-midnight; ⓜSultanahmet) The limos outside Balıkçı Sabahattin pay testament to its enduring popularity with the city's establishment, who join cashed-up tourists in enjoying its limited menu of meze and fish. The food here is excellent, though the service is often harried. You'll dine in a wooden Ottoman house or under a leafy canopy in the garden.

Çiğdem Pastanesi CAFE €
(Map p62; Divan Yolu Caddesi 62a; cappuccino ₺5, tea ₺2, pastries ₺1-4; ☺8am-11pm; ⓜSultanah-

FISH SANDWICHES

The city's favourite fast-food treat is undoubtedly the *balık ekmek* (fish sandwich), and the most atmospheric place to try one of these is at the Eminönü end of the Galata Bridge. Here, in front of fishing boats tied to the quay, are a number of **stands** (Map p76) where mackeral fillets are grilled, crammed into fresh bread and served with salad; a generous squeeze of bottled lemon is optional but recommended. A sandwich will set you back a mere ₺5 or so, and is delicious accompanied by a glass of the *şalgam* (sour turnip juice) sold by nearby pickle vendors.

There are plenty of other places around town to try a *balık ekmek* – head to any *iskele* (ferry dock) and there's bound to be a stand nearby. Alternatively, **Fürreyya Galata Balıkçısı** (Map p84), a tiny place opposite the Galata Tower, serves an excellent versions for ₺7.

met) Strategically located on the main drag between Aya Sofya Meydanı and the Grand Bazaar, Çiğdem has been serving locals since 1961 and is still going strong. Pop in for a quick cup of tea or coffee accompanied by a cake, *börek* or *acma* (Turkish-style bagel).

Sefa Restaurant   TURKISH €
(Map p62; Nuruosmaniye Caddesi 17; portions ₺7-12, kebaps ₺12-18; ⊙7am-5pm; 🍴; 🚇Sultanahmet) Locals rate this place near the bazaar highly. It describes its cuisine as Ottoman, but what's really on offer here are *lokanta* (ready-made) dishes and kebaps at extremely reasonable prices. You can order from an English menu or choose daily specials from the bain-marie. Try to arrive early-ish for lunch because many of the dishes run out by 1.30pm. No alcohol.

Hocapaşa Pidecisi   PIDE €
(Map p62; www.hocapasa.com.tr; Hocapaşa Sokak 19, Sirkeci; pides ₺8-14; ⊙10am-10pm Mon-Sat; 🚇Sirkeci) If you're in the Sirkeci neighbourhood at lunchtime, join the locals in Hocapaşa Sokak, a pedestrianised street lined with cheap eateries. Here, *lokantas* serve *hazır yemek* (ready-made dishes), *köftecis* dish out flavoursome meatballs, *kebapçis* grill meat to order and this much-loved *pidecisi* (it opened in 1964) offers piping-hot pides accompanied by pickles. For more about eating in Sirkeci check http://sirkecirestaurants.com.

Caferağa Medresesi
Lokanta & Çay Bahçesi   TURKISH €
(Map p62; Soğukkuyu Çıkmazı 5, off Caferiye Sokak; soup ₺4, portions ₺10; ⊙8.30am-4pm; 🚇Sultanahmet) In Sultanahmet, it's rare to eat in stylish surrounds without paying through the nose for the privilege. That's why the small *lokan-*

ta in the gorgeous courtyard of this Sinan-designed *medrese* near Topkapı Palace is such a find. The food isn't anything to write home about, but it's fresh and inexpensive. You can enjoy a tea break here, but it's an alcohol-free zone.

Karadeniz Aile
Pide ve Kebap Salonu   PIDE, KEBAP €
(Map p62; Biçki Yurdu Sokak, off Divan Yolu Caddesi; pides ₺8-12; ⊙11am-11pm; 🚇Sultanahmet) This long-timer off Divan Yolu serves a delicious *mercimek* (lentil soup) and decent pides. You can claim a table in the utilitarian interior, but in warm weather most people prefer those on the cobbled lane. No alcohol.

BAZAAR DISTRICT

TOP CHOICE Fatih Damak Pide   PIDE €
(Büyük Karaman Caddesi 48, Zeyrek; pide ₺8-12; ⊙11am-11pm; 🚇Aksaray) It's worth making the trek to this *pidecesi* overlooking the İtfaiye Yanı Park Karşısı (Fire Station Park) near the Aqueduct of Valens. Its reputation for making the best Karadeniz (Black Sea)–style pide on the Historic Peninsula is well deserved, and the free pots of tea served with meals are a nice touch. Great pide, great staff, great choice!

Toppings are pretty well standard (the *sucuklu-peynirli* option is particularly tasty), but there's also an unusual *bafra pidesi* (rolled-up pitta-style pizza) on offer. There's also an organic open buffet brunch on weekends costing a mere ₺12.50 per person. No alcohol.

TOP CHOICE Hamdi Restaurant   KEBAPS €€
(Map p76; ☎212-528 8011; www.hamdirestorant .com.tr; Kalçın Sokak 17, Eminönü; mezes ₺7-15, kebaps ₺20-28, dessert ₺7-15; 🚇Eminönü) Hamdi Arpacı arrived in İstanbul in the 1960s and

almost immediately established a street stand near the Spice Bazaar where he grilled and sold tasty kebaps made according to recipes from his hometown Urfa, in Turkey's southeast. His kebaps became so popular with locals that he soon acquired this nearby building, which has phenomenal views from its top-floor terrace.

A meal here offers views of the Old City, Golden Horn and Galata, as well as tasty food and a bustling atmosphere. It's always busy, so make sure you book, and don't forget to request a rooftop table with a view (outside if the weather is hot). If you arrive early, you might be able to score one of these without booking.

TOP CHOICE **Siirt Fatih Büryan** TURKISH €

(İtfaiye Caddesi 20a, Zeyrek; büryan ₺11, perde pilavi ₺10; 🚇Aksaray) Those who enjoy investigating regional cuisines should head to this eatery in the Kadın Pazarı (Women's Market) near the Aqueduct of Valens. It specialises in two dishes that are a specialty of the southeastern city of Siirt: *büryan* (lamb slow-cooked in a pit) and *perde pilavi* (chicken and rice cooked in pastry). Both are totally delicious.

The *büryan* here is meltingly tender and is served on flat bread with crispy bits of lamb fat and a dusting of salt. *Perde pilavi* is made with rice, chicken, almonds and currants that are encased in a thin pastry shell and then baked until the exterior turns golden and flaky. Order either of these with a glass of frothy homemade *ayran* (salty yoghurt drink) and you'll be happy indeed. No alcohol.

Sur Ocakbaşı KEBAP €€

(📞212-533 8088; www.surocakbasi.com; İtfaiye Caddesi 27; kebaps ₺11-20; 🚇Aksaray) Indulge in some peerless people-watching while enjoying the grilled meats at this popular local eatery. The square is always full of locals shopping or enjoying a gossip, and tourists were a rare sight before Anthony Bourdain filmed a segment of *No Reservations* here and blew Sur's cover. No alcohol, but there's homemade *ayran*.

Dönerci Şahin Usta KEBAP €

(Map p80; Kılıççılar Sokak 7, Nuruosmaniye; döner kebab ₺10; ⊙10am-3pm Mon-Sat; 🚇Çemberlitaş) Turks take family, football and food seriously. And when it comes to food, few dishes are sampled and assessed as widely as the humble *döner kebap*. Ask any shopkeeper in the Grand Bazaar about who makes the best *döner* in the immediate area, and they are likely to give the same answer: 'Şahin Usta, of course!' Only available to go.

Bahar Restaurant TURKISH €

(Map p80; Yağcı Han 13, off Nuruosmaniye Sokak, Nuruosmaniye; soup ₺4, dishes ₺9-15; ⊙11am-4pm Mon-Sat; 🗹; 🚇Çemberlitaş) Our favourite eatery in the Grand Bazaar precinct, tiny Bahar ('Spring') is popular with local shopkeepers and is always full, so arrive early to score a table. Dishes change daily and with the season – try the delicious lentil soup, tasty *hünkar beğendi* or creamy macaroni. The latter is made only once per week. No alcohol.

Onur Et Lokantası TURKISH, KEBAP €

(Map p76; Shop 7, Ali Baba Türbe Sokak 21, Nuruosmaniye; dishes ₺9-16; ⊙8am-4pm Mon-Sat; 🚇Çemberlitaş) Another excellent neighbourhood eatery, Onur grills succulent kebaps to order and displays an array of daily dishes in its bain-marie. Of these, the aubergine dishes are particularly tasty. No alcohol.

Fes Cafe CAFE €€

(Map p76; www.fescafe.com; Ali Baba Türbe Sokak 25, Nuruosmaniye; sandwiches ₺12-19, salads ₺16-18, pasta ₺17-19; ⊙closed Sun; 🗹; 🚇Çemberlitaş) After a morning spent trading repartee with the touts in the Grand Bazaar, you'll be in need of a respite. Fortunately, this stylish cafe just outside the Nuruosmaniye Gate is an excellent place to relax over lunch or a coffee. Popular choices include Turkish coffee (served with a piece of *lokum*), homemade lemonade and generously proportioned bowls of pasta.

There's another **branch** (Map p80; 📞212-527 3684; Halıcılar Çarşışı Sokak 62, Grand Bazaar; ⊙9.30am-6.30pm Mon-Sat; 🚇Beyazıt-Kapalı Çarşı) located inside the Bazaar.

Burç Ocakbaşı KEBAP €

(Map p80; off Yağlıkçılar Caddesi, Grand Bazaar; kebaps ₺7-25; ⊙9am-6pm Mon-Sat; 🚇Beyazıt-Kapalı Çarşı) The *üsta* (master chef) at this simple place presides over a charcoal grill where choice cuts of southeastern-style meats are cooked. You can claim a stool or ask for a *dürüm kebap* (meat wrapped in bread) to go.

Another place to source good, similarly priced kebaps in the bazaar is **Kara Mehmet** (Map p80; İç Cebeci Han 92, Grand Bazaar) in the İç Cebeci Han.

Kuru Fasülyeci
Erzincanlı Ali Baba TURKISH €

(Map p76; www.kurufasulyeci.com; Prof Sıddık Sami Onar Caddesi 11, Süleymaniye; beans with pilaf & pickles ₺10; ⏰7am-7pm; 🅿; 🚇Laleli-Üniversite) Join the crowds of hungry locals at this long-time institution located opposite the Süleymaniye Mosque. It's been dishing up its signature *kuru fasulye* (Anatolian-style white beans cooked in a spicy tomato sauce) since 1924 and they're delicious when accompanied by pilaf (rice) and pickles. Next-door **Kanaat Fasülyeci** is nearly as old and serves up more of the same. No alcohol.

Havuzlu Restaurant TURKISH €€

(Map p80; Gani Çelebi Sokak 3, Grand Bazaar; dishes ₺8-18, kebaps ₺17-20; ⏰11.30am-5pm Mon-Sat; 🅿; 🚇Beyazıt-Kapalı Çarşı) After a morning spent in the Grand Bazaar, many visitors choose to park their shopping bags at this well-known *lokanta*. A lovely space with a vaulted ceiling, Havuzlu (named after the small fountain at its entrance) serves up simple but tasty fare to hungry hordes of tourists and shopkeepers – go early when the food is freshest.

The restaurant also has a clean toilet, something quite rare in the bazaar. No alcohol though.

Namlı DELICATESSEN €

(Map p76; www.namlipastirma.com.tr; Hasırcılar Caddesi 14-16; ⏰6.30am-7pm Mon-Sat; 🅿; 🚇Eminönü) Namlı's mouth-watering selection of cheeses, *pastırma* (air-dried beef) and meze are known throughout the city. Fight your way to the counter and order a tasty fried *pastırma* roll or a takeaway container of meze. You can also grab a light lunch in the upstairs cafeteria. There's another **branch** (Map p84; www.namligida.com.tr; Rıhtım Caddesi 1, Karaköy; ⏰7am-10pm; 🅿; 🚇Karaköy) in **Karaköy**.

WESTERN DISTRICTS

TOP CHOICE **Asitane** OTTOMAN €€€

(🅿212-635 7997; www.asitanerestaurant.com; Kariye Oteli, Kariye Camii Sokak 6, Edirnekapı; starters ₺12-18, mains ₺26-42; ⏰11am-midnight; 🅿; 🚇31E, 32, 36K & 38E from Eminönü, 87 from Taksim) This elegant restaurant next to the Kariye Museum (Chora Church) serves Ottoman dishes devised for the palace kitchens at Topkapı, Edirne and Dolmabahçe. Its chefs have been tracking down historic recipes for years, and the menu is full of versions that will tempt most modern palates. There's a comfortable indoor space and an outdoor courtyard for summer dining.

TOP CHOICE **Kömür Turk Mutfağı** TURKISH €

(www.komurturkmutfagi.com; Fevzi Paşa Caddesi 18, Fatih; veg dishes ₺6-7, meat dishes ₺9-13, grills ₺10-18; ⏰lunch; 🅿; 🚇31E, 32, 336E, 36KE & 38E from Eminönü, 87 from Taksim) Located amid the wedding-dress shops on Fatih's main drag is this five-floor *Türk mutfağı* (Turkish kitchen) where brides-to-be join businessmen and worshippers from the nearby Fatih Mosque for lunch. The gleaming ground-floor space has a huge counter where ready-made dishes are displayed and where fresh meat and fish can be cooked to order.

BEYOĞLU & AROUND
A recent local-government ban on outdoor drinking in Beyoğlu has had a sorry impact on this neighbourhood's restaurant and bar scene, sending some venues with streetside seating broke and causing the interior dining spaces of others to become unpleasantly crowded. We, like many locals, can only hope that good sense prevails and that the ban is rescinded in the near future.

The only enclave to escape the ban was Nevizade Sokak behind the Balık Pazarı, which continues to host boisterous crowds on weekend evenings.

TOP CHOICE **Asmalı Cavit** TURKISH €€

(Asmalı Meyhane; Map p84; 🅿212-292 4950; Asmalımescit Sokak 16, Asmalımescit; mezes ₺6-20, mains ₺18-24; 🚇Karaköy, then funicular to Tünel) Cavit Saatcı's place is quite possibly the best *meyhane* in the city. The old-fashioned interior gives no clue as to the excellence of the food on offer. Standout dishes include *yaprak ciğer* (liver fried with onions), *patlıcan salatası* (eggplant salad), *muska böreği* (phyllo stuffed with beef and onion) and *kalamar tava* (fried calamari). Bookings essential.

TOP CHOICE **Lokanta Maya** MODERN TURKISH €€

(Map p84; 🅿212-252 6884; www.lokantamaya.com; Kemankeş Caddesi 35a, Karaköy; mezes ₺11-28, mains ₺26-35; ⏰lunch Mon-Sat, dinner Tue-Sat, brunch Sun; 🅿; 🚇Karaköy) Critics and chowhounds alike are raving about the dishes created by chef Didem Şenol at her stylish restaurant near the Karaköy docks.

DON'T MISS

BALIK PAZARI

Accessed off İstiklal Caddesi, Galatasaray's **fish market** (Map p84; Şahne Sokak off İstiklal Caddesi, Galatasaray;) is full of small stands selling *midye tava* (skewered mussels fried in hot oil), *kokoreç* (grilled sheep's intestines stuffed with peppers, tomatoes, herbs and spices) and other snacks. You'll also find shops selling fish, caviar, fruit, vegetables and other produce; most of these are in Duduodaları Sokak on the left (southern) side of the market.

Many of the shops here have been here for close on a century and have extremely loyal clienteles – check out **Sütte Şarküteri** (Map p84; 212-293 9292; Duduodatarı Sokak 13, Balık Pazarı, Galatasaray; 8am-10pm; Kabataş, then funicular to Taksim) for its delicious charcuterie, *kaymak* (clotted cream) and take-away sandwiches; **Tarihi Beyoğlu Ekmek Fırını** (Map p84; Duduodaları Sokak 5, Balık Pazarı, Galatasaray; Kabataş, then funicular to Taksim) for fresh bread, **Üç Yıldız Şekerleme** (Map p84; 212-293 8170; www.ucyildizsekerleme.com; Duduodaları Sokak 7, Balık Pazarı, Galatasaray; 7am-8.30pm Mon-Sat, 9am-6pm Sun; Kabataş, then funicular to Taksim) for jams, *lokum* and sweets; **Petek Turşuları** (Map p84; Duduodaları Sokak 6, Balık Pazarı, Galatasaray; Kabataş, then funicular to Taksim) for pickles; and **Reşat Balık Market** (Map p84; 212-293 6091; Sahne Sokak 30, Balık Pazarı, Galatasaray; Kabataş, then funicular to Taksim) for caviar and the city's best *lakerda* (strongly flavored salted kingfish).

The author of a successful cookbook focusing on Aegean cuisine, Didem creates food that is light, flavoursome, occasionally quirky and always assured – everyone eats well here. You'll need to book for dinner; lunch is cheaper and more casual.

TOP CHOICE Zübeyir Ocakbaşı KEBAPS €€
(Map p84; 212-293 3951; www.zubeyirocakbasi.com; Bekar Sokak 28; mezes ₺4-6, kebaps ₺10-20; noon-1am; Kabataş, then funicular to Taksim) Every morning, the chefs at this popular *ocakbaşı* (grill house) prepare the fresh, top-quality meats to be grilled over their handsome copper-hooded barbecues that night: spicy chicken wings and Adana kebaps, flavoursome ribs, pungent liver kebaps and well-marinated lamb *şiş kebaps*. Their offerings are famous throughout the city, so booking a table is essential.

TOP CHOICE Meze by Lemon Tree MODERN TURKISH €€€
(Map p84; 212-252 8302; www.mezze.com.tr; Meşrutiyet Caddesi 83b, Tepebaşı; mezes ₺8-25, mains ₺26-36; Karaköy, then funicular to Tünel) Chef Gençay Üçok creates some of the most interesting – and delicious – modern Turkish food seen in the city. Come to his small restaurant opposite the Pera Palace Hotel to sample triumphs such as the monkfish casserole or grilled lamb sirloin with baked potatoes and red beets; both are sure to be holiday highlights. Bookings are essential.

Karaköy Güllüoğlu SWEETS, BÖREK €
(Map p84; www.karakoygulluoglu.com; Kemankeş Caddesi, Karaköy; baklava ₺4-7, börek ₺6; 8am-11pm; Karaköy) This Karaköy institution has been making customers deliriously happy and dentists obscenely rich ever since 1947. Head to the register and order a *porsiyon* (portion) of whatever baklava takes your fancy (*fıstıklı* is pistachio, *cevizli* walnut and *sade* plain), preferably with a glass of tea. Then hand your ticket over to the servers. The *börek* here is good, too.

Karaköy Lokantası TURKISH €€
(Map p84; 212-292 4455; Kemankeş Caddesi 37a, Karaköy; mezes ₺6-10, portions ₺7-12, grills ₺11-16; dinner daily, lunch Mon-Sat; ; Karaköy) Known for its gorgeous tiled interior, genial owner and bustling vibe, Karaköy Lokantası serves tasty and well-priced food to its loyal local clientele. It functions as a *lokanta* during the day, but at night it morphs into a *meyhane*, with slightly higher prices. Bookings are essential for dinner.

Antiochia ANATOLIAN €€
(Map p84; 212-292 1100; www.antiochiaconcept.com; Minare Sokak 21a, Asmalımescit; mezes ₺8-10, mains ₺13-27; lunch Mon-Fri, dinner Mon-Sat; Karaköy, then funicular to Tünel) Dishes from the southeastern city of Antakya (Hatay) are the speciality at this tiny (read cramped) restaurant. Mezes are dominated by wild thyme, pomegranate syrup, olives, walnuts and tangy

homemade yoghurt, and the kebaps are equally flavoursome – try the succulent *şiş et* (grilled lamb) or *dürüm* (wrap filled with minced meat, onions and tomatoes). There's a 20% discount at lunch.

Ca' d'Oro
ITALIAN €€

(Map p84; ☎212-243 8292; www.istanbuldoors .com; Bankalar Caddesi 11, Galata; starters ₺10-29, pizzas ₺15-21, mains ₺18-55; ⊘lunch & dinner Tue-Sun; ☑; ☒Karaköy) The glamorous rooftop restaurant at the SALT Galata cultural centre serves *molto buono* Italian staples such as pasta, pizza and risotto, but is most memorable for its extraordinary view over the Golden Horn to the historic peninsula. Vegetarians will appreciate the generous array of suitable options on the menu.

Journey
INTERNATIONAL, CAFE €€

(Map p84; www.journeycihangir.com; Akarsu Yokuşu 21a, Cihangir; sandwiches ₺14-19, soups ₺7-9, mains ₺15-39; ⊘9am-2am; ☑; ☒Kabataş, then funicular to Taksim) This bohemian lounge-cafe located in the expat enclave of Cihangir serves a great range of Mediterranean comfort foods including sandwiches, soups, pizzas and pastas. Most of the dishes use organic produce and there's a decent array of vegetarian options. The crowd is 30-something, the music is alternative and the ambience is laid-back. Great stuff.

Mikla
MODERN TURKISH €€€

(Map p84; ☎212-293 5656; www.miklarestaurant.com; Marmara Pera Hotel, Meşrutiyet Caddesi 15, Tepebaşı; appetisers ₺25-38, mains ₺51-79; ⊘dinner; ☒Karaköy, then funicular to Tünel) Local celebrity chef Mehmet Gürs is a master of Mod Med, and the Turkish accents on the menu here makes his food memorable. Extraordinary views, luxe surrounds and professional service complete the experience. Try the delicious Trakya Kıvırcık lamb dishes, consider a finale of the pistachio and *helva* ice cream and be sure to have a drink at the bar beforehand.

İstanbul Modern Cafe/Restaurant
INTERNATIONAL €€€

(Map p84; ☎212-292 2612; Meclis-i Mebusan Caddesi, Tophane; pizzas ₺19-28, pasta ₺19-33, mains ₺28-55; ⊘10am-midnight; ☑; ☒Tophane) The cafe-restaurant at İstanbul's pre-eminent contemporary art museum offers an 'industrial arty' vibe and great views over the Bosphorus when there are no cruise ships moored in front. The pasta is homemade, the

pizzas are Italian-style and service is slick – all of which make for a happy lunch experience. For a table on the terrace you'll need to book ahead.

Sofyalı 9
TURKISH €€

(Map p84; ☎212-245 0362; Sofyalı Sokak 9, Asmalımescit; mezes ₺2.50-10, mains ₺13-25; ⊘closed Sun; ☒Karaköy, then funicular to Tünel) Tables at this *meyhane* are hot property on a Friday or Saturday night, and no wonder. The food is fresh and tasty, and the atmosphere is convivial. Stick to mezes rather than ordering mains – choose cold dishes from the waiter's tray and order hot ones from the menu – the *kalamar* (calamari) and *Anavut ciğeri* (Albanian fried liver) are delicious.

Kafe Ara
CAFE €€

(Map p84; Tosbağ Sokak 8a, Galatasaray; sandwiches ₺15-20, salads ₺15-23, grills ₺19-24; ⊘7.30am-midnight Mon-Thu, to 1am Fri & Sat, to 10pm Sun; ☒Kabataş, then funicular to Taksim) This casual cafe is named after its owner, legendary local photographer Ara Güler. It occupies a converted garage with tables and chairs spilling out into a wide laneway opposite the Galatasaray Lycée and serves an array of well-priced salads, sandwiches and Turkish staples such as *köfte* (meatballs) and *sigara böreği* (pastries filled with cheese and potato). No alcohol.

Fasuli Lokantaları
ANATOLIAN €

(Map p84; www.fasuli.com.tr; Tophane İskele Caddesi 10-12, Tophane; beans & rice ₺13; ☒Tophane) There are two types of *fasulye* (bean dishes) served in Turkey: Erzincan-style beans cooked in a spicy tomato sauce, and Black Sea–style beans cooked in a red gravy full of butter and meat. This *lokanta* next to the nargile joints in Tophane serves its beans Black Sea–style, and they are truly delicious. There's another **branch** (Map p62; www.fasuli.com.tr; Muradiye Caddesi 35-37, Sirkeci; beans & rice ₺13; ☒Sirkeci) in Sirkeci.

Asmalı Canım Ciğerim
ANATOLIAN €

(Map p84; Minare Sokak 1, Asmalımescit; 5 skewers ₺12; ☒Karaköy, then funicular to Tünel) The name means 'my soul, my liver', and this small place next to the Ali Hoca Türbesi specialises in grilled liver served with herbs, *ezme* (spicy tomato sauce) and grilled vegetables. If you can't bring yourself to eat offal, fear not – you can substitute the liver with lamb if you so choose. No alcohol, but *ayran* is the perfect accompaniment.

Zencefil
VEGETARIAN €

(Map p84; Kurabiye Sokak 8; soup ₺7-9, mains ₺9-17; ◎10am-11pm Mon-Sat, noon-10pm Sun; ◪; ◙Kabataş, then funicular to Taksim) We're not surprised that this vegetarian cafe has a loyal following. Its interior is comfortable and stylish, with a glassed courtyard and bright colour scheme, and its food is 100% homemade, fresh and varied. Dishes are also available in small and large sizes. Be warned that one chicken dish always features on the otherwise strictly vegetarian menu.

'Zencefil' means 'ginger' in Turkish, and the cafe makes its own ginger beer and ginger ale. You can also order wine by the glass and fresh *limonata* served with Absolut vodka.

Galata Konak Patisserie Cafe
CAFE €€

(Map p84; www.galatakonakcafe.com; Hacı Ali Sokak 2, Galata; ◎10am-10pm; ◙Karaköy) After checking out the pastries and cakes on sale in the ground-floor patisserie, make your way up the stairs to the rooftop terrace cafe, where you can order anything that has taken your fancy downstairs and enjoy it with a tea or coffee. The view from the terrace encompasses the Sultanahmet skyline, the Bosphorus and the Golden Horn.

Datlı Maya
BAKERY €

(Map p84; www.datlimaya.com; Türkgücü Caddesi 59, Cihangir; cakes & pastries ₺2-5; ◎8am-10pm; ◙Kabataş, then funicular to Taksim) Dilara Erbay is an exciting if unpredictable player on the city's culinary scene, and her latest venture, a tiny cafe-bakery located behind the Firuz Ağa Mosque in Cihangir, is as popular as it is fashionable. Her wood-fired oven produces cakes, *lahmacuns* (Arabic-style pizzas), pides, *böreks* and breads, all of which are enjoyed with glasses of tea dispensed from a battered old samovar.

Demeti
TURKISH €€

(Map p84; ◪212-244 0628; www.demeti.com.tr; Şimşirci Sokak 6, Cihangir; mezes ₺5-20, mains ₺16-25; ◎4pm-2am Mon-Sat; ◙Kabataş, then funicular to Taksim) This modern *meyhane* has a friendly feel and simple but stylish decor. Reservations are a must if you want one of four tables on the terrace, which have an unimpeded Bosphorus view. There's occasional live music.

Jash
ANATOLIAN €€

(Map p84; ◪212-244 3042; www.jashistanbul.com; Cihangir Caddesi 9, Cihangir; mezes ₺8-20, mains ₺20-42; ◎lunch & dinner; ◙Kabataş, then funicular to Taksim) Amenian specialities such as *topik* (a cold meze made with chickpeas, pistachios, onion, flour, currants, cumin and salt) make an appearance on the menu of this bijou *meyhane* in trendy Cihangir. Come on the weekend, when an accordian player entertains diners and unusual dishes including *harisa* (chicken with a hand-forged wheat and butter sauce) are on offer.

Helvetia Lokanta
TURKISH €

(Map p84; General Yazgan Sokak 8-12, Asmalımescit; soup ₺5, portions ₺5-12; ◎8am-10pm Mon-Sat; ◪; ◙Kabataş, then funicular to Tünel) This tiny *lokanta* is popular with locals (particularly of the vegetarian and vegan variety), who pop in here for inexpensive soups, salads and stews that are cooked fresh each day. No alcohol and cash only.

ORTAKÖY & KURUÇEŞME

Eateries on and around the Golden Mile (along Muallim Naci and Kuruçeşme Caddesis in Ortaköy and Kuruçeşme) can get pricey, and if you're on a tight budget you should probably limit yourself to brunch – as most young locals do.

On weekends, the stands behind the Ortaköy Mosque do brisk business selling *gözlemes* (savoury pancakes) and *kumpir* (baked potatoes filled with your choice of sour cream, olive paste, cheese, chilli or bulgur).

Sıdıka
TURKISH €€

(◪212-259 7232; www.sidika.com.tr; Şair Nedim Caddesi 38 , Beşiktaş; cold mezes ₺3-14, hot mezes ₺15-20, fish ₺16-18; ◎5pm-midnight Mon-Sat; ◙Akaretler) Come to this out-of-the-way *meyhane* for simply prepared but absolutely sensational fish and vegetable mezes, best sampled in the mixed cold plate (₺30). Follow with some fried fish, a bowl of pasta or – if it's a Friday – a tasty bowl of fish soup.

Zuma
JAPANESE €€€

(Map p90; ◪212-236 2296; www.zumarestaurant.com; Salhane Sokak 7, Ortaköy; veg mains ₺11-26, fish mains ₺28-65, sushi & sashimi ₺39-89; ◎lunch & dinner; ◪; ◙Kabataş Lisesi) Good Izakaya-style food and a stunning waterside location make the local branch of this London favourite a safe bet. There's a bar and lounge on the top floor and a sushi bar and *robata* grill downstairs.

House Cafe
INTERNATIONAL €€€

(Map p90; İskele Meydanı 42; breakfast platters ₺24, sandwiches ₺15-26, pizzas ₺17.50-27.50, mains ₺16.50-29.50; ⊙9am-1am Mon-Thu, to 2am Fri & Sat, to 10.30pm Sun; ⊜Kabataş Lisesi) This casually chic cafe is one of the best spots in town for Sunday brunch. A huge space right on the waterfront, it offers a good-quality buffet spread for ₺45 between 10am and 2pm. Food at other times can be disappointing, though that doesn't deter the locals, who flock here every weekend.

ÜSKÜDAR

Kanaat Lokantası
TURKISH €

(Selman-i Pak Caddesi 25; portions ₺7-17, kebaps ₺10-15; ⊙6.30am-11pm; ⊜Üsküdar) This barn-like place near the *iskele* has been serving up competent *hazır yemek* since 1933, and is particularly fancied for its desserts, including a house-made ice cream made from sheep's milk and salep (ground orchid root). Its understated but pleasing decor features framed photographs of old street scenes.

KADIKÖY

Kadı Nimet Balıkçılık
FISH €€

(☑216-348 7389; Serasker Caddesi 10a, Kadıköy; mezes ₺6-15, fish mains ₺10-30; ⊙noon-midnight; ⊜Kadıköy) Locals love this casual place tucked among the fish stalls in the produce market. It serves some of the freshest seafood in the city and is always busy, so you'll need to book for dinner. Try the *levrek dolma* (stuffed sea-bass meze).

Çiya Sofrası
ANATOLIAN €€

(www.ciya.com.tr; Güneşlibahçe Sokak 43; portions ₺10-15; ⊙11am-11pm; ⊜Kadıköy) Known throughout the culinary world, Musa Dağdeviren's *lokanta* showcases dishes from the region surrounding the chef owner's home city of Gaziantep. While standards in the kitchen seemed to have fallen in recent times, it's still a great place to try Turkish regional specialities. Its next-door *kebapçı* (kebaps ₺15 to ₺35) sells a huge variety of tasty meat dishes. Neither sells alcohol.

Baylan Pastanesi
SWEETS €

(☑216-336 2881; www.baylanpastanesi.com.tr; Muvakkithane Caddesi 9; ⊙7am-10pm; ⊜Kadıköy) Baylan Pastanesi has been serving its excellent espresso coffee, decadent ice-cream sundaes and delicious cakes and pastries to appreciative İstanbullus since 1923. This branch dates from 1925, but had its last (very funky) facelift in 1961, making it a true time capsule.

BOSPHORUS SUBURBS

 MüzedeChanga
MODERN TURKISH €€€

(☑212-323 0901; www.changa-istanbul.com; Sakıp Sabancı Müzesi, Sakıp Sabancı Caddesi 42, Emirgan; starters ₺18-29, mains ₺37-49; ⊙10.30am-1am Tue-Sun) Operated by Changa, one of the city's top restaurants, this venue in the Sakıp Sabancı Museum has a terrace with Bosphorus views, an ultra-stylish interior fitout and a delicious menu. It's extremely popular for weekend lunch or brunch. If you don't feel like visiting the museum, door staff will waive the entry fee and point you towards the restaurant.

Mama
ITALIAN €€

(www.mamapizzeria.com; Baltalimanı Caddesi 4, Rumeli Hisarı; pizzas ₺16-33, pastas ₺18-29; ⊙10am-11.30pm Mon-Sat, from 9am Sun; ⊜22, 22RE & 25E from Kabataş, 40, 40T & 42T from Taksim) The resort decor and wide range of Italian dishes will make you feel as if you're relaxing in a trattoria on the Amalfi Coast rather than here in İstanbul. Great pizzas and pastas, a good range of drinks (including excellent fresh *limonata*) lavish Sunday brunch choices and a kids' menu all go towards making Mama as loved as its namesake.

Sütiş
CAFE €

(Sakıp Sabancı Caddesi 1, Emirgan; ⊙6am-1am; ⊜22, 22RE & 25E from Kabataş, 40, 40T & 42T from Taksim) The Bosphorus branch of this popular chain has an expansive and extremely comfortable terrace overlooking the water. It's known for serving all-day breakfasts and milk-based puddings – we recommend the *simit* with honey and *kaymak* (clotted cream). Watching the valet parking ritual on weekends is hilarious.

🍸 Drinking

It may be the biggest city in a predominantly Islamic country, but let us assure you that İstanbul's population likes nothing more than a drink or three. If the rakı (aniseed brandy)-soaked atmosphere in the city's *meyhanes* isn't a clear enough indicator, a foray into the thriving bar scene will confirm it.

The city's bohemian and student set tends to gravitate to the bars in Beyoğlu's Cihangir, Asmalımescit and Nevizade enclaves or head over the water to grungy Kadife Sokak in the suburb of Kadıköy on the city's Asian side. This is known to everyone as Barlar Sokak (Bar Street).

DON'T MISS

CRAZY ABOUT KEYİF

Tea and nargile go together like Posh and Becks. And the best setting in which to try out this particularly magic combo is the traditional *çay bahçesi* (tea garden), of which İstanbul has many. These *çay bahçesis* are where the locals go to practise *keyif*, the Turkish art of quiet relaxation. To emulate them, follow the smell of apple tobacco to these faves.

» Tophane Nargile (p115)

» Erenler Çay Bahçesi (p115)

» Lale Bahçesi (p115)

» Derviş Aile Çay Bahçesi (p114)

Alternatively, you can check out the alcohol-free, atmosphere-rich *çay bahçesis* or *kahvehanes* (coffee houses) dotted around the Old City. These are great places to relax and sample that great Turkish institution, the nargile, accompanied by a cup of *Türk kahve* (Turkish coffee) or çay. It will cost around ₺2 for a tea, ₺6 for a Turkish coffee and ₺15 to ₺25 for a nargile at all of the places listed here.

SULTANAHMET & AROUND

Set Üstü Çay Bahçesi TEA GARDEN
(Map p62; Gülhane Park, Sultanahmet; ☺9am-10.30pm; ⊕Gülhane) Come to this terraced tea garden to watch the ferries plying the route from Europe to Asia, while at the same time enjoying an excellent pot of tea accompanied by hot water (such a relief after the usual fiendishly strong Turkish brew). Add a cheap *tost* (toasted cheese sandwich) and you'll be able to make a lunch of it.

Yeni Marmara NARGILE CAFE
(Map p62; Çayıroğlu Sokak, Küçük Ayasofya; ☺10am-1am; ⊕Sultanahmet) This is the genuine article: a neighbourhood teahouse frequented by backgammon-playing regulars who slurp tea and puff on nargiles. The place has loads of character, featuring rugs, wall hangings and *fasıl* music on the CD player. In winter a wood stove keeps the place cosy; in summer patrons sit on the rear terrace, which overlooks the Sea of Marmara.

Derviş Aile Çay Bahçesi TEA GARDEN
(Map p73; Mimar Mehmet Ağa Caddesi; ☺9am-11pm Apr-Oct; ⊕Sultanahmet) Superbly located directly opposite the Blue Mosque, the Derviş beckons patrons with its comfortable cane chairs and shady trees. Efficient service, reasonable prices and peerless people-watching opportunities make it a great place for a leisurely tea, nargile and game of backgammon.

Cafe Meşale NARGILE CAFE
(Map p73; Arasta Bazaar, Utangaç Sokak, Cankurtaran; ☺24hr; ⊕Sultanahmet) Located in a sunken courtyard behind the Blue Mosque, Meşale is a tourist trap par excellence, but still has loads of charm. Generations of backpackers have joined locals in claiming one of its cushioned benches and enjoying a tea and nargile. There's sporadic live Turkish music and a bustling vibe in the evening.

Türk Ocağı Kültür ve Sanat Merkezi İktisadi İşletmesi Çay Bahçesi TEA GARDEN
(Map p62; cnr Divan Yolu & Bab-ı Ali Caddesis; ☺8am-midnight; ⊕Çemberlitaş) Tucked into the rear right-hand corner of a shady courtyard filled with Ottoman tombs, this enormously popular tea garden is a perfect place to escape the crowds and relax over a çay and nargile. You can even score a cheap and tasty *gözleme* (filled with cheese, spinach or potato) here.

Hotel Nomade Terrace Bar BAR
(Map p62; www.hotelnomade.com; Ticarethane Sokak 15, Alemdar; ☺noon-11pm; ⊕Sultanahmet) The intimate terrace of this boutique hotel overlooks Aya Sofya and the Blue Mosque. Settle down in a comfortable chair to enjoy a glass of wine, beer or freshly squeezed fruit juice. The only music that will disturb your evening's reverie is the Old City's signature sound of the call to prayer.

Denizen Coffee CAFE
(Map p62; Şehit Mehmet Paşa Yokuşu 8; ☺8.30am-10pm Mon-Sat; ⊕Sultanahmet) Ken Weimar and Earl Everett opened this American-style coffee shop in 2011 and describe it simply ('for us, it's all about the coffee'). Come here for espresso, decaf, hot chocolate and hot white chocolate served in a welcoming space decorated with Ken's photos of Sultanahmet and Beyoğlu. There are pastries, panini, salads and mezes available too.

Yeşil Ev BAR, CAFE
(Map p73; Kabasakal Caddesi 5; ☺noon-10.30pm; ⊕Sultanahmet) The elegant rear courtyard of this Ottoman-style hotel is a true oasis for those wanting to enjoy a quiet drink.

In spring, flowers and blossoms fill every corner; in summer the fountain and trees keep the temperature down. You can order a sandwich, salad or cheese platter if you're peckish.

BAZAAR DISTRICT

Lale Bahçesi   TEA GARDEN
(Map p76; Şifahane Caddesi, Süleymaniye; ⊙9am-11pm; ⧉Laleli-Üniversite) In a sunken court-yard that was once part of the Süleymaniye *külliye*, this charming outdoor teahouse is always full of students from the nearby theological college and İstanbul University, who come here to sit on cushioned seats under trees and relax while watching the pretty fountain play. It's one of the cheapest places in the area to enjoy a çay and nargile.

Erenler Çay Bahçesi   TEA GARDEN
(Map p76; Yeniçeriler Caddesi 35, Beyazıt; ⊙7am-midnight; ⧉Beyazıt-Kapalı Çarşı) Set in the vine-covered courtyard of the Çorlulu Ali Paşa Medrese, this nargile cafe near the Grand Bazaar is a favourite with students from nearby İstanbul University.

Kahve Dünyası   CAFE
(Map p62; Nuruosmaniye Caddesi 79; ⊙7.30am-9.30pm) The name means 'Coffee World', and this coffee chain has the local world at its feet. The secret of its success lies with the huge coffee menu, reasonable prices, delicious chocolate spoons (yes, you read that correctly), comfortable seating and free wi-fi. The filter coffee is better than its espresso-based alternatives.

There's another **branch** (Map p76; Kızılhan Sokak 18, Eminönü; ⧉Eminönü) near the Spice Market.

Pandeli   CAFE
(Map p76; www.pandeli.com.tr; Spice Bazaar, Eminönü; ⊙noon-4pm Mon-Sat; ⧉Eminönü) Pandeli's three salons are encrusted with stunning turquoise-coloured İznik tiles and furnished with chandeliers and richly upholstered banquettes. Though its location above the main entrance to the Spice Bazaar makes it a popular lunch spot for tourists (locals wouldn't dream of eating here), we suggest visiting for a tea or coffee after the main lunch service instead.

BEYOĞLU & AROUND

⧉TOP⧉ Tophane Nargile Cafes   NARGILE CAFE
CHOICE
(Map p84; off Necatibey Caddesi, Tophane; ⊙24hr; ⧉Tophane) This atmospheric row of nargile cafes behind the Nusretiye Mosque

is always packed with locals enjoying tea, nargile and snacks. Follow your nose to find it – the smell of apple tobacco is incredibly enticing. It's great fun to watch live *Süper Lig* football matches on the televisions here, as patrons and waiters like to make their allegiances clear.

⧉TOP⧉ Mikla   BAR
CHOICE
(Map p84; www.miklarestaurant.com; Marmara Pera Hotel, Meşrutiyet Caddesi 15, Tepebaşı; ⊙from 6pm Mon-Sat summer only; ⧉Karaköy, then funicular to Tünel) It's worth overlooking the occasionally uppity service at this stylish rooftop bar to enjoy what could well be the best view in İstanbul. After a few drinks, consider moving downstairs to eat in the classy restaurant.

Manda Batmaz   COFFEEHOUSE
(Map p84; Olivia Geçidi 1a, off İstiklal Caddesi; ⊙9.30am-midnight; ⧉Karaköy, then funicular to Tünel) He's been working at this tiny coffee house for two decades, so Cemil Pilik really knows his stuff when it comes to making Turkish coffee. The name translates as 'so thick that even a water buffalo won't sink in it', and Cemil's brew is indeed as viscous as it is smooth. You'll find it behind the Barcelona Cafe & Patisserie.

Mavra   CAFE
(Map p84; Serdar-ı Ekrem Caddesi 31a, Galata; ⊙8am-midnight; ⧉Karaköy, then funicular to Tünel) Serdar-ı Ekrem Caddesi is one of the most interesting streets in Galata, full of ornate 19th-century apartment blocks, avant-garde boutiques and laid-back cafes and bars. Mavra is the best of these, offering tasty cheap food and good tea and coffee amid thrift-shop chic decor. There's always good music on the turntable here, too.

Leb-i Derya   BAR
(Map p84; www.lebiderya.com; 6th fl, Kumbaracı Yokuşu 57, Galata; ⊙4pm-2am Mon-Thu, to 3am Fri, 10am-3am Sat, to 2am Sun; ⧉Karaköy, then funicular to Tünel) On the top floor of a dishevelled building off İstiklal, Leb-i Derya has wonderful views across to the Old City and down the Bosphorus, meaning that seats on the small outdoor terrace or at the bar are highly prized. There's also food on offer.

Litera   BAR
(Map p84; www.literarestaurant.com; 5th fl, Yeniçarşı Caddesi 32, Galatasaray; ⊙11am-4am; ⧉Karaköy, then funicular to Tünel) Occupying the 5th floor of the handsome building downhill from Galatasaray Meydanı, Litera

revels in its expansive views of the Old City, Asian side and Bosphorus. It hosts plenty of cultural events, as befits its location in the Goethe Institute building,

360
BAR

(Map p84; www.360istanbul.com; 8th fl, İstiklal Caddesi 163; ⊙noon-2am Mon-Thu & Sun, 3pm-4am Fri & Sat; 🚇Karaköy, then funicular to Tünel) İstanbul's most famous bar, and deservedly so. If you can score one of the bar stools on the terrace you'll be happy indeed – the view is truly magnificent. It morphs into a club after midnight on Friday and Saturday, when a cover charge of around ₺40 applies.

Baylo
BAR, RESTAURANT

(Map p84; www.baylo.com.tr; Meşrutiyet Caddesi 107a, Tepebaşı; ⊙6.30pm-1am Mon-Thu, to 2.30am Fri & Sat; 🚇Karaköy, then funicular to Tünel) The much anticipated reopening of the Pera Palace Hotel in the lower section of Asmalımescit has been accompanied by a boom in glamorous bistro-bars in its immediate vicinity. Of these, Baylo is undoubtedly the best. The elegant interior provides a perfect backdrop for the 30-something bankers, architects and other professionals who head here after a busy day at the office.

5 Kat
BAR, RESTAURANT

(Map p84; www.5kat.com; 5th fl, Soğancı Sokak 7, Cihangir; ⊙10am-1am; 🚇Kabataş) This İstanbul institution is a great alternative for those who can't stomach the style overload at Mikla, 360 and the like. In winter, drinks are served in the boudoir-style bar on the 5th floor; in summer, action moves to the outdoor roof terrace. Both have great Bosphorus views.

Hazzo Pulo Çay Bahçesi
TEA GARDEN

(Map p84; Tarihi Hazzo Pulo Pasaji, off İstiklal Caddesi; ⊙9am-midnight; 🚇Karaköy, then funicular to Tünel) There aren't as many traditional teahouses in Beyoğlu as there are on the historic peninsula, so this picturesque cobbled courtyard full of makeshift stools and tables is beloved of local 20-somethings. Order from the waiter and then pay at the small cafe near the narrow arcade entrance. The next-door cafe Grand Bouevard offers more of the same.

Cafe Susam
CAFE, BAR

(Map p84; Susam Sokak 11, Cihangir; ⊙9am-2am; 🚇Kabataş, then funicular to Kabataş) Susam is the epitome of a great neighbourhood cafe. The expats and arty İstanbullus who call Cihangir home come here to drink good cof-

fee, take advantage of the free wi-fi, snack on sandwiches and drink mean mojitos on weekend evenings.

Münferit
BAR

(Map p84; Yeni Çarşı Caddesi 19, Galatasaray; 🚇Kabataş, then funicular to Taksim) When this book went to print, this upmarket bar and restaurant designed by the Autoban Design Partnership was the most glamorous watering hole in town. Though the restaurant's take on nouvelle *meyhane* food lacks assurance, the bar is fabulous, serving expertly made cocktails and good wine by the glass to a formidably fashionable crowd.

Le Fumoir
BAR

(Map p84; www.georges.com; Georges Hotel, Serdar-ı Ekrem Caddesi 24, Galata; ⊙8am-1am; 🚇Karaköy) *Ô là là'!* This atmospheric but small bar in the French restaurant of the same name is an elegant venue for an aperitif or nightcap. It's also a good spot for breakfast, as the French-style pastries and coffee are excellent.

Urban
BAR, CAFE

(Map p84; www.urbanbeyoglu.com; Kartal Sokak 6a, Galatasaray; ⊙11am-1am; 🚇Kabataş, then funicular to Taksim) A tranquil bolthole in the middle of İstiklal's mayhem, Urban is where the pre-club crowd congregates at night and where many of them can be found kicking back over a coffee during the day. The vaguely Parisienne interior is a clever balance of grunge and glamour.

X Bar
BAR

(Map p84; www.xrestaurantbar.com; 7th fl, Sadı Konuralp Caddesi 5, Şişhane; ⊙9am-midnight Sun-Wed, to 4am Thu-Sat) High culture meets serious glamour on the top floor of the İstanbul Foundation for Culture and Arts (İKSV) building. Our meals here haven't been worth their hefty price tags, so we suggest limiting yourself to a sunset aperitif or two – the Golden Horn view is simply wonderful.

Sensus Wine Bar
WINE BAR

(Map p84; www.sensuswine.com; Büyük Hendek Sokak 5, Galata; ⊙10am-10pm; 🚇Karaköy, then funicular to Tünel) Set in a stone basement lined with wine bottles, this new bar underneath the Anemon Galata Hotel has a great concept, but needs to work on its customer service. There are close to 300 bottles of local wine to choose from, but when we visited staff were unable or unwilling to offer any wine-related information or drinking suggestions.

Atölye Kuledıbı BAR, CAFE

(Map p84; Galata Kulesi Sokak 4, Galata; ☺10am-midnight Mon-Fri, to 2am Fri & Sat; ⛴Karaköy, then funicular to Tünel) Great music (sometimes live jazz) and a welcoming atmosphere characterise this bohemian place near Galata Tower.

Club 17 GAY

(Map p84; Zambak Sokak 17; ☺11pm-5am; ⛴Kabataş, then funicular to Taksim) Rent boys outnumber regulars at this narrow bar. At closing time, the crowd spills out into the street to make final hook-up attempts possible. It's quiet during the week but jam-packed late on Friday and Saturday.

Bigudi Cafe GAY

(Map p84; www.bigudiproject.net; terrace fl, Mis Sokak 5; ☺11pm-4am Fri & Sat; ⛴Kabataş, then funicular to Taksim) The first lesbian-exclusive venue in Turkey, Bigudi is frequented by lipstick lesbians on Saturday nights and is resolutely off-limits to non-females. Fridays are open to gay men and the transgendered. To find it, look for the Altin Plak cafe on the ground floor.

KADIKÖY

TOP CHOICE **Fazıl Bey** COFFEEHOUSE

(www.fazilbey.com; Serasker Caddesi 3, Kadıköy; ☺daily; ⛴Kadıköy) Head to the centre of the Kadıköy produce market to find this tiny cafe-coffee roastery, which has been serving İstanbul's best Turkish coffee since 1923.

BOSPHORUS SUBURBS

TOP CHOICE **Pierre Loti Café** CAFE

(Gümüşsuyu Balmumcu Sokak 1, Eyüp; ☺8am-midnight; ⛴Eyüp) Many visitors head to this hilltop cafe after visiting the Eyüp Sultan Mosque (p95). Named for the famous French novelist who is said to have come here for inspiration, it offers lovely views across the Golden Horn and is a popular weekend destination for locals, who relax over tea, coffee, ice cream and nargiles.

To find the cafe, walk out of the mosque's main gate and turn right. Walk around the complex (keeping it to your right) until you see a set of stairs and a cobbled path going uphill into the Eyüp Sultan Mezarlığı (Cemetery of the Great Eyüp), where many important Ottomans are buried. It's a 15-minute walk up the steep hill. Alternatively, take the cable car (p129) that links the waterfront with the top of the hill.

Sade Kahve CAFE

(www.sadekahve.com; Yahya Kemal Caddesi 36; ☺8am-10pm) Cheap and cheerful it may well be, but this casual terrace cafe near the fortress of Europe is also a favourite weekend brunch spot for power brokers, celebrities and their entourages. It serves soup and an array of sandwiches at lunch.

☆ Entertainment

It's rare to have a week go by when there's not a special event, festival or performance somewhere in town.

For an overview of what's on, make sure you pick up a copy of *Time Out İstanbul* magazine when you hit town, and also check its *Istanbul Beat* blog (www.istanbulbeatblog.com). Tickets for major events are available through the **Biletix** (☎216-556 9800; www.biletix.com) website.

Nightclubs

The best nightclubs are in Beyoğlu and on the 'Golden Mile' between Ortaköy and Kuruçeşme on the Bosphorus. To visit any of the venues on this sybaritic strip you'll need to dress to kill and be prepared to outlay loads of lira – drinks start at ₺25 for a beer and climb into the stratosphere for wine, imported spirits or cocktails. Booking the restaurants at these venues is a good idea, because it's usually the only way to get past the door staff – otherwise you'll be looking at a lucky break or a tip of at least ₺100 to get the nod.

The Beyoğlu clubs are cheaper, more avant garde and relatively attitude-free. All venues are busiest on Friday and (especially) Saturday nights, and the action doesn't really kick off until 1am or 2am.

BEYOĞLU & AROUND

TOP CHOICE **MiniMüzikHol** CLUB, LIVE MUSIC

(MMH; Map p84; www.minimuzikhol.com; Soğancı Sokak 7, Cihangir; ☺Wed-Sat 10pm-late; ⛴Kabataş, then funicular to Taksim) The mothership for inner-city hipsters, MMH is a small, slightly grungy venue near Taksim that hosts live sets by local and international musicians midweek and the best dance party in town on weekends. It's best after 1am.

Kiki CLUB, CAFE

(Map p84; www.kiki.com.tr; Sıraselviler Caddesi 42, Cihangir; ☺closed Sun; ⛴Kabataş, then funicular to Taksim) Cool cafe by day and hip bar-club by night, Kiki has a loyal clientele who enjoy its pizzas, burgers, drinks and music (DJs

REINHARD DIRSCHERL / GETTY IMAGES ©

Imperial Hall, Topkapı Palace (p67)

grand, domed hall in the Harem where the sultan would receive his guests.w

Kariye Museum (Chora Church; p82)

he interior of the Kariye Museum studded with superb Byzantine osaics and frescoes.

Blue Mosque (p60)

his mosque is known for the blue es adorning its walls.

İstiklal Caddesi (p87)

tanbul's 'Independence Avenue' in eyoğlu is a lively, popular place to roll and shop.

IZZET KERIBAR / GETTY IMAGES ©

and live sets). Regulars head to the rear courtyard and budget drinkers appreciate the happy hour, held between 7pm and 9pm from Monday to Thursday (Monday and Wednesay half-price drinks, Tuesday and Thursday free tapas).

Dogzstar
CLUB
(Map p84; www.dogzstar.com; Kartal Sokak 3, Galatasaray; ⊘closed Sun; 🚇Kabataş, then funicular to Taksim) It's a three-storey affair, but the compact size (300 persons maximum) makes for an acoustic powerhouse. The crowd comprises budding fans or hardcore followers of featured up-and-coming bands or DJs. The owners give the collected (modest) cover charges to performers and also charge reasonable drink prices. Bravo! There's a terrace where clubbers cool off in summer.

Love Dance Point
GAY
(www.lovedp.net; Cumhuriyet Caddesi 349, Harbiye; ⊘11.30pm-5am Fri & Sat; 🚇Kabataş, then funicular to Taksim) Going into its second decade, Love DP is easily the most Europhile of the local gay venues, hosting gay musical icons and international circuit parties. Hard-cutting techno is thrown in with gay anthems and Turkish pop. This place attracts the well travelled and the unimpressionable, as well as some straight hipsters from nearby Nişantaşı.

Indigo
CLUB
(Map p84; www.livingindigo.com; 1st–5th fl, Mısır Apt, 309 Akarsu Sokak, Galatasaray; ⊘10pm-5am Fri & Sat, closed summer; 🚇Kabataş, then funicular to Taksim) This is Beyoğlu's electronic music temple, and dance-music enthusiasts congregate here on weekends for their energetic kicks. The program spotlights top-notch local and visiting DJs or live acts. Check the website for schedules and cover charges.

Off Pera
CLUB
(Map p84; Gönül Sokak 14a, Asmalımescit; 🚇Karaköy, then funicular to Tünel) You'll need to squeeze your way into this tiny club, but once inside your persistence is sure to pay off. The DJs perch on a balcony over the bar and the multi-aged crowd spills out onto the street to smoke and catch their breath. Go on a Tuesday night, when Turkish pop dominates the sound system after midnight.

Araf
CLUB
(Map p84; www.araf.com.tr; 5th fl, Balo Sokak 32; ⊘5pm-4am Tue-Sun; 🚇Kabataş, then funicular to

Taksim) Grungy English teachers, Erasmus exchange students and Turkish language students have long claimed this as their favoured destination, listening to world music (including the live in-house gypsy band) and swilling some of the cheapest club beer in the city.

ORTAKÖY & KURUÇEŞME

Reina
CLUB
(Map p90; ☑212-259 5919; www.reina.com.tr; Muallim Naci Caddesi 44, Ortaköy; cover charge Sat & Sun ₺50, Mon-Fri free; ⊘daily summer, Sat & Sun winter; 🚇Ortaköy) According to its website, Reina is where 'foreign heads of states discuss world affairs, business people sign agreements of hundred billions of dollars and world stars visit'. In reality. it's where Turkey's C-list celebrities congregate, the city's nouveaux riches congregate and an occasional tourist gets past the doorman to ogle the spectacle. The Bosphorus location is truly extraordinary.

Sortie
CLUB
(Map p90; ☑212-327 8585; www.eksenistanbul.com; Muallim Naci Caddesi 141, Kuruçeşme; cover charge Fri & Sat ₺50, Mon-Thu & Sun free; ⊘summer only; 🚇Şifa Yurdu) Sortie has long vied with Reina as the reigning queen of the Golden Mile, nipping at the heels of its rival dowager. It pulls in the city's glamourpusses and poseurs, all of whom are on the lookout for the odd celebrity guest.

Supperclub
CLUB
(Map p90; ☑212-261 1988; www.supperclub.com; Muallim Naci Caddesi 65; admission free; ⊘summer only; 🚇Ortaköy) With an all-white decor and a location close to the Bosphorus, Supperclub has an unmistakable resort feel. Customers lounge or dine in oversized beach beds in lieu of tables and chairs, enjoying the atmospheric lighting, live shows, imported DJ talents and highly creative cuisine.

Live Music & Dance

SULTANAHMET

Hocapaşa Culture Centre
PERFORMING ARTS
(Hodjapasha Culture Centre; Map p62; ☑212-511 4626; www.hodjapasha.com; Hocapaşa Hamamı Sokak 3b, Sirkeci; adult/child under 12yr whirling dervish show ₺50/30, Turkish dance show ₺60/40; 🚇Sirkeci) Occupying a beautifully converted 550-year-old hamam near Eminönü, this cultural centre stages a one-hour whirling-dervish performance for tourists on Friday, Saturday, Sunday, Mon-

day and Wednesday evenings at 7.30pm, and a 1½-hour Turkish dance show on Tuesday and Thursday at 8pm and Saturday and Sunday at 9pm. Note that children under seven are not admitted to the whirling-dervish performance.

BEYOĞLU & AROUND

TOP CHOICE **Babylon**   LIVE MUSIC, CLUB

(Map p84; www.babylon.com.tr; Şehbender Sokak 3, Asmalımescit; ⊙9.30pm-2am Tue-Thu, 10pm-3am Fri & Sat, closed summer; ⊡Karaköy, then funicular to Tünel) İstanbul's pre-eminent live music venue has been packing the crowds in since 1999 and shows no sign of losing its allure. The eclectic program often features big-name international music acts, particularly during the festival season. Most of the action occurs in the concert hall, but there's also a lounge with DJ. Cover charge varies. Book at Biletix or at the venue's box office.

Munzur Cafe & Bar   LIVE MUSIC

(Map p84; www.munzurcafebar.com; Hasnun Galip Sokak, Galatasaray; ⊙1pm-4am Tue-Sun, music from 9pm; ⊡Kabataş, then funicular to Taksim) Hasnun Galip Sokak in Galatasaray is home to a number of *Türkü evleri*, Kurdish-owned bars where musicians perform live, emotion-charged *halk meziği* (folk music). The best of these is probably Munzur, which is nearly two decades old and still going strong. It has a great line-up of singers and expert *bağlama* (lute) players. Nearby **Toprak** (Map p84; ☎212-293 4037; www.toprak turkubar.tr.gg/ana-sayfa.htm; Hasnun Galip Sokak, Galatasaray; ⊙4pm-4am, show from 10pm) offers more of the same.

Galata Mevlevi Museum   PERFORMANING ARTS

(Galata Mevlevihanesi Müzesi; Map p84; Galipdede Caddesi 15, Tünel; ₺40; ⊙performances 4pm Sun; ⊡Karaköy, then funicular to Tünel) The 15th-century *semahane* at this *tekke* is the venue for a *sema* (ceremony) held most Sundays during the year. Tickets are only available on the day of the performance and often sell out – your best bet is to head to the museum and purchase tickets well ahead of the performance (the ticket office opens at 9am),

Nardis Jazz Club   JAZZ

(Map p84; ☎212-244 6327; www.nardisjazz.com; Kuledibi Sokak 14, Galata; ⊙9.30pm-12.30am Mon-Thu, 9.30pm-1.30am Fri & Sat, closed Aug; ⊡Karaköy) Named after a Miles Davis track, this intimate venue near the Galata Tower is run by jazz guitarist Önder Focan and his wife Zuhal. Performers include gifted amateurs, local jazz luminaries and visiting international artists. It's small, so you'll need to book if you want a decent table. Cover charge varies.

Salon   LIVE MUSIC

(Map p84; ☎212-334 0700; www.saloniksv .com; İstanbul Foundation for Culture & Arts, Nejat Eczacıbaşı Building, Sadi Konuralp Caddesi 5, Şişhane; ⊡Karaköy, then funicular to Tünel) This intimate performance space in the İstanbul Foundation for Culture & Arts (İKSV) building hosts live contemporary music (mainly jazz), lectures and theatrical performances; check the website for program and booking details. Before or after the show, be sure to have a drink at X Bar (p116), in the same building.

ORTAKÖY & KURUÇEŞME

İstanbul Jazz Center   JAZZ

(Map p90; ☎212-327 5050; www.istanbuljazz .com; Salhane Sokak 10, Ortaköy; ⊙from 7pm, live sets 9.30pm & 12.30am Mon-Sat, closed summer; ⊡Kabataş Lisesi) JC's plays regular host to members of the jazz world's who's who. Cover charge varies. Its location in the Golden Mile accounts for the steep bill for dinner plus music and drinks.

Sport

There's only one spectator sport that really matters to Turks: football (soccer). Eighteen teams from all over Turkey compete from August to May, and three of the top teams – Fenerbahçe, Galatasaray and Beşiktaş – are based in İstanbul. The top team of the first division plays in the European Cup.

Matches are usually held on weekends, normally on a Saturday night. Almost any Turkish male will be able to tell you which is the best match to see. Tickets are sold at the clubhouses at the *stadyum* (stadium) or through Biletix, and usually go on sale between Tuesday and Thursday for a weekend game. Open seating is reasonably priced; covered seating – which has the best views – can be expensive. If you miss out on the tickets you can get them at the door of the stadium, but they are usually outrageously overpriced.

To join local supporters watching a broadcast of the match, head to the Tophane Nargile Cafes (p115).

İSTANBUL ENTERTAINMENT

🔒 Shopping

If you love shopping you've come to the right place. Despite İstanbul's big-ticket historic sights, many travellers are surprised to find that the highlight of their visit was shopping, particularly searching and bartering for treasures in the city's atmospheric bazaars. The best of these are the Grand Bazaar and Arasta Bazaar, which specialise in carpets, jewellery, textiles and ceramics.

For Turkish musical instruments, check out the shops along Galipdede Caddesi, which runs between Tünel Meydanı and Galata Tower in Beyoğlu. For designer fashions, head to the upmarket shopping area of Nişantaşı, and for avant-garde fashion go to Serdar-ı Ekrem Caddesi in Galata. Antique hunters should wander through the streets of Çukurcuma in Beyoğlu.

Come energised, come with maximum overdraft and – most importantly – come with room in your suitcase.

SULTANAHMET

TOP CHOICE Cocoon CARPETS, TEXTILES

(Map p62; www.cocoontr.com; Küçük Aya Sofya Caddesi 13; ⊙8.30am-7.30pm; 🚇Sultanahmet) There are so many rug and textile shops in İstanbul that choosing individual shops to recommend is incredibly difficult. We had no problem whatsoever in singling this one out, though. Felt hats, antique costumes and textiles from central Asia are artfully displayed in one store, while rugs from Persia, central Asia, the Caucasus and Anatolia adorn the other. There's a third shop in the Arasta Bazaar and another in the **Grand Bazaar** (Map p80; Halıcılar Çarşışı Sokak 38, Grand Bazaar; ⊙9am-7pm Mon-Sat; 🚇Beyazıt-Kapalı Çarşı).

Jennifer's Hamam BATHWARE

(Map p73; www.jennifershamam.com; 43 & 135 Arasta Bazaar; ⊙9am-10.30pm Apr-Sep, 9am-7.30pm Oct-Mar; 🚇Sultanahmet) Owned by Canadian Jennifer Gaudet, the two Arasta Bazaar branches of this shop stock top-quality hamam items including towels, robes and *peştemals* (bath wraps) produced on old-style shuttled looms. It also sells natural soaps and *kese* (coarse cloth mittens used for exfoliation).

Mehmet Çetinkaya Gallery CARPETS, TEXTILES

(Map p62; www.cetinkayagallery.com; Tavukhane Sokak 7; ⊙9.30am-7.30pm; 🚇Sultanahmet) Mehmet Çetinkaya is known as one of the country's foremost experts on antique oriental carpets and kilims. His flagship store-cum-gallery stocks items that have artistic and ethnographic significance, and is full of treasures. There's a second shop selling rugs, textiles and objects in the Arasta Bazaar.

Yilmaz Ipekçilik TEXTILES

(Map p73; www.yilmazipekcilik.com/en; İshakpaşa Caddesi 36; ⊙9am-9pm Mon-Sat, to 7pm in winter; 🚇Sultanahmet) Well-priced hand-loomed silk textiles made in Antakya are on sale in this slightly out-of-the-way shop. Family-run, the business has been operating since 1950 and specialises in producing good-quality scarves, shawls and *peştemals*.

Khaftan ART, ANTIQUES

(Map p62; www.khaftan.com; Nakilbent Sokak 33; ⊙9am-8pm; 🚇Sultanahmet) Owner Adnan Cakariz sells antique Kütahya and İznik ceramics to collectors and museums here and overseas, so you can be sure that the pieces he sells in his own establishment are top-notch. Gleaming Russian icons, delicate calligraphy (old and new), ceramics, Karagöz puppets and contemporary paintings are all on show in this gorgeous shop.

Tulu HOMEWARES

(Map p62; www.tulutextiles.com; Üçler Sokak 7; 🚇Sultanahmet) One of the new breed of contemporary homeware stores taking İstanbul by storm, Tulu is owned by American Elizabeth Hewitt, a textile collector and designer who produces a stylish range of cushions, bedding and accessories inspired by textiles from Central Asia. These are sold alongside an array of furniture, textiles and objects sourced from countries including Uzbekistan, India, Japan and Indonesia.

BAZAAR DISTRICT

Yazmacı Necdet Danış TEXTILES

(Map p80; Yağlıkçılar Caddesi 57, Grand Bazaar; ⊙9am-7pm Mon-Sat; 🚇Beyazıt-Kapalı Çarşı) Fashion designers and buyers from every corner of the globe know that, when in İstanbul, this is where to come to source top-quality textiles. It's crammed with bolts of fabric of every description – shiny, simple, sheer and sophisticated – as well as *peştemals*, scarves and clothes. Next-door Murat Danış is part of the same operation

Derviş TEXTILES, BATHWARE

(Map p80; www.dervis.com; Keseciler Caddesi 33-35, Grand Bazaar; ⊙9am-7pm Mon-Sat; 🚇Beyazıt-

Kapalı Çarşı) Gorgeous raw cotton and silk *peştemals* share shelf space here with traditional Turkish dowry vests and engagement dresses. If these don't take your fancy, the pure olive-oil soaps and old hamam bowls are sure to step into the breach. There's another **store** (Map p80; Halıcılar Çarşışı Sokak 51) further north in the Bazaar.

Abdulla Natural Products   TEXTILES, BATHWARE
(Map p80; Halıcılar Çarşışı Sokak 62, Grand Bazaar; ☺9am-7pm Mon-Sat; 🚇Beyazıt-Kapalı Çarşı) The first of the Western-style designer stores to appear in this ancient marketplace, Abdulla sells top-quality cotton bed linen and towels, handspun woollen throws from Eastern Turkey, cotton *peştemals* and pure olive-oil soap. There's another store in the Fes Cafe (p108) in Nuruosmaniye.

Ak Gümüş   HANDICRAFTS
(Map p80; Gani Çelebi Sokak 8, Grand Bazaar; ☺9am-7pm Mon-Sat; 🚇Beyazıt-Kapalı Çarşı) Specialising in Central Asian tribal arts, this delightful store stocks an array of felt toys and hats, as well as jewellery and other objects made using coins and beads.

Sevan Bıçakçı   JEWELLERY
(Map p76; www.sevanbicakci.com; Gazi Sinan Paşa Sokak 16, Nuruosmaniye; ☺10am-6pm Mon-Sat; 🚇Çemberlitaş) Inspired by the monuments and history of his much-loved İstanbul, flamboyant jeweller Sevan Bıçakçı creates wearable art that aims to impress. His flagship store is in the Kutlu Han near the Grand Bazaar's Nuruosmaniye Gate.

Dhoku   CARPETS
(Map p80; www.dhoku.com; Takkeçiler Sokak 58-60, Grand Bazaar; ☺9am-7pm Mon-Sat; 🚇Beyazıt-Kapalı Çarşı) One of the new generation of rug stores opening in the bazaar, Dhoku (meaning 'texture') sells artfully designed wool kilims in resolutely modernist designs. Its sister store, **EthniCon** (Map p80; www.ethnicon.com; Takkeçiler Sokak, Grand Bazaar), opposite this store, sells similarly stylish rugs in vivid colours and can be said to have started the current craze in contemporary kilims.

Muhlis Günbattı   TEXTILES
(Map p80; www.muhlisgunbatti.net; Perdahçılar Sokak 48, Grand Bazaar; ☺9am-7pm Mon-Sat; 🚇Beyazıt-Kapalı Çarşı) One of the most famous stores in the bazaar, Muhlis Günbattı specialises in *suzani* fabrics from Uzbekistan. These beautiful bedspreads, tablecloths and

wall hangings are made from fine cotton embroidered with silk. As well as the textiles, it stocks top-quality carpets, brightly coloured kilims and a small range of antique Ottoman fabrics richly embroidered with gold. Its second shop at **Tevkifhane Sokak** (Tevkifhane Sokak 12; 🚇Sultanahmet) in Sultanahmet sells a wider range of costumes at stratospheric prices.

Serhat Geridönmez   JEWELLERY
(Map p80; Şerifağa Sokak 69, Old Bazaar, Grand Bazaar; ☺9am-7pm Mon-Sat; 🚇Beyazıt-Kapalı Çarşı) There are plenty of jewellers in the Grand Bazaar, but few sell objects as gorgeous as the expertly crafted copies of Hellinistic, Roman and Byzantine pieces on offer at this tiny store.

Sofa   ART, JEWELLERY
(Map p76; www.kashifsofa.com; Nuruosmaniye Caddesi 53, Nuruosmaniye; ☺9.30am-7pm Mon-Sat; 🚇Çemberlitaş) Investigation of Sofa's artfully arranged clutter reveals an eclectic range of pricey jewellery, prints, textiles, calligraphy, Ottoman miniatures and contemporary Turkish art.

Vakko İndirim   CLOTHING, ACCESSORIES
(Vakko Sale Store; Map p62; Yeni Camii Caddesi 13; ☺9.30am-6pm Mon-Sat; 🚇Eminönü) This remainder outlet of İstanbul's famous fashion store should be on the itinerary of all bargain hunters. Top-quality men's and women's clothing – often stuff that's been designed and made in Italy – is sold here for a fraction of its original price.

Ali Muhiddin Hacı Bekir   FOOD
(Map p62; www.hacibekir.com.tr/eng; Hamidiye Caddesi 83, Eminönü; ☺8am-8pm Mon-Sat; 🚇Eminönü) It's obligatory to sample *lokum* while in İstanbul, and one of the best places to do so is at this historic shop, which has been operated by members of the same family for over 200 years. Buy it *sade* (plain), or made with *cevizli* (walnut), *fıstıklı* (pistachio), *badem* (almond) or *roze* (rose-water). There's another store in **Beyoğlu** (Map p84; İstiklal Caddesi 83; 🚇Kabataş, then funicular to Taksim Meydanı).

BEYOĞLU & AROUND

TOP CHOICE **Dear East**   ARTS & CRAFTS
(Map p84; www.deareast.com; Lüleci Hendek Sokak 35, Tophane; ☺10.30am-7pm Mon-Sat; 🚇Tophane) Interior designer Emel Güntaş is one of İstanbul's style icons, and her recently

opened shop in Tophane is a favourite destination for the city's design mavens. The stock includes cushions (including a new range by fashion designer Rifat Özbek), carpets, kilims, silk scarves, woollen shawls, porcelain, felt crafts, paintings and photographs. Everything here is artisan-made, and absolutely gorgeous.

A La Turca
CARPETS, ANTIQUES

(Map p84; www.alaturcahouse.com; Faikpaşa Sokak 4, Çukurcuma; ⊙10.30am-7.30pm Mon-Sat; ⊠Kabataş, then funicular to Taksim) Antique Anatolian kilims and textiles are stacked alongside top-drawer Ottoman antiques in this fabulous shop in Çukurcuma. This is the best area in the city to browse for antiques and curios, and A La Turca is probably the most interesting of its retail outlets. Ring the doorbell to gain entrance.

Tezgah Alley
CLOTHING

(Map p84; Terkoz Cikmazı, off İstiklal Caddesi; ⊙closed Sun; ⊠Karaköy, then funicular to Tünel) Put your elbows to work fighting your way to the front of the *tezgah* (stalls) in this alleyway off İstiklal Caddesi, which are heaped with T-shirts, jumpers, pants and shirts on offer for under ₺10 per piece. Turkey is a major centre of European clothing manufacture, and the items here are often factory run-ons from designer or high-street-chain orders.

SIR
CERAMICS

(Map p84; www.sircini.com; Serdar-i Ekrem Sokak 66, Galata; ⊙closed Sun; ⊠Karaköy, then funicular to Tünel) Ceramics produced in İstanbul can be pricey, but the attractive hand-painted plates, platters, bowls and tiles sold at this small atelier are exceptions to the rule.

Lâl
HANDICRAFTS

(Map p84; www.lalistanbul.com; Camekan Sokak 4c, Galata; ⊙10.30am-8pm; ⊠Karaköy) Lâl is one of the new breed of handicraft shops in Turkey, selling items such as bags, scarves, clothing and Anatolian lace and braid jewellery made by traditional artisans but featuring a contemporary design aesthetic. The well-priced T-shirts with appliqué decoration are particularly desirable.

Hammam
BATHWARE

(Map p84; www.hammam.com.tr; Kule Çıkmazı, Galata; ⊙11am-8pm; ⊠Karaköy) The wonderful smell of naturally scented soap greets shoppers as they enter this small shop hidden in a street under the Galata Tower. The traditional laurel- and olive-oil soaps on offer are very well priced, as are the attractive cotton and silk *peştemals* and bath robes.

Bahar Korçan
CLOTHING

(Map p84; www.baharkorcan.org; Serdar-ı Ekrem Sokak 9, Galata; ⊙closed Sun; ⊠Karaköy) Bahar Korçan was in the vanguard of the design community's move into Galata, and her shop with its lofty ceiling, chandeliers and always-arresting window display is one of the most beautiful in Serdar-ı Ekrem Sokak. Her collections are characterised by their ultrafeminine designs, whimsical touches and delicate fabrics.

Arzu Kaprol
CLOTHING

(Map p84; www.arzukaprol.net; Serdar-ı Ekrem Sokak 22, Galata; ⊠Karaköy) Parisian-trained Arzu Kaprol is lauded throughout Turkey for her exciting designs. Her collections of women's clothing and accessories feature in Paris Fashion Week and are stocked by international retailers including Harrods in London. This store showcases her sleek prêt-à-porter range.

İroni
HOMEWARES

(Map p84; www.ironi.com.tr; Camekan Sokak 4e, Galata; ⊙10.30am-8pm; ⊠Karaköy) Güney İnan's range of silver-plated Turkish-style homewares includes plenty of options for those wanting to take home a souvenir of their trip. The tea sets (tray, glasses with holders, sugar bowls) are extremely attractive, as are the light fittings.

Robinson Crusoe
BOOKS

(Map p84; www.rob389.com; İstiklal Caddesi 389; ⊙9am-9.30pm Mon-Sat, 10am-9.30pm Sun; ⊠Karaköy, then funicular to Tünel) There are few more pleasant fates than being marooned here for an hour or so. With its classy decor, good magazine selection and wide range of English-language novels and books about İstanbul, it's one of the best bookshops in the city. There's another branch specialising in art books on the ground floor of SALT Beyoğlu (p88).

Lale Plak
MUSIC

(Map p84; Galipdede Caddesi 1, Tünel; ⊙9.30am-7.30pm Mon-Sat, 10.30am-7pm Sun; ⊠Karaköy, then funicular to Tünel) This small shop is crammed with CDs including a fine selection of Turkish classical, jazz and folk music. It's a popular hang-out for local musicians.

Selda Okutan JEWELLERY
(Map p84; www.seldaokutan.com; Ali Paşa Değirmeni Sokak 10a, Tophane; ⊘closed Sun; 🚇Tophane) Selda Okutan's sculptural pieces featuring tiny naked figures have the local fashion industry all aflutter. Come to her design studio in Tophane to see what all the fuss is about.

BEŞİKTAŞ, ORTAKÖY & KURUÇEŞME
The shops around fashionable W Hotel near Dolmabahçe Palace are among the most glamorous in the city. Marni, Chloé, Marc Jacobs and Jimmy Choo are just a few of the labels that draw the city's moneyed elite here to shop.

[TOP CHOICE] **Lokum** FOOD
(www.lokumistanbul.com; Kuruçeşme Caddesi 19, Kuruçeşme; ⊘9am-7pm Mon-Sat; 🚇Kuruçeşme) *Lokum* is elevated to the status of artwork at this boutique in Kuruçeşme. Owner-creator Zeynep Keyman aims to bring back the delights, flavours, knowledge and beauty of Ottoman-Turkish products such as *lokum, akide* candies (traditional boiled sweets, sometimes made with nuts and dried fruits), cologne water and scented candles. The gorgeous packaging makes for perfect gifts.

Haremlique HOMEWARES
(www.haremlique.com; Şair Nedim Bey Caddesi 11, Beşiktaş; ⊘Mon-Sat; 🚇Akaretler) The shops around the fashionable W Istanbul are among the most glamorous in the city. Among the international labels that are based here is this local business, which sells top-drawer bed linen and bathwares. Come here to source items such as boudoir cushion-covers featuring Ottoman rococo prints – they're certain to wow your guests back home.

❶ Information

Dangers & Annoyances

İstanbul is no more nor less safe a city than any large metropolis, but there are a few dangers worth highlighting:

» Some İstanbullus drive like rally drivers, and there is no such thing as a generally acknowledged right of way for pedestrians.

» Bag-snatchings and muggings occasionally occur on Beyoğlu's side streets.

» There has been a recent police crackdown on gay venues in the city, especially hamams and saunas. Many have closed but those that remain open are in constant danger of being raided by police for 'morality' reasons.

» Males travelling alone or in pairs should be wary of being adopted by a friendly local who is keen to take them to a club for a few drinks – many such encounters end up at *pavyons*, sleazy nightclubs run by the mafia where a drink or two with a female hostess will end up costing hundreds – sometimes thousands – of euros. If you don't pay up, the consequences can be violent.

Emergency
Ambulance (☑112)
Fire (☑110)
Police (☑155)
Tourist Police (☑212-527 4503; Yerebatan Caddesi 6) Across the street from the Basilica Cistern.

Media
Time Out İstanbul Published monthly, the English edition of this magazine has a large listings section and is the best source for details about upcoming events – you can pick it up at the airport, at newspaper booths in Sultanahmet and at some bookshops. It costs ₺6.

The Guide İstanbul The online edition of this advertising-driven listings magazine is more useful than its printed counterpart.

Medical Services
Although they are expensive, it's probably best to visit one of the private hospitals listed here if you need medical care when in İstanbul. Both accept credit-card payments and charge around ₺200 for a standard consultation.

Universal Taksim Alman Hastanesi (Universal German Hospital; ☑212-293 2150; www.uhg .com.tr; Sıraselviler Caddesi 119; ⊘8.30am-6pm Mon-Fri, 8.30am-5pm Sat) This hospital is a few hundred metres south of Taksim Meydanı on the left-hand side. It has eye, dental and pediatric clinics and staff speak English.

Vehbi Koç American Hospital (Amerikan Hastanesi; ☑212-444 3777 ext 9, 212-311 2000; www.americanhospitalistanbul.org /ENG; Güzelbahçe Sokak 20, Nişantaşı; ⊘24hr emergency department) About 2km northeast of Taksim Meydanı, this hospital has English-speaking staff and a dental clinic.

Money
ATMs are everywhere in İstanbul and include those conveniently located near Aya Sofya Meydanı in Sultanahmet, in the Grand Bazaar and all along İstiklal Caddesi in Beyoğlu.

The 24-hour *döviz bürosus* (exchange bureaux) in the arrivals hall at Atatürk International Airport offer rates comparable to those offered by city bureaux. Other exchange bureaux can be found on Divan Yolu in Sultanahmet, near the Grand Bazaar and around Sirkeci station in Eminönü.

Post

İstanbul's central PTT (post office) is in a convenient location between Sirkeci Train Station and the Spice Bazaar.

Telephone

If you are in European İstanbul and wish to call a number in Asian İstanbul, you must dial ☎216, then the number. If you are in Asian İstanbul and wish to call a number in European İstanbul dial ☎212, then the number. Don't use the area codes if you are calling a number on the same shore.

Tourist Information

When this book was being researched, the Ministry of Culture & Tourism was operating four tourist information offices around town; a fifth was scheduled to open in the Atatürk Cultural Centre on Taksim Meydanı when renovations there were complete. To be frank, none of the offices are particularly helpful.

Tourist Information Desk – Atatürk Airport (☎212-465 3451; International Arrivals Hall, Atatürk International Airport; ⏰9am-10pm)

Tourist Information Office – Karaköy (Karaköy International Passenger Terminal, Kemankeş Caddesi, Karaköy; ⏰9.30am-5pm Mon-Sat)

Tourist Information Office– Sirkeci (☎212-511 5888; Sirkeci Train Station, Ankara Caddesi, Sirkeci; ⏰9.30am-6pm summer, 9am-5.30pm rest of yr; 🚇Sirkeci)

Tourist Information Office – Sultanahmet (☎212-518 8754; Hippodrome, Sultanahmet; ⏰9.30am-6pm mid-Apr–Sep, 9am-5.30pm Oct–mid-Apr; 🚇Sultanahmet)

ℹ Getting There & Away

İstanbul is the country's foremost transport hub.

Air

Atatürk International Airport (IST, Atatürk Havalimanı; ☎212-463 3000; www.ataturkairport.com) Located 23km west of Sultanahmet. The *dış hatlar* (international terminal) and *iç hatlar* (domestic terminal) are side by side. There are car-hire desks, money-exchange offices, a tourist information desk, a pharmacy, ATMs and a PTT in the international arrivals hall and a 24-hour supermarket on the walkway to the metro. The left-luggage service (₺18 to ₺25 per suitcase per 24 hours) is to your right as you exit customs.

Sabiha Gökçen International Airport (SAW, Sabiha Gökçen Havalimanı; ☎216-588 8888; www.sgairport.com) Located 50km east of Sultanahmet, on the Asian side of the city, and popular with cut-price European carriers. There are car-hire desks, exchange offices, a pharmacy, a minimarket and a PTT here.

SERVICES FROM İSTANBUL'S OTOGAR

DESTINATION	FARE (₺)	DURATION (HR)	DISTANCE (KM)
Alanya	60	12	860
Ankara	38-43	6	450
Antakya	70	2	1107
Antalya	60	12½	740
Bodrum	70	12½	860
Bursa	25-30	4	230
Çanakkale	45	6	340
Denizli (for Pamukkale)	40-50	10	665
Edirne	25	2½	235
Fethiye	70	12	820
Göreme	65	11	725
İzmir	50	9	575
Kaş	75	13	1090
Konya	50	11	660
Kuşadası	60	12	555
Marmaris	70	12½	805
Selçuk	60	11	181
Trabzon	70-80	17	1110

Boat

Karaköy The **Karaköy International Maritime Passenger Terminal** (☑212-249 5776) is just near Galata Bridge.

Yenikapı The dock for the İstanbul Deniz Otobüsleri (p131) fast ferries across the Sea of Marmara to Bursa, Yalova and Bandırma (from where you can catch a train to İzmir). These carry both passengers and cars.

Bus

The Büyük İstanbul Otogarı is the city's main bus station for both intercity and international routes. Called simply the otogar (bus station), it's in the western district of Bayrampaşa, just south of the expressway and about 10km west of Sultanahmet. There's an ATM here and a few cafes.

The metro from Aksaray stops here (otogar stop) on its way from the airport; you can then connect with a tram to Sultanahmet. If you're going to Beyoğlu, bus 830 leaves from the centre of the otogar every 15 minutes between 5.50am and 8.45pm and takes approximately one hour to reach Taksim Meydanı. Bus 910 leaves for Eminönü every 15 to 25 minutes between 6am and 8.45pm; the trip takes approximately 50 minutes. Both trips cost ₺2. A taxi will cost approximately ₺30 to Sultanahmet, ₺35 to Taksim.

There's a smaller bus station on the Asian shore of the Bosphorus at Harem, south of Üsküdar and north of Haydarpaşa train station. If you're arriving in İstanbul by bus from anywhere on the Anatolian side of Turkey, it's always quicker to get out at Harem and take the car ferry to Sirkeci/Eminönü (₺2, every 30 minutes from 7am to 10.30pm); if you stay on the bus until the otogar, you'll add at least an hour to your journey. If you're going the other way, you may want to catch your bus here, instead of at the otogar; if your destination is serviced by frequent buses (eg Ankara or Antalya) you should have no trouble arriving at the Harem otogar and buying a ticket on the spot; if there are fewer services (eg Cappadocia) you should reserve your ticket by calling the bus line ahead of time, requesting that you board at Harem instead of the Büyük Otogarı.

Car & Motorcycle

The E80 Trans-European Motorway (TEM) from Europe passes about 10km north of Atatürk International Airport then, as Hwy 02, takes Fatih Bridge across the Bosphorus to Asia, passing some 1.5km north of Sabiha Gökçen International Airport. This will be your main route for getting to and from İstanbul, but try to avoid rush hours (7am to 10am and 3pm to 7pm Monday to Saturday) as the traffic is nightmarish and the Bosphorus bridges come to a standstill.

If you want to hire a car for your travels, we recommend you hire it from either of the airports on your way *out* of İstanbul, minimising the amount of time you'll need to spend navigating İstanbul's manic roads in an unfamiliar vehicle.

Train

At the time of our research, only one international service – the daily Bosfor/Balkan Ekspresi between İstanbul and Bucharest, Sofia and Belgrade – was operating in and out of İstanbul. Check **Turkish State Railways** (TCDD; ☑444 8233; www.tcdd.gov.tr) for details.

Services from İstanbul to cities within Turkey were also severely curtailed, largely due to an extensive upgrade to the rail link between it and Ankara. When this line reopens in 2014, it will feature high-speed trains that will depart from a new railway hub in Üsküdar, on the Asian shore.

ℹ️ Getting Around

To/From the Airport

ATATÜRK INTERNATIONAL AIRPORT

Bus If you are staying near Taksim Meydanı, the Havataş (Havaş) Airport Bus from Atatürk International Airport is even more convenient. This departs from outside the arrivals hall. Buses leave every 30 minutes between 4am and 1am; the trip takes between 40 minutes and one hour, depending on traffic. Tickets cost ₺10 and the bus stops outside the Havaş ticket office on Cumhuriyet Caddesi, just off Taksim Meydanı. A public bus service (no 96T) travels from a stop next to the Havataş buses and travels to Taksim Meydanı, but passengers must have an İstanbulkart (travelcard) to travel, and these are not available at the airport.

Metro There's an efficient metro service from the airport to Zeytinburnu, from where it's easy to connect with the tram to Sultanahmet, Eminönü and Kabataş. From Kabataş, there's a funicular to Taksim Meydanı. The metro station is on the lower ground floor beneath the international departures hall – follow the 'Metro/Subway' signs down the escalators and through the underground walkway. A token costs a mere ₺2 and services depart every 10 minutes or so from 5.40am until 1.40am. When you get off the metro, the tram platform is right in front of you. You'll need to buy another token (₺2) to pass through the turnstiles. The entire trip from the airport takes around 50 to 60 minutes to Sultanahmet, 60 to 70 minutes to Eminönü and 85 to 95 minutes to Taksim.

Shuttles Many hotels will provide a free pick-up service from Atatürk airport if you stay with them for three nights or more. There are also a number of cheap (but very slow) shuttle-bus

İstanbul Public Transport

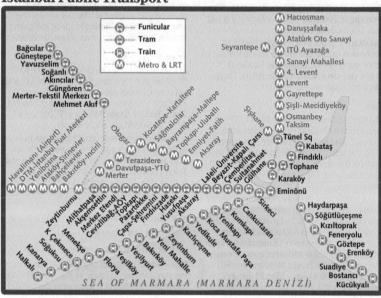

İSTANBUL GETTING AROUND

services from hotels to the airport for your return trip. Check details with your hotel.

Taxi Around ₺40 to Sultanahmet, ₺50 to Taksim Meydanı and ₺70 to Kadıköy.

SABIHA GÖKÇEN INTERNATIONAL AIRPORT

Bus The Havataş (Havaş) Airport Bus travels from the airport to Taksim Meydanı between 5am and midnight; after midnight there are shuttle services 30 minutes after every flight arrival. Tickets cost ₺12 and the trip takes approximately 90 minutes. If you're heading towards the Old City, you'll then need to take the funicular to Kabataş and the tram from Kabataş to Sultanahmet. A public bus service (no E10) goes from the airport to Kadıköy, from where ferries travel to Eminönü. Another (E3) goes to Levent, from where it's possible to transfer to a metro heading to Taksim Meydanı. Unfortunately, passengers must have an İstanbulkart (travelcard) and these are not available at the airport.

Taxi Around ₺90 to Taksim and ₺120 to Sultanahmet.

Bus

İstanbul's bus system is extremely efficient. The major bus stations are at Taksim Meydanı, Beşiktaş, Eminönü, Kadıköy and Üsküdar. Most services run between 6.30am and 11.30pm. Destinations and main stops on city bus routes are shown on a sign on the kerbside of the *otobus* (bus) or on the electronic display at its front.

İstanbul Elektrik Tramvay ve Tünel (www.iett .gov.tr) buses are run by the city and you must have a ticket (₺2) before boarding. You can buy tickets from the white booths near major stops or from some nearby shops for a small mark-up (look for 'İETT *otobüs bileti satılır*' signs). Think about stocking up on a supply to last throughout your stay in the city, or buying an İstanbulkart. Blue private buses regulated by the city, called Özel Halk Otobüsü, run the same routes; these accept cash (pay the conductor) and transport cards.

Dolmuş

A public bus service (no E10) goes Dolmuşes are privately run minibuses working defined routes. As a short-term visitor to the city, you won't have much, if any, cause to use them.

Ferry

The most enjoyable and efficient way to get around town is by ferry. *Jetons* (transport tokens) for most trips cost ₺2 and it's possible to use İstanbulkarts on all routes. **İstanbul Şehir Hatları** (İstanbul City Routes; www.sehirhatlari .com.tr) has fare and timetable information.

The main ferry docks are at the mouth of the Golden Horn (Eminönü and Karaköy) and at Beşiktaş, a few kilometres northeast of Galata Bridge, near Dolmabahçe Palace. There are also busy docks at Kadıköy and Üsküdar on the Asian (Anatolian) side. Ferries travel many routes around the city, but the following routes are those commonly used by travellers.

Beşiktaş–Kadıköy Every 30 minutes from 7.45am to 9.15pm.

Eminönü–Anadolu Kavağı Take the *Uzun Boğaz Turu* (Long Bosphorus Tour); between one and three services per day.

Eminönü–Kadıköy Approximately every 15 to 20 minutes from 7.30am to 9.10pm.

Eminönü–Üsküdar Approximately every 20 minutes from 6.35am to 11pm.

Kabataş–Kadıköy–Kınalıada–Burgazada–Heybeliada–Büyükada The Adalar (Princes' Islands) ferry; approximately every hour from 6.50am to 7.40pm.

Karaköy–Kadıköy Approximately every 20 minutes from 6.10am to 11pm.

Üsküdar–Eminönü–Kasımpaşa–Hasköy–Ayvansaray–Sütlüce–Eyüp The *Haliç* (Golden Horn) ferry; approximately every hour from 10.45am to 8pm, earlier on weekdays.

Funicular Railway

The Tünel was built in the late 19th century to save passengers the steep walk from Karaköy up the hill to İstiklal Caddesi in Beyoğlu. The three-minute service still runs today from 7am to 9pm Monday to Friday (from 7.30am on weekends), every five or 10 minutes, and the fare is ₺1.40.

A modern funicular railway runs through a tunnel from the Bosphorus shore at Kabataş, where it connects with the tram, up the hill to the metro station at Taksim Meydanı. The three-minute service runs around every three minutes and costs ₺2.

A **cable car** (₺1.50 each way, Akbil accepted) runs between the waterside at Eyüp to the Pierre Loti Café (p117).

İstanbulkarts can be used on all three services.

Metro

One service connects Aksaray with the airport, stopping at 15 stations including the otogar along the way. Services depart every 10 minutes or so from 5.40am until 1.40am and tickets cost ₺2. There are plans to eventually extend this service to Yenikapı.

Another line connects Şişhane, near Tünel Meydanı in Beyoğlu, and Hacıosman, northeast of Taksim. Unfortunately, it's not possible to travel between the two points in one trip – one metro runs between Şişhane and Taksim Meydanı; another runs between Taksim and Hacıosman, stopping at nine stations along the way. The full trip takes around one hour. Services run every five minutes or so from 6.15am to midnight. Tickets cost ₺2.

İstanbulkarts can be used on both lines.

Works are currently underway to extend the Taksim–Şişhane route over the Golden Horn via a new metro bridge and under the Old City to Yenikapı via stops at Unkapanı and Şehzadebaşı. It will then connect with the metro to Aksaray and with a transport tunnel being built under the Bosphorus as part of the Marmaray project. This tunnel will include a metro connection between Yenikapı, Sirkeci, Üsküdar and Söğütlüçesme. Other works underway include construction of a 16-stop metro line running between Kadıköy and Kartal on the Asian side of town.

 İSTANBULKARTS

İstanbul's public transport system is excellent, and for many years the Akbil system was one of its best features. These small electronic tags could be purchased with a refundable deposit, recharged with cash and then used to access easy discounted travel across the system. The Akbil system is in the process of being slowly phased out, and is being replaced by the İstanbulkart,a rechargable travel card similar to London's Oyster Card, Hong Kong's Octopus Card and Paris' Navigo.

İstanbulkarts are simple to operate: as you enter a bus or pass through the turnstile at a ferry dock or metro station, swipe your card for entry and the fare will automatically be deducted from your balance. The cards offer a considerable discount on fares (₺1.75 as opposed to the usual ₺2, with additional transfers within a two-hour journey window ₺1) and they can be used to pay for fares for more than one traveller (one swipe per person per ride).

The cards can be purchased for a refundable deposit of ₺10 and charged with amounts between ₺5 and ₺150. Unfortunately, they are a bit difficult to access – you need to find a kiosk displaying an 'Akbil' or 'Istanbulkart' sign. The most conveniently located kiosk for travellers is at the bus station at Eminönü.

Cards can be recharged at machines at ferry docks, metro stations and bus stations. Note that, in our experience, machines will only accept ₺10 or ₺20 notes – not ₺50.

Taxi

» Taxi rates are very reasonable – from Sultanahmet to Taksim Meydanı will cost around ₺15 and there are no evening surcharges. Ignore taxi drivers who insist on a fixed rate as these are much higher than you'd pay using the meter.

» Few of the city's taxis have seatbelts.

» If you take a taxi over either of the Bosphorus bridges it is your responsibility to cover the toll. The driver will add this to your fare.

» Locals usually round up the fare to the nearest 0.5₺.

Train

İstanbul has two *banliyö treni* (suburban train lines), but neither are of interest to the average traveller.

Tram

An excellent *tramvay* (tramway) service runs from Bağcılar, in the city's west, to Zeytinburnu (where it connects with the metro from the airport) and on to Sultanahmet and Eminönü. It then crosses the Galata Bridge to Karaköy (to connect with the Tünel) and Kabataş (to connect with the funicular to Taksim Meydanı). In the future, it will be extended from Kabataş to the ferry dock at Beşiktaş. Services run every five minutes from 6am to midnight. The fare is ₺2; *jetons* are available from machines on every tram stop and İstanbulkarts can be used.

AROUND İSTANBUL

Princes' Islands

Most İstanbullus refer to the Princes' Islands as 'The Islands' *(Adalar)*. The group lies about 20km southeast of the city in the Sea of Marmara and makes a great destination for a day's escape, particularly as the ferry ride here is so enjoyable.

In Byzantine times, refractory princes, deposed monarchs and others who had outlived their roles were interned on the islands (rather like Abdullah Öcalan, the ex-PKK leader, marooned today on İmralı Island in the Sea of Marmara). A ferry service from İstanbul was started in the mid-19th century and the islands became popular summer resorts with Pera's Greek, Jewish and Armenian business communities. Many of the fine Victorian villas built by these wealthy merchants survive today.

You'll realise after landing that there are no cars on the islands, something that comes as a welcome relief after the traffic mayhem of the city. Except for the necessary police, fire and sanitation vehicles, transport is by bicycle, *fayton* (horse-drawn carriage) and foot, as in centuries past.

All of the islands are extremely busy in summer, particularly on weekends, so we recommend avoiding a Sunday visit.

◉ Sights & Activities

There are nine islands in the group and the ferry stops at four of these. Year-round there are 15,000 permanent residents scattered across the six islands that are populated, but numbers swell to 100,000 or so during the summer months when İstanbullus – many of whom have holiday homes here – come here to escape the city heat.

After boarding the ferry at Kabataş, try to find a seat on the right side of the ferry so that you can view the various islands as the ferry approaches them.

MARMARAY PROJECT

Marmaray (www.marmaray.com) is an ambitious public transport project aimed at relieving İstanbul's serious traffic congestion. Its name comes from combining the name of the Sea of Marmara, which lies just south of the project site, with *ray*, the Turkish word for rail.

The project will see the Halkalı–Sirkeci rail line, which runs alongside the historical peninsula's coastline, going underground at Yedikule and travelling to a huge underground transport hub at Yenikapı before continuing to Sirkeci and then on to a 5km tunnel being built under the Bosphorus. This will link the historical peninsula with another new underground transport hub in Üsküdar on the Asian side of the city. From there, the rail line will return to ground level at Söğütlüçeşme, 2km east of Kadıköy, where it will connect with the Gebze Anatolian rail line.

The project's original completion date was to be 2010, but important archaeological finds made during excavation works have slowed the process down. These include the site of a Byzantine harbour complete with wooden boats at Yenikapı and an ancient port and bazaar at Üsküdar. It's now hoped that the new rail line will open in June 2015.

Heading towards the Sea of Marmara, passengers are treated to fine views of Topkapı Palace, Aya Sofya and the Blue Mosque on the right and Kız Kulesi, Haydarpaşa Railway Station and the distinctive minaret-style clock towers of Marmara University on the left.

After a quick stop at Kadıköy, the ferry makes its way to the first island in the group, Kınalıada. This leg takes 30 minutes. After this, it's another 15 minutes to the island of Burgazada and another 15 minutes again to Heybeliada, the second-largest of the islands. Buyukada is another 15 minutes from here.

HEYBELİADA

Heybeliada (Heybeli for short and Halki in Greek) is popular with day trippers, who come here on weekends to walk in the pine groves and swim from the tiny (but crowded) beaches. The island's major landmark is the hilltop Haghia Triada Monastery, which is perched above a picturesque line of poplar trees in a spot that has been occupied by a Greek monastery since Byzantine times. The current monastery complex dates from 1844 and housed a Greek Orthodox theological school until 1971, when it was closed on the government's orders. The Ecumenical Patriarchate of Constantinople is waging an ongoing campaign to have it reopened. The complex includes a small church with an ornate altar, as well as an internationally renowned library, which is home to many old and rare manuscripts. To visit the library, you'll need to gain special permission from the abbot, Metropolitan Elpidophoros. A *fayton* will charge ₺25 to bring you here from the centre of town.

The delightful walk from the *iskele* up to the Merit Halki Palace (☑351 0025; www .halkipalacehotel.com; Refah Şehitleri Caddesi 94; s €80-180, d €125-320; @🛜🕿) hotel at the top of Refah Şehitleri Caddesi passes a host of large wooden villas set in lovingly tended gardens. Many laneways and streets leading to picnic spots and lookout points are located off the upper reaches of this street. To find the hotel, turn right as you leave the ferry and head past the waterfront restaurants and cafes to the plaza with the Atatürk statue. From here walk up İşgüzar Sokak, veering right until you hit Refah Şehitleri Caddesi. If you don't feel like walking up to the hotel (it's uphill but not too steep), you can hire a bicycle (₺5 per hour, ₺15 per day) from one of the shops in the main street or a *fayton* to take you around the island. A

PUBLIC TRANSPORT OPERATORS

İstanbul Elektrik Tramvay ve Tünel (İETT, Istanbul Electricity, Tramway and Tunnel General Management; www.iett .gov.tr) is responsible for running public buses, funiculars and historic trams in the city. Its website has useful timetable and route information in Turkish and English. Metro and tram services are run by İstanbul Ulaşım (www.istanbul-ulasim.com.tr), ferry services are run by İstanbul Şehir Hatları (p128), and seabus and fast ferry services are operated by İstanbul Deniz Otobüsleri (İDO; ☑212-444 4436; www.ido.com.tr).

25-minute tour *(küçük tur)* costs ₺40 and a one-hour tour *(büyük tur)* costs ₺50; the *fayton* stand is behind the Atatürk statue. Some visitors spend the day by the pool at the Merit Halki Palace, which is a good idea, as the waters around the island aren't very clean. Towels and chaise longues are supplied, and there's a pleasant terrace restaurant for meals or drinks. There is a charge for nonguests using the pool (weekdays/ weekends ₺40/60).

BÜYÜKADA

The largest island in the group, Büyükada (Great Island), is impressive viewed from the ferry, with gingerbread villas climbing up the slopes of the hill and the bulbous twin cupolas of the Splendid Otel providing an unmistakable landmark.

The ferry terminal is an attractive building in the Ottoman Revival style; it dates from 1899. Inside there's a pleasant tile-decorated cafe with an outdoor terrace.

The island's main drawcard is the Greek Orthodox Monastery of St George, located in the 'saddle' between Büyükada's two highest hills. To walk here, head from the ferry to the clock tower in İskele Meydanı (Dock Square). The shopping district (with cheap eateries) is left along Recep Koç Sokak. Bear right onto 23 Nisan Caddesi, then head along Çankaya Caddesi up the hill to the monastery; when you come to a fork in the road, veer right. The walk, which takes at least one hour, takes you past a long progression of impressive wooden villas set in gardens. About a quarter of the way up on the left is the

Around İstanbul

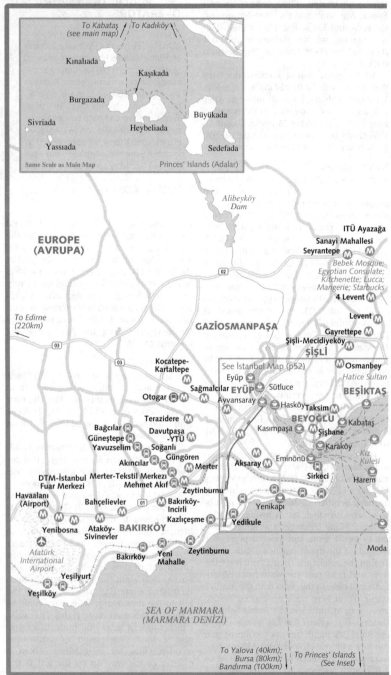

To Kabataş (see main map) To Kadıköy

Kınalıada

Kaşıkada

Burgazada

Büyükada

Sivriada

Heybeliada

Yassıada

Sedefada

Same Scale as Main Map

Princes' Islands (Adalar)

Alibeyköy Dam

EUROPE (AVRUPA)

ITÜ Ayazağa

Sanayi Mahallesi
Seyrantepe

*Bebek Mosque;
Egyptian Consulate;
Kitchenette; Lucca;
Mangerie; Starbucks*

4 Levent

To Edirne (220km)

Levent

Gayrettepe

Şişli-Mecidiyeköy

GAZİOSMANPAŞA

ŞİŞLİ

Osmanbey

See İstanbul Map (p52)

Hatice Sultan

Kocatepe-
Kartaltepe

Eyüp

Sağmalcılar

Sütluce

EYÜP

BEŞİKTAŞ

Otogar

Ayvansaray

Hasköy

Taksim

Terazidere

BEYOĞLU

Bağcılar

Davutpaşa
-YTÜ

Kasımpaşa

Şişhane

Kabataş

Güneştepe
Yavuzselim

Soğanlı

Karaköy

Akıncılar

Güngören

*Kız
Kulesi*

DTM-İstanbul
Fuar Merkezi

Merter-Tekstil Merkezi

Merter

Aksaray

Eminönü

Mehmet Akif

Sirkeci

Harem

Havaalanı
(Airport)

Bahçelievler

Zeytinburnu

Bakırköy-
Incirli

Yenikapı

Yenibosna

Ataköy-
Sivinevler

BAKIRKÖY

Kazlıçeşme

Yedikule

Moda

*Atatürk
International
Airport*

Bakırköy

Yeni
Mahalle

Zeytinburnu

Yeşilyurt

Yeşilköy

*SEA OF MARMARA
(MARMARA DENİZİ)*

To Yalova (40km);
Bursa (80km);
Bandırma (100km)

To Princes' Islands
(See Inset)

Büyükada Kültür Evi, a charming spot where you can enjoy a tea or coffee in a garden setting. After 40 minutes or so you will reach a reserve called 'Luna Park' by the locals. The monastery is a 25-minute walk up an extremely steep hill from here. As you ascend, you'll sometimes see pieces of cloth tied to the branches of trees along the path – each represents a prayer, most made by female supplicants visiting the monastery to pray for a child.

There's not a lot to see at the monastery. A small and gaudy church is the only building of note, but there are fabulous panoramic views from the terrace, as well as the pleasant Yücetepe Kır Gazinosu (p134) restaurant. From its tables you will be able to see all the way to İstanbul and the nearby islands of Yassıada and Sivriada.

The new **Museum of the Princes' Islands** (Adalar Müzesi Hangar Müze Alanı; www .adalarmuzesi.org; Aya Nikola Mevkii; admission ₺5, Wed free; ⊙9am-6pm Tue-Sun, to 4pm winter) is also worth a visit, with exhibits covering local lifestyle, famous residents and local food. It's hard to locate, so we recommend taking a *fayton* (₺20).

Bicycles are available for rent in several of the town's shops (₺5 per hour, ₺15 per day), and shops on the market street can provide picnic supplies. The *fayton* stand is to the left of the clock tower. Hire one for a long tour of the town, hills and shore (₺50, one hour) or a shorter tour of the town (₺40). It costs ₺20 to be taken to Luna Park.

✖ Eating

Unfortunately, most of the restaurants on the islands are unremarkable and pricey.

HEYBELİADA

⌈TOP⌉
⌊CHOICE⌋ **Heyamola Ada Lokantası** TURKISH €€
(Mavi Marmara Yalı Caddesi 30b, Heybeliada; cold mezes ₺5-8, hot mezes ₺17-21, mains ₺15-30, set brunch ₺25; ⊙lunch & dinner Mon-Fri, brunch & dinner Sat & Sun, closed Mon Nov-Apr; ⛴Heybeliada) Until recently, there were few decent places to eat on the Adalar. Fortunately, Basir Seving remedied that situation by opening this restaurant opposite the İDO dock. Heyamola wows customers with a huge array of mezes (try the baked saganaki), delicious fish mains (order *mezgit* if it's on offer) and an interesting and affordable wine list featuring plenty of boutique labels.

BÜYÜKADA

Yücetepe Kır Gazinosu
Restaurant   TURKISH €
(www.yucetepe.com; Monastery of St George, Büyükada; mezes ₺5-8, mains ₺12-15; ☺daily Apr-Oct, Sat & Sun only Nov-Mar) At the very top of the hill where the Monastery of St George is located, this simple place has benches and chairs on a terrace overlooking the sea and İstanbul. Dishes are simple but delicious – the *köfte* is particularly tasty. You can also enjoy a beer or glass of tea here.

Büyükada Kültür Evi   CAFE €
(Çankaya Caddesi 21, Büyükada; sandwiches ₺8-14, grills ₺16; ☺daily Apr-Oct, Sat & Sun only Nov-Mar) Occupying a villa dating from 1878, this garden cafe serves breakfast, lunch and dinner in its terraced garden. Service can be desultory and the food's not up to much, but it's an undeniably pretty setting and a great spot for a morning glass of tea or a late-afternoon beer.

❶ Getting There & Away

At least eight ferries run to the islands each day from 6.50am to 7.40pm (to midnight mid-June to mid-September), departing from the Adalar İskelesi at Kabataş. The most useful departure times for day trippers are 10.40am and noon (8.30am, 9.30am, 10.30am and 11.30am mid-June to mid-September). On summer weekends, board the vessel and grab a seat at least half an hour before departure time unless you want to stand the whole way. The trip costs ₺4 (₺3 with an İstanbulkart) to the islands and the same for each leg between the islands and for the return trip. To be safe, check the timetable at www.sehirhatlari.com.tr, as the schedule often changes.

Ferries return to İstanbul every two hours or so. The last ferry of the day leaves Büyükada at 8pm and Heybeliada at 8.15pm (10.40pm and 10.55pm mid-June to mid-September).

Thrace & Marmara

Includes »

Best Places to Eat

» Melek Anne (p141)

» Yalova (p160)

» Doyuranlar Gözleme (p154)

» Tavern (p163)

» Zindanaltı Meyhanesi (p141)

Best Places to Stay

» Gallipoli Houses (p153)

» Zeytindali Hotel (p163)

» Anemos Otel (p163)

» Hotel Crowded House (p154)

» Hotel Edirne Palace (p141)

Why Go?

The Thracian isthmus is a former Balkan stronghold that adds an important chapter to the Turkish narrative. On the beautiful, pine-strewn Gallipoli (Gelibolu) Peninsula, nationalism spread its wings in World War I and Atatürk became a legend incarnate. Today the Dardanelles are less imposing; in Çanakkale, on the Anatolian side of the straits, Antipodean pilgrims lend the city's night spots a cosmopolitan feel.

Centuries earlier, the great city of Edirne was the base from which Mehmet the Conqueror (Mehmet Fatih) seized Constantinople (İstanbul); today the Tunca River flows past mosque and palace complexes that capture human brilliance. The city's 650-year-old Historic Kırkpınar Oil Wrestling Festival recalls the days of Ottoman–Byzantine clashes.

Fifteen miles due west of the mainland is Gökçeada island, a time-worn landscape where Greek settlements cling to a valley slowly waking up to the outside world.

When to Go

Edirne

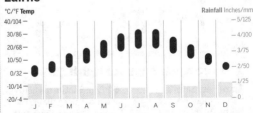

May Red poppies bloom on Gökçeada island.

Jun & Jul Oily Goliaths grapple at the Historic Kırkpınar Oil Wrestling Festival, Edirne.

Sep Autumn on the Gallipoli Peninsula.

Edirne

☎ 0284 / POP 144,531

Tucked away in the northwest corner of the country – and consequently overlooked by most travellers – Edirne is a small, dreamy city with magnificent Ottoman architecture and an old Roman district that over centuries has only changed its signage and the dress of its residents.

Edirne is close to the Greek and Bulgarian border, which lends the former Ottoman capital a frontier mentality. The streets here are livelier than in most similar-sized Turkish cities and visitors pour in every summer for a famous oil wrestling tournament.

History

Emperor Hadrian made Hadrianopolis (later Adrianople) the main centre of Roman Thrace in the early 2nd century AD. In the

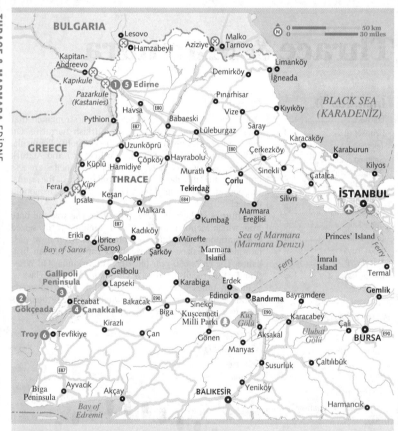

Thrace & Marmara Highlights

❶ Witness Sinan's architectural legacy at **Edirne** (p136) a former Ottoman capital near the Bulgarian border.

❷ Get lost on the dramatic, windswept reaches of **Gökçeada** (p161), Turkey's largest island.

❸ Contemplate the horrors of warfare along the eerily bucolic **Gallipoli Peninsula** (p146).

❹ Party across the straits in youthful **Çanakkale** (p156), a popular base for the region.

❺ Watch the slippery fun at Edirne's annual **Historical Kırkpınar Oil Wrestling Championships** (p140).

❻ Explore the ruins of **Troy** (p164) where literary legends were made.

mid-14th century the nascent Ottoman state began to grow in size and power. In 1363 its army crossed the Dardanelles, skirted Constantinople and captured Adrianople, which the Ottomans made their capital.

For a century, Edirne was the city from which the Ottoman sultan launched campaigns in Europe and Asia. Mehmet the Conqueror set out for Constantinople from here.

When the Ottoman Empire collapsed after WWI, the Allies handed Thrace to the Greeks and declared Constantinople (now İstanbul) an international city. In the summer of 1920 Greek armies occupied Edirne, only to be driven back by forces under the command of Atatürk. The Treaty of Lausanne (1923) ceded Edirne and eastern Thrace to the Turks.

◉ Sights & Activities

Selimiye Camii
MOSQUE

(Selimiye Mosque; Mimar Sinan Caddesi) Great Ottoman architect Mimar Sinan designed Edirne's grandest mosque (built 1569–75) for Sultan Selim II (r 1566–74). The mosque is smaller but more elegant than Sinan's Süleymaniye Camii in İstanbul, and it is said that he considered this to be his finest work. Lit up at night, the complex is a spectacular sight.

Enter the mosque through the courtyard to the west, as the architect intended. You don't need to buy a plastic bag for your shoes from the ladies in the courtyard.

The broad, lofty dome – at 31.3m, marginally wider than that of İstanbul's Aya Sofya – is supported by eight unobtrusive pillars, arches and external buttresses, creating a surprisingly spacious interior. As they only bear a portion of the dome's weight, the walls are sound enough to hold dozens of windows, the light from which brings out the interior's colourful calligraphic decorations.

The delicately carved marble *mimber* (pulpit), with its conical roof of İznik tiles, and the *şadırvan* (ablutions fountain) beneath the central prayer-reader's platform are particularly exquisite.

Part of the Selimiye's striking effect comes from its four 71m-high minarets, which Sinan fluted to emphasise their height. Each tower also has three *şerefes* (balconies), Sinan's respectful nod, perhaps, to his predecessor, the architect of the Üç Şerefeli Cami.

Medreses
MUSEUMS

(Selimiye Camii) The *medrese* (seminary) in the southern corner of the Selimiye complex houses the **Selimiye Foundation Museum** (Selimiye Vakıf Müzesi; ☑212 1133; admission free; ⊙9am-5pm Tue-Sun), with displays covering the restoration of the mosque, metalwork, İznik tiles and seminary education. The *medrese* in the eastern corner houses the **Turkish & Islamic Arts Museum** (Türk-İslam Eserleri Müzesi; Dilaver Bey Park; admission €1.10; ⊙8am-noon & 1-5.30pm Tue-Sun), which opened in 2012 and is understated by Ottoman standards.

Edirne Archaeology & Ethnography Museum
MUSEUM

(Edirne Arkeoloji ve Etnografya Müzesi; ☑225 1120; Mimar Sinan Caddesi; admission TL3; ⊙9am-5pm Tue-Sun) Facing a garden of janissary gravestones behind the Selimiye Camii, this museum has displays covering embroidery, textiles, calligraphy and jewellery. The Ottoman technique of lacquering wood, cardboard and leather was developed in Edirne. There are several reconstructions of Ottoman houses, including bridal and circumcision rooms.

The archaeological section features exhibits from prehistory, with finds from the Macedonian Tower and the Taşlıcabayır tumulus near Kırklareli to the east: the terracotta sarcophagi (6th century BC) from Enez (Aenus) in southwest Thrace; the 1st- and 2nd-century terracotta figures; and the bronze figures from a millennium earlier are exquisite. The grounds contain all kinds of jars, sculptures, menhirs (standing stones), a dolmen and a Roman tomb.

Üç Şerefeli Cami
MOSQUE

With its four strikingly different minarets, the Üç Şerefeli Cami dominates Hürriyet Meydanı (Freedom Sq). The name refers to the three balconies on the tallest minaret. The second-tallest minaret has only two.

The mosque was built between 1437 and 1447 in a design halfway between the Seljuk Turkish-style mosques of Konya and Bursa and the truly Ottoman style, which would later reach its pinnacle in İstanbul. In the Seljuk style, smaller domes are mounted on square rooms, whereas here the 24m-wide dome is mounted on a hexagonal drum and supported by two walls and two massive hexagonal pillars. The designs under the domes and central *şadırvan* in

Edirne

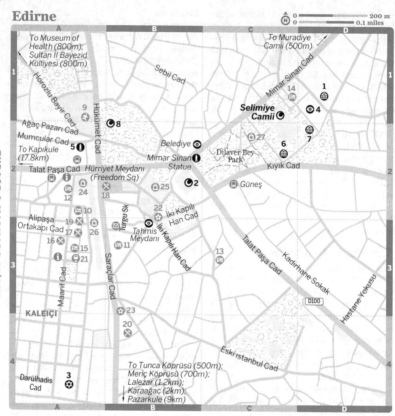

To Museum of Health (800m); Sultan II Bayezid Külliyesi (800m)

To Muradiye Camii (500m)

Horozlu Bayır Cad

Sebil Cad

Mimar Sinan Cad

Selimiye Camii

Ağaç Pazarı Cad

Mumcular Cad

To Kapıkule (17.8km)

Hükümet Cad

Belediye

Mimar Sinan Statue

Dilaver Bey Park

Kıyık Cad

Talat Paşa Cad

Hürriyet Meydanı (Freedom Sq)

Güneş

Alipaşa

Ortakapı Cad

Turan Sk

Saraçlar Cad

Tahmis Meydanı

İki Kapılı Han Cad

İki Kapılı Han Cad

Talat Paşa Cad

Kadirhane Sokak

D100

Hastane Yokuşu

KALEİÇİ

Darülhadis Cad

To Tunca Köprüsü (500m); Meriç Köprüsü (700m); Lalezar (1.2km); Karaağaç (2km); Pazarkule (9km)

Eski Istanbul Cad

---

the partially covered courtyard – another innovation that came to be standard – are fantastic.

Makedonya Kulesi
TOWER

Southwest of the hamam stands the restored Macedonian Tower, part of the city fortifications dating back to Roman times. Around its base, recent excavations have uncovered parts of the old city wall, a necropolis and the remains of a Byzantine church.

Eski Cami
MOSQUE

The Old Mosque (1403–14) exemplifies one of the two classic mosque styles used by the Ottomans in their earlier capital, Bursa. Like Bursa's Ulu Cami, the Eski Cami has rows of arches and pillars supporting a series of small domes. Inside, there are striking red, white and black geometric patterns on the domes, and a marvellous *mimber;* huge calligraphic inscriptions cover the walls.

Kaleiçi
HISTORIC AREA

The Kaleiçi area, framed by Saraçlar Caddesi, Talat Paşa Caddesi, the railway line and the Tunca River, was the original medieval town. You could start exploring by walking south from the tourist office along Maarif Caddesi, which takes you past some fine examples of ornate wooden houses with attractive Edirnekari woodwork and finishes at Edirne's derelict **Great Synagogue** (Büyük Sinagog; Maarif Cadessi 10), which was built in 1906. Cumhuriyet Caddesi, running perpendicular to Maarif Caddesi, is another interesting street with wooden houses.

Sokollu Mehmet Paşa Hamam
HAMAM

(wash & massage ₺30; ⊙men 7am-10pm, women 10am-6pm) Mimar Sinan designed this atmospheric hamam for Grand Vizier Sokollu Mehmet Paşa in the 16th century. It's one of the best in Turkey.

Edirne

THRACE & MARMARA EDİRNE

NORTH OF THE CENTRE

TOP CHOICE **Museum of Health**   MUSEUM
(Sağlık Müzesi; ☎224 0922; admission ₺5; ⊙9am-5.30pm) Part of the Sultan Bayezid II Külliyesi complex, this museum has scooped European tourism awards for its illustrations of the therapy and teaching that took place here. One of the most important Ottoman hospitals, it operated from 1488 to 1909, and music therapy was employed from 1652 – when mentally ill people were still being burnt alive in Europe. A 10-piece band played different 'modes' to treat ailments from paralysis to palpitations. Because all healing work was carried out in one room (the *şifahane* – healing room), the hospital required fewer staff. This created the first centralised hospital system. The sound of water was also used, and the gurgling fountain in the high-ceilinged hall is certainly soothing after a long walk from the centre.

The museum continues into the *medrese*, where dioramas cover aspects of Ottoman medicine, including cauterisation – a popular operation at that time – and the development of antidotes (coaxing a viper to bite a chicken).

Approach via the Ottoman Yalnızgöz Köprüsü (Lone Eye Bridge; 1570) over the Tunca River. Buses to Yenimaret ('Y. Maret') from opposite the tourist office pass the complex (₺1, 10 minutes); a taxi costs about ₺7.

Sultan II Bayezid Külliyesi   MOSQUE
(Beyazit Mahallesi) Standing in splendid isolation north of the centre, this mosque complex was built by Ottoman architect Hayreddin for Sultan Bayezid II (r 1481–1512) between 1484 and 1488. In style, the mosque lies midway between the Üç Şerefeli and Selimiye models: its large prayer hall has one large dome, similar to the Selimiye, but it also has a courtyard and fountain, like the earlier Üç Şerefeli. The interior has a rough, almost unfinished feel to it.

The extensive complex includes a *tabhane* (travellers hostel), bakery, *imaret* (soup kitchen), *tımarhane* (asylum), *medrese* and *darüşşifa* (hospital).

Sarayiçi   HISTORIC AREA
The Inner Palace is actually an island that was once the private hunting reserve of the Ottoman sultans. Today it's the site of the famous Kırkpınar oil wrestling matches.

Near the modern stadium, which is flanked by uberbutch *başpehlivan* (champions) in bronze, stands the Adalet Kasrı (Justice Hall; 1561), a stone tower with a conical

SLIP-SLIDING AWAY IN EDİRNE

One of the world's oldest and most bizarre sporting events, in which muscular men, naked except for a pair of heavy leather shorts, coat themselves with olive oil and throw each other around, takes place annually in late June/early July in northern Edirne. It's called the **Tarihi Kırkpınar Yağlı Güreş Festivali** (Historic Kırkpınar Oil Wrestling Festival; www.kirkpinar.com).

The origins of this oleaginous contest go back 6½ centuries to the early days of the Ottoman Empire. Shortly before the conquest of Edirne in 1363, Sultan Orhan Gazi sent his brother Süleyman Paşa with 40 men to conquer the Byzantine fortress at Domuz in Rumelia, the European part of the Ottoman Empire. The two-score soldiers were all keen wrestlers, and after their victory challenged each other to bouts. Two of them were so evenly matched that they fought for days without any clear result, until both of them finally dropped dead. When the bodies were buried under a nearby fig tree, a spring mysteriously appeared. The site was given the name Kırkpınar ('40 Springs'), in the wrestlers' honour.

The original Kırkpınar is now the village of Samona, just over the border in Greece; the annual three-day contest has been held outside Edirne since the birth of the republic. Wrestlers, who are classed not by weight but by height, age and experience, compete in 13 categories – from *minik* (toddler) to *baş* (first class) – and dozens of matches take place simultaneously in the Sarayiçi stadium. Bouts are now capped at 30 or 40 minutes, after which they enter 'sudden death' one-fall-wins overtime. When all the fights are decided, prizes are awarded for gentlemanly conduct and technique, as well as the coveted and hotly contested *başpehlivan* (head wrestler) title.

You can buy tickets to the wrestling from **Biletix** (www.biletix.com) for about ₺60. Transport and accommodation fill up fast around the festival.

For more information visit **Kırkpınar Evi** (Kırkpınar House; ☑212 8622; www.kirkpinar .com; ☒10am-noon & 2-6pm), with displays about oil wrestling, or check out its website and www.turkishwrestling.com.

roof that dates from the time of Süleyman the Magnificent. In front of it are two square columns: on the Seng-i Hürmet (Stone of Respect) to the right, people would place petitions to the sultan, while the Seng-i İbret (Stone of Warning) on the left displayed the heads of high-court officers who had managed to anger the sultan.

Behind the Justice Hall is the small **Fatih Köprüsü** (Conqueror Bridge; 1452). Across it and on the right is a sombre **Balkan Wars memorial**; straight ahead and to the left are the scattered ruins of **Edirne Sarayı** (Edirne Palace). Begun by Sultan Murat II in 1450, the palace once rivalled İstanbul's Topkapı Palace in size and luxury, though you'd be hard-pressed to visualise it nowadays.

To get here, walk north along Hükümet Caddesi and cross the Tunca River on Saraçhane Köprüsü (Saddler's Bridge); or head north on Mimar Sinan Caddesi and Saray Yolu, and cross the river on Saray Köprüsü (Palace Bridge; 1560). Alternatively, it's a scenic 1km walk along the road to the north of the river from the Sultan Bayezid II complex.

Muradiye Camii　　　　　　　　MOSQUE
A 15-minute walk northeast of Selimiye Mosque along Mimar Sinan Caddesi brings you to the Muradiye Mosque, built for Sultan Murat II and topped with an unusual cupola. Note the massive calligraphy on the exterior. Built between 1426 and 1436, it once housed a Mevlevi (whirling dervish) lodge. The mosque's T-shaped plan, with twin *eyvans* (vaulted halls) and fine İznik tiles, is reminiscent of Ottoman work in Bursa.

The small **cemetery** on the east side contains the grave of Şeyhülislâm Musa Kâzım Efendi, the Ottoman Empire's last chief Islamic judge, who fled the British occupation of İstanbul after WWI and died here in 1920.

SOUTH OF THE CENTRE

To reach the quiet south from the centre, follow Saraçlar Caddesi under the railway line and cross the **Tunca Köprüsü**, an Ottoman stone humpback bridge dating back to 1615, and the equally graceful **Meriç Köprüsü** (1847). The area around the bridges is packed with restaurants, tea gardens and bars, all great places to come for a drink or a meal in warm weather. The best ones are those on the southern side of the Meriç River, which offer perfect sunset river vistas.

A taxi back to the centre costs ₺8; a horse and cart, ₺10.

🛏 Sleeping

Most of Edirne's budget and midrange hotels are on Maarif Caddesi, where parking is a nightmare.

TOP CHOICE Hotel Edirne Palace   HOTEL €€€
(☎214 7474; www.hoteledirnepalace.com; Vavlı Cami Sokak 4; s/d ₺120/200) This formidable new business hotel is regularly booked out with commercial travellers and well-heeled tour groups. Don't be discouraged by the pokey back streets en route; the welcome is thoroughly professional and the rooms are large, stylish and by far the best in Edirne.

Efe Hotel   BOUTIQUE HOTEL €€
(☎213 6166; www.efehotel.com; Maarif Caddesi 13; s/d ₺100/150; ❄@) The off-red Efe stands out for its atmospheric, archival lobby with tartan carpets and polished wood. The chaotic retro patterns in the small rooms is brought together by heavy furniture and soft lighting. There's an English pub open outside the summer months and a decent bar-restaurant called Patio.

Selimiye Taşodalar   BOUTIQUE HOTEL €€€
(☎212 3529; www.tasodalar.com.tr; Selimiye Arkası Hamam Sokak 3; s/d from ₺160/210; ❄@) The location next to Selimiye Mosque and the 14th-century Sultan Selim Saray Hamam is the most obvious reason to stay at this 15th-century Ottoman house. Unfortunately the old-world charm does not quite compensate for the interiors. The shared spaces have an air of elegance, but the dusty kitsch in the rooms doesn't quite cut it. The tea garden is pleasant and shady.

Grand Altunhan Hotel   HOTEL €€
(☎213 2200; www.altunhanhotel.com; Saraçalar Caddesi; s/d ₺80/130) Opened in 2007, the Grand Altunhan is located on a popular shopping strip and provides a friendly midrange hotel experience. The rooms are modern, with flats-creen TVs, colourful furniture and brightly tiled bathrooms.

Tuna Hotel   HOTEL €€
(☎214 3340; fax 214 3323; Maarif Caddesi 17; s/d ₺70/110; ❄) A recent paint job and energetic young manager have lifted the 'Danube' above a few similar hotels in the area. The small burgundy rooms are comfortable with small TVs and clean bathrooms. Breakfast is served in a small courtyard by the back annexe. Street noise is a concern.

Hotel Antik   HOTEL €€
(☎255 1555; www.edirnehotelantik.com; Maarif Caddesi 6; s/d ₺60/100) This two-storey mansion has friendly staff and an enormous upstairs sitting area, even if it does cry out for a makeover. Still, the rooms are comfy with plenty of nanna-esque furniture and the showers are hot and spacious. Breakfast is bland.

🍴 Eating

There's a wide assortment of eateries along Saraçlar Caddesi. Most of the riverside restaurants south of the centre are open only in summer and are often booked solid at weekends.

The city's dish of choice is *Edirne ciğeri*, which is thinly sliced calf's liver deep fried and eaten with crispy fried red chillies and yoghurt.

TOP CHOICE Melek Anne   CAFE €
(☎213 3263; Maarif Caddesi 18; mains ₺7) Popular with students and foodies, 'Angel' Anne's is still the most interesting place to eat in Edirne. The 120-year-old house serves a rotating menu of homemade dishes, including unusual salads and hearty vegetarian choices. The spacious courtyard is a relief from the noisy streets.

Lalezar   MODERN TURKISH €€
(☎223 0600; Karaağaç Yolu; mains ₺9-20) On pretty grounds down by the Tunca, Lalezar is a delightful family restaurant with an extensive bilingual menu featuring *lahmaçun* (thin pizza), salads, fried fish and spicy *içli köfte* (stuffed meatball). Ask for a table on the raised platforms among the trees.

Osman Köfteci   TURKISH €€
(☎212 7725; Saraçalar Caddesi 3; main ₺8-15; ⊙11am-10pm) Widely recommended by locals for its tasty meat dishes, attentive service and prime location at the top of the main drag, Osman is a stalwart of the Edirne dining scene; just ask the friendly old touts who hurl slogans at passers-by.

Zindanaltı Meyhanesi   TURKISH €€
(☎212 2149; Saraçlar Caddesi 127; meze ₺6, mains ₺10) There's loads of fun to be had at this three-storey Turkish pub overlooking pedestrianised Saraçlar Caddesi. The food is fairly

typical Turkish fare, but the beer is ice cold and the brazen Turkish pop tunes get your cutlery a-tapping.

Niyazi Usta
KEBAP €€

(☑213 3372; Alipaşa Ortakapı Caddesi; ciğeri ₺9) This bright, modern fast-ish food joint is perhaps the safest place to try the Edirne-style calf's liver. There's a smaller branch on the far side of the florist.

Penaltı
CAFE €

(Alipaşa Ortakapı Caddesi; mains ₺7) Its walls hung with photos of soccer stars, 'Pen-alty' snack bar is the local tip for Turkish *kahvaltı* (breakfast).

🍷 Drinking & Entertainment

Tea gardens cluster around the Mimar Sinan statue in the city centre, and there's a row of bars between the two bridges south of the centre.

TOP CHOICE Café Pena
BAR

(Alipaşa Ortakapı Caddesi 6) Edirne's pulse is found on the long shared tables and the jumbled upstairs rooms at this lively bar and cafe. Good coffee, Tuborg on tap and stiff cocktails are served under the steady gaze of American film stars.

London Café
BAR, CAFE

(Saraçlar Caddesi; mains ₺5) This unexpected pleasure on two floors serves non-Turkish staples such as pasta and sandwiches, but its raison d'être is the dispensing of booze.

Kahve Rengi Bistro
BAR, CAFE

(☑214 4210; Orhaniye Caddesi 14) A fun little cafe with a courtyard that morphs into a drinking den after sunset, Rengi has good service and an interesting clientele.

Barfly
LIVE MUSIC

(☑212 1881; Tahmhis Meydanı 13) An excellent basement venue for local and international rock, pop, folk music, glammed-up divas and tattoed lotharios.

Deep Club
NIGHTCLUB

(☑214 7918; Saraçalar Caddesi 91) The hottest club in Edirne shoots lasers by the mother-load and features pretty good local and inter-national DJs on Friday and Saturday nights.

🛍 Shopping

Traditional Edirne souvenirs include *meyve sabunu* (fruit-shaped soaps) scented with at-tar of roses, and *badem ezmesi* (marzipan).

Ali Paşa Covered Bazaar
BAZAAR

(☉7am-sunset) Mimar Sinan designed this atmospheric bazaar in 1569. Off Saraçlar Caddesi.

Bedesten
MARKET

(☉sunrise-sunset) Across a little wooden bridge from the Eski Cami, this market dates from 1418. Off Talat Paşa Caddesi.

Selimiye Arastası
MARKET

(Selimiye Arcade; ☉sunrise-sunset) Also known as Kavaflar Arastası (Cobblers' Arcade), this is below Selimiye Mosque.

Keçecizade
FOOD & DRINK

(Saraçlar Caddesi 50) Branches throughout the centre, including one opposite the post of-fice, sell *lokum* (Turkish delight) and *badem ezmesi*.

ℹ Information

Banks are found in the area around the tourist office.

Araz Döviz (Talat Paşa Caddesi, Ali Paşa Bazaar; ☉9am-7pm Mon-Sat) One of the only places to change cash and travellers cheques on Saturdays.

Post Office (PTT; Saraçlar Caddesi) The only place to change money on Sundays.

Tourist Office (☑213 9208; Talat Paşa Cad-desi; ☉9am-6pm) Very helpful, with English-language brochures and a city map.

ℹ Getting There & Around

Bus & Dolmuş

Edirne's otogar (bus station) is 9km southeast of the centre on the access road to the E80.

ÇANAKKALE (₺30, four hours) Regular buses.

İSTANBUL (₺12, 2½ hours) Frequent buses, but demand is high so book ahead.

KAPIKULE (₺5, 25 minutes) Dolmuşes run to this Bulgarian border crossing, 18km north-west, from outside Şekerbank, opposite the tourist office on Talat Paşa Caddesi.

KEŞAN Hourly minibuses (₺10, 1½ hours), run by **Güneş** (☑213 2105; Kadirhane Sokak), leave from the company's office northwest of the hospital. A cheaper service leaves from the otogar (₺7, 2½ hours).

PAZARKULE The nearest Greek border post is 9km southwest of Edirne. Catch a dolmuş (₺1, 20 minutes) straight there from near the tourist office, or change in Karaağac.

UZUNKÖPRÜ (₺7, one hour) Güneş minibuses to Keşan stop here, as does the cheaper serv-ice from the otogar (₺4, 1¾ hours).

KIYIKÖY

One of European Turkey's handful of settlements on the Black Sea, Kıyıköy (formerly Salmidesos) is a popular getaway for İstanbullus, but can be just as easily reached from Thrace. Come here for the sandy **beach**, north of the village, where you can hire pedal-boats and meander around the river mouth; the remains of the 6th-century **Kıyıköy Castle** (Kıyıköy Kalesı); and the **market** on Tuesday.

Hotel Endorfina (☑388 6364; www.hotelendorfina.com; Manastır Üstü; half-board per person ₺160; @☒), found on a bluff above the main beach and river, has a fantastic terrace and white cubist rooms, each with a private balcony. The managers are skilled at handling fussy customers. The setting is sublime, but the hotel has lagged a touch. Activities, a fish restaurant and pick-ups from Saray are added attractions. Another excellent option is **Kıyıköy Marina** (☑365 6400; www.kiyikoymarina.com; Sümbül Sokak 3; per person ₺50) which has good value, mini-apartment rooms, though it's not as close to the water as the name suggests. The organic breakfast is a highlight.

The best of the basic pensions are **Midye Pansiyon** (☑388 6472; s/d excl breakfast ₺40/80), just east of the main square, and the cliff-top **Deniz Feneri** (☑388 6073; d ₺100), at the eastern end of the village. You can also camp by both beaches.

You can eat at **Son Tango** (☑388 6283; mains ₺10), a good choice for breakfast; **Marina** (☑388 6058; mains ₺10), where dishes include *mantı* (Turkish ravioli), *köfte* and breakfast; and **Kösk** (☑0536 475 8169; mains ₺15), which has good meze and fish. All have terraces with prime sundowner potential.

There's one direct bus a day from İstanbul (₺17, three hours) at 4pm year-round, and to İstanbul from Kıyıköy at 8am and 12.15pm. Alternatively, buses run every two to three hours to/from Saray (₺5, 30 minutes), 30km southwest, which is linked to İstanbul (₺14, 2½ hours, hourly), Tekirdağ (₺9, 1½ hours, regular) and Edirne (₺13, two hours, twice daily).

Car

The toll from Edirne to İstanbul on the E80 is under ₺10. You can hire a vehicle from **Turizm Rent A Car** (☑214 8478; Talat Paşa Caddesi) for about ₺120 per day for a small car.

Train

Edirne train station is 4km southeast of the Eski Cami. To get to the station from the centre, dolmuşes and city buses travelling southeast on Talat Paşa Caddesi, including bus 3, pass Migros supermarket – you should get off here and walk down İstasyon Caddesi. A taxi costs around ₺10.

İSTANBUL (₺13, four to 6½ hours) The *Edirne Ekspresi* leaves Edirne at 7.30am and 4pm, and the *Bosfor Ekspresi* leaves at 3.50am. From İstanbul, the former service leaves at 8.30am and 3.15pm, and the latter at 10pm.

EUROPE The *Bosfor Ekspresi* leaves Edirne at 2.32am for Bucharest (Romania).

Uzunköprü

☑0284 / POP 40.620

About 63km southeast of Edirne on the E87/D550, the farming town of Uzunköprü (Long Bridge) sits on the banks of the Ergene River. Amazingly, the 1392m-long Ottoman bridge (1426–43), after which the town is named,

is still standing with all of its 174 arches intact. It remains on the town's main access road from the north, an impressive feat after nearly six centuries of continuous use.

ℹ️ Getting There & Away

Uzunköprü is the border crossing town on the rail line connecting İstanbul with Greece; the *Dostluk-Filia Ekspresi* leaves for Thessaloniki at 1.20am, and for İstanbul at 4am. The station is 4km north of town – if you take an Edirne-bound bus from the station by the bridge, ask the driver to drop you off, or take a taxi (₺8).

Tekirdağ

☑0282 / POP 147.490

Famous for its grapes – used to produce wines and rakı (aniseed brandy) – and cherries, Tekirdağ overlooks an attractive bay on the northern shore of the Sea of Marmara. It's not worth a trip in itself, but the city makes a reasonable pit stop en route to/from Greece or the Gallipoli Peninsula. Once known as Rodosto, it has interesting architecture, including some lovely old wooden *yalı* (seafront mansions), and three diverse museums. Tekirdağ is also known for its gypsy musicians, who entertain drinkers and diners on and around the waterfront promenade.

The small **tourist office** (☑261 1698; ☺9am-6pm Mon-Fri year-round, 10am-7pm Sat & Sun Jun-Sep) is near the *iskele* (jetty).

◉ Sights

Waterfront
SEAFRONT

This is the most pleasant part of the city, with a long promenade running round the bay, centred on the *iskele* and nearby playground, tea gardens, bars and restaurants.

TOP CHOICE Rákóczi Museum
MUSEUM

(Rakoczi Müzesi; ☑263 8577; Hikmet Çevik Sokak 21; admission ₺3; ☺9am-noon & 1-5pm Tue-Sun) This unusual museum is devoted to Prince Ferenc (Francis) II Rákóczi (1676–1735), the courageous leader of the first Hungarian uprising against the Habsburgs between 1703 and 1711. Forced into exile, the Transylvanian eventually turned up in Turkey and was given asylum by Sultan Ahmet III; he settled in Tekirdağ in 1720 and lived here until his death. In 1906 Rákóczi's remains were returned to Kassa in Hungary (now Košice in Slovakia), along with the interior fittings from the house. Almost 80 years later, however, these were painstakingly reproduced and put on display in a surprisingly informative museum that is something of a pilgrimage site for visiting Magyars.

The three floors contain portraits, weapons, kitchen equipment, ceramics and even a water well. The finest room is the 2nd-floor reception, with stained-glass windows, walls painted with Hungarian folk motifs, and a chair made by the good prince himself. Look out for the writing room of Kelemen Mikes (an 18th-century Transylvanian essayist); his fictitious letters to an imaginary aunt in Constantinople described life in the exiled court. To get here from the *iskele,* walk or catch a dolmuş (₺1) west along the waterfront for about 1km until you see the large wooden Namık Kemal House above you. The museum is further up the slope on the left.

FREE Tekirdağ Museum
MUSEUM

(Tekirdağ Müzesi; ☑261 2082; Barbaros Caddesi; ☺9am-5pm Tue-Sun) Housed in a fine late-Ottoman building, the town museum contains finds from several local tumuli (burial mounds) and from a site at Perinthos (Marmara Ereğlisi). The most striking exhibits are the marble chairs and the table set with bronze bowls from the Naip tumulus dating back to the early 5th century BC; and a wonderful pottery brazier in the form of a mother goddess from the Taptepe tumulus (4300 BC). Also interesting are the poignant inscriptions from a number of Roman gravestones translated into English. Read them and weep; they are timeless.

FREE Namık Kemal House
MUSEUM

(Namık Kemal Evi; Namık Kemal Caddesi 9; ☺8.30am-noon & 1-5pm Mon-Fri, 9.30am-3.30pm Sat) In a gingerbread-like wooden house, this small ethnographical museum is dedicated to Tekirdağ's most famous son, who was born nearby. A nationalist poet, journalist and social reformer, Kemal (1840–88) had a strong influence on Atatürk, who called him 'the father of my ideas'. The two-storey house is beautifully restored; don't miss the music room, the kitchen with its Turkish utensils, and the beautiful coffered ceilings. Climb the steps at the east end of the *köfte* restaurants; it's on the far right-hand side of the square.

Rüstem Paşa Külliyesi
MOSQUE

(Mimar Sinan Caddesi 19) Just before the waterfront, this small, square mosque is on the right. The great Mimar Sinan designed it in 1546.

Orta Camii
MOSQUE

Turn left at the top of the steps at the east end of the *köfte* restaurants and head uphill to find this brown stone mosque (1855) with a single minaret.

Hüseyin Pehlivan
MONUMENT

This chunky statue commemorates another famous Tekirdağan, a great oil wrestler (1908–82).

✦✦ Festivals & Events

Kiraz Festivali
CULTURAL FESTIVAL

Tekirdağ's red-letter event is the Kiraz Festivali (Cherry Festival) in early June, a week-long orgy of cherry gobbling and judging, as well as music concerts and oil wrestling matches.

⛌ Sleeping

Golden Yat Hotel
HOTEL €€

(☑261 1054; www.goldenyat.com; Yalı Caddesi 42; s/d/tr/ste from ₺90/130/160/210; ☀) The Yat has 54 kind-of-classy rooms by the harbour, all with starry carpets. Slightly overpriced, but popular with business folk, it's the pick of a very lean bunch.

THREE CHEERS FOR RAKI

Turkey's unofficial national drink is rakı (rah-*kuh*), an aniseed-flavoured distillation not unlike French pastis. Like pastis, it is drunk with water and ice, but unlike the French tipple, which is an appetiser, rakı is often consumed with food.

Turkey is the world's third-largest producer of grapes, a high percentage of which are grown around Tekirdağ. About a third of these grapes are consumed fresh, but much of the remainder goes into making rakı.

It's a long, complicated process, involving fresh grapes or well-preserved raisins that are mashed, shredded, mixed with water and steamed. Next, anise is added and the product goes through a double-distillation process. It is then watered down to an alcoholic strength of about 45% and aged for between 60 and 75 days. The most common brand is Yeni Rakı (New Rakı), but arguably the best is Tekirdağ Rakısı, which has a distinctive flavour thanks to the artesian water it uses from Çorlu, a town to the northeast of Tekirdağ. Turks drink what they call *aslan sütü* ('lion's milk', possibly because of the milky white it turns when water is added) with anything, but it's best with cold meze, white cheese and melon, and fish.

Rodosto Hotel   HOTEL **€€**
(263 3701; info@rodostohotel.com.tr; İskele Caddesi 34; s/d ₺70/130; ❊) This converted house on the waterfront is looking weary and the 'period' furniture has turned to tack. It's a bit friendlier than the Yat though, and solo travellers can save money with the boxy 'economy single' (₺50).

✖ Eating

Buses often pause for lunch in Tekirdağ, pulling up opposite the promenade at the row of restaurants serving *Tekirdağ köftesi*, a spicy version of *köfte*, eaten with rice and peppers. Alternatively, grab a *balık ekmek* (fish kebap, ₺4) across the road on the waterfront.

Meşhur Köfteci Ali Usta   KÖFTE **€**
(261 1621; Atatürk Bulvarı 24; mains ₺10) With four branches in the area, the 'Famous Master Ali Köfte Restaurant' serves a good range of dishes, including four types of *köfte*.

❶ Getting There & Away

Buses for İstanbul (₺18, 2½ hours), Edirne (₺14, two hours), Eceabat (₺27, three hours) and Çanakkale (₺30, 3½ hours) stop at the otogar and along the waterfront.

Gelibolu

☎0286 / POP 30,273

The largest town on the Gallipoli Peninsula is almost 50km from the main battlefield sites and is less appealing than Çanakkale as a base for the region. Yet it does contain a number of historical points of interest. Just about everything you'll need – hotels, restaurants, banks, tea-sipping layabouts – is clustered around the harbour.

◉ Sights

Gallipoli War Museum   MUSEUM
(Gelibolu Savaş Müzesi; 566 1272; Sahil Yolu; admission ₺3; ◷9am-noon & 1-6pm Tue-Sun) On the main road into town, this museum evokes the battlefield experience through the sandbags and barbed wire outside and the many displays inside. Artefacts range from a letter home (on pink paper) to photos of the excavations and dedications carried out in the present day.

FREE **Piri Reis Museum**   MUSEUM
(Piri Reis Müzesi; ◷8.30am-noon & 1-5pm Fri-Wed) Overlooking the harbour walls, this stone tower is all that remains of the Greek settlement of Callipolis, which gave the present town and peninsula their name. Inside, the small museum honours the swashbuckling admiral and cartographer Piri Reis (1470–1554), whose statue stands in the harbour on the way to the ferry pier. There's a large, shallow well and an upstairs chamber displaying copies of Reis' famous maps.

Shrine of Ahmed-i Bican Efendi   MONUMENT
In a small park 800m uphill from the harbour walls is this pretty shrine.

FREE **Tomb of Mehmed-i Bican Efendi**   TOMB
(Mehmed-i Bican Efendi Turbesi; ◷24hr) The tomb of Bican, the author of *Muhammadiye*, a commentary on the Koran, is opposite the Shrine of Ahmed-i-Bican Efendi.

FREE Hallac-i Mansur Türbesi   TOMB
(Tomb of Hallac-i Mansur; ☉24hr) Easily mistaken for a mosque.

FREE Bayraklı Baba Türbesi   TOMB
(Flag Father Tomb; ☉24hr) This tomb contains mortal remains of one Karaca Bey, an Ottoman standard bearer who, in 1410, ate the flag in his keeping piece by piece rather than let it be captured by the enemy. The entrance and the tomb itself are decked out with hundreds of Turkish flags; the attendant will sell you one to add to the collection.

FREE Azebler Namazgah   MOSQUE
(Soldiers' Open-Air Prayer Area; ☉24hr) This unusual, vaguely Mogul-looking mosque (1407) has a white marble *mihrab* (niche indicating the direction of Mecca) and *mimber*.

FREE French Cemetery   CEMETERY
(☉24hr) A tall modern bell tower marks this cemetery from the Crimean War (1854–56) – what the French call the Guerre d'Orient. It houses the bones of 11 Senegalese soldiers who died in the Gallipoli campaign and were buried here between 1919 and 1923.

FREE Saruca Paşa Türbesi   TOMB
(Tomb of Saruca Pasa; ☉24hr) This tomb of a late-14th-century Ottoman military hero is next to the French Cemetery.

Hamzakoy   BEACH
At the resort part of town, there is a thin strip of rough sandy beach and a small cafe.

FREE Deniz Kuvvetleri Kültür Park   PARK
(Sea Forces Culture Park) This small park, just east of the centre, is full of spent torpedoes, mines, and even a tiny submarine standing on end.

🛏 Sleeping & Eating

Oya Hotel   HOTEL €
(☑566 0392; Miralay Şefik Aker Caddesi 7; r ₺70-80, ste ₺100) Tired and green, with a small collection of naval memorabilia in the lobby, Oya is the best of Gelibolu's central options, which are mostly found near the Piri Reis Museum.

Düş Evi   CAFE €
(☑566 2628; Aker Caddesi; sandwich ₺5) This liberal, cultured cafe on the road through town serves excellent coffee and light lunches.

İlhan Restaurant   RESTAURANT €€
(☑566 1124; mains ₺15) The best of Gelibolu's harbourside restaurants, where you can tuck into local *sardalya* (sardines) cooked in a clay dish. Friendly İlhan is right on the *iskele,* with both sea and harbour views.

❶ Getting There & Away

The otogar is 500m southwest of the harbour, past the war museum on the main road to Eceabat.

ECEABAT (₺5, 50 minutes) Hourly minibuses run from the ferry pier, and continue to Kilitbahir (₺5, one hour).

EDIRNE (₺25, three hours, hourly)

İSTANBUL (₺35, 4½ hours)

LAPSEKİ The ferry (per person ₺2, motorbikes ₺8, cars ₺20, 30 minutes) leaves every hour on the hour, in either direction.

Gallipoli (Gelibolu) Peninsula
☑0286

For a millennium, the slender peninsula that forms the northwestern side of the Dardanelles has been the key to İstanbul: any navy that could break through the strait had a good chance of capturing the capital of the Eastern European world. Many fleets have tried to force open the strait, but most, including the mighty Allied fleet mustered in WWI, have failed.

Today the Gallipoli battlefields are peaceful places, covered in brush and pine forests. But the battles fought here nearly a century ago are still alive in many memories, both Turkish and foreign, especially in those of Australians and New Zealanders, who view the peninsula as a place of pilgrimage. The Turkish officer responsible for the defence of Gallipoli was one Mustafa Kemal – the future Atatürk – and the Turkish victory is commemorated in Turkey on 18 March.

On Anzac Day (25 April), a dawn service marks the anniversary of the Allied landings, attracting thousands of travellers from Down Under and beyond. In recent years an increasing number of Turkish visitors are being bussed in by municipal councils to better understand the Turkish side of the story.

The most convenient base for visiting the Gallipoli battlefields is Eceabat, on the western shore of the Dardanelles, although Çanakkale, on the eastern shore, has a wider range of accommodation and restaurants, and a more vibrant nightlife.

The southern third of the peninsula is given over to a national park. Even if you're not well up on the history, it's still worth visiting for the area's rugged natural beauty.

History

Not even 1500m wide at its narrowest point, the Strait of Çanakkale (Çanakkale Boğazı), better known as the Dardanelles or the Hellespont in English, has always offered the best opportunity for travellers – and armies – to cross between Europe and Asia Minor.

King Xerxes I of Persia forded the strait with a bridge of boats in 481 BC, as did Alexander the Great a century and a half later. In Byzantine times it was the first line of defence for Constantinople, but by 1402 the strait was under the control of Sultan Bayezid I (r 1390–1402), which allowed his armies to conquer the Balkans. Mehmet the Conqueror fortified the strait as part of his grand plan to conquer Constantinople (1453), building eight separate fortresses. As the Ottoman Empire declined during the 19th century, Great Britain and France competed with Russia for influence over this strategic sea passage.

In a bid to seize the Ottoman capital, then First Lord of the Admiralty Winston Churchill organised a naval assault on the strait early in 1915. In March a strong Franco-British fleet tried to force them without success. Then, on 25 April, British, Australian, New Zealand and Indian troops landed on Gallipoli, and French troops landed near Çanakkale. Turkish and Allied troops fought desperately, devastating one another. After nine months of ferocious combat but little headway, the Allied forces withdrew.

The outcome at Gallipoli was partly due to bad luck and leadership on the Allied side, and partly due to reinforcements to the Turkish side brought in by General Liman von Sanders. But a crucial element in the defeat was that the Allied troops landed in a sector where they faced Lieutenant Colonel Mustafa Kemal.

A relatively minor officer, the future Atatürk had managed to guess the Allied battle plan correctly when his commanders did not, and he stalled the invasion in spite of bitter fighting that wiped out his regiment (see Chunuk Bair, p151). Although suffering from malaria, Kemal commanded in full view of his troops throughout the campaign, miraculously escaping death several times. At one point a piece of shrapnel hit him in the chest, but was stopped by his pocket watch. His brilliant performance made him a folk hero and paved the way for his promotion to *paşa* (general).

The Gallipoli campaign lasted until January 1916, and resulted in a total of more than half a million casualties, of which 130,000 were deaths. The British Empire saw the loss of some 36,000 lives, including 8700 Australians and 2700 New Zealanders. French casualties numbered 47,000 (making up over half the entire French contingent); 8800 Frenchmen died. Half the 500,000 Ottoman troops were casualties, with almost 86,700 killed. Despite the carnage, the battles here are often considered a 'gentleman's war', with both sides displaying respect towards their enemy.

Tours

Unless you have some knowledge of the peninsula's history, a guided tour is by far the best way to experience the peninsula. The recommended tour providers generally offer five- or six-hour afternoon tours, including transport by car or minibus, guide and picnic lunch. Tours from Eceabat typically cost ₺60, as opposed to ₺90 from Çanakkale. Tours do not cover the less-visited sites at Cape Helles and the more northerly Suvla Bay; to do that, you have to hire a guide for a private tour, which costs over ₺120 even if you have your own vehicle. Condensed tours from İstanbul are available, but these can be exhausting as they involve visiting the battlefields straight after a five-hour bus ride. The best agencies in Eceabat and Çanakkale:

Crowded House Tours TOUR
(☑814 1565; www.crowdedhousegallipoli.com; Eceabat) Led by the ever-popular Oz Bülent 'Bill' Yılmaz Korkmaz, Hotel Crowded House is the most reputable mob for informative, engaging tours. Also on offer is a morning snorkelling tour (₺35, including transportation and equipment) to a WWI shipwreck at North Beach, and private tours. One- and two-day packages involve a transfer from accommodation in İstanbul to the otogar, then a night in Eceabat before the tour.

Hassle Free Travel Agency TOUR
(☑213 5969; www.anzachouse.com; Çanakkale) Run by Anzac House in Çanakkale, these tours are forthright and frequent, with both Australian and Turkish guides on offer. Readers have only good things to say about the level of knowledge and professionalism

Gallipoli Peninsula

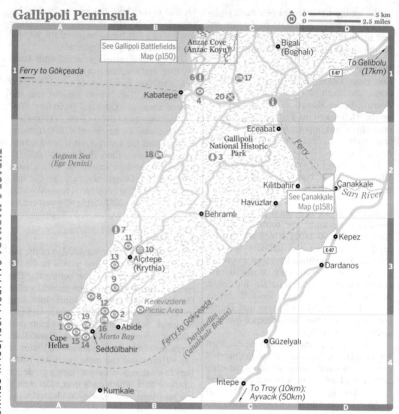

of this long-running outfit. Boat trips are also available.

Kenan Celik PRIVATE TOURS
(☑217 7468; www.kcelik.com) Excellent private tours available from one of Turkey's foremost experts on Gallipoli and the battlefields.

⊙ Sights

Gallipoli National Historic Park (Gelibolu Yarımadası Tarihi Milli Parkı; Map p148) encompasses 335 sq km of the peninsula and all of the significant battle sites. There are several different signage systems in use: normal Turkish highway signs; national park administration signs; and wooden signs posted by the Commonwealth War Graves Commission. This can lead to confusion because the foreign and Turkish troops used different names for the battlefields, and the park signs don't necessarily agree with those

erected by the highway department. We've used both English and Turkish names.

There are currently three dozen Allied war cemeteries in the national park, with about another 20 Turkish ones. The principal battles took place on its western shore, around Anzac Cove (Anzac Koyu), 12km northwest of Eceabat, and in the hills east of the cove.

The peninsula is a fairly large area to tour, especially without your own transport; it's over 35km as the crow flies from the northernmost battlefield to the southern tip of the peninsula. If time is tight or you're touring by public transport, head to Anzac Cove or Lone Pine and Chunuk Bair first.

For extra information, head to **Kilye Bay Information Centre** (Kilye Koyu Ana Tanıtım Merkezi; admission free; ⊙9am-noon & 1-5pm). Popular with Turkish visitors, this modern centre includes an information centre with interactive displays, exhibition areas, a memorial, cinema, library and cafeteria. It's about 3km

Gallipoli Peninsula

north of Eceabat, some 200m off the İstanbul highway.

The **Kabatepe Information Centre & Museum** (Kabatepe Müzesi ve Tanıtma Merkezi; Map p148; admission ₺3; ⊙9am-1pm & 2-6pm), roughly 1km east of the village of Kabatepe, was completely overhauled and scheduled to reopen in 2012 with more interactive exhibits.

NORTHERN PENINSULA

About 3km north of Eceabat, the road to Kabatepe heads west into the park past the Kilye Bay Information Centre. We describe the sites in the order most walkers and motorists are likely to visit them.

KABATEPE VILLAGE

The small harbour here was probably the object of the Allied landing on 25 April 1915. In the predawn dark it is possible that uncharted currents swept the Allies' landing craft northwards to the steep cliffs of Arıburnu – a bit of bad luck that may have sealed the campaign's fate from the start. Today there's little in Kabatepe except for a campground, cafe and dock for ferries to Gökçeada island.

The road uphill to Lone Pine (Kanlısırt) and Chunuk Bair begins 750m northwest of the Kabatepe Information Centre & Museum. Anzac Cove is another 3km north.

ANZAC COVE

Heading northwest from the information centre, it's 3km to **Beach (Hell Spit) Cemetery** (Map p150). Before it, a rough track cuts inland to Lone Pine (1.5km) and, across the road from the car park at the cemetery, another track heads inland to **Shrapnel Valley Cemetery** (Map p150) and **Plugge's Plateau Cemetery** (Map p150).

Following the coastal road for another 400m from the turn-off, or taking the footpath from Beach Cemetery past the WWII bunker, brings you to Anzac Cove, beneath and just south of the Arıburnu cliffs, where the ill-fated Allied landing began on 25 April 1915. Ordered to advance inland, the Allied forces at first gained some ground, but later in the day met with fierce resistance from the Ottoman forces under the leadership of Mustafa Kemal, who had foreseen where they would land and disobeyed an order to send his troops further south to Cape Helles.

In August of the same year a major offensive was staged in an attempt to advance beyond the beach up to the ridges of Chunuk Bair and Sarı Bair. It resulted in the battles at Lone Pine and The Nek, the bloodiest of the campaign, but little progress was made.

Another 300m along is the **Arıburnu Sahil Anıtı** (Arıburnu Coastal Memorial; Map p150), a moving Turkish monument with Atatürk's famous words of peace and reconciliation, spoken in 1934:

> To us there is no difference between the Johnnies and the Mehmets...You, the mothers, who sent your sons from faraway countries, wipe away your tears; your sons are now lying in our bosom... After having lost their lives in this land, they have become our sons as well.'

Just beyond the memorial is **Arıburnu Cemetery** (Map p150) and, 750m further north, **Canterbury Cemetery** (Map p150). Between them is the **Anzac Commemorative Site** (Anzac Tören Alanı; Map p150), where dawn services are held on Anzac Day.

Gallipoli Battlefields

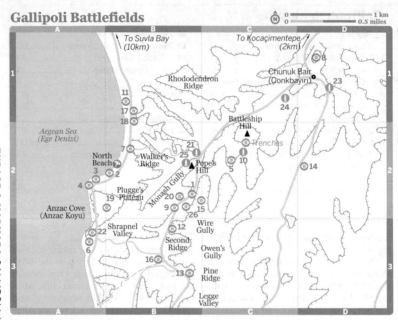

0 ___ 1 km
0 ___ 0.5 miles

Gallipoli Battlefields

◎ Sights

1 57 Alay Cemetery B2	14 Kemalyeri Turkish HQ......................D2
2 Anzac Commemorative Site B2	15 Kesikdere Cemetery B2
3 Arıburnu Cemetery........................A2	16 Lone Pine Cemetery B3
4 Arıburnu Sahil Anıtı A2	Mesudiye Topu............................. (see 5)
5 Baby 700 Cemetery C2	17 New Zealand No 2 Outpost
6 Beach (Hell Spit) Cemetery................A3	Cemetery B1
7 Canterbury Cemetery B2	18 No 2 Outpost Cemetery......................B1
8 Chunuk Bair New Zealand	19 Plugge's Plateau Cemetery.................B2
Cemetery & Memorial D1	20 Quinn's Post Cemetery........................B2
9 Courtney's & Steele's Post	21 Sergeant Mehmet Monument...............B2
Cemetery.................................. B2	22 Shrapnel Valley Cemetery....................A3
10 Düztepe Monument C2	23 Suyatağı Anıtı D1
11 Embarkation Pier Cemetery...............B1	24 Talat Göktepe Monument C1
12 Johnston's Jolly B3	25 The Nek...B2
13 Kanlısırt Kitabesi...................................B3	26 Yüzbaşı Mehmet Şehitliği....................B2

Look up and you can easily make out the image in the sandy cliff face nicknamed 'the Sphinx' by young 'diggers' (Aussie infantrymen) who had arrived from Australia via Egypt.

Less than 1km further along the seaside road on the right-hand side are the cemeteries at **No 2 Outpost** (Map p150), set back inland from the road, and **New Zealand No 2 Outpost** (Map p150). The **Embarkation**

Pier Cemetery (Map p150) is 200m beyond the New Zealand No 2 Outpost on the left.

TOWARDS LONE PINE

Returning to the Kabatepe Information Centre & Museum, you can follow the signs just under 3km uphill for Lone Pine.

En route, the first monument you'll come to, **Mehmetçiğe Derin Saygı Anıtı** (Map p148) on the right-hand side of the road about 1km from the junction, is dedicated to 'Mehmetçik'

(Little Mehmet, the Turkish 'tommy' or 'digger') who carried a Kiwi soldier to safety.

Another 1200m brings you to the **Kanlısırt Kitabesi** (Bloody Ridge Inscription; Map p150), which describes the battle of Lone Pine from the Turkish viewpoint.

LONE PINE

Lone Pine (Kanlısırt; Map p150), 400m uphill from Kanlısırt Kitabesi, is perhaps the most moving of all the Anzac cemeteries. Australian forces captured the Turkish positions here on the afternoon of 6 August 1915, and 7000 men died, in an area the size of a soccer field, in just four days. The trees that shaded the cemetery were swept away by a fire in 1994, leaving only one: a lone pine planted from the seed of the original solitary tree, which stood here at the beginning of the battle and gave the battlefield its name. Reforestation of the park is proving successful.

The tombstones carry touching epitaphs and the cemetery includes the grave of the youngest soldier to die here, a boy of just 14. The remains of trenches can be seen just behind the parking area.

From here, it's another 3km up the one-way road to the New Zealand Memorial at Chunuk Bair.

JOHNSTON'S JOLLY TO QUINN'S POST

Progressing up the hill from Lone Pine, the ferocity of the battles becomes more apparent; at some points the trenches are only a few metres apart. The order to attack meant certain death to those who followed it, and virtually all did as they were ordered on both sides.

The road marks what was the thin strip of no-man's land between the two sides' trenches, as it continues to the cemeteries **Johnston's Jolly** (Kırmızı Sırt; Map p150), 200m on the right beyond Lone Pine, **Courtney's & Steele's Post** (Map p150), roughly the same distance again, and **Quinn's Post** (Map p150), 100m uphill. Almost opposite Quinn's Post is the **Yüzbaşı Mehmet Şehitliği** (Captain Mehmet Cemetery; Map p150).

57 ALAY & KESİKDERE CEMETERIES

About 1km uphill from Lone Pine, across the road from the statue of Little Mehmet, is the **cemetery** (Map p150) and monument for the Ottoman 57th Regiment, which was led by Mustafa Kemal, and sacrificed by him to halt the first Anzac assaults. The cemetery has a surprising amount of religious symbolism for a Turkish army site, as historically the republican army has been steadfastly

secular. The statue of an old man showing his granddaughter the battle sites represents Hüseyin Kaçmaz, who fought in the Balkan Wars, the Gallipoli campaign and at the fateful Battle of Dumlupınar during the War of Independence. He died in 1994, aged 111, the last surviving Turkish Gallipoli veteran.

Down some steps from here, the **Kesikdere Cemetery** (Map p150) contains the remains of another 1115 Turkish soldiers from the 57th and other regiments.

SERGEANT MEHMET MONUMENT & THE NEK

About 100m uphill past the 57th Regiment Cemetery, a road goes west to the **Sergeant Mehmet Monument** (Map p150), dedicated to the Turkish sergeant who fought with rocks and his fists after he ran out of ammunition, and **The Nek** (Map p150). It was at The Nek on the morning of 7 August 1915 that the 8th (Victorian) and 10th (Western Australian) Regiments of the third Light Horse Brigade vaulted out of their trenches into withering fire and were cut down before they reached the enemy line, an episode immortalised in Peter Weir's film *Gallipoli*.

BABY 700 CEMETERY & MESUDİYE TOPU

About 200m uphill on the right from the access road to The Nek is the **Baby 700 Cemetery** (Map p150) and the Ottoman cannon called the **Mesudiye Topu** (Map p150). Named after its height above sea level in feet, Baby 700 was the limit of the initial attack, and the graves here are mostly dated 25 April.

DÜZTEPE & TALAT GÖKTEPE MONUMENTS

The **Düztepe Monument** (Map p150), uphill from the Baby 700 Cemetery, marks the spot where the Ottoman 10th Regiment held the line. Views of the strait and surrounding countryside are superb. About 1km further on is a **monument** (Map p150) to a more recent casualty of Gallipoli: Talat Göktepe, chief director of the Çanakkale Forestry District, who died fighting the devastating forest fire of 1994.

CHUNUK BAİR & AROUND

At the top of the hill, some 500m past the Talat Göktepe Monument, turning right at the T-junction takes you east to the **Suyatağı Anıtı** (Watercourse Monument; Map p150). Having stayed awake for four days and nights, Mustafa Kemal spent the night of 9–10 August here, directing part of the counterattack to the Allied offensive. Further south is **Kemalyeri** ('Kemal's Place'; Map p150) at Scrubby Knoll,

THRACE & MARMARA GALLIPOLI (GELIBOLU) PENINSULA

his command post, and the road back to the Kabatepe Information Centre & Museum.

Back at the T-junction, turn left for Chunuk Bair, the first objective of the Allied landing in April 1915, and now the site of the **Chunuk Bair New Zealand Cemetery and Memorial** (Conkbayırı Yeni Zelanda Mezarlığı ve Anıtı; Map p150).

As the Anzac troops made their way up the scrub-covered slopes on 25 April, Mustafa Kemal, the divisional commander, brought up the 57th Infantry Regiment and gave them his famous order: 'I am not ordering you to attack, I am ordering you to die. In the time it takes us to die, other troops and commanders will arrive to take our places'. The 57th was wiped out, but held the line and inflicted equally heavy casualties on Anzac forces below.

Chunuk Bair was also at the heart of the struggle for the peninsula from 6 to 10 August 1915, when some 30,000 men died on this ridge. The peaceful pine grove of today makes it difficult to imagine that blasted wasteland, when bullets, bombs and shrapnel mowed down men as the fighting went on day and night. The Anzac attack from 6 to 7 August, which included the New Zealand Mounted Rifle Brigade and a Maori contingent, was deadly, but the attack on the following day was of a ferocity that, according to Mustafa Kemal, 'could scarcely be described'.

To the east a side road leads to the Turkish **Chunuk Bair Mehmet Memorials** (Conkbayırı Mehmetçik Anıtları), five giant tablets, like the fingers of a hand praying to god, with Turkish inscriptions describing the battle.

SOUTHERN PENINSULA
Fewer travellers visit the southern peninsula, where there are more British, French and Turkish memorials than Anzac sites. During low-season, it's a good place to escape the traffic and tour groups, although the Çana-

---

GALLIPOLI UNDER THREAT

It seems a world away from the early 1980s, when Australian film director Peter Weir spent two days scampering over the hills of the Gallipoli Peninsula and saw not a living soul. The numbers of visitors have grown by leaps and bounds since then and they're not just foreigners. Since 2004, when 81 students from the 81 provinces in Turkey made the patriotic pilgrimage to where national hero Mustafa Kemal led their nation to victory, *belediyes* (town and city councils) from Edirne to Van have been sending their citizens in by the busload. According to Turkish official sources, domestic visitors numbered two million in 2007, up from between 400,000 and 500,000 five years before. And the buses continue to increase.

This increased popularity has made conservation of the national park particularly challenging, and many people feel that the local government and park administration don't always handle the situation effectively. In recent years the flow of bus and coach traffic has become extremely heavy, particularly around the most-visited Turkish cemeteries and monuments. Supposed 'improvements' such as car parks and road-widening schemes have caused considerable damage to some areas, most shockingly at Anzac Cove. The beach there is now little more than a narrow strip of sand.

Crowds of travellers turn up for the dawn Anzac Day memorial service, one of the most popular events in Turkey for foreign visitors, and almost a rite of passage for young Australians in particular. In 2005 more than 20,000 people came to mark the 90th anniversary of the Gallipoli landings, and this overwhelmed the peninsula's modest infrastructure. Just as many people are expected in 2015, the 100th anniversary; tours and cruises are already being marketed. Local operators estimate that about 5000 people usually visit around Anzac Day. Traffic still reaches all-day jam proportions the day before, some people coming in from as close as Çanakkale don't always arrive in time for the service, and many bed down at the Anzac Commemorative Site to be sure that they'll make it.

Some 50,000 Turks turn up on 18 March to celebrate what they call the Çanakkale Naval Victory (Çanakkale Deniz Zaferi), when Ottoman cannons and mines succeeded in keeping the Allied fleet from passing through the Dardanelles in 1915. It's easier to appreciate Gallipoli's poignancy and beauty at almost any other time than around this event and Anzac Day, and many visitors find their emotional experience completely different if they take the time to explore at leisure away from the crowds.

kkale Şehitleri Anıtı in particular is becoming increasingly popular with Turkish groups.

From Kabatepe it's about 12km to the village of **Alçıtepe**, formerly known as Krithia. A few metres north of the village's main intersection is the **Salim Mutlu War Museum** (Map p148; admission ₺1; ⊙8am-8pm), a hodgepodge of rusty finds from the battlefields, giving a sense of just how much artillery was fired. Past the souvenir stands, the more-ambitious **Gallery of the Gallipoli Campaign** (Map p148; admission ₺3; ⊙8am-8pm) takes a more illustrative approach, with photos and artefacts enhanced by mock-ups, dioramas and sound effects. At the main intersection, a sign points right to the Turkish **Sargı Yeri Cemetery** (Map p148), approximately 1.5km away, with its enormous statue of 'Mehmet' and solid **Nuri Yamut Monument** (Map p148). Take the first left for the **Twelve Tree Copse Cemetery** (Map p148), 2km away, and the **Pink Farm Cemetery** (Map p148), which is 3km away.

From Pink Farm, the road passes the **Lancashire Landing Cemetery** (Map p148). Turn right 1km before Seddülbahir village for the **Cape Helles British Memorial** (Map p148), a commanding stone needle honouring the 20,000-plus Britons and Australians who perished in this area and have no known graves. The initial Allied attack was two-pronged, landing on 'V' Beach at the tip of the peninsula as well as Anzac Cove. **Yahya Çavuş Şehitliği** (Sergeant Yahya Cemetery; Map p148) remembers the Turkish officer who led the resistance to the Allied landing here, causing heavy casualties. **'V' Beach Cemetery** (Map p148) is visible 500m downhill.

Seddülbahir is a sleepy farming village with a few pensions and restaurants, a war museum and the ruins of an Ottoman/Byzantine fortress overlooking a small harbour.

North of the village, the road divides; the left fork leads to the **Skew Bridge Cemetery** (Map p148), followed by the **Redoubt Cemetery** (Map p148). Turn right and head east, following signs for Abide or Çanakkale Şehitleri Anıtı at Morto Bay, and you'll pass the **French War Memorial & Cemetery** (Map p148). French troops, including a regiment of Africans, attacked Kumkale on the Asian shore in March 1915 with complete success, then re-embarked and landed in support of their British comrades-in-arms at Cape Helles, where they were virtually

wiped out. The French cemetery is rarely visited but is quite moving, with rows of metal crosses and five white concrete ossuaries each containing the bones of 3000 soldiers.

The **Çanakkale Şehitleri Anıtı**, also known as the Abide monument, is a gigantic four-legged, almost-42m-high stone table that commemorates all the Turkish soldiers who fought and died at Gallipoli. It's surrounded by landscaped grounds, including a rose garden planted to commemorate the 80th anniversary of the conflict in 1995.

🛏 Sleeping & Eating

There are some good accommodation options inside the park itself, but most are around Seddülbahir and can be tricky to get to without your own transport.

TOP CHOICE Gallipoli Houses BOUTIQUE HOTEL €€€
(Map p148; ☑814 2650; www.thegallipolihouses.com; d half-board from ₺240; ❄) Blending in seamlessly with a small Turkish village, Gallipoli Houses is the intelligent choice for travel to the peninsula. Eric, the Belgian co-host, and his Turkish wife, Ozlem, are equally at ease preparing home-cooked Turkish cuisine as tailoring a visit or recounting a little-known skirmish on a map. The 10 rooms are split between the original stone house and a purpose-built section with sublime field views. Kocatepe, on the 1st floor, is the grandest.

Mocamp PENSION €€
(Map p148; ☑862 0056; www.seddulbahirmocamp.com; s/d/tr ₺75/100/130) Next to 'V' Beach Cemetery near Seddülbahir village is a franchise of this popular camping ground. The blue rooms are a good option if you tire of roughing it.

Pansiyon Helles Panorama PENSION €
(Map p148; ☑862 0035; hellespanorama@hotmail.com; s/d without bathroom ₺35/70) This is the best place to stay if you want to be close to the Cape Helles section of the battlefield. Run by an ex-warden with a vast memory for war history, it has seven decent pension rooms and plenty of garden space. Both Çanakkale Şehitleri Anıtı and the Cape Helles British Memorial are visible from its elevated position just west of Seddülbahir village.

Hotel Kum HOTEL €€€
(Map p148; ☑814 1455; www.hotelkum.com; s/d/tr/ste half-board ₺110/180/225/275, 4-person caravan ₺30; ⊙Apr-Oct; ❄❄) The Kum is a large,

scratchy two-storey hotel on a decent patch of tree-filled turf just 50m from the beach. The camping facilities (and the rooms) are very tired though and the caravans look better placed in a horror film set.

Abide Motel
PENSION €€

(Map p148; ☑862 0010; motelabide@hotmail.com; s/d ₺45/90) Undergoing a renovation when we visited, Abide has basic rooms and a big terrace restaurant, set in scruffy grounds near the French Cemetery.

Doyuranlar Gözleme
TURKISH €

(Map p148; ☑814 1652; mains ₺6) The village women in charge of this roadside restaurant have a sophisticated business model. There's *köfte, menemen* (a type of omelette) and breakfast on offer, but a hot, crisp *gözleme* (savoury pancake) washed down with spicy peppers and a jug of *ayran* (salted yoghurt) is the smart order.

❶ Information

For good general information, head to Kilye Bay Information Centre and Kabatepe Information Centre & Museum.

Further Information

Defeat at Gallipoli Using letters and diaries, Peter Hart and Nigel Steel tell the soldiers' stories.

Gallipoli Award-winning Australian historian and journalist Les Carlyon's 2001 book is considered a modern classic.

Gallipoli: A Battlefield Guide By Australians Pam Cupper and Phil Taylor.

Gallipoli Association (www.gallipoli-association.org)

Gallipoli Battlefield Guide (Çanakkale Muharebe Alanları Gezi Rehberi) An excellent bilingual (and most historically accurate) reference book by Gürsel Göncü and Şahin Doğan, available at some bookshops in Çanakkale and Eceabat.

Gallipoli Peninsula National Historic Park Guide Map (Gelibolu Yarımadası Tarihi Milli Parkı Kılavuz Harita) Park information centres sell this very detailed map.

Visit Gallipoli (www.anzacsite.gov.au)

Many accommodation options in Eceabat and Çanakkale screen at least one of the following every night.

Gallipoli Peter Weir's 1981 film is an easy way to get an overview of the campaign.

Gallipoli (Gelibolu) A 2005 documentary by Tolga Örnek.

Gallipoli: The Fatal Shore Harvey Broad-

bent's documentary is quite dated (1987), but includes interviews with veterans of the campaign.

❶ Getting There & Around

With your own transport, you can easily tour the northern battlefields in a day. Trying to do both the northern and southern parts of the peninsula is possible within one day, provided you get an early start. Touring by public transport is tricky; dolmuşes serve only a few sites and villages. The most important group of monuments and cemeteries, from Lone Pine uphill to Chunuk Bair in the northern peninsula, can be toured on foot.

Ferry

You can cross the Dardanelles between Çanakkale and Eceabat or Kilitbahir on the peninsula.

Taxi

Drivers in Eceabat will run you around the main sites for about ₺120, but they take only two to 2½ hours, and few speak English well enough to provide a decent commentary. An organised tour is a better idea.

Eceabat

☑0286 / POP 5293

Eceabat (Maydos) is an unremarkable waterfront town just over the Dardanelles from Çanakkale. The only reason to stay here is for proximity to the main Gallipoli battlefields. Ferries dock by the main square (Cumhuriyet Meydanı), which has hotels, restaurants, ATMs, a post office, bus company offices, and dolmuş and taxi stands.

Like most of the peninsula, Eceabat is swamped with students and tour groups over weekends from 18 March to mid-June, and again in late September.

🛏 Sleeping

Hotel Crowded House
HOSTEL €

(☑814 1565; www.crowdedhousegallipoli.com; Hüseyin Avni Sokak 4; dm/s/d ₺20/50/65; ❋@) Eceabat's most congenial digs are in a four-storey building just off the main square. This is no ordinary backpacker joint. Guests of all budgets and persuasions will find real comfort, professionalism and a truly accommodating staff led by Ringo. The three dorms are faultless, while the small double rooms, recently updated with prints and flatscreen TVs, represent excellent value. The addition of a beer garden for summer barbecues is inspired.

BRIAN HUMPHRIES: TOUR GUIDE

There's a beautiful coastal walk that commences north of Salt Lake (Tuz Gölü) at Sulva Point. From Sulva Point follow any of the trails up towards the cliff edge to the left of the road. There are clear trails running just back from the edge of the cliff. After a short distance these trails drop below the cliff line to the right with views over to Salt Lake. Slightly over a kilometre from the start – and after a gradual descent – the trail leads to a gully coming down from the cliff edge. Before arriving at the gully, a clear trail can be seen running parallel with it, up to what now has become the ridge line. Turn left to follow this broader trail up to pass over the ridge and turn right to continue on a broad trail just below the ridge line on the seaward side for about 5km (not followed all the way but clearly visible). Just before the trail dips down to a saddle and at a large rounded cairn, the trail passes back over the ridge and descends to merge with a broader trail below. It would be possible to turn right onto this broader trail and follow it all the way back well below the ridge line to the starting point.

By turning left at the broader path and descending further, the trail will arrive at a large spring from where it is a short distance across fields to gain the vehicular road coming from the road junction below before Sulva Point. A little further along the road there is a Turkish War Cemetery at Ta35 on the map. From the cairn it is also possible to pick up a trail leading to an equally large cairn visible a little further below and then all the way down to the coastline where there is access to coves (not investigated but visible).

For more information, visit www.cultureroutesinturkey.com.

Hotel Ejder
HOTEL €€

(☏8023 8757; Ataturk Caddesi 5; s/d ₺60/120; 🅿🏠) The mayor has a silent interest in this new yellow hotel on a busy road just off the bay. The rooms have floorboards and tiled bathrooms, but are also quite small and lack furniture aside from the firm beds. The pluses here are the terrace views, huge breakfast, mezzanine and the friendly staff.

Hotel Boss Business
HOTEL €

(☏814 1464; www.heyboss.com; Cumhuriyet Meydanı 14; s/d ₺40/70; 🅰@) This narrow building's pale yellow facade hides a cool, compact hotel, with a black-and-white themed reception and some of Eceabat's best rooms. The helpful staff here speak a little English and the hotel may appeal to travellers who want to forego staying at a backpackers.

Grand Eceabat Hotel
HOTEL €€

(☏814 2458; www.rsltour.com; Cumhuriyet Meydanı 2; s/d ₺80/160; 🅿🅰🏠) Close to the ferry terminal, this large hotel is functional and popular with tour groups and familes. It's a little stuffy compared to Eceabat's alternatives but the service is keen. The lobby is a 1980s period set and there is an excellent rooftop dining area.

Eating

Liman Restaurant
SEAFOOD €€

TOP CHOICE

(☏814 2755; İstiklal Caddesi 67; mains ₺12) Worthy of a ferry ride from Canakkale, 'Harbour' is a humble and extremely popular fish restaurant with a delightful covered terrace. Service is sharp and unobstrusive.

Maydos Restaurant
INTERNATIONAL €€

(☏814 1454; İstiklal Caddesi; mains ₺8-15) A common stopping point on the Hassle Free Tour itinerary, Maydos has views across the Dardanelles and a very long, meaty menu. The meze (₺3.50 to ₺12) are fresh and there's a good list of wines and rakı. It's 500m south of the centre.

Meydan Lokantası
TURKISH €

(☏814 1357; mains ₺7) Meydan offers relatively good service and dishes including the recommended *tavuk şiş* (roast chicken kebap).

🍷 Drinking

Boomerang Bar
BAR

(Cumhuriyet Caddesi 102) Run by an eccentric Turk who knows how to host any crowd, the Boomerang is a kitschy beach shack that somehow makes the perfect place for a beer after touring the battlefields. It's past the tourist office at the town's north entrance. Free camping is unofficially available.

WINES OF THRACE & MARMARA

The sunny and windy conditions of northwest Turkey have been highly suited to winemaking for centuries, yet only in recent years has the industry gained the attention of foreign palates. Bozcaada is well known for its wines, but there are a few lesser-known vineyards worth a visit:

Suvla, Eceabat The pick of the region, the showroom is in town. To reach the *bağevi* (vineyard house), follow the road to Gokceada then, 2km after turning for Alçıtepe, follow the sign to Bozokbağ.

Arcadia, Luüleburgaz Makes fine rosés and whites. It's in a small town with a Sinan-made mosque.

Sevelin, Mürefte Their most famous winery is near the İzmir airport at Menderes, but this smaller cellar on the beach near Mürefte in Tekirdağ province is worth a visit for the seafront location and ambience.

Melen, Hösköy A boutique winery a little further along the Sea of Marmara.

Büyülübag, Avşa Adası In the Sea of Marmara, reached via ferry from tiny Ermek, you'll need a drink at this recommended winery in package-tourist hell.

Kafe'e' CAFE
(Cumhuriyet Caddesi 72; ⊘9am-10pm) Entered through Eceabat Cultural Centre or the neighbouring internet cafe, this cafe has sweeping views of the Dardanelles. Drinks, including beer and çay, are available.

❶ Information

Tourist Office (Cumhuriyet Caddesi 72; ⊘8am-5pm) Very little English is spoken.

❶ Getting There & Away

ÇANAKKALE Gestaş (☑444 0752; www .gestasdenizulasim.com.tr) ferries cross the Dardanelles in both directions (₺2, car ₺23, 25 minutes) every hour on the hour between 7am and midnight, and roughly every two hours after that.

GELİBOLU Hourly buses or minibuses (₺5, 50 minutes) are available.

İSTANBUL Buses leave hourly (₺40, five hours).

KABATEPE In summer there are several dolmuşes daily to Kabatepe ferry dock (₺2.50, 15 minutes) on the western shore of the peninsula; in winter they meet the ferries. The dolmuşes can drop you at the Kabatepe Information Centre & Museum, 750m southeast of the bottom of the road up to Lone Pine and Chunuk Bair.

KİLİTBAHİR Dolmuşes frequently run down the coast (₺1.50, 10 minutes).

Kilitbahir

Just across the Narrows from Çanakkale and accessible by ferry, Kilitbahir (Lock of the Sea) is a tiny fishing harbour dominated by a massive **fortress** (admission ₺3; ⊘8am-5pm Tue-Sun winter, to 7.30pm summer). Built by Mehmet the Conqueror in 1452 and given a grand seven-storey interior tower a century later by Süleyman the Magnificent, the castle is well worth a quick look around. Climb the rail-less staircase onto the walls if your nerves will stand it (people suffering from heart disease, hypertension and vertigo are warned not to do so and you'll soon see why).

At the end of one of the castle walls, the **Sarı Kule** (admission ₺1) houses a small war museum, and overlooks the **Namazgah Tabyası** (Namazgah Redoubt), a mazelike series of 19th-century defensive bunkers.

The small, privately run ferry to/from Çanakkale (₺2, car ₺18, 20 minutes) can carry only a few cars and waits until it is full before departing. From the ferry, dolmuşes and taxis run to Eceabat and Gelibolu, as well as to the Turkish war memorial at Abide, although you may have to wait for them to fill up.

Çanakkale

☑0286 / POP 104,321

With its large student population, sweeping waterfront promenade and close proximity to Gallipoli and Troy, Çanakkale has rightfully grown in stature as a travel destination. The nightlife here is legitimately raucous and international visitors often rate a night out here as far more intimate and friendly than some more famous Turkish party towns.

For a more cultured fix, there are good museums, a famous wooden horse and an active old town replete with original hamams and mosques.

During the summer, try to plan your visit for midweek unless you like to mix it with hordes of Turks on vacation.

Sights & Activities

Military Museum MUSEUM
(213 1730; Çimenlik Sokak; admission ₺4; 9am-5pm Tue, Wed & Fri-Sun; P) A park in the military zone at the southern end of the quay houses the Military Museum, also known as the Dardanelles Straits Naval Command Museum (Çanakkale Boğaz Komutanliği Deniz Müzesi). It's free to enter the park, which is open every day and is dotted with guns, cannons and military artefacts.

A sea-facing late-Ottoman building contains informative exhibits on the Gallipoli battles and some war relics, including fused bullets that hit each other in mid-air. Apparently the chances of this happening are something like 160 million to one, which gives a chilling idea of just how much ammunition was being fired.

Nearby is a **replica of the Nusrat minelayer** (Nusrat Mayın Gemisi), which played a heroic role in the sea campaign. The day before the Allied fleet tried to force the straits, Allied minesweepers proclaimed the water cleared. At night the *Nusrat* went out and picked up and relaid loose mines. Three Allied ships struck the *Nusrat*'s mines and were sunk or crippled.

Mehmet the Conqueror built the impressive **Çimenlik Kalesi** (Meadow Castle) in 1452, and Süleyman the Magnificent repaired it in 1551. The cannons surrounding the stone walls are from French, English and German foundries. Inside are some fine paintings of the battles of Gallipoli.

Trojan Horse MONUMENT
Along the waterfront promenade north of the main ferry pier, don't be surprised to see this larger-than-life model, as seen in the movie *Troy* (2004). The model of the ancient city and information displays beneath it are better than anything you'll find at Troy for now.

Archaeology Museum MUSEUM
(Arkeoloji Müzesi; 217 6565; 100-Yıl Caddesi; admission ₺5; 8am-5pm; P) Just over 1.5km south of the otogar, just off the road to Troy, is the Archaeology Museum, also called the Çanakkale Museum (Çanakkale Müzesi).

The best exhibits here are those from Troy and Assos, although the finds from the tu-mulus at Dardanos, an ancient town some 10km southwest of Çanakkale, are also noteworthy. There's quite a bit on display in the small garden.

Dolmuşes heading down Atatürk Caddesi towards Güzelyalı or Troy will drop you off near the museum for ₺1.

Clock Tower LANDMARK
The five-storey Ottoman *saat kulesi* (clock tower) near the harbour was built in 1897. It was paid for by an Italian consul and Çanakkale merchant who left 100,000 gold francs in his will for this purpose.

FREE **Korfmann Library** LIBRARY
(Korfmann Kütüphanesi; 213 7212; Tifli Sokak 12; 10am-6pm Tue-Sat) Housed in a 19th-century former school in the old town, this library, opposite the Tifli Mosque, was the bequest of the late Manfred Osman Korfmann (1945–2005), archaeological director at Troy from 1988 to 2003. It contains 6000 volumes on history, culture, art and archaeology.

Çanakkale Pot MONUMENT
Behind the WWI cannons is an oversized copy of this 19th-century style of pot, which is slowly regaining popularity.

Yalı Hamam HAMAM
(Çarşı Caddesi 5; men 6am-11pm, women 8am-6pm) In this 17th-century hamam, the full works costs ₺30. The women's entrance is just around the corner on Hapishane Sokak.

Festivals & Events

Çanakkale is almost unbearably overcrowded around the following events.

Çanakkale Naval Victory COMMEMORATION
(Çanakkale Deniz Zaferi) Turks celebrate this day on 18 March.

Anzac Day COMMEMORATION
Australians and New Zealanders descend on the Gallipoli Peninsula to mark this day, on 25 April.

Sleeping

If you intend to be in town around 25 April (Anzac Day), book well in advance and check prices carefully.

TOP CHOICE **Hotel Limani** HOTEL €€
(217 4090; www.hotellimani.com; Yalı Caddesi 12; ₺130-180; ﹡@) A renovation and a name change has seen the Hotel 'Harbour' emerge

Çanakkale

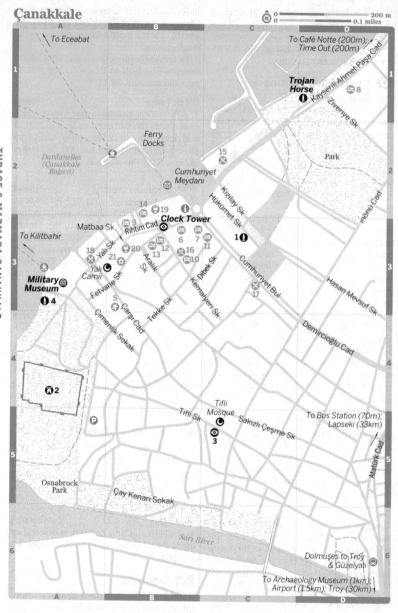

N 0 _____ 200 m
0 _____ 0.1 miles

To Eceabat

To Café Notte (200m);
Time Out (200m)

Trojan Horse 1

Kayserili Ahmet Paşa Cad

Ziveriye Sk

8

Park

Ferry Docks

Dardanelles
(Çanakkale
Boğazı)

15

Cumhuriyet
Meydanı

Kızılay Sk

Hükümet Sk

İnönü Cad

14 19

Clock Tower

Matbaa Sk   Rıhtım Cad

9

1

To Kilitbahir

18   6   7

21 20   13 12   11

Yalı Sk

Arlık Sk

Yalı
Camii

Fetvane Sk

16

10

Dibek Sk

Cumhuriyet Bul

Hasan Mevsuf Sk

**Military
Museum** 4

5

Çarşı Cad

Çimenlik Sokak

Tekke Sk

Kemalyeri Sk

17

Demircioğlu Cad

P

2

Tifli
Mosque

Tifli Sk

3

Sakızlı Çeşme Sk

To Bus Station (70m);
Lapseki (33km)

Atatürk Cad

Osnabruck
Park

Çay Kenarı Sokak

Sarı River

Dolmuşes to Troy
& Güzelyalı

To Archaeology Museum (1km);
Airport (1.5km); Troy (30km)

as the most popular option in Çannakale. Rooms are smallish, but thoughtfully fitted with quality linens, pillows, drapery wallpaper and polished floorboards. It's worth spending a little extra for a sea view. The staff are genuinely helpful too, especially the erudite owner. Don't miss a cocktail in the superb lobby restaurant.

Hotel Des Etrangers   BOUTIQUE HOTEL €€€
(📞214 2424; www.yabancilaroteli.com; Yali Caddesi 25-27; s/d ₺180/240; ❄️🛜) An old French hotel

Çanakkale

(Schleiman himself once stayed here) has found new life thanks to a dedicated local couple who reopened its gilt-edged doors in 2010. The lobby is grand and the rooms are country-style Ottoman by the sea. Walls and ceilings are whitewashed in the Seljuk fashion. Yali Caddesi is just busy enough to balance the convenience-versus-quiet ledger.

Hotel Kervansaray — BOUTIQUE HOTEL €€
(☏217 8192; www.otelkervansaray.com; Fetvane Sokak 13; s/d/tr ₺100/170/200; ❅@) In an Ottoman house once owned by an early-20th-century judge, the Kervansaray is the only half-historic hotel in town. The smell of yesteryear may permeate the older rooms, but the dowdiness is kind of fun. Rooms in the newer section have bath-tubs instead of showers, but the garden en route is a little oasis.

Hotel Grand Anzac — HOTEL €€
(☏216 0016; www.grandanzachotel.com; Kemalyeri Sokak 11; s/d from ₺80/100) Strongly recommended by readers, the Grand Anzac is great value for money. The rooms feel slightly prefab (and noisy as a result) but are bright and spacious, and include small desks and TVs. Service and location are both excellent.

Anzac Hotel — HOTEL €€
(☏217 7777; www.anzachotel.com; Saat Kulesi Meydanı 8; s/d/tr ₺75/90/120; ❅@) The Anzac is a very dependable hotel run by the same crowd as Kervansaray. Its position by the

clock tower is pivotal for garnering errant travellers, and staff are trained to please. There's a mezzanine area for hanging out and the rooms are all well presented with good-sized bathrooms.

Hotel Helen Park — HOTEL €€
(☏212 1818; www.helenhotel.com; Tekke Sokak 10; s/d ₺90/120; ❅) Helen Park and her sister hotel, plain old Helen, each have sizeable rooms with mod cons and earthy hues. It's hospitable enough, like a midday movie when you're sick on the couch. The buffet breakfast is plentiful and overlooks a quiet street.

Hotel Akol — HOTEL €€€
(☏217 9456; www.hotelakol.com.tr; Kayserili Ahmet Paşa Caddesi; s/d/ste ₺150/200/370; ❅❅) This old orange mare near the wooden horse is enormous and antiquated. Popular with tour groups, it's well serviced and ideal for anonymity. There's a roof bar that gets pretty loose on weekends.

Anzac House Hostel — HOSTEL €
(☏213 5969; www.anzachouse.com; Cumhuriyet Meydanı 59; dm/s/d without bathroom & excl breakfast ₺20/30/45; @) The base of **Hassle Free Travel Agency** (☏213 5969; Cumhuriyet Meydanı 61) is the only genuine backpackers in Çanakkale. It's a little drab and militant upstairs in and around the dorm rooms, but the bright colours and friendly staff go some way to alleviating the cramped confines.

✗ Eating

The waterfront is lined with licensed restaurants. For cheaper fare, street stalls along the *kordon* (waterfront promenade) offer corn on the cob, mussels and other simple items. A local speciality is *peynir helvası*, a dessert made with soft white village cheese, flour, butter and sugar, and served natural or baked.

 Yalova SEAFOOD €€
(☎217 1045; www.yalovarestaurant.com; Gümrük Sokak 7; mains ₺15-20) Yalova restaurant is infinitely more exciting than its namesake on the Marmara Sea. This is a pure seafood restaurant that combines impeccable service with the best produce and preparation in Çanakkale. Ask for a tour of the 2nd floor where you can select your own fish. Starters include all crustaceans and cephalopods, lightly oiled and herbed. Wine is matched to order.

Cafe du Port RESTAURANT €€
(☎217 2908; Yalı Caddesi 12; ⊙8am-11pm) The restaurant at Hotel Limani is popular for good reason. The glass-fronted building on the *kordon* is stylish and inviting, the chefs are the most versatile in Çanakkale and the service is brilliant for a regional city. Specialities include steaks, salads, pastas and whatever else inspires the manager on his regular gallivants to İstanbul. If nothing else, buy a cocktail.

Anafartalar Kebap KEBAP €€
(☎214 9112; İskele Meydanı; mains ₺10; ⊙8am-11.30pm) In the glass-walled lobby of an established large hotel, Anafartalar is the best place for an İskender kebap (döner kebap on fresh pide, with tomato sauce, browned butter and yoghurt) and other sloppy meat genius.

Gülen Pide KEBAP, PIDE €€
(☎212 8800; Cumhuriyet Bulvarı 27; kebaps ₺9-19; ⊙11am-10.30pm) Locals recommend this *kebapçı* (kebap restaurant) strip, and Gülen is a good choice with a clean, white-tiled floor and an open kitchen producing pide and *lahmacun* (Arabic-style pizza; ₺3 to ₺9).

Gülen Pizza ITALIAN €
(Hükümet Sokak; pizzas from ₺6) On the other side of the park from Gülen Pide, this place serves all the pizza classics.

Edem Dondurma CAFE €
(☎213 1620; 1225 Sokak 4; milkshakes ₺7) Ice-cream cafes are all the rage in Turkey. Join the throngs of young men and women nailing pancakes, triple-scoops and milkshakes by the gallon.

Çonk Coffee CAFE €
(Kemalyeri Sokak; snacks ₺2.50) Old coins and cameras adorn this friendly cafe, which serves Turkish coffee, sandwiches and *tost* (toasted sandwiches).

♟ Drinking & Entertainment

Çanakkale has a frenetic bar and club scene. Most of the busiest places are clustered around Matbaa and Fetvane Sokaks.

Benzin BAR, CAFE
(Eski Balıkhane Sokak 11; ☎) Friendly staff make this grungy waterfront bar-cafe, done out in 1960s decor, a relaxing spot for a drink and a bite (pizzas ₺8 to ₺12.50). Heaves at weekends.

Makkarna Bistro BAR
(Matbaa Sokak 8; beer ₺6) One of the drinking dens on this buzzing pedestrianised lane, Makkarna serves cocktails and the traditional Turkish 'beer bong' (₺15).

Time Out LIVE MUSIC
(Kayserili Ahmet Paşa Caddesi; beer ₺6) A rock club of the stylish (rather than dingy) variety, with pictures of Elvis et al, and outside tables.

Yalı Hanı Bar PERFORMANCE SPACE, BAR
(Fetvane Sokak 26) Upstairs in the 19th-century Yalı Han, this is a popular performance space that opens and closes at whim. The outside gallery overlooks an equally popular courtyard tea garden.

Lodos NIGHTCLUB
This thumping club at the northern end of the seaside is a stalwart of the rotating electronic music scene.

ⓘ Information

Çanakkale is centred on its harbour, with a PTT (Post, Telegraf, Telefon) booth, ATMs and public phones right by the docks, and hotels, restaurants, banks and bus offices all within a few hundred metres.

Araz Internet (Fetvane Sokak 21; per hr ₺1.50; ⊙9am-midnight) Internet access in the centre.

Çanakkale.com.tr (www.canakkale.com.tr) A good source of information.

Tourist Office (✆217 1187; Cumhuriyet Meydanı; ⏰8am-7pm Jun-Sep, 8.30am-5.30pm Oct-May) Some 150m from the ferry pier, with brochures and bus timetables.

❶ Getting There & Away

Air

Turkish Airlines (www.thy.com) flies to/from İstanbul (55 minutes) three times a week. A Turkish Airlines shuttle bus (₺7) links central Çanakkale with the airport, 2km southeast; otherwise a taxi costs about ₺10.

Boat

BOZCAADA (₺20 per person, 35 minutes, several daily)

ECEABAT (₺3/25 per person/car, 15 minutes, several daily)

GÖKÇEADA (₺3/25 per person/car, 2½ hours, once at 5pm)

KİLİTBAHİR (₺2/20 per person/car, 10 minutes, several daily)

Bus

Çanakkale's otogar is 1km inland of the ferry docks, beside a large Carrefour supermarket, but most buses pick up and drop off at the bus company offices near the harbour. If you're coming from İstanbul, hop on a ferry from Yenikapı to Bandırma and then take a bus to Çanakkale. It's easier than trekking out to İstanbul's otogar for a direct bus.

ANKARA (₺45, 10 hours, several daily)

AYVALIK (₺25, 3½ hours, hourly)

BANDIRMA (₺20, 2½ hours, hourly)

BURSA (₺30, 4½ hours, hourly)

EDİRNE (₺30, 4½ hours, several daily)

İSTANBUL (₺35, six hours, several daily)

İZMİR (₺35, 5½ hours, hourly)

Car

Car parks throughout the centre charge ₺3 per hour.

Dolmuş

TROY Dolmuşes to Troy (₺4, 35 minutes, hourly) leave on the half-hour between 9.30am and 4.30pm (7pm in summer, and less frequently at weekends) from a station at the northern end of the bridge over the Sarı River, and drop you by the ticket booth. Coming back, dolmuşes leave on the hour between 7am and 3pm (5pm in summer).

GELİBOLU Take the ferry to Eceabat (or Kilitbahir) and pick up a minibus; or take a bus or minibus from Çanakkale otogar to Lapseki (₺5, 45 minutes) and then take the ferry across the Dardanelles.

Gökçeada

✆0286 / POP 5937

A steady number of travellers make the effort to reach 'Heavenly Island', a spectacular outpost just north of the entrance to the Dardanelles, and few leave disappointed. Running 30km from east to west, Gökçeada is a stoney, windswept paradise with a steep valley running through the centre and an empty coastline that rivals any for sheer drama and isolation. The presence of a military base ensures Gökçeada will never fall prey to mass tourism, but you best hurry up and get here all the same.

Gökçeada was once a predominantly Greek island called Imbros. During WWI it was an important base for the Gallipoli campaign; indeed, Allied commander General Ian Hamilton stationed himself at the village of Aydıncık (then Kefalos) on the island's southeast coast. Along with its smaller island neighbour to the south, Bozcaada, Gökçeada was retained by the new Turkish Republic in 1923 but was exempted from the population exchange. However, in the 1960s when the Cyprus conflict flared up, the Turkish government put pressure on local Greeks, who numbered about 7000, to leave; today only a few hundred pensioners remain.

Gökçeada's inhabitants mostly earn a living through fishing, sheep- and cattle-rearing, farming the narrow belt of fertile land around Gökçeada town, and tourism. Apart from its semi-deserted Greek villages, olive groves and pine forests, the island boasts fine beaches and craggy hills.

◎ Sights & Activities

TOP CHOICE Greek Villages   HISTORIC AREA

Heading west from Gökçeada town, you'll pass **Zeytinli** (Aya Theodoros) after 3km, **Tepeköy** (Agridia), another 7km on, and **Dereköy** (Shinudy), another 5km west. All were built on hillsides overlooking the island's central valley to avoid pirate raids. Many of the houses are deserted and falling into disrepair, particularly at Dereköy, which is reminiscent of the Mediterranean ghost town of Kayaköy. However, thanks to a couple of inspired accommodation options, Zeytinli and Tepeköy are discovering the benefits of small-scale tourism, and both are worth a visit. Tepeköy is absolutely gorgeous, surrounded by green-grey scree-covered hills, with views over valleys and a large reservoir,

Gökçeada

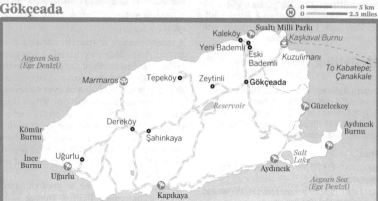

plus a dash of Greek heritage in its main square and taverna.

Kaleköy
SEAFRONT, RUINS
Although the views are dented by the presence of the military, the Gökçeada Resort Hotel and a large yacht marina, Kaleköy (formerly Kastro) exudes an infectious seaside contentment. Above the tiny public beach and rocks are a hillside old quarter, a lovely whitewashed former Greek church and the remains of an Ottoman-era castle. The coastline between Kaleköy and Kuzulimanı forms a **sualtı milli parkı** (national marine park).

Beaches
BEACHES
The sand beach at **Aydıncık** is the best on the island, and is adjacent to **Tuz Gölü** (Salt Lake). Further west on the stunningly picturesque southeast coast, there are smaller beaches at **Kapıkaya** and **Uğurlu**.

Windsurfing
WINDSURFING
(per hr/day ₺20/50) Aydıncık beach and Tuz Gölü, respectively offering flat water and waves, are popular for windsurfing and kitesurfing. Otel Gökçeada Surf (p163) offers equipment rental and tuition (one hour from ₺50).

Festivals & Events

Yumurta Panayırı
FOOD
During the Yumurta Panayırı (Egg Festival) in the first week of July, many former Greek inhabitants return to the island, along with the Orthodox Patriarch of İstanbul.

Sleeping & Eating

It's not unusual for locals to approach and offer you a spare room in their house (*ev pansiyonu*) for considerably less than the prices charged by pensions and hotels.

GÖKÇEADA TOWN

Restaurants are clustered around the main square.

Hotel Kale Palace
HOTEL ₺₺₺
(☑888 0021; www.hotelkalepalace.com; Atatürk Caddesi 54; s/d ₺120/200; P❋⛄) The Palace is an overpriced but nonetheless impressive new 'luxury' hotel, a short walk from the town square back from whence the ferry came. Choose between a street or a mountain view from your bettter-than-standard three-star hotel room.

Otel Taşkın
HOTEL ₺
(☑887 3266; www.taskinotel.com; Zeytinli Caddesi 3; s/d ₺40/80) This unassuming small hotel is still excellent value though the rooms are tiring by the season. The private balconies, courtyard and light-filled communal spaces lift it above the dreary pensions on the square. It's the one with the brown-tiled mosaic.

Gül Hanım Mantı Evi
TURKISH ₺
(☑887 3773; Atatürk Caddesi 23; mains ₺6) The *mantı* steals the show, but moussaka and chicken and spinach are also recommended at this simple home-cooking eatery.

Asmalı Konak Birhanesi
CAFE, BAR ₺
(☑887 2469; Çarşı Sokak 5; mains ₺7) At this female-friendly side-street bar, the menu

includes calamari, *köfte,* meze, and fish netted by the proprietor.

Meydanı Café PATISSERIE €

(☏887 4420; Atatürk Caddesi 35) This big, airy cafe attracts a young crowd for excellent snacks and shop-made desserts.

KALEKÖY

TOP CHOICE **Anemos Otel** BOUTIQUE HOTEL €€€

(☏887 3729; www.anemos.com.tr; Yukarı Kaleköy Önü; s/d from ₺180/280; ❃❅❆❈) The pick of the 'high-end', Anemos is a stylish stone hotel conceived by a Greek travel photographer with a passion for the Gökçeada landscape. The rooms are very comfortable, if a tad modest for the price, but really it's the views, service, food and swimming pool that make it so memorable. The huge, light-filled lounge area is like a scene from a coffee-table book.

Club Masi Hotel BOUTIQUE HOTEL €€

(☏887 4619; www.hotelmasi.com; Eski Bademli; r ₺150-200; ❃@❆) Also with a branch in İstanbul, Masi is a reliable luxury hotel with superb views of Kaleköy castle and the Aegean from the terrace. Rooms are modern but slightly faded. It's located above the Gökçeada–Kaleköy road.

Kalimerhaba Motel PENSION €

(☏887 3648; erayda@msn.com; Barbaros Caddesi 28; s/d ₺50/70; ❃) Of the row of waterfront hotel-restaurants, Kalimerhaba is the mainstay for its big, light reception and vine-covered terrace, more than the sterile rooms.

Kale Otel PENSION €

(☏887 4404; www.kalemotel.com; Barbaros Caddesi 34; s/d excl breakfast ₺50/80; ❃) The Kaleköy branch of the Kale Otel is less appealing than the newer town version, but the Dağınık family still ekes out every last drop of the waterfront charm from their fading hotel.

Yakamoz RESTAURANT €

(☏887 2057; www.gokceadayakamoz.com; Yukarı Kaleköy; ❂lunch & dinner) For a sundowner with million-dollar views over the bay and hills, climb to Yukarı Kaleköy (Upper Kaleköy) and the terrace restaurant at Yakamoz Motel.

AYDINCIK

Şen Camping CAMPING GROUND €

(☏898 1020; s/d ₺35/70, camping per person excl breakfast ₺9; ❂) The most remote of Turkey's

well-known camping grounds, the sandy site is neat and spacious. The reed-roofed restaurant has a mellow party vibe in high season. There are basic rooms if your tent has holes in it. Breakfast is extra (₺5).

Otel Gökçeada Surf RESORT €€

(☏898 1022; www.surfgokceaada.com; Çınarlı Mah; s/d ₺80/150) Next to Şen Camping is a wonderful new windsurfing resort with a friendly communal vibe and sympathetic stone rooms. The finishing touches were still being applied when we visited, but there was enough evidence in the spacious entertainment areas, knowledgeable staff and sublime end-of-the-Earth locale to suggest this place will excel.

ZEYTİNLİ

TOP CHOICE **Zeytindali Hotel** BOUTIQUE HOTEL €€€

(☏887 3707; www.zeytindalihotel.com; s/d ₺180/220; ❂May-Oct; ❃) Two rebuilt Greek stone houses above the old village showcase supreme island style and comfort. The 16 rooms – each named after a Greek god – combine French beds and wooden floors with a contemporary colour scheme and mini-courtyards. The ground-floor seafood restaurant is worth a detour for nonguests.

TEPEKÖY

Barba Yorgo PENSION €€

(☏887 3592; www.barbayorgo.com; r per person ₺45; ❂May-Sep) 'Papa George' is the big-spirited owner of this humble taverna and guest house that spreads across a number of buildings in the village. The cute rooms – with stone walls, blue linen and wooden floorboards – have mountain views that belie the cheap room rate.

TOP CHOICE **Tavern** TURKISH €€

(mains ₺10-20; ❂May-Sep) The atmospheric village restaurant, run by Barba Yorgo's family, serves goat stew, forbidden boar, platefuls of meze and local retsina to knock your teeth out. Seek it out for a rare culinary experience.

UĞURLU

Gül Pansiyon PENSION €

(☏897 6144; s/d ₺40/70) The friendly 'Rose Pension' overlooks the grassy central square. It has bright rooms with small, clean bathrooms, and a restaurant (*köfte* ₺7) on its covered verandah.

🛍 Shopping

Gökçeada is committed to becoming the first Turkish community to produce only organic foodstuffs; at present its 120,000 trees produce an annual 2000 tonnes of oil, most of which is organic. At the forefront of this endeavour is **Elta-Ada** (⌚887 3287; www .elta-ada.com.tr), a farm that produces organic olive oil, dairy products (soft white cheeses, yoghurt and butter) and assorted fruits and vegetables. Shops around the main square in Gökçeada town sell organic fruit, vegetables and produce, including Elta-Ada's **kiosk** (Cumhuriyet Meydanı; ☺8am-9pm summer), opposite the Pegasus Otel, and **Ekozey** (Atatürk Caddesi), near Gül Hanım Mantı Evi. If you visit Gökçeada in May/June, don't miss its organic black cherries.

ℹ Information

The ferry docks at Kuzulimanı, but facilities such as an internet cafe, taxis, bank, ATMs and post office are found inland at Gökçeada town, where most of the island's population lives.

Tourist Office (⌚887 2800; Cumhuriyet Meydanı; ☺10am-8pm Jun-Sep) In a kiosk on Gökçeada town's main square.

ℹ Getting There & Away

Check departure times, because they do change.

ÇANAKKALE Ferries run at weekends, leaving Çanakkale (per person ₺2, cars ₺23, two hours) at 9am on Friday and 5pm on Sunday, and returning from Gökçeada at 6pm on Friday and 7pm on Sunday.

GALLIPOLI PENINSULA Gestaş (⌚444 0752; www.gestasdenizulasim.com.tr) runs daily ferries to/from Kabatepe (per person ₺2, cars ₺20, 1½ hours) on the western side of the peninsula, leaving the mainland at 10am, 3pm and 7pm and departing the island at 7.15am, noon and 5pm. Tickets are also valid for the Eceabat–Çanakkale ferry, so you don't have to pay again to cross the strait.

ℹ Getting Around

BUS & DOLMUŞ Ferries dock at Kuzulimanı, where buses and dolmuşes should be waiting to drive you the 6km to Gökçeada town (₺1.50, 15 minutes), or straight through to Kaleköy, 5km further north (₺2.50, 25 minutes). A bus runs between Kaleköy, Gökçeada and Kuzulimanı roughly every hour; it doesn't always stick to the timetable, but is generally reliable for catching the ferry.

CAR Gökçeada Rent-A-Car (⌚218 2869; Atatürk Caddesi; per day ₺80) is fine but the only petrol station is 2km from Gökçeada town centre on the Kuzulimanı road.

TAXI You can take a taxi from Gökçeada town to Kaleköy (₺7, five minutes), Kuzulimanı (₺14, 10 minutes), Zeytinli (₺10, 10 minutes), Tepeköy (₺13, 20 minutes) and Uğurlu (₺25, 30 minutes).

Troy (Truva) & Tevfikiye

☑0286

History

The first inhabitants lived here during the early Bronze Age. The cities called Troy I to Troy V (3000–1700 BC) had a similar culture, but Troy VI (1700–1250 BC) took on a different Mycenae-influenced character, doubling in size and trading prosperously with the region's Greek colonies. Archaeologists argue over whether Troy VI or Troy VII was the city of King Priam who engaged in the Trojan War. Most believe it was Troy VI, arguing that the earthquake that brought down the walls in 1250 BC hastened the Achaean victory.

Troy VII lasted from 1250 BC to 1000 BC. An invading Balkan people moved in around 1190 BC, and Troy sank into a torpor for four centuries. It was revived as a Greek city (Troy VIII, 700–85 BC), then as a Roman one (Novum Ilion; Troy IX, 85 BC to AD 500). Before eventually settling on Byzantium, Constantine the Great toyed with the idea of building the capital of the eastern Roman Empire here. As a Byzantine town, Troy didn't amount to much.

The Fourth Crusaders sometimes claimed that their brutal behaviour in Turkey was justified as vengeance for the Trojan War, and when Mehmet the Conqueror visited the site in 1462 he, in turn, claimed to be laying those ghosts to rest. After that, the town simply disappeared from the records.

Discovering Troy

Until the 19th century, many historians doubted whether Troy was a real place at all. One man who was convinced of its existence – to an almost obsessive level – was the German businessman Heinrich Schliemann (1822–90), who in 1871 received permission from the Ottoman government to excavate a hill near the village of Hisarlık, which archaeologists had previously identified as a possible site for the city. This was to be no slow, forensic excavation, however. Schliemann was more of an eager treasure

Troy (Truva)

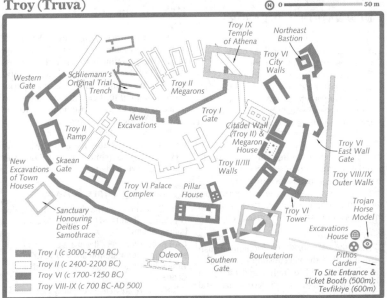

N 0 ————————— 50 m

Troy IX Temple of Athena
Northeast Bastion
Troy VI City Walls
Western Gate
Schliemann's Original Trial Trench
Troy II Megarons
Troy I Gate
New Excavations
Troy II Ramp
Citadel Wall (Troy II) & Megaron House
Troy VI East Wall Gate
New Excavations of Town Houses
Skaean Gate
Troy II/III Walls
Troy VIII/IX Outer Walls
Troy VI Palace Complex
Pillar House
Trojan Horse Model
Sanctuary Honouring Deities of Samothrace
Troy VI Tower
Excavations House
Odeon
Southern Gate
Bouleuterion
Pithos Garden

Troy I (c 3000-2400 BC)
Troy II (c 2400-2200 BC)
Troy VI (c 1700-1250 BC)
Troy VIII-IX (c 700 BC-AD 500)

To Site Entrance & Ticket Booth (500m); Tevfikiye (600m)

hunter than a methodical archaeologist and he quickly tore open the site, uncovering the remains of a ruined city, which he confidently identified as the Troy of Homeric legend; and a great cache of gold artefacts, which he named, with typical understatement, 'Priam's Treasure'. These discoveries brought Schliemann world fame, but also greater scrutiny of his slapdash approach, prompting criticism and revealing that not all of his findings were quite as he presented them.

In his haste, Schliemann had failed to appreciate that Troy was not a single city, but rather a series of settlements built successively, one on top of the other, over the course of about 2500 years. Subsequent archaeologists have identified the remains of nine separate Troys, large sections of which were damaged during Schliemann's hotheaded pursuit of glory. Furthermore, it was soon established that his precious treasures were not from the time of Homer's Troy (Troy VI), but from the much earlier Troy II.

Schliemann's dubious attitude towards archaeological standards continued after the excavation when he smuggled part of 'Priam's Treasure' out of the Ottoman Empire. Much of it was displayed in Berlin, where it was seized by invading Soviet troops at the end of WWII. Following decades of denials about their whereabouts, the treasures were eventually found hidden away in the Pushkin Museum in Moscow, where they remain while international wrangles over their true ownership continue.

Tours

The travel agencies we've listed in Çanakkale and Eceabat offering afternoon tours of the Gallipoli battlefields also offer morning trips to Troy (around ₺60 per person); worth considering if you want a guided tour of both sites at an affordable rate.

Sleeping & Eating

Most visitors stay in Çanakkale and visit Troy on a day trip. However, the village of Tevfikiye, 1km from the ruins, makes a pleasant change from the hassle of Çanakkale.

Troia Pension   PENSION €

(☑283 0571; www.troiapension.com; Truva Mola Noktası Tevfikiye; s/d ₺30/60, camping ₺15; P❄️📶) This newish guesthouse, a short walk from the entrance to the ruins, has four rooms facing onto a pretty patch of garden. Each contains two beds (that can be shoved together for the sake of marital harmony) and the showers have a hot,

DON'T MISS

NEW NATIONAL TREASURE

Turkey's new national archaeological and history museum has been commissioned to be built along the road to Troy. It's an exciting development for the region that saw a host of top international architectural firms compete for the honour. Expect something bold, innovative and open by 2015.

steady stream. Camping here is hugely popular during summer. It's run by the experienced, English-speaking guide Urvan Savas. Next door is the family-run gift shop and simple restaurant. Opposite is the site of a new national museum.

Varol Pansiyon
PENSION €

(✆283 0828; s/d ₺50/80) Overlooking a lush garden behind the village shop in Tevfikiye, Varol is clean and lovingly cared for by an older couple. Rooms are a decent size, and guests can use the kitchen.

Hotel Hisarlık
HOTEL €

(✆283 0026; www.thetroyguide.com; s/d/tr €25/35/50) This basic but comfortable hotel is run by local guide Mustafa Askin's family. Some 500m from the ruins, it's a good spot for watching country life once the coaches have disappeared. The restaurant, which serves Turkish home cooking, is ideal for energising yourself before or after a Trojan tour.

Bandırma

✆0266 / POP 138,206

An undistinguished 20th-century *betonville* (concrete city), the port town of Bandırma marks the junction between ferries across the Sea of Marmara from İstanbul, and İzmir-bound trains. Taking a ferry from central İstanbul to Bandırma is a quick and pleasant way to get to Anatolia, or to the Gallipoli Peninsula via Çanakkale.

The otogar is 2km uphill from the ferry terminal, out on the main highway and served by *servis* (shuttle buses). The train station is next to the ferry terminal.

❶ Getting There & Away

BUS Bandırma is midway between Bursa (₺15, two hours, 115km) and Çanakkale (₺20, 2¾ hours, 195km).

CAR A local company, if you are planning a short trip, is **Viraj Rentacar** (✆718 2102; virajotokiralama@hotmail.com; Mehmetçik Caddesi 29).

FERRY There are at least two daily fast ferries that are run by **İstanbul Deniz Otobüsleri** (İDO; ✆455 6900; www.ido.com.tr; per pedestrian/car/passenger ₺32/125/27), connecting Bandırma with İstanbul's Yenikapı docks (two hours). It's a comfortable service, with assigned seats, refreshments available, a business-class lounge and a lift for disabled passengers.

TRAIN There are daily express trains to/from İzmir (₺17, six hours), leaving at 2.20pm and 4pm. Apart from Tuesday, there are also services at 9.50am/9.25am, and these trains coordinate with the ferry to/from İstanbul.

İzmir & the North Aegean

Best Places to Eat

» Asma Yaprağı (p205)
» Sakız (p196)
» Sandal Restaurant (p170)

Best Places to Stay

» Vintage Boutique Hotel (p204)
» Key Hotel (p195)
» Lola 38 (p189)
» Assos Alarga (p173)

Why Go?

İzmir is Turkey's third-largest city – a buzzing, Eurocentric metropolis with an attractive bazaar and *kordon* (seafront) – and the short stretch of coast running north is a colossus for history buffs. The hilltop ruins of Bergama and Behramkale are breathtaking sites of antiquity, while others lie hidden along peninsulas inhabited by descendants of the Turkmen nomads.

The Greek influence in this region is inescapable. Many towns experienced the great population exchange of the early twentieth century and today, in places like Ayvalık and on the island of Bozcaada, the architecture, music and food seem like bittersweet echoes from across the horizon.

Beaches along the Ege Deniz (Aegean Sea) and the Biga Peninsula are superb (and often empty), while on the Çeşme Peninsula, Alaçatı offers world-class windsurfing.

When to Go

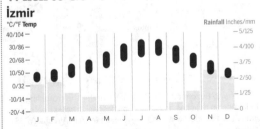

İzmir

May Cruise in a traditional wooden boat on the Çeşme Peninsula without crowds.

Jul International İzmir Festival brings music and dance to the region.

Sep Bozcaada's wine festival is on the viticultural Aegean island.

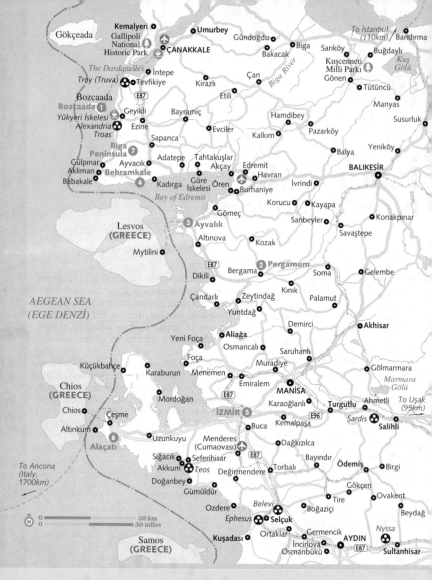

İzmir & the North Aegean Highlights

1 Ferry to **Bozcaada** (p169) to lounge on beaches and indulge in fine local wine and dining

2 Take a cable car to **Pergamum** (Bergama; p181), one of the country's finest ancient sites

3 Wander the crumbling, atmospheric backstreets of the old town in **Ayvalık** (p176)

4 Climb the cobbled streets of Behramkale to the amazing **Temple of Athena** (p172) with its glorious sea views

5 Enjoy the liberal atmosphere of **Alsancak** (p195) in İzmir, Turkey's third-largest city

6 Windsurf by day and party by night in **Alaçatı** (p204), the glamour town of the Çeşme peninsula

7 Take a road trip around the **Biga Peninsula** (p173), with its ruins, villages and sleepy beaches

Bozcaada

☎0286 / POP 2472

This stylish Aegean island is still relatively unknown outside the smart Turkish travel set. Every summer it seems a new batch of expatriate İstanbullus open up another wine bar or pension, but even at capacity it's still all charm, with a warren of picturesque, vine-draped old houses and cobbled streets huddling beneath a huge medieval fortress.

Windswept Bozcaada has always been known to Anatolian wine connoisseurs, and vineyards still blanket its sunny slopes. The island is small (about 5km to 6km across) and easy to explore. Lovely unspoilt sandy beaches line the coast road to the south.

Be warned that outside the school-holiday period (mid-June to mid-September) many businesses shut down; some, particularly eating and drinking options, open their doors at weekends and on Wednesdays, when a market fills the main square.

◉ Sights

Fortress FORTRESS
(admission ₺2; ⊙10am-1pm & 2-6pm) Although Bozcaada is a place for hanging out rather than doing anything specific, there is one official tourist attraction: Bozcaada town's impressive castle. It dates to Byzantine times, but most of what you see are later Venetian, Genoese and Ottoman additions. Inside the double walls are traces of a mosque, ammunition dumps, a barracks, an infirmary and Roman pillars. It sits right next to the ferry terminal.

Beaches BEACH
The best beaches – Ayana, Ayazma, Sulu-bahçe and Habbele – straggle along the southwest coast, although Tuzburnu, which is to the east, is also passable. Ayazma is by far the most popular and best equipped, boasting several cafes (offering the usual Turkish fare) as well as a small, abandoned Greek monastery uphill. In summer you can rent umbrellas and deckchairs at Ayazma, which also hosts good parties.

Bozcaada Local History Museum MUSEUM
(Bozcaada Yerel Tarih Müzesi; ☎0532 215 6033; Lale Sokak 7; adult/child ₺5/3; ⊙10am-8pm late May-Sep) A treasure trove of island curios – maps, prints, photographs, seashells and day-to-day artefacts. Next door, a small private gallery sells island scenes. Located 100m west of the ferry terminal (and well signposted).

THE EVIL ALL-SEEING EYE

However short your trip to Turkey, you can't fail to notice the famous 'evil eye' watching you wherever you go. Belief in the evil eye is still widespread throughout the country; the beads, pendants and other artefacts emblazoned with the eye are made as much for the local market as for tourists. In a nutshell, certain people are thought to carry within them a malevolent force that can be transmitted to others via their eyes. Charms, resembling eyes, known as *nazar boncuk*, are used to reflect the evil look back to the originator. The majority of the evil-eye production takes place in the Aegean region.

Church CHURCH
(20 Eylül Caddesi) The church, in the old Greek neighbourhood to the west of the fortress, is sadly rarely open.

⌂ Sleeping

BOZCAADA TOWN

Headscarf-wrapped ladies may greet you at the *iskele* (pier) and offer you their spare room; if not, wander through the old Greek quarter west of the castle and an offer will be forthcoming. The following are located in the old Greek neighbourhood.

TOP CHOICE Dokuz Oda BOUTIQUE HOTEL €€€
(☎0532 427 0648; www.dokuzoda.com; Eylül Caddesi 43; s/d ₺130/190) Greek-owned 'Nine Rooms' is essentially two renovated buildings either side of a pretty cobblestone street in the old quarter. It's a short walk west of the ferry terminal. Kosta, a Bozcaada native, has conceived a clean-lined island retreat. Polished floorboards, earthy colours and the odd objet d'art help keep the calm.

Kale Pansiyon PENSION €€
(☎697 8617; www.kalepansiyon.net; s/d ₺60/120) Reached via a steep climb from the old quarter, and with impressively commanding views from the top of town, the family-run Kale Pansiyon has 14 simple but fastidiously clean rooms and a terrace on the lane for breakfast. Of its two houses, the one on the right has better bathrooms; light wooden floors and kilims are found throughout.

Bozcaada

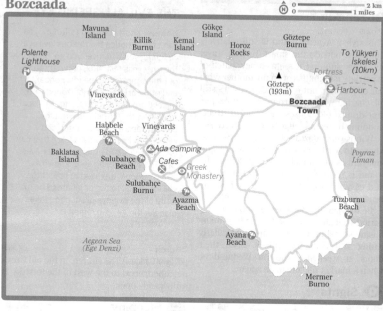

Göztepe (193m)

Polente Lighthouse

Mavuna Island

Killik Burnu

Kemal Island

Gökçe Island

Horoz Rocks

Göztepe Burnu

To Yükyeri İskelesi (10km)

Fortress

Harbour

Bozcaada Town

Vineyards

Habbele Beach

Vineyards

Baklataş Island

Sulubahçe Beach

Ada Camping

Cafes

Greek Monastery

Sulubahçe Burnu

Ayazma Beach

Poyraz Liman

Tuzburnu Beach

Aegean Sea (Ege Denzi)

Ayana Beach

Mermer Burno

Otel Kaikias   BOUTIQUE HOTEL €€€

(☑697 0250; www.kaikias.com; s/d ₺175/230; ❄) Overlooking a tiny seaside square near the castle, this artful hotel is an attraction in itself – from the reception's plant ceiling to the antiques and artefacts, such as a bookcase of flaking tomes behind protective glass.

Adahan Otel   PENSION €€

(☑697 0004; www.adahanpansiyon.com; Eylül Caddesi 20; r ₺150) Adahan has two premises in Bozcaada near the old primary school. The discreet hotel far outpoints the pension in both comfort and value, with three single and six double rooms, all combining original stone foundations with mod cons across three floors. Smart choice.

Ergin Pansiyon   PENSION €€

(☑697 0038; www.erginpansiyon.com; s/d ₺40/80; ❄) The delicious Turkish breakfast served in the courtyard, and the rooftop terrace with its castle view, almost make up for the rooms at Ergin Pansiyon. The decorative disasters include mixing green walls and orange blankets, but Ergin is nonetheless one of Bozcaada town's cheaper options.

SOUTHWEST & EAST COASTS

Ada Camping   CAMPGROUND €

(☑697 0442; senayalir@mynet.com; Eski Kule Mevkii; per person ₺15) This scrappy campsite, 200m inland from Sulubahçe beach, has a kitchen, a barbecue and tents for hire (per person ₺20).

✖ Eating

Check the price of fish before ordering. There have been complaints from travellers about the exorbitant costs in some restaurants.

Sandal Restaurant   SEAFOOD €€€

TOP CHOICE

(☑697 0278; Alsancak Sokak; mains ₺20-25; ☑lunch & dinner; ☎) The former Turkish president Turgut Erzal's manservant dotes on customers who travel from afar for the meze and fish dishes. Sandal is the one with the boat hanging on the wall and the crowds filling the pavement.

Ada Café   CAFE €€

(☑697 8795; Çınar Çeşme Sokak 4; mains ₺8-17.50, wine from ₺14; ☑8.30am-midnight May-Sep) Melih and Semra have presided over this popular cafe and gourmet larder since İstanbul was a faraway city. Ada serves wholesome, simple food such as fresh thyme salad and a crispy house *börek* (filled pastry). In summer try a frothy sherbet drink.

Koreli
SEAFOOD €€

(☏697 8098; Yali Caddesi 12; mains ₺15) Nearly five decades of plundering the ocean and frying it in a pan has seen the harbourside Koreli maintain the island's best reputation for fresh seafood.

Café at Lisa's
CAFE €€

(☏697 0182; Kurtulus Caddesi; mains ₺15; ☏) Lisa is an Australian expat and community media mogul who runs the cutest cafe on the island. This place is a sure thing for good coffee, cake and pasta. Grab an outside table beneath the big tree. Next door you'll find a great Turkish-language bookshop.

Gülüm Ocakbaşı
TURKISH €€

(☏697 8567; Sakarya Sokak 5; mains ₺12; ☏lunch & dinner) Next to Tüketim Market, this *ocakbaşı* (grill house) serves a wide range of delicious Turkish classics, including kebaps, *köfte* (meatballs) and pide (Turkish-style pizza).

Tüketim Market
FOOD MARKET €€

(Alsancak Sokak 20; ☏8am-1am high season, 9am-9pm low season) Popular store on the main square, with fresh bread and fruit, cheeses and meats – great for getting up a picnic.

Ali Baba
CAFE €

(☏697 0207; mains ₺5; ☏) One of the better eateries at Ayazma beach.

Drinking

Bakkal
BAR, CAFE

(Lale Sokak) Opened by an İstanbullu restaurateur, this super-cool cafe serves Corvus wine (glass ₺8), smoothies, espressos and delectable sandwiches (₺18 to ₺25). Seating is at little tables on the lane or inside, among products such as De Cecco pasta and organic skin toner.

Bar Ali
BAR, RESTAURANT

(Çınar Çarşı Caddesi; ☏8am-4am high season) The waterfront seating area overlooks the fortress and, festooned with cushions, beanbags and deckchairs, is the place to wind down at the end of the day. Inside there's a more formal area where you can tuck into wines and cheese, plus a mezzanine with comfy leather chairs.

Polente
BAR

(Yali Sokak 41; ☏8pm-2am; ☏) Polente, off the main square, plays an eclectic mix of music, including Latin and jazz, and attracts an equally eclectic mix of locals and visitors (mostly 20- and 30-somethings).

❶ Information

Captain Internet Kafe (Çınar Çarşı Caddesi; per hr ₺2; ☏9.30am-11pm)

Information booth (İskele Caddesi) In addition to this wooden hut near the *iskele*, you can pick up a map from some of the accommodation and cafes, including Ada Café and Cafe at Lisa's.

Ziraat Bankası This branch and other ATMs are on the main square in Bozcaada town, near the PTT.

İZMİR & THE NORTH AEGEAN BOZCAADA

FINE WINE

Bozcaada has been one of Turkey's great wine-growing regions since ancient times, when enormous quantities of wine were used to fuel the debauchery at festivals for Dionysus, the Greek god of wine. Nobody is quite sure why, but some magical alchemy of the island's climate, topography and soil make-up perfectly suits the growing of grapes. The island's four main winemakers are Corvus, Talay, Ataol and Yunatçılar.

Corvus (www.corvus.com.tr; Çınar Çarşı Caddesi), which has a shop next to Lodos restaurant, is the work of the famous Turkish architect Reşit Soley. Its wines, such as Karga (named after the island's many crows) and Zeleia Vasilaki, have impressed wine critics internationally.

The **Talay shop** (www.talay.com.tr), behind the ATMs on the main square in Bozcaada town, offers tastings of its reds, whites and rosés (₺9 to ₺25). You can also visit the winemaker's fermentation tanks, behind the Ziraat Bankası.

Çamlıbağ (www.camlibag.com.tr) is an excellent smaller winery that makes a delightful merlot-kuntra blend and a decent rosé.

If travelling in September, try to coincide with the annual **Wine Festival**, which offers free tastings, tours of the wine houses and lectures on the processes of viticulture.

ℹ️ Getting There & Away

BOAT **Gestaş** (☎ 444 0752; www.gdu.com.tr) ferries run daily to Bozcaada from Yükyeri İskelesi (Yükyeri harbour; return per person/car ₺5/45, 30 minutes), 4km west of Geyikli, south of Troy, leaving the mainland at 10am, 2pm and 7pm and departing the island at 7.30am, noon and 4pm. Hydrofoils also sail from Çanakkale (per person ₺10, one hour) on Wednesday (departs at 9am, returns at 8pm), Saturday (departs at 8am and 8pm, returns at 9.30am and 9.30pm) and Sunday (departs at 9am, returns at 9.30pm). It's worth checking departure times, as they do change.

BUS Hourly dolmuşes (minibuses) link Çanakkale otogar (bus station) with Geyikli (₺8) via Ezine, with connections to Yükyeri İskelesi (₺2). Dolmuşes meet the ferry from Bozcaada and run to Geyikli and to Ezine (₺4), from where there are services to Çanakkale and destinations to the south such as Behramkale/Assos and Gülpınar.

ℹ️ Getting Around

BICYCLE You can hire mountain bikes (one hour/day ₺10/25) at **İskele Sancak Café** (☎ 0532 443 8999), on the right when you disembark from the ferry.

DOLMUŞ Hourly dolmuşes leave from near the *iskele* in Bozcaada town to Ayazma beach (₺4). In the summer, more-frequent dolmuşes also serve Ayazma via Ada Camping and Sulubahçe beach, and there's a service to **Polente feneri** (lighthouse) on the west coast for watching sunsets.

TAXI A taxi from Bozcaada town to Ayazma costs ₺25 to ₺30.

Behramkale & Assos
☎ 0286

The twin villages of Behramkale and Assos are a breathtaking double act. The former Greek settlement spreads out around the ancient temple to Athena (Behramkale); and, at the bottom of the steep hill, a former working harbour has a small pebble beach, where the old stone buildings and warehouses have been transformed into hotels and fish restaurants (Assos).

Try to avoid visiting on weekends and public holidays from the beginning of April to the end of August, when tourists pour in by the coach load. Locals often refer to the two areas as Assos *liman* (harbour) and *köyü* (village). In Behramkale there are few facilities other than an ATM and a pharmacy.

History

The Mysian city of Assos was founded in the 8th century BC by colonists from Lesvos, who later built its great temple to Athena in 530 BC. The city enjoyed considerable prosperity under the rule of Hermeias, a one-time student of Plato who also ruled the Troad and Lesvos. Hermeias encouraged philosophers to live in Assos, and Aristotle himself lived here from 348 to 345 BC and ended up marrying Hermeias' niece, Pythia. Assos' glory days came to an abrupt end with the arrival of the Persians, who crucified Hermeias and forced Plato to flee.

Alexander the Great drove the Persians out, but Assos' importance was challenged by the ascendancy of Alexandria Troas to the north. From 241 to 133 BC the city was ruled by the kings of Pergamum.

St Paul visited Assos briefly during his third missionary journey, walking here from Alexandria Troas to meet St Luke before taking a boat to Lesvos.

In late Byzantine times the city dwindled to a village. Turkish settlers arrived and called the village Behramkale. Only the coming of tourism revived its fortunes.

👁️ Sights & Activities

Temple of Athena RUINS
(☎ 217 6740; admission ₺8; ⏰ 8am-7.30pm) Right on top of the hill in Behramkale village is this 6th-century-BC Ionic temple. The short tapered columns with plain capitals are hardly elegant, and the concrete reconstruction hurts more than helps, but the site and the view out to Lesvos are spectacular and well worth the admission fee.

Villagers set up stalls all the way up the hill to the temple, touting local products from bags of dried herbs or mushrooms to linen and silverware.

Hüdavendigar Camii MOSQUE
Beside the entrance to the Temple of Athena, this 14th-century mosque is a simply constructed Ottoman mosque – a dome on squinches set on top of a square room – built before the Turks had conquered Constantinople and assimilated the lessons of Sancta Sophia. It's one of just two remaining Ottoman mosques of its kind in Turkey (the other is in Bursa).

Other Ruins RUINS
Scramble down the hill from the Temple of Athena, or walk along the road to Assos, to find the **necropolis**. Assos' sarcophagi

WORTH A TRIP

BİGA PENINSULA

With your own transport, the isolated Biga Peninsula, with its assorted, all-but-forgotten ruins, makes a good day trip.

Ten kilometres south of Geyikli lie the ruins of **Alexandria Troas** (☑0532 691 3754), scattered around the village of Dalyan. After the collapse of Alexander the Great's empire, Antigonus (one of his generals) took control of this land, founding the city of Antigoneia in 310 BC. This site feels blessedly secret, with rarely another traveller among its great grass-strewn ruins. Much of it remains buried, but there are some wonderful relics to see, such as stone arches and crystal-clear inscriptions.

A little further south is Gülpınar, a one-street farming village once the ancient city of **Khrysa**, famous for its 2nd-century-BC Ionic temple to Apollo – and for its mice. An oracle had told Cretan colonists to settle where 'the sons of the earth' attacked them. Awaking to find mice chewing their equipment, they decided to settle here and built a temple to Smintheion (Lord of the Mice). The 5m-tall cult statue of the god, of which only a fragment remains, had marble mice carved at its feet.

The ruins of the **Apollon Smintheion** (incl museum ₺5; ⊙8am-5pm) lie 300m down a side road at the bottom of the village (look for the brown sign on the right if you're coming from the north). Wonderful reliefs and column drums with illustrated scenes from the *Iliad*, which recounts the Apollo Smintheon priest Chryse's feud with Agamemnon, were found among the ruins.

From Gülpınar, a road heads 9km west past a few coastal developments to Babakale, the westernmost point of mainland Turkey. It's a sleepy place that seems almost overawed by the 18th-century **fortress**, the last Ottoman castle built in present-day Turkey.

Above the harbour, the **Uran Hotel** (☑747 0218; s/d ₺50/100; ※) has simple but sea breeze–fresh rooms with tiny bathrooms and small balconies overlooking the castle and sea. There's also a delightful terrace and a good and reasonably priced **fish restaurant** (mains ₺15).

There are buses from Gülpınar (₺2, 15 minutes) and daily services from Ezine (₺7, two hours).

(from the Greek, 'flesh-eaters') were famous. According to Pliny the Elder, the stone was caustic and 'ate' the flesh off the deceased in 40 days. Other ruins include the remains of a late-2nd-century-BC **theatre** and **basilica**.

Ringing the hill are stretches of the **city walls** of medieval Assos, which are among the most impressive medieval fortifications in Turkey.

🛏 Sleeping

Peaceful Behramkale village has the more atmospheric accommodation, though Assos harbour has a bit more energy. In high season, virtually all the hotels around the harbour insist on *yarım pansiyon* (half-board), though you could try negotiating.

BEHRAMKALE

TOP CHOICE **Assos Alarga**   BOUTIQUE HOTEL €€€
(☑721 7260; www.assosalarga.com; Berhamkale 88; r from ₺200; P※🌐🏊) Located in the quiet end of the village, just behind the temple ruins, this is a fabulous place to stay. Alarga may only have three rooms, but this ensures stellar service from Ece, the owner. 'Orsa' has the floorboards, beautiful bookshelves and desk. All rooms have amazing views over the mountains and very cool bathrooms. There's a deluxe outdoor pool, garden, sauna and pool table.

Assosyal Otel   BOUTIQUE HOTEL €€€
(☑721 7046; www.assosyalbutikotel.com; Alan Meydanı 8; s/d ₺160/260) Opposite Alarga is this new addition to the Behramkale hotel scene. Contemporary lines arc across old stone, vine-clad walls. Tea in the courtyard feels timeless. The rooms are minimally furnished, with deluxe, raised beds and stunning mountain-facing terraces. The tin sculpture upon entry sets the playful mood.

Biber Evi   BOUTIQUE HOTEL €€€
(☑721 7410; www.biberevi.com; d ₺300-340; ※) 'Chilli House' is the pride of Lütfi, a former theatre director who has long had eyes for Assos. The entrance to the stone property, which sits in the middle of the village, is charming and the living area is pinned with artefacts and a subdued romanticism.

The six rooms' bathrooms – modern versions of the Ottoman *gusülhane* (cupboard bathroom) – feature underfloor heating. Breakfast on the terrace includes views of the temple and coast.

Eris Pansiyon
PENSION €€

(☑721 7080; www.erispansiyon.com; s/d incl tea ₺70/120) This guesthouse has three pleasant rooms; those facing the sea are less impressive inside. Lovingly prepared afternoon tea is served on a terrace with spectacular views over the hills, and there's an extensive library and book exchange. It's at the eastern end of the village. Call ahead out of season.

Dolunay Pansiyon
PENSION €€

(☑721 7172; s/d ₺50/100; ❄) In the centre of the village on the main square, this basic family-run place has six spotless rooms. There's also a pretty terrace with sea views where you can have a scenic breakfast.

Tekin Pansiyon
PENSION €€

(☑721 7099; assostekinpansiyon@hotmail.com; s/d ₺50/100; ❄) Offers the basic pension requirements, and even though the rooms face away from Behramkale's panoramic views, the little tables on the balcony overlook village goings-on.

ASSOS

Çakır Restaurant and Yelken Camp offer accommodation in wooden huts (single/double including half-board from ₺60/100).

Hotel Kervansaray
HOTEL €€€

(☑721 7093; www.assoskervansaray.com; s/d with sea view ₺140/180; ❄❄) Probably the most reliable place to stay down by the ancient harbour, but something of an oddity all the same. A 19th-century acorn store, the Kervansaray is pretty good value in its newer 'Butik' section, but the popularity of the restaurant can detract from the guest experience. The hotel's smart rooms have small bathrooms and plasma-screen TVs concealed in wooden cases; some have balconies. The outdoor pool almost laps into the sea.

Yıldız Saray Hotel
PENSION €€

(☑721 7025; www.yildizsaray-hotels.com; s/d/f ₺100/140/220; ❄) The Star Palace is drifting into post-retro territory in its tired decor, but it's friendly, the upstairs terrace is sublime and the family apartment with two doubles and a jacuzzi is good value. Breakfast is served on a floating platform. The owners also operate another hotel, just east along the coast at Kadırga.

Dr No Antik Pansiyon
PENSION €

(☑721 7397; www.assosdrnoantikpansiyon.com; s/d ₺40/80; ❄) No sign of an evil conspiracy at this simple, friendly pension with cramped rooms and a pleasant outdoor area. It's the best budget option near the sea.

Hotel Nazlıhan
HOTEL €€€

(☑721 7385; www.assosnazlihanspahotel.com; d from ₺180) Remodelled as a spa resort (where a decent treatment is available), the Nazlıhan's older section has two floors of musty rooms facing an internal courtyard, while the newer section is actually pretty flash. Tacky trimmings aside, these are very comfortable four-star hotel rooms with wood-panelled bath-tubs at the foot of garish beds, and very small, tiled bathrooms. The hotel caters mostly to tour groups, so service to independent travellers can be a bit ordinary.

✖ Eating & Drinking

Proximity to the sea accounts for higher prices at the harbour. Be sure to check the cost of fish and bottles of wine before ordering.

BEHRAMKALE

TOP CHOICE Ehl-i Keyf
TURKISH €

(☑721 7106; www.assosehlikeyf.com.tr; gozleme ₺5; 🛜) This multilevel restaurant combines excellent, fresh food with attentive service and a very pleasant outlook. Choose from a long menu of *izgara* (grills) and *gozlemeles* (savoury pancake) amid flowering plants and wheeled mini-gazebos. Also good for cocktails, coffee and ice cream. They have also recently opened a guesthouse.

Panorama Restaurant
RESTAURANT €€

(☑721 7037; mains ₺10) A friendly family restaurant en route to the ruins, Panaroma serves excellent mezes such as *börülce* (black-eyed peas), stuffed pumpkin flowers and *avcı boreği* (hunter's *börek;* pastry filled with meat or cheese).

Mantı & Börek Evi
TURKISH €

(☑721 7050; mains ₺7; ⊗8am-7pm) Serving *mantı* (Turkish ravioli), *avcı boreği* and a good range of mezes, this *lokanta* (eatery serving ready-made food) has a small terrace overlooking the main square. It's one of the only eateries on the hill offering beer.

Aile Çay Bahçesi
TEA GARDEN

(tea ₺1, soft drinks ₺3; 🛜) For a coffee or Coke on the main square, this place has a pleasant shaded terrace offering attractive views.

ASSOS

TOP CHOICE Uzunev   SEAFOOD €€

(☑721 7007; mains ₺15-20; ☺lunch & dinner)
Uzunev is the pick of the non-hotel restaurants and garners the most lively crowd, especially on weekends in high season. Blue wooden chairs line the terrace, while inside it feels like a warm Turkish pub. Try the succulent speciality, sea bass à l'Aristotle (steamed in a special stock), or the delicious seafood meze (₺10).

Çakır Restaurant   SEAFOOD €€

(☑721 7048; mains ₺12-15) About as chilled out as dining can get, the Çakýr brothers' restaurant overlooks a pebble beach and rickety wooden platforms above the water. You can pick meze and mains such as *kalamar* (squid) and *köfte* from the fridge.

Yelken Camp   BAR

(☑721 7433; ☎) Yelken attracts those who want the bare essentials: good tunes, cold beer and a sofa by the sea.

🛈 Getting There & Away

BAY OF EDREMİT In the summer, dolmuşes connect Behramkale with Küçükkuyu (₺4, one hour); otherwise a taxi costs ₺40 to ₺45.

BİGA PENINSULA Dolmuşes run to Behramkale from Gülpınar (₺3, one hour).

ÇANAKKALE Regular buses run from Çanakkale (₺12, 1½ hours) to Ayvacık, where you can pick up a dolmuş to Behramkale (₺$, 20 minutes). Some dolmuşes make a second stop down in Assos (₺4) in summer, but some don't, obliging you to switch to the shuttle service. In low season, dolmuşes run less frequently. Try to get to Ayvacık as early in the day as you can to catch a dolmuş to Behramkale. If you miss the last one, Ayvacık has a couple of hotels, or a taxi to Behramkale will cost around ₺30.

🛈 Getting Around

In summer, there's a shuttle service throughout the day between Behramkale and Assos (₺1, every 30 minutes). In winter, dolmuşes occasionally run between Assos and Behramkale (₺8).

Ayvacık

☑0286 / POP 7600

Heading to or from Behramkale you may have to transit in Ayvacık, which has a big **Friday market** where women from the surrounding villages sell fruit, vegetables and baskets. Those in long satiny overcoats or brightly coloured headscarves are the descendants of Turkmen nomads who settled in this area.

Ayvacık is famous for its diminutive carpets, and some 20 villages and Turkmen communities in the region still produce them. Two kilometres out of Ayvacık, opposite the Total garage on the main road to Çanakkale, is the **Doğal Boya Arıştırma ve Geliştirme Projesi** (Natural Dye Research & Development Project; ☑712 1274; ☺9am-6pm), which was set up in 1982 to encourage villagers to return to weaving carpets from naturally dyed wool. The prices charged by the village women are cheaper than those found in big-city bazaars. The great majority of carpets are exported, and the prices are not extravagant considering what goes into the process: every stage – shearing, carding, spinning, weaving, knotting and dyeing – is done by hand. The upstairs exhibition hall may be empty out of season, but there are a few displays and some coffee-table books for sale. Phone ahead to organise a village tour.

Bay of Edremit

About 25km from Behramkale, the road meets the highway, which runs east along the north shore of the Bay of Edremit.

Turn left here, towards Ayvacık, and head 4km northwest into the hills to reach the village of **Yeşilyurt**, set among pine forests and olive groves. The many restored houses' yellow stone walls have been beautifully enhanced by red brick and wood, and the village offers plenty of boutique hotels and restaurants.

Back on the coastal highway, you could pause in Küçükkuyu to inspect the **Adatepe Zeytinyağı Museum** (☑0286-752 1303; ☺9am-7pm), housed in an old olive-oil factory and explaining the process of making olive oil.

From Küçükkuyu, head 4km northeast into the forested hills to visit the pretty village of **Adatepe**, a cluster of restored stone houses below a lizard-like rock formation. The area is great for walking, with waterfalls, plunge pools for swimming and, near the falls at Başdeğirmen, a Roman bridge. At the top of Adatepe you'll find the blissfully tranquil **Hünnap Han** (☑0286-752 6581; www.hunnaphan.com; s/d half-board ₺190/250), a restored country pile with traditionally decorated rooms, a lovely garden and stone courtyard.

Buses stop in Küçükkuyu, which has Metro and Truva offices, every hour en route to Çanakkale (₺18) and İzmir (₺28). A taxi from Küçükkuyu to Adatepe or Yeşilyurt costs ₺10. In the summer, dolmuşes run to Behramkale (₺4, one hour); otherwise a taxi costs ₺40 to ₺45.

The road continues east, past a string of holiday villages, hotels and second-home developments aimed at domestic tourists. Just before Güre İskelesi, follow the brown signpost and head 2.5km north into the hills to find the **Etnografya Galerisi** (Ethnographic Gallery; ☑0266 387 3340; admission ₺2; ☺8am-8pm) in Tahtakuşlar village. Exhibits such as a domed tent give an insight into the local villages inhabited by descendents of Turkmen people who moved here in the 15th century.

Demre Tour, a travel agency based in Akçay, 10km west of Edremit, runs **jeep safaris** (☑0266-384 8586; incl lunch ₺50, incl night in a Turkmen tent & 3 meals ₺125; ☺Jun-Sep) in Mount Ida National Park (Kazdağı Milli Parkı).

There is a good lunch stop near the seafront in Akçay. Turn right off the main street just after Ömür Lokanta to find the multi-coloured **Zeyyat Lokanta** (mains ₺10; ☺8am-10pm), which has outside seating and dishes up home-cooking such as *balık* (fish) with peppers.

A new airport has opened at Edremit. Bora Jet and Anadolu Jet fly daily to İstanbul and Ankara.

❶ Getting There & Away

Regular buses run to/from Çanakkale (₺10, 1½ hours). There are also regular buses or dolmuşes to Ayvacık from Ezine, Behramkale and Küçükkuyu.

Ayvalık

☑0266 / POP 37,182

Ayvalık is an attractive, work-a-day fishing town with a secret. Distinctively free of the tourist hustle, the palm-tree-lined waterfront and smattering of fish restaurants are much like elsewhere on the Aegean, but wander a few streets back to find an old Greek village in spirited abandon. Cars are squeezed out of the narrow, cobblestone lanes by horses, carts and market-faring locals. Colourful, shuttered doors conceal all-day cafes and craft stores, time lapses in the afternoon sun and visitors slow down and join in the languid atmosphere.

Olive-oil production is the traditional business around here, and is still thriving, with lots of shops selling the end product. The broken chimney next to **Tansaş supermarket** in the town centre belongs to a now-abandoned olive-oil factory. Ayvalık is also well known as a gateway to local islands, including Alibey, just offshore, and Lesvos, Greece.

◉ Sights & Activities

Old Town HISTORIC AREA

There are few specific sights but Ayvalık's old town is a joy to wander around, with its maze of cobbled streets lined with wonderfully worn-looking Greek houses. You can pick up a map with information about sights, including the former Greek Orthodox churches, at Tarlakusu Gurmeko cafe and Çöp Madam craftshop. There are plans to turn the broken-chimneyed former olive-oil factory just northwest of Taklakusu Gurmeko into a local museum.

Markets MARKET

Thursday sees one of the region's largest and most vibrant markets, and stalls seem to fill the whole town. Seek out the **köy pazarı** (village market), which takes place next to the main **pazar yeri** (bazaar). The daily **Balık Pazarı** (fish market) also takes place on the waterfront next to the terminal for the ferry to Alibey.

Beaches BEACH

There are a number of good, sandy beaches a few kilometres to the south. **Sarımsaklı Plaj** (Garlic Beach) is the most famed and will inevitably be the most crowded, as this is package-holiday territory. Stay on the bus a bit longer until you reach Badavut to the west and you'll find some quieter stretches.

🛏 Sleeping

TOP CHOICE **İstanbul Pansiyon** PENSION €

(☑312 4001; www.istanbulpansiyonayvalik.com; Neşe Sokak Aralığı 4; s/d ₺35/70; P❄🐾) This lovely pension on the edge of the bazaar opens onto a quiet public square. The pretty blue and pink exterior gives way to six spacious rooms, four facing the courtyard. Breakfast is a delight in the lush garden, among flowers and ceramic jugs or under a green canopy.

Ayvalık

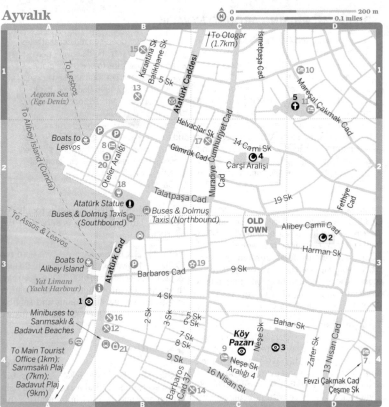

Ayvalık

DIVING & CRUISING AROUND AYVALIK

The waters around Ayvalık are famed among divers for their deep-sea red coral at sites like Deli Mehmet and Kerbela. Another boon for the industry was the discovery of a wrecked jet in 2009. Dive companies in Ayvalık can organise trips to see these places and their attendant marine life, including moray eels, grouper, octopus and sea horses. One of the better options is the **Korfez Diving Center** (☑312 4996, 0532 266 3589; www.korfezdiving.com; Atatürk Bulvari Özaral Pasaji 61; ☺Mar-Nov), which moors its boat by the fish market. A day's diving costs ₺90 and dive courses are ₺500.

In addition to the dive sites and summer ferries to Lesvos, cruises head around the bay's islands, including Alibey, and stop here and there for swimming, sunbathing and walking. They generally depart at 11am and return by 6.30pm and cost around ₺50 per person, including lunch. **Jale Tour** (☑331 3170; www.jaletour.com; Yeni Liman Karsisi) also cruises to Assos (₺60), leaving at 10.30am and returning by 7.30pm.

Kelebek Pension
PENSION €€

(☑312 3908; www.kelebek-pension.com; Mareşal Çakmak Caddesi 108; s/d/tr ₺60/100/135; 🌢) A management re-shuffle has not detracted from this colourful seven-room pension where you can see the sea from your bedroom. The white-and-blue building has a terrace for having breakfast in the fresh air. Bikes are available to rent.

Taksiyarhis Pension
PENSION €€

(☑312 1494; www.taksiyarhispension.com; Mareşal Çakmak Caddesi 71; per person without bathroom ₺45; 🌢) This 120-year-old Greek house, behind the eponymous church, is one of the more stylish in Ayvalık. There's a vine-shaded terrace with sweeping views across the city, a communal kitchen and a decent book exchange. Rooms are period chic with exposed wooden beams and areas that beckon for an afternoon nap. Breakfast costs ₺10 extra.

Ayazma Butik Otel
HOTEL €€

(www.ayzamaotel.com; Ataturk Bulvari 69; s/d ₺60/100; 🌢🌢) This former 19th-century stone residence is the pick of the underwhelming seafront hotels. The six rooms upstairs are comfortable, with good bathrooms and large beds; the best two share a balcony. The courtyard facing Ataturk Bulvari is a lovely place for breakfast or a beer, and often fills with high-school students looking for a cheap lunch. The basement restaurant serves local delicacies.

Bonjour Pansiyon
PENSION €€

(☑312 8085; www.bonjourpansiyon.com; Fevzi Çakmak Caddesi, Çeşme Sokak 5; s/d without bathroom ₺60/100; 🌢) This 300-year-old mansion is well run, but there's an overwhelming sense of sentimentality in the ageing furniture and 1st-floor, bathroom-less rooms. An excellent buffet breakfast is served in the courtyard.

Hotel Ayvalık Palas
HOTEL €€€

(☑312 1064; www.ayvalikpalashotel.com; Gümrük Meydanı Oteller Aralığı; s/d ₺100/180; 🅿🌢🌢) Not the prettiest seafront hotel, but the location is spot on and it's anonymous and serviceable, plus there's a huge car park, a luxury in Ayvalık.

🍴 Eating

Balıkçı
SEAFOOD €€

(☑312 9099; Balıkhane Sokak 7; mains ₺17; ☺dinner) Run by a local association of fishermen and marine environmentalists, this is a fine place to sample seafood and settle into the tiled terrace or sit inside for a better view of the Turkish troubadours, who get a singalong going from 8.30pm onwards.

Tarlakusu Gurmeko
CAFE €€

(☑312 3312; Cumhuriyet Caddesi 53; ☺8.30am-8.30pm; 🌢) This artsy coffee house is very urbane for Ayvalık (the owners hail from İzmir) and the brew they make is top notch. Lounge on soft armchairs, browse the painting exhibits or purchase from the larder. Nibbles include cookies, brownies, soup, salads, cheese plates and *börek* (₺4.50).

Cafe Caramel
CAFE

(Barbaros Caddesi 37) Beautiful Yasemin fronts this nostalgic cafe in the old town. With a jazz soundtrack, an extensive cake and dessert menu, homemade soda and simple meals done well, Caramel hits the sweetest spot.

Deniz Kestanesi
SEAFOOD €€

(☑312 3262; Karantina Sokak 9; mains ₺15; ☺10am-midnight) The 'sea urchin' is a flash indoor/outdoor affair, right on the waterfront, with wooden floors, high ceilings, leather chairs and great views of Alibey's twinkling lights. Meat dishes are available in addition to meze (₺8 to ₺16) and *balık* including bass, bream, shark and mullet.

Hatipoğlu Pastaneleri
PATISSERIE €

(Atatürk Caddesi 12; tea/Turkish coffee ₺1/2; ☺7am-1am; ❋) With a great selection of traditional Turkish puds, pastries and cakes, this friendly patisserie makes a terrific breakfast or tea stop. Try the Ayvalık speciality, *lok* (sponge oozing honey; ₺3) and go on, add a scoop of *dondurma* (ice cream).

Palmiye Cafe
CAFE €

(☑312 1188; Atatürk Caddesi 78; börek ₺4; ☺9am-9pm) A very friendly new cafe serving delicious pastries, both sweet and savoury. The back section is popular with young lovers. The owner speaks good English and her daughters like to practise.

Drinking & Entertainment

White Knight Café
BAR

(☑312 3682; Cumhuriyet Meydanı 13; beer ₺4; ☺9am-2am; ☎) Popular cafe by the statue of Atatürk, overseen by Ahmet and his British wife, Anthea. The vibe is mellow, except when major football matches are shown, and it sells English-language magazines and yesterday's newspapers.

Sanat Fabrikası
THEATRE

(☑312 3045; www.sanatfabrikasi.com.tr; Barbaros Caddesi 4, Sokak 1-3) The 'arts factory' is a newly opened hub for live performance that attracts an appreciative, youthful crowd to its cosy theatre. The attached bar is ideal for a drop-in drink before, after, or during a show and can get rowdy on weekends.

Studio Organic
CINEMA, COURSES

(☑312 3312; Cumhuriyet Caddesi 53) The studio above Tarlakusu Gurmeko cafe offers a cinema club (₺2) on Wednesday evenings, plus night classes – yoga on Mondays, drawing on Tuesdays, photography on Tuesdays and Thursdays, and tango and salsa on Fridays.

🛍 Shopping

Çöp Madam
CRAFTS

(☑312 6095; Alibey Cami Caddesi 2; ☺9am-5pm) A cooperative for unemployed women who make colourful bags and jewellery out of recycled materials. Next to a popular teahouse, 250m east of the ferry terminal.

Antikacılar Çarşısı
ANTIQUE MARKET

(Otelier Aralığı; ☺9am-6pm) Buy old coins, jewellery and bric-a-brac, plus retro magazines and posters in this quaint covered market.

ℹ Information

Post Office (Atatürk Caddesi) At the northern end of town on the main street.

Tourist Office Main Branch (☑312 2122; Yat Limanı Karşısı; ☺8am-noon & 1-5pm Mon-Fri) The main tourist office is beyond the yacht marina, but in high season you can get information from the **kiosk** (Yat Limanı; ☺Jun-Sep) on the waterfront south of the main square.

ℹ Getting There & Away

Boat

LESVOS From May to September, boats sail daily except Sunday to Lesvos, Greece (passenger one way/return ₺60/70, car ₺120/130, 1½ hours) at 5pm, and to Ayvalık on the same days at 8.30am. From October to May, boats sail to Lesvos and Ayvalık at the same times on Tuesday, Thursday and Saturday.

Note that times do change and you must make a reservation (in person or by telephone) 24 hours before departure. When you pick up your tickets, bring your passport. For information and tickets, contact Jale Tour (p178).

FAST FOOD – AYVALIK STYLE

Ayvalık may have made its name as an olive-oil producer, but these days it's better known throughout Turkey for a rather less refined culinary offering – *Ayvalık tost* (Ayvalık toast). The town's take on fast food is essentially a toasted sandwich, crammed with all manner of ingredients, including cheese, *sucuk* (spicy veal sausage), salami, pickles and tomatoes. These goodies are, of course, lathered in ketchup and mayonnaise (unless you specifically request otherwise). It's available at cafes and stalls throughout town, but **Avşar Büfe** (Atatürk Caddesi; ☺24hr high season, 7am-3am low season) and the surrounding eateries are good places to take the *tost* challenge. *Tost* typically costs just ₺4 (or ₺3 for just cheese) but take note – it's a fast-food feast in a sandwich.

GHOSTS FROM THE PAST

The early 1920s hold mixed memories for Ayvalık. Pride over its role in the Turkish War of Independence – it was here that the first shots were fired – is tempered by what happened afterwards. The Ottoman Greeks, who made up the majority of the population, were forced to abandon the land of their birth and relocate to the Greek island of Lesvos, while the Turks from that island were, in turn, compelled to start new lives in Ayvalık. Despite the enormous distress this must have caused, the Ayvalık–Lesvos exchange is nonetheless regarded as one of the least damaging episodes of the period. The reasons why the exchange caused less tumult than many others had much to do with the proximity of the two communities, which enabled people from both sides to continue visiting their former homes – mixed though their emotions must have been during those trips. Furthermore, both communities were involved in the production of olive oil, and so would have found much that was familiar in the other.

Today, whispers from the past are everywhere. Some elderly locals can speak Greek and many of the town's former Greek Orthodox churches remain standing, albeit converted into mosques. The Ayios Ioannis, which in 1923 became the **Saatlı Camii** ('Clock Mosque', so named for its clock tower), still serves as a church for Ayvalık's expat community on Sunday mornings. The former Ayios Yioryios is today the **Çınarlı Camii**, named after the *çınar* (plane trees) that grew here, one of which remains. One of the grandest of all the old Greek churches, the **Taksiyarhis** church, was never converted. However, it no longer functions as a church either, but rather sits empty and forlorn, waiting to be renovated at some unspecified future date.

Bus

BERGAMA It is possible to make a day trip to Bergama (₺7, 1¾ hours, 45km). Hourly Bergama buses leave the otogar between 8am and 7pm and drive slowly south through town, so you can jump on at the main square.

ÇANAKKALE Coming from Çanakkale (₺15, 3¼ hours, 200km), five a day) smaller companies may drop you on the main highway, from where you'll have to hitch to the centre. Larger companies, such as Ulusoy, provide *servis* (shuttle buses) to their offices in the centre.

EDREMİT Regular dolmuşes go from Ayvalık otogar (₺7, one hour).

İZMİR There are hourly buses to/from İzmir (₺16, three hours, 150km).

Car

BERGAMA The inland route to Bergama, via Kozak, is much more scenic and only marginally slower than the coast road, winding through idyllic pine-clad hills. Backtrack north towards Gömeç then turn right.

ℹ Getting Around

Bus & Dolmuş

TOWN CENTRE Dolmuş taxis (white with red stripes running around them) serve the town centre, stopping to put down and pick up passengers along a series of short set routes. You can catch them at the main square. Destinations include Armutçuk, 1km to the north of town; fares are typically ₺2.

OTOGAR Ayvalık *belediyesi* (town) buses (₺2 to ₺3) run through town between the otogar and the main square.

SOUTH *Belediyesi* buses continue from the main square to the tourist office and the beaches around Sarımsaklı. Minibuses (₺1.50 to ₺2) also depart for the beaches from beside the Tansaş supermarket sign south of the main square.

Car

Navigating Ayvalık old town's fiendishly narrow lanes can be an extremely stressful experience. You'd be better off parking at one of the car parks along the waterfront. They generally cost ₺8/12 per day/night.

Taxi

A taxi from the otogar to the town centre costs ₺7.

Alibey Island

Named after a hero of the Turkish War of Independence, Alibey Island, known to the locals as Cunda, lies just offshore, facing Ayvalık across the water. It's linked to the mainland by a causeway and is generally regarded as a quieter extension of Ayvalık itself, with residents of both communities regularly shuttling back and forth between the two. Accessible both by dolmuş taxi and the more pleasant option of the ferry, the island makes for a fine day trip from Ayvalık.

The ferry will drop you at a small quay, in front of which is a long line of fish restaurants. Behind these sits a small, distinguished-looking town made up of old (and in parts rather dilapidated) Greek stone houses. As with Ayvalık, the people here were compelled into a population exchange in the early 1920s; in this instance with Muslims from Crete.

Just to the right of the ferry stop is the town's main square. There are ATMs on the seafront and an information board with maps in the car park at the eastern end of the esplanade. Behind the square is a small tourist market with stalls selling jewellery and other trinkets.

One of the most famous relics of the town's Greek past, the **Taksiyarhis church** (not to be confused with the church of the same name in Ayvalık), perches on a small hill, just inland from the tourist market. Though it avoided being turned into a mosque, the church suffered severe damage during an earthquake in 1944, and today stands in picturesque decrepitude. Inside are some faded and rather forlorn-looking frescoes.

The nicest parts of the island are west, where there are good beaches for sunbathing and swimming, and to the north, much of which is taken up by the **Pateriça Nature Reserve**. This has good walking routes and, on the north shore, the ruins of the Greek **Ayışığı Manastırı** (Moonlight Monastery).

🛏 Sleeping

Tutku Pansiyon PENSION €€
(✆327 1965; www.tutkupansiyon.com; Sahil Restorantları ve Taşkahve Arkası; s/d ₺40/80; ❄🛜) Alibey's best pension, 'Passion' is located in the heart of Cunda, beside a cool wine house and a few streets back from the water. It has five small, fragrant, simple rooms with red tiled floors, small TVs and fridges. The owner is relaxed and hospitable.

Ada Kamping CAMPING GROUND €
(✆327 1211; www.adacamping.com; camp site per person ₺15, caravan/bungalow per person ₺50/70; ☺Apr-Nov) This large, well-equipped camping ground lies 3km to the west of town. The air-conditioned bungalows are simple but spotless, although the caravans and the grounds are a little worn-looking. The site boasts its own beach and waterside restaurant (mains ₺15), plus a kitchen for guest use.

🍴 Eating & Drinking

Lal Girit Mutfağı CRETAN €
(✆327 2834; Altay Pansiyon Yanı 20; meze ₺6, beer ₺6; ☺dinner) At this *mutfak* (restaurant serving home cooking) and local hang-out, Emine serves delicious *Girit* (Cretan) dishes learnt from her grandmother, including *peynirli kabak* (courgette with feta cheese) and *briam* (vegetable stew). You can even BYO fish and they'll cook it for you (₺10).

Lezzet Diyarı SEAFOOD €€
(✆327 1016; Çarşı Caddesi 17; meze ₺6-12; ☺1-11pm) Even by Turkish standards, the fridge in this small blue-and-white restaurant is heaving with meze. Hot dishes include Aegean staples such as octopus casserole.

TOP CHOICE **Taş Kahve** BAR, CAFE
(Sahil Boyu 20; tea ₺0.75, beer ₺6; ☺7am-midnight) It's worth the trip just to sip tea and talk fishing in this cavernous venue adorned with period photos and artwork on its cracked concrete walls. Here it's backgammon inside, children outside, and everyone else in between.

ℹ Getting There & Away

BOAT Boats to Alibey Island (₺4, 15 minutes, every 15 minutes, June to early September) leave from a quay behind the tourist kiosk just off the main square in Ayvalık.

CAR & DOLMUŞ On the other side of the road, you can pick up a dolmuş taxi across the causeway to the island (₺2, 20 minutes). They run between 6am and midnight, and drop off at the eastern end of Alibey esplanade, where there's also a car park (₺4).

TAXI These typically cost ₺25 between the island and central Ayvalık.

Bergama (Pergamum)

✆0232 / POP 60,559

Bergama, a laid-back market town, is the modern successor to the once-powerful ancient city of Pergamum. Unlike Ephesus, which heaves with tourists year-round, Pergamum is a site of quiet, classical splendour. Those who do make it here are invariably enamoured with the uncrowded access to the Asclepion, ancient Rome's pre-eminent medical centre, and the staggering mountainside Acropolis.

There has been a town here since Trojan times, but Pergamum's heyday was during the period between Alexander the

IZMIR & THE NORTH AEGEAN BERGAMA (PERGAMUM)

Great and the Roman domination of all Asia Minor, when it was one of the Middle East's richest and most powerful small kingdoms.

History

Pergamum owed its prosperity to Lysimachus, one of Alexander the Great's generals, who took control of much of the Aegean region when Alexander's far-flung empire fell apart after his death in 323 BC. In the battles over the spoils Lysimachus captured a great treasure, estimated at over 9000 gold talents, which he entrusted to his commander in Pergamum, Philetarus, before going off to fight Seleucus for control of Asia Minor. But Lysimachus lost the battle and was killed in 281 BC, whereupon Philetarus set himself up as governor.

Philetarus, a eunuch, was succeeded by his nephew Eumenes I (263–241 BC), who was in turn followed by his adopted son, Attalus I (241–197 BC). Attalus declared himself king, expanding his power and forging an alliance with Rome.

During the reign of Attalus' son, Eumenes II (197–159 BC), Pergamum achieved its greatest glory. Rich and powerful, Eumenes founded a library that would in time rival that of Alexandria, Egypt, then the world's greatest repository of knowledge. He also added the Altar of Zeus to the buildings already crowning the Acropolis, built the 'middle city' on terraces halfway down the hill, and expanded and beautified the Asclepion. Inevitably, much of what the Pergamese kings built hasn't survived the ravages of the centuries (or the acquisitive enthusiasm of Western museums), but what has survived is impressive, dramatically sited and well worth visiting.

Eumenes' brother Attalus II kept up the good work but under his son, Attalus III, the kingdom began to fall apart again. With no heir, Attalus III bequeathed his kingdom to Rome, and the kingdom of Pergamum became the Roman province of Asia in 129 BC.

◉ Sights & Activities

Bergama's attractions open from 8.30am to 6.30pm daily between June and September and 8.30am to 5.30pm in low season (except the museum, which is closed on Monday). Of the four main sights, only the museum is in the town centre. The two main archaeological sites are on top of steep hills, several kilometres out of town.

Acropolis   RUINS

(Akropol; admission ₺20) The road up to the Acropolis winds 5km from the Red Basilica to a car park (₺3) at the top, with some souvenir and refreshment stands nearby. A short cut shaves a couple of kilometres from the walk; opposite the Red Basilica, take Mahmut Şevket Paşa Sokak, the narrow lane between Aklar Gıda groceries and a carpet shop, which leads to the Lower Agora.

A line of rather faded (and in some places completely obliterated) blue dots marks a suggested route around the main structures, which include the **library** as well as the marble-columned **Temple of Trajan**, built during the reigns of the emperors Trajan and Hadrian and used to worship them as well as Zeus. It's the only Roman structure surviving on the Acropolis, and its foundations were used as cisterns during the Middle Ages.

Immediately downhill from the temple, descend through the tunnel to the vertigo-inducing, 10,000-seat **theatre**. Impressive and unusual, its builders decided to take advantage of the spectacular view, and conserve precious space on top of the hill, by building the theatre into the hillside. In general, Hellenistic theatres are wider and rounder than this, but at Pergamum the hillside location made rounding impossible and so it was increased in height instead.

Acropolis

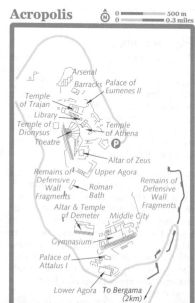

Ⓝ 0 ———— 500 m
0 ———— 0.3 miles

Arsenal
Barracks
Palace of Eumenes II
Temple of Trajan
Library
Temple of Dionysus
Temple of Athena
Theatre
Ⓟ
Altar of Zeus
Remains of Defensive Wall Fragments
Upper Agora
Roman Bath
Remains of Defensive Wall Fragments
Altar & Temple of Demeter
Middle City
Gymnasium
Palace of Attalus I
Lower Agora
To Bergama (2km)

Asclepion

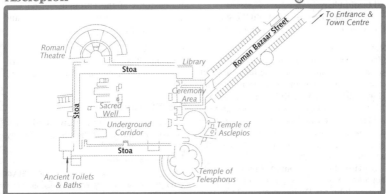

N   0 ▬▬▬▬ 50m

To Entrance &
Town Centre

Roman Bazaar Street

Roman
Theatre

Library

Stoa

Ceremony
Area

Stoa

Sacred
Well

Underground
Corridor

Temple of
Asclepios

Stoa

Ancient Toilets
& Baths

Temple of
Telesphorus

Above the stage is the ruined **Temple of Dionysus**, while below the theatre is the **Altar of Zeus**, which was originally covered with magnificent friezes depicting the battle between the Olympian gods and their subterranean foes. However, 19th-century German excavators were allowed to remove most of this famous building to Berlin, leaving only the base behind.

Piles of rubble on top of the Acropolis are marked as palaces, including that of **Eumenes II**, and you can see fragments of the once-magnificent defensive **walls**.

To escape the crowds and get a good view of the theatre and Temple of Trajan, walk downhill behind the Altar of Zeus, or turn left at the bottom of the theatre steps, and follow the sign to the *antik yol* (antique street). Ruins, including a gymnasium, sprawl down the hill to a building on the site of the **Middle City** protecting part of a peristyle court and some fantastic **mosaic floors**; look for the grotesque faces at the far end. With sights beyond including the **Lower Agora**, from here you could ruin hop back to the foot of the hill, taking the short cut suggested in the opposite direction.

Asclepion
RUINS

(Temple of Asclepios; admission/parking ₺15/3) An ancient medical centre, the Asclepion was founded by Archias, a local who had been cured at the Asclepion of Epidaurus (Greece). Treatments included mud baths, the use of herbs and ointments, enemas and sunbathing. Diagnosis was often by dream analysis.

Pergamum's centre came to the fore under Galen (AD 131–210), who was born here and studied in Alexandria, Greece and Asia Minor before setting up shop as physician to Pergamum's gladiators. Recognised as perhaps the greatest early physician, Galen added considerably to knowledge of the circulatory and nervous systems, and also systematised medical theory. Under his influence, the medical school at Pergamum became renowned. His work was the basis for Western medicine well into the 16th century.

The Asclepion is 2km uphill from the town centre as the crow flies (but it's a winding road), signposted from Cumhuriyet Caddesi just north of the tourist office and PTT. A second road runs from Böblingen Pension, southwest of town. It's closed to motorists and we don't recommend walking it, as it passes through a large military base; if you do, be off it by dusk and don't take photos.

A Roman **bazaar street**, once lined with shops, leads from the entrance to the centre, where you'll see the base of a column carved with snakes, the symbol of Asclepios (Aesculapius), god of medicine. Just as the snake sheds its skin and gains a 'new life', so the patients at the Asclepion were supposed to 'shed' their illnesses. Signs mark a circular **Temple of Asclepios**, a **library** and, beyond it, a **Roman theatre**.

You can take a drink from the **sacred well**, although the plastic tube out of which the water flows doesn't look particularly inviting, and pass along the vaulted underground corridor to the **Temple of Telesphorus**, another god of medicine. Patients slept in the temple hoping that Telesphorus would send a cure or diagnosis in a dream. The names of Telesphorus' two daughters,

Hygeia and Panacea, have passed into medical terminology.

Soft drinks are available from the stalls by the Asclepion car park, albeit at a premium.

Red Basilica   RUINS

(Kınık Caddesi; admission ₺5) The cathedral-sized Red Basilica was originally a giant temple to the Egyptian gods Serapis, Isis and Harpocrates, built in the 2nd century AD. It's still an imposing-looking place, though rather scattered and battered-looking these days. Be careful as you make you way around as several sections of the basilica's high walls are severely damaged.

During its pagan pomp, this must have been an awe-inspiring place. In his Revelation, St John the Divine wrote that this was one of the seven churches of the Apocalypse, singling it out as the throne of the devil. Look for a hole in the podium in the centre, which allowed a priest to hide and appear to speak through the 10m-high cult statue. The building is so big that the Christians didn't convert it into a church but built a basilica inside it. The most intact section, the southern rotunda, was used for religious and cult rituals; once covered in marble panels, it is now just red brick.

Along with the glass-topped northern rotunda, the curious red flat-brick walls of this large, roofless structure are visible from midway down the roads to the Acropolis and town centre. You can easily walk to the Red Basilica, or stop your taxi here on your way to/from the Acropolis.

Archaeology Museum   MUSEUM

(Arkeoloji Müzesi; ☑631 2884; Cumhuriyet Caddesi; admission ₺5) Right in the centre of town, the Archaeology Museum boasts a small but substantial collection of artefacts, including Greek, Roman and Byzantine gravestones, busts and pillars. Most interestingly, it features a collection of statues from the 4th century BC that formed part of the so-called 'Pergamum School', when sculptors, breaking with the more grotesque and stylised traditions of previous centuries, first began to represent the gods as recognisably human with expressive features. Other finds from the surrounding sites include a smashed Roman tablet listing city laws, discovered at the Lower Agora on the Acropolis.

Look out, too, for the scale replica of the Altar of Zeus (the original is in Berlin) and, in the main hall, finds from the nearby, and now underwater, site of Allianoi. The ethnography gallery focuses on the crafts and customs of the Ottoman period with dioramas representing folk dancing and carpet weaving.

Hacı Hekim Hamamı   HAMAM

(Cumhuriyet Caddesi; ⏰6am-11pm) This 16th-century hamam charges ₺40 for the full works.

🛏 Sleeping

The northern end of Cumhuriyet Caddesi, in the old part of town, is the best area to stay.

TOP CHOICE Hera Boutique
Hotel   BOUTIQUE HOTEL €€€

(☑631 0634; www.hotelhera.com; Tabrak Körpü Caddesi 21; d from ₺200; P❄🛜) A pair of 200-year-old Greek houses have been converted into Bergama's newest and most sophisticated accommodation. Each of the 10 rooms, named after mythological Greek deities, features timber ceilings, parquetry floorboards and curios handpicked by the erudite couple in charge. Zeus is a beauty, with two balconies, while Nike, in the second buliding, just does it. The breakfast spread comes highly recommended.

Odyssey Guesthouse   PENSION €

(☑631 3501; www.odysseyguesthouse.com; Abacıhan Sokak 13; dm ₺20, s/d from ₺45/50, s/d without bathroom from ₺35/45) This grand old house is still a good choice, with superb views of the Red Basilica from the upstairs terrace. The main building has some basic doubles, with excellent showers. Self-caterers enjoy the small kitchenette and separate sleeping area. There's a book exchange, and a copy of Homer's *Odyssey* in every room.

Citi Hostel   HOSTEL €

(☑830 0668; Bankalar Caddesi 10; dm/s/d ₺30/35/60; ❄🛜) Beside the hamam is this great new, old-school hostel run by the friendly and irrepressible Imdat (translation: *help*), a Turkish-Australian chap with decades of travel experience. Basic, spotless rooms on two levels encircle a spacious courtyard filled with bright green, fake grass, orange furniture and two large trees.

Les Pergamon   BOUTIQUE HOTEL €€€

(☑632 3935; www.lespergamon.com; Taksim Caddesi 35; d from ₺200; P❄🛜) Another recently opened boutique hotel is this gorgeous stone property that served as a Greek school in a previous life. The rooms have high ceilings,

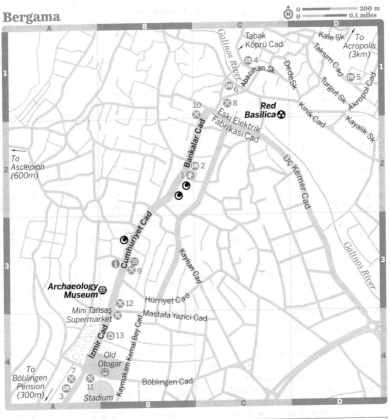

Bergama

⊚ Top Sights

Archaeology Museum	B3
Red Basilica	C1

⊕ Activities, Courses & Tours

1 Hacı Hekim Hamamı	B2

🛏 Sleeping

2 Citi Hostel	C2
3 Gobi Pension	A4
4 Hera Boutique Hotel	C1
5 Les Pergamon	D1
6 Odyssey Guesthouse	C1

⊗ Eating

Bergama Sofrası	(see 2)
7 Kervan	A4
8 Paksoy Pide	C1
9 Sağlam Restaurant	B3
10 Sarmaşık Lokantası	C1
11 Simge Pastanesi ve Simit Dünyasi	A4
12 Zıkkım	B3

🛍 Shopping

13 Yanikoğlu Supermarket	B4

wooden floors and black or white bedspreads and rugs. Some bathrooms are in original stone. 'King Zeus' is a touch more regal. If you don't stay, splurge on a meal in the garden restaurant.

Gobi Pension　　　　　　　　PENSION €
(☎633 2518; www.gobipension.com; İzmir Caddesi 18; s/d ₺40/65, s/d without bathroom ₺25/45; ❄@) This very popular family-run place has 12 bright rooms of varying quality. Those at the front have double glazing to keep the

ℹ PERGAMUM CABLE CAR

To spend more time enjoying the ruins, and avoid the steep ascent, take the **cable car** (one way ₺4) up to the Acropolis, and then walk back down via the oft-overlooked **gymnasium**.

traffic noise out and those at the back overlook a garden; some have balconies. It's well set up for travellers, with a kitchen, laundry service and help on hand from English-speaking Mustafa.

✗ Eating

TOP CHOICE Kervan TURKISH €€

(☎633 2632; İzmir Caddesi; mains ₺12; ✳) Kervan is popular among locals for its large outdoor terrace and excellent food. The menu features a good range of kebaps, pide, *çorba* (soup) and, for dessert, *künefe* (syrup-soaked dough and sweet cheese sprinkled with pistachios). It's cheap but prices are not listed.

Bergama Ticaret Odası Sosyal Tesisleri RESTAURANT €€

(☎632 9641; Ulucamii Mahallesi; mains ₺15; ☉9am-midnight) Run by the municipality, this is the best restaurant serving alcohol. The outdoor terrace and school cafeteria–style interior have panoramic views and reasonable food. It's located in a park 300m up the hill behind the main street. Avoid walking in the area at night.

Sağlam Restaurant RESTAURANT €€

(☎667 2003; Yeni Otogat Yanı; mains ₺12; ☉11.30am-3pm & 6pm-midnight) This Bergama favourite has moved out of town to the Opet garage by the otogar. Despite the proximity of the petrol pumps, it has a pleasant dining environment and an unlimited buffet. Beer, meze, pide and kebaps are also offered.

Simge Pastanesi ve Simit Dünyasi BAKERY €

(İzmir Caddesi; baklava & ice cream ₺4; ☉24 hr) Along with the neighbouring Simgecan Pastanesi, run by the same family, this is considered the best patisserie in town.

Paksoy Pide PIDE €

(İslamsaray Mahallesi; pide ₺3.50-5.50) Pint-sized Paksoy is clean and patronised by locals. Watch the chef rolling and flipping the pide classics in front of the oven.

Sarmaşik Lokantası TURKISH €

(☎632 2741; Istiklal Meydani 6; mains ₺8) One of the more dependable local restaurants on the main street, with a heavy rotation of village stews, soups and rice dishes.

Zıkkım CAFE €

(Cumhuriyet Caddesi; mains ₺5-9; ☉10.30am-1am) With shady garden seating just off the main road, Zıkkım makes a welcome midtown pit stop, offering cheap *köfte* and salads (white-bean salad ₺4).

Bergama Sofrası TURKISH €

(☎631 5131; Bankalar Caddesi 44) Sit outside next to the hamam or inside the diner-like interior, with its clean surfaces and open kitchen under bright lights. The spicy *köfte* (₺8) is the speciality. Best to eat here at lunch when the food is still fresh.

Market MARKET

(☉8am-6pm) Bergama has a bustling Monday market, which stretches from the old otogar to past the Red Basilica. It's great for fresh fruit and veg. Böblingen Caddesi and the area around the old bus station are good for picnic provisions. Cheese, olives, fresh bread and dried fruit are all sold.

Yanikoğlu Supermarket SUPERMARKET

(İzmir Caddesi; ☉8am-midnight) A supermarket stocking all the essentials.

ℹ Information

Modern Bergama lies spread out either side of one long main street, along which almost everything you'll need can be found, including hotels, restaurants, banks, the PTT and museum.

Tourist Office (☎631 2851; İzmir Caddesi 54; ☉8.30am-noon & 1-5.30pm) Just north of the museum, the board outside has useful information such as bus and minibus times.

ℹ Getting There & Away

Bus

Bergama's *yeni* (new) otogar lies 7km from the centre, at the junction of the İzmir–Çanakkale highway and the main road into town. Between 6am and 7pm, a free *servis* shuttles between there and the *eski* (old) otogar in the town centre. Outside these hours you will have to take a taxi (about ₺25). Some buses from Çanakkale drop you at the junction near the otogar, from where you can walk to the bus station and pick up the *servis*.

ANKARA ₺55, eight to nine hours, 480km, nightly

AYVALIK ₺8, 1¼ hours, 60km, every hour

İSTANBUL (via Bursa) ₺50, 11 hours, 250km, nightly with additional morning services in high season

İZMİR ₺10, two hours, 110km, every 45 minutes

Dolmuş

In the early morning and evening, half-hourly dolmuşes to Ayvalık and Çandarlı leave from the old otogar; in between, they leave from the new otogar.

❶ Getting Around

Bergama's sights are so spread out that it's hard to walk around them all in one day. The Red Basilica is over 1km from the tourist office, the Asclepion is 2km away and the Acropolis is over 5km away.

BUS Between 6am and 7pm, half-hourly buses run through town between the old otogar and the market area (₺2), 200m past the Red Basilica at the foot of the road up to the Acropolis.

TAXI A convenient option is to book a 'city tour'. From the centre to the Asclepion, Red Basilica and Acropolis, with 30 minutes at the first two sights and an hour at the last, should cost around ₺50. Taxis wait around some of the mosques and the otogars. Individual fares from the taxi rank near Köy Evi are about ₺8 to the Asclepion, and ₺15 to the Acropolis.

Çandarlı

📞 0232

The small and tranquil resort town of Çandarlı (ancient Pitane) sits on a peninsula jutting into the Aegean, 33km southwest of Bergama. It's dominated by a small but stately 14th-century restored Genoese **castle** (admission free; ⏰ 24hr Jul & Aug) and has a sandier beach than some of its neighbours.

Local tourism fills most of the pensions in high summer. From late October to April/May it's pretty much a ghost town.

Shops, internet cafes and the PTT are in the centre, 200m behind the seafront. The castle, pensions and restaurants line the seashore. Market day is Friday.

🛏 Sleeping

Most of the hotels and pensions lie west of the castle, facing a thin strip of coarse sand.

Otel Samyeli   HOTEL €€
(📞 673 3428; www.otelsamyeli.com; s/d/tr ₺45/90/130; ❄) Right on the beachfront, Otel Samyeli has simple, spotless and cheerful rooms (number 11, which is a triple, has

KALEM ISLAND

Located just 450m from the shore near Bademli village, 18km northwest of Çandarlı, lies Kalem Adası (Kalem Island), a small island of great natural beauty. It's possible to swim there, otherwise local fishermen are your best bet.

There's an overpriced **resort** (www .olivieraresort.com) that arranges **boat trips**, but we recommend a day trip instead. Some travellers claim you can camp wild on the far side of the island, but much of the island is private property so tread carefully.

a sofa and a sea view) and a seafront fish restaurant (mains ₺15). Reserve in advance (a week in summer).

Emirgan Beach Hotel   HOTEL €
(📞 673 2500; www.otelsamyeli.com; Sahil Plaj Caddesi; s/d ₺50/80; ❄) Operated by the same owners as Otel Samyeli, the Emirgan is 150m to the west and right on the beach. It's older than Samyeli but has more character, with long white balconies leading to the quiet rooms.

🍴 Eating & Drinking

For fresh fruit, the daily çarşı (market), in the shadow of the town mosque, is a good place to replenish. There's also a Tanşaş supermarket, and ice-cream stalls on the seafront east of the castle.

Köşem Lokantası   TURKISH €
(📞 673 2132; PTT Sokak 3; mains ₺4-9; ⏰ 10am-10pm) A big hit at lunchtime, this lokanta serves a plethora of eats including pide, köfte, İskender kebap and daily specials. It's 200m behind Otel Samyeli on the left, across the main road from the park.

Deniz Restaurant   SEAFOOD €€
(📞 673 3124; Sahil Plaj Caddesi; mains ₺12; ⏰ 11am-11pm) With tables right on the seafront, the 'Sea Restaurant' is friendly and good value, serving all the usual meze and fish dishes plus meat options.

❶ Getting There & Away

Frequent buses run between Çandarlı and İzmir (₺12, 1½ hours) via Dikili (₺3, 15 minutes). At least six dolmuşes run daily to and from Bergama (₺4, 30 minutes).

Yeni Foça

☑ 0232 / POP 3470

This small resort town set around a harbour boasts a strip of coarse beach, and a wealth of crumbling Ottoman mansions and old Greek stone houses. Long discovered by second-home hunters, Yeni Foça now has its fair share of modern monstrosities alongside the aged marvels. There are some more secluded beaches to the south towards Foça (Eski Foça).

The best hotel in town is the **Griffon Boutique Hotel** (☑ 814 77 77; www.griffonbutik otel.com; Fabrika Sokak 2; s/d ₺120/200), situated in a former olive-press factory and run by astute, all-female staff. A cobblestone laneway splitting two wings fills with guests during the summer months. Rooms are dotted with 1930s-era furniture and the restaurant is excellent.

In an attractive one-storey stone building, **Kıvanç Café & Restaurant** (☑ 814 7857; Sahil Caddesi 67; mains ₺10) offers a good mix of meat and fish dishes, including chicken şiş kebap (recommended), pizzas and pide. Seating is on the covered terrace or underneath a fat palm tree by the beach.

The town has a PTT, internet cafe and ATMs. Buses leave every half-hour to İzmir (₺10, 1¾ hours) and every three hours to Foça (₺4). Taxis to Foça cost around ₺40.

Foça

☑ 0232 / POP 28.629

Sometimes called Eski Foça (Old Foça) to distinguish it from its newer neighbour (Yeni Foça) over the hill, this happy-go-lucky holiday town straddles both Büyük Deniz (Big Sea) and the picturesque Küçük Deniz (Small Sea). Its Ottoman-Greek houses are among the finest on the Aegean coast and open onto a storybook esplanade where children fish and couples stroll from pension to restaurant in the shadows of Beskipılar castle.

Foça was once the site of ancient Phocaeai, which takes its name from the seals basking offshore at Siren Rocks and was founded before 600 BC. During their golden age (5th century BC), the Phocaeans were great mariners, sending swift vessels powered by 50 oars into the Aegean, Mediterranean and Black Seas. They were also keen colonists, founding Samsun on the Black Sea, as well as towns in Italy, Corsica, France and Spain.

More recently, this was an Ottoman-Greek fishing and trading town. It's now a prosperous, middle-class resort, with holiday villas gathered on the outskirts and a thin, dusty beach with some swimming platforms. There are some more secluded beaches to the north towards Yeni Foça.

The otogar is just inland from the Büyük Deniz. Heading north from here, with the Büyük Deniz and its accompanying tour boats on your left, takes you through the centre of town to the Küçük Deniz. You will pass the tourist office, the PTT and banks, before reaching the harbour after around 350m. Continue north along the Küçük Deniz's right-hand (eastern) side to find the pensions.

◎ Sights & Activities

FREE Ancient Phocaea Ruins   RUINS
Little remains of the ancient Ionian city: a ruined theatre, remains of an aqueduct near the otogar, an *anıt mezarı* (monumental tomb) which is 7km east of town on the way to the İzmir highway on the left, and traces of two shrines to the goddess Cybele.

Temple of Athena   RUINS
In recent years, the townsfolk made this exciting discovery above the outdoor sanctuary of Cybele. The site was found to contain, among other things, a beautiful griffin and a horse's head believed to date to the 5th century BC. Excavations are undertaken there every summer; visits should be possible by the time you read this.

Beşkapılar   FORTRESS
(Five Gates) If you continue past the outdoor sanctuary of Cybele, you'll come to the city walls and the partially rebuilt Beşkapılar castle, built by the Byzantines, repaired by the Genoese and the Ottomans in 1538–39, and clearly much restored since.

Dışkale   FORTRESS
(External Fortress) Guarding the town's southwestern approaches, the 17th-century Dışkale is best seen from the water (on a boat trip) as it's inside a military zone.

Boat Trips   CRUISE
Between late April and early October, boats leave daily at about 11am from both the Küçük Deniz and Büyük Deniz for day trips around the outlying islands with various swim stops en route, returning about 6.30pm. Most visit Siren Rocks, and typically cost ₺30, including lunch and tea. One

FOÇA'S SEALS

Foça's offshore islands provide some of the last remaining homes to the endangered Mediterranean monk seal, once common throughout the region. There are thought to be fewer than 400 left in the world, so you shouldn't bank on seeing one. Thankfully, much of Foça's offshore area is now a protected zone, the extent of which was increased in 2007. For more information on the Mediterranean monk seal, contact the Ankara-based **SAD-AFAG** (Underwater Research Society-Mediterranean Seal Research Group; ☑0312 443 0581; www.sadafag.org), which oversees protection programs on the coast.

The seals' habit of basking on rocks and their wailing plaintive cries are believed to have been the inspiration for the legend of the Sirens, as featured in Homer's *Odyssey*.

According to legend, the sirens were strange creatures, half-bird, half-woman, who lived on rocky islands. They used their beautiful, irresistible singing voices to lure sailors towards their perilous perches, where the ships would be dashed against the rocks, and the sailors killed. Odysseus, so the story goes, only managed to resist their entreaties by having himself lashed to his ship's mast.

Appropriately enough, one of the seals' favourite modern basking spots is the Siren Kayalıkları (Siren Rocks) on Orak Island, just off Foça's shore, although these days it is the seals' lives, rather than those of local sailors, that are in danger.

İZMİR & THE NORTH AEGEAN FOÇA

of the better operators is **Valinor: Lord of the Boats** (☑798 6317; info@valinortour.com; Büyük Deniz).

Belediye Hamamı HAMAM
(☑812 1959; 115 Sokak 22; ⊗8am-midnight) Treatments cost ₺15 to ₺30 at this tourist-friendly hamam.

🛏 Sleeping

A lot of accommodation is pretty shabby here, especially in summer, but a few nicer options have popped up recently.

There are camping grounds on the coast north of Foça.

TOP CHOICE Lola 38 Hotel HOTEL €€€
(☑812 3809; www.lola38hotel.com; Reha Midilli 140; d ₺180-350) If you have a hard-core doll fetish, a penchant for Marie Antionette, or a love of living inside a wedding cake, here's a novel place. Lola 38 is a sweet, converted Greek stone house on the quiet end of the smaller bay that employs overstatement and fairy dust as its chief design principles. Lots of fun, quite posh and supremely comfortable, this is a must for kinky honeymooners and those tired of the humdrum hotel room.

Bülbül Yuvası Hotel BOUTIQUE HOTEL €€€
(Nightingale's Nest; ☑812 5152; www.bulbulyuvasi.com.tr; 121 Sokak 20; r ₺250-400; P❋🐕) The 'Nightingale's Nest' is a designer refuge in sleepy little Foça. The seven rooms are beautifully appointed, and feature heavy drapery and wooden floors. Caria and Veria are a little pokey for the price, while the sea views from

the two Alalia rooms lift them up a category. It's down a dead-end lane, so silence abounds.

Siren Pansiyon PENSION €
(☑812 2660; www.sirenpansiyon.com; 161 Sokak 13; s/d ₺40/80) Popular with German and British travellers, the Siren was undergoing a welcome makeover at the time of research. The location is excellent, tucked off the promenade, and return guests continually rave about Remzi's hospitality and the breakfast on the roof terrace.

İyon Pansiyon PENSION €€
(☑812 1415; www.iyonpansion.com; 198 Sokak 8; s/d ₺60/100) İyon is a great choice for independent travellers. The mood on the two terraces is unobtrusive, yet communal. The rooms are simple, but recently renovated, and those downstairs open onto a shared courtyard. There are sea views from an upstairs room and the reception-breakfast area.

🍴 Eating

Foça's dining scene is mostly Turkish pescatarian. There is a decent Tuesday market, which is a good place to stock up for a picnic, and various grocery stores.

TOP CHOICE Fokai Restaurant RESTAURANT €€
(☑812 2186; 121 Sokak 8; mains ₺8-20; ⊗10am-midnight) Overlooking Büyük Deniz, Fokai is the most dependable restaurant in town. The atmosphere is understated and the service is sincere. In summertime, the terrace fills with Turks and foreign tourists chowing

down yummy, fresh meze like *pancar* (beetroot) and *brokoli*, superb seafood grills and casseroles and pretty good pizza.

Çarşı Lokantası
TURKISH €€

(☑812 2377; Küçük Deniz Caddesi 18; mains ₺8-18) This *lokanta* is the best place in town for lunch. A mixed plate (with meat) typically includes *köfte*, stew, *kalamar* and half a dozen vegetables and starches, sprinkled with herbs and spices by the friendly Mesut. Treat yourself to a pudding with ice cream; you won't regret it.

Letafet
TURKISH €€

(☑812 1191; 197 Sokak 3; mains ₺15-30) This new restaurant is hidden behind a white wall in the old town, but the giveaway is the loud music and the din of ambient noise and clinking cutlery. Happy diners enjoy classic Turkish cuisine at reasonable prices.

Harika Köfte Evi
KÖFTE €

(Wonderful Köfte House; ☑812 5409; Belediye Karşısı; mains ₺8) In addition to four types of *köfte* – reputedly the best in town – the Wonderful Köfte House serves *çorba* and *tavuk şiş* (roast skewered chicken kebap).

Ülker Pastanesi
BAKERY €

(☑814 7119; Nayap Dinçer Caddesi 25; pastries from ₺2) This flash patisserie on a charming corner is perfect for stocking up on cakes and biscuits before hitting the road or the beach.

🍷 Drinking

Keyif
BAR, CAFE

(Sahil Caddesi 42a; beer ₺7) Funky for Foça – it's got a glitter ball – Keyif offers both Western music and live Turkish performers; dancing has been known to take place inside.

❶ Information

Fokai 2 Internet Café (194 Sokak; per hr ₺1.50; ⊙8.30am-midnight) Just off the main square.
Tourist Office (☑812 1222; fax 812 1222; Cumhuriyet Meydanı; ⊙8.30am-noon & 1-5.30pm Mon-Fri, 10am-7pm Sat Jun-Sep) Very helpful, with lots of brochures.

❶ Getting There & Around

Bus

BERGAMA Take the bus to Menemen/İzmir, jump off on the highway and flag down any bus heading north.

İZMİR & MENEMEN Between 6.30am and 9.15pm (11pm in summer) half-hourly buses run to İzmir (₺8, 1½ hours, 86km), passing through Menemen (for connections to Manisa).

YENİ FOÇA Three to five city buses run daily to/from Yeni Foça (₺4, 30 minutes, 22km); the timetable is in the otogar. These buses pass the pretty, small coves, beaches and camping grounds north of Foça.

Car

If you're staying in the area for a few days you could hire a car from **MNB Oto Kiralama** (☑812 1987; www.mnbrentacar.com; 123 Sokak 6; 1 day ₺85), behind the police station on the Büyük Deniz.

İzmir

☑0232 / POP 2.8 MILLION

The grand port city of İzmir, Turkey's third-largest, is a proudly liberal, long-time centre of commerce that has emerged as a smart alternative base for travel in the west of the country. Formerly the famed Greek city of Smyrna, İzmir lives by its *kordon* (seafront) which, especially around leafy Alsancak, is as fetching and lively as any large seaside city in the world.

With its Levantine and Jewish heritage, İzmir is proudly distinct from the rest of Turkey; indeed, its fellow countrymen sometimes still regard İzmiris with a degree of suspicion. That's certainly not to say there aren't Turkish flags aplenty between the palms, but İzmir does have a liberal, laid-back feel. During Ramazan, when some bars in İstanbul and elsewhere close, it's business as usual in the countless watering holes on the balmy *kordon*.

İzmir is also developing a reputation for its cultural and civic foresight. The International Arts Festival in June is adventurous and vast, while a number of decrepit industrial bulidings have found new life as communal and creative spaces.

History

İzmir was once Smyrna, a city founded by colonists from Greece sometime in the early part of the 1st millennium BC. Over the next 1000 years it would grow in importance as it came under the influence of successive regional powers: first Lydia, then Greece, and finally Rome. By the 2nd century AD it was, along with Ephesus and Pergamum, one of the three most important cities in the Roman province of Asia. Under Byzantine rule, however, its fortunes declined as the focus of government turned north to Constantinople. Things only began to look up again when the Ottomans took control in 1415, after which Smyrna rapidly became Turkey's most sophisticated commercial city.

After the collapse of the Ottoman Empire at the end of WWI, the Greeks invaded, but were eventually expelled following fierce fighting which, along with a subsequent fire, destroyed most of the old city. The day that Atatürk recaptured Smyrna (9 September 1922) marked the moment of victory in the Turkish War of Independence, and it's now the biggest local holiday. The events of 1922 are commemorated in the rather top-heavy monument gracing the waterfront.

◉ Sights

Kordon & Alsancak   SEAFRONT, NEIGHBOURHOOD
It's difficult to imagine life in İzmir without its iconic boulevard. A triumph of urban renewal, the *kordon*'s pedestrianised confines are home to a great selection of bars and restaurants that attract droves of people at the end of the day to watch the picture-perfect sunsets. Inland, the Alsancak district is now the focus of the city's nightlife and fashion.

Konak Meydanı   SQUARE
On a pedestrianised stretch of Cumhuriyet Bulvarı, this wide plaza, named after the Ottoman **government mansion** (*hükümet konağı*), pretty much marks the heart of the city; signs pointing to the centre simply say 'Konak'. It's the site of a late Ottoman clock tower (*saat kulesi*) built in 1901 to mark the 25th anniversary of Sultan Abdül Hamit II's coronation. Its ornate Orientalist style may have been meant to atone for Smyrna's European ambience. Beside it is the lovely **Konak Camii**, dating from 1755, which is covered in Kütahya tiles.

Agora   RUINS
(Agora Caddesi; admission ₺8; ⊘8.30am-7pm, to 5.30pm Sat; P) The ancient Agora, built for Alexander the Great, was ruined in an earthquake in AD 178, but rebuilt soon after by the Roman emperor Marcus Aurelius. Colonnades of reconstructed Corinthian columns, vaulted chambers and arches give you a good idea of what a Roman bazaar must have looked like. Later, a Muslim cemetery was built on the site and many of the old tombstones can be seen around the perimeter of the Agora. The site is entered on the south side, just off Gazi Osman Paşa Bulvarı.

FREE Old Gas Factory   CULTURAL CENTRE
The site of the mid-19th-century Ottoman Gas Company has found new life as İz-

mir's latest cultural precinct. Two beautiful brick storage buildings now house art exhibitions and workshops. In summertime there's an outdoor cinema in the courtyard and a hip cafeteria in the foundry. It's located opposite the Alsancak football stadium, about 1km northeast of Alsancak train station.

Archaeology Museum   MUSEUM
(Arkeoloji Müzesi; ☑489 0796; Bahri Baba Parkı; admission ₺8; ⊘9am-5pm Tue-Sun) İzmir's Archaeology Museum is a little dry, but look out for the beautifully decorated sarcophagi, the head of a gigantic statue of Domitian that once stood at Ephesus, and the impressive frieze from the mausoleum at Belevi (250 BC). It's a short walk up the hill from Konak.

FREE Ethnography Museum   MUSEUM
(Etnografya Müzesi; ☑489 0796; ⊘8.30am-6.30pm Tue-Sun) The Ethnography Museum occupies the former St Roche Hospital, beside the Archaeology Museum. This lovely old four-storey stone building houses colourful displays (including dioramas, photos and information panels) demonstrating local arts, crafts and customs. You'll learn about everything from camel wrestling, pottery and tin-plating to felt-making, embroidery and weaponry.

Fatih Camii   MOSQUE
(Birleşmis Milletler Caddesi) Above the museums, this reconstructed, blue-tiled mosque has a small tea garden with a view down the hill, and a beautiful interior. The tiles inside show the difference between İznik designs and more-colourful, vibrant İzmir tiles with large, flowing motifs (above the windows and on the domed ceiling).

Kemeraltı Bazaar   BAZAAR
(⊘8am-5pm) İzmir's Kemeraltı Bazaar is the city's heart and soul, and a great place to get lost for a few hours. There are bargains galore, especially leather goods, clothing and jewellery. Seek out the flower and bead markets, then stop for a reviving shot of Turkish coffee in one of the delightful cafes at its core.

Anafartalar Caddesi rings the main bazaar area and is its principal thoroughfare.

Within the main bazaar, the glorious **Kızlarağası Han** (⊘8am- 5pm) is a much smaller, calmer version of İstanbul's famous Grand Bazaar. It's touristy, with many items from the far end of the Silk Road (China),

İzmir

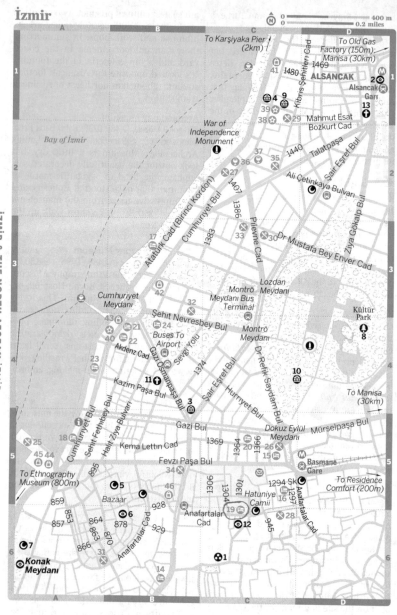

but good for a wander. There's a cafe in the courtyard, where merchants once tethered their camels.

The bazaar also contains the city's largest mosque – **Hisar Camii**. The interior is quintessentially İzmiri: the blue-and-gold motifs on the domed ceiling are simpler and less Oriental than classic Ottoman designs. Be sure to also look out for the roses and grapes carved along the bottom of the women's gallery and the designs on the stone staircase.

İzmir

Kültür Park
PARK

Much of the inland centre of town, between Alsancak and Basmane, was heavily damaged in the 1922 fire, and is now taken up by the Kültür Park. The park injects a little greenery into the city and attracts strolling couples and joggers – who have their own dedicated track. Specific attractions include a 50m parachute tower, a gorgeous Ferris wheel, some contemporary sculptures on the west side of the pond, and exhibition halls for events including the International İzmir Festival.

Museum of History & Art
MUSEUM

(Tarih ve Sanat Müzesi; ☑445 6818; Kültür Park; admission ₺3; ◷8.30am-5.30pm Tue-Sun) Containing three separate departments (Sculpture, Ceramics and Precious Artefacts), this museum gives a good overview of the region's artistic heritage. Look out for the 2nd-century-AD high relief of Poseidon and Demeter from the Agora, the late Neolithic anthropomorphic vase, and the cute sitting Aphrodites from the Roman period.

Atatürk Evi
HISTORIC BUILDING

(Atatürk Caddesi; ◷9am-noon & 1-5.15pm Tue-Sun) During İzmir's 19th-century heyday the *kordon* was lined with stately offices and fine houses. Built by a carpet merchant, this is perhaps the city's best preserved residence. Atatürk stayed here intermittently between 1930 and 1934.

Kadifekale
FORTRESS

(Rakım Elkutlu Caddesi) In the 4th century, Alexander the Great chose a secure site for Smyrna on Kadifekale (Mt Pagus), southeast of the modern city centre, erecting the fortifications that still crown the hill. The view from the 'Velvet Fortress' is magnificent, especially just before sunset. You may see Kurdish women, migrants from southeastern Anatolia, hard at work on horizontal carpet looms.

Bus 33 from Konak will carry you up the hill. Don't walk here alone near dark, as the surrounding neighbourhood is notoriously rough. Tourists have been attacked. At the time of writing, space was being cleared for a viewing park.

Şıfalı Lux Hamam   HAMAM
(☑445 2209; Anafartalar Caddesi 660; bath & massage from ₺30; ⊙8am-10pm men, 7am-6pm women) This clean hamam has a lovely domed and marble interior.

Mask Museum   MUSEUM
(☑465 3107; www.izmirmaskmuzesi.com; Cumbalı Sokak 22; ₺5; ⊙10.30am-7pm) Tucked away in an old house on a street filled with bars, this new museum has an interesting collection of ceremonial and decorative masks from around the world.

★ Festivals & Events

From mid-June to mid-July the annual **International İzmir Festival** offers performances of music and dance in Çeşme and Ephesus as well as İzmir (in the Kültür Park). Check www.iksev.org for program and ticket information.

🛏 Sleeping

İzmir's waterfront is dominated by large high-end business hotels, while inland are more budget and midrange options, particularly around Kemeraltı Bazaar and Basmane train station.

BAZAAR & BASMANE

Just southwest of Basmane train station, 1294 Sokak and 1296 Sokak boast many options that occupy restored Ottoman houses. However, this is an unsalubrious area after dark. If you want a budget hotel, we recommend heading instead to 1368 Sokak, west of the station.

Met Boutique Hotel   BOUTIQUE HOTEL €€€
(☑483 0111; www.metotel.com; Gazi Bulvari 124; d from ₺180; ꔛꔛꔛ) Met is indicative of the increased popularity of İzmir for both travel and business. The new boutique hotel in the CBD has sleek rooms with soothing colour schemes and streamlined furniture, but

could do with stand-alone desks or a little extra space. Still, the lobby cafe area is genuinely funky and the service is worthy of the world's great cities.

Hotel Baylan Basmane   HOTEL €€
(☑483 1426; www.hotelbaylan.com; 1299 Sokak 8; s/d ₺80/140) The newer Baylan is Basmane's best option. The entrance via the huge car park is a little disconcerting, but inside is a spacious and attractive hotel with a welcoming terrace out the back. All rooms have polished floorboards and large bathrooms. Management speak little English.

Konak Saray Hotel   BOUTIQUE HOTEL €€
(☑483 7755; www.konaksarayhotel.com; Anafartalar Caddesi 635; s/d ₺70/120; ꔛꔛ) Visitors should treat the Konak Saray Hotel as the best opportunity to stay in a beautifully restored old Ottoman house in İzmir. It's located in a less touristy part of the bazaar, and the inward-facing small rooms are modern (minibars, plasma screens) and well priced. There's also a great top-floor restaurant.

Residence Comfort   APARTMENT €€
(☑425 9503; www.comfortresidence.com; Gaziler Caddesi 206; s/d from €55/70; ꔛꔛ) A short taxi ride east of the city, this popular business hotel is good value and the 25 large suites are perfect for longer stays or families with small kids. The bathrooms are huge and the furniture ample for a big night in. The location is a drawback – overlooking noisy Gaziler Caddesi – but all west-bound buses go to Konak Pier.

Güzel İzmir Oteli   HOTEL €
(☑483 5069; www.guzelizmirhotel.com; 1368 Sokak 8; s/d ₺40/70) One of Basmane's better choices, the Good İzmir is friendly, safe and terribly convenient for bus and train access. The rooms are nothing special – avoid the small and damp few – but it's good value for money at the low end.

Agora Konak Saray Hotel   HOTEL €€€
(☑484 1424; www.konaksarayhotel.com/agorakonaksarayhotel; Kestelli Caddesi 113; s/d ₺150/250; ꔛꔛꔛ) Popular with tour groups, the second branch of Konak Saray is a recently renovated Ottoman home high above the Agora. The small rooms are modern and certainly lack any design pretensions, with drab brown and white colour schemes. There's a lobby restaurant. When we visited, service was flippant.

COSMOPOLITAN İZMİR

Between the early 17th and early 20th centuries, İzmir had one of the Ottoman Empire's largest populations of Levantines. The international expat community was drawn here when İzmir was one of the empire's principal trading hubs, and its influence can still be seen. Areas such as Bornova, northeast of the centre, have whole streets of Levantine houses, which reveal the various nationalities' different temperaments. French- and British-built houses have open balconies, as their owners didn't mind being glimpsed from the street, whereas the more-conservative Italians had closed balconies and the Greeks had no balconies. Visit www.levantineheritage.com for more information. Levantine sights in the centre include the following:

Alsancak train station (Ziya Gökalp Bulvarı) The 19th-century station is colonial in style, with stained-glass windows and a steam train outside.

St John's Church (Ziya Gökalp Bulvarı) This Anglican-Episcopal church was consecrated in 1902.

Jackson's (✆422 6045; Gazi Kadınlar Sokak 17; mains ₺12; ☉lunch & dinner) This restaurant was a British consular residence; the rack behind the bar was used for displaying china.

Apikam (City Museum & Archive; ✆293 3900; Şair Esref Bulvarı 1; ☉8.30am-5.30pm Mon-Sat) Formerly a fire station, built by the British in 1923, it has displays on İzmir's history and a courtyard cafe.

Konak Pier (Atatürk Caddesi) Gustave Eiffel, who designed Paris' famous tower, also designed the site of today's shopping centre in 1890.

Konak clock tower Designed by the Levantine French architect Raymond Charles Père.

Sen Polikarp church (Saint Polycarpe; Vali Kazım Dirik Caddesi) Charming murals are the highlight of this late-17th-century Catholic church.

İzmir's Levantine community is fast disappearing, but it is still has a sizeable Jewish community, mostly in Alsancak, and it is possible to tour some of the city's beautiful old **synagogues** (guided tours €35). The tours usually take in some of the restored synagogues in Karataş, and the Old Jewish Quarter (3km south of the centre of town) including the **Bet Israel**, which has a museum on its upper floor, and lies near the Asansör (p197), an elevator built in 1907 to enable trade between Karataş and the Turkish Halil Rifat Paşa neighbourhood – the alternative is 155 steps. At the foot of the lift, a plaque marks the typical old İzmir house where Darío Moreno, the late Jewish singer of *Canım İzmir* (My dear İzmir), was born. Other highlights include the three Ottoman-style synagogues on Havra Sokak in the bazaar, the remainder of nine that used to stand here. To arrange a tour, call the tourist office (p198).

ALSANCAK & SEAFRONT

North of Gazi Bulvarı is safer and more pleasant, although the hotels here are firmly in midrange and top-end territory.

TOP CHOICE **Key Hotel** BOUTIQUE HOTEL €€€
(✆482 1111; www.keyhotel.com; Mimar Kemalettin Caddesi 1; d ₺270; P❋☎) Key Hotel is a black, gold and brown masterpiece down by Konak Pier. Located in a former bank building, the original vault is now a glass-topped atrium while the hotel includes glass elevators, a superb ground-floor restaurant and concierge service. The rooms have hi-tech touches, rain showers and king-size beds. The owner is a local soft-drink magnate who plans to replicate the hotel elsewhere in Turkey.

MyHotel BOUTIQUE HOTEL €€€
(✆445 5241; www.myhotel.com.tr; Cumhuriyet Bulvarı 132; s/d ₺160/220; ❋☎) In a brilliant location just a street back from the sea, MyHotel is a low-key alternative to the fancier chain hotels nearby. The lobby bar and restaurant are super cool and the spacious rooms are still in decent shape since their decade-old imagining.

Swissôtel Grand Efes HOTEL €€€
(✆414 0000; www.swissotel.com.tr; Gazi Osman Paşa Bulvarı 1; s/d €140/160; P❋@☆) Swissôtel has adapted well to the Turkish

market, and this Izmir branch is no exception. Occupying a prime location overlooking Cumhuriyet Meydanı and the bay, the Grand Efes is the choice location for business and glamour travel. The underwater restaurant is excellent, while the day spa (open to nonguests) was recently voted the best in the world.

Mövenpick Hotel LUXURY HOTEL €€€
(☑488 1414; Cumhuriyet Bulvarı 138; s/d ₺180/290; P❄✳️) The modestly posh Swiss luxury hotel has landed flush in the middle of Konak to serve up the expected 4½-star hotel experience. Ask for an upgrade to a sea-view room (you never know your luck). The restaurant, Margeaux, has an impressive European menu (and is popular with visiting foodies).

Otel Kilim HOTEL €€€
(☑484 5340; www.kilimotel.com.tr; Atatürk Caddesi; s/d ₺125/165; ✳️@) This trusty upmarket hotel in the Pasaport section of the *kordon* is a good value option that attracts a swathe of return visitors. The rooms are generous (both in dimensions and minibar contents) with lovely showers and vintage photos of İzmir. Half a dozen rooms face the sea; the others have good side views.

İzmir Palas Oteli HOTEL €€
(☑465 0030; www.izmirpalas.com.tr; Atatürk Caddesi; s/d from ₺120/165; P✳️) Established in 1927 and rebuilt in '72, the 138-room Palas is a storied beast, but it's popular and quite comfortable, and the location is tremendous, overlooking the bay, with fine fish restaurants on the doorstep.

✖ Eating

The *kordon* restaurants have outside tables with views of the bay – some serve excellent food. On and around Kıbrıs Şehitleri Caddesi in Alsancak, you'll lose the sunset views but gain on atmosphere; in particular try 1453 Sokak.

For fresh fruit and veg, freshly baked bread and delicious savoury pastries, head for the canopied market, just off Anafartalar Caddesi.

TOP CHOICE Sakız MODERN TURKISH €€
(☑484 1103; Şehit Nevresbey Bulvarı 9a; mains ₺12-25; ⊙noon-2pm & 7.30-10pm Mon-Sat) With a wooden terrace and red-and-white tablecloths, Sakız is informal and fabulous. Its fresh meze includes recommended sar-

dines, octopus and *köz patlıcan* (smoked aubergine with tomatoes and peppers); the unusual mains include sea bass with asparagus and stir-fried fish with artichoke. Live traditional guitar music sets the scene on weekends.

Reyhan PATISSERIE €
(☑444 7946; Dr Mustafa Bey Enver Caddesi 24; cheesecake ₺6.75) This institution is serious about sweet stuff, with a professional taster and headset-wearing waiters. Decadent delights like strawberry cheesecake and almond-cream cake with pineapple and almonds sit alongside favourites such as carrot cake and a yummy Turkish breakfast.

Veli Usta Balık Pişiricisi SEAFOOD €€€
(☑464 2705; Atatürk Caddesi 212; mains ₺20; ⊙noon-10.30pm) This relaxed, quality seafood restaurant outstrips the strip thanks to the maroon-sweater-clad staff, and dishes like fresh, good value *dil şiş* (grilled sole). The crowd is abundant and friendly.

Deniz Restaurant SEAFOOD €€€
(☑464 4499; Atatürk Caddesi 188; mains from ₺17; ⊙11am-11pm) This old favourite on the *kordon* trades a little on its reputation – and it's far from good value – but the mezes such as octopus in oregano and baked sardines are worth the snobby service. The house speciality is *tuzda balık* (fish baked in a block of salt that's broken at your table; suitable for three or four people).

Ankara Lokantası TURKISH €
(☑445 3607; Anafartalar Caddesi 779; dishes ₺6-12) Near the Basmane train station is this humble eatery that fills with local workers during the week and a relaxed drop-in crowd on weekends. It's a traditional 'point-and-pick' joint with loads of meat, rice and vegetable dishes.

Kırçiçeği KEBAP €€
(☑464 3090; Cumhuriyet Bulvarı; kebaps ₺11-18; ⊙24 hr) İzmir's poshest soup kitchen also serves great pide (₺8) – including *ıspanaklı peynirli* (cheese and spinach) and *kuşbaşılı kaşarlı* (bird's heads; the bits of meat supposedly resemble them) – and kebaps. The *ayran* (yoghurt drink) brand, Eker, from Bursa, is not widely available elsewhere.

Apropo GRILL €€€
(☑259 7070; www.leventmarina.com; Haydar Aliyev Bulvarı 4; mains ₺15-30; P✳️❄) Apropo is one of the more interesting, opportune restaurants at the flashy, somewhat generic new

Levant Marina complex to the south of the centre. The menu is essentially a choice of grilled meats, cooked to order, served on heaters alongside vegies and fries. The casual wood and tiled tables and chairs overlooking the water keep it family-friendly yet trendy all the same.

Sir Winston Tea House
CAFE €

(☑421 8861; Dr Mustafa Bey Enver Caddesi 20; sandwiches ₺13, tea ₺4-8) On a street known for its cafes, this is one of the best, serving dozens of teas, hot and cold coffees, good salads and pastas. There's shady seating outside. There's a second branch behind the Swissôtel.

Asansör
RESTAURANT €€€

(☑261 2626; Darío Moreno Sokağı; mains ₺15-30; ⊘9am-midnight; P) Asansör is a 'destination' restaurant rising high above the old Jewish quarter and accessed via a charming historic elevator. Inside is a formal, white-tablecloth venue with superb set menus on weekends (₺60 per person). Perhaps more charming though is a light meal and a beer on the terrace, especially in summer when the crowd comes to escape the Alsancak kerfuffle. It's about 2km from the town centre.

Tuğba
SWEETS €

(Gazi Osman Paşa Bulvarı 56; ⊘8.30am-11pm) Power up for a visit to the bazaar with dried fruit, nuts, baklava and Turkish delight. There's an Alsancak branch (Kıbrıs Şehitleri Caddesi) at the southern end of Kıbrıs Şehitleri Caddesi.

%100
RESTAURANT, CAFE €€€

(☑441 5593; Konak Pier, Atatürk Caddesi; mains ₺22) Down the end of Konak Pier, %100 has a huge menu, with steak, sushi and pizza highly recommended by our table. It's a great place for a lazy cocktail (₺20) or mid-shop coffee by the water's edge. Service is excellent.

Mennan
BAKERY €

(899 Sokak 30; cornet ₺3.50) This cafe in the bazaar is known for its excellent homemade ice cream.

Rıza Aksüt
PATISSERIE €

(863 Sokak 66; cake ₺3; ⊞) In the Baş Durak area of the bazaar, try the *peynir tatlısı* (sponge dessert made with cheese), preferably *kaymaklı* (with cream), at this dessert shop.

🍷 Drinking & Entertainment

The row of bars around Balık Pişiricisi Restaurant are particularly popular. Alsancak plays host to the city's hottest nightlife, particularly in the clubs and bars on side streets such as Sokak 1482.

Sunset Cafe
BAR

(☑463 6549; Ali Çetinkaya Bulvarı 2A) On the edge of the boulevard, Sunset Cafe makes a great sunset drinking hole, with colourful booths on the street and a relaxed, youthful crowd. The cheap beer flows freely, but the one-toilet bathroom gets a little tight.

Tyna
BAR

(Ali Çetinkaya Bulvarı 5; beer ₺4) The outside tables are hot property at this pizzeria on a small square. Most just come for a beer; pizzas cost ₺6.

Aksak Lounge
BAR

(1452 Sokak 10) In a typical İzmir mansion with high ceilings, balconies and a courtyard garden, Aksak attracts a cultured crowd to its jazz nights on Tuesday and Sunday.

Beyaz Cafe
LIVE MUSIC

(White Cafe; ☑422 6645; www.beyazcbr.com; 1452 Sokak 4) Near the plaque to poet Can Yücel, the White Cafe is a folk-music haunt with excellent Turkish cuisine. Perfect for a good, honest night on the tiles.

Passport Cafe & Bar
CAFE

(☑489 9299; Atatürk Caddesi 140; ⊘8am to 2pm) One of the more modern of the many seafront cafes running south from the police station.

1888
NIGHTCLUB

(☑421 6690; www.1888.com.tr; Cumhuriyet Bulvarı 248) This newish nightclub around an old Ottoman courtyard hosts everything from film and cultural festivals to frantic disco parties.

Kybele
CLUB

(Sokak 1453; admission ₺20; ⊘Fri & Sat) Rock bands entertain the dance floor in this small club occupying an old İzmir house with stone walls and ornate decor. Pretty much a 'dare-you-to-leave' policy on weekends.

Cine Bonus
CINEMA

(www.cinebonus.com.tr; Konak Pier, Atatürk Caddesi; adult ₺12.50) Five screens; films in English with Turkish subtitles.

TRAVEL CARDS

İzmir has two travel cards, covering bus, metro and ferry; available at stations, piers and shops with the Kent Kart sign:

Kent Kart (City Card) You pay a ₺5 deposit when you buy this and put credit on it. When you use the card ₺1.55 is debited from it, then every journey you make for the next 90 minutes is free.

Üç-beş (Three-five) This card with three credits, each valid for a single journey, costs ₺5.75.

Shopping

İzmir's shopping scene spans all sections of the market – from the bazaar (p191), with its crowded intensity, its haggling and its old-world commercial exuberance, to the Konak Pier shopping centre, a bright, shiny, modern mall jutting out over the water and filled with big-name chains.

Dösim (Cumhuriyet Bulvarı 115) is geared towards tourists and its prices are a little high, but the quality is dependable and it stocks a wide range of items – from slippers to necklaces (from ₺50).

The branch of **Remzi Kitabevi** (Konak Pier, Atatürk Caddesi) has a large selection of English-language books for both adults and children.

Konak Pier Shopping Centre   SHOPPING CENTRE

On the jetty built by Gustav Eiffel, this modern mall is spacious and stylish. There's a cinema, good Turkish fashion stores and two smart waterside cafes.

Sipahi Okey   SOUVENIRS

(446 0830; Anafartalar Caddesi 447) For traditional Turkish souvenirs, try this place with lovely *tavla* (backgammon sets), strings of Turkish chillies to cheer up your kitchen or your cuisine, and lovely beaded jewellery.

Arma Kitap & Cafe   BOOKSHOP

(465 0771; Atatürk Caddesi No 312) Not the widest selection of English language titles at this very popular bookshop and cafe but plenty of good international magazines and some sweet tunes to fill out a lazy afternoon near the sea.

Artı Kitabevi   BOOKS

(421 2632; Cumhuriyet Bulvarı 142B) English-speaking, friendly bookshop with a good selection of English-language and speciality art books.

Information

Banks, ATMS, internet cafes and wi-fi networks are found all over the centre.

İzmir Döviz (441 8882; Fevzi Paşa Bulvarı 75; 8am-7pm Mon-Sat) Money changer where no commission is charged.

Post Office (522 8181; Fevsi Pasa Bulvari 170) The main post office is a short walk east of Cankaya station.

Tourist Office (483 5117; 1344 Sokak 2) Inside the ornately stuccoed İl Kültür ve Turizm Müdürlüğü building just off Atatürk Caddesi. Has English-, German- and French-speaking staff.

Dangers & Annoyances

Like any big city, İzmir has its fair share of crime. However, the main tourist routes are fairly safe, with the notable exceptions of the Kadifekale neighbourhood and the area around Basmane train station, which is something of a red-light district – lone women should take special care. Do not enter Kemeraltı Bazaar after dark, and be alert to pickpockets and thieves there during the day.

Getting There & Away

Air

There are many flights to İzmir's **Adnan Menderes Airport** (455 0000; www.adnanmenderesairport.com) from European destinations.

Turkish Airlines (484 1220; www.thy.com; Halit Ziya Bulvarı 65) Offers direct flights from İstanbul (both airports), Adana, Ankara, Antalya, Diyarbakır, Erzurum, Gaziantep, Kayseri Kars, Malatya, Samsun, Sivas, Trabzon and European destinations.

Other airlines serving İzmir:

Atlasjet (www.atlasjet.com)

Izair (www.izair.com.tr)

Onur Air (www.onurair.com.tr)

Pegasus Airlines (www.flypgs.com)

Sun Express (www.sunexpress.com.tr)

Bus

İzmir's mammoth otogar lies 6.5km northeast of the city centre. For travel on Friday or Saturday to coastal towns to the north of İzmir, buy your ticket a day in advance; in the high season, two days in advance. Tickets can also be purchased from the bus companies' city-centre offices, mostly found at Dokuz Eylül Meydanı in Basmane.

Long-distance buses and their ticket offices are found on the lower level; regional buses (eg Selçuk, Bergama, Manisa, Sardis) and their ticket offices are on the upper level. City buses and dolmuşes leave from a courtyard in front of the lower level.

Short-distance buses (eg the Çeşme Peninsula) leave from a smaller local bus terminal in Üçkuyular, 6.5km southwest of Konak. They now pick up and drop off at the otogar as well.

Details of daily bus services to important destinations are listed in the table below.

Train

Most intercity services arrive at **Basmane Garı**, although **Alsancak Garı** is being vamped up and is set to receive more trains. For northern or eastern Turkey, change at Ankara.

ANKARA There are daily trains to/from Ankara (₺27, 15 hours), leaving in both directions at 5.50pm and 7.45pm and travelling via Eskişehir (₺21, 11 hours).

BANDIRMA There are daily trains to/from Bandırma (₺18, six hours) at 2.20pm/4pm. Apart from Tuesday, there are also services at 9.25am/9.50am, and these trains coordinate with the ferry to/from İstanbul.

MANISA Every day but Tuesday, there are six trains to/from Manisa (₺3 to ₺8, 1¾ hours).

SELCUK Six daily trains travel to Selcuk, leaving between 8am and 7pm (₺4.75, 1½ hours).

❶ Getting Around

To/From the Airport

The airport is 18km south of the city on the way to Ephesus and Kuşadası.

BUS On the hour every hour, buses 200 and 202 run between both arrivals terminals and the Swissôtel (formerly Efes Otel) via Üçkuyular; bus 204 runs between both arrivals terminals and the otogar via Bornova metro. Both cost two credits.

SHUTTLE Hourly Havaş buses (₺10, 30 minutes) leave from Gazi Osman Paşa Bulvarı near the Swissôtel between 3.30am and 11.30pm; and go to the Swissôtel from domestic arrivals, leaving 25 minutes after flights arrive.

To/From the Bus Stations

If you've arrived at the main otogar on an intercity bus operated by one of the larger bus companies, a free *servis* shuttle is provided to the centre, normally Dokuz Eylül Meydanı. If you arrive on a local bus, you can catch a dolmuş (₺2, 25 minutes) that runs every 15 minutes between the otogar and both Konak and Basmane Garı, or you can take buses 54 and 64 (every 20 minutes) to Konak or 505 to Bornova metro (every 30 minutes). Passes can be bought at the bus stop.

To get to the otogar, the easiest way is to buy a ticket on an intercity bus at Dokuz Eylül Meydanı and take the bus company's *servis*. However, if you're catching a local bus from the otogar (eg to Salihli), take the metro to Bornova then pick up bus 505.

To get to Üçkuyular bus station, catch bus 554 or 169 from the Konak bus terminal.

Boat

The most pleasant way to cross İzmir is by **ferry** (◷6.40am-11.40pm). Roughly half-hourly

SERVICES FROM İZMIR'S OTOGAR

DESTINATION	FARE (₺)	DURATION (HR)	DISTANCE (KM)	FREQUENCY (PER DAY)	VIA
Ankara	40	8	550	hourly	Afyon
Antalya	45	7	450	hourly	Aydın
Bergama	10	2	110	frequent	Menemen
Bodrum	25	3¼	286	every 30min in high season	Milas
Bursa	25	5	300	hourly	Balıkesir
Çanakkale	35	6	340	hourly	Ayvalık
Çeşme	15	1¾	116	frequent	Alaçatı
Denizli	25	3¼	250	hourly	Aydın
Foça	8	1½	86	frequent	Menemen
İstanbul	45	9	575	hourly	Bursa
Konya	35	8	575	every 2 hours	Afyon
Kuşadası	15	1¼	95	frequent	Selçuk
Manisa	8	1	45	frequent	Sarnıc
Marmaris	38	4	320	hourly	Aydın
Salihli	10	1½	90	frequent	Sardis
Selçuk	9	1	80	frequent	Belevi

timetabled services, with more at the beginning and end of the working day, link the piers at Karşiyaka, Bayraklı, Alsancak, Pasaport, Konak and Göztepe. *Jetons* (transport tokens) cost ₺3 each.

Bus

City buses lumber along the major thoroughfares, although stops are infrequent. Montrö Meydanı, by the Kültür Park, is a major terminal or transfer point. Routes 86 and 169 run down Şair Eşref Bulvarı then pass Montrö Meydanı, the bazaar and Agora (and serve the same route in reverse after terminating in Balçova, past Üçkuyular in southwest İzmir); route 269 runs down Talatpaşa Bulvarı and Cumhuriyet Caddesi to Konak Meydanı.

Car

Large international car-hire franchises, including Budget, Europcar, Hertz, National Alamo and Avis, and smaller companies have 24-hour desks at the airport, and some have an office in town. Green Car (p673) is one of the largest car-hire companies in the Aegean region.

Metro

İzmir's **metro** (jeton ₺1.80; ⊙6.30am-11.30pm) is clean and quick. There are currently 10 stations running from Üçyöl to Bornova via Konak, Çankaya and Basmane, although there are plans to expand the network.

Taxi

You can either hail a taxi, or pick one up from a taxi stand or outside one of the big hotels. Fares start at ₺3.75 then cost ₺0.30 per 100m. Make sure the meter is switched on.

Manisa

📞 0236 / POP 301,218

Backed by mountains, the modern town of Manisa was once the ancient town of Magnesia ad Sipylus. The early Ottoman sultans left Manisa many fine mosques, but retreating Greek soldiers wreaked terrible destruction during the War of Independence. The main reasons to visit are to inspect the mosques

---

WORTH A TRIP

SARDIS (SART)

Sardis was once the capital of the wealthy Lydian kingdom that dominated much of the Aegean before the Persians arrived. Its ruins, scattered around the village of Sartmustafa, 90km east of İzmir, make a particularly worthwhile excursion.

The **Ruins of Sardis** (admission ₺3; ⊙8am-5pm, to 7pm high season) lie at the eastern end of the village, immediately north of the road. Information panels dot the site.

You enter the site along a Roman road, past a well-preserved Byzantine latrine and, backing onto a synagogue, rows of Byzantine shops, which belonged to Jewish merchants and artisans.

Turn left from the Roman road to enter the impressive *havra* (synagogue), with its beautiful decoration: fine geometric mosaic paving and coloured stone on the walls.

Beside the synagogue is the grassy expanse of what was once the hamam and gymnasium. This complex was probably built in the 2nd century AD and abandoned after a Sassanian invasion in 616.

Right at the end is a striking two-storey building called the Marble Court of the Hall of the Imperial Cult, which, though heavily (and unattractively) restored, gives an idea of the former grandeur of the building.

Across the road from the enclosed site, continuing excavations have uncovered a stretch of the Lydian city wall and a Roman house with painted walls right on top of an earlier Lydian residence.

A sign points south down the road beside the tea houses to the **Temple of Artemis** (admission ₺3; ⊙8am-5pm), just over 1km away. Today, only a few columns of the once-magnificent but never-completed building still stand. Nevertheless, the temple's plan is clearly visible and very impressive.

As you head back to İzmir, look to the north of the highway and you'll see a series of softly rounded tumuli, the burial mounds of the Lydian kings.

Half-hourly buses to Salihli (₺10, 1½ hours, 90km) leave from İzmir otogar, and pass Sartmustafa. You can also catch dolmuşes to Sartmustafa (₺1, 15 minutes, 9km) from the back of Salihli otogar.

Buses can be hailed along the highway from Salihli to Manisa (₺5, one hour), making it possible to visit both Manisa and Sardis in the same day.

and the finds from Sardis in the museum, or to take in the Mesir Şenlikleri festival.

👁 Sights & Activities

Of Manisa's many old mosques, the **Muradiye Camii** (1585), the last work of the famous architect Mimar Sinan, has the most impressive tile work. The adjoining building, originally constructed as a soup kitchen, is now **Manisa Museum** (☏231 3685; admission ₺3; ⊘9am-noon & 1-5pm Tue-Sun), which houses some fine mosaics from Sardis.

More or less facing the Muradiye, the **Sultan Camii** (1522) features some gaudy paintings. The **hamam** (☏232 3347; admission ₺15; ⊘10am-9pm) next door has separate entrances for men and women. Above the town centre is the **Ulu Cami** (1366), ravaged by the ages and not as impressive as the view from its hillside perch.

🎊 Festivals & Events

Mesir Şenlikleri   CULTURAL
If you're able to visit during the four days around the spring equinox, you can catch the Mesir Şenlikleri, a festival in celebration of *mesir macunu* (power gum).

According to legend, over 450 years ago a local pharmacist named Müslihiddin Celebi Merkez Efendi concocted a potion to cure Hafza Sultan, mother of Sultan Süleyman the Magnificent, of a mysterious ailment. Delighted with her swift recovery, the queen mother paid for the amazing elixir to be distributed to the local people.

These days townsfolk in period costumes re-enact the mixing of the potion from sugar and 40 spices and other ingredients, then toss it from the dome of the Sultan Camii. Locals credit *mesir* with calming the nerves, stimulating the hormones and immunising against poisonous stings.

ℹ Getting There & Around

It's easiest to get to Manisa by half-hourly buses from İzmir (₺8, 50 minutes, 30km), although trains also run. From Manisa, buses to Salihli pass Sardis (₺5, one hour). To get to Manisa's historic mosques, take a dolmuş from in front of the otogar to Ulu Parkı (₺1).

Çeşme

☏0232 / POP 21,394
With its long seafront, hilltop castle and winding, busy market streets, Çeşme makes a pleasant base for exploring the surrounding peninsula. As the exit point for the Greek island of Chios, 8km across the water, it's a good place for a summer farewell party as it's far less pretentious than Alaçatı. Inevitably, it's popular with weekending İzmiris and can get busy during the school holidays, when prices rise accordingly.

👁 Sights & Activities

FREE **Çeşme Castle**   FORTRESS
The Genoese fortress, whose dramatic walls dominate the town centre, was built in 1508 and repaired by Sultan Beyazıt, son of Sultan Mehmet the Conqueror (Mehmet Fatih), to defend the coast from attack by pirates. Later, the Rhodes-based Knights of St John of Jerusalem also made use of it. The battlements offer excellent views of Çeşme, and it's good to walk around inside – under arches, up and down steps, and through towers with exhibits on subjects including the area's naval history.

Çeşme Museum   MUSEUM
(Çeşme Müzesi; admission ₺3; ⊘9am-7pm Tue-Sun) Housed in the castle's Umur Bey tower, this museum displays archaeological finds from nearby Erythrae.

Statue of Cezayirli Gazi Hasan Paşa   MONUMENT
Facing İskele Meydanı, with its back to the fortress, is a statue of this great Ottoman admiral (1714–90), who was sold into slavery but became a grand vizier. He is shown accompanied by a lion; he famously brought one to Turkey from Africa.

Orthodox Church of Ayios Haralambos   CHURCH
(İnkılap Caddesi) North of the castle, this imposing but redundant 19th-century church is used for temporary exhibitions of arts and crafts during the summer months.

Beach   BEACH
At the far northern end of the waterfront esplanade is a small, sandy beach – worth a quick dip.

Boat Trips   CRUISE
From late May to September, *gülets* (traditional Turkish wooden yachts) offer one-day boat trips to nearby Black Island, Donkey Island and Wind Bay, where you can swim and snorkel. Browse the waterfront to compare prices and negotiate; they should cost around ₺35 to ₺45, including lunch. Boats usually leave around 10am and return around 5pm.

İZMİR & THE NORTH AEGEAN ÇEŞME

Çeşme

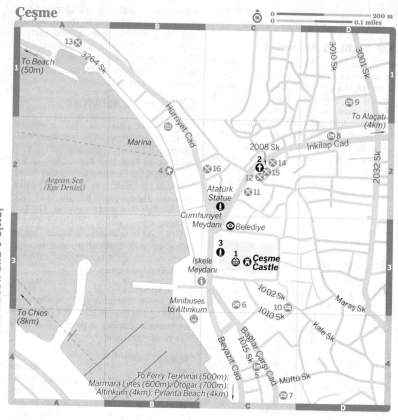

🛏 Sleeping

TOP CHOICE **Levant Apart Otel** APARTMENTS €€
(☎712 6553; www.cesmelevantaparts.com; 105 Sokak 23; 1/2-bedroom apt ₺135/250; P❄️🅿️) Levant has raced ahead of Çeşme's otherwise humble digs with its slick designer apartments one street back from the sea. The 35-sq-metre studios are bright and cool, with plasmas, wi-fi, hairdryers, cute bathrooms and self-catering facilities. The desk is open around the clock and the leafy terrace kicks off in summer. All in all, terrific value. It's well signposted, 100m south along Baglar Carsi Caddesi, past the ruins of a hamam.

Nese Hotel HOTEL €
(☎712 6543; www.neseotel.net; Inkilap Caddesi, 3025 Sokak; s/d ₺40/80; P❄️🅿️) A hit with readers, Nese is a charming white and blue hotel set a few streets back from the sea. Rooms are tiled and pastel, cool and clean. The canopied restaurant is lovely in summer. Excellent value and popular with İzmiris.

Işik Pansiyon PENSION €
(☎712 6305; 1021 Sokak 8; s/d ₺30/60; ❄️) The sunny courtyard and hospitable, elderly owners make this basic little pension better than others in the price range. Rooms are dark, but all have small TVs and huge fridges. Off Baglar Caddesi, 150m south of the marina.

Kanuni Kervansaray Hotel HISTORIC HOTEL €€€
(☎712 0630; www.cesmekervansaray.com.tr; Çarşı Mevki 5; r ₺200) Ostentatious in presentation and pricing, this 'historic' hotel is nonetheless very novel and perfectly located. The 16th-century facade impresses from afar; inside the rooms are large and bland, but we'll put it down to teething problems. Per-

haps stick to the restaurant, which is good, though service is slow.

Yalçın Otel　　　　　　　　　　　HOTEL €
(⌨712 6981; www.yalcinotel.com; 1002 Sokak 10; s/d ₺60/80; ⊙May-Oct) Perched on the hillside overlooking the harbour, the Yalçın Otel has 18 spotless and well-maintained rooms. The biggest drawcards are the two large terraces, both of which have sunbeds and fabulous views, and its midrange quality for a budget price. Out of season, call in advance.

Antik Ridvan Otel　　　　　　　HOTEL €€
(⌨712 9772; www.antikridvanotel.com; 1015 Sokak 10; d ₺70) This odd, brown-orange place near the old hamam feels half-finished, but the open-air courtyard is welcome in summer and the rooms are clean and comfortable enough (some with sea views). The owner is very friendly.

Uz Pansiyon　　　　　　　GUESTHOUSE €
(⌨712 6579; Sokak 3010 11; s/d ₺30/60; ✭) Close to the bus station and 450m from the centre, this is one of Çeşme's cheapest, but it's spotless and terrific value.

✖ Eating

The most touristy restaurants are all along the waterfront. For cheaper, more locally oriented places, head to İnkılap Caddesi.

Rumeli　　　　　　　　　　　　BAKERY €
(İnkılap Caddesi; ⊙8am-8pm) Occupying an Ottoman stone house, this 65-year-old *pastane* (patisserie) sells great ice cream (₺1.50 per scoop) from its side window, and stocks all manner of local jams, pickles and preserves.

Tiko's Cafe　　　　　　　　　　TURKISH €
(2008 Sokak 8A; mains ₺8-12; ⊙6am-3am winter, 24 hr summer) This new, Ottoman-feeling establishment rams with locals at lunchtime and with sailors and partygoers through summer when soup is served 24 hours. The regular menu includes seafood and grilled meat and a revolving display of fresh meze.

Pasifik Otel Restaurant　　　SEAFOOD €€
(⌨712 1767; Tekke Plajı Mevkii 16; mains ₺10-20; ⊙noon-midnight) If you fancy a walk and some fish, head to this hotel restaurant at the far northern end of the seafront, where you can enjoy a great fish casserole behind a ceiling-high glass window overlooking a small beach.

Kumrucu Tani　　　　　　　FAST FOOD €
(⌨712 1149; 2008 Sokak No 4; kebap ₺5-10; ⊙11am-11pm) Run by a local sporting identity who fraternises with İzmir's B-list, this is a friendly, straight-up kebap joint with delicious, healthy sides.

İmren Lokantası Restaurant　　TURKISH €€
(⌨712 7620; İnkılap Caddesi 6; mains ₺15; ⊙noon-9pm) Çeşme's first restaurant, opened back in 1960, is set in a bamboo-roofed atrium with a fountain and plants. It's famous locally for its traditional, high-quality Turkish food, including stews.

Yelken Restaurant　　　　　　TURKISH €€
(⌨712 9077; Kutludağ Sokak 16; mains ₺12-25) Under new ownership, the Yelken has returned to Turkish grills alongside mezes such as *patlican* (aubergine) and tomatoes, and the house speciality *kabak çiçeği dolması* (stuffed courgette flowers).

☕ Drinking & Entertainment

Some of the restaurants along the marina morph into live-music venues during the summer.

ℹ️ Information

The **tourist office** (☑712 6653; fax 712 6653; İskele Meydanı 4; ⊙8.30am-noon & 1-5.30pm Mon-Fri), ferry and bus ticket offices, banks with ATMs, restaurants and hotels are all within two blocks of Cumhuriyet Meydanı, the main square near the waterfront with the inevitable Atatürk statue. You can access the internet at **Sahil Net** (Hürriyet Caddesi; per hr ₺2; ⊙9am-1am).

ℹ️ Getting There & Away

Bus

You have to transit through İzmir to travel between Çeşme and most places (and through Çeşme to get to other parts of the peninsula). Çeşme otogar is almost 1km south of Cumhuriyet Meydanı, although you can pick up dolmuşes in town.

ANKARA Same details as İstanbul.

İSTANBUL ₺50, 11 hours; there are morning and evening services with Metro; in the summer other companies offer additional buses.

İZMİR Buses run every 15 minutes to İzmir's main otogar (₺12, 1¾ hours) and the city's smaller, western Üçkuyular terminal (₺10, 1½ hours, 85km).

Dolmuş

ALAÇATI & ILICA Dolmuşes (₺3.50) leave every five minutes in summer, half-hourly in winter, from the corner of İnkılap Caddesi and 2052 Sokak.

ALTINKUM Dolmuşes (₺3.50) leave half-hourly from Çeşme otogar, and pick up on the main street 20m south of the tourist office.

Ferry

As times (and destinations) change every year, check the websites listed below.

CHIOS Ferries sail to/from the nearby Greek island (one way/return ₺65/100, car ₺150/260, 1½ hours) once or twice a day between mid-May and mid-September. Outside that period, ferries sail to Chios on Friday and Saturday and return on Saturday and Sunday. Tickets can be bought directly from **Ertürk** (☑712 6768; www.erturk.com.tr; Beyazıt Caddesi 6; ⊙9am-7.30pm); you don't need to purchase your ticket in advance unless you have a car.

Taxi

ALAÇATI To Alaçatı centre costs about ₺35.

Pırlanta Beach & Altınkum

Southwest of Çeşme, the aptly named **Pırlanta (Diamond) Beach** is good for kite-surfing (as well as windsurfing). Two companies rent equipment here; **Adrenaline Sports** (☑0541 803 9733; www.adrenalinesports .com.tr; ⊙May-Sep) also offers tuition.

Back on the main road from Çeşme, turn right to reach the increasingly built-up resort of **Altınkum**, which boasts a series of delightful sandy coves. There's a cafe with sunloungers on a clean beach with turquoise water right where the dolmuşes stop.

Half-hourly dolmuşes run from Çeşme to Altınkum (₺3.50) via Pırlanta Beach (₺2.50).

Alaçatı

☑0232

Alaçatı is the hottest destination for Turkey's trend-seeking middle class. Two decades ago this rather unremarkable old Greek village, a few kilometres southeast of both Çeşme and the sea, was known mostly for its decent olive oil and tobacco stores and its world-class windsurfing. Yet thanks to some forward-thinking hoteliers, who turned the dilapidated *taş* (stone) buildings into high-end boutique accommodation, Alaçatı has spawned an impressive culinary and social scene.

Aside from a shoulder-to-shoulder high season stroll along Kemalpaşa Caddesi, there are not a lot of activities on offer or sights to tick off. But that's all the more reason to don your designer sunglasses and join the flashy İstanbullus for a glass of wine, some chilled out electronica and a comprehensive lesson in Turkish chic.

🛏️ Sleeping

Prices drop sharply out of season, although most hotels (and restaurants) open only from mid-May to mid-October and for Christmas and New Year. Reservations are essential in the high season. For more boutique hotels, visit www.charmingalacati.com.

TOP CHOICE **Vintage Boutique Hotel** BOUTIQUE HOTEL €€€
(☑716 0716; www.vintagealacati.com; 3046 Sokak 2; ₺250-400; ⸋✳️🛜) The interior of the hip Vintage is aesthetically more modern than some may want in an historic neighbourhood, but its confidence and popularity are indicative of Alaçatı's maturing hotel scene. The rooms are all white and feature high-

MELEK TORAMAN: PROFESSIONAL WINDSURFER

How long have you been windsurfing? For nine years and I've lived in Alaçatı for the past six years.

Career highlights? In the 2012 World Championships I finished 9th. My wish was to be in the top 10, so I'm happy about my result. I was also second in Turkey for women.

What's your next goal? I want to do well at the World Championships at the end of August in Alaçatı-Çeşme.

How is the windsurfing scene here? In Turkey windsurfing is very popular and we have really good spots for it. Alaçatı is special for the beginners because it's very easy to learn here.The water is not so deep, so you can stand.

Describe your perfect summer weekend on the Çeşme peninsula. Windsurf all day, maybe see flying fish around me while I surf, then party on the beach at night with cool DJs like Bob Sinclair and singers like Buika and Zaz.

İZMİR & THE NORTH AEGEAN ALAÇATI

end beauty products and linen. The restaurant serves a generous breakfast, while owners Akin and Yeliz have quickly established a reputation for first-class service (and a mean cocktail).

Alaçatı Taş Otel BOUTIQUE HOTEL €€€
(Stone Hotel ; ☑716 7772; www.tasotel.com; s/d incl afternoon tea from ₺150/200; ❄☀) The Stone Hotel is the oldest in Alaçatı and continues to lead the boutique scene. Owner Zeynep, who has a knack for determining guests' needs, designed all seven understated rooms overlooking a walled garden. The poolside afternoon teas are lavish, featuring freshly baked cakes. Open year-round.

Tash Mahal Otel BOUTIQUE HOTEL €€€
(☑716 0122; www.tashmahalotel.com; 1005 Sokak 68; r ₺300-400) This 150-year-old former wine house is one of Alaçatı's most enchanting small hotels. Hidden down a back street, the Tash avoids the heavy foot traffic of some of its rivals. It's hard to pick a favourite from the eight rooms: 'Romance' has marble walls and storybook windows, while 'Provence', a former warehouse with a suspended floor, opens onto the hotel gardens and the signature eagle-headed mosaic.

Çiprika Pansiyon PENSION €
(☑716 7303; 3046 Sokak 4; ☎) An old Alaçatı family presides over this humble pension that competes admirably with the more glamorous opposition. Çiprika is one of a few real pensions in the town, offering decent, though daggy, stone rooms, with wi-fi, TVs and small writing tables. The big plus is the huge corner garden for watching the crowds stroll by.

İncirliev BOUTIQUE HOTEL €€€
(Fig Tree; ☑716 0353; www.incirliev.com; Mahmut Hoca Sokak 3; r incl afternoon tea from ₺260; ❄) The eight rooms at the century-old Fig Tree showcase Aegean interior design; our favourites are the Blue Room in a former stable and the stone Terrace Room with floor-length windows. Guests will long recall feasting beneath the leafy namesake with the charming owners Sabahat and Osman.

Sailors Hotel Meydan BOUTIQUE HOTEL €€€
(☑716 8765; www.sailorsotel.com; Kemalpaşa Caddesi 66; r ₺200; ❄) One of four Sailors properties in Alaçatı, this hotel occupies an old Greek house on the main square, above a buzzing streetside cafe. Rustic but refined, the blue-and-white rooms have closed balconies. The downstairs cafe-restaurant is a local meeting place.

✖ Eating

There are few better places to eat in the whole Aegean than Alaçatı. Most restaurants target the smart set, with mains typically starting at around ₺20. Many restaurants close for lunch, when everyone heads to the beach, and open only at weekends (if at all) in low season.

The expensive but soulless Alaçatı marina has a number of new restaurants, including the excellent fish restaurant **Ferdi Baba** (☑568 6034; mains ₺20-35).

TOP CHOICE Asma Yaprağı AEGEAN €€
(☑716 0178; 1005 Sokak No.50; meze ₺10-15) Communal meals in this one-room restaurant are an Alaçatı experience for gastronomes and lucky stragglers. Tin-plated meze

WINDSURFING IN ALAÇATI

Alaçatı was 'discovered' as a windsurfer's paradise in the 1970s by a handful of intrepid German campers. Its strong, consistent northerly winds – blowing at a steady 16 to 17 knots – make it a big hit with the surfing community. Alaçatı Surf Paradise (the main windsurfing beach) is now generally recognised as one of the prime destinations outside Europe for windsurfing, on a par with the likes of Dahap in Egypt.

'The wind comes from the land to the sea, leading to few waves and flat water, which is easy for beginners and fun for pros – it's a sideshore wind', explains Ali Palamutcu of Myga Surf City, one of the schools at Alaçatı Surf Paradise. 'You can touch the sea floor and walk, so it feels secure and comfortable to learn.'

Sadly, although Alaçatı might still be just another Aegean backwater if the surfers hadn't discovered it, the windsurfing beach has suffered in recent years. The construction of a marina cannibalised 1km of the beach, reducing it to 2km and leading to fears for the surfers' safety with boats motoring past. The road there is now lined with large new houses, which are part of the ongoing Port Alaçatı residential development.

The town won't become the next Bodrum or Fethiye; the Ministry of Tourism has demarcated the whole peninsula as an upscale tourism destination, and houses with more than two storeys are banned in Alaçatı. However, with the Alaçatı Preservation Society and the Alaçatı Tourism Society both defunct, there are concerns that the quality of service offered to visitors may suffer if development continues unchecked. 'The genie is out of the bottle and we're trying to squeeze it back in', says one hotelier.

For now, windsurfing continues largely unhindered, with the main season running from mid-May to the beginning of November (many operators close outside that time). The Windsurf World Cup takes place here in August. With seven schools at Alaçatı Surf Paradise (and one across the bay), more than 5000 people start windsurfing here every year.

ASPC and Myga are the largest operators. English-speaking instructors are normally available at the following centres, as are kitesurf boards. Hiring boards for longer periods lowers daily rates.

ASPC (Alaçatı Surf Paradise Club; ☎716 6611; www.alacati.info) This Turkish-German operation offers good courses and high-quality equipment, charging ₺80 to ₺140 for a package (board, wetsuit, harness and shoes) for one day. Booking ahead lowers the daily rates. JP/Neil Pryde, Tabou/Gaastra and, for beginners, Tabou Coolrider/Gaastra Freetime boards are available. A starter course consisting of five hours (10 hours for three students or more) across three days costs ₺400.

Myga Surf Company (☎716 6468; www.myga.com.tr) Myga has a range of equipment, charging ₺90 to ₺160 for a package for one day. It also hires out paddle boards. A five-hour starter course (7½ hours for two students, 10 hours for three or more), which can be spread across a few days, costs ₺400.

Active Alaçatı Windsurf Centre (☎716 6383; www.active-surf.com) Recommended by readers, Active charges ₺80 to ₺120 for a package for one day. A starter course offering a similar amount of instruction to those above costs ₺420.

alternate weekly, but expect plenty of fresh herbs, lashings of olive oil, Aegean vegetables and vine leaves. Dessert is a mastic appreciation ceremony. It's at the mosque-end of the antique district.

Cafe Agrilia
GOURMET RESTAURANT €€€
(☎716 8594; Kemalpaşa Caddesi 75; mains ₺25-70; ⊙breakfast & dinner) This long-running alternative to traditional Turkish fare specialises in creative pasta fusion dishes and Argentine grilled meats. It occupies a former olive-oil factory beyond the bottom of Kemalpaşa Caddesi, with a high ceiling and courtyard. Service can be a little aloof.

Su'dan Restaurant
RESTAURANT, BAR €€€
(☎716 7797; Mithat Paşa Caddesi 22; mains ₺28-42; ⊙9am-1pm & 7-11pm) This former gambling den is now a far more salubrious culinary destination in the Hicimesiş neighbourhood. Experiment with appetisers like hummus and squid or a yummy peach salad. Recommended mains include the mussels in white wine. If nothing else, come for the fruit-and-herb-laden cocktails in the secret garden.

Kaptan'nın Yeri
SEAFOOD €€

(☑716 8030; Garaj İçi; fish ₺15; ☺9am-midnight)
The dining scene in Alaçatı can get a little
la-di-da, but the Captain's Place is one of the
cheapest spots to eat good fish in Alaçatı.
The squid and mussels are exemplary and
the service is warm and friendly. It's just below the car park.

Yusuf Usta Ev Yemekleri
TURKISH €

(☑716 8823; Zeytinci İş Merkezi 1; mains ₺9) On
the ring road near the main entrance to
Alaçatı, the ₺4 salad bar and *bain marie*
with meat and vegetable mains are popular
at lunchtime. This is cheap traditional food
done well.

Rasim Usta'nin Yeri
MODERN TURKISH €€€

(☑716 8420; Kemalpaşa Caddesi 54; mains ₺15-30;
☺11am-11pm) Rasim is one of the oldest, most
dependable restaurants in town. Choose
from delicious soups and salads, and a few
meat and pasta dishes rotating daily. Ask the
grill chef to turn the fish and chicken to order. It's just above the main square.

Café Eftalya
CAFE €

(Cami Arkası Sakarya 3; gözleme ₺6) In the line
of cafes next to the mosque, Eftalya's *gözleme*, packed with cheese and greens, is
a hearty breakfast choice. Homemade lemonade, meat-filled *çiğ börek* and *mantı* are
also available.

Ciğerci Hasan
STREET FOOD €

(Mektep Caddesi; köfte ₺6-8) On the thoroughfare leading from Kemalpaşa Caddesi to
the mosque, this *ciğerci* (liver *köfte* sales-
man) sells the goods, seasoned with fresh
thyme and served with cumin, onions and
tomatoes.

🍷 Drinking & Entertainment

At many bars Efes is not available and bottles of imported beer costing over ₺10 are offered instead. Try a number of bars to garner
the vibe. In summer, the İstanbul megaclub
Babylon (www.babylon.com.tr) organises regular beach parties.

Gizem Café
BAR, CAFE

(Mystery Café; Cumhuriyet Meydanı; beer ₺7) Although its prices follow the Alaçatı trend
and shoot up at the height of summer, Mystery Café is one of the best-value places for
a drink.

Âlâ
BAR, RESTAURANT

(Mektep Caddesi; beer ₺8) With tables on the
thoroughfare leading from Kemalpaşa Caddesi to the mosque, this bar-restaurant occupies a former bakery.

Makah
BEACH BAR

(☑716 6611; Cark Mevkii 1; ☺10am-late) İstanbul's
famous 11:11 club has opened on Makah
Beach, in the heart of the windsurfing scene.
Outside of high season, it's a great place for
a beer and a burger. In high season, it's party
time.

ℹ️ Getting There & Around

BICYCLE ASPC rents out mountain bikes (per
day/week from €10/60).

BUS Metro has an office by the car park, selling
tickets to nationwide destinations (normally
via İzmir).

CAR You can rent cars from **Işıltı** (☑716 8514;
Uğur Mumcu Caddesi 16; 1 day ₺70).

DOLMUŞ Frequent dolmuşes run to/from
Çeşme (₺3.50, 10 minutes, 9km) and İzmir
(₺12, one hour, 75km). Between mid-May and
November, dolmuşes run to/from Alaçatı Surf
Paradise (₺2), which is 4km south of town on
the western side of the *liman* (harbour).

Sığacık
☑0232

Sığacık is an isolated port village clustered
around a crumbling 16th-century castle.
With no beach, there's not much to do here
except stroll the picturesque waterfront,
take a boat trip and watch the fishermen
returning with their famous *kalamar* and
barbun (red mullet).

🛏️ Sleeping & Eating

To find Sığacık's pensions, head towards the
harbour then follow the waterfront promenade to the right beside the city walls.

Beyaz Ev
PENSION €€

(☑598 1760; www.sigacikpansiyon.net; s/d €40/80;
❄️) This four-bedroom White House has been
recently converted into a fine pension, with
a large terrace overlooking Sığacık Beach.
Rooms are spacious and bright, with thin
wooden floorboards and curious furniture.

Teos Pansiyon
PENSION €€

(☑745 7463; www.teospension.com; 126 Sokak 14;
d ₺100; ❄️) With a nice family feel and spacious, attractive rooms, Teos Pansiyon is
good value. Sofas, sea views and big white
beds all feature. You can buy fresh fish from
the market and ask the obliging family to
cook it for you.

Dağ Motel
MOTEL **€**

(Mountain Motel; ☑761 9549; www.dagmotel.net; r ₺60) The Mountain Motel, with its newly renovated rooms, has the best location on the north side of the bay and its fine restaurant (mains ₺20) is part of the regional Slow Food movement. Service is prompt.

Liman
SEAFOOD

(☑745 7011; Liman Meydanı 19; mains ₺15) The Liman doesn't disappoint with its fresh fish and seafront views.

ⓘ Getting There & Away

ÇEŞME You have to travel via İzmir.

İZMİR Take a bus or dolmuş to Seferihisar from İzmir's Üçkuyular otogar (₺4.50, 50 minutes, every 30 minutes). From Seferihisar, half-hourly dolmuşes run to Sığacık (₺1.50, 10 minutes, 5km).

Akkum & Teos
☑0232

Two kilometres over the hill from Sığacık is **Akkum**. A protected cove, it used to attract windsurfers in their thousands in summer but has been eclipsed by Alaçatı. Today, it's quieter and cheaper than Alaçatı and has larger waves.

Of its two smooth, sandy beaches, Büyük Akkum has the better facilities – windsurfing, sea kayaking and diving equipment and instruction are available – but Küçük Akkum is likely to be quieter.

Before Akkum, turn left to reach the scattered ruins at **Teos**, 5km from Sığacık. It's primarily a few picturesque fluted columns, left over from a temple to Dionysus and re-erected amid grass and olive groves. Teos was once a vast Ionian city, and you can roam the fields in search of other remnants (including a theatre used for Dionysian festivals). It's a good place to come for a picnic.

🛏 Sleeping & Eating

There are pensions just after the Teos turn-off and camp sites further on, although we recommend staying in Sığacık instead.

On the road to the ruins, 1km from the turn-off, is **Teos Park**, a forestry department picnic grove. Here you can buy snacks and cold drinks to enjoy beneath shady pine trees overlooking the sea.

Above Küçük Akkum, **Yakamoz** (☑745 7599; 3216 Sokak 8; mains ₺18) has a great terrace, serving seafood and Turkish classics as well as international dishes such as English breakfasts and fajitas.

ⓘ Getting There & Away

BICYCLE Bikes are generally available at Sığacık's pensions.

DOLMUŞ In summer, frequent dolmuşes run to Teos from Seferihisar (₺2, 20 minutes) via Sığacık and Akkum.

TAXI A taxi from Sığacık to Akkum costs about ₺6; a return trip to Teos (including waiting time) costs about ₺20.

Ephesus, Bodrum & the South Aegean

Best Places to Eat

» La Pasión (p247)
» Lemon Tree (p250)
» Terzi Mustafa (p256)
» Ship Ahoy (p257)
» Zekeriya Sofrası (p266)

Best Places to Stay

» Atilla's Getaway (p223)
» Su Otel (p246)
» Maçakızı (p256)
» Mavi Konak (p263)
» Villa Aşina (p265)

Why Go?

Turkey's sparkling Aegean coast boasts 4000 years of civilisation – and it's got the ruins to prove it, the most famous being ancient sites such as Ephesus, Priene, Miletus and Didyma, where excavations continue to yield astonishing new treasures every year.

In summer, the coast's population swells as millions of foreign and Turkish tourists descend on Marmaris, Kuşadası and, especially, Bodrum, the most glamorous of all Anatolia's seaside getaways. Yet despite the nonstop partying, this whitewashed town beneath a castle somehow preserves a unique air of refinement, while new boutique hotels and elegant eateries keep springing up, both here and in the exclusive (but easily visited) coastal villages of the Bodrum Peninsula.

Nevertheless, all of the commotion aside, it's still possible to experience the elemental pleasures of rugged terrain, village life and spectacular Aegean views on the more remote Bozburun and Datça Peninsulas. The coast is most peaceful in spring or autumn (when prices drop, too).

When to Go

Selçuk

°C/°F Temp — Rainfall Inches/mm

May & Jun Tour ancient sites while it's splendidly sunny but not yet oppressive.

Jul & Aug Party with the Turkish jet set and foreign hoi polloi at hot spots Bodrum and Marmaris.

Sep & Oct Enjoy the coastal villages' fish restaurants and beaches, with the Aegean waters at their warmest.

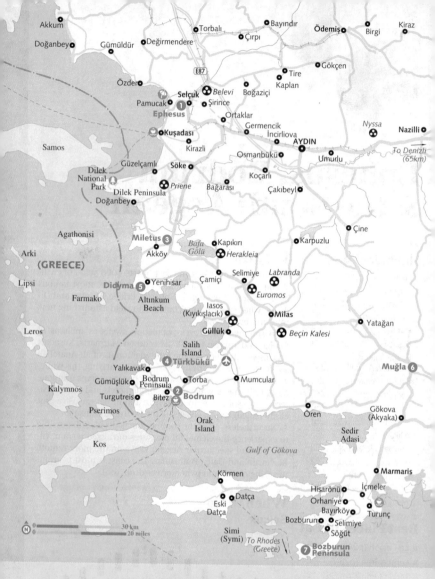

Ephesus, Bodrum & the South Aegean Highlights

❶ Join the masses in bringing new life to **Ephesus** (p211), Europe's best-preserved ancient city

❷ Indulge in sophisticated dining and nightlife in **Bodrum** (p242), with its castle and evocative harbour

❸ Learn how the Romans bathed, and see priceless antiquities, at the ruins and museum of **Miletus** (p235)

❹ Party with the Turkish glitterati at the beach bars of **Türkbükü** (p256), on the Bodrum Peninsula

❺ Gape in awestruck wonder at the soaring columns of Didyma's **Temple of Apollo** (p238)

❻ Wander the white-plastered old town, and savour the traditional cafes and shops in friendly **Muğla** (p262)

❼ Get your motor running on a scooter trip down the spectacular coastline of **Bozburun Peninsula** (p264), near Marmaris

History

Understanding the south Aegean coast's history requires visualising bays and peninsulas where they no longer exist – otherwise, the (now, inland) location of key ancient cities Ephesus, Priene and Miletus would make no sense. Before the lazy Meander River gradually silted things up, these were economically and strategically significant port cities, fully integrated into the wider Greco-Roman culture back when the Mediterranean Sea was dubbed a 'Roman lake'. With geographical changes, however, the Aegean coast's power and commerce centres would move to accommodate the subcontinent's evolving contours.

Mycenaeans and Hittites were the region's earliest recorded peoples (from 1200 BC). More important, however, were the Ionian Greeks who came after fleeing Greece; they founded Ephesus, Priene and Miletus. South of Ionia was mountainous Caria – site of the great King Mausolus' tomb. This, the Mausoleum of Halicarnassus (today's Bodrum), became one of the Seven Wonders of the Ancient World.

Under the Romans, Ephesus prospered, becoming the capital of Asia Minor, while the temples of Artemis here (and the one of Apollo at Didyma) were spectacular pagan pilgrimage sites. As Christianity spread, an intriguing mix of pagans, Jews and Christians coexisted peacefully in the big towns. Most famously, St John reputedly brought the Virgin Mary to Ephesus, where tradition attests his gospel was written.

During subsequent Byzantine rule, the coastal communities maintained their traditional social, cultural and economic links with the facing Greek islands. While the precise territorial divisions changed frequently, the general division of the themes (Byzantine military regions) here was between Thracesion (in the north and central coastal region) and Kibyrrhaeoton (in the south). The latter included some Aegean islands and was an important base for the Byzantine navy, especially when Arab fleets menaced.

In the late 11th and 12th centuries, overland Seljuk expansion coincided with Crusaders on the move to the Holy Land – along with the disastrous decline of the Byzantine navy, which allowed Italian fleets to eventually rule the Mediterranean. In 1402 the Knights of St John (who then owned much of the Greek Do-

decanese islands) built a grand castle in Halicarnassus – scandalously, using stone from the ancient mausoleum – and they renamed the town Petronium. After Süleyman the Magnificent's 1522 conquest of Rhodes, the Templars' Petronium was ceded to the Ottomans (thus the Turkicised name 'Bodrum'). Although the coast would be Turkish-controlled thereafter, it remained significantly populated by Greeks; their traditional knowledge of sailing, shipping and shipbuilding would prove crucial to the empire's maritime commerce and naval success.

After Turkey's Independence War, the 1923 Treaty of Lausanne decreed the great Greek–Turkish population exchanges – terminating three millennia of Greek coastal civilisation with one stroke of the pen. Although Turkey was officially neutral in WWII, the Aegean coast's curving bays provided cover for Greek resistance ships harassing the Germans.

Despite the eminently peaceful holiday atmosphere here today, this frontier's strategic significance remains as vital now as it's always been – Greek and Turkish fighter pilots engage almost daily in mock dogfights over the coast (fatalities are rare). The two countries' long-standing dispute over territorial waters and sovereign territory almost caused a war in January 1996, when Turkish commandos briefly stormed the uninhabited Greek islet of Imia (Kardak in Turkish), causing frantic diplomatic activity in Western capitals. Today, you can gaze at this distant, hazy speck of rock from the beachfront cafes of laid-back Gümüşlük, on the Bodrum Peninsula, and wonder what all the fuss was about.

EPHESUS & AROUND

Ephesus (Efes)

More than anywhere else, the Greco-Roman world comes alive at **Ephesus** (☑892 6010; admission/parking ₺25/7.50; ⊙8am-6.30pm May-Oct, to 4.30pm Nov-Apr). After almost 150 years of excavation, the city's recovered and renovated structures have made Ephesus the most complete classical metropolis in Europe – and that's with 82% of the city still to be unearthed.

As capital of Roman Asia Minor, Ephesus was a vibrant city with a population of over

Ephesus (Efes)

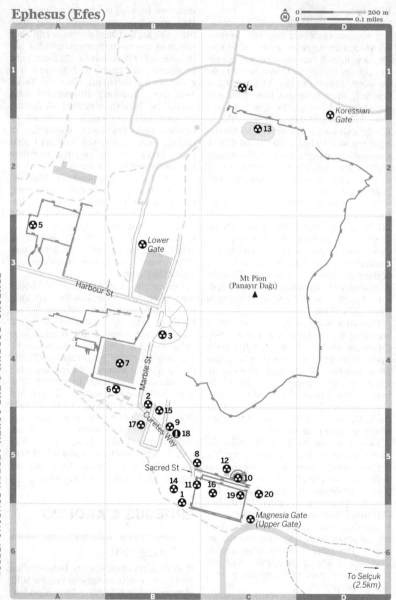

250,000 inhabitants. Counting traders, sailors and pilgrims to the Temple of Artemis, these numbers were even higher, meaning that in Ephesus one could encounter the full diversity of the Mediterranean world and its peoples. So important and wealthy was

Ephesus that its Temple of Artemis was the biggest on Earth, and one of the Seven Wonders of the Ancient World.

In 2011, Ephesus ticket prices jumped when the site was privatised – a Turkish company won a minority share, taking some

Ephesus (Efes)

of the profits too. Hopefully, this will also mean better services in future. On the site, Austrian and German archaeologists still lead summer digging.

History

EARLY LEGEND

According to legend, 10th-century-BC Dorian incursions forced Androclus, Ionian prince of Athens, to seek a safer settlement. First, however, he consulted the famed Delphic oracle, which foresaw 'the fish, the fire and the boar' as markers of the new Ionian city.

After crossing the Aegean, Androclus and his crew rested on the Anatolian shore and cooked a freshly caught fish – so fresh, in fact, that it jumped out of the pan. The toppled coals set the nearby forest ablaze, smoking out a wild boar that Androclus chased down and killed; on that very spot, he resolved to build Ephesus (near today's ruins of the Temple of Artemis). Later on, Androclus reportedly died in battle while defending Priene (another Ionian city) against the Carians.

ALLEGIANCE TO ARTEMIS

Androclus and his Ionian followers had been preceded on the coast by the Lelegians, who worshipped the Anatolian maternal fertility goddess Cybele. The Ionians fused Lelegian ritual with their own, making the Artemis of Ephesus a unique fertility goddess (rather than one of the hunt). However, a 7th-century-BC flood damaged the temple, and the city (and temple) were then razed by Cimmerian invaders around 650 BC. Nevertheless, the Artemis cult continued, and the determined population kept rebuilding the temple following each setback.

CROESUS & THE PERSIANS

Ephesus' massive wealth, accumulated from maritime trade and pilgrims to the Temple of Artemis, aroused the envy of Lydia's King Croesus, who attacked in around 560 BC. Autocratic Croesus relocated the populace inland, where the new Ephesus was built (near the temple's southern edge). However, the Lydian king also respected the cult, funding its reconstruction – a 10-year project overseen by famed Cretan architect Chersiphron and his son, Metagenes.

Everyday life continued as the Ephesians paid tribute to Lydia and, later, to Persian invaders. Ephesus revolted in 498 BC, sparking the Greco-Persian War, which briefly drove out the eastern invaders, and Ephesus joined Athens and Sparta in the Delian League. However, in the later Ionian War, Ephesus picked the losing side and again was ruled by Persia.

On 21 July in 356 BC, a young notoriety-seeker, Herostratus, burned down the Temple of Artemis, to ensure his name would resound forever. The disgusted Ephesian elders executed Herostratus and declared that anyone who mentioned his name would also be killed. A new temple, bigger and better than anything before, was immediately envisioned. In 334 BC, an admiring Alexander the Great offered to pay for construction – if the temple would be dedicated to him. But the Ephesians – who were fiercely protective of their goddess – cleverly declined, pointing out that it was unfitting for one god to make a dedication to another. When finished, the temple was recognised as one of the Seven Wonders of the Ancient World.

FROM LYSIMACHUS TO THE ROMANS

Upon Alexander's death, Lysimachus (one of his generals) took Ionia. However, by then

ℹ️ **EPHESUS: HOW TO MAKE THE MOST OF IT**

Tourists come from across Turkey (and from the high seas) to visit Ephesus. If making a day trip from a distant town or cruise ship, your tour will be prearranged; in such cases, try to ascertain that your guide is licensed and well informed before going, and understand exactly how much time you'll get on-site, compared to how much time will be spent on 'detours' to local shops.

Noticing how such practices were irritating time-sensitive independent travellers, the enterprising Mehmet Esenkaya and his Australian wife Christine started **No-Frills Ephesus Tours** (☑️892 8838; www.nofrillsephesustours.com; Sen Jean Caddesi 3A ; ⊘8am-8pm summer, 9am-5pm winter). Other tours may be cheaper, but this is often because their prices are being subsidised by expected commission on carpet-shop sales after the tour, which can translate into pressure on tourists to buy, as well as wasted time.

No-Frills offers half-day (₺79) and full-day (₺99) Ephesus tours that include transport, and that are led by entertaining and well-informed guides – without any side trips to tacky souvenir shops. Find the office prominently signposted halfway up on the left-hand side of Sen Jean Caddesi in Selçuk (look for the 'Sea Spirit Travel' sign). Tours run daily from 1 April to 31 October.

For a totally different take on Ephesus, see it from above with **Selcuk Ephesus Sky-Diving** (☑️892 2262; www.selcukephesus.com/skydiving; flights ₺120-400) in a two-seater microlight out of Selçuk Airport, just east of Ephesus. Your journey will take you over the main sights of Selçuk and Ephesus, before looping over the Kuşadası coast for sea views.

silt from the River Cayster (Küçük Menderes, or 'Little Meander', in Turkish) had already started to block Ephesus' harbour. The population was moved to today's Ephesus site, strategically set between two hills. Lysimachus built a 10km-long defensive wall (little remains today) and a lighthouse. However, the Ephesians revolted again, and Lysimachus' Seleucid rivals invaded, leading to a messy period of conquest and reconquest that only ended when Ephesus became Roman in 133 BC.

While taxes increased under the Romans, Augustus' decision to make Ephesus capital of Asia Minor in 27 BC proved a windfall for the city; its population grew to around 250,000, drawing immigrants, merchants and imperial patronage. The annual festival of Artemis (Diana to the Romans) became a month-long spring party drawing thousands from across the empire. Yet Ephesus also attracted Christian settlers, including St John, who supposedly settled here with the Virgin Mary and wrote his gospel here. St Paul also lived in Ephesus for three years (probably in the AD 60s).

END OF ANCIENT EPHESUS & ITS BYZANTINE EPILOGUE

Despite efforts by Attalus II of Pergamum, who rebuilt the harbour, and Nero's proconsul, who dredged it in AD 54, the harbour continued to silt up. A century later, Emperor Hadrian tried diverting the Cayster, but eventually the sea was forced back to to-

day's Pamucak. Malarial swamps developed, the port was lost, and Ephesus' increasingly Christian composition meant diminished funds for the Artemis/Diana cult. In AD 263, Germanic Goths sacked Ephesus, burning the temple yet again.

Nevertheless, Ephesus' association with two disciples of Christ (not to mention his mother), and its status as one of the seven churches of Asia in the Book of Revelations, meant that pious Byzantine emperors were determined to salvage what they could. Fourth-century Emperor Constantine the Great thus rebuilt many public buildings, with additional works overseen by Arcadius (r 395–408). And 6th-century Emperor Justinian I built a basilica dedicated to St John on Ayasuluk Hill (in today's Selçuk).

The fortress settlement there later became known as Agios Theologos (the 'Holy Theologian' in Greek) – hence the later Turkicised name, Ayasuluk. Amusingly, medieval Crusaders versed in the classics were befuddled, when passing through, to find a forlorn village here, rather than the epic ancient city they had expected.

👁️ Sights

Ephesus takes 1½ to two hours (add 30 minutes if visiting the Terraced Houses – an extra ₺15 per person). Visit in the morning or late afternoon to avoid crowds and the bright midday sun. Take a hat, sunglasses, sunscreen and water; overpriced shops at the top entrance sell some of these. The site lacks restrooms.

Starting from the Magnesia Gate (Upper Gate) in Upper Ephesus, follow the Curetes Way straight down – all sights are close and easily accessible. Sunny mornings provide ideal photo opportunities. For good guided-tour options, see the box text opposite. The random guides lurking at the entrances aren't recommended. If you haven't a guide, multilingual yet uninformative audio guides (₺10) are sold on-site. Otherwise, most individual ruins have English-language signage, with the Terraced Houses' lengthy placards being the most detailed.

Upper Ephesus   RUIN

First you'll encounter the **Varius Baths** – as in other ancient cities, situated at the main entrances so that visitors could wash before entering. Greco-Roman baths also had a social function as a meeting and massage destination.

Next comes the **Upper Agora**, a large square used for legislation and local political talk. The structure was originally flanked by grand columns and filled with polished marble. In the middle was a small **Temple of Isis** – a testament to the strong cultural and trade connections between Ephesus and Alexandria in Egypt. The agora's columns would later be reused for a Christian basilica, which was a typically Byzantine three-nave structure with a wooden roof. From here, there are several archways in the distance, once food-storage houses.

Ephesus had one of the ancient world's most advanced aqueduct systems, and there are signs of this in terracotta piping for water, along the way to the **Odeon**, a 5000-seat theatre. Primarily used for municipal meetings, this once-lavish building boasts marble seats and carved ornamentation.

Further on, two of six original Doric columns mark the entrance to the ruined **Prytaneum** (town hall) and city treasury. Here and elsewhere, guides may discuss the differences between the Ionian Greeks' heavily ornamented, spiralling columns, and the smooth, unadorned ones of the Romans – both coexist randomly across the site, due to ancient retrofitting and modern relocations. Another difference is notable in arches: the genius of the single-material, harmoniously balanced Ionian Greek ones, and the pragmatic use of mortar cement by the Romans.

The Prytaneum also hosted the **Temple of Hestia Boulaea**, where the city's eternal flame was tended to by vestal virgins, and was fronted by a giant Artemis statue. The fertility goddess was carved with huge breasts and welcoming arms extending from her body, though her hands (probably crafted from gold) are long gone. Many of the statues of deities, emperors and other luminaries here originally had precious gemstones for eyes – another indicator of Ephesian wealth.

A side street called the Sacred Street led to Ephesus' **Asclepion** (hospital). Protected by the god Asclepius and his daughter Hygieia, doctors used the Asclepian snake symbol, often etched into the stone. The snake's symbolic meaning was its ability to shed its skin and renew itself, while the ancients also knew that snake venom had curative powers, and Ephesus was famous for its medical school.

Nearby is the ruined **Temple of Domitian**. Domitian (r AD 81–96) was the tyrant who banished St John to Patmos (where he wrote the Book of Revelations), and executed his own nephew for showing interest in Christianity. Although the unpopular ruler demanded a temple be made in his honour, it was promptly demolished when he died.

Finally, the **Pollio Fountain** and **Memius Monument** hint at the lavish nature of ancient Ephesus' fountains, which filled the city with the relaxing sound of rushing water, again indicating its wealth.

Curetes Way   RUIN

Named for the demigods who helped Lena give birth to Artemis and Apollo, the Curetes Way was Ephesus' main thoroughfare, ringed by statuary, great buildings, and rows of shops selling incense, silk and other goods.

Walking this street is the best way to understand Ephesian daily life. There are many subtle details to look for along the Way. Regular circular depressions and linear grooves are sporadically gouged into the marble, to keep pedestrians from slipping on the slick surface. This was important not only during winter rains, but also during the searing summer heat; shopkeepers would regularly douse the slippery marble street with water from the fountains to cool the air.

Flowering trees that once flanked the street and shops also created shade and coolness. Right under where they stood, there are occasional stone abutments adorned with 12

Ephesus

A DAY IN THE LIFE OF THE ANCIENT CITY

Visiting Ephesus might seem disorienting, but meandering through the city that was once second only to Rome is a highlight of any trip to Turkey. The illustration shows Ephesus in its heyday – but since barely 18% of Ephesus has been excavated, there's much more lurking underfoot than is possible to depict here. Keep an eye out for archaeologists digging away — exciting new discoveries continue to be made every year.

A typical Ephesian day might begin with a municipal debate at the Odeon **1** . These deliberations could then be pondered further while strolling the Curetes Way **2** to the Latrines **3** , perhaps marvelling on the way at imperial greatness in the sculpted form of Emperor Trajan standing atop a globe, by the Trajan fountain. The Ephesian might then have a look at the merchandise on offer down at the Lower Agora, before heading back to the Terraced Houses **4** for a leisurely lunch at home. Afterwards, they might read the classics at the Library of Celsus **5** , or engage in other sorts of activities at the Brothel **6** . The good citizen might then supplicate the gods at the Temple of Hadrian **7** , before settling in for a dramatic performance at Ephesus' magnificent Great Theatre **8** .

FACT FILE

» Ephesus was famous for its female artists, such as Timarata, who painted images of the city's patron goddess, Artemis.

» The Great Theatre could hold up to 25,000 spectators.

» According to ancient Greek legend, Ephesus was founded by Amazons, the mythical female warriors.

» Among Ephesus' 'native sons' was the great pre-Socratic philosopher, Heraclitus.

Brothel

As in other places in the ancient Mediterranean, a visit to the brothel was considered rather normal for men. Visitors would undertake progressive stages of cleansing after entering, and finally arrive in the marble interior, which was decorated with statues of Venus, the goddess of love. A foot imprint on the pavement outside the rubble indicates the way in.

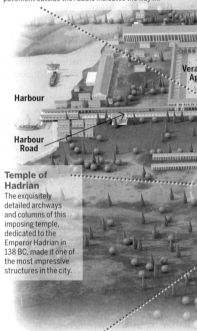

Vera
Ap

Harbour

Harbour Road

Temple of Hadrian

The exquisitely detailed archways and columns of this imposing temple, dedicated to the Emperor Hadrian in 138 BC, made it one of the most impressive structures in the city.

Library of Celsus

Generations of great thinkers studied at this architecturally advanced library, built in the 2nd century AD. The third-larges library in the ancient world (after Alexandria and Pergamum) it was designed to guard its 12,000 scrolls from extremes of temperature and moisture.

Great Theatre

Built into what is today known as Payanir Mt, the Great Theatre was where Ephesians went to enjoy works of classical drama and comedy. Its three storeys of seating, decorated with ornate sculpture, were often packed with crowds.

Latrines

A fixture of any ancient Greco-Roman city, the latrines employed a complex drainage system. Some wealthier Ephesians possessed a 'membership', which allowed them to reserve their own seat.

Odeon

The 5000-seat Odeon, with its great acoustics, was used for municipal meetings. Here, debates and deliberations were carried out by masters of oratory – a skill much prized by ancient Greeks and Romans.

Lower Agora

 8

6

3 **Trajan Fountain**

Hercules Gate

7

5 2

4

1

Upper Agora

Terraced Houses

These homes of wealthy locals provide the most intimate glimpse into the lives of ancient Ephesians. Hewn of marble and adorned with mosaics and frescoes, they were places of luxury and comfort.

Curetes Way

Ephesus' grandest street, the long marble length of the Curetes Way, was once lined with buzzing shops and statues of local luminaries, emperors and deities.

circular depressions – boards for games of chance that ancient Ephesians would play for fun, and even bet on: the contest was known in Latin as *ludus duodecim scriptorum*, or the 'game of twelve markings'.

There's a rather patchwork look to the Way's marble blocks – it's because many are not in their original places, due to ancient and modern retrofitting. An intriguing element in some blocks underfoot are the tiny, carved Greek-language initials; they denoted the name of the specific builder responsible for the relevant section. This helped labourers collect their pay, as it proved they had actually worked.

Several structures along the Way have occasional oval depressions in the walls – these held the oil lamps that lent a magical glow to the city's main thoroughfare by night.

Halfway down Curetes Way is the honorary **Trajan Fountain**. It was originally fronted by a huge statue of the great emperor, grasping a pennant and standing on a globe; the fountain inscription reads, 'I have conquered it all, and it's now under my foot.' The fountain's water flowed under the statue, spilling onto and cleaning the Way.

Next up are the **men's latrines**, a square structure with toilet 'seats' along the back walls. Although wealthy men would have had private home bathrooms, they'd also use the public toilets – some even paying a membership fee to claim a specific seat. Turning in to the structure's entrance, you'll note a small aperture; here stood the clerk, who collected fees from visitors. While the whole experience was indeed a public one, the flowing Roman toga would have provided a modicum of privacy.

A bit further down Curetes Way are the **brothel** ruins. Unsurprisingly, the site is eagerly anticipated by tourists, though the rather dishevelled state of the place makes envisioning its allegedly licentious nature a challenge. In fact, some experts believe that visiting sailors and merchants simply used it as a guesthouse and bath, which of course would not necessarily exclude prostitution services on demand.

Whatever the brothel's fundamental purpose, its administrators reputedly required visitors to this windowless structure to undergo various degrees of cleansing before entering into the inner areas, which were adorned with little statues of Aphrodite. While Ephesus' current management is keen to downplay the possible existence of a secret underground tunnel connecting the brothel to the Library of Celsus opposite, you may encounter locals who swear to have walked through it as recently as 15 to 20 years ago.

Next is the ornate, Corinthian-style **Temple of Hadrian**, successor of Trajan. Ephesus' second-most famous attraction after the Library of Celsus, the temple originally had a wooden roof and doors. Note its main arch; supported by a central keystone, this architectural marvel remains perfectly balanced, with no need for cement or mortar. Temple designers also covered the structure with intricate decorative details and patterns – Tyche, goddess of chance, adorns the first arch, while Medusa wards off evil spirits on the second. Sailors and traders particularly invoked Tyche, to protect them on their long journeys. After the first arch, in the upper-left corner, is a relief of a man on a horse chasing a boar – a representation of Ephesus' foundation myth. At shoulder-height are backwards swastikas representing the nearby Meander River.

Terraced Houses   RUIN

(Yamaç Evleri; admission ₺15) Across from the Temple of Hadrian, the Terraced Houses cost an additional ₺15, but they're worth it. The whole residential area was used originally as a graveyard – the Romans built the actual terraces for their homes over this and other Hellenistic structures. The roofed complex here contains (at present) seven well-preserved Roman homes. As you ascend the snaking stairs throughout the enclosure, detailed signs explain each structure's evolving use during different periods. In dwelling 2, keep an eye out for wall graffiti: these hand-scrawled images include everything from pictures of gladiators and animals to names and love poems. Dwelling 6 once contained a huge marble hall, which has been partly restored, as well as remarkable hot and cold baths (calderium and frigidarium, respectively), dating from the 3rd century AD. Even if you aren't a history buff, the colourful mosaics, painted frescoes and marbles provide breathtaking insight into the lost world of Ephesus and its aristocracy.

Library of Celsus   RUIN

The early-2nd-century-AD governor of Asia Minor, Celsus Polemaeanus, was commemorated in this magnificent library. As a Greek and Latin inscription on the front staircase attests, Celsus' son, Consul Tiberius Julius

Aquila, built it in 114 to honour his deceased father, who was buried under the library's western side.

Capable of holding 12,000 scrolls in its wall niches, the Celsus was the third-largest ancient library (after Alexandria and Pergamum). The valuable texts were protected from temperature and humidity extremes by a 1m gap between the inner and outer walls. Originally built as part of a complex, the library looks bigger than it actually is: the convex facade base heightens the central elements, while the central columns and capitals are larger than those at the ends.

Facade niches hold replica statues of the Greek Virtues: Arete (Goodness), Ennoia (Thought), Episteme (Knowledge) and Sophia (Wisdom). The originals are in Vienna's Ephesus Museum (the library was restored by the Austrian Archaeological Institute).

Marble Street   RUIN
This was the third-largest street in Ephesus, and connected the Library of Celsus and the Great Theatre (it remains closed due to excavations). Instead, you'll cross the Lower Agora – a 110-sq-metre former textile and food market that once had a massive colonnade.

After exiting, you'll see the Great Theatre. Originally built under Hellenistic King Lysimachus, it was reconstructed by the Romans between AD 41 and AD 117. However, they incorporated original design elements, including the ingenious shape of the *cavea* (seating area). Seating rows are pitched slightly steeper as they ascend, meaning that upper-row spectators still enjoyed good views and acoustics – useful, considering that the theatre could hold 25,000 people. Indeed, Ephesus' estimated peak population (250,000) is supported by the archaeologists' method of estimation: simply multiply theatre capacity by 10.

Harbour Street   RUIN
Formally the Arcadian Way, Harbour St was built by Byzantine Emperor Arcadius (r AD 395–408) in a late attempt to revive the fading city. At the time, it was Ephesus' most lavish thoroughfare, illuminated at night by 50 streetlights on its colonnades, while water and sewerage channels ran beneath its marble flagstones. It greeted visitors after they patronised the Harbour Baths. Look for the high column at the arcade's end to see how far inward the sea reached in those days.

After exiting the Lower Gate, the ruined Gymnasium of Vedius (2nd century AD) had exercise fields, baths, toilets, covered exercise rooms, a swimming pool and a ceremonial hall. Further along is the contemporaneous Stadium, stones from which were later used for the Byzantine Ayasuluk Hill castle.

While here, look out for new surprises as archaeologists continue to dig. In 2007 a gladiator's cemetery was discovered near the Stadium, and Roman-era synagogue remains reportedly lie behind the library; these are among several areas where new discoveries may be made.

In the future, Turkish authorities are planning for war against the silt accumulation that defeated all previous Ephesian civilizations. If accomplished, their marvellous idea of dredging a canal to the Aegean would allow visitors to come to Ephesus by boat, or to gaze out from it onto the sea, thus bringing back the city's original identity as a romantic port.

ℹ Getting There & Away

Most visitors to Ephesus sleep in neighbouring Selçuk (3km away), Kuşadası on the coast (19km away), or touristy mountain hamlets such as Şirince. Technically, hotels cannot take you to Ephesus, so take a taxi, car or tour.

Ephesus' two entry points are 3km apart. The Upper Gate (Magnesia Gate) is most logical, allowing you to walk downhill to the Lower Gate.

Alternatively, Pamucak and Kuşadası minibuses pass the Ephesus turn-off (₺4, five minutes, 3km), a 20-minute walk to the Lower Gate's ticket office. A taxi from Selçuk runs at ₺20.

Around Ephesus

Most Ephesus tours also visit the nearby sites of Meryemana and Grotto of the Seven Sleepers, though ask in advance.

⦿ Sights

Meryemana (Mary's House)   HISTORIC BUILDING
(☏894 1012; per person/car ₺12.50/5, Turkish citizens ₺3; ⏰8am-7pm May-Oct, to 4.30pm Nov-Apr) Although legend has long attested that St John brought the Virgin Mary to Ephesus near the end of her life (AD 37–45), it took until the 19th century for conditions to be right for commercialisation. In 1881, French priest Julien Gouyet claimed to have found Mary's

house based on the visions of a 'mystic', bed-ridden German nun, Catherina Emmerich. Since then, four popes have visited (most recently, Benedict XVI in 2006). Although the Vatican has not taken an official position on the case, the late John Paul II did declare Emmerich a saint in 2004, during the frenzy of last-minute sanctifications before his death.

The ruined house foundations discovered by the French priest are from the 6th century AD (though certain elements are older), and lie on the wooded slope of Bülbül Dağı (Mt Coressos) near Ephesus. Atop these foundations, the enterprising Turks let a chapel be built, which sees continuous mobs of bussed-in pilgrims and curious tourists.

You may not have space to see much inside the tiny chapel through all the tourists, but do note the pale red line on the chapels' side after exiting – everything beneath it is from the original foundation. Multilingual information panels exist; *Mary's House* by Donald Carroll has details. Brochures and booklets (€3) are available.

A 'wishing wall' below the chapel is covered in bits of rags, indicative of Turkic folk custom that visitors have imitated by tying their own bits of cloth, paper, plastic (or anything at hand) to a frame and making a wish.

A formal Catholic mass is held at 7.15am Monday to Saturday (evening service at 6.30pm), and at 10.30am on Sunday. A special service to honour Mary's Assumption is held every 15 August. 'Appropriate dress' is required.

Café Turca (Meryemana Evi; mains ₺4-10; ⊘breakfast, lunch & dinner) at the entrance sells drinks, and the leafy site is good for a picnic.

The site is 8.5km from Ephesus' Lower (northern) Gate and 7km from the Upper (southern) Gate. Dolmuşes don't go, and taxis run ₺50 return from Selçuk's otogar (bus station), if you're not driving or going with a tour.

FREE **Grotto of the Seven Sleepers** RUIN
The road from Mary's House to Ephesus passes a turn-off to the Grotto of the Seven Sleepers, seven legendary Christians persecuted by Emperor Decius in 250 AD. Having refused to recant their beliefs, they gave their possessions to the poor and went to pray in a cave on Mt Pion. They soon fell asleep, and Decius had the cave sealed.

When the men were awoken centuries later by a landowner seeking to use the cave, the story goes, they felt they had slept but a day, and warily sent someone into pagan Ephesus. The dazed young emissary was just as surprised to find Christian churches there as the Ephesians were to find someone presenting 200-year-old coins. The local bishop, Stephen, met the seven sleepers, who later died and were buried in their cave. The bishop quickly proclaimed the miracle (in around 450), immediately creating a Byzantine pilgrimage cult that would last for over 1000 years. The legend became famous as far away as France and England, and there's even a Koranic variant.

Grotto excavation began in 1927; intriguingly, it has unearthed hundreds of 4th- and 5th-century terracotta oil lamps, decorated with Christian and in some cases pagan symbols. Regardless of the legend's verisimilitude, it's clear from these finds and the scores of rock-carved graves in this necropolis that the area was very important to many people for many years.

Walk 200m from the car park (1.5km from Ephesus) to see the **tombs**, following the hill path. Although the grotto itself is fenced off, a large hole in the fence allows entry. Near the site, vendors sell drinks and snacks such as *gözleme* (savoury pancake).

Selçuk
📞0232 / POP 28,158

Were it not for nearby Ephesus, Selçuk might be just another provincial Turkish town; that said, it does have more than the usual number of attractions, from graceful Byzantine aqueduct ruins to the foundations of St John's Basilica and Ayasuluk Fortress – for centuries the town's guardian, and now finally open to visitors.

Like all similarly small places catering to short-term visitors, there's plenty of competition (bordering on downright enmity) between everyone in the local tourism trade, which can result in both good deals for visitors and less-welcome pressure tactics. Yet all in all, Selçuk remains a likeable, down-to-earth town, with a decent selection of places to eat, sleep and drink, and all the necessary services (such as a post office, for sending home those Ephesus postcards). Selçuk is also well connected by bus and train to important destinations, making it a good and inexpensive base for regional adventures.

◉ Sights

Temple of Artemis RUIN

(Artemis Tapınağı; ⊘8.30am-5.30pm) Just beyond Selçuk's western extremities, in an empty field, stands a solitary reconstructed pillar. All that remains of the massive Temple of Artemis, one of the Seven Wonders of the Ancient World, it's now just a 20-second photo opportunity.

At its height, the structure had 127 columns; today, the only way to get any sense of this grandeur is to see the better-preserved Temple of Apollo, in Didyma (it had 122 columns originally).

Artemis' Temple underwent many reconstructions, being damaged by flooding and various invaders over a 1000-year lifespan. But it was always rebuilt – a sign of the great love and attachment Ephesians felt for their fertility avatar, the cult of which brought tremendous wealth to the city from pilgrims and benefactors who included the greatest kings and emperors of the day.

Ephesus Museum MUSEUM

(☑892 6010; Uğur Mumcu Sevgi Yolu Caddesi; admission ₺5; ⊘8.30am-6.30pm summer, to 4.30pm winter) This museum holds artefacts from Ephesus' Terrace Houses, including scales, jewellery and cosmetic boxes, plus coins, funerary goods and ancient statuary. The famous effigy of Phallic god Priapus, visisble by pressing a button, draws giggles, and a whole room is dedicated to Eros in sculpted form. The punters also get a rise out of the multi-breasted, egg-holding marble Artemis statue, which is by any estimation a very fine work indeed.

Finds from a gladiators' cemetery excavation are also displayed, with commentary on their weaponry, training regimes and occupational hazards. Also worth seeing is the frieze from Hadrian's Temple that shows four heroic Amazons with their breasts cut off – early Greek writers attributed Ephesus' founding to them.

Visit the museum after touring Ephesus. After midday, it gets crowded with cruise crowds being rushed through.

Basilica of St John RUIN

(St Jean Caddesi; admission ₺5; ⊘8.30am-6.30pm summer, to 4.30pm winter) Even despite a century of restoration, this once-great basilica of Byzantine Emperor Justinian (r 527–65) is still but a skeleton of its former self. Nevertheless, it makes for a pleasant stroll and warm-up to Ayasuluk Fortress, and the hilltop views are excellent.

The on-site information panel's plan and drawing highlight the building's original grandeur, as do the marble steps and monumental gate. Over time, earthquakes and attackers ruined Justinian's church, which was inspired by the local connection with St John, who reportedly visited Ephesus twice. The first (between AD 37 and AD 48) was with the Virgin Mary; the second (in AD 95) was when he wrote his gospel, on this very hill. These legends, and the existence of a 4th-century tomb supposedly housing John's relics, inspired Justinian to build the basilica here. In Byzantine times, the site drew thousands of pilgrims, and tourists still flock to it today.

Ayasuluk Fortress CASTLE

(St Jean Caddesi; admission €8; ⊘8.30am-6.30pm summer, to 4.30pm winter) Finally opened in September 2012 after years of (still ongoing) excavation, Selçuk's crowning achievement is accessed via the Basilica of St John – and on the same ticket. The digs here, begun in 1990, have proven that the castle peak hosted not only the original Ephesian settlement, but also settlements going back to the Neolithic age. The partially restored fortress' remains date from Byzantine and Ottoman times.

One section of the castle, the mostly ruined **Fortress Mansion**, made waves when excavated in 2009, because it had last been mentioned by a British traveller, John Covell, in 1670. Built for a ruling Ottoman family, the structure was probably created by the same architects responsible for İsa Bey Camii in town.

Recent excavations of the Inner Fortress here have also uncovered the remains of three houses in the Kale Mosque, an area comprised of 15 bedrooms now dubbed the **Southern Terrace**. Since 2010, more than 100m of the western walls and towers have been restored using original materials; archaeologists will continue restoring the former citadel's grandeur in the years ahead.

İsa Bey Camii MOSQUE

(St Jean Caddesi) At the base of Ayasuluk Hill (but very much within town), the imposing İsa Bey Camii (1375) was built by the Emir of Aydın in a post-Seljuk/pre-Ottoman transitional style, and contains a bust of İsa Bey. It's open to visitors, except at prayer times.

Selçuk

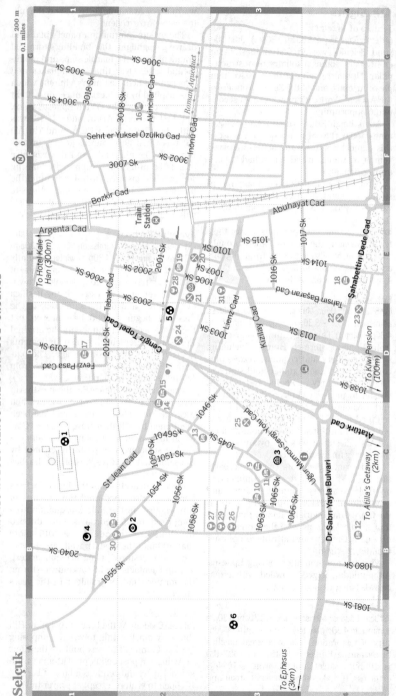

200 m
0.1 miles

To Hotel Kale Han (300m)

Argenta Cad

3005 Sk
3018 Sk
3004 Sk
3008 Sk
Akıncılar Cad
Roman Aqueduct
3006 Sk
İnönü Cad
16
3007 Sk
3002 Sk
Şehit er Yuksel Özülkü Cad

Bozkir Cad
Train Station
Abuhayat Cad

2006 Sk
Tabak Cad
2002 Sk
2003 Sk
2001 Sk
1010 Sk
1015 Sk
1017 Sk
Şahabettin Dede Cad
1014 Sk
Tahsin Başaran Cad
1016 Sk
18

Fevzi Paşa Cad
2019 Sk
17
Cengiz Topel Cad
2012 Sk
28
19
20
1007 Sk
1006 Sk
31
Lienız Cad
1013 Sk
22
23
Kızılay Cad

24
21
1003 Sk

5
7

St Jean Cad
14
15
1046 Sk
1045 Sk
13
25
Uğur Mumcu Sevgi Yolu Cad
Atatürk Cad
To Kiwi Pension (100m)
1038 Sk

1
9
3
11
To Atilla's Getaway (2km)

8
2
4
30
1050 Sk
1049 Sk
1051 Sk
1054 Sk
1056 Sk
1058 Sk
10
1065 Sk
1063 Sk
1066 Sk
Dr Sabrı Yayla Bulvarı
12

2040 Sk
1055 Sk
27
29
26
1080 Sk

1081 Sk

6

To Ephesus (3km)

Selçuk

◉ Sights
1 Basilica of St John C1
2 Crisler Library... B2
3 Ephesus Museum C3
4 İsa Bey Camii...B1
5 Roman Aqueduct.................................... D2
6 Temple of Artemis A3

◉ Activities, Courses & Tours
7 No-Frills Ephesus Tours........................ D2

🛏 Sleeping
8 Akay Hotel..B1
9 Alihan Guesthouse C3
10 Australia & New Zealand
   Guesthouse C3
11 Barım Pension C3
12 Canberra Hotel.. B4
13 Homeros Pension C2
14 Hotel Bella.. C2
15 Naz Han D2

16 Nur Pension... F2
17 Tuncay Pension D1
18 Vardar E4
19 Wallabies Aquaduct Hotel.................... E2

🍴 Eating
20 Ejder Restaurant E2
21 Eski Ev... E2
22 Market..D4
23 Selçuk Köftecisi......................................D4
24 Sişçı Yaşarın Yeri....................................D2
25 St John's Café..C3
   Wallabies Aquaduct Restaurant...(see 19)

🍷 Drinking
26 Amazon...B3
27 Anton..B3
28 Denis Café E2
29 Destina Cafe & Bar..................................B3
30 Odeon Beer Garden B1
31 Pink...E3

Roman Aqueduct RUIN
Running east–west intermittently along Namık Kemal Caddesi and İnönü Caddesi, the long and tall Roman/Byzantine aqueducts are now festively adorned with the huge nests of migrating storks, who stand guard from March through September. The outdoor restaurants and cafes beside the attractively lit central aqueduct arches make for atmospheric and romantic summer dining.

Çetin Museum MUSEUM
(☏894 8116; admission ₺3; ◷9am-5pm) Located 300m beyond the Pamucak-Kuşadası roundabout, this small museum details Anatolian life in the 1950s with a costumed doll collection and folk-dancing exhibit.

Crisler Library NOTABLE BUILDING
(☏892 8317; www.crislerlibraryephesos.com; Prof Anton Kallinger Caddesi 40; admission ₺5; ◷9am-5pm Mon-Fri) If you're keen on Ephesian history, visit this relaxing library – it also offers information on other aspects of ancient, classical, biblical and Islamic history, holds a lecture program for visiting archaeology students, and keeps conference facilities, a bookshop and cafe. It was created by the bequest of distinguished American biblical scholar, archaeologist and Harvard graduate, B Cobbey Crisler.

Çamlık Steam Locomotive Museum MUSEUM
(☏894 8116; admission ₺5; ◷8am-7pm summer, to 5pm winter) An open-air museum several kilometres from Selçuk on the Aydın road, the Çamlık displays over 30 steam locomotives, including the British C-N2 (1887). When headquartered here during the Independence War, Atatürk kept his special white train here; his memory is preserved with photos, portraits, newspaper articles and an antique desk.

🛏 Sleeping

Selçuk specialises in good-value, family-run pensions, though more upscale hotels exist, too; it's by no means a 'budget ghetto'. However, with all of the attentive service, free extras, bus station pick-ups and eager assistance, there can be pressure to buy (carpets, tours etc), which some travellers find stressful. You should be OK at the places listed here.

TOP CHOICE **Atilla's Getaway** HOSTEL €
(☏892 3847; www.atillasgetaway.com; Acarlar Köyü; camp site per person/dm/s/d incl breakfast & dinner €13/17/24/40; ❄🛜🏊) This friendly 'backpacker's resort' is probably the only reason to linger in Selçuk after seeing the sights. Located 2.5km south of town (but linked to the otogar by regular free shuttles),

Atilla's offers basic rooms and spacious (no bunk beds) dorms spread around an outdoor pool, itself flanked by a billiards table, a 'chill-out area' of floor pillows and low wood tables, plus an outdoor bar and dining area.

Campers can use the lower lawn, beside the sand volleyball court. Planned renovations include separate washrooms for campers and generally warmer interiors for off-season visits. Air-conditioning in private rooms costs an extra ₺7. Delicious home-cooked dinners crafted from Atilla's familial vegetable patch are included (if eating out instead, deduct €5 from the given prices).

Akay Hotel
HOTEL €€

(✆892 3172; www.hotelakay.com; 1054 Sokak 7; s/d/tr from €30/50/80; ✳@🛜✉) The quality of this smart, Swiss-run hotel near İsa Bey Camii shows in the impeccable service and attention to detail. Enclosed from the outside street, Akay preserves a quiet elegance with its stone foundations, white walls and green doors. The well-appointed rooms overlook an inviting turquoise pool and patio. Dinners (mains ₺12 to ₺15) are on the relaxing roof terrace.

Homeros Pension
PENSION €€

(✆892 3995; www.homerospension.com; 1048 Sokak 3; s/d/tr ₺50/80/110; ✳🛜) Friendly Homeros is a long-time favourite on the pension scene. It offers a dozen rooms, unique for their colourful hanging textiles and handcrafted furniture made by the owner, a carpenter and antiques collector. Enjoy good views, coffee and dinners (₺15) from the roof terraces. There are ₺5 discounts if you share a bathroom.

Wallabies Aquaduct Hotel
HOTEL €

(✆892 3204; www.wallabiesaquaducthotel.com; Cengiz Topel Caddesi 2; s/d/tr from ₺50/70/105; ✳🛜) Right beside the aqueducts in Selçuk centre, recently renovated Wallabies has clean, modern rooms, some with great views into the storks' nests atop the ruins. It's a busy area, but double-glazed windows keep noise out. There's a great buffet breakfast, and the ground-floor restaurant is among the town's best. Prices are slightly higher than those given here for the upper, renovated rooms, though they plan to finish renovating all of them soon, so check ahead. Owner Mehmet (aka 'Jeff'), his wife Filiz and hard-working parents are extraordinarily kind and helpful.

Barım Pension
PENSION €€

(✆892 6923; barim_pansiyon@hotmail.com; 1045 Sokak 34; s/d ₺40/80; ✳🛜) This 12-room pension stands out for its unusual and winding wire art crafted by the owners, two friendly metalworking brothers. The pension itself occupies a 140-year-old stone house, and there's a leafy back garden for breakfasts and coffees.

Villa Dreams
PENSION €€

(✆892 3514; ephesusvilladreams@gmail.com; Zafer Mah. 3046 Sokak 15; r €35-50; 🛜✉) A brand new pension 1km above town, Villa Dreams offers great views, an outdoor swimming pool and communal kitchen. It has modern standard rooms and two big family rooms with shiny wood floors and balconies. The rooftop terrace affords fantastic castle views, and there's parking. Alternatively, use the free shuttle from the centre (call ahead for pick-up).

Australia & New Zealand Guesthouse
HOSTEL €

(✆892 6050; www.anzguesthouse.com; 1064 Sokak 12; dm/s/d/q from €9/20/25/38; ✳@🛜) The long-established ANZ remains a dependable and very international backpacker's choice in the backstreets. It offers clean but small rooms and standard dorms (though bathrooms for the latter are two flights away). There's a flowery courtyard, relaxed nooks for hanging out and decent breakfast. Barbecue dinners are served on the rooftop terrace, which also has nice views.

Hotel Bella
HOTEL €€€

(✆892 3944; www.hotelbella.com; St Jean Caddesi 7; s/d from €80/120; ✳@🛜) Well situated near St John's Hill, this posh little hotel comes complete with a pricey carpet and jewellery shop, and caters primarily to an older American and British clientele. The well-designed rooms have Ottoman flourishes in the decor, and the relaxing roof terrace offers refined dinners (₺25).

Naz Han
PENSION €€

(✆892 8731; www.nazhan.net; 1044 Sokak 2; r €60-80; ✳@) A hotel with boutique aspirations by St John's Hill, Naz Han occupies a century-old Greek house; both the rooms and the relaxing courtyard are abundantly decorated with artefacts and antiques. There's also a small roof terrace with views.

Kiwi Pension
PENSION €

(Alison's Place; ✆892 4892; www.kiwipension.com; 1038 Sokak 26; s/d/tr/q €25/34/42/48; ✳🛜✉)

This cheerful place near the centre has bright modern rooms and a small private pool out back. Deduct €10 to €15 from the given prices if your room shares a bathroom.

Alihan Guesthouse
PENSION €

(☎892 9496; www.alihanguesthouse.com; 1045 Sokak 34; s/d ₺40/65; ❋🔊) Behind the town's museum, and a two-minute walk from the bus station, the Alihan has friendly owners and clean, renovated rooms, plus a kitchen for self-caterers.

Hotel Kale Han
HOTEL €€

(☎892 6154; www.kalehan.com; Atatürk Caddesi; s/d from ₺100/140; ❋🔊☀) Near Selçuk's entrance, somewhat overpriced Kale Han does have an outdoor pool lined with flowering trees, and well-kept rooms, with traditional charm lent by the decor (black-and-white photographs and scattered antiques). There's also a good restaurant.

Vardar
PENSION €

(☎892 4967; www.vardar-pension.com; Şahabettin Dede Caddesi 9; s/d from ₺35/50; ❋@🔊) This simple but well-kept pension has clean rooms and a lovely roof terrace offering views. There's no pool, but the public one is a two-minute walk, and both train and bus stations are close by, too.

Nur Pension
PENSION €

(☎892 6595; www.nur-pension.com; 3004 Sokak 20; dm/s/d €10/20/39; ❋🔊) This pension past the train station has small rooms (the dorm particularly), but they're fine.

Tuncay Pension
PENSION €

(☎892 6260; www.tuncaypension.com.tr; 2015 Sokak 1; s/d/tr €25/50/60; ❋🔊) This richly carpeted fallback is somewhat pricey (for what you get), though the fan-cooled rooms are slightly cheaper than the air-con ones (listed here). For both, the price includes a Turkish breakfast, and staff can accommodate different dietary needs.

Canberra Hotel
HOTEL €

(☎892 7688; www.hotelcanberra.net; Atatürk Bulvari 15; s/d/tr €25/35/45; ❋@🔊) A fallback option, the midsized Canberra has clean but cramped rooms and a rooftop deck with good views.

✕ Eating

Selçuk offers dependable and reasonably priced Turkish fare. Pensions and hotels also offer good meals at prices consistent with their room rates.

Ejder Restaurant
ANATOLIAN €€

(Cengiz Topel Caddesi 9e; mains ₺7-17) Roughly opposite the Byzantine aqueduct, this tiny but time-tested local favourite serves delicious Turkish dishes – if you can't decide, take the whole sizzling Anatolian meat platter. The kind owners, Mehmet and his wife Rahime, are proud to show off the guest books and memorabilia, which include photos from the Clinton family's visit and a touching guest entry from the late, great Steve Irwin.

Wallabies Aquaduct Restaurant
TURKISH €€

(☎892 3204; Cengiz Topel Caddesi 2; mains ₺10-16) Beneath the hotel of the same name, this recently refurbished restaurant spills out onto the square beneath the Byzantine aqueduct, guaranteeing atmospheric summer dining. The traditional Anatolian fare is complemented by more international offerings, including vegie dishes and fish. Definitely try the house speciality, *krep tavuk sarması* – a specially seasoned chicken dish, baked under a ridge of mashed potatoes sprinkled with bechamel sauce. Incredibly delicious.

Selçuk Köftecisi
KÖFTE €

(Şahabettin Dede Caddesi; mains ₺6-9) This classic *köfte* (meatball) joint, family-run since 1959, offers great but small meat portions and tasty side salads.

Sişçi Yaşarın Yeri
KÖFTE €

(Atatürk Caddesi; mains from ₺6) A popular spot for *köfte* and kebaps, this stall has tables.

St John's Café
MEDITERRANEAN €

(www.stjohns-cafe-ephesus.com; Uğur Mumcu Sevgi Yolu Caddesi 4c; mains ₺8-13; 🔊) Despite, or perhaps because, it being Selçuk's most touristy cafe-shop, St John's has the town's widest coffee selection, various toasts and other international snacks. There's a play area for restless youngsters, too.

Eski Ev
ANATOLIAN €

(Old House Restaurant; 1005 Sokak 1a; mains ₺6-11; ☼breakfast, lunch & dinner) Rather touristy, but with an undeniably pleasing courtyard set amid fruit trees, the 'Old House' offers varied Turkish fare.

Market
MARKET €

(Şahabettin Dede Caddesi; ☼9am-5pm Sat winter, 8am-7pm Sat summer) Self-caterers (and sightseers) will enjoy Selçuk's Saturday market, behind the bus station. This and the Wednesday market (behind the train station) offer fruits, veg and cheeses from village farms.

🍷 Drinking

While seaside Kuşadası has wild nightlife, Selçuk's desultory bar-cafe scene exists mainly to help local males watch televised football matches out of their homes. Drinking with fellow travellers and your hosts back at your pension is generally more worthwhile.

If you do go out, you'll find the action concentrated along Prof Anton Kallinger Caddesi and Siegburg Caddesi, with a few scattered cafes near İsa Bey Camii as well. While near-identical, **Destina** (Prof Anton Kallinger Caddesi 24; ⊘10am-3am) and **Amazon** (Prof Anton Kallinger Caddesi 22; 🕿) are two aesthetically pleasing central places. The nearby **Anton** (Prof Anton Kallinger Caddesi) and **Denis** (Cengiz Topel Caddesi 20; ⊘10am-2am) are more simple. Also downtown is **Pink** (Siegburg Caddesi 24; ⊘10am-2am Sun-Thu, to 3am Fri & Sat), Selçuk's oldest and most nightclub-like bar.

Opposite İsa Bey Camii, the new **Odeon Beer Garden** (1054 Sokak 1; ⊘6am-midnight) is one of a few laid-back places for a drink on Selçuk's northern side.

ℹ Information

Banks with ATMs and exchange offices line Cengiz Topel and Namık Kemal Caddesis.

Selçuk Hospital (☑892 7036; Dr Sabri Yayla Bulvarı)

Tourist Office (www.selcuk.gov.tr; Agora Caddesi 35; ⊘8am-noon & 1-5pm daily summer, Mon-Fri winter)

Dangers & Annoyances

Look out for conniving 'coin-men': although savvy travellers won't fall for it, there are apparently still enough naive tourists willing to part with a couple of hundred euros or dollars to make it worthwhile for locals to tinker with coin molds, base metals and household chemicals to create pieces of supposedly ancient numismatic treasure. Besides the clear illegality of trying to purchase antiquities on the street, it's a total waste of your money. The fraudsters are most often found around St John's Hill or the gates of Ephesus.

ℹ Getting There & Around

Bus & Dolmuş

Buses serve İzmir (₺9, one hour) every 40 minutes from 6.30am to 9pm (less frequent in winter). Going by bus to İzmir's airport involves being dropped off at a highway turn-off, from where it's a 2km walk or a ₺10 taxi ride. Taking the direct Selçuk–airport train is a far simpler and cheaper way to travel between the two.

Three daily summer buses serve Bodrum (₺25, 3¼ hours). A direct daily bus to Pamukkale leaves at 9.30am and returns at 5pm. Otherwise, two direct buses serve Denizli (₺25, 4½ hours), for transfers to Pamukkale or coastal stops such as Fethiye and Antalya. For İstanbul (₺45 to ₺50, 10 hours) direct buses (three night-time and one daytime) operate via Bursa.

For coastal Kuşadası (₺5, 30 minutes) and Pamucak (₺2.50, 10 minutes) dolmuşes run every 20 to 30 minutes from 6.55am to 10pm during summer, fewer in winter. In summer, the last Kuşadası–Selçuk dolmuş runs at midnight (8pm in low season).

The Priene, Miletus and Didyma ruins are best accessed by car (₺80 to ₺100 per day plus petrol), or with a tour, which can be cheaper and is definitely more informative.

Taxi

You won't usually need in-town taxis, but if so it's around ₺5 to ₺8. For Ephesus, figure ₺20, for Mary's House expect ₺50 return. İzmir airport taxis run ₺130, but again the direct train is a much better option.

Train

The direct train to İzmir's Adnan Menderes Airport (₺4.50, 55 minutes) is the best way to get there. Services start at 6.25am and finish at 7.30pm. Note that from the train's airport stop, it's a 15 to 20 minute stroll to the departures terminal.

Three daily trains serve Denizli (₺14.70, 4½ hours). For İstanbul, a popular train-boat combination route involves taking a train from Selçuk to Bandarma, and then a ferry service to İstanbul – more interesting than the long slog by bus. Note that advance ticket purchase doesn't guarantee a seat.

Şirince

☑0232 / POP 960

Once a Greek-populated mountain village, Şirince's clustered stone-and-stucco homes, bucolic wooded setting and long winemaking tradition have made it popular for foreign and Turkish tourists. While the deluge has affected its original charms, it remains a beautiful place and fun day trip. It's much more tranquil by night, and a handful of rather precious (and overpriced) boutique pensions have sprung up to cater to well-heeled tourists.

While Şirince was probably settled when Ephesus was abandoned, today's remains date to the 19th century. Legend says that freed Greek slaves in the 15th century resettled here, calling it Çirkince (Ugliness) to keep others away. However, by at least the 19th century it had become Kirkinje. Under the new republic in the 1920s, the name Şirince (Pleasantness) came with the exodus of the Greeks, who largely moved to a village they called Nea Ephesos (New Ephesus) in northern Greece.

Şirince was repopulated by Turks also from northern Greece; they built a mosque, but retained the local alcohol trade, and today you can sample their unique wines (made from raspberry, peach, black mulberry and pomegranate) in local restaurants and cafes. That said, if ordering expensive wine, ask for it to be poured in front of you. Local miscreants have been known to give refills of cheap house wine, presuming (correctly) that tourists will never know the difference.

👁 Sights

Crowds dissipate by evening; 1pm to 3pm is busiest. There's a gauntlet of souvenir stands, but past them you can enjoy the cool, crisp air and lovely old houses from the cobbled lanes on high.

A couple of generally well-kept public toilets (₺1) are near the main sights.

Church of St John the Baptist　　CHURCH
(🕙8am-8pm summer, 8.30am-6.30pm winter) The Church of St John the Baptist (1805) has been sadly neglected by modern Turkey, with an American charitable society being largely responsible for its upkeep. Despite the faded Byzantine frescoes on some walls, preservation is nonexistent, birds flit through the barren windows and Turkish-language graffiti is scrawled across where the altar once was.

If you have a spare kuruş or two, there's a shallow wishing well before the church entrance.

🛏 Sleeping

Rooms tend to be named after colours or vegetation in Şirince's lovely but overpriced rustic hotels – it's just that kind of place.

Terrace Houses　　BOUTIQUE HOTEL €€€
(🕿0532 263 7942; www.ephesushousessirince
.com; r from ₺215, cottage ₺275; ❀🖥) These three lovingly adorned traditional houses are in the quieter streets above the mosque, away from the tourist bustle. Choose from the Grapevine, Olive and Fig Houses, each of which differs slightly in capacity; some include poster beds and bath-tubs, while all

enjoy relaxing views over the village. Breakfast is in the enclosed outdoor terraces.

Güllü Konak　　BOUTIQUE HOTEL €€€
(🕿898 3131; www.gullukonak.com; Şirince Köyü 44; r ₺340-420; ❀@) This collection of 12 spacious and individually decorated rooms occupies two sturdy white-and-brown mansions, and feature a tranquil private garden.

Kırkınca Pansiyon　　BOUTIQUE HOTEL €€€
(🕿898 3133; www.kirkinca.com; s/d ₺130/250; ❀) Up the hill opposite the bazaar, the Kırkınca constitutes several restored, 250-year-old houses with elegantly appointed rooms. Some have four-poster beds, and one has a mini-hamam. The main building's shaded roof terrace offers great views.

İstanbul Pansiyon　　PENSION €€
(🕿898 3189; www.istanbulpension.com; İstiklal Mah 13; d ₺150; ❀) A sumptuous, restored old house, the İstanbul has five well-decorated traditional rooms.

🍴 Eating

Artemis Şirince
Şarap Evi Restaurant　　ANATOLIAN €€
(🕿898 3240; www.artemisrestaurant.com; mains ₺9.50-28) At the village entrance, Artemis occupies the former Greek schoolhouse and has great views from its outside terrace and garden.

Şirincem Restaurant & Cafe　　ANATOLIAN €€
(🕿898 3180; mains ₺7-14) This rustic restaurant under shady foliage is strong on meats. The fruit-farming owner makes his own wines (but offers 'mainstream' reds and whites, too).

ℹ Getting There & Away

Minibuses (₺3) leave Selçuk for Şirince every 30 minutes in summer, hourly in winter.

Tire & Kaplan
🕿0232

Inland day trips (ideally, by car) reach less touristy places; Tire, located amid farmland under the Bozdağlar Mountains, is one of these, except during its popular **Tuesday market**. The 8.30am Islamic market prayer over the loudspeaker provides a certain exotic touch for the bussed-in tourist crowds. The foodstuffs on sale at this day-long event are undeniably delicious, and the market provides a slice-of-life view into rural Turkey.

Tire clings to its traditional felt-making industry, with three felt-makers, including Keçeci (☑512 2391; www.tireconkece.com; ⊙8.30am-7.30pm Mon-Sat), still working on blends of teased cotton and wool. You'll be shown the design-making process, which involves creating patterns, dousing with water, adding cotton and finally pressing the material for a full hour.

Nearby Tire, Kaplan village offers the excellent **Kaplan Dağ Restorant** (☑512 6652; www.kaplandag.com; mains ₺10-12; ⊙1-9.30pm Tue-Sun), which serves traditional local *köfte*, a variety of mezes and Turkish mains. Try the local blackberry juice, and book ahead on Tuesdays and weekends.

Hourly minibuses serve Tire from Selçuk (₺6). Tire–Kaplan taxis cost ₺20.

Pamucak

☑0232

Popular Pamucak, 7km west of Selçuk, is your nearest beach day trip, though better beaches exist further down the coast (ask locally). On weekends, Turkish families flock here, often leaving their trash behind, so it's not the cleanest stretch of sand, but still fine for a swim. From February to March, flamingos visit the estuary wetlands (a 15-minute walk from the beach).

Accommodation is limited. Try **Dereli** (☑893 1205; www.dereli-ephesus.com; d ₺70-100), which offers palm-fronted, beach-facing bungalows. Camping grounds (₺15 per person) are also available.

Half-hourly summer minibuses run from Selçuk (₺2.50, 10 minutes), hourly in winter. To/from Kuşadası, go to Selçuk first. Dolmuşes pass Dereli (and Ephesus).

Kuşadası

☑0256 / POP 68,225

Coastal Kuşadası is a popular package-tour destination for Northern Europeans and, as the gateway to Ephesus, has become the Med's fourth-busiest cruise port. It's a place that could, and should, be better than it is, but lacking the sights and ambience of Bodrum or the size of Marmaris, it remains a distant runner-up on the Aegean coast's party scene, though the plethora of Irish pubs and discos do make an effort.

If you want nightlife, or simply like being near the sea, this is a good base, though Selçuk offers better value for money.

⊙ Sights & Activities

Kuşadası town's small artificial beach is eclipsed by **Kadınlar Denizi** (Ladies Beach), 2.5km south and served by regular dolmuşes. It's nice, but gets very crowded with package tourists from the big nearby hotels. Further south are several small beaches, again backed by big hotels.

Kuşadası's main attraction is a minor stone **fortress** on causeway-connected **Güvercin Ada** (Pigeon Island). It exhibits handicrafts and features pigeon coops on stilts, but is mostly just a nice place for a seaside stroll.

East of here are the cruise-ship docks; immediately in the line of sight of a disembarking cruiser starts the main **bazaar** area, where 'genuine fake watches', leathery apparel, cheap jewellery and the like are sold.

If Kuşadası is your base for Aegean manoeuvres, local travel agencies offer trips to Ephesus (full day with lunch for €45), Priene, Miletus and Didyma (€50), or more distant places such as Pamukkale (€45).

Belediye Hamamı　　　　　　HAMAM

(☑614 1219; Yildirim Caddesi 2; admission €14; ⊙9am-7pm Apr-Oct) Kuşadası's emancipated hamams offer mixed bathing (with towels). The Belediye, which dates back 600 years, is a restored, clean and atmospheric bath up from Bar St.

🛏 Sleeping

Kuşadası centre has pensions and business hotels, none terribly atmospheric, while package-tour resorts cover the outlying coasts.

Liman Hotel　　　　　PENSION €€

(Mr Happy's; ☑614 7770; www.limanhotel.com; Kıbrıs Caddesi, Buyral Sokak 4; s/d €25/38; ❄@🛜) Independent travellers will feel good vibes here; from owner Hasan ('Mr Happy') right through to the cooks and cleaners, everyone is friendly and helpful. It's a budget hotel, so not particularly fancy, but the rooms are clean and spacious enough, while the rooftop terrace/bar has great views and is the place for the buffet breakfast. It's in a tall old building opposite the cruise port. Hasan and company are full of local information and can help arrange trips to the local sites and Samos.

Hotel Ilayda　　　　BUSINESS HOTEL €€

(☑614 3807; www.hotelilayda.com; Atatürk Bulvarı 46; s/d ₺80/140; ❄@🛜) This shiny, renovated seaside option has nice design touches and a good restaurant. It has all mod cons, and

EPHESUS, BODRUM & THE SOUTH AEGEAN PAMUCAK

GETTING WET IN KUŞADASI

Adaland (☑618 1252; www.adaland.com; Çamlimanı Mevkii; adult/child ₺50/40; ☉10am-6pm May-Oct), just north of Kuşadası near Pamucak, calls itself one of the world's top 10 water parks, while **Aqua Fantasy** (☑893 1111; www.aquafantasy.com; Kuşadası beach; adult/child €22/13; ☉10am-6pm), by Kuşadası's beach, claims to be Europe's largest. Both have myriad slides, rides, pools and so on. Kids under three can enter free at both. Aqua Fantasy offers a 10% discount if booking online, and also has a hotel and spa centre on its sprawling, 18-hectare grounds.

Scuba-diving lessons, and actual dives, are offered by **Aquaventure Diving Center** (☑612 7845; www.aquaventure.com.tr; Miracle Beach Club; ☉8am-6pm); located by Ladies Beach, it offers PADI open-water courses (€250) and reef dives (from €30). Call for free pick-up from most local hotels.

great views from some rooms, and from the rooftop terrace.

Sezgin Hotel Guest House   HOSTEL €
(☑614 4225; www.sezginhotel.com; Arslanlar Caddesi 68; s/d/tr/f €25/35/50/60; ✴@☏≋) A solid budget pick, Sezgin offers clean rooms with big, comfortable beds and small balconies overlooking a garden and pool. There's a self-catering family room (though note the pension is near loud bars). Call for free port or bus-station pick-up.

Club Caravanserail   HISTORIC HOTEL €€
(☑614 4115; www.kusadasihotelcaravanserail.com; Atatürk Bulvarı 2; s/d/ste €80/100/150; ✴☏) A grand 17th-century stone caravanserai, this photogenic structure is lit at night, and accessed by giant stairs leading to a secluded inner courtyard. The rooms' Ottoman decor is authentic, the kitschy 'Turkish nights' less so.

Villa Konak   BOUTIQUE HOTEL €€
(☑612 6318; www.villakonakhotel.com; Yıldırım Caddesi 55; s/d from €40/60; ✴@☏≋) In Kuşadası's quieter old quarter, Villa Konak offers periodpiece rooms in a restored 140-year-old stone house. The leafy courtyard-garden has a pool, ancient well, scattered Roman ruins and shady magnolias. Children under six aren't allowed.

Charisma   LUXURY HOTEL €€€
(☑618 3266; www.charismahotel.com; Akyar Mevkii 5; s/d/ste €165/220/850; ✴@☏≋) North of the centre on its own beach, Charisma is as posh as Kuşadası gets, and seems to draw an older American crowd. There's an atmospheric wood-beamed verandah overlooking the water, and the rooms (which have all the amenities one could need) each have sea views. There's also a specially fitted room for disabled travellers.

Kısmet   LUXURY HOTEL €€€
(☑618 1290; www.kismet.com.tr; Gazibeğendi Bulvarı 3; s/d/ste €99/129/339; ☉Apr–mid-Nov; ✴@☏≋) On a verdant promontory on Kuşadası's northern side, Kısmet is owned by a descendent of the last Ottoman sultan; it boasts a fittingly regal look, with manicured gardens, romantic candlelit dinners on the waterfront terrace restaurant, and a private beach. While rooms are not as opulent as one might expect, they do all come with balconies (try for a sea-facing one).

Hotel Stella   PENSION €
(☑614 1632; www.hotelstellakusadasi.com; Bezirgan Sokak 44; s/d ₺40/70; ✴@≋) Central Hotel Stella, on a hillly street, makes a good budget fallback, with tidy rooms offering sea-and-city views. Rates are negotiable for longer stays.

✕ Eating

Waterfront dining is atmospheric but can be expensive – verify seafood prices before ordering. If ambience isn't important, head inland for cheaper but tasty kebap shops. Kaleiçi, Kuşadası's old quarter, offers characterful backstreet eats and some fun, more Turkish cafes.

Ferah   SEAFOOD €€€
(☑614 1281; İskele Yanı Güvercin Parkı İçi; mains ₺15-25; ☉lunch & dinner) This waterfront restaurant is one of the classier options, with great sunset sea views and good-quality mezes and seafood.

Bebop   INTERNATIONAL €€
(☑618 0727; www.bebopjazzclub.com; mains from ₺9; ☉lunch & dinner) Located within the marina itself, Bebop actually offers something different, with breakfasts, a pool to laze by over drinks, and generous portions

Kuşadası

EPHESUS, BODRUM & THE SOUTH AEGEAN KUŞADASI

200 m
0.1 miles

To Bebop (50m);
Kismet (500m);
Charisma (1km)

Istiklal Cad

Gençlik Cad

Topiani Sk

Ülgen Sk

Sevgi Sk

Candan Tarhan Bul

Demiroğlu Sk

Dolmuşes for Selçuk
via Pamucak

Atatürk Bulvarı

50 Yıl Cad

Tavaslı Sk

Bahçearası Sk

Ismet İnönü Bulvarı

Ismet İnönü Bul

Atatürk Bul

Kemal Arıkan cad

Oğe Sk

Sevgi Sk

Sağlık Cad

Emek Sk

Bus Company
Offices

Old Bazaar

Zafer Sk

Kışla Sk

Kaleiçi Sk

Cephanı Sk

Bahar Sk

KALEICI

Monumental
Arch

Mosque

İbrahim
Camii

Yıldırım Cad

Kuşadası
Cruise
Terminal

Scala
Nuova

Ferry to
Samos

Meander
Travel

Barbaros Hayrettin
Bulvarı

Bazaar

Deniz Sk

Arslanlar Cad

Anıt Sk

Kıbrıs Cad

Bezirgan Sk

Aydınlık Sk

Sultan İmam Sk

To Samos

Güvercin Ada Cad

Atatürk
Monument

To Jade
(700m)

To Samos

Kuşadası

of Turkish and international fare – often followed by late-night live jazz.

Saray INTERNATIONAL €€€
(☎0544 921 6224; Bozkurt Sokak 25; mains ₺15-35; ☷) Saray does international fare and some decent Turkish choices, plus good vegetarian options. It can get kitschy during evening singalongs and on Wednesday's 'Turkish Night', though.

Köfteci Ali KÖFTE €
(Arslanlar Caddesi 14; mains ₺5; ☷24hr summer, 9am-midnight winter) This Bar St kebap booth caters to both well-mannered Turks and drunken foreign louts, when the clubs are closing. The spicy wrapped-pide kebap here is nourishing.

Cimino ITALIAN €€
(Atatürk Bulvarı 56b; mains ₺5-19; ☷lunch & dinner) Opposite the seafront and featuring jazz music, Cimino is the best local option for Italian food and coffees.

Kazim Usta Restaurant SEAFOOD €€€
(☎614 1226; Liman Caddesi 4; meze ₺5-12, mains ₺15-30) Opposite the tourist office by the water, Kazim Usta opened in 1950 and since then has become known as Kuşadası's top fish restaurant. Salad, and fish soup or calamari for an appetiser, followed by sea bream and a drink, will run about ₺55 per person. Waterfront tables require advance booking in summer.

🍷 Drinking & Entertainment

Kuşadası's nightlife scene comprises three areas: Barlar Sokak (Bar St), a cacophonous central zone patronised by tourists and fronted by loquacious touts; the more laid-back old cafes of Kaleiçi, preferred by Turks; and Cape Yılancı on the southern coast, with its giant bar-club-concert complexes. Basically private beaches by day, these transform by night into slick bars, dance clubs, and live-music stages on the water.

Jimmy's Irish Bar PUB
(Barlar Sokak 8; ☷Apr-Nov) The oldest and most famous of several local joints inexplicably evoking the Emerald Isle, Jimmy's is situated right at the Bar St entrance. Like the others, it does everything loud, from the music to the karaoke to the beamed-in football for visiting lager louts.

Another Bar BAR
(Tuna Sokak 10) On the site of an old citrus orchard, Another Bar has tables and stools dotted among the remaining trees, but less harmoniously, a huge screen and dance floor, too.

Jade CLUB
(www.jadebeachclub.com; weekday/weekend ₺25/30) West of the marina, Jade is Kuşadası's full-on entertainment venue, boasting a pool, sand volleyball, beachside loungers and relaxed drinks by day, and dance floors, bars and concerts; it's all palm trees, wraparound couches, mood lighting and mojitos.

Orient Bar LIVE MUSIC
(www.orientbar.com; Kaleiçl Kışla Sokak 14 & 17) On a side street, this perennial favourite in an atmospheric old stone house has trellises across the lattice roof. Unlike Bar St's sonic screeching, here you'll get mellower sounds, such as live acoustic guitar.

Bizim Meyhane MEYHANE
(Kışla Sokak) This characterful and slightly eccentric place, marked by low beams, stone walls and hung instruments, is popular with Turks and foreign tourists. They do good live Turkish music here.

ℹ️ Information

ATM-equipped banks are on Barbaros Hayrettin Bulvarı.

Özel Kuşadası Hastanesi (📞613 1616; Anıt Sokak) Excellent, English-speaking private hospital 3km north of the centre (Selçuk road).

Post Office (Barbaros Hayrettin Bulvarı 23-25; ⏱8.30am-12.30pm & 1.30-5.30pm Mon-Sat winter, 8am-midnight daily summer)

Tourist Office (Liman Caddesi, İskele Meydanı; ⏱8am-noon & 1-5pm Mon-Fri) Near the cruise-ship dock, and under the walls. Kind staff, but they only provide maps.

ℹ️ Getting There & Away

Boat

Meander Travel (www.meandertravel.com; Kıbrıs Caddesi 1; ⏱9am-9pm), by the dock, operates the ferry to Samos, and sells tickets (like all other Kuşadası travel agencies). From 1 April to 31 October, boats depart daily from Kuşadası at 8.30am. Tickets cost €35 for a single, €40 for a same-day return and €55 for an open return (this includes port tax).

Staying overnight in Samos incurs a €10 tax for leaving Greece, and another €10 tax for re-entering Turkey. Ask ahead if you want a ticket that includes these fees (they may also be discounted or waived). Arrive 45 minutes before departure for immigration formalities. Returning to Kuşadası could prove problematic if your Turkish visa is not multi-entry. So think ahead, lest your friends someday demean you as the idiot who ruined their vacation.

Bus

Kuşadası's otogar is at Kahramanlar Caddesi's southern end, on the bypass highway. Bus companies on İsmet İnönü Bulvarı sell tickets and offer free *servis* (shuttle minibuses) to it. Dolmuşes leave from centrally located Adnan Menderes Bulvarı, and from the otogar.

Three daily summer buses serve Bodrum (₺25, 2½ hours, 151km); in winter, take a dolmuş

to Söke (₺5, at least every 30 minutes year-round).

Dolmuşes run every 20 to 30 minutes to Selçuk (₺5, 30 minutes); grab this line for Pamucak beach or Ephesus' gate on the way.

ℹ️ Getting Around

Kuşadası lacks direct links to İzmir's airport. Either take a bus to İzmir otogar and switch to the local shuttle service, or make the short trip to Selçuk – the train from there goes directly to the airport. Otherwise, a taxi costs around ₺160.

Şehiriçi minibuses (₺1.50) run every few minutes in summer (every 15 to 20 in winter) from Kuşadası otogar to the centre, and along the coast. Kadınlar Denizi minibuses serve Ladies Beach.

Dilek Peninsula

About 26km south of Kuşadası, the Dilek Peninsula juts westwards into the Aegean, almost touching Samos. West of Güzelçamlı, **Dilek National Park** (Dilek Milli Parkı; www.dilekyarimadasi.com; per person/car ₺4/10; ⏱7am-7.30pm Jun-Sep, 8am-5pm Oct-May) is a mountainous reserve with walking trails, stunning vistas, azure coves for swimming, and secret military installations you will never see.

A brown sign outside the entrance points to **Zeus Mağarası** (the 'Cave of Zeus'), where the water's refreshingly cold in summer and warm in winter.

After the Dilek National Park entry gate, four rounded bays with pebble beaches lie below. The road then tapers off at a high-security military compound covering the peninsula's end, from where men in uniform can train their binoculars at the frolicking tourists on opposing Samos.

Accessing the first cove, **İçmeler Köyü** (1km past the entrance), involves a steep

'PMD' TOURS

The ancient settlements of Priene, Miletus and Didyma run in a line south of Kuşadası. Visiting all three in one day is easily done by rental car (₺80 to ₺100 per day, plus petrol) or, if you want more details, on a so-called 'PMD' (Priene, Miletus and Didyma) tour with travel agencies in Selçuk and Kuşadası. Tours usually require at least four participants, and cost around €35 for transport, lunch and an hour at each site. Ascertain in advance where you'll go and for how long (make sure the tour operator will take you to Miletus' newly opened museum, which is sometimes forgotten but definitely worthwhile).

Going via public transportation is difficult, as dolmuşes don't serve Miletus. However, the dolmuş from Söke does serve Priene and Didyma (you must return to Söke to switch minibuses in between). Highway turn-offs to the ruins are marked with big brown signs.

KİRAZLİ

Some 10km east of Kuşadası, on a back road, the white houses and terracotta roofs of traditional Turkey rise from a bowl in the hills at Kirazli, the 'Place of Cherries'. Enjoy breakfast here at **Köy Sofrası** (☑667 1003; www.koysofrasi.com; mains ₺5-15), set in an old orchard. It's a relaxed restaurant with rustic charm, serving good local mezes.

With only 600 inhabitants, Kirazli has retained its agricultural ways, but the recent arrival of tourists (and a few foreign home-buyers) has caused a re-think; Kirazli now plays up its organic produce, sold at a Sunday **farmers market**. The enterprising locals also now rent (and sell) traditional villas, targeting artistic and writerly sorts. Prices for self-catering villas start at around ₺90 per night. For information, visit www.kirazlivillage.com.

---

walk down to the sandy but somewhat dirty beach. The road above has great views from designated pullover points.

About 3km beyond İçmeler Köyü, an unpaved turn-off heads 1km downhill to **Aydınlık Beach**. This quieter, 800m-long pebble-and-sand strand is backed by pines, and is busy enough to warrant a lifeguard station.

Less than 1km further along, after the *jandarma* (provincial police) station turn-off, the signposted **kanyon** appears on the left. If you think it's worth the 15km walk down a forest trail, **Doğanbey** village has a museum of stuffed animals. The path's first 6km are open to all, but after that you need a permit or to be with a guide.

Dilek's third bay, **Kavaklı Burun**, has a sand-and-pebble surf beach. As at Aydınlık, there's a second entrance 1km further down. The final visitable beach, **Karasu Köyü**, is the most placid, and enjoys revelatory views of mountainous Samos rising from the sea. If you're lucky, you might even see a dolphin.

Camping is forbidden – the party's over at closing time. All four beaches have free wood-slatted chairs, which are quickly taken. An umbrella with two fold-out chairs costs ₺20. Each bay has a restaurant shack (mains ₺8 to ₺25), serving everything from steak to sea bass.

❶ Getting There & Away

In season, dolmuşes run from Kuşadası every 15 minutes for Dilek (₺5, 40 minutes), but only to the third bay (Kavaklı Burun). For the fourth, the driver will need an additional ₺2. Güzelçamlı–Kuşadası buses run until midnight in summer. The Dilek National Park entrance fee is paid on the bus.

PRİENE, MİLETUS, DİDYMA & AROUND

Priene

☑0256

Like Ephesus, Priene was once a sophisticated port city. Although its relative lack of spectacular ruins leaves more to the imagination, Priene does enjoy a commanding position high on Mt Mykale (near Güllübahçe), giving it a certain natural grandeur missing at Ephesus. Priene also offers plenty of shady trees and fewer crowds, making the trip cooler and more relaxing.

While up on these craggy peaks, try to imagine the sea below you, instead of today's fields. Before the Meander River silted over, Priene had two harbours, and was famed for its shipbuilding industry and sailing tradition. Digging only started here in the late 19th century, led by British and German archaeologists. Plenty of marble statues and other antiquities ended up in their museums – in some cases, short-sighted sultans actually traded them for 'useful' things such as trains and technology.

Priene was important by 300 BC (when the League of Ionian Cities held congresses and festivals here), peaking between then and 45 BC. Still, it was smaller than nearby Miletus, and the Romans made fewer modifications to its Hellenistic buildings, which has preserved its uniquely 'Greek' look. By the 2nd century AD, however, the silt had won, and most of the population relocated to Miletus. Amid the rubble, a tiny Greek village, Samson (later populated by Turks also), existed until 1923, when the Greeks were expelled and the Turks moved to the greener pastures of Güllübahçe.

Priene

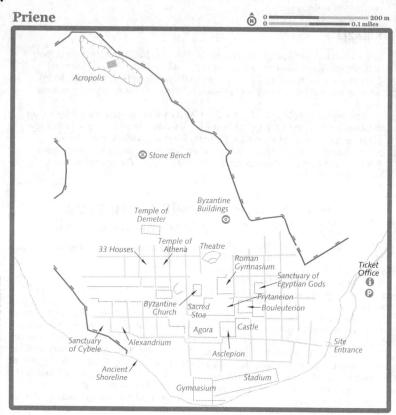

Acropolis

Stone Bench

Temple of
Demeter

Byzantine
Buildings

33 Houses

Temple of
Athena

Theatre

Roman
Gymnasium

Sanctuary of
Egyptian Gods

Ticket
Office

Byzantine
Church

Sacred
Stoa

Prytaneion

Bouleuterion

Agora

Castle

Sanctuary
of Cybele

Alexandrium

Asclepion

Site
Entrance

Ancient
Shoreline

Gymnasium

Stadium

After the ticket booth, walk up the steep path to the ruins. Note that the streets meet at right angles – a system invented by Hippodamus (498–408 BC), an architect from nearby Miletus. Creator of the 'grid system' of urban planning, Hippodamus became influential, and his system was used not only in Miletus and Priene, but also in Rhodes, Piraeus (the port of Athens in Greece), and even ancient Greek Thurii, in southern Italy. As at Ephesus, Priene's marble streets also have gouged lines and notches to prevent slipping.

On a high bluff backed by stark mountains and overlooking what was once the sea, stands the ruined **Temple of Athena**. Once Priene's biggest and most important structure, it was designed by Pythius of Priene, who also designed the Mausoleum at Halicarnassus (today's Bodrum). An original inscription, now in the British Museum, states that Alexander the Great funded the temple.

Unlike urban-planner Hippodamus, whom Aristotle recalled as being rather the free spirit (he never cut his hair and wore the same clothes year-round), Pythius was a strict stickler for detail; he saw his Classical Ionian temple design as solving the 'imperfections' he perceived in preceding Doric design. Today's five re-erected columns give some sense of its original look, though many others lie in unruly heaps around it. (The temple was destroyed by earthquake, not plundered.)

At the time of research, archaeologists hoped to excavate a **Hellenistic Synagogue** near the temple – check while you're there.

Priene's **theatre** (capacity 6500) is among the best-preserved Hellenistic theatres anywhere. Whistle to test the acoustics, and slip your fingers between the lion's-paw indentations on the finely carved VIP seats in front.

Also see the nearby **bouleuterion** (council chamber), built to hold 250 interlocutors; from here a narrow path leads down to the ruined medical centre, the **Asclepion** (once thought to be a Temple of Zeus). Remains of a **gymnasium** and **stadium** are also around. In an unexcavated area nearby lie **Byzantine church** ruins.

Right at the parking, under a ruined Byzantine aqueduct overflowing with water that cools the hot air, **Selale Restaurant** (mains ₺10) has a big basin with (cookable) trout. The adjoining shaded courtyard is perfect for a relaxed coffee or juice after seeing the site.

ⓘ Getting There & Away

Visit Priene by car or on a tour – it's not as well signposted as Ephesus, so having a professional guide will help you get much more out of your visit.

Otherwise, dolmuşes run every 15 minutes between Priene (Güllübahçe; ₺4, 17km) and Söke; the last one back to Söke leaves Priene at 7pm. The dolmuş stops at the aqueduct and restaurant (250m from the entrance).

Miletus (Milet)

☑ 0256

Ancient Miletus, 22km south of Priene amid rich cotton fields, was once a great port city. It's often (but unfairly) disparaged as dull compared to Priene and Didyma, but you should definitely not skip it – Miletus' mixed Hellenistic-Roman architecture is impressive, and its small but fascinating new museum illustrates the original relationship between all three places.

Although Miletus' distant origins are unclear, it's likely that Minoan Cretans came in the Bronze Age (the word Miletus is of Cretan origin). Ionian Greeks consolidated themselves from 1000 BC, and Miletus became a leading centre of Greek thought and culture over the following centuries; most significantly, the Milesian School of philosophy (from the 6th century BC) featured great thinkers such as Thales, Anaximander and Anaximenes. Their observations

EPHESUS, BODRUM & THE SOUTH AEGEAN MILETUS (MILET)

Miletus (Milet)

Ancient Ruins

Eternally the crossroads of diverse civilisations, Turkey is bursting with ancient sites. Wherever you go, you're bound to stumble across something epic.

Priene

1 Lovely Priene (p233), tucked up into a mountain, was among the first planned cities in history. The largely overgrown city is divided by a grid system of streets originally built to have 90-degree-angle corners.

Ephesus

2 Home to 250,000 citizens in its heyday, Ephesus (p211) remains the best-preserved ancient city in Europe. Structures such as the Library of Celsus and Temple of Hadrian are architectural marvels, and the restored Terraced Houses provide a window into ancient Ephesian life.

Mt Nemrut (Nemrut Dağı)

3 The remote summit of Nemrut Dağı (p572) is littered with giant sculptures of a pre-Roman king. Earthquakes have now separated most of the heads from the bodies.

Hierapolis

3 Ancient Anatolia's premier 'spa getaway', Hierapolis (p296) enjoys the most photogenic position of any ancient city – atop the glittering calcite travertines of Pamukkale, running over with warm mineral waters.

Afrodisias

4 Once famed for its school for marble sculptors, Afrodisias (p301) preserves its Roman identity in its museum's magnificent sculpted friezes. The sprawling city's most awesome sight, however, is its vast stadium, which once held gladiators, beasts and roaring masses.

Clockwise from top left
1 Seat for a dignitary in the ancient theatre at Priene
2 Library of Celsus, Ephesus 3 Stone statues on the eastern terrace of Mt Nemrut

of nature emphasised rational answers rather than recourse to mythical explanations, making the Milesians essentially the world's first scientists.

Like the other coastal cities, Miletus was fought over by Athens and Persia, and finally freed by Alexander the Great in 334 BC. Rome later took over, and a small Christian congregation developed following St Paul's visits (around 57 AD). In Byzantine times, Miletus was an archbishopric. Unlike other coastal cities, enough of its port was free from silt build-ups, and Seljuks still used it for maritime trade through the 14th century. (The Meander has since pushed Miletus 10km inland.)

As at Priene, you'll notice on the streets the right-angle grid plan of local son Hippodamus. Approaching from the south, see the **Great Theatre**, Miletus' commercial and administrative centre from 700 BC to AD 700. This 15,000-seat Hellenistic theatre had majestic sea views. The Romans reconstructed it in the 1st century AD.

East of the theatre, beyond a vanished ancient commercial centre, the ruined **Temple of Apollo** had great significance, marking the start of a 15km-long sacred road to Didyma's oracle and temple of Apollo. Almost as if by magic, the laurel trees that Greeks considered sacred to Apollo still cast their shade by the Milesian temple ruins.

Above the theatre, ruined **Byzantine castle ramparts** provide views of the former harbour (called **Lion Bay**, after the lion statues that guarded it) to the left. Look right for the **stadium** and the northern, western and southern **agoras**, and between them, **bouleuterion** ruins.

The final ancient site, the vast **Baths of Faustina**, were constructed for Marcus Aurelius' wife, and are worth entering. The massive walls and inner floors of the two spacious structures still survive. The designers' ingenious plan used an underground system of hot-water pipes (known as 'hypocausts') and *tubuli* (terracotta wall flues), which kept the bath interior hot. Next to it was a refreshing cold bath. Note the reproduction statue of river god Meander in repose (the original is in the on-site museum). At the time of research, archaeologists were digging deeper, so more from this remarkable structure should be unveiled soon.

South of the ancient ruins is the post-Seljuk **İlyas Bey Camii** (1404), with an intricate doorway.

Just beyond on the Didyma road, the recently reopened **Miletus Museum** (admission ₺3; ☉8.30am-4.30pm) exhibits ancient glass, pottery and votive stelae, statues, numerous classical, Roman and Byzantine coins, and exquisite gold pendants, necklaces and rings from ancient tombs.

Crucially, the museum has informative wall placards, geographical maps and city plans of the original Miletus and Priene settlements; these help visitors understand these cities, and to appreciate just how different the Anatolian coast looked before river silt deformed it.

ℹ Getting There & Away

Dolmuşes are very infrequent – rent a car or join a tour (make sure the museum is included, too).

Didyma (Didim)

☑0256

Unlike Priene and Miletus, Didyma wasn't a city, but its astonishing **Temple of Apollo** (☑811 0035; admission ₺3; ☉9am-7.30pm mid-May–mid-Sep, to 5.30pm mid-Sep–mid-May) was the ancient world's second-largest, its 122 original columns only five fewer than Ephesus' Temple of Artemis. Since the latter has only one lonesome column today, visiting Didyma really helps travellers visualise the lost grandeur of Artemis' temple, too.

In Greek, Didyma means 'twin' (here, referring to the twin siblings Apollo and Artemis). Didyma's oracle of Apollo had an importance second only to the Oracle of Delphi. Although destroyed by Persians in the early 5th century BC, Alexander the Great revitalised it in 334 BC and, about 30 years later, Seleucid rulers planned to make it the world's largest temple; however, it was never completely finished and Artemis' temple in Ephesus took the record instead.

In 303 AD, the oracle allegedly supported Emperor Diocletian's harsh persecution of Christians – the last such crackdown, since Constantine the Great soon thereafter made the empire a Christian polity. The now unpopular oracle was silenced by Emperor Theodosius I (r 379–395), who closed other pagan temples like the Delphic Oracle.

The impressive temple site is surrounded by souvenir shops and a couple of small pensions (being an archaeological site, building modifications aren't allowed). Entering from the ticket booth, clamber up the wide steps to marvel at the massively thick and towering columns.

Behind the temple porch, oracular poems were inscribed on a great doorway and presented to petitioners. Covered ramps by the porch lead down to the *cella* (inner room), where the oracle prophesied after drinking from the sacred spring. A sacred path, lined by ornate statues (relocated to the British Museum in 1858), once led to a bygone harbour.

After Didyma, the sandy **Altınkum Beach** is a popular package-tour destination, and you can buy snacks here.

🛏 Sleeping & Eating

Didyma has basic eating and dining options, though there's little reason to stay. It gets 'neo-pagan' Greek visitors seeking a moonlit night at the temple – you'll see the odd paean to 'Greek-Turkish friendship' written here and there. To really feel the ancient vibes, a couple of cheap (and very ramshackle) pensions flank the temple itself.

Medusa House   PENSION €€
(📞811 0063; www.medusahouse.com; d €60) This is a restored 150-year-old stone home offering five nice rooms in an attractive garden. To get there from the main entrance, leave the temple on your left and take the slightly right-hand turn 50m down.

Olio   INTERNATIONAL €€
(Apollon Temple Restaurant & Bar; mains ₺12-36; ⊙lunch & dinner) Housed in a charming stone cottage opposite the temple, this restaurant offers a wide selection of international dishes. The wooden rooftop terrace has great views.

Kamacı   BUFFET €€
(📞811 0028; buffet ₺10-15; ⊙lunch) Located behind the temple, Kamacı is a big buffet hall for tour groups. It's cheap, filling and the mezes are suprisingly tasty.

ℹ Getting There & Away

Frequent dolmuşes run from Söke to Didyma (₺8, one hour) and Altınkum (₺8, 1½ hours). Didyma–Akköy dolmuşes also operate (₺3.50, 30 minutes).

Herakleia & Lake Bafa

📞0252
Landlocked (but 50% saltwater) **Bafa Gölü** (Lake Bafa) constitutes the last trace of the

Aegean's former inland reach. It's a peaceful place, dotted by traditional villages such as **Kapıkırı**, 10km off the highway at the lake's far eastern shore, near ruined **Herakleia**. Bygone Byzantine hermitages and churches abound in the Bafa hills, and the lake itself is great for bird-watchers: over 220 avian species are represented, including eagles, flamingos, pelicans and cormorants.

Above Kapıkırı rises **Beşparmak Dağı** (Five-Fingered Mountain; 1500m), known as Mt Latmos in the ancient Greek myth of Endymion. Although the ancient sources tell different versions, the most salacious is that this handsome shepherd boy was put into an eternal sleep by his father, Zeus, at the request of the rather smitten moon goddess, Selene. Every night, she would visit the perfectly preserved Endymion, whose nocturnal emissions were apparently sufficiently abundant to father Selene's 50 daughters.

Herakleia's ruins sprawl throughout the village, which is populated by roving chickens, donkeys and old women forcefully hawking trinkets and crafts. Since the ruins are less exciting than elsewhere, this rustic scene and the lakeside setting comprise most of the experience. If the attendant is around, you'll pay ₺8 for parking.

◉ Sights & Activities

For sublime lake views, follow the road past the rock-hewn **Temple of Endymion**, and past the ruined **Byzantine castle**, which overlooks its **necropolis'** rock tombs.

From the beach and a ruined **Byzantine church**, note the island just opposite – its base conceals ancient building foundations. It's sometimes possible to walk there, when waters recede.

The large **Temple of Athena**, accessed on a westward path behind the agora car park, occupies a promontory overlooking the lake. Only three walls remain, but the perfectly cut blocks (no mortar) are impressive. Other signposted paths lead eastwards to the **agora**, the **bouleuterion** and (several hundred metres across the pastures) to the unrestored **theatre**, with barely a few seating rows remaining. Also nearby are stretches of **city walls** (c 300 BC).

🛏 Sleeping & Eating

Pension owners speak mostly German. Pensions can provide two-hour boat tours (₺50 per boat) and can organise afternoon hikes to Neolithic caves and ruins (₺90 for two people). Whole house rental runs ₺2100 to ₺250 per night.

Bafa's unusual saltwater-freshwater composition means restaurants cook sea and lake fish taken from the same waters.

Karia Pansiyon & Restaurant   PENSION €€
(☑543 5490; www.kariapension.com; s/d incl half-board ₺90/140; ❄) This placid pension has clean rooms decorated with hand-woven carpets. There is a roof terrace with lake views, and a tasty restaurant.

Agora Pansiyon   PENSION €€
(☑543 5445; www.agora.pansiyon.de; s/d incl half-board from ₺110/150; ❄@) Nestled between gardens and a shaded terrace with hammocks, this relaxing place has decent rooms and wood bungalows. It offers hiking, bouldering and bird-watching trips.

Selene's Pension   PENSION €€
(☑543 5221; www.bafalake.com; d incl half-board ₺130-180; ❄@☀) Bafa's original pension, Selene's offers 11 well-kept rooms and a breezy restaurant serving local fish and other specialities. Find it 50m from the beach, at the village's far end.

Club Natura Oliv   HOTEL €€
(☑519 1072; www.clubnatura.com; s/d incl half-board €35/53; ❄@) Some 10km north of the Herakleia turn-off, this slightly posh hotel occupies an old olive plantation, and makes its own oil. It also has great lake views, and offers various guided nature walks.

❶ Getting There & Away
Buses passing the Herakleia turn-off will drop you off, but it's still 10km from there to Kapıkırı. Dolmuşes (₺5) are rare. Taxis run ₺20. One 8am dolmuş goes from Kapıkırı to the highway turn-off, returning around noon. If calling ahead, your pension may provide a free pick-up.

Milas & Around
☎0252 / POP 54,068
Mylasa (Milas) was ancient Caria's royal capital, except for during Mausolus' reign from Halicarnassus (present-day Bodrum). While this agricultural town is most interesting for the Tuesday farmers market, its outlying region conceals unique historic sites.

◉ Sights
Milas' best sights are within a 20km radius. In-town ruins include Baltalı Kapı (Gate with an Axe), a well-preserved Roman gate. Up a steep path from Gümüşkesen Caddesi, see Gümüşkesen ('That Which Cuts Silver' or 'Silver Purse'), a 2nd-century-AD Roman tomb possibly modelled on the Halicarnassus Mausoleum.

Euromos   RUIN
(admission ₺8; ⊙8.30am-7pm May-Sep, to 5pm Oct-Apr) Ancient Euromos stood 12km northwest of Milas and 1km from Selimiye village. Founded in the 6th century BC, Euromos peaked between 200 BC and AD 200, under Hellenistic and then Roman rule. Its indigenous deity had earlier been subsumed by that of Zeus, and indeed the partially restored Temple of Zeus is all that survives.

To get here, take a Milas–Söke bus or dolmuş and ask to get off at the ruins, 200m from the highway.

Iasos (Kıyıkışlacık)   RUIN
(admission ₺2; ⊙8.30am-5.30pm) Seaside Kıyıkışlacık village contains ancient Iasos, a Carian city that was once an island and prospered from fishing and the unique red-and-white marble in the nearby hills. A member of the ancient Delian League, Iasos participated in the Peloponnesian Wars, but later weakened. Nevertheless, it was definitely a Byzantine bishopric from the 5th to the 9th centuries. Iasos was finally abandoned in the 15th century.

Today, the hillside walled acropolis-fortress stands opposite fishing docks. Excavations have revealed ruins of a bouleuterion, agora and Roman temple of Artemis Astias (AD 190), among other structures. Enjoy fresh fish and good views of the wave-soaked ruins at Iasos Deniz Restaurant (fish from ₺10; ⊙10am-midnight).

In summer, an hourly Iasos–Milas dolmuş runs (₺4.75); less frequently in winter. The village turn-off is marked on the highway 10km northwest of Milas. A 20km-long road ends at Iasos.

Labranda   RUIN
(admission ₺8; ⊙8am-5pm) The hillside site of ancient Labranda, surrounded by pines, occupies the area that supplied Mylasa's drinking water. Labranda's local deity was worshipped since at least the 6th century BC, subsequently becoming a sanctuary of Zeus, under Mylasa's control. The great Temple of Zeus honours the god's war-like aspect (Stratius, or Labrayndus means 'Axe-Bearing'). Festivals and Olympic games

occurred at Labranda, which possibly possessed an oracle.

Northwest of Milas, towards Söke, you'll see the Labranda turn-off. It's 14km to the site from here; unless you're driving, take a Milas taxi (₺40, including an hour of waiting).

Beçin Kalesi · RUIN
(Beçin Castle; admission ₺3; ⊙8am-dusk) After 1km on the Milas–Ören road, a signposted right-hand turn accesses Beçin Kalesi, on a rocky outcropping. Originally a Byzantine fortress, it was remodelled by the short-lived, 14th-century Menteşe Empirate.

The high castle walls, topped by a giant Turkish flag, offer great views of Milas below. A hill 500m away has other Menteşe-era structures, including the Kızılhan (Red Caravanserai), the Ahmet Gazi tomb and the restored medrese.

❶ Getting There & Away
Milas' otogar is 1km from the centre, on the Bodrum–Söke road. Dolmuşes from Bodrum (₺15, one hour) serve the centre, where a small dolmuş station (Köy Tabakhane Garaji) has timetabled Iasos minibus services (₺4.75).

BODRUM PENINSULA

The Bodrum Peninsula, named for the summer hot spot of Bodrum, offers a mix of exclusive resorts and laid-back coastal villages where you can enjoy good swimming and stylish eats. Despite the visible inroads of modern tourism, tradition and tranquillity are partially preserved by local open-air vegetable markets and the rugged coastline, overlooked by almost unpopulated hills in the peninsula's centre. The area has a remarkably well-run and inexpensive public transport system, and if you plan to linger for more than a few days, you can find quality accommodation at reasonable rates with just a little planning.

❶ Getting There & Away
Air
Bodrum International Airport(BJV), 36km from Bodrum town, was expanded in 2012, doubling flight capacities. It's served by almost 50 airlines, mostly charters and budget airlines working in summer. Along with having offices in Bodrum town, Turgutreis and Yalıkavak, **Turkish Airlines** (THY; www.thy.com; Kıbrıs Şehitler Caddesi) is in Bodrum's Oasis Shopping Centre (2km from town on the Gümbet road).

Dolmuşes (₺1.75) go here from the otogar – ask for 'Oasis'. **AtlasJet** (www.atlasjet.com)offers direct İstanbul flights. Turkish budget carrier **Pegasus Airlines** (www.flypgs.com) often has good deals.

Take Turkish Airlines' Havaş bus (₺19) from the Bodrum otogar two hours before departure (if flying with them). It also meets flights and drops passengers in central Bodrum. Otherwise, an expensive taxi (₺90 from the city centre; ₺100 from the airport) is your only option. Do check, though, as other airlines may start their own shuttle buses.

Boat
Bodrum's cruise port accommodates large liners and smaller ferries for Datça and the Greek islands of Kos and Rhodes. Contact the **Bodrum Ferryboat Association** (☑316 0882; www.bodrumferryboat.com; Kale Caddesi Cümrük Alanı 22; ⊙8am-8pm), on the dock past the Castle of St Peter's western entrance, in person or by phone, as its website departure info isn't always reliable.

For Kos, ferries (one way or same-day return €32, open return €60, one hour) leave Bodrum daily year-round (weather permitting) at 9.30am, returning at 4.30pm from Kos. A cheaper Kos ferry (one way €12, return €20) is operated by the nearby **Bodrum Express Lines** (☑316 1087; www.bodrumexpresslines.com; Kale Caddesi 18; ⊙8am-6pm). Usually, a Monday to Saturday hydrofoil departs at 9.30am, returning at 5pm.

For Rhodes, hydrofoils (one way and same-day return €60, open-day return €120, 2¼ hours) leave Bodrum from June to September at 8.30am on Monday and Saturday and return at 5pm.

For Datça, ferries (single/return/car ₺25/40/70, two hours) leave Bodrum at 9am daily from June to mid-September. In April, May, early June and October departures are at 9.30am on Tuesday, Thursday, Saturday amd Sunday. Same-day returns aren't possible. The ferry docks at Körmen on the peninsula's northern coast, and the fare includes the 15-minute bus ride to Datça.

Ferries for Kalymnos from Turgutreis (€20, 45 minutes) usually run from May through October; they weren't running at time of research, though, so check ahead.

Car & Motorcycle
Neyzen Tevfik Caddesi in Bodrum has car-rental agencies. **Avis** (☑316 2333; www.avis.com; Neyzen Tevfik Caddesi 92a) and **Neyzen Travel & Yachting** (☑316 7204; www.neyzen.com.tr; Kibris Sehitleri Caddesi 34) rent automatics and manuals (€45 to €65 per day). Motorcycles and scooters run €15 to €30 per day.

ℹ Getting Around

Bodrum dolmuşes are colour-coded: orange buses serve central Bodrum (₺2 to ₺3), turquoise ones reach peninsula coastal spots (₺4 to ₺9), and lime-green dolmuşes go to Gümbet (₺3.50). The terminus name is printed or painted on the minibus. From Bodrum otogar, two main lines traverse the peninsula. The first (west) serves Gümbet, Bitez, Ortakent, Turgutreis, Gümüşlük and Yalıkavak. The second (north) serves Torba, Türkbükü and Yalıkavak.

Turgutreis, Gümüşlük and Yalıkavak also get a separate dolmuş. From Yalıkavak to Bodrum takes one hour or so; estimate 15 minutes between each bay.

During summer, dolmuşes run nonstop, and between 7am and 11pm in the low season. For trips between, say, Bitez and Ortakent, solicit a passing dolmuş and go 'indi bindi' (₺2.50) to the next bay. Some bays, such as Yalıkavak and Türkbükü, traditionally aren't connected by minibus service, requiring a return to Bodrum in between, but check for any changes.

Bodrum

☏ 0252 / POP 34,866

Although more than one million tourists flock to its beaches, boutique hotels and clubs each summer, Bodrum (Halicarnassus in ancient times) never loses its cool; more than any other Turkish seaside getaway, it has an enigmatic elegance that pervades it, from the town's grand crowning castle and glittering marina to its flower-filled cafes and white-plastered backstreets. Even in the most hectic days of high summer, you can still find little corners of serenity, in the town and especially in its outlying coastal villages.

Only in the past few decades has Bodrum come to be associated with pleasure, paradisical beaches and glittering summertime opulence. Previously, it was a simple fishing village, and old-timers can still remember when everything was in a different place or didn't exist at all. Long before the palmed promenades and elaborate eateries, Bodrum wasn't even desirable – it was actually the place where dissidents against the new Turkish republic were sent into exile.

Ironically, all that started to change after one of the inmates took over the prison. Writer Cevat Şakir Kabaağaçlı (aka the 'Fisherman of Halicarnassus') was exiled to sleepy Bodrum in 1925, and quickly fell in love with the place. After serving his time, he proceeded to turn on a whole generation of Turkish intellectuals, writers and artists to Bodrum's charms in the mid-1940s.

From then on, there was no going back: by the 1980s, well-heeled foreigners were starting to come, and today Bodrum is a favourite getaway for everyone from European package tourists to Turkey's prime movers and shakers. But it was Kabaağaçlı's early influence, giving the town its arty identity, which saved it from the ignominious fate of other Turkish fishing-villages-turned-resorts.

Urban planners have also sought to preserve Bodrum's essential character. Laws restrict buildings' heights, and the whitewashed houses with bright-blue trim evoke a lost era. The evocative castle, numerous museums and Ottoman mosques also help keep Bodrum a discerning step above the rest.

◉ Sights

Castle of St Peter   MUSEUM
(☏ 316 2516; www.bodrum-museum.com; admission ₺10, Glass Wreck Hall ₺5, Carian Princess Hall ₺5; ⊙9am-noon & 1-7pm Tue-Sun summer, 8am-noon & 1-5pm winter, Glass Wreck Hall 10-noon & 2-4pm Tue-Fri, Carian Princess Hall 10am-noon & 2-4pm Tue-Sun) Tamerlane's Mongol invasion of Anatolia (1402) not only gave Byzantine Constantinople a reprieve from Turkish besiegers, it also allowed the Knights Hospitaller, based in Rhodes, to build a castle at ancient Halicarnassus, using marble and stones from the famed mausoleum. They named the city Petronium (hence the Turkicised 'Bodrum').

By 1437 they had finished the Castle of St Peter, adding new defensive features (moats, walls, cisterns etc) right up until 1522, when Süleyman the Magnificent captured Rhodes. The Knights were forced to cede St Peter's castle, and the victorious Muslim sultan promptly built a mosque in it. For centuries, the castle was never tested, but French shelling in WWI toppled the minaret (the Turkish government re-erected it in 1997).

Renovations started in the 1960s, and the underwater archaeology treasures amassed therein became Bodrum's **Museum of Underwater Archaeology** in 1986. This attractively lit and informative museum has reconstructions and multimedia displays to complement the antiquities, and takes about two hours to see.

The castle battalions offer splendid views. Heading in, you'll pass a carved

Bodrum Peninsula

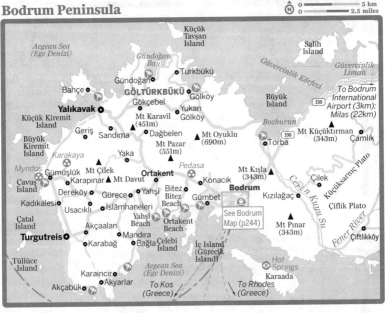

marble **Crusader coats of arms**. Next is the castle's main court, centred on an ancient mulberry tree. Here too is a massive **amphorae collection**, with pieces from the 14th century BC to modern times, all recovered from southern-coast waters. The adjoining courtyard cafe, adorned with ancient statuary, adjoins a small **glassblowing workshop**, where you can watch artisans create glass bottles and jewellery resembling those found on ancient and medieval underwater wrecks.

A tiny model, and a full-sized reconstruction of a late-Roman ship's stern discovered off Yassıada are displayed in the chapel. Walk the decks, take the helm and inspect the galley and wine casks below.

Left of here and up the towers is the **Glass Wreck Hall**. It houses a 16m-long, 5m-wide ship that sank in AD 1025, while carrying 3 tonnes of glass between Fatimid Syria and a Byzantine glass factory in the Danube or Black Sea. Archaeologists and historians were excited by the find not only for what it revealed about ship construction at the time, but also for what it indicated about Fatimid glass production and design.

Next, the small **Glass Hall** exhibits finds from the 15th century BC to the 14th century AD, and include Mycenean beads, Roman glass bottles and Islamic weights. Ancient coins (including from Croesus' Caria) are displayed next door.

Beyond, the **French Tower** has finds from the *Tektaş Burnu*, the world's only fully excavated Classical Greek shipwreck (dating from 480 BC to 400 BC). Amphorae, talismanic marble discs and kitchen utensils from the vessel are displayed, plus 2001 excavation photos taken at the Çeşme Peninsula site.

Next door, the **Carian Princess Hall** exhibits a gold crown, necklace, bracelets, rings and an exquisite wreath of gold myrtle leaves. Popularly associated with the last Carian queen, Ada (reinstated by Alexander the Great after annexing Halicarnassus in 334 BC), these belonged to an unknown woman of status.

Guarding the castle's southeast corner, the **English Tower** was built during the reign of King Henry IV of England (1399–1413). In 1401 Henry became the first (and only) English monarch to host a Byzantine emperor, Manuel II Palaeologos, and he took seriously Manuel's warning about the Muslim threat to Christian Europe posed by the Turks. The English Tower was thus a symbol of support for their common cause.

Bodrum

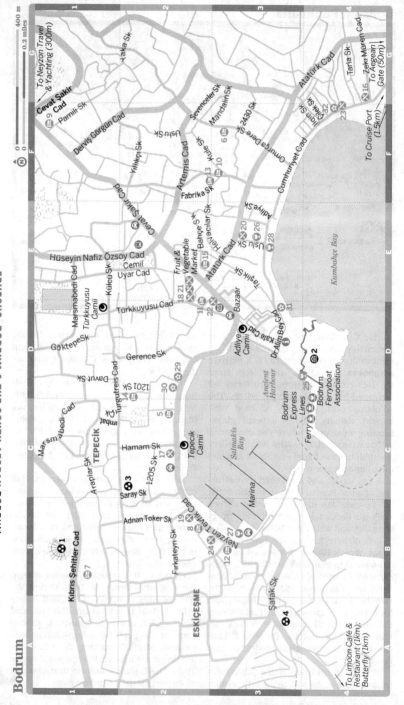

Bodrum

Today, however, museum organisers have belied this heritage. The room has been fitted out as a medieval refectory with a long dining table surrounded by suits of armour, stag horns and the standards of the Knights Hospitaller and their Turkish adversaries, with piped-in medieval music completing the farcical picture of a knightly theme restaurant.

To the north, the **Uluburun Wreck Hall** contains extraordinary **Bronze Age shipwrecks**, including the world's oldest excavated wreck, the 14th-century-BC *Uluburun*. Full-size replicas of the interior and the wreck site exist. The nearby **Treasure Room** displays Canaanite gold jewellery, bronze daggers, ivory cosmetic boxes, wooden writing boards and Egyptian Queen Nefertiti's golden scarab.

Further north, enter the dungeons at **Gatineau Tower**, where the Knights imprisoned, and sometimes tortured, their enemies from 1513 until 1523. The inner gate's chilling inscription sums up the dungeon as being *Inde Deus abest* ('Where God does not exist'). A sign warns that the torture implements exhibit mightn't be suitable for children.

Mausoleum
RUIN
(Turgutreis Caddesi; admission ₺8; ⊘8.30am-5.30pm Tue-Sun) One of the Seven Wonders of the Ancient World, the Mausoleum was the greatest achievement of Carian King Mausolus (r 376–353 BC). Although Caria had existed for at least 700 years, with a capital in Mylasa (Milas), Mausolus moved it to Halicarnassus. Before his death, the king had planned his own tomb, to be designed by Pythius (architect of Priene's Temple of Athena). When Mausolus finally died, his wife (and sister), Artemisia, oversaw the completion of this enormous, white-marble tomb topped by stepped pyramids.

Incredibly, the Mausoleum stood relatively intact until the Knights Hospitallers needed building material for the Castle of St Peter; between 1406 and 1522, almost all of it was reused or ground into powder for walls. Luckily, the more impressive ancient friezes were incorporated into the castle walls, while original statues of Mausolus and Artemisia were sent to the British Museum.

Despite thus being non-existent, the site has relaxing gardens, with excavations to the right and a covered arcade to the left – the latter contains a copy of the famous frieze in the British Museum. Four original fragments displayed were discovered more recently. Models, drawings and documents indicate the grand dimensions of the original Mausoleum. A scale model of Mausolus' Halicarnassus and the Mausoleum also stands.

Today, the only ancient elements to survive are the pre-Mausolean stairways and tomb chambers, the Mausolean drainage system, the entry to Mausolus' tomb chamber, precinct wall bits and some large fluted marble column drums.

Myndos Kapısı   RUIN
(Turgutreis Caddesi) The restored remains of Myndos Kapısı (Myndos Gate), the only surviving gate from King Mausolus' 4th-century-BC 7km-long walls, stand in west Bodrum. Before them are the remains of a moat that took the lives of many of Alexander the Great's soldiers in 334 BC.

Ancient Theatre   RUIN
(Kıbrıs Şehitler Caddesi) On the Gümbet road, ancient Halicarnassus' restored theatre (capacity 13,000) lies in the hillside rock, and still functions for summer concerts.

Shipyard   RUIN
(Şafak Sokak; ⏰9am-6pm) The recently restored Ottoman shipyard stands just beyond the marina. In 1770, Russia destroyed the entire Ottoman fleet at Çeşme; rebuilding it occurred in boatyards like this. It was fortified when pirates menaced in the 19th century. Although the shipyard's tower occasionally hosts art exhibitions, it's essentially a children's playground. Old tombstones, dating from the period when the Latin alphabet was replacing Arabic, are kept above. There are good views from here, too.

🏃 Activities

Blue Cruises   BOAT TOUR
Countless excursion boats are moored along Neyzen Tevfik Caddesi; a 'blue cruise' on board one of these is a fun day trip. Like the ferry companies, some even access peninsula bays, saving you a sweaty minibus ride (check locally). **Karaada** (Black Island), with hot-spring waters gushing from a cave, is a popular destination where you can swim and loll in supposedly healthful orange mud.

Book cruises at your hotel, or on the moored excursion boats, ideally a day ahead. Group tours start from €12.

Neyzen Travel & Yachting   BOAT TOUR
(📞316 7204; www.neyzen.com.tr; Kibris Sehitleri Caddesi 34) Neyzen offers *gület* trips, including a nice circular tour of the Gulf of Gokova, down to Knidos and hugging the coast all the way back to Bodrum.

🛏 Sleeping

It's more expensive than other coastal resorts, but if you're keen on a Bodrum-area base, try to plan in advance: many hotels offer discounted rates for advance bookings.

Also increasingly popular is apartment and villa rental near gorgeous coastal beaches, which allows you the option of self-catering from the many farmers markets operating daily.

In high summer, places fill up fast so be prepared to pound the pavement if you haven't booked ahead. The marina-area hotels get the most noise from the clubs and bars. If arriving by bus, you may be harassed by touts offering 'budget accommodation' – it's best to ignore them.

TOP CHOICE Su Otel   BOUTIQUE HOTEL €€€
(📞316 6906; www.bodrumsuhotel.com; Turgutreis Caddesi, 1201 Sokak; s/d/ste from €70/95/115; ❄🛜🏊) Epitomising Bodrum's traditional white-and-bright-blue decor, the Su has sun-filled bedrooms, some with balconies overlooking the terraced gardens and inviting pool. The friendly management helps with all local activities; out of high season, it even runs a cooking class.

Kaya Pension   PENSION €€
(📞316 5745; www.kayapansiyon.com.tr; Eski Hükümet Sokak 14; s/d/tr ₺100/120/140; ❄🛜) One of Bodrum's better pensions, Kaya has clean, simple rooms in town and a beautiful flowering courtyard for breakfast and drinks. Reception has a safe for valuables, and the helpful staff can arrange activities.

Otel Atrium   HOTEL €€
(📞316 2181; www.atriumbodrum.com; Fabrika Sokak 21; s/d incl half-board from ₺100/120; ❄🛜🏊) This midsize hotel amid tangerine trees has bright and fairly spacious rooms. It's good value for families and independent travellers. There's a pool (with separate kids' section), a poolside bar, two restaurants and free parking. It's a five- to 10-minute walk to both centre and beach.

Marmara Bodrum   LUXURY HOTEL €€€
(📞999 1010; www.themarmarahotels.com; Suluhasan Caddesi 18; r/ste from €180/600; ❄@🏊) The upmarket Marmara, high on a bluff, has great views and elegant rooms (try for one with sea views). It's part of a five-star chain, and facilities include tennis, spa, gym and two pools. A free shuttle accesses a private

beach in Torba. The rooftop 'party animal suite' has a big jacuzzi, two balconies and a private roof terrace for throwing your own all-nighter.

Bahçeli Ağar Aile Pansiyonu   PENSION €€
(☑316 1648; 1402 Sokak 4; s/d €50/65) This friendly little pension has small but spotless rooms with balconies, some overlooking a vine-draped courtyard. It's also good value because there's a kitchen.

Anfora   PENSION €
(☑316 5530; www.anforapansiyon.com; Omurça Dere Sokak 23; s/d from ₺45/70; ❄️🛜) Rooms are well kept and clean (though can be cramped) at this friendly pension, a worthy budget contender. Although Bar St's a few blocks away, it's not too loud at night.

Butterfly   B&B €€€
(☑313 8358; Ünlü Caddesi, 1512 Sokak 24; d €165-275; ❄️🛜💺) High on the headland between Bodrum and Gümbet, quiet Butterfly is an immaculately clean six-room B&B, run by a friendly American expat. Gaze down on the bay from the tranquil infinity pool.

Antik Tiyatro Hotel   BOUTIQUE HOTEL €€€
(☑316 6053; www.antiquetheatrehotel.com; Kıbrıs Şehitler Caddesi 169; r €120-375; ❄️💺) By the ancient theatre, this opulent place enjoys great castle and sea views, and has a big outdoor pool and one of Bodrum's best hotel restaurants. Original artwork and antiques adorn the rooms, which each have an individual character, though the suites are arguably overpriced.

Marina Vista   RESORT €€€
(☑313 0356; www.majesty.com.tr; Neyzen Tevfik Caddesi 226; r from €180; ❄️@💺) In a courtyard off the coast road, the Marina Vista preserves some individual character despite its size (almost 200 beds), splashing modern art and vivid colours across the good old blue-and-white Aegean background. Its Argentine restaurant, Tango, offers a sophisticated foreign alternative to local fare.

El Vino Hotel   BOUTIQUE HOTEL €€€
(☑313 8770; www.elvinobodrum.com; Omurça Mahallesi Pamili Sokak; r from €140; ❄️🛜💺) This rustic place behind a stone wall in the backstreets has large and well-appointed rooms with wooden floors. Try for a room with views of the pool and garden area (where breakfast is served). The rooftop restaurant also affords nice views.

Albatros Otel   PENSION €€
(☑316 7117; www.albatrosotel.net; Neyzen Tevfik Caddesi, Menekşe Sokak 6; s/d ₺90/130; ❄️@🛜) This marina-side pension has a good location and friendly service, making it a worthwhile pick for independent travellers and small families (extra cots aren't available, but one child under seven can stay for free).

Aegean Gate   BOUTIQUE HOTEL €€€
(☑316 7853; www.aegeangatehotel.com; Guvercin Sokak 2; s/d/tr €70/110/140; ❄️🛜💺) One kilometre east of Bodrum harbour on a quiet hill, Aegean Gate has sparkling rooms and a relaxing pool with bar. The catch? A minimum two-night stay is required, and credit cards aren't accepted. It's 50m from a 24-hour taxi rank, has a nearby dolmuş connection to the centre, and is a 15-minute walk to Bodrum's main party strip.

Hotel Güleç   PENSION €
(☑316 5222; www.hotelgulec.com; Üçkuyular Caddesi 22; s/d from €30/50; ❄️@) This good-value little pension has a central location and simple but bright and clean rooms. There's also a relaxing, quiet garden.

Turunç Pansiyon   PENSION €
(☑316 5333; www.turuncpansiyon.com; Atatürk Caddesi, 1023 Sokak 4a; s/d from ₺50/70; ❄️@) This town pension offers rather plain accommodation, and English is hit-or-miss, but staff are helpful with local information.

✖ Eating

Like all harbourside resorts, Bodrum's waterfront has pricey, big-menu restaurants (not all bad), but also discreet backstreet contenders, fast-food stalls and a famous fish market and seafood-restaurant scene on Cevat Şakir Caddesi, which is also the site of the fruit and veg market.

Generally, Bodrum's western bay eateries are more upscale, while the eastern bay has more informal fare marketed to the dizzy patrons of the adjacent bars and nightclubs.

TOP CHOICE · La Pasión   SPANISH €€
(Restaurante Español; www.lapasion-bodrum.com; cnr Atatürk Caddesi & Uslu Sokak; set menus ₺18-35; ⏰lunch & dinner) To see just how far Bodrum has come in its quest to join the ranks of international seaside sophistication, try this refined Spanish restaurant down a side street off Cumhuriyet Caddesi. The lunch menus change weekly

and, given the intricacy of the entrees and desserts, are surprisingly good value (appetiser, mains, dessert and first drink are ₺18 per person). The restaurant occupies an old stone home with a flowering courtyard, and there's Spanish music wafting through the breeze.

Fish Market
SEAFOOD ₺₺

(Cevat Şakir Caddesi; meze from ₺4, fish ₺20; ☉dinner Mon-Sat) Bodrum's fish market (sometimes called *manavlar* for the fruit stands at the entrance to this small network of back alleys) offers a unique sort of direct dining: you choose between myriad fresh fish and seafood on ice at fishmongers' tables and, having paid there, have them cooked (about ₺6 extra) at any adjoining restaurant. If in doubt, waiters can help you decide – options run from top-end catches to cheaper farm fish.

Aside from the admirably high degree of choice, this direct-purchase system also prevents people from complaining that they were cheated (the number-one complaint about seafood restaurants, anywhere in the world).

The plain restaurants spill across the small streets, which get incredibly crowded and have zero atmosphere, save maybe for the people-watching. If indecisive, pick the busiest-looking place – locals are fiercely loyal to their favourites. **Meyhane Deniz Feneri** (☎316 3534; Belediye Gıda Çarşısı 12; fish ₺18-35) is the area's oldest restaurant, and many long-time residents still consider it the best. Dinner for two with a few mezes, drinks and fish will run at least ₺100 here. In any fish-market restaurant, book ahead for evening dining.

Marina Köftecisi
KÖFTE ₺₺

(☎313 5593; Neyzen Tevfik Caddesi 158; mains ₺10-17) With a waterfront view, this is an excellent spot for various traditional *köfte* recipes – try the *kaşarlı köfte* (meatballs with cheese from sheep's milk), served with pita bread drizzled with tomato sauce and yoghurt.

Urfa Diyarı
KEBAP ₺₺

(☎317 0031; Oasis Shopping Center; kebaps ₺12-17; ☉9am-11pm) Locals come to this cosy openair place behind two palm trees on the Oasis Shopping Center's lower level for the filling kebaps – whether you want spicy or not spicy, Adana, Urfa or other, the kebap creations are succulent.

Döner Tepecik
KEBAP ₺

(Neyzen Tevfik Caddesi; kebaps from ₺6) Across from the eponymous mosque, this local favourite does tasty kebaps on homemade bread.

Orfoz
SEAFOOD ₺₺₺

(☎316 4285; Cumhuriyet Caddesi 177B; mains from ₺26; ☉dinner) Orfoz is often listed as one of Turkey's best seafood restaurants. While the meze portions are small, the fish mains are excellent.

Gemibaşı
SEAFOOD ₺₺₺

(Neyzen Tevfik Caddesi; meze from ₺5, mains ₺20-30; ☉lunch & dinner) A popular fish restaurant, this features the blue-and-white decor of a Greek taverna, shady sea views, and fresh meze and fish.

Sünger
PIZZERIA ₺

(Neyzen Tevfik Caddesi 218; mains ₺8-30) Excellent pizzas and fast-food fare are cooked at this popular joint.

Berk Balık Restaurant
SEAFOOD ₺₺

(☎313 6878; Cumhuriyet Caddesi 167; meze ₺6-12, fish from ₺12; ☉lunch & dinner) A lively seafood spot, Berk Balık is refreshingly untouristy, which has kept prices down. Young locals liven up the bright upstairs terrace. An imposter shop with a similar name has opened nearby, so look for the orginal.

Nazik Ana
TURKISH ₺

(Eski Hukumet Sokak 7; mains ₺5-9; ☉closed Sun winter) This simple back-alley place offers prepared dishes hot and cold (viewable at the front counter), letting you sample different Turkish traditional dishes at knockdown prices.

Limoon Cafe & Restaurant
TURKISH ₺

(www.limooncaferestaurant.com; Cafer Paşa Caddesi 10; mains ₺8-12) On shady grounds in western Bodrum, Limoon offers cheap appetisers and soups (₺4 to ₺5), plus mains – the chicken with mushrooms is excellent.

🍷 Drinking & Entertainment

Bodrum's varied nightlife scene caters to its diverse clientele. The Turkish jet set fills the western-bay clubs, while the foreign masses frequent the loud waterfront bars and clubs of Bar St (Dr Alim Bey Caddesi and Cumhuriyet Caddesi). Many more bars and clubs of varied styles line the coastal villages.

The castle and antique theatre host opera, ballet and rock performances; for upcoming event schedules, visit www.biletix.com.

Marina Yacht Club BAR
(☑316 1228; Neyzen Tevfik Caddesi 5; ☺8am-late) Although Marina also does meals (Italian and Turkish flavours, average ₺22 per person), its primary identity is as a big, breezy waterfront night spot. Merrymakers congregrate around the extended, wrap-around bar or at the scattered tiny tables dotting the way to the water-facing deck, where cover bands liven things up nightly in summer. Domestic beer prices (₺4 to ₺5) are unexpectedly good, and there's a wide cocktail selection.

Hadigari BAR
(www.hadigari.com.tr; 1025 Sokak 2; ☺7pm-5am) Bodrum's oldest bar, Hadigari rocks on from its auspicious location under the Castle of St Peter.

Körfez BAR
(www.korfezbar.com; Uslu Sokak 2; ☺9pm-5am summer) This unpretentious old favourite (not the like-named western-bay eatery) does rock, with a dark-wood atmosphere to match. Sunday is '80s night.

Moonlight BAR
(www.moonlightbodrum.com; Cumhuriyet Caddesi 60b) Chilled-out Moonlight, off a side street of Cumhuriyet Caddesi, has a somewhat contemplative vibe, making it good for a relaxed, water-view drink.

Küba Bar CLUB
(Neyzen Tevfik Caddesi 62; ☺7pm-4am) Bodrum's poshest and most popular address for Turkish clubbers, Küba has all the plasma screens, disaffected DJs, shiny poles and laser beams one would expect. It does good international fare by evening.

Helva CLUB
(www.helvabodrum.com; Neyzen Tevfik Caddesi 54; ☺2pm-3am) Just a bit less snobby than nearby Küba, Helva is also less frenetic but attracts a similarly slick Turkish crowd – more lounging and less dancing.

Mavi Bar LIVE MUSIC
(Cumhuriyet Caddesi 175; ☺6pm-6am) Inviting Mavi specialises in great live acts five nights weekly. It's busiest after 1am.

Marine Club Catamaran CLUB
(www.clubcatamaran.com; Dr Alim Bey Caddesi; weekday/weekend ₺35/40; ☺10pm-4am mid-May–Sep) Bodrum's party boat, this floating nightclub sails at 1.30am, keeping the licentiousness offshore for a good three hours. Its transparent dance floor can pack in 1500 clubbers plus attendant DJs. A free shuttle operates every 15 minutes to the eastern bay.

ⓘ Information

ATMs line Cevat Şakir Caddesi and harbour-front streets.

Post Office (Cevat Şakir Caddesi; ☺8.30am-5pm, telephone exchange 8am-midnight)

SERVICES FROM BODRUM'S OTOGAR

DESTINATION	FARE (₺)	DURATION (HR)	DISTANCE (KM)	FREQUENCY (PER DAY)
Ankara	55	11	689	1 nightly
Antalya	42	7½	496	2 (9.30am, 10.30pm)
Denizli (for Pamukkale)	25	4½	250	1
Fethiye	30	5	265	3 (9.30am, 12.30pm, 5.15pm)
İstanbul	68	12	851	10 nightly
İzmir	25	3½	286	hourly
Konya	45	12	626	6
Kuşadası	20	2½	151	4 (all after midday)
Marmaris	15	3	165	hourly
Milas	15	1	45	every 15min
Muğla	13	2	149	hourly

Tourist Office (Kale Meydanı; ⊘8am-6pm Mon-Fri, daily summer)

Getting Around

Most everything is in walking distance downtown. There's an intra-city dolmuş service (₺1.75), which is frequently stuck in traffic. Drivers should note that most roads follow a clockwise one-way system – missing your turn necessitates an irritating repetition of the process.

Gümbet

✆0252

Since it's just 5km from Bodrum, party-palace Gümbet got debased faster than other peninsula villages. Now more or less a British colony, Gümbet is an outpost of neon, cheap cocktails, energy drinks and table-dancing. In winter, the place is derelict.

Package-tour operators have a firm grip, and most accoms are fairly uniform. However, a few places, such as **Fuga** (✆319 6500; www.fuga.com.tr; Adnan Menderes Cad; d incl full board ₺350; ⊘May-Oct; ❄@≋), have a more arty boutique feel. Despite (or perhaps because of) the fact that Gümbet isn't a family destination, Fuga allows kids under six to stay free, while those aged seven to 12 stay for half-price.

Bitez

✆0252

Less hectic than Gümbet just east, Bitez is still a major centre of coastal nightlife in summer, and draws more foreigners than Turks. However, it's an actual village, framed by lovely orchards, so it doesn't go into total hiberation in winter. The fine sandy beach here is good for swimming, packed with umbrellas and loungers, satellites of the restaurants and cafes behind them on the narrow road.

For some cultural edification, visit the ruins of **Pedasa**, located on the main peninsula road near the Bitez turn-off. A relic of the lost Lelegian civilisation that predated the Carians, this small site features defensive wall foundations and ruins, probably of a temple.

🛌 Sleeping

Okaliptüs Otel   PENSION €€€
(✆363 7957; www.okaliptus.com.tr; Bitez Yalısı; s/d incl half-board ₺200/260; ❄🛜≋) Behind the homonymous restaurant and a big banyan

tree, the Okaliptüs features accommodation hidden around a series of alcoves and flower-filled trellises. Although the rooms are simply furnished, they're spotless, with gleaming marble baths. There's a swimming pool, and private pebble-and-sand beach, from where a range of wild water sports are organised. The hotel's large yacht is used for various day trips.

Şah Hotel   BOUTIQUE HOTEL €€€
(✆363 7721; www.sahhotel.com; Şah Caddesi; s/d ₺230/300; ❄🛜≋) Although prices have risen considerably, the Şah remains a good choice, with breezy, well-furnished rooms inside a courtyard on the beach boardwalk, enclosing well-maintained grounds and an inviting pool.

✖ Eating

Bitez has a few good eateries working year-round. Seafront restaurants' weekend brunch buffets have become rather the local tradition in recent years.

 Lemon Tree   INTERNATIONAL €€€
(✆363 9543; Sahil Yolu 28; mains ₺18-30; ⊘8am-late) Right at the beach, near the small Yalı Mosque, this hugely popular place marked by breezy white-and-green decor lets you eat, drink and enjoy at shaded tables or on its loungers on the sand. There's an appetising blend of Turkish and international fare (try the house 'Lemon Tree chicken' – a light take on chicken sweet-and-sour). Even locals come for the ridiculously massive and varied buffet brunch (₺17.50, from 10am to 2pm on weekends), which rivals that of any Bodrum luxury hotel. It's a lively watering hole by night, too.

Bağarası   SEAFOOD €€€
(✆358 7693; Pınarlı Caddesi 59; meze from ₺6, fish from ₺20; ⊘lunch & dinner, closed Mon Nov-Apr) Popular with locals, Bağarası sits tucked away in a residential garden, and serves varied Turkish specialities, such as *kıtır mantı* (crispy Turkish pasta with meat sauce and cream), plus mezes and fresh fish.

Bitez Mantıcı   TURKISH €
(Atatürk Bulvarı 40; mains ₺4-13; ⊘lunch & dinner) This unassuming place does excellent versions of Turkey's extended carbohydrates family, from *mantı* (Turkish pasta) to pastries such as *börek* and buttery-rich *gözleme* (savoury pancakes).

Black Cat
TURKISH €€

(Mart Kedileri; www.martkedileri.com; mains ₺7-15) One block behind Bitez beach near the Şah Hotel, the Black Cat is a whimsical place with no fixed menu, but you can count on the local Turkish dishes-of-the-day to be fresh and flavourful.

Ortakent
📞0252

Just beyond Bitez, Ortakent is becoming more popular as the relentless wave of summer-home building continues to gouge out the peninsula hillside with alarmingly uniform giant white cubes. Ortakent's 3km sand beach is mostly the domain of packed lounge chairs by summer, but the water here is nevertheless among the peninsula's cleanest (and coldest), due to wave action. The eastern Scala Beach (www.scalabeach.net) is quieter.

🛏 Sleeping

Satsuma Suites
APARTMENT €€€

(📞348 4249; www.satsumasuites.com; Eren Sokak 17; r €105-125; ❀☎) While the adults-only policy makes Satsuma decidedly not family-friendly, for couples looking to escape the noise of Bodrum, these luxe suites with elegantly appointed baths, and set around flowering trees and a welcoming pool, are ideal, and the breakfast is solid as well.

✗ Eating

Adasofra
MEDITERRANEAN €€€

(📞358 7414; www.adasofra.com; Kule Sokak 29, Mustafa Paşa Kulesi; mains ₺16-35; ⊘dinner) This restored ancient watchtower, effortlessly turned into an upscale, escapist restaurant, serves a colourful array of gourmet Mediterranean specialities.

Palavra
SEAFOOD €€€

(📞358 6290; www.palavrabalik.com; Yahşi Beldesi; meze ₺5-15, fish ₺20; ⊘8am-midnight) This popular fish restaurant follows the peninsula custom of dining right on the sand, with a delicious range of home-cooked mezes and fish dishes to complement the local wine.

Gebora
SEAFOOD €€

(📞348 3340; Yahşi Beldesi; meze ₺5-15, fish ₺20; ⊘9am-midnight) On the main beachfront boardwalk near Yalı Camii, Gebora is a straightforward, much-loved old standby for fresh fish, mezes and home-grown salads.

Turgutreis
📞0252

Once a sponge-diving centre, Turgutreis has turned its sights on tourism, particularly longer-term villa and apartment rentals, and this does make some logistical sense for visitors. As the second-largest village on the peninsula, Turgutreis has more services, shops and concrete than other places; the workaday Saturday market resembles dusty middle Anatolia more than an Aegean retreat. (Indeed, the waterfront statue of a pregnant woman holding an olive branch is meant to represent the health, peacefulness and diversity of Anatolia.)

In 1972 the village, then called Karatoprak, was renamed after Ottoman Admiral Turgut Reis, who was born here in 1485 and led many maritime battles before dying in the 1565 siege of Malta.

Turgutreis has 5km of sandy beaches and over a dozen tiny islets. Its new marina offers ferries for both Bodrum town and Kos in Greece, meaning it's one of the few peninsula bases allowing you to largely avoid road transport.

Gümüşlük
📞0252

Unlike other fishing villages that got hijacked by modern tourism, Gümüşlük has been preserved from the worst of it because it lies around the ruins of ancient Carian Myndos; as a protected archaeological zone, the village legally cannot be overdeveloped, at least not on the waterfront where the ruins disappear into the sea, continuing out to the facing Rabbit Island, which can be reached by foot when the tide's low.

Accessible from the main coastal road down a dirt track, Gümüşlük has an escapist feel, and it's good for a swim and drink or fresh fish meal at simple yet stylish eateries on the beach. All of this authenticity has however made it more than a bit precious, and the prices have risen to match the village's increasingly upscale passers-by.

It's said that famed Carian King Mausolus built Myndos (which largely awaits excavation) due to its strategic position and harbour – indeed, the sea just north of Rabbit Island is very deep. Look straight across these waters to see a hazy speck of rock, Kardak (Imia in Greek), the ownership of which almost sparked a war between

Beaches

Turkey's beaches range from vast, sandy stretches backed by resort hotels to tiny azure coves accessible only by boat. With four seas to choose from (Mediterranean, Aegean, Marmara and Black), the options are endless.

Patara

1 Flanked by tall sand dunes, and at 18km Turkey's longest beach, Patara (p335) is not just a pretty face but also a nesting ground for sea turtles, a stage of the Lycian Way hiking trail and one of the richest archaeological sites on the Mediterranean.

Kabak

2 This delightful pebble beach (p329), overlooked by two high cliffs, is backed by a remote and very chilled collection of campgrounds and bungalows, accessible via a steep track.

Ölüdeniz

3 A long spit of sandy beach (p327) wrapping itself around a blue lagoon, Ölüdeniz is one of the most photographed spots in all of coastal Turkey. And with good reason – it's nothing short of stunning.

Pamucak

4 The closest place to cool off in the sea near ancient Ephesus, Pamucak (p228) is a stretch of sand sloping around 7km of prime Aegean waterfront. Churning surf makes it a great place to battle the waves.

Ayazma

5 This popular sand beach (p169) heaves with people at the height of summer – all there to lap up the vast southward views and crystal-clear water, and feast on watermelon, fresh fish and local *şarap* (wine).

Clockwise from top left

1 Long stretch of sand at Patara beach 2 Mountain biker on a dirt track overlooking the beach at Kabak 3 Lagoon beach at Ölüdeniz

Greece and Turkey in January 1996, following gratuitous flag-planting exchanges and a more serious but brief Turkish commando occupation. Today, the area is strictly off-limits.

A municipal car park (₺3 per day) is 300m from the waterfront, though you may find the back road that brings you closer to the beach, and free parking.

🛏 Sleeping

Gümüşlük is getting expensive, but family-run pensions still exist – book ahead.

Villa rentals can be great value; for an idea of the going rates, check out local Teldolap restaurant, which rents fully-furnished apartments by the day (₺150 to ₺300, including breakfast) or by the month (₺1500 to ₺3000, which includes housekeeping). If self-catering at least some of the time, such offers constitute seriously good deals for those seeking extended sojourns on the secluded Bodrum coast, without breaking the bank.

Otel Gümüşlük   RESORT €€
(☑394 4828; www.otelgumusluk.com; Yalı Mevkii 28; d ₺130-220; ❄@☀) Away from the water, this two-storey, ranch-style hotel has airy, minimalist rooms and a pool. It's a three-minute walk to the dolmuş stop. It also rents a fully equipped villa and apartment (useful for groups or self-caterers), and guests can use the hotel's facilities.

Club Hotel Zemda   RESORT €€€
(☑394 3151; www.clubhotelzemda.com; s/d/ste with half-board €88/120/140; ❄@☀) At the bay's southern end, this resort-style hotel is the place for activities; what it lacks in creative decor it makes up for in the tennis lessons, windsurfing and paddling classes and other water sports. There's also a pool and bar.

Liman Motel   PENSION €€
(☑394 3302; www.limanmotelrestaurant.com; r ₺100-160; ❄) In central Gümüşlük, Liman overlooks the action, with especially sublime sunset views. The simple, white rooms have a suitably Aegean feel.

🍴 Eating & Drinking

Gümüşlük's atmospheric little beach restaurants and cafes are excellent for eating, drinking or just whiling away the time.

Cash-carrying self-caterers can greet the incoming fisherfolk on the docks (from 8am to 10am) to relieve them of some of their burden, otherwise destined for local restaurants.

Mimoza   SEAFOOD €€€
(☑394 3139; www.mimoza-bodrum.com; meze from ₺20, mains from ₺40; ☺lunch & dinner mid-Jun–Aug) Popular Mimoza, on the beach's north end, has cheery white tables perched above the sea, boats bobbing in the secluded bay opposite. These splendid attributes have made it a favourite of the Turkish upper-crust, and prices become rather hard to justify on objective merits alone. Nevertheless, it does do a good variety of mezes and seafood dishes. Book ahead for evening dining.

Limon   SEAFOOD €€
(☑394 4044; www.limongumusluk.com; meze ₺14-28; ☺lunch & dinner mid-Jun–mid-Sep; 🍴) Above Gümüşlük on the old Myndos Rd to Yalıkavak, Limon sprawls around Roman bath and Byzantine chapel ruins. It's great for vegetarians, with unique mezes such as seaweed slathered in olive oil and garlic, stuffed zucchini flowers, and a house take on the famous *sigara böreği* (with potatoes and egg, plus the usual cheese). The restaurant's also famous for its unique cocktails – a perfect complement to the long Aegean sunset views.

Teldolap   TURKISH €€
(☑394 3729; www.teldolaprestaurant.com; Sarıcayer Mevkii 2, Küme Evleri 85/2; mains ₺15-28) High in the hills behind Gümüşlük (you need a car), Teldolap has great views, good Turkish fare and ample home-cooked breakfasts.

Ali Ruza'nin Yeri   SEAFOOD €€€
(☑394 3097; www.balikcialirizaninyeri.com; meze ₺8-20, mains from ₺20; ☺lunch & dinner) Run by a fishing family, this Gümüşlük classic serves expertly prepared fresh fish dishes on the water's edge.

Soğan~Sarmısak   TURKISH €€€
(☑394 3087; mains from ₺22; ☺lunch & dinner mid-Jun–Aug) This waterfront restaurant has become trendy (and the prices have risen), but it's still a great choice for its atmosphere and eclectic decor. Reserve for the Sunday brunch (11am to 2pm).

Gözleme Shack   GÖZLEME €
(gözleme ₺4) If in search of a cheap snack, visit this unassuming place near the beach road car-park junction. It serves spinach,

cheese, mince and potato varieties of *gözleme*, and drinks.

Mandarina BAKERY €

(poğaça ₺1; ⏱6.30am-6.30pm) South of the road for the car park, Mandarina's good for breakfast snacks, particularly the *poğaça* (puff pastry).

Yalıkavak

☑0252

A former fishing and sponge-diving village, Yalıkavak has played up its relative remoteness from Bodrum to attract a more exclusive and Turkish clientele. However, it hasn't escaped the holiday-home-construction craze, and is known too for its upmarket private beaches – **Xuma Beach Club** and **Dodo Beach Club** are the most popular.

Nearby abandoned Yakaköy (outside of Yalıkavak), the **Dibek Sofrası** (www.dibeklihan.com; Yakaköy Çilek Caddesi; ⏱May-Oct) complex contains a restaurant, art gallery, museum, boutique hotel and vineyard. It exhibits Ottoman antiques such as jewelled daggers, antique fountain pens and ornate coffee cups collected by the owners.

Sleeping

4 Reasons Hotel BOUTIQUE HOTEL €€€

(☑385 3212; www.4reasonshotel.com; Bakan Caddesi 2; r from €158-290; ❋⏾⏾) This friendly and intimate hillside retreat features elegant and spotless rooms with lots of little designer touches. The friendly owners sanction bocce in the garden (free) and yoga classes (₺30), and there's a nice pool. The on-site restaurant serves excellent pan-Mediterranean cuisine.

Pink Life APARTMENT €€€

(☑385 5838; www.pinklifehotel.com; Aratepe Mevkii; apt ₺320; ⏱May-Oct; ❋⏾) These self-catering apartment blocks are great value, and come with a shared swimming pool. The large two-bedroom apartments come with an equipped kitchen and simple tropical-style furnishings. Air-conditioning works only in the living rooms, though.

Sandima 37 Suites BOUTIQUE HOTEL €€€

(☑385 5337; www.sandima37suites.com; Atatürk Caddesi 37; ste ₺240-400; ❋@⏾) Seven stylish suites set around a lush garden comprise Sandima's essential character; however, the restored stone cottage back by the pool has the most ambience.

Lavanta Hotel HOTEL €€€

(☑385 2167; www.lavanta.com; Begonvil Sokak 17; s/d from €105/130; ❋⏾) This country retreat with a pool features individually designed rooms furnished with antiques, surrounded by vine-draped gardens and connected by winding stone paths. It's up in the hills, so the view is slightly marred by the glare of white vacation homes mushrooming up.

✖ Eating

Geriş Altı (Yalıkavak's western district, towards Gümüşlük) is the place for the day's fishing catch. Thursday is market day at Çınaraltı.

Kavaklı Köfteci KÖFTE €

(Merkez Çarşı İçi; köfte ₺6-8) Around 50m inland, the distinctively smoky-flavoured, spicy Yalıkavak *köfte* is served here with garlic bread.

Deniz Kızı SEAFOOD €€€

(The Mermaid; ☑385 2600; Gerişaltı; mains ₺16-24; ⏱lunch & dinner) Along the seafront, this classic fish restaurant has tables by the docks and in the cosy indoor confines, and serves good seafood mezes.

Ali Baba SEAFOOD €€€

(İskele Meydanı 166; fish ₺20; ⏱lunch & dinner) Another seafront eatery, Ali Baba has a varied but somewhat expensive seafood menu, and nourishing grills, too.

Gündoğan

☑0252

Placid Gündoğan Bay, surrounded on both sides by hills glistening with wealthy villas, offers good swimming right in the centre and stays relatively sedate at night: most of its part- or full-time occupants are retirees of status from İstanbul or Ankara who, despite their secularist proclivities, have just not been able to get the local imam to turn down the volume at the mosque – about the only noise that could jolt you out of bed here. Apartments and villas are available in Gündoğan for long-term stays, and some new hotels are coming, too.

In 1961 the village's original Greek name (Farilya) was changed to Gündoğan. Settlement here probably began around AD 1100, though an earlier Roman town, Vara, had preceded it nearby. Although Gündoğan gets little attention on the historical-tours circuit, its backhills contain **Lelegian rock tombs** and, a 15-minute boat trip from town, **Apostol Island**, crowned by a fairly well-preserved Byzantine church with frescoes – ask locally to arrange trips.

🛏 Sleeping

Villa Joya
APARTMENT **€**

(☏387 8841; www.villajoyabodrum.com; villa for 4 €75; ❄️🐕) One of several family-run businesses renting to self-caterers, the Joya offers three apartments with kitchens and lovely gardens. While each apartment sleeps four, there's only one master bedroom (the other two beds are pull-out sleepers in the living room). Still, the price is hard to beat.

Hamak
BOUTIQUE HOTEL **€€€**

(☏387 9840; Kızılburun Mevkii, Casa Costa Sitesi; d €160-290; ❄️🐕) This seafront hotel has cheery, colourful rooms, most enjoying great views of hills and sea. A long, wood-slatted sundeck lined with white chaise longues extends into the lapping waters.

🍴 Eating

TOP CHOICE Terzi Mustafa
SEAFOOD **€€**

(☏387 7089; www.terzimustafaninyeri.com; Atatürk Caddesi 10; fish ₺16-24) Right on the sand at the central waterfront, this local favourite serves marine delicacies from shrimp to sea bream and sea bass, cooked to perfection and sprinkled with herbs and olive oil. There's no noise save for the wind and waves, no lights save for the moon and stars – ideal for those seeking great food and quiet conversation.

Reana
SEAFOOD **€€€**

(☏387 7117; Yalı Mevkii, Limaniçi; fish ₺20; ⏱dinner) A notable local seafood place, the white-walled Reana does excellent seafood mezes and fresh fish.

Türkbükü
☏0252

Türkbükü's reputation as Turkey's poshest beach getaway is kept alive by the Turkish celebrities, politicians and business moguls who flock here each summer. Thus considering that better beaches exist elsewhere on the peninsula, visiting this privileged cove might actually be best understood as a sociocultural experience.

Indeed, even in a place where women go to the beach in high-heels, sporting diamond-encrusted sunglasses, tongue-in-cheek reminders of social divisions remain; the tiny wooden bridge that crosses the two halves of Türkbükü's beach is jokingly understood by Turks as separating the 'Europe side' to the west from the 'Asia side' to the east – a reference to İstanbul, and an insinuation of the wealth gap between the ultra-posh homes and hotels on the western shores, and the ever-so-slightly less-expensive ones to the east.

At the time of research, the cross-peninsula road to Bodrum was being widened, making it now only a 15-minute drive between the two.

🛏 Sleeping

Türkbükü accommodation is unsurprisingly pricey, but you'll certainly have some interesting neighbours. Note that the rockin' summer clubs keep things loud until late.

TOP CHOICE Maçakızı
BOUTIQUE HOTEL **€€€**

(☏377 6272; www.macakizi.com; Kesire Buğlu Mevkii; r from ₺400; ❄️@🐕) Ground zero for Türkbükü's chic summer crowd, this luxurious place combines a resort feel with boutique trimmings and minimalist decor. There's a sociable restaurant and lively bar, but the real eyecatcher is the long wood-slatted boardwalk extending into the languid sea, replete with cosy pillow-beds.

Kaktüs Çiçeği
PENSION **€€€**

(☏377 5254; www.kaktuscicegi.com.tr; Atatürk Caddesi 119; d €120; ❄️🐕🐕) If the resorts are too hectic (or pricey) for your taste, try this small pension – with only 18 artfully designed rooms, it has a cosy feel, and a private beach and waterfront restaurant too. It's on the 'other' side of the small wood bridge near the Divan Hotel. Prices dip considerably outside of high season.

YU
BOUTIQUE HOTEL **€€€**

(☏377 5275; www.yu-otel.com; Bağarası Caddesi 26; r €150-180; ❄️🐕🐕) YU shoots for a boutique-chic look as disaffected as Türkbükü's visitors are, and it hits the mark with compact, cubic and clinical accommodation. But hey, there's a pool and some rooms have jacuzzis built directly into the bedding.

Maki Hotel
HOTEL **€€€**

(☏377 6105; www.makihotel.com.tr; Keleşharımı Mevkii; d/ste from €170/280; ❄️@🐕) Next to Maçakızı, and a little more laid-back, the Maki has two pools, a big wooden deck for lounging on throw pillows, and a lively bar – actually, the whole place is an ongoing party during summer.

Life Co
RESORT €€€

(📞377 6310; www.thelifeco.com; 136 Sokak 2, Bağ Arası Mahallesi; s/d €180/360; ❄@☀) There's no limit to the kind of people you can meet at a Turkish 'detoks centre by the sea', as Life Co decribes itself. A one-day detox program plus accommodation runs €180 (four-, seven- and 10-day packages are also available). The program includes yoga, diet seminars, massages and fruit smoothies – in short, everything that could help counteract the ageing process abetted by late nights at local bars. For better or for worse, colon irrigation is self-service.

5 Oda
BOUTIQUE HOTEL €€€

(Beş Oda; 📞377 6219; www.otel5oda.com; İnönü Caddesi 161; r €450; ☺May-Oct; ❄🛜) Apparently the law of supply and demand has worked out well for this eclectic boutique spot – the prices for its five fresh, seafacing rooms have almost doubled in just two years. But the striking natural stone-and-wood design impresses, and service is prompt and professional.

Divan Hotel
HOTEL €€€

(📞377 5601; Keleşharım Caddesi 6; d €125-260; ❄@☀) One of Türkbükü's older, and now slightly less-posh choices, the Divan (pronounced *Di*-wan) and its pool are popular with primarily Turkish vacationers. Rooms are adequate but not amazing, considering the price.

✗ Eating & Drinking

Deluxe hotels have excellent (and exorbitantly priced) restaurants, while other establishments are clustered by the waterfront; some turn into standing-room-only open bars for the glitterati. Book ahead.

Fidèle
RESTAURANT, BAR €€€

(📞377 5081; www.fidelehotel.net; mains from ₺20) Spreading responsibilities evenly between its dining and drinking duties, this posh place cooks delicacies such as seafood risotto and octopus carpaccio. Later in the evening, it transforms into a popular nightclub.

Casita
TURKISH €€

(www.casita.com.tr; mains from ₺15; ☺lunch & dinner) İstanbul's famous *mantı* (Turkish ravioli) restaurant graces the shores of Türkbükü, giving its summer guests a taste of home. By day it offers comfortable chaise longues for unwinding.

🏆 Ship Ahoy
BAR, RESTAURANT

(📞377 5070; Yalı Mevkii; mains ₺17-16; ☺May-Aug) Nothing says power like understated Ship Ahoy: essentially just a wide dock extending over the water, it's the antithesis of the lavish nightclub concept of entertainment, and the first port of call for Türkbükü's richest and most famous summer guests. While the average traveller could not even approach a beach bar frequented by Hollywood hotshots and Western politicos, in Turkey you can even reserve a table. Do it for the experience.

Gölköy
📞0252

Gölköy Bay exists in Türkbükü's shadow, and is thus often overlooked. However, it has great nightlife, beaches and (slightly) cheaper digs. Well-known Turkish bands sometimes play **Bianca Beacha** (www.biancabeach.com; Akdeniz Caddesi 35; ☺10am-5am May-Oct), an open-air club on the beach.

Only 50m from the centre and 1km from Türkbükü, **Villa Kılıc Hotel** (📞357 8118; www.villakilic.com; Sahil Sokak 22; r/ste from ₺350/550; ❄@☀) offers 33 lavishly designed rooms with hardwood floors and marble accents, while the suites have jacuzzis. There's a big pool and good restaurant, or you can recline on Gölköy's largest bathing platform (300 sq metres), where DJs play in summer.

Torba
📞0252

Despite being a short ride from Bodrum, Torba has stayed quieter and more family-oriented. It has a slightly escapist touch and a nice beach, though it lacks the seclusion of places on the peninsula's more distant corners.

🛏 Sleeping

Casa Dell'Arte
LUXURY HOTEL €€€

(📞367 1848; www.casadellartebodrum; Kilise Mevkii Mutlu Sokak; ste €460-980; ❄🛜☀) True to its name, Casa Dell'Arte is a veritable collection of valuable paintings and other works of art. The 12 rooms (not counting a separate family wing) are each named for a zodiac sign. The lighting around the pool and common spaces is understated and sublime. Luxuriate on the jetty over the sea, or escape the breeze in the 'silent pool' in the well-maintained grounds.

La Boutique Alkoçlar
BOUTIQUE HOTEL €€€

(⌖367 1970; www.alkoclar.com.tr; Hoşgörü Sokak 1; r/ste incl full board from ₺250/350; ❋@�❄☲) Run by the Turkish Alkoçlar hotel chain, this place shows promise, with plenty of boutique charm. Rooms are tastefully appointed with creamy colours and light wooden trim.

Izer Hotel & Beach Club
RESORT €€€

(⌖367 1910; www.izerhotel.com; d incl full board from €180; ☺May-Oct; ❋❄☲) This recently renovated, family-friendly option has myriad amenities and big twisting waterslides for kids (other water sports are available, too). It's a cheery, colourful place to bring the family, far from the other coves' dens of iniquity.

✗ Eating

Gonca Balık
SEAFOOD €€€

(fish ₺20; ☺lunch & dinner) With wooden tables strung along the ebbing waves, this is Torba's top place for a fish-and-meze meal.

Da Vittorio
ITALIAN €€

(⌖346 7002; Manastır Mevkii, Hoşgörü Sokak 5; mains ₺10-20; ☺lunch & dinner) Housed on the Marmara Bodrum's private beach, this excellent Italian eatery is open to the public day and night.

Eastern Peninsula
⌖0252

Bodrum's eastern bays are less well known, in some cases because hotels have swallowed them whole.

🛏 Sleeping

Kempinski Barbaros Bay
LUXURY HOTEL €€€

(⌖311 0303; www.kempinski.com; Yalıçiftlik; r from €380; ❋❄@☲) Bodrum's branch of the famed international chain, the Kempinski Barbaros Bay is cradled within a sea-facing cliff, isolated from any outside disturbances, with its own private beach and docks. The modern rooms have all of the expected amenities, and there are three restaurants, a bar and the Six Senses spa centre. However, the real marvel is the massive, elliptical outdoor pool, possibly Turkey's biggest.

Hapimag Sea Garden
RESORT €€€

(⌖311 1280; www.hapimag-seagarden.com; Yalıçiftlik; r per person incl full board from €104; ❋@☲) The sprawling Sea Garden is the answer for parents seeking to appease young children, with its all-inclusive hotel-and-apartment units dedicated to family fun.

MARMARIS & AROUND

Marmaris
⌖0252 / POP 31,397

Marmaris owes its debatable desirability to the industrial-tourism concept, and it does deliver by providing a nonstop party atmosphere for its British, Scandinavian and Russian summer tourists, most of them packaged. Still, the sprawling town does have a pretty harbour, crowned by a castle and lined with wood-hulled yachts and the vessels of visiting sailors.

Nevertheless, without the refinement of Bodrum, coarser Marmaris is essentially a sort of Kuşadası on steroids. Not many Turks you will encounter here actually come from the area, and few cultural attractions remain.

Nevertheless, Marmaris' immediate surroundings – including the rugged and relatively unvisited peninsulas of Bozburun and Datça – are spectacular, and the town makes a good base for *gület* cruises, diving in pristine waters, and for visiting the Greek isle of Rhodes. And hey, there's always the nightlife.

◉ Sights & Activities

Behind İskele Meydanı are Marmaris' (very) few remaining classic buildings. Inland from here, the mostly covered *çarşı* (bazaar) sells everything from haircuts to hats for concealing them.

Marmaris Castle & Museum
FORTRESS, MUSEUM

(Marmaris Kalesi ve Müzesi; ⌖412 1459; admission ₺3; ☺8am-noon & 1-5pm Tue-Sun) Marmaris' hilltop castle (1522) was Süleyman the Magnificent's assembly point for 200,000 troops, used to capture Templar-held Rhodes. The castle hosts **Marmaris Museum**, which exhibits amphorae, glassware, coins and other finds, including from Knidos and Hisarönü. Saunter the castle's **walls** and gaze down on the bustling marina.

Beaches
BEACH

Marmaris' narrow, pebbly town beaches allow decent swimming, but much better are **İçmeler** and **Turunç** (10km and 20km southwest, respectively). Dolmuşes by the new fountained square (₺3.25 and ₺7) access them.

From May to October, hourly water taxis docked around the **Atatürk statue** also serve İçmeler and Turunç (₺13, 45 minutes).

Marmaris

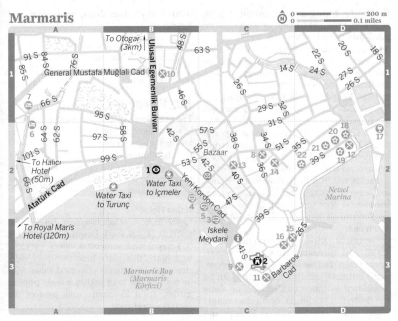

Marmaris

The beach at **Günlücek Park**, a forest park reserve 3.5km southeast of Marmaris, is also accessible by dolmuş from the new fountained square.

Armutalan Hamamı   HAMAM
(Pear Field Hamam; ☑ 417 5374; 136 Sokak 1; bath & scrub ₺20, with massage ₺40; ☺ 9am-10pm Apr-Oct) The enormous, full-serve Armutalan Hamamı is behind the government hospital,

off Datça Caddesi (2km west of the centre). After 6pm it's quietest, as the tour groups are gone. A free shuttle (Armutalan No 4) is near the new fountained square.

Boat Trips   BOAT TOUR
(4 people incl all meals & soft drinks €300) While Marmaris Bay dolmuş-boat day trips (₺30 to ₺35) offer eye-opening views and inviting swimming holes, you can really take things

further by hiring a yacht, together with your own group of friends, or with random new ones, which offers the pleasure of a 'blue voyage' down the coast. So many old salts advertise tours that their yachts are practically bumping and grinding into one another on the docks. Blue cruises offered by the long-established **Yeşil Marmaris Travel and Yachting** (☎412 2290; www.yesil marmaris.com; Barbaros Caddesi 13; 4 people around €300; ☉7am-11.30pm Mon-Sat high season, 8.30am-6.30pm low season) are recommended. As for the rest, compare prices, ask around and negotiate.

Yachts sail from May to October, departing between 9.30am and 10am and returning around 6pm to 6.30pm. Before signing up, confirm all details (exact boat, itinerary, lunch etc).

Overnight trips, plus two-day (from €700) and three-day trips (from €1200) often reach Dalyan and Kaunos. Longer, more intimate yachting adventures can be negotiated to Datça and Knidos, or along the Bozburun Peninsula, or on the original 'blue voyage' route south to Fethiye and beyond.

Diving

Several harbourside companies along Yeni Kordon Caddesi offer scuba-diving excursions and courses (April through October).

As with the numerous boat tours, many dive boats operate, so choose carefully. Since diving is potentially more life-endangering than lounging on a yacht, ask whether the company is licensed by the Turkish Underwater Federation. Also, ask whether your dive leader will be a certified instructor or an 'assistant instructor' – the latter often being a simple deckhand in scuba gear, not ideal for one's safety underwater. And do be responsible by reporting any medical conditions in advance.

Marmaris Diving Center DIVING
(aytac.ozan@hotmail.com) This professional outfit offers different dive packages in a big vessel run by Emre and Ozan Aytaç (the captain and the dive manager, respectively). A day's diving (starting at 10am) includes equipment, two dives of 20 to 30 minutes each, with lunch in between (₺70). Free pick-up from your hotel is included.

Deep Blue Dive Center DIVING
(☎0541 374 5881, 0506 614 6408; www.sealung.com) Deep Blue offers a three-day PADI open-water course (€240). Day excursions (€30) include two dives, equipment and lunch.

Professional Diving Centre DIVING
(☎0533 456 5888; www.prodivingcentre.com) This company charges €25 to €30 for two dives, equipment and lunch on the water.

🛏 Sleeping

The prevalence of package tourists (typically, sequestered in big outlying beach hotels) means that good central options are limited to a handful of options. Dimly lit, seedier pensions lurk around darker corners, propping up the bottom end of Marmaris' sex-tourism industry.

Halıcı Hotel HOTEL €€
(☎412 3626; www.halicihotel.com; Sokak 1; s/d ₺80/130; P❄@🛜🏊) Despite being a big (174-room) and somewhat dated package-tour hotel, this place near the quiet side-street canal is actually very good value, with its big outdoor pool within a leafy tropical garden. It's a 10-minute walk west of the central waterfront.

Maltepe Pansiyon PENSION €
(☎412 1629; www.maltepepansiyon.com; 66 Sokak 9; s/d/tr/q ₺35/75/90/120; ❄@) A small pension in a shady garden, the Maltepe offers small but spotless rooms (most en suite). You can use the kitchen.

Bariş Motel & Pansiyon PENSION €
(☎413 0652; www.barismotel.com; 66 Sokak 10; s/d ₺50/70; ❄) Opposite the canal, the Bariş is a friendly little place with spartan but clean rooms. Breakfast costs ₺6. If you're planning to stay out after midnight, ask for a key to get back in. If coming by taxi, specify that you mean this one, and not a similarly named apartment complex elsewhere in Marmaris.

Royal Maris Hotel HOTEL €€€
(☎412 8383; www.royalmarishotel.com; Atatürk Caddesi 34; s/d/tr ₺130/170/210; P❄🏊) Although it claims a gym, two pools and a private beach, this is definitely a glorified city hotel, not a resort, and these extras are so humble that it's hard to justify the price. However, the rooms are clean and modern (though those overlooking the palm-lined waterfront get considerable noise from the busy boulevard below). It's a 10- to 15-minute walk from the centre along the water.

✗ Eating

Ney
TURKISH €€
(☑412 0217; 26 Sokak 24; meze ₺5-6, mains ₺15-20) Up from the western marina, little Ney has atmosphere, in a 250-year-old Greek house. The home-cooked specialities include *tavuklu mantı böreği* (Turkish ravioli with chicken; ₺14).

Liman Restaurant
SEAFOOD €€
(☑412 6336; 40 Sokak 38; mains ₺10-20; ⊙8am-1am) Inconspicuously set in the bazaar, this old favourite run by the gracious Ömer Yüce serves excellent mezes and fish dishes, such as grilled sea bass (₺22), fish soup and calamari. Landlubbers will enjoy the *kavurma* (stir-fried lamb). Just check prices in advance to keep the bill under control.

Panorama Restaurant & Bar
INTERNATIONAL €€
(☑413 4835; Hacı İmam Sokağı 40; mains ₺10-15; ⊙9am-1am) The marina-view terrace here is more famous than the food, though it's still a nice place for pizza or pasta and sunset drinks.

İdil Mantı Evi
TURKISH €€
(☑0534 296 4410; 39 Sokak 140; meze ₺5-6, mains ₺8-20; ⊙4pm-5am) This Bar St shop keeps the punters upright with rich *gözleme* and other alcohol-soak-up snacks.

Aquarium Restaurant
INTERNATIONAL €€€
(☑413 1522; Barbaros Caddesi; mains ₺15-30; ⊙9am-midnight) A port-side restaurant with sublime views, this is a good spot for large grills and steaks.

Meryemana
TURKISH €
(☑412 7855; 35 Sokak 5b; mains ₺5-6; 🛜) The nourishing traditional tastes here, including mezes, spicy dips and homemade bread, draw a Turkish crowd as well as visitors. Try the *mantı* (₺6).

Fellini
ITALIAN €€€
(☑413 0826; Barbaros Caddesi 71; mains ₺15-25; ⊙9am-2am) Film-themed and specialising in Italian fare, this waterfront restaurant serves great thin-crust pizzas (₺18 to ₺22) and pasta (₺15 to ₺24).

Alin's Cafe & Restaurant
INTERNATIONAL €€
(☑413 2525; www.alins.com.tr; 36 Sokak 23; mains ₺5.90-14.90; ⊙8am-12.30am; 🛜) This Turkish chain does inexpensive and healthy grills, burgers and filled baked potatoes.

Doyum
KEBAP €€
(☑413 4977; Ulusal Egemenlik Bulvarı 14; mains ₺4-12; ⊙24hr) Ample breakfasts (₺7) and a good salad selection complement the tasty kebaps here.

🍷 Drinking & Entertainment

Marmaris by night offers more neon than Vegas, and almost as many drunks certain they're just one shot away from the big score. It's geared towards consumption on premises that spill out onto the street – 39 Sokak or 'Bar St', as this raucous stretch of licentiousness is known. If you like laser beams, dance music, liquored-up louts, tequilas by the half-dozen and the odd foam party, this is pretty much it.

As the night wears on, Bar St becomes a veritable cacophony, as each place tries to drown out its neighbours by cranking up the volume. This strip consists of both small and large bars, with the one or two 'clubs' being rather modest. Most open from 7pm to 4am daily. Beers cost ₺7 to ₺10, and spirits ₺10 to ₺15 (though 'happy hours' and other corrective incentives are offered).

Since Bar St establishments are so close and so interchangeable, they're best understood as a single amorphous mass. Cavernous **Joy Club** (☑412 6572; 39 Sokak 99) is shiny and sinful, while neighbouring **B52** (☑413 5292; 39 Sokak 120) comprises both a full-on club and a standing-room-only outdoor cocktail bar, across the street.

Nearby **Back Street** (☑412 4048; 39 Sokak 123) is also popular, as is **Arena** (39 Sokak 125), with two bars around a large dance floor. **Crazy Daisy** (☑412 4856; 39 Sokak 119) has raised terraces and is Brit-packed. Further towards the water is the strip's only rock bar, **Davy Jones's Locker** (☑412 1510; 39 Sokak 156), which has live bands in summer. A couple of lesser-visited (by foreigners, at least) Turkish-music bars are here, too.

Alternatively, quiet drinks with water views are had at **Panorama Restaurant & Bar** (☑413 4835; Hacı İmam Sokağı 40; ⊙9am-1am), or **Keyif Bar** (☑412 1061; Netsel Marina Çarşısı; ⊙8.30am-4am), a glassed-in lounge bar perched above the marina (beyond the footbridge).

ℹ Information

Akasya Internet (☑413 6906; 2nd fl, Ulusal Egemenlik Bulvarı 6; per hr ₺2; ⊙9am-midnight) Above the main north–south thoroughfare.

Mavi Internet (413 4979; 26 Sokak 8; per hr ₺2; 9am-11pm) Near the Ney restaurant in the old town.

Tourist Office (412 1035; İskele Meydanı 2; 8am-noon & 1-5pm Mon-Fri mid-Sep–May, daily Jun–mid-Sep) Below the castle, but not very helpful.

❶ Getting There & Away

Air

Dalaman Airport is 92km southeast of Marmaris. It gets many summer charters, and Turkish budget companies such as Pegasus Airlines sometimes have great deals. Turkish Airlines runs an airport bus (the Havaş bus; ₺25) from Marmaris otogar, departing three hours before each Turkish Airlines flight. Otherwise, Marmaris Coop's buses serve Dalaman (₺14); from there, it's a short, expensive taxi ride (₺42).

Boat

From April to October, daily catamarans serve Rhodes (one-way/same-day return/open-return including port tax €45/55/65, 50 minutes) from the pier 1km southeast of Marmaris. They depart at 9am, returning from Rhodes at 4.30pm. Cars cost €110/130/190 for a one-way/same-day return/open-return ticket.

Greek catamaran companies also do the Rhodes–Marmaris run, but are generally 10% more expensive. They leave Rhodes at 8am daily, returning from Marmaris at 4.30pm.

Turkish cargo boats (78 passenger capacity) serve Rhodes weekly in summer for similar prices, though the trip takes two hours. Departures are usually at 11.30am; in low season, when there's no catamaran competition, they go two to three times weekly at 9am (weather permitting). These ferries typically make same-day returns, but might stay in Rhodes for two or three days. (Greek ferries don't sail in low season.) The Sunday morning service runs only sporadically in June and July.

Travel agencies sell tickets, including Yeşil Marmaris Travel & Yachting (p260). Book ahead at least one day (if driving, more) and bring your passport. Be at the ferry dock one hour before departure for immigration formalities. Some agencies provide free pick-up service from hotels.

Bus

Marmaris' small otogar is 3km north of the centre. Dolmuşes serve it along Ulusal Egemenlik Bulvarı very frequently in the high season.

Hourly summer buses serve Bodrum (₺15, three hours, 165km), every two hours in low season. Four daily buses serve İstanbul (₺70, 13 hours, 810km) year-round. Hourly buses also serve İzmir (₺32, 4¼ hours, 270km), Göcek (₺18, 2¼ hours, 98km) and Dalaman (₺15, 1½ hours, 90km); Fethiye (₺20, three hours, 138km)

is served half-hourly in summer. Antalya (₺40, six hours, 365km) gets one daily bus. Nearby Muğla (₺9, one hour, 53km) gets half-hourly (hourly in low season) buses.

For Datça (₺12, 1¾ hours, 71km) hourly summer dolmuşes (every two hours in low season) run from the otogar. For Köyceğiz (₺8, 50 minutes, 63km), take the Fethiye bus. For Dalyan, also take the Fethiye bus, but change at Ortaca (₺10, 1½ hours, 84km) for the dolmuş. Five daily summer dolmuşes serve Selimiye and Bozburun (₺8, 55 minutes, 44km).

❶ Getting Around

Frequent dolmuşes canvas the bay, from near the new fountained square on Ulusal Egemenlik Bulvarı. Green dolmuşes serve Uzunyalı (₺2.50, 3km) and Turban-Siteler (₺4, 6km), and orange ones serve İçmeler (₺6, 10km).

Muğla

0252 / POP 62,635

While Muğla (*moo-*lah) is often overlooked by tourists eager to break for the coast, it's well worth a visit. With its whitewashed Ottoman quarter, traditional shops, historic structures and museums, Muğla has plenty of cultured charm and, as a small university city, offers relaxing and aesthetically pleasing cafes and restaurants to while away the hours amid the click of backgammon and rustling of Mediterranean foliage.

◉ Sights & Activities

Old Town   HISTORIC AREA
From Cumhuriyet Meydanı, the traffic roundabout with Atatürk's statue, walk north along Kurşunlu Caddesi to **Kurşunlu Cami**, the white 'Lead-Covered Mosque' (1493). Its minaret and courtyard were added in 1900.

Continue to the **bazaar**, its narrow lanes jammed with artisans' shops, confectioners and restaurants. Muğla's 18th- and 19th-century **Ottoman houses** and the **Ulu Cami** (1344) are up the hill; the mosque was built by Menteşe emirs (though 19th-century repairs altered its look). Nearby, the **clock tower** (*saatli kule*), Greek-built in 1905, sounds a church bell on the hour. Further up, the recently renovated Ottoman **Sekibaşı Hamamı** hosts occasional art exhibits. But the intricate architecture alone, with branching side rooms and central marble bath-table, make it worth a peek.

Zahire Pazarı
HISTORIC BUILDING

(Zahire Pazarı; ☺8am-11pm) This carefully restored bazaar, overlooked by a mosque, features lazy cafes spilling across a leafy cloistered courtyard dotted with 14 traditional craft shops; the city pays their rents to subsidise traditions such as marbled paper and art, hand-woven items and intricate painted boxes. Even if you're not shopping, come for an atmospheric drink.

Muğla Museum
MUSEUM

(☏214 6948; Postane Sokak; admission ₺3; ☺8am-noon & 1-5pm Tue-Sun) This courtyard lined with rooms boasts Greek and Roman antiquities, a **Gladiator Room** (with mock-ups, weapons and stone carvings), and a traditional arts and crafts section. It's opposite the beautiful **Konakaltı Kültür Merkezi** (Mustafa Muğlalı Caddesi 51), a traditional complex turned cultural centre in eastern Muğla.

Vakıflar Hamamı
HAMAM

(Foundations Hamam; ☏214 2067; Mustafa Muğlalı Caddesi 1; bath & scrub ₺20, with massage ₺40; ☺7am-11pm) This mid-14th-century hamam, for men and women, is still in operation.

📏 Sleeping

TOP CHOICE Mavi Konak
BOUTIQUE HOTEL €€

(☏214 7007; www.mavi-konak.eu; Kusular Çıkmazı 13; s €35-45, d €60-75; @) Originally a 19th-century Greek residence, the old-town 'Blue Mansion' offers five lovely guest rooms around a leafy courtyard. Run by a kind German couple, Claudia and Dieter (he's behind the handcrafted wood furniture), it has a modern kitchen/laundry for guests' use. There's only one en-suite room, but the shared bathroom (once a hamam) is cavernous. It's a bit hard to find – look for the big door with a tiny sign. There's a short cut through Zahire Pazarı.

İzethan Hotel
HOTEL €€

(☏212 2700; www.izethanhotel.net; Abdi İpekçi Bulvarı 75-77; s/d ₺60/90; ❄🛜) This businessy hotel has almost 200 modern rooms with all mod cons. Although it's a 15-minute walk northwest of Atatürk's statue, near Nazim Hikmet Parki, it's fantastic value and boasts a restaurant, bar, hamam and sauna.

Petek Hotel
BUSINESS HOTEL €€

(☏214 3995; www.petekhotel.com; Marmaris Bulvarı 27; s/d/tr ₺70/100/120; 🅿❄🛜) The comfortable and well-run Petek is a big af-

fair, with 64 rooms, and so fairly uniform; find it on the busy boulevard southeast of Cumhuriyet Meydanı.

🍴 Eating & Drinking
Market day in Muğla is Thursday.

Konak Kuzine
TURKISH €€

(☏213 1000; Kurşunlu Caddesi 13; mains ₺8.50-16; ☺10am-10pm) Excellent pide (₺5 to ₺9) and grills are served in this stylish 19th-century Greek mansion opposite Kurşunlu Cami.

Mavi Sofra
KÖFTE €€

(☏212 5250; Kurşunlu Çıkmazı 4/2; mains ₺8-15; ☺9am-11pm) Down a small alleyway opposite Kurşunlu Cami, this local favourite serves delicious kebaps and *köfte*.

Muğla Lokantası
TURKISH €

(☏212 3121; İsmet İnönü Caddesi 53; mains ₺3-6; ☺6.30am-10pm) The selection here is straightforward – a row of prepared Turkish dishes to choose from – and excellent.

Muğla Belediyesi Kültür Evi
CAFE

(Muğla Council Culture House; ☏212 8668; İsmet İnönü Caddesi 106; ☺8am-7.30pm) This 200-year-old house with a restored garden is a tranquil place for breakfast (₺5) or coffee.

Çakarkeyf
CAFE

(☏212 0048; Zahire Pazarı; ☺8am-11pm) This laid-back cafe in Zahire Pazarı offers tables under a balcony and in the adjoining stone courtyard. It's myriad traditional coffees are all superb. Some come with extra flourishes – try the *cilveli kahve* ('flirtatious coffee'), flecked by almond bits and with aromatic spices, served in a cup covered by a copper lid and set on a soft cupholder resembling a pasha's hat.

Sobe
CAFE, BAR

(☏212 6271; Mustafa Muğlalı Caddesi 43; ☺8am-1am) This delightful place, with large grassy courtyard and live music on weekends, is popular with Muğla's university students.

ℹ️ Information
Tourist Office (☏214 1261; www.mugla-turizm.gov.tr; Marmaris Bulvarı 22a; ☺8am-5pm Mon-Fri) About 600m southeast of Cumhuriyet Meydanı. Provides free town and province maps.

ℹ️ Getting There & Away
Muğla's otogar is about 750m southwest of the main square via Marmaris Bulvarı, then left on Zübeyde Hanım Caddesi. Buses leave

half-hourly (hourly in low season) to Marmaris (₺9, one hour, 53km) and Bodrum (₺13, two hours, 149km). If heading east along the coast, change in Marmaris.

Note that your car (or bus) might be randomly stopped at the hidden *jandarma* (police) hut on the Marmaris road – unless you're peddling drugs, there's nothing to worry about, but try to have your passport with you.

Akyaka (Gökova)

☑ 0252 / POP 2500

Tucked between pine-clad mountains and a grey sand beach on the Gulf of Gökova, Akyaka is a relaxing alternative to hectic Bodrum and Marmaris. It's sometimes called Gökova (also the name of a different town, several hundred kilometres inland).

The northward road from Muğla crosses the Sakar Pass (Sakar Geçidi; 670m), popular with paragliders. It offers breathtaking views of the water.

Çinar Beach, 2km from town, has the best swimming. When heading towards the marina, turn right at the school and take the high road right to get there. **Boat tours** (₺50) are offered by the local sailing club.

Akyaka gets steady summertime winds, making it ideal for windsurfing and kiteboarding. Beachside **Rüzgar Sports Center** (☑ 243 4217, 0505 918 3600; www.gokovaruzgar .com; Sahil Sokak 2; ⊙9am-7pm) rents equipment and offers lessons, and also rents sea kayaks, canoes, sailboats and mountain bikes.

🛏 Sleeping

Susam Hotel   HOTEL €€
(☑ 243 5863; www.susamhotel.com; Lütfiye Sakıcı Caddesi 30; s ₺50-100, d ₺70-120; ❉ 🕸) Susam has 10 immaculate rooms (most with balconies) and a small garden with pool. It's a five-minute walk from the water, on the main beach road.

Yücelen Hotel   RESORT €€€
(☑ 243 5108; www.yucelen.com.tr; s/d ₺120/190; ❉ 🕸 ❄ 🛋) This big (125-room) classic near the beach is a popular family resort and has indoor and outdoor pools, a fitness centre and a sauna.

Okaliptüs Apart   APARTMENT €€
(☑ 243 4370; www.tomsanokaliptus.com; Volkan Sokak 2i; 2-bedroom apt €60-90, 3-bedroom €80-140; ❉ 🕸 🛋) Self-caterers get great value at these fully furnished apartments; one's just 300m from the beach.

Gökova Park Camping   CAMPING GROUND €
(☑ 243 4055; per person/tent/car ₺5/10/15, bungalow up to 6 people ₺195) Beside the Yücelen Hotel on the beach; offers tent pitches, bungalows, mobile homes and cottages.

🍴 Eating

Among the beach restaurants, try pier-side **Şıkıdam** (☑ 243 5738; İncir Sokak 8; mains ₺5-20; ⊙8am-2am) for fresh fish, and the somewhat posher **Spica** (☑ 243 4270; Sanat Sokak 4; mains ₺11-19; ⊙8am-midnight), on the opposite western side, with a breezy seafront terrace.

Wednesday is **market day** in Akyaka, while on Saturday it's near Gökova Bay.

Golden Roof Restaurant   INTERNATIONAL €€
(☑ 243 5392; Karanfil Sokak 1; meze ₺5, mains ₺12-20; ⊙8am-1am) This family-run institution does good pizza and pasta, plus home-cooked Turkish dishes. The affable host is a good source of local information.

Tıkın House   KEBAP €
(☑ 243 5444; Lütfiye Sakıcı Caddesi; dishes ₺3.50-8.50; ⊙8.30am-11pm) Opposite the Susam Hotel, this popular kebap joint also does great mezes, grills, omelettes and salads.

ⓘ Getting There & Away

Minibuses serve Muğla (₺4, 30 minutes, 26km) half-hourly, and Marmaris (₺6, 30 minutes, 31km) twice daily (in summer). Otherwise, Marmaris minibuses drop you at the highway junction (2.5km from the beach) – walk or catch a random passing minibus from there.

Datça & Bozburun Peninsulas

Far from the madding crowds of Marmaris, a more elemental and tranquil experience awaits on its outlying peninsulas, Datça (occasionally called Reşadiye) and Bozburun (or Hisarönü) just south. They unwind wonderfully for over 100km into the Aegean Sea, and feature stunning azure coves, hidden archipelagos, and craggy, thickly forested peaks overlooking it all.

Despite having developed some tourism presence, these rugged shores are far less built up than the Bodrum Peninsula, and as such are reserved for escapists and anyone seeking simple village life or a sail in secluded waters. The scattered antiquities here include the ruins of ancient Knidos, at the Datça Peninsula's tip.

DATÇA
☑ 0252 / POP 14,800

Some 70km from Marmaris, down a winding road dotted with traditional windmills, Datça is the peninsula's major harbour town. Datça is more workaday and boxy than it should be, given its location close to the sea, but it has three lovely beaches; **Kumluk Plajı** (Sandy Beach), tucked behind the main street (Atatürk Caddesi) shops; **Hastanealtı** (literally 'Below the Hospital'), the bigger, eastern-shore beach; and **Taşlık Plajı** (Stony Beach) at harbour's end.

If you can ignore the downtown and stay focused on the beaches, Datça makes a nice place to stay, and it's the closest town to ancient Knidos' ruins. Yet if you've made the long trek all the way out here, chances are high that you'll prefer Eski Datça (Old Datça) 2km away, past remote coves, which has largely preserved the traditional feel that Datça has lost.

If you are planning to take the Datça–Bodrum ferry, check locally or phone the Bodrum Ferryboat Association office (p267) office in advance, as its website's itineraries are not always up to date.

🛏 Sleeping

Basic but decent budget pensions are available before the small roundabout with a big tree, along Atatürk Caddesi, and above the harbour near the square.

Renting villas and apartments in Datça or nearby villages can be good value; check locally or via websites such as www.hidden datca.com.

TOP CHOICE **Villa Aşina**　　BOUTIQUE HOTEL **€€€**
(**☑** 712 0443; www.villaasina.com.tr; İskele Mahallesi 24 Sokak 10 ; s/d/ste ₺130/210/230; **※♨**) Several kilometres west of the centre, this lovely spot has 17 rooms (all with sea views), notable for their intricate carved ceilings, oval beds and local embroideries. There are two sparkling beaches, and the friendly owners serve complimentary tea and sweets daily at 5pm. Kids under six sleep free, and paying in cash gets you a 5% discount. To get here from Atatürk Caddesi (by the mosque),

---

BOZBURUN PENINSULA BY SCOOTER

The mountainous, deeply indented Bozburun (or Hisarönü) Peninsula is the perfect place to escape the madness of Marmaris. For a real off-the-beaten-track adventure, kick-start a motorbike and roll down the winding country roads, into a natural paradise and villages that modernity forgot.

On the way, you'll pass through fragrant pine forests on a high plateau inland from Turunç; they give way to the steep and rocky hillsides as you approach Bozburun. Although the main road reaches Bozburun, it's much more exciting to cruise the village roads and circle back onto the main one.

Leaving Marmaris, head for İçmeler to the southwest, via Atatürk Caddesi and the coastal road. In İçmeler the main road branches; take the right-hand street around the back of the town and then up a steep, winding road towards Turunç. Before reaching it, an unpaved, right-hand road passes through the pine forest; it narrows and gets steeper, slowly winding down to Bayırköy, an inland village with rustic houses. The village square, shaded by an ancient plane tree, has atmospheric terraced restaurants with views into the valley. After Bayırköy the landscape becomes arid, and the hills drop away into inaccessible azure coves. From tiny Söğüt the road is relatively level all the way to Bozburun, which also has several nourishing lunch spots.

From Bozburun, a good road leads back along the peninsula's western side, past the idyllic bays of Selimiye, Orhaniye and Hisarönü, before rejoining the main Datça–Marmaris road. Between the first two, about 3km southeast of tiny Turgutköy, a waterfall sparkles, cooling the air (follow the sign for 'şelale'). You can also jump in the frigid pools here for more cool relief.

This circular peninsula tour covers about 120km of driving distance; plan for about six hours of travel, which includes rests, swims and photo stops. Marmaris scooter rentals average ₺45 per day in high season. Considering the steep and winding roads, and Turkey's relatively high rate of road traffic accidents, do wear a helmet. If not the full biker gear, try to wear clothes that would at least protect your skin if you skid out.

Fill up before you go, as the peninsula's only petrol stations are at Bozburun and Turunç.

follow the road that branches right and proceed for 3km; it's signposted on the left.

Villa Tokur
BOUTIQUE HOTEL €€€

(🖉712 8728; www.hoteltokur.com; Koru Mevkii; d/ste €83/115; 🕸🕸) This quiet hilltop hotel with a garden and well-groomed grounds overlooking the sea offers 15 nicely furnished rooms. It's a 10-minute walk uphill from Taşlık Plajı.

Tunç Pansiyon
PENSION €

(🖉712 3036; www.tuncpansiyon.com; Buxerolles Caddesi; s/d/apt ₺50/80/140; 🕸@) This pension in the roundabout area (look for the Öğür taxi stand) has basic but sunny and spotless rooms with balconies, as well as an apartment sleeping up to five. The rooftop deck offers great views. One-day car excursions for up to three persons to Knidos are offered – you're charged just for the petrol (₺45).

Bora Hotel
HOTEL €€

(🖉712 2040; www.borahotel.com.tr; Atatürk Caddesi; s/d ₺70/120; 🕸) This hilltop hotel overlooking the harbour has 18 bright, airy rooms with balconies, and friendly (if a bit slow) service.

Ilıca Camping
CAMPING GROUND €

(🖉712 3400; www.ilicacamping.com; Taşlık Plajı; tent & campervan per couple ₺35, 2-bed bungalow with/without bathroom ₺110/60, 3-bed bungalow ₺150/120; 🕸@) On Taşlık Plajı, this well-run camping ground shaded by eucalyptus trees has a great open grassy pitch and facilities.

✕ Eating

Datça's *keşkek* (lamb mince and coarse, pounded wheat) is its speciality.

TOP CHOICE Zekeriya Sofrası
KÖFTE, KABAP €

(🖉712 4303; Atatürk Caddesi 60; dishes ₺7-9; ⊘8am-11pm; 🖋) Sometimes simple is better, and that's the case at this nondescript main-street eatery, run by its friendly namesake. The home-cooked dishes and made-to-order fare are incredibly delicious and nourishing, and great value, too. Vegetarians will be happy with the stuffed aubergine offerings (among much else), and the great meat dishes include *inegöl köfte* (mixed meat spicy meatballs) made with Zekeriya's own secret recipe.

Papatya Restaurant & Bar
SEAFOOD €€

(🖉712 2860; Kargı Yolu Caddesi 4; mains ₺12-20; ⊘8.30am-5am) This stone-house marina restaurant, with its vine-covered terrace, exudes atmosphere. Try the *karides güveç şarapli fırında* (shrimps oven-baked in wine; ₺23);

simpler dishes such as *köfte* and kebaps are available, too. Find it where the main road branches to the west from the mosque.

Emek Restaurant
SEAFOOD €€

(🖉712 3375; Yat Limanı; mains ₺10-22) Datça's oldest and most reliable seafood joint on the marina, Emek serves good grilled fish, at better prices than most.

Culinarium
INTERNATIONAL €€€

(🖉712 9770; www.culinarium-datca.com; Yat Limanı; mains ₺20-35) Beside Emek Restaurant, the posher Culinarium has flair, ambience and a three-course set menu (₺40), with a unique all-Turkish wine list.

▼ Drinking & Entertainment

Datça's nightlife centres on the harbour. **Bolero** (🖉712 3862; Yat Limanı; beer ₺5; ⊘8am-2am; 🛜) is a central and lively place; **Mojo** (🖉712 4868; Yat Limanı; beer ₺5; ⊘7.30am-2am), at the end of the bar strip, is popular with hip young Turks.

🛍 Shopping

Datça Köy Ürünleri
FOOD & DRINK

(🖉712 8318; Atatürk Caddesi 51a; ⊘9am-5pm, to 1am Jun-Sep) Datça's three main products (honey, almonds and olive oil) are sold here.

ℹ Information

Karnea Turizm (🖉712 8842; İskele Mahallesi Atatürk Caddesi 54b) Run by the helpful Beycan Uğur, this travel agency on the main street provides useful local info, books flights, rents cars and runs local trips, such as a half-day Knidos tour (₺60 per person).

ℹ Getting There & Away

Hourly summer dolmuşes serve Marmaris (₺13, 1¾ hours, 71km, every two hours in low season) from Cumhuriyet Meydanı, the main square (five times daily in low season). Change there for other destinations. Note that the bus from Marmaris leaves you on the main street, but 500m before the square and harbourside pensions.

From May to September, hydrofoils serve Rhodes (single/return ₺90/180, 45 minutes) and Symi (single/return ₺60/120, 15 minutes) on Saturday, normally at 4pm, but check locally.

A *gület* cruise to Symi runs two to three times weekly (₺140, 70 minutes) at 9am. It requires at least eight people.

Knidos Yachting (🖉712 9464; Yat Limanı 4a), next to Emek Restaurant, sells hydrofoil, ferry and *gület* tickets. For Rhodes and Symi, bring your passport at 11am on the Saturday of departure; for the *gület*, you can reserve by phone. Knidos also organises diving trips (₺80/110 for one/two dives).

From June to mid-September, daily ferries serve Bodrum (passenger single/return ₺25/40, car and driver ₺70, extra passenger ₺10, two hours) from Körmen harbour at Karaköy (5km northwest of Datça). In May, departures are on Monday, Wednesday and Friday at 9.30am, and on Tuesday, Thursday, Saturday and Sunday at 5.30pm. In April and October they run on Monday, Wednesday and Friday (returning the same days). From Bodrum, they return on Tuesday, Thursday, Saturday and Sunday at 9.30am, and the rest of the week at 5.30pm.

Tickets are sold at the **Bodrum Ferryboat Association** (☑712 2143; fax 712 4239; Turgut Özal Meydanı), by the mosque. Confirm details there or phone them beforehand (the website may be out of date). Or ask at the **Ulusoy bus office** (☑712 9598; Atatürk Caddesi 25; ☻8am-10pm), near the square, where tickets are sold. A free shuttle takes you from Datça to Karaköy harbour at 9am. If staying in Eski Datça, a free shuttle will also collect you from there before the ferry (with prior notice).

ESKİ DATÇA
☑0252 / POP 8000

'Old Datça', capital of an Ottoman district stretching into today's Greece, is much more atmospheric than its 'new' counterpart. Its cobbled streets and old stone houses make for a blissful escape into the untroubled coast of yesteryear.

🛏 Sleeping & Eating

Yağhane Pansiyon PENSION ₺₺
(☑712 2287; www.suryaturkey.com; Karaca Sokak 42; s/d ₺70/130) In the Surya Yoga Centre, this seven-room pension is ideal for chilling out, but for those interested, yoga (hatha and iyengar) and ayurvedic massage are available, too. The compact rooms have non-allergenic wooden floors and fans, though two share facilities.

Mehmet Ali Ağa Konağı HISTORIC HOTEL ₺₺₺
(☑712 9257; www.kocaev.com; stone house r €180-300, stone house ste €350-420, mansion r €385-425, mansion ste €625-700; ✱@☒) Just north of Eski Datça, in Reşadiye (formerly Elaki), this opulent boutique hotel is among the most beautiful of any around. Its 18 historically furnished rooms sprawl across four buildings set amid lush rose and citrus gardens. The owners of this property, which was once a wealthy Ottoman dynastic mansion, have restored the hamam to its original spa function (special spa packages are available). The hotel's celebrated restaurant, Elaki, cooks creative Med flavours (mains €25 to €40).

Dede Garden Hotel HOTEL ₺₺₺
(☑712 3951; Can Yücel Sokak; s/d ₺180/230; ✱☒) This 150-year-old stone manor tucked within a walled garden has a pool and relaxed bar. The seven individually designed rooms come with kitchens.

Datça Sofrası TURKISH ₺
(☑712 4188; Hurma Sokak 16; mains ₺6-10) This stylish bistro beneath a vine-clad pergola specialises in one of the vegetables Turks do best (aubergines), and serves good grilled fish and meat.

Antik Cafe CAFE ₺₺
(☑712 9176; Can Yücel Sokak 1; dishes ₺5-12; ☻8.30am-1am Apr-Sep) This simple cafe and arts and crafts centre serves fresh chilled juices and good Turkish coffees.

🛍 Shopping

Olive Farm FOOD & DRINK, HOMEWARES
(☑712 8377; Güller Dağı Çiftliği 30; ☻8am-7pm) Olive-grove tours, tastings and a shop will placate lovers of liquid gold. It's 600m before the main road's Datça turn-off.

ℹ Getting There & Away

Hourly Eski Datça–Datça minibuses (₺2.50) depart, wait 30 minutes, and return (May to October). In low season, it's every two hours.

KNİDOS

Knidos, a once-prosperous Dorian port city dating to 400 BC, lies in scattered ruins covering 3km of the Datça Peninsula's tip. Here, dramatic and steep hillsides, terraced and planted with groves of olive, almond and fruit trees, rise above two idyllic bays where yachts drop anchor.

The peninsula edge's unpredictable winds meant that ancient ships often had to wait for favourable winds at Knidos (also known by the Latinised name, Cnidus); this boosted the ship-repairs business, hospitality and general trade. St Paul, en route to Rome for trial in AD 50 or 60, was one of many maritime passengers forced to wait out the storm here.

Although little remains, the city paths are well preserved. The round **Temple of Aphrodite** once contained the world's first freestanding female statue, while the 5000-seat Hellenistic **lower theatre** and a 4th-century-BC **sundial** comprise other ancient attractions. Fine carvings from an erstwhile Byzantine church exist, too.

An on-site restaurant offers great views.

❶ Getting There & Away

Datça's Karnea Turizm (p266) offers a half-day Knidos tour (₺60 per person). Knidos Taxi, near Cumhuriyet Meydanı, will take up to three persons for ₺100 (including two hours of waiting).

If you have more time, Datça harbour excursion boats also serve Knidos, at around 9am or 9.30am, returning in the early evening (₺30 per person).

SELİMİYE

☎0252 / POP 4900

This former traditional boat-builders' village on the Bozburun Peninsula remains blissfully detached from the outside world, despite being just an hour from Marmaris. Popular with yachtspeople, Selimiye's barely a tiny promenade lined with restaurants, pensions and bars on a calm bay, beneath a few toppled ruins.

🛏 Sleeping

Nane Limon Pansiyon PENSION €€
(☎446 4146; www.nanelimonpansiyon.com; s/d ₺100/150; ❄) This attractive, blue-shuttered white guesthouse has 10 breezy rooms, many with balconies. A garden path accesses the beachfront bar and its swaying hammocks.

Sardunya Bungalows HOTEL €€
(☎446 4003; www.sardunya.info; s/d incl half-board ₺130/160; ❄@) These family-friendly stone 'bungalows' actually offer hotel amenities for reasonable rates. It's behind the beach, with a nice garden.

Bahçe Apart Otel HOTEL €€
(☎446 4235; bahceapart@hotmail.com; s/d/apt ₺100/120/140; ❄@) This simple hotel's three rooms may be spartan, but they're clean and it's literally by the water. Four larger apartments are also available.

🍴 Eating & Drinking

Falcon Restaurant TURKISH €€
(☎446 4105; mains ₺10-18) This fun place does traditional Turkish, as well as international fare such as pasta. The stone-oven pide and *tandir* (clay oven) dishes are excellent.

Özcan Restaurant SEAFOOD €€
(☎446 4233; mains ₺10-14) Friendly Özcan's serves excellent meze (₺4 to ₺6) and fish – try the tasty grilled squid (₺15).

Aurora Restaurant SEAFOOD €€
(☎446 4097; mains ₺10-15) Fish and meze at good rates are the specialities at this antique stone house with an intimate shaded terrace and seafront tables.

Cafe Ceri CAFE
(coffee ₺3, frappés ₺4.50; ⊗8.30am-11pm) A laid-back marina cafe for drinking with both local and foreign sea dogs.

❶ Getting There & Away

Dolmuşes serve Marmaris (₺9, 1¼ hours, 43km) every two hours. The Marmaris–Bozburun bus stops on the main road at Selimiye's northern end. Drivers should take the Bozburun road about 9km south of Orhaniye and follow the signs.

BOZBURUN

☎0252 / POP 2000

Bozburun, 12km down the peninsula on Sömbeki Körfezi (Sömbeki Bay), retains its rustic farming-and-fishing roots, though tourism (mostly from maritime visitors) has arrived too. It's an agreeable spot far from the masses, and you can swim in brilliantly blue waters just around the harbour to the left, from the rocks (just watch out for sea urchins). Local charter boats venture into the idyllic surrounding bays.

🛏 Sleeping

Yilmaz Pansiyon PENSION €
(☎456 2167; www.yilmazpansion.com; İskele Mahallesi 391; s/d ₺60/90; ❄) Around 100m east of the marina, this friendly little pension is great value: 10 simple but cheerful rooms, a modern shared kitchen, and a vine-covered terrace just metres from the sea. It also arranges local boat cruises.

Pembe Yunus PENSION €€
(Pink Dolphin; ☎456 2154; www.bozburunpembeyunus.com; Kargı Mahallesi 37; s/d incl half-board ₺80/160; ❄) Located 700m from the marina, the 'Pink Dolphin' is a friendly, rustic place, with some rooms enjoying huge terraces with vast sea views. The home-cooked three-course set dinners cost ₺25. The hotel uses its private boat for Symi trips.

Sabrinas Haus LUXURY HOTEL €€€
(☎456 2045; www.sabrinashaus.com; d from €375, ste from €750) Reachable by boat (a liveried skipper picks up guests in a speedboat *Hawaii Five-O*–style) or a half-hour walk along the bay's eastern shore, Sabrinas Haus is the ultimate pamperific, get-away-from-it-all place. There are 14 tastefully designed rooms (think lots of natural woods and shades of white) in three buildings hidden in a beautiful mature garden. The infinity pool and seafront deck and bar are super and the spa has

massage and myriad treatments. Note that a credit card deposit is required, and that kids under 14 aren't allowed.

✖ Eating & Drinking

Fisherman House   SEAFOOD **€€**
(☑456 2730; İskele Mahallesi 391; meze ₺4, seafood meze ₺12-15, fish per 500g ₺20-30) Fresh fish at honest prices is served at this place run by the fisherman who owns Yilmaz Pansiyon.

Kandil Restaurant   SEAFOOD **€€**
(☑456 2227; İskele Mahallesi 3; mains ₺10-12) This square-side local favourite serves cheap mezes, and varied fish and grills.

Marin Cafe Bar   CAFE, BAR
(☑456 2181; Atatürk Caddesi 56; beer ₺5) Very chilled-out cafe-bar, near the Pembe Yunus.

❶ Getting There & Away

Six daily summer minibuses serve Marmaris (₺10, 1½ hours, 55km) via Selimiye.

Western Anatolia

Includes »

Best Places to Eat

» Kaplıkaya Kocamanlar Et Balık Restaurant (p282)

» Passage (p289)

» Seki Döner (p282)

» Café Del Mundo (p289)

Best Places to Stay

» Kitap Evi (p281)

» Abacı Konak Otel (p289)

» Charly's Pension (p305)

Why Go?

Durable, diverse and down-to-earth, Western Anatolia combines everything from ancient sites and spectacular mountain terrain to some of Turkey's heartiest food and friendliest people.

The region's diversity of civilisations can be experienced directly: hike the rock-carved Phrygian valley, pound the marbled pavement of the ancient cities of Sagalassos and Afrodisias, or take a woodland pilgrimage on St Paul's Trail. Original Ottoman capital Bursa, meanwhile, is a cornerstone of Turkish identity, with mosques, imperial mausoleums and the İskender kebab. The shimmering travertines of Pamukkale, on the other hand, are just great for splashing in.

The region's lesser-known attractions constitute its secret weapon, however: escapist Eğirdir, set on a tranquil lake, is perfect for kayaking, hiking, or doing nothing at all, while vibrant Eskişehir, a student city with a sublime old town, offers river gondola rides, cultural events and happening restaurants and bars.

When to Go

Bursa

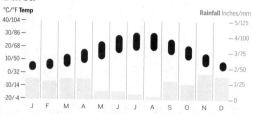

Jan & Feb Take in the fresh forest air while skiing on Uludağ, near Bursa.

Jul & Aug Escape the heat at Lake Eğirdir, tucked between mountains.

Sep Enjoy Pamukkale's crystal travertines, without the crowds.

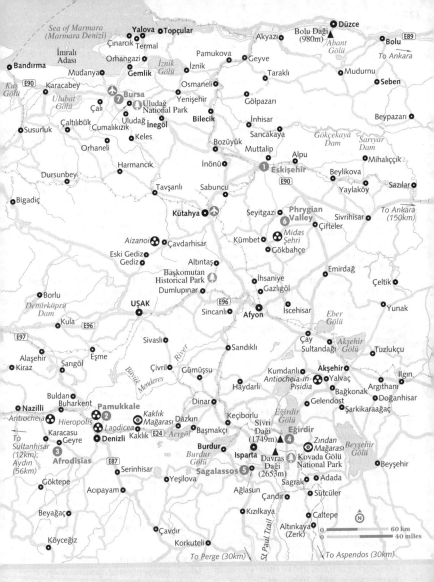

Western Anatolia Highlights

1 Indulge in the nightlife, old-town ambience and all-around good vibes of **Eskişehir** (p286)

2 Laze in calcite travertine pools on the snow-white ridges of **Pamukkale** (p295), beneath the ruins of ancient Hierapolis

3 Channel the fated exhilaration of the Roman gladiator, gazing from the tunnel onto **Afrodisias'** (p301) vast stadium

4 Find B&B bliss by the idyllic lake of **Eğirdir** (p303), and tackle St Paul's Trail through the Taurus Mountains

5 Ascend the lonely heights of **Sagalassos** (p308), a ruined mountain city with a magnificent rebuilt fountain

6 Hike deep into a civilisation lost in the desolate, rock-hewn **Phrygian Valley** (p285)

7 Marvel at the early Ottoman rulers' elaborate mausoleums and mosques in **Bursa** (p275), and shop for hand-woven silks

İznik

📞 0224 / POP 22.661

Turks are proud of İznik's Ottoman tile-making tradition, though its Byzantine incarnation as Nicaea was more significant – church councils in this fortress town shaped the future of all Christianity. Sadly, modern socio-political trends have suppressed this heritage, and İznik today lingers as a rundown collection of tile shops, teahouses and handicraft parlours, though the fortress ruins and lakeside setting make visiting worthwhile.

History

Founded around 1000 BC, İznik got its classical Greek name (Nikaea, Westernised to Nicaea) when one of Alexander the Great's generals, Lysimachus, captured it in 301 BC and named it after his wife, Nikaea. Nicaea became capital of Bithynia, a kingdom along the Marmara Sea. By 74 BC the city was Roman, though Gothic and Persian invasions ruined it by AD 300.

In 325, Emperor Constantine the Great chose Nicaea for the first Ecumenical Council – uniting ecclesiastical leaders from across Christendom and setting a precedent for future councils. Huge differences then existed between different Christian sects, and the council (which considered Christ's divinity, the calculation of Easter and other issues) resulted in the Nicene Creed, enabling bishops and priests to speak in an authoritative and unified way – and thus, for the religion to expand. Four centuries later, the seventh Ecumenical Council was held in Nicaea's Aya Sofya church.

Under Justinian I (AD 527–65), Nicaea's buildings and defensive walls were renovated, thwarting later Arab attackers. In 1204, when Constantinople fell to Venetian-bankrolled conquerors (the perfidious Fourth Crusade), Nicaea became a Byzantine empire-in-exile, one of three successor states (along with Trebizond/Trabzon on the Black Sea and Epiros in Greece).

In 1331 Sultan Orhan conquered the city, establishing İznik's first Ottoman *medrese* (seminary). In 1514 Sultan Selim I captured Persian Tabriz, bringing its artisans to İznik. The Persian craftsmen were skilled tile-makers, and soon İznik's kilns were producing faience (tin-glazed earthenware) unequalled even today. Since 1993, the İznik Foundation has revitalised İznik's tile-making tradition.

◉ Sights & Activities

Most attractions are within the fortifications.

Aya Sofya   RUIN

(Church of the Divine Wisdom; cnr Kılıçaslan & Atatürk Caddesi; admission ₺7; ⊙9am-7pm Tue-Sun) Originally a great Justinianic church, Aya Sofya is now a crumbling, neglected ruin slumbering in a rose garden. The building encompasses ruins of three different structures. A mosaic floor and mural of Jesus, Mary and John the Baptist survive from the original church. Destroyed by a 1065 earthquake, it was later rebuilt with the mosaics set into the walls. The Ottomans made it a mosque, but a 16th-century fire again destroyed it. Reconstruction supervised by the great architect Mimar Sinan added İznik tiles to the decoration.

Yeşil Cami   MOSQUE

Built between 1378 and 1387 under Sultan Murat I, Yeşil Cami (Green Mosque) has Seljuk Turkish proportions, influenced by Seljuk homeland Iran. The minaret's green-and-blue-glazed zigzag tiles foreshadowed the famous local industry.

İznik Museum   MUSEUM

(İznik Müzesi; 📞757 1027; Müze Sokak; admission ₺3; ⊙9am-7pm Tue-Sun) The city museum is housed in a soup kitchen that Sultan Murat I built for his mother, Nilüfer Hatun, in 1388. Born a Byzantine princess, Nilüfer was given to Sultan Orhan to cement a diplomatic alliance.

The museum's grounds contain marble statuary, while the lofty whitewashed halls contain original İznik tiles, with their milky bluish-white and rich 'İznik red' hues. Other displays include 8000-year-old finds from a nearby *tumulus* (burial mound) at Ilıpınar.

Opposite, see the restored **Şeyh Kutbettin Camii**.

City Walls & Gates   RUIN

İznik's once-imposing Roman walls, renovated by the Byzantines, no longer dominate, though they remain impressive. Four main gates – İstanbul Kapısı, Yenişehir Kapısı, Lefke Kapısı and Göl Kapısı – still transect the walls, while remains of 12 minor gates and 114 towers stand.

The most impressive walls, reaching 10m to 13m in height, stand between **Yenişehir Gate** and the eastern **Lefke Gate**. The latter comprises three Byzantine gateways, and offers good views. The imposing **İstanbul Gate** features huge stone carvings of heads facing

İznik

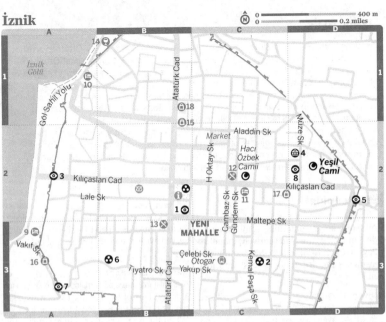

İznik

outwards. The **Göl (Lake) Gate** has scant remains, like the **Saray (Palace) Gate** to the southwest. Sultan Orhan (r 1326–61) had a palace nearby. Adjacent walls contain a ruined 15,000-seat **Roman theatre**.

Within the big walls, traces of the minor **Horoz (Rooster) Gate** remain, as do the blown-up foundations of the **Church of the Koimesis** (in Greek, Dormition of the Mother of God) on the western side of Kaymakam S Taşkın Sokak. Built around 800 and re-

constructed after a mid-11th-century earthquake, it's İznik's only church that was never converted into a mosque; unsurprisingly, it was dynamited by victorious Turks after the Independence War. Byzantine emperor Theodore I (Lascaris), who established the Empire of Nicaea after the Crusaders' 1204 conquest, was buried here. Lascaris also built Nicaea's outer walls, which were then supported by over 100 towers and protected by a wide moat.

İZNİK TILES

Peaking from the 15th to 17th centuries, İznik's tile-making was a unique Ottoman artistic tradition. However, the decreased demand for significant public works in post-Ottoman Turkey caused a rapid decline. To revive this craft, the İznik Foundation has worked with historians, university laboratories and trained craftspeople from across Turkey.

Made of 85% quartz from the local quarries, the tiles' unique thermal properties keep buildings warm in winter and cool in summer. Reflected sound waves create perfect acoustic qualities – all reasons why Ottoman mosques used them.

In a sunny atelier above the foundation's kilns, designers meticulously design the pristine white tiles – following tradition, only floral cross-sections are painted. Today, all the designers are women. It takes up to 70 days to complete larger works, such as İstanbul's metro system and the World Bank in Ankara.

🛏 Sleeping

İznik's best hotels are near the lake. The İznik Foundation sometimes rents its snug, old-fashioned rooms. Alternatively, Çamoluk village (10km from İznik) has family-run pensions – inquire at the tourist information kiosk.

Cem Otel   HOTEL €€
(☎757 1687; www.cemotel.com; Göl Sahil Yolu 34; s/d ₺70/90; ❋) Well-situated near the lake and walls, the Cem offers good value and friendly service. The suites are family-friendly, but the standard ones are a bit tight. Cem also has a tasty terrace restaurant.

Çamlık Motel   HOTEL €€
(☎757 1632; www.iznik-camlikmotel.com; Göl Sahil Yolu; s/d ₺80/100; ❋) Despite an unpromising exterior, the Çamlık is actually quite nice, with spacious (if uniform) rooms and good baths. It's near the lakefront's southern end, and has a water-facing, banquet-style restaurant often used for events.

Kaynarca Pansiyon   HOSTEL €€
(☎757 1753; www.kaynarca.net; cnr Kılıçaslan Caddesi & Gündem Sokak 1; dm/s/d ₺40/70/90) The Kaynarca has simple but clean, fan-only rooms, but it's not as good value as previously. They've stopped accepting phone or email reservations due to no-shows, so you'll have to hope there's room when arriving. The owners may ask couples to show marriage certificates.

🍴 Eating & Drinking

İznik's fish dishes and *köfte* (meatballs) are excellent. Enjoy sunset dining at one of the lakeside restaurants. **Bim supermarket** (Atatürk Caddesi; ⊙9.30am-9.30pm Mon-Sat, 9.30am-9pm Sun) has various foodstuffs for picnics.

Köfteci Yusuf   KÖFTE €
(Atatürk Caddesi 75; köfte ₺7-10; ⊙lunch & dinner) Köfteci Yusuf is a good local joint for *köfte*, served with thick-cut bread and hot green peppers.

Çamlık Restaurant   SEAFOOD €€
(Göl Sahil Yolu; meze ₺5-8, mains from ₺10; ⊙lunch & dinner) Part of the Çamlık Hotel, this lake-facing restaurant is a local favorite for fish. When the weather's good, enjoy a meze and drink in the lakeside garden, as the yawning interior can seem lonesome (unless, of course, a wedding party's going on).

Karadeniz   PIDE €
(cnr Kılıçaslan Caddesi & Cambaz sokok; mains from ₺5; ⊙lunch & dinner) On İznik's main street, Karadeniz specialises in simple pide and *lahmacun* (Arabic-style meat pizza) – good for a mid-afternoon snack.

Artı Bar   BAR
(Göl Sahil Yolu) Shaded by willows, this simple garden bar's nice for a sunset drink.

🛍 Shopping

Artisan shops sell İznik's unique, multi-coloured tiles. The **İznik Foundation** (☎757 6025; www.iznik.com; Vakıf Sokak 13) offers free tours (with advance booking), showing off its patient tile painters hard at work. For handicrafts, city-centre **Nilüfer Haltun** (⊙8.30am-8.30pm), across the street from Seyh Kutbettin Camii, sells stylish earrings and pendants in a cedar complex dotted with tea tables. **Sultan Hamamı** (⊙9am-9pm), in another restored building, has craft shops and an art gallery.

ℹ Information
Internet Cafe (per hr ₺1; ⊙9am-11pm)

Tourist Information Kiosk (⊘9am-7pm mid-May–mid-Sep, 8am-5pm mid-Sep–mid-May) At Aya Sofya.

ⓘ Getting There & Away

Hourly buses serve Bursa (₺10, 1½ hours) until 7pm, plus there's frequent buses to Yalova (₺9, one hour).

Bursa

◢0224 / POP 1,704,441

Modern, industrial Bursa is built around the mosques, mausoleums and other sites from its incarnation as first Ottoman capital. Despite being built-up and somewhat chaotic, its durable Ottoman core and abundant parks keep it remarkably placid in places. For some fresh air after pounding the old-town pavement, the soaring peaks of Mt Uludağ (Turkey's premier ski resort) and its national park are 22km away.

As with Konya, Bursa's historic contributions to Islamic development has given it an austere reputation; you'll see a majority of head-scarved women and devout prayer in overflowing mosques. Yet locals are kind and welcoming, and you can take the occasional photo inside historic religious structures (just be respectful).

Bursans take pride in their contribution to Turkish cuisine: the İskender kebap, a giant, semi-spicy pot of meat simmering in its own juices, was created here in the 19th century, and is known nationwide as the 'Bursa kebap'. Bursa's also famous for its *kestane şekeri* (sweet candied chestnuts) and its silks – both are widely available in shops.

History

Bursa was mentioned (by both Aristotle and ancient geographer Strabo) as a Greek city, Kios. In 202 BC, Macedonian King Philip V bequeathed it to his Bithynian counterpart, Prusias, who promptly renamed it after himself (hence the origin of the modern name). After 128 years and Bithynia's demise, Prousa became Roman.

Under Byzantine rule, and especially under Justinian I, Prousa grew in stature, while Çekirge's thermal baths were developed. However, tumultuous events such as the 1075 Seljuk occupation (which lasted 22 years until Crusaders rolled through) initiated a cycle of conquest and reconquest. Prousa's proximity to Nicaea (today's İznik) cemented their ties; not long after the 40-year-reign of Manuel I Komnenos ended in 1180, the cities revolted during a lurid dynastic struggle. In one of Byzantine history's more gruesome scenes, the sadistic Emperor Andronikos I Komnenos (r 1183–85) attacked Prousa, hanging rebellious Greeks from its lovely chestnut trees, in a frenzy of mutilations, eye-gouging and impalement.

Amid such instability, Prousa was easy pickings for Seljuk conquerors. Small principalities arose around warlords such as Ertuğrul Gazi and, in 1317, Prousa was besieged by his son Osman – founder of the Ottoman line. By 1326, Prousa had been starved into submission, becoming Osman's capital. His successor, Orhan Gazi (r 1326–59), gradually expanded the empire towards Constantinople, during yet another Byzantine civil war.

Sultan Orhan opened the first Ottoman mint, and eventually could dictate to Byzantine leaders, among them John VI Cantacuzene, who became his father-in-law and

---

SHADOW PUPPETS

Originally a Central Asian Turkic tradition, Karagöz shadow puppet theatre developed in Bursa and spread throughout the empire. These camel-hide puppets, made translucent after oil treatment and then painted, are manipulated by puppeteers behind a white cloth screen onto which their images are cast by backlighting.

Legend attests that Ulu Camii's foreman, Karagöz the Hunchback, distracted the workforce with the humorous antics he carried out with 'straight man' Hacivat. An infuriated sultan executed the comic slackers, whose joking became immortalised in Bursa's Karagöz shadow puppetry. In 2006, Ezel Akay revived this legend in comic film *Hacivat & Karagöz* (*Killing the Shadows* in English), starring Haluk Bilginer and Beyazit Öztürk.

Bursa's Şinasi Çelikkol has championed Karagöz puppetry, helping to establish the **Karagöz Museum** (Karagöz Müzesi; ◢232 3360; Çekirge Caddesi 59; ⊘9am-5pm), opposite the Karagöz monument. The collection includes magnificent Uzbek puppets. English-speaking apprentice puppeteers can guide you through.

Bursa

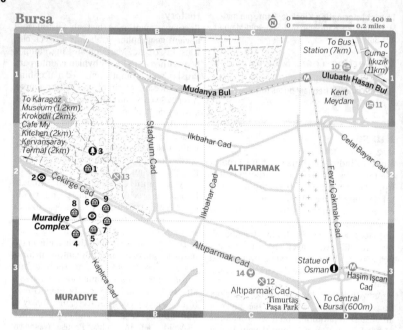

ally. Although Edirne (then Hadrianople, near today's Bulgaria and Greece) became the capital in 1402, Bursa remained important. Both Osman and Orhan are buried here, and Muslim tourists flock to their tombs to pray and exalt their legacy. Throughout Ottoman times, Bursa's silk production was legendary and much sought-after by Turkish nobles.

Population changes began in the late 19th century, when Balkan Muslims arrived with the Ottoman Empire's decline there. In a sadly appropriate twist, the city's Greek residents chose Kios – Bursa's original iteration – when naming their new village in Greece, after the 1923 population exchanges.

After the Independence War, Bursa developed industrially and has been a major automotive producer since the 1960s, when Fiat (Tofaş) and Renault built factories here – today, bus factories predominate.

Sights & Activities

Sprawling Bursa has three civic sections – Yıldırım, Osmangazi and Nilüfer (where Çekirge lies).

YILDIRIM

East of Heykel, at Setbaşı, Namazgah Caddesi crosses the Gök Deresi (Gök Stream), which tumbles through a gorge. Just after the stream, Yeşil Caddesi veers left to Yeşil Camii and Yeşil Türbe, then changes names, becoming Emir Sultan Caddesi.

Yeşil Camii   MOSQUE

(Green Mosque; Map p278; Yeşil Caddesi) Built for Mehmet I between 1419 and 1424, Yeşil Camii represents a departure from the previous, Persian-influenced Seljuk architecture. Exemplifying Ottoman stylings, it contains a harmonious facade and beautiful carved marblework around the central doorway. Diverse calligraphy exists on the main door's niches.

Entering you'll pass beneath the sultan's apartments and into a domed central hall with a 15m-high *mihrab* (niche indicating the direction of Mecca). The mosque was named for the interior wall's greenish-blue tiles – fragments of a few original frescoes remain. A narrow staircase leads to the sumptuously tiled *hünkar mahfili* (sultan's private box), above the main door. The sultan stayed here (the harem and household staff enjoyed less plush digs on either side) whenever in town. The mosque's a short walk uphill from Setbaşı.

FREE Yeşil Türbe   HISTORIC BUILDING

(Green Tomb; Map p278; ⏰8am-noon & 1-5pm) In a cypress-trimmed park surrounding the

Bursa

mosque is Yeşil Türbe, the mausoleum of Mehmed I Çelebi (and several of his children). During his short rule (1413–21), the fifth Ottoman sultan reunited a fractured empire following the Mongols' 1402 invasion. Despite its name, the *türbe* isn't green (the blue Kütahya tiles outside postdate an 1855 earthquake). The structure has a sublime, simple beauty, the original interior tiles exemplifying 15th-century decor. There's also an impressive tiled *mihrab*.

Yıldırım Beyazıt Camii   MOSQUE
(Mosque of Sultan Beyazıt I) Across the valley from Emir Sultan Camii rises the twin-domed Yıldırım Beyazıt Camii, built by Mehmed I Çelebi's father, Bayezıt from 1391 to 1395 (it's also referred to as the Bayezıt Camii). Its adjoining *medrese* is now a medical centre. The mosque houses tombs of Sultan Beyazıt I and his other son, İsa.

Emir Sultan Camii   MOSQUE
An early Ottoman mosque, the 14th-century Emir Sultan was named for Sultan Bayezıt I's Persian son-in-law and adviser, a Persian scholar-dervish. Today's structure reflects renovations made after a 1766 earthquake, and the then-fashionable baroque style. Renovated by Selim III in 1805, it was damaged by the 1855 earthquake and rebuilt by Sultan Abdülaziz in 1858. In the 1990s, it received more touch-ups.

Emir Sultan Camii echoes the romantic decadence of Ottoman rococo style – rich in wood, curves and outer painted arches. The interior is surprisingly plain, but enjoys a nice setting beside a tree-filled cemetery overlooking the valley. The oldest of several refreshing and historic fountains here dates to 1743.

Dolmuşes and buses marked 'Emirsultan' travel here. Walking from Yeşil Camii and Yeşil Türbe, another cemetery on the way contains the **grave of İskender Usta**, creator of the Bursa kebap.

Turkish & Islamic Arts Museum   MUSEUM
(Map p278; Yeşil Caddesi; admission ₺3; ◷8am-noon & 1-5pm) Housed in Yeşil Camii's former *medrese*, this museum contains pre-Ottoman İznik ceramics, the mosque's original door and *mihrab* curtains, jewellery, embroidery, calligraphy and dervish artefacts.

Irgandı Sanat Köprüsü   HISTORIC BUILDING
(Irgandı Bridge; Map p278) Across the river, north of the Setbaşı road bridge, this restored Ottoman structure houses shops, cafes and touristy artisans' workshops.

Tofaş Museum of Anatolian Carriages   MUSEUM
(☎329 3941; Kapıcı Caddesi; ◷10am-5pm Tue-Sun) Old cars and horse-drawn carts are housed in this former silk factory with gardens. It's a short walk uphill south from Setbaşı, along Sakaldöken Caddesi.

CENTRAL BURSA (OSMANGAZİ)
Central Cumhuriyet Alanı (Republic Sq) is also called Heykel (statue), after its large **Atatürk monument** (Map p278). Atatürk Caddesi runs west from Heykel through the commercial centre to Ulu Cami (Great Mosque). Further west, **Zafer Plaza shopping centre** (Map p278) is a blue-glass pyramid, which is a useful landmark.

Bursa City Museum   MUSEUM
(Bursa Kent Müzesi; Map p278; ☎220 2486; www.bursakentmuzesi.gov.tr; 8 Atatürk Caddesi; admission ₺1.50; ◷9.30am-5.30pm Tue-Sat)

Central Bursa

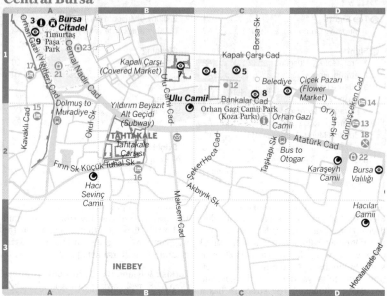

Central Bursa

Chronicling Bursa's history from the earliest sultans to War of Independence relics and cultural and ethnographic collections, this museum also offers multimedia touch screens on notable 20th-century local actors and musicians, plus films showing old-fashioned artisans at work.

Ulu Camii　　　　　　　　　　MOSQUE

(Map p278; Atatürk Caddesi) This enormous Seljuk-style shrine (1396) is Bursa's most dominant and durable mosque. Sultan Beyazıt I built it in a monumental compromise – having pledged to build 20 mosques after defeating the Crusaders in the Battle of Nicopolis, he settled for one mosque, with

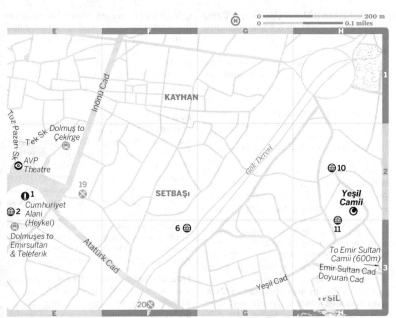

20 small domes. Outside, a massive minaret augments the domes, while giant square pillars and portals within are similarly impressive. The *mimber* (pulpit) boasts fine wood carvings, and the walls feature intricate calligraphy. Bursa's Karagöz shadow puppet theatre reportedly began with Ulu Camii's construction.

Central Markets
MARKET

Behind Ulu Camii, Bursa's sprawling **Kapalı Çarşı** (Covered Market; Map p278; Kapalı Çarşı Caddesi) contains two historic markets: the 14th-century *bedesten* (covered market), built by Sultan Beyazıt I, and reconstructed after the 1855 earthquake, plus the **Eski Aynalı Çarşı** (Old Mirrored Market; Map p278; Kapalı Çarşı Caddesi) (Old Mirrored Market) – originally the Orhangazi Hamam (bathhouse of the Orhan Camii Külliyesi). Built in 1335, it features a domed ceiling with skylights. Karagöz shadow puppets and other traditional items are sold here.

Kapalı Çarşı extends across surrounding streets – find the gateway into the Koza Han (p283), built in 1490, for expensive *ipek* (silk) shops. A small courtyard mosque (1491) honours Beyazıt.

Silk purveyors also sell at the **Emir Han** (Map p278; Kapalı Çarşı Caddesi), near Ulu Cami. Bursa was on the Silk Road, and camel caravans lodged here, their precious cargo stored in the ground-floor rooms while the drovers and merchants slept and did business upstairs. The courtyard tea garden has a fine old fountain.

Bursa Citadel
CASTLE

(Osman Gazi ve Orhan Gazi Türbeleri; Map p278; tombs & tower by donation) Some ramparts and walls still survive on the steep cliff, the site of Bursa's citadel and oldest neighbourhood. From Ulu Cami, walk west and up Orhan Gazi (Yiğitler) Caddesi, to reach the Hisar (Fortress) or Tophane. On the summit, a park contains the **Tombs of Sultans Osman & Orhan** (Osman Gazi ve Orhan Gazi Türbeleri; Timurtaş Paşa Park; admission by donation), the Ottoman Empire's founders. Although the tombs were ruined in the 1855 earthquake, Sultan Abdülaziz rebuilt them in baroque style in 1868. Osman Gazi's tomb is the more richly decorated. Remove shoes before entering.

The six-storey **clock tower**, the last of four that also served as fire alarms, adjoins a **tea garden** where families and couples gaze out over the valley and snap photos.

MURADİYE COMPLEX
This relaxing **complex** (Map p276) contains a shady park, a cemetery with historic tombs,

and the **Sultan II Murat (Muradiye) Camii** (Map p276; ⊘8.30am-noon & 1-5pm). Imitating Yeşil Cami's painted decorations, it features an intricate *mihrab*.

The adjacent cemetery's 12 **tombs** (Map p276) from the 15th and 16th centuries include that of Sultan Murat II (r 1421–51). Although his son, Mehmet II, would capture Constantinople, Murat did all the earlier hard work, annexing territories from enemy Islamic states during his reign. Like other Islamic dynasties, the Ottoman's did not practise primogeniture – any royal son could claim power upon his father's death, which unsurprisingly resulted in numerous bloodbaths. The Muradiye Complex preserves this macabre legacy in its tombs – all the *şehzades* (imperial sons) interred here were killed by close relatives. While many tombs are ornate and trimmed with beautiful İznik tiles, others are simple and stark, such as that of the ascetic, part-time dervish Murat II.

The nearby **Ulumay Museum of Ottoman Folk Costumes & Jewellery** (Osmanlı Halk Kıyafetleri ve Takıları Müzesi; Map p276; İkincimurat Caddesi; admission ₺6; ⊘9am-7pm), originally the Sair Ahmet Paşa *medrese* (1475), exhibits around 70 costumes and over 350 different pieces of jewellery. A similar museum, the **Ottoman House Museum** (Osmanlı Evi Müzesi; Map p276; admission ₺2; ⊘hr vary) opposite the mosque is rarely open. The 15th-century **Muradiye Medresesi** (Map p276), west of the tombs, was a tuberculosis clinic in the 1950s.

Uphill behind the **Sultan Murat II Hamam** (Map p276), the Ottoman **Hüsnü Züber Evi** (Map p276; Uzunyol Sokak 3; admission ₺3; ⊘10am-noon & 1-5pm Tue-Sun) is signposted (but sporadically open). Beyond here lie winding alleys, shops and crumbling Ottoman houses.

KÜLTÜR PARKI & AROUND

North of Muradiye and down the hill, Bursa's leafy **Culture Park** (Kültür Parkı; Map p276) boasts fine lawns and flowers. Families enjoy its tea gardens, playgrounds and restaurants. The **Archaeology Museum** (Arkeoloji Müzesi; Map p276; admission ₺5; ⊘8.30am-12.30pm & 1.30-5pm Tue-Sun), with mostly classical finds from local sites, is also here.

FREE **Atatürk House**   NOTABLE BUILDING
(Atatürk Evi; Map p276; ☎236 4844; Çekirge Caddesi; ⊘8.30am-12.30pm & 1.30-5pm Tue-Sun) West of the Archaeology Museum, and across the Çekirge road, Atatürk House (1895) commemorates the great leader in a pine-scented garden setting. The restored structure contains mostly original furnishings from when Atatürk stayed here, while visiting Bursa.

Any bus or dolmuş from Heykel going to Altıparmak, Sigorta or Çekirge passes the Culture Park and Atatürk House.

ÇEKİRGE

Heading northwest on Atatürk Caddesi the road leads to Çekirge, Bursa's spa suburb. Mt Uludağ's warm mineral-rich waters bubble up here and have been valued since ancient times for their curative powers. Hotels here usually have private mineral baths, but several independent *kaplıcalar* (thermal baths) exist too.

Çekirge's main street is I Murat Caddesi (Birinci Murat Caddesi). A 10-minute bus or dolmuş ride (₺2) from Heykel or Atatürk Caddesi reaches Çekirge or SSK Hastanesi.

I Murat (Hüdavendigar) Camii   MOSQUE
The unusual I Murat Camii, features a barrel-vaulted Ottoman T-square design, and includes ground-floor *zaviye* (dervish hostel) rooms. The only visible part of the 2nd-floor facade gallery (originally a *medrese*) is the sultan's *loge* (box), above the mosque's rear.

Sarcophagus of Sultan Murat I   TOMB
Sultan Murat I (r 1359–89), most famous for the Battle of Kosovo that claimed his life, is interred in this huge sarcophagus opposite the mosque. Murat's remains were brought from Kosovo by his son, Bayezıt I.

Eski Kaplıca   HAMAM
(☎233 9300; Fevzi Yakmak Caddesi; men/women ₺55/50; ⊘7am-10.30pm) The restored Eski Kaplıca, on Çekirge's eastern outskirts is run by the adjacent Kervansaray Termal Hotel. The bath is hewn of marble, and the hot rooms have plunge pools. Prices include soap, shampoo, sauna and massage. Take Yeni Yalova Bulvar south from the centre.

Yeni Kaplıca   HAMAM
(☎236 6955; Mudanya Caddesi 10; ⊘6am-11pm) Northwest of the Culture Park lies Bursa's 'new' bath – it's actually its oldest, founded by 6th-century Emperor Justinian I, and renovated in 1522 by Süleyman the Magnificent's grand vizier, Rüstem Paşa. Here too are the women-only *kaynarca* (boiling) baths, and the family-oriented Karamustafa baths. Last admission is 10pm; 30-minute massages cost ₺30.

☞ Tours

Karagöz Travel Agency TOUR
(Map p278; ☑221 8727; www.karagoztravel.com; cnr Kapalıçarşı & Eski Aynalı Çarşı 4) Offers interesting local tours, including city excursions.

★☆ Festivals & Events

Uluslararasi Bursa Festival MUSIC
(www.bursafestivali.org) Bursa's June–July music and dance festival lasts three weeks, and features diverse regional and world music, plus an international 'star' headliner or two. Tickets for top acts are around ₺20.

**Golden Karagöz
Dance Festival** DANCE
In July this dance festival draws international groups.

Karagöz Festival PUPPETRY
Every November, this five-day festival attracts Karagöz shadow puppeteers, Western puppeteers and marionette performers for fun and performances.

🛏 Sleeping

Despite its historical sights, Bursa's primarily a business tourist destination – hotels are priced accordingly. If sensitive to smoke, check the room first. Newer options are near Kent Meydanı, just beyond the centre. For R&R, try a thermal hotel in Çekirge (3km southwest of central Bursa).

TOP CHOICE Kitap Evi BOUTIQUE HOTEL €€
(Book House; Map p278; ☑225 4160; www.kitapevi.com.tr; cnr Kavaklı Mahallesi & Burç Üstü 21; s/d/ste €100/140/230; ❋@) Kitap Evi is a refreshing change from Bursa's industrial-strength business hotels. This former Ottoman house, once a bookshop, draws an artistically inclined clientele attracted by its eclectic decor (the 12 rooms each have their own style; room 1 boasts a marble-lined hamam). Well-polished wood fixtures, and little touches like artwork and stained glass, complement the rows of bookshelves and empty leather suitcases that welcome guests. The hotel restaurant is excellent.

Hotel Gönlüferah LUXURY HOTEL €€
(☑233 9210; www.gonluferah.com; Murat Caddesi; s/d €90/120; ❋@🌐⛱) Dating from 1890 and a hotel since the early 20th century, the hilltop Gönlüferah in Çekirge has hosted many a famous guest and definitely looks the part, combining old-world charm with modern luxuries such as spa packages and an opulent bar. Rooms range from standards to the 'Prince' and 'Sultan' suites, featuring plush headboards and a crescendo of overlapping curtains, with sophisticated baths. This is ideal for visitors to Çekirge's thermal springs, and the day-use spa packages (₺30 per person) are available for non-guests too.

Hotel Karakaya BUSINESS HOTEL €€€
(Map p276; ☑253 7575; http://www.karakayahotel.com.tr; Ulubatlı Hasan Bulvarı 33; s/d ₺100/180; ❋@🌐) This sleek modern business hotel has trendy modern rooms with big comfy beds, plasma TVs and numerous extras (from 24-hour room service to sauna and massage). There's a busy restaurant and bar too.

Safran Otel PENSION €€
(Map p278; ☑224 7216; www.safranotel.com; Orta Pazar Caddesi; s/d ₺90/150; ❋🌐) The Safran occupies an elegant restored Ottoman house near the Osman and Orhan tombs, in a historic district. Although its exterior partly includes a Byzantine wall, the 10 rooms are thoroughly modern, spacious and well-lit (with a hint of the Ottoman retained in its distinctive carpets).

Otantik Club Hotel BOUTIQUE HOTEL €€
(☑211 3280; www.otantikclubhotel.com; Soğanlı Botanik Park; s/d €85/120, ste from €160; ❋🌐⛱) If you crave fresh air, head 7km from Central Bursa to the Soğanlı botanical gardens, and the Otantik Club. Its faux-Ottoman interior contains beaded canopied beds with ethnic rugs and rich wood ceilings. There are two restaurants – including the Şifne – and an indoor and outdoor swimming pool (the latter contrasts somewhat with the recreated Ottoman architecture, but it all works out). The gardens make for a wonderfully relaxing environment away from built-up Bursa.

Hotel Çeşmeli HOTEL €€
(Map p278; ☑224 1511; Gümüşçeken Caddesi 6; s/d ₺80/120; ❋) Run by two sisters (and employing only women), this is a good spot for female travellers and it's close by the bustling market. Although the rooms are a bit dated, they're spacious enough and the Çeşmeli remains a friendly central spot, located behind the public fountain for which it's named.

Tuğcu Hotel BUSINESS HOTEL €€
(Map p276; ☑256 4500; www.tugcuhotel.com; Karşış Celal Bayar Caddesi 195; s/d €100/135; ❋🌐)

In the center near Kent Meydanı, Tuğcu's a business hotel with all mod cons and neat underground parking. The restaurant offers an ample buffet breakfast and serves Turkish specialities by night.

Hotel Efehan
BUSINESS HOTEL €€

(Map p278; ☑225 2260; www.efehan.com.tr; Gümüşçeken Caddesi 34; s/d ₺110/140; ❄@) The central Efehan offers good value, good service and fresh standard (and a handful of family-sized) rooms, equalling the best price-value ratio in downtown Bursa. The top-floor breakfast hall offers good views of the city. Avoid the south-facing suite – it gets blasted by the neighbouring mosque's call to prayer.

Otel Güneş
HOSTEL €

(Map p278; ☑222 1404; İnebey Caddesi 75; s/d ₺35/50) The Güneş has seen better days but remains the only true budget accommodation in Bursa's centre, and is run by a kind family. Rooms are on the small side, though clean (you can choose between those with regular and 'Turkish traditional' toilets).

🍴 Eating & Drinking

Bursa's famous for its rich İskender kebap, and its modest dessert, fashioned from candied chestnuts (*kestane şekeri*; also called *maron glacé*).

TOP CHOICE Kaplıkaya Kocamanlar Et Balık Restaurant
SEAFOOD €€

(☑366 7878; Siteler Mahalessa Kaplıkaya Cazibe Merkezi Akvaryum 3; fish dishes 10-18₺) With tables surrounded by a 300-sq-metre aquarium, this colossally unique new place lets you watch giant fish as they watch you eat other fish. The gracious owner is a fishmonger, so fresh and inexpensive seafood from three seas is guaranteed. With a big grassy expanse and tropical birds twittering outside, and men in scuba gear diving in tanks for reasons unknown, Kaplıkaya's also a spectacle for children. No alcohol. It's 6km from the centre, in the mountainside Kaplıkaya district. Take a taxi (₺15) or city bus (numbers 98, 53 and 25A to the last station, Kaplıkaya).

Seki Döner
KEBAP €

(İhsaniye Mahalessi Cami Sokak 46, Nilüfer; Mains ₺9-14) It's worth the 10-minute drive to the suburb of Nilüfer to feast on Bursa's famed İskender kebap at this unpretentious hole-in-the-wall place on a quiet street. Although they are sold in many Turkish kebap shops, the quality can be uncertain so keep an eye out for the 'Seki' sign. The enormous portions, served in terra-cotta pots and accompanied by complimentary light salads, are awesome.

Arap Şükrü
SEAFOOD €€

(Map p276; Sakarya Caddesi; meze ₺7-20; ⊙lunch & dinner) Situated in a cobblestoned lane in the former Jewish quarter, about a 10-minute walk from Ulu Camii, this historic restaurant is named for its founder, an Independence War hero whose descendents still run it. From seafood meze to main courses, all the dishes are excellent and fresh. Try the *karides güveç* (shrimp casserole), excellent grilled octopus, and rakı with melon. Similar restaurants line the same street, frequently regaled by accordion-wielding Roma bands.

Kebapçı İskender
KEBAP €€

(Map p278; Ünlü Caddesi 7; iskender kebap ₺18; ⊙lunch & dinner) This refuge for serious carnivores is known nationwide – it's where the legendary İskender kebap was created in 1867. This is the main branch of approximately 12 other eponymous eateries around Bursa; there's a good one in the Soğanlı botanical garden too, which has a 'museum' dedicated to the iconic dish.

İskender
KEBAP €€

(Map p278; Atatürk Caddesi 60; mains ₺16; ⊙lunch & dinner) This central spot (which also claims to have created the İskender kebap) does hearty versions of the local favorite, at slightly cheaper prices.

Cafe My Kitchen
INTERNATIONAL €€

(☑234 6200; Çekirge Caddesi 114; pizza ₺11-18, mains ₺17-24; ⊙lunch & dinner; ☎) This 'international' restaurant, fashionable among up-and-coming young Bursans, is somewhat upscale and does excellent pastas and salads. Fleshed out with eclectic modern decor, its wine bar is also good for a drink.

Mahfel Mado
RESTAURANT, BAR €

(Map p278; Namazgah Caddesi 2; mains ₺5-10; ⊙breakfast, lunch & dinner) Bursa's oldest cafe is known for its *dondurma* (ice cream), and has a nice shady ravine setting.

Krokodil
ITALIAN €€€

(Çekirge Meydanı, Zübeyde Hanım Caddesi; mains ₺18-30; ⊙breakfast, lunch & dinner) At the main roundabout in Çekirge, Krokodil's an old favourite for its Italian fare and wide selection of wines

Yusuf
RESTAURANT €€

(Map p276; Kültür Parkı; meze ₺4-14; ⊘lunch & dinner) In Bursa's Culture Park, this old-school teahouse is a good spot for a çay (or meze and rakı) alongside gesticulating local elders and families.

Oylum
RESTAURANT, BAR €€

(Ovlu Caddesi; mains ₺13-22; ⊘lunch & dinner; 🛜) Located 1.5km down the hill from Çekirge, and 200m from the Paşa Çiftliği metro station, this restaurant-nightclub complex does everything from fast-food to Turkish specialities.

Gren
BAR, CAFE

(Map p276; 🗹223 6064; www.grencafe.com; Sakarya Caddesi 46) Unusually hip for a workaday city, Gren is Bursa's 'photography cafe', with regular exhibitions, workshops and other events matching its antique-camera decor and arty young clientele.

 Shopping

Bursa's massive market system runs underground, overground and all around, hawking everything from fish and veg to sharp suits, home appliances and veritable mountains of silver and gold.

For the most renowned item (silk), try the central Koza Han (Cocoon Caravanserai; Map p278; ⊘8.30am-8pm Mon-Sat, 10.30am-6pm Sun), or boutiques both underground and in the open-air square for scarves and other garments. Ensure that you're buying real silk, not a cheap synthetic product.

For handicrafts, visit Bali Bey Han (Map p278) near Zafer Plaza. The local candied chestnut sweet (kestane şekeri) is everywhere – try Kafkas (Map p278; www.kafkas. com; ⊘7am-11.30pm), on Atatürk Caddesi.

 Information

Post office, payphones, and ATMs are on Atatürk Caddesi; for exchange offices visit the Covered Market.
Tourist Office (⊘9am-5pm Mon-Fri, to 6pm Sat) Beneath Atatürk Caddesi, in the shop row at Orhan Gazi Alt Geçidi's northern entrance.

Dangers & Annoyances
Bursa is heavily built-up, crowded and, with its constant traffic, stacked overpasses and lack of street lights, can seem bewildering. Cross Atatürk Caddesi by the alt geçidi (pedestrian underpasses). Disabled people can use the lift at Atatürk Alt Geçidi (the underpass nearest to Heykel) – the nearby florist has the key.

BURSA SILK

Bursa's ancient silk tradition is owed to both local production and its position on the Silk Road that brought Chinese and Persian silk to Europe via Anatolia. Today, silk is Bursa's prime local handicraft, and some villagers still cultivate silk worms, buying them each April from cooperatives, and letting them gorge themselves on mulberry leaves back home.

Once the worms have spun their cocoons they're sold at the Koza Han. To witness some of Bursa's 14,000 silkworm breeders haggling over huge sacks of precious white cocoons, visit in June or September.

ⓘ Getting There & Away
Air
Flights from **Yenişehir Airport** (www.yenisehir .dhmi.gov.tr) are so limited, locals say, because Bursa's powerful bus manufacturing lobby owns the politicians. Whatever the case, you're lucky to find even an Ankara flight these days. Check with **Turkish Airlines** (www.thy.com).

Bus
Bursa's otogar is 10km north of the centre on the Yalova road.

For İstanbul, the metro-bus combo – to Mudanya and then the **İDO fast ferry** (🗹444 4436; www.ido.com.tr) – is quickest. Ferries also link İstanbul to Yalova nearby. Otherwise, the karayolu ile (by road) buses there wind around the Bay of İzmit (four to five hours). Better are those designated feribot ile (by ferry), transitting through Topçular, east of Yalova, and continuing by ferry to Eskihisar.

ⓘ Getting Around
To/From the Bus Station
City bus 38 connects the centre with the otogar (₺3, 45 minutes). Wait at stop 4 on Atatürk Caddesi for the otogar. From it, bus 96 also serves Çekirge (₺3, 40 minutes).

Otogar to–centre taxis run ₺25 to ₺30.

Bus
City buses (BOİ; ₺2) have their destinations and stops visible. Lined-up yellow bus stops, with clear signs marking the destinations and drop-offs, are opposite Koza Parkı on Atatürk Caddesi. These destinations include the Botanik Parkı and otogar.

City buses are prepay – buy single or multiuse tickets from kiosks or shops near most bus stops (look for the BuKART sign).

SERVICES FROM BURSA'S OTOGAR

DESTINATION	FARE (₺)	DURATION (HR)	DISTANCE (KM)	FREQUENCY (PER DAY)
Afyon	33	5	290	8
Ankara	35	6	400	hourly
Bandırma	15	2	115	12
Çanakkale	40	5	310	12
Denizli	48	9	532	several
Eskişehir	19	2½	155	hourly
İstanbul	24	3	230	frequent
İzmir	30	5½	375	hourly
İznik	10	1½	82	hourly
Kütahya	20	3	190	several
Yalova	9	1¼	76	half-hourly

Dolmuş

Cars and minibuses operate as dolmuşes, with destinations indicated by an illuminated rooftop sign. Dolmuşes are as cheap as buses, faster and more frequent, especially to Çekirge, accessed via the Culture Park, Eski Kaplıca and I Murat Camii from a major dolmuş terminal south of Heykel. Other dolmuşes wait by Koza Parkı. Figure ₺2 from Heykel to Çekirge.

Metro

The metro (₺2) is useful for Mudanya's İstanbul ferry connections.

Taxi

Heykel to Muradiye is about ₺5; ₺10 to Çekirge.

Around Bursa

MUDANYA

📞0224 / POP 54,301

Mudanya is a lively seaside town most known for its Istanbul ferry. Strategically set on the Sea of Marmara, it's where the Armistice of Moudania was signed by Italy, France, Britain and Turkey on 11 October 1922 (Greece reluctantly signed three days later). Under it, all lands from Edirne eastward, including Istanbul and the Dardanelles, became Turkish. A prominent white house in Mudanya's west end exhibits historic Armistice-related photos.

🛌 Sleeping

Montania   LUXURY HOTEL €€€
(📞554 6000; www.montaniahotel.com; İstasyon Caddesi; s/d/ste ₺160/240/300; ※@�) Mudanya's most famous hotel sits in the old French customs house (1849). The various structures include a private swimming club – a plus, as the rooms are not as inspiring as the price would warrant.

Golden Butik Hotel   HOTEL €€
(📞554 6464; www.goldenbutikotel.com; Mustafa Kemalpaşa Caddesi 24; s/d ₺80/120; ※@) This lovely little place, marked by extensive wood fixtures, period furniture and historic photos, mixes Ottoman touch with modern baths and amenities. There's a shaded back terrace for breakfast or coffee. It's up from Eski Camii.

❶ Getting There & Away

Take Bursa's metro (₺2) to the final stop, then continue by public bus (₺3) for the Mudanya–İstanbul ferry (www.ido.com.tr).

ULUDAĞ

📞0224

Close to İstanbul, Bursa and Ankara, Uludağ (Great Mountain; 2543m), is Turkey's favourite ski resort. It's 22km from Bursa, but the *teleferik* (cable car) runs up to Sarıalan, 7km from Uludağ town and and its assorted hotels, only really busy from December through March. In summer, come for the views and clean, cool air, or hike the summit (three-hour hikes).

Sarıalan cable-car terminus has snack stands and a campground. The www.uludaghotels.com website provides useful accommodation options for ski season. Prominent Turkish chains such as Anemon cater to an increasingly international ski crowd.

If simply seeking a city break in cooler climes, head 7km from Bursa toward the mountain, to tiny **Inkaya** and its celebrated,

600 year-old plane tree, the çinar – its wildly curving, thick branches are supported partly by sturdy metal braces. Enjoy a relaxing tea and snacks at the Inkaya Tarihi Çinaraltı Çay Bahcesi (☎239 5969; ⊙8am-midnight) under the abundant foliage. Bursa bus 1C also serves the village hourly.

ⓘ Getting There & Away

Take a city bus from stop 1 or dolmuş marked 'Teleferik' (₺2) from behind the city museum to the cable-car lower terminus (a 15-minute ride from Heykel). The cable cars (₺8 return, 30 minutes) depart every 40 minutes between 8am and 10pm in summer and between 10am and 5pm in winter, wind and weather permitting. In season, they go whenever they fill up (30 people).

The Teleferik stops first at Kadıyayla, then continues upwards to the Sarıalan terminus (1635m).

Dolmuşes from central Bursa to Uludağ (₺8) and Sarıalan (₺12) run several times daily in summer (more frequently in winter).

At the 11km marker begins the **Uludağ National Park** (per car ₺5). The hotel zone is 11km further from here.

Public transport is infrequent in summer, making taxis more expensive, but in winter try bargaining.

Phrygian Valley

Anatolia's mysterious ancient Phrygians once inhabited this rock-hewn valley (Frig Vadisi), running haphazardly past Kütahya, Eskişehir and Afyon, southeast of Bursa. Although an increasingly popular hiking destination, it's still relatively untouched, and offers spectacular Phrygian relics. The rugged terrain is exhilarating and highly photogenic. The Afyon-area ruins are best-preserved, and the Eskişehir-area ruins also impress, while Kütahya's are less abundant.

For all things Phrygian, check out the **Phrygian Way Project** (www.frigyolu.com). The website has detailed information about Phrygian history and hiking options. The project team, led by passionate hiker Dr Hüseyin Sarı, recently finished a 400km-long marked trail – making Phrygian lands accessible at last.

⊙ Sights

Eskişehir Ruins   RUINS
Through Yazılıkaya Valley, heading from Seyitgazi to Afyon, turn south after 3km down the road marked with a brown sign pointing to Midas Şehri. Further along this rough road a sign leads right 2km to the Doğankale (Falcon Castle) and Deveboyukale (Camel-Height Castle), both riddled with formerly inhabited caves.

Further south, another rough track leads 1km to the Mezar Anıtı (Monumental Tomb), and a restored, rock-carved tomb. Continuing south, you'll find another temple-like tomb, Küçük Yazılıkaya (Little Inscribed Stone).

Midas Şehri, several kilometres from Küçük Yazılıkaya, is called Midas Şehri (Midas City) by archaeologists, though it's actually Yazılıkaya (Inscribed Rock), 32km south of Seyitgazi. Entry costs ₺3, and the ticket-man has helpful 'Highlands of Phrygia' brochures. Another brochure (produced in Eskişehir) has good Phrygian Valley maps, and Yazılıkaya details.

The Midas Tomb is a 17m-high relief carved into volcanic tufa, and covered in geometric patterns resembling a temple facade. During festivals, an effigy of Cybele was displayed in the bottom niche. Phrygian-alphabet inscriptions – one bearing Midas' name – circle the tomb.

A path behind it leading to a tunnel passes a second, smaller tomb, unfinished and high in the rock. Continue upwards to the high mound, where there stood an acropolis. The stepped altar stone, possibly used for sacrifices, remains along with traces of walls and roads. Interestingly, the first evidence of water collection comes from here – carved holes with slatted steps that trapped rainwater for the dry season.

Afyon Ruins   RUINS
The Afyon-area ruins include examples from Phrygian up to Turkish times. Doğer village's *han* (caravanserai) dates to 1434 (you can get the key at the municipality building opposite). From here, dirt tracks lead to lily-covered Emre Gölü (Lake Emre), overlooked by a small stone building once used by dervishes; and a rock formation with a rough staircase, the Kirkmerdiven Kayalıkları (Rocky Place with 40 Stairs). The dirt track then continues 4km to Bayramaliler and Üçlerkayası, with rock formations called *peribacalar* (fairy chimneys), resembling Cappadocia's.

After Bayramaliler, Göynüş Valley (Göynüş Vadisi) is a 2km walk from the Eskişehir–Afyon road, with fine Phrygian rock tombs decorated with lions.

PHRYGIANS

A mysterious Thracian tribe arriving around 2000 BC, the Phrygians spoke an Indo-European language, used a Greek alphabet, and ruled from Gordion (106km west of Ankara). The Phrygians dominated during the 8th and 7th centuries BC, under the royal lineages of Midas and Gordias. Phrygian culture continued under Cimmerian (and subsequently Lydian) overlords.

When hearing the word 'Phrygian', music-lovers today might first think of modal jazz, and indeed this mysterious ancient tribe reportedly invented numerous instruments, like the double clarinet, flute, lyre, syrinx (Pan pipes), triangle and cymbals. No doubt the caves in which these Greek- and Hittite-influenced people lived had great acoustics to test them in.

Phrygian civilisation peaked around 585 to 550 BC, when the rock-cut monuments at Midas Şehri – the most impressive surviving Phrygian stonework – were carved. Phrygian relics in museums provide fascinating insights into a lost culture that transformed Anatolia and the Aegean.

At **Ayazini** village there once stood a rock settlement, Metropolis, also like Cappadocia: behold the Byzantine **church**, apse and dome hewn from the rock face, and several rock-cut tombs with carvings of lions, suns and moons.

Around Alanyurt, more caves exist at **Selimiye**; and there's more fairy chimneys at Kurtyurdu, Karakaya, Seydiler and İscehisar, including the bunker-like rock **Seydiler Castle** (Seydiler Kalesi).

☞ Tours

Day trips depart from Eskişehir (see its tourist office for info), though many full-service travel agencies in towns ranging from Pamukkale to Selçuk now offer excursions. In Afyon, the **Ceba** (☑213 2715; A. Türkeş Bulvarı C/2 Erçelik Sitesi) and **Aizanoi** (☑213 1080; Ordu Bulvarı, Çamlı 62/31) travel agencies offer trips. Again, serious hikers should contact the folks at the **Phrygian Way Project** (www.frigyolu.com) – these are Turkey's best-informed people for all Phrygian developments.

❶ Getting There & Around

For exploring, rent a car or motorbike. Afyon's **Arhan** (☑213 1080; Ordu Bulvarı Camii 62/31) and **Kaya** (☑212 5100; Dumlupinar Mh Süleyman Çarış Caddesi Ozgün Sitesi C Blok Altı 27) rental companies offer insured vehicles for ₺90 to ₺120 per day. (With your own insurance, figure around ₺70.) Otherwise, Afyon dolmuşes serve Ayazini (on the Afyon–Eskişehir road). From the church drop-off, walk 500m for Metropolis. From Ayazini, take the dolmuş back towards Afyon, but disembark at Gazlıgöl, then take a dolmuş headed to Döğer.

Eskişehir

☑0222 / POP 648,396

Eskişehir may well be the happiest city in Turkey – and, with a massive university population, it's certainly among its liveliest. An oasis of liberalism in austere middle Anatolia, Eskişehir's increasingly popular with weekenders from elsewhere in Turkey, and even boasts a small community of dedicated foreigners.

Eskişehir's progressive spirit is associated with mayor Yilmaz Büyükerşen, who freed up the local Porsuk River, adding walking bridges and a sand beach, while building pedestrian thoroughfares and an award-winning light rail system. (In summer, you can even navigate local waterways by gondola or ferry.)

The cumulative result is Turkey's most liveable city, and a place where you can engage with the friendly and open-minded locals. With an atmospheric old quarter, roaring nightlife, cultivated cuisine, two parks and a brand-new science centre for kids, Eskişehir truly has much on offer.

History

Although regional relics date to Palaeolithic times, traces of Eskişehir's first settlements date to the Bronze Age (3000–2000 BC). Hittites came, and later Phrygians, making it an important base until the 7th-century-BC Cimmerian conquest. Alexander the Great later captured the town; subsequently a Hellenistic, Roman and Byzantine city, it was known by the Greek name Dorylaion. The 6th-century Emperor Justinian had a summer palace here, and Dorylaion flourished as a bishopric.

Dorylaion's strategic location along military routes was tested by marauding Arabs in the 8th century and later by Seljuk expansion across Anatolia. In the Battle of Dorylaion (1097), Crusaders defeated Seljuk forces, but revenge was exacted in 1147. By contrast, the Greeks (who hadn't been eager to let Crusaders through in the first place) and Seljuks lived peacefully. However, their long non-aggression pact ended by 1180, when Seljuk authority was confirmed. Ottoman records attest to Dorylaion's continued importance as a garrison, its fortress being referenced in records of sultans like Mehmet II and Suleyman the Magnificent. The modern name Eskişehir ('old city') – also found in historical texts as Eskihisar ('old castle') – referred to the ruined Dorylaion castle (in today's Şarhöyük suburb).

Modern Eskişehir's formative developments began with the arrival of Crimean Tatars and Caucasus natives, diversifying the population in the late 19th century, while the Istanbul railroad's completion in 1892, and later development of factories and trade, invigorated the economy. Locals are proud of their ancestors' role in the Independence War, with important battles fought nearby. Their resolute stance toward wartime occupiers (Greeks, and even Brits) was often mentioned by Atatürk when he visited.

◉ Sights & Activities

New attractions have increased Eskişehir's appeal to everyone from kids to history buffs. And, as 'cultural capital of the Turkic world' for 2013, Eskişehir is offering tons of extra events.

Each October/November, the **International Eskişehir Festival** brings numerous Turkish and foreign artists, musicians and performers for nine days of concerts, exhibitions and plays. For details, see the city's official website, www.eskisehir.gov.tr.

Ottoman Quarter
(Odunpazarı)   HISTORIC AREA

The Ottoman district (Odunpazarı) features elegant, pastel-shaded traditional homes with distinctive overhanging stories and wood-framed shutters, set around narrow stone lanes – a real aesthetic treat. Here you'll find an excellent hotel, a restaurant and museums, along with mosques and other historic structures. This was Eskişehir's first Turkish district, and it features Ottoman and even Seljuk structures. *Odun* means 'firewood' (the area was once a firewood bazaar). Today it comprises several neighbourhoods, many enjoying protected heritage status, to preserve the legacy of centuries past.

Kurşunlu Külliyesi Complex   HISTORIC AREA
(Mücellit Sokak, Odunpazarı; ⊘8am-10pm) This sublime old-town complex was built between 1517 and 1525 by a leading master of classical Ottoman architecture, Acem Ali, though internal structures were built and rebuilt in following centuries. The vaulted **imaret** (almshouse) and adjacent, domed **aşevi** (kitchen) were the culinary quarters, and the dining hall, kitchen and alcoved oven partly remain. The Ottoman **caravansarai**, built after 1529, is used for weddings.

Other sites include the 1492 **Kurşunlu Mosque** – as its name would suggest, it boasts a leaden dome. Running parallel with it and the former **medrese** (Islamic school), is the four-domed **tabhane** – a guesthouse that may also have been a harem. The *medrese* today houses the **Museum of Meerschaum** (☑233 0582; ⊘8am-10pm), which pays homage to the region's weird and wonderful white rock, in its artistically crafted form.

Archaeological Museum   MUSEUM
(☑230 1371; Akarbaşı Mahallesi Atatürk Bul 6; ⊘8am-5pm daily) Combining elements of a museum of natural history (note the prehistoric elephant tusks) and more common archaeological fare, this intriguing place showcases fossilised flora and fauna, prehistoric artefacts, items from Hittite, Phrygian and Classical Antiquity, plus many Greek, Byzantine and Ottoman coins, religious items and household possessions.

Museum of the
Republican History   MUSEUM
(Cumhuriyet Müzesi; ☑335 0580; Paşa Mahallesi Atatürk Bul 11; ⊘10am-6pm Tue-Sun) Despite the ravages of time and recent political intrigues designed to dilute both secularism and the legacy of Atatürk, Eskişehir remains defiantly respectful of Turkey's national hero. History buffs will enjoy the hundreds of photos, paintings and collages covering seminal events like the battles of Gallipoli, Sakarya and Dumlupınar, along with the models of Turkish WWI warships. Over 50 portraits of Atatürk are displayed, and visitors can watch an Atatürk documentary. The imposing building itself (built 1915) reflects the mores of contemporaneous Western European structures, and remains a striking example of Turkey's First National Period of architecture.

WESTERN ANATOLIA ESKİŞEHİR

FREE ETOSANAT ART GALLERY
(2 Eylül Caddesi 28/7, Eskişehir Ticaret Odası; ⊙8am-6pm Mon-Fri) This neat new art gallery, located downtown in Eskişehir's Chamber of Commerce (Ticaret Odası), features an intriguing combination of works both contemporary and inspired by Turkish myth and tradition. Chamber president Harun Karacan opened it, and still organises different exhibitions monthly by noted Turkish painters.

FREE Museum of Contemporary Glass Art MUSEUM
(☑235 3734; Akarbaşı Mahallesi Türkmen Hoca Sokak 45; ⊙10am-7pm Tue-Sun) Turkey's first such museum, this Old Town house keeps a unique glasswork collection donated by about 70 Turkish and foreign artists. The tradition of melting and fusing glass dates to the pharaohs, and a local Egyptologist (and university professor) revived the art and opened a studio here too.

Atlıhan Complex HISTORIC BUILDING
(Pazaroğlu Sokak 8; ⊙9am-10pm) Eskişehir is famous for its 'white gold', or meerschaum (lületaşı in Turkish) – a light, porous white stone, mined locally and shaped into pipes and other objects. The Atlhan Complex hosts the shops of several local artisans, such as Ak-Tas (☑220 6652; Pazaroğlu Sokak 8; ⊙9am-6pm), which has a workshop that allows visitors to watch and even, if you're in the mood, to participate.

Kent Park PARK
Beautiful 'City Park' is a civic masterpiece full of enticing sights and activities. The man-made sandy beach is packed in summer (sunbeds cost ₺4), and there is a stable that offers horse-riding lessons and city carriage rides (₺10 per ride). There are also gondola rides on the river (₺10 per boat). Paths perfect for a romantic stroll exemplify Eskişehir's chosen path as Turkey's 'Aşkşehir' (City of Love).

Sazova Park PARK
Just beyond the centre of town, in an area of cleared cane (sazova means 'cane field'), Sazova is Eskişehir's newest park. In it is the biggest Japanese garden outside of Japan, which provides a calm space in which to relax. Further, above a small lake, stands a giant kids' castle, while an enormous Calyon pirate ship is moored below. These kid-friendly offerings are enhanced by the new science centre and planetarium next door. A taxi from the centre costs ₺10, though the expanding metro line should soon reach it.

Eskişehir Science & Experiment Centre SCIENCE CENTRE
(Eskişehir Bilim Deney Merkezi; ☑448 236; http://www.eskisehirbilimdeneymerkezi.com; cnr Sazova Çiftlik Yolu & Ulusal Egemenlik Bulvari; adult/student ₺2/1; ⊙10am-5pm Tue-Sun) At Sazova Park, this colourful and hugely entertaining complex illustrates the history of science and scientific principles through hands-on experiments (led by guides) and interactive areas (like the straw-strewn room of roaring, lunging dinosaurs). The real marvel, though, is the 'planetarium' which offers different shows (30 to 40 minutes) for kids and adults; even if you can't understand Turkish, the 3D animation is spectacular. At the time of research, an adjoining zoo and aquarium were planned.

THE CAR THAT JUST WOULDN'T GO

In 1961, the Turkish nation was bursting with pride: President Cemal Gürsel's stirring call for technological progress in domestic industry was soon to be answered – with the Devrim (Revolution). Turkey's first car, it had been designed and manufactured in just 130 feverish days in Eskişehir, and sent by train to Ankara for the ceremonial first drive around parliament on Republic Day.

Crowds watched in eager anticipation as the president settled in and the car roared to life. However, after 100m, it sputtered to a halt – apparently, someone had forgotten to fill up the petrol.

Legend has it that the infuriated president ordered the car – one of only four ever produced – to be imprisoned in a glass case in Eskişehir, as a monumental reminder against ineptitude. Whatever the facts, today only one Devrim survives, and you can see this classic throwback, splendidly preserved at Eskişehir's TÜLOMSAŞ locomotive factory.

🛏 Sleeping

There aren't (yet) standout budget options, but Eskişehir does have excellent midrange and top-end accomodation. Book ahead if possible as it can get suddenly (and unexpectedly) full.

TOP CHOICE Abacı Konak Otel
HISTORIC HOTEL €€

(☏333 0333; www.abaciotel.com; Akarbaşı Mahallesi Türkmen Hoca Sokak 29; s/d/ste ₺120/160/220; ❄⊕?) With clustered pastel heritage homes enclosed around a flowering, fountained courtyard, staying at the Abacı Konak is like having your own personal Ottoman quarter. Being in the old town, it's legally a heritage site, so nothing can be changed – the vintage furnishings, wood floors and ceilings are all original, and the tasteful, subdued decor matches. Take your coffee in the sunny courtyard, or in the excellent on-site **restaurant** (mains ₺18-35; ☺restaurant breakfast, lunch & dinner). The kind manager, Nazım Yeniova, is keen to explain each room's unique history. Book ahead if possible – the hotel is very popular with Turkish groups (especially on weekends). It's easy to find in the old town, and the closest tram stop is Atatürk Lisesi, on the first tram line (SSK).

Grand Namlı Otel
HOTEL €€

(☏322 1515; www.namliotel.com.tr; Üniversite Caddesi 14; s/d ₺110/160; ❄@?) This excellent, 'business-like' hotel up towards Anadolu University has spacious modern rooms with big beds, fluffy pillows and well-done baths. Service is friendly and there's a good buffet breakfast, and a nearby light-rail stop. As with other local hotels, try to book ahead.

Roof Garden Hotel
HOTEL €€€

(☏239 4050; www.roofgardenhotel.com; Büyükdere Mahallesi Sanlar Sokak 4; s/d/ste ₺129/169/269; ❄?) This stylish new place has a minimalist feel with its dark surfaces, curling floral prints and subdued backlighting in the well-appointed rooms. Service is helpful and attentive, and there's an excellent top-floor restaurant with views. Guests can use the tennis courts opposite. It's next to the Osmangazi Üniversitesi tram stop.

Ibis Hotel
HOTEL €€€

(☏211 7700; www.ibishotel.com; Siloönü Sokak 5; s/d ₺120/200; ❄?) Well located near the train station, the Ibis is a modern business hotel with a restaurant, and marked by kind service. Unlike some of the others, public areas are entirely nonsmoking.

🍴 Eating

Eskişehir's vast and varied restaurant scene caters to its diverse community of locals, university students and expats.

TOP CHOICE Passage
INTERNATIONAL €€

(www.eskisehirpassage.com; Kızılcıklı Mahmut Pehlivan Caddesi 15/B; mains ₺11-17; ☺breakfast, lunch & dinner) Eskişehir's most creative food is served at this spacious place offering everything from coffees and rich cakes to wraps, big salads, pastas and contemporary Turkish flavours. There's an open kitchen where the chefs are on display – join them for special chocolate-making courses. From the İsmet İnönü tram stop (on the first line), turn left on Kızılıklı Mahmut Pehlivan Caddesi; it's a 200m walk.

TOP CHOICE Café Del Mundo
INTERNATIONAL

(Siloönü Sokak 3; mains ₺11-17) This friendly and welcoming place, which is mostly a popular bar (p289), serves varied international cuisine (ranging from Thai to Mexican) on the ground floor,

Acıktım Kafedeyiz
INTERNATIONAL €€

(www.aciktimkafedeyiz.com; İsmet İnönü 52/C; mains ₺12-20; ☺breakfast, lunch & dinner) This trendy central place, famous for its big breakfasts, serves a varied menu including salads, perfectly seasoned steaks and rich desserts. The creation of passionate owner Bülent Şarlar, Acıktım has a hip interior marked by high stools, long tables and stone-and-wood columns that fit its uptempo rhythms. It's near the İsmet İnönü stop on the first tram line.

Has Kırım Çibörekçisi
ANATOLIAN €

(Atalar Caddesi 20/A; mains ₺4-8; ☺10.30am-9pm) Eskişehir's historic Crimean Tatar population has contributed to local cuisine with several traditional restaurants – visit this simple spot to sample the signature Tatar dish, *çiğ börek* (a puffed pastry pocket shaped like a bell and filled with meat). Has Kırım Çibörekçisi is at Mahmure tram station. There is another branch in Kent Park.

Birsen Kebap
TURKISH €

(Universite Caddesi 7B; mains ₺5-9; ☺lunch & dinner) Not far from Anadolu Universitesi, this student fave serves up quick and inexpensive platefuls of *köfte*, *şiş kebap* and salads, with outdoor and indoor seating.

Mezze
SEAFOOD €€

(☑230 3009; 15A Nazım Hikmet Sokak 2; mains ₺11-18; ⊘lunch & dinner) Popular for seafood, Mezze offers a great mixture of Turkish appetizers and full fish dinners. It enjoys a breezy, open-air setting on the lively pedestrian street, at the corner of Pehlivan Caddesi).

Osmanlı Evi
TURKISH €€

(Yeşil Efendi Sokak 22; mains ₺3.50-14, brunch ₺12.50; ⊘breakfast, lunch & dinner) The 'Ottoman House' has operated for two centuries (Atatürk even stayed during his military campaigning). A good selection of Turkish traditional fare is served in the historic, renovated confines of this former inn.

♟ Drinking & Entertainment

⌐TOP⌐ Café Del Mundo
CHOICE
BAR, RESTAURANT

(Siloönü Sokak 3; mains from ₺11-17) This cosy and colourful bar – created by travellers, for travellers – is the friendliest spot in town. Del Mundo's three levels are splendidly decorated with assorted international memorabilia (ranging from license plates, tickets, travel books, and many billowing flags) gathered from over 70 countries by young owners Yekta, Murat and Canlis. International cuisine is available, while the upstairs bars are filled by night with merry students and foreigners. The first drink's free when you show a passport on Mondays. İsmet İnönü, on the first tram line, is the closest stop – from there, walk towards the university and it's on the first right-hand street.

222 Park
CLUB

(www.222park.com; Pehlivan Caddesi 15A; ⊘8am-4pm) Housed in an enormous former wood factory, 222 (as pronounced in English) is Eskişehir's party colosseum, hosting more than 2000 revellers between its nightclub, live stage, and assortment of cafes and restaurants and summer wine terrace. During the daytime 222 is a smart destination for a drink or meal, but cranks it up by night. The owners run a tight ship, so under-18s can't enter the nightclub section, where entry is ₺30 (₺20 with a student card). It's across from the Espark shopping mall.

Eskişehir Municipal Symphony Orchestra
MUSIC

(☑220 4232; Manure Mah, İsmail Gaspıralı Caddesi 1) Since picking up its baton in 2002, Eskişehir's symphony orchestra has become one of Turkey's best, and now offers weekly concerts for an enthusiastic local audience. It also provides backup for operas and ballets. Works performed here run the gamut from classical masters to modern musicals, plus kids' shows. The orchestra tours widely abroad and cooperates with visiting musicians too.

ℹ Information

Eskişehir's **tourist office** (☑230 1752) is in the Valiliği (regional government) building on the southwest side of İki Eylül Caddesi. Helpful maps (produced by the city and by its chamber of commerce) are freely available at the bus and train stations and in most hotels.

Wi-fi is abundant in cafes, restaurants and hotels; internet cafes and ATMs are at the southern end of Hamamyolu Caddesi.

The city's official website (www.eskisehir.gov .tr) has regularly updated info on local events and activities in Turkish, English, German and Russian.

ℹ Getting There & Around

Turkish Airlines (www.thy.com) has details on flights to Bursa or Ankara.

From the otogar regular buses serve Afyon (three hours), Ankara (3¼ hours), Bursa (2½ hours), İstanbul (six hours), and Kütahya (1½ hours). The light rail metro serves the otogar.

Eskişehir train station has various services from İstanbul (four to six hours) and Ankara (2½ to four hours), among others. The train station is northwest of the centre; the otogar is 3km east. Trams and buses run from the otogar to Köprübaşı, the central district just north of Hamamyolu Caddesi.

Prepaid tickets (₺2) are used for public transport – buy from a booth or kiosk where the green-and-yellow circular sign reading *Es Karti* is visible. Light rail trams, buses and dolmuşes serve the otogar; look for signs saying 'Terminal' or 'Yeni Otogar'. A taxi from Köprübaşı costs around ₺10.

The light rail system, ESTram, starts at the otogar and, after the central Belediye stop, branches out to the northwest (line one, for Anadolu Universitesi and beyond), and to the southwest (for Osmangazi Universitesi). This second line also snakes northeast through the central artery and across to Belediye Konser Salonu (the concert hall). It can be confusing to identify which train is which at certain crossover stops, so ask if unsure.

In summer months, a regular ferry (seating 40 to 50 persons) runs from the center (at Köprübaşı) to Kent Park (₺3).

Taxis are plentiful, and there are electronic signal buttons on some street corner posts that you can press to hail one.

Kütahya

📞 0274 / POP 214.286

Dusty Kütahya is a provincial town with Phrygian roots, though it's unique historically as the bygone capital of the Germiyan Emirate (1302–1428), before it was swallowed up by the Ottoman Empire. There are certainly historical attractions here, but little else, making Kütahya better for a day trip than a place to stay overnight.

Kütahya's association with industrial porcelain and tile production dates to the capture of Tabriz in 1514, when Selim I relocated its tile-making artisans to Kütahya and İznik. Kütahya museums showcase its kiln-fired past, and the July Dumlupınar handicrafts fair is worth seeing.

◉ Sights & Activities

Zafer (Belediye) Meydanı, Kütahya's square, is marked by a huge, vase-shaped fountain and overlooked by the *vilayet* (provincial government building) and *belediye* (town hall). Running southwest is main commercial street Cumhuriyet Caddesi, which continues to Ulu Cami (1410), a cavernous structure notable for its riot of colourful Arabic-language calligraphy.

Archaeology Museum   MUSEUM
(Arkeoloji Müzesi; 📞 224 0785; admission ₺3; ⊘ 9am-1pm & 2-5.45pm Tue-Sun) Beside Ulu Cami in the Vacidiye Medresesi (1314), this museum exhibits Phrygian Valley finds and Roman votive stelae, plus a masterpiece Roman sarcophagus from Aizanoi's Temple of Zeus, carved with scenes of battling Amazons. The structure was built by Umur bin Savcı of the Germiyan clan.

FREE **Tile Museum**   MUSEUM
(Çini Müzesi; 📞 223 6990; ⊘ 9am-6.45pm Tue-Sun) Opposite Ulu Cami, the (nonworking) İmaret Cami hosts Kütahya's tile museum, with pottery by masters like Hacı Hafız Mehmet Emin Efendi (who also worked on İstanbul's Haydarpaşa station), plus some İznik tiles and local embroidery. The 14th-century, blue-tiled tomb of Yakup Bey (r 1390–1409), one of the Germanid Sultanate's last leaders, is also here.

Dönenler Camii   MOSQUE
Built in the 14th century and later used as a *mevlevihane* (home to a Mevlevi dervish group), the Dönenler Camii evokes the Seljuk past with its galleried *semahane* (large hall where Sufi ceremonies are held) with paintings of tall Mevlevi hats on the columns.

FREE **Kossuth House**   HISTORIC BUILDING
(Kossuth Evi; 📞 223 6214; ⊘ 9am-1pm & 2-5.45pm Tue-Sun) Signposted behind Ulu Cami, the Kossuth House, also called Macar Evi (Hungarian House), is at once Kütahya's oldest house and oddest attraction. This stately whitewashed building once housed dissident Hungarian parliamentarian Lajos Kossuth (1802–94). After demanding independence from the Austrian-dominated Hapsburg Empire, he and others were expelled – in Lajos' case, from one empire to another, being taken in by the Ottomans here, in 1850–51.

More than just a setting for an historical anecdote, however, the house exemplifies upper-class Kütahyan life in the mid-19th century. Along with period furnishings, the 1st-floor verandah overlooks a rose garden and statue of Kossuth.

FREE **Kütahya Fortress**   CASTLE
Looming over Kütahya, this originally Byzantine fortress was restored by the Seljuks, the Germiyan emirs and the Ottomans (through the 15th century). Dozens of round tower ruins indicate its former strength. It's a long uphill walk, or a taxi costs ₺15; afterwards take the steep path down to Ulu Cami.

🛏 Sleeping

Ispartalılar Konağı   HISTORIC HOTEL €€
(📞 216 1975; www.ispartalilarkonagi.com.tr; Germiyan Caddesi 58; s/d ₺90/150; @) This restored, 180-year-old house is laden with Ottoman antiques and hand-woven rugs. It's the most atmospheric place in town, though toilets are snug. Its restaurant serves decent international fare (mains ₺8 to ₺18), and (unlike many other places) alcohol.

Hilton Garden Inn   BUSINESS HOTEL €€€
(📞 229 5555; www.kutahya.hgi.com; Atatürk Bulvarı 21; s/d €120/160; ❋ @) Yes, it's a chain, with all the patented mattresses and standard furnishings that come with it, but the Hilton offers the best business digs around. Service is sharp and the colourful local tiles have been

WESTERN ANATOLIA KÜTAHYA

AİZANOİ – TEMPLE OF ZEUS

Visit rural Çavdarhisar (60km southwest of Kütahya) to see Aizanoi – one of Anatolia's best-preserved Roman remains. Its **Temple of Zeus** (admission ₺3; ⏱8am-6.30pm), built under Hadrian (r AD 117–138), was dedicated to both the king of the Olympian gods and Anatolian fertility goddess Cybele.

The temple was founded on a broad terrace (now a meadow). Its north and west faces have intact, double-rowed Ionic and Corinthian columns, while the south and east rows are toppled. The cella (inner room) walls illustrate the imposing original dimensions. Good sculpture finds are exhibited, with some English-language signage. See the cryptlike sanctuary of Cybele beneath.

Çavdarhisar's on the Kütahya–Gediz road. From 11.30am to 7.20pm minibuses serve Çavdarhisar from Kütahya otogar (₺6, one hour), dolmuşes return from 8.30am to around 6pm. Buses for Gediz or Emet transit Çavdarhisar.

used very impressively in the lounge decor. Rates can fluctuate depending on various offers, so check ahead.

Qtahya Otel HOTEL €€
(☑226 2010; www.q-tahya.com; Atatürk Bulvarı 56; s/d ₺90/140; ❄@☎) Well located for otogar arrivals, the Qtahya is a reliable modern place with friendly service and a restaurant like a wedding banquet hall – arguably overpriced, though it comes with the territory.

🍴 Eating & Drinking

Karavan Gözleme PIDE €
(www.karavangozleme.com; Atatürk Bulvarı 12/A; mains ₺3.50-8) From 15 types of *gözleme* to tasty pide and *lahmacun*, Karavan is great for breakfast or a snack. Similar, but more upscale, is **Hammam-I Ziyafe** (Sevgi Yolu Tarihi Küçük Hamam; mains ₺7-15).

Döner Restaurant KEBAP €€
(mains ₺10-16; ⏱lunch & dinner) This tasty kebap spot inside the ruined fortress can (somewhat unusually) rotate, and has good views.

Kütahya Konağı KEBAP €€
(mains ₺7-14; ⏱breakfast, lunch & dinner) A central kebap shop, the Konağı has a reputation for its excellent and well-apportioned döners.

ℹ Information

Tourist Information Kiosk (☑223 6213; Zafer Meydanı; ⏱9am-6pm) Little English spoken, but good maps.

ℹ Getting There & Away

Kütahya has services to Afyon (1½ hours), Ankara (five hours), Bursa (three hours), Denizli (five hours), Eskişehir (1½ hours), İstanbul (six hours) and İzmir (six hours).

Minibuses to Çavdarhisar, for Aizanoi (₺7, one hour), leave from the otogar's local bus stand.

Afyon (Afyonkarahisar)

☑0272 / POP 179,344

Like nearby Kütahya, Afyon is a provincial place lying under an ancient castle, one which has had myriad occupants between Hittite and Ottoman times. And like its dusty counterpart, despite having a university it remains a workaday, fairly conservative place where the only noise at night comes from the mosques, tea-drinking cafes tuned into televised football matches, and the occasional passing motorbike or horse-drawn cart.

Despite its prosaic qualities, Afyon (officially now 'Afyonkarahisar') does have a fine museum, magnificent mosques and Ottoman houses befitting its long history. But it's Afyon's role in the War of Independence, when Atatürk briefly made it his headquarters before routing the Greeks in the 1922 Battle of Dumlupınar, that makes Turks most proud. Lest there be any doubt, note the giant statue of a muscular man beating another into the ground, at the main square (Hükümet Meydanı).

◉ Sights & Activities

FREE **Citadel** CASTLE
The *kale* or *hisar* (citadel) overlooks Afyon from a craggy rock and the 570-step path up is signposted in a laneway opposite Ulu

Cami. If you're not keen, take a taxi (₺15). The strenuous approach passes Ottoman guard towers on what was quite the formidable defensive structure.

Hittite King Mursilis II built the first castle here, c 1350 BC. Since then, various rulers have restored the original *kara hisar* (black citadel) – most recently the Turkish government, with unorthodox white masonry. The state's desire to emphasise the castle's role was shown by Afyon being officially renamed as Afyonkarahisar ('Black Citadel of Opium').

Although the castle is empty, the views from the 226m-high summit are spectacular. However, by night it's unlit, so don't leave it too late if walking down.

Photo opportunities from below are best from the terrace of the **Kültür ve Semt Evi** (Zaviye Türbe Caddesi), a restored hamam.

FREE **Archaeological Museum** MUSEUM
(Arkeoloji Müzesi; ☑215 1191; Kurtuluş Caddesi 96; ◷8.30am-5.30pm) Hittite, Phrygian, Lydian and Roman antiquities, including an impressive marble Hercules statu, are exhibited here. The nearby marble quarry of Dokimeon (now İscehisar) was used for much of the statuary displayed. To get here, take a dolmuş along Kurtuluş Caddesi, the continuation of Bankalar Caddesi – it's near the İsmet İnönü Caddesi intersection.

THE CURSE OF CROESUS & THE LYDIAN HOARD

Envy, imprisonment, paralysis, madness, suicide, murder. For decades, these are just some of the woes to have befallen those cursed by the glittering riches of the Lydian Hoard, a collection of 363 gold and silver antiquities from the 7th and 6th centuries BC – the era of legendary Lydian King Croesus, whose name has become synonymous with ridiculous wealth.

Today, the treasure is kept in unassuming **Uşak**, at the local **Archaeology Museum** (Doğan Sokak; admission ₺3; ◷8.30am-1pm & 2-5.45pm Tue-Sun), though the eternal strife for possession hasn't abated. The government tried to snatch it away not long ago, after local workers tried to steal the originals by replacing them with fakes. Yet in the morality tale of Croesus's treasure, Turks are hardly the only ones with loot on their hands.

The sordid story begins in 1965, when avaricious treasure-hunters from the Uşak-area village of Güre dug and (finally, dynamited) open the tomb of a Lydian princess who had been sleeping peacefully for 2600 years. The stupendous wealth of gold and silver jewellery entranced the men, whose greed would sure enough incur enmity and ruin. These and many other illicitly found local items were smuggled to the USA via İzmir and Amsterdam, soon reaching New York's Metropolitan Museum of Art – with a provenance listed as 'Greek'.

Although the smugglers were betrayed to police by one of their own (naturally, after a dispute about profit-sharing) the story might have ended there had not *Boston Globe* journalists investigated in the 1970s. This inspired Turkish reporter Özgen Acar, who in 1984 caught up with the hoard in New York, sparking a legal battle between Turkey and the museum; it ended in 1993, when the latter admitted that it had knowingly purchased 'hot' items back in the 1960s.

In September 2011, Turkish daily *Today's Zaman* recounted the whole saga, noting that 'one of the thieves had lost three of his sons, one of whom was gruesomely murdered with his throat slit. His two other sons died in two separate traffic accidents and in different countries'. Other tomb raiders suffered bitter divorces, paralysis, and insanity; the İzmir middleman endured wretched suffering before an agonising death.

Although it's unknown whether the American buyers suffered similar fates, the saga of the Lydian Hoard is a stark reminder that Western pillaging of other peoples' antiquities is not a tale relegated to the mists of the colonial past. Sadly, the well-heeled and ostensibly 'civilised' representatives of European and American private collectors, auction houses and museums still today have the biggest appetite for black-market antiquities from Turkey, Greece and the Balkan states.

Visiting the Uşak Archaeology Museum is easy, via regular buses from Afyon (₺14, 1½ hours), and periodic ones from İzmir (₺25, 2½ hours). If you're dropped on the highway (Dörtyol), follow the signs for the *şehir merkezi* (city centre), where the museum stands off the main square. Otogar–centre taxis run ₺12.

WESTERN ANATOLIA AFYON (AFYONKARAHİSAR)

Mevlevihane Camii
MOSQUE

(Zaviye Caddesi) This 13th-century Seljuk creation was a dervish lodge when Sultan Veled
(son of dervish founder Celaleddin Rumi)
made Afyon the empire's second-most important Mevlevi centre after Konya. Today's
mosque (1908), rebuilt for the ill-fated Sultan Abdülhamid II, has twin domes and
twin pyramidal roofs above its courtyard.
The free museum brings the mystical dervish ways to life.

İmaret Cami
MOSQUE

Afyon's major mosque complex (south
of the roundabout, down Bankalar Caddesi) was built for Gedik Ahmet Paşa in
1472. The blue-tiled, spiral-fluted minaret
decorations indicate Seljuk preferences,
though Ottoman stylings are apparent. The
eastern entrance, like an *eyvan* (vaulted
hall), accesses a double-domed sanctuary
(as in mosques at early Ottoman capitals
Bursa and Edirne). The adjoining İmaret
hamam (☉men 5am-midnight, women 8am-
8pm) retains its original stone basins and
is still used.

Ulu Cami
MOSQUE

Although among the most important surviving Seljuk mosques, the opulent Ulu Cami
(1273) is generally open only during prayers.
It's supported by 40 soaring wooden columns with stalactite capitals and features a
flat-beamed roof. Local green tiles decorate
the minaret.

Ottoman Houses
HISTORIC AREA

Around Ulu Cami several Ottoman wooden
houses lend an atmospheric touch, with
some serving now as restaurants.

🛏 Sleeping

Afyon has worthwhile sleeping options, and
thermal spa hotels dot the Afyon–Kütahya
road.

Şehitoğlu Konaği
HISTORIC HOTEL €€€

(☎214 1313; www.sehitoglukonagi.com; Kuyulu
Sokak 2-6; s/d ₺125/190) Afyon's best 'restoration hotel,' this renovated Ottoman house
has warm and inviting rooms, some with
attractive wood balconies. Baths are appropriately done up in local tiles. Its restaurant (mains ₺10 to ₺20) specialises in local
fare, particularly the *sucuk* (spicy sausage)
and cheeses that accompany a variety of salads. Bucking the no-alcohol trend, they also
make a decent house wine.

Çakmak Marble Otel
HOTEL €€

(☎214 3300; www.cakmakmarblehotel.com; Süleyman Gonçer Caddesi 2; s/d ₺95/160, ste ₺280;
✳🐾📶☻) One block east of Hükümet Meydanı,
the Çakmak Marble offers more than just
well-done business-style rooms: there's an
indoor swimming pool and jacuzzi, hearty
breakfast (with views, from the 8th floor)
and a working bar. There's a room package
with dinner in the on-site restaurant included (add ₺20 to ₺30 to the room price).

Hotel Soydan
HOTEL €€

(☎215 2323; www.soydanhotel.com/; Turan Emeksiz
Caddesi 2; s/d ₺55/90) Rooms at the Soydan
are decidedly less posh than at the other local contenders, but are decent and clean, and
most have balconies – good value if you'd
rather forgo the niceties to save a little money.

🍴 Eating & Drinking

Afyon's famous for its *sucuk* and local cheeses, both of which you'll see festively hung/
stacked in shop windows, and on restaurant
menus. Alas, conservative Afyon is practically a dry town, though the more upscale
hotels sell alcohol.

Altınay
SWEETS €€

(Millet Caddesi 5; ☉6.30am-9pm) This well-
known confectioner's shop has mastered
Afyon's unique version of Turkish delight,
which includes *kaymak* (cream); though
the cream's made partly from the opium
plant, for better or for worse, it will not leave
you in a narcotic stupor.

Mihrioğlu Konağı
ANATOLIAN €

(mains ₺5-12; ☉breakfast, lunch & dinner) Set in
an old Ottoman-style home and run by the
family who owns it, Mihrioğlu clicks the culinary clock back a few centuries with its menu
of traditional food mixed with current local
faves (Afyon kebap, *mantı* etc). Crinkled civic
photos line the walls while antique tagines
and sewing machines fill the corners. A rustic
garden provides summer seating out back.

Osmanlı Yeniçeri Lokantası
TURKISH €€

(☎213 1550; Ambaryolu Caddesi; mains ₺12-15)
Although the only notable decor is the odd
assortment of plastic domesticated animals
against the walls, this clean, well-lit modern
restaurant is a safer bet than the numerous
fast-food kebap shops. It offers both prepared dishes and cooked-to-order Turkish
foods (the chicken *şiş* with savoury pilaf is
a winner). It's on a central side street (opposite the TEB Bank).

SERVICES FROM DENIZLI'S OTOGAR

DESTINATION	FARE (₺)	DURATION (HR)	DISTANCE (KM)	FREQUENCY (PER DAY)
Afyon	22	4	240	8
Ankara	35	7	480	frequent
Antalya	25	5	300	several
Bodrum	25	4½	290	several
Bursa	42	9	532	several
Eğirdir	25	2½	180	2
Fethiye	25	5	280	several
Isparta	17	3	175	several
İstanbul	40-65	12	665	frequent
İzmir	21	4	250	frequent
Konya	35	6	440	several
Marmaris	23	3	185	several
Nevşehir	40	11	674	at least 1 nightly
Selçuk	20	3	195	several, or change at Aydın

ℹ️ Information

Tourist Office (☏ 213 5447; Hükümet Meydanı; ⊙8am-noon & 1.30-5.30pm Mon-Fri) Has useful maps, but little English spoken.

ℹ️ Getting There & Away

Afyon is well connected with major destinations. Buses serve Ankara (four hours), Antalya (five hours), Denizli/Pamukkale (four hours), Eskişehir (three hours), Isparta (three hours), İstanbul (eight hours), İzmir (5½ hours), Konya (3¾ hours) and Kütahya (1½ hours).

As with most everywhere else, free *servis* dolmuşes go to and from the centre (show your bus ticket). The dolmuş to the otogar stops regularly at bus stops along the main drag. Otogar–centre cabs run ₺15.

PAMMUKALE REGION

The glittering white of Pamukkale's calcite cliffs jumps straight out of many Turkey tourism brochures, and day-waders do indeed come from far and wide to indulge in the warm waters of these dazzling travertines. Above them stand the ruins of ancient Hierapolis, whose inhabitants did much the same thing 2000 years ago. Other, more impressive, ancient ruins sprawl across a green plain at lesser-visited Afrodisias, the museum of which easily surpasses that of Ephesus.

While Pamukkale's village is modest, it has good budget digs (some with thermal water pools from the travertines), and thus makes a relaxing base for a few days of absent-minded lounging (with rudimentary nightlife). The ancient ruins of Laodicea and Aphrodisias provide culturally edifying day-trip opportunities.

Industrial **Denizli** is a big city, but for most travellers it's merely a transport hub – the place where you take the bus or dolmuş to Pamukkale or other more interesting towns.

ℹ️ Getting There & Away

Air

Turkish Airlines (www.thy.com) has daily connections to Denizli from İstanbul. From Denizli airport a Turkish Airlines shuttle will drop you at the otogar on request. Airport–centre taxis cost ₺60 and around ₺85 to Pamukkale.

Bus

From Denizli's otogar, buses and minibuses (₺3) serve Pamukkale every 15 minutes. But remember that if you've booked a room ahead, Pamukkale pension owners will usually save you the hassle by picking you up at the otogar.

Pamukkale

☏ 0258 / POP 2630

Although Pamukkale itself is barely a three-street village, it's been eternally famous for the gleaming white calcite shelves overrunning with warm, mineral-rich waters on the mountain above it – the so-called 'Cotton Castle' (*pamuk* means 'cotton' in Turkish).

While many visitors are content to laze in the travertines, just above them lies Hierapolis, once a Roman and Byzantine spa city which has considerable preserved ruins and a museum (a single ticket allows access to both the travertines and Hierapolis). Unesco World Heritage status (granted in 1988) has brought more extensive measures to protect the glistening bluffs. Yet though the days of freely traipsing around everywhere are long gone (and with them, much of the local nightlife), Pamukkale remains one of Turkey's singular experiences, even if costs have risen and bathing has been restricted.

While the photogenic travertines get busloads of day trippers passing through for a quick soak and photo op, staying overnight is useful for those wishing to see the very worthwhile ancient ruins of Laiodikeia and Aphrodisias. Such sites are off the tourist trail, meaning you'll have a relaxing time, whether going independently or with an (inexpensive and hassle-free) day tour from Pamukkale.

⊙ Sights & Activities

Pamukkale's double attractions – the shimmering white travertines/terraces and the adjacent ruins of ancient Hierapolis – are a package deal. Both are accessed on the same ticket and comprise their own national park, located on a whitewashed hill right above Pamukkale village.

Of the site's three main entrances, the southern one is most practical. It's just over 2km from Pamukkale, on the hill at the entrance to Hierapolis, meaning you see both attractions while walking downwards, finishing up back in the village. The second entrance is in nearby Karahayıt village, and is thus more useful for those based in luxury spa hotels there.

The third, 'northern' entrance, at the edge of Pamukkale itself, is at the base of the terraced mountain, meaning you walk uphill over the travertines before even reaching Hierapolis, and then also have to find a way back down. However, if you're just after a little R&R in the pools, this is a quick and easy option. The northern gate is located just east of the Beyaz Cennet public park in town, and down a path along Mehmet Akif Ersoy Bulvarı, and opposite the junction with Atatürk Caddesi.

Since the ever-increasing ticket price (₺30) includes both, however, get a lift to the south gate via minibus, taxi or (in many cases) a free lift provided by your local pension. Additional fees apply for the archaeological museum and antique swimming pool (though you can arguably get enough out of the experience without shelling out more lira for these). Previously, one ticket granted access for a 24-hour period – local tourism providers lament how ending this policy diminished their business. Nevertheless, you can stay inside as long as you like (the park works during daylight hours), and for most people a single visit is just fine.

Travertines
NATURE RESERVE

These saucer-shaped travertines (or terraces, as they're also called) wind sideways down the powder-white mountain, providing stunning contrast to the clear blue sky and green plain below. To protect the unique calcite surface, guards oblige you to go barefoot, so if planning to go down and continue out, be prepared to carry your shoes with you.

Although the ridges look rough, in reality the constant water flow keeps the ground mostly soft, even gooey in places, and the risk of slipping is greater than that of cutting your feet. (If still concerned, just leave your socks on). The constant downward motion can be hard on the knees. To walk straight down without stops takes between 30 to 45 minutes.

Although the terrace pools aren't particularly deep, you can get fully submerged if you try. If you don't have a bathing suit or shorts, or otherwise don't wish to get too wet, however, there are plenty of dry sections leading down. Also note that going at midday means crowds and sharp sunlight reflecting off the dazzling white surface; later afternoon is a better time to go.

Hierapolis
RUINS

Hierapolis' location atop the tourist magnet that is the 'Cotton Castle' seems to have blessed it with a budget rather more ample than that of most Turkish archaeological sites. The orderly paved pathways, well-trimmed hedges, flower-filled expanses, wooden bridge walkways and array of shady park benches make Hierapolis far more genteel than Ephesus (or anywhere else in

Turkey). Wild and raw it is not, but for those wishing, or needing, to see an ancient site on flat and well-maintained terrain, this is the place.

The curvaceous mountaintop means that the city's ruins are relatively compact, with the main sites easily accessible. The ruins evoke life in a bygone era, in which Greeks, Romans and Jews, pagans and Christians, and spa tourists peacefully coexisted.

Indeed, Hierapolis became a curative centre when founded around 190 BC by Eumenes II of Pergamum. It prospered under the Romans, even more so under the Byzantines, when large Jewish and Orthodox Christian communities comprised most of the population. However, recurrent earthquakes brought disaster, and Hierapolis was finally abandoned after a 1334 tremor.

Entering at the southern gate, start near the Archaeology Museum for the ruined **Byzantine church** and **Temple of Apollo** foundations. As at Didyma and Delphi, eunuch priests tended the temple's oracle. Its alleged power derived from an adjoining spring, the Plutonium (named after the underworld god Pluto). Apparently only the priests understood the secret of holding one's breath around the toxic fumes that billowed up from Hades, immediately killing the small animals and birds they sacrificed.

To see this lethal spring, walk towards the **Roman theatre**, enter the first gate in the right-hand fence, then follow the right-hand path down. At the big, block-like temple on the left, a small subterranean entrance is closed with a rusted grate, with a sign reading 'Tehlikelidir Zehirli Gaz' (Dangerous Poisonous Gas). Here the gases can indeed be heard bubbling up from below.

The spectacular Roman theatre, built in stages by emperors Hadrian and Septimius Severus could seat over 12,000 spectators. The stage mostly survives, along with some decorative panels and the front-row, VIP 'box' seats.

From the theatre, rough tracks lead uphill to the less-visited but fascinating **Martyrium of St Philip the Apostle**, an intricate octagonal structure on terrain where St Philip was supposedly martyred. The arches of the eight individual chapels, marked with crosses, originally had heptagonal interiors.

Differing accounts from ancient sources have created confusion over precisely

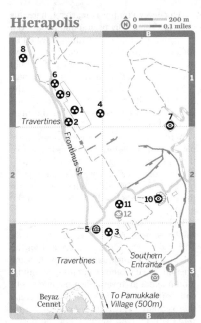

Hierapolis

⊙ **Sights**

which Philip was commemorated here – if it really was Jesus' apostle, he was allegedly hung upside down from a tree after challenging the pagan snake-worshippers at their nearby temple. An apocryphal ancient source claims that at Philip's death, a yawning abyss opened in the earth, swallowing up the Roman proconsul, the snake-worshippers, their temple and about 7000 hapless bystanders. Righteous!

Whichever Philip was martyred here, his body has reportedly been found about 40m away, in a Byzantine structure excavated by Italian archaeologists. The sensational news of August 2011 revived interest in St Philip and Hierapolis. Considering that his martyrium clearly suffered fire damage in the 5th century, it's possible that the unearthed body was indeed relocated from the martyrium then.

Across the western hillside is the completely ruined **Hellenistic theatre**, above the 2nd-century **agora**. One of the largest ever discovered, it was surrounded by marble porticoes with Ionic columns on three sides, and closed by a basilica on the fourth.

Walking downhill through the agora, you'll re-emerge on the ridgeline main path. Turn right towards the northern exit for the colonnaded **Frontinus Street**, with some original paving and columns remaining. Monumental archways once bounded both ends of this, the city's main commercial thoroughfare. The ruined **Arch of Domitian**, with its twin towers, is at the northern end; just before them, the large **latrine** building has two floor channels, for sewage and for fresh water.

Beyond the Arch of Domitian are the ruined **Roman baths**, and further past these, Hierapolis' Appian Way. An extraordinary **necropolis** (cemetery) extends several kilometres northwards. The clustered circular tombs here probably belonged to the many ancient spa tourists whom Hierapolitan healers failed to cure.

Hierapolis Archaeology Museum   MUSEUM
(admission ₺3; ⊙9am-12.30pm & 1.30-7pm Tue-Sun) Housed in former Roman baths, this excellent museum has three separate sections, one housing spectacular sarcophagi, another with small finds from Hierapolis and Afrodisias. The third exhibits friezes and Roman-era statuary from Afrodisias' famous school. Those depicting Cybele's lover Attis and a priestess of Egyptian goddess Isis, are especially fine.

Antique Pool   SWIMMING
(admission ₺25, public pool ₺7.50; ⊙9am-7pm, public pool 9am-8pm) The sacred pool – nowadays, the separate-ticket swimming pool in the Antique Pool spa's courtyard – has submerged sections of original fluted marble columns to lounge against. The water, which is abun-

dant in minerals and a more-than-balmy at 36°C, was thought to have restorative powers in antiquity, and may still. In summer, it's busiest from 11am to 4pm. Budget-wary travellers can enjoy the faux-travertines at the **public pool** at the base of the hill by Pamukkale.

🛏 Sleeping

Pamukkale's numerous pensions and small hotels offer good value for money. Many places have pools (with water from the travertines or other springs). The stiff competition translates into good service, tips and assistance.

If you have a preference, and especially in high summer, try and book ahead – whatever the season, this often scores you a free lift from Denizli's otogar or train station. (Generally you'll find rooms just showing up, though). Campers are usually welcome to pitch their tent on the premises for a small fee.

If not the loudest in all Turkey, Pamukkale's mischievous mosque is right up there, so don't be surprised if you're blasted from your bed at 5am.

TOP
CHOICE Artemis Yoruk Hotel   HOSTEL €
(☑272 2073; www.artemisyorukhotel.com; Atatürk Caddesi; dm/s/d from ₺15/40/50; ❄@🛜🏊) Appealing to independent budget travellers, the centrally located Artemis Yoruk Hotel offers simple rooms with balconies set around a palm-lined outdoor swimming pool, flanked by cushioned nooks and overlooked by an open terrace-bar. The smaller indoor pool, heated by Pamukkale's mineral-rich waters, opens until late. There's a sauna and Turkish bath, where massages (₺50 to ₺80) are available. The mixed Turkish–Australian staff are friendly and helpful. Find the hotel under the UN-like display of flags.

Melrose Hotel   PENSION €
(☑272 2250; www.melrosehousehotel.com; Vali Vekfi Ertürk Caddesi 8; s/d/tr €31/37/43; ❄@🛜🏊) Clearly a step above the average Pamukkale pension (but pricier, too), the Melrose has an array of sumptuously decorated big modern rooms with wood floors, ranging from singles to suites and family rooms – the deluxe room (€60) even has a jacuzzi and bar. There's a good on-site restaurant and pool.

Pamukkale

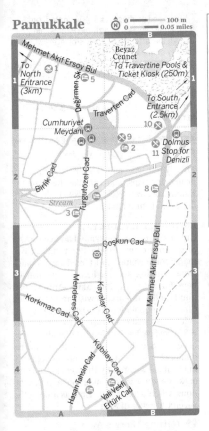

places, but some have balcony views of the travertines, and there's a relaxing pool. An added benefit is that it's a very short walk to the park's north (lower) gate.

Beyaz Kale Pension PENSION €
(☏272 2064; www.beyazkalepension.com; Menderes Caddesi; s/d €25/35; ✻🛜🌊) This central, family-run place, also not far from the park entrance, has unpretentious but spotless rooms and a pool, plus some of the best local pension fare – served on the relaxing rooftop terrace.

Hotel Dört Mevsim PENSION €
(☏272 2009; www.hoteldortmevsim.com; Hasan Tahsin Caddesi 19; s/d/q from ₺35/55/70; ✻🛜🌊) The 'Four Seasons' is a welcoming place downtown with bright, clean rooms. Set on a quiet lane, it offers extras like a game room, babysitting and laundry services, making it quite family-friendly. Pets are allowed too (OK, maybe not in the pool). The homemade food is excellent and staff are eager to assist. Breakfast costs ₺5.

Ozbay HOSTEL €
(☏272 2126; Mehmet Akif Ersoy Bulvarı 37; s/d ₺40/60; ✻@) There's no pool and the rooms are spartan, but Ozbay is situated across from the lower travertines entrance and staff are very friendly. Enjoy free tea and coffee during (and long after...) the excellent breakfast.

🍴 Eating & Drinking

Pamukkale's restaurants are unremarkable – your pension likely offers better fare. Nightlife is lacklustre, but during high season a

Venüs Hotel PENSION €
(☏272 2152; www.venushotel.net; Hasan Tahsin Caddesi; s/d/tr €25/35/42; ✻@🛜🌊) The rooms here (some with travertine views from the balconies) are just part of the package; the traditional Turkish poolside restaurant is excellent, and quiet corners for reading or chatting with fellow travellers abound. The kind family owners also arrange day trips to the major local sites at good prices.

Hotel Hal-Tur HOTEL €€
(☏272 2723; www.haltur.net; Mehmet Akif Ersoy Bulvarı 71; s/d/tr from €40/60/85; ✻@🌊) The Hal-Tur has fantastic travertine views, and clean and well-kept (if a bit dated) rooms. The excellent pools (with separate kids' section) and ping-pong table make it family-friendy.

Kervansaray Pension PENSION €
(☏272 2209; www.kervansaraypension.com; İnönü Caddesi; s/d ₺45/60; ✻@🌊) The rooms here are not as impressive as other midrange

couple of decent cafe-bars get lively (as do some pension/hotel 'house' bars).

Kayaş
RESTAURANT, BAR €

(Atatürk Caddesi 3; mains ₺5-14; ☺lunch & dinner) This central place has a long bar and opposing big TV (for football matches, generally). It's probably the friendliest spot for drinks, but it also has decent Turkish food at better prices than other places. The *Imam bayildi* (braised aubergine stuffed with garlic, onion and tomatoes) and *çiğ börek* (a crunchy, cheese-filled appetizer) are among the tasty treats prepared by the chef, Melahat.

Mustafa's
INTERNATIONAL €€

(Atatürk Caddesi 22; mains ₺8-15; ☺breakfast, lunch & dinner) This streetside place doesn't have views, but does have good pizzas, wraps and salads.

Mehmet's Heaven
TURKISH €€

(Atatürk Caddesi 25; mains ₺12-20; ☺breakfast, lunch & dinner) Long-established Mehmet's has an interior with wide cushions and a back terrace with travertine views. The Turkish fare is decent but Mehmet's heaven is now somewhere in purgatory as prices have crept up.

❶ Information

Pensions offer advice, maps and assistance. As with any claustrophobically small tourist town, most have their own favourite travel providers and disparage everyone else, so compare offers. The **tourist office** (☺8am-7pm Mon-Sat) is by the upper Hierapolis gate.

ATMs exist; Denizli has banks.

Hermosa Tours (☎272 2666; Atatürk Caddesi 5/A) On the main street near the square, this full-service travel agency offers tours, bus tickets (from major Turkish company Kamil Koc – look for the sign) and activities like tandem paragliding from Hierapolis (₺100 for a 20-minute flight, weather permitting). Prices are not the cheapest, but staff is friendly and well informed.

❶ Getting There & Away
Bus

Most Pamukkale services involve changing in Denizli. In summer direct buses serve Selçuk (₺27) and Kuşadası (₺30). Pamukkale lacks an otogar, so buses drop off passengers by places like Cumhuriyet Square's ticket office. Eager touts hawking pensions and hotels sometimes lie in wait, but you can make up your own mind.

Buses and dolmuşes (₺5, 40 minutes) run frequently between Denizli and Pamukkale, though the latter particularly stop everywhere in the city on the way, slowing down the trip. Most people choose advance hotel booking to get the free lift to Pamukkale (and often, back again).

Taxi

If required, Denizli–Pamukkale taxis cost ₺50 to ₺60.

Around Pamukkale

The Afrodisias and Laodikya ruins are prime day trips. You can also head to the Kaklık Mağarası (Kaklik Cave), a sort of underground Pamukkale.

LAODİCEA (LAODİKYA)

Only 8km from Pamukkale, Laodicea was a prosperous commercial city straddling two major trade routes, and famed for its black wool, banking and medicines. Cicero lived here for a time before Mark Antony had him liquidated. Large Jewish and Orthodox Christian populations coexisted here.

The spread-out **ruins** (admission ₺5; ☺8.30am-5pm Tue-Sun) indicate Laodicea was once big. See the **stadium** outlines and remains of two **theatres**; upper-tier seats remain in the second. By the **agora** are ruins of the **basilica church** mentioned in Revelations, where Laodicea is listed as among the Seven Churches of Asia.

❶ Getting There & Away

The Pamukkale–Denizli bus passes Korucuk village, where a sign leads to Laodicea (1km). An infrequent dolmuş also runs (₺3). Alternatively, tours run from Pamukkale.

Hermosa Tours offers a three-hour guided tour (₺40 per person) that includes transport and lunch. Pensions also arrange trips, and sometimes multi-site trips can be organised for negotiable rates.

KAKLIK MAĞARASI (KAKLIK CAVE) & AK HAN

Near Pamukkale, the **Kaklık Mağarası** (admission ₺2) cave lies under a field, and gushes with calcium-rich water. The flow, into a large sinkhole, creates a bright, white pyramid with warm travertine pools below. Bathe in the outside (but non-aesthetic) pool.

Just 1km past the Pamukkale turn-off on the Denizli–Isparta highway, **Ak Han** (c 1251) is a well-preserved Seljuk *han* with a beautifully carved gateway.

Pamukkale tours are better than bus, though buses and dolmuşes (₺5) from Denizli to Afyon, Isparta or Burdur pass by. A sign in Kaklık village points left (north) 4km to the cave – walk the shadeless road or flag down a farm vehicle.

Afrodisias

The relative remoteness of Afrodisias (incl museum entry ₺8; ⊙9am-7pm May-Sep, 9am-5pm Oct-Apr), set amid Roman poplars, green fields and warbling birds, safeguards its serenity from the masses. While compact Ephesus boasts finer individual ruins, Afrodisias outdoes it for sheer scale, while its on-site museum is more impressive too (erstwhile European excavators relocated much Ephesian treasure to their own museums).

Also unlike Ephesus, Afrodisias is largely overgrown, with many side paths passing through thickets and bramble. While this lends a certain exotic feel, it's sensible to wear long pants and good shoes. For much of the year, some Afrodisian ruins are surrounded by (or even filled by) brackish pools of black water from where frogs ominously croak, and the area's generally marshy quality means that unexpected soft patches may lurk underfoot. Try to keep upwind of the occasional roving tractors, from which workmen spray unknown chemicals at the weeds flanking the pathways.

History

Afrodisias' acropolis began as a prehistoric mound (around 5000 BC). Its later temple was a pilgrimage site from the 6th century BC. By the 2nd or 1st century BC, Aphrodisias had become large and prosperous, due to its rich marble quarry and imperial favour. In the 3rd century AD, this 150,000-strong city became the provincial capital of Roman Caria.

Early Byzantine Afrodisias developed into an Orthodox city, with the Temple of Aphrodite being transformed into a church, while the stone from other buildings was re-used for defensive walls (c AD 350). By the 7th century, Afrodisias had been renamed Stavroupolis (City of the Cross), and historical sources attest to the prescence of Byzantine bishops here through the 10th century. It remained a Byzantine titular bishopric through the 15th century. Oddly enough, in 1693 the Vatican took over this role (any aspiring titular bishops should note that the post is currently vacant).

Sometime after the city's 12th-century abandonment, a Turkish village developed here; called Geyre, it was ruined by

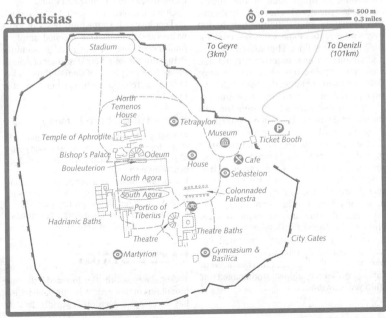

a 1956 earthquake and relocated, allowing archaeologists to work on the site. The trailblazing Kenan T Erim, a Turkish professor from New York University, oversaw excavations here from 1961 to 1990; he was honoured by being buried here. Erim's book *Afrodisias: City of Venus Aphrodite* (1986) is comprehensive.

◉ Sights

From the parking lot (₺5, if you're driving), a tractor will tow you 500m to the entrance in its connected open train car. A cafe, shop and toilets are inside the entrance, opposite the museum. Take the circular site tour first, then dry your sweat over a drink, saving the (cooler) indoor museum for last. You have two route choices, but the counter-clockwise route elaborated here is less affected by the occasional midmorning package-tour groups.

Turn right beside the museum for the grand **house** with Ionic and Corinthian pillars on the left. Further on the left, the elaborate **tetrapylon** (monumental gateway) once greeted pilgrims coming to the Temple of Aphrodite. (It's been reconstructed using 85% of the original blocks). The tomb of Professor Erim is on the lawn.

Continue on the straight footpath, and turn right across the grassy field for the 270m-long **stadium**. One of the biggest and best preserved classical stadiums, this massively long structure has 30,000 overgrown seats (some were reserved for individuals or guilds). The eastern end was a gladiatorial arena; entering through the dark and curving tunnels onto the huge field, you can imagine the fear, exhilaration and sheer adrenaline these ancient warriors would have felt, striding towards imminent death amid a raucous crowd demanding blood.

A gentler site, accessible from the main path, is the erstwhile **Temple of Aphrodite**, goddess of love. When converted into a basilica (c AD 500), its *cella* was removed, its columns shifted to form a nave, and an apse was added. It's thus hard to visualise the original structure. Near the temple-church, the **Bishop's Palace** is a grand house that previously accommodated Roman governors. Just beyond, an eastward path leads to the beautiful marble **bouleuterion**, preserved almost undamaged for 1000 years by mud.

South of the odeum was the **north agora**, now a grassy field. The path leads through the early 2nd-century-AD **Hadrianic Baths** to the **south agora**, with a long, partially excavated pool, and the grand **Portico of Tiberius**.

Stone stairs up the earthen, prehistoric mound access the white marble **theatre**, a 7000-capacity auditorium complete with stage and individually labelled seats. Just south was the large **theatre baths** complex.

The path then turns to the **Sebasteion**: originally a temple to the deified Roman emperors, it was visually spectacular, with a three-storey-high double colonnade decorated with friezes of Greek myths and imperial exploits.

To understand the magnitude here, see approximately 70 (of the once-existing 190) reliefs in the elegant **museum**. They occupy opposing sides of the main interior hall. The unique combination of friezes acknowledge a Greek culture and mythology underpinning the worldly achievements of the pragmatic Romans. So, along with the statues illustrating mythical heroes, you'll see statues of robust emperors. Note how subjugated nations are always presented in the female form – for example, Trajan rips open the shirt of chaste Dacia, while Nero has his way with a trembling Armenia. You don't want to know what Claudius does to blushing Britannia.

Other marbles here include Aphrodite's 2nd-century cult statue, and busts of great writers and thinkers. One, labelled simply, 'a philosopher', may be the great 3rd-century Peripatetic philosopher, Alexander of Aphrodisias. See sculptures of Caius Julius Zoilos, Octavian's freed slave who became a wealthy local benefactor.

❶ Getting There & Away

Afrodisias is 55km southeast of Nazilli and 101km from Denizli. Tours from Pamukkale usually run ₺70 per person, though this fluctuates depending on the number of participants and the operator. Generally, a four-person minimum is required. You'll have around 2½ hours on-site. Otherwise, car rental (₺80 per day, plus ₺70 for petrol) or taxis are options for small groups. There's an ATM at the site entrance.

LAKE DISTRICT

Tucked away within the forested hills and mountains of inner Anatolia, the lake region has an escapist, even otherworldly, feel. At

ST PAUL TRAIL

Almost two millennia ago, the Apostle Paul trekked northwards from Perge (near the coast and Antalya) through the Anatolian wilds to today's Yalvaç, near Eğirdir. The winding route – which runs from sea level to a 2200m peak – passes crumbling ancient ruins. Although some hikers start from the south, you'll have more options and a more realistic shot if you're based in Eğirdir. For more information, see the trail's website (www.stpaultrail .com) and Kate Clow's authoritative book, *St Paul Trail*.

its heart is Eğirdir, a placid town overlooked by Davraz Dağı (Mt Davraz; 2635m). It's an excellent base for hiking, climbing and seeing regional sites – or for simply relaxing by the tranquil lake surrounding it.

Along with the lake, its water activities and tasty fish, the Eğirdir area offers year-round action, including the rose harvests in May and June, autumn apple harvests and winter skiing. History-loving hikers can explore the St Paul Trail, while ancient sites such as the lonesome, mountaintop ruins of Sagalassos remain reserved for the initiated alone. But it's the extraordinarily kind hospitality of the locals, unaffected by mass tourism, that perhaps makes visiting most worthwhile.

Eğirdir

☎ 0246 / POP 19.417

Enigmatic Eğirdir, surrounded by shimmering Eğirdir Gölü (Lake Eğirdir) and ringed by steep mountains, lies hidden away from the heat and dust of Anatolia like some secret treasure. Indeed, with its Byzantine fortress, unique Seljuk structures and crumbling old quarter ringed by beaches and fishing boats, the place has just about everything except a mythical lake monster.

Eğirdir makes an excellent base for regional sites and outdoors activities, with inexpensive lodging provided by family-run pensions offering hearty, home-cooked meals. All the info you need about activities and local attractions is found quickly

and easily, with no carpet-selling or other distractions.

Like all lake towns, Eğirdir has much going on under the surface, and it does attract a varied population. The mountain above it hosts a special-forces mountain warfare training base, while a distant western shore conceals its underwater equivalent. In summer, Muslim devotees of the quasi-mystical Nur movement mass in Barla village, not far away. At summer's end, Yürük mountain nomads descend to do business, while autumn's influx of apple wholesalers stimulates certain dens of iniquity on Eğirdir-connected island, Yeşilada. Through it all, the town's dependable news source – a public loudspeaker – crackles on, reporting who has died or what utility bills are overdue.

History

Originally Hittite (c 1200 BC), the town was successively occupied by Phrygians and Lydians, captured by Persians and then Alexander the Great, finally becoming Roman Prostanna. The modern mountain warfare base occupies the ancient settlement; the archaeological identity of this formerly large and prosperous town thus remains unexplored.

The Byzantines renamed it Akrotiri (Steep Mountain), making it a bishopric. Seljuks captured it in 1204, and later the Turkish Hamidoğulları tribe came; by the mid-14th century, the name had been debased to 'Akridur.' In 1417, the Ottomans conquered, though the population (especially on Yeşilada) remained mostly Greek until the 1923 population exchange.

The name Akrotiri/Akritur eventually became Eğridir, meaning 'crooked' or 'bent'. In the 1980s, to end the jokes, it was officially renamed Eğirdir, meaning 'she is spinning'. It partly refers to a folk tale about a queen who sat at her loom, unaware that her son was dead.

◎ Sights & Activities

Hızır Bey Camii   MOSQUE

Originally a Seljuk warehouse in 1237, this simple stone structure became a mosque in 1308 under Hamidoğulları Emir Hızır Bey. It features a clerestory (an upper row of windows) above the central hall and new tiles around the *mihrab*. Note the finely carved wooden doors, and the minaret's blue tile trim.

Eğirdir

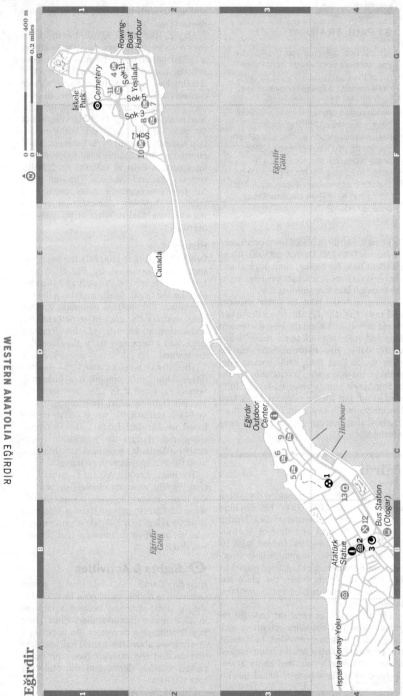

0   0.2 miles
0   400 m

Eğirdir Gölü

Rowing-Boat Harbour

Yeşilada

Cemetery

İskele Park

Sok 11

Sok 4

Sok 5

Sok 7

Sok 3

Sok 8

Sok 1

Canada

Eğirdir Outdoor Center

Harbour

Eğirdir Gölü

Atatürk Statue

Bus Station (Otogar)

Isparta Konay Yolu

Eğirdir

Dündar Bey Medresesi HISTORIC BUILDING
In 1285, Hamidoğulları Emir Felekeddin Dündar Bey turned this grand stone structure (then a 67-year-old Seljuk caravanserai) into a *medrese*. If you plan to form your own paramilitary unit, the on-site bazaar sells camouflage gear, high-powered rifles and plenty of ammo.

Castle RUINS
A few hundred metres down the peninsula stand the massive walls of Akrotiri's ruined castle, which allegedly dates back to 5th-century-BC Lydian King Croesus. At the time of research, some restoration was happening, but there's nothing to enter.

Beaches & Boat Trips
From the western shore by the castle, to the peninsula's tip at Yeşilada, several relaxing small **beaches** exist, some with changing cabins and food stalls. Out of town, at Yazla (under 1km down the Isparta road) is sandy **Belediye Beach**. Several kilometres further is pebbly **Altınkum Beach**. In summer, dolmuşes run every 15 minutes (₺1.50) from the otogar. Taxis cost ₺12. Further north, 11km towards Barla, is the long, sandy **Bedre Beach**. Cycle or catch a taxi (₺15).

Some of Eğirdir's best swimming spots are accessible only by **boat trips** (per person around €17), which let you relax, try some fishing, and generally bliss out on the lake's breezy blue waters and in its verdant lagoons. Boat trips run during summer and have traditionally provided a second income for fishermen and pension owners. However, the ever-declining number of fishermen means that prices have soared – if you solicit a boat-owner at random, expect to pay ₺35 to ₺40 per person, for only one hour on the lake.

It's wiser to arrange a trip through your pension or the Eğirdir Outdoor Center (p306), which charges ₺50 per person for a seven-hour excursion. The trip involves visiting hidden coves, swimming, sunbathing and a fresh fish lunch prepared by expert captain (and fisherman) Mustafa. Trips run from 15 June to 15 September.

🛏 Sleeping
When looking for a place to stay, be sure to check that your bedroom windows have screens – Eğirdir's harmless but extremely irritating little lake bugs will fly towards any lit area, but they can't get through a screen (they're less of a nuisance when the wind is up).

Eğirdir's family-run pensions cluster around the castle ruins (a close walk to the centre) and at the peninsula's far end, on the road-attached island of Yeşilada (1.5km north of centre). Air-conditioning is generally not provided (nor needed, given that evenings are cool and breezy).

TOP CHOICE Charly's Pension PENSION €
(☎311 4611; www.charlyspension.com; Kale Mahallesi 4 Nolu Sokak; s/d/tr ₺35/55/65; 🕸) This family-run getaway, in a restored Ottoman-era house braced by the castle's western wall, offers a handful of cheerfully painted rooms with weathered wood floors and luminous curtains. The placid back balcony overlooking the lake has two levels – a covered one, where breakfast and dinner are served, and a lower one for sunbathing. The entertaining combination of backpackers, families and mountaineering sorts fosters a fun and laid-back atmosphere. A small beach lies below. Breakfast is ₺6.

Mavigöl Hotel HOTEL €€
(☎425 1020; www.mavigolhotel.com; s/d ₺60/100; @🕸🛷) If you seek swimming pools, safes and satellite TV, try Mavigöl, Eğirdir's only real hotel. Service is very kind and attentive, and rooms are spotless. Billiards and table tennis add to the attractions for youngsters.

WESTERN ANATOLIA EĞİRDİR

Ali's Pension
PENSION €

(☑311 2547; www.alispension.com; Yeşilada; s/d ₺45/60; @) If you're keen on staying out on Yeşilada, Ali's is a great choice, with handsomely furnished and spotless rooms and excellent hospitality. The home-cooked breakfasts and dinners are abundant and very tasty. Call in advance for free bus station pick-up.

Lale Pension
PENSION, HOSTEL €

(☑311 2406; www.lalehostel.com; Kale Mahalessi 5 Sokak 2; dm/s/d without breakfast ₺20/45/65; ✳@) Near the castle, the long-established Lale is divided into two completely separate buildings: the quiet pension, with well-maintained modern rooms and rooftop lounge offering lake views, and the hostel, with clean if basic dorms. Breakfast is not included in the price, but meals can be enjoyed in sister hotel Charly's Pension, a short walk away.

Şehsuvar Peace Pension
PENSION €

(☑311 2433; www.peacepension.com; s/d ₺40/60) Another island pension, near Yeşilada's inland *meydan* (square), this quieter choice has a shaded terrace with grapevines and well-maintained rooms. The owners, Huseyin and Esma, also rent rowboats and bicycles. The restaurant serves excellent fish (you can join Huseyin to help bring in the day's catch). Call in advance for free pick-up from the bus station.

Göl Pension
PENSION €€

(☑311 2370; ahmetdavras@hotmail.com; r ₺80-100; @) Another family-run place out on Yeşilada, this pension has spacious, clean and well-maintained rooms. Those on the top floor enjoy great lake views from the private terrace.

Choo Choo Pension
PENSION €€

(☑311 4926; www.choochoopension.com; Yeşilada Mahallesi 2; d/tr/qd/apt ₺105/130/160/225) This Yeşilada pension is run by an old fishing clan, who also run the neighbouring Halikarnas restaurant on the lakefront. Room prices here are rather dear by local standards, but they are spacious and modern. Call in advance for free bus pick-up.

Çetin Pansiyon
PENSION €

(☑311 2154; s/d/tr ₺50/60/70) Also near the castle, this quiet place has six bright rooms up a narrow staircase, four of which have excellent views across the lake to Mt Barla. Breakfast is an additional ₺10.

✗ Eating

Pension dinners are tasty, convenient, and great for meeting fellow travellers. Local specialities include *istakoz* (crayfish) and the lake carp and other fish. Yeşilada has good fish restaurants.

The somewhat rundown inland part of town has average fast food and kebap shops, like **Kemer Lokantasi** (Sahil Yolu 20; mains ₺6-9; ☺lunch & dinner) near the mosque. For a variety of caffeinated drinks, visit the Eğirdir Outdoor Center for a drink on the eastern waterfront.

Eğirdir Market
MARKET

Thursday market is held by the castle. If around on any Sunday between August and October, buy apples, cheese, yoghurt or even a goat from the Yörük Turks, who descend from their mountain redoubts to hawk their wares and stock up for winter. In the old days, wily Yörük mothers would use these public events to negotiate marriages for their children.

❶ Information

The tourist information office remains closed. ATMs and banks are near the Hotel Eğirdir.

Eğirdir Outdoor Center (☑311 6688; www.egirdiroutdoorcenter.com; Ata Yolu Üzeri) This all-in-one info centre, cafe, and activities planner overlooks the eastern waterfront (you'll see the cafe sign and lined-up mountain bikes out front). Owned by outdoor-sports enthusiast and pension owner Ibrahim Ağartan, this is an excellent place for arranging local adventures, enjoying the town's widest coffee selection, meeting fellow travellers, or even doing laundry.

The Center provides free info on how to tackle local attractions such as the St Paul Trail, and rents mountain bikes (₺5/45 per hour/day) and kayaks (₺25 per hour). It runs half-day and full-day boat trips (₺35 to ₺50), and sunset cruises (₺20). Finally, the Center offers group-rate transport for day trips to Sütçüler (₺130), Zindan Cave (₺60), Çandır Kanyon/Yazılı Canyon Nature Park (₺150), Lake Kovada National Park (₺60), Antiocheia-in-Pisidia (₺150) and Sagalassos (₺180).

❶ Getting There and Away

Eğirdir has frequent connections to İstanbul (₺55), Bursa, Antalya, Konya (₺30), Nevsehir (₺40) and Goreme (₺45) in Capaddocia, Denizli for Pamukkale (₺20) and İzmir (₺35). The frequency of long-haul buses is greater from nearby Isparta, accessible by frequent minibuses (₺6, 30 minutes).

From the bus station, pensions by the castle are within walking distance, whereas Yeşilada is 1.5km north (₺10 by taxi, or ₺1 by dolmuş). However, regardless of where you're staying, most pension owners will retrieve you for free if you call ahead.

Around Eğirdir

Within an 80km radius of Eğirdir exist numerous interesting destinations, most along the St Paul Trail; they're listed here in a south-to-north fashion.

Trips can be arranged by the Eğirdir Outdoor Center or by your pension. Otherwise, drive or take a taxi (₺50 to ₺100, destination depending). Sütçüler and Yalvaç are served by dolmuş (₺10 to ₺14) in summer.

SÜTÇÜLER

Sütçüler is a hiking base up a winding mountain road. Traipse the Roman road of Adada, where a ruined agora and Trajan's temple are visible. There's no real need to stay but if you do, the Otel Karacan (☑351 2411; www.karacanotel.com; Atatürk Caddesi 53; half-board ₺40-50; @) has 25 spacious rooms (some without bathroom) and an indoor restaurant, with garden terrace overlooking the hills. Book ahead in summer.

ZINDAN MAĞARASI (ZINDAN CAVE)

Roughly 30km southeast of Eğirdir, and about 1km north of Aksu by a Roman bridge, is the entrance to the kilometre-long Zindan Cave; it features Byzantine ruins, stalactites and stalagmites, and the so-called 'Hamam' room.

YAZILI CANYON NATURE PARK & ÇANDIR KANYON

The Yazılı Canyon Nature Park (Yazılı Kanyon Tabiat Parkı; admission ₺1, car ₺2), 73km south of Eğirdir, protects a forested gorge deep in the Taurus Mountains, which separate the Lake District (ancient Pisidia) and the Antalya region (Pamphylia), and their unique climatic zones. At the parking area you pay the admission ticket, then follow a path 1km upstream through the glorious Çandır Kanyon. There are shady bathing spots, filled with catharticly cold alpine water. It's busy in summer, but otherwise tranquil.

LAKE KOVADA NATIONAL PARK

Lake Kovada National Park (Kovada Gölü Milli Parkı) surrounds a small lake connected to Lake Eğirdir by a channel. It's nice for hikes, picnicking and flora, especially at the nearby Kasnak Forest, which is full of butterflies and rare mountain flowers.

DAVRAZ DAĞI (MT DAVRAZ)

Mt Davraz (2635m), rising between three lakes, has great skiing from mid-December to March. There's nordic and downhill skiing, plus snowboarding here, and the 1.2km-long chairlift is fast and modern. A day pass (includes equipment hire and lift ticket) costs around €50; summit treks and paragliding are also possible.

WORTH A TRIP

ISPARTA'S ROSE TOURS

While apparently just an unassuming transport hub, Isparta is famous for its attar of roses, a valuable oil for perfumes. Each May and June, when the flowers bloom in surrounding villages, the process starts anew.

At daybreak, rose petals are plucked and placed in copper vats. The steam then passed over them is drawn off and condensed, leaving the water's surface covered with a thin layer of oil that's skimmed off and bottled. The 'extra' rosewater is also sold, and there's plenty (it takes 100kg of petals to produce just 25g of attar of roses).

In season, Eğirdir pension owners can organise factory tours (₺40 per person). Or, you can arrange a trip directly with a manufacturer. Gülbirlik is the world's biggest rose-oil producer, with four processing plants handling 320 tonnes of petals daily. If you haven't time for touring, local shops (and bus stations) sell all rose-related creams and perfumes.

From the Çarşı terminal downtown, half-hourly buses and dolmuşes serve Eğirdir (30 minutes) while less frequent ones serve Ağlasun (for Sagalassos). Further afield, buses also serve Antalya (two hours), Burdur (45 minutes), Denizli (three hours), İzmir (six hours) and Konya (five hours).

The ski centre has basic accommodation, and there's the five-star **Sirene Davraz Mountain Resort** (www.sirene.com.tr/sirene davras.asp), though staying in Isparta or Eğirdir is cheaper and not difficult.

ANTIOCHEIA-IN-PISIDIA

About 2km from Yalvaç is **Antiocheia-in-Pisidia** (admission ₺3; ⊘9am-6pm), a largely unexcavated ancient Pisidian city. St Paul of Tarsus visited several times (as recorded in the Bible's Acts of the Apostles). On the strategic borderland of ancient Phrygia and Pisidia, it became an important Byzantine city, but was abandoned in the 8th century after Arab attacks.

After the gate, a Roman road leads up past triumphal-arch foundations, then turns right to the **theatre**. Further uphill, on a flat area surrounded by a semicircular rock wall, is the main **shrine**. Originally dedicated to the Anatolian mother goddess Cybele, and later to the moon god Men, it became an imperial Roman cult temple of Augustus. Leftwards you'll see the **nymphaeum**, once a spring.

Several Antiocheian **aqueduct arches** are visible across the fields. Downhill from the nymphaeum, the ruined **Roman baths** feature several excavated large chambers, and a largely intact original ceiling. The foundations of **St Paul's Basilica** also remain.

Nearby **Yalvaç Museum** (Yalvaç Müzesi; admission ₺3; ⊘8.30am-5.30pm Tue-Sun) has maps and a modest artefact collection.

Sagalassos

To visit the sprawling ruins of **Sagalassos** (admission ₺5; ⊘7.30am-6pm), high amid the jagged peaks of Ak Dağ (White Mountain) is to approach myth; indeed, the urban ruins set in stark mountains seem to illuminate the Sagalassian perception of a sacred harmony between nature, architecture and the great gods of antiquity.

The very antithesis of the 'Ephesus experience', Sagalassos has neither tour buses nor crowds; sometimes the visiting archaeologists or sheep wandering the mountains outnumber tourists. This is a place for getting perspective, for feeling the raw Anatolian wind on your face, and of course, for seeing some very impressive ancient sites. Thus, while you can rush

through in about 90 minutes, take the time to linger, and take it all in from on high.

Sagalassos is among the Mediterranean's largest archaeological projects. Although repeatedly devastated by earthquakes, it was never pillaged, and reconstruction is slowly moving ahead. After visiting, see the Burdur Museum, where the important finds are kept.

History

Sagalassos was founded about 1200 BC by a warlike tribe of 'Peoples from the Sea' seeking defensive positioning. A large swamp (perhaps even a lake) probably covered part of the lowland where today's village stands. Ancient Sagalassos would thus have been protected on three sides by mountains, and on the other by water.

Sagalassos later became second only to Antiocheia-in-Pisidia in Pisidian society. The locals adopted Greek cultural, linguistic and religious mores. Alexander the Great claimed it in 333 BC, and its oldest ruins date from the Hellenistic period he opened. Although most surviving structures are Roman, inscriptions are in Greek (the ancient world's lingua franca).

Sagalassos prospered under the Romans. Its grain export, mountain springs and iron ore making it economically important and self-sufficient. Despite the high elevation, Sagalassos was well-integrated into Rome's Anatolian road system. In the 4th century, the city became a Christian, Byzantine outpost. However, plague and disasters (like the 590 earthquake) damaged the city's sophisticated structures and dispersed its surviving population. After a massive 7th-century quake, Sagalassos was abandoned; survivors moved to villages or occupied fortified hamlets amid the rubble.

Seljuk warriors defeated the last Byzantine defenders in the mid-13th century, though the remote and largely ruined city would have little strategic value for the Ottomans. And so it slumbered for centuries, guarded by sheep and birds, until 1706, when a French traveller commissioned by King Louis XIV 'discovered' it. Yet it was not until 1824 that the ancient city's actual name was finally deciphered, by a British reverend and antiquarian, FVJ Arundell.

Visiting the Site

At the ticket booth, request the key to the oft-closed Neon Library. From the entranceway you can turn up to the right, starting from the top and working your way down-hill (a somewhat steeper approach), or proceed from the bottom and work your way up and around.

Following the latter route, see the marble colonnaded street that marked the city's southern entrance from the lowland valleys. The lack of wheel indentations suggests that mainly pedestrians used this street, which is the spine and central axis of Sagalassos, stretching upwards through it.

From the bottom, it appears that the city's terraced fountains are actually one triple-tiered tower of water – an impressive optical illusion. Passing through the Tiberian gate see the lower agora, and the massive reconstructed Roman baths complex to the right. At the agora's rear, the Hadrianic nymphaeum stands flanked by the mountainside. The well-preserved former fountain here contains elaborate sculptures of four (mostly headless) mythic Nereids and Muses. A ruined Odeon sits just beyond.

Next is the Upper Agora, once the main civic area and political centre. Thanks to recent restoration, it boasts Sagalassos' most impressive attraction: the Antonine Nymphaeum, a huge fountain complex some 9m high and 28m across. Originally wrought from seven different kinds of stone, the fountain was ornately decorated with Medusa heads and fish motifs. Although it collapsed in the 590 earthquake, the rubble lay clustered, aiding modern restorers. The impressive result is a massive structure supported by rows of thick columns (including bright blue marble ones in the centre), through which huge sheets of water gush into a lengthy receptacle. The fountain is bedecked by statues, including a large marble Dionysus replica (the original is in the Burdur Museum).

The agora's western edge is flanked by the bouleuterion; some of its seating remains intact. Rising over the fountain in the north-west corner is a 14m-high heroon (hero's monument). In 333 BC, Alexander the Great had a statue of himself erected here (it's now in the Burdur Museum too). From here, peer over the agora's southern edge to spot the macellon (food market), dedicated to Emperor Marcus Aurelius, with its trademark Corinthian columns. Note the tholos in the middle; the deep fountain was used to sell live fish.

WORTH A TRIP

BURDUR MUSEUM

Try to add the **Burdur Museum** (Burdur Müzesi; admission ₺5; ⏰9am-6pm Tue-Sun) to your Sagalassos adventure (otherwise, hourly minibuses serve Burdur in 45 minutes from Isparta's otogar for ₺6). Along with Sagalassos' most important Hellenistic and Roman statues, the museum exhibits Neolithic finds from the nearby Hacılar and Kuruçay mounds, exquisitely carved ancient sarcophagi and more.

Since only unimportant ruins lay scattered westward, turn right and up into the hills for the late-Hellenistic Doric fountain-house (its piping is now reattached to its original Roman-era source). A bit further is Sargalassos' only restored covered building, the Neon Library, with its fine mosaic floor. In the darkness at rear, an original Greek inscription commemorates Flavius Severianus Neon, a noble who funded the library in AD 120. The back podium contained curving and rectangular niches for storing reading material. The library was modified over following centuries, with the striking mosaic of Achilles' departure for Troy having been commissioned during the brief reign of Emperor Julian (361–363), whose unsuccessful attempt to restore paganism to the Orthodox empire augured his demise.

Finally, atop the hill is Sagalassos' 9000-seat Roman theatre. Earthquakes have damaged the seating rows, but it's still among Turkey's most complete of such structures. Just above its top steps, walk parallel with the theatre through its eery tunnel, where performers and contestants once entered (note that it's dark, strewn with debris and has a very low exit point). The bluff east of here offers stunning panoramic views over the city, mountains and plains.

❶ Information

Since Sagalassos sprawls upwards across steep, prickly terrain, wear sturdy shoes and long pants. Even on hot and sunny days it's often windy, and clouds can suddenly arrive (bring an extra shirt or sweater). In summer, start early to avoid the midday sun on this treeless and exposed site. Parking's free, but driving the final 7km up is on a narrow, winding road without guard rails – you may feel safer on an organised excursion.

It takes from 1½ to 3½ hours to do Sagalassos. Signage is excellent, with detailed and colourful representations of the various structures. From Monday to Thursday in summer, Belgian and British archaeologists will gladly show you around. Out of season, it's basically all yours.

The ticket office has informative pamphlets and sells drinks, but for shops and services visit **Ağlasun** (7km below). Ağlasun has a few small eateries for a quick lunch before you head home – try the excellent pide at **Tadim Pide ve Kebap Salonu** (Fatih Caddesi; pide ₺5-9; ☺9am-7pm) halfway down the main street.

❶ Getting There & Away

An organised trip or shared taxi from Eğirdir costs from ₺50 to ₺80 per person. Inquire at your pension, or the lakefront Eğirdir Outdoor Center (p306), which offers different packages.

Otherwise, a one-hour dolmuş ride from Isparta's Çarşı terminal serves Ağlasun hourly from 6am to 5pm. (In summer, the last Ağlasun–Isparta dolmuş leaves at 8pm.)

From Ağlasun, it's a steep and winding 7km trip up the mountain just to reach the ticket office. The dolmuş driver might accept an extra ₺25 to bring you up and wait an hour, but anything longer will cost you more. Again, organising the trip from Eğirdir is recommended.

Antalya & the Turquoise Coast

Includes »

Best Places to Eat

» İkbal (p345)
» Dalyan La Vie (p316)
» Levissi Garden (p331)
» Reis (p324)
» Çiftlik (p341)

Best Places to Stay

» Hoyran Wedre Country House (p350)
» Hotel Villa Mahal (p337)
» Tuvana Hotel (p356)
» Happy Caretta (p314)
» Myland Nature (p352)

Why Go?

Turkey's Turquoise Coast is a huge region of endless azure sea, lined with kilometres of sandy beaches and backed by mountains rising up to almost 3000m. It's a winning combination no matter how you look at it, but add to that a surfeit of ancient ruins strewn through the aromatic scrub, pine forests, and a large selection of sports and activities, and you've hit pay dirt.

By far the most dramatic way to see this stretch of coastline is by skimming through the crystal waters aboard a *gület* (traditional wooden yacht) or by following sections of the 500km-long Lycian Way on foot, high above what the Turks call the Akdeniz (literally, 'White Sea').

When to Go
Antalya

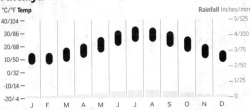

Mar & Apr See the hills come alive with colourful spring bulb flowers.

Jul & Aug It's peak season and packed, but there's lots of fun to be had, especially for families.

Dec & Jan Cool but mostly bright, sunny days are perfect for walking in the hills.

Antalya & the Turquoise Coast Highlights

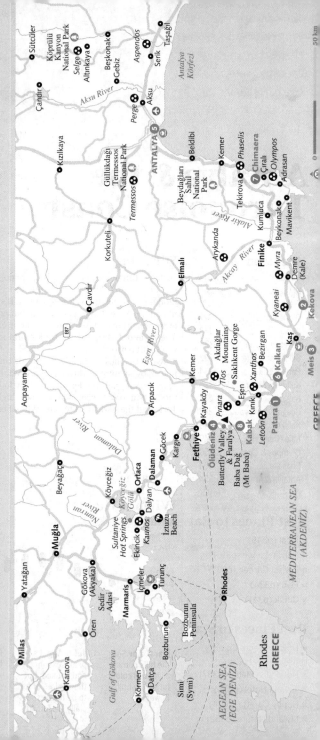

1 Potter around the ruins of **Patara** (p335) before diving into the Mediterranean from its 20km-long beach

2 Kayak over the sunken city of **Üçağız** (p347) in Kekova

3 Experience 'instant Greece' in **Meis** (p346) just a shortboat ride from Kaş

4 Sample a stage of the Lycian Way long-distance

walking trail from the cliffs above **Ölüdeniz** (p327)

5 View the Ottoman splendour of **Kaleiçi** (p354), Antalya's historic quarter, and

stroll through a world-class museum

6 Dine in **Kalkan** (p338) an epi(curean)-centre of Mediterranean and Modern Turkish cooking

7 Marvel at the timeless **Chimaera** (p352), still ablaze after on the slopes of Mt Olympos

8 Chill and centre yourself while lux-camping at **Kabak** (p329)

Dalyan

☑0252 / POP 4865

Once a sleepy farming community and now increasingly a package-tour destination, river-side Dalyan has somehow managed to retain its peaceful, almost laid-back atmosphere. It makes an excellent base for exploring the surrounding fertile waterways, in particular Lake Köyceğiz and the turtle nesting grounds at İztuzu Beach. Dalyan's most famous feature is the impressive cliff-side ruins of ancient Kaunos, but you won't be alone when visiting; summer afternoons bring a virtual armada of excursion boats in from Marmaris and Fethiye.

◉ Sights & Activities

Kaunos   RUINS
(admission ₺8; ☉8.30am-7pm May-Oct, 8.30am-5.30pm Nov-Apr) Founded in the 9th century BC, Kaunos (or Caunus) was an important Carian city by 400 BC. Right on the border with Lycia, its culture reflected aspects of both empires. The famous **Kings' Tombs** in the cliffs southwest of the centre, for instance, are largely Lycian style. If you don't take a boat excursion to the site, walk south from town along Maraş Caddesi to the western end of Kaunos Sokak to view the tombs across the Dalyan River.

Apart from the clifftop tombs, the **theatre** is very well preserved; nearby there are parts of an **acropolis** and other structures, such as baths, fountains, a temple and defensive walls. The curious wooden structures in the river are fishing weirs *(dalyanlar)*, from where the town and its river takes their name. Two-hour guided boat trips cost around ₺20. Alternatively, a private rowing boat moored next to the Saki (p316) restaurant will take you across the river from where you can walk to Kaunos in 20 minutes.

İztuzu Beach   BEACH
(İztuzu Kumsalı) An excellent swimming beach 13km south of Dalyan's centre and accessible via road and the Dalyan River, 4.5km-long İztuzu (or Turtle) Beach is one of the Mediterranean nesting sites of the loggerhead turtle, and special rules to protect it are enforced. Although the beach is open to the public during the day, night-time visits – 8pm to 8am – are prohibited from May to September. A line of wooden stakes on the beach indicates the nest sites, and visitors are asked to keep behind them to avoid disturbing the nests. At the southern end of the beach is the headquarters of the **Sea Turtle Research, Rescue & Rehabilitation Centre** (Deniz Kaplumbağaları Araştırma, Kurtarma ve Rehabilitasyon Merkezi, DEKAMER; ☑289 0077; http://caretta.pamukkale.edu.tr; ☉10am-6pm), established in 2009 largely through the influence of June Haimoff (Kaptan June, see p317) whose reconstructed *baraka* (beach hut) now serves as a small museum to her life and work. The centre, which can be visited daily by guided tour (donations welcome), has saved and returned to the sea dozens of loggerhead and green turtles, and you'll see various creatures injured by fishing hooks and nets, as well as by boat propellers, being treated. Highly recommended. Minibuses (₺3.50, 20 minutes) run to the beach from the **main mosque** (Cumhuriyet Meydanı) in the centre of Dalyan every half-hour in high season.

Boat Excursions   CRUISE
You can save yourself a lot of money and hassle by taking boats run by the **Dalyan Kooperatifi** (☑284 2094), whose members moor on the river southwest of the main square. It's a fairly easy process, but if you need help, ask for Eddy (or call him on ☑0541 505 0777).

Boats usually leave the quayside at 10am or 10.30am to cruise to Lake Köyceğiz (p317) and the Sultaniye hot springs (p318), the ruins of Kaunos and İztuzu Beach on the Mediterranean. These good-value tours, including lunch, cost ₺30 per person.

If you can drum up a team of like-minded folk, you can hire a passenger boat that holds from eight to 12 people. A two-hour tour just to Kaunos costs ₺80 for the boat; if you want to visit the Sultaniye hot springs as well, count on three hours and ₺130.

Boats belonging to the cooperative also operate a river dolmuş service between the town and İztuzu Beach, charging ₺8 to ₺10 for the return trip. In high summer boats head out every 20 minutes from 10am or 10.30am to 2pm and return between 1pm and 6pm. Avoid any trips advertising themselves as 'turtle-spotting' tours.

Kaunos Tours   ADVENTURE SPORTS
(☑284 2816; www.kaunostours.com; Sarısu Sokak 1/A) On the main square opposite the landmark **sea turtles statue**, Kaunos Tours offers any number of organised activities both on and off the water, including sea

Dalyan

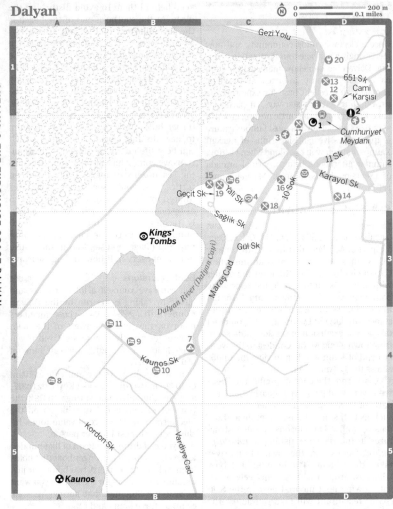

kayaking and canoeing (each ₺70), trekking (from ₺40), canyoning (₺70) and jeep safari (₺65). Prices include lunch.

Ethos Dalyan Dive Centre DIVING
(☑0555 412 5438, 284 2332; www.dalyandive.com; Yalı Sokak 5) Other agencies in Dalyan offer snorkelling and diving trips but why not stick with the pros? A day-long excursion including two dives and lunch is around ₺125.

🛏 Sleeping

Happy hunting grounds for hotels and pensions is Maraş Caddesi, a 1km-long road running north–south that ends at a sharp bend in the river and carries on as Kaunos Sokak.

TOP CHOICE **Happy Caretta** HOTEL €€
(☑0532 645 8400, 284 2109; www.happycaretta .com; Kaunos Sokak 26; s/d ₺120/170; ❄@❋) National Geographic staff have stayed here in the past and you may too, enjoying the magical garden of cypress trees, palms and caged songbirds. The 14 rooms are simple and on the small side, but comfortable, quiet and stylishly decorated with natural materials. The lovely boat and leisure dock waiting for you to take the plunge is a plus, and

Dalyan

the view of the illuminated Kings' Tombs by night is priceless. Affable owners İlknur and Münir make their own plum and fig jams from their fruit trees and lay on a superb four-course home-cooked meal (₺45) when pre-ordered.

Kilim Hotel　　　　　　　　　　HOTEL €€
(☑0532 645 8400, 284 2253; www.kilimhotel.com; Kaunos Sokak 7; s/d/f ₺60/100/120; ※@🛜🌊) Dynamic owners Becky and Emrah preside over this property with 20 rooms in both a kilim- and art-filled midrange hotel and a more rustic annexe across the road and near the river. There's a ramp for wheelchair access; Pilates workouts three times a week cost ₺10.

Kamarca House Hotel　　　BOUTIQUE HOTEL €€€
(☑0532 283 9001, 284 4517; www.kamarcahotel.com; Tepearası Köyü; r €160, suite €470; ※🛜🌊) If you're seeking luxury amidst absolute tranquillity head for this boutique hotel in Tepearası, a tiny village set in lush vegetation some 8km northeast of Dalyan. The five rooms and suites are contained in a main building and annexe and are wonderfully decorated in a tactile mix of natural wood and stone, antique furnishings and original artwork. Hostess Kamer's cooking is legendary; she ran her own restaurant in the USA. For full board add €75.

Midas Pension　　　　　　　PENSION €€
(☑284 2195; www.midasdalyan.com; Kaunos Sokak 32; s/d €35/40; ※🛜) Selçuk and Saadet Nur are the welcoming hosts of this family-friendly riverside pension complete with wa-

terside deck-cum-dock and groovy outside bar. The 10 rooms are smartly furnished, with private bathrooms attached. It's almost at the end of Kaunos Sokak.

Bahaus Resort Dalyan　　　　HOSTEL €
(☑0533 688 2988, 284 5050; www.bahausresort.com; İztuzu Yolu 25; d €12-18, tw €25, dm €30; ※@🛜🌊) A 'hostel resort' may sound like the ultimate oxymoron, but this is the real McCoy. About 8km from the centre along the road to İztuzu Beach, the Bahaus Resort is spread over an enormous farmlike property and has both dormitory (rooms with four to 10 beds) and private en-suite accommodation. The pool is a delight, food at breakfast locally sourced, and we love the telescope in the common room just begging for a little moon-gazing.

Dalyan Resort　　　　　　　RESORT €€€
(☑0530 665 990, 284 5499; www.dalyanresort.com; 114 Sokak 12; s/d/ste €75/120/150; ※🛜🌊) This snazzy 58-room hotel is on its own little peninsula that juts into the river about 1200m from the town centre. The service is discreet and there are full views of the Kings' Tombs from the classy pool. The health centre and spa are excellent; try the elegant Turkish hamam (full treatment €20).

Çınar Sahil Otel　　　　　　HOTEL €€
(☑0555 507 3035, 284 2402; www.cinarsahilhotel.com; Yalı Sokak 14; s/d ₺70/90; ※🛜) Fronting the river and surrounded by plane trees, this simple but very central pension has 10 impeccably clean and renovated rooms and a terrace with possibly the best views in town.

Ask for one of the four rooms with balcony and river view. Barbecues are organised in season, and there's a boat accommodating up to four people for rent (₺90).

Dalyan Camping
CAMPING GROUND €

(☑0506 882 9173, 284 5316; www.dalyancamping .net; Maraş Caddesi 144; per person tent/caravan ₺10/30, bungalow s ₺15-40, d ₺20-70; ☺Apr-Oct) Owner Servet will welcome you to this compact, well-shaded site centrally located by the river and opposite the tombs. The nine bungalows come in three sizes; note that the smallest have no en-suite bathrooms. The largest (No 7) has a loft and the Old Village House (No 2) is downright luxurious. Laundry costs ₺10 per load.

✗ Eating & Drinking

Dalyan's restaurant scene swings between high quality and touristy/ordinary, so follow our advice. Saturday is market day in Dalyan. There are a host of bars and other drinking spots along Maraş Caddesi.

TOP CHOICE Dalyan La Vie
MODERN TURKISH €€€

(☑284 4142; www.dalyanlavie.com; Sağlik Sokak 5; mains ₺18-32) What was the tired Riverside Restaurant has metamorphosed into one of the most exciting new restaurants on the Turquoise Coast – perhaps because most of the kitchen staff have been imported from İstanbul. The seafood dishes, especially the casseroles, are highly recommended, desserts are Turkish traditional with a twist, and the location on the river is enviable.

Saki
MEZE €€€

(☑284 5212; Geçit Sokak; mains ₺12-28; ☺10am-11pm) With a brilliant (and breezy) location right on the riverfront just over from Dalyan La Vie (they're friends), this very authentic eatery serves some of the most wholesome Turkish food in Dalyan. There's no menu; choose from the glass cabinet of homemade meze (₺7 to ₺12) as well as meat and fish dishes.

Kordon
SEAFOOD €€€

(☑284 2261; Çarşi İçi 2; fish mains ₺20-25) Dalyan's long-established (since 1987!) fish restaurant, the Kordon has a commanding position on the river just up from where the excursion boats moor. Ichtyphobes can choose from a large selection of steaks and grills, and there are a half-dozen vegetarian choices on offer.

Atay Dostlar Sofrasi
PIDE €

(☑284 2156; Camı Karşısı 10; mains ₺6-8; ☺7am-midnight) You'll find competent staff and unbeatable prices at this local workers' restaurant where visitors are greeted warmly and fed well. There's a point-and-pick counter and dishes are fresh daily. It's opposite the mosque and information centre.

Mai Steakhouse
RESTAURANT €€

(☑284 2642; Sulungur Caddesi 1; ₺12-20) This new eatery in the heart of Dalyan is making quite a name for itself locally. But it is not always what it seems. There's lots more than steak available and though decorated bright blue-and-white, Mai's heart is Turkish, not Greek.

Chinatown
CHINESE, INDIAN €€

(☑284 4478; Gülpınar Caddesi 16; mains ₺10-28) OK, it ain't going to win any culinary awards but if you need the occasional fix of Asian-style rice and/or noodles (₺8 to ₺15), this place can assist. There's a good choice of vegetarian dishes and – something new – a stab at Indian food.

Dalyan İz
CAFE €€

(☑0542 451 5451; www.dalyaniz.com; sandwiches & salads ₺10-15, cakes ₺5-8; ☺9.30am-7pm) This excellent addition to Dalyan's social scene is an art gallery and shop selling hand-painted ceramics and tiles as much as a garden cafe. It's hugely popular with expats in Dalyan and a great source of local information.

Demet Pastanesi
CAFE €

(Maraş Caddesi 39; coffee ₺2; ☺7.30am-midnight) With excellent pastries and tantalising Turkish desserts (₺4.50), this is also a great place for breakfast and picnic supplies. The hazelnut and walnut tart (₺5) is to die for.

Jazz Bar Dalyan
COCKTAIL BAR

(www.jazzbardalyan.com; Gülpınar Caddesi) Facing the harbour just north of the centre, this lively place is where to head for jazz, live or canned, till the wee hours (open daily till 3am). Cocktails deftly shaken and/or stirred by expert mixologists.

❶ Information

Hadigari Internet Cafe (Karayol Sokak 25/A; per hr ₺2; ☺10am-2am) East of Maraş Caddesi and just up from the Dalyan İz cafe.
Tourist Office (☑284 4235; Cumhuriyet Medanı; ☺8am-noon & 1-5.30pm Mon-Fri) Keeps banker's hours in a modern glass-walled kiosk on the main square just off Çarşi İçi north of the mosque.

LOCAL KNOWLEDGE

KAPTAN JUNE: MARINE ENVIRONMENTALIST

Sea turtles were the last thing on Briton June Haimoff's mind when she sailed into Dalyan on her boat *Bouboulina* in 1975. But after 'Kaptan June' - as the locals had affectionately dubbed her – set up house in a *baraka* (hut) on İztuzu Beach, got to observe the *caretta caretta* (loggerhead turtles) at ground level and fended off, with the help of a number of Turkish and foreign environmentalists, plans to develop the beach into a 1800-bed Marmaris-style hotel resort, they became her life's work. Kaptan June set up the **Sea Turtles Conservation Foundation** (www.dalyanturtles.com) and was awarded an MBE in 2011 at age 89.

What is the greatest threat at present to the sea turtles? Humans. The proliferation of dams and roads has devastated lots of the Mediterranean coast. The turtles' habitats are being destroyed for the sake of tourist development. As for injuries to the turtles, more than 90% are human-inflicted and come from fishing hooks and nets and, most commonly, boat propellers.

What steps has the foundation taken to reduce these? Our first project was to give away 90 locally manufactured propeller guards to excursion boats on the Dalyan River and there are plans to hand out another 100. We are now looking into sourcing and distributing biodegradable fishing line which won't harm the turtles if they happen to ingest it.

How can visitors to İztuzu Beach reduce their impact? The urge to see a turtle in nature is not easily satisfied; they only come out at night during mating season and the beach is closed then. Some boat companies offer 'turtle-spotting' tours by day and attract the turtles by feeding them their favourite crab or chicken, which is not suitable for them. Avoid these at all costs. Only join tours run by boats with propeller guards; these can be identified by a a flag bearing the foundation's logo. The boat cooperative, especially the younger captains, has been very supportive. Once visitors use the services of these captains exclusively, others will follow suit.

❶ Getting There & Away

Minibuses stop in Cumhuriyet Meydanı, near the main mosque. There are no direct minibuses from here to Dalaman. First take a minibus to Ortaca (₺3.5, every 25 minutes in high season, every hour in low season, 14km) and change there. At the Ortaca otogar, buses go to Köyceğiz (₺6, 25 minutes, 22km) and Dalaman (₺5, 15 minutes, 9km). A taxi to Dalaman airport from Dalyan costs ₺80.

Köyceğiz

📞0252 / POP 8900

A short distance off the D400, the main coastal highway, this hardscrabble county seat lies on the northern side of Köyceğiz Gölü, the large and serene 'Lake Köyceğiz' linked to the Mediterranean by the Dalyan River. As beautiful (and ecologically significant) as it is, a brackish lake is not major competition for the Med, and this farming community attracts only modest tourism, depending still on citrus fruits, pomegranates, honey and and a bit of cotton for its livelihood. The region is also famous for its Oriental sweetgum trees *(Liquidambar orientalis)*, the sap of which is used to produce frankincense.

◉ Sights & Activities

Köyceğiz (keuy-*jay*-iz) is a town for strolling. Hit the lakeshore promenade called Kordon Boyu and walk past the pleasant town park, shady tea gardens and waterfront restaurants. Most pensions have bicycles available free for guests, so take a ride out to the surrounding orchards and farmland. The road along the western shore of the lake to the Sultaniye mud pools offers superb views. It's 26km by road to the springs or you can take a boat excursion from the promenade. The **Köyceğiz-Dalyan Nature Reserve** has a growing reputation among outdoor types for its excellent hiking and cycling.

Köyceğiz Waterfall   WATERFALL

There's a small waterfall 7km northwest of town where locals go to swim in the warm weather. Take any minibus heading west towards Marmaris and Muğla and tell the driver you want to get off at the *şelale* (shay-*lah*-lay) or 'waterfall'. It's about a 15-minute walk from the highway.

Sultaniye Hot Springs
SPRING

(Sultaniye Kaplıcaları; admission ₺8) For some good (and dirty) fun, head for the Sultaniye Hot Springs, on the southeast shore of Lake Köyceğiz, which are accessible from both Köyceğiz and Dalyan. These bubbling hot mud pools (temperatures can reach 39°C) contain mildly radioactive mineral waters that are rich in chloride, sodium, hydrogen sulphide and bromide; drinking and bathing in the water is said to have a relaxing and beneficial effect on sufferers of rheumatism, skin disorders and bronchitis. At the smaller baths just before the Dalyan River joins the lake, pamper yourself with a restorative body-pack of mud in a steaming sulphur pool. To get here from Köyceğiz, take the bus headed for Ekincik (₺6) at 9.30am, which will drop you off at the springs. From Dalyan, take a dolmuş boat (₺10, 30 minutes), which leaves when full (every half-hour or so in summer, every hour otherwise) from the riverfront.

Boat Excursions
BOAT TOUR

You can take boat trips across the lake south to Dalyan and the Kaunos ruins for ₺15 to ₺30 per person including lunch.

🛏 Sleeping

Most pensions and hotels are either on or just off Kordon Boyu along the lake.

TOP CHOICE Flora Hotel
HOTEL €€

(☑0535 320 8567, 262 4976; www.florahotel .info; Kordon Boyu 96; s/d ₺50/90, 2/4-person apt ₺120/200; ❄@🖤) This backpacker favourite gets our vote as the best place in Köyceğiz, mostly because of its enthusiastic and very 'green' owner Alp, who can arrange walks into the nearby Gölgeli Mountains for bird-watching (almost 150 species have been spotted) as well as fishing trips in the lake (catch and release) and on the sea. Some of the 16 rooms have balconies with views to the lake and the four apartments include a kitchenette. There are a couple of kayaks and 10 bicycles for guests' use.

Hotel Alila
HOTEL €

(☑262 1150; www.hotelalila.com; Emeksiz Caddesi 13; s/d ₺45/65; ❄🖤) Full of character, the bougainvillea-bedecked Alila has two dozen simple rooms, 16 of which have direct views of the lake from small balconies. The friend-

ly owner Ömer runs the place professionally and attends to every detail (right down to the swan-folded towels).

Kaunos Hotel
HOTEL €

(☑262 3730; www.kaunoshotel.com; Ali İhsan Kalmaz Caddesi 29; s/d €40/55; ❄@🖤) This newly opened salmon-coloured colossus commands a prominent position on the waterfront, with full views of the lake from 50 of the 73 rooms. The rooms, all of which have balconies and showers, are comfortable and pin-neat rather than remarkable. Spend most of your time at the huge terrace pool.

Tango Hostel & Pension
HOSTEL, PENSION €

(☑0533 811 2478, 262 2501; www.tangopension.com; Ali İhsan Kalmaz Caddesi 112; dm/s/d ₺25/40/60; ❄@🖤) Managed by Sahin, the local school sports teacher, this place is big on activities including boat trips (₺20), trekking (₺25) and rafting (₺60). Prices include lunch. The 26 rooms (including six dorms with a half-dozen beds each) are bright, cheerful and well maintained, and there's a pleasant garden. It's away from the water and very much a party place. Bikes are free.

Fulya Pension
PENSION €

(☑262 2301; fulyapension@mynet.com; Ali İhsan Kalmaz Caddesi 88; s/d ₺20/40; ❄@🖤) This brilliant budget option, set back from the lake, has 16 spick-and-span rooms with balconies, and there's a large roof terrace with a bar and occasional live music. Bikes are available free of charge, and boat trips (₺20, including lunch) to the local attractions are a bargain. Guests love the breakfasts here.

🍴 Eating

There are several predominantly fish restaurants bunched up along the lake and lots of cheap and cheerful eateries off the main square. You'll find several places selling *köyceğiz lokması,* a local speciality of fried dough drenched in syrup.

The local market is held every Monday near the police station opposite the tourist office at the southern end of Atatürk Bulvarı.

Colıba
MODERN TURKISH €€

(☑262 2987; Cengiz Topel Caddesi 64; mains ₺8-17; ◷10am-midnight) In this very stylish restaurant, cool-headed staff serve delicious *or-dövr* (mixed meze platter; ₺10) and *alabalık* (trout; ₺15), though the grills (₺12) are more of a bargain. Whitewashed and wooden, the Colıba has a shaded terrace with views of the lake. Warm welcome.

Thera Fish Restaurant   SEAFOOD €€
(☑0541 833 6154; Cengiz Topel Caddesi; mains ₺12-15; ☺9am-midnight) On the other side of the Coliba you can pick your fish from a large tank on the waterfront terrace here. The red mullet fillets (₺16) are excellent, as is the sea bream (₺15). The grilled prawns (₺30) are ideal for a special occasion and to share.

Mutlu Kardeşler   PIDE €
(☑262 2482; Fevzipaşa Caddesi; köfte & kebap ₺8, pide ₺4-6; ☺7am-11pm) This simple and exceptionally friendly place off the main square, much loved by locals, has tables on a little shaded terrace.

ⓘ Information
Tourist Office (☑262 4703; ☺8.30am-5pm Mon-Fri) South of the main square and almost on the lake; stocks brochures and photocopies of a simple hand-drawn map.

ⓘ Getting There & Away
The otogar serving Köyceğiz is just off the main highway, about 2km from the lake; dolmuşes (₺1) run every 15 minutes or so into town.
Buses go to Dalaman (₺6, 30 minutes, 26km), Marmaris (₺10, one hour, 63km), Ortaca (₺5, 25 minutes, 22km) and Fethiye (₺10, two hours, 65km) hourly.

Dalaman
☑0252 / POP 24,600
Little has changed for this agricultural town since the ever-expanding international airport was built on the neighbouring river delta, with most arrivals moving on immediately.

It's just over 5km from the airport to the town of Dalaman and another 5km from there to the D400 coastal highway. Besides seasonal flights to many European cities, there are between four and six daily flights from Dalaman to İstanbul year-round, costing around ₺85 one way. In high season, Havaş buses meet incoming Turkish Airlines flights. The fare to Fethiye is ₺20 and to Marmaris ₺25. A taxi into Dalaman town is an extortionate ₺30 to ₺35.

From Dalaman's otogar, near the junction of Kenan Evren Bulvarı and Atatürk Caddesi, you can catch buses to Antalya (₺30, four hours, 335km), Köyceğiz (₺8, 30 minutes, 26km) and Marmaris (₺15, 1½ hours, 90km). All routes north and east pass through either Muğla (₺14, two hours, 87km) or Fethiye (₺8, one hour, 46km).

Göcek
☑0252 / POP 4160
Göcek (*geuh*-jek) is the western Mediterranean's high-end yacht spot and the attractive bay makes a relaxing alternative to Fethiye despite all the building going on in the hills surrounding the town. There's a small but clean swimming beach at the western end of the quay, and boat-charter companies scattered throughout the town.

🛌 Sleeping
Villa Danlin   HOTEL €€
(☑645 1521; www.villadanlin.com; Çarşı İçi; s €55-70, d €65-80; ❄️🛜☀️) This hotel, in a charming little building you'll pass on the main street, only contains a lobby and three rooms; the other 10 are in a modern extension out in the back, looking onto a generous-sized pool. Almost but not quite 'boutique', the Danlin is tantalisingly close to the sea but offers no views.

Efe Hotel   LUXURY HOTEL €€€
(☑645 2646; www.efehotelgocek.com; 38 Sokak; s/d €80/90, ste €100-130; ❄️🛜☀️) Hidden in a lush garden about 200m north of the Skopea Marina, Göcek's most ambitious hotel to date has 19 large and bright rooms, a half-Olympic-sized pool and restful mountain views. The garden bar is a delight.

Tufan Pansiyon   PENSION €
(☑0546 921 7460, 645 1334; Belediye Marina; s & d ₺50-60; ❄️) In the centre and just 25m from the sea, the family-run Tufan has eight small but spotless and rather sweet rooms, half of which have sea views from a shared balcony.

A&B Home Hotel   HOTEL €€
(☑0532 255 2025, 645 1820; www.abhomehotel.com; Turgut Özal Caddesi; s €50-70, d €60-80; ❄️🛜☀️) The 11 smallish rooms here all contain wrought-iron bedsteads and are decorated in various shades of yellow, but the real boon here is the medium-sized pool on the attractive front terrace. A good breakfast buffet is served. Sea views from room 201.

Göcek Dim Hotel   HOTEL €€
(☑0532 796 2798, 645 1294; www.dimhotel.com; Sokak 14; r €30-60; ❄️🛜☀️) With 15 simple but well-furnished rooms and a pleasant terrace, medium-sized pool and a location just opposite the beach, this hotel to the west of the

centre offers good value. All rooms have a fridge and TV.

Eating & Drinking

Can Restaurant
SEAFOOD €€

(☑645 1507; Skopea Marina; mains ₺14-27; ⊘7am-midnight) Set back from the seafront but with a lovely terrace shaded by an old yucca tree and beachside seating, this local favourite serves a great selection of meze (₺6 to ₺9, seafood meze ₺10 to ₺20), some of them rather unusual. The house speciality is *tuzda balık* (fish baked in salt); expect to pay from ₺75 per kilogram.

West Cafe & Bistro
INTERNATIONAL €€

(☑645 2794; www.westcafegocek.com; Turgut Özal Caddesi; mains ₺9-21; 🛜) As the name suggests, it's Western in cuisine and feel, with bacon for breakfast (₺8 to ₺14) – supposedly the best English breakfast in town – and tarts for tea. If you're tired of kebaps it makes a nice change. There's comfortable alfresco seating too, with award-winning views.

Kebab Hospital Antep Sofrası
KEBAP €€

(☑645 1873; Turgut Özal Caddesi; mains ₺14-18; ⊘8am-midnight) Apparently this simple place (backing on to the water) is where everyone in Göcek comes for their kebaps (and pide and pizza and *lahmacun*), whether or not they're ailing. Service is friendly and efficient.

Dice Cafe
BAR, CAFE

(☑620 8514; Safı Villalar Önü; 🛜) Snappy little bar on the waterfront to the west has good mojitos (₺15) and free wireless connection. It's a great place for a sundowner.

Shopping

Muse Jewellery
JEWELLERY

(☑0533 361 6054; Turgut Özal Caddesi) Amid all the chandlers and shops selling boat supplies is this uberposh bling shop selling antique Ottoman jewellery. And with most of the baubles priced in euros with at least five digits, you'll almost have to be a sultan to afford them.

Getting There & Away

Buses drop you at the petrol station on the main road, from where it's a 1km walk to the centre. Minibuses drive into the main square, with its requisite bust of Atatürk, a PTT and ATMs. Minibuses depart every half-hour for Fethiye (₺5, 45 minutes, 30km). For Dalyan, change at Ortaca (₺4, 25 minutes, 19km, hourly).

Fethiye

☑0252 / POP 81,500

In 1958 an earthquake levelled the seaside city of Fethiye (feh-*tee*-yeh), sparing only the remains of the ancient city of Telmessos. More than half a century on and it is once again a prosperous, growing hub of the western Mediterranean. Fethiye is also incredibly low-key for its size, due mostly to the restrictions on high-rise buildings and the transitory nature of the *gület* gangs.

Fethiye's natural harbour is perhaps the region's finest, tucked away in the southern reaches of a broad bay scattered with pretty islands, in particular Şövalye Adası, glimpsed briefly in the new James Bond film *Skyfall*. About 15km south is Ölüdeniz, one of Turkey's seaside hot spots, and the surrounding countryside has many interesting sites to explore, including the ghost town of Kayaköy (or Karmylassos), waiting patiently and in silence just over the hill.

Sights

Telmessos
RUINS

Fethiye's most recognisable sight is the mammoth **Tomb of Amyntas** (admission ₺8; ⊘8am-7pm May-Oct, to 5pm Nov-Apr), an Ionic temple facade carved into the sheer rock face in 350 BC, in honour of 'Amyntas son of Hermapias'. Located south of the centre, it is best visited at sunset. Other, smaller rock tombs lie about 500m to the east.

Behind the harbour in the centre of town are the partly excavated remains of a Roman **theatre** dating from the 2nd century BC. Only about a quarter of its 6000 seats have been excavated.

In town you'll see curious **Lycian stone sarcophagi** dating from around 450 BC. There's one north of the **belediye** (city hall). All were broken into by tomb robbers centuries ago.

On the hillside above (and south of) the town and along the road to Kayaköy, you can't miss the ruined tower of a **Crusader fortress**, built by the Knights of St John at the start of the 15th century on earlier (perhaps Lycian, Greek and Roman) foundations.

Fethiye Museum
MUSEUM

(www.lycianturkey.com/fethiye-museum.htm; 505 Sokak; admission ₺3; ⊘8am-5pm) Focusing on Lycian finds from Telmessos as well as the ancient settlements of Tlos and Kaunos, this museum exhibits pottery, jewellery, small statuary and votive stones (including the im-

ON THE DEEP BLUE SEA

For many travellers a four-day, three-night cruise on a *gület* (traditional sailing boat) along the Turquoise Coast – known as a 'blue voyage' *(mavi yolculuk)* – is the highlight of their trip to Turkey. Although advertised as a voyage between Fethiye and Olympos, the boats usually start (or stop) at Demre and the trip to/from Olympos (1¼ hours) is by bus. From Fethiye, boats usually call in at Ölüdeniz and Butterfly Valley and stop at Kaş, Kalkan and/ or Kekova, with the final night at Gökkaya Bay opposite the eastern end of Kekova. A less common (but perhaps prettier) route is between Marmaris on the Aegean Sea and Fethiye.

Food is usually included in the price, but you sometimes have to pay for water and soft drinks and always for alcohol. All boats are equipped with showers, toilets and smallish but comfortable double and triple cabins (usually between six and eight of them). Most people sleep on mattresses on deck as the boats are not air-conditioned.

A blue voyage is not cheap – depending on the season, the price is usually between €165 and €195 (though some reach as high as €275 in midsummer – so it makes sense to shop around. Here are some suggestions to avoid getting fleeced:

» Ask for recommendations from other travellers.

» Avoid touts at the bus stations and go straight to agencies (see those listed below).

» Bargain but don't necessarily go for the cheapest option because the crew will skimp on food and services.

» Check out your boat if you are on-site and ask to see the guest list.

» Ask whether your captain and crew speak English.

» Don't go for gimmicks such as free water sports; they often prove to be empty promises and boats rarely have insurance for them in case of accidents.

» Confirm whether the boat ever actually uses the sails (though most don't in any case) rather than relying on a diesel engine.

» Avoid buying your ticket in İstanbul, as pensions and commission agents there take a healthy cut.

» Book well ahead – both in high season (July and August) when spaces are in great demand and low season when far fewer boats take to the water.

We recommend the following owner-operated outfits because they run a much tighter ship than some others. Boats depart at least daily between late April and October.

Before Lunch Cruises (☏0535 636 0076; www.beforelunch.com) Run out of Fethiye by an experienced Turkish and Australian duo who set their own itinerary and are more expensive than most but apparently worth it!

Ocean Yachting (☏0252-612 4807; www.bluecruise.com) Based at the marina in Fethiye.

Olympos Yachting (☏0242-892 1145; www.olymposyachting.com) Popular Olympos-based outfit.

V-Go Yachting & Travel Agency (☏0252-612 2113; www.bluecruisesturkey.com) Based in Fethiye with a branch at Olympos.

portant Grave Stelae and the Stelae of Promise). Its most prized significant possession, however, is the so-called Trilingual Stele from Letoön, dating from 358 BC, which was used partly to decipher the Lycian language with the help of ancient Greek and Aramaic. The garden surrounding the museum contains an excellent lapidary of mostly Lycian sarcophagi and Roman tombstones, some of them portraying early Christian symbols and angels.

Activities

Ocean Yachting
Travel Agency   ADVENTURE SPORTS
(☏612 4807; www.oceantravelagency.com; İskele Meydanı 1; ⊙9am-9pm Apr-Oct) Next to the tourist office, Ocean Yachting sells boat tickets and organises parasailing (₺180 for 45 minutes), day-long rafting trips (₺85) and half-day horse-riding excursions (₺50) along with lots of other water sports, including so-called blue voyages (see p321).

Fethiye

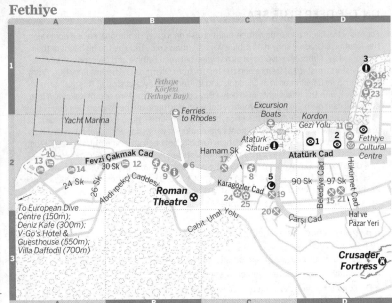

European Diving Centre   DIVING
(☑614 9771; www.europeandivingcentre.com; Fevzi Çakmak Caddesi 133) The British-owned and operated European Diving Centre, west of the main harbour in Karagözler, organises diving trips (per person ₺100 for beginners; two dives, all equipment and lunch per person ₺125 for advanced divers) and three-day PADI courses (₺700).

Seven Capes   KAYAKING
(☑0537 403 3779; www.sevencapes.com) One of the best ways to see the Med up close is in a sea kayak. A very experienced outfit, Seven Capes has both daily tours (€40), including an excellent four-hour trip between Ölüdeniz and Kabak via Butterfly Valley (€50), and 'night paddling' (€45) under the stars from sunset to midnight. Surreal.

Old Turkish Bath   HAMAM
(Tarihi Fethiye Hamamı; ☑614 9318; www.oldturkishbath.com; Hamam Sokak 2-4; bath & scrub ₺35, massage ₺20-50; ☉7am-midnight) Low-key and small, the Old Turkish Bath in Paspatur, the oldest section of Fethiye, dates to the 16th century. All manner of massage is available. Open to men and women.

Çalış, Beach   BEACH
About 5km northeast of the centre is Çalış, a narrow stretch of gravel beach lined with mass-produced hotels as well as pubs and chip shops patronised by resident British expats. Dolmuşes depart for Çalış (₺1.50, 10 minutes) from the minibus station every five to 10 minutes throughout the day.

🕝 Tours

Many travellers to Fethiye not joining longer cruises opt for the **12-Island Tour** (per person incl lunch ₺30-35, on sailboat ₺50; ☉10.30am-6pm mid-Apr–Oct), a boat trip around Fethiye Bay (Fethiye Körfezi). The boats usually stop at five or six islands and cruise by the rest, but either way it's idyllic (if a little crowded). Travel agencies sell tickets or you can deal directly with the boat companies at the marina. One reliable company based along the promenade is **Kardeşler Daily Boat Company** (☑612 4241, 0542 326 2314; www.kardesler.com).

The normal tour visits **Yassıcalar** (Flat Island) for a stop and a swim, then **Tersane Adası** (Shipyard Island) for a dip and a visit to the ruins, followed by **Akvaryum** (Aquarium) for lunch, a swim and a snorkel. **Cennet Koyu** (Paradise Bay) is next for a plunge, followed by **Kleopatra Hamamı**

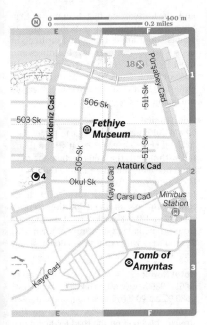

N 0 ————————— 400 m
   0 ————————— 0.2 miles

Fethiye

(Cleopatra's Bath) and finally **Kızılada** (Red Island) with its beach and mud baths.

If you have another day or so, excellent boat tours of the same length go to or include **Butterfly Valley** (per person ₺25) via Ölüdeniz and allow you to walk, swim and visit ruins. There's also the **Saklıkent Gorge Tour** (per person ₺45), which includes the ruins at Tlos and a trout lunch; and the **Dalyan Tour** (per person ₺50; ⊙9am -6.30pm), which includes a shuttle to Dalyan, a tour of Köyceğiz Gölü (Lake Köyceğiz), the Sultaniye mud baths, Kaunos ruins and İztuzu Beach.

🛏 Sleeping

The bulk of accommodation options are up the hill behind the marina in Karagözler or further west. Many pensions will organise transport from the otogar, but the area is also served by minibus.

TOP CHOICE Yildirim Guest House   PENSION, HOSTEL €
(☎614 4627, 0543 779 4732; www.yildirimguest house.com; Fevzi Çakmak Caddesi 21; dm/d/tr ₺25/80/90; ❄@🛜) Our favourite budget option in Fethiye, this shipshape hostel-cum-pension just opposite the marina includes three dorms (two by gender and one mixed) with four to six beds and a half-dozen spotless rooms, some facing the harbour. Nothing is too difficult for well-travelled host Omer Yapis – from excursions and pick-ups to laundry and evening meals (₺15). Saturday hikes on the Lycian Way walking trail are ₺10 and bikes are free for guests.

Villa Daffodil
HOTEL €€

(☎614 9595; www.villadaffodil.com; Fevzi Çakmak Caddesi 115; s/d ₺85/120; ❋🛜🏊) This large Ottoman-styled and flower-bedecked guest house is one of the few older buildings to survive the earthquake, and development and has now expanded into the house on the hill behind it. The 41 rooms have stylish furnishings and a homely feel; the best ones (such as room 204 in front, 502 and 602 in back) have balconies and sea views. The terrace in front, with an ancient carriage and pool in the back, are the centres of activity.

Ferah Pension
PENSION, HOSTEL €

(☎0532 265 0772, 614 2816; www.ferahpension .com; Orta yol 23; dm €15, d €20-25, €35-38; ❋@🏊) Love, love, love this place with its leafy and covered lobby terrace and tiny swimming pool, paintings by owner Monica and 'sexy dinners' (₺20) by same. The 10 sizeable, very tidy rooms include a dorm with five beds. Two of the rooms at the top have views of the harbour to die for.

Yacht Classic Hotel
BOUTIQUE HOTEL €€€

(☎612 5067; www.yachtclassichotel.com; Fevzi Çakmak Caddesi 1; s/d/ste ₺150/250/350; ❋🛜🏊) This 35-room boutique hotel is a symphony in white with all the mod cons, including just about the most stylish hotel hamam on the Med coast. The large pool terrace overlooking the harbour is a pleasing feature of this efficient and friendly large hotel, but we will fight (and die) for one of the half-dozen rooms on the 3rd and 4th floors with huge terraces above the sea, complete with jacuzzi.

Duygu Pension
PENSION €

(☎614 3563, 0535 736 6701; www.duygupension .com; Orta Yol 54; s/d/tr ₺40/60/90; ❋@🏊) A very appealing and welcoming budget option at the western end of the harbour, the salmon-coloured 'Feeling' has colourful stencils and carpets brightening up its 10 spick-and-span rooms. It includes a small pool and a rooftop terrace with bar and blinding views of the harbour. Birol is your man and a great source of information.

V-Go's Hotel & Guesthouse
PENSION, HOSTEL €€

(☎612 5409, 614 4004; www.v-gohotel.com; Fevzi Çakmak Caddesi 109; dm €10, r per person €20, f €60; ❋@🛜🏊) This super-modern hostel-cum-guesthouse at the western end of Karagözler has become a firm favourite with budget travellers. The 28 rooms – four are dorms with four to eight beds – are spread over two buildings and most look out to the sea (rooms 204 and 205) or pool. There's a great terrace with chill-out chairs and a bar with self-service music and DVDs.

Hotel Kemal
HOTEL €€

(☎614 5010; www.hotelkemal.com; Kordon Gezi Yolu; s/d ₺60/100; 🅿❋@🛜) It's four floors tall with no lift, the colour scheme is mud and chocolate, and the lobby – though it's been somewhat freshened up – feels more Eastern European than western Mediterranean. But it's all about location (repeat, repeat) and the Kemal is right on the seafront promenade in the centre of town with 21 rooms (18 with sea-facing balconies) and very affordable rates.

Hotel Doruk
HOTEL €€

(☎614 9860; www.hoteldoruk.com; Yat Limanı; s ₺80-95, d ₺120-150; ❋@🏊) Quieter and more private than many places to stay on this stretch, this hotel on the road leading down the marina offers a well-maintained medium-sized pool with a view. At least half of the 28 rooms have balconies overlooking the bay; room 103 on the side is especially well-placed. Avoid the mansard rooms on the top floor, which can feel claustrophobic.

Tan Pansiyon
PENSION €

(☎0546 711 4559, 614 1584; tanpansiyon@hotmail .com; 30 Sokak 41; s ₺35-45, d ₺50-65; ❋🛜) If the backpacker grind wears a bit thin, try this charmingly 'lived-in' pension run by the charming Öztürk family in Karagözler. The nine rooms are small (the bathrooms even smaller). But it's sparkling clean and quiet. It's also good for self-caterers; there's a kitchen for guests' use on the stunning roof terrace.

✖ Eating

Fethiye's enormous **market** takes place on Tuesday along the canal between Atatürk Caddesi and Pürşabey Caddesi next to the stadium.

⌜TOP⌝
⌞CHOICE⌟ Reis
SEAFOOD €€

(☎0532 472 5989, 612 5368; www.reisrestaurant .com; Hal ve Pazar Yeri 62; mains ₺12-20; ⊙10am-midnight) One way to taste Fethiye's fabulous fish is to buy your own (₺18 to ₺25 per kilogram) from the circle of fishmongers in the central covered market, then take it to one of the restaurants opposite to have them cook it the way you like it. Our favourite is Reis, which charges ₺5 per head for cooking the fish, plus a green salad, bread with garlic butter, a sauce to accompany the fish and fruit. They also do their own meze and meat dishes. You should book.

İskele Ocakbaşı
BARBECUE ₺₺

(☎614 9423; Şehit Feti Bey Parkı; meze ₺6-19, grills ₺12-26; ⊙9am-1am) Our favourite grill restaurant in Fethiye overlooks the water and a small park (outside seating), and serves excellent meat dishes from its central *ocakbaşı* (barbecue). Non-Turkish dishes (₺18 to ₺40) are available as well.

Meğri Lokantasi
TURKISH ₺₺

(☎614 4047; www.megrirestaurant.com; Çarşı Caddesi 26; mains ₺7-13, mixed plates ₺17-25; ⊙8am-11.30pm low season, 8am-1am high season) Looking for us at lunchtime in Fethiye? We're usually here. Packed with locals who spill onto the streets, the Meğri offers excellent and hearty home-style cooking at very palatable prices. Choose from the huge glass display window of meze and savoury mains or try one of their many types of *güveç* (casserole; ₺20 to ₺25).

Deniz Restaurant
SEAFOOD ₺₺

(☎612 0212; Uğur Mumcu Parkı Yanı 10/1; mains ₺15-30) Probably the best seafood restaurant in Fethiye outside of the fish market, the 'sea' restaurant exhibits everything alive and swimming in tanks (the grouper is best) and excels in making unusual meze. Try the excellent *semizotu* (purslane) in yoghurt and the ceviche (fish preserved in lemon juice).

Paşa Kebab
KEBAP ₺

(☎614 9807; Çarşı Caddesi 42; meze ₺4-7 pide ₺6-10, kebaps ₺11.50-22.50; ⊙9am-1am) This spruced-up place has a well-priced menu complete with useful little photos of dishes. Try the Paşa Special (₺16), a gigantic (and delicious) concoction of beef, tomato and cheese. There's also pizza (₺12.50 to ₺16.50).

Duck Pond
TURKISH ₺₺

(☎614 7429; Eski Cami Sokak 41; mains ₺18-25) A lively place surrounded by a pond replete with fountain and a battalion of quackers, the Duck Pond may be a bit touristy but is always fun. It serves mostly traditional Turkish food such as Adana kebap (₺15) that is straightforward and wholesome.

Ceyazir Usta
KEBAP ₺₺

(Hal ve Pazar Yeri; dishes ₺7.50-15; ⊙8am-9pm Mon-Sat) For ichthyophobes who find themselves in the fish market (what WERE you thinking?), 'Master Ceyazir' wil fix you up with some of the best kebaps and *dürüm* (grilled wraps, for lack of a better description) served from his tiny hole in the wall.

Nefıs Pide
PIDE, KEBAP ₺

(☎614 5504; Eski Cami Sokak 9; pide ₺4-9, köfte ₺11, kebap ₺15; ⊙9am-midnight) Stark and simple but sparkling clean, this popular place right next to the old mosque serves delicious pide, pizza and döner but no alcohol.

🍷 Drinking & Entertainment

The lion's share of Fethiye's bars and nightclubs stand cheek-by-jowl along Hamam Sokak, which runs north–south between Karagözler Caddesi and Atatürk Caddesi in the old town. Another happy hunting ground for bars is along Dispanser Caddesi, south of the Martyrs' Monument.

Kismet
BAR, CABARET

(☎0545 922 2301; Uğur Mumcu Parkı Yanı) This welcoming bar and cabaret (shows most Friday nights in season – phone for an update) off Dispanser Caddesi is open all day and until the wee hours. Good crowd, good for a sundowner or something cold much later.

Val's Cocktail Bar
BAR

(☎612 2363; Uğur Mumcu Parkı Yanı; ⊙9am-1am) Englishwoman Val has been keeping the local expat community well informed and happily quenched for a score of years now. Her little bar stocks a mean selection of poison and suitably strong coffee, has a free lending library with more than 2000 books, and hosts a resident grey parrot.

Deniz Kafe
BAR, CAFE

(2 Karagözler Kürek Yarışları; ⊙9am-11pm) This little makeshift cafe-bar has tables right up to the edge of the water and even one or two on a small pier west of the marina. It's a great place to while away a lazy afternoon.

Car Cemetery
BAR, CLUB

(☎612 7872; Haman Sokak 25; ⊙10am-4am) British boozer-cum-club, this place with the whacko deco and live rock music at the weekend is particularly popular with locals, when it will be standing (or falling down) room only.

CELAL COŞKUN: CARPET SELLER

Celal Coşkun learned to make carpets and weave kilims at his grandmother's knee in Malatya in southeastern Anatolia before apprenticing himself as a carpet repairer in İstanbul and opening his shop, Old Orient Carpet & Kilim Bazaar in Fethiye. We asked this 30-year veteran of the trade for his top tips on buying and caring for carpets and kilims.

» Know the basics: a carpet is wool or silk pile with single (Persian) or double (Turkish) knots; a kilim is a flat weave and reversible; a *cicim* is a kilim with one side embroidered.

» Establish in advance your price range and what you want in terms of size, pattern and colour.

» Deal only with a seller who you feel you can trust, be it through reputation, recommendation or instinct.

» Counting knots is only important on silk-on-silk carpets, though a double-knotted wool carpet will wear better than a single-knotted one.

» Most reputable carpet shops can negotiate discounts of between 5% and 10%, depending on how you may pay; anything higher than that and the price has been inflated in the first place.

» To extend the life of a carpet, always remove your shoes when walking on it and never beat a carpet as this breaks the knots and warp (vertical) and weft (horizontal) threads.

» If professional cleaning is too expensive and the traditional method – washing it with mild soap and water and drying it on wood blocks to allow air to circulate beneath it – is too much like hard work, lay the carpet face (pattern) side down for a few minutes in fresh snow (if available!).

» Anything made by hand – including a carpet – can be repaired by hand.

Kum Saati Bar   BAR, CLUB
(Haman Sokak 31) What looks like just another joint along Fethiye's most raucous street after dark, the 'Hour Glass' keeps good time thoughout the day as a bar and turns into a club with music and dancing at night.

Shopping

Sister's Place   HERBALIST
(⏺0536 614 3877; Hal ve Pazar Yeri; ⏱7.30am-9.30pm, to 5pm in winter Mon-Sat) This tiny Aladdin's Cave of herbs, essential oils and – for real – magic potions is where everyone comes for a cure and a spell. You're in good hands with Nesrin and her brother Tarık – trust us.

Old Orient Carpet & Kilim Bazaar CARPETS
(⏺0532 510 6108; c.c_since.1993@hotmail.com; Çarşı Caddesi 5) As solid as Gibraltar and reliable as rain, this shop is where the discerning buy their carpets and kilims, following the sage advice of carpet seller Celal Coşkun.

Information

Millennium Internet Cafe (503 Sokak 2/A; per hr ₺1.50; ⏱8am-midnight) Three dozen computers southeast of the Martyrs' Monument.

Tourist Office (⏺614 1527; İskele Meydanı; ⏱8am-7pm Mon-Fri, 10am-5pm Sat & Sun May-Sep, 8am-noon & 1-5pm Mon-Fri Oct-Apr) Helpful information centre for Fethiye and surrounding areas opposite the marina.

Getting There & Away

Fethiye's busy otogar is 2.5km east of the town centre, with a separate station for minibuses 1km east of the centre near the petrol station.

Buses from the otogar to Antalya (₺28, 6½ hours, 285km) head east along the coast at least every hour in high season, stopping at Kalkan (₺11, 1½ hours, 83km), Kaş (₺13, two hours, 107km) and Olympos (₺35, 4¾ hours, 228km). The inland road to Antalya (₺20, 3½ hours, 200km) is much quicker.

Minibuses destined for places in the vicinity depart from the stops near the mosque. Destinations include Faralya and Kabak (₺5.50), Göcek (₺5), Hisarönü (₺3.50), Kayaköy (₺4), Ovacık (₺3.50), Ölüdeniz (₺5), Saklıkent (₺7.50) and Tlos (₺8).

Catamarans sail daily to Rhodes in Greece (one-way/same-day return/open-return €50/60/75, 1½ hours) from the pier opposite the tourist office. They run from late April to October, departing from Fethiye at 9am Wednesday, Thursday and Friday (and sometimes Saturday in high season), returning from Rhodes at 4.30pm. Tickets are available near the pier from Ocean Yachting Travel Agency (p321) and **Yeşil Dalyan** (☑ 612 4015; www.yesildalyantravel .com; Fevzi Çakmak Caddesi 35b).

❶ Getting Around

Minibuses (₺1.50) ply the one-way system along Atatürk Caddesi and up Çarşı Caddesi to the otogar, as well as along Fevzi Çakmak Caddesi to the Karagözler pensions and hotels. They also go to Çalış Beach. A taxi from the otogar to the pensions west of the centre costs about ₺5, to the otogar ₺20 and the Dalaman airport between ₺80 and ₺100.

A couple of agencies in town, including **Levent Rent a Car** (☑ 614 8096; www.leventrentacar .net; Fevzi Çakmak Caddesi 37b), hire out scooters for ₺30 per day.

Ölüdeniz

☑ 0252 / POP 4595

With its sheltered (and protected) lagoon beside a lush national park, a long spit of sandy beach and Baba Dağ (Mt Baba) casting its shadow across the sea, Ölüdeniz (*eu-leu-den-eez*), some 15km south of Fethiye, is a tourist association's dream come true. Problem is, like most beautiful destinations, everyone wants to spend time here and a lot of people think package tourism has turned the motionless charms of the 'Dead Sea' into a Paradise Lost. But Ölüdeniz remains a good place to party before continuing on to the less-frenetic Butterfly Valley or Kabak. And it's a good starting point for the wonderful Lycian Way walking trail, which runs past some of the nicer hotels, high above the fun and frolic.

🏃 Activities

Ölüdeniz Beach & Lagoon   BEACH
The beach is very much the centre of things here; it's at the bottom of the hill past the package-tour colonies of Ovacik and Hisarönü. Near the junction of the road with a *jandarma* (police) post and opposite the post office is the guarded entrance to **Ölüdeniz Tabiat Parkı** (Ölüdeniz Nature Park; Ölüdeniz Caddesi; adult/student ₺4.50/2; ☉ 8am-8pm) and its lagoon, still a lovely place to while away a few hours on the beach with mountains soaring above you. There are showers, toilets and cafes here too.

Boat Excursions   CRUISE
Throughout the summer, boats set out to explore the coast, charging between ₺15 and ₺25 for a day trip (including lunch). A typical cruise might take in Gemile Bay, the Blue Cave, Butterfly Valley and St Nicholas Island, with some time for swimming included. Ask the tourist office for more information.

Paragliding   PARAGLIDING
Daniel Craig jumps off 1960m-high Baba Dağ in the latest James Bond film *Skyfall* and so can you. The descent from the mountain can take up to 40 minutes, with amazing views over the Blue Lagoon, Butterfly Valley and, on a clear day, as far as Rhodes.

Various companies offer tandem paragliding flights, but prices can vary between ₺120 and ₺150. Just ensure the company has insurance and the pilot has the appropriate qualifications. Reliable companies include **Easy Riders** (☑ 617 0114; www.easy ridersparagliding.com; Han Camp Ölüdeniz) and **Pegas Paragliding** (☑ 617 051; Çetin Motel Ölüdeniz). Parasailing (₺100) on the beach is also possible.

🛏 Sleeping

Ölüdeniz has everything from plush boutique hotels to camping grounds that are almost like budget resorts, with comfortable and stylish bungalows as well as tent pitches.

Sugar Beach Club   CAMPING GROUND, RESORT €
(☑ 617 0048; www.thesugarbeachclub.com; Ölüdeniz Caddesi 20; campsite per person/car/caravan ₺15/15/15, bungalows per person ₺50-140; ✸ @ 🛜) About 500m north of the entrance to the park, this ultra-chilled spot with campsites and bungalows, run by affable Erkin, is the pick of the crop in Ölüdeniz for backpackers. The design is first class – a strip of beach shaded by palms and lounging areas, with a waterfront bar and restaurant and backed by two-dozen colourful bungalows with bathrooms and air-conditioning. There's free entry to the beach, canoes and pedalos can be hired, and special events like barbecues are a regular occurrence. If you're not staying here but want to hang out, it costs ₺7 to use the sun lounges, parasols and showers.

Oyster Residences   BOUTIQUE HOTEL €€€
(☑ 617 0765; www.oysterresidences.com; Belcekiz 1 Sokak; d €110-150, tr €160-200; ✸ 🛜 ☀) This delightful boutique hotel, inspired by old

Fethiye-style houses, was built in 2004 but looks at least a century older. It has 26 bright and airy rooms done up in a kind of neo-tropo style that will have most mortals swooning. The walk-in wardrobes are room-sized, the wooden basins are antique and the French doors open on to lush gardens that creep all the way up to the beach. Stunning stuff.

Paradise Garden
RESORT €€€

(☑617 0545; www.paradisegardenhotel.com; Ölüdeniz Yolu; s/d €90/130; ❋@☒) Situated up the hill to the right as you make the descent some 2km to the centre of Ölüdeniz, this Eden-like place is not misnamed. Set in a 6-hectare garden with three buildings, it boasts spectacular views, two pools (including a natural spring in the mouth of a cave and one shaped like a heart), a menagerie with peacocks, and a cafe and gourmet restaurant. The 27 rooms are large and very tastefully furnished.

Blue Star Hotel
HOTEL €€

(☑617 0069; www.hotelbluestaroludeniz.com; Mimar Sinan Caddesi 8; s & d ₺70-160; ❋☜☒) Quite attractively designed and well maintained, this family-run place was one of the first on the block when it opened just 60m from the beach in 1985. Though they're not large, the 42 rooms contained in three buildings are light, bright and airy and most have balconies. The two-storey wooden cabin beside the swimming pool is a unique place to stay.

Sultan Motel
HOTEL €€

(☑616 6139; www.sultanmotel.com; Ölüdeniz Yolu; s/d ₺50/80; ❋☜☒) Just off the main road on the left as you descend from Hisarönü into Ölüdeniz, the Sultan is at a trailhead of the Lycian Way and is a favourite of walkers and trekkers. Its 16 rooms and five apartments, which also have kitchens for self-catering, are in stone chalets. Some have excellent views down to Ölüdeniz.

Seahorse Beach Club
CAMPING GROUND, RESORT €€

(☑0532 691 4375, 617 0123; www.seahorsebeachclub.com; Ölüdeniz Caddesi; campsite per person ₺15-20, caravan d ₺80-140; ❋) Gazing out onto Ölüdeniz Bay but not quite as chilled as other camping grounds in the area, Seahorse nonetheless has two-dozen blue-and-white caravans with all the mod cons, a restaurant and bar in a lofted wooden cabin and its very own beach a very short stroll away. They will discount longer stays.

✗ Eating & Drinking

Buzz Beach Bar Grill
INTERNATIONAL €€€

(☑617 0526; www.buzzbeachbar.com; Belcekız 1 Sokak; mains ₺18.50-35.50; ☺restaurant 8am-midnight, bar noon-2am) With a commanding position on the waterfront, this two-level place offers a wide menu from pasta and pizza (₺11.50 to ₺17.50) to fillet steak and seafood.

Oba Motel Restaurant
INTERNATIONAL €€

(☑617 0158; www.obamotel.com.tr/Erestaurant.asp; Mimar Sinan Caddesi; mains ₺15-25; ☺8am-midnight) Partly housed in a wooden cabin, the restaurant of the leafy Oba Motel has a great reputation for home-style food at palatable prices. It also does great Turkish/European breakfasts (from ₺12) including homemade muesli with mountain yoghurt and local pine honey. The menu offers everything from snacks to full-on mains, including a half-dozen vegie options.

Sun Cafe
INTERNATIONAL, MEXICAN €€€

(☑617 0630; Bellcekız Beach; dishes ₺18.50-30.50) This open-fronted bar and eatery is especially popular with expats, and it's imediately apparent why. There's a great terrace, a pool table, aquarium and, in the colder months, an open fire. And the food? A mixed feedbag of Mexican, international and (some) Turkish favourites seems to go down well.

Help Lounge Bar
BAR

(☑617 0650; Belcekız 1 Sokak; beer ₺6.50; ☺9am-4am) The most happening place in town, this funky joint has a large terrace with a bar right on the seafront with comfy cushioned benches, colourful murals on the walls and the front end of a Chevy coming through the wall. Happy hour (cocktails ₺15) is from 6pm to 8pm and again from 10.30pm till midnight.

ℹ Information

Tourist Office (☑617 0438; www.oludeniz.com.tr; Ölüdeniz Caddesi 32; ☺8.30am-11pm May-Aug, to 7pm Sep & Oct, Apr & May, to 5pm Nov, Mar-Apr) Helpful information booth and booking service in the centre.

ℹ Getting There & Away

In high season, minibuses leave Fethiye (₺5, 25 minutes, 15km) for Ölüdeniz roughly every five to 10 minutes, passing through Ovacık and Hisarönü. In low season they go every 15 to 20 minutes by day and hourly at night. You can reach Faralya and Kabak on six minibuses a day in summer. A taxi to Kayaköy costs ₺20. To Fethiye it's ₺40 to ₺45.

Butterfly Valley & Faralya

Tucked away on the Yedi Burun (Seven Capes) coast a dozen kilometres from Ölüdeniz is the village of Faralya (population 150), also called Uzunyurt. Below it is the paradise-found of Butterfly Valley, with a fine beach and some lovely walks through a lush gorge. It is home to the unique Jersey tiger butterfly, from where it takes its name.

There are two ways to reach Butterfly Valley: via boat from Ölüdeniz or on foot via a very steep path that wends its way down a cliff from Faralya. If you choose the latter, be sure to wear proper shoes and keep to the marked trail (indicated with painted red dots). It usually takes 30 to 45 minutes to descend and closer to an hour to come back up. There are fixed ropes along the path in the steepest or most dangerous parts. Faralya is on a stage of the Lycian Way (see p35).

🛏 Sleeping

Butterfly Valley　　　BUNGALOW, CAMPING GROUND €€
(Kelebekler Vadisi; ☑0555 632 0237; www.kelebek lervadisi.org; incl half-board per person tent ₺35-55, dormitory ₺40-50, bungalow ₺55-65) Accommodation in Butterfly Valley itself is simple: pitches for tents (rent or bring your own) and bungalows on stilts with mattresses on the floor. Be warned that these rooms bake during the summer. For those who prefer their creature comforts, there are lots more places to stay above the valley in Faralya.

George House　　　PENSION, CAMPING GROUND €
(☑0535 793 2112, 642 1102; www.georgehouse faralya.com; incl half-board per person tent ₺30, bungalow with/without bathroom ₺50/40; ✳@☀) Run by the eponymous George's enthusiastic son Hasan, this Faralya institution offers mattresses in the main house and 16 bungalows (half with air-conditioning) on tented platforms. There are also four new tree houses, raised woden platforms with cushions for lounging and a bar near the path leading down to Butterfly Valley. There's a spring-water source that feeds a lovely pool.

Melisa Pansiyon　　　PENSION €€
(☑0535 881 9051, 642 1012; www.melisapension .com; s/d ₺50/100; ✳✳☀) Offering as warm a welcome as you'll find anywhere along the Yedi Burun, the Melisa has four very well-maintained and cheerful rooms, a pretty garden and vine-bedecked terrace overlooking the valley. The owner, Mehmet, speaks English and is a good source of local information. Home-cooked vegetarian/meat-based meals (₺15/25) are offered, though guests are welcome to use the kitchen.

Die Wassermühle　　　LUXURY HOTEL €€€
(The Watermill; ☑642 1245; www.natur-reisen.de; incl half-board per person r/ste €55/70; ✳) More 'country' than 'luxury', this incredibly tasteful resort property, owned by a longtime German resident Brigitte, is hidden within a wooded slope to the left as you enter Faralya and is the coolest (in both senses) place around. The seven suites and two doubles within a 150-year-old mill and newer building are spacious and use all-natural materials. Suites have kitchenettes. The views from the restaurant and spring-water pool terraces are commanding.

Onur Motel　　　BUNGALOW €€
(☑0538 260 8734, 642 1162; www.onurmotelfaralya .com; incl half-board per person ₺50-60; ✳✳) This place above the road in Faralya offers accommodation in 10 modern and somewhat stylish bungalows on a hill at the end of the village. The choicest ones are the three fronting the street. Excellent food, nice garden with pool. Popular with walkers on the Lycian Way.

❶ Getting There & Away

You can take a tour of Butterfly Valley from Fethiye or Ölüdeniz, or board the shuttle boat (₺20 return), which departs from Ölüdeniz daily at 11am, 2pm and 6pm (with additional sailings at noon, 4pm and 6.30pm mid-June to mid-September). From Butterfly Valley back to Ölüdeniz, it leaves at 9.30am, 1pm and 5pm (and, in high season, at 10.30am, 3pm and 6pm as well).

Six daily minibuses (₺6, 35 minutes, 26km) from June to September (three in spring and two in winter) link Fethiye and Faralya via Ölüdeniz. If you should miss the bus, a taxi back to Fethiye should cost ₺40.

Kabak

☑0252

The relatively remote beach community of Kabak has grown in size in recent years; it now counts 14 camping grounds, including the enormous Sea Valley one fronting the beach. But regardless of how you get down the steep track to Kabak – by high-suspension vehicle (15 minutes) or on foot (half-hour) – you'll be rewarded with a spectacular beach flanked by two long cliffs. Six kilometres south of Faralya – and worlds away from everywhere else – Kabak is for the camping and trekking enthusiast, yoga devotee or any fan of untapped beauty.

🛏 Sleeping & Eating

Accommodation in Kabak consists of camping or tented platforms and bungalows. All include half-board in the price – there are no restaurants as such on Gemile Beach, only on the road to/from Faralya. Most camps open from April to October, and most can organise transport down; phone, email or text ahead.

🌿 Reflections Camping   CAMPING GROUND €€
(📞0539 872 5650, 642 1020; www.reflection scamp.com; per person own tent/camp tent ₺40/45, bungalow with/without bathroom ₺80/60; @) Built from scratch by American Chris, this comfortable place with pitches and 14 bungalows (including two built of bamboo within the trees and four made of earth compacted in bags) offers some of the best sea views in Kabak. (The outlook from one toilet, with a 'living' roof planted with ferns and ginger plants, is nothing short of awesome.) Reflections is higher and more green than most.

Turan Hill Lounge   CAMPING GROUND €€
(📞0532 490 4073, 642 1227; www.turancamp ing.com; d bungalow ₺170-190, without bathroom ₺110-120, boutique ₺230-285; @≋) The first accommodation to open in Kabak and still a trendsetter, this place has hiked its prices considerably in recent years. Still, it boasts 17 very different bungalows (including four beautiful decorated and furnished 'boutique' ones) as well as a half-dozen unusual tent platforms. It also has lovely views and lots of mellow lounging areas; yoga courses are held regularly on the enormous platform in the valley below. Owner Ece is always on hand to help.

Shambala   CAMPING GROUND €€
(📞0532 496 0870, 642 1147; www.theshambala .com; per person Indian tent ₺50-60, tree house ₺60-90, bungalow ₺60-190; @≋) This vaguely Indian-themed place halfway down the valley has 17 bungalows in three categories, including some that are verging on the luxurious. Those on a stricter budget will opt for the spacious tree houses and breezy Indian tents with the ultimate sea view. There's also a swimming pool, bar, fabulous hammocks and suspension chairs for

relaxing, and a centre for 'shamanic healing' therapy.

Olive Garden   BUNGALOW €€
(📞0536 439 8648, 642 1083; www.olivegar denkabak.com; s/d ₺75/130) Oozing with charm, the Olive Garden is not in Kabak but down a side track 100m from the Faralya road. With gorgeous views from the cosy hillside platforms, it's a wonderful place to stay. Accomodation is in a dozen bungalows with toilet and shower. The owner, Fatih, is a former chef and the ingredients come from his family's 15 hectares of fruit trees, olive groves and vegetable gardens. Popular with walkers.

Mamma's Restaurant   RESTAURANT €€
(📞6421071; mains ₺10-15) Above Kabak and near the dolmuş stop are a couple of decent restaurants, including Mamma's. It offers a couple of simple but hearty dishes as well as *gözleme* (₺5) and Mama's own homemade *ayran* (yoghurt drink; ₺3).

❶ Getting There & Away

The tortuous 6km road from Faralya is as memorable for its views as for its knuckle-whitening corners. There are eight daily minibuses to/from Fethiye (₺6) between 8.30am and 8.30pm.

Kayaköy

📞0252 / POP 2200
About 9km south of Fethiye is Kayaköy (ancient Karmylassos), an eerie ghost town of 4000-odd abandoned stone houses and various other structures that once made up the Greek town of Levissi. Today they form a memorial to Turkish-Greek peace and cooperation.

Levissi was deserted by its mostly Greek inhabitants in the general exchange of populations supervised by the League of Nations in 1923 after the Turkish War of Independence. Most Greek Muslims came to Turkey and most Ottoman Christians moved from coastal Turkey to Greece. The abandoned town was the inspiration for Eskibahçe, the setting of Louis de Bernières' 2004 novel, *Birds Without Wings*.

As there were far more Ottoman Christians than Greek Muslims, many Turkish towns were left unoccupied after the population exchange. Also, Kayaköy, or Kaya as it is known locally, was badly damaged by an earthquake in 1957.

With the tourism boom of the 1980s, a development company wanted to restore Kayaköy's stone houses and turn the town into a holiday village. Scenting money, the local inhabitants were delighted, but Turkish artists and architects were alarmed and saw to it that the Ministry of Culture declared Kayaköy a historic monument, safe from unregulated development. What remains is a timeless village set in a lush valley with some fine vineyards nearby. In the evening, when the stone houses are spotlit, Kayaköy is truly surreal.

◎ Sights

Kayaköy (Levissi) Abandoned Village
RUINS

(admission ₺5, after closing free; ⊗8.30am-6.30pm May-Oct, 8am-5pm Nov-Apr) Frankly, there's not not a whole lot to see that's still intact but two churches are prominent: the Kataponagia in the lower part of the town and the Taxiarkis further up the slope. Both retain some of their painted decoration and black-and-white pebble mosaic floors. There's an ossuary with the mouldering remains of the long-dead in the churchyard behind the former.

🛏 Sleeping & Eating

TOP CHOICE Günay's Garden
BOUTIQUE HOTEL €€€

(⏰0537 231 7648, 618 033; www.gunaysgarden.com; Gümrük Sokak; villa high season ₺300, low season ₺90; ❄@🕏🖵) This positively scrumptious boutique resort consists of a half-dozen villas with two and three bedrooms hidden within lush gardens and set around a shimmering pool. Host Rebecca organises art and yoga courses and literary events – Louis de Bernières, author of *Birds Without Wings* has stayed and read here – while husband Tolga is in command of the kitchen at the excellent Izela restaurant, located in the grounds. Some of the villas have both front and back balconies, and the views of the abandoned village are evocative.

Villa Rhapsody
GUEST HOUSE €€

(⏰0532 337 8285, 618 0042; www.villarhapsody.com; s/d ₺70/105; 🕏🖵) This welcoming place has 16 comfortable rooms with balconies overlooking a delightful walled garden and a swimming pool. Atilla and Jeanne, the Turkish and Dutch owners, can offer local advice and sketch maps for walking in the area as well as organise bike hire. Set meals are available on request (₺25 to ₺40). Fans keep the rooms cool.

Doğa Apartments
APARTMENT €€

(⏰0532 684 2514, 618 0373; www.dogaapartments.com; apt ₺150-210; ❄🕏🖵) Just 200m from the main entrance to the abandoned village, the six self-contained apartments at the 'Natural' are housed in two old farm buildings, one of which dates back more than 200 years. They're well equipped, with bedroom, living room with sofa bed and kitchen, and sleep up to four people. The poolside bar is a delight.

Selçuk Pension
PENSION €

(⏰0535 275 6706, 618 0075; istanbulrestaurant@hotmail.com; s/d/apt ₺30/60/80; ❄) Set amid flower and vegetable gardens, the Selçuk has a dozen rooms that are a bit worn but spotless, quite spacious and homely; four have lovely views of abandoned Kaya. Guests can use the swimming pool of the nearby İstanbul restaurant and the affable owner Engin is eager to please.

TOP CHOICE Levissi Garden
MODERN TURKISH €€€

(⏰0533 247 5934, 618 0108; www.levissigarden.com; Eski Köy Sokak; mains ₺25-44) A 400-year-old stone building houses a stunning wine house and somewhat costly restaurant, with a cellar that stocks 12,000 bottles of Turkey's finest tipple. From its original stone oven, the Levissi produces a slow-cooked lamb stew (₺38) and mouth-watering *klevtiko* (leg of lamb cooked in red wine, garlic and herbs; ₺38), and some of the meze (₺8 to ₺20) are unique. Book to avoid disappointment.

Izela Restaurant
MEDITERRANEAN, TURKISH €€€

(⏰0537 231 7648, 618 033; www.gunaysgarden.com/restaurant.asp; mains ₺26-35) Kayaköy's top gourmet restaurant is located in the lush grounds of Günay's Garden (p331). It specialises in Mediterranean dishes, with more than a tip of the hat toward modern Turkish cuisine. Almost everything is sourced locally (as in the farm next door) – from olive oil and vegetables to chickens, ducks and turkeys. The wine list is exemplary and the decor – all stone and wood – is both warm and of the moment.

Cin Bal
BARBECUE, KEBAP €€

(⏰618 0066; www.cinbal.com; mains ₺15-20) Arguably the most celebrated grill restaurant in the region, Cin Bal specialises in lamb *tandir* (clay oven) dishes and kebaps, and seats 300 people both inside and in its garden courtyard under the grapevines. It's just down a narrow lane from the abandoned village and is always heaving (and smoking!).

İstanbul Restaurant RESTAURANT €€

(☑618 0148; mains ₺15-25; ◷8am-midnight) Run by the same people from the Selçuk Pension, this place serves up excellent homestyle grills and meze made from the produce of the surrounding vegetable gardens and orchards. It's a delightful spot for dinner, and the traditional Turkish dishes are delicious. Free pick-up.

❶ Getting There & Away

Minibuses run to Fethiye (₺4, 20 minutes, 8km) every half-hour or so from May to October and every couple of hours in low season. A taxi there costs ₺35. Two or three daily minibuses go to Hisarönü (₺2, 15 minutes, 6km) from where minibuses leave every 10 minutes for Ölüdeniz. Taxi to Hisarönü is ₺18. It's about a one-hour walk downhill through pine forest from Hisarönü to Kayaköy. You can also follow a very pretty trail to Ölüdeniz that takes two to 2½ hours (8km).

Tlos

☑0252

On a rocky outcrop high above a pastoral plain, Tlos was one of the most important cities of ancient Lycia. So effective was its elevated position that the well-guarded city remained inhabited until the early 19th century.

As you climb the winding road to the **ruins** (admission ₺5; ◷8.30am-8.30pm May-Oct, 8am-6pm Nov-Apr), look for the **acropolis** topped with an **Ottoman fortress** on the right. Beneath it, reached by a narrow path, are **rock tombs**, including that of the warrior Bellerophon of Chimaera fame. It has a temple-like façade carved into the rock face and to the left a fine bas-relief of our hero riding Pegasus, the winged horse.

The **theatre** is 100m further up the road from the ticket kiosk. It's in excellent condition, with most of its marble seating intact, and the stage wall is being rebuilt. Look among the rubble of the stage building for blocks carved with an eagle, a player's mask and garlands. Just across the road are ruins of the ancient **baths** (note the apothecary symbol – snake and staff – carved on an outer wall on the south side).

Set in a pretty garden with a stream, a pool, lots of shade, seating areas and birdsong, **Mountain Lodge** (☑638 2515, 0532 577 0191; www.tlosmountainlodge.com; r per person €22-42; ✹@☲) is a peaceful and attractive place with accommodation in four

buildings designed to look like old stone houses. The eight themed rooms (think birds) are comfy and homely (rates vary according to size and position), each has a balcony or verandah and there is a pool set on a terrace with views. The charming Mel (short for Melahat) offers three-course home-cooked set menus (₺30 to ₺35) and makes her own oil, jams and bread.

❶ Getting There & Away

From Fethiye, minibuses go to Saklıkent (₺7, 45 minutes) every 20 minutes via Güneşli, the departure point for Tlos, which is 4.5km north up the road. Mountain Lodge is halfway up; either walk the 2km to Yaka Köyü or call Mel for pick-up.

Saklıkent Gorge

☑0252

Some 12km after the turn-off to Tlos heading south, this spectacular **gorge** (adult/student ₺4.50/2; ◷8am-6pm) is really just a fissure in the Akdağlar, the mountains towering to the northeast. Some 18km long, the gorge is too narrow in places for even sunlight to squeeze through. Luckily *you* can, but prepare yourself for some very cold water year-round – even in summer.

You approach the gorge along a wooden boardwalk towering above the river. On wooden platforms suspended above the water, you can relax, drink tea and eat fresh trout while watching other tourists slip and slide their way across the river, hanging onto a rope, and then dropping into the gorge proper. Good footwear is essential, though plastic shoes and helmets can be rented (₺5).

Across the river from the car park is **Saklıkent Gorge Club** (☑659 0074, 0533 438 4101; www.gorgeclub.com; camp site ₺20, dm on platform incl half-board ₺25, tree house without bathroom s/d ₺35/60; @☲), a rustic backpacker-oriented camp with basic but very real tree houses (all have little fridges), a pool, bar and restaurant. Bathrooms are shared.

The club can organise various activities such as rafting (₺30/60 for 45 minutes/three hours), canyoning (₺20/100/200 for trips of three hours/one day/two days and one night, minimum four people), fishing (₺10 including guide and equipment, two hours), and trekking (₺10, three hours). Also available are jeep safaris (₺50 including lunch and guide) and tours of Tlos and Patara (₺20 each).

❶ Getting There & Away

Minibuses run every 20 minutes between Fethiye and Saklıkent (₺7, one hour). The last one back is at 8.30pm.

Pınara

Some 46km southeast of Fethiye along the D400 is a turn-off for Pınara and its spectacular **ruins** (admission ₺8, guide ₺20; ☺8.30am-8.30pm May-Oct, to 5pm Nov-Apr). The road wends through citrus orchards and across irrigation channels for 3.5km to just before the village of Minare, then takes a sharp left turn to climb a steep slope for another 2km.

Pınara was one of the six highest-ranking cities in ancient Lycia, but although the site is vast, the actual ruins are not the region's most impressive. Instead it's the sheer splendour and isolation that makes it worth visiting.

Rising high above the site is a sheer column of rock honeycombed with **rock tombs**; archaeologists are still debating as to how and why they were cut here. Other tombs are within the ruined city itself. The one to the southeast called the **Royal Tomb** has particularly fine reliefs, including several showing walled Lycian cities. Pınara's **theatre** is in good condition, but its **odeon** and **temple** to Aphrodite (with heart-shaped columns) are badly ruined. Note the enormous (and anatomically correct) phallus, a kind of early graffiti carved on the steps of the latter by builders.

Infrequent minibuses from Fethiye (₺8, one hour) in high season drop you at the start of the Pınara road, from where you can walk to the site. Eşen, a village 3km southeast of the Pınara turn-off from the highway, has a few shops and basic restaurants.

Letoön

Sharing a place with the Lycian capital Xanthos on Unesco's World Heritage List since 1988, Letoön is home to some of the finest **ruins** (admission ₺5; ☺8.30am-7pm May-Oct, 9am-5.30pm Nov-Apr) on the Lycian Way. Located about 17km south of the Pınara turn-off, this former religious centre is often considered a double-site with Xanthos but Letoön has its own romantic charm.

Letoön takes its name and importance from a large shrine to Leto who, according to legend, was Zeus's lover and bore him Apollo and Artemis. Unimpressed, Zeus's wife Hera commanded that Leto spend eternity wandering from country to country. According to local folklore she passed much time in Lycia and became the national deity; the federation of Lycian cities then built this very impressive religious sanctuary to house her statue.

The site consists of three **temples** standing side by side and dedicated to Apollo (the Doric one on the left), Artemis (the Ionian in the middle) and Leto (the Ionian on the right and now partially reconstructed). The Apollo temple has a fine mosaic showing a lyre, a bow and arrow and floral centre. The permanently flooded **nymphaeum** (ornamental fountain with statues), inhabited by frogs (said to be the shepherds who refused Leto a drink from the fountain), is appropriate as worship of Leto was associated with water. To the north is a large Hellenistic **theatre** dating from the 2nd century BC.

❶ Getting There & Away

Minibuses run from Fethiye via Eşen to Kumluova (₺7, one hour, 60km) every half-hour or so. Get out here and walk the few kilometres to Letoön.

Letoön is just outside the village of Kumluova. If driving from Pınara, turn right off the highway, go 4km and bear right at the signpost 'Letoön/Karadere'. After another 3.5km, turn left at the T-junction, then right after 100m and proceed a kilometre – all signposted – to the site through fertile fields and orchards and hectares of polytunnels full of tomato plants.

Xanthos

Up on a rock outcrop at Kınık, 63km southeast of Fethiye, are the **ruins** (admission ₺5; ☺9am-7pm May-Oct, 8am-5pm Nov-Apr) of ancient Xanthos, once the capital and grandest city of Lycia, with a fine **Roman theatre** and pillar **tombs**.

It's a short uphill walk to the site past the city gates and the plinth where the fabulous **Nereid Monument** (now in the British Museum in London) once stood. For all its grandeur, Xanthos had a chequered history of wars and destruction. At least twice, when besieged by clearly superior

ANCIENT LYCIA 101

The Lycian civilisation was based in the Teke peninsula, the bump of land jutting out into the sea and stretching from Dalyan in the west to Antalya in the east (pretty much the exact extent of this chapter).

The Lycian people date back to at least the 12th century BC, but they first appear in writing in the *Iliad* when Homer records their presence during an attack on Troy. It is thought they may have been descended from the Lukkans, a tribe allied with the ancient Hittites. A matrilineal people, they spoke their own unique language – which has still not been fully decoded.

By the 6th century BC the Lycians had come under the control of the Persian Empire. Thus began a changing of the guard that occurred as regularly as today's guard at Buckingham Palace. The Persians gave in to the Athenians, who were defeated in turn by Alexander the Great, the Ptolemaic Kingdom in Egypt and then Rhodes.

Lycia was granted independence by Rome in 168 BC, and it immediately established the Lycian League, a loose confederation of 23 fiercely independent city-states. Six of the largest ones – Xanthos, Patara, Pınara, Tlos, Myra and Olympos – held three votes each, the others just one or two. The Lycian League is often cited as the first proto-democratic union in history and the *bouleuterion* (council chamber) among the ruins of Ancient Patara (p335) has been dubbed the 'world's first parliament'.

Partly as a result of this union, peace held for over a century but in 42 BC the league made the unwise decision not to pay tribute to Brutus, the murderer of Caesar, whom Lycia had supported during the Civil War. With his forces, Brutus besieged Xanthos, and the city-state's outnumbered population, determined not to surrender, committed mass suicide.

Lycia recovered under the Roman Empire but in AD 43 all of Lycia was amalgamated into the neighbouring province of Pamphylia, a union that lasted until the 4th century when Pamphylia became part of Byzantium.

Lycia left behind very little in the way of material culture or written documents. What it did bequeath to posterity, however, was some of the most stunning funerary monuments from ancient times. Cliff tombs, 'house' tombs, sepulchres and sarcophagi – the Teke peninsula's mountains and valleys are littered with them, and most are easily accessible on foot and/or by car.

enemy forces, the city's population committed mass suicide.

You'll see the Roman theatre with the **agora** opposite the open car park. The **acropolis** is badly ruined. As many of the finest sculptures (eg the Harpies Monument) and inscriptions were carted off to London by Charles Fellows in 1842, most of the inscriptions and decorations you see today are copies of the originals.

Follow the path in front of the snazzy new ticket office to the east along the colonnaded street to find some excellent **mosaics**, the attractive **Dancers' Sarcophagus** and **Lion Sarcophagus** as well as some excellent **rock tombs**.

Minibuses run to Xanthos from Fethiye (₺8, one hour, 63km) about once an hour, and some long-distance buses may stop along the highway if you ask.

Patara

📞 0242 / POP 950

Patara, on the coast 8km south fo Xanthos, can claim Turkey's longest uninterrupted beach as well as some of Lycia's finest ruins; its village, laid-back little Gelemiş, is the perfect spot to mix ruin-rambling with some dedicated sun worship. Once very much on the hippy trail, Gelemiş is almost never filled with travellers these days – a miracle given its obvious charms – and traditional village life still goes on.

Patara's lofty place in history is well documented. It was the birthplace of St Nicholas, the 4th-century Byzantine bishop of Myra who later passed into legend as Santa Claus. Before that, Patara was celebrated for its temple and oracle of Apollo, of which little remains. It was Lycia's major port – which explains the large storage granary still standing. And according to Acts 21:1–2, Sts Paul and Luke changed boats here while on their third mission from Rhodes to Phoenicia.

◉ Sights & Activities

Ancient Patara   RUINS
(admission ₺5; ☺9am-7pm May-Oct, 8am-5pm Nov-Apr) From the highway turn-off, Gelemiş is 2km to the south and it's another 1.5km to the **ruins**, which includes admission to the beach. If you'll be staying longer than a day ₺7.50 allows you 10 entries over 10 days. You'll pass under a 2nd-century triple-arched **triumphal arch** at the entrance to the site with a necropolis containing a number of **Lycian tombs** nearby. Next is a **Harbour Baths complex** and the remains of a **Byzantine basilica**.

You can climb to the top of the 5000-seat **theatre** for a view of the site; note the stones at orchestra level carved with gladiator dress and equipment. On top of the hill to the south are the foundations of a Temple of Athena and an unusual circular **cistern**, cut into the rock with a pillar in the middle.

Just north of the theatre is the *bouleuterion* (council cahmber), ancient Patara's 'parliament' where it is believed members of the Lycian League met. Following a two-year, ₺8.5 million reconstruction, the *bouleterion* was opened by members of the Turkish National Assembly in May 2012. Nearby is the **colonnaded agora**, which leads to a dirt track and a **lighthouse** built by Emperor Nero and only recently excavated and reconstructed. Look among the nearby blocks for some amusing carvings. Across the ancient harbour (now a reedy wetland) is the enormous **Granary of Hadrian** for cereals and olive oil and a Corinthian-style **temple tomb**.

Patara Beach   BEACH
Backed by large sand dunes, this splendid, 18km-long sandy beach is unique for the region. You can get here by following the road for a kilometre past the ruins, or by turning right at the Golden Pension and following the track waymarked with blue arrows, which heads for the sand dunes along the western side of the archaeological section. Between late May and October, wagons pulled by tractors (₺2) trundle down to the beach from the village.

On the beach, which is hardly ever crowded (even in high season), you can rent umbrellas (₺4) and sunbeds (₺3) and there is a refreshment stand providing shade and sustenance. Depending on the season, parts of the beach are off-limits as it is an important nesting ground for sea turtles (see p377). It always closes at dusk and camping is prohibited.

Kirca Travel   CANOEING, HORSE RIDING
(☏843 5298; www.kircatravel.com) Based at the Flower Pension (p336), Kirca specialises in six-hour canoeing trips (₺50) on the Xanthos River but also offers three-hour horse-riding trips (₺70) through the Patara dunes, including lunch.

Patara Jeep Safari   DRIVING TOUR
(☏0554 393 2699; www.patarajeepsafari.com; tours ₺60) If you'd like to tour the Patara dunes (well away from the protected sea-turtle areas, of course), Xanthos and the Saklıkent Gorge at greater speed and on four wheels, talk to Patara Jeep Safari based in the centre.

🛏 Sleeping

As you come into Gelemiş the hillside on your left contains various hotels and pensions. A turn to the right at the Golden Pension takes you to the village centre, across the valley and up the other side to more pensions.

TOP CHOICE Patara View Point Hotel   HOTEL €€
(☏0533 350 0347, 843 5184; www.pataraview point.com; s/d ₺70/100; ❄@🛜🏊) Up the hill from the main road, the *très* stylish Patara View (owner Muzaffer was a French teacher) has a nice swimming pool, an Ottoman-style cushioned terrace, 27 rooms with balconies and, as its name suggests, killer views over the valley (though check out garden room 108). You'll find old farm implements inside and out, including a 2000-year-old olive press, an ancient beehive, charcoal forge and a shahoof, a distinctive sweep-pole well. They've even got their own newly carved Lycian tomb. There's a tractor-shuttle to and from the beach daily at 10am and 3pm.

Akay Pension   PENSION €
(☏0532 410 2195, 843 5055; www.pataraakay pension.com; s/d/tr ₺45/60/80; ❄@) Run by keen-to-please Kazım and his wife, Ayşe, the Akay has a total of 13 very well-maintained rooms and comfortable beds with balconies overlooking citrus groves, and comfy Ottoman-style lounge. Ayşe's cooking is legendary; sample at least one set meal (from ₺18) while here.

Flower Pension PENSION €
(☎0530 511 0206, 843 5164; www.pataraflowerpension.com; s/d ₺45/60, 4-/6-person apt ₺100/150; ❄@📶) On the road before the turn to the centre, the Flower has nine simple and airy rooms with balconies overlooking the garden as well as five kitchen-equipped (including fridges) studios and apartments accommodating four to six people. There's a free shuttle to the beach and owner, Mustafa, and his son, Bekir, are founts of local information.

Golden Pension PENSION €
(☎843 5162; www.pataragoldenpension.com; s/d ₺50/75; ❄@) With 16 homely rooms (all with balconies and new showers) and a friendly owner (Arif, the village mayor), Patara's original pension is peaceful despite its very central location on a crossroads. Day-long boat trips are available for ₺50, and there's a popular restaurant with a pretty shaded terrace. Choose a room with a garden view.

Zeybek 2 Pension PENSION €
(☎0532 683 5845, 843 5086; www.zeybek2pension.com; s ₺40-45, d ₺45-55, apt ₺85-100; ❄@) This family-run pension with a slightly rural feel has nine clean and sunny rooms and kitchen-equipped apartments with balconies, bedecked with traditional rugs. For the best view in town, climb up to the roof terrace that boasts 360-degree vistas of the hills and the ancient harbour. We love the dedicated internet room and tea at (precisely) 5pm.

Hotel Sema HOTEL €
(☎0537 428 9661, 843 5114; www.semahotel.com; r per person ₺25-30, apt ₺70-90; ❄@📶) The Sema is not luxurious but ideal for those who want to spend time with warm locals like Ali and Hanife, the proprietors. The large hotel sits in a garden above Patara where the dozen rooms and studios with kitchens are basic but spotless, cool and mosquito-free. Great views from up here too.

Eating & Drinking

Tlos Restaurant TURKISH €€
(☎843 5135; meze ₺3-6, pide ₺6-15, mains ₺12-20; ⏰8am-midnight) Run by the moustached and smiling chef-owner Osman, the Tlos has an open kitchen by the centre under a large plane tree. The *guveç* (₺15) – Turkish goulash for lack of a better term – is recommended. It's BYO.

Lazy Frog INTERNATIONAL €€
(☎843 5160; mains ₺15-25; ⏰8am-1am) With its very own kitchen garden, this central, popular place offers steaks as well as various vegetarian options and *gözleme* on its relaxing terrace.

SimBar BAR, CAFE
(☎0539 674 7849, 843 5214; ⏰11am-late) Patara's first seriously chilled-out cafe-bar has arrived, with lounge, garden and hammocks strung between the trees. German-Turkish owners Selina and Süha plan at least one special night (eg salsa) each week.

Medusa Bar BAR
(☎843 5193; ⏰9am-3am) Laid-back with cushioned benches and walls hung with old photos and posters, the Medusa plays music until the wee hours.

Gypsy Bar BAR
(⏰9am-3am) Tiny but traditional and much loved locally, the Gypsy has live Turkish music from 10pm a couple of nights each week.

Getting There & Away

Buses on the Fethiye–Kaş route drop you on the highway 4km from the village. From here dolmuşes run to the village every 30 to 40 minutes. In high season, minibuses depart from the beach via Gelemiş to Fethiye (₺12, 1½ hours, 73km), Kalkan (₺7.50, 20 minutes, 15km) and Kaş (₺10, 45 minutes, 40km). There's also a daily departure to Saklıkent Gorge (₺10, one hour, 52km) at 10am.

Kalkan

☎0242 / POP 3250

Kalkan is a well-to-do harbourside town built largely on hills that look down on an almost perfect bay. It's as justly famous for its excellent restaurants as its small but central beach. Just be aware that Kalkan is far more touristed, expat and expensive than most other places on the coast, including neighbouring Kaş.

A thriving Greek fishing village called Kalamaki until the 1920s, Kalkan is now largely devoted to high-end tourism. Development continues up the hills, with scores of new villas appearing each season. But look for Kalkan's charms in the compact old town.

Sights & Activities

Most people use Kalkan as a base to visit the Lycian ruins or engage in the many activities in the surrounding area. But it's an excellent place for a day-long boat trip. One recommended vessel is Ali Eğriboyun's **Anıl Boat** (☎844 3030, 0533 351 7520; jacksonvictoria@ hotmail.com), which costs ₺45 per person (or about ₺500 for the whole boat accommodating up to eight people), including an excellent lunch. Apart from the beach near the marina and **Kaputaş**, a perfect little sandy cove with a beach about 7km east of Kalkan on the road to Kaş, options for getting wet include **swimming platforms** at various hotels and pensions such as the Caretta Boutique Hotel and Hotel Villa Mahal, open to the public for a nominal fee. Kaş may have a better reputation for diving but there are a couple of wrecks and a fair amount of sealife to the west of Kalkan harbour. Contact **Dolphin Scuba Team** (☎844 2242, 0533 815 9236; www.dolphin scubateam.com; beginner & experienced divers from £37, PADI courses £47-240) on the harbour.

🛏 Sleeping

With private villas the dominant form of accommodation in Kalkan and many of the hotels block-booked by travel agencies and wholesalers, Kalkan doesn't offer quite the wide range of places to stay usually found in Turkish resort towns. The high season here is May to October.

TOP CHOICE **Hotel Villa Mahal** LUXURY HOTEL **€€€**
(☎0532 685 2136, 844 3268; www.villamahal.com; d €200-300, ste €550; ✳🛰☒) One of the most elegant and stylish hotels in all of Turkey lies atop a cliff on the western side of Kalkan Bay, about 2km by road from town. The 13 rooms, all individually designed in whiter-than-white minimalist fashion with azure splashes here and there, have breathtaking views of the sea and sunsets from the walls of windows that open onto private terraces. The sail-shaped infinity pool is spectacularly suspended on the edge of the void, but a mere 180 steps will take you to the sea and a bathing platform. There's a free water taxi into the centre; a normal taxi to/from Kalkan costs about ₺15. Sailboats (two Lasers and a Topper) can be hired for ₺50 per hour.

Caretta Boutique Hotel HOTEL **€€**
(☎0505 269 0753, 844 3435; www.carettaboutique hotel.com; İskele Sokak 6; s €45-58, d €69-85; ✳@) A perennial local favourite for its isolated swimming platforms, excellent home-style cooking and warm welcome from owners Gönül and her son, Murat, the Caretta has metamorphosed from pension caterpillar to boutique butterfly with 13 bright and sunny

rooms (three with jacuzzi). For a total away-from-it-all experience, try to nab one of the two terrace rooms away from the main house and down the steps along the cliff. There's a free boat service from below the lighthouse in the marina.

White House Pension PENSION **€€**
(☎0532 443 0012, 844 3738; www.kalkanwhite house.co.uk; Süleyman Yılmaz Caddesi 24-26; s/d ₺100/150, f ₺175; ✳@) Situated on a quiet corner at the top of the hill, this attentively run pension has 10 compact, breezy rooms – four with balconies – in a spotless family home. The real winner here, though, is the view from the terrace. Sharing the garden is the White House's sister property, the **Courtyard Hotel Kalkan** (☎844 3738, 0532 443 0012; www.courtyardkalkan.com; Süleyman Yılmaz Caddesi 24-26; s & d ₺350), cobbled out of a couple of 19th-centuury village houses, with original marble fireplaces, wooden ceilings and floors and a 'cave bath' that served as a water cistern 400 years ago.

Türk Evi PENSION **€€**
(☎0533 335 3569, 844 3129; www.kalkanturkevi .com; Şehitler Caddesi 19; s €40, d €45-55; ✳🛰) An excellent midrange choice, the attractive stone 'Turkish House', dating from the 1950s and surrounded by lush garden, houses nine larger-then-average rooms individually decorated with period furniture and colourful kilims. Some of the rooms upstairs have wonderful sea views.

Zinbad Butik Hotel HOTEL **€€**
(☎844 3475; www.zinbadhotel.com; Mustafa Koca Kaya Caddesi 26; s/d ₺60/100; ✳🛰) It's hard to see what makes this old stalwart 'boutique': its 21 rooms, some sponged Mediterranean blue and with balconies (room 302) looking to the sea, are just as cheerful and comfortable as before. It's close to the waterfront and central. Lovely welcome.

Kelebek Hotel & Apartments HOTEL, APARTMENT **€**
(☎0543 375 7947, 844 3770; www.butterflyholi days.co.uk; Mantese Mahallesi 4; s ₺45-50, d ₺70-85, 1-/2-bedroom apt ₺75/125; ✳@☒) Though slightly away from the action to the north of the centre, and a couple of hundred metres off the D400, the blue-and-white, family-run 'Butterfly' offers remarkably good value for Kalkan. Choose from among 22 rooms in the main building – with a pool table in the tiled lobby, and fronted by a large swimming pool – and eight apartments with

Kalkan

kitchens in a separate block. One room with a stunning harbour view is 202.

Gül Pansiyon
PENSION €

(☏0533 216 8487, 844 3099; www.kalkangulpan siyon.com; Şehitler Caddesi 7 Sokak; s/d ₺50/75, 2-/3-/5-person apt ₺90/110/180; ❄@) Our favourite recent budget find is the 'Rose', with six rooms and three apartments (the latter with kitchens and washing machines). Try to bag one of the rooms on the top (3rd) floor for the views, the balcony and the light. Owner Ömer is a welcoming host.

Holiday Pansiyon
PENSION €

(☏844 3154; Süleyman Yılmaz Caddesi 2; s/d ₺50 /80; ❄) Though the seven rooms here are simple, they're spotless and charming. The three in the older Ottoman section are particularly atmospheric, with wooden beams, lacy curtains and delightful balconies with good views. It's run by the charming Ahmet and Şefıka, who make delicious breakfast jams. Five rooms have air-con, the rest have fans.

Çelik Pansiyon
PENSION €

(☏844 2126; www.celikpansiyon.com; Süleyman Yılmaz Caddesi 9; s/d ₺50/70; ❄) One of Kalkan's very few cheap guest houses, open year-round, the Çelik has eight rooms with balconies that are spartan but spotless and quite spacious. The two mansard rooms at the top look over the rooftops and marina, as does the roof terrace. Best views are from rooms 6 and 7.

✖ Eating

Kalkan's main market day is Thursday, though there is a much smaller one in the Akbel district to the northwest on Sunday. In season, it's wise to book ahead no matter where you plan to eat in Kalkan.

Kalkan

Korsan Fish Terrace
SEAFOOD €€€

(844 3076; www.korsankalkan.com/FishTerrace.htm; Atatürk Caddesi; mains ₺26-40; 10am-midnight) On the roof of the 19th-century Patara Stone House, this restaurant is among the finest seafood experiences in Kalkan. Its homemade lemonade is legendary and there's live jazz on Tuesday and Saturday from 8.30pm. Ichthyophobes need not be concerned; hosts Uluç and Claire have come up with an alternative menu of modern Turkish and international dishes that are fishless.

Guru's Place
ANATOLIAN €€

(0536 331 1016, 844 3848; www.kalkanguru.com; Kaş Yolu; meze plate ₺20, mains ₺9-28; 8am-11pm) Affable Hüseyin and his family, who have been in the area for four centuries, have been running this restaurant by the sea for 20 years. Food is authentic and fresh, coming from their own garden. The menu is often limited to daily specials such as the lamb shanks. It's a bit out of town on the road to Kaş, so a free transfer service is provided. It's well worth the short journey.

Hünkar Ocakbaşı
TURKISH €€

(844 2077; Şehitler Caddesi 38e; mains ₺9-17) At long last, Kalkan gets its own authentic ocakbaşı (grill restaurant) serving all the traditional favourites. They also do pide (₺6 to ₺9) and pizzas (₺8 to ₺11) as well as five kinds of guveç (casserole), including a vegetarian one.

Mussakka
TURKISH €€€

(0537 493 2290, 844 1576; İskele Sokak 41; mains ₺24-40; 9.30am-1am) This new kid on the harbourfront is making quite a splash with its oh-so-pink decor and signature moussaka (₺26), which they insist is Turkish (it's all Greek to us). A boon for vegetarians, it offers five meatless mains (₺16 to ₺21). We love the great views and the big comfortable bar in front.

Marina Restaurant
TURKISH €€€

(0535 380 0970, 844 3384; İskele Sokak; mains ₺23-35; 8am-1am) Just below the landmark Pirat Hotel, our favourite grill restaurant by the water is dearer than it used to be – what isn't? – but still does excellent grills and fish dishes. It excels with pide (₺10 to ₺15) cooked in a stone oven in all its infinite variety. Ask Hikmet to recommend from the more than a dozen meze made daily.

Öz Adana
KEBAP €€

(0537 440 74 08, 844 1140; Şehitler Caddesi 1; mains ₺8-19) Despite its move close to the road to Kaş, the 'Original Adana' remains just that and serves some of the best kebaps, pide and lahmacun (Turkish pizza) in town.

Zeytinlik
MODERN TURKISH €€€

(Olive Grove; 844 3408; Hasan Altan Caddesi; mains ₺23-36;) Another winning British-Turkish joint venture under the guidance of Fathi and Rebecca, the rooftop Olive Grove serves some of the most adventurous Turkish food around – try the fish dolmas, the samosa-like minced lamb in filo pastry triangles or any of the several vegetarian options.

Kalamaki
MODERN TURKISH, BAR €€€

(☎844 1555; Hasan Altan Caddesi 43; mains ₺27-39) A modern venue with a very stylish minimalist pub on the ground floor and restaurant above offers superb Turkish dishes with a European twist. Try the scrumptious lamb with plums (₺31) or the generous vegetarian casserole (₺22). Host Tayfur takes it all in his stride – even when celebs like Gordon Ramsay come a-calling (for real).

Trio
SEAFOOD €€€

(☎0533 388 9713, 844 3380; www.triokalkan.com; İskele Sokak; mains ₺31-44; ☯7am-2am) Perennial favourite of expat Brits (just try to get in here on New Year's Eve!), this waterfront restaurant and bar serves excellent fish dishes (eg grouper with samphire) but not exclusively. It's a great place for a mid-afternoon cocktail while sprawled on one of the comfy wicker lounges.

Foto's Pizza
PIDE €€

(☎844 3464; www.fotospizza.com; İskele Sokak; pizza ₺13-23.50) Listing a pizza joint in a town of such culinary repute seems sacrilegious, but (a) Foto's has always been more pide than pizza for us and (b) the views from the terrace make it hard to overlook. It's just past the taxi rank on the way down the steep incline that locals call Heart Attack Hill. There's pasta (₺11 to ₺17), omelettes and casseroles too.

Aubergine
MODERN TURKISH, INTERNATIONAL €€€

(Patlıcan; ☎844 3332; www.kalkanaubergine.com; İskele Sokak; mains ₺19-36; ☯8am-3am) With tables right on the marina, as well as cosy seats inside, this restaurant that also goes by the name Patlıcan ('eggplant' in Turkish) is a magnet for its location alone. But add to that specialities like its slow-roasted wild boar (₺35) and swordfish fillet served in a creamy vegetable sauce (₺30) and you have a winner.

Merkez Cafe
CAFE, INTERNATIONAL €€

(☎844 2823; Hasan Altan Caddesi 17; pizza ₺9-17; ☯8am-1am) This very central (the meaning of its name) cafe that has recently got all dolled up makes superb pastries and cakes, including a gorgeous chocolate baklava (₺7) and coconut and almond macaroons (₺4). More substantial fare includes pizzas (₺9 to ₺17) and pasta.

Ada Patisserie
CAFE €

(☎844 2536; Kalamar Yolu; cakes ₺5-10; ☏) Charming little cafe-patisserie at the start of the Kalamar road, with shop-made delectables and wi-fi.

🍷 Drinking

Lighthouse
TEA GARDEN, CAFE

(☎844 3752; Yat Limanı; beer ₺6; ☯8.30am-2.30am) The closest thing Kalkan has to a tea garden, the erstwhile Fener ('lighthouse' in Turkish – and no prizes for guessing its location) is as popular with locals as it is with expats and visitors. Looking for someone in Kalkan? Try here first.

Parc Kalkan
BAR, PUB

(☎844 1634; www.kalkanparc.com; Şehitler Caddesi 36) As much an eatery (snacks ₺7 to ₺11, mains ₺14 to ₺26) as it is a bar, this garden-like place under a marquee on the main road into town is the expat watering hole of choice. Quiz nights are a regular feature.

Moonlight Bar
BAR

(☎844 3043; Süleyman Yılmaz Caddesi 17; beer ₺7; ☯9am-4am) Just down from the post office, Kalkan's oldest boozer is still its most 'happening', though a good percentage of people sitting at the tables outside – or on the small dance floor inside – are visitors.

🛍 Shopping

Just Silver
JEWELLERY

(☎844 3136; Hasan Altan Caddesi 28) Just about the most famous shop in Kalkan has gals and dolls lining up for ear, nose, neck, finger and toe baubles.

ℹ Information

Kalkan Turkish Local News (KTLN; http://kalkan.turkishlocalnews.com) Independent, comprehensive and reliable website on all things Kalkan run by a well-informed British expat.
Mavi Bilgisaya Internet Cafe (Hasan Altan Caddesi 2; per hr ₺3; ☯8.30am-5pm, until 9pm May-Oct) On the 3rd floor of the old *belediye* (town hall) building with a handful of terminals and wi-fi.

ℹ Getting There & Away

Minibuses connect Kalkan with Fethiye (₺11, 1½ hours, 83km) and Kaş (₺5, 35 minutes, 29km) via the beach at Kaputaş (₺3, 15 minutes, 7km). Some eight minibuses also run daily to Patara (₺5, 25 minutes, 15km).

Around Kalkan

İSLAMLAR

This alpine former Greek village in the mountains is a favourite escape from Kalkan, 8km south. The attractions here are a temperature that is 5°C cooler than in Kalkan in summer, and the dozen or so trout restaurants that make use of icy mountain streams to fill their tanks. In the village square, have a look at one of two working mills that still use waterpower and a great millstone to turn local residents' grain into flour. Due south along a rough track is our favourite restaurant, **Çiftlik** (☑838 6055, 0537 421 6129), where fresh trout (₺8) and a variety of meze, salads and chips won't cost much more than ₺15 per person. The nearby **Değirmen** (☑838 6295, 0532 586 2734) is a posher but still authentic eatery that makes it own tahina from sesame picked from the fields and ground in the basement. Enjoy the views from both!

If you just can't tear yourself away there's a mini-paradise called **Grapevine Cottage** (☑838 6078, 0534 744 9255; verydeb@gmail.com; d ₺100), set among citrus groves and vineyards just east of the Çiftlik restaurant. Run by Briton Deborah, the place has two bedrooms decorated with Mexican tiles (Deborah has a house in Mexico). The views down to the sea from the breakfast terrace are priceless, and Deborah makes her own bread and jams. Transport to/from Akbel, a suburb to the northwest of the centre of Kalkan, can be arranged but getting here by public transport is not possible. It's right on the Lycian Way, so ideal for walkers.

BEZİRGAN

In an elevated valley some 17km northeast of Kalkan sits the beautiful village of Bezirgan, a timeless example of Turkish rural life. Towering some 725m above the fruit orchards and fields of sticky sesame are the ruins of the Lycian hilltop citadel of **Pirha**.

Accommodation is available at **Owlsland** (☑837 5214; www.owlsland.com; r per person ₺95, incl half-board ₺140), a 150-year-old farmhouse idyllically surrounded by fruit trees and run by a charming Turkish-Scottish couple. Erol, a trained chef, turns out traditional Turkish dishes made with locally grown produce and Pauline makes her own jams and ginger cake. The three rooms are simple but cosy, contain most of their original features and are decorated with old farm implements.

The upstairs room with balcony and traditional decor is especially nice.

ℹ Getting There & Away

Hourly minibuses between Kınık and Elmalı go via the Akbelin in Kalkan (₺4) and will drop you off in Bezirgan. There's also a direct bus to/from Antalya.

If you're under your own steam head north from Kalkan, cross over the D400 linking Fethiye and Kaş and follow the signs for Sütleğen and Elmalı. The road climbs steadily, with stunning views across the sea, and heads further up the mountain, past the Turkish home of one of the authors. Once the road crests the pass, you can see Bezirgan below. Ignore the first exit for Bezirgan and take the second. The signposted turning for Owlsland is just before the road begins climbing again to Sütleğen.

Kaş

☑0242 / POP 7200

A more workaday destination than Kalkan, Kaş – pronounced (roughly) 'cash' – may not sport the finest beaches in the region, but it's a yachties' haven and the atmosphere of the town is wonderfully mellow. The surrounding areas are ideal for day trips by sea or scooter, and a plethora of adventure sports are on offer, in particular some excellent wreck diving.

Extending to the west of the old town is the 6km-long Çukurbağ Peninsula. At the start of it you'll find a well-preserved ancient theatre, about all that's left of ancient Antiphellos, the name of the original Lycian town here. Above the town several Lycian rock tombs in the mountain wall can be seen even at night when they are illuminated.

Lying just offshore is the geopolitical oddity of the Greek island of Meis (Kastellorizo), which can be visited.

◉ Sights & Activities

Antiphellos Ruins   RUIN

Walk up hilly Uzun Çarşı Sokak, the Roman-era road that locals call Slippery Street, to the east of the main square to reach the **King's Tomb**, a superb example of a 4th-century-BC Lycian sarcophagus, which is mounted on a high base and has two lions' heads on the lid.

Antiphellos was a small settlement and the port for Phellos, the much larger Lycian town further north in the hills. The small Hellenistic **theatre**, 500m west of the main

Kaş

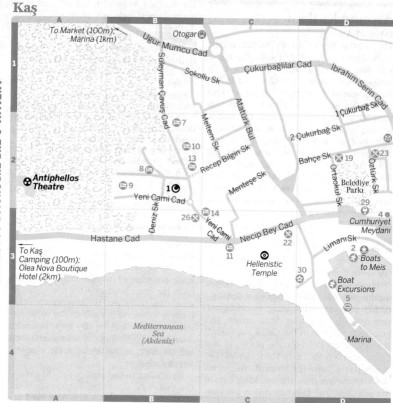

square, could seat some 4000 spectators and is in very good condition. You can also walk to the **rock tombs** cut into the sheer cliffs above town, which are illuminated at night. The walk is strenuous so go at a cool time of day.

Beaches
BEACH

Büyük Çakıl (Big Pebble) is a relatively clean beach about a kilometre from the town centre while **Akçagerme Plajı** is a public beach opposite the exit to Gökseki, along the main road west to Kalkan. **İnceboğaz** is a shingle beach at the start of the peninsula. But the best idea is to hop on one of the water taxis (₺10) in the harbour and head for one of three beaches on the peninsula opposite at **Liman Ağzı**.

Diving
DIVING

Kaş is the regional centre for diving in the Mediterranean and there are wrecks and a lot more underwater life than you'd expect below the surface. A number of companies offer their services, including **Subaqua Diving Centre** (☎0532 221 0129; www.subaquadive .com) in the habour and **Sundiving** (☎0532 254 0710, 836 2637; www.sundiving.com) at Kaş Camping. An introductory dive costs around €35, it's €50 for two dives and lunch for experienced divers, and three-day open-water PADI courses start at €285.

Tours

Most companies offer more or less the same journeys, but you can always tailor your own for a negotiated price.

Among the stalwarts, the three-hour **bus and boat trip** (₺40 to ₺50) to Üçağız and Kekova is a fine day out, and includes time to see several interesting ruins as well as swim.

Other standard tours go to the Mavi Mağara (Blue Cave), Patara and Kalkan or to Longos

Olympica Travel Agency — TRAVEL AGENCY

(☑0532 498 8228, 836 2049; www.olympicatravel .com; Cumhuriyet Meydanı, Necip Bey Caddesi 14) This place specialises in 'build your own activity packages' according to clients' time, interests and budget.

Xanthos Travel — OUTDOOR ACTIVITIES

(☑0533 561 0710, 836 3292; www.xanthostravel .com; İbrahim Serin Caddesi 5/A) An affable group that can organise any number of activities and excursions such as sea kayaking in Kekova (₺60 to ₺70, or ₺90 including Aperlae).

✹ Festivals & Events

Kaş Lycia Festival — FESTIVAL

The annual Kaş Lycia Festival runs for three days at the end of June. It features prominent folk-dancing troupes and musicians – and an international swimming race – and works to foster an improved relationship between Greece and Turkey.

🛏 Sleeping

Most – but not all – affordable accommodation in Kaş is west and northwest of the centre along the waterfront and up the hill around the Yeni Cami (New Mosque).

TOP CHOICE Hideaway Hotel — HOTEL €€

(☑0532 261 0170, 836 1887; www.hotelhideaway .com; Eski Kilise Arkası Sokak 7; s ₺40-60, d ₺60-120; ❈@🛰🏊) The aptly named Hideaway, located at the far end of town on a quiet street, has just got even better. Run by the unstoppable Ahmet, a fount of local information, the Hideaway counts 19 comfortable rooms, all with balcony and a half-dozen facing the sea. The recently renovated white-on-white rooms with rain showers and ceiling fans are positively luxurious. There's a smallish pool and a roof terrace with terminals, DVD player, honour-system bar, and views over the water and amphitheatre. Full meals as cheap as ₺15 are available. A real coffee machine too!

Hotel Hadrian — RESORT €€€

(☑836 2856; www.hotel-hadrian.de; Doğan Kaşaroğlu Sokak 10; s €80-100, d €125-140, ste from €160; ❈🏊) About halfway out on the peninsula, the German-owned Hadrian is a tropical oasis with 14 rooms and suites (though the faux-classical statues add a touch of Teutonic kitsch). The large seawater pool and private swimming platform are excellent, and we could spend most of the rest of

and several small nearby islands. There are also overland excursions to Saklıkent Gorge.

A great idea is to charter a boat from the marina. A whole day spent around the islands of Kaş should cost from ₺200 to ₺250 for the entire boat, accommodating up to eight people.

There are several good tour companies:

Bougainville Travel — OUTDOOR ACTIVITIES

(☑836 3737; www.bougainville-turkey.com; İbrahim Serin Sokak 10) A long-established English-Turkish tour operator with a solid reputation and much experience in organising any number of activities lasting a full day, including canyoning (₺110); mountain biking (₺90); paragliding (₺210 for flights lasting 20 to 30 minutes); scuba diving (₺55 per dive including all equipment, ₺80 for a first dive); and sea kayaking (₺70). They are also experts on Lycian Way trekking and designing tailor-made tours for all of Turkey.

Kaş

our lives propped up at the terrace bar with wow-factor views. Choicest room/suite? Room 110 and apartment A3.

White House Pension   PENSION €€
(☎0532 550 2663, 836 1513; www.orcholiday.com; Yeni Cami Caddesi 10; s ₺60-85, d ₺100-140; ✴🅰) Decked out in wood, wrought iron, marble and terracotta paint, this is a stylish little gem with eight attractive rooms and a pretty terrace. Ask for the attic room towards the back with the lovely balcony. Very warm welcome.

Anı Pension & Guesthouse   PENSION €
(☎0533 326 4201, 836 1791; www.motelani.com; Süleyman Çavuş Caddesi 12; dm ₺25, s ₺30-50, d ₺50-60; ✴🅰🛜) Unstoppabe host Ömer continues improving his pension with 15 smallish but spotless rooms with balconies and new bathrooms. There's a book exchange, a relaxing roof terrace with DVD player, köşk (lounge area) with cushions and water pipes and a bar. Guests can also use the kitchen (occasional barbecues for ₺15) and Ömer will lend you a chaise longue and umbrella for the beach.

Olea Nova Boutique Hotel   BOUTIQUE HOTEL €€€
(☎836 2660; www.oleanova.com.tr; Demokrasi Caddesi 43; s & d €90-150; ✴🅰🛜🏊) This stunning new 19-room boutique hotel, on the peninsula about 2km from the centre and built within a one-time teachers' holiday home, is set amid olive groves on a hill above the sea, with views straight to the Greek island of Meis. The kidney-shaped pool with terrace bar is convenient, but we prefer the bathing platform 100m down the hill. Rooms have ceiling fans and aircon; some of the superior ones boast views from the bathroom.

Santosa Pansion   PENSION €
(☎0535846 3584, 836 1714; www.santosapension .com; Recep Bilgin Sokak 4; s ₺50-60, d ₺60-90; ✴🅰) Clean, quiet and cheap is how best to describe this backpacker hang-out. The 11 rooms are simple but attractively decorated with floral stencilled patterns, and are excellent for the price. The couple who run the show are cooks – try one of their barbecues (₺25) or vegetarian set meals (₺15).

Narr Hotel   BOUTIQUE HOTEL €€
(📞836 2024; www.narrhotelcom; Hükümet Caddesi; s ₺60-100, d ₺85-140; ❄️🛜📶) This narrow white-and-cream boutique hotel with 15 rooms, just opposite Little Pebble Beach and its bathing platforms, is good value for its location and style. Seven rooms (including 201 and 202) look directly at the sea and the Greek island of Meis.

Ateş Pension   PENSION €
(📞0532 492 0680, 836 1393; www.atespension .com; Amfitiyatro Sokak 3; dm ₺25-30, s ₺40-60, d ₺60-80; ❄️@) Well run by Recep and Ayşe, this is a friendly place with 17 smallish rooms including a dorm with four beds, new bathrooms and a pleasant roof terrace where barbecues (₺20) are held. Guests get to use the pool at the nearby Hideaway Hotel.

Kaş Otel   HOTEL €€
(📞0533 223 5913, 836 1271; www.myhotelkas .com; Hastane Caddesi 15; s/d ₺100/150; ❄️) The 22 rooms are simple here but you're paying for one of the best locations on the water. In fact, the sea is so close you can hear it lapping from the terrace or the balconies of 10 rooms – and there's a swimming platform. The dozen rooms set back from the water are not as nice.

Hilal Pansiyon   PENSION €€
(📞0532 615 1061, 836 1207; www.korsan-kas.com; Süleyman Yıldırım Caddesi 8; s €19-22, d €28-35, tr €36-45; ❄️@🛜) Run by the friendly Süleyman, the Hilal offers 16 unexceptional rooms and a leafy terrace that sometimes hosts barbecues (₺15) and boasts extravagant views. The travel agency below it offers guests 10% discounts on activities including kayaking, diving and trips to Saklıkent. Bikes are free for guests.

Kaş Camping   CAMPING GROUND €
(📞836 1050; www.kaskamping.com; Hastane Caddesi 3; campsite ₺20-40, standard/deluxe bungalow ₺65/160; ❄️@) Located on an attractive rocky outcropping at the start of the peninsula 800m west of town, this popular site is 100m from the sea and features a lively terrace bar. Deluxe bungalows have bathrooms and air-conditioning.

✗ Eating

Kaş doesn't offer quite the dining scene that Kalkan does, though you'll find some excellent restaurants to the southeast of the main square, especially around Sandıkçı Sokak.

There's a big outdoor market along the old road to Kalkan on Friday.

TOP CHOICE İkbal   MODERN TURKISH €€€
(📞836 3193; Sandıkçı Sokak 6; mains ₺20-34; ⏰9am-midnight) Arguably Kaş's best restaurant and run by Vecdi and his German wife, Barbara, İkbal serves excellent prepared fish dishes and the house speciality, slow-cooked leg of lamb, from a small but well-chosen menu. We appreciate the good selection of Turkish wines from Mediterranean vineyards.

Şaraphane   TURKISH €
(📞0532 520 3262, 836 2715; Yeni Cami Caddesi 3; mains ₺12-25) Excellent new kid on the block in the old part of Kaş, the 'Wine House' emphasises the fruit of the vine amid cosy surrounds with an open kitchen, bleached wooden floors and a roaring fire in the cooler months. It's very much home style but has a great atmosphere and there are nice touches like complimentary homemade meze. Great service.

Köşk   MEZE €€
(📞836 3857; Gürsoy Sokak 13; mains ₺14-25) In a lovely little square off a cobbled street just up from the water, Köşk occupies a rustic, 150-year-old house with two terraces and seating in the open courtyard. They serve good grills and gorgeous meze (₺6 to ₺KL7) – a full three dozen of them, in fact.

Blue House   MEZE €€
(📞836 1320; Sandıkçı Sokak 8; mains ₺20-34) This restaurant, with its distinctive blue doorway and balcony, has a great ambience and lovely views. The meze are good and the main reason for coming. It's a family affair; the ladies work from the kitchen of their own house, which you have to pass through to get to the terrace.

Bi Lokma   MEZE €€
(📞836 3942; www.bilokma.com.tr; Hükümet Caddesi 2; mains ₺13-21; ⏰9am-midnight) Also known as 'Mama's Kitchen', this place has tables meandering around a terraced garden overlooking the harbour. Sabo – the 'mama' in question – turns out great traditional dishes including eight meze and her famous *mantı* (₺13) and *börek* (filled pastry; ₺13).

Cafe Mola   CAFE €€
(📞836 1994; Emin Erdem Meydanı 3/B; dishes ₺7-12; ⏰8.30am-11pm) Our home away from home in Kaş, this convivial cafe is great for

MEIS EXPRESS

The **Meis Express** (www.meisexpress.com; one-way or same-day return ₺40) fast ferry sails throughout the year to the tiny Greek island of Meis (Kastellorizo) at 10am (10.30am in winter) and returns at 4pm (3pm in winter); the voyage takes just 20 minutes. Meis is a simple fishing village with a sprinkling of restaurants, a superb bakery, a duty-free shop selling Greek wine and pork, some excellent walks over the hill and a decent photo museum in the old church. It's possible to spend the night in Meis, or continue onwards into Greece proper. There are regular ferries to Rhodes (€18, 4½ hours) three times a week and a high-speed catamaran (€32, 2½ hours) in summer. Meis even has a tiny landing strip from where you can fly to Rhodes (€30, 30 minutes) at 5.30pm Friday to Wednesday. On Meis your best source of information is **Papoutsis Travel** (☑+30 22460 49 286; www.greeklodgings.gr).

Tickets for Meis can be bought from Meis Express in the harbour or any travel agency, such as Olympica (p343). Make sure you arrive a half-hour before sailing in order to complete immigration formalities.

Turkish breakfast (₺12), sandwiches (₺7) or *mantı* (₺10). It has an espresso machine, and staff make award-winning fresh lemonade with mint (₺5).

Sultan Garden Restaurant
ANATOLIAN €€€

(☑836 3762; www.sultangarden.co.uk; Hükümet Caddesi; mains ₺20-32) This very leafy place, with a terrace overlooking the harbour and a functioning ancient cistern, is a perennial favourite offering excellent service and both traditional and more inventive Turkish dishes. Try the Sultan's Delight (₺24), spiced stewed lamb on aubergine puree.

Havana Balık Evi
SEAFOOD €

(☑836 4111; Öztürk Sokak 7; mains ₺6-14; ⊙9am-midnight) The Cuban reference is lost on us, but we come to this place not for its more complex mains but for *balık ekmek* (₺6), the simple fish sandwich that is a staple in coastal Turkey. It's BYO.

Chez Evy
FRENCH €€€

(☑836 1253; Terzi Sokak 4; mains ₺25-40; ⊙7pm-midnight) This French restaurant, a Kaş institution, is run by the indefatigable Evy and tucked in the back streets above town. Evy serves such classics as *gigot d'agneau* and *filet de boeuf sauce béarnaise* as well as a lot of salads. It's expensive for what it is but an experience unique to Kaş.

Enişte'nin Yeri
TURKISH €

(☑836 4404; Necip Bey Caddesi; dishes ₺5-15) Just opposite Yapı Kredi bank, 'Brother-in-Law's Place' has very good (and cheap) pide, grills, soups and salads, with a pretty courtyard and a lovely air-conditioned room for the warmer months.

Bahçe Restaurant
TURKISH €€

(☑836 2370; Uzun Çarşı Sokak 31; mains ₺15-30) This restaurant opposite the monumental King's Tomb has a pretty garden and serves excellent dishes at decent prices, including a terrific range of meze (₺6 to ₺7). The fish wrapped in paper (₺24) gets good reviews.

Çınarlar Pide & Pizza House
PIDE €€

(☑836 2860; İbrahim Serin Sokak 4; pide ₺8.50-14, pizza ₺12-20; ⊙8am-1am) Perennially popular with Kaş' young bloods, who come for the affordable pide, pizza and and pop music, Çınarlar has a pleasant courtyard tucked away off the street.

Cafe Corner
CAFE, BAR €€

(☑836 3661; İbrahim Serin Sokak 20; meze ₺5, dishes ₺12-18; ⊙8am-1am) This well-positioned cafe-bar has a nice relaxed atmosphere and well-priced drinks. It does decent snacks as well as light meals and breakfast (₺9)

🍷 Drinking & Entertainment

Giorgio's Bar
BAR

(☑0544 608 8687; Cumhuriyet Meydanı) Facing the main square, Georgio's has great music (played live several times a week) and service. Drinks prices are not bad (cocktails from ₺18) when you consider the key location.

Hideaway Bar & Cafe
BAR, CAFE

(☑836 3369; Cumhuriyet Meydanı 16/A; beer ₺6-8; ⊙4pm-3am) Well named, this enchanting cafe and bar is secreted in a garden accessible from the street via a secret doorway. Turkish breakfast (₺20) and Sunday brunch is offered, as well as snacks and cakes.

Moon River BAR

(☑836 4423; İbrahim Serin Sokak 1/D; beer ₺5; ⊙8am-3am; 🔊) The erstwhile Harry's Bar has reinvented itself as a lounge with frequent live music throughout the week. It has very good coffee, and drinks are reasonably priced.

Echo Cafe & Bar BAR, CLUB

(☑836 2047; www.echocafebar.com; Limanı Sokak; ⊙8am-4am) Hip and stylish, this lounge near an ancient (5 BC, anyone?) cistern on the harbour has Kaş high society sipping fruit daiquiris to both live and canned jazz. The airy gallery upstairs has nice little balconies overlooking the water.

 Shopping

Turqueria ANTIQUES, HANDICRAFTS

(☑836 1631; Uzun Çarşı Sokak 21) Run by Orhan and Martina, a charming Turkish-German couple long resident in Kaş, Turqueria is an Aladdin's cave, with everything from old prints and advertisements to rare Turkish puppets handcut from leather.

Gallery Anatolia CERAMICS

(☑836 1954; www.gallery-anatolia.com; Hükümet Caddesi 2; ⊙9am-11pm) This very upmarket gallery along the marina has locally designed ceramic pieces.

ℹ Information

Computer World (☑836 2700; Bahçe Sokak; per hr ₺3; ⊙9am-11pm) Computer shop opposite the post office has 13 terminals.

Tourist Office (☑836 1238; Cumhuriyet Meydanı; ⊙8am-5pm daily May-Oct, 8am-noon & 1-5pm Mon-Fri Nov-Apr) Marginally helpful office on the main square has town plans and a few brochures.

ℹ Getting There & Away

The **otogar** is along Atatürk Bulvarı 350m north of the centre. From here there are daily buses to İstanbul (₺65, 15 hours, 985km) at 6.30am. There are direct buses to İzmir (₺40, 8½ hours, 440km). To reach Ankara (₺50, 11 hours, 740km), you must change at Fethiye.

Closer to home there are dolmuşes every half-hour to Kalkan (₺5, 35 minutes, 29km), Olympos (₺18, 2½ hours, 109km) and Antalya (₺23, 3½ hours, 188km) and hourly to Fethiye (₺15, 2½ hours, 107km). Services to Patara (₺7.50, 45 minutes, 40km) run every half-hour in high season, and hourly at other times. You can also reach Saklıkent Gorge (₺12.50, one hour, 52km) from here.

Üçağız & Kekova

☑0242 / POP 400

Declared off-limits to development, Üçağız (ooch-eye-iz) is a Turkish fishing and farming village in an absolutely idyllic setting on a bay amid islands and peninsulas. Little has changed here over the years aside from the steady trickle of visitors, most of whom leave by the end of the day. There's not a lot to do – the water isn't especially good for swimming – but it's a regular stop on the gület circuit, and a final taste of the mainland before visiting the sunken city at Kekova or secluded Kaleköy.

A few words about where you are and what's what: the village you enter from the coastal highway is Üçağız, ancient Teimiussa, with its own Lycian necropolis. Across the water on the peninsula to the southeast is Kaleköy (called Kale locally), a protected village on the site of the ancient city of Simena.

South of the villages and past the channel entrance is the long island of Kekova with its famous underwater ruins; local people generally use this name to refer to the whole area. To the west on the Sıcak Peninsula is Aperlae, an isolated and very evocative ancient Lycian city on the Lycian Way.

🛏 Sleeping & Eating

Üçağız's pensions all offer free boat service to the beaches on Kekova Island. They are excellent bases for hiking sections of the Lycian Way.

Onur Pension PENSION €€

(☑0536 675 0717, 874 2071; www.onurpension.com; s ₺50-80, d ₺70-100; ❄@) With a picturesque setting right on the harbour, this well-run pension combines charm with attentive service. Locally born Onur can give great trekking advice and act as a guide. Four of the eight rooms, kept shipshape by Onur's Dutch wife, Jacqueline, have full sea views (though the mansard ones at the top are a little cramped).

Likya Pension PENSION €

(☑0533 462 8554, 874 2090; www.likyacennet .com/; s/d ₺50/70; ❄@🔊) Just up the steps from the harbour, gregarious carpet seller Mehmet runs this comfortable eight-room pension in an ancient stone complex hidden within lush gardens. His snazzy new branch, the Likya Cennet Pension (☑0533 462 8854, 874 2090; www.likyacennet.com; s/d ₺60/80) next door, has five newly renovated rooms with everything.

MAKING SENSE & CENTS IN KEKOVA

Given the difficulty of getting to Kekova by public transport, most people end up taking a boat tour of the area from Kaş or Kalkan, which starts with a bus ride to Üçağız where you'll board the boat for Kekova.

Along the northern shore of Kekova are ruins, partly submerged 6m below the sea and referred to as the Batık Şehir (Sunken City). These ruins are the result of a series of severe earthquakes in the 2nd century AD; most of what you can still see is a residential part of ancient Simena. Foundations of buildings, staircases and moorings are also visible. It is forbidden to anchor or swim around or near the Sunken City.

After the visit to Kekova you'll have lunch on the boat and then head on to Kaleköy, passing a couple of submerged (and very photo-worthy) Lycian tombs just offshore. There's usually about an hour to explore Kaleköy and climb up to the hilltop fortress.

Tours from Kaş, which cost ₺50 per person, generally leave at 10am and return around 6pm. A similar tour organised in Üçağız will cost about ₺40 per person; a boat for the day accommodating four/eight people costs from ₺180/250. We like Mehmet Tezcan's **Kumsal** (☎0532 685 2401; kumsal_boat.hotmail.com) or you could try Captain Turgay Poyraz at the **Onur Pension** (☎874 2071; www.onurpension.com).

The closest you'll get to the underwater ruins is on a sea-kayaking tour (₺60 per person, or ₺90 with Aperlae, including transfers and lunch) run by one of the Kaş travel agencies such as Bougainville Travel (p343).

Kekova Pansiyon
PENSION €€

(☎0532 658 8517, 874 2259; www.kekovapansiyon .com; d ₺70-120; ❄@☀) Set in splendid isolation on the far end of the waterfront, this pension is in a handsome old stone building with a terrace dotted with flowerpots. The eight rooms are comfortable and share a lovely verandah with cushioned benches and views over the water.

Kordon Restaurant
SEAFOOD €€

(☎874 2067; meze ₺5-6, grills & fish per 500g ₺15-17.50; ☉9am-midnight) With an attractive and breezy terrace overlooking the marina and fresh fish – try the excellent grilled sea bass – the Kordon is one of the better restaurants in town. Set lunch is a snip at ₺20 to ₺25.

Kekova Fish House
SEAFOOD €€

(☎0542 848 8545; www.kekovarestaurant.com; mains ₺12-16) This excellent, newly opened fish restaurant right on the harbour also has accomodation in five basic rooms (singles ₺40 to ₺60, doubles ₺70 to ₺100), some of which are perched right over the water.

ℹ️ Getting There & Away

A tricky place to reach... One dolmuş leaves Antalya for Üçağız daily at 2.30pm (₺20, 3½ hours) and returns at 8am. Dolmuşes also run every hour or so from Antalya to Demre (₺12, three hours), from where you can get a taxi (₺50) to Üçağız.

Taxi is the only option from Kaş (₺60). In summer, you might hitch a lift with one of the boat companies making daily tours to Üçağız (one way ₺30, two hours).

From Demre, one dolmuş a day goes to Üçağız (₺5, 30 minutes) at 5pm. It leaves Üçağız at 8am.

Kaleköy (Kale)

☎0242 / POP 150

The watery paradise of Kaleköy is one of the western Mediterranean's truly delightful spots, home to the ruins of ancient **Simena** and an impressive Crusader **fortress** (admission ₺8) perched above a hamlet looking out to sea. Within the fortress, the ancient world's tiniest **theatre** is cut into the rock, and nearby you'll find ruins of several temples and public baths. From the top you can look down upon a field of **Lycian tombs**, and the old **city walls** are visible on the outskirts. The stately mansion, with the helipad overlooked by the castle, is owned by the Koç family, Turkey's richest.

Kaleköy is accessible from Üçağız only by motorboat (10 minutes) or on foot (45 minutes) along a rough track.

🛏️ Sleeping & Eating

TOP CHOICE **Mehtap Pansiyon**
PENSION €€

(☎0542 593 1006, 874 2146; www.mehtappansiyon. com; campsite ₺20, s ₺90-150, d ₺140-180; ❄🛜) Kaleköy has a couple of pensions, but your first choice should be the 10-room Mehtap, with spectacular views over the harbour and submerged Lycian tombs below. Four rooms are in a 200-year-old stone house so quiet and tranquil you may start snoozing as you check in; another four are in a building dating back a millennium and there's two more in a purpose-built wood cottage. İrfan and his son, Saffet, are warm and knowledgeable hosts. Saffet's wife, Nazike, grows her own vegetables and is an excellent cook (set meal ₺40).

Kale Pansiyon
PENSION €€

(☑0532 244 1163, 874 2111; www.kalepansiyon.com; s ₺80-100, d ₺150-170; ❄) Down by the harbour, the eight homely rooms of the Kale Pansiyon all have balconies with direct views that are so close to the sea you can hear the water lapping. The family's holdings spread to the similarly priced **Olive Grove** (☑874 2025), which is set back from the harbour and costs the same. It's a gorgeous 150-year-old Greek stone house (look out for the lovely mosaic on the verandah). The four rooms of the house are simple but elegant and share a large verandah with sea views.

Hassan Deniz Restaurant
SEAFOOD €€

(☑874 2101; www.hassandeniz.com; mains ₺10-20) One of about five restaurants along the seafront, Hassan Deniz is much favoured by yachties and their crews for its fresh fish, great meze and reliable wi-fi. It's at the end of a long pier.

Ankh
CAFE €

(☑874 2171; www.ankhpansion.com; ice cream ₺8) Ankh, a cafe at a pension, makes its own peach, banana and hazelnut ice cream and boasts million-dollar views from its terrace.

Kale (Demre)

☑0242 / POP 16,200

Officially 'Kale' but called by its old name 'Demre' by just about everyone, this sprawling, dusty town was once the Lycian (and later Roman) city of Myra. By the 4th century it was important enough to have its own bishop – most notably St Nicholas, who went on to catch the Western world's imagination in his starring role as Santa Claus. In AD 60, St Paul put Myra on the liturgical map by changing boats at its port, Andriake, while on his way to Rome (or so Acts 27: 4–6 tell us).

Once situated on the sea, Demre moved further inland as precious alluvium – deposits of clay, silt, sand and gravel – flowed from the Demre stream. That silting is the foundation of the town's wealth, and it remains a major centre for the growing and distribution of fruit and vegetables.

The street going west from the main square to the Church of St Nicholas is pedestrian Müze Caddesi and is lined with cafes and shops. Alakent Caddesi leads 2km north to the Lycian rock tombs of Myra while the street going south from the square passes the otogar (100m).

◉ Sights

St Nicholas Church & Museum
CHURCH, MUSEUM

(Müze Caddesi; admission ₺10; ⊙9am-7pm Apr-Oct, to 5pm Nov-Mar) Not vast like Aya Sofya or brilliant with mosaics like İstanbul's Kariye Museum (Chora Church), the Church of St Nicholas is nonetheless a star attraction for pilgrims and tourists alike. Nowadays almost all of them are Russian (Nicholas is the patron saint of Russia). The remains of the eponymous saint were laid here upon his death in AD 343.

The bare earthen church features some interesting Byzantine frescoes and mosaic floors. It was made a basilica when it was restored in 1043. Italian merchants smashed open the sarcophagus in 1087 and supposedly carted off St Nicholas' bones to Bari.

Restorations sponsored by Tsar Nicholas I of Russia in 1862 changed the church by building a vaulted ceiling and a belfry – something unheard of in early Byzantine architecture. More recent work by Turkish archaeologists is aiming to protect it from deterioration.

There are a couple of statues of the saint – one of them the height of kitsch as Santa Claus – in the square in front of the church. St Nick's feast day (6 December) is a very big event here.

Myra
RUINS

(admission ₺15; ⊙9am-7pm Apr-Oct, to 5pm Nov-Mar) If you only have time to see one striking honeycomb of Lycian rock tombs, then choose the memorable ruins of ancient Myra. Located about 2km inland from Demre's main square, they are among the finest in Lycia. There's a well-preserved **Roman theatre** here, which includes several theatrical masks carved on stones lying in the nearby area. The so-called **Painted Tomb** near the river necropolis portrays a man and his family in relief both inside and out. A taxi ride from the square will cost about ₺10.

Andriake
RUINS

About 5km southwest of the centre is the seafront settlement of Çayağzı, called Andriake by the Romans at a time when the port was an important entrepot for grain on the sea route between the eastern Mediterranean and Rome.

The ruins of the ancient town are strewn over a wide area to the north and south of the access road approaching Çayağzı, which is little more than a half-dozen boat-building yards and a few beach front cafes. Much of the land is marshland (great bird-watching!) so the great granary built by Hadrian and completed in AD 139, to the south of the road, can be difficult to reach in wet weather. In 2009 the ruins of the first synagogue found in ancient Lycia were uncovered here.

Dolmuşes run sporadically out to Çayağzı; your best bet is probably a taxi (₺15).

🛏 Sleeping & Eating

Most visitors travel to Demre by day and sleeping options in the town centre are virtually nonexistent. If you're driving and get hungry, about 2km east of Demre, at the end of a long pebble beach, are several shacks serving freshly caught crab with chips and salad.

TOP CHOICE Hoyran Wedre Country House
BOUTIQUE HOTEL ₺₺₺

(☑ 0532 291 5762, 875 1125; www.hoyran.com; s/d/ste €80/100/130; @ 🔊 🕿 🕿) A destination hotel if ever there was one, this complex of old and new stone buildings made to look antique is a rural oasis 18km west of Demre. Some 500m up in the Taurus Mountains, with views of Kekova and minutes away from an important Lycian acropolis (which owner Süleyman will gladly guide you through), Hoyran Wedre counts 17 rooms and suites done in traditional fashion (wattle-and-daub plastered walls) and decorated with antiques sourced in İstanbul. We love the pool shaped like a traditional cattle trough, Canan's set meals (€20) prepared entirely from locally grown produce (though some rooms have kitchens if you prefer to self-cater) and high teas at 5pm. It's 3km south of Davazlar, off the D400.

Gaziantep Restaurant
KEBAP ₺

(☑ 871 2812; Eynihal Caddesi; pide ₺4-7, kebap ₺9-15; ☉ 7am-10pm) Just opposite the square with the Church of St Nicholas and its accompanying faux-icon shops, this simple but spotless place with outside seating is a local favourite.

Akdeniz Restaurant
TURKISH ₺

(☑ 871 5466; Müze Caddesi; pide ₺4, köfte ₺8, dishes ₺5-7; ☉ 7am-11pm) This welcoming eatery on the main square, west of the church has a large array of tasty precooked dishes as well as pide and *köfte* (meatballs).

Sabancı Pastaneleri
CAFE, CONFECTIONER ₺

(☑ 871 3020; Eynihal Caddesi; fresh orange juice ₺3, pastries ₺1.50-3; ☉ 6am-11pm) This pleasingly modern place near the market is great for breakfast or a snack. It also serves ice cream (₺2 per scoop).

❶ Getting There & Away

Buses and dolmuşes travel to/from Kaş (₺8, one hour, 45km) hourly and less frequently to/from Olympos and Çıralı (₺10, 1½ to two hours) and Antalya (₺15, 2½ to three hours).

Olympos & Çıralı

☑ 0242

About 65km northeast of Demre, past Finike and Kumluca, a road leads southeast from the main highway (veer to the right then follow the signs for 11km) to Olympos. This is yet another ancient city bearing that name; this particular one was absorbed by Rome in AD 43. On the other side of the mountain and over the narrow Ulupınar Stream is Çıralı, a holiday hamlet with dozens of hotels and pensions that may look like it was born yesterday but contains that most enigmatic of classical icons: the eternal flame of the Chimaera.

OLYMPOS

An important Lycian city in the 2nd century BC, Olympos devoutly worshipped Hephaestus (Vulcan), the god of fire, which may have been inspired by the Chimaera, an eternal flame that still burns from the ground not far from the city. Along with the other Lycian coastal cities, Olympos went into a decline in the 1st century BC. With the arrival of the Romans here and at its larger neighbour, Phaselis, at the end of the 1st century AD, things improved, but in the 3rd century renewed pirate attacks brought decline. In the Middle Ages the Venetians and Genoese built fortresses along the coast but by the 15th century the site had been abandoned.

Set inside a deep shaded valley that runs directly to the sea, the ruins (admission ₺3, 10 entries to ruins & beach ₺7.50); ☉ 9am-7.30pm May-Oct, 8am-6pm Nov-Apr) of ancient Olympos appear 'undiscovered' among the vines and

ARYKANDA

Some 29km northeast of Demre is the unremarkable provincial centre of Finike, where there's an exit off the D400 leading north for another 30km to the ancient city of **Arykanda** (admission ₺10; ⏱9am-7pm Apr-Oct, to 5pm Nov-Mar). Built on five terraces into a south-facing hillside, it is one of the best preserved – and dramatically situated – archaeological sites in Turkey.

One of the oldest sites on the peninsula, Arykanda was part of the Lycian League from its inception in the 2nd century BC but was never a member of the 'Big Six' group of cities that commanded three votes each. This may have been due to its profligate and free-wheeling ways as much as anything else. Arykanda was apparently the party town of Lycia and forever deeply in debt. Along with the rest of Lycia it was annexed by Rome in AD 43 and survived as a Byzantine settlement until the 9th century when it was abandoned.

Arykanda's most outstanding feature is its two-storey **baths** complex, standing some 10m tall, next to the gymnasium on the lowest terrace. Following a path northwards to the next terrace you'll come to a large **agora** colonnaded on three sides. Its northern arches lead into a small **odeon**; have a look at the relief of the Emperor Hadrian over the portal. Above that is a fine **theatre** dating from the 2nd century and a **stadium**. Other notable constructions on upper terraces to the northwest are another agora, a *bouleterion* and a large cistern (not all easy to reach).

Dolmuşes (₺8) headed for Elmalı (₺12) from Demre will drop you off at the foot of the hill leading to the site entrance or in the village of Ariif, about a kilometre to the north, from where a signposted path leads to the ruins. A taxi will cost about ₺85 from Demre.

flower trees. A rare treat is rambling along the trickling Ulupınar Stream that runs through a rocky gorge down to the beach, with nary a tour bus in sight.

You can swim at the beach that fronts the site or engage in any of the numerous activities available from agencies and camps in Olympos. The **Adventure Centre** (☎892 1316; ⏱8.30am-10pm) at Kadır's Tree Houses, for example, can organise the following (prices are per person): boat cruises (full-day trip ₺45 with lunch); canyoning (full-day trip ₺80, with lunch at trout farm); mountain biking (four hours ₺40); diving (₺60 to ₺90 for two dives with equipment and lunch); sea kayaking (half-day trip ₺45 with lunch); hiking (six hours ₺45 with lunch); and rock climbing (₺45 for two climbs on a natural wall). Some of the best and most difficult rock climbing is at Hörguc, a wall opposite Olympos.

Sleeping & Eating

Staying in an Olympos 'tree house' at one of the dozen or so camps that line the 1.5km-long track along the valley down to the ruins and beach has long been the stuff of travel legend. The former hippy-trail hot spot has gentrified considerably in past years and is today pretty overcrowded and institution-alised. But, love it or hate it, Olympos still offers good value and an up-for-it party at-

mosphere in a lovely setting. Just remember that 'tree house' is a misnomer; few huts are actually up in the trees.

Unless specified otherwise, the prices for accommodation at the camps listed here is per person and includes half-board (ie breakfast and dinner); all drinks cost extra. Bathrooms are generally shared, though some bungalows have en-suite rooms and some even have air-conditioning. Not all tree houses have reliable locks, so store valuables at reception.

Be extra attentive to personal hygiene while staying at Olympos. In summer, particularly, the huge numbers of visitors can stretch the camps' capacity for proper waste disposal to the limit, so be vigilant about where and what you eat. Every year some travellers wind up ill.

Şaban Pansion   CAMPING GROUND, PENSION €
(☎0532 457 3439, 892 1265; www.sabanpansion.com; dm ₺25-30, tree house ₺35-40, bungalow ₺45-50; ❄@) A personal favourite, this is the place to come if you want to snooze in a hammock or on cushions in the shade of orange trees. In the words of the charming manager Meral: 'It's not a party place'. Instead it sells itself on tranquillity, space and great home cooking. There's an internet room and room 7 really is a tree house. Capacity for 120 guests.

Kadır's Tree Houses
CAMPING GROUND, PENSION €

(☑0532 347 7242, 892 1250; www.kadirstreehouses .com; dm ₺20-30, bungalow ₺40-65; ❄@) The place that put Olympos on the map looks like a Wild West boom town that just kept a-growin' and not the Japanese POW camps that some others resemble. There are pillows in wooden bungalows, cabins and dorm rooms for 350 heads, the Bull and Hangar bars are the liveliest in the valley and the Adventure Centre (p351) is on-site.

Bayrams
CAMPING GROUND, PENSION €

(☑0532 494 7454, 892 1243; www.bayrams.com; dm ₺30-35, tree house ₺35-40, bungalow with air-con ₺45-60, without air-con ₺40-55; ❄@) Here guests relax on cushioned platforms, playing backgammon or reading in the garden or puffing away on a nargile (water pipe) at the bar. Come here if you want to socialise but not necessarily party. High-ceilinged rooms shelter beds for 150.

Orange Pension
CAMPING GROUND, PENSION €

(☑0532 492 2284, 892 1317; www.olymposor angepension.com; dm ₺25-30, r ₺40-60, without bathroom ₺35-50, bungalow ₺40-60; ❄@) A bit edgier than most, this long-standing favourite has morphed in size in recent years, but Apo still runs a pretty good show. The wooden en-suite rooms upstairs feel like a Swiss Family Robinson future, and some deluxe bungalows even have TVs. Lovely gardens. There's room for 180 people.

Varuna Pansiyon
RESTAURANT €€

(☑0532 602 7839, 892 1347; www.olymposvaruna. com; mains ₺10-15; ⊗8am-11pm) This popular restaurant serves a fair range of snacks and mains including pide (₺7 to ₺9), trout (₺15) and şiş kebaps (roast skewered meat; ₺10 to ₺12.50) in an attractive open dining room. There's also accomodation here in 11 bungalows with 20 rooms costing between ₺30 and ₺60, depending on the season.

ÇIRALI

Çıralı (cher-ah-luh) is a relaxed, family-friendly hamlet of upscale pensions and hotels leading down to and along a beach lined with a dozen restaurants, including the Orange Home Restaurant (☑825 7293; meze ₺6-7, mains ₺12-25). It makes an excellent alternative to the backpackers' 'paradise' down the beach at Olympos. And it's close to the magical and mystical Chimaera.

Known in Turkish as Yanartaş or 'Burning Rock', the Chimaera (admission ₺4, torch/flashlight rental ₺3) is a cluster of flames that blaze spontaneously from crevices on the rocky slopes of Mt Olympos. At night it looks like hell itself has come to pay a visit, and it's not difficult to see why ancient peoples attributed these extraordinary flames to the breath of a monster – part lion, part goat and part snake – which had terrorised Lycia. The mythical hero Bellerophon supposedly killed the Chimaera by mounting the winged horse Pegasus and pouring molten lead into the monster's mouth.

Today gas still seeps from the earth and bursts into flame upon contact with the air. The exact composition of the gas is unknown, though it is thought to contain methane. Although a flame can be extinguished by covering it, it will reignite close by into a new and separate flame. At night the 20 or 30 flames in the main area are clearly visible at sea.

The best time to visit is after dinner. From Çıralı, follow the road along the hillside marked for the Chimaera until you reach a valley and walk up to a car park. From there it's another 20- to 30-minute climb up a stepped path to the site; bring or rent a torch. It's a 7km walk from Olympos, but most pensions will run you there for ₺5. Agencies organise three-hour 'Chimaera Flame Tours' for ₺15, departing at 9pm (an hour earlier from Olympos).

🛏 Sleeping

Çıralı may look at first like just two dirt roads lined with pensions, but it's a delightful beach community for nature lovers and post-backpackers. Driving in, you cross a small bridge where a few taxis wait to run people back up to the main road. Continue across the bridge and you'll come to a junction in the road with innumerable signboards – there are about 60 pensions here. Go straight on for the pensions nearest to the path up to the Chimaera. Turn right for the pensions closer to the beach and the Olympos ruins.

Myland Nature
PENSION €€€

(☑0532 407 9656, 825 7044; www.mylandnature .com; s ₺113-167, d ₺168-225, tr ₺205-279; ❄⊛) This is an artsy, holistic and very green place that is sure to rub you up the right way (massage, free yoga and meditation workshops available). The 13 spotless and spacious wooden bungalows are set around a pretty garden, and the food (vegetarian set meal ₺20) garners high praise. Bikes are available (free for one hour, ₺7 all day).

Hotel Canada
HOTEL €€

(📞0532 431 3414, 825 7233; www.canadahotel.net; d €55-60, 4-person bungalow €85-90; ✳@🅿❄) This is a beautiful place to stay, offering pretty much the quintessential Çıralı experience: warmth, friendliness and house-made honey. The garden is filled with hammocks, citrus trees, a pool and 11 bungalows (some ideal for families with bedroom and bunk beds), and the very comfortable main building has 26 rooms. Canadian Carrie and foodie husband Şaban are impeccable hosts; excellent set meals (€10) are served in the covered outdoor dining room. The Canada is 750m from the beach; grab a free bike and pedal on down.

Sima Peace Pension
PENSION €€

(📞0532 238 1177, 825 7245; www.simapeace .com; s/d/tr ₺80/120/140; ✳@) A comfortable throwback to the 1960s (dig the peace sign logo), this Çıralı stalwart has moved to a new location just down from the beach and now has five rooms and two delightful bungalows hidden in a pretty (and fragrant) orange grove. Aynur is the consummate host and cooks like a dream (evening buffet ₺15 to ₺20), while Koko the parrot adds a tropo feel to the place.

Olympos Lodge
RESORT €€€

(📞825 7171; www.olymposlodge.com.tr; s €140-160, d €175-195; ✳@🅿) Just about the poshest place in Çıralı, the Olympos Lodge is not only situated right on the beach but also boasts over 1.5 hectares of cool citrus orchards, manicured gardens and strutting peacocks. It's professionally managed and the 13 rooms in five separate villas are peaceful and very luxurious (rooms 1 and 2 have sea views). The breakfasts here are legendary, and there's a lovely winter garden open in the cooler months. Bikes available.

Orange Motel
PENSION €€

(📞825 7327; www.orangemotel.info; s €40-50, d €50-65, 2-bedroom bungalow €80-100; ✳@) A smart and reasonably priced choice, the Orange is smack dab in the middle of an orange grove; come here in spring and you'll never forget the overwhelming scent. The garden is hung with hammocks and the wrought-iron circular stairs lead to 14 relatively large rooms and bungalows. The evening meal is good value at ₺20.

❶ Getting There & Away

Virtually any bus taking the coastal road between Fethiye and Antalya will drop you off or pick you up at the stops near the Olympos and Çıralı junctions. Just make sure you specify which one you want. From there, minibuses (₺5) leave for both destinations.

For Olympos (9km from the D400), minibuses depart every half-hour between 8am and 7pm from May to October. Returning, minibuses leave Olympos at 9am, then every half-hour until 8pm, picking up passengers along the road. After October they will wait until enough passengers arrive, but usually depart once an hour.

To Çıralı (7km) there are minibuses every two hours between 9am and 7pm but they usually don't depart until they are full. They usually do a loop along the beach road, then pass the turn-off to the Chimaera and head back along the edge of the hillside.

Most of the places to stay listed here will pick you up from the highway (₺20 to ₺25) if you book in advance.

Phaselis

About 6km north of the exits for Olympos and Çıralı from the D400 is the romantically sited ancient Lycian port of Phaselis. Founded by colonists from Rhodes as early as the 7th century BC on the border between Lycia and Pamphylia, its wealth came from the shipment of timber, rose oil and perfume, which continued up until the early Middle Ages.

Shaded by pines, the **ruins** (admission ₺8; ⏱9am-7pm Apr-Oct, 8.30am-5pm Nov-Mar) of Phaselis are arranged around three small, perfectly formed bays, each with its own diminutive beach. The ruins are extensive and well worth exploring, but most date from Roman and Byzantine times. Look out for **Hadrian's Gate** (the Roman emperor visited in 129 AD), the **agora** at the South Harbour and the wonderful **colonnaded street** running down from the North Harbour.

The site entrance is about 1km from the D400. It's another 1km to the ruins and the sea.

If you're keen to sit on top of the world and look down on creation, a cable car called the **Olympos Teleferik** (📞814 3047, 242 2222; www.olymposteleferik.com; adult/child 7-16yr ₺50/25; ⏱9am-6pm May-Sep, 10am-5pm Oct-Apr) climbs almost to the top of 2375m-high **Tahtalı Dağ** (Wooded Mountain), the centrepiece of **Olympos Beydağları National Park** (Olimpos Beydağları Sahil

Milli Parkı). The turn-off from the highway is about 3km before Phaselis. A well-paved but steep road then carries on for 7km to the cable-car's lower station at 725m. The gondolas seat 80 people and depart every half-hour in summer and hourly in winter. The trip takes 12 minutes.

❶ Getting There & Away

Frequent buses on the highway from Antalya (₺8, 45 minutes, 58km) and Kemer (₺5, 20 minutes, 15km) pass both the exits for Phaselis and the Olympos Teleferik. The cable-car company also lays on a bus to/from Antalya (₺35) and Kemer (₺25), which you must book in advance.

Antalya

0242 / POP 964,000

Once seen simply as the gateway to the Turkish Riviera, Antalya is today very much a destination in its own right. Situated directly on the Gulf of Antalya (Antalya Körfezi), the largest Turkish city on the western Mediterranean coast is both classically beautiful and stylishly modern. It boasts the wonderfully preserved ancient district of Kaleiçi – literally 'within the castle' – a splendid Roman-era harbour and one of Turkey's finest museums.

Boutique hotels have sprung up in Antalya in recent years like mushrooms after rain and are of an international standard and good value. For partygoers, there are a number of excellent bars and clubs, while the opera and ballet season at the Aspendos (p363) amphitheatre continues to draw critical attention.

History

Antalya was named Attaleia after its 2nd-century founder Attalus II of Pergamum. His nephew Attalus III ceded the town to Rome in 133 BC. When the Roman Emperor Hadrian visited the city more than two centuries later, in 130 AD, he entered the city via a triumphal arch (now known as Hadrian's Gate), built in his honour.

There followed a succession of new 'landlords': the Byzantines took over from the Romans, followed by the Seljuk Turks in the early 13th century. The latter gave Antalya both a new name and an icon – the Yivli Minare (Fluted Minaret).

The city became part of the Ottoman Empire in 1391. After WWI, the empire collapsed and Antalya was ceded to Italy. In 1921 it was liberated by Atatürk's army and made the capital of Antalya province.

◉ Sights & Activities

Yivli Minare   LANDMARK
(Map p358) Antalya's symbol is the Yivli Minare, a handsome and distinctive 'fluted' minaret erected by the Seljuk sultan Aladdin Keykubad I in the early 13th century. The adjacent mosque (1373) is still in use. Within the Yivli Minare complex is a heavily restored **Mevlevi Tekke** (whirling dervish monastery, which probably dates from the 13th century). Nearby to the west are two **türbe** (tombs), one from the late 14th century and the other from 1502. The broad plaza to the west with the equestrian **statue of Atatürk** is Cumhuriyet Meydanı.

Kaleiçi   HISTORIC AREA
(Map p358) Antalya's historical district begins at the main square called **Kale Kapısı** (Fortress Gate), which is marked by an old stone **clock tower** (*saat kalesi*) and a **statue of Attalus II**, the city's founder. To the north is the **İki Kapılar Hanı**, a sprawling covered bazaar dating to the late 15th century.

Walk south along Uzun Çarşı Sokak, the street that starts opposite the clock tower. Immediately on the left is the 18th-century **Tekeli Mehmet Paşa Camii**; Uzun Çarşı Sokak), a mosque built by then Beylerbey (Governor of Governors) and repaired extensively in 1886 and 1926. Note the beautiful calligraphy in the coloured tiles above the windows.

Wander further into this protected zone; many of the gracious old **Ottoman houses** have been restored and converted into pensions, boutique hotels and shops. To the east and at the top of Hesapçi Sokak is the monumental **Hadriyanüs Kapısı** (Hadrian's Gate, also known here as Üçkapılar or the 'Three Gates'), erected for the Roman emperor's visit to Antalya in 130 AD.

The **Roman harbour** at the base of the slope was Antalya's lifeline from the 2nd century BC until late in the 20th century, when a new port was constructed about 12km to the west, at the far end of Konyaaltı Plajı. The harbour was restored during the 1980s and is now a marina for yachts and excursion boats.

In the southern reaches of Kaleiçi is the **Kesik Minare** (Truncated Minaret), a stump of a tower marking the ruins of a

Antalya

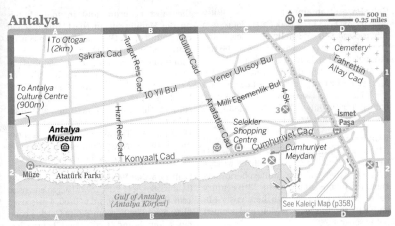

substantial building that played many roles over the century. Built originally as a 2nd-century Roman temple, it was converted into the Byzantine Church of the Virgin Mary in the 6th century and then a mosque three centuries later. It became a church again in 1361 but fire destroyed most of it in the 19th century. You can still see bits of Roman and Byzantine marble from the outside.

At the southwestern edge of Kaleiçi, on the corner with **Karaalioğlu Parkı** (Atatürk Caddesi), a large, attractive, flower-filled park with good views, rises **Hıdırlık Kalesi** (Kaleiçi), a 14m-high tower that may once have served as a lighthouse in the 2nd century AD.

Suna & İnan Kıraç Kaleiçi Museum   MUSEUM
(Map p358; ☎243 4274; www.kaleicimuzesi.org; Kocatepe Sokak 25; admission ₺2; ☺9am-noon & 1-6pm Thu-Tue) In the heart of Kaleiçi, just off Hesapçı Sokak, this small but well-formed ethnography museum is housed in a lovingly restored Antalya mansion. The 2nd floor contains a well-executed series of life-size dioramas depicting some of the most important rituals and customs of Ottoman Antalya. Much more impressive is the collection of Çanakkale and Kütahya ceramics found in the exhibition hall behind, the former Greek Orthodox church of Aya Yorgi (St George), which has been fully restored and is worth a look in itself.

Antalya Museum   MUSEUM
(Map p355; ☎236 5688; www.antalya-ws.com/english/museum; Konyaaltı Caddesi 1; admission ₺15; ☺9am-7pm Tue-Sun mid-Apr–Oct, 8am-5pm Tue-

Antalya

◉ Top Sights
Antalya Museum A2

✘ Eating
1 Can Can Pide ve Kebap Salonu D2
2 Club Arma C2
3 Güneyliler C1

Sun Nov–mid-Apr) On no account should you miss this comprehensive museum which is about 2km west of the centre and accessible on the old-fashioned *tramvay* (tram). The museum is large, with exhibitions in 14 big halls that cover everything from the Stone and Bronze Ages to Byzantium, so allow sufficient time. Unmissable are the Hall of Regional Excavations, which exhibits finds from ancient cities in Lycia (eg Patara and Xanthos) and Pamphylia; the Marble Portraits Hall, with evocative busts bearing incredibly realistic expressions and emotions; and the sublime Hall of Gods. Even those not especially interested in Greek mythology will be moved by this collection, which includes representations of some 15 Olympian gods, many of them in near-perfect condition. Most of the statues, including the sublime Three Graces, were found at Perge.

Upstairs are coins and other gold artefacts recovered from Aspendos, Side and some Byzantine sites. Taking pride of place is the so-called Elmalı Treasure of almost 2000 Lycian coins looted from Turkey in 1984 and returned from the USA some 15 years later.

Balık Pazarı Hamamı
HAMAM

(Map p358; ☎243 6175; Balık Pazarı Sokak; bath ₺15, package ₺40; ☺8am-11pm) Kaleiçi is a great place to experience the joys of the traditional Turkish hamam, most notably at the 700-year-old Balık Pazarı Hamamı (Fish Market Bath) where a bath, a peeling, and a soap and oil massage costs ₺40 (₺15 for a bath and scrub only). There are separate sections for men and women.

Sefa Hamamı
HAMAM

(Map p358; ☎0532 526 9407, 241 2321; www.sefa hamam.com; Kocatepe Sokak 32; bath ₺18, package ₺40; ☺9.30am-10pm) The atmospheric Sefa Hamamı retains much of its 13th-century Seljuk architecture. A bath here costs ₺18 and ₺40 for the works. Men and women bathe separately.

Boat Excursions
CRUISE

(Map p358) Excursion yachts tie up in the Roman harbour, now used as a modern marina, in Kaleiçi. Some trips go as far as Kemer, Phaselis, Olympos, Demre and even Kaş. You can take one-/two-hour trips (₺20/35) or a six-hour voyage (₺80 with lunch) which visits Kemer and Phaselis, the Gulf of Antalya islands and some beaches such as Konyaaltı Plajı for a swim.

★★ Festivals & Events

Golden Orange Film Festival
FILM

(Altın Portakal Film Festivalı; www.altinportakal.org .tr) Antalya's annual red-letter event is the Golden Orange Film Festival, held in the first half of October.

Antalya International Piano Festival
MUSIC

(Antalya Uluslararası Piyano Festivalı; www.an talyapiyanofestivali.com) Internationally recognised, the Antalya International Piano Festival is held at the Antalya Cultural Centre (Antalya Kültür Merkezi; ☎238 5444; Atatürk Kültür Parkı, 100 Yıl Bulvarı) west of the city centre.

⊨ Sleeping

The best place to stay in Antalya is the old town of Kaleiçi, a virtually vehicle-free district that has everything you need. Kaleiçi's winding streets can be confusing to navigate, although signs pointing the way to most pensions are posted on street corners.

TOP CHOICE Tuvana Hotel
BOUTIQUE HOTEL €€€

(Map p358; ☎247 6015; www.tuvanahotel.com; Karanlık Sokak 18; r €140-300; ❋🞀🖭) Among the most beautiful and intimate hotels on the Mediterranean coast, this discreet compound of six Ottoman houses has been converted into a refined city hotel with 46 rooms and suites. The Tuvana's sophistication is personified by hosts Nermin and Aziz, who look after this 'Special Class' hotel with precision and grace. Rooms are suitably plush, with kilims, linen and brass light fittings as well as such mod cons as DVD players. The swimming pool is a bonus in the warmer months and the main restaurant Seraser (p358) is world-class.

White Garden Pansiyon
PENSION €

(Map p358; ☎241 9115; www.whitegardenpansion .com; Hesapçı Geçidi 9; s/d ₺40/60, 4-person apt ₺120; @🞀) The 15-room White Garden combines tidiness and class beyond its price level, with impeccable service from Metin and his staff. The building itself is a fine restoration; the courtyard is particularly charming. Guests get to use the pool at the Secret Palace (Map p358; ☎244 1060; www.secretpalace pansion.com; Fırın Sokak 10; s/d ₺50/70; ❋@🞀), an Ottoman conversion in the same stable behind the White Garden with 11 rooms that have fridges.

Hotel Hadrianus
HOTEL €€

(Map p358; ☎244 0030; www.hadrianushotel.com; Zeytin Çıkmazı 4; s ₺65-80, d ₺80-120; ❋🞀) No doubt named after the city's first bona-fide tourist, the Roman emperor who visited in 130 AD, this 10-room 'almost boutique' hotel is set in 750 sq metres of garden, a veritable oasis in Kaleiçi. Rooms at the top are larger and contain faux-antique and Ottoman-style furnishings. Good value.

Mediterra Art Hotel
BOUTIQUE HOTEL €€

(Map p358; ☎244 8624; www.mediterraart.com; Zafer Sokak 5; s €50-80, d €70-120; ❋@🞀) This upscale masterpiece of wood and stone once housed a Greek tavern (see the 19th-century frescoes and graffiti on the restaurant wall). The Mediterra offers sanctuary by a cutting-edge pool, a marvellous winter dining room and 28 small, though modestly luxurious, rooms spread over four buildings. On the top floor, via ancient stone steps, is a small art gallery.

Sabah Pansiyon
PENSION €

(Map p358; ☎0555 365 8376, 247 5345; www. sabahpansiyon.com; Hesapçı Sokak 60; dm ₺25, s/d without shower ₺35/45, s/d with shower ₺40/55, 2-bedroom apt ₺200; ❋🞀🖭) Long one of the first ports of call for budget travellers to Antalya, the Sabah has 22 rooms that vary greatly so ask to see a couple. The Sabah brothers run the place with aplomb while Mama takes care of the kitchen. A real attraction is the shaded courtyard, perfect for hooking up with other travellers. Another is the five new villas (with a pool nearby) that can accomodate six people. Great for families.

Villa Perla   PENSION €€
(Map p358; ☑248 4341; www.villaperla.com; Hesapçı Sokak 26; s/d €50/70; ❄🛜🏊) We love this authentic Ottoman place hidden in a courtyard (with pool and tortoises) off Hesapçı Sokak. The 10 comfortable rooms are at the top of a staircase that starts with a 12th-century stone step, the wooden ceilings are the real deal and some of the renovated (and named) rooms have four-poster beds and folk-painted cupboards. Mama Perla makes all the meze (plate ₺19) at her in-house restaurant and offers, unusually, a full nine rabbit dishes (from ₺19).

Kaleiçi Lodge   HOTEL €€
(Map p358; ☑243 2270; www.kaleicilodge.com; Hesapçı Sokak 37; s/d ₺70/110, ste ₺240; ❄@) This very central, 14-room hotel is a stylish and excellent-value choice. The rather stark lobby opens onto to a courtyard crammed with curiosities, and hallways lead to red-draped, sharp-lined rooms, with lots of wrought iron and old wood. Choose corner room 206 or 207. The top-floor suite with two bedrooms is filled with antiques and has a jacuzzi.

Hotel Blue Sea Garden   HOTEL €€
(Map p358; ☑0537 691 4164, 248 8213; www.hotelblueseagarden.com; Hesapçı Sokak 65; s/d €35/50; ❄@🏊) The plus here is the swimming pool in a leafy courtyard – vital in the heat of summer. The 16 rooms are not really special (with small bathrooms), though the ones higher up are more peaceful and we hear good things about the in-house restaurant.

Mavi & Anı Pansiyon   PENSION €
(Map p358; ☑247 0056; www.maviani.com; Tabakhane Sokak 26; s €22-28, d €32-38, f from €35; ❄@) This restored Ottoman house has 15 rooms, some of which are loft-style and some Turkish style (beds on the floor); try to bag a single or double room with attached terrace and sea view. The common areas are decorated in old Anatolian furniture and bric-a-brac and there's a large family room on the top floor with a terrace and views to both sea and mountains.

La Paloma Hotel   HOTEL €€
(Map p358; ☑244 8497; www.lapalomapansion.com; Tabakhane Sokak 3; s €30-40, €40-55; ❄@🏊) Slightly away from the action and all the more attractive (and quiet) for that, La Paloma has 13 surprisingly large rooms for a single converted Ottoman building. The best of the lot face inwards to the infinity-shaped swimming pool. Some rooms have ceiling fans.

Atelya Art Hotel   HOTEL €€
(Map p358; ☑241 6416; www.atelyahotel.com; Civelek Sokak 21; s/d/tr €40/50/60; ❄@) Timelessness is hard to pin down, but the Atelya makes a bold effort in this eccentric art-inspired 30-room hotel contained in two old buildings (room 104 is great) and two newer ones. The owner displays his diverse portfolio on the walls, but it's the Ottoman splendour of richly coloured fabrics and beautiful furniture cast in beams of sunlight that best capture the spirit of the past. It's an excellent midrange choice.

Otantik Butik Otel   BOUTIQUE HOTEL €€€
(Map p358; ☑244 8530; www.otantikbutikotel.com; Hesapçı Sokak 14; s €49-99, d €59-109; ❄@) In a class of its own among Ottoman houses converted into boutique hotels, the Otantik is, well, 'authentic' in that the 10 named rooms are stylish – we love the old chests – but simple and on the small side (though three have jacuzzis). The restaurant with cosy fireplace has a particularly well-stocked wine cellar. A 16-room addition, with pool, is planned just opposite.

✗ Eating

A nearly endless assortment of cafes and eateries is tucked in and around the harbour area. For cheap eating, walk east to the **Dönerciler Çarşısı** (Market of Döner Makers; Map p358; Atatürk Caddesi) along Atatürk Caddesi, or north to the rooftop kebap places around Kale Kapısı (p354).

TOP CHOICE Vanilla   INTERNATIONAL €€
(Map p358; ☑247 6013; www.vanillaantalya.com; Zafer Sokak 13; mains ₺22-40) Another indicator of Antalya's rising stock is this outstanding, ultra-modern restaurant led by British chef Wayne and his Turkish wife, Emel. Banquettes, glass surfaces and cheery orange bucket chairs provide a streamlined and unfussy atmosphere, allowing you to concentrate on the menu: Meditearranean-inspired international dishes like rosemary and

Kaleiçi

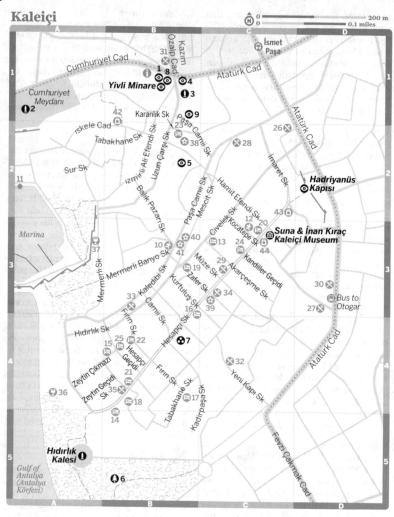

caramalised onion focaccia, goat's cheese salad, duck confit and sea scallops with foie gras.

Seraser MEDITERRANEAN, MODERN TURKISH €€€
(Map p358; ☑247 6015; www.seraserrestaurant.com; Karanlık Sokak 18, Tuvana Hotel; mains ₺29-50; ☺1pm-midnight) The signature restaurant at the Tuvana Hotel and among Antalya's best, Seraser offers international dishes with a Mediterranean twist – try the seabass wrapped in vine leaves or the quail with mustard honey glaze – in especially fine Ottoman surrounds. (We love the pasha-style chairs and the glass-bead chandelier.) The Turkish coffee crème brûlée is legendary.

Sim Restaurant MEZE €€
(Map p358; ☑248 0107; Kaledibi Sokak 7; mains ₺12.50-20) A choice of seated areas makes this simple but charming restaurant a unique experience. When the weather's fine, dine underneath the canopy in the narrow passageway at the front, wedged against ancient Byzantine walls. Inside, global graffiti on the ground floor gives it a youthful – if somewhat dated – feel, while upstairs, eclec-

Kaleiçi

tic antiques complement *köfte*, a choice of six meze and glorious *çorbalar* (soups).

Parlak Restaurant ANATOLIAN €€
(Map p358; ☑241 6553; www.parlakrestaurant. com; Kazım Özlap Caddesi 7; mains ₺10-24) Opposite the jewellery bazaar and just off pedestrian Kazım Özlap Caddesi is this sprawling open-air patio restaurant in an old caravanserai favoured by locals. It's famous for its charcoal-grilled chicken (one-half ₺10) and excellent meze.

Gül Restoran MEZE €€
(Map p358; ☑243 2284; Kocatepe Sokak 1; mains ₺9-24) On the edge of Atatürk Caddesi is this very blue intimate garden restaurant, shaded by a grove of Antalya's famous orange trees and popular with visiting German couples. The buffet of meze (₺8) – there are eight different ones each day – are well known.

Hasanağa Restaurant RESTAURANT €€
(Map p358; ☑247 1313; Mescit Sokak 15; mains ₺9-25) Expect to find the garden dining area here packed on the nights when traditional Turkish musicians and folk dancers entertain from 8pm onwards. Dishes are predictable – *köfte*, mixed grills and the like – although the cooks do produce some vegie dishes (around ₺15).

Club Arma SEAFOOD €€€
(Map p355; ☑244 9710; www.clubarma.com.tr; İskele Caddesi 75; mains ₺19-42) Housed in a former oil depot built right into the cliffside above the harbour, this upmarket *balık evi* (fish restaurant) specialises in meze (brought to you properly on a tray to choose from) and seafood in its infinite variety. If dining *en plein air* be careful not to fall off the fabulous open terrace or you'll literally end up in the drink.

7 Mehmet Restaurant
MODERN TURKISH €€€

(☑238 5200; www.7mehmet.com; Atatürk Kültür Parkı, Dunmlupınar 201; meze ₺6-20, mains ₺10-35) Antalya's most famous eatery is a couple of kilometres west of the centre, and its spacious indoor and outdoor dining areas occupy a hill overlooking Konyaaltı Plajı and the city. The menu of grilled mains, fish and meze is unsurprising but of very high quality. Ask for a peek in the enormous kitchen.

LeMan Kültür
CAFE, RESTAURANT €€

(Map p358; ☑243 7473; www.leman.com.tr; Atatürk Caddesi 44; mains ₺11.50-20; ☺9am-midnight) This garden cafe south of Hadrian's Gate takes as its theme cartoons and caricatures (they're all done by patrons) and is vastly popular with students. It's open for breakfast, lunch and dinner and is always packed. This is where you'll meet young Turks, for certain.

Yemenli
TURKISH €€

(Map p358; ☑247 5346; Zeytin Sokak 16; mains ₺14.50-17.50) A Sabah brothers (p356) venture so it's bound to be good, the name of this new restaurant recalls the land of their father's birth but sticks to tried-and-true Turkish fare. It's in a charmingly renovated stone house.

Can Can Pide ve Kebap Salonu
KEBAP €

(Map p355; ☑243 2548; Arık Caddesi 4/A; pide & dürüm ₺8; ☺7am-midnight Mon-Sat) Looking for something very cheap and cheerful? Fantastically prepared *çorba*, pide and Adana *dürüm* (beef kebap rolled in pitta) are here at bargain prices as are *mantı*, a kind of Turkish ravioli. It's opposite the landmark Antalya 2000 building and its Plaza Cinema.

Güneyliler
KEBAP €€

(Map p355; ☑241 1117; 4 Sokak 12/A; meals ₺9-12) With its cafeteria-style interior, this reasonably priced locals-only joint isn't much to look at. But the wood-fired *lahmacun* (₺3 to ₺6) and expertly grilled kebaps are served with so many complimentary extras, you'll want to return. If you get lost, ask for directions at the landmark Best Western Khan Hotel at Kazım Özlap Caddesi 55.

Paul's Place
CAFE €

(Map p358; ☑244 3375; www.spccturkey.com; Yeni Kapı Sokak 24; latte ₺5, cakes ₺4.50, köfte ₺5-7; ☺9am-6pm Mon-Fri; ☺) The good word comes in coffee cups at this informal cafe run by Christian expats in the St Paul Cultural Center. Regardless of your faith, you'll enjoy the espresso or filter coffee (₺1 to ₺5) and scrumptious baked goods. There's a well-stocked lending library too.

Hotel Alp Paşa
BUFFET €€

(Map p358; ☑247 5676; www.alppasa.com; Hesapçı Sokak 30; buffet €17; ☺7.30-9.30pm) Frankly the only time we visit this rather overwrought Ottoman-style hotel is to chow down at the nightly all-you-can-eat buffet that lasts just two hours. If you're very hungry and can masticate like a master, this is the place for you.

🍷 Drinking & Entertainment

Kaleiçi has a lot to offer after dark. There are buzzy beer gardens with million-dollar views, live music venues with everything from rock to *türkü* (Turkish folk music) and raunchy clubs where drinks are pricey and Russian prostitutes are in full force.

Castle Café
BAR

(Map p358; ☑248 6594; Hıdırlık Sokak 48/1; beer ₺7.50; ☺8am-11pm) Our favourite place along the cliff's edge just opposite the Hıdırlık Kalesi, the appropriately named Castle is buzzy, affordable and a good place to mix with a younger crowd of Turks.

Kale Bar
BAR

(Map p358; ☑248 6591; Mermerli Sokak 2; beer ₺9; ☺11am-midnight) This patio bar attached to the CH Hotels Türkevi may very well command the most spectacular harbour and sea view in all of Antalya. Cocktails are priced accordingly (from ₺21).

The Lounge
BAR, CAFE

(Map p358; ☑247 6013; Zafer Sokak 13; ice cream ₺3.50, cakes ₺10; ☺9am-1am; ☺) Next door to the Vanilla restaurant and under the same management, this very slick cafe-bar offers imported ice cream (it's Mövenpick) and a genuine Lavazza espresso machine for those weary of Turkish coffee. Panini and pizza (₺10 to ₺18) are available, and there's live music on Friday and Saturday nights.

Dem-Lik
LIVE MUSIC

(Map p358; ☑247 1930; Zafer Sokak 6; beer ₺5, coffee ₺4; ☺noon-midnight) Dem-Lik is located (mostly) in a large garden behind high stone walls, where Antalya's university crowd reshapes the world between ice-cold beers while listening to (mostly) jazz, reggae and blues (live at the weekend).

Kralın Bahçesi LIVE MUSIC

(Map p358; ✆0535 480 6834; Paşa Camii Sokak 33; ⊗9am-3am) A cafe (including amply supplied water pipes) by day and live-act *türku* venue by night, the 'King's Garden' is a regal act any time of day. Music starts at 9pm.

Filika Cafe-Bar LIVE MUSIC

(Map p358; ✆244 8266; Mescit Sokak 46; ⊗8pm-5am) This venue with live pop and rock music (above Mescit Sokak in the centre of Kaleiçi) attracts a way-cool young Turkish crowd.

Bar Rock Cafe CLUB, LIVE MUSIC

(Map p358; ✆0532 695 3291; off Uzun Çarşi Sokak; ⊗noon-4am) This dark tavern with a large open garden features local guitar bands playing covers of alt-rock classics. Located down an alleyway directly across the street from the Akdeniz clothing shop on Uzun Çarşi Sokak. Look for the archaeological excavation site – ah, Turkey! – on the left.

🛍 Shopping

Owl Bookshop BOOKS

(Map p358; ✆0532 632 3275; Kocatepe Sokak 9; ⊗9am-7pm Mon-Sat) Second-hand bookshop stocked mostly with travellers' hand-me-downs under the care of literary larrikin, Kemal Özkurt, who doles out heartfelt reading and other advice (requested or otherwise).

Osmanlı Sultan Çarık SHOES

(Map p358; ✆0532 677 0642, 247 1540; www.osmanlicarik.com; Hesapçı Sokak 3) The 'Ottoman Sultan Slipper' shop will whip you up a pair of hand-stitched pointy-toed slippers in dyed ox and buffalo leather for ₺90 to ₺160. Sandals (₺60 to ₺80) and boots (₺270 to ₺30) are also available.

ℹ Information

Internet Access

Megi Internet Cafe (www.megicafe.com; 46 Sokak; per hr ₺1) Super-modern internet cafe just north of Cumhuriyet Meydanı has 40 terminals.

Solemar İnternet Kafe (Arık Caddesi 13/C; per hr ₺1; ⊗8am-11pm) Some 15 computers in a small space just east of Hadrian's Gate.

Tourist Information

Tourist Office (✆241 1747; Cumhuriyet Meydanı; ⊗8am-6pm May-Oct, 8.30am-5.30pm Nov-Mar) Tiny but relatively helpful information office just west of the Yivli Minare.

Websites

Antalya Guide (www.antalyaguide.org) Comprehensive site with info on everything from climate to TV channels.

ℹ Getting There & Away

Air

Antalya's busy airport is 10km east of the city centre on the D400 highway. There's a tourist information desk and a number of car-hire agencies have counters here as well. Turkish Airlines and its regional budget airline AnadoluJet (www.anadolujet.com) have about a dozen daily nonstop flights year-round to/from İstanbul (₺75 to ₺120 one way) and several to/from Ankara (₺50 to ₺170).

Bus

Antalya's otogar, about 4km north of the city centre on highway D650, consists of two large terminals fronted by a park. Looking at the otogar from the main highway or its parking lot, the Şehirlerarası Terminalı (Intercity Terminal), which serves long-distance destinations, is on the right. The İlçeler Terminalı (Domestic Terminal), serving nearby destinations such as Side and Alanya, is on the left.

ℹ Getting Around

Antalya's original 6km-long single-track old-style *tramvay* (₺1.25) has 10 stops and provides the simplest way of crossing town. It runs every half-hour between 7.30am and 9pm. You pay as you board and exit through the rear door. The tram runs from the Antalya Museum (Müze stop) along Konyaaltı Caddesi, Cumhuriyet Caddesi, Atatürk Caddesi and Isıklar Caddesi.

A sleek, double-track tram line with 16 stations called AntRay, which opened in 2009, links northern areas of the city to the south and the coast, and is really only helpful for visitors getting to/from the otogar. The two tram lines are not linked at present though the İsmet Paşa stop on the AntRay is a short walk from the central Kale Kapısı stop on the *tramvay*.

To/From the Airport

To reach the airport, catch bus 600 (₺2), which can be boarded along 100 Yıl. A taxi will cost you about ₺35.

To/From the Bus Station

Bus 45 (₺1.75) heads for Atatürk Caddesi in the town centre every 20 minutes or so from the bus shelter near the airport taxi stand and takes about an hour. To get to the otogar from Kaleiçi, go out of Hadrian's Gate, turn right and wait at any of the bus stops along Atatürk Caddesi.

The AntRay has a stop called Otogar at the bus station that is eight stops from the central

SERVICES FROM ANTALYA'S OTOGAR

DESTINATION	FARE (₺)	DURATION (HR)	DISTANCE (KM)	FREQUENCY (PER DAY)
Adana	52	11	565	every 2 hr
Alanya	19	3	135	every 20 min
Ankara	50	8	555	frequent
Çanakkale	65	12	770	daily at 4.30pm
Denizli (Pamukkale)	25	4	225	several
Eğirdir	25	3½	195	hourly
Fethiye (coastal)	25	7½	285	several
Fethiye (inland)	18	4	200	frequent
Göreme/Ürgüp	40	9	485	frequent
İstanbul	65	11½	785	frequent
İzmir	40	8	470	several
Kaş	20	3½	188	frequent
Kemer	10	1½	55	every 15 min
Konya	38	5	305	several
Marmaris	40	6	365	several
Olympos/Çıralı	13	1½	80	several minibuses & buses
Side/Manavgat	13	1½	65	every 20 min in high season

İsmet Paşa stop just outside Kaleiçi. It takes 20 minutes and costs ₺1.50.

A taxi between the otogar and Kaleiçi should cost ₺25.

Around Antalya

Antalya is an excellent base for excursions to the ancient sites of Phaselis, Termessos, Perge, Aspendos and Selge. If you're travelling strictly along the coast, however, substantial time can be saved by visiting Phaselis on your way to or from Olympos or Kaş. Likewise, visiting Perge and Aspendos is easiest when travelling to or from Side or Alanya.

There's a huge array of travel agencies in Antalya's Kaleiçi area offering tours, including **Nirvana Travel Service** (Map p358; ☑0532 521 6053, 0242-244 3893; www.nirvanatour.com; İskele Caddesi 38/4). A full-day tour to Termessos with a stop at the Düden Şelalesi (Düden Falls) costs ₺100 including lunch. Tours to Perge and Aspendos with a side trip to Manavgat waterfall cost ₺115. There are plenty of car-rental agencies here including **Gaye Rent a Car** (☑0242-247 1000; www.gayerentacar.com; İmaret Sokak 1), hiring out cars for ₺50 to ₺90 (scooters ₺30 to ₺40) per day.

ASPENDOS

People come in droves to this ancient site near the modern-day village of Belkıs for one reason: to view the awesome **theatre** (admission ₺15, parking ₺5; ☺9am-7pm Apr-Oct, 8am-5pm Nov-Mar), which is considered the best preserved Roman theatre of the ancient world.

The theatre was built by the Romans during the reign of Emperor Marcus Aurelius (AD 161–80), and used as a caravanserai by the Seljuks during the 13th century. But while Aspendos' golden age only stretched from the 2nd to 3rd centuries AD, the history of the city goes all the way back to as far as the Hittite Empire (800 BC).

After touring the area in the early 1930s, Atatürk declared Aspendos too fine an example of classical architecture to stay unused. Following a restoration that didn't please a lot of historians, the 15,000-seat theatre began to stage operas, concerts and other events and does so to this day. The acoustics are excellent and the atmosphere at night sublime.

The ruins of the ancient city are extensive and include a **stadium**, **agora** and 3rd-century **basilica**, but they offer little to look at. To reach them follow the trail to the right of the theatre exit. To the north are the remains of the city's **aqueduct**.

✦✦ Festivals & Events

Aspendos Opera & Ballet Festival FESTIVAL
(Aspendos Opera ve Bale Festivalı; www.aspendos festival.gov.tr) The internationally acclaimed Aspendos Opera & Ballet Festival is held in the Roman theatre in June and again in September. Tickets can be bought online, from the kiosk opposite the theatre and from travel agents in Antalya.

ⓘ Getting There & Away

Aspendos lies 47km east of Antalya. If driving, immediately on your right as you exit the D400 for Aspendos is a restored Seljuk-era switchback bridge with seven arches spanning the Köprü River. It dates from the 13th century but was built on an earlier Roman bridge.

From Antalya, minibuses (₺8) headed for Manavgat will drop you at the Aspendos turn-off, from where you can walk (45 minutes) or hitch the remaining 4km to the site. Taxis waiting at the highway junction will take you to the theatre for an outrageous ₺20, or you can join an excursion from Antalya for ₺115, stopping at Perge along the way. A taxi tour will cost about ₺160.

TERMESSOS

Hidden high in a rugged mountain valley, 34km northwest of Antalya, lies the ruined but still massive ancient city of **Termessos** (admission ₺5; ⊙9am-7pm Apr-Oct, 8am-5pm Nov-Mar). Neither Greek nor Lycian, the inhabitants were Pisidian, fierce and prone to warring. They successfully fought off Alexander the Great in 333 BC, and the Romans (perhaps wisely) accepted Termessos's wishes to remain independent and an ally in 70 BC.

Termessos is spread out and requires much scrambling over loose rocks and up steep though well-marked paths. Allow a minimum of two hours to explore, and bring plenty of drinking water.

The first remains you'll come across at the end of the access road (King's Rd) are within the car park. The portal on the hillock to the west was once the entrance to the **Artemis-Hadrian Temple** and **Hadrian Propylaeum**. From here follow the steep path south; you'll see remains of the lower city walls on both sides and pass through the **city gate** before reaching, in about 20 minutes, the **lower gymnasium** and **baths** on your left. A short distance further on your right are the **upper city walls** and the **colonnaded street**. Next the **upper agora** and its five large **cisterns** is an ideal spot to

explore slowly and to catch a bit of shade. Push on to the nearby **theatre**, which enjoys a positively jaw-dropping position atop a peak, surrounded by a mountain range; you can see Antalya on a clear day. Walk southwest from the theatre to view the cut-limestone **bouleuterion**, but use caution when scrambling across the crumbled **Temple of Artemis** and **Temple of Zeus** south of it. The **southern necropolis** is at the very top of the valley, 3km – or one hour's walk – up from the car park.

Güllükdağı Termessos National Park (Termessos Milli Parkı), which surrounds the site, abounds in wildlife including mountain goats, speckled deer, golden eagles and 680 species of plant (80 of them endemic). At the entrance, the small **Flora and Fauna Museum** (included in the entry price) contains a bit of information about the ruined city, as well as about the botany and zoology of the immediate area.

ⓘ Getting There & Away

Taxi tours from Antalya cost around ₺150; organised or group excursions are cheaper. An even cheaper option is to catch a bus from Antalya otogar bound for Korkuteli (₺12) and alight at the entrance to the national park. Taxis waiting here in the warmer months will run you up the 9km-long King's Rd to the ruins and back for about ₺25.

Termessos

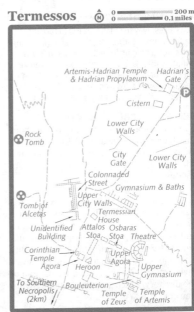

ⓝ 0 _____ 200 m
0 _____ 0.1 miles

Artemis-Hadrian Temple & Hadrian Propylaeum
Hadrian's Gate
Cistern
Lower City Walls
Rock Tomb
City Gate
Lower City Walls
Colonnaded Street
Gymnasium & Baths
Tomb of Alcetas
Upper City Walls
Termessian House
Unidentified Building
Attalos Stoa
Osbaras Stoa
Theatre
Corinthian Temple
Heroon
Upper Agora
Upper Gymnasium
Agora
To Southern Necropolis (2km)
Bouleuterion
Temple of Zeus
Temple of Artemis

PERGE

Some 17km east of Antalya and 2km north of Aksu on highway D400, **Perge** (admission ₺15; ☉9am-7pm Apr-Oct, 8am-5.30pm Nov-Mar) was one of the most important towns of ancient Pamphylia. It experienced two golden ages: during the Hellenistic period in the 2nd and 3rd centuries BC and under the Romans in the 2nd and 3rd centuries AD (from which most of the ruins here date). Turkish archaeologists first began excavations here in 1946 and a selection of the statues discovered – many in magnificent condition – can be seen at the Antalya Museum.

The **theatre** and **stadium**, each of which sat 12,000 spectators, appear along the access road before you reach the site itself; both were closed at the time of writing. Inside the site, walk through the massive **Roman Gate** with its four arches; to the left is the **southern nymphaeum** and well-preserved **baths**, and to the right the large square-shaped **agora**. Beyond the **Hellenistic Gate**, with its two huge towers, are the fine **colonnaded street**, where an impressive collection of columns still stands.

The water source for the narrow concave channel running down the centre of the colonnaded street was the **northern nymphaeum**, which dates to the 2nd century AD. From here it's possible to follow a path to the ridge of the hill with the **acropolis**.

ℹ Getting There & Away

The easiest way to reach Perge is to take the AntRay tram to the last southern stop (Maydan) and catch a dolmuş from there to Aksu (₺3, 30 minutes, 15km). You can easily walk the remaining 2km north to the ruins. An excursion to both Perge and Aspendos from Antalya should cost around ₺115. A taxi tour will be about ₺160.

SELGE & KÖPRÜLÜ KANYON

The ruins of ancient Selge are strewn about the Taurus-top village of Altınkaya, 12km above spectacular Köprülü Kanyon and within a national park with peaks up to 2500m.

As you wander through the village and its ruins, consider that Selge once counted a population of more than 20,000. Because of the city's elevated position, its city walls and surrounding ravines, approaching undetected wasn't a simple task and the city was able to ward off most invaders. Nevertheless, the Romans eventually took hold of the territory, which survived into the Byzantine era.

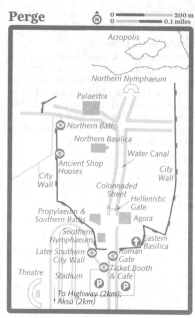

Perge

About 350m of the city wall still exists, but its most striking monument is its **theatre** restored in the 3rd century AD. Close by is the **agora**.

At the foot of the ascent, you'll discover two Roman-era bridges. The first (and smaller) is the **Bürüm Bridge** and the second the dramatically arched **Oluk Bridge** spanning 14m across a deep canyon of the ancient Eurymedon (now Köprü) River. It has been in service since the Romans put it here in the 2nd century AD.

🏃 Activities

HIKING

Around the Oluk Bridge, you'll find villagers keen to guide you on hikes up from Köprülü Kanyon (Bridged Canyon) along the original Roman road, about two hours up (1½ hours down), for about ₺60. An excellent qualified guide who knows the area inside and out is Adem Bahar, who can be reached on ☎0535 762 8116 or via the Köprülü Kanyon Restaurant. He also organises rafting trips.

You can also arrange two-day mountain treks for groups to Mt Bozburun (2504m) and other points in the Kuyucak Dağları (Kuyucak Range) for about ₺120. There is a three-day walk through the Köprülü Kanyon on the St Paul's Trail.

RAFTING

There are more than two-dozen companies offering rafting trips in the canyon, including larger outfits like **Medraft** (☏0242-312 6296, in UK +44 20 8150 0687; www.medraft.com) and **Gökcesu Rafting** (☏0242-765 3384, 0533 522 3205; www.gokcesu.net) and smaller ones such as **Antalya Rafting** (☏0530 776 1607; www.antalya-rafting.net), based at the the Köprülu Kanyon Restaurant about 100m down from the eastern side of Oluk Bridge. An excursion on the excellent intermediate rapids is about ₺30, which includes a lesson, a two- to three-hour trip and lunch.

🛏 Sleeping

There are a couple of waterfront pensions with restaurants on the west side of the Köprü River, about 4km past the modern Karabük Bridge. The first is the rather rustic **Selge Pansiyon** (☏0242-765 3244, 0535 577 9475; www.selgepansiyon.com; s/d ₺30/60, incl full board ₺60/120; @), with 11 rooms right on the river. It offers excellent value and perhaps is best for families. A larger and more modern option is **Perge Pansiyon** (☏0242-765 3074, 0533 475 8108; www.facebook.com/Pergepansion; campsit per person ₺15, bungalow s/d ₺40/80, incl

full board ₺70/140; ❄@🛜), which has 14 comfortable timber bungalows with good bathrooms and a decent restaurant right on the edge of a pond fed by rapids. For accommodation in Altınkaya, just minutes from the Selge ruins, contact **Adem Bahar** (☏0535 762 8116; per person incl full board ₺40).

ⓘ Getting There & Away

Köprülü Kanyon Milli Parkı and Selge are included in tours from Antalya for about ₺100 per person. Unless you're under your own steam, this is your only option.

If you do have a vehicle, however, you can visit in half a day, though it deserves a lot more time. The turn-off to Selge and Köprülü Kanyon is about 5km east of the Aspendos road (51km from Antalya) along highway D400. Another 30km up into the mountains the road divides, with the left fork marked for Karabük and the right for Beşkonak. If you take the Karabük road along the river's west bank, you'll pass most of the rafting companies and the two pensions. About 11km from the turn-off is the graceful old Oluk Bridge. From here the paved road marked for Altınkaya climbs some 13km to the village and the Selge ruins through increasingly dramatic scenery.

If you follow via Beşkonak, it is 6.5km from there to the canyon and the bridge.

Eastern Mediterranean

Best Places to Eat

» Antakya Evi (p394)
» İskele Sofrası (p374)
» Ova Ev Yemekleri (p387)
» Öz Asmaaltı (p387)

Best Places to Stay

» Hotel Bosnalı (p386)
» Beach House Hotel (p369)
» Centauera (p373)
» Konak Efsus (p385)

Why Go?

Turkey's eastern Mediterranean has long lived in the shadow of its more fashionable neighbour to the west. And why not? That's razzle-dazzle and this is 'real' Turkey, where enormous vegetable farms and fruit orchards work overtime between the mountains and stunning coastline, and timeless hillside villages peek down onto large industrial cities with nary a tourist in sight. Here you'll be rewarded with modern, secular and very friendly locals, as well as all the requisite fun things to see and do: ancient Hittite settlements, Crusader castles, trekking. To some visitors, though, it is the abundance of important Christian sites, places where the Apostles actually preached the Gospel and made converts to the new religion, that make this a chosen destination. Others will be fascinated by the peninsula that faces southward to Syria, an area offering one of Turkey's most fascinating mixes of cultures, religions, languages and foods.

When to Go
Antakya

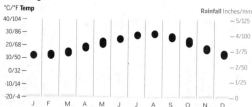

Mar & Apr
Spring, after the rain and before the crowds, is an ideal time to visit.

Jul & Aug
Steaming hot days, though offshore breezes help temper the furnace.

Nov–Feb Positively balmy along most of the coast, but often wet and the sea is chilly.

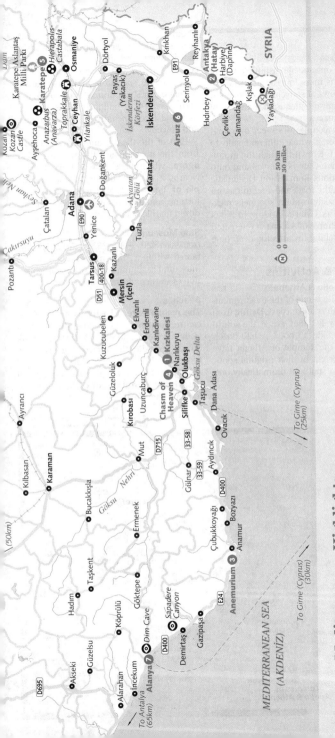

Eastern Mediterranean Highlights

1 Swim to the offshore **Kız-kalesi Castle** (p381) at Kızkalesi, and hike to the isolated reliefs at **Adamkayalar** (p382)

2 View the finest mosaics in the world at the **Hatay**

Archaeology Museum (p391), and climb to St Simeon's mountain-top **monastery** (p395)

3 Re-enact past glories in the Byzantine city of **Anemurium** (p376)

4 Descend into the massive **Chasm of Heaven** (p382) near Silifke, where Zeus is said to have held the monster Typhon captive

5 Go way back in time at the Hittite ruins at **Karatepe** (p390), in the national park

6 Take a break from the ruins at **Arsuz** (p391), down the coast from İskenderun

7 Enjoy the unbridled hedonism of the throbbing, laser-shooting nightclubs of **Alanya** (p374)

Side

🕿 0242 / POP 11,400

To some, the once-docile fishing town of Side (see-day) is mass tourism at its worst, with endless rows of souvenir peddlers and matching restaurant menus in a variety of European languages.

But move a couple of streets over and you'll encounter a whole different side to Side. Entering the town through the monumental Vespasian Gate is like walking onto a film set: glorious Roman and Hellenistic ruins mark out the road, and a rebuilt agora could just as easily contain shoppers picking over togas as T-shirts. Adding to Side's appeal is the Temple of Athena, a re-created colonnade marching towards the deep blue sea.

👁 Sights & Activities

Temples of Apollo & Athena   RUIN

This compact site is one of the most romantic on this Mediterranean coast. Dating from the 2nd century BC, they are at the southwestern tip of Side harbour. A half-dozen columns from the Temple of Athena have been placed upright in their original spots, and after dark a spotlight dramatically outlines their form.

Theatre   RUIN

(admission ₺10; ⊙9am-7.30pm mid-Apr–mid-Oct, 8am-5.30pm mid-Oct–mid-Apr) Built in the 2nd century AD, Side's spectacular theatre seats up to 20,000 spectators and rivals nearby Aspendos for sheer drama. Look to the wall of the *skene* (stage building) for reliefs of figures and faces, including those of Comedy and Tragedy.

East of the theatre and across the road from the museum are the remains of an **agora**, which once held a slave market. Nearby is the ruined circular-shaped **Temple of Tyche** dedicated to the goddess of fortune, and an arresting **latrine** with two-dozen marble seats.

Side Museum   MUSEUM

(admission ₺10; ⊙9am-7.30pm Tue-Sun) Contained within a 5th-century bathhouse, the museum has an impressive (if small) collection of statues and sarcophagi.

Beaches   BEACHES

The main **Western Beach** is north of the centre; follow the main road out of town (Side Caddesi) and turn left at Şarmaşık Sokak opposite the otogar (bus station). Closer is the smaller **Eastern Beach** off Barbaros Caddesi. On the way here you'll pass the large **State Agora**. There's a much longer **beach** further east.

Side

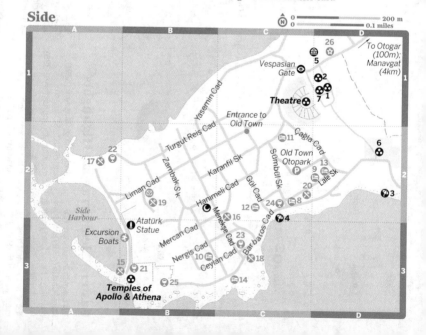

✦ Festivals & Events

The **Aspendos Opera & Ballet Festival** runs in June, and is held at the Gloria Aspendos Arena, which is en route to Antalya. A multimedia spectacle called the **Fire of Anatolia** is performed at the same venue on a seasonal basis. A second spectacle based on the legend of Troy is performed on some nights. For more information, see www.anadoluatesi.com.

Tickets for both the festival and spectacles can be purchased in season at the **ticket office** next to the museum.

🛏 Sleeping

Vehicular entrance to the old town is restricted, and if you're driving you'll need a reservation at an old-town hotel or pension to gain access. If you're just visiting for the day, you'll be steered to park in the old town otopark.

TOP CHOICE **Beach House Hotel**   HOTEL €€

(☎753 1607; www.beachhouse-hotel.com; Barbaros Caddesi; s/d ₺50/100; ❄@🛜) Once the celebrated Pamphylia Hotel, a magnet for celebrities in the 1960s, the Beach House's prime seafront location and welcoming staff lures a loyal band of regulars. Most of the 22 rooms face the sea and all have balconies. The roof terrace with jacuzzi is a delight, and we love the ruins of a Byzantine villa (and the rabbits) in the garden.

Özden Pansiyon   PENSION €

(☎0534 552 3328, 753 1337; www.yoga-holidays-turkey.com; Gül Sokak 50; s/d ₺30/60; 🛜) Simple but stylish wood-lined rooms frame a leafy courtyard that's a tranquil retreat from the souvenir-shop buzz just outside. Independent travellers are welcome, and the pension is also home base for Jo and Murat Özden's Yoga Holidays Turkey. One week yoga holidays cost £395 per person. Some early morning classes take place near the towering columns of the Temples of Apollo and Athena.

Onur Pansiyon   PENSION €

(☎753 2328; www.onur-pansiyon.com; Karanfil Sokak 3; s/d ₺50/80; ❄@🛜) This excellent family-owned operation has regular guests year-round who return for its seven bright and cosy rooms – and (in cooler months) cocktails by the fireplace. The friendly manager is helpful with advice and local lore.

Hotel Lale Park   HOTEL €€

(☎753 1131; www.hotellalepark.com; Lale Sokak 5; s ₺85-120, d ₺120-170; ❄🛜❄) One of Side's nicest small hotels, the 'Tulip Park' has manicured lawns, flower beds and a pretty pool. Roman columns and stone walkways frame an alfresco garden bar, and some rooms have Ottoman-style balconies. Dinner (₺25) is a good-value alternative to Side's other restaurants, and is open to outside guests. You'll need to book by noon.

Side

Yalı Hotel
HOTEL €€

(☏753 1011; www.yalihotel.com; Barbaros Caddesi 50; s/d ₺100/140; ❄@🛜⛱) We've always wondered why this place, dramatically perched above the sea (literally for rooms 208, 209, 308 and 309), isn't constantly packed. It's true the 25 rooms are fairly spartan, but staff are keen to please, the restaurant boasts killer views and the swimming pool is a welcome addition.

Side Doğa Pansiyon
PENSION €€

(☏753 6246; www.sidedoga.com; Lale Sokak 8; s/d ₺60/110; ❄🛜) A short distance from Side's Theatre, this exceptionally laid-back, nine-room pension is conveniently located across the street from a car park. Expect colourful and tidy rooms in an old stone house surrounded by an attractive courtyard garden.

Hotel Sevil
HOTEL €€

(☏753 2041; www.hotelsevil.com; Zambak Sokak 32; s ₺50-70, d ₺120-130; ❄🛜) Set around a miniforest of mulberry trees and palms, this midrange option features a smart little bar and a chilled vibe. The 15 rooms are heavy on wood panelling; those upstairs have balconies, some with sea views.

✗ Eating

Ottoman Restaurant
SEAFOOD €€€

(☏753 1434; mains ₺20-35) Host Rasim and the terrace high above Side's main (and always busy) drag are the main reasons for dining at this excellent restaurant off Liman Caddesi, which serves a lot of fish. Indian and Mexican flavours also make an appearance.

Emir
TURKISH €€

(☏753 2224; Menekşe Caddesi; meze ₺8-10, mains ₺16-25) The Emir almost leans on the ruins of the Roman baths where Cleopatra is said to have dallied. The open kitchen produces some excellent meze, grills and a generous array of vegetarian dishes.

Karma
RESTAURANT, BAR €€€

(Turgut Reis Caddesi; mains ₺25-35) Welcome to a sleek and cosmopolitan slice of trendy Bodrum transplanted to Side. The town's newest restaurant and bar combines bold architectural stylings with a trendy alfresco garden area and oceanfront seating. The diverse menu channels a Mediterranean and Pan-Asian vibe.

Balık & Köfte Ekmek
SANDWICHES €

(sandwiches ₺7) Bobbing away gently in Side's sheltered harbour, this converted fishing boat serves up good-value fish and köfte (meatball) sandwiches. Meze platters are also available, and in a tourist town with uniformly expensive restaurants, it's a thrifty haven for travellers watching their lira.

Moonlight Restaurant
SEAFOOD €€€

(☏753 1400; Barbaros Caddesi 49; mains ₺15-30) The waterfront Moonlight, in business since 1983, offers an extensive Turkish wine list and professional but unfussy service. The mostly seafood offerings are well presented and very fresh. The biggest drawcard is the romantic back terrace, which is regularly filled with happy couples.

Soundwaves Restaurant
INTERNATIONAL €€€

(☏753 1059; Barbaros Caddesi; mains ₺20-30) This long-running Side eatery is in the same family as the Beach House Hotel, so the vibe is friendly and relaxed. A small, focused menu is delivered by an experienced chef, and there are regular seafood specials. Ask if the excellent swordfish kebaps are available, and kick off with a few meze and a cold beer.

🍷 Drinking & Entertainment

Apollonik
BAR, CAFE

(Liman Yolu) Hidden within the ruins around the Temples of Apollo and Athena, the Apollonik is a laid-back bar that's perfect for an early evening start to a big night out. It does good food too, with mains (mostly grills) from ₺18 to ₺26. Even if Side is quiet early in the season, the Apollonik will still be full of satisfied punters.

Beyaz Bar
BAR

(Turgut Reis Caddesi) Beyaz translates to 'white' in Turkish, and the interior of this restored Ottoman house near the harbour is most definitely 'beyaz'. Inside is a romantic confection of white walls and tables, a stylish and classy backdrop to regular performances of Turkish music.

Stones Rock Bar
BAR

(Barbaros Caddesi 119) Undergoing a shimmering all-white Eurochic makeover when we visited, this dance bar with spectacular views is an excellent pre-club venue while the sun is still going down.

Mehmet's Bar
BAR

(Barbaros Caddesi) This ever-popular spot opposite the beach might be better suited to a tropical island than a Turkish promontory. Pop in for a quiet drink and ask them to crank up the reggae.

Kiss Bar BAR

(Barbaros Caddesi 64) This neon-lit, open bar located just up from the water is a great spot for people-watching.

ℹ️ Getting There & Away

Side's otogar is east of the ancient city. In summer, an open-top bus (₺1) shuttles visitors from the otogar to near the entrance to the old town.

Frequent minibuses connect Side otogar with the Manavgat otogar (₺2), 4km to the northeast, from where buses go to Antalya (₺10, 1½ hours, 75km), Alanya (₺10, 1½ hours, 60km) and Konya (₺25, four hours, 230km). Coming into Side, most buses either drop you at the Manavgat otogar or stop on the highway so you can transfer onto a free *servis* (shuttle bus) into Side. A taxi from Side to Manavgat otogar costs about ₺15.

In summer Side has direct bus services one to three times daily to Ankara (₺35, 10 hours, 625km), İzmir (₺40, 8½ hours, 540km) and İstanbul (₺55, 13 hours, 850km).

Alanya

📞 0242 / POP 103,700

In just a few short decades, Alanya has mushroomed from a sparsely populated highway town fronting a sandy beach to a densely populated tourist haven for predominantly Dutch and Scandinavian visitors. At night, the city can resemble 'Vegas by the Sea', and aside from taking a boat cruise or stroll along the waterfront, many visitors shuffle only between their hotel's pool and all-inclusive buffet restaurant, and then frequent the laser-shooting nightclubs after dark.

However, Alanya has something up its ancient sleeve: looming high above the promontory to the south of the modern centre is an impressive fortress complex, with the remains of a fine Seljuk castle, some atmospheric ruins, and even something of a small traditional village.

◉ Sights

Alanya Castle FORTRESS

(Alanya Kalesı; admission ₺10; ⏱9am-7pm Apr-Oct, 8am-5pm Nov-Mar) The sole 'must-see' site in Alanya is the awesome Seljuk-era castle overlooking the city, Pamphylian plain and Cilician mountains.

Before reaching the entrance to the castle, the road passes a turn-off for the village of Ehmedek, which was the Turkish quarter during Ottoman and Seljuk times. Today a number of old wooden houses still cluster around the fine 16th-century **Süleymaniye Camii**, the oldest in Alanya. Also here is a former Ottoman **bedesten** (vaulted covered market) and the **Akşebe Türbesi**, a distinctive 13th-century mausoleum.

At the end of the road is the entrance to the **İç Kale** (Inner Fortress), where you'll mostly find poorly preserved ruins, including a half-dozen **cisterns** and the shell of an 11th-century **Byzantine church**.

The winding road to the fortress – Kaleyolu Caddesi – is 3.5km long and uphill. Catch a bus from Hürriyet Meydanı (₺1.25, hourly from 9am to 7pm) or opposite the tourist office (15 minutes past the hour and, in summer, also 15 minutes before the hour). Taxis are around ₺15 each way.

Red Tower HISTORIC BUILDING

(Kızılkule; admission ₺4; ⏱9am-7pm Apr-Oct, 8am-5pm Nov-Mar) This five-storey octagonal defence tower, measuring nearly 30m in diameter, more than 30m in height and with a central cistern within for water storage, looms over the harbour at the lower end of İskele Caddesi. Constructed in 1226 by Seljuk Sultan Alaeddin Keykubad I (who also built the fortress), it was the first structure erected after the Armenian-controlled town surrendered to the sultan. There's a small **ethnographic museum** here and some 85 steps lead to a roof terrace with views of the harbour. To the south is the only Seljuk-built **tersane** (shipyard) remaining in Turkey.

Alanya Museum MUSEUM

(İsmet Hilmi Balcı Caddesi; admission ₺3; ⏱9am-7pm Tue-Sun Apr-Oct, 8am-5pm Tue-Sun Nov-Mar) Alanya's small museum is worth a visit for its artefacts, which include tools, jugs and jewellery collected from other Pamphylian sites in the area.

Cleopatra's Beach BEACH

(Kleopatra Plajı) Sandy and quite secluded in low season, and with fine views of the fortress, Cleopatra's Beach is the city's best. Alanya's main beaches are also decent, although east of the centre they're fronted by a busy main road.

Dripstone Cave CAVE

(Damlataş Mağarası; adult/child ₺4.50/2.25; ⏱10am-7pm) Close to Cleopatra's Beach, this stalactite-studded cave has humidity levels of 95% and is said to produce a certain kind of air that, if inhaled and exhaled long enough, has the ability to relieve asthma sufferers.

EASTERN MEDITERRANEAN ALANYA

Alanya

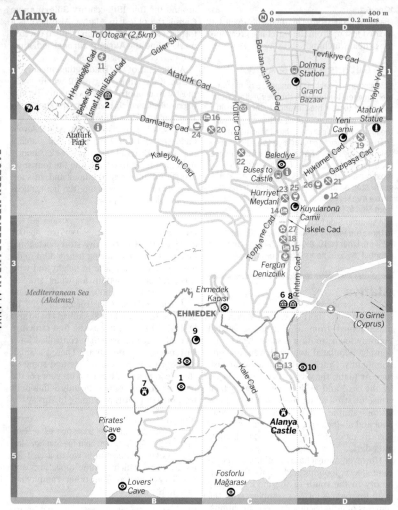

Activities

Damlataş Aqua Centre   AMUSEMENT PARK
(İsmet Hilmi Balcı Caddesi 62; adult/child ₺25/12;
⊙9am-6pm) Alanya boasts an impressive
water park close to the centre.

Tours

Many local operators organise tours to the
ruins along the coast west of Alanya and to
Anamur. A typical tour to Aspendos, Side
and Manavgat will cost around ₺75 per
person, while a 4WD safari visiting villages
in the Taurus Mountains will cost about

₺60 per person. Some tours also take in the
Sapadere Canyon (p376).

Excursion Boats   BOAT TOUR
(per person incl lunch ₺35) Every day at around
10.30am, boats leave from near Rıhtım Caddesi for a six-hour voyage around the promontory, visiting several caves, as well as Cleopatra's Beach. Other cruises include sunset
jaunts around the harbour (from ₺20).

Sleeping

Alanya has hundreds of hotels and pensions, almost all of them designed for

groups and those in search of *apart otel-ler* (self-catering flats). A few independent places can be found along İskele Caddesi, and two new boutique hotels have opened in restored Ottoman houses in the Tophane district under the castle.

Centauera TOP CHOICE BOUTIQUE HOTEL €€€
(☑519 0016; www.centauera.com; Andızlı Camii Sokak 4, Tophane; r €110-140; [P][❉][🛜]) A 10-minute stroll from the harbour, the romantic Centauera fills a restored Ottoman house in the Tophane district under Alanya castle. Views take in the elegant sweep of Alanya bay, and birdsong from the surrounding heritage neighbourhood may be the only sound you hear most mornings. Dinner is available on request and for outside guests.

Villa Turka BOUTIQUE HOTEL €€€
(☑513 7990; www.hotelvillaturka.com; Kargı Sokak 7, Tophane; r €84-130; [❉][@][🛜]) Villa Turka showcases a restored Ottoman house in the Tophane neighbourhood. Each of the 10 rooms features quality bedlinen, honey-toned cedar decor and antique furniture, and views take in the Taurus Mountains and the nearby Red Tower. Breakfast often incorporates organic goodies from farms surrounding Alanya, and dinner is also available.

Seaport Hotel BUSINESS HOTEL €€
(☑513 6487; www.hotelseaport.com; İskele Caddesi 82; s/d ₺120/200; [❉]) The business-style Seaport Hotel, the last on the İskele hotel strip and just steps from the Red Tower, offers efficient service and brilliant sea views from half of its rooms. The 65 rooms are not huge but are very well appointed. Rates include a breakfast and dinner buffet, but be warned that the food can be a little disappointing.

Temiz Otel HOTEL €€
(☑513 1016; http://temizotel.com.tr; İskele Caddesi 12; s/d ₺65/120; [❉]) The refreshingly named 'Clean Hotel' is nothing short of that. Its 32 rooms are spacious, and the ones facing the sea with balconies offer a bird's-eye view of the thumping club and bar action down below.

Tayfun Pansiyon PENSION €
(☑513 0938; Tolupaşa Sokak 17a; s/d ₺20/30) Tucked away in a central residential neighbourhood, the Tayfun Pansiyon is one of the last cheap sleeps in Alanya. Rooms are definitely basic, but they're clean and spacious enough, and there's an adjacent leafy garden for end-of-day relaxing. Breakfast isn't included in the price, but there are plenty of cafes around the corner on Damlataş Caddesi.

✗ Eating

Most of the restaurants listed here will pick you up from and bring you back to where you are staying.

TOP CHOICE İskele Sofrası SEAFOOD €€
(Tophane Caddesi 2b; meze ₺6-8, mains ₺15-30) Eschew the glitzier harbour restaurants and head for this intimate place just off İskele Caddesi. Run by the friendly Öz family, the menu includes more than 70 meze, including *girit ezmesi,* an unforgettable mash of feta, walnuts and olive oil. The terrace with harbour views is a delight, perfect with a cold beer and the shrimp *güveç* (seafood casserole).

Ottoman House TURKISH €€€
(☑511 1421; www.ottomanhousealanya.com; Damlataş Caddesi 31; mains ₺20-32) Inside a 100-year-old stone villa surrounded by lush gardens, Ottoman House is Alanya's most atmospheric eatery. The *beğendili taş kebabı* (₺32), a traditional Ottoman combination of sautéed lamb and aubergine purée, and grilled seafood dishes (₺24 to ₺29) are all good to try. Visit on Thursday or Sunday night for all-you-can-eat barbecue (€15). Meanwhile on Tuesdays there's a meze buffet (€15) and lively Turkish dancing.

Lokanta Su MEDITERRANEAN €€€
(☑512 1500; www.lokantasu.com; Damlataş Caddesi 14a; mains ₺20-35) From Italy to the Middle East, Lokanta Su's pricey menu covers the best of the Mediterranean, but the beautiful courtyard of this restored Ottoman house (originally the residence of the Governor of Alanya) is also a lovely spot to come for a drink from one of the best wine lists in town. The pizza menu (₺19-28) showcases some innovative touches.

Sofra ANATOLIAN €€
(İskele Caddesi 8a; mains ₺8-16) Sofra delivers a modern spin on the traditional Turkish eatery with tasty kebaps, *mantı* (Turkish ravioli), and eastern Anatolian *içli köfte* (ground lamb and onion in a bulgur wheat shell). The complimentary self-serve salad bar is both healthy and good value, and you can peruse the interesting black-and-white photographs of historic Alanya while waiting for your meal.

Köyüm Gaziantep Başpınar ANATOLIAN €€€
(☑513 5664; Hükümet Caddesi; meze ₺10-13, mains ₺20-30) For something more adventurous than the usual grills, this is one of central Alanya's best traditional (if somewhat pricey) Turkish options. Dishes from the eastern city of Gaziantep (Antep) are on offer; try the *patlıcan kebabı* (aubergine kebaps) or the *beyti sarması* (spicy meatballs wrapped in flat bread).

Mahperi Restaurant INTERNATIONAL €€€
(☑512 5491; http://www.greenbeachclub.com/en-mahperi; Rıhtım Caddesi; mains ₺25-35) Quite a feat in fly-by-night Alanya, this classy waterfront fish and steak restaurant has been in operation since 1947 and offers a good selection of international dishes.

♟ Drinking & Entertainment

Alanya features some of the most bawdy, bright and banging nightclubs in all of Turkey. It's all good fun – so long as you don't have to sleep within a kilometre of the blistering tech stompers. More restrained entertainment options also feature.

Ehl-i-Keyf NARGILE CAFE
(Damlataş Caddesi 32) The shaded garden of this restored Ottoman residence is a trendy hangout for Alanya's bright young things, and a great antidote to the more touristy bars and cafes around town. Enjoy a relaxing combo of tea, nargile (water pipe) and backgammon, or a freshly-squeezed juice. Note that only alcohol-free beer is available (we found out the hard way).

Cello LIVE MUSIC
(İskele Caddesi 36) Cello is a rustic wooden bar showcasing 'protest & folk music' (their words, not ours) and is a top spot for an acoustic-fuelled night combining rakı or a few beers. Friendly locals crowd in, escaping the boom-boom-boom manufactured beats in the super clubs down by the harbour. Gigs kick off at 9.30pm most nights.

Red Tower Brewery Restaurant BREWERY
(www.redtowerbrewery.com; İskele Caddesi 80) It's fusion confusion at this multistorey pleasure palace with harbour views. The ground-floor brew pub serves two decent beers, there's an international restaurant on the 1st floor, Turkish dishes on the 3rd floor, and sushi and live guitar music on the 6th floor Sky Lounge. Our pick is a pint of the authentically hoppy pilsner on Red Tower's alfresco deck.

ARMENIAN KINGDOM OF CİLİCİ7A

During the early 11th century the Seljuk Turks swept westwards from Iran, wresting control of much of Anatolia from a weakened Byzantium and pushing into the Armenian highlands. Thousands of Armenians fled south, taking refuge in the rugged Taurus Mountains and along the Mediterranean coast, where in 1080 they founded the kingdom of Cilicia (or Lesser Armenia) under the young Prince Reuben.

While Greater Armenia struggled against foreign invaders and the subsequent loss of its statehood, the Cilician Armenians lived in wealth and prosperity. Geographically, they were in the ideal place for trade and they quickly embraced European ideas, including its feudal class structure. Cilicia became a country of barons, knights and serfs, the court at Sis (today's Kozan) even adopted Western-style clothing. Latin and French became the national languages. During the Crusades the Christian armies used the kingdom's castles as safe havens on their way to the Holy Land.

This period of Armenian history is regarded as the most exciting for science and culture, as schools and monasteries flourished, teaching theology, philosophy, medicine and mathematics. It was also the golden age of Armenian ecclesiastical manuscript painting, noted for its lavish decoration and Western influences.

The Cilician kingdom thrived for nearly 300 years before it fell to the Mamluks of Egypt. The last Armenian ruler, Leo V, spent his final years wandering Europe trying to raise support to recapture his kingdom, before dying in Paris in 1393.

James Dean Bar BAR, CLUB
(Gazipaşa Caddesi) The embodiment of 'the most bawdy, bright and banging' club in the land, this homage to the long-dead American film star is all about bubbles, boobs and, err, pulling. If you can't get a date here, go home or head to one of the other bars shimmering and shaking along Gazipaşa Caddesi. Subtle it ain't.

Robin Hood Bar BAR, CLUB
(Gazipaşa Caddesi 12) Supposedly the biggest club in Alanya, the first two floors of this all-singin', all-dancin', all-flashin' monstrosity are decked out in (you guessed it) a Sherwood Forest theme. Upstairs is the even louder Latin Club for South American beats.

ℹ Information

Alanya Guide (www.alanya.tv) Useful website for Alanya and surrounds. Another good online resource is www.sunsearch.info.

Tourist Office (☑513 1240; Damlataş Caddesi 1; ⊗8am-5pm May-Oct, closed Sat & Sun Nov-Apr) Opposite the Alanya Museum.

Tourist Office (Damlataş Caddesi; ⊗9am-6pm Mon-Fri) Smaller branch near Alanya's *belediye* (town hall).

ℹ Getting There & Away

Boat
There are services to Girne (Kyrenia) in Northern Cyprus operated by **Fergün Denizcilik** (☑511 5565, 511 5358; www.fergun.net; İskele Caddesi 84). Boats leave Alanya at noon on Monday and Friday, returning from Girne at 11am on Thursday and Sunday. Services usually commence in June.

Buy a ticket and present your passport at least a day before departure for immigration formalities. Not included in the ₺77/127 one-way/return ticket prices (students ₺65/110) is a ₺15 harbour tax from Alanya and a whopping ₺33 one from Girne.

Bus
The otogar is on the coastal highway (Atatürk Caddesi), 3km west of the centre. Most services are less frequent off-season, but buses generally leave hourly for Antalya (₺15, two hours, 115km) and eight times daily to Adana (₺40, 10 hours, 440km), stopping at a number of towns along the way. Buses to Konya (₺25, 6½ hours, 320km) take the Akseki–Beyşehir route.

ℹ Getting Around

Dolmuşes (minibuses that stop anywhere along their prescribed routes) to the otogar (₺1.50) can be picked up near the mosque behind the Grand Bazaar, north of Atatürk Caddesi. From the otogar, walk out towards the coast road and the dolmuş stand is on the right. A taxi to the otogar from the centre costs ₺12.

Around Alanya

Around 30km west towards Side and just after Incekum beach is a turning for a road leading north for 9km to **Alarahan**, a 13th-century *han* (caravanserai), which can be explored with a torch. At the head of the valley nearby are the 13th-century ruins of **Alara Castle** (Alara Kalesi).

East from Alanya, the twisting clifftop road occasionally descends to the ocean to pass through the fertile delta of a stream, planted with bananas, or crowded with greenhouses. It's a long drive to Anamur, but it's a beautiful procession of sea views and cool pine forests.

This region was ancient Cilicia Tracheia (Rugged Cilicia), a somewhat forbidding part of the world because of the mountains and fearsome pirates, who preyed on ships from the hidden coves.

There are several notable attractions on or just north of the D400 as you travel west from Alanya, including the seldom-visited ancient sites of **Laertes** and **Syedra**. A turn-off near the 11km marker leads northward for 6km to **Dim Cave** (Dim Mağarası; admission ₺9.50; ⊗low season 9am-5pm, high season to 8pm), with a 360m-long walkway leading past spectacular stalactite and stalagmite formations and a crystal-clear pool. Dolmuşes headed for Kestel from Alanya (hourly in season) will drop you off near the entrance to the cave. A return taxi will cost about ₺70. Dim Cave is often included on organised tours to Sapadere Canyon.

A turning at 27km and another road leading 18km northeast takes you to beautiful **Sapadere Canyon** (Sapadera Kanyonu; adult/child ₺4/2; ⊗low season 9am-5pm, high season to 8pm). Access for walkers is along a 750m-long path. A return taxi from Alanya is around ₺120, and tours from Alanya are ₺60 per person.

Anamur

📞0324 / POP 35,100

Close to the massive Byzantine city of Anemurium, and with a pretty good beach, Anamur is a great place to relax. At the other end of town is the impressive Mamure Castle.

Anamur is also the centre of Turkey's banana-growing industry, and you'll see local *muzler* (bananas; shorter and sweeter than imported ones) on sale everywhere.

◉ Sights

Anamur lies north of highway D400. About 2.5km southeast of the main roundabout is İskele, a popular waterfront district with hotels and restaurants. Anemurium is 8.5km west while Mamure Castle is 7km east.

Anemurium   RUIN

(Anemurium Ancient City; admission ₺3; ⊗8am-7pm Apr-Oct, to 5pm Nov-Mar) Although founded by the Phoenicians in the 4th century BC, most of the ruins visible at Anemurium today date from the late Roman period through to the Byzantine and medieval eras. The site is both sprawling and eerily quiet, with ruins stretching 500m to the pebble beach, and massive city walls impossibly scaling the mountainside.

A number of devastating setbacks included an attack in AD 52 by a vicious Cilician tribe, and archaeologists have uncovered evidence that a massive earthquake destroyed the city in about 580.

From the car park and sprawling **necropolis**, walk southeast past a 4th-century **basilica**; look behind it for a pathway of mosaic tiles leading to the sea. Above the church is one of two **aqueducts**. Opposite the **theatre** dating from the 2nd century AD is the more complete **odeon**, with 900 seats and a tile floor. The best-preserved structure in Anemurium is the **baths complex**; look for the coloured mosaic tiles that still decorate portions of the floor.

Approaching Anamur from the west or down from the Cilician Mountains, a sign points south towards the ruins of Anemurium Antik Kenti. The road then bumps along for 2km to the *gişe* (ticket kiosk); it's another 500m to the car park.

Mamure Castle   FORTRESS

(Mamure Kalesi; admission ₺3; ⊗8am-7.30pm Apr-Oct, to 5pm Nov-Mar) This tremendous castle, with its crenellated walls, 39 towers and part of its original moat still intact, is the biggest and best-preserved fortification on the Turkish Mediterranean coast. The rear of the castle sits directly on the beach, where sea turtles come in summer to lay their eggs, while its front end almost reaches the highway.

Mamure Castle dates from the 13th century; it was constructed by the rulers of the Armenian kingdom of Cilicia on the site of a Roman fortress dating from the 3rd century AD. Mamure was taken by Karamanoğlu Mehmet Bey and his troops in 1308 and alterations began, including the addition of a **mosque** in the eastern courtyard. Here you'll also see remnants of an **aqueduct** that brought water from the mountains 5km away, a **stable** that looks like a garage, and the holes in the walls that served as the **guards' barracks**. To the west is the **kaleiçi**

TURTLES AT RISK

The beach at Anamur is one of a dozen nesting sites of the loggerhead turtle (*Caretta caretta*) along Turkey's Mediterranean coast.

The loggerhead (Turkish: *deniz kaplumbağası*) is a large, flat-headed turtle coloured reddish brown on top and yellow-orange below that spends most of its life in the water. An adult can weigh up to 200kg.

Between May and September, females come ashore at night to lay their eggs in the sand. Using their back flippers they scoop out a nest about 40cm deep, lay between 70 and 120 soft-shelled white eggs the size of ping-pong balls, then cover them over. If disturbed, the turtles may abandon the nests and return to the sea.

The eggs incubate in the sand for some 60 days and the temperature at which they do determines the gender of the hatchlings: below 30°C and all the young will be male, above 30°C they will be female. At a steady 30°C a mix is assured.

As soon as they're born (at night when it's cool and fewer predators are about), the young turtles make their way towards the sea, drawn by the reflected light. If hotels and restaurants are built too close to the beach (as is often the case in the western Mediterranean), their lights can confuse the youngsters, leading them to move up the beach towards danger – in Anamur's case the D400 highway.

The loggerhead turtle also nests on the beaches at Demirtaş and Gazipaşa, both southeast of Alanya, and in the Göksu Delta. In the western Mediterranean, important nesting grounds are at Dalyan, Fethiye, Patara, Demre (Kale), Kumluca and Tekirova (both northeast of Demre), and Belek (east of Antalya).

(castle interior), where the castle commander and other top brass lived.

Climbing the castle's **towers**, especially the one with a dungeon within, is something of an adventure, although some stairs are pretty crumbled, so use extreme caution. Your reward is an astounding view of the sea and the ruins of **Softa Castle** (Softa Kalesi), another fortress built by the Armenian rulers of Cilicia, near Bozyazı some 18km to the east.

FREE **Anamur Museum** MUSEUM
(Anamur Müzesi; Adnan Menderes Caddesi 3; ⊙8.30am-5pm) Highlights of this museum are archaeological finds from Anemurium, including frescoes from private houses, bathhouse mosaics, an unusual clay sarcophagus, plus jewellery, oil lamps and early Christian religious objects. Look for the iron scales in the shape of a woman, her bulging eyes staring emptily into space.

🛌 Sleeping

The popular İskele (harbour) district is where most visitors to Anamur end up. Pensions and hotels run along Fevzi Çakmak Caddesi (or İskele Yolu) down to the harbour and around İnönü Caddesi, the main street running along the waterfront. Dolmuşes stop at the main intersection.

Hotel Esya HOTEL €
(☎0539 491 0211, 816 6595; hotel_esya@mynet.com; İnönü Caddesi 55; s/d ₺50/80; ❀🍃) Quite possibly Anamur's friendliest family runs this excellent hotel just a short walk from the beach. Breakfast in the garden usually includes freshly cooked *sigara böreği* (fried filo and cheese pastries), and the rooms are simple but spacious. Often the family's English-speaking son is on hand, but loads of smiles create a warm welcome even if he's not around.

Hotel Luna Piena HOTEL €€
(☎814 9045; www.hotellunapiena.com; Süleyman Bal Sokak; s ₺60-80, d ₺90-110; ❀🍃) A comfortable hotel in a six-storey block just paces from the beach, the 'Full Moon' offers 32 rooms with parquet floors, balconies with full sea views, spacious showers and a preference for sparkling white decor.

Hotel Tayfun HOTEL €
(☎0536 217 9878, 814 1161; www.tayfunotel.com; Fevzi Çakmak Caddesi 176; s/d/tr ₺50/80/110; ❀🍃) Run by a chatty and welcoming English-speaking owner, the eponymous Tayfun is around 300m from the beach. The 28 rooms have views of the street to the front, or of greenhouses to the back. Good breakfasts (included) and dinners are served in a breezy downstairs restaurant.

Yan Hotel
HOTEL €

(☑814 2123; www.yanhotel.com; Adnan Menderes Caddesi ; s/d ₺50/80; ❄@🏠) Try for a front room with seaviews at this cheap and cheerful hotel in leafy surroundings. The beach is only 30m away, and the downstairs bar is a good place to meet Turkish tourists.

🍴 Eating & Drinking

İskele Sofrası
TURKISH €€

(Sokak 1909; mains ₺8-12) Just one block back from the beach, this popular family eatery turns out top-notch meze and heaving grills: order the *patlıcan* (aubergine) kebap, and try not to feed the very patient Labrador usually parked outside. Good fish dishes and Anamur's best pide round out the menu, and cold beer is also available.

Mare Vista Restaurant
INTERNATIONAL, ITALIAN €€

(☑814 2001; İnönü Caddesi 28; mains ₺10-15) Reasonably priced, considering its location opposite the beach, the 'Sea View' has international and some Italian-themed dishes (including the ubiquitous pizza), as well as salads and sandwiches. Service can be slow, so count on ordering a second beer. Keep an eye on the noticeboard out front for details of occasional live music.

Masalim
TEA GARDEN

(İnönü Caddesi) Anamur's seafront has recently been enlivened with sand-between-your-toes tea gardens. Run by a couple of friendly sisters, the Masalim is the best of them, and highlights include cheap eats and a couple of kilim-bedecked day beds. Fire up a nargile session, or order a cold beer and listen to the bouncy Turkish pop music cascading over nearby waves.

ℹ️ Information

Tourist Office (☑814 5058; ⏲8am-noon & 1-5pm Mon-Fri) In the otogar complex behind the police station.

ℹ️ Getting There & Away

Several buses daily to Alanya (₺25, three hours, 130km), Taşucu/Silifke (₺25, three hours, 140km) and Adana (₺35, six hours, 305km).

ℹ️ Getting Around

Anamur's otogar is on the intersection of the D400 highway and 19 Mayıs Caddesi. Buses and dolmuşes to İskele depart from a small stand behind the otogar (₺1.50, every 30 minutes). A taxi between İskele and the otogar costs ₺12.

Dolmuşes to Ören (₺2, half-hourly) also leave from next to the mosque, over the road from the otogar, and can drop you off at the Anemurium turn-off on the main highway, from where it's a 2.5km walk. Expect to pay ₺60 for a taxi to Anemurium and back, with an hour's waiting time.

Frequent dolmuşes headed for Bozyazı (₺2) will drop you off outside Mamure Castle.

Taşucu
☑0324 / POP 8800

The working port of nearby Silifke, but a destination in its own right, Taşucu (tah-*shoo*-joo) is a low-key resort with a decent city beach. Ferries and hydrofoils for both walk-on passengers and cars travel to/from Girne in Northern Cyprus. The beach is fronted by Sahil Caddesi, which stretches east from the ferry pier and has several good pensions. Around the harbour, excursion boats depart for day trips (per person ₺30) along the coastline and to nearby islands.

🛏️ Sleeping

Holmi Pansiyon
PENSION €

(☑0545 948 3806, 741 5378; www.holmipansiyon. com; Sahil Caddesi 23; r ₺40-90; ❄@🏠) The covered front porch at this 11-room pension around the corner from the beach is particularly nice for relaxing on a hot day. Around half the rooooms have sea views, and a shared guests' kitchen is also available. Refurbishment aplenty was taking place when we last dropped by.

Lades Motel
HOTEL €€

(☑741 4008; www.ladesmotel.com; İsmet İnönü Caddesi 45; s/d €39/54; ❄@🏠⊞) This hotel on the road into Taşucu is a favourite of birdwatchers who flock to the nearby Göksu Delta. The two-dozen rooms, set around a large pool, are nothing to write home about, but there are wonderful harbour views from the balconies. The lobby and public spaces are well designed for comparing 'twitching' notes with fellow birders in residence.

Otel Olba
PENSION €€

(☑0545 277 8721, 741 4222; www.otelolba.net; Sahil Caddesi; s/d ₺65/130; ❄🏠) Cheek-by-jowl with Meltem Pansiyon and directly on the sea, the Olba is tidy and well run. The huge 2nd-floor terrace (where breakfast is served each morning) offers wonderful sea views.

Meltem Pansiyon PENSION €
(☑0533 360 0726, 741 4391; www.meltempansiyon.
net; Sahil Caddesi 75; s ₺40-80, d ₺60-100; ❄@⊜)
This family-run pension right on the beach
is affordable and very friendly. Some eight of
the 20 modest rooms face the sea, and breakfast is served on the delightful back patio.

✕ Eating & Drinking

For a good-value seafood fix, head to one of
the excursion boats lining the harbour. They
also double as restaurants with fish sandwiches (₺5) and grilled seafood.

Denizkızı Restaurant SEAFOOD €€
(☑741 4194; İsmet İnönü Caddesi 62c; mains ₺12-
18) The 'Mermaid' is good for meze, fish and
grills, and as a cooling haven on the lovely
roof terrace on a hot afternoon. The cost for
seafood varies by weight, so check the price
when you're ordering.

Baba Restaurant SEAFOOD €€
(☑741 5991; İsmet İnönü Caddesi 43; mains ₺15-25)
Regarded as the area's best eatery, the Baba's
terrace is a beautiful place to sip a cold beer
or slurp Italian *gelato* (₺4 to ₺6). It's the excellent food that really lures diners though,
especially the tempting meze (₺3 to ₺5).

❶ Getting There & Away

Akgünler Denizcilik (☑741 2303; www.akgun
ler.com.tr; İsmet İnönü Caddesi) runs *feribotlar*
(car ferries) and/or *ekspresler* (hydrofoils) between Taşucu and Girne in Northern Cyprus. It
has a daily hydrofoil at 11.30am (one way/return
₺69/114) and a car ferry (passenger one way/
return ₺59/99, car ₺150/300) leaving at midnight from Sunday to Thursday. The hydrofoil
leaves Girne at 9.30am daily while the car ferry
leaves at noon Monday to Friday only.

Hydrofoils are faster (two hours) but the ride
can be stomach-churning on choppy seas. Tickets cost less on the car ferry, but the trip can take
anywhere from four to 10 hours, depending on
the weather. Not included in the fares is the harbour tax: ₺10 out of Taşucu and ₺33 from Girne.

Dolmuşes drop you at the petrol station to
the north of town; it's a five-minute walk to the
beach. There are frequent dolmuşes between
Taşucu and Silifke (₺2), where you can make
long-distance connections.

Silifke

☑0324 / POP 54,800
Silifke is a riverside country town with a
long history. A striking castle towers above
the mineral-rich blue-green Göksu River,

dubbed the Calycadnus in ancient times.
In the vicinity are other archaeological and
natural sights that deserve a visit.

Seleucia ad Calycadnum, as Silifke was
once known, was founded by Seleucus I
Nicator in the 3rd century BC. He was one
of Alexander the Great's most able generals
and founder of the Seleucid dynasty that
ruled Syria after Alexander's death.

The town's other claim to fame is that
Emperor Frederick Barbarossa (r 1152–90)
drowned in the river near here while leading his troops on the Third Crusade. It was
apparently the weight of his armour that
brought him down.

Silifke's accommodation options are mediocre at best, and the town is best visited as
a day trip from nearby Taşucu.

◉ Sights

FREE **Fortress** FORTRESS
The Byzantine hilltop fortress, with its
moat, two dozen towers and vaulted underground chambers was once Silifke's
command centre. Keep an eye out for the
friendly Ahmet Kulali. He speaks excellent
English and knows all about local history.
Tip him well – he's worth it.

FREE **Tekir Ambarı** HISTORIC BUILDING
From the fortress it's possible to see the Tekir Ambarı, an ancient cistern carved from
rock that can be entered via a spiral staircase. To reach the cistern, head to the junction of İnönü Caddesi and Menderes Caddesi, then walk up the steep road to the left of
the Küçük Hacı Kaşaplar butcher shop. An
alternative to a long and hot walk up the hill
to the castle are the motorcycle drivers who
wait at this corner. Expect to pay around
₺20 per person.

FREE **Necropolis** RUIN
To the south of Tekir Ambarı is ancient Silifke's necropolis. In the centre, the rather
sad ruins of the Roman **Temple of Jupiter**,
its columns used by storks as nesting posts,
sits right along the side of very busy İnönü
Caddesi. The temple dates from the 2nd
century AD, but was turned into a Christian
basilica sometime in the 5th century.

Silifke Museum MUSEUM
(Taşucu Caddesi 29; admission ₺3; ⊘8am-5pm
Tue-Sun) To the east of the centre, Silifke's
museum showcases Roman figures and
busts. The collection also includes ancient

EASTERN MEDITERRANEAN SILIFKE

coins and jewellery, amphora and pottery, and tools and weapons from the Roman and Hellenistic eras.

Merkez Camii
MOSQUE

(Central Mosque; Fevzi Çakmak Caddesi) Also called the Alaeddin Camisi, or Aladdin's Mosque, the Seljuk-era Merkez Camii dates from 1228, although it's seen many renovations over the centuries.

Reşadiye Camii
HISTORIC BUILDING

(İnönü Caddesi 138) Built by the Ottomans, the Roman columns supporting the back and front porticoes were originally from the Temple of Jupiter.

Stone Bridge
BRIDGE

The stone bridge over the Göksu dates back to AD 78 and has been restored many times, including twice in the last century (1922 and 1972).

✗ Eating & Drinking

Try the *Silifke yoğrdu* – a local yoghurt famous throughout Turkey.

Gözde Restaurant
KEBAP €€

(Balıkçılar Sokak 7; mains ₺8-15) This kebap and *lahmacun* (Arabic-style pizza) joint also serves up delicious soups, meze and grills in a shaded outdoor dining area down a small street.

Kale Restaurant
KEBAP, PIDE €€

(mains ₺8-12) This eatery below the towers of the castle has simple dishes at reasonable prices, and is the best place within kilometres for a sundowner.

Göksu Pastanesi
TEA GARDEN €

(pastries from ₺1.50) A large and shaded terrace off Cavit Erdem Caddesi, perched atop the rumbling Göksu River and close to the stone bridge.

❶ Information

Tourist Office (☎714 1151; Veli Gürten Bozbey Caddesi 6; ◷8am-5pm Mon-Fri) Just north of Atatürk Caddesi, with a surprisingly good array of English-language info on the region.

❶ Getting There & Away

Buses depart hourly for Adana (₺20, 2½ hours, 165km). Other frequent services include Mersin (₺10, two hours, 95km), Alanya (₺35, six hours, 265km) and Antalya (₺40 nine hours, 395km).

Dolmuşes to Taşucu (₺2) depart every 20 minutes from opposite the Lezzet Dünyası restaurant and east of the otogar, or from a stand on the south bank of the Göksu. A taxi to Taşucu costs ₺25.

Around Silifke

Just southeast of Silifke are the lush salt marshes, lakes and sand dunes of the **Göksu Delta**, an important wetland area and home to some 332 bird species. To the north and northeast, the slopes of the maquis-covered **Olba Plateau** stretch along the coast for about 60km before the Cilician plain opens into an ever-widening swathe of fertile land. It is one of Turkey's richest areas for archaeological sites and includes many destinations more easily accessed from Kızkalesi.

UZUNCABURÇ

The impressive **ruins** (admission ₺3; ◷8am-8pm Apr-Oct, to 5pm Nov-Mar) at Uzuncaburç, in the mountains some 30km northeast of Silifke, are well worth the trip. They sit within the ancient Roman city of Diocaesarea, originally a Hellenistic city known as Olba, home to a zealous cult that worshipped Zeus Olbius.

The **Temple of Zeus Olbius**, with two dozen erect columns, lies to the left of a **colonnaded street**. Just before the entrance is a Roman **theatre**. Important Roman structures include a **nymphaeum** (2nd or 3rd century AD), an arched **city gate**, and the **Temple of Tyche** (1st century AD) with five Corinthian columns. Look around the Zeus temple for **sarcophagi** bearing reliefs (such as of Medusa).

To view a Hellenistic structure built before the Romans sacked Olba, head north through the village, where you'll pass a massive, five-storey **watch tower** with a **Roman road** behind it. Another 600m down into the valley leads to a long, roadside **necropolis** of **rock-cut tombs** and more **sarcophagi**.

On the road to Uzuncaburç some 8km out of Silifke at Demircili – ancient Imbriogon – you'll pass several superb examples of Roman **monumental tombs** that resemble houses.

❶ Getting There & Away

Minibuses to Uzuncaburç (₺6) leave from a side street near the Silifke tourist office at 10am, noon, 2pm, 4pm and 6pm. They usually depart Uzuncaburç in the morning before noon, though there is one at 4.30pm.

Hiring a taxi costs ₺120 return, usually incorporating a visit to the tombs at Demircili.

Kızkalesi

📞 0324 / POP 1750

Kızkalesi boasts not only one of the region's loveliest beaches, but also two castles, one of which seems to be floating at sea. It's also a springboard for the Olba Plateau, a virtual open-air museum of ruins.

The scene here is more inclusive than you'd expect of a typical Turkish coastal village, due to the easygoing locals and the prevalence of foreign archaeology buffs strolling the foreshore.

◉ Sights

Kızkalesi Castle FORTRESS
(Maiden's Castle; admission ₺3 to 5pm May-Oct) Lying 300m from the shore, Kızkalesi Castle is like a suspended dream. Check out the **mosaics** in the central courtyard and the vaulted **gallery**, and climb one of the four **towers** (the one at the southeast corner has the best views). It's possible to swim to the castle, but most people catch the boat (₺5) from in front of the Albatross restaurant. Another option is to rent a dolphin-themed pedalo (around ₺10).

Corycus Castle FORTRESS
(Korykos Kalesi; admission ₺3; ⊗8am-8pm Apr-Oct, to 5pm Nov-Mar) At the northern end of the beach, Corycus Castle was either built or rebuilt by the Byzantines, briefly occupied by the Armenian kingdom of Cilicia and once connected to Kızkalesi by a causeway. Walk carefully to the east, where a ruined tower affords a fine view of the Kızkalesi castle.

Ruins RUIN
Across the highway from Corycus Castle is a **necropolis**, once the burial ground for tradespeople. Tombs and rock carvings include a 5th-century relief of a warrior with a raised sword.

Some 4km northeast of Kızkalesi at Ayaş, are the extensive but badly ruined remains of ancient **Elaiussa-Sebaste**, a city dating back to the early Roman period and perhaps even to the Hittite era. Important structures on the left (west) side include a 2300-seat hilltop **theatre**, the remains of a **Byzantine basilica**, a **Roman temple** with floor mosaics of fish and dolphins, and a total-immersion cruciform **baptistery**. The ruins on the eastern side are unstable and entry is forbidden.

🛏 Sleeping

Rain Hotel HOTEL €€
(📞523 2782; www.rainhotel.com; per person €40-70; ❄@) With a friendly vibe set by manager Mehmet, the Rain is a perennially popular choice. Run by the same people as Cafe Rain and its attached travel agency, it's got a similar anything-is-possible ethos, including scuba diving excursions and day trips around the area. The 18 spotless and spacious rooms are sparingly decorated and, with fridges, conducive to long stays.

Yaka Hotel HOTEL €€
(📞0542 432 1996, 523 2444; www.yakahotel.com.tr; s/d/tr ₺70/110/130; ❄@🛜) Yakup Kahveci, the Yaka's multilingual and quick-witted owner, runs the most welcoming hostelry in Kızkalesi. The 17 rooms are impeccably tidy, breakfast (or specially ordered dinner) is eaten in the attractive garden, and there's nothing in the area Yakup doesn't know and/or can't organise. The Yaka is also a great place to meet travellers, especially those interested in archaeology.

Hotel Hantur HOTEL €
(📞523 2367; www.hotelhantur.com; s ₺60/80; ❄@🛜) The Hantur has a front-row seat on the sea and the 20 colourful rooms are cool, and comfortable. All have balconies, but try to grab one facing the sea (for example, room 301). The breezy front garden is another bonus, as is the helpful and friendly management.

🍴 Eating & Drinking

Another option is a 10-minute bus ride (₺2) to the seafood restaurants at Narlıkuyu.

Cafe Rain INTERNATIONAL €€
(📞523 2234; mains ₺15-25) The rainbow decor here complements the cheery menu of tasty, good-value international favourites as well as what might be the finest *börek* (pastry filled with cheese or meat) on the eastern Mediterranean. In the evenings, travellers transform it into a companionable cocktail bar.

Paşa Restaurant KEBAP €€
(📞523 2230; Plaj Yolu 5; mains ₺8-16) Just off central Cumhuriyet Meydanı, this large open spot has grills and meze at better prices than the beachfront restaurants. Keeping things super-competitive is the adjacent and equally good value **Tanem** ('Sweetheart') restaurant.

Villa Nur
CAFE €€

(☏523 2340; mains ₺10-18) Readers have written raving letters about the meals served at this seafront pension owned by a Turkish–German couple. The European-style cakes are exceptional.

Turkish Turtles Club
BAR

Exposed bricks and giant beer cans make this the funkiest place in town. You may be keeping company with Turkish teenagers from Adana or Mersin, proudly showing off the newly-inked tattoos they've just scored around the corner.

Albatross
BAR, RESTAURANT

The Albatross is a restaurant as well, but visit here for sundowners around the outdoor bar, with full views of the Kızkalesi castle. They've been known to overcharge travellers, so check prices when you order your drinks.

Getting There & Away

Frequent buses link Kızkalesi with Silifke (₺4, 30 minutes, 24km) and Mersin (₺7, 1½ hours, 60km).

Around Kızkalesi

There are several places to the southwest and northeast of Kızkalesi that are of genuine historical interest and importance. They include everything from an idyllic seaside village with an important mosaic to a descent into the very bowels of the earth.

NARLIKUYU

On a cove 5km southwest of Kızkalesi, Narlıkuyu has popular fish restaurants, a mosaic of singular beauty and other-worldly mountain caves nearby.

Inside the village's **Mosaic Museum** (Mozaik Müzesi), in a compact 4th-century Roman bath, is a wonderful mosaic of the Three Graces – Aglaia, Thalia and Euphrosyne – the daughters of Zeus.

Absolute waterfront restaurants include the **Kerim** (mains ₺15-25) near the museum, and the **Narlıkuyu** (mains ₺15-25) on the opposite side of the cove.

Frequent dolmuşes run between Kızkalesi and Silifke via Narlıkuyu (₺2).

CAVES OF HEAVEN & HELL

Near Narlıkuyu, a road winds north for 3km to several **caves** (admission ₺5; ☺8am-7pm) – sinkholes carved out by a subterranean river and places of great mythological significance.

The **Chasm of Heaven** (Cennet Mağarası) – an underground cavern 200m long, 90m wide and 70m deep – is reached via 450-odd steps to the left of the car park. Near a landing not far from the cave mouth is the 5th-century Byzantine **Chapel of the Virgin Mary**, used for a short time in the 19th century as a mosque.

Running off this large cavern is the **Cave of Typhon** (Tayfun Mağarası), a damp, devilish theatre. Locals believe this to be a gateway to the eternal furnace and Strabo mentions it in his *Geography*. According to legend, the cave's underground river connects with the hellish River Styx.

Up the hill from the Chasm of Heaven is the **Cave-Gorge of Hell** (Cehennem Mağarası), with almost vertical walls and a heart-stopping viewing platform extending over a 120m-deep pit. This charred hole is supposedly where Zeus imprisoned the 100-headed, fire-breathing monster Typhon after defeating him in battle.

Around 600m west is **Asthma Cave** (Astim Mağarası), which supposedly relieves sufferers of the affliction.

ADAMKAYALAR

Tricky to get to but well worth the effort is Adamkayalar (Men Rock Cliff), some 17 Roman-era reliefs carved on a cliff face about 8km north of Kızkalesi. They are part of a 1st century AD necropolis and immortalise warriors wielding axes, swords and lances, and citizens, sometimes accompanied by their wives and children.

At the necropolis opposite Corycus Castle a sign points west to the site. Follow the road uphill for 5km and, at another sign, turn left; the car park is just under 3km down this road. Follow the painted blue arrows down a rather tricky incline into the glen for about 750m and don't go alone: you might fall and be stranded.

KANLIDİVANE

About 8.5km northeast of Kızkalesi at Kumkuyu is the road leading 3km to the frightening **ruins** (admission ₺5; ☺8am-8pm Apr-Oct, to 5pm Nov-Mar) of Kanlıdivane, the ancient city of Kanytelis. Near the carpark is a 17m **Hellenistic tower** built to honour Zeus.

Central to Kanlıdivane ('Bloody Place of Madness'), is a 60m-deep chasm where criminals were tossed to wild animals.

Ruins ring the pit including four **Byzantine churches**, and a **necropolis** along a Roman road to the northeast, with a stupendous 2nd-century **temple tomb**. On the cliff walls are reliefs of a six-member family (southwest) and a Roman soldier (northwest).

Mersin (İçel)

📞 0324 / POP 860,000

Mersin was earmarked a half-century ago as the seaside outlet for Adana and its rich agricultural hinterland. Today it is the largest port on the Turkish Mediterranean and for the most part a sprawling, soulless place that most people leave quickly. But Mersin, whose official new name İçel (also the name of the province of which it is capital) is ignored by most everyone, does have its moments. Some of the streets near the sea almost have a Marseilles feel to them, and there are definitely worse ways to while away an afternoon than a lazy seafood lunch on the excursion boats lining the harbour.

◉ Sights & Activities

FREE **Atatürk Evi**   MUSEUM
(Atatürk House; Atatürk Caddesi 36; ◷8am-7pm Mon-Sat Apr-Oct, 9am-noon & 1-4.30pm Mon-Sat Nov-Mar) Along the pedestrianised section of Atatürk Caddesi is a museum in a beautiful seven-room villa where Atatürk once stayed.

FREE **Archaeology & Ethnography Museum**   MUSEUM
(Cumhuriyet Meydanı 62; ◷8am-noon & 1-7pm Apr-Oct, to 4pm Nov-Mar) Mersin's archaeology museum has finds from nearby tumuli (burial mound) sites (including Elaiussa-Sebaste near Kızkalesi), a great bronze of Dionysus and curious odds and ends such as a Roman-era glass theatre 'token' on the ground floor.

Greek Orthodox Church   CHURCH
(◷divine liturgy 9-11.15am Sun) Next to Mersin's Archaeology & Ethnography Museum, the walled 1852 church is still in use and has a lovely *iconostasis*. To gain entry, go to the left side of the church facing 4302 Sokak and ring the bell.

🛏 Sleeping

Budget and midrange hotels huddle around the otogar.

Kardelen Hotel   HOTEL €€
(📞337 2798; www.kardelenotel.com.tr; Mesudiye Fasih Kayabak Caddesi ; s/d ₺60/100; ❄❀🐸) This newish hotel is around 300m from the city's otogar. Modern decor combines with flat-screen TVs and spotless bathrooms for a hassle-free way to break your travels. Central Mersin and the city's main restaurant area is around 600m away.

Nobel Oteli   HOTEL €€
(📞237 2210; www.nobelotel.com; İstiklal Caddesi 73; s/d ₺90/130; ❄🐸) A smart choice in the heart of the city, the Nobel has 74 big and comfortable rooms with some deft design touches and satellite TV. The foyer is a hive of business activity, and the adjoining restaurant is popular at lunch.

Hotel Gökhan   HOTEL €€
(📞232 4665; www.otelgokhan.com; Soğuksu Caddesi 20; s/d ₺60/90; ❄🐸) The decor of the public areas of this two-star hotel is vaguely art deco – though we don't know how the large aquarium fits in. The 28 airy rooms include satellite TV and minibar. Opt for one with a balcony.

✖ Eating & Drinking

Mersin's local speciality is *tantuni* kebap: chopped beef sautéed with onions, garlic and peppers, and wrapped in pita-like *lavaş ekmek*. *Tantuni* is often accompanied by *şalgam suyu*, a crimson-coloured juice made by boiling turnips and adding vinegar. For something sweet, try *cezerye*, a semigelatinous confection made from carrots and packed with walnuts.

Deniz Yıldızı   SEAFOOD €€
(📞237 7124; 4701 Sokak 10b; mains ₺12-20) The 'Starfish' is the best of several fish restaurants around Silifke Caddesi. For a cheaper seafood fix, try the floating fish restaurants around the harbour. Fish sandwiches and a beer are both around ₺5.

Hacıbaba   TURKISH €€
(📞238 0023; İstiklal Caddesi 82; mains ₺7-14) Opposite the Nobel Oteli, the delightful Hacıbaba does excellent *zeytinyağlı biber dolması* (stuffed peppers), and there are good kebaps, *lahmacun* and pide too.

Piknik   BAR, CAFE
(5218 Sokak) This bar-cum-cafe-cum-teahouse is one of a collection of humming little working-class drinking venues in the

Taşhan Antik Galerya on a street between İsmet İnönü Caddesi and Uray Caddesi.

ℹ Information

Tourist Office (📞238 3271; İsmet İnönü Bulvarı; ⊙8am-noon & 1-5pm Mon-Fri) Near the harbour at the eastern end of town.

ℹ Getting There & Away

Bus

Mersin's otogar is on the city's eastern outskirts. To get to the centre, leave by the main exit, turn right and walk up to the main road (Gazi Mustafa Kemal Bulvarı). Cross to the far side and catch a bus travelling west (₺1.50). Buses from town to the otogar leave from outside the train station, as well as from a stop opposite the Mersin Oteli.

Frequent buses run to Adana (₺12, 1½ hours, 75km), Silifke (₺15, two hours, 85km, three per hour) and Alanya (₺45, 8½ hours, 375km, eight per day).

Train

There are rail services to Tarsus (₺3) and Adana (₺5) between 6am and 10.30pm.

Tarsus

📞0324 / POP 242,000

Should Tarsus' most famous son return two millennia after his birth, St Paul would hardly recognise the place through the sprawl of concrete apartment blocks. But although the appeal of Tarsus is largely historic, a stroll through the back lanes leading to early Christian and Old Testament sites is reason enough to linger.

◉ Sights & Activities

Cleopatra's Gate   GATE

The Roman Kancık Kapısı, literally the 'Gate of the Bitch', but better known as Cleopatra's Gate, has nothing to do with the Egyptian queen, although she is thought to have had a rendezvous with Mark Antony here in 41 BC. Heavy-handed restoration has robbed it of any sense of antiquity.

St Paul's Well   RUIN

(St Paul Kuyusu; admission ₺3; ⊙8am-8pm Apr-Oct, to 5pm Nov-Mar) A kilometre north of Cleopatra's Gate (signs point the way) are the ruins of St Paul's house, his supposed birthplace, which can be viewed underneath sheets of plexiglass.

Old City   HISTORIC AREA

The Old City (Antik Şehir) lies a couple of hundred metres south and southeast of St Paul's Well. It includes a wonderful 60m-long stretch of **Roman road**, and **historical Tarsus houses**, one now housing the Konak Efsus boutique hotel.

Southeast of the Old City are several historical mosques, including the **Eski Camii** (Old Mosque), a medieval structure that was originally a church dedicated to St Paul. Adjacent looms the barely recognisable brickwork of a huge old **Roman bath**. Across Atatürk Caddesi is the late-19th-century **Makam Camii** (Official Mosque), and to the east is believed to be the **tomb of the Prophet Daniel**. To the west is the 16th-century **Ulu Camii** (Great Mosque), sporting a curious 19th-century minaret moonlighting as a clock tower. Adjacent is the 19th-century **Kırkkaşık Bedesten** (Forty Spoons Market), still used as a covered bazaar.

Church of St Paul   CHURCH

(St Paul Kilisesi; admission ₺3; ⊙8am-8pm) South of the Kırkkaşık Bedesten (Forty Spoons Market), parts of the Church of St Paul date from the 18th century.

Tarsus Museum   MUSEUM

(Muvaffak Uygur Caddesi 75; admission ₺3; ⊙8am-7.30pm Apr-Oct, to 5pm Nov-Mar) About 750m southwest of the city centre, the museum showcases ancient statuary and coins, one from the 6th century BC.

Waterfall   WATERFALL

Catch a dolmuş (₺1.5) in front of the Eski Cami to a cooling waterfall on the Tarsus River (the Cydnus River in ancient times), some 3km to the north. There are tea gardens and restaurants nearby.

A PLACE OF PILGRIMAGE

Jewish by birth, Paul (born Saul) was one of early Christianity's most zealous proselytisers and during his lifetime converted hundreds of pagans and Jews to the new religion throughout the ancient world. After his death in Rome about AD 67, the location of his birthplace became sacred to his followers. Today pilgrims still flock to the site of his ruined house in Tarsus to take a drink from the 30m-deep well on the grounds.

🛏 Sleeping & Eating

Konak Efsus BOUTIQUE HOTEL €€
(✆614 0807; www.konakefsus.com; Tarihi Evler Sokak 31-33; s/d ₺90/160; ❃@🛜) Tarsus' best accommdation is this delightful boutique hotel converted from a traditional Ottoman house. The eight rooms, with stone walls, antique furniture and 21st-century plumbing, are all unique and bear different names. The Cleopatra Suite is especially fine, as is the lovely patio. It's very popular, especially at weekends, so booking ahead is recommended.

Antik Cafe CAFE
(✆0538 866 6565; Tarihi Evler Sokak; 🛜) This pretty little cafe in a 200-year-old house opposite the Konak Efsus is a cooling haven when Tarsus is hot and dusty.

ℹ Information

Tourist Office (✆613 3888; Cumhuriyet Alanı; ☺8am-5pm Mon-Sat) In front of the Roman road.

ℹ Getting There & Away

Tarsus' otogar is 3km east of the centre. A taxi is ₺10 and a bus or dolmuş (₺1.25). Buses and dolmuşes connect Tarsus with Mersin (₺3.50, 29km) and Adana (₺4, 42km).

The train station, with regular services to Mersin (₺3) and Adana (₺4), is northwest of the tourist office at the end of Hilmi Seçkin Caddesi.

Adana

✆0322 / POP 1.61 MILLION

Turkey's fourth-largest city is more or less cut in two by the D400 highway. It's a thoroughly modern affair with some decent sights, pretty good cafes and bars, and good transportation links. If you've been travelling lazily along the Med, the city's urban buzz may surprise you.

North of the city's main road, Turan Cemal Beriker Bulvarı running west to east and over Kennedy Köprüsü (Kennedy Bridge), are leafy and well-heeled districts. South of the trendy high-rise apartments and sidewalk bars and cafes, the mood deepens, and housing starts to sprawl. The Seyhan River delimits the city centre to the east.

◉ Sights & Activities

Mosques MOSQUE
The attractive 16th-century **Ulu Camii** (Great Mosque; Abidin Paşa Caddesi) is reminis-

cent of mosques found in northern Syria, with black-and-white banded marble and elaborate window surrounds. The tiles in the *mihrab* (prayer niche) came from Kütahya and İznik.

The central **Yeni Camii** (New Mosque; Özler Caddesi) dating from the early 18th century, follows the general square plan of the Ulu Camii, with 10 domes. The 16th-century **Yağ Camii** (Oil Mosque; Ali Münif Caddesi), with its imposing portal to the southeast, started life as the church of St James.

Most imposing of all, though, is the six-minaret **Sabancı Merkez Camii** (Sabancı Central Mosque; Turan Cemal Beriker Bulvarı), on the left bank of the river beside the Kennedy Bridge. The largest mosque between İstanbul and Saudi Arabia, it was built by the late industrial magnate Sakıp Sabancı (1933–2004), who was a philanthropist and founder of the second-richest family dynasty in Turkey. The mosque is covered top to tail in marble and gold leaf, and can accommodate an estimated 28,000 worshippers.

Archaeology Museum MUSEUM
(Fuzuli Caddesi 10; admission ₺5; ☺8am-5pm Tue-Sun) Next door to the Sabancı Merkez Camii, the Archaeology Museum is rich in Roman statuary from the Cilician Gates, north of Tarsus. These 'gates' were the main passage through the Taurus Mountains and an important transit point as far back as Roman times. Note especially the 2nd-century Achilles sarcophagus, decorated with scenes from the *Iliad*. Hittite artefacts and Hellenistic monuments are also on display.

Adana Ethnography Museum MUSEUM
(Ziyapaşa Bulvarı 143; admission ₺3; ☺8am-5pm Tue-Sun) Just off İnönü Caddesi, this museum is housed in a former Crusader church that later served as a mosque. It was closed for restoration at the time of writing, but a late 2012 reopening was planned to once again showcase its array of carpets and kilims (pileless woven rugs), weapons, manuscripts and funeral monuments.

Stone Bridge BRIDGE
Taşköprü, a Roman-era stone bridge over the Seyhan at the eastern end of Abidin Paşa Caddesi, was built under Hadrian (r 117–138) and repaired in the 6th century. The 300m-long span has 21 arches but you can only see 14 – the rest are underwater.

Adana

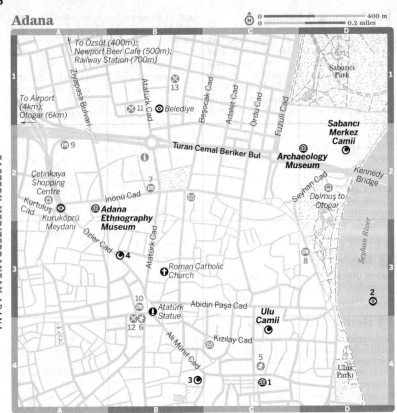

To Özsüt (400m);
Newport Beer Cafe (500m);
Railway Station (700m)

To Airport
(4km);
Otogar (6km)

Sabancı
Park

Belediye

Turan Cemal Beriker Bul

Sabancı
Merkez
Camii

Archaeology
Museum

Kennedy
Bridge

Çetinkaya
Shopping
Centre

Kurtuluş
Cad

Kuruköprü
Meydanı

Adana
Ethnography
Museum

İnönü Cad

Özler Cad

Seyhan River

Dolmuş to
Otogar

Roman Catholic
Church

Abidin Paşa Cad

Atatürk
Statue

Ali Münif Cad

Kızılay Cad

Ulu
Camii

Ulus
Parkı

Great Clock Tower   HISTORIC BUILDING

(Büyük Saat Kulesi) Near Adana's sprawling **covered market** (*kapalı çarşı*), the Great Clock Tower dates back to 1881.

Hamams   HAMAM

(per person ₺15-20) There are two traditional hamams in the town centre where you can go for a soak and a scrub: **Mestan Hamamı** (Merry Hamam; Pazarlar Caddesi 3; ⏰5am-11pm), next to the Öz Asmaaltı restaurant, and the **Çarşı Hamamı** (Market Hamam; Ali Münif Caddesi 145; ⏰men 5-9am & 4-10pm, women 9am-3.30pm) opposite the Great Clock Tower.

🛌 Sleeping

TOP CHOICE Hotel Bosnalı   BOUTIQUE HOTEL €€€

(☑359 8000; www.hotelbosnali.com; Seyhan Caddesi 29; s/d €75/85, ste €130-160; ❄🌐) This lovely boutique hotel is housed in a private mansion built in 1889. Stone-tile floors, hand-carved wooden ceilings and antique Ottoman furnishings create a unique heritage ambience, and the views from the rooftop restaurant are breathtaking. The staff are uniformly friendly and professional, making the Bosnalı a splurge-worthy treat, and one of eastern Turkey's best places to stay.

Ibis Hotel   BUSINESS HOTEL €€

(☑355 9500; www.ibishotel.com; Turhan Cemal Beriker Bulvari 49; r ₺100; ⊖❄🌐) This brand-new opening has a perfect location, bridging the compelling chaos of old Adana and the wide avenues, cafes and bars of the newer part of the city. In true Ibis style, the compact rooms are chic and modern with all mod cons, and we also applaud their decision to incorporate non-smoking floors.

Otel Mercan   HOTEL €€

(☑351 2603; www.otelmercan.com; Küçüksaat Meydanı 5; s/d ₺60/100; ❄🌐) Recent renovations have created what is quite probably

Adana

Adana's chicest hotel lobby, but unfortunately the hip vibe is not transferred to the more prosaic, but still comfortable, rooms. That said, the rebooted Mercan still boasts a great location, right opposite the city's best spot for Adana kebap, and the surrounding fabric bazaar area features plenty of local colour.

Akdeniz Oteli   HOTEL **€€**
(☑363 1510; fax 363 1510; İnönü Caddesi 22; s/d ₺70/100; ❋🛜) Centrally located near lots of restaurants, the clean and smartly decorated two-star Akdeniz Oteli has 30 rooms. Don't miss the psychedelic mirrored staircase leading from the lobby to the 2nd-floor bar.

✗ Eating & Drinking

Famous worldwide is Adana kebap: minced beef or lamb mixed with powdered red pepper and grilled on a skewer. It is served with sliced onions dusted with the slightly acidic herb sumac and barbecued tomatoes.

TOP CHOICE **Ova Ev Yemekleri**   TURKISH **€**
(off Atatürk Caddesi; soups & rice ₺3, mains ₺6-11; ⦿Lunch) Ignore the incongruous car park location, and join the loyal band of regulars who crowd this bustling eatery for its changing daily menu. The emphasis is on *yöresel yemekler* (hearty renditions of traditional homestyle recipes), so you're guaranteed an authentic and filling lunch. There's always a few soups and rice dishes on offer, so mix and match away with main courses such as *patlıcan biber dolma* (stuffed aubergines and peppers). Next to a building called Ticaret Borsası.

TOP CHOICE **Öz Asmaaltı**   KEBAP **€€**
(☑351 4028; Pazarlar Caddesi 9; mains ₺15-20) Just opposite the Otel Mercan, this local favourite is just about the best restaurant of its class in Adana. It's a fairly spartan place, but the mains and meze are delightful. This is *the* place to try Adana kebap, but don't leave without also trying the dessert of *kadayıf* (dough soaked in syrup and topped with clotted cream).

Şen   TURKISH **€**
(62001 Sokak; mains ₺7-12) From Ataturk Caddesi, turn right into 62002 Sokak and then left into 62001 Sokak to find this relaxed neighbourhood *lokanta* (eatery serving ready-made food) popular with desk jockeys from nearby offices and featuring loads of vegetarian options. The best place to sit is on the terrace shaded by a rambling arbor. There's no menu, so check out what looks good.

Newport Efes Beer Cafe   PUB
(Şinasi Efendi Caddesi 23) Retro Americana decor, an outdoor terrace, plus a range of draught beers are the key attractions for a young and cosmopolitan crowd at this bustling pub, tucked away in a leafy, upmarket neighbourhood. Look for the red British-style phone booth out front. Hearty food comes with a Turkish, Italian or Mexican accent. Alfresco bars and cafes dot the surrounding streets.

Özsüt   CAFE **€**
(Ziyapaşa Bulvarı 15c; cakes ₺4.50-8; ⦿8am-midnight) Cakes, puddings and a delightfully delicious assortment of ice creams are available at this branch of a popular chain.

➊ Information

Tourist Office (☑363 1448; Atatürk Caddesi 7; ⦿8am-noon & 1-5pm Mon-Sat) One block north of İnönü Caddesi, with excellent city maps and pretty good English spoken.

SERVICES FROM ADANA'S OTOGAR

DESTINATION	FARE (₺)	DURATION (HR)	DISTANCE (KM)	FREQUENCY (PER DAY)
Adıyaman (for Nemrut Dağı)	30	6	335	7 buses
Alanya	35	10	440	up to 8 buses
Ankara	40	7	475	hourly
Antakya	20	3½	190	hourly
Antalya	40	11	565	2 or 3 buses
Diyarbakır	50	8	535	several
Gaziantep	25	3	220	several
İstanbul	60	12	920	hourly
Kayseri	20	6	355	several
Konya	40	6	335	frequent
Şanlıurfa	20	6	360	several
Silifke	20	2½	165	14 buses
Van	80	15	910	at least 1 bus

❶ Getting There & Away

Adana's airport (Şakirpaşa Havaalanı) is 4km west of the centre on the D400. The otogar is 2km further west on the north side of the D400. The otogar is at the northern end of Ziyapaşa Bulvarı, 1.5km north of İnönü Caddesi.

Bus

Adana's large otogar has direct bus and/or dolmuş services to just about everywhere in Turkey. Note that dolmuşes to Kadirli (₺10, two hours, 108km) and Kozan (₺8, one hour, 72km) leave from the Yüreği otogar, on the right bank of the Seyhan River.

Train

Sleeper trains link the ornate *gar* (station) at the northern end of Ziyapaşa Bulvarı with Ankara (₺55, 12 hours). Departures are at 7.30pm daily. There are trains almost twice an hour between 6am and 11.15pm to Mersin (₺4) via Tarsus (₺3).

❶ Getting Around

A taxi from the airport into town costs ₺10 to ₺15. A taxi from the city centre to the Yüreği otogar will cost ₺7.50.

Around Adana

Inland from the Bay of İskenderun (İskenderun Körfezi) are the remains of castles and settlements connected with the Armenian kingdom of Cilicia, including its capital, Sis at Kozan. Some, such as Anavarza, date back to Roman times or earlier.

KOZAN

This large market town and district seat 72km northeast of Adana via route No 815 was once Sis, the capital of the kingdom of Cilicia and the linchpin of a cavalcade of castles overlooking the expansive (and hard-to-defend) Çukurova plain. Towering above the plain is stunning **Kozan Castle** (Kozan Kalesi; admission free), built by Leo II (r 1187–1219), stretching some 900m along a narrow ridge.

Along the kilometre-long road to the castle are the ruins of a church, locally called the *manastır* (monastery). From 1293 until 1921 this was the seat of the Katholikos (Patriarchate) of Sis, one of the two senior patriarchs of the Armenian Church.

Inside the castle is a mess of ruined buildings, but continue upward to the many-towered keep on the right. On the left is a massive tower, which once held the royal apartments. There are 44 towers and lookouts and the remains of a *bedesten* (warehouse).

Kozan has some lovely old houses and makes a good day trip by minibus from Adana (₺8, one hour). An old house dating from 1890 is now a quirky inn called **Yaver'in Konağı** (Yaver's Mansion; ☏515 0999; www.yaverinkonagi.com; Manastır Sokak 5; s/d ₺60/90; ❋@☎), and features 13 rustic but comfortable rooms in a traditional three-storey house, and two newer outbuildings at the bottom of the ascent to the castle. There's a good restaurant, serving superb *lahmacun* baked in an open-air stone oven.

YILANKALE

Yılankale (Snake Castle) was built in the mid-13th century when this area was part of the Armenian kingdom of Cilicia. It's said to have taken its name from a serpent that was once entwined in the coat of arms above the main entrance. It's 38km east of Adana and just over 3km south of the D400 highway. From the car park there's a well-laid path for 100m then a rough trail. Reaching the castle's highest point requires a 20-minute steep climb over the rocks, past gatehouse, cisterns, vaulted chambers and even a dungeon.

ANAZARBUS (ANAVARZA)

When the Romans moved into this area in 19 BC, they built this fortress city on top of a hill dominating the fertile plain and called it Caesarea ad Anazarbus. Later, when Cilicia was divided in two, Tarsus remained the capital of the west and Anazarbus the main seat in the east. It changed hands at least 10 times over the centuries, falling to the Persians, Arabs, Byzantines, the Hamdanid princes of Aleppo, the Crusaders, a local Armenian king, the Byzantines again, the Turks and the Mamluks. When that last group finally swept away the Armenian kingdom of Cilicia in 1375, the city was abandoned.

Some 5km after leaving the highway, you reach a T-junction and a large **gateway** set in the city walls; beyond this was the ancient city, now just fields strewn with ancient stones. Turn right and you'll soon reach the house of the *bekçi* (watchman); look for the blue gate. His own property contains **Roman sarcophagi** (one with the face of the 3rd-century Emperor Septimius Severus) and pools with glorious **mosaics** of Titus and dolphins, fish and sea birds. A guided walk (be generous), will showcase the stadium, theatre, baths and, of course, the hilltop **castle** (up a trek of 400 steps). Make sure you see the dedication stone of the ruined 6th-century **Church of the Apostles** in the field, with a carved cross and the alpha and omega symbols; the very rare Roman **vaulted stables** south of the castle; and the **main aqueduct** with several arches still standing.

ℹ️ Getting There & Away

If driving from Yılankale, return to the D400 highway and take the exit to route 817 (Kozan/Kadirli) north for 27km to the village of Ayşehoca, where a road on the right is marked for Anavarza/Anazarbus, 5km to the east. If you're in a dolmuş or minibus you can get out here and hitch a ride. From Kozan follow route 817 south for 28km and turn left at Ayşehoca.

İskenderun

📞 0326 / POP 184,600

İskenderun (Alexandretta in ancient times) is a modern industrial city with a working port and is the gateway to the province of Hatay.

Strategically located, the town has changed hands more than once. Alexander the Great took charge in 333 BC, and it was occupied by the British in 1918. The following year the French took charge until 1938. In 1939 the Republic of Hatay voted to join the nascent Turkish Republic.

With an attractive waterfront and an excellent museum, İskenderun is a handy stopover between Adana and Antakya. It's also a springboard to the beach town of Arsuz.

The main road along the waterfront is Atatürk Bulvarı. Şehir Pamir Caddesi is İskenderun's 'high street', running north from the waterfront and the massive monument to Atatürk and friends.

İskenderun Museum of the Sea MUSEUM
(İskenderun Deniz Müzesi; Atatürk Bulvarı; adult/child ₺4/1.30; ⊙9am-5pm Wed-Sun) This excellent private museum fills a restored colonial mansion with an interesting showcase of Turkish naval history. There's plenty of English language translations, and highlights include a mini-armada of model ships, the story of the sea battles of the Gallipoli campaign (essential for Aussie and Kiwi visitors) and a room covering the fascinating role of the Hatay region in Turkish history. The museum is around 600m west on Atatürk Bulvarı, to the right if you're facing inland.

🛏️ Sleeping

Altındişler Otel HOTEL €
(📞617 1011; www.altindislerotel.com; Şehir Pamir Caddesi 11; s/d ₺50/80; ❄️🔊) This good-value hotel has colourful prints and a large picture window in the 1st-floor lobby. Its 30 rooms are slightly more prosaic, but still clean and spotless, and there's a friendly English-

WORTH A TRIP

KARATEPE

Archaeology buffs should make a beeline for the **Karatepe-Aslantaş Open-Air Museum** (Karatepe-Aslantaş Açık Hava Müzesi; admission ₺3; ☺8am-noon & 1-7pm Apr-Oct, to 5pm Nov-Mar) within the national park of that name. The ruins date from the 8th century BC, when this was a summer retreat for the neo-Hittite kings of Cilicia, the greatest of whom was named Azitawatas. The forested hilltop site overlooks Lake Ceyhan (Ceyhan Gölü), an artificial lake used for hydroelectric power and recreation.

Karatepe was defended by 1km-long walls, traces of which are still evident in the landscape. A visit to the Hittite remains is in guided groups (you may have to wait) and begins at the southwest **Palace Gate**, which is protected by representations of lions and sphinxes and lined with fine reliefs, including one showing a relaxed feast at Azitawatas' court, complete with sacrificial bull, musicians and chariots. A circular path leads to the **Lower Gate** in the northeast with even better stone carvings, including reliefs of a galley with oarsmen, warriors doing battle with lions, a woman suckling a child under a tree and the Hittite sun god. There is an excellent **indoor museum** with items unearthed in the area and a scale model of the site, which helps put everything into perspective.

Karatepe is a tricky spot to reach without your own transport. If you're driving from Kozan, follow route 817 for 18km to Çukurköprü and then head east for another 18km to Kadirli, from where a secondary road leads for 22km to the site. It's easier to reach Karatepe along route 80-76 from Osmaniye, 30km to the southeast, which is served by dolmuşes from Adana (₺10, 1½ hours, 95km) and İskenderun (₺10, 1½ hours, 105km).

If carless, your best bet is to organise a taxi from Osmaniye. A return trip to Karatepe (two hours) with an hour's stop at the ruined Hellenistic city of Hierapolis-Castabala will cost around ₺120.

speaking welcome at reception. Note that a nearby mosque kicks off the day with the call to prayer around 4.30am.

Hataylı Oteli   BUSINESS HOTEL €€
(☎614 1590; www.hataylioteli.com; Mete Aslan Bulvarı; s ₺100-110, d ₺150-180; ❉🌐) This three-star hotel with all mod cons is ideally located near the water at the eastern end of Atatürk Bulvarı. The excellent lobby bar has a mildly equine theme, and the 62 rooms are huge and handsome. The terrace restaurant offers a glorious breakfast vista across the Med.

İmrenay Hotel   HOTEL €€
(☎613 2117; www.imrenayhotel.com; Şehir Pamir Caddesi 5; s/d ₺75/120; ❉🌐) At first this hotel is a tad gloomy, with dark brown parquet floors at reception, but the 33 smallish rooms have recently been renovated and are light and airy. The early-morning call to prayer of the nearby mosque is a factor to consider when staying here. Reception brings an open mind to negotiation.

✖ Eating

Kücük Kervan   TURKISH €€
(19 Sokak 7/3; meze ₺2-4, mains ₺8-12) Compile a meze platter at this excellent local eatery

serving locals for over 40 years. Kebaps include a mini-mountain of fresh herbs and salad. It's located off a sleepy square seemingly transplanted from Naples or Marseille. Find Kücück Kervan two blocks inland from Atatürk Bulvarı and two blocks west from Şehir Pamir Caddesi; to the right when facing inland.

Sirinyer   SEAFOOD €€€
(☎641 3050; www.sirinyerrestaurant.com; Akdeniz Caddesi 113; mains ₺15-25) Reputed to have some of the Turkish Mediterranean's freshest fish, this upmarket destination restaurant with a lovely seafront terrace is around 5km southwest of the centre, on the old road to Arzus. Beer, rakı and wine mix freely with the nautical atmosphere, and it's a perfect splurge-worthy opportunity if you haven't seen the coast much during your eastern Turkey travels.

Petek   SWEETS €
(Mareşal Çakmak Caddesi 16; cakes ₺4-8) Stylish Petek has been serving very fine *künefe* (layers of kadayıf cemented together with sweet cheese, doused in syrup and served hot with a sprinkling of pistachio) since 1942; pair with espresso to offset the

exceptional sweetness. Find it one block inland from Atatürk Bulvarı and three blocks west from Şehir Pamir Caddes; to the right when facing inland.

❶ Getting There & Away

There are frequent minibus and dolmuş connections to Adana (₺10, 2½ hours, 135km), Antakya (₺5, one hour, 58km) and Osmaniye (₺8, one hour, 66km).

Regular dolmuşes scoot down the coast to Uluçınar (₺4, 30 minutes, 33km), better known as Arsuz.

Antakya (Hatay)

☏ 0326 / POP 213.300

Built on the site of ancient Antiocheia ad Orontem, Antakya, officially known as Hatay, is a prosperous and modern city near the Syrian border. Under the Romans, Antioch's important Christian community developed out of the already large Jewish population that was at one time led by St Paul. Today Antakya is home to a mixture of faiths – Sunni, Alevi and Orthodox Christian – and has a cosmopolitan and civilised air. Locals call their hometown Barış Şehri (City of Peace), and that's just what it is.

The Arab influence permeates local life, food and language; indeed, the city only became part of Turkey in 1939 after centuries conjoined in some form or another to Syria. Most visitors come to Antakya for its archaeology museum or as pilgrims to the Church of St Peter. Be sure to take time to stroll along the Orontes (Asi) River and through the bazaars and back lanes of a city we rate as an underrated jewel of the Turkish Mediterranean.

◉ Sights

Hatay Archaeology Museum   MUSEUM
(Hatay Arkeoloji Müzesi; Gündüz Caddesi 1; admission ₺8; ◷9am-6.30pm Tue-Sun Apr-Oct, 8.30am-noon & 12.30-4.30pm Nov-Mar) This museum contains one of the world's finest collections of Roman and Byzantine mosaics, covering a period from the 1st century AD to the 5th century. Many were recovered almost intact from Tarsus or Harbiye, what was Daphne in ancient times, 9km to the south. And while Gaziantep's newly built mosaics museum (p556) is becoming deservedly popular, Antakya's only slightly less impressive collection is also definitely worth a visit.

Salons I to IV are large, naturally lit rooms with high ceilings, perfect for displaying mosaics of tiles so tiny that at first glance you may mistake them for paintings. Be sure to see the full-body mosaic of **Oceanus & Thetis** (2nd century; Salon 4) and the **Buffet Mosaic** (3rd century; Salon 2) with dishes of chicken, fish and eggs. As well as the standard scenes of hunting and fishing (eg **Thalassa & the Nude Fishermen**, with kids riding whales and dolphins, in Salon 4), there are stories from mythology, including the fabulous 3rd-century mosaics of **Narcissus** (Salon 2) and **Orpheus** (Salon 4). Other mosaics have quirkier subjects: don't miss (all in Salon 3) the happy hunchback with an oversized phallus, the black fisherman or the mysterious portrayal of a raven, a scorpion, a dog and a pitchfork attacking an 'evil eye'.

EASTERN MEDITERRANEAN ANTAKYA (HATAY)

ARSUZ

For a little R&R between exploring the dusty remains of the Armenian kingdom of Cilicia, head for Arsuz (Uluçınar), a delightful fishing town jutting out into the sea, 33km southwest of İskenderun. Relaxing highlights include swimming, gazing at the distant mountains, or trying your luck fishing in the nearby river.

Accommodation of choice is at the **Arsuz Otel** (☏643 2444; www.arsuzotel.com; s/d from ₺100/150; 🐕), a rambling 'olde worlde' (though really only 50 years old) hotel fronting the sea, with its own beach and 50 spacious and airy rooms. Splash out and take something over-the-top like room 28, a two-bedroom suite called Cennet (Paradise), with a huge balcony. The lobby, with its old-fashioned tiles and piano, has a vague south of France ambience to it, and the restaurant features grilled *mercan* (Red Sea bream) and local Hatay meze including *oruk* (spicy beef croquette) and *sürk* (soft cheese flavoured with dried red pepper).

Dolmuşes link Arsuz and İskenderun (₺4, 30 minutes) throughout the day.

Antakya (Hatay)

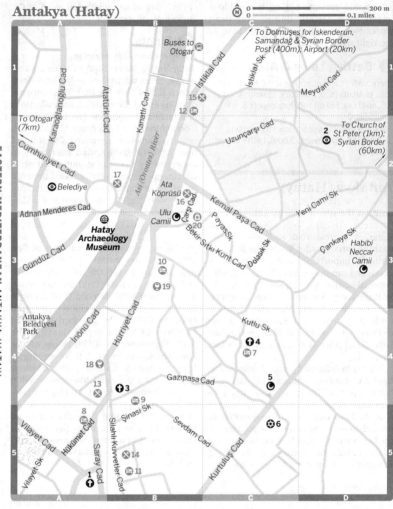

Other rooms contain artefacts recovered from various mounds and tumuli in the area, including a Hittite one near Dörtyol, 16km north of İskenderun. Taking pride of place in one room is the so-called **Antakya Sarcophagus** (Antakya Lahdı), an impossibly ornate tomb with an unfinished reclining figure on the lid.

Church of St Peter   CHURCH

(St Pierre Kilisesi; admission ₺8; ⊙9am-noon & 1-6pm Apr-Oct, 8am-noon & 1-5pm Nov-Mar) This early Christian church cut into the slopes of Mt Staurin (Mountain of the Cross) is thought to be the earliest place where the newly converted met and prayed secretly. Tradition has it that this cave was the property of St Luke the Evangelist who was born in Antioch, and that he donated the cave to the burgeoning Christian congregation. Both Peter and Paul lived in Antioch for a few years; they almost certainly preached here. When the First Crusaders took Antioch in 1098, they constructed the wall at the front and the narthex, the narrow vestibule along the west side of the church.

Antakya (Hatay)

E A S T E R N   M E D I T E R R A N E A N   ANTAKYA (HATAY)

To the right of the altar faint traces of an early fresco can be seen, and some of the simple mosaic floor survives. The water dripping in the corner is said to cure disease.

Just 2.5km northeast of town, the church is accessible on foot in about half an hour along Kurtuluş Caddesi.

Bazaar   BAZAAR
A sprawling market fills the back streets north of Ulus Alanı and Kemal Paşa Caddesi. The easier way to see it is to follow Uzunçarşı Caddesi, the main shopping street.

Around the 7th-century **Habib Neccar Camii** on Kurtuluş Caddesi you'll find most of Antakya's remaining **old houses**, with carved stone lintels or wooden overhangs, and courtyards within the compounds. The priests at the Catholic church believe St Peter would have lived in this area between AD 42 and 48, as it was then the Jewish neighbourhood.

Other Houses of Worship   NOTABLE BUILDINGS
In the ecumenical city of Antakya you'll find at least five different religions and sects represented within a couple of blocks of one another. Most of the city's 1200-strong Christians worship at the fine **Orthodox church** (Hürriyet Caddesi 53; ⊙divine liturgy 8.30am & 6pm). Rebuilt after a devastating earthquake in 1900 with Russian assistance, the church is fronted by a lovely courtyard up some steps from the street and contains some beautiful icons, an ancient stone lectern and valuable church plate.

The Italian-ministered **Roman Catholic church** (Kutlu Sokak 6; ⊙10am-noon & 3-5pm, mass 8.30am daily & 6pm Sun) was built in 1852 and occupies two houses in the city's old quarter, with the chapel in the former living room of one house. Next door is the **Sermaye Camii** (Capital Mosque; Kurtuluş Caddesi 56), with a wonderfully ornate *şerefe* (balcony) on its minaret.

Just south is the underutilised **synagogue** (Kurtuluş Caddesi 56). And there's even the relatively new Korean-ministered Methodist **Antioch Protestant Church** (Saray Caddesi; ⊙9am-6pm), just south of the Antik Beyazıt Hotel.

🛏 Sleeping

Belkis Konuk Evi ve Pansiyon   PENSION €€
(☎212 1511; www.belkisev.com; Gazipasa Caddesi, Güllübahçe Sokak; s/d ₺60/120; ❋) Rooms in the cute family-run Belkis Konuk Evi ve Pansiyon frame a whitewashed inner courtyard dotted with leafy trees. Expect decor that merges rustic with chintzy, and a warm welcome from the friendly and talkative owner (who doesn't speak a word of English). Bathrooms are definitely on the compact side, but breakfast in the shaded and dappled courtyard is a great way to start a Hatay day.

Liwan Hotel   BOUTIQUE HOTEL €€€
(☎215 7777; www.theliwanhotel.com; Silahlı Kuvetler Caddesi 5; s/d ₺130/200; ❋🖵) This 1920s, eclectic-style building was once owned by the president of Syria, and contains two dozen tastefully furnished rooms

GOOD EATING IN ANTAKYA

Arab – particularly Syrian – influences permeate Hatay's local cuisine. Handfuls of mint and wedges of lemon accompany kebaps, hummus is readily available, and the unique *kekik salatası* (fresh thyme salad made with spring onions and tomatoes) is a zingy treat.

Be sure to try the following: *muhammara*, a meze dip of crushed walnuts, red pepper and olive oil (also called *cevizli biber*, or walnutty peppers); *oruk*, a torpedo-shaped croquette of spicy minced beef encased in bulgur wheat flour and fried that is not unlike Lebanese *kibbeh*; and *sürk*, a tangy soft cheese flavoured with dried red pepper.

For dessert, you can't miss *künefe*, a cake of fine shredded wheat laid over a dollop of fresh mild cheese, on a layer of sugar syrup topped with chopped walnuts. Several places near the Ulu Camii make a mean one for around ₺4, including **Kral Künefe** (Çarşı Caddesi 7).

across four floors. The restaurant is in an open courtyard (once an internal garden with ogee arches) that becomes a covered courtyard with the flick of a switch. The atmospheric stone bar features live music from 11pm to 2.30am most weekends, and note that not all rooms have windows, so check when you book.

Antakya Catholic Church Guesthouse
GUEST HOUSE €

(☏215 6703; www.anadolukatolikilisesi.org/anta kya; Kutlu Sokak 6; per person ₺30; ✸) A positively delightful place to stay (if you can get in), this guesthouse run by the local Catholic church has eight tidy double rooms wrapped around a leafy (and suitably reflective) courtyard. Guests are invited (though not required) to attend daily mass in the church opposite.

Mozaik Otel
HOTEL €€

(☏215 5020; www.mozaikotel.com; İstiklal Caddesi 18; s/d ₺85/130; ✸🅰) This 'almost boutique' hotel is an excellent midrange choice north of central Ulus Alanı and near the bazaar. The two dozen rooms are decorated with folksy bedspreads and mosaic reproductions, and the excellent Sultan Sofrası restaurant is just next door. One of Antakya's most central hotels, it's also one of the city's quietest.

Antik Beyazıt Hotel
BOUTIQUE HOTEL €€

(☏216 2900; www.antikbeyazitoteli.com; Hükümet Caddesi 4; s/d ₺100/130; ✸🅰) Housed in a pretty French Levantine colonial house (1903), Antakya's first boutique hotel is looking a bit frayed, though the antique furnishings, Oriental carpets and ornate chandelier in the lobby still evoke a more elegant past. The 27 rooms are fairly basic; the ones in the

rear have loft-style bedrooms and access to a back studio.

Hotel Saray
HOTEL €

(☏214 9001; Hürriyet Caddesi 3; s/d ₺40/60; ✸🅰) A bit rugged and definitely not what its name suggests, the 'Palace' has 35 good-sized rooms, some even with tiny balconies and mountain views. Look forward to a super-central location near the bazaar and good restaurants.

🍴 Eating & Drinking

There are many restaurants south of Ulus Alanı, either on or just off Hürriyet Caddesi. Good places to relax over a drink and a snack are the tea gardens in the riverside Antakya Belediyesi Parkı, on the left bank of the Asi (Orontes) southwest of the museum.

Antakya Evi
TOP CHOICE / TURKISH €€

(Silahlı Kuvvetler Caddesi 3; mains ₺7-12) Antakya Evi is in an old villa decorated with photos and antique furniture. There are loads of spicy Hatay specialties, local meze (₺6 to ₺8) and robust grills. Look forward to live Turkish folk music on Friday and Saturday night.

Hatay Sultan Sofrası
TURKISH €€

(www.sultansofrasi.com; İstiklal Caddesi 20a; mains ₺10-16) Antakya's premier spot for affordable local meals, this place turns out dishes at a rapid pace. The articulate manager loves to guide diners through the menu, and it's a top spot for a diverse array of meze, spicy local kebabs, and (just maybe) Hatay's best *künefe*.

Anadolu Restaurant
TURKISH €€

(Hürriyet Caddesi 30a; mains ₺8-35) Popular with families, the local glitterati and the expense-account brigade, Antakya's culinary hot spot serves a long list of fine meze (₺6 to ₺12) on gold-coloured tablecloths in a splendid alfresco garden, where the palm trees push through the roof. Meat dishes include Anadolu kebap (₺15) and the special *kağıt*, or 'paper' kebap (₺12).

Cabaret
BAR, CAFE

(Hürriyet Caddesi) This local student hangout with brick walls and shuttered windows is an atmsopheric spot for a tea, coffee or something stronger. There's occasional live music, cheap snacks aplenty, and tucked around the back is an even cosier private courtyard.

Özsüt
CAFE €

(Cumhuriyet Alanı 2; snacks ₺5-7) Occupying a restored heritage building, Özsüt is perfect for mid-morning coffee and cake. Make your way through the colourful and trendy decor to the slim, crescent-shaped balcony offering the town's best views of central Antakya's compelling panorama.

Vitamin Shop Center
JUICE BAR

(Hürriyet Caddesi 7; juice from ₺2) This friendly place is where to go for a classic 'atom shake' (₺6), a regional speciality of banana, pistachio, honey, apricot and yoghurt that will keep you full for half a day.

🛍 Shopping

Doğal Defne Dünyası
HOMEWARE, TEXTILES

(Çarşı Caddesi 16) High-quality soaps from ancient Daphne (now Harbiye to the south), as well as gorgeous silk scarves woven and block-printed by hand are sold here.

ℹ Getting There & Around

Air

Antakya's Hatay airport is 20km north of the city. A taxi is around ₺30, and Havaş run a regular bus (₺10) into central Antakya.

Pegasus Airlines (www.flypgs.com) Regular flights to/from İstanbul (from ₺60) and İzmir (from ₺70).

Turkish Airlines (www.turkishairlines.com) Regular flights to/from İstanbul (from ₺75) and Ankara (from ₺65).

BUS Antakya's intercity otogar is 7km to the northwest of the centre. A taxi to/from the centre will cost ₺15. Ask about *serviş* transfers from central Antakya. Buses 2, 9 and 17 (₺2) run from just outside the otogar to the western bank of the Orontes river, central to hotels.

Direct buses go to Ankara, Antalya, İstanbul, İzmir, Kayseri and Konya, usually travelling via Adana (₺20, 3½ hours, 190km). There are also frequent services to Gaziantep (₺25, four hours, 262km) and Şanlıurfa (₺30, seven hours, 400km). Minibuses and dolmuşes for İskenderun (₺8, one hour, 58km) and Samandağ (₺5, 40 minutes, 28km) leave near the Shell petrol station along Yavuz Sultan Selim Caddesi, at the top of İstiklal Caddesi.

Around Antakya

MONASTERY OF ST SIMEON

The remains of the 6th-century **Monastery of St Simeon** (Aziz Simon Manastırı; admission free) sit atop a mountain 18km southwest of Antakya on the road to Samandağ. The cross-shaped monastery contains the ruins of three churches. Fragments of mosaics can be seen in the floor of the first (north) church, but the central **Church of the Holy Trinity**, is the most beautiful. The south church is more austere.

The site's most interesting item is the octagonal base of a **pillar**, atop which Saint Simeon Stylite the Younger (521–597), imitating a 5th-century Syrian predecessor deemed the 'Elder', would preach against the iniquities of Antioch.

ℹ Getting There & Away

The turn-off is just past the village of Karaçay, reachable by a Samandağ dolmuş (₺3, 20 minutes)

ⓘ ONWARD TRAVEL TO SYRIA

In the past it was possible to catch direct buses from Antakya to Aleppo and Damascus in Syria. Another option was to go by dolmuş via the Turkish border town of Yayladağı, and then on to Lattakia in Syria. At the time of writing, however, the US, UK and many other governments have recalled their ambassadors from, and advise against all travel in, Syria, urging any of their nationals in the country to leave. When the situation changes – though no one knows when that will be – the country will still present risks to travellers. You are advised to exercise caution and be sure to check the security situation before travelling.

from Antakya. After travelling 5km through a wind turbine farm, the road branches, and the monastery remains are 2km up the right hand road. A taxi from Antakya and back with an hour at the site will cost about ₺120.

ÇEVLİK

The scant ruins of **Seleuceia in Pieria** at Çevlik, Antioch's port in ancient times 5km northwest of Samandağ, are hardly impressive, but they include the **Titus & Vespasian Tunnel** (Titüs ve Vespasiyanüs Tüneli; admission ₺3; ⊙9am-7pm Apr-Oct, 8am-5pm Nov-Mar), an astonishing feat of Roman engineering. Seleucia lived under the constant threat of flooding from a stream that descended from the mountains and flowed through the town. To counter this threat, 1st-century Roman emperors Titus and Vespasian ordered that a 1.4km-long channel be cut through the solid rock to divert the stream.

From the *gişe* (ticket kiosk), follow the trail along an irrigation canal and past some shelters cut into the rock, finally arriving at a Roman arch spanning the gorge and the entrance to the tunnel. Bring a torch as the path can be slippery. At the far end of the channel an inscription provides a date for the work carried out by sailors and prisoners from Judea. About 100m from the tunnel are a dozen Roman **rock tombs** with reliefs, including the excellent **Beşikli Mağarası** (Cave with a Crib).

✦ Getting There & Away

Dolmuşes run between Antakya and Samandağ (₺8, 40 minutes, 28km), where you can change for another bound for Çevlik (₺3, 15 minutes).

Ankara & Central Anatolia

Why Go?

Somewhere between the cracks in the Hittite ruins, the fissures in the Phyrgian burial mounds and the scratches in the Seljuk caravanserais, the mythical, mighty Turks raced across this highland desert steppe with big ideas and bad-ass swords. Nearby, Alexander the Great cut the Gordion knot, King Midas displayed his deft golden touch and Julius Caesar came, saw and conquered. Atatürk forged his secular revolution along dusty Roman roads that all lead to Ankara, an underrated capital city and geo-political centre. Further north through the nation's fruitbowl, in Safranbolu and Amasya, 'Ottomania' is still in full swing. Here wealthy weekenders sip çay with time-rich locals who preside over dark timber mansions. Central Anatolia is the meeting point between the fabled past and the prosperous present – a sojourn here will enlighten and enchant.

Best Places to Eat

» Konak Konya Mutfağı
(p440)
» Münire Sultan Sofrası (p418)
» Zenger Paşa Konağı
(p405)
» Balıkçıköy (p407)

Best Places to Stay

» Gül Evi (p414)
» Angora House Hotel (p404)
» Efe Backpackers Pension
(p414)
» Deeps Hostel (p404)
» Derviş Otel (p438)

When to Go

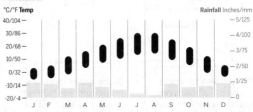

Ankara

May & Jun Fruit harvest: cherries the size of a baby's fist, apricots sweeter than a baby's face...

Jun Summer storms light up the twin Ottoman towns of Safranbolu and Amasya.

Dec The Mevlâna Festival in Konya is a Sufi spectacular of extraordinary human spirit.

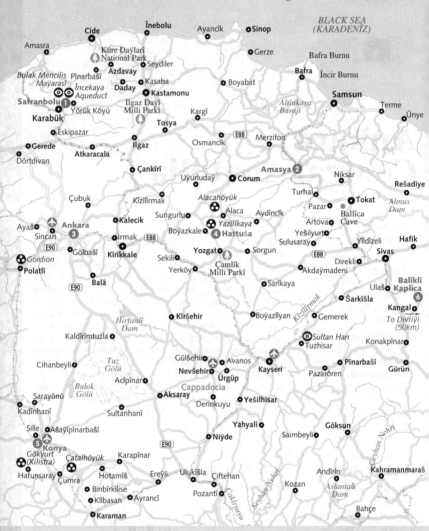

Ankara & Central Anatolia Highlights

1 Turn back the clocks among the cobblestones and creaky timber-framed mansions in Ottomanised **Safranbolu** (p411)

2 Ponder the Pontic tombs that poke out from craggy cliffs in ancient **Amasya** (p424)

3 Join the cafe-hopping crowd in **Ankara's** trendy Kızılay and Kavaklıdere neighbourhoods (p399), then discover Turkey's roots at the **Museum of Anatolian Civilisations** (p399)

4 Hit the Hittite hills at **Hattuşa** (p419) and get your head around ancient history

5 Pay homage to Rumi at the **Mevlâna Museum** (p434), then soak up **Konya's** (p434) blue-tiled Seljuk splendour.

6 Dip your toes in eastern Turkey and have your travel-weary feet exfoliated by the fish at **Balıklı Kaplıca** (p434)

7 Knock once on the divine doors at **Divriği** (p435)

ANKARA

☑0312 / POP 4.5 MILLION

Turkey's 'other' city may not have any showy Ottoman palaces or regal facades but Ankara thrums to a vivacious, youthful beat unmarred by the tug of history. Drawing comparisons with İstanbul is pointless – the flat, modest surroundings are hardly the stuff of national poetry – but the civic success of this dynamic and intellectual city is assured thanks to student panache and foreign-embassy intrigue.

The country's capital has made remarkable progress from a dusty Anatolian backwater to today's sophisticated arena for international affairs. Turkey's economic success is reflected in the booming restaurant scene around Kavaklıdere and the ripped-jean politik of Kızılay's sidewalk cafes, frequented by hip students, bums and businesspeople alike. And while the dynamic street-life is enough of a reason to visit, Ankara also boasts two extraordinary monuments central to the Turkish story – the beautifully conceived Museum of Anatolian Civilisations and the Anıt Kabir, a colossal tribute to Atatürk, modern Turkey's founder.

History

Although Hittite remains dating back to before 1200 BC have been found in Ankara, the town really prospered as a Phrygian settlement on the north–south and east–west trade routes. Later it was taken by Alexander the Great, claimed by the Seleucids and finally occupied by the Galatians around 250 BC. Augustus Caesar annexed it to Rome as Ankyra.

The Byzantines held the town for centuries, with intermittent raids by the Persians and Arabs. When the Seljuk Turks came to Anatolia, they grabbed the city but held it with difficulty. Later, the Ottoman sultan Yıldırım Beyazıt was captured near here by Central Asian conqueror Tamerlane and subsequently died in captivity. Spurned as a jinxed endeavour, the city slowly slumped into a backwater, prized for nothing but its goats.

That all changed when Atatürk chose Angora, as the city was known until 1930, to be his base in the struggle for independence. When he set up his provisional government here in 1920, the city was just a small, dusty settlement of some 30,000 people. After his victory in the War of Independence, Atatürk declared it the new Turkish capital, and set about developing it. From 1919 to 1927,

BAHAR TEGIN: SHOP OWNER, SAMANPAZARI

How should a traveller spend a morning in the citadel? Start with a local coffee served the Ottoman way, with syrup and *lokum* (Turkish delight). It's good fuel for the Museum of Anatolian Civilisations.

Best lunch? Definitely Çengelhan, then visit Rahmi m Koç Industrial Museum while you're there.

What next? Drop by the nearby art galleries to buy paintings, sculpture and designer jewellery.

Time to go home? Not before you see the copperware and kilim (rug) shops in the small streets around Samanpazarı. Pick up a bag of nuts and spices for the walk and end your day on a high.

Atatürk never set foot in İstanbul, preferring to work at making Ankara top dog.

◉ Sights

TOP
CHOICE **Museum of Anatolian Civilisations** MUSEUM
(Anadolu Medeniyetleri Müzesi; Map p402; ☑324 3160; Gözcü Sokak 2, Ulus; admission ₺15; ⊗Apr-Oct 8.30am-7pm, Nov-Mar 8.30am-5pm; MUlus) The superb Museum of Anatolian Civilisations is the perfect introduction to the complex weave of Turkey's ancient past, housing artefacts cherry-picked from just about every significant archaeological site in Anatolia.

The museum is housed in a beautifully restored 15th-century *bedesten* (warehouse). The 10-domed central marketplace houses reliefs and statues, while the surrounding hall displays exhibits from the earlier Anatolian civilisations: Palaeolithic, Neolithic, Chalcolithic, Bronze Age, Assyrian, Hittite, Phrygian, Urartian and Lydian. The downstairs sections hold classical Greek and Roman artefacts and a display on Ankara's history. Get there early to avoid the flood of tour groups and school parties.

The exhibits are chronologically arranged in a spiral: start at the Palaeolithic and Neolithic displays in the room to the right of the entrance, then continue in an anticlockwise direction, visiting the central room last.

Items from one of the most important Neolithic sites in the world – Çatalhöyük,

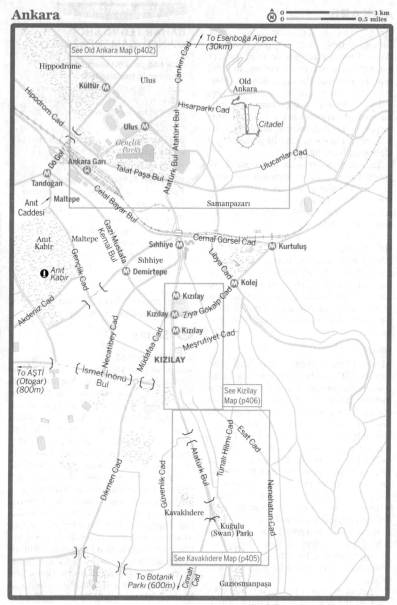

Ankara

N

0 ——— 1 km
0 ——— 0.5 miles

See Old Ankara Map (p402)

Hippodrome

Kültür Ⓜ

Ulus

To Esenboğa Airport (30km)

Çankırı Cad

Old Ankara

Hipodrom Cad

Ulus Ⓜ

Hisarparkı Cad

Citadel

Gençlik Parkı

Atatürk Bul

Atatürk Bul

Ulucanlar Cad

Dö Göl

Ankara Garı

Talat Paşa Bul

Tandoğan Ⓜ

Maltepe

Celal Bayar Bul

Samanpazarı

Anıt Caddesi

Anıt Kabir

Maltepe

Gazi Mustafa Kemal Bul

Sıhhiye Ⓜ

Cemal Gürsel Cad

Kurtuluş Ⓜ

❶ Anıt Kabir

Gençlik Cad

Sıhhiye

Ⓜ Demirtepe

Libya Cad

Ⓜ Kolej

Akdeniz Cad

Ⓜ Kızılay

Kızılay Ⓜ Ziya Gökalp Cad

Ziya Gökalp Cad

Necatibey Cad

Müdafaa Cad

Ⓜ Kızılay

Meşrutiyet Cad

To AŞTİ (Otogar) (800m)

İsmet İnönü Bul

KIZILAY

See Kızılay Map (p406)

Dikmen Cad

Güvenlik Cad

Atatürk Bul

Tunalı Hilmi Cad

Esat Cad

Nenehatun Cad

Kavaklıdere

Kuğulu (Swan) Parkı

See Kavaklıdere Map (p405)

To Botanik Parkı (600m)

Cinnah Cad

Gaziosmanpaşa

southeast of Konya – are displayed here. There's a mock-up of the inside of a dwelling typical of those uncovered at the site, one of the most famous mother goddess sculptures unearthed from the excavations and wall paintings of hunting scenes.

Also on show are many finds from the Assyrian trading colony Kültepe, one of the world's oldest and wealthiest bazaars. These include baked-clay tablets found at the site, which dates to the beginning of the 2nd millenium BC.

One of the striking Hittite figures of bulls and stags in the next room used to be the emblem of Ankara. The Hittites were known for their relief work, and some mighty slabs representing the best pieces found in the country, generally from around Hattuşa, are on display in the museum's central room.

Most of the finds from the Phrygian capital Gordion, including incredible inlaid wooden furniture, are on display in the museum's last rooms. The exhibits also include limestone blocks with still-indecipherable inscriptions resembling the Greek alphabet, and lion- and ram-head ritual vessels that show the high quality of Phrygian metalwork.

Urartian artefacts are also on display here. Spurred by rich metal deposits, the Urartians were Anatolia's foremost metalworkers, as the knives, horse-bit, votive plates and shields on display demonstrate. There are also terracotta figures of gods in human form, some revealing their divine powers by growing scorpion tails, and neo-Hittite artefacts.

Downstairs, classical-period finds and regional history displays provide a local picture. Excavations have unearthed a Roman road near the Column of Julian, and Ankara has its own 'missing link', the 9.8-million-year-old *Ankarapithecus* (a 30kg, fruit-eating primate).

TOP CHOICE Citadel
NEIGHBOURHOOD

(Ankara Kalesi; Map p402; M Ulus) The imposing *hisar* is the most interesting part of Ankara to poke about in. This well-preserved quarter of thick walls and intriguing winding streets took its present shape in the 9th century AD, when the Byzantine emperor Michael II constructed the outer ramparts. The inner walls date from the 7th century.

Opposite the main **Parmak Kapısı** (Finger Gate ; Map p402) entry is the beautifully restored **Çengelhan** which houses the **Rahmi M Koç Industrial Museum** (Map p402; 309 6800; www.rmk-museum.org.tr; Depo Sokak 1 ; adult/child ₺6/3; 10am-5pm Tue-Fri, 10am-6pm Sat-Sun). Inside are three floors covering subjects as diverse as transport, science, music, computing, Atatürk and carpets; some displays have interactive features.

After you've entered Parmak Kapısı, and passed through a gate to your left, you'll see **Alaettin Camii** (Map p402; Alitaş Sokak) on the left. The citadel mosque dates from the 12th century but has been extensively rebuilt. To

your right a steep road leads to a flight of stairs that leads to the **Şark Kulesi** (Eastern Tower; Map p402), with panoramic city views. Although it's much harder to find, a tower to the north, **Ak Kale** (White Fort), also offers fine views.

Inside the citadel local people still live as they would in a traditional Turkish village, and you'll see women beating and sorting skeins of wool. Broken column drums, bits of marble statuary and inscribed lintels are incorporated into the walls.

TOP CHOICE Anıt Kabir
MONUMENT

(Atatürk Mausoleum and Museum; Gençlik Caddesi; admission free, audio guide ₺5; 9am-5pm May-Oct, to 4pm Nov-Apr; M Tandoğan) The monumental mausoleum of Mustafa Kemal Atatürk (1881–1938), the founder of modern Turkey, sits high above the city with its abundance of marble and air of veneration. You enter via the **Lion Rd**, a 262m walkway lined with 24 lion statues – Hittite symbols of power used to represent the strength of the Turkish nation. The path leads to a massive courtyard, framed by colonnaded walkways, with steps leading up to the huge tomb on the left.

To the right of the tomb, the extensive **museum** displays Atatürk memorabilia, personal effects, gifts from famous admirers, and recreations of his childhood home and school. Just as revealing as all the rich artefacts are his simple rowing machine and huge multilingual library, which includes tomes he wrote.

Downstairs, extensive exhibits about the War of Independence and the formation of the republic move from battlefield murals with sound effects to over-detailed explanations of post-1923 reforms. At the end, a gift shop sells Atatürk items of all shapes and sizes.

As you approach the tomb itself, look left and right at the gilded inscriptions, which are quotations from Atatürk's speech celebrating the republic's 10th anniversary in 1932. Remove your hat as you enter, and bend your neck to view the ceiling of the lofty hall, lined in marble and sparingly decorated with 15th- and 16th-century Ottoman mosaics. At the northern end stands an immense marble **cenotaph** cut from a single piece of stone weighing 40 tonnes. The actual tomb is in a chamber beneath it.

It takes around two hours to see the whole site. It is virtually a pilgrimage site, so arrive

Old Ankara

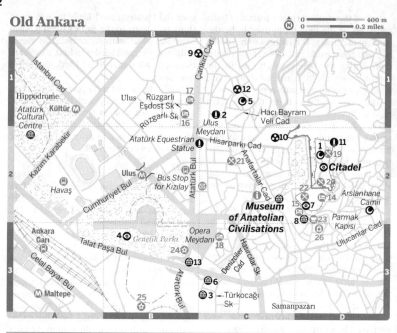

0 ——————— 400 m
0 ——————— 0.2 miles

Old Ankara

early to beat the crowds; school groups frequently drop by midweek, especially in May, June and September.

The memorial straddles a hill in a park about 2km west of Kızılay and 1.2km south of Tandoğan, the closest Ankaray-line metro station to the entrance. A free shuttle regularly zips up and down the hill from the entrance; alternatively, it's a pleasant walk to the mausoleum (about 15 minutes). Note that security checks, including a bag scan, are carried out on entry.

FREE **Vakıf Eserleri Müzesi** MUSEUM
(Ankara Museum of Religious Foundation Works; Map p402; Atatürk Bulvarı, Ulus; ⊘9am-5pm Tue-Sun ; MUlus) The tradition of carpets being gifted to mosques has helped preserve many of Turkey's finest specimens. This extensive collection – which once graced the floors of mosques throughout the country – spent years languishing in the depots of the nation's *Vakıf* (religious foundation) for safekeeping and was finally put on display to the public in 2007. A must for anyone interested in Turkish textiles, the exhibits also include a fascinating Ottoman manuscript collection, tilework, metalwork and intricately carved wood panels. All of it is superbly displayed with detailed information panels explaining the history of Turkish crafts.

Ethnography Museum MUSEUM
(Etnografya Müzesi; Map p402; Türkocağı Sokak, Samanpazarı; admission ₺3; ⊘8.30am-12.30pm & 1.30-5.30pm; MUlus) The Ethnography Museum is housed inside a white marble post-Ottoman building (1927) that served as Atatürk's mausoleum until 1953.

Past the equestrian statue out the front, the mausoleum is preserved in the entrance hall. Around the walls are photographs of Atatürk's funeral. The collection is superb, with displays covering henna ceremonies, Anatolian jewellery, rug-making, Seljuk ceramics, early-15th century doors and (opposite the anxious-looking mannequins in the circumcision display) coffee. Also of interest is the ethnography collection of writer and scientist Besim Atalay, who translated the Koran into Turkish.

FREE **Painting &
Sculpture Museum** MUSEUM
(Resim ve Heykel Müzesi; Map p402; Türkocağı Sokak, Samanpazarı; ⊘9am-noon & 1-5pm; ⊞; MUlus) The Painting & Sculpture Museum showcases the cream of Turkish artists. Ranging from angular war scenes to society portraits, the pieces demonstrate that 19th- and 20th-century artistic developments in Turkey paralleled those in Europe, with increasingly abstract form.

Roman Ruins RUINS
(MUlus) Ulus has a smattering of Roman-era ruins that can be easily seen in half a day.

At the sprawling 3rd-century **Roman Baths** (Roma Hamaları; Map p402; Ulus Çankırı Caddesi; admission ₺3; ⊘8.30am-12.30pm & 1.30-5.30pm) ruins, the layout is still clearly visible; look for the standard Roman *apoditerium* (dressing room), *frigidarium* (cold room), *tepidarium* (warm room) and *caldarium* (hot room). A Byzantine tomb and Phrygian remains have also been found here.

Except for a couple of imposing, inscribed walls, not much remains of the **Temple of Augustus & Rome** (Map p402; Hacı Bayram Veli Caddesi; admission ₺3) (AD 25), built to honour the Roman Emperor Augustus.

The **Column of Julian** (Jülyanus Sütunu; Map p402; Çam Sokak) was erected in honour of Roman Emperor Julian the Apostate's visit to Ankara. In a square ringed by government buildings, it is usually topped by a stork's nest.

Along Hisarparkı Caddesi, you can see the remains of a **Roman theatre** (Map p402; Hisarparkı Caddesi) from around 200 to 100 BC.

Hacı Bayram Camii MOSQUE
(Map p402; Hacı Bayram Veli Caddesi, Ulus; MUlus) Ankara's most revered mosque is Hacı Bayram Camii. Hacı Bayram Veli was a Muslim 'saint' who founded the Bayramiye dervish order around 1400. Ankara was the order's centre and Hacı Bayram Veli is still revered by pious Muslims. The mosque was built in the 15th century, with tiling added in the 18th century. Surrounding shops sell religious paraphernalia (including wooden toothbrushes as used, supposedly, by the Prophet Mohammed).

Kocatepe Camii MOSQUE
(Map p406; Bankacı Sokak, Kızılay; MKızılay) The huge outline of Kocatepe Camii is the symbol of Ankara. It is one of the world's largest mosques but it is also very new (it was built between 1967 and 1987).

✪ Festivals & Events

Ankara Film Festival FILM
(www.filmfestivalankara.com.tr) Kicks off each March, hosting a selection of both local and foreign cinema.

Ankara Music Festival MUSIC
(www.ankarafestival.com) Three weeks of classical performances in April.

FREE **Büyük Ankara Festivali** MUSIC, FAMILY
Week-long event in July that exists somewhere between a summer concert series and carnival.

🛏 Sleeping

ULUS

★TOP CHOICE Angora House Hotel
HISTORIC HOTEL €€

(Map p402; ☎309 8380; www.angorahouse.com.tr; Kalekapısı Sokak 16; s/d/tr €50/69/75; ⓢ; Ⓜ Ulus) Be utterly charmed by this restored Ottoman house, which oozes subtle elegance at every turn. The six spacious rooms are infused with loads of old-world atmosphere, featuring dark wood accents, creamy 19th-century design textiles and colourful Turkish carpets, while the walled courtyard garden is the perfect retreat from the citadel streets. Delightfully helpful staff add to the appeal.

Divan Çukurhan
HISTORIC HOTEL €€€

(Map p402; ☎306 6400; www.divan.com.tr; Depo Sokak 3, Ankara Kalesi; s/d €130/150, ste €180-400; ✴ⓢ; Ⓜ Ulus) Opened in 2011, this distinctive hotel offers guests a chance to soak up the historical ambience of staying in the 16th-century Çukurhan caravanserai. Set around a dramatic glass-ceilinged interior courtyard, each individually themed room blends ornate decadence with sassy contemporary style. Ankara's best bet for those who want to be dazzled by oodles of sumptuous luxury and sleek service.

Otel Mithat
HOTEL €

(Map p402; ☎311 5410; www.otelmithat.com.tr; Tavus Sokak 2; s/d/tr €25/40/50; ✴ⓢ; Ⓜ Ulus) Revamped with groovy carpeting and sleek neutral bed linen, the Mithat's rooms are fresh and modern. The teensy bathrooms do let the side down somewhat but this is a minor complaint about what is, overall, an excellent budget choice. Non-smokers will be pleased that unlike most Ankara hotels in this price range, the Mithat takes their no-smoking policy seriously.

Hotel Taç
HOTEL €€

(Map p402; ☎324 3195; Çankırı Caddesi 35; s/d/tr ₺70/90/110; ✴ⓢ; Ⓜ Ulus) It may not look like much from outside, but the Taç really delivers in the midrange hotel stakes. Cute floral rugs and nice art inject a bit of personality into the rooms, which all come with extras such as a kettle, hair dryer and flat-screen TV. Light sleepers should avoid the front rooms if possible.

Hotel Oğultürk
HOTEL €€

(Map p402; ☎309 2900; www.ogulturk.com; Rüzgarlı Eşdost Sokak 6; s/d/tr €40/55/70; ✴ⓢ; Ⓜ Ulus) The alleyway outside may be slightly seedy but inside the Oğultürk it's smart-

ness itself. The efficient staff speak English and the decent-sized rooms are decked out in soft pastels.

KIZILAY

★TOP CHOICE Deeps Hostel
HOSTEL €

(Map p406; ☎213 6338; www.deepshostelankara.com; Ataç Sokak 46; dm/s/d without bathroom €10/18/32; ⓢ; Ⓜ Kızılay) Ankara's best budget choice, friendly Deeps opened in early 2012 and owner Şeyda is spot on with knowing what budget travellers want. There are colourful, light-filled rooms, a spacious dorm, and squeaky-clean, modern shared bathrooms. It's all topped off by a fully equipped kitchen (although breakfast isn't included) and a cute communal area downstairs where you can swap your Turkish travel tales in comfort.

Hotel Eyüboğlu
HOTEL €€

(Map p406; ☎417 6400; www.eyuboglu.com; Karanfil Sokak 73; s/d €69/89; ✴ⓢ; Ⓜ Kızılay) Although lacking in character, this great value option is wonderfully efficient. There's tinkly piano music in the lobby, staff that go out of their way to help (despite a shortage of English), and no-nonsense, neutral toned rooms boasting beds so comfy you'll be tempted to hit the snooze button.

Hotel Gold
HOTEL €€

(Map p406; ☎419 4868; www.ankaragoldhotel.com; Güfte Sokak 4; s/d ₺90/130; ✴ⓢ; Ⓜ Kızılay) Swish in a jazzy kind of way with super-smooth service to match. Think subtly sparkly textured wallpaper and beds festooned with a mountain of silky cushions; the perfect haven after a hard day's cafe-hopping in Kızılay.

Otel Elit
HOTEL €€

(Map p406; ☎417 5001; www.elitotel.com.tr; Olgunlar Caddesi 6; s/d ₺100/140/170; ⓢ; Ⓜ Kızılay) The lobby looks like it was teleported out of a 1970s Swiss chalet and the rooms haven't been refurbished for a few decades, but it's all rigidly clean and the staff are sweet.

KAVAKLIDERE

Gordion Hotel
HISTORIC HOTEL €€€

(Map p405; ☎427 8080; www.gordionhotel.com; Büklüm Sokak 59; s/d €85/110; ✴ⓢ⚡) This independent hotel is a fabulously cultured inner-city residence that remains remarkably empty much of the year. In the middle of Kavaklıdere, guests will lap up the basement swimming pool, the Vakko textiles in the lobby, the centuries-old art engravings, the

Kavaklıdere

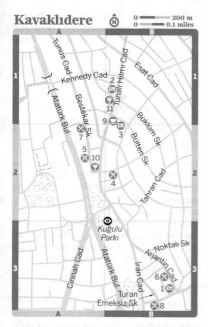

conservatory restaurant, the beautiful beds and the extensive DVD library. At night, the Gordion looks a picture.

Hotel Aldino
HOTEL €€

(Map p405; www.hotelaldino.com; Bülten Sokak 22; s/d €60/80; 🛜) Good-sized rooms and professional service make this business-style hotel a Kavaklıdere bargain. Everything is spotlessly clean, the staff speak English and you can't beat the location. Just look past their fondness for granny-ish dried flower arrangements and floral bed linen.

Argentum Hotel
HOTEL €€€

(Map p405; www.hotelargentum.com; Borazan Sokak 11; s/d/ste €80/120/140; ❄🛜) While the large rooms at the Argentum boast classic soft furnishings galore and super modern bathrooms, it's the panoramic views from the top-level restaurant that really make this hotel a winner.

✖ Eating

ULUS

Most Ulus options are basic. The southern end of Anafartalar Caddesi is the perfect hunting ground for cheap and cheerful *kebapçis* (kebap eateries). If self-catering seems like a good option, **Ulus Hali food market** (Map p402) is the place to pick up provisions, from oversized chilli peppers to jars of honey.

🏆 Zenger Paşa Konağı
ANATOLIAN €€

(Map p402; 🕿311 7070; www.zengerpasa.com; Doyran Sokak 13; mains ₺12-17; Ⓜ Ulus) Crammed with Ottoman ephemera, the Zenger Paşa at first looks like a deserted ethnographic museum, but climb up the rickety stairs and you'll find views of the city that are worth a visit alone. Wealthy Ankaralıs love the pide (Turkish-style pizza), meze and grills, still cooked in the original Ottoman oven. We adore lazily grazing on its fine mezes while gazing over the sweep of cityscape below.

And Evi Cafe
MODERN TURKISH €€

(Map p402; 🕿312 7978; İçkale Kapısı; mains ₺12-24; Ⓜ Ulus) Even if the food was so-so this cafe set into the citadel walls would be a winner for the cosy Ottoman-style interior and incredible panoramic views of the city from the terrace. Luckily, the food is great. Tuck into a lunchtime crepe (₺11), sample a slice of its divine carrot cake (₺6) with a latte for afternoon tea, or choose one of its pasta dishes for dinner. It's all good.

Çengelhan
MODERN TURKISH €€€

(Map p402; 🕿309 6800; Depo Sokak 1; mains ₺16-30; ⊙Tue-Sun ; Ⓜ Ulus) Inside an old caravanserai, the Rahmi M Koç Industrial Museum restaurant offers sleek dining in novel surroundings, with tables nestled between museum displays of vintage cars and Ottoman paraphernalia. A top choice to sample traditional Turkish dishes with a contemporary twist. Reservations are essential.

Kınacızade Konağı
TURKISH €€
(Map p402; ☎324 5714; www.kinacizadekonagi.
com; Kale Kapısı Sokak 28; mains ₺6-23 ; Ⓜ U-
lus) This Ottoman house serves up a range
of typical Turkish kebap dishes alongside
cheaper pide and *gözleme* (savoury pancakes). Eat in the shady courtyard, enclosed
by picturesque timber-framed facades in
various states of higgledy-piggledy disrepair.

KIZILAY
It's all about street-side eating and cafe-hopping in the trendy hangouts here. You'll find
everything from stalls serving döner kebap
(spit-roasted lamb slices) and corn on the cob
to hip bistros blasting pop tunes, their tables
graced by cooler-than-thou student-types.

TOP CHOICE Le Man Kültür
INTERNATIONAL €€
(Map p406; ☎310 8617; Konur Sokak 8; mains ₺6-
16; Ⓜ Kızılay) Named after a cult Turkish comic strip – and decorated accordingly – this is
still the pre-party pick for a substantial feed

and for spotting beautiful young educated
things. Drinks are reasonably priced and
the speakers crank everything from indie-
electro to Türk pop.

Çomlek Ev Yemekleri
TURKISH €
(Map p406; Konur Sokak ; Set menu ₺6; Ⓜ Kızılay)
This unpretentious place is crammed with
students who slurp down simple but filling
daily lunch specials. Choose the *güveç* (meat
and vegetable stews cooked in a terracotta
pot) for a tasty, wholesome meal.

Cafe Tarçın
INTERNATIONAL €€
(Map p406; Karanfıl Sokak ; mains ₺5-11; Ⓜ Kızılay)
If you're having trouble choosing from the
massive menu of *gözleme* (savoury pancakes), kebaps, pizza, salads and sandwiches
then just opt for the daily special. The hearty
meal of *çorba* (soup), a main dish and rice
(₺8) is sure to fill you up. Afterwards, relax
on the comfy sofa seating with your complimentary çay.

Cafe Sobe
CAFE €€
(Map p406; ☎425 1356; Konur Sokak 19; mains
₺5-10; Ⓜ Kızılay) Board games and cool tunes
make this buzzing cafe-restaurant a popular
hang-out. The *tereyağında* (trout) and sautéed *biftek* (steak) are among the favourite
menu picks.

Urfalı Kebap
KEBAP €€
(Map p406; ☎418 9495; Karanfıl Sokak 69; mains
₺5-10) Urfalı is fast and friendly and seats

80-plus hungry diners, from merry students to three generations of one family. The *urfa kebap* (a mild version of the Adana kebap, served with lots of onion and black pepper) won't disappoint.

KAVAKLIDERE

TOP CHOICE Balıkçıköy   SEAFOOD €€€

(Map p405; ☎466 0450; Abay Kunanbay Caddesi 4/1; mains ₺18-22; ☉noon-midnight) This is the third instalment of Ankara's favourite seafood restaurant. Take the waiter's recommendations for the cold meze (the pickled whitebait, ₺6, is a favourite), then take your pick of the fried and grilled fish, all perfectly cooked and quick to the table. The skewered prawns were among the finest tastes on our travels. Book ahead to avoid disappointment.

Hayyami   RESTAURANT, BAR €€€

(Map p405; ☎466 1052; Bestekar Sokak 82B; mains ₺12-25; ☉noon-late) Named after the renowned Sufi philosopher, this thriving wine house/restaurant attracts a hobnobbing crowd to its lowered courtyard for *salçalı sosis* (barbecued sausage) and devilishly large cheese platters, among other less booze-worthy plates. The liquor and fortified wine list is very long.

Mezzaluna   ITALIAN €€€

(Map p405; ☎467 5818; Turan Emeksiz Sokak 1; mains ₺21-37; ☉noon-11pm) The capital's classiest Italian restaurant is busy busy busy, with chefs slapping pizzas on the counter for apron-clad waiters to deliver. The choices include antipasti, risotto, wood-fired pizzas and seafood (a better bet than the steaks).

Günaydın   STEAKHOUSE €€€

(Map p405; ☎468 5353; Arjantin Caddesi 18/A; mains ₺20-30) Ankara's favourite steakhouse seriously knows its meat. This carnivore heaven serves up T-bones, Porterhouse and beef ribs with snappy, professional service.

Guangzhou Wuyang   CHINESE €€

(Map p405; ☎427 6150; Bestekar Sokak 88/B; mains ₺12-24) Sometimes all you need is a half-decent Chinese meal and a half-dozen beers. Luckily this busy place is more than half decent, with delicious seafood and vegetarian options available.

Drinking

Kızılay is Ankara's cafe central, with terraces lining virtually every inch of space south of Ziya Gökalp Caddesi.

Aylak Madam   CAFE

(Map p406; ☎419 7412; Karanfıl Sokak 2, Kızılay; ☉10am-late) A super cool French bistro/cafe with a mean weekend brunch (from 10am to 2.30pm), plus sandwiches, head-kicking cappuccinos, and a laid-back jazz-fusion soundtrack. Postgraduates and writers hang out here, hunched over their laptops or with pens tapping against half-finished manuscripts.

Kirit Cafe   CAFE

(Map p402; Koyunpazarı Sokak, Ankara Kalesi) With a fun felt shop on the ground floor and quirky local art gracing the walls of the cafe upstairs, this place is a lovely find. They brew a decent coffee if you just want a drink but their burgers, pasta and cheesecake hit the spot as well.

Bibar   BAR

(Map p406; Inkılap Sokak 19, Kızılay) Bibar attracts everyone from pale-faced student goths, alternative rockers and people who just want to boogie. The music can be as mixed as the crowd on the right night.

Café des Cafés   CAFE

(Map p405; ☎428 0176; Tunalı Hilmi Caddesi 83, Kavaklıdere; ☉8.30am-11pm) Quirky vintage styling and comfy sofas make Café des Cafés a popular Kavaklıdere haunt. Pull up a chair on the tiny streetside terrace and sharpen up your people-watching skills. The orange and cinnamon hot chocolate is bliss in a glass.

Papsi   BAR, CAFE

(Map p405; Tunalı Hilmi Caddesi, Kavaklıdere; ☉noon-late) Papsi is a chilled out and friendly choice for an afternoon beer. The stereo belts out decent rock and indie tunes, the clientele tends to be international and the service is swift.

Edge   BAR

(Map p405; ☎426 0516; Tunus Caddesi, Kavaklıdere; ☉noon-late) Generous happy-hour drink specials between noon-6pm, good indie music and a mixed crowd make this corner spot popular throughout the week.

☆ Entertainment

For a night out with Ankara's student population, head to Kızılay – particularly Bayındır Sokak, between Sakarya and Tuna Caddesis. The tall, thin buildings pack in up to five floors of bars, cafes and *gazinos* (nightclubs). Many of the clubs offer live

Turkish pop music, and women travellers should feel OK in most of them.

Ankara State Opera House   PERFORMING ARTS
(Opera Sahnesi; Map p402; 324 6801; www.dobgm.gov.tr; Atatürk Bulvarı 20, Ulus) This venue plays host to all the large productions staged by the Ankara State Opera and Ballet. The season generally runs from September to June and it's worthwhile trying to catch a performance if you're in town at that time.

Cer Modern   GALLERY
(Map p402; 310 0000; www.cermodern.org; Altunsoy Caddesi 3; ☉10am-6pm Tue-Sun) Located in an old train depot, this huge new artists park and gallery exhibits modern art from across Europe, plus there's a really cool cafe and shop.

🛍 Shopping

To see what fashionable Turkey spends its money on, head south along Tunalı Hilmi Caddesi where lots of local stores stand alongside more familiar names such as the British department store **Marks & Spencer**. There are several massive malls outside of the central city including the **AnkaMall**, easily accessed by alighting at Akköprü metro station.

Hisar Area   HANDICRAFTS
(Map p402) The alleyways southwest of the Parmak Kapısı entrance to the citadel were traditionally the centre for trading in angora wool. Walk downhill from the dried-fruit stalls in front of the gate, and you'll come across copper-beaters and craftspeople carrying on their age-old trades, as well as

---

ANGORA WOOL

Can you tell the difference between a goat and a rabbit? It's not as easy as you think – or at least not if all you have to go on is the wool. One of the most popular misconceptions about Ankara's famous angora wool is that it comes from angora goats, a hardy breed believed to be descended from wild Himalayan goats. Not so: the soft, fluffy wool produced from these goats is correctly known as mohair. Angora wool in the strictest sense comes from angora rabbits, also local but much cuter critters whose fur, weight for weight, was once worth as much as gold.

---

plenty of carpet and antique stores, small galleries and craft shops that are good for a rummage.

Dost Kitabevi   BOOKS
(Map p406; 418 8327; Karanfıl Sokak, Kızılay) Head downstairs at this buzzing book store to browse its large (and very decently priced) selection of English-language novels.

ℹ Information

Internet Access
There are many internet cafes in Ulus and Kızılay, particularly around Ulus Meydanı and Karanfıl Sokak, but they are scarcer in Kavaklıdere. Wi-fi is widely available in hotels, cafes and bars.

Medical Services
Pharmacists take it in turns to open around the clock; look out for the *nobetçi* (open 24 hours) sign.

Bayındır Hospital (428 0808; Atatürk Bulvarı 201, Çankaya) An up-to-date private hospital.

City Hospital (466 3838; Büklüm Sokak 72, Çankaya) Has a women's health centre (kadın sağlığı merkezi).

Hospital Information Hotline (444 0911) Turkish-language service only.

Money
There are lots of banks with ATMs in Ulus, Kızılay and Kavaklıdere. To change money, *döviz bürosu* (currency-exchange offices) generally offer the best rates, often without commission.

Post & Telephone
The **Main Post Office** (Atatürk Bulvarı) is in Ulus. There are also PTT branches in Kızılay. All have phone booths nearby.

Tourist Information
Tourist Office (310 8789; Gazi Mustafa Kemal Bulvarı; ☉9am-5pm Mon-Fri, 10am-5pm Sat) Staff are reasonably helpful and have lots of brochures available. There are also (usually unmanned) branches at AŞTİ (the otogar; see p409) and at the train station.

ℹ Getting There & Away

Air
Although domestic and international budget carriers serve Ankara's **Esenboğa airport** (590 4000; www.esenbogaairport.com; Özal Bulvarı, Esenboğa), İstanbul's airports offer more choice. Even flying domestically, it may save you time and money to travel via İstanbul.

Lufthansa, Pegasus Airlines and Qatar Airways offer international connections while Turkish

LONG-DISTANCE SERVICES FROM ANKARA GARI (2013 TO 2014)

DESTINATION	VIA (MAJOR STOPS)	TRAIN NAME	DURATION (HR)	DEPARTURE TIME
Adana	Kayseri	Çukurova Mavi Tren	11	Daily, 8.05pm
Diyarbakır	Kayseri, Sivas, Malatya	Eylül Mavi Tren	22¼	Daily, 3.10pm
İzmir	Eskişehir	İzmir Mavi Tren	13¼	Daily, 7.50pm
Kars	Kayseri, Sivas, Erzurum	Doğu Ekspresi	27¾	Daily, 6.30pm
Kurtalan	Kayseri, Sivas, Malatya, Diyarbakır	Güney/Kurtalan Ekspresi	26¾	Mon, Wed, Thu, Fri, Sat, 1.33am
Tatvan (for ferry to Van)	Kayseri, Sivas, Malatya	Vangölü Ekspresi	36	Tue, Sun, 1.33am

Airlines' subsidiary, **Anadolu Jet** (www.anadolu jet.com; THY Office, Atatürk Bulvarı 211), has direct flights between Ankara and destinations including Adana, Antalya, Bodrum, İstanbul, İzmir and Van.

Bus

Every Turkish city or town of any size has direct buses to Ankara. The gigantic otogar (bus station), also referred to as **AŞTİ** (Ankara Şehirlerarası Terminali İşletmesi; Mevlâna Bulvarı), is at the western end of the Ankaray underground train line, 4.5km west of Kızılay.

Buses to/from İstanbul (₺40, six hours), Antalya (₺40, eight hours), İzmir (₺45, eight hours) and other major destinations leave numerous times daily. Buses to Cappadocia (₺30, five hours) often terminate in Nevşehir. Be sure your ticket states your *final* destination (eg Göreme, Ürgüp).

Because there are so many buses to many parts of the country, you can often turn up, buy a ticket and be on your way in less than an hour. Don't try this during public holidays, though.

The *emanet* (left-luggage room) on the lower level charges ₺4 per item stored; you'll need to show your passport.

Train

All train services between **Ankara Train Station** (Ankara Garı; Talat Paşa Bulvarı) and İstanbul have all been cancelled until at least 2014 due to the rail network being completely overhauled to support high-speed rail links. Because of this maintenance some cross-country services have been suspended completely, while others run on a limited schedule.

The new high-speed train services to Eskişehir (economy/business class ₺25/35, 1½ hours, 10 daily) and Konya (economy/business class ₺25/35, two hours, eight daily) are comfortable, fast and efficient.

The Trans-Asia train to Iran leaves at 10.25am every Wednesday, pulling into Tehran Station on Friday at 8.20pm.

ℹ Getting Around

To/From the Airport

Esenboğa airport is 33km north of the city. **Havaş** (☑ 444 0487; www.havas.net; Gate B, 19 May Stadium, Kazım Karabekir Caddesi, Ulus) airport buses depart every half-hour between 2am and 10pm daily (₺10, 35 minutes). After 10pm buses leave according to flight departure times.

The same buses link the airport and AŞTİ (₺10, 60 minutes), leaving the otogar every half-hour between 1.30am and 9.30pm from in front of the passenger arrival lounge. Havaş has an information booth at the otogar, near the main exit on the ground floor.

Buses from the airport leave 25 minutes after each flight arrival. Don't pay more than ₺60 for a taxi between the airport and the city.

To/From the Bus Station

The easiest way to get into town is on the Ankaray metro line, which has a station at AŞTİ. Get off at Maltepe for the train station (a 10-minute walk), or go to Kızılay for midrange hotels. Change at Kızılay (to the metro line) for Ulus and cheaper hotels.

A taxi costs about ₺20 to the city centre.

To/From the Train Station

Ankara Train Station is about 1km southwest of Ulus Meydanı and 2km northwest of Kızılay. Many dolmuşes head northeast along Cumhuriyet Bulvarı to Ulus, and east on Talat Paşa Bulvarı to Kızılay.

It's just over 1km from the station to Opera Meydanı; any bus heading east along Talat Paşa Bulvarı will drop you within a few hundred metres if you ask for Gazi Lisesi.

Bus

Ankara has a good bus, dolmuş and minibus network. Signs on the front and side of the vehicles are better guides than route numbers. Buses marked 'Ulus' and 'Çankaya' run the length of Atatürk Bulvarı. Those marked 'Gar' go to the train station, those marked 'AŞTİ' to the otogar.

Standard ₺3.50 transport cards (valid for two journeys) are available at metro stations and major bus stops or anywhere displaying an EGO Bilet sign. They work on most buses as well as the metro. These tickets are not valid on express buses, which are the longer buses with ticket counters halfway down the vehicle.

Car

Driving within Ankara is chaotic and signs are inadequate; it's easier to ditch your car and use public transport.

If you plan to hire a car to drive out of Ankara, there are many small local companies alongside the major international firms; most have offices in Kavaklıdere along Tunus Caddesi, and/or at Esenboğa airport.

Metro

Ankara's underground train network is the easiest way to get between Ulus and Kızılay and the transport terminals. There are currently two lines: the Ankaray line running between AŞTİ in the west through Maltepe and Kızılay to Dikimevi in the east; and the Metro line running from Kızılay northwest via Sıhhiye and Ulus to Batıkent. The two lines interconnect at Kızılay. Trains run from 6.15am to 11.45pm daily.

A one-way fare costs ₺1.75. Tickets are available at all stations for two journeys (₺3.50) and five journeys (₺8.75).

Taxi

Taxis are everywhere and they all have meters, with a ₺2.25 base rate. It costs about ₺10 to cross the centre; charges rise at night and the same trip will cost well over ₺15.

AROUND ANKARA

You don't have to go far from Ankara to hit some major pieces of Anatolian history, but if it's a leisurely day trip you're after rather than an overnighter, consider the Phrygian archaeological site at Gordion or the small Ottoman town of Beypazarı.

Gordion

The capital of ancient Phrygia, with some 3000 years of settlement behind it, Gordion lies 106km west of Ankara in the village of Yassıhöyük.

Gordion was occupied by the Phrygians as early as the 9th century BC, and soon afterwards became their capital. Although destroyed during the Cimmerian invasion, it was rebuilt before being conquered by the Lydians and then the Persians. Alexander the Great came through here and famously cut the Gordian knot in 333 BC, but by 278 BC the Galatian occupation had effectively destroyed the city.

The moonscape-like terrain around Yassıhöyük is dotted with tumuli (burial mounds) that mark the graves of the Phrygian kings. Of some 90 identified tumuli, 35 have been excavated; you can enter the largest tomb, and also view the site of the Gordion acropolis, where digs revealed five main levels of civilisation from the Bronze Age to Galatian times.

◉ Sights

Midas Tumulus & Gordion Museum RUINS
(admission incl museum ₺3; ◷8.30am-5.30pm) In 1957 Austrian archaeologist Alfred Koerte discovered Gordion, and with it the intact **tomb** of a Phrygian king, probably buried some time between 740 and 718 BC. The tomb is actually a gabled 'cottage' of cedar surrounded by juniper logs, buried inside a tumulus 53m high and 300m in diameter. It's the oldest wooden structure ever found in Anatolia, and perhaps even in the world. The tunnel leading into the depths of the tumulus is a modern addition, allowing you to glimpse some of the interior of the fenced-off tomb.

Inside the tomb archaeologists found the body of a man between 61 and 65 years of age, 1.59m tall, surrounded by burial objects, including tables, bronze *situlas* (containers) and bowls said to be part of the funerary burial feast. The occupant's name remains unknown (although Gordius and Midas were popular names for Phrygian kings).

In the **museum** opposite, Macedonian and Babylonian coins show Gordion's position at the centre of Anatolian trade, communications and military activities, as do the bronze figurines and glass-bead jewellery from the Syro-Levantine region of Mesopotamia.

Acropolis RUINS
Excavations at the 8th century BC acropolis yielded a wealth of data on Gordion's many civilisations.

The lofty main gate on the city's western side was approached by a 6m-wide ramp. Within the fortified enclosure were four *megara* (square halls) from which the king and his priests and ministers ruled the empire. The mosaics found in one of these halls, the so-called Citadel of Midas, are on display outside the Gordion Museum.

ℹ Getting There & Away

Baysal Turizm buses connect Ankara's otogar (ticket counter 28) with Polatlı every half-hour (₺5, one hour). Once in Polatlı, you can travel the last 18km to Yassıhöyük in a minibus (₺3), but this involves a 1.5km walk across town to the minibus stand, and services depart sporadically. A taxi will charge about ₺50 to drive you to the main sites and back to Polatlı otogar.

Beypazarı

☎ 0312 / POP 36,334

A considered approach from a proactive town mayor has turned this picturesque Ottoman town, set high above the İnönü Vadisi, into the weekend destination *du jour* for Ankara's escapees. More than 3000 Ottoman houses line the narrow streets in the hilltop old quarter, where 500-plus buildings and some 30 streets have been restored. Coppersmiths and carpenters beaver away, shopkeepers flog model Ottoman houses in little bags to Ankaralı day-trippers, and the 200-year-old market recalls Beypazarı's position on the Silk Road.

Occupying a sizeable Ottoman mansion, **Beypazarı Museum** (Beypazarı Tarih ve Kültür Evi; admission ₺1.50; ⊙10am-6pm Tue-Sun) is good for nosing around to a classical music soundtrack. Exhibits range from Roman and Byzantine pillars to an Ottoman depiction of an elephant, and the characteristic cupboard-bathrooms are still intact.

On the first weekend in June, the local food festival **Havuç Guveç** celebrates the humble carrot (the area grows more than half of the carrots consumed in Turkey). Additional attractions, if any are needed, include craftwork markets and Ottoman house tours.

While you're here try the local delicacies, which include *havuç lokum* (carrot-flavoured Turkish delight), clumpy *cevizli sucuğu* (walnuts coated in grape jelly) and Beypazarı mineral water, bottled here and swigged throughout the country.

ℹ Getting There & Away

From Ankara, take a Metro train to Akköprü and cross the motorway, heading away from the Ankamall. Walk to your left, away from the flyover, until you reach the area between the M Oil garage and the pedestrian bridge, where you can hail passing Beytaş Turizm minibuses to Beypazarı (₺6, 1½ hours). In the Beytaş Turizm office across the road from the town centre bus stop (decorated with an Ottoman mural), you can check the time of the last bus back to Ankara.

Safranbolu

☎ 0370 / POP 41,954

Turkey's most thoroughly preserved Ottoman town is so gloriously dinky, it's as if it slid off the lid of a chocolate box. Safranbolu's Çarşı (old town) is a vision of red-tiled roofs and meandering alleys chock-a-block full of candy stores and cobblers. Having first found fame with traders as an isolated source of the precious saffron spice, people flock here today to recapture the heady scent of yesteryear within the muddle of timber-framed mansions now converted into quirky boutique hotels. Spending the night here is all about soaking up the enchanting Ottoman scene – all creaky wooden floors, exuberantly carved ceilings and traditional cupboard-bathrooms. A day at the old hamam, browsing the market shops, and revelling in the cobblestone quaintness is about as strenuous as it gets, but if history begins to feel a bit like old news, then hiking in the wondrous Yenice Forest nearby, remapped and rediscovered, will show you exactly why Unesco stamped this region as a World Heritage Site in 1994.

History

During the 17th century, the main Ottoman trade route between Gerede and the Black Sea coast passed through Safranbolu, bringing commerce, prominence and money to the town. During the 18th and 19th centuries, Safranbolu's wealthy inhabitants built mansions of sun-dried mudbricks, wood and stucco, while the larger population of prosperous artisans built less impressive but similarly sturdy homes. Safranbolu owes its fame to the large numbers of these dwellings that have survived.

The most prosperous Safranbolulus maintained two households. In winter they occupied town houses in the Çarşı district, which is situated at the meeting point of

ANKARA & CENTRAL ANATOLIA BEYPAZARI

Safranbolu - Çarşı

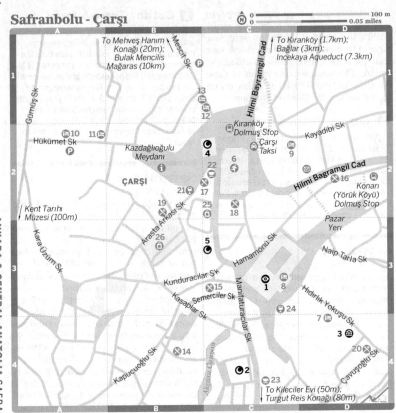

three valleys and so protected from winter winds. During the warm months they moved to summer houses in the garden suburb of Bağlar (vineyards). When the iron- and steelworks at Karabük were established in 1938, modern factory houses started to encroach on Bağlar, but Çarşı has remained virtually untouched.

During the 19th century about 20% of Safranbolu's inhabitants were Ottoman Greeks, but most of their descendants moved to Greece during the population exchange after WWI. Their principal church, dedicated to St Stephen, was converted into Kıranköy's Ulu Cami (Great Mosque).

◎ Sights & Activities

TOP CHOICE **Ottoman Houses**   ARCHITECTURE

Just walking through Çarşı is a feast for the eyes. Virtually every house in the district is an original, and what little modern

development there is has been held in check. Many of the finest historical houses have been restored, and as time goes on, more and more are being saved from deterioration and turned into hotels, shops or museums.

Kaymakamlar Müze Evi   MUSEUM

(Hıdırlık Yokuşu Sokak; admission ₺3; ⊙9am-6pm) This typical Safranbolu home has all the classic features of Ottoman houses. It was owned by a lieutenant colonel and still feels like an address of note as you climb the stairs towards the wooden ceiling decoration. Tableaux (featuring some rather weary mannequins) recreate scenes such as bathing in a cupboard and a wedding feast.

Kileciler Evi   MUSEUM

(Manifaturacılar Sokak; adult/student ₺2/1; ⊙9am-6pm) Built in 1884, this mansion also has 1950s period pieces among the family heir-

Safranbolu - Çarşı

looms in its cupboards. The whitewashed interior has been attractively renovated, with exhibits including family photos, carpets and mannequins clad in traditional clothes. As the information sheet explains, the 99 cupboards symbolise the 99 names of God.

Cinci Hanı ARCHITECTURE
(Eski Çarşı Çeşme Mahalessi; admission ₺1) Çarşı's most famous and imposing structure is this brooding 17th-century caravanserai that's now a hotel. Climb up to the rooftop for red-tiled roof panoramas over the town. On Saturdays a market takes place in the square behind it.

İzzet Paşa Camii MOSQUE
(Manifaturacılar Sokak) One of the largest mosques constructed during the Ottoman Empire, built by the grand vizier (prime minister) in 1796 and restored in 1903. Its design was influenced by European architecture.

Kent Tarıhı Müzesi MUSEUM
(☎712 1314; Çeşme Mahallesi Hükümet Sokak; admission ₺3; ⊙9am-7pm Apr-Oct, 9am-5pm Nov-Mar) Inside the *eski hükümet konağı* (old government building), these museum exhibits are a decent introduction to local life.

Just behind is the **clock tower** (1797), built by grand vizier İzzet Mehmet Paşa.

Köprülü Mehmet Paşa Camii MOSQUE
(Manifaturacılar Sokak) This beefy, helmet-roofed building beside the *yemeniciler arastası* (a row of shops beside a mosque)

dates to 1661. The metal sundial in the courtyard was added in the mid-19th century.

Cinci Hamam HAMAM
(☎712 2103; Kazdağlıoğulu Meydanı; full works ₺35; ⊙for men 6am-11pm, for women 9am-10pm) One of the most renowned bathhouses in all of Turkey, with separate baths for men and women.

🎊 Festivals & Events

Geleneksel Sezzetler Şenliği FOOD
A popular May food festival run by the Association of Anatolian Cuisine.

FREE **Safranbolu Architectural Treasures & Folklore Week** TRADITIONAL CULTURE
In September, with exhibitions and performances across town.

🛏 Sleeping

Safranbolu is very popular with Turkish tourists during weekends and holidays. Prices may rise at particularly busy times, and it can be worth booking ahead. Splashing out a bit is virtually an obligation, as you may never get another chance to sleep anywhere so authentically restored.

If you'd rather stay in a family home than a hotel, the tourist office has a list of 25 basic pensions (the *Safranbolu'daki Ev Pansiyonları Listesi*). These are cheaper than hotels, though often of lower quality, and generally cost about ₺30 per person.

Gül Evi
HISTORIC HOTEL €€€

(☑725 4645; www.canbulat.com.tr; Hükümet Sokak 46; s €75-90, d €100-120, ste €135-180 ; ☞) Eminent architect-design couple İbrahim and Gül are wholly responsible for Safranbolu's most striking reinterpretation of the Ottoman aesthetic. 'Rose House' is an affordable masterpiece where urban luxury mingles seamlessly with traditional Ottoman design. Amid a shaded, grassy garden, the rooms (spread over three houses) are all soft colours, gorgeous wood panelling and Turkman carpets, set off by wonderfully flamboyant artistic touches. Guests lucky enough to stay here can enjoy a drink in the tiny underground cave bar (once the treasury of the house) or dine at the private restaurant where the pick of local produce is on the menu.

Efe Backpackers Pension
PENSION €

(☑725 2688; www.backpackerspension.com; Kayadibi Sokak 8; dm/s/d/tr ₺20/45/70/80 ; ☞) This place dishes up all of Safranbolu's Ottoman charm at a smidgen of the cost of other hotels. Efe is a new breed of hostel, where being on a budget doesn't mean scrimping on quality, cleanliness or friendly efficiency. There's a basic dorm for those really saving their Lira, but upstairs the snug private rooms are packed full of local character with sparkly new bathrooms to boot. Yasemin, the polyglot matriarch, runs a tight ship with a host of extras on offer such as free otogar transfers, cheap dinners (₺10) and daily tours. The stunning views over town from the terrace top it all off.

Kahveciler Konağı
HISTORIC HOTEL €€

(☑725 5453; www.kahvecilerkonagi.com; Mescit Sokak 7; s/d ₺60/₺120; ☞) The large, minimalist-decorated rooms here have whitewashed walls, glorious wood-panel ceilings and lovely views of red-tiled roofs. Amiable host Erşan has transformed his grandfather's house into a comfortable home-from-home. As a bonus for those less agile, the bathrooms are big by Safranbolu standards and require no climbing into cupboards.

Selvili Köşk
HISTORIC HOTEL €€

(☑712 8646; www.selvilikosk.com; Mescit Sokak 23; s/d/tr ₺100/160/200; ☞) From the engraved banisters to the carved ceilings, this wonderful restoration job offers a regal-feeling, romantic retreat. Dazzling carpets cover every inch of floor and are layered over the *sedirs* (bench seating that runs along the walls). Ingeniously hidden bathrooms are found through opening cupboard doors, and local embroidered linen graces the beds in sun-drenched rooms. One of the most authentically Ottoman places in town.

Bastoncu Pansiyon
PENSION €€

(☑712 3411; www.bastoncupension.com; Hıdırlık Yokuşu Sokak; dm/s/d/tr ₺25/60/90/120 ; ☞) In a 300-year-old building, Bastoncu is a Safranbolu institution with a superb higgledy-piggledy feel. Connected by a labyrinth of staircases, rooms and dorms have all their original wood panelling, jars of dried flowers, and some cupboard bathrooms. It's run by a friendly couple who speak English and Japanese and appreciate travellers' needs.

Mehveş Hanım Konağı
HISTORIC HOTEL €€

(☑712 8787; www.mehveshanimkonagi.com; Mescit Sokak 30 ; s ₺80, d ₺100-120; ☞) With every nook and cranny crammed with curios and Ottoman paraphernalia, the Mehveş manages to walk the fine line between quaint and kitschy and come out on top. Run with cheerful competency, the spacious rooms have intricately carved wooden ceilings, *sedir* seating and teensy cupboard bathrooms.

Turgut Reis Konağı
HISTORIC HOTEL €

(☑725 1301; www.turgutreiskonak.com; Akpınar Sokak 27; r €35; ☞) Boasting a quiet position and some of Safranbolu's nicest views, this friendly hotel is one of the best deals around. The shiny red bedspreads sit rather incongruously with the otherwise simple decor but the vast amount of dark wood panelling on the walls fills the place with a lovely old-world appeal.

Imren Lokum Konak
HISTORIC HOTEL €€

(☑725 2688; www.imrenkonak.com; Kayyim Ali Sokak; s/d ₺70/140; ☞) This lovely new mansion attracts a sociable crowd to its large open courtyard and spacious, good value Ottoman rooms. The friendly, laid-back service ensures a holiday vibe.

Cinci Hanı
HISTORIC HOTEL €€

(☑712 0680; www.cincihan.com; Eski Çarşı Çeşme Mahalessi; s/d/tr ₺55/100/140; ✲☞) It's worth taking the chance to sleep in this Silk Road caravanserai, if only for the stony sense of history. Rooms are smallish and a bit plain but the cave-like acoustics are a bit of kick and it's a short stumble from the local bars.

Havuzlu Asmazlar Konağı
HISTORIC HOUSE €€

(☑725 2883; www.safranbolukonak.com; Çelik Gülersoy Caddesi 18; s/d weekday ₺120/160, weekend from ₺160/210; ❄) The tiny bathing pool in the lobby is the first of many audacious quirks in this beautiful house set in a garden filled with trees, flowers and summer bees. The rooms are beautifully furnished with brass beds, *sedirs* and kilims. An unusual and undeniably beautiful hotel, it's often booked solid.

✗ Eating

Taşev MODERN TURKISH €€
(☑712 0680; www.tasevsanatvesarapevi.com; Hıdırlık Yokuşu Sokak 14; mains ₺11-23) Visitors to Safranbolu now have a bonafide contemporary dining option that delivers on thick steaks and creamy pasta dishes. The Turkish cheese platter (₺15) is a must for cheese-lovers. Service is more aloof than elsewhere in town, but the alluring wall art, multi-purpose exhibition space and extensive wine menu make this a long-overdue change from Ottoman-inspired dining.

Çızgı Cafe ANATOLIAN €€
(Arasta Arkası Sokak ; mains ₺7-15) Eat on the cushioned benches outside and watch the world go by, or dine inside in one of the cosily intimate cubby-hole dining areas. Çızgı is an easygoing place where local dishes such as *cevizli yayım* (macaroni topped with walnuts) and *mantı* (Turkish ravioli) are on the small menu, and it's all about wasting hours talking over coffee and nargile afterwards.

Bizım Cafe ANATOLIAN €
(Çeşme Mahallesi; mains ₺5-8) Deep in the old shopping district is this welcoming little family-run restaurant that serves whatever's on the stove, which luckily is always pretty good, including *dolmades* rolled on the street and deliciously spicy soups. Locals love it.

Kadıoğlu Şehzade Sofrası TURKISH €€
(☑712 5657; Arasta Sokak 8; mains ₺11-23; ⊙11.30am-10.30pm) It's all traditional Ottoman-style seating at this converted mansion restaurant. The huge, steaming hot pide, *çorba*, grills and *zerde* (saffron dessert) are all recommended. The rooms are tacky but pretty large and service is swift.

Hanım Sultan ANATOLIAN €
(mains ₺5-10) Squirreled away down a little alleyway, this place rustles up rustic, wholesome cooking. Try the divine pot of *eth dolma* (vine leaves stuffed with meat) for a hearty, delicious lunch.

Bestemi Gözleme TURKISH €
(Kapucuoğlu Sokak; mains ₺4) Cheap and cheerful, this family-run restaurant may not be big on atmosphere but it delivers big portions of flavourful Turkish favourites at bargain prices. The *mantı* is worth the wait.

Çevrikköprü 3 TURKISH €€
(☑725 2586; Hilmi Bayramgil Caddesi ; mains ₺8-18) Huge plates of traditional food at cheekily cheap prices. The service is keen and the menu the length of a novella.

☕ Drinking

Sade Kahve CAFE
(Manifaturacılar Caddesi 17; coffee ₺4-6, desserts ₺4-8) Opposite a slew of tinkerers and metal-benders, this is a fabulous little find run by coffee fanatics who make a mean brew, Turkish or otherwise, and the most delicious waffles in town. From the cappuccinos to the complimentary cake, Sade is smooth.

Türkü Cafe BAR
(Musalla Hallesi Han Arkası Sokak 16) On Safranbolu's equivalent of a bar strip, this friendly place is run by a cool mother-and-daughter team who pour ice-cold Efes with smiley efficency. Türkü also hosts regular live music in the form of locals belting out pop tunes.

Meydan NARGILE CAFE
(Arasta Arkası Sokak; snacks ₺2.50-6) Pull up a pew on the pavement, order a nargile and a çay, and listen to the slap of counter-tiles at nearby tables as the backgammon battles begin at this popular central hang-out.

Arasna Pension BAR
(☑712 4170; Arasta Arkası Sokak 5) A lively bar with regular live music. Its atmospheric stone walls are illuminated by electric candles.

🛍 Shopping

Safranbolu is a great place to pick up handicrafts – especially textiles, metalwork, shoes and wooden artefacts – whether locally made or shipped in from elsewhere to supply coach tourists.

Yemeniciler Arastası MARKET
(Peasant Shoemaker's Bazaar; Arasta Arkası Sokak) The restored Yemeniciler Arastası is the best place to start looking for crafts, although the makers of the light, flat-heeled shoes who used to work here have long since moved out. The further you go

from the *arasta* the more likely you are to come across shops occupied by authentic working saddle-makers, felt-makers and other artisans.

Safrantat FOOD

(Manifaturacılar Sokak) Although Safranbolu is so packed with sweet shops that you half expect the houses to be made out of gingerbread, Safrantat is one of the top picks for sugary delights. Don't leave without trying the regional speciality, *yaprak helvası* – delicious chewy layers of white *helva* (halva) spotted with ground walnuts. You can also visit the Safrantat factory behind the petrol station in Kıranköy to see how *lokum* is made.

 Information

Çarşı has a bank, with an ATM, on Kazdağlıoğlu Meydanı.

Tourist Office (☑712 3863; www.safranbolu. gov.tr; Kazdağlıoğlu Meydanı; ☺9am-5.30pm) One of Turkey's most helpful tourist information offices. Informed, multilingual staff can provide loads of tips and advice, and will even help with booking bus tickets.

 Getting There & Away

Most buses stop in Karabük first and then finish at Kıranköy otogar (upper Safranbolu), from where minibuses or a *servis* (shuttle bus) can deposit you in central Kıranköy, near the dolmuş stand for Çarşı.

There are several bus company offices along Sadrı Artunç Caddesi and just off Adnan Menderes Caddesi in Kıranköy, where you can buy tickets to destinations including Ankara (₺25, three hours), İstanbul (₺40, seven hours) and Kastamonu (₺15, two hours).

Şavaş Turizm (☑712 7480; Adnan Menderes Caddesi, Kıranköy) runs buses to Amasra (₺15,

two hours) roughly every two hours between 8.15am and 6.30pm. Or take their hourly bus to Bartın (₺10, 1½ hours) and change there.

If you're driving, exit the Ankara–İstanbul highway at Gerede and head north, following the signs for Karabük/Safranbolu.

There is a direct train from Karabük to Ankara, but the bus is a much easier option.

 Getting Around

Dolmuşes (₺1.50) ply the route from Çarşı's main square, over the hills, and into central Kıranköy every 15 minutes. From the last stop you can catch another minibus to Karabük. You only have to pay the bus fare once if you're going all the way. A taxi from Çarşı to Kıranköy will cost you ₺10.

Around Safranbolu

YÖRÜK KÖYÜ

Along the Kastamonu road, 15km east of Safranbolu, Yörük Köyü (Nomad Village) is a beautiful settlement of crumbling old houses once inhabited by the dervish Bektaşi sect. The government forced the nomads to settle here so it could tax them, and once they'd put down roots these new villagers grew rich from their baking prowess.

Sipahioğlu Konağı Gezi Evi (Leyla Gencer Sokağı; admission ₺4; ☺8.30am-sunset) is one of the village's enormous Ottoman houses. The builder's warring sons divided the mansion in two, and you tour the *selamlık* (male quarters) and *haremlik* (female quarters) separately.

Nearby in Cemil İpekçi Sokağı is the 300-year-old *çamaşırhane* (laundry), with arched hearths where the water was heated in cauldrons. Ask at Sipahioğlu Konağı Gezi Evi for the key.

WORTH A TRIP

YENİCE FOREST

Yenice is an adorable district 35km west of Karabük and surrounded by the breathtaking **Yenice Forest**. With roughly 85% of Yenice composed of wild forest, Governor Nurullah Çekır (elected in 2009) pressed his love of nature upon locals in a bid to provide an alternative to the logging industry. His results are impressive, as the forest now has 396km of walking trails through sublime, lush countryside, an impeccable hiking guidebook (available in Safranbolu and Karabük), and a loghouse built on approach to Şeker Canyon. Three national parks (Çitdere Nature Reserve, Kavaklı Nature Reserve and Gökpınar Site Arboretum) converge in Yenice – one of Turkey's most accessible wilderness areas, fed by cool springs and containing an array of flora and fauna.

The Zonguldak-bound slow train to Yenice from Karabük (₺5, 1½ hours, four daily) passes through 16 tunnels and a deep valley where the Filyos River flows deep.

Getting There & Away

There is no direct bus service from Safranbolu to Yörük Köyü, but dolmuşes to the nearby village of Konarı (five daily, ₺1.50) can drop you at the Yörük Köyü turn-off on the main road. From there it's a 1km walk to the village. Some dolmuş drivers may have to diverge off their route and drop you/pick you up from the village if you ask them.

Çarşı Taksi (☏725 2595; Hilmi Bayramgil Caddesi) charges ₺35 return, including waiting time, to Yörük Köyü and many hotels can organise tours.

BULAK MENCİLİS MAĞARASI

Deep in the Gürleyik hills 10km northwest of Safranbolu, the impressive **Bulak Mencilis Mağarası** (adult/child ₺4/2; ☾9am-7.30pm) cave network opened to the public a decade ago, although troglodytes may have lived here many millennia before that. You can walk through 400m of the 6km-long network, enough to reveal a fine array of stalactites and stalagmites with inevitable anthropomorphic nicknames. There are steps up to the cave and you should wear sturdy shoes as the metal walkway inside can be slippery and wet. A taxi from Safranbolu costs ₺35 return.

İNCEKAYA AQUEDUCT

Originally built in Byzantine times but restored in the 1790s by İzzet Mehmet Paşa, **İncekaya Aqueduct** (Su Kemeri) is just over 7km north of Safranbolu. Its name means 'thin rock' and the walk across it, high above the beautiful **Tokatlı Gorge**, would not suit sufferers of vertigo. A taxi from Safranbolu costs ₺30 return.

Kastamonu

☏0366 / POP 93,380

A town where they still need signs to stop tractors trundling down the main street doesn't seem immediately promising, but veer into the helter-skelter of alleyways off bustling Cumhuriyet Caddesi and you'll discover decaying remnants of former glory at every turn. A wealth of Ottoman mansions slowly slumping and sliding into picturesque abandon line Kastamonu's lanes, while market streets throng with locals on a bargain-hunt. It's a glimpse of provincial Turkey yet to be trussed up for the tourists. Just out of town, Kasaba's intricately carved and painted wooden mosque provides enough of a reason to spend the night.

History

Kastamonu's history has been as chequered as that of most central-Turkish towns. Archaeological evidence suggests there was a settlement here as far back as 2000 BC, but the Hittites, Persians, Macedonians and Pontic (Black Sea) kings all left their mark. In the 11th century the Seljuks descended, then the Danışmends. The 13th-century Byzantine emperor John Comnenus tried to hold out here, but the Mongols soon swept in, followed by the Ottomans.

Kastamonu's modern history is inextricably linked to headgear: Atatürk launched his hat reforms here in 1925, banning the fez due to its religious connotations and insisting on the adoption of European-style titfers.

Sights

Archaeology Museum MUSEUM

(☏214 1070; Cumhuriyet Caddesi; admission ₺3; ☾8.30am-12.30pm & 1.30pm-5.30pm Tue-Sun) South of Nasrullah bridge, this small museum has beautifully displayed exhibits and detailed information panels in English. The central hall is devoted to Kastomonu's role in Atatürk's sartorial revolution, while the lefthand room houses Hellenic and Roman finds. Upstairs are Hittite and Bronze Age exhibits from regional excavations.

Nasrullah Meydanı SQUARE

(off Cumhuriyet Caddesi) Leading off from Nasrullah bridge, the square centres on the Ottoman **Nasrullah Camii** (1506). Poet Mehmet Akif Ersoy delivered speeches in this mosque during the War of Independence. The former **Münire Medresesi** (seminary) at the rear houses craft shops. West of the square are old market buildings, including the **Aşirefendi Hanı** and the 15th-century **İsmail Bey Hanı**.

FREE Castle CASTLE

(Kale; ☾9am-5pm) One block south of the Archaeology Museum, turn right onto Şeyh Şaban Veli Caddesi and follow the road up to the scant remains of Kastamonu's castle. Parts of the building date from Byzantine times, but most belong to Seljuk and Ottoman reconstructions.

Ethnography Museum MUSEUM

(☏214 0149; Sakayra Caddesi 5; admission ₺3; ☾8.30am-5.30pm Tue-Sun) South of Nasrullah bridge on Cumhuriyet Caddesi, turn right after Gazi Paşa school to reach the restored 1870 Liva Paşa Konağı, with its upstairs salons furnished as it would have been in Ottoman times.

🛏 Sleeping

Most of the hotels are clustered around Nasrullah Bridge. The bus companies' offices and internet cafes are in the same area.

Uğurlu Konakları   HISTORIC HOTEL €€
(☑212 8202; www.kastamonukonaklari.com; Şeyh Şaban Veli Caddesi 47-51; s/d ₺100/150; ☜) A short walk from the castle, these two houses have been faithfully restored with Indian carpets, red-brown trimmings and a private garden. Rooms in the front house are more appealing, leading off from atmospheric communal salons.

Osmanlı Sarayı   HISTORIC HOTEL €€
(Ottoman Palace; ☑214 8408; www.osmanlisarayi. tr.cx; Belediye Caddesi 81; s/d ₺50/100; ☜) Atatürk once visited this grand building in its former incarnation as Kastamonu's town hall. Breathe in the history in the high-ceilinged rooms, which have authentic fittings and cupboard-bathrooms.

Kurşunluhan Hotel   HISTORIC HOTEL €€
(☑214 2737; www.kursunluhanotel.com; Nasrullah Camii Karşısı; s/d ₺90/140; ☜) This 15th-century *han* (caravanserai), beside Nasrullah Meydanı, has been fully restored. Its dome-ceilinged rooms are set around a courtyard that for centuries was the centre of Kastamonu's commercial bustle.

🍴 Eating & Drinking

The winding streets to the west of Nasrullah Meydanı are great for a wander and a çay.

Münire Sultan Sofrası   ANATOLIAN €€
(Nasrullah Meydanı; mains ₺7-14) Tucked inside the Münire Medresesi complex, we like this place for its local specialities. Try *banduma* (chicken and filo pastry drenched in butter and chopped walnuts) and order a glass of *eğşi* (sour plum drink) to wash it all down.

Eflanili Konağı   ANATOLIAN €€
(☑214 1118; Gazipaşa İlköğr Yanı; mains ₺5-12) Signposted off Cumhuriyet Caddesi, there's a warren of upstairs dining rooms in this finely restored Ottoman house and the menu is packed with local flavour.

Canoğlu   CAFE €
(☑213 9090; Cumhuriyet Caddesi; ⊗6am-8pm) A couple of blocks north of Nasrullah Bridge, this patisserie is Kastamonu's premier catch-up spot.

❶ Getting There & Away

Kastamonu's **otogar** (Kazım Karabekir Caddesi) offers regular departures for Ankara (₺30, four hours), İstanbul (₺50, eight hours), Karabük (₺15, two hours), Samsun (₺35, 5½ hours) and Sinop (₺25, three hours).

Minibuses for İnebolu (₺10, two hours) also leave from the otogar.

Around Kastamonu

KASABA

Amid rolling hills and fertile fields, the tiny hamlet of Kasaba, 17km northwest of Kastamonu, is a pretty but unlikely place to find one of Turkey's finest surviving wooden mosques. The restored interior of **Mahmud Bey Camii** (1366) has four painted wooden columns, a wooden gallery and finely painted ceiling rafters. You can climb some rough ladders to the third storey of the gallery to look at the ornate beam-ends and interlocking motifs topping the pillars.

A return taxi from Kastamonu, with waiting time, costs ₺40. A cheaper option is to take the Pınarbaşı bus and jump off at the Kasaba turn-off, but it is a 4km walk to the village from there.

PINARBAŞI

Pınarbaşı is the main access point for the 37,000-hectare **Küre Dağları National Park** (Küre Dağları Milli Parkı; ☑0366-771 2465; www. ked.org.tr/empty.html). Despite some marketing efforts made by the local government, the Küre Mountains are still largely undiscovered by tourists and you will likely have the park to yourself. Spots worth seeking out include the Ilgarini 'Inn' and Ilıca 'Hamam' caves, Ilıca waterfall and Horma Canyon.

The dinky pine cabins at **Park Ilıca Turizm Tesisi** (☑0366-771 2357; www.parkilica.com; Ilıca Köyü, Pinarbaşı; per person ₺80) near the Ilıca waterfall make a great base for exploring the park. There's an on-site restaurant and thermal springs to soak in nearby.

There are a couple of minibuses a day from Kastamonu to Pınarbaşı, but you really need your own transport to move around the park. For ₺150, a taxi will take you there and spend the afternoon touring the park before returning to Kastamonu.

Boğazkale, Hattuşa & Yazılıkaya

Out in the centre of the Anatolian plains, two Unesco World Heritage Sites evoke a vital historical moment at the height of Hittite civilisation. Hattuşa was the Hittite capital, while Yazılıkaya was a religious sanctuary with fine rock carvings.

The best base for visiting the sites around here is Boğazkale, a farming village 200km east of Ankara. Boğazkale has simple traveller services; if you want or need something fancier you'll need to stay in Çorum or, if you get going early enough in the morning, Ankara.

BOĞAZKALE

 0364 / POP 1300

The village of Boğazkale has ducks, cows and wheelbarrow-racing children wandering its cobbled streets, farmyards with Hittite and Byzantine gates, and a constant sense that a once-great city is just over the brow. Most visitors come solely to visit Hattuşa and Yazılıkaya, which can be accessed on foot if it's not too hot, but there is more to explore. Surrounded by valleys with Hittite caves, eagles' nests, butterflies and a neolithic fort, the area around Hattuşa is ripe for hiking. Head 4km east of Yazılıkaya and climb Yazılıkaya Dağı to watch the sun set on the sites, or head to the swimming hole (locally known as *hoşur*) on the Budaközü river to cool off after a long day in the ruins.

Late in the day, the silence in Boğazkale is broken only by the occasional car kicking up dust on the main street, and the rural solitude may tempt you to stay an extra night. Apart from the accommodation options, the village's only facilities are some small shops, a post office and bank with an ATM.

Unsurprisingly, Hittite artefacts dominate the small **Boğazkale Museum** (free audio guides are available; ⊘8am-5pm Tue-Sun). The pride of the collection are the two sphinx statues that once stood guard at Hattuşa's Yer Kapı gate. They were only returned to Boğazkale in 2011, having previously been on display in Berlin and İstanbul.

HATTUŞA

The mountainous, isolated site of **Hattuşa** (adult/student ₺5/free, also valid for Yazılıkaya; ⊘9am-5pm) was once the capital of the Hittite kingdom which stretched from Syria to Europe. At its epoch this was a busy and impressive city of 15,000 inhabitants with defensive walls more than 6km in length, some of the thickest in the ancient world, studded with watchtowers and secret tunnels.

As you climb down out of the village to the site, an evocative reconstruction of a section of city wall comes into view. Imagine the sense of purpose that drove the Hittites to haul stone to this remote spot, far from oceans and trade routes, and build an engineering masterpiece that launched a mighty empire.

A word of warning: some touts and carpet sellers have begun posing as 'compulsory guides' around the Hattuşa site and outside the entrance to Yazılıkaya. Remain firm, as this is clearly a con.

⊙ Sights

Büyük Mabet   TEMPLE

(Great Temple) The vast complex of the Büyük Mabet, dating from the 14th century BC and destroyed around 1200 BC, is the best preserved of Hattuşa's Hittite temple ruins, but you'll need plenty of imagination.

As you walk down the wide processional street, the administrative quarters of the temple are to your left. The well-worn cube of green nephrite rock here is thought to

---

ⓘ VISITING HATTUŞA

» The ruins are an easy, and extremely pretty, walk from town.

» Arrive early in the morning to tour the ruins before the 21st century intrudes in the form of coaches and souvenir sellers.

» Enter the Büyük Mabet temple ruins from the trail uphill of Hattuşa's ticket kiosk, opposite the remains of a house on the slope.

» The circuit is a hilly 5km loop; if you want to walk, wear sturdy shoes and take enough water (there is no shop on site).

» There is very little shade so don't forget a hat and sunblock.

» Your Hattuşa ticket is also valid for Yazılıkaya.

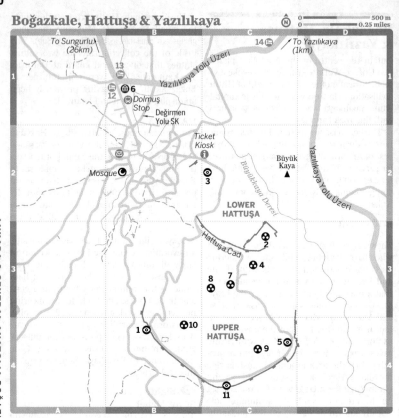

have played a significant role in the Hittite religion.

The main temple, to your right, was surrounded by storerooms thought to be three storeys high. In the early 20th century, huge clay storage jars and thousands of cuneiform tablets were found in these rooms. Look for the threshold stones at the base of some of the doorways to see the hole for the hinge-post and the arc worn by the door's movement. The temple is believed to have been a ritual altar for the deities Teshub and Hepatu; the large stone base of one of their statues remains.

Sarı Kale & Yenice Kale   RUIN
About 250m south of the Büyük Mabet, the road forks; take the right fork and follow the winding road up the hillside. On your left in the midst of the old city you can see several ruined structures. The rock-top ruins of the Sarı Kale (Yellow Fortress) may be a Phrygian fort on Hittite foundations. On another rock

outcrop are the remains of the Yenice Kale which may have been a royal residence or small temple. You can climb to the summit from the east side.

Aslanlı Kapı   GATE
(Lion's Gate) At Aslanlı Kapı two stone lions (one rather poorly reconstructed) protect the city from evil spirits. This is one of at least six gates in Hattuşa's defensive walls, though it may never have been completed. You can see the best-preserved parts of Hattuşa's fortifications from here, stretching up the ridge southeast to Yer Kapı and from there to Kral Kapı. These 4000-year-old walls illustrate the Hittites' engineering ingenuity, which enabled them to either build in sympathy with the terrain or transform the landscape, depending on what was required. Natural outcrops were appropriated as part of the walls, and massive ramparts were built to create artificial fortresses.

Boğazkale, Hattuşa & Yazılıkaya

Yer Kapı   GATE

(Earth Gate) The Yer Kapı is Hattuşa's most impressive gate, with an artificial mound pierced by a 70m-long tunnel. The Hittites built the tunnel using a corbelled arch (two flat faces of stones leaning towards one another), as the 'true' arch was not invented until later. Primitive or not, the arch has done its job for millennia, and you can still pass down the stony tunnel as Hittite soldiers did, emerging from the postern. Afterwards, re-enter the city via one of the monumental stairways up the wide stone glacis and pass through the **Sphinx Gate**, once defended by four great sphinxes. One is still in situ, two are in the Boğazkale museum and the other has been lost. There are wonderful views over the **upper city temple district** from here.

Kral Kapı   GATE

(King's Gate) Kral Kapı is named after the regal-looking figure in the relief carving. The kingly character, a Hittite warrior god protecting the city, is a copy; the original was removed to Ankara for safekeeping.

Nişantaş & Güney Kale   RUINS

At **Nişantaş** a rock with a faintly visible Hittite inscription cut into it narrates the deeds of Suppiluliuma II (1215–1200 BC), the final Hittite king.

Immediately opposite, a path leads up to the excavated **Güney Kale** (Southern Fortress) with a fine (fenced-off) **hieroglyphics chamber** with human figure reliefs.

Büyük Kale   RUIN

(Great Fortress) Although most of the Büyük Kale site has been excavated, many of the older layers of development have been recovered to protect them, so what you see today can be hard to decipher. This fortress held the royal palace and the Hittite state archives.

YAZILIKAYA

Yazılıkaya (Yazılıkaya Yolu Üzeri; admission included in Hattuşa ticket) means 'Inscribed Rock', and that's exactly what you'll find in these outdoor rock galleries, just under 3km from Hattuşa. There are two galleries: the larger one, to the left, was the Hittite empire's holiest religious sanctuary; the narrower one, to the right, has the best-preserved carvings. Together they form the largest known Hittite rock sanctuary, sufficiently preserved to make you wish you could have seen the carvings when they were new.

In the larger gallery, **Chamber A**, the fast-fading reliefs show numerous goddesses and pointy-hatted gods marching in procession. Heads and feet are shown in profile but the torso is shown front on, a common feature of Hittite relief art. The lines of men and women lead to some large reliefs depicting a godly meeting. Teshub stands on two deified mountains (depicted as men) alongside his wife Hepatu, who is standing on the back of a panther. Behind her, their son and (possibly) two daughters are respectively carried by a smaller panther and a double-headed eagle. The largest relief, on the opposite wall, depicts the complex's bearded founder, King Tudhaliya IV, standing on two mountains. The rock ledges were probably used for offerings or sacrifices and the basins for libations.

On the way into **Chamber B**, you should supposedly ask permission of the winged, lion-headed guard depicted by the entrance before entering. The narrow gallery is thought to be a memorial chapel for Tudhaliya IV, dedicated by his son Suppiluliuma II. The large limestone block could have been the base of a statue of the king. Buried until a century ago and better protected from the elements, the carvings include a procession of 12 scimitar-wielding underworld gods. On

ANKARA & CENTRAL ANATOLIA BOĞAZKALE, HATTUŞA & YAZILIKAYA

HITTITES

While the name may evoke images of skin-clad barbarians, the Hittites were a sophisticated people who commanded a vast Middle Eastern empire, conquered Babylon and challenged the Egyptian pharaohs more than 3000 years ago. Apart from a few written references in the Bible and Babylonian tablets, there were few clues to their existence until 1834 when a French traveller stumbled upon the ruins of the Hittite capital of Hattuşa.

In 1905 excavations turned up notable works of art and the Hittite state archives, written in cuneiform on thousands of clay tablets. From these tablets, historians and archaeologists were able to construct a history of the Hittite empire.

The original Indo-European Hittites swept into Anatolia around 2000 BC, conquering the local Hatti, from whom they borrowed their culture and name. They established themselves at Hattuşa, the Hatti capital, and in the course of a millennium enlarged and beautified the city. From about 1375 to 1200 BC Hattuşa was the capital of a Hittite empire that, at its height, shared Syria with Egypt and extended as far as Europe.

The Hittites worshipped over a thousand different deities; the most important were Teshub, the storm or weather god, and Hepatu, the sun goddess. The cuneiform tablets revealed a well-ordered society with more than 200 laws. The death sentence was prescribed for bestiality, while thieves got off more lightly provided they paid their victims compensation.

Although it defeated Egypt in 1298 BC, the empire declined in the following centuries, undone by internal squabbles and new threats such as the Greek 'sea peoples'. Hattuşa was torched and its inhabitants dispersed. Only the city states of Syria survived until they, too, were swallowed by the Assyrians.

the opposite wall, the detailed relief of Nergal depicts the underworld deity as a sword; the four lion heads on the handle (two pointing towards the blade, one to the left and the other to the right) double as the deity's knees and shoulders.

Tours

Hattuşas Taxi CULTURAL TOUR
(☑0535 389 1089; www.hattusastaxi.com) A mine of Hittite information, Murat Bektaş runs excellent tours in Hattuşa and around the surrounding area. For those with little time, his full day Hittite tour of Hattuşa, Yazılıkaya and Alacahöyük (₺70 per person) is highly recommended.

Sleeping & Eating

The following offer camping for about ₺10 per person, including the use of electricity and hot water.

Aşıkoğlu Hotel & Pension HOTEL €€
(☑452 2004; www.hattusas.com; Sungurlu Asfalt Caddesi; pension s/d ₺20/40, hotel s/d/tr ₺60/100/120; 🕸) The friendly service sets this place apart and the simple, spick-and-span rooms are just the ticket for resting your head after visiting Hattuşa. There are lovely views from the upstairs terrace and a cosy Ottoman-style cafe. Hittite documen-

taries are shown on a cinevision screen in the evening and there's an information office brimming with free maps and brochures about the site. On the pension side of the building, rooms are small and basic but you still get to use all the facilities of the hotel. Dishes at the restaurant cost from ₺5 to ₺20. If you ring ahead the hotel can organise taxi transfers from Sungurlu otogar for ₺20, and from Yozgat for ₺40.

Hittite Houses HOTEL €€
(☑452 2004; www.hattusas.com; Sungurlu Asfalt Caddesi; s/d ₺50/80; 🕸) Behind a mocked-up Hittite wall-facade, this hotel has plain but light-filled rooms. It's run by the knowledgeable owners of Aşıkoğlu Hotel, so guests have access to all the facilities and services there.

Kale Hotel HOTEL €€
(☑452 3126; www.bogazkoyhattusa.com; Yazılıkaya Yolu Üzeri; s/d ₺50/80 ; ☺Apr-Oct) Kale's colourful rooms have cheery floral linen and decent beds; the top ones at the front have good views and some have balconies. The restaurant, with its adjoining terrace, mostly caters to groups.

ℹ Getting There & Away

To get to Boğazkale by public transport, you'll need to go via Sungurlu. Many of the buses from

Ankara to Sungurlu (₺12, three hours, hourly) are run by Mis Amasya (counter 23 at Ankara's otogar). From Sungurlu otogar your bus should provide a *servis* to the Boğazkale dolmuş stand, 1km from the otogar near the soccer stadium. There is no set dolmuş schedule (₺3) but there are more in the morning and they run until about 5.30pm. Taking a taxi may be your only resort at the weekend; don't pay more than ₺30. Travellers coming from Cappadocia should note that there are no dolmuşes between Boğazkale and Yozgat, 41km southeast. You're better off going via Sungurlu.

❶ Getting Around

To get around Hattuşa and Yazılıkaya without your own transport you'll need to walk or hire a taxi. It's 1km from the Aşıkoğlu Hotel to the Hattuşa ticket kiosk. From there the road looping around the site from the ticket kiosk (not including Yazılıkaya) is another 5km. The walk itself takes at least an hour, plus time spent exploring the ruins, so figure on spending a good three hours here.

Alacahöyük

The tiny farming hamlet of Alacahöyük is 36km north of Boğazkale and 52km south of Çorum. The site is very old but the excavation area is small and most of the movable monuments are now in Ankara's Museum of Anatolian Civilisations, so it's really only worth the effort if you've got some spare time after Hattuşa.

The **museum** (including excavation area admission ₺5; ⊗8am-7pm) is beside the ruins, displaying artists' impressions of the site at various points in its history, as well as finds dating back to the Chalcolithic and Old Bronze ages.

At the ruins, the **monumental gate** has two eyeless sphinxes guarding the door. The detailed reliefs (copies, the originals are in Ankara) show musicians, a sword swallower, animals for sacrifice and the Hittite king and queen – all part of festivities and ceremonies dedicated to Teshub, shown here as a bull. Once through the gate, the main excavations on the right hand side are of a Hittite palace/temple complex.

To the left, protected under plastic covers, are the pre-Hittite royal shaft graves. Dating to 2300 to 2100 BC, each skeleton was buried individually along with a variety of personal belongings and several oxen skulls, which archaeologists presume to be the leftovers of a funereal meal.

On the far left of the back of the site is an underground tunnel. Walk through it and look down at the fields to see how the site was built up over the millennia.

❶ Getting There & Away

There's no public transport between Alacahöyük and Boğazkale so the best way to reach the site is by taxi or with your own transport. If you're really keen, you could take a bus or dolmuş from Çorum to Alaca and another from Alaca to Alacahöyük (one or two services per day, none at weekends).

Çorum

☑0364 / POP 225,927

Set on an alluvial plain on a branch of the Çorum river, Çorum is an unremarkable provincial capital, resting on its modest fame as the chickpea capital of Turkey. The town is full of *leblebiciler* (chickpea roasters) and sacks upon sacks of the chalky little pulses, sorted according to fine distinctions obvious only to a chickpea dealer.

The Çorum museum is excellent preparation for Hattuşa and the other Hittite sites to the southeast, and the busy and bustling town centre offers some glimpses of provincial Turkish life.

◉ Sights

Çorum Museum   MUSEUM

(admission ₺4; ⊗9am-5pm Tue-Sun) On the far side of Anitta Otel from the otogar, this excellent museum is well worth a visit before heading to Hattuşa. Impressive exhibits display Anatolian history from the Bronze Age to the Roman period with a major focus on Hittite history. The centrepiece is a reconstruction of the royal tomb at Alacahöyük, with bull skulls and a crumpled skeleton clad in a crown, and there are some incredible artefacts such as a Hittite ceremonial jug with water-spouting bulls around its rim and a good collection of Hittite cuneiform tablets.

🛏 Sleeping & Eating

Grand Park Hotel   HOTEL €€

(☑212 3044; www.grandpark.com.tr; İnönü Caddesi 60; s/d ₺60/95; ❄☺) This fine business-style hotel has spacious rooms with light modern decor and shipshape, sparkling clean bathrooms. The friendly staff and lightning-bolt fast wi-fi are a bonus. It's 250m up the road from the otogar.

Anitta Otel
LUXURY HOTEL €€€

(☑213 8515; www.anittahotel.com; İnönü Caddesi 80; s/d/tr ₺135/185/245; ❋ ☷) Grand in a slick, ultra-modern way, this mammoth block towers over the otogar. Rooms are decked out with a profuse pizzazz of mirrors and glass, plasma screens and all manner of slightly over-the-top contemporary design features.

Katipler Konağı
OTTOMAN €€

(☑224 9651; Karakeçili Mahallesi, 2 Sokak 20; mains ₺6-11; ◷11am-9pm) This restaurant is spread across two floors of a restored Ottoman house. Highlights include the mulberry juice and filling local starters such as çatal aşı (lentil and wheat soup) and keşkek (roasted wheat, chicken, red pepper and butter). To find it, turn left on İnönü Caddesi after Hotel Sarıgül, cross the road and turn right; turn right on to the side street behind the mosque, then turn left and it's on the right.

❶ Getting There & Away

Being on the main Ankara–Samsun highway, Çorum has good bus connections. Regular buses go to Alaca (₺4, 45 minutes), Amasya (₺8, two hours), Ankara (₺20, four hours), Kayseri (₺35, 4¾ hours), Samsun (₺20, three hours) and Sungurlu (₺5, 1¼ hours).

Amasya
☑0358 / POP 90,665

Amasya is a tale of two shores. On the north of the Yeşilırmak river, rows of half-timbered Ottoman houses sit squeezed together like chocolate cakes in a patisserie window. To the south, the newer, more modern Turkey tries to get on with things in an outward-looking ode to the succession of empires that reigned in this narrow, rocky valley. Towering above the minarets and the medreses are pockmarks of Pontic tombs etched into the highrise bluff and guarded by a lofty citadel. Amasya's setting may evoke high drama, but life here unfolds as slowly as the train takes apples out of town via a mountain tunnel. In local folklore, these tunnels were dug by Ferhat, a star-crossed lover who was tragically in love with Şirin, the sister of a sultan queen.

History

Called Hakmış by the Hittites, the Amasya area has been inhabited continuously since around 5500 BC. Alexander the Great conquered Amasya in the 4th century BC, then it became the capital of a successor kingdom ruled by a family of Persian satraps (provincial governors). By the time of King Mithridates II (281 BC), the Kingdom of Pontus entered a golden age and dominated a large part of Anatolia from its Amasya HQ. During the latter part of Pontus' flowering, Amasya was the birthplace of Strabo (c 63 BC to AD 25), the world's first geographer.

Amasya's golden age continued under the Romans, who named it a 'first city' and used it as an administrative centre for rulers such as Pompey. It was Julius Caesar's conquest of a local town that prompted his immortal words 'Veni, vidi, vici' – 'I came, I saw, I conquered'.

After the Romans came the Byzantines, the Danışmend Turks, the Seljuks, the Mongols and the national republic of Abazhistan. In Ottoman times, Amasya was an important military base and testing ground for the sultans' heirs; it also became a centre of Islamic study, with as many as 18 medreses and 2000 theological students by the 19th century.

After WWI, Atatürk met his supporters here and hammered out the basic principles of the Turkish struggle for independence, which were published in the Amasya Circular.

◉ Sights
NORTH OF THE RIVER

TOP CHOICE Tombs of the Pontic Kings
TOMBS

(Kral Kaya Mezarları; admission ₺3; ◷8.30am-6.30pm May-Oct, to 4.45pm Nov-Apr) Looming above the northern bank of the river is a sheer rock face with the conspicuous cut-rock Tombs of the Pontic Kings. The tombs, cut deep into the limestone as early as the 4th century BC, were used for cult worship of the deified rulers. There are more than 20 (empty) tombs in the valley and they're at their most striking when viewed from the southern river bank.

Climb the steps from the souvenir stalls to the ticket office. Just past the office the path divides: turn right to view the most impressive tombs, with good panoramas of Amasya. Turn left to find the remnants of the Baths of the Maidens Palace, built in the 14th century and, through a rock-hewn tunnel, a couple more tombs.

Hatuniye Mahallesi
HISTORIC NEIGHBOURHOOD

The Hatuniye Mahallesi is Amasya's wonderful neighbourhood of restored Ottoman

Amasya

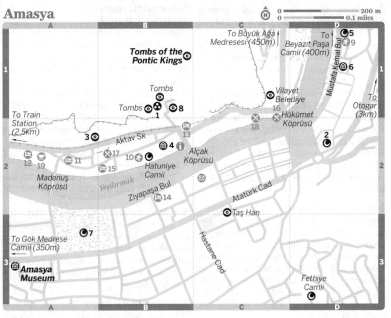

N
0   200 m
0   0.1 miles

Amasya

houses, interspersed with good modern reproductions to make a harmonious whole.

The **Hazeranlar Konağı** (Hazeranlar Sokak; admission ₺3; ⊙8.30am-noon & 1pm-4.45pm Tue-Sun), constructed in 1865 and restored in 1979, was built by Hasan Talat, the accountant of governor-poet Ziya Paşa, for his sister, Hazeran Hanım. The restored rooms are beautifully furnished in period style, with a refined feel to their chandeliers and

carved wood, and have mannequins to illustrate their use. The Directorate of Fine Arts gallery in the basement has changing exhibitions.

FREE **Harşena Castle**   CITADEL
(Kale) Perched precariously atop rocky Mt Harşena, the *kale* offers magnificent views down the valley. The remnants of the walls

date from Pontic times, perhaps around King Mithridates' reign, but a fort stood here from the early Bronze Age. Destroyed and repaired by several empires, it had eight defensive layers descending 300m to the Yeşilırmak river, and a tunnel with 150 steps cut into the mountain.

Although the *kale* is popular with families, travellers of either sex are advised not to go up unaccompanied later in the day. To reach the castle turn left when you get to the Büyük Ağa Medresesi and follow the road for about 1km to a street on the left marked 'Kale'. It's 1.7km up the mountainside to a car park, then another steep 15-minute climb to the summit.

Büyük Ağa Medresesi   MEDRESE

The impressive Büyük Ağa Medresesi (1488) has an octagonal layout, rarely seen in Ottoman *medrese* architecture. It was built by Sultan Beyazıt II's chief white eunuch Hüseyin Ağa, also known as Grandagha. It still serves as a seminary for boys who are training to be *hafız* (theologians who have memorised the entire Koran) and is not open to the public.

SOUTH OF THE RIVER

TOP
CHOICE **Amasya Museum**   MUSEUM

(☏218 4513; Atatürk Caddesi; admission ₺3; ⊙8.15am-noon & 1-4.45pm) The first floor of this superb museum packs in beautifully laid out exhibits detailing Amasya and the surrounding area during the Bronze Age, Hittite, Pontic and Roman eras. Look out for the famous Statuette of Amasya, a bronze figure of the Hittite storm god Teshub, with a conical hat and almond-shaped eyes. All the displays have detailed information panels in English. Upstairs the extensive collection continues into later periods, with unwieldy manuscripts, Ottoman artefacts and an armoury of flintlock guns among the displays. In the middle of the room, the original wooden doors from Amasya's Gök Medrese Camii show the progression between Seljuk and Ottoman carving.

Also upstairs is the highlight of the museum. Housed in a separate room is a unique collection of mummies dating from the 14th-century İlkhan period. The bodies, mummified without removing the organs, were discovered beneath the Burmalı Minare Camii. Be warned that none of it is suitable for squeamish or young eyes.

Sabuncuoğlu History of Medicine Museum   MUSEUM

(Darüşşifa; Mustafa Kemal Bulvarı; admission ₺4; ⊙Tue-Sun 9am-5pm) Built as a mental hospital in 1309 by Ilduş Hatun, wife of the İlkhanid Sultan Olcaytu, the Darüşşifa (or Bimarhane) may have been the first place to try to treat pychiatric disorders with music. The İlkhans were the successors to Genghis Khan's Mongols, who had defeated the Anatolian Seljuks. Their architecture reflects motifs borrowed from many conquered peoples, and the building is based on the plan of a Seljuk *medrese*.

The building was used as a hospital until the 18th century. One of the most important physicians who worked here was Serefedin Sabuncuoğlu; the rooms surrounding the courtyard are dedicated to exhibits of his work. The small collection includes surgical equipment and some fascinating (and rather graphic) illustrations of treatments and surgeries to cure reproductive illnesses.

Sultan Beyazıt II Camii   MOSQUE

(Ziyapaşa Bulvarı) The graceful Sultan Beyazıt II Camii (1486) is Amasya's largest *külliye* (mosque complex), with a *medrese*, fountain, *imaret* (soup kitchen) and library. The mosque's main door, *mihrab* (niche in a minaret indicating the direction of Mecca) and pulpit are made of white marble and its windows feature *kündekari* (interlocking wooden carvings).

Gök Medrese Camii   MOSQUE

(Mosque of the Sky Blue Seminary; Atatürk Caddesi) The Gök Medrese Camii was built from 1266 to 1267 for Seyfettin Torumtay, the Seljuk governor of Amasya. The *eyvan* (vaulted recess) serving as its main portal is unique in Anatolia, while the *kümbet* (domed tomb) was once covered in *gök* (sky blue) tiles, hence the name.

Mehmet Paşa Camii   MOSQUE

(Mustafa Kemal Bulvarı) The pretty Mehmet Paşa Camii was built in 1486 by Lala Mehmet Paşa, tutor to Şehzade Ahmet, the son of Sultan Beyazıt II. Don't miss the beautiful marble *mimber* (pulpit). The complex originally included the builder's tomb, an *imaret*, *tabhane* (hostel), hamam and *handan* (inn).

Beyazıt Paşa Camii   MOSQUE

(Mustafa Kemal Bulvarı) This early Ottoman mosque (1419) follows a twin-domed plan that was a forebear in style to the famous

Yeşil Cami in Bursa. It's closed except at prayer times, but its most interesting features are external anyway.

Gümüşlü Cami
MOSQUE

(Silvery Mosque; Meydanı, Atatürk Caddesi) The Gümüşlü Cami (1326) is the earliest Ottoman mosque in Amasya but has been rebuilt several times; in 1491 after an earthquake, in 1612 after a fire and again in 1688. It was added to in 1903 and restored again in 1988.

Activities

Hamams
HAMAMS

Amasya has several venerable hamams that are still in operation. The Yıldız Hamamı (Star Hamam; Hazeranlar Sokak; wash & massage ₺13) was built by a Seljuk commander in the 13th century and restored in the 16th century. On the southern side of the river is the Ottoman Mustafa Bey Hamamı (Mustafa Kemal Bulvarı; wash & massage ₺12), built in 1436. Both are open from about 6am to 10am and 4pm to 11pm for men; from 10am to 4pm for women.

Sleeping

TOP CHOICE Gönül Sefası
GUEST HOUSE €€

(☏212 9461; Yalıboyu Sokak 24; s/d/tr ₺60/100/120) Antique farming equipment decorates the courtyard while Ottoman curios swing from every nook in the little restaurant, adding lots of local character to this family-run hotel. Upstairs the four large rooms are kept elegantly simple with comfy beds and modern bathrooms. Grab one of the two hosting teensy balconies over the Yeşilırmak river to make the most of this delightfully dinky place.

Emin Efendi Konağı
HISTORIC HOTEL €€

(☏213 0033; www.eminefendikonaklari.com; Hazeranlar Sokak 66-85; s/d ₺80/130/150; ❀🛜) Brought to life by one of Amasya's oldest families, the Emin Efendi is the hot hotel for northern Turkey's weekend elite. The lobby is a picture of stately elegance though the rooms (eight have river views) are a mixed bag of classic and modern styling that doesn't really gel. The courtyard restaurant (mains ₺9 to ₺19) is the place for fine dining.

Şükrübey Konağı
GUESTHOUSE €€

(☏212 6285; www.sukrubeykonagi.com.tr; Hazeranlar Sokak 55; s/d ₺60/120) A sweet family choice with simple, cosy rooms set around a courtyard, Şükrübey is a winner for its genuinely warm and welcoming atmosphere. Rooms lead out to narrow balconies with views of either the courtyard or the Yeşilırmak river.

Harşena Otel
HISTORIC HOTEL €€

(☏218 3979; www.harsenaotel.com; Hatuniye Mahallesi; new house s/d/tr ₺95/160/180, old house s/d ₺180/220 ; ❀) Well-maintained and comfortable though the old house, backing onto the Yeşilırmak river, is the real star.

Konfor Palas Hotel
HOTEL €

(☏218 1260; www.konforpalas.com; Ziyapaşa Bulvarı 2c; s/d/tr ₺40/65/85) Comfortable enough if you overlook the stained carpets and minor design flaws.

Eating & Drinking

Amasya's best eating is found in its hotels but there are a few reasonable cafes and restaurants in Hatuniye Mahallesi and a smattering of more basic options around town. Amasya is famed for its apples, which give autumn visitors one more thing to sink their teeth into.

Strabon Restaurant
MODERN TURKISH €€

(☏212 4012; Teyfik Havız Sokak ; mains ₺7-16) Our favourite riverside deck in Amasya. The hot or cold mezes (₺5 to ₺9) are tasty and fresh; the meat grills and grilled *balik* (fish) are low on oil and literally fall off big serving plates. If you're not hungry, Strabon doubles as a fun venue for drinking booze.

Amasya Şehir Derneği
TURKISH €€

(Teyfik Havız Sokak; mains ₺8-16) Beloved by a suited-and-booted clientele, this popular restaurant has three tiers to choose from and a menu of typical Turkish grills. The balcony is the place to be, especially in the evening when the river views provide a respite from the live music 'entertainment' inside.

Eylül Buğusa Avlu
TURKISH €€

(Hazeranlar Sokak ; mains ₺8-15) It may have no view, but this shaded courtyard is a pleasant spot for a meal or a couple of beers. The menu sticks to Turkish staples and the soundtrack is a blast-from-the-past of '80s hits.

Ali Kaya Restaurant
TURKISH €€

(☏218 1505; Çakallar Mevkii; mains ₺12; ⏱noon-11pm) Perched on a hill, this simple, licensed restaurant is perfect for sunset dining, when you can recharge with meze after the steep climb while taking in views of the town and the tombs. Taxis will ferry you up for ₺8.

Seyran Cafe
NARGILE CAFE

(Hazeranlar Sokak) The coveted seating is on the tiny balcony of this mellow cafe.

ℹ Information

Tourist Office (Alçak Köprüsü)

ℹ Getting There & Away

The **otogar** (Atatürk Caddesi) has daily services to locations including Ankara (₺30, five hours), Çorum (₺8, two hours), İstanbul (₺50, 11 hours), Kayseri (₺45, eight hours), Nevşehir (₺50, nine hours), Samsun (₺15, 2½ hours), Sivas (₺30, 3½ hours) and Tokat (₺15, two hours).

Amasya **train station** (☑218 1239; İstasyon Caddesi ; ⊙4am-10pm) is served by daily local trains to Samsun (₺6, three hours, 4.55am and 8.40am) and Sivas (₺11, 5½ hours, 2.25pm).

Tokat

☑0356 / POP 132,300

Locals claim you can hear the steps of civilisations creeping up behind you in Tokat, where history buffs gorge themselves on the mosques, mansions, hamams and *hans* in this ancient town at the heart of Anatolia. Others come for the famed Tokat kebap – a delectable mess of lamb and vegetables – then wash their greasy hands in the river that splits the town in two.

Physically on the rise due to seven centuries of sodden silt, Tokat's booming antique trade and architectural treats guarantee the town won't sink into obscurity any time soon.

You can easily spend a day rummaging through the *yazma* (headscarf) and copperware stalls, or getting knuckled by Tokat's notorious masseurs.

◉ Sights & Activities

TOP CHOICE Gök Medrese
HISTORIC BUILDING

(Blue Seminary; GOP Bulvarı; admission ₺3; ⊙8am-noon & 1-5pm Tue-Sun) Constructed after the fall of the Seljuks and the coming of the Mongols by Pervane Muhinedin Süleyman, a local potentate, the 13th-century Gök Medrese has also served as a hospital, a school and, today, Tokat's museum.

Very few of the building's *gök* (sky blue) tiles are left on the facade, but there are enough on the interior courtyard walls to give an idea of what it must have looked like in its glory days.

Although the courtyard is the highlight of the museum, the collection packs in Roman tombs, Seljuk carpets, Hellenic jewellery and local folkloric dresses, with informative signs in English. Look out for Bronze Age and Hittite artefacts, icons and relics from Tokat's churches (including a Greek Orthodox representation of John the Baptist with his head on a platter) and dervish ceremonial tools and weapons.

The seminary contains the **Tomb of 40 Maidens** (Kırkkızlar Türbesi; 1275), actually an assembly of 20 tombs, possibly of the seminary's founders, though another theory is that they are the tombs of 40 nurses who worked here.

FREE Mevlevihane
MUSEUM

(Bey Sokağı; ⊙9am-5pm) Turn left on GOP Bulvarı just before Latifoğlu Konağı and cross the canal to get to this restored dervish lodge, built in 1613 by Muslu Ağa, vizier to Sultan Ahmet I (r 1603-17). One of the most tranquil corners of Tokat, the building is set inside a small garden compound in a neighbourhood of cobbled streets and Ottoman houses buckling under the weight of years.

The exhibits inside include metalwork, illustrated Korans and prayer carpets gathered from mosques throughout the region. The *semahane* (where whirling ceremonies were held) is upstairs. The room contains an interesting collection of dervish paraphernalia but the effect is unfortunately tarnished by the tacky mannequins illustrating the *sema*.

Follow the garden path round to the back of the building to get to **Muslu Ağa Köşkü**, which the vizier used as his family residence.

Just outside, back across the canal, is Tokat's **Ottoman Clock Tower**; the numbers on its faces are in Arabic.

FREE Sulusokak Caddesi
NEIGHBOURHOOD

Many of Tokat's old buildings still survive, though in ruins, along Sulusokak Caddesi, which was the main thoroughfare before the perpendicular Samsun–Sivas road was improved in the 1960s.

Sulusokak Caddesi runs west from the north side of Cumhuriyet Meydanı on GOP Bulvarı, past **Ali Paşa Camii** (1572), which has classical Ottoman features on its grand central dome. Continue along the road and on the right you'll see the tiny **Ali Tusi Türbesi** (1233), a brick Seljuk work that incorporates some fine blue tiles.

AUBERGINE DREAM

The Tokat kebap is made up of skewers of lamb and sliced aubergine (eggplant) hung vertically, then baked in a wood-fired oven. Tomatoes and peppers, which take less time to cook, are baked on separate skewers. As the lamb cooks, it releases juices that baste the aubergine. All these goodies are then served together with a huge fist of roasted garlic, adding an extra punch to the mix.

It's almost worth coming to Tokat just to sample the dish, and in fact you might have to; it's inexplicably failed to catch on in places much further afield than Sivas or Amasya, and Tokat's chefs do it best anyway. Standard aubergine döners that crop up are a far cry from the glorious blow-out of the original.

Further on, on the same side of the road, the brick-and-wood **Sulu Han** is still in use with its interior painted turquoise and white. This 17th-century Ottoman caravanserai provided accommodation for merchants visiting the **Arastalı Bedesten** (covered market) next door, which has been superbly reconstructed. Right after the *bedesten* is the 16th-century **Takyeciler Camii**, displaying the nine-domed style of great Ottoman mosques.

Across the road from the *bedesten* are two spectacular buildings that are currently being restored: the **Yağıbasan Medresisi** (1152), one of Anatolia's first open-domed *medreses*, and beside it the enormous bulk of the 16th-century Ottoman **Deveciler Hanı**, one of Tokat's finest caravanserais.

Carry on up the road and you'll come to the tiny 14th-century **Kadı Hasan Camii** and the Ottoman **Paşa Hamamı** (1434).

FREE **Taş Han & Around**   ARCHITECTURE
(GOP Bulvarı; ⏰8am-8pm) Virtually next door to the Gök Medrese is the 17th-century Taş Han, an Ottoman caravanserai and workshop with a cafe in the courtyard. Two floors of shops sell a mixture of local garb and copperware, and paintings of sailboats and doe-eyed puppies.

Behind the Taş Han are streets lined with old half-timbered **Ottoman houses**. There are more shops in this area; some of the designs you see on *yazmas*, kilims and carpets were assimilated from Afghan refugees who settled here during the Soviet invasion of Afghanistan in the 1980s.

In the fruit and vegetable market, across GOP Bulvarı from the Taş Han, stand the **Hatuniye Camii** and ruined *medrese*, dating from 1485 and the reign of Sultan Beyazıt II.

A few hundred metres north of the Taş Han, behind some plastic sandal stands on the same side of the street, look out for **Sümbül Baba Türbesi** (1291), an octagonal Seljuk tomb. Beside it a road leads up for around 1km to the **citadel**, built in the 5th century and restored during the Seljuk and Ottoman eras. Little remains but the fine view, and women travellers should not go up alone.

FREE **Latifoğlu Konağı**   MUSEUM
(GOP Bulvarı) Two blocks south of Cumhuriyet Meydanı, the splendid 19th-century Latifoğlu Konağı is a fine example of baroque architecture in the Ottoman style. The rooms have been restored to their former finery with elaborately carved wood ceilings and intricately embellished plasterwork detail.

Ali Paşa Hamam   HAMAM
(GOP Bulvarı; ⏰5am-11pm for men, 9am-5pm for women) These baths, under domes studded with glass bulbs to admit natural light, were built in 1572 for Ali Paşa, one of the sons of Süleyman the Magnificent. They have separate bathing areas for men and women, and the full works should cost around ₺15.

🛏 Sleeping

Otel Yeni Çınar   HOTEL €€
(📞214 0066; GOP Bulvarı 167; s/d/tr ₺60/100/120; ❄🛜) We get the feeling the owner likes blue. Rooms big enough to throw a party in harbour turquoise-painted furniture and navy carpets. Some have unique features such as fat columns slap bang in the middle of the room which may or may not have some structural use. Maybe the owner just likes columns too? A good choice, with helpful staff, as long as you don't mind the obvious wear and tear – and aren't feeling blue.

Çavuşoğlu Otel HOTEL €
(213 0908; GOP Bulvarı 168; s/d ₺45/80; ❄🌐) The price is right at this central bargain. Large rooms have had a fresh lick of paint so they aren't looking too tired. There's fast wi-fi, hairdryers in the bathrooms and the towels are nice and new.

✖ Eating & Drinking

Yeşil Köşe Restaurant TURKISH €€
(GOP Bulvarı; mains ₺5-12) One of the best places to try a Tokat kebap, this friendly, popular joint also does a fine line in other kebaps, moussaka and çorba. It's next to the Ali Paşa Hamam.

Hocaoğlu Kebap KEBAP €€
(Cumhuriyet Meydanı; meal ₺14) You'll have to be rolled out of this cheerful kebapçı which serves up fresh and crunchy salad meze before presenting you with your massive main. It's next to Metro bus office.

Konak Café CAFE
(214 4146; GOP Bulvarı; mains ₺4-15; ⊙9am-11pm) At the rear of the Latifoğlu Konağı, this friendly cafe has multilevel outdoor shaded seating to lounge out on after stomping all those historic streets. The menu does the usual köftes and kebaps but it's a good place to just chill out with a juice and puff on a nargile as well.

❶ Information

Tourist Office (211 8252; Taş Han, GOP Bulvarı 138/I; ⊙8am-5pm) An informative Tokat brochure and map in English is available.

❶ Getting There & Away

Tokat's small **otogar** (Gültekin Topçam Bulvarı) is about 1.7km northeast of the main square. Bus companies should provide a *servis* to ferry you to/from town; otherwise, if you don't want to wait for a dolmuş, a taxi will cost about ₺10.

Several bus companies have ticket offices around Cumhuriyet Meydanı.

There are regular buses to Amasya (₺15, two hours), Ankara (₺45, 7½ hours), İstanbul (₺60, 12 hours), Samsun (₺25, three hours) and Sivas (₺15, 1½ hours).

Local minibuses leave from the separate İlçe ve Köy terminal, one block east from the Taş Han.

Around Tokat

The **Ballıca Cave** (Ballıca Mağarası; 0356-261 4236; adult/child ₺4/2; ⊙daylight hr), 26km west of Tokat, is one of Turkey's most famous caves. The limestone labyrinth, 3.4-million-years-old and 8km long (680m is open to the public), bristles with rock formations such as onion-shaped stalactites and mushroom-like stalagmites. Smugglers used to live here and the squeaks of the current residents, dwarf bats, add to the atmosphere created by dripping water.

Unfortunately, the ambience is quickly lost if you share the metal walkways with many others and with its copious lighting and signposts, the cave can feel like an underground theme park.

The views from the cafe at the entrance are stunning, but its toilets are not the cleanest in Anatolia.

Returning, pause in Pazar to inspect the beautiful remains of a Seljuk han on the way out of town on the Tokat road. You can wait outside it for minibuses to Tokat.

❶ Getting There & Away

To get to Ballıca, take a minibus from Tokat's İlçe ve Köy minibus terminal to Pazar (₺2.50, 40 minutes), where a taxi will be waiting to run you up the winding country road to the cave (8km). Drivers exploit their captive audience and you may have to pay as much as ₺30 return (including an hour's waiting time). If you are driving from Amasya, Pazar is signposted 14km south of the main road to Tokat.

Sivas

0346 / POP 310,647
With a colourful, sometimes tragic history and some of the finest Seljuk buildings ever erected, Sivas is a good stopover en route to the wild east. The city lies at the heart of Turkey politically as well as geographically, thanks to its role in the run-up to the War of Independence. The Congress building resounded with plans, strategies and principles as Atatürk and his adherents discussed their great goal of liberation. The Turkish hero commented: 'Here is where we laid the foundations of our republic'. At night, as the red flags on the meydan (town square) compete for attention with the spotlit minarets nearby, İnönü Bulvarı might be central Anatolia's slickest thoroughfare outside Ankara. The occasional horse and cart gallops down the boulevard, past the neon lights, like a ghost of Anatolia's past.

History
The tumulus at nearby Maltepe shows evidence of settlement as early as 2600 BC, but

Sivas

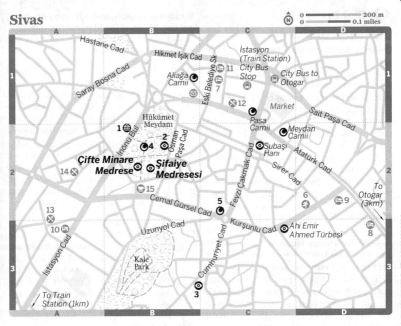

N   0 ———————— 200 m
    0 ———————— 0.1 miles

Sivas

◎ Top Sights

Çifte Minare Medrese	B2
Şifaiye Medresesi	B2

◎ Sights

1 Atatürk Congress & Ethnography Museum	B2
2 Bürüciye Medresesi	B2
3 Gök Medrese	B3
4 Kale Camii	B2
5 Ulu Cami	C2

✦ Activities, Courses & Tours

6 Kurşunlu Hamam	D2

▣ Sleeping

7 Eray Pansiyon	C1
8 Hotel Nevv	D3
9 Otel Fatih	D2
10 Sivas Büyük Otel	A3
11 Sultan Otel	C1

✕ Eating

12 Büyük Merkez Lokantası	C1
13 Perde Café	A2
14 Sema Hanımın Yeri	A2

☕ Drinking

15 Sıla Cafe	B2

Sivas itself was probably founded by the Hittite king Hattushilish I around 1500 BC. It was ruled in turn by the Assyrians, Medes and Persians, before coming under the sway of the kings of Cappadocia and Pontus. Eventually the city fell to the Romans, who called it Megalopolis; this was later changed to Sebastea, then shortened to Sivas by the Turks.

The Seljuks and the Danışmends slogged it out for supremacy here between 1152 and 1175 until the Seljuks finally prevailed, only to be dispossessed by the Mongol invasion of 1243. The İlkhanids succeeded the Mongols, and the city was then grabbed by the Ottomans (1398), Tamerlane (1400) and the Ottomans again (1408).

More recently Sivas was the location for the famous Sivas Congress in September 1919. Seeking to consolidate Turkish resistance to the Allied occupation and partition of his country, Atatürk arrived here from Samsun and Amasya, and gathered delegates to confirm decisions made at the Erzurum Congress. The two congresses heralded the War of Independence.

⊙ Sights

TOP CHOICE **Şifaiye Medresesi** MEDRESE

(Hükümet Meydanı; admission free) Built in 1218, this was one of the most important medical schools built by the Seljuks and was once Anatolia's foremost hospital.

Look to the right as you enter the courtyard to see the porch that was walled up as a tomb for Sultan İzzettin Keykavus I, who commissioned the building before he died of tuberculosis.

The decoration features stylised sun/lion and moon/bull motifs, beautiful blue Azeri tile work and a poem in Arabic composed by the sultan. The main courtyard has four *eyvans* (vaulted halls), with sun and moon symbols on either side of the eastern one.

TOP CHOICE **Çifte Minare Medrese** MEDRESE

(Seminary of the Twin Minarets; Hükümet Meydanı; admission free) Commissioned by the Mongol-İlkhanid vizier Şemsettin Güveyni after defeating the Seljuks at the battle of Kösedağ, the Çifte Minare Medrese (1271) has a *çifte* (pair) of mighty minarets. In fact, that's about all that is left, along with the elaborate portal and facade. Stand on the path between the Çifte and Şifaiye medreses to see the difference made by half a century and a shift in power.

FREE **Kale Camii &
Bürüciye Medresesi** HISTORIC BUILDINGS

(Hükümet Meydanı) The squat Ottoman **Kale Camii** (Hükümet Meydanı; 1580) was constructed by Sultan Murat III's grand vizier Mahmut Paşa.

Just east of the Kale Camii, reached through a monumental Seljuk gateway, is the **Bürüciye Medresesi** (Hükümet Meydanı), built to teach 'positive sciences' in 1271 by Iranian businessman Muzaffer Bürücerdi, whose tiled tomb is inside. The tea garden in the courtyard, where exhibitions are held, is good for a çay in the evening, when spotlights illuminate the building.

Gök Medrese MEDRESE

(Sky Blue Seminary; Cumhuriyet Caddesi) Although it's currently undergoing restoration, you can still view the twin minarets and facade of the glorious **Gök Medrese** from outside. It was built in 1271 at the behest of Sahib-i Ata, the grand vizier of Sultan Gıyasettin Keyhüsrev III, who funded Konya's Sahib-i Ata mosque complex. The facade is exuberantly decorated with tiles,

brickwork designs and carvings, covering not just the usual inlaid portal but the walls as well. The blue tile work on the minarets gave the school its name.

Ulu Cami MOSQUE

(Great Mosque; Cemal Gürsel Caddesi) The Ulu Cami (1197) is Sivas' oldest significant building, and one of Anatolia's oldest mosques. Built by the Danışmends, it's a large, low room with a forest of 50 columns. The superfat leaning brick minaret was added in 1213. Inside, 11 handmade stone bands surround the main praying area and the ornate *mihrab* was discovered during renovations in 1955. It has a certain old-Anatolian charm, slightly marred by modern additions.

**Atatürk Congress &
Ethnography Museum** MUSEUM

(Atatürk Kongre ve Etnografya Müzesi; İnönü Bulvarı; admission ₺3; ⊗8.30am-noon & 1.30-5pm Tue-Sun) This imposing Ottoman school building hosted the Sivas Congress in 1919. Today it's a museum with an extensive Ottoman ethnographical collection (enter via the rear).

🏃 Activities

Kurşunlu Hamam HAMAM

(☑for men 222 1378, for women 221 4790; Kurşunlu Caddesi; soak & scrub ₺15; ⊗7am-11pm for men, 9am-6pm for women) Built in 1576 this huge, multiple-domed structure had the indignity of being put to work as a salt warehouse for 30 years before it was restored to its former glory and put back into service as a hamam. There are separate men's and women's sections.

🛏 Sleeping

TOP CHOICE **Sultan Otel** HOTEL €€

(☑221 2986; www.sultanotel.com.tr; Eski Belediye Sokak 18; s/d/ste ₺95/160/220; ❄🛜) A recent revamp puts the Sultan miles ahead of other hotels in town. Rooms have been brushed up with swanky fixtures and furnishings in soft sage and neutral tones, while bathrooms are sparkling and modern. It's all squeaky-clean and professionally run with a rooftop bar-restaurant and extensive breakfast buffet to add to the mix.

Hotel Nevv HOTEL €€

(☑221 6363; www.hotelnevv.com.tr; Atatürk Caddesi 96; s/d/tr ₺90/140/180 ; ❄🛜) Except for the odd crack in the uneven paintwork, the Nevv is a good deal. Rooms are brightened by lots of green accents and are decent-sized, modern bathrooms to boot.

SİVAS MASSACRE

Sivas' Otel Madımak was the site of one of modern Turkey's worst hate crimes, on 2 July 1993, when 37 Alevi intellectuals and artists were burned alive in a mob arson attack. The victims, who had come for a cultural festival, included Aziz Nesin, the Turkish publisher of Salman Rushdie's *Satanic Verses*. A crowd of 1000 extreme Islamist demonstrators gathered outside the hotel after Friday prayers to protest about the book's publication, and in the ensuing chaos the hotel was set alight and burned to the ground.

Despite continual calls from the victim's families for the site to be turned into a memorial, the Madımak was reopened and run as a hotel and kebap shop until 2010 when the government purchased the building. In 2011 it reopened as a children's science and cultural education centre with a small memorial corner that lists the names of those who died.

The scars from the tragedy show no signs of fading, though. Every year, on the anniversary, demonstrators gather at the site in remembrance and many of the victim's families and supporters still say that justice has yet to be served. In March 2012 five further suspects in the attack had the case against them dropped due to the statute of limitations. Of the 190 people initially charged for their role in the attack only 31 are still in prison, serving sentences of life imprisonment.

Sivas Büyük Otel   LUXURY HOTEL €€€
(📞225 4763; www.sivasbuyukotel.com; İstasyon Caddesi; s/d/ ₺150/240; ❈ 🛜) The city's original luxury hotel is a seven-storey block with its own hamam and rooms of old-fashioned, regal elegance. Unfortunately service lets the side down by being a tad frosty.

Otel Fatih   HOTEL €
(📞223 4313; www.fatihoteli.com; Kurşunlu Caddesi; s/d/ ₺60/75; 🛜) Amid a row of cheap hotels, the Fatih wouldn't win any style awards, but its decent-sized rooms come with good bathrooms and staff are used to seeing the occasional foreigner walk through the door.

Eray Pansiyon   PENSION €
(📞223 1647; www.eraypansiyon.com; Eski Belediye Sokak 12; dm per person ₺20; 🛜) One of few communal dorm rooms in Central Anatolia. Sturdy brown doors lead to clean six-bed dorms, which are often unoccupied. The friendly owner speaks German.

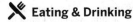 **Eating & Drinking**

TOP 🏆 **Sema Hanımın Yeri**   ANATOLIAN €
(📞223 9496; İstaasyon Caddesi Öncu Market; mains ₺3.50-6; ⏰8am-midnight) In this rustic, wood-panelled restaurant, the welcoming Madame Sema serves home-cooked food such as *içli köfte* (meatballs stuffed with spices and nuts).

Perde Café   CAFE €
(📞223 2321; İstasyon Caddesi; snacks ₺3-7; ⏰10am-11pm) This two-storey hangout for university students feels like a fun secret everybody's keeping. Milkshakes, boardgames, burgers and waffles are the favourites.

Büyük Merkez Lokantası   TURKISH €
(📞223 2354; Atatürk Caddesi; mains ₺7; ⏰4am-midnight) This popular *lokanta* gets packed out at lunchtime. Try the house speciality, *sebzeli Sivas kebapı* (a local take on the Tokat kebap, ₺14).

Sıla Cafe   CAFE
(Hükümet Meydanı) This tiny cafe pumps out good music and serves up coffee to arty university types.

ℹ Information
Toraman İnternet (off Hükümet Meydanı; per hour ₺1; ⏰10am-late)

ℹ Getting There & Away
Bus
Bus services from Sivas aren't all that frequent. From the otogar (₺10 from the city centre by taxi) there are fairly regular services to Amasya (₺20, 3½ hours), Ankara (₺35, seven hours), İstanbul (₺60, 13 hours), Kayseri (₺20, three hours), Samsun (₺30, six hours) and Tokat (₺15, 1½ hours).

Buses should provide a *servis* into the city centre. Otherwise, catch any city bus heading to the city centre from their terminal, next to the otogar. Buses head up Atatürk Caddesi and end their run just uphill from the Paşa Camii.

Train
Sivas **train station** (📞221 7000; İstasyon Caddesi) is a major rail junction for both east–west and north–south lines. The main express services are the Doğu Ekspresi (to Kars,

daily, 16 hours) and the 4 Eylül Mavi Tren (to Diyarbakır, daily, 12 hours). There are also local services to Kangal, Divriği and Amasya.

Around Sivas

The place where the fish-pedicure craze has it origins, bathing at **Balıklı Kaplıca** (Hot Springs with Fish; ☑469 1151; www.balikli.org; visitor/patient ₺7.50/50; ☉8am-5pm) is a satisfyingly unusual experience. According to local lore a shepherd boy discovered the healing qualities of the local mineral water here, high in the dermatologically curative element selenium, and noticed that the warm water was inhabited by 'doctor fish' which sloughed dead skin off any body part you offered them. The fish supposedly favour psoriasis-inflicted skin and the spa attracts patients from all over the world, but the swarming school happily gets stuck into any patch of flesh. It is wonderfully therapeutic to dangle your feet in the water and feel nature giving you a thorough pedicure, with the nippers tickling and then soothing like tiny vacuum cleaners.

The spa complex has six segregated pools set amid trees, a cafe above the mineral water and the **Balıklı Kaplıca Hotel** (☑469 1151; www.balikli.org; s/d ₺110/140; ❄☎❄) with a buffet restaurant. Rates depend on whether you define yourself as 'visitor' or 'patient'; the recommended course for genuine patients is eight hours a day in the pool for three weeks. About 12km southwest of the resort is the tiny service town of Kangal which gave its name to the black-faced, pale-bodied Kangal dogs seen throughout Turkey.

Dolmuşes from the terminal beside Sivas' otogar run to Kangal (₺5, one hour); from there you can take a taxi to the resort (₺20). Balıklı Kaplıca offers group transfers from Sivas.

Konya

☑0332 / POP 1,073,791

Turkey's equivalent of the 'Bible Belt', Konya treads a delicate path between its historical significance as the home town of the whirling dervish orders and a bastion of Seljuk culture, and its modern importance as an economic boom town. The city derives considerable charm from this juxtaposition of old and new. Ancient mosques and the maze-like market district rub up against contemporary Konya around Alaaddin Tepesi, where hip-looking university students talk religion and politics in the tea gardens. If you are passing through this region, say from the coast to Cappadocia, bear in mind that the Mevlâna Museum is one of Turkey's finest and most characteristic sights.

History

Almost 4000 years ago the Hittites called this city 'Kuwanna'. It was Kowania to the Phrygians, Iconium to the Romans and then Konya to the Turks. Iconium was an important provincial town visited several times by Saints Paul and Barnabas.

From about 1150 to 1300 Konya was the capital of the Seljuk Sultanate of Rum, which encompassed most of Anatolia. The Seljuk sultans endowed Konya with dozens of fine buildings in an architectural style that was decidedly Turkish, but had its roots in Persia and Byzantium. Traditionally Konya lay at the heart of Turkey's rich farming 'bread basket', but these days light industry and pilgrimage tourism are at least as important.

◉ Sights

TOP CHOICE **Mevlâna Museum**   MUSEUM
(☑351 1215; admission ₺3, audio guide ₺5; ☉9am-5pm Tue-Sun, 10am-5pm Mon) For Muslims and non-Muslims alike, the main reason to come to Konya is to visit the Mevlâna Museum, the former lodge of the whirling dervishes.

Celaleddin Rumi, the Seljuk Sultanate of Rum, produced one of the world's great mystic philosophers. His poetry and religious writings, mostly in Persian, the literary language of the day, are among the most beloved and respected in the Islamic world. Rumi later became known as Mevlâna (Our Guide) to his followers.

Rumi was born in 1207 in Balkh (Afghanistan). His family fled the impending Mongol invasion by moving to Mecca and then to the Sultanate of Rum, reaching Konya by 1228. His father, Bahaeddin Veled, was a noted preacher, known as the Sultan of Scholars, and Rumi became a brilliant student of Islamic theology. After his father's death in 1231, he studied in Aleppo and Damascus, returning to live in Konya by 1240.

In 1244 he met Mehmet Şemseddin Tebrizi (Şemsi Tebrizi or Şems of Tabriz), one of his father's Sufi (Muslim mystic) disciples. Tebrizi had a profound influence on Rumi but, jealous of his overwhelming influence on their master, an angry crowd of Rumi's dis-

DON'T MISS

DIVINE DOORS OF DİVRİĞİ

The quadruplet of 780-year-old stone doorways on Divriği's **Ulu Cami & Darüşşifa** (Grand Mosque & Hospital; ⊘8am-5pm) complex are so intricately carved that some say their craftmanship proves the existence of god.

Although the sleepy settlement of Divriği seems an obscure place for one of Turkey's finest old religious structures, this was once the capital of a Seljuk *beylik* (principality), ruled over by the local emir Ahmet Şah and his wife, Melike Turan Melik, who founded the adjoining institutions in 1228.

The entrances to both the Ulu Cami and the Darüşşifa are truly stupendous, their reliefs densely carved in such minute detail that it's hard to imagine the stone started out flat. It's the tasteful Seljuk equivalent of having a cinema in your house, the sort of thing only a provincial emir with more money than sense could have dreamt of building.

Entered through the 14m-high **Darüşşifa Gate**, the hospital (one of the oldest in Anatolia) is pervaded by an air of serenity. The vast domed inner courtyard is centred around an octagonal pool with a spiral run-off, which allowed the tinkle of running water to break the silence of the room and soothe patients' nerves. A platform raised above the main floor may have been for musicians who likewise soothed the patients. The building was used as a *medrese* from the 18th century.

Next door, the **West Gate** of the mosque is a riot of kilim motifs, rosettes and textured effects. Note the carvings of the two-headed eagles on the far sides of the gate. Inside the mosque is very simple with an intricately carved wooden *minbar* (a pulpit in a mosque) and unique *mihrab* (niche in a minaret indicating the direction of Mecca). On the northern side of the mosque is the spectacular **North Gate**, a dizzying cornucopia of floral designs, Arabic inscriptions, and a wealth of geometric patterns and medallions. Climb the stairs to the eastern side to view the smaller **Shah's Gate**.

Dolmuş services from Sivas leave from the terminal beside Sivas otogar at 9am, noon, 3pm and 5pm (₺15, 2½ hours), and from Divriği back to Sivas at 5am, 8.30am, noon and 4.30pm. All stop in Kangal. It is possible to see Balıklı Kaplıca and Divriği on the same day using public transport as long as you take the 9am bus and visit Balıklı Kaplıca first.

A return taxi from Sivas, stopping in Balıklı Kaplıca and Divriği, costs about ₺200. Take ID as there is sometimes a police checkpoint after Kangal.

Drivers should note that there's no through road to Erzincan from Divriği, forcing you to head northwest to Zara and the highway before you can start driving east.

---

ciples put Tebrizi to death in 1247. Stunned by the loss, Rumi withdrew from the world to meditate, and wrote his greatest poetic work, the 25,000-verse *Mathnawi* (*Mesnevi* in Turkish). He also wrote many aphorisms, *ruba'i* and *ghazal* poems, collected into his 'Great Opus', the *Divan-i Kebir*.

Tolerance is central to Mevlâna's teachings, as in this famous verse:

Come, whoever you may be,
Even if you may be
An infidel, a pagan, or a fire-worshipper, come.
Ours is not a brotherhood of despair.
Even if you have broken
Your vows of repentance a hundred times, come.

Rumi died on 17 December 1273, the date now known as his 'wedding night' with Allah. His son, Sultan Veled, organised his fol-lowers into the brotherhood called the Mevlevi, or whirling dervishes.

In the centuries following Mevlâna's death, over 100 dervish lodges were founded throughout the Ottoman domains. Dervish orders exerted considerable conservative influence on the country's political, social and economic life, and numerous Ottoman sultans were Mevlevi Sufis (mystics). Atatürk saw the dervishes as an obstacle to advancement for the Turkish people and banned them in 1925, but several orders survived on a technicality as religious fraternities. The Konya lodge was revived in 1957 as a 'cultural association' intended to preserve a historical tradition.

For Muslims, this is a very holy place, and more than 1.5 million people visit it a year, most of them Turkish. You will see many people praying for Rumi's help. When entering,

Konya

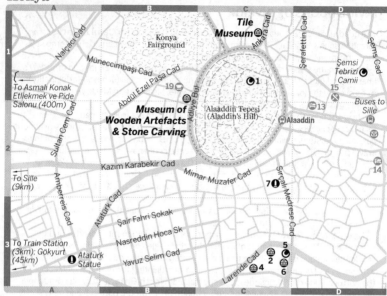

Konya

⦿ Top Sights

Mevlâna Museum	F2
Museum of Wooden Artefacts & Stone Carving	B1
Tile Museum	C1

◎ Sights

1	Alaaddin Camii	C1
2	Archaeological Museum	C3
3	Aziziye Camii	E2
4	Ethnographic Museum	C3
5	Sahib-i Ata Külliyesi	C3
6	Sahib-i Ata Vakıf Müzesi	C3
7	Sırçalı Medresi	C2

🛏 Sleeping

8	Derviş Otel	F2
9	Hotel Rumi	F2
10	Mevlâna Sema Otel	E2
11	Otel Derya	F2
12	Otel Mevlâna	E2
13	Selçuk Otel	D2
14	Ulusan Otel	D2

✕ Eating

15	Aydın Et Lokantası	D1
16	Gülbahçesi Konya Mutfağı	F2
17	Konak Konya Mutfağı	F3
18	Şifa Lokantası	E2

☕ Drinking

19	Osmanlı Çarşısı	B1

🛍 Shopping

20	Bazaar	E2
21	Ikonium	E2

women should cover their heads and shoulders, and no one should wear shorts.

The lodge is visible from some distance, its fluted dome of turquoise tiles one of Turkey's most distinctive sights. After walking through a pretty garden you pass through the *Dervişan Kapısı* (Gate of the Dervishes) and enter a courtyard with an ablutions fountain in the centre.

Remove your shoes and pass into the *Tilavet* (Koran reading room), also known as the calligraphy room due to its calligraphic displays.

At the entrance to the mausoleum, the Ottoman silver door bears the inscription, 'Those who enter here incomplete will come out perfect'. Entering the mausoleum, look out for the big bronze *Nisan tası* (April

The small mosque and *semahane* to the left of the sepulchral chamber contain exhibits such as musical instruments, the original copy of the *Mathnawi*, Mevlâna's prayer rug, and a 9th-century gazelle-skin Christian manuscript. There is a casket containing strands of Mohammed's beard, and a copy of the Koran so tiny that its author went blind writing it. Look to the left of the *mihrab* for a *seccade* (prayer carpet) bearing a picture of the Kaaba at Mecca. Made in Iran of silk and wool, it's extremely fine, with some three million knots (144 per square centimetre).

The *matbah* (kitchen) of the lodge is in the southwest corner of the courtyard. It is decorated as it would have been in Mevlâna's day, with mannequins dressed as dervishes. Look out for the wooden practice board, used by novice dervishes to learn to whirl. The dervish cells (where the dervishes lived) run along the northern and western sides of the courtyard. Inside are a host of ethnographical displays relating to dervish life.

Beside the museum is the **Selimiye Camii**, built between 1566 and 1574 when Sultan Selim II was the governor of Konya.

TOP CHOICE / **Tile Museum**　　　　MUSEUM
(Karatay Medresesi Çini Müzesi; ☑ 351 1914; Alaaddin Meydanı; admission ₺3; ⊙9am-5pm) Gorgeously restored, the interior central dome and walls of this former Seljuk theological school (1251) showcase some finely preserved blue and white Seljuk tilework. There is also an outstanding collection of ceramics on display including exhibits of the octagonal Seljuk tiles uneartherd during excavations at Kubad Abad Palace on Lake Beyşehir. Emir Celaleddin Karatay, a Seljuk general, vizier and statesman who built the *medrese*, is buried in one of the corner rooms.

TOP CHOICE / **Museum of Wooden Artefacts & Stone Carving**　　MUSEUM
(Taş ve Ahşap Eserler Müzesi; ☑ 351 3204; Adliye Bulvarı; admission ₺3; ⊙Tue-Sun 9am-5pm) The İnce Minare Medresesi (Seminary of the Slender Minaret), now the Museum of Wooden Artefacts and Stone Carving, was built in 1264 for Seljuk vizier Sahip Ata. Inside, many of the carvings feature motifs similar to those used in tiles and ceramics. The Seljuks didn't heed Islam's traditional prohibition of human and animal images: there are images of birds (the Seljuk double-headed eagle, for example), humans, lions and leopards.

bowl) on the left. April rainwater, vital to the farmers of this region, is still considered sacred and was collected in this 13th-century bowl. The tip of Mevlâna's turban was dipped in the water and offered to those in need of healing. Also on the left are six sarcophagi belonging to Bahaeddin Veled's supporters who followed him from Afghanistan.

Continue through to the part of the room directly under the fluted dome. Here you can see **Mevlâna's Tomb** (the largest), flanked by that of his son Sultan Veled and those of other eminent dervishes. They are all covered in velvet shrouds heavy with gold embroidery, but those of Mevlâna and Veled bear huge turbans, symbols of spiritual authority; the number of wraps denotes the level of spiritual importance. Bahaeddin Veled's wooden tomb stands on one end, leading devotees to say Mevlâna was so holy that even his father stands to show respect. There are 66 sarcophagi on the platform, not all visible.

Mevlâna's tomb dates from Seljuk times. The mosque and *semahane,* where whirling ceremonies were held, were added later by Ottoman sultans (Mehmet the Conqueror was a Mevlevi adherent and Süleyman the Magnificent made charitable donations to the order). Selim I, conqueror of Egypt, donated the Mamluk crystal lamps.

The octagonal minaret in turquoise relief outside is over 600 years old and gave the seminary its popular name. If it looks short, this is because the top was sliced off by lightning.

Sahib-i Ata Külliyesi MOSQUE COMPLEX
(Larende Caddesi; ⊘9am-noon & 1-5pm) Behind its requisite grand entrance with built-in minaret is the Sahib-i Ata Camii, originally constructed during the reign of Alaaddin Keykavus. Destroyed by fire in 1871, it was rebuilt in 13th-century style. The *mihrab* is a fine example of blue Seljuk tile work.

Around the corner, in the old dervish lodge, is the Sahib-i Ata Vakıf Müzesi (Sırçalı Medrese Caddesi; ⊘9am-5pm) with its red-brick and blue-tiled interior now home to an interesting collection of religious artefacts.

FREE **Sırçalı Medresi** MONUMENT
(Glass Seminary; Sırçalı Medresi Caddesi; ⊘8.30am-5.30pm) Sponsored by the Seljuk vizier Bedreddin Muhlis, the 13th-century Sırçalı Medrese was named after its tiled exterior. The *eyvan* on the western side of the courtyard was used for classes; it is decorated with blue tiles and its arch has a band of particularly fine calligraphic tile work.

Archaeological & Ethnographic Museums MUSEUMS
The rather dusty Archaeological Museum (☑351 3207; Larende Caddesi; admission ₺3; ⊘9am-12.30pm & 1.30-5pm Tue-Sun) houses finds from Çatalhöyük, including the skeleton of a baby girl, clutching jewellery made of stone and bone. Other artefacts range across the millennia, from Chalcolithic terracotta jars to Hittite hieroglyphs, an Assyrian oil lamp shaped like a bunch of grapes, and bronze and stone Roman sarcophagi, one narrating the labours of Hercules in high-relief carvings. Nearby, the little-visited Ethnographic Museum (Larende Caddesi; admission ₺3; ⊘8.30am-noon & 1.30-5.30pm Tue-Sun) has a good collection of Ottoman craftwork, including some keys the size of 21st-century doors.

FREE **Koyunoğlu Museum** MUSEUM
(Kerimler Caddesi 25; ⊘8.30am-5.30pm Tue-Sun) This curious museum contains the legacy of railway inspector Izzet Koyunoğlu who built up his esoteric collection of rare, er, collectables on his travels through Turkey. Our heart goes out to the tired-looking stuffed pelican, but there is a wonderful variety of exhibits, encompassing prehistoric bones, rhinoceros horn rosaries, boxwood spoons bearing words of wisdom about food, 19th-century carriage clocks, and old photos of Konya. Ask the guards to unlock the recreated Koyunoğlu Konya Evi, which shows how a well-heeled Konyalı family lived a century ago. Izzet lived in the original building with US$3 million of art around him.

Alaaddin Camii MOSQUE
(⊘8.30am-5.30pm) Konya's most important religious building after the Mevlâna shrine, this Seljuk mosque bestrides Alaaddin Tepesi. You may be able to wander in outside the listed opening hours. Built for Alaeddin Keykubad I, Sultan of Rum from 1219 to 1231, the rambling 13th-century building was designed by a Damascene architect in Arab style. Over the centuries it was embellished, refurbished, ruined and restored. The grand original entrance on the northern side incorporates decoration from earlier Byzantine and Roman buildings.

Aziziye Camii MOSQUE
Originally built in the 1670s and destroyed in a fire, this was rebuilt in 1875 in late Ottoman, baroque and rococo styles. Located in the bazaar, it has twin minarets with sheltered balconies, and a sign pointing out its interesting features.

✯✯ Festivals & Events

Mevlâna Festival FESTIVAL
(☑353 4020) The annual Mevlâna Festival runs for a fortnight, culminating on 17 December, the anniversary of Mevlâna's 'wedding night' with Allah. Tickets (and accommodation) should be booked well in advance; contact the tourist office for assistance. If you can't get a ticket, other venues around town host dancers during the festival, although they are not of the same quality.

🛏 Sleeping

There's certainly no shortage of hotels in Konya, but the steady flow of pilgrims can lead to high prices.

TOP CHOICE **Derviş Otel** BOUTIQUE HOTEL €€
(☑350 0842; www.dervishotel.com; Güngör Sokak 7; s/d/tr ₺100/160/210; ❄☎) This airy, light-filled 200-year-old house has been converted into a rather wonderful boutique hotel which has a taste of local character without scrimping on modern luxuries. All of the spacious seven rooms

WATCHING THE WHIRLING DERVİSHES

The Mevlevi worship ceremony, or *sema,* is a ritual dance representing union with God; it's what gives the dervishes their famous whirl, and appears on Unesco's third Proclamation of Masterpieces of the Oral and Intangible Heritage of Humanity. Watching a *sema* can be an evocative, romantic, unforgettable experience. There are many dervish orders world-wide that perform similar rituals, but the original Turkish version is the smoothest and purest, more of an elegant, trancelike dance than the raw energy seen elsewhere.

The dervishes dress in long white robes with full skirts that represent their shrouds. Their voluminous black cloaks symbolise their worldly tombs, their conical felt hats their tombstones.

The ceremony begins when the *hafız,* a scholar who has committed the entire Koran to memory, intones a prayer for Mevlâna and a verse from the Koran. A kettledrum booms out, followed by the plaintive sound of the *ney* (reed flute). Then the *şeyh* (master) bows and leads the dervishes in a circle around the hall. After three circuits, the dervishes drop their black cloaks to symbolise their deliverance from worldly attachments. Then one by one, arms folded on their breasts, they spin out onto the floor as they relinquish the earthly life to be reborn in mystical union with God.

By holding their right arms up, they receive the blessings of heaven, which are communicated to earth by holding their left arms turned down. As they whirl, they form a 'constellation' of revolving bodies, which itself slowly rotates. The *şeyh* walks among them to check that each dervish is performing the ritual properly.

The dance is repeated over and over again. Finally, the *hafız* again chants passages from the Koran, thus sealing the mystical union with God.

It's worthwhile planning your Konya trip to be here on a Saturday when the *sema* ceremony is performed at the **Mevlâna Culture Centre** (Whirling Dervish Performance; Aslanlı Kışla Caddesi; ☉9pm Sat). Those interested in learning more about the philosophy and beliefs of Sufis (Muslim mystics) can also attend a lecture on the teachings of Mevlâna beforehand at 8pm. There's usually no need to book but you might want to arrive early to guarantee your seat.

have lovely soft colour schemes with local carpets covering the wooden floors, very comfortable beds and super-modern bathrooms to boot. With enthusiastic management providing truly personal service this is a top-notch alternative to Konya's more anonymous hotels.

TOP CHOICE Ulusan Otel HOTEL €
(☎351 5004; Çarşi PTT Arkasi 4; s/d without bathroom ₺30/60; ☎) This little gem is the pick of the Konya cheapies. The rooms may be totally basic but they're bright and spotlessly clean. Shared bathrooms are immaculately kept (some rooms have private bathrooms) and the communal area is full of homely knick-knacks. The real bonus though is owner Ahmet, an enthusiastic and graceful host who really endeavours to please. An all-round gold-star backpacker choice.

Hotel Rumi HOTEL €€€
(☎353 1121; www.rumihotel.com; Durakfakih Sokak 5; s/d/tr/ste €60/90/110/130; ☀☎) Rooms at the Rumi are a tad on the small side but

are elegantly styled in soft mauves and sage green. Staff seem to delight in offering genuine service and the top-level breakfast room has killer views over to the Mevlâna Museum, across the road. An oasis of calm in central Konya.

Mevlâna Sema Otel HOTEL €€
(☎350 4623; www.semaotel.com; Mevlâna Caddesi 67; s/d ₺60/90; ☀☎) We're not sure what the decorators were thinking when they stuck the strange plaster mouldings all over the room walls, but if you can deal with that this is a safe, solid choice with a great location and friendly staff. Ask for a rear-facing room to avoid the din of the main road.

Otel Mevlâna HOTEL €
(☎352 0029; Cengaver Sokak 2; s/d/tr ₺50/70/90, s/d without bathroom ₺20/30 ; ☎) This budget bonanza has rooms with firm beds, a clutter of unmatched furniture, TV, kitchy paintings on the walls, and a fair amount of wear and tear. Across the road, the rooms without bathroom are seriously bare-bones basic.

Selçuk Otel
HOTEL €€

(☎353 2525; www.otelselcuk.com.tr; Babalık Sokak 4; s/d/tr €45/70/100; ✳🖥🛜) This grand old 4-star could do with a refurbishment but staff are super smiley and the large, old-fashioned rooms, decked out in shades of subtle cream and green, have a yesteryear charm.

Otel Derya
HOTEL €€

(☎352 0154; Ayanbey Sokak 18; s/d/tr ₺65/100/120; ✳🖥🛜) Undergoing some seriously snazzy-looking renovations when we visited, the Derya's rooms are sleekly comfortable with funky grey and chocolate accents and modern walk-in showers.

🍴 Eating & Drinking

Konya's speciality is *fırın* kebap, slices of (hopefully) tender, fairly greasy oven-roasted mutton served on puffy bread. The city bakers also make excellent fresh pide topped with minced lamb, cheese or eggs, but in Konya pide is called *etli ekmek* (bread with meat). Some restaurants around the Mevlâna Museum have great views, but their food is not recommended. The fast-food restaurants on Adilye Bulvarı, competing with the golden arches, are lively places for a snack, but check that the swift grub is thoroughly cooked.

TOP CHOICE Konak Konya Mutfağı
ANATOLIAN €€

(☎352 8547; Piriesat Caddesi 5; mains ₺8-16; ⏰11am-10pm) This excellent traditional restaurant is run by well-known food writer Nevin Halıcı, who puts her personal twist on Turkish classics. Grab an outside table to rub shoulders with vine-draped pillars and a fragrant rose garden. Aubergine aficionados shouldn't miss the *sebzeli közleme* (a grill of smoked aubergine and lamb) and sweet-tooths should definitely save room to try the unusual desserts.

Şifa Lokantası
KEBAP €

(☎352 0519; Mevlâna Caddesi 29; mains ₺6-14) Super-fast and super-friendly service keep this cheap and cheerful restaurant a surefire favourite. The pide is filling, fresh and tasty, and the kebaps are succulent and flavourful.

Gülbahçesı Konya Mutfağı
TURKISH €€

(☎351 0768; Gülbahçe Sokak 3; mains ₺8-18; ⏰8am-10pm) One of Konya's best restaurants, mostly because of its upstairs terrace with views of the Mevlâna Museum. Dishes include *yaprak sarma* (stuffed vine leaves), Adana kebab and *etli ekmek*.

Aydın Et Lokantası
TURKISH €

(☎351 9183; Şeyh Ziya Sokak 5e; mains ₺4.50-7) The fake oak tree, with ailing goldfish in the pool at its base, may be gaudy but a good array of Turkish staples are on offer and the menu has English translations.

Asmalı Konak Etliekmek ve Pide Salonu
TURKISH €

(☎322 7175; Babalık Mahallesi, Yahya Çavuş Caddesi 11/B; mains ₺3-6; ⏰8am-10pm) This tiny backstreet eatery rightfully claims the mantle of best *köfte* in Konya. The pides and salads aren't far behind either.

Osmanlı Çarşısı
CAFE

(☎353 3257; İnce Minare Sokak) An atmospheric early-20th century house with terraces, pavement seating and cushions galore where students talk politics while sucking on nargile.

🛍 Shopping

Bazaar
MARKET

Konya's bazaar sprawls back from the PTT building virtually all the way to the Mevlâna Museum, cramming the narrow streets with stalls, roving vendors and the occasional horse-drawn cart. There's a concentration of shops selling religious paraphernalia and tacky souvenirs at the Mevlâna Museum end.

Ikonium
HANDICRAFTS

(☎350 2895; www.thefeltmaker.net; Bostan Çelebi Sokak 12a) Konya was traditionally a felt-making centre but the art is fast dying out in Turkey. Passionate *keçeki* (felt-maker) Mehmet and his Argentinean wife Silvia offer treats including op-art–style patterns and what might be the world's largest hand-decorated piece of felt.

ℹ Information

Anadolu Net (Mimar Müzafer Caddesi; per hr ₺1; ⏰10am-11pm) One of several internet cafes along this street.

Tourist Office (☎353 4020; Aslanı Kışla Caddesi ; ⏰8.30am-5.30pm Mon-Sat) Gives out a city map and a leaflet covering the Mevlâna Museum; can also organise guides for the museum and has information on the weekly whirling dervish shows.

Dangers & Annoyances

Konya has a long-standing reputation for religious conservatism. Not that this should inconvenience you, but take special care not to upset the pious and make sure *you're* not an annoyance. If you visit during Ramazan be aware that many restaurants will be closed during the daylight fasting hours; as a courtesy to those who are fasting, don't eat or drink in public during the day.

Non-Muslim women seem to encounter more hassle in this bastion of propriety than in many other Turkish cities, and dressing conservatively will help you avoid problems. Men can wander around in shorts without encountering any tension, but may prefer to wear something longer to fit in with local customs.

Male travellers have reported being propositioned in the Tarihi Mahkeme Hamamı.

ⓘ Getting There & Away

Air

Both **Turkish Airlines** (☑321 2100; Ferit Paşa Caddesi; ◷8.30am-5.30pm Mon-Fri, 8.30am-1.30pm Sat) and **Pegasus Airlines** operate three daily flights to and from Istanbul.

The airport is about 13km northeast of the city centre; ₺40 by taxi.

Depending on flight arrival/departure times, **Havaş** (☑444 0487; www.havas.net; Turkish Airlines (THY) Office, Ferit Paşa Caddesi) airport buses run five to seven shuttle-bus services between the airport and central Konya per day (₺9, 30 minutes). Buses leave from outside the Turkish Airlines office.

Bus

Konya's **otogar** (İstanbul Caddesi) is about 7km north of Alaaddin Tepesi, accessible by tram from town. Regular buses serve all major destinations, including Ankara (₺18, 3½ hours), Antalya (₺30, five hours), İstanbul (₺45, 11½ hours), Kayseri (₺30, four hours) and Sivas (₺50, seven hours). There are lots of ticket offices on Mevlâna Caddesi and around Alaaddin Tepesi.

The **Karatay Terminal** (Eski Garaj; Pırıeasat Caddesi), 1km southwest of the Mevlâna Museum, has bus and dolmuş services to local villages.

Train

The **train station** (☑332 3670; Alay Caddesi) is about 3km southwest of the centre. There are eight high-speed train links between Konya and Ankara daily (adult/child ₺25/12.50, 1¾ hours).

ⓘ Getting Around

To get to the city centre from the otogar take any tram from the east side of the station to Alaaddin Tepesi (30 minutes); tickets, which cover two journeys, cost ₺3. Trams run 24 hours a day, with one per hour after midnight. A taxi costs around ₺25.

There are half-hourly minibuses from the train station to the centre. A taxi from the station to Hükümet Meydanı costs about ₺15.

Innumerable minibuses and city buses ply Mevlâna Caddesi. Buy an electronic ticket from the booths beside the bus stands (₺3, valid for two journeys).

Around Konya

ÇATALHÖYÜK

No, this isn't a hallucination brought on by the parched Konya plain. Rising 20m above the flatlands, the East Mound at Çatalhöyük (◷8am-5pm) is left over from one of the largest neolithic settlements on earth. About 9000 years ago, up to 8000 people lived here, and the mound comprises 13 levels of buildings, each containing around 1000 structures.

Little remains of the ancient centre other than the excavation areas, which draw archaeologists from all over the world. If you visit between June and September, when the digs mostly take place, you might find an expert to chat to. At other times, the **museum** does a good job of explaining the site and the excavations, which began in 1961 under British archaeologist James Mellaart and have continued with the involvement of the local community. Mellaart's controversial theories about mother-goddess worship here caused the Turkish government to close the site for 30 years.

Near the museum entrance stands the **experimental house**, a reconstructed mudbrick hut used to test various theories about neolithic culture. People at Çatalhöyük lived in tightly packed dwellings that were connected by ladders between the roofs instead of streets, and were filled in and built over when they started to wear out. Skeletons were found buried under the floors and most of the houses may have doubled as shrines. The settlement was highly organised, but there are no obvious signs of any central government system.

From the museum you can then walk across the mound to the dome-covered **north shelter** where excavation work has uncovered the remains of several buildings with their outlines still visible. A short trail then leads to the **south area**. With 21m of archaeological deposits, many of the site's most famous discoveries were made here. The lowest level of excavation, begun by Mellaart, is the deepest at Çatalhöyük and holds deposits left more than 9000 years ago. There are information panels on the viewing platforms of both excavation areas which help you decipher the site.

Getting There & Away

To get here by public transport from Konya, 33km northwest, get the Karkın minibus, which leaves the Karatay Terminal at 7am, 9.30am and 4.50pm. Get off at Kük Koy (₺2.50, 45 minutes) and walk 1km to the site, or you may be able to persuade the driver to take you the whole way. Going back, minibuses leave Kük Koy at 7.15am, 3pm and 7pm.

A taxi from Konya to the site and back will cost about ₺90.

GÖKYURT (KILISTRA, LYSTRA)

A little piece of Cappadocia to the southwest of Konya, the landscape at Gökyurt is reminiscent of what you'll see in Güzelyurt or the Ihlara Valley: a gorge with dwellings and medieval churches cut into the rock face, but without the crowds.

St Paul is thought to have stayed here on his three Anatolian expeditions and the area has long been a Christian pilgrimage site; especially for the 12 months from June 2008 after the year was declared by Pope Benedict XVI as 'the year of St Paul' to celebrate the 2000th anniversary of the saint's birth.

There's one particularly fine church cut completely out of the rock, but no frescoes. A trip out here makes a lovely half-day excursion, and the surrounding landscape is simply stunning.

Getting There & Away

The easiest way to get here from Konya, 45km away, is by car or taxi; the latter will charge ₺120 return (including waiting time). There are several daily buses from Konya's Karatay Terminal to Hatunsaray, 18km from Gökyurt, but taxis there are actually more expensive than from Konya as the drivers make the most of their captive audience.

Driving, you should take the Antalya road, then follow signs to Akören. After about 34km, and a few kilometres before Hatunsaray, look for a tiny brown and white sign on the right (marked 'Kilistra-Gökyurt, 16km'). Cyclists need to watch out for sheepdogs roaming about.

SİLLE

🖉 0332 / POP 2000

If you're looking for an excursion from Konya, head to the pretty village of Sille, where a rock face full of cave dwellings and chapels overlooks bendy-beamed village houses in several states of decay and a few bridges across the dry river.

The domed Byzantine St Helen's Church (Ayaelena Kilisesi), near the last bus stop, was reputedly founded by Empress Helena, mother of Constantine the Great. It was closed for restoration when we visited but

if it opens by the time you visit, check out the vandalised and fast-fading frescoes that date from 1880.

On the hill to the north stands a small ruined chapel, the Küçük Kilese (also under restoration); it's worth the scramble up for the views over the village.

Getting There & Away

Bus 64 from Mevlâna Caddesi (near the post office) in Konya leaves every half-hour or so for Sille (25 minutes).

Karaman

🖉 0338 / POP 138,135

After the fall of the Seljuk Empire, central Anatolia was split into several different provinces with different governments, and for some time Karaman served as a regional capital. Although little visited these days, it boasts a selection of fine 13th- and 14th-century buildings and makes a base for excursions to Binbirkilise.

The Hacıbeyler Camii (1358) has a magnificent squared-off entrance, with decoration that looks like a baroque variant on Seljuk art. The Mader-i Mevlâna (Aktepe) Cami (1370) is the burial place of the great Mevlâna's mother and has a dervish-style felt hat carved above its entrance. The adjacent hamam is still in use.

The tomb of the great Turkish poet Yunus Emre is beside the Yunus Emre Camii (1349). Extracts from his verses are carved into the walls of a poetry garden to the rear of the mosque.

The slightly disorganised Karaman Museum (Turgut Özal Bulvarı; admission ₺3; ⊘8am-noon & 1-5pm Tue-Sun) contains cave finds from nearby Taşkale and Canhasan and has a fine ethnography section. Next door, the magnificent Hatuniye Medresesi (1382), whose ornate portal is one of the finest examples of Karaman art, now houses a restaurant.

If you get caught in Karaman overnight, the two-star Nas Hotel (🖉 214 4848; İsmetpaşa Caddesi 30; s/d ₺50/80) is low on luxury but comfortable, welcoming to travellers of both sexes and close to the sights.

Getting There & Away

Regular buses link Karaman with Konya (₺12, two hours) and Ereğli (₺15, two hours). Getting to Karaman from Nevşehir (Cappadocia) is more time-consuming, as you must change in Niğde and Ereğli. The İç Anadolu Mavi trains stop here between Konya and Adana.

SILK ROAD SPLENDOUR AT SULTANHANI

The highway between Konya and Aksaray crosses quintessential Anatolian steppe: flat grasslands as far as the eye can see, with only the occasional tumbleweed and a few mountains in the distance breaking the monotony. The Seljuks built a string of *hans* (caravanserais) along this Silk Road route and, 110km from Konya, 42km from Aksaray, the dreary village of Sultanhanı is home to one of the most stunning *hans* still standing.

The largest in Anatolia, the **Sultanhanı** (admission ₺3; ⊙7am-7pm) was constructed in 1229, during the reign of the Seljuk sultan Alaaddin Keykubad I, and restored in 1278 after a fire (when it became Turkey's largest *han*). Through the wonderful carved entrance in the 50m-long east wall, there is a raised *mescit* (prayer room) in the middle of the open courtyard, which is ringed with rooms used for sleeping, dining and cooking. A small, simple doorway leads to the atmospheric *ahır* (stable), with arches, domes and pillars in the pigeon-soundtracked gloom.

The site is a popular stop for tour groups, and you may field invitations to visit the nearby carpet-repair workshop. If you resist such offers, you could easily explore Sultanhanı in half an hour.

Regular buses run from Aksaray's otogar from Monday to Friday (₺5, 45 minutes); there are fewer services at weekends. Leaving Sultanhanı, flag down a bus or village minibus heading to Aksaray or Konya on the main highway. If you start out early you can hop off the bus, see the *han* and be on your way again an hour or so later.

Binbirkilise

Just before WWI, the great British traveller Gertrude Bell travelled 42km northwest of Karaman and recorded the existence of a cluster of Byzantine churches set high on a lonely hillside and rather generously known as Binbirkilise (1001 Churches). Later Irfan Orga came here in search of the last remaining nomads, a journey recorded in his book *The Caravan Moves On*. You won't see any nomads around these days, or indeed much to mark the ruins out as churches, but half a dozen families live around the ruins (and in them, in the case of some of their animals) and the site is a rural alternative to busier attractions.

It's easiest to reach the churches with your own transport. Drive out of Karaman on the Karapınar road and follow the yellow signs. The first sizeable ruin pops up in the village of Madenşehir, 36km north, after which the road becomes increasingly rough. There are fantastic views all along the road, which is just as well, as you'll have to come back the same way.

A taxi from Karaman's otogar should cost around ₺100 for the return trip; the drivers know where the churches are.

Cappadocia

Why Go?

As if plucked from a whimsical fairytale and set down upon the stark Anatolian plains, Cappadocia is a geological oddity of honeycombed hills and towering phallic boulders of otherworldly beauty. Fashioned through lashings of volcanic ash, moulded by millennia of rain and river flow, this fantastical topography is equally matched by the human history here. People have long utilised the region's soft stone, seeking shelter underground, leaving the countryside scattered with the fresco-adorned rock-cut churches of early Christians, cavernous subterranean refuges, and villages half-burrowed into the earth itself.

Cappadocia woos both outdoor enthusiasts who revel in the lunarscape and the cultured set more likely to enjoy the panoramas from the balcony of their boutique cave-hotel with fine local wine in hand. Whatever your tastes, this region's accordion-ridged valleys, shaded in a palette of dusky orange and cream, are an epiphany of a landscape – the stuff of psychedelic daydreams.

Best Places to Eat

» Köy Evi (p456)

» Ziggy's (p473)

» Seten Restaurant (p456)

» Topdeck Cave Restaurant (p456)

Best Places to Stay

» Esbelli Evi (p471)

» Hezen Cave Hotel (p468)

» Kelebek Hotel & Cave Pension (p453)

» Koza Cave Hotel (p453)

» Serinn House (p472)

When to Go

Kayseri

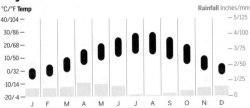

Apr & May Wild flowers shock the valley moonscapes into a photogenic riot of colour.

Jul–Sep Listen to classical music concerts in natural outdoor rock venues.

Dec–Mar Disperse the snow bunnies atop Erciyes Daği (Mt Erciyes), a rugged Turk ski spot.

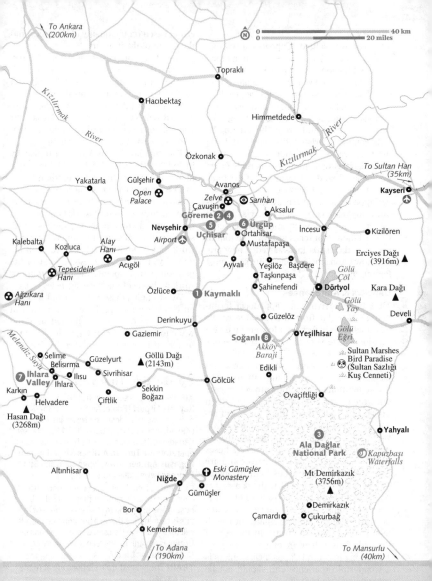

Cappadocia Highlights

1 Delve downwards into the Byzantine tunnels of underground cities, such as **Kaymaklı** (p478)

2 Examine the fresco-covered finery of churches in the **Göreme Open-Air Museum** (p448)

3 Tackle nature in the waterfalls and trails of **Ala Dağlar National Park** (p481)

4 Seek out hidden churches, amid cliffs and fairy chimneys in **Göreme's** labyrinthine valleys (p449)

5 Clamber atop **Uçhisar Castle** (p458) to gaze over a surreal panorama of rock

6 Munch on multiple mezes in chic **Ürgüp** (p469)

7 Stroll between verdant fields and soaring cliffs, seeking rock-cut churches, in **Ihlara Valley** (p482)

8 Trek through a secluded monastic settlement in **Soğanlı** (p479)

History

The Hittites settled Cappadocia (Kapadokya) from 1800 BC to 1200 BC, after which smaller kingdoms held power. Then came the Persians, followed by the Romans, who established the capital of Caesarea (today's Kayseri). During the Roman and Byzantine periods, Cappadocia became a refuge for early Christians and, from the 4th to the 11th century, Christianity flourished here; most churches, monasteries and underground cities date from this period. Later, under Seljuk and Ottoman rule, Christians were treated with tolerance.

Cappadocia progressively lost its importance in Anatolia. Its rich past was all but forgotten until a French priest rediscovered the rock-hewn churches in 1907. The tourist boom in the 1980s kick-started a new era, and now Cappadocia is one of Turkey's most famous and popular destinations.

Dangers & Annoyances

Most buses arriving in Cappadocia terminate in Nevşehir from where a free *servis* (shuttle bus) will ferry you to your final destination. Make sure that your ticket states that it is for Göreme, Ürgüp etc, not just 'Cappadocia'. Be aware that tour companies based at Nevşehir otogar (bus station) have a bad reputation for attempting to get tourists onto their private shuttle buses, and then proceeding to hard-sell them tours and accommodation in Nevşehir. We suggest that you avoid any dealings with the tour agents here. The official bus company *servis* buses usually meet your bus as it arrives and are clearly marked with the bus company logo.

If you do find yourself without a *servis* or a taxi and you have booked a hotel, it is worth phoning it for assistance; Nevşehir's otogar has long been problematic for travellers and the tourist industry in the rest of Cappadocia is well aware of it.

Walking in central Cappadocia's valleys is a wonderful experience and should not be missed, but solo travellers who do not want to hire a guide to explore should buddy-up before venturing into the more isolated areas. It's also advised to avoid the valleys and unlit roads between villages during the evenings.

Tours

Travel agents abound in Cappadocia. Prices are usually determined by all operators at the beginning of each season. Make your decision based on the quality of the guide and the extent of the itinerary.

Most tour companies offer both full-day tours (to destinations such as the Ihlara Valley, the underground cities, and Soğanlı) and guided day hikes in the Cappadocian valleys.

Guided day hikes are usually in the Güllüdere (Rose), Kızılçuker (Red), or Meskendir Valleys. Costs vary according to the destination, degree of difficulty and length.

The full-day Ihlara Valley trip usually includes a short guided hike in the gorge, lunch and a trip to an underground city; most operators charge about ₺90.

Most itineraries finish at a carpet shop, onyx factory or pottery workshop, but it is still worth taking a tour. It is interesting to see a traditional Cappadocian craftsman at work, but make it clear before the trip begins if you are not interested. Most of the pensions either operate their own tours or work with one of the travel agencies.

We strongly advise you to avoid booking an expensive tour package upon arrival in İstanbul. If your time is limited and you want to take a tour in Cappadocia, you're better off booking a tour directly from an agent in Cappadocia itself.

Getting There & Away

AIR Two airports serve central Cappadocia: **Kayseri Airport** (Erkilet Airport; ✆0352-337 5494; Kayseri Caddesi) and **Nevşehir Airport** (Kapadokya Airport; ✆0384-421 4451; Nevşehir Kapadokya Havaalanı Yolu, Gülşehir). The main operators are **Turkish Airlines** (www.thy.com), **Pegasus Airlines** (www.flypgs.com) and **Sun Express** (www.sunexpress.com).

BUS Buses from İstanbul to Cappadocia travel overnight (in high summer there may also be day buses) and bring you to Nevşehir, where (if the bus is terminating there) a bus company *servis* will take you on to Uçhisar, Göreme, Avanos or Ürgüp. From Ankara you can travel more comfortably during the day.

TRAIN The nearest train stations are at Niğde and Kayseri.

Getting Around

TO/FROM THE AIRPORT The easiest solution is to request your hotel or pension in Cappadocia to book an airport shuttle bus for you. You can also book directly with the shuttle bus service. There are a few different companies but **Cappadocia Express** (✆0384-271 3070; www.cappadociatransport.com; Iceridere Sokak 3, Göreme; per passenger ₺20) is the pick of the bunch as its service operates for all flights coming in

CAPPADOCIA FROM ABOVE

If you've never taken a flight in a hot-air balloon, Cappadocia is one of the best places in the world to try it. Flight conditions are especially favourable here, with balloons operating most mornings throughout the year. It's a truly magical experience and many travellers judge it to be the highlight of their trip.

Flights take place just after dawn. Unfortunately, due to demand, even most of the reputable companies now offer a second, later-morning flight as well. Winds can become unreliable and potentially dangerous later in the morning so you should always book the dawn flight. Transport between your hotel and the balloon launch site is included in the hefty price, as is a champagne toast.

You'll quickly realise that there's a fair amount of hot air between the operators about who is and isn't inexperienced, ill-equipped, underinsured and unlicensed. Be aware that hot-air ballooning can be dangerous. It's your responsibility to check the credentials of your chosen tour operator carefully and make sure that your pilot is experienced and savvy – even if it means asking to see their licences and logbooks. And don't pick the cheapest operator if it means they might be taking short cuts with safety or over-filling the balloon baskets.

It's important to note that the balloons travel with the wind, and that the companies can't ensure a particular flight path on a particular day. All companies try to fly over the fairy chimneys, but sometimes – albeit rarely – the wind doesn't allow this. Occasionally, unfavourable weather conditions mean that the pilot will cancel the flight for the day for safety reasons; if this happens you'll be offered a flight on the next day or will have your payment refunded. Although this may be an inconvenience it is preferable to the pilot being made to fly in dangerous conditions. All passengers should take a warm jumper or jacket and women should wear flat shoes and trousers. Children under seven will not be taken up by most companies.

The following agencies have good credentials:

Butterfly Balloons (☑271 3010; www.butterflyballoons.com; Uzundere Caddesi 29, Göreme) This seamless operation has an excellent reputation, with superlative pilots Mustafa, the first Turkish citizen to gain a US pilot's licence, and Englishman Mike, who has vast international experience and is a fellowship member of the Royal Meteorological Society. Standard flights (one hour, up to 16 passengers) cost €175 a pop.

Royal Balloon (☑271 3300; www.royalballoon.com; Dutlu Sokak 9) Seasoned pilot Suat Ulusoy heads up this reputable balloon operation with a staff of local and international pilots. Standard flights (one hour, up to 20 passengers) cost €175.

Voyager Balloons (☑271 3030; www.voyagerballoons.com; Müze Caddesi 36/1, Göreme) Recommended for their multilingual pilots and professional service. Standard flights cost €160.

and going out of both airports and will pick up from and drop off to hotels in Avanos, Cavasin, Göreme, Nevşehir, Ortahisar, Uçhisar and Ürgüp.

CAR & MOTORCYCLE Cappadocia is great for self-drive visits. Roads are often empty and their condition is reasonable. There is ample parking space but pulling up outside some cave hotels might be tricky.

PUBLIC TRANSPORT Belediye Bus Corp dolmuşes (minibuses; ₺2.50 to ₺3 depending on where you get on and off) travel between Ürgüp and Avanos via Ortahisar, the Göreme Open-Air Museum, Göreme, Çavuşin and (on request) Paşabağı and Zelve. The services leave Ürgüp at 10am, noon, 4pm and 6pm, and Avanos (going the opposite way) at 9am, 11am, 1pm, 3pm and

5pm. You can hop on and off anywhere along the route.

There's also an hourly *belediye* (municipal council) bus running between Avanos and Nevşehir (₺4) via Çavuşin (10 minutes), Göreme (15 minutes) and Uçhisar (30 minutes). It leaves Avanos from 7am to 7pm.

The Ihlara Valley in southwest Cappadocia can be visited on a day tour from Göreme. If you want to visit it independently plan to spend the night, as bus changes in Nevşehir and Aksaray prolong travelling time.

TAXI Taxis are a good option for moving from town to town. Meters operate but a negotiated price is also welcome.

Göreme

🎫 0384 / POP 2138

Surrounded by epic sweeps of lunarscape valleys, this remarkable honey-coloured village, hollowed out of the hills, may have long since grown out of its farming hamlet roots but its charm has not diminished. In the back alleys, new boutique cave hotels are constantly popping up but tourists still have to stop for tractors, which trundle up narrow winding roads where elderly ladies dally for hours on sunny streetside stoops doing their knitting. Nearby, the Göreme Open-Air Museum is an all-in-one testament to Byzantine life, while if you wander out of town into the golden-hued valleys you'll find storybook landscapes and little-visited rock-cut churches at every turn. With its easygoing allure and stunning setting, it's no wonder Göreme continues to send travellers giddy.

👁 Sights

 Göreme Open-Air Museum MUSEUM
(Göreme Açık Hava Müzesi; 🎫 271 2167; admission ₺15, Karanlık Kilise ₺8; ⏱ 8am-5pm) One of Turkey's World Heritage sites, the Göreme Open-Air Museum is an essential stop on any Cappadocian itinerary and deserves at least a two-hour visit. First an important Byzantine monastic settlement that housed some 20 monks, then a pilgrimage site from the 17th century, the cluster of rock-cut churches, chapels and monasteries is 1km uphill from the centre of Göreme.

From the ticket booth, follow the cobbled path until you reach **Aziz Basil Şapeli**, the

> ### ℹ VISITING THE MUSEUM
>
> » Arrive early in the morning, at midday, or near closing to bypass tour groups.
>
> » Avoid weekends if possible.
>
> » Don't skimp on Karanlık Kilise – it's worth the extra ₺8.
>
> » Your ticket is valid all day if you want to leave and come back.
>
> » The museum is an easy 1km walk from town.
>
> » Beware the sun – this is an 'open-air' museum.

chapel dedicated to Kayseri-born St Basil, one of Cappadocia's most important saints. The grate-covered holes in the floor were the graves of the chapel's architects and financiers; the small boxes contained less-affluent folks' bones. In the main room, St Basil is pictured on the left; a Maltese cross is on the right, along with St George and St Theodore slaying a (faded) dragon, symbolising paganism. On the right of the apse, Mary holds baby Jesus, with a cross in his halo.

Above Aziz Basil Şapeli, bow down to enter the 12th-century **Elmalı Kilise** (Apple Church), overlooking a valley of poplars. Relatively well preserved, it contains both simple, red-ochre daubs and professionally painted frescoes of biblical scenes. The Ascension is pictured above the door. The church's name is thought to derive from an apple tree that grew nearby or from a misinterpretation of the globe held by the Archangel Gabriel, in the third dome.

Byzantine soldiers carved the **Azize Barbara Şapeli** (Chapel of St Barbara), dedicated to their patron saint, who is depicted on the left as you enter. They also painted the mysterious scenes on the roof – the middle one could represent the Ascension; above the St George representation on the far wall, the strange creature could be a dragon, and the two crosses, the beast's usual slayers. The decoration is typical of the iconoclastic period, when images were outlawed – red ochre was painted on the stone without any images of people or animals.

Uphill, in the **Yılanlı Kilise** (Snake Church or Church of St Onuphrius), the dragon is still having a bad day. To add insult to its fatal injuries, it was mistaken for a snake when the church was named. The hermetic hermaphrodite St Onuphrius is pictured on the right, holding a genitalia-covering palm leaf. Straight ahead, the small figure next to Jesus is one of the church's financiers.

The museum's most famous church, the stunning, fresco-filled **Karanlık Kilise** (Dark Church), is definitely worth the extra outlay. The supplementary fee is due to its costly renovation, and an attempt to keep numbers down and preserve the frescoes. One of Turkey's finest surviving churches, it took its name from the fact that it originally had very few windows.

Just past the Karanlık Kilise, the small **Azize Katarina Şapeli** (Chapel of St Cather-

WALKING IN THE VALLEYS AROUND GÖREME

Göreme village is surrounded by the magnificent Göreme National Park. The valleys are easily explored on foot; each valley needs about one to three hours. Most are interconnected, so you could easily combine several in a day, especially with the help of the area's many dolmuşes (minibuses). Don't forget to take a bottle of water and sunscreen.

Some of the most interesting and accessible valleys:

Bağlıdere (White Valley) From Uçhisar to Göreme.

Görkündere (Love Valley) Trailheads off Zemi Valley and from Sunset View Hill in Göreme; particularly spectacular rock formations.

Güllüdere (Rose Valley) Trailheads just north of Göreme, at Çavuşin, and Kızılçukur viewpoint (opposite the Ortahisar turn-off); superb churches and panoramic views.

Güvercinlik (Pigeon Valley) Connecting Göreme and Uçhisar; colourful dovecotes.

İçeridere Running south from İçeridere Sokak in Göreme.

Kılıçlar (Swords Valley) Running off the Göreme Open-Air Museum road.

Kızılçukur (Red Valley) Running between Güllüdere and Meskendir Valleys; great views and vibrant dovecotes.

Meskendir Trailhead next to Kaya Camping; tunnels and dovecotes.

Zemi Valley Trailhead running west off the Göreme Open-Air Museum road.

A word of warning: although many of the valleys now have trailhead signposts and signage has been put up at strategic points along the paths of Güllüdere and Kızılçukur Valleys, many of the trails remain only basically marked and there's no detailed map of the area available. It's quite easy to get lost if you don't stick to the trails.

ine) has frescoes of St George, St Catherine and the Deesis.

The 13th-century **Çarıklı Kilise** (Sandal Church) is named for the footprints marked in the floor, representing the last imprints left by Jesus before he ascended to heaven. The four gospel writers are depicted below the central dome; in the arch over the door to the left is the Betrayal by Judas.

Downhill, the cordoned-off **Rahibeler Manastırı** (Nun's Convent) was originally several storeys high; all that remains is a large plain dining hall and, up some steps, a small chapel with unremarkable frescoes.

When you exit the museum, don't forget to cross the road and visit the **Tokalı Kilise** (Buckle Church), 50m down the hill towards Göreme. Covered by the same ticket, it is one of Göreme's biggest and finest churches, with an underground chapel and fabulous frescoes painted in a narrative (rather than liturgical) cycle. Entry is via the 10th-century 'old' Tokalı Kilise, through the barrel-vaulted chamber with frescoes portraying the life of Christ. Upstairs, the 'new' church, built less than a hundred years later, is also alive with fres-

coes on a similar theme. The holes in the floor once contained tombs, taken by departing Christians during the population exchange.

Güllüdere Valley Churches CHURCHES
The trails that loop around Güllüdere (Rose) Valley are easily accessible to all levels of walkers and provide some of the finest fairy-chimney-strewn vistas in Cappadocia. As well as this though, they also hide fabulous, little-visited, rock-cut churches boasting vibrant fresco fragments and intricate carvings hewn into the stone.

Follow the signs from the Güllüdere Valley trailhead to the **Kolonlu Kilise** (Columned Church). The rock facade here is easily overlooked. Take the trail through the orchard and the steps that lead off to the left to clamber onto the nondescript rock face. Once you've scrambled through the entrance and the lower chamber you'll find a white stone nave studded with sturdy columns carved out of the rock. From here, backtrack through the orchard and follow the main trail to the **Haçlı Kilise** (Church of the Cross), where the shady cave-cafe at the entrance is the perfect

Göreme

To Uçhisar (4km);
Nevşehir (12km)

Adnan Menderes Cad

To Avanos
(8km)

To Güllüdere and
Kızılçukur Valley
Trailheads (50m)

Ragıp Üner Cad

Posta Sk

Direk

Dolmuş Stop
for Çavuşin,
Zelve & Avanos

Dolmuş stop
for Ürgüp

Müze Cad (Open-Air Museum Rd)

To Göreme
Open-Air Museum (500m);
Kaya Camping &
Meskendir Valley (2.2km)

5

2

1

3

24

39
15
40
41
45
50
10
51

Müze Cad

Fatih Sk

Sağlık Sk

Park Sk

İlkokul Sk

27
30
42

Karşıbucak Cad

Uzundere Cad

Aslan Sk

Adnan

23

29

4
7

25
18

Hafız Abdullah
Efendi Sk

44
33
35
31

32
43

Aydınlı Sk

Çakmaklı Sk

22

20

Kale Cad

İsali Cad

Müze Cad

Hafız Şükrü Sk

Cappadocia
Express

17

38

19

Müdür Sk

Ünlü Sk

11

Otogar

12

13
6
8

14
49
46
9
47
48
16
37
36

Cami Sk

Konak Sk

Dolmuş
stop for Uçhisar
& Nevşehir

21
26
34

0   200 m
0   0.1 miles

Göreme

pit stop for a walking break. The church, accessed by a rickety wooden staircase, has frescoes dating to the 9th-century on its apse and a large cross carved into its ceiling. Head north from here and take the right-hand path to reach the **Üç Haçlı Kilise** (Church of the Three Crosses), with its stunning ceiling relief and damaged frescoes featuring an enthroned Jesus.

El Nazar Kilise   CHURCH
(Church of the Evil Eye; admission ₺8; ⊙8am-5pm) Carved from a ubiquitous cone-like rock formation, the 10th-century El Nazar Kilise has been restored, although its frescoes are not in the best condition. To find it, take the signposted trail off Müze Caddesi.

Saklı Kilise   CHURCH
(Hidden Church) A yellow sign points the way off Müze Caddesi to the Saklı Kilise. When

you reach the top of the hill, follow the track to the left and look out for steps leading downhill to the right.

🏃 **Activities**

Mehmet Güngör   WALKING
(📞0532 382 2069; www.walkingmehmet.com; Noriyon Cafe, Müze Caddesi; four hours/full day €60/80) Mehmet Güngör's nickname 'Walking Mehmet' says it all. Göreme's most-experienced local walking guide has an encyclopaedic knowledge of the surrounding valley trails and can put together itineraries to suit all interests and levels of fitness. Highly recommended.

Elis Kapadokya Hamam   HAMAM
(📞271 2974; Adnan Menderes Caddesi; soak, scrub & massage €25; ⊙10am-midnight) Unwind after the chimney-spotting and treat yourself

LOCAL KNOWLEDGE

MEHMET GÜNGÖR: CAPPADOCIA'S WALKING GURU

Mehmet Güngör (aka Walking Mehmet) has been guiding visitors through the maze of valley trails surrounding Göreme for the past 14 years. We asked him for his top tips for DIY hikers.

Best morning walk? Görkündere Valley is perfect for early morning walks as the sun's angle at this time highlights the rock formations perfectly.

Best walk if you only have one day? Güllüdere and Kızılçukur Valleys are my absolute favourite walks. Every corner reveals a different frame. For the best light, walk here in the afternoon.

Best adventurous walk? Walk from Zelve, via Paşabağı, to Çavuşin and take the trails opposite the old village ruins which lead up to the Boztepe ridge. Hike all the way along here to the Kızılçukur viewpoint then walk down through the Kızılçukur and Güllüdere Valleys.

Best walk to escape the crowds? Zemi Valley still sees very few visitors and is extremely pretty. Further away from Göreme, Gomeda Valley (between Ürgüp and Mustafapaşa) and Çat Valley (trailhead near Gülşehir's Open Palace ruin) are rarely visited.

Which church should walkers not miss? The Kolonlu Kilise (p449) always surprises people as it's very well hidden and in the middle of nowhere.

to a thorough massage at the beautiful Elis Kapadokya Hamam, which has mixed and women-only areas.

Kelebek Turkish Bath Spa HAMAM
(271 2531; Kelebek Hotel, Yavuz Sokak; soak & scrub €30) Cappadocia's most luxurious hamam experience with a full-range of spastyle added extras.

Topdeck Cave Restaurant Cooking Classes COOKING COURSE
(271 2474; Hafız Abdullah Efendi Sokak 15; €40; ⊙classes 9am-11am) Mustafa Ciftçi runs recommended Turkish cooking classes (reservation-only) from his family home and restaurant. All the fiddly chopping and sweating over the stove is worth it for the slap-up lunch afterwards when you get to eat your creations.

☞ Tours

The following tour businesses have been recommended by Lonely Planet readers or can be vouched for by us. However, the list is by no means exhaustive.

Middle Earth Travel ADVENTURE TOUR
(271 2559; www.middleearthtravel.com; Cevizler Sokak 20) The adventure-travel specialist offers climbing and treks ranging from local, one-day expeditions (€35 to €60 per person) to one-week missions through Ala Dağlar National Park, along the Lycian Way or St Paul's Trail, through the Kaçkar Mountains or up Mt Ararat.

Heritage Travel GUIDED TOUR
(271 2687; www.turkishheritagetravel.com; Uzundere Caddesi) Local tours with the knowledgeable Mustafa at Heritage Travel are highly recommended (group tours €45 per person, or €100 per person for a private tour). The company also offers more offbeat tours such as photography jeep safaris (€125 per person) and tailor-made Turkey packages.

Yama Tours GUIDED TOUR
(271 2508; www.yamatours.com; Müze Caddesi 2) Yama Tours has a range of one-day Cappadocia group tours to choose from and also three-day trips to Nemrut Dağı, which leave on Monday and Thursday. An excellent choice of tour with friendly owner-guide, Mehmet.

Neşe Tour GUIDED TOUR
(271 2525; www.nesetour.com; Avanos Yolu 54) Offers Cappadocian day tours and trips to Nemrut Dağı (Mt Nemrut) lasting between two and four days.

Nomad Travel GUIDED TOUR
(271 2767; www.nomadtravel.com.tr; Belediye Caddesi) Nomad Travel offers an excellent Soğanlı tour.

New Göreme Tours GUIDED TOUR
(271 2166; www.newgoreme.com) Fun and friendly private tours. Close to the otogar, off Belediye Caddesi.

⚶ Festivals & Events

Klasik Keyifler CLASSICAL MUSIC
(☏0532 614 4955; www.klasikkeyifler.org)
Klasik Keyifler is an innovative organisation run by an American musician that holds chamber-music concerts by Turkey's brightest stars in intimate natural settings. The summer series hits Cappadocia in July and August, when you can hear the sounds of Schumann bouncing off the Hidden Valley walls. Workshops run in conjunction with the performance.

FREE **Kapadokya Caz Günleri** JAZZ
(Cappadocia Jazz Days; www.kapadokyacazgunleri.com) Begun in 2010, Kapadokya Caz Günleri brings some of Turkey's most acclaimed jazz musicians to the region for one week in late November and early December. Free concerts are hosted at venues throughout Cappadocia and are accompanied by a series of workshops.

🛏 Sleeping

If you're visiting between October and May, pack warm clothes as it gets very cold at night and pension owners may delay putting the heating on. Ring ahead, too, to check that your choice is open. This is only a small sample of the huge number of rock-cut retreats in this fairy-chimney-punctured village.

TOP CHOICE **Kelebek Hotel & Cave Pension** HOTEL €€
(☏271 2531; www.kelebekhotel.com; Yavuz Sokak 31; fairy chimney s/d €40/50, deluxe €52/65, ste s €64-144, ste d €80-180; 🖀🖾) It's reassuring to know the oldie is still the goodie. Local guru Ali Yavuz leads a charming team at one of Göreme's original boutique hotels that has seen a travel industry virtually spring from beneath its stunning terrace. Spread over two gorgeous stone houses, each with fairy chimneys protruding skyward, rooms exude Anatolian inspiration at every turn. It's refreshing to see a hotel that doesn't rest on its laurels and Kelebek continues to innovate; now offering complimentary village garden breakfast visits to every guest. It's no wonder people leave smitten.

TOP CHOICE **Koza Cave Hotel** HOTEL €€
(☏271 2466; www.kozacavehotel.com; Cakmaklı Sokak 49; s/d €75/90, ste €115-140 ; 🖀) Bringing a whole new level of eco-inspired chic to Göreme, Koza Cave is a master-class in stylish sustainable tourism. Passionate owner Derviş spent decades living in Holland and has incorporated Dutch ecosensibility into every cave crevice of the 10 stunning rooms. Grey water is reused, and recycled materials and local handcrafted furniture are utilised in abundance to create sophisticated,

CAPPADOCIA GÖREME

EKREM ILHAN

When Persia ruled Turkey, Katpatuka (Cappadocia) was famous throughout the empire for its beautiful horses. In Iran's Persepolis palace, among the reliefs depicting delegates from Persia's subject states, visitors from Katpatuka are pictured with equine offerings.

It seems appropriate, then, that present-day Göreme has a horse whisperer. Ekrem Ilhan brings wild horses to Göreme from Erciyes Dağı (Mt Erciyes), where a tribe of 400 has grown as local farmers have replaced them with machinery.

'They are in shock when they arrive here, but when their eyes open they see me, talking and giving them sweet things', he says. 'People teach animals to bite and kick, because they are angry with them. But when you're friends, and you talk to them and give them some carrot and cucumber, you don't have any problems.'

Looking like a Cappadocian Clint Eastwood in a hat brought from America by a carpet-dealing friend, Ilhan tells a story about two pregnant mares he returned to Mt Erciyes to give birth. 'One year later, I went into the mountains, among the 400 horses, and called their names and they came directly to me.'

Ilhan treats the 11 horses in his cave stable using homemade remedies, such as grape water to extract parasites, and olive oil, mint and egg for indigestion. He has started a horse-trekking company, called **Dalton Brothers** (☏0532 275 6869; Müze Caddesi ; 1 hr ₺45, 2 hr ₺90), at the suggestion of a Canadian traveller and *Lucky Luke* fan. 'People like wild horses because it's difficult riding in the mountains, it's rocky, and the horses are used to it', he says.

Many of the horses are not suitable for first-time riders. If you are not an experienced rider please make sure you specify this before signing up.

LOCAL KNOWLEDGE

PAT YALE: OLD GÖREME RESTORATION FUND MEMBER

Once upon a time Old Göreme was full of lovely honey-coloured cave houses that blended gently into the background so that they looked almost as if they had sprung straight out of it. Today the village is a conservation area but over the decades a lot of incidental ugliness has developed as people used breeze blocks and other cheap materials to carry out repairs and extensions. The **Old Göreme Restoration Fund** (OFRF; www.goremecharity.com) was set up in 2007 to pay for small improvements to the visual environment, in particular to replace some of the concrete with natural stone. With funding from Intrepid Travel in Australia and other generous individuals it has refaced breeze-block walls, cleaned up old fountains and reopened viewpoints that had been blocked. To raise money it holds twice-yearly 'Open House' events, when visitors are able to see some of the privately owned homes. It's a rare chance to see how carefully the old houses were designed to suit a lifestyle in which almost all foodstuffs were laboriously homemade.

Until the 1970s most Göreme residents made their living from farming and kept pigeons so that their droppings could be used for manure. The arrival of chemical fertilisers put an end to the pigeons, and the coming of tourism saw most people abandoning their fields too. The OGRF has now cleaned out some of the old pigeon houses, and invested in a new generation of pigeons. The hope is to restart some farming here and then perhaps sell produce such as organic apricot jam to the hotels. Ultimately this might make it possible to provide some work other than in tourism for the village.

Pat Yale works for OGRF and is a resident of Göreme.

elegant spaces which prove you don't have to sacrifice comfort in the pursuit of responsible tourism. Highly recommended.

Aydınlı Cave House HOTEL €€
(☑271 2263; www.thecavehotel.com; Aydınlı Sokak 12; r from €70-140; ⊛) Lovely Aydınlı gets it right on every level. Proprietor Mustafa has masterfully converted his family home into a haven for honeymooners and those requiring a little rock-cut style with their solitude. Guests rave about the warm service and immaculate, spacious cave rooms, formerly used for drying fruits, storing wheat and making wine. If children are in tow, take the family suite, which includes an active tandoor oven and antique kitchen utensils.

The Dorm Cave HOSTEL €
(☑271 2770; www.travellerscave.com; Hafız Abdullah Efendi Sokak 4; dm/d/tr €10/30/45; ⊛) Just when you thought Göreme had forgotten about its budget-traveller roots along comes this superb new hostel that shuns the boutique craze in favour of backpacker-friendly-priced beds. Three spacious cave rooms are home to the dorm beds and share small, but modern, bathrooms across a pretty courtyard. Upstairs a couple of snug, private rooms also offer brilliant value.

Kismet Cave House HOTEL €€
(☑271 2416; www.kismetcavehouse.com; Kağnı Yolu 9; d €75; ⊛) Kismet's fate is assured as guests consistently hail the intimate experience created by the unobtrusive Faruk and his family at this honest-to-impending-greatness Anatolian cave house. The rooms host local antiques, colourful rugs and quirky artwork while communal areas are home to cosy cushion-scattered nooks.

Fairy Chimney Inn HOTEL €€
(☑271 2655; www.fairychimney.com; Güvercinlik Sokak 5-7; r from €55-111; ⊛) This highbrow retreat is run by Dr Andus Emge and his lovely wife, who offer academic asides to their wonderful hospitality. The views from the garden and various peepholes are magnificent, while the rooms temper the senses with simple furniture and traditional textiles. Communal meals in the tranquil garden area will invariably induce happiness.

Taşkonak HOTEL €€
(☑270 2680; www.taskonak.net; Güngör Sokak 23; d/ste/f €40/80/110; ⊛) Angela and Yılmaz provide huge helpings of hospitality at this intimate and highly relaxed hideaway. The spacious cave suites are among the best value deals in town while killer views from the terrace and a breakfast

feast of homemade spreads, freshly baked delights and proper coffee leave guests grinning at their good fortune.

Travellers' Cave Pension
PENSION €

(☑271 2707; www.travellerscave.com; Güngör Sokak 11; s/d/tr €25/40/50, deluxe d/tr €50/60; 🛜) Friendly, efficient management and super-clean, comfortable rooms set around a tree-shaded courtyard ensure that Travellers' continues to be one of Göreme's most popular pensions. The attentive staff speak good English and can swiftly arrange all sorts of tours.

Köse Pension
HOSTEL €

(☑271 2294; www.kosepension.com; Ragıp Üner Caddesi; dm/d/tr ₺12.50/80/90, s without bathroom ₺25; 🛜🏊) It may have no cave-character but this traveller's favourite, Köse Pension, provides a range of spotless rooms that all feature brilliant bathrooms, bright linens and comfortable beds. The excellent breakfast options (not included in the price, ₺5 to ₺6 extra) set you up for the day while the swimming pool is an added bonus after a long hot hike.

Arch Palace
HOTEL €€

(☑271 2575; www.archpalace.com; Ünlü Sokak 14; d/f €60-70/85; 🛜) Arch Palace has many fans and owner Mustafa has a reputation for being a helpful and knowledgeable host. For those who don't fancy the idiosyncrasies of cave-living, or can't manage climbing up hills to their hotel, the arched stone rooms here, all with recently modernised bathrooms, are the perfect compromise.

Kemal's Guest House
PENSION €

(☑271 2234; www.kemalsguesthouse.com; Karşıbucak Caddesi; dm/d/tr/q €13/40/57/70; 🛜) This homely pension brims with old-fashioned hospitality. Kemal is a terrific cook and his Dutch wife Barbara knows her way around the region's hiking trails like perhaps no other hotelier. Pull up a comfy sofa in reception, grab a dog-eared book off the shelf and thumb your nose at your 'boutique' friends.

Flintstones Cave Hotel
HOSTEL €

(☑271 2555; www.flintstonescave.com; Uzundere Caddesi, Karşıbucak Sokak 3; dm/d/tr/f ₺25/80 /120/150; 🛜🏊) The old Flintstones Cave outlives its party reputation to outshine many budget rivals. The dorm is still a musty, squashy affair but the minimally furnished privates are spacious and comfortable. Staff are fun and professional and the large swimming pool is the best in town.

Shoestring Cave Pension
PENSION €

(☑271 2450; www.shoestringcave.com; Aydınlı Mahallesi; dm/s/d/ste €10/30/60, d €35-50; 🛜🏊) A recent renovation has seen the double rooms at this old-school backpacker paradise get jazzed-up while the funky cave dorm means those counting their kuruş still have a dependable place to crash. The courtyard picnic tables and cool rooftop swimming-pool area provide a real communal feel and are packed with travellers jousting over the merits of their respective itineraries.

Cappadocia Cave Suites
LUXURY HOTEL €€€

(☑271 2800; www.cappadociacavesuites.com; Ünlü Sokak 19; r €135-275; ❄🛜) Uncomplicated service, spacious, modern-meets-megalithic suite rooms and cool, converted stables. Fairy Chimney 1 is our pick for its cosy living room, ideal for balloon viewing.

Elysee Pension
HOTEL €€

(☑271 2244; www.elyseegoreme.com; Mizraz Sokak 18; budget s/d €30/45, d/tr/q €60/75/85; 🛜) Highly recommended by readers is this restored farmhouse, which has a range of rooms for all budgets and is run by charismatic manger Cengiz.

Divan Cave House
HOTEL €€

(☑271 2189; www.divancavehotel.com; Aydınlı Mahallesi; s/d/tr €45/60/80, ste €100-120; 🛜) This tranquil hotel offers traditionally styled cave and stone rooms that surround a flower-filled, spacious courtyard.

Saksağan Cave Hotel
PENSION €€

(☑271 2165; www.cavehotelsaksagan.net; Okul Sokak 1; s/d €30/45, fairy chimney d €55; 🛜) We like this cheerful family-run pension for its friendly Anatolian hospitality and simple but spick-and-span rooms.

Travel Inn Cave Hotel
HOTEL €€

(☑271 2622; www.travelinncavehotel.com; Harım Sokak 39; s €30, d €50-60, ste €75; 🛜) With bags full of local character and more eclectic bric-a-brac than you could shake a stick at, the warren of rooms here are a wonderfully atmospheric choice.

Gerdiş Evi Guesthouse
GUEST HOUSE €€

(☑271 2221; www.gerdisevi.com; Goynuk Sokak 5/B; s/d/tr €30/40/45, deluxe €65-80; 🛜) A great range of rooms for all budgets, no trudging up hills, and friendly service make this newcomer shine on the Göreme hotel scene.

Kaya Camping CAMPING GROUND €
(☑343 3100; Göreme Yolu; campsites per adult/child ₺15/10; 🛜🏊) This impressive campsite has magnificent views and top-notch facilities such as clean bathrooms, plentiful hot water, a restaurant, supermarket, communal kitchen and washing machines. It's 2.5km from the centre of Göreme, uphill from the Göreme Open-Air Museum.

✕ Eating

TOP CHOICE **Köy Evi** ANATOLIAN €€€
(☑271 2008; Aydınkırağı Sokak 40; set menu ₺25; ☑) The simple, wholesome, tasty flavours of village food are the main act at this brilliant set-menu restaurant where highly charming staff serve up a taste-bud tour of Göreme while the hard-working lady-chefs shovel out more steaming hot bread from the *tandır* (oven). Inside, the warren of cave rooms have been kept authentically basic which adds to the homespun appeal. Bring your appetite and prepare to feast on the soul-food that fuelled Cappadocian farmers for centuries.

TOP CHOICE **Seten Restaurant** MODERN TURKISH €€€
(☑271 3025; www.setenrestaurant.com; Aydınlı Sokak; mains ₺16-40) Brimming with an artful Anatolian aesthetic, Seten is a feast for the eye as well as for the stomach. Named after the old millstones used to grind bulgur wheat, this restaurant is an education for newcomers to Turkish cuisine and a treat for well-travelled tongues. Signature chefs and attentive service complement classic dishes done right and a dazzling array of mezes done differently enough to keep you coming back. Göreme's most sophisticated dining experience.

TOP CHOICE **Topdeck Cave Restaurant** ANATOLIAN €€€
(☑271 2474; Hafız Abdullah Efendi Sokak 15; mains ₺15-20; ⊙dinner only; ☑) If it feels like you're dining in a family home, it's because you are. Talented chef Mustafa (aka Topdeck) and his gracious family have transformed an atmospheric cave room in their house into a cosy restaurant. Here the kids pitch in with the serving and diners dig into hearty helpings of Anatolian favourites,

often with a spicy twist. Make sure you choose the mixed meze plate for a flavour-packed blowout your stomach will thank you for.

Nazar Börek BÖREKÇISI €
(☑271 2441; Müze Caddesi; gözleme & börek ₺6-9; 🛜) Head to Nazar Börek for supremely tasty traditional Turkish staples, which are served up by friendly Rafik and his team. Nazar remains our long-standing favourite for its hearty plates of *gözleme* (savoury pancakes) and *sosyete böregi* (stuffed spiral pastries served with yoghurt and tomato sauce). The atmosphere here is extremely convivial, and encourages diners to linger long after their meals have finished.

Dibek ANATOLIAN €€
(☑271 2209; Hakkı Paşa Meydanı 1; mains ₺10-22; ☑) Diners sprawl on cushions and feast on traditional dishes and homemade wine at this family restaurant, located inside a 475-year-old building. Many book ahead (at least three hours in advance) for the delicious slow-cooked *testi kebap* meal ('pottery kebap', with meat or mushrooms and vegetables cooked in a sealed terracotta pot, which is broken at the table; ₺28).

Fırın Express PIDE €
(☑271 2266; Eski Belediye Yanı Sokak; pide ₺4-8; ☑) Simply the best pide in town is found in this local haunt. The cavernous wood oven fires up meat and vegetarian options and anything doused with egg. We suggest adding an *ayran* (yoghurt drink) and a *çoban salatası* (shepherd's salad) for a delicious bargain feed.

Local Restaurant MODERN TURKISH €€
(☑271 2629; Müze Caddesi 38; mains ₺11-32) New owners have brought in a creative chef and enthusiastic staff to give this old-timer a fresh lease of life. The steak dishes are scrumptious by themselves but don't forget to order the *patlican* (aubergine) salad which is gloriously smoky perfection on a plate.

Orient Restaurant INTERNATIONAL €€€
(☑271 2346; Adnan Menderes Caddesi; mains ₺16-40) Juicy steaks and a stack of flavoursome pasta dishes head up the impressive, meaty menu which romps from traditional Turkish to continental cuisine with ease. The outside seating, among blooming roses, and service are delightful.

Meeting Point Café
INTERNATIONAL €

(Müze Caddesi; mains ₺10) Missing your favourite comfort foods? Cenap and Anniesa, a Turkish–South African couple, dish up curries, burgers, fruit smoothies, filter coffee and home-baked cakes from their cabin-like restaurant.

Drinking

Fat Boys
BAR, RESTAURANT

(☎0535 386 4484; Belediye Caddesi; beer ₺7, mains ₺8-16; ⏰noon-late; 📶) This lounge-style bar is a winner. We love the terrace, strewn with fat cushions, and curling up on the comfortable couches inside. The hungry can order from a global pub-grub menu which stars Aussie-style pies, as well as burgers, nachos and Vegemite on toast. While the pool table and board games are tempting diversions it's the friendly staff and well-stocked bar that make this place so popular.

Cafe Şafak
CAFE

(Müze Caddesi; coffee ₺5-7, mains ₺7-18; 📶) Hands down the best coffee in Göreme. With an exposed-brick interior, displaying quirky art, Şafak is a little slice of New York cafe-cool that delivers in the caffeine-hit stakes. There's a good menu as well if you're feeling peckish.

Mydonos Cafe
CAFE

(Müze Caddesi 18; drinks ₺3-8) Subdued jazzy background music and wall displays of old vinyl dust jackets fill the interior of Mydonos Cafe with subtle bohemian flair while the balcony is the perfect pit stop for sunny Cappadocian afternoons. We love the decadent hot chocolate and aromatic French-press coffee.

Red Red Wine House
BAR

(☎271 2183; Müze Caddesi; glass of wine ₺10) In a former stable with arched ceilings, this seductive local feels like an ancient bootlegger's secret mixing den decorated by lovers of adult contemporary. A steady chain of guests smoke fruity pipes and sip increasingly palatable Cappadocian wines.

Noriyon Cafe
CAFE

(Müze Caddesi; beer ₺7) This brightly painted, cruisy cafe rustles up a mean *türk kahve* (Turkish coffee) and has a roaring fire to set the scene outside in the evenings. It's also the meeting point for the guided walks run by Mehmet Güngör (p451).

RUDE BOYS

The *peribacalar* (fairy chimneys) that have made Cappadocia so famous were formed when erosion wiped out the lava covering the *tuff* (consolidated volcanic ash), leaving behind isolated pinnacles. They can reach a height of up to 40m, have conical shapes and are topped by caps of harder rock resting on pillars of softer rock. Depending on your perspective, they look like giant phalluses or outsized mushrooms. The villagers call them simply *kalelar* (castles).

Red Rock Bar
BAR

(Uzendere Caddesi; ⏰5pm-late) Set in a beautifully atmospheric and cavernous cave, Red Rock's party scene doesn't really get going until late.

Shopping

Tribal Collections
CARPETS

(☎271 2400; Müze Caddesi 24; ⏰9am-8pm) As well as being home to some mighty fine rugs, owners Ruth and Faruk are known for their highly recommended educationals (a kind of carpets 101) which explain the history and artistry of these coveted textiles.

Argos
CERAMICS

(☎271 2750; Cevizler Sokak 22) A classy selection of handmade ceramics, both modern and Asian-inspired, as well as unusual stone pieces.

Information

Internet Access

There are a couple of internet cafes in the village centre including **Internet Call Shop** (Belediye Caddesi; per hr ₺1.50; ⏰9am-late), which also has printing/photocopying facilities and a book swap, and sells memory cards.

Money

There are standalone ATM booths in, and around, the otogar. Some of the town's travel agencies will exchange money, although you're probably better off going to the post office (PTT) or **Deniz Bank** (Müze Caddesi 3).

Post

The **post office** (Posta Sokak) has phone, fax and money-changing services.

Tourist Information

There's an information booth at the otogar that is open when most long-distance buses arrive,

SERVICES FROM GÖREME'S OTOGAR

DESTINATION	FARE (₺)	DURATION (HR)	FREQUENCY (PER DAY)
Adana	30	5	1 morning
Ankara	30	4½	2 morning & 2 afternoon
Antalya	45	9	2 evening
Çanakkale	70	16	1 evening
Denizli (for Pamukkale)	45	11	2 evening
Fethiye	55	14	1 evening
İstanbul	40-50	11-12	1 morning & 2 evening
İzmir	40	11½	1 evening
Konya	20	3	2 morning & 3 evening
Marmaris/Bodrum	60	13	2 evening
Selçuk	50	11½	1 evening

but it's run by the **Göreme Turizmciler Derneği** (Göreme Tourism Society; ☑271 2558; www .goreme.org). This coalition of hotel and restaurant owners is solely aimed at directing travellers to accommodation in the village, and staff can't supply any meaningful information. They give out free maps and sell one for ₺5.

ⓘ Getting There & Away

There are daily long-distance buses to all sorts of places from Göreme's **otogar** (bus station), although normally you're ferried to Nevşehir's otogar to pick up the main service (which can add nearly an hour to your travelling time). Note that the morning bus to İstanbul goes via Ankara, so takes one hour longer than the evening bus. For Aksaray, change in Nevşehir.

Göreme has good connections to the other Cappadocian villages; the Ürgüp–Avanos dolmuş and Avanos–Nevşehir bus both pick up/ drop off passengers on their way through town. There is also a regular dolmuş from Göreme to Nevşehir via Uçhisar (₺2.50, every 30 minutes between 8am and 7pm).

ⓘ Getting Around

There are several places to hire mountain bikes, scooters, cars and the objectionable quads, including **Hitchhiker** (☑271 2169; www.cappa dociahitchhiker.com; Uzundere Caddesi) and **Oz Cappadocia** (☑271 2159; www.ozcappadocia .com; Uzundere Caddesi) which are both near the otogar entrance. It pays to shop around, as prices vary dramatically.

As a rule, mountain bikes cost about ₺25 for a day while mopeds and scooters go for ₺45 to ₺55. A small Renault or Fiat car costs ₺90 to ₺130 for a day, with features such as air-con, automatic gears and a diesel engine available.

Since there are no petrol stations in Göreme and the rental companies will hike petrol prices, refill your tank in Nevşehir, Avanos or Ürgüp, or at one of the garages on the main road near Ortahisar and Ibrahimpaşa.

Uçhisar

☑0384 / POP 3801

Pretty little Uçhisar has undergone rapid development since the heady Club Med days. The French love affair with the clifftop village continues each summer as busloads of Gallic tourists unpack their *joie de vivre* in trendy hotels at the foot of Uçhisar Castle. The royal rectangular crag, visible from nearby Göreme, is the dramatic centrepiece of a stylish Cappadocian aesthetic, albeit at times a touch manufactured. If you need respite from the many shades of sun-kissed rock, divert your gaze to the white peaks of **Erciyes Dağı** (Mt Erciyes; 3916m), which is a wild world away from your shaded terrace. Uçhisar remains a quieter alternative to Göreme as a base for exploring the region.

There are Vakif Bank and Garanti Bankası ATMs on the main square, and an **internet cafe** (per hr ₺1; ⊙9am-midnight) and a **PTT** (Adnan Menderes Caddesi) nearby.

⊙ Sights & Activities

Watching the sun set over the Rose and Pigeon Valleys from the wonderful vantage point of **Uçhisar Castle** (Uçhisar Kalesi; admission ₺3; ⊙8am-8.15pm) is a popular activity. A tall volcanic-rock outcrop riddled with tunnels and windows, the castle is visible for miles around. Now a tourist attraction complete with terrace cafes at its entrance, it provides panoramic views of the Cappadocian countryside. Unfortunately, many of the bus groups that visit leave rubbish, which diminishes the experience. The lack of barriers means you should be very careful – one photographer died when he fell over the edge after stepping back to get a good shot.

There are some excellent **hiking** possibilities around Uçhisar, with trailheads to both Bağlıdere Vadısı (White Valley) and Güvercinlik Vadısı (Pigeon Valley) on the outskirts of town. See p449 for more information.

🛏 Sleeping

TOP CHOICE · Kale Konak   HOTEL €€€
(☑219 2828; www.kalekonak.com; Kale Sokak 9; s/d/ste €90/110/140; ☎) Take a handful of minimalist retreat-chic, blend it with touches of artistic flair and balance it all out with wads of Ottoman style and you get this effortlessly elegant hotel. Spacious rooms lead out through underground passageways to comfortable reading corners, communal areas strewn with fat cushions, and shady terraces in the shadow of Uçhisar's craggy *kale* (castle). The marble hamam tops off what has to be Uçhisar's most super-sophisticated place to stay. The epitome of casual luxury.

TOP CHOICE · Şira Hotel   HOTEL €€€
(☑219 3037; www.hotelsira.com; Göreme Caddesi 87; s/d €125/135; ☎) Multilingual Filiz and her family have created a beautiful retreat where modern comfort and traditional architecture sit in harmony side-by-side. The panoramic views from the terrace may be enough to tempt you never to leave but the real bonus is the management's appreciation for wine, food and nature; all on show in the restaurant which dazzles with flavourful feasts. Grape-harvesting tours and culinary workshops are also available on request.

Kilim Pension   PENSION €€
(☑219 2774; www.sisik.com; Tekelli Mahallesi; s/d/tr ₺70/130/170; ☎) The pride of fun-loving, multilingual 'Şişik', Kilim Pension is an unpretentious home-away-from-home with a glorious vine-draped terrace and cosy restaurant that dishes up first-class local fare. Spacious rooms are smartly simple, light-filled and airy, with swish bathrooms as an added bonus. The complimentary chaperoned hikes into the valleys are highly recommended.

Taka Ev   HOTEL €€
(☑0532 740 4177; www.takaev.net; Kayabaşi Sokak 43; r from €70; ☎) Run by friendly Murat, charmingly cute Taka Ev is an intimate place festooned with flower pots and colourful *suzani* embroideries. The seven light-filled rooms have tonnes of local character and homely touches, along with swanky bathrooms that host powerful showers.

Argos   LUXURY HOTEL €€€
(☑219 3130; www.argosincappadocia.com; Kaya başi Sokak; r €160-240, ste €400-600; ✳☎) This is a new level of designer-luxury from the İstanbul advertising firm with its fancy feet now in the hotel game. Spilling over the hillside are some of the finest rooms in Cappadocia, all sporting renowned architect Turgur Cansever's sympathetic restorative edge. Take refuge in the subterranean tunnels and old cellars then rise to the manicured lawns. On-site is Bezirhane, a former linseed press and now an acoustic hall staging regular music performances and private parties.

Uçhisar Pension   PENSION €
(☑219 2662; www.uchisarpension.com; Göreme Caddesi; s/d/tr €25/40/55; ☎) Mustafa and Gül dispense lashings of old fashioned Turkish hospitality in their cosy pension. Simple rooms are spick-and-span with white-washed walls, fresh linen and small but squeaky-clean bathrooms. A couple have cave features. In summer swing from the rooftop hammock and pinch yourself for your luck on finding million-dollar views for budget prices.

Les Maisons de Cappadoce   APARTMENT €€€
(☑219 2813; www.cappadoce.com; studios €140-190, villas €240-980) If only all real-estate barons could use French architect Jacques Avizou's tasteful expansion policy, then maybe we could all live in places like Les Maisons de Cappadoce in the old quarters of ancient towns with little breakfast baskets hanging on our door every morning. These intelligently designed serviced villas range from studios to sublime family fun houses.

Anatolia Pension   PENSION €€
(☑219 2339; www.anatoliapension.com; Hacialibey Caddesi; d/tr ₺100/130; ☎) Anatolia has 15 bright, spotless rooms inside a sturdy stone house. Manager Ahmet is a charming host who provides discerning travel advice and services. Traditional Turkish meals are available.

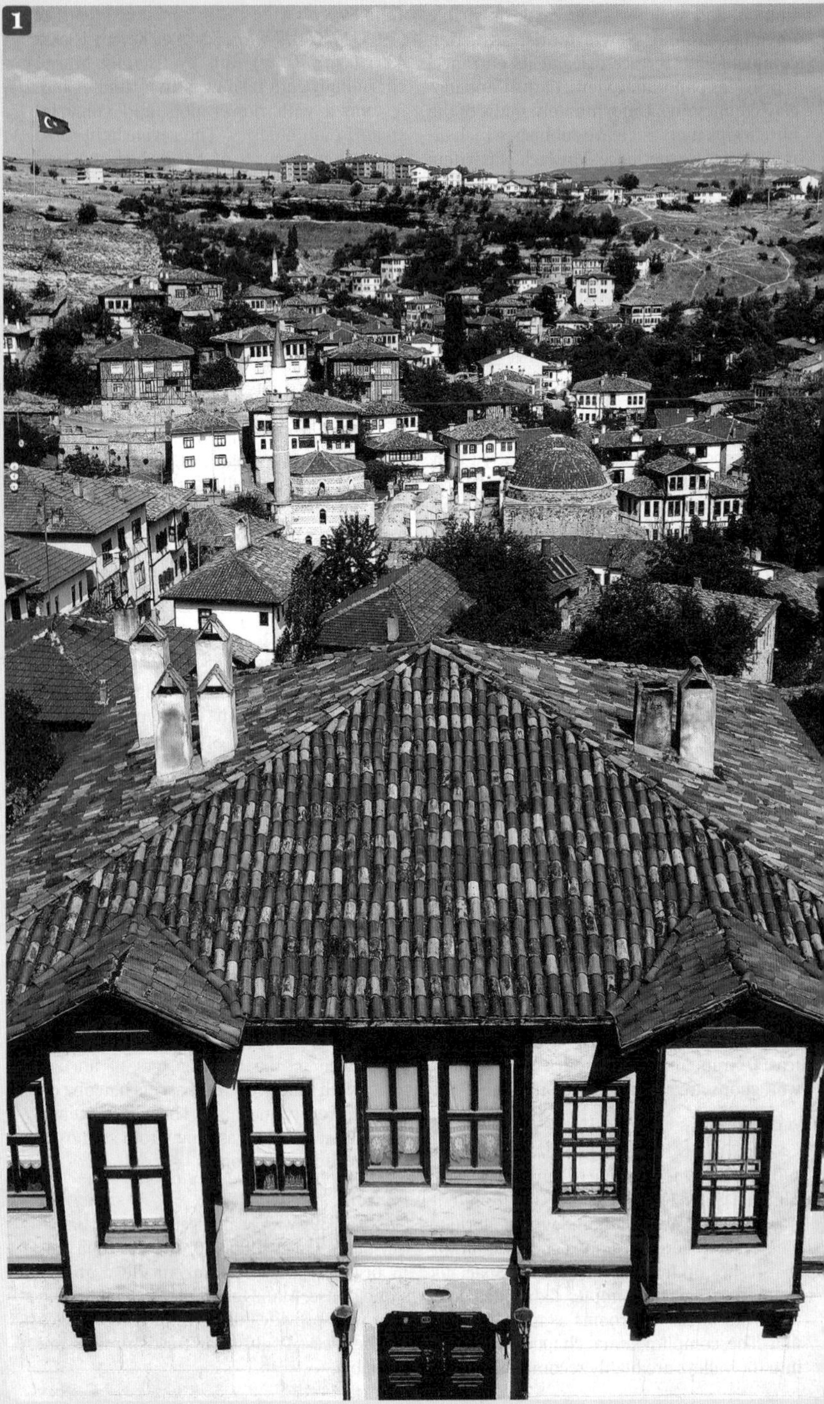

1. Safranbolu architecture (p411)
Turkey's most well-preserved Ottoman town is a vision of red-tiled roofs and meandering alleys.

2. İshak Paşa Palace (p548)
The epitome of romance, this palace is perched on a small plateau near the base of Mt Ararat.

3. Turkish delight, Spice Bazaar (p79)
İstanbul's Spice Bazaar is one of the many places where you can sample *lokum*.

4. Waterfront, Bozcaada town (p169)
Charming and stylish, the Aegean island of Bozcaada is a picturesque holiday spot.

Lale Saray
HOTEL €€€

(☑219 2333; www.lalesaray.com; Göreme Caddesi; s/d/ste €100/130/150; 🛜) Large stone-vaulted rooms, decked out in muted oranges and pinks and jazzed up by wrought iron and tilework accents, offer a comfortably modern alternative to cave-living.

✖ Eating

TOP CHOICE Elai
TURKISH €€€

(☑219 3181; www.elairestaurant.com; Eski Göreme Yolu; mains ₺24-45; ⊙10.30am-2.30pm & 6.30-11pm) This prime example of an emerging Cappadocian style is as far removed from the desert communities it once served as the Turkish fusion menu is from original Anatolian cuisine. In a converted cafe, where the gossiping old men have been replaced by a sharp dining room with velvety curtains and exposed beams, guests can kick off with a drink on the terrace, with its magnificent view, before moving inside to sample dishes ranging from duck confit to grilled jumbo shrimp. Dishes travel around the world but really shine when they are Turkish in inspiration.

Center Café & Restaurant
TURKISH €€

(☑219 3117; Belediye Meydanı; mains ₺10-25) A former top-notch Club Med chef now presides over this humble town-square cafe-restaurant. The verdant garden setting hums with satiated locals, and young glamour pusses coo over *dondurma* (ice cream) and crispy salads. We almost wish this place was still secret.

Restaurante du Mustafa
TURKISH €€

(Kale Sokak; gözleme ₺5, mains ₺15-30) It may not be as flashy as other restaurants in town but Mustafa's delivers on fresh, local flavour serving up Turkish favourites with unpretentious flair.

Le Mouton Rouge
BAR, RESTAURANT

(☑219 3000; Belediye Meydanı; mains ₺10-20) Inside a courtyard adorned with hammocks which inspire lazy hours of drinking, this is Uçhisar's most convivial place for a sun-soaked afternoon beer or a long evening on the *rakı* (aniseed brandy).

🔒 Shopping

Göreme Onyx
JEWELLERY

(Güvercinlik Vadisi Karşısı) The full gamut of precious stones is on offer in this large shop on the outskirts of Uçhisar.

ℹ Getting There & Away

The Nevşehir–Avanos bus and the Nevşehir–Göreme dolmuş both pass through Uçhisar and drop off/pick up passengers on the main road.

Dolmuşes to Nevşehir (₺2.50) leave from outside the *belediye* on the main square every half-hour between 7am to 7.30pm.

A taxi to Göreme costs ₺15 and to Ürgüp ₺35.

Çavuşin
☑0384

Midway between Göreme and Avanos is little Çavuşin, dominated by a cliff where a clutter of abandoned houses spills down the slope in a charming jumble. The main hive of activity is the clutch of souvenir stands at the cliff base, which spring into action when the midday tour buses roll into town. When the last bus has left for the day, Çavuşin resets the snooze button and resumes its slumber. The village has no bank or ATM.

⊙ Sights & Activities

Çavuşin is the starting point for scenic hikes to the southeast, through Güllüdere Vadısı (Rose Valley), Kızılçukur Vadısı (Red Valley) and Meskendir Valley. You can even go as far as the Kızılçukur viewpoint (6.5km), then walk out to the Ürgüp–Ortahisar road and catch a dolmuş back to your base.

Çavuşin Church
CHURCH

(Big Pigeon House Church; admission ₺8; ⊙8am-5pm) Just off the highway on the northern edge of Çavuşin you'll find this church, accessed via a steep and rickety iron stairway. Cappadocia's first post-iconoclastic church, it served as a pigeon house for many years and is home to some fine frescoes.

Old Village Ruins
RUINS

Walk up the hill through the new part of Çavuşin and continue past the main square to find the old village ruins. Here you can explore a steep and labyrinthine complex of abandoned houses cut into a rock face, as well as one of the oldest churches in Cappadocia, the **Church of John the Baptist**, which is located at the top of the cliff path.

☞ Tours

Mephisto Voyage
ADVENTURE TOURS

(☑532 7070; www.mephistovoyage.com) Based at the İn Pension, this group has a very good reputation. It's been operating for over a decade and offers trekking and camping packages ranging from a two-day local wander to a 14-day trip around Cappadocia and the Taurus Mountains (€500). It also rents out bicycles and offers tours by bike, horse and cart and, for mobility-impaired people, the Joëlette system.

🛏 Sleeping & Eating

Village Cave Hotel
HOTEL €€

(✆532 7197; www.thevillagecave.com; r from €80; 🔊) The most interesting lodging in Çavuşin is this restored 18th-century stone house with six bedrooms carved on two floors in view of the gorgeous tumble of the old village. Decorated with minimalist chic, the seriously quirky cave shapes here are the stand-out feature. Friendly host Halim is the third generation to manage the property.

Turbel Cave Hotel
HOTEL €€

(✆532 7084; www.turbelcavehotel.com; r from ₺150; 🔊) With just four rooms this is a wonderfully intimate choice. Choose from either the stone rooms with their airy vaulted ceilings or the snug cave rooms. All are comfortably furnished with tea/coffee making facilities, plasma TVs and fridges, and boast fantastic walk-in showers. The pretty breakfast terrace has prime-time views of Çavuşin's old village.

İn Pension
PENSION €

(✆532 7070; www.pensionincappadocia.com; old wing s/d €25/30, new wing s/d/tr €35/40/50; 🔊) This little pension by the main square comes with built-in travel advice courtesy of owner Mephisto Voyage. Some rooms have been spruced up with new linen and white paint, though beds and bathrooms are pretty small.

Panorama Pension
PENSION €

(✆532 7002; r per person ₺30) A cheap and cheerful option for those looking to save their lira. Basic rooms (some without bathrooms) are balanced out by friendly management, a lovely garden setting and cute restaurant out the front.

Ayse & Mustafa's Place
TURKISH €

(mains ₺5-10; ⊙9am-5pm) Sitting under the plum trees, Ayse's home-cooked *gözleme* and *menemen* (scrambled eggs with peppers, tomatoes and cheese) are a hit with the lunchtime tour-bus crowd.

❶ Getting There & Away

Çavuşin is on the route of both the hourly Nevşehir–Avanos bus and the Ürgüp–Avanos dolmuş service (see p465).

Zelve

The road between Çavuşin and Avanos passes a turn-off to the **Zelve Open-Air Museum** (admission ₺8, parking ₺2; ⊙8am-7pm Apr-Oct, 8am-5pm Nov-Mar), where three valleys of abandoned homes and churches converge. Zelve was a monastic retreat from the 9th to the 13th century. It doesn't have as many impressive painted churches as the Göreme Open-Air Museum, but its sinewy valley walls with rock antennae could have been made for poking around. An impressive new walking trail which loops around the valleys has vastly improved access to the site, although erosion continues to eat into the valley structures and certain areas are cordoned off due to rockfalls.

The valleys were inhabited until 1952, when they were deemed too dangerous to live in, and the villagers were resettled a few kilometres away in Aktepe, also known as Yeni Zelve (New Zelve). Remnants of village life include the small, unadorned, rock-cut **mosque** in Valley Three and the old *değirmen* (mill), with a grindstone and graffitied wooden beam, in Valley One.

Beyond the mill, the **Balıklı Kilise** (Fish Church) has fish figuring in one of the primitive paintings. Adjoining it is the more impressive **Üzümlü Kilise** (Grape Church), with obvious bunches of grapes. In Valley Two what's left of the **Geyikli Kilise** (Church with Deer) is worth seeing.

There are cafes and *çay bahçesi* (tea gardens) in the car park outside.

Paşabağı, a valley halfway along the turn-off road to Zelve near a fairy-chimney *jandarma* (police station), has a three-headed formation and some of Cappadocia's best examples of mushroom-shaped fairy chimneys. Monks inhabited the valley and you can climb up inside one chimney to a monk's quarters, decorated with Hellenic crosses. Wooden steps lead to a chapel where three iconoclastic paintings escaped the Islamic vandals; the central one depicts the Virgin holding baby Jesus.

❶ Getting There & Away

The Ürgüp–Avanos dolmuş stops at Paşabağı and Zelve. If you're coming from Ürgüp, Göreme or Çavuşin and tell the driver that you want to go to Paşabağı or Zelve, the bus will turn off the highway past Çavuşin, let you off and then go up to Aktepe and on to Avanos. If no one wants Paşabağı or Zelve, the bus will not make this detour.

Returning dolmuşes from Avanos to Ürgüp all stop at Zelve. If you don't want to wait for the dolmuş you can walk the 3.5km from the site to the main highway, from where you can flag down a bus going towards either Göreme or Avanos.

Devrent Valley

Look, it's a camel! Stunning Devrent Valley's volcanic cones are some of the best-formed and most thickly clustered in Cappadocia, and looking at their fantastic shapes is like gazing at the clouds as a child. See if you can spot the dolphin, seals, Napoleon's hat, kissing birds, Virgin Mary and various reptilian forms.

Most of the rosy rock cones are topped by flattish, darker stones of harder rock that sheltered the cones from the rain until all the surrounding rock was eaten away, a process known as differential erosion.

To get to Devrent Valley (also known as Imagination Valley) from Zelve, go about 200m back down the access road to where the road forks and take the right road, which is marked for Ürgüp. After about 2km you'll come to the village of Aktepe (Yeni Zelve). Bear right after this and follow the Ürgüp road uphill for less than 2km. The Ürgüp–Avanos dolmuş can drop you off at Aktepe.

Avanos

📞 0384 / POP 11,800 / ELEV 910M

The Kızılırmak (Red River) is the slow-paced pulse of this provincial town and the unusual source of its livelihood, the distinctive red clay that, mixed with a white, mountain mud variety, is spun to produce the region's famed pottery. Typically painted in turquoise or the earthy browns and yellows favoured by the Hittites, the beautiful pieces are traditionally thrown by men and painted by women. Aside from the regulation tour groups (who quicker than an eye blink, get bussed into the pottery workshops and then bussed out again) Avanos is relatively devoid of foreign visitors, leaving you alone to meander the alleys which snake up the hillside, lined with gently decaying grand Greek houses. Occasional (and slightly incongruous) Venetian-style gondolas now ply the river, but riverside is still the place to ponder the sunset as you sip your umpteenth çay.

⊙ Sights

Tour groups are shuffled into the pottery warehouses outside of town. Others should patronise one of the smaller **pottery workshops** in the centre, most of which will happily show you how to throw a pot or two. These are located in the small streets around the main square and in the group of shops opposite the PTT. Our favourite is **Le Palais du Urdu**, a unique drum-making and pottery studio that caused a minor stir in ceramic circles with a recent TV appearance. Also worth a visit is **Chez Galip** (Firin Sokak 24; ⊙10am-8pm), an extensive pottery gallery with the infamous 'Hair Museum', a creepy collection of 16,000 samples of women's hair.

☞ Tours

Kirkit Voyage   GUIDED TOURS
(☎511 3148; www.kirkit.com; Atatürk Caddesi 50) This company has an excellent reputation and friendly multilingual staff. As well as the usual guided tours, it can arrange walking, biking, canoeing, horse-riding and snowshoe trips and can arrange airport transfers (reservation essential). The highly-recommended guided horse-riding treks range from €35 for two hours to €70 for a full day and include proper riding equipment.

🛏 Sleeping

🏆 Kirkit Pension   HOTEL €€
CHOICE
(☎511 3148; www.kirkitpension.com; Genç Ağa Sokak; s/d/tr €40/50/70; 🎐) This Avanos institution, right in the centre of town, is a rambling stone house with rooms set between a lovingly restored courtyard filled with plants and quirky antique pieces. With just 15 rooms looked after by incredibly knowledgeable and helpful management, Kirkit is the perfect low-key base for trips around Cappadocia. Kilims, old black-and-white photographs, intricately carved cupboards and *suzani* bedspreads spark up the simple-yet-perfectly-comfortable rooms which are all different shapes and sizes. Guests can dine in the super-atmospheric cave restaurant below (dinner €10) on feasts full of local flavour.

Sofa Hotel   HOTEL €€
(☎511 5186; www.sofahotel.com; Gedik Sokak 9; s/d/ste €40/50/70; 🎐) The Sofa Hotel is a higgledy-piggledy wonderland for adults struck by wanderlust. Resident artist Hoja has spent a fair chunk of his life purchas-

ing and redesigning this collection of Ottoman houses that now welcomes guests to live among the beautiful madness. Rooms merge eclectic-chic and traditional decoration with a tasteful ease. Service is a little more aloof here than elsewhere but it's not often you get to stay somewhere so lavishly offbeat.

Günay Stone House Hotel
HOTEL €€

(☑511 5255; www.gunaystonehouse.com; Büyük Dere Caddesi; s/d €50/70; ☎) Right at the top of the hill from Avanos main square, with splendid red-tiled-roof views over town, this welcoming hotel has comfortable, modern rooms with just a touch of local character.

Tokmak Konuk Evi
GUESTHOUSE €€

(☑511 4587; www.tokmakkonukevi.com; Cami Sokak 11; s/d/tr ₺70/100/150; ☎) A friendly place with small rooms that have a whiff of the Swiss Alps about them. There's pinewood detail in abundance and ultra-high beds. It's up the hill from Avanos, main square.

Ada Camping
CAMPING GROUND €

(☑511 2429; www.adacampingavanos.com; Jan Zakari Caddesi 20; campsites per person incl electricity ₺10; ☎) Take the Nevşehir road and bear right to reach this large, family-run camping ground, in a superb setting near the river. The toilet block could be cleaner but there's lots of shade and grass, a restaurant and a cold but inviting swimming pool.

✖ Eating

The grassy banks of the Kızılırmak River have recently been spruced up and are prime picnicking territory. There are also some shady riverside cafes to relax in.

🔝CHOICE Dayının Yeri
KEBAP €€

(☑511 6840; Atatürk Caddesi; pide ₺7-8, mains ₺13-20) Locals may grumble that it's not as cheap as it used to be but this shiny, modern ocakbaşı (grill restaurant), right beside Taş Köprü (the town's main bridge), is one of Cappadocia's best. As long as you steer clear of the meze selection it's also still good value. All the kebabs here are sensational but we love the Beyti Kebap (lamb wrapped in lavaş bread and smothered in garlic sauce). Don't even think of leaving without sampling the freshly prepared künefe (layers of kadayıf cemented together with sweet cheese, doused in syrup and

served hot with a sprinkling of pistachio). No alcohol is served.

Bizim Ev
INTERNATIONAL €€€

(☑511 5525; Baklacı Sokak 1; mains ₺15-25) The cave wine cellar could easily tempt you into a few lost hours of tasting tipples but if you can make it upstairs the terrace is the place for atmospheric dining. Service is sleekly unobtrusive and the menu ranges from steaks to kebaps to casseroles.

Hanım Eli
ANATOLIAN €

(Atatürk Caddesi; mains ₺7-10) This modest little diner serves up wholesome local dishes packed full of fresh, local flavour. This is home-style cooking executed brilliantly and without pretentious flourish. The mantı (Turkish ravioli) we had here was the best in Cappadocia.

Avanos Kadın Girişimciler Koop Restaurant
ANATOLIAN €€

(Avanos Women's Cooperative Restaurant; Uğur Mumcu Caddesi; mains ₺10-15) Want to sample içli köfte (ground lamb and onion with a bulgur coating, often served as a hot meze) the way a Turkish mamma does it? The industrious women of Avanos have got together to offer a taste of village home-cooking in this restaurant just off Avanos' main square. Portions are on the small side.

ℹ Information

The **tourist office** (☑511 4360; Atatürk Caddesi; ◷8.30am-5pm), which doesn't always stick to its opening hours, is based in a beautifully restored Ottoman house opposite Taş Köprü (Avanos' main bridge). Several ATMs are on or around the main square.

ℹ Getting There & Around

Buses from Avanos to Nevşehir (₺3) leave every 30 minutes between 7am and 7pm. Services departing on the hour travel via Çavuşin, Göreme and Uçhisar (₺2.50); the half-hour departures take the direct route.

Dolmuşes to Ürgüp (₺3) leave at 9am, 11am, 1pm, 3pm and 5pm, travelling via Zelve, Paşabağı, Çavuşin, Göreme and Göreme Open-Air Museum.

All these services stop at the bus stands along Atatürk Caddesi.

Monday to Friday there is a dolmuş service to Özkonak underground city hourly between 8.30am and 4.30pm. The dolmuşes leave from behind the PTT near the main square.

Kirkit Voyage hires out mountain bikes for ₺25 per day or ₺15 for half a day.

Around Avanos

SARIHAN

Built in 1249, the Sarıhan (Yellow Caravanserai; admission ₺3; ⊙9am-midnight) has an elaborate gateway with a small mosque above it. Having been restored in the late 1980s, it's one of the best remaining Seljuk caravanserais. Gunning down the highway towards it makes you feel like a 13th-century trader, ready to rest his camels and catch up with his fellow dealers.

Inside, you also have to use your imagination in the bare stone courtyard. Visitors are allowed on the roof, but the main reason to come here is the 45-minute whirling dervish ceremony (sema; ☑511 3795; admission €25; ⊙9.30pm Apr-Oct, 9pm Nov-Mar). You must book ahead – most hotels in Göreme, Ürgüp, Avanos and Uçhisar will be able to arrange it for you. Be aware that the price may vary according to how much commission your tour agent or hotel is skimming off the top.

Though the setting is extremely atmospheric, the *sema* is nowhere near as impressive as those staged at the Mevlevi Monastery in İstanbul's Beyoğlu. If you've seen one of those you should probably give this a miss.

❶ Getting There & Away

Getting to the Sarıhan, 6km east of Avanos, without your own transport is difficult, as there are no dolmuşes and few vehicles with which to hitch a ride. An Avanos taxi driver will probably want around ₺30 to take you there and back, including waiting time.

ÖZKONAK UNDERGROUND CITY

About 15km north of Avanos, the village of Özkonak hosts a smaller version of the underground cities of Kaymaklı and Derinkuyu, with the same wine reservoirs and rolling stone doors. Although Özkonak underground city (admission ₺8; ⊙8.30am-5.30pm) is neither as dramatic nor as impressive as the larger ones, it is much less crowded.

The easiest way to get there is by dolmuş from Avanos (₺1.50, 30 minutes, hourly between 8.30am and 4.30pm). There are no services on the weekend. Ask to be let off for the *yeraltı şehri* (underground city); the bus stops at the petrol station, a 500m stroll from the entrance.

Nevşehir

☑0384 / POP 86,000 / ELEV 1260M

According to local lore, if you set eyes on the beautiful view from Nevşehir's hilltop castle, you will be compelled to stay here for seven years. The legend must be very old, because the provincial capital is an ugly modern town that offers travellers little incentive to linger. Nevşehir's accommodation is also pretty bleak. Even if you arrive here in the middle of the night, we recommend that you make your way to nearby Göreme, where the accommodation is better value and infinitely superior.

◎ Sights

Nevşehir Museum   MUSEUM

(☑213 1447; Türbe Sokak 1; admission ₺3; ⊙8am-noon & 1pm-5pm Tue-Sun) This tiny museum is housed in an ugly building 1km from the centre. The collection includes an archaeological room with Phrygian, Hittite and Bronze Age pots and implements, as well as Roman, Byzantine and Ottoman articles. Upstairs, the dusty ethnographic section is less interesting.

⌸ Sleeping & Eating

Hotel Safir   HOTEL €€

(☑214 3545; www.otelsafir.com; Paşa Bulvarı 27; s/d ₺70/110; ▣⊛) Finally, a half-decent hotel in Nevşehir with large, tiled, spotless rooms, a swanky lift and keen-enough staff.

Nevşehir Konaği   ANATOLIAN €

(☑213 6183; Aksaray Caddesi 46; mezes ₺2.50, mains ₺7-15; ⊙9am-9.30pm) There is one good reason to visit Nevşehir. This municipal restaurant, in an Ottoman-style building in the park of the Kültür Merkezi (City Cultural Centre), 1.5km southwest of the centre, serves Cappadocian specialities such as *bamya çorba* (okra soup) and *dolma mantı*.

❶ Getting There & Away

Turkish Airlines (www.thy.com) has two flights per day from İstanbul to Nevşehir (₺79 to ₺249 one way). Airport shuttle buses run between the airport and villages of central Cappadocia and must be pre-booked.

Nevşehir is the main regional transport hub. If your bus terminates in Nevşehir but your ticket's final destination states Göreme (or any of the other villages) your bus company should provide a free *servis* to your destination.

HACI BEKTAŞ VELİ & THE BEKTAŞI SECT

Born in Nishapur in Iran in the 13th century, Hacı Bektaş Veli inspired a religious and political following that blended aspects of Islam (both Sunni and Shi'ite) with Orthodox Christianity. During his life he is known to have travelled around Anatolia and to have lived in Kayseri, Sivas and Kırşehir, but eventually he settled in the hamlet that is now the small town of Hacıbektaş.

Although not much is known about Hacı Bektaş himself, the book he wrote, the *Makalât*, describes a mystical philosophy less austere than mainstream Islam. In it he laid out a four-stage path to enlightenment (the Four Doors). Though often scorned by mainstream Islamic clerics, Bektaşi dervishes attained considerable political and religious influence in Ottoman times. Along with all the other dervishes, they were outlawed by Atatürk in 1925.

The annual pilgrimage of Bektaşi dervishes is an extremely important event for the modern Alevi community. Politicians tend to hijack the first day's proceedings, but days two and three are given over to music and dance.

The **otogar** (Aksaray Nevşehir Yolu) is 2.5km southwest of the city. Dolmuşes pass by the otogar and can drop you off at the central bus stand on Osmanlı Caddesi in the city centre. From here you can pick up a dolmuş to Göreme (₺2.50, every 30 minutes from 8am to 7.30pm); Uçhisar (₺2, every 30 minutes from 7.30am to 6pm); Niğde (₺7, every two hours from 7.30am to 6pm) via Kaymaklı and Derinkuyu; and Ürgüp (₺3.50, every 15 minutes from 7am to 10.30pm). If you want to go to Ortahisar, all the Nevşehir–Ürgüp dolmuşes can drop you at the turn-off on the main highway, a 1km walk from the town centre. There are two services to Avanos: one leaves every half-hour and goes direct and the other leaves on the hour and travels via Göreme and Çavuşin. Both operate from 7am to 7pm and charge ₺3.

A taxi to Göreme should cost around ₺35. See p446 for further information.

Around Nevşehir

If you're heading for Ankara, consider stopping off to see Gülşehir and especially Hacıbektaş along the way. While this is easily done if you have your own vehicle, it's not too hard by public transport either.

GÜLŞEHIR

☏ 0384 / POP 8961

This small town 19km north of Nevşehir has two rocky attractions on its outskirts that are worth visiting if you're passing through.

Four kilometres before Gülşehir's town centre you'll find the **Open Palace** (Açık Saray; ◷ 8am-5pm), a fine rock-cut monastery dating from the 6th and 7th centuries. It includes churches, refectories, dormitories and a kitchen, all of which are cut into fairy chimneys.

Two kilometres closer to town, just before the turning to the centre, is the rock-cut **Church of St John** (Karşı Kilise; admission ₺8; ◷ 8am-5pm). A five-minute walk down a signed road on the left of the highway, it's signposted 'Church of St Jean/Karşı Kilise'. This 13th-century church on two levels has marvellous frescoes, including scenes depicting the Annunciation, the Descent from the Cross, the Last Supper, the Betrayal by Judas, and the Last Judgment (rarely depicted in Cappadocian churches). The frescoes are particularly well preserved due to the fact that until restoration in 1995 they were covered in a layer of black soot.

Dolmuşes to Gülşehir (₺1.50, 15 minutes, every 30 minutes) from Nevşehir depart from a dolmuş stand on Lale Caddesi, just north of the Alibey Camii. Ask to be let off at the Açık Saray or Karşı Kilise to save a walk back from town. Returning, just flag the bus down from the side of the highway. Onward buses to Hacıbektaş leave from Gülşehir's small otogar opposite the Kurşunlu Camii (₺2, 30 minutes, hourly).

HACIBEKTAŞ

Not to be confused with the town's normally closed Ethnographic Museum, the **Hacıbektaş Museum** (Hacıbektaş Müze; admission ₺3; ◷ 8am-noon & 1-5pm Tue-Sun) contains the tombs of Hacı Bektaş Veli and his followers. Pilgrims carry out superstitious activities such as hugging a pillar, kissing door frames and tying ribbons around a mulberry bush known as *dilek ağacı* (wish tree). Several rooms are arranged as they might have been when the Bektaşi order lived here, with exhibits such as photos of the dervishes and earrings worn by celibate members of the sect.

Hacıbektaş has limited hotel options. The unremarkable **Evrim Hotel** (☑441 2900; s/d ₺30/70) or the slightly more popular **Hünkar Otel** (☑441 3344; s/d ₺25/50), on the *meydanı* (town square) between the shrine and the otogar, offer basic rooms with blue and yellow furniture and reasonable bathrooms. Prices should be negotiable except in August, when it's booked solid. Eating options are limited to the basic *lokantas* (eateries serving ready-made food), *pastanes* (patisseries) and *kebapçıs* (kebap eateries) on the main street.

Dolmuşes from the centre of Nevşehir to Hacıbektaş (₺3, 45 minutes, 11 daily between 7.30am and 6.15pm on weekdays, fewer services on weekends) depart from just in front of the Alibey Camii on Lale Caddesi. The last bus from Hacıbektaş' otogar to Nevşehir leaves at 5pm (4.45pm on weekends).

Ortahisar

☑0384 / POP 3617

When Cappadocia's cartographers first got together, the farming village of Ortahisar must have been left off the tourist map. Known for its jagged castle that gives the town its name, Ortahisar is the epitome of the rural town where craggy-faced men lean listlessly against craggy houses and work storing citrus fruit in underground caves. The cobbled streets which wind around the gorge are lined by gorgeously worn stonehouse ruins, and the evening silence is only broken by out-of-sync cockerels and the odd whining dog. Change is in the air though. A handful of off-beat and beautiful boutique hotels have started to pop up as visitors searching for the Cappadocia-of-old begin to discover Ortahisar's beguiling, arcadian beauty.

If you need information head to 'Crazy Ali's' antique shop (which is next to the castle). The loquacious poet, Ali, who speaks some English, French and German, says he was given his nickname when he drove an ox cart to the moon, and can help with walking directions into the surrounding valleys.

There is a standalone ATM in the main square and you can check your email at **Antiknet** (Huseyin Galif Efendi Caddesi; per hr ₺1; ◷8am-midnight) on the main road between the square and the PTT.

◉ Sights & Activities

FREE **Castle** FORTRESS
(◷9am-6pm) There are no monuments in Ortahisar other than the castle, an 18m-high rock used as a fortress in Byzantine times. It is not recommended that you climb it as the structure has been deemed unstable by the authorities.

Culture Folk Museum MUSEUM
(Kültür Müzesi; Cumhuriyet Meydanı 15; admission ₺5; ◷9am-7pm) Located on the main square near Ortahisar's castle, the Culture Folk Museum gets bombarded with tour groups but is nevertheless a good place to get to grips with the basics of local culture. In the dioramas, with their multilingual interpretive panels, mannequins dressed in headscarves and old men's *şapkas* (hats) make *yufka* (thinly rolled, unleavened bread), *pekmez* (syrup made from grape juice) and kilims.

Hallacdere Monastery MONASTERY
The atmospheric columned church of this large rock-cut monastery complex contains unusual decorative features. Look for the animal heads on the column capitals and the human figure sculpted onto the wall. The complex also contains several other rooms which would have been used by the monks for eating and sleeping. The monastery is 1km northeast of Ortahisar.

Cemal Ranch HORSE RIDING
(☑0532 291 0211; cemalhome50@hotmail.com; İsak Kale; 1/2hr ₺40/75, half-day ₺150) One kilometre from Ortahisar centre, this ranch offers riding excursions in the surrounding countryside. Camping and meals at the ranch, with its stunning valley views, can also be arranged.

🛏 Sleeping

TOP CHOICE **Hezen Cave Hotel** HOTEL €€€
(☑343 3005; www.hezenhotel.com; Esentepe Mahallesi, Tahir Bey Sokak 87; s/d/ste €110/140/190; 🛜) We think we've fallen in love. From the recycled *hezen* (telegraph poles) which form the statement-piece ceiling of the foy-

er to the gourmet feast laid on at breakfast, every detail at this truly gorgeous design hotel has been thought through. A riot of quirky turquoises, yellows and reds dust doors, window frames and fixtures, shining a shot of contemporary chic over cave rooms that exude an atmosphere of effortless cool. The honesty bar, complimentary goodies and free shuttle service just top off an experience where you wonder if you've mistakenly wandered into a VIP's daydream. Don't pinch us. We don't want to wake up.

Hotel Cave Deluxe　　　　HOTEL €€
(☑343 3393; www.cavedeluxe.com; Esentepe Mahallesi, Tahir Bey Sokak 14; s/d €80/94; ☎) This elegant affair sits at the bottom of Ortahisar's gorge, its ample verdant gardens and terraces surrounded by village views. Intricately crafted doors lead to spacious caves where fine textiles, pretty ceramics and luxurious bathrooms blend to create an atmosphere steeped in tradition but far from stuffy.

AlkaBris　　　　HOTEL €€€
(☑343 3433; www.alkabris.com; Cedid Mahallesi, Ali Reis Sokak 23; d/ste €100/140; ☎) Hosts Sait and Kamer have carved out a special five-room retreat sporting views of both Ortahisar castle and Erciyes Dağı. All are named after figures from Hittite history with mosaic-tile details and soft colours throughout. Breakfast is plentiful and lovingly prepared, and dinner (€25) is pricey but good.

✖ Eating

Süreyya Restaurant　　　　ANATOLIAN €€€
(☑343 2030; Selimbey Sokak 11; meals ₺40) Carnivore heaven, Cappadocian style. Ortahisar's famed *kasap* (butcher) family – 90 years and still top of the trade – have now opened a restaurant where all that flesh is turned into hearty traditional dishes. There's only ever one choice but it's always good. Reservations essential – book at least two hours beforehand.

Ciğerci Bilalin Yeri　　　　ANATOLIAN €
(Huseyin Galif Efendi Caddesi; meals ₺10; ☺Apr-Aug) The normally Mersin-based chef opens up his second operation in Ortahisar to feed the citrus-fruit workers when they're in town. Grab a table at the cubbyhole diner during these months and you're guaranteed plates of perfectly grilled meat skewers, served with a mountain of fresh *lavaş* bread and crunchy salad. It's on the main road just uphill from the main square.

Tandır Restaurant　　　　ANATOLIAN €€
(☑477 8575; Esentepe Mahallesi, Manzara ve Kültür Park; mains ₺10-15; ☑) Inside a lovely park (on the road between Hezen Cave Hotel and AlkaBris), with gorgeous views over a tumble of village houses, hides this traditional restaurant where dishes such as *kabak çiçeği dolması* (stuffed zucchini flowers) and *tandır kuzu* (lamb tandoor) are served up with gracious aplomb.

Park Restaurant　　　　TURKISH €
(☑343 3361; Tepebaşı Meydanı; pides ₺6-9, mains ₺9-15) Overlooking Ortahisar main square, this attractive garden is a perfect spot to recharge with a meat pide and green salad, accompanied by a beer or glass of 'energy drink' (fresh orange juice).

❶ Getting There & Away

Dolmuşes make the 5km run between Ortahisar and Ürgüp every 30 minutes from 8am to 5pm Monday to Saturday (₺1.50). All services stop next to the Culture Folk Museum on the main square. There are buses to Nevşehir, but it may be quicker to walk 1km to the Ortahisar turn-off on the main highway, as passing buses pick up passengers there. From the turn-off you can also catch the Ürgüp–Avanos dolmuş as it goes by.

Bus companies including Metro, Kent and Nevşehir have offices in the village.

Ürgüp

☑0384 / POP 18.631
When the Greek settlement was evicted from Ürgüp in 1923, there must have been buckets of tears shed at the borders. Nearly 90 years later and tourists from all over the world are pained to disperse from their temporary boutique residences. Ürgüp is elegant without even trying, like your favourite Turkish aunt who visits once a year. Better still, there's not a lot to do, no obligatory sights to see, just a few restaurants, a fabulous hamam, an up-and-coming winery and, outside of town, valley views that taste like honey on a stick. Perhaps Turkey's hippest rural retreat, Ürgüp is the connoisseurs' base for exploring the geographical heart of Cappadocia.

Ürgüp

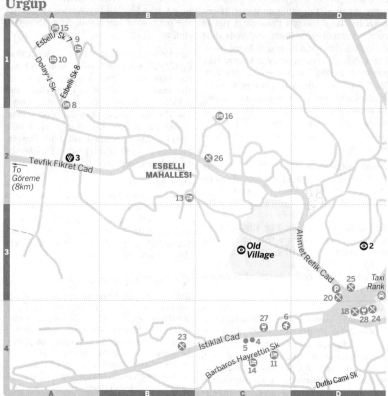

◉ Sights & Activities

TOP CHOICE Old Village　　　ARCHITECTURE
The back alleys of Ürgüp are home to many fine examples of the traditional stone architecture of this region, and are well worth a stroll.

Temenni Wishing Hill　　　VIEWPOINT
(☉9am-11pm) Home to a saint's tomb and a cafe, this viewpoint has 360-degree views over Ürgüp.

FREE Museum　　　MUSEUM
(Kayseri Caddesi; ☉8am-noon & 1-5pm Tue-Sun) The museum features some 10-million-year-old teeth from a forerunner of the elephant, unearthed at Mustafapaşa, but the overall collection is uninspiring.

Turasan Winery　　　WINERY
(☑341 4961; Tevfik Fikret Caddesi; vineyard tour & wine tasting €5; ☉8.30am-7pm) The abundant sunshine and fertile volcanic soil of Cappadocia produce delicious sweet grapes, and several wineries carry on the Ottoman Greek winemaking tradition. You can sample some of the local produce.

Tarihi Şehir Hamamı　　　HAMAM
(☑341 2241; İstiklal Caddesi; soak, scrub & massage ₺25; ☉7am-11pm) Partly housed in what was once a small church, the hamam offers mixed but respectable bathing.

☞ Tours
Several Ürgüp-based travel agents run tours around Cappadocia.

Argeus Tours　　　GUIDED TOUR
(☑341 4688; www.argeus.com.tr; İstiklal Caddesi 47) Offers three- to nine-day packages, including a nine-day mountain-biking option, as well as day tours, flights and car hire. They're Ürgüp's Turkish Airlines representative.

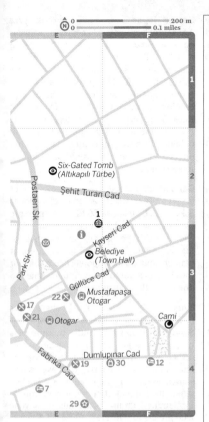

CAPPADOCIA ÜRGÜP

Peerless Travel Services   GUIDED TOUR
(☎341 6970; www.peerlessexcursions.com; İstiklal Caddesi 41) A range of one-day private tours as well as two- to six-day Cappadocia packages. Can also arrange car rental, airport transfers and tours throughout Turkey.

🛌 Sleeping

Ürgüp has a glut of luxury boutique hotels, mostly on and around Esbelli hill. If you're looking for a good range of midrange and budget options you're better off in Göreme. Some hotels close down between November and March when Ürgüp's weather keeps locals indoors and travellers elsewhere.

TOP CHOICE Esbelli Evi   BOUTIQUE HOTEL €€€
(☎341 3395; www.esbelli.com; Esbelli Sokak 8; d €120, ste €150-235; ❄️🛜) Jazz in the bathroom, whiskey by the tub, secret tunnels to secluded walled gardens covered in vines, this is the pick of accommodation in Cappadocia. A lawyer who never practised, Süha Ersöz instead (thank God) purchased the 12 surrounding properties over two decades and created a highly cultured, yet decidedly unpretentious hotel that stands out on exclusive Esbelli hill. The 14 detailed rooms feel more like first-class holiday apartments for visiting dignitaries, from

the state-of-the-art family room with fully decked kids' room to the raised beds and provincial kitchens in the enormous cave suites. The breakfast spread is organic and delicious, while an enchanting evening on the terrace is an education in local history, humility and grace.

TOP CHOICE Serinn House
BOUTIQUE HOTEL €€€

(☑341 6076; www.serinnhouse.com; Esbelli Sokak 36; d €120-140; ☎) Jetsetter hostess Eren Serpen has truly set a new standard for hotel design in Cappadocia with this contemporary effort that seamlessly merges İstanbul's European aesthetic with Turkish provincial life. The six minimally furnished rooms employ dashes of colour, and feature Archimedes lamps, signature chairs, hip floor rugs and tables too cool for coffee. The toiletries are top shelf, breakfasts feature Eren's fabulous home-baking, and relaxing on the sun-drenched courtyard leaves guests in no doubt that their kind has evolved from that staid old prehistoric cave life.

Melekler Evi
BOUTIQUE HOTEL €€

(☑341 7131; www.meleklerevi.com.tr; Dere Sokak 59; d €90-115, ste 145; ☎) Architectural duo Muammer and Arzu have created a sweet little hideaway that brims with inspired artistic flourishes. Each room is an individual piece of interior-design heaven, where hi-fi music and hi-tech shower systems merge with smatterings of winged sculpture, grand old stone fireplaces and touches of homespun whimsy. Delectable meals are prepared each day on request in a former stable, as enchanted residents come and go with a handmade map in one hand and a glass of local şarap (wine) in the other.

Yunak Evleri
LUXURY HOTEL €€€

(☑341 6920; www.yunak.com; Yunak Mahallesi; s/d €130/140, ste 160-200; ☎) Warranting its own postcode, Yunak is a labyrinth of good taste cut into the cliffside itself. This regal hotel, its structure in some parts dating back to the 5th century, unfurls itself in a string of Arabic lights that guide guests to its carved stone chambers. From the brass beds and handcrafted wooden furniture to the wireless entertainment systems, this is a hotel for connoisseurs of exceptional travel.

Sacred House
LUXURY HOTEL €€€

(☑341 7102; www.sacred-house.com; Barbaros Hayrettin Sokak 25; d €200-500; ☎) Yezim and her all-female team have raided Ottoman jumble sales and objet d'art stores in search of the right pieces to fill the 12 rooms at this haute-couture hotel that employs a maximum-design philosophy. Luckily the service lacks pretension, while the ostentatious statues, pillars and chandeliers will have you contemplating what our Greek ancestors would've made of modern man.

Cappadocia Palace
HOTEL €€

(☑341 2510; www.hotel-cappadocia.com; Mektep Sokak 2; s/d €30/44, cave €60/88; ☎) An Ürgüp old-timer with helpful management and a choice of either enormous cave rooms hosting bathrooms big enough to boogie in, or plainer (and smaller) motel-style rooms for those who aspire to the boutique scene but don't have the budget to match.

Evinn
APARTMENT €€€

(☑341 4353; www.evinncappadocia.com; Esbelli Sokak 7; ste €130) This little treasure of a hideaway has just two spacious suites furnished with traditional flair and opening out onto a leafy courtyard. Upstairs the shared lounge and fully equipped kitchen make this the perfect boutique compromise for families, groups of friends or anyone who prefers to self-cater.

Hotel Assiana
HOTEL €€€

(☑341 4960; www.assianahouse.com; Dolay Sokak 1; d/ste €100/120; ☎) It may not be as polished as neighbouring hotels but Assiana has an old-fashioned charm. Interiors have hints of country-house grandeur with gilded mirrors, stately armchairs, stone fireplaces and sedir seating.

Hotel Elvan
PENSION €€

(☑341 4191; www.hotelelvan.com; Barbaros Hayrettin Sokak 11; s/d/tr ₺50/100/150 ; ☎) Set around an internal courtyard filled with colourful pot plants, the 20 neat rooms feature daisy bedspreads, pinewood floors and tiny bathrooms, all kept sparkling clean.

Hotel Kilim
HOTEL €€

(☑341 3131; www.hotelkilim.com; Dumlupinar Caddesi 50; s/d/tr ₺60/90/120; ❁☎) The friendly staff more than make up for this hotel's lack of character. Bright rooms boast fresh paint jobs, private balconies and new linen.

✖ Eating

The range of restaurants in Ürgüp is more limited than in Göreme. If you're passing through the otogar, there are plenty of *pastanes* and cafes right outside.

TOP CHOICE **Ziggy's** MODERN TURKISH €€€
(☎341 7107; Yunak Mahallesi, Teyfik Fikret Caddesi 24; mezes ₺6-12, set menus ₺45, mains ₺25; 🖊) This tribute to the adored pet dog (and a camp David Bowie) of charismatic hosts Selim and Nuray, who is often decked in her beautiful handmade jewellery available downstairs, is a luscious success. With the finest meze menu in Cappadocia, and a two-tiered terrace that fills day and night with humming tunes, strong cocktails and a hip clientele, Ziggy's backs up its glowing reputation with professional service and an innovative menu.

Han Çirağan Restaurant RESTAURANT, BAR €€€
(☎341 2566; Cumhuriyet Meydanı; mains ₺15-25; 🖊) The Han is our favourite Ürgüp restaurant for atmospheric yet casual dining. Service is super-friendly and the menu is a meander through Turkish favourites with a modern twist. After dinner, retire to the cool bar downstairs, under the vine trellis, that has a city atmosphere, an excellent wine list, and serves up mean Martinis.

Restaurant 68 MODERN TURKISH €€€
(☎341 6468; İstiklal Caddesi 68; mains ₺15-25) We like dining on the breezy terrace and the casual-yet-refined atmosphere which lends this place a sophisticated air. The mixed meze plates are creative and delicious and the desserts decadent enough to warrant a splurge. Tuesday is fish night, which makes a nice change if you're suffering kebap overload.

Cafe In INTERNATIONAL €€
(Cumhuriyet Meydanı; mains ₺13-17; 🖊) If you're hankering after a decent plate of pasta this wee cafe should be your first port of call. Servings are on the generous side, service is swift and they also do some excellent, inventive salads.

**Develili Deringöller
Pide ve Kebap Salonu** PIDE €
(Dumlupınar Caddesi; pide ₺6-8; 🖊) Shush. We're going to tell you a secret the locals have been trying to hide for years. Develili Deringöller Pide ve Kebap Salonu makes hands-down the best pide in Cappadocia.

Cappadocia Restaurant TURKISH €€
(Cumhuriyet Meydanı; meals ₺20) Savvy travellers join the locals packing out the pavement tables here, sampling generous helpings of Cappadocian flavour.

**Şömine Cafe
& Restaurant** MODERN TURKISH €€€
(Cumhuriyet Meydanı; mains ₺15-25) Stylish Şömine is big on pristine napery and fancy service. We like the tasty *kiremits* (meat or vegetable dishes baked on a tile in a traditional oven) but the kebaps are succulent as well.

Teras Cafe TURKISH €€
(☎341 2442; Cumhuriyet Meydanı 42; mains ₺9-18) The outdoor area features comfy couches under giant, colourful umbrellas while inside smiley staff dish up decently priced Turkish staples including kebaps and spicy soups.

Ocakbaşı TURKISH €€
(☎341 3277; Güllüce Caddesi 44; mains ₺8-13) This massive restaurant serves delectably oily mezes and huge plates of grilled meat and rice to grinning locals who slosh down beer and fresh *ayran*, often in the same gulp.

Merkez Pastane ve Dondurma ICE CREAM €
(Güllüce Caddesi; scoop ₺2) Cappadocian locals have been known to drive to Ürgüp just to buy a *dondurma*. Check out the honey and almond flavour and you'll see why.

⚱ Drinking & Entertainment

The main square is the best place to grab an alcoholic or caffeinated beverage at an outside table and watch Cappadocia cruise by. Bookended by carpet shops, the pedestrian walkway running northeast from Ehlikeyf restaurant is full of cafes, bars and old men playing backgammon.

By far the most convivial and relaxed place for a drink in Ürgüp is at the bar in Han Çirağan but if you want to go exploring there are a few other places that pass muster.

Ailanpa Wine House WINE BAR
(☎341 6927; İstiklal Caddesi; wine ₺10) Often the traditional Turkish wine houses are musty affairs filled with shamefaced drinkers sitting on piles of sour grapes. This trendy number happily breaks the mould, thanks to chatty staff, comfy red velvet seating and a decent soundtrack.

SERVICES FROM ÜRGÜP'S OTOGAR

DESTINATION	FARE (₺)	DURATION (HR)	FREQUENCY (PER DAY)
Adana (via Nevşehir)	30	5	2 morning, 1 evening
Ankara	30	4½	7
Antalya	45	10	2 evening (& 1 morning in summer)
Çanakkale	70	17	1 evening
İstanbul	50	11	1 morning, 2 evening
İzmir & Selçuk	50	11½	2 evening
Kayseri	8	1¼	hourly 7am to 7.30pm (to 5.30pm in winter)
Konya	25	4	6
Marmaris/Bodrum/ Pamukkale	70	11-15	1 evening (only in summer)

Angel Café Bistro BAR, RESTAURANT
(☑341 6894; Cumhuriyet Meydanı) Straight from the big city comes this incongruously cool bar where Ürgüp's bright young things lounge around on the red beanbags out the front and hip-hop blasts from the stereo. It comes into its own after dark.

Barfiks LIVE MUSIC
(☑341 8442; Fabrika Caddesi) The downstairs cave bar is a wonderfully atmospheric setting for soulful, traditional tunes from local musicians. Don't expect to be able to have a conversation because it really is loud.

🛍 Shopping

Kavruk Kuruyemiş FOOD
(Dumlupınar Caddesi) The juiciest dried apricots, crunchiest nut mixes and most delectable Turkish delight.

ℹ Information

There are several banks with ATMs on or around the main square, Cumhuriyet Meydanı.

The **post office** (PTT; Postaen Sokak) is northeast of the square.

The helpful **tourist office** (☑341 4059; Kayseri Caddesi 37; ◷8am-5.30pm Mon-Fri) gives out a town map and has a list of Ürgüp's hotels.

For internet head to **Eftelya** (per hr ₺1.50; ◷9.30am-11pm) at the otogar.

ℹ Getting There & Away

From the **otogar** (Güllüce Caddesi), dolmuşes travel to Nevşehir every 15 minutes from 7am to 10.30pm (₺2.50). A service runs between Ürgüp and Avanos (₺3) via the Ortahisar turn-

off, the Göreme Open-Air Museum, Göreme village, Çavuşin and Zelve at 10am, noon, 4pm and 6pm.

Dolmuşes to Mustafapaşa leave roughly every 30 minutes between 8am and 8.30pm (₺2); and to Ortahisar every 30 minutes between 8am and 7pm. Both these services leave from the **Mustafapaşa otogar** (Güllüce Caddesi), next to the main otogar.

ℹ Getting Around

If you don't fancy the steep walk from the centre of town up to Esbelli Mahallesi you can catch a **taxi** (₺5) from the rank on the main square.

Ürgüp is a good base for hiring a car, with most agencies located on the main square or İstiklal Caddesi. Rates hover around ₺90 to ₺100 per day for a small manual sedan such as a Fiat Palio, and climb to ₺120 to ₺140 for a larger automatic. Companies include **Europcar** (☑341 8855; İstiklal Caddesi 10), **National** (☑341 6541; Cumhuriyet Meydanı), **Avis** (☑341 2177; İstiklal Caddesi 19) and **Astral** (☑341 3344; www.astralrentacar.com; İstiklal Caddesi 19).

Several outlets rent mopeds and motorcycles from ₺50 a day, and bicycles from ₺25.

Ayvalı
☑0384 / POP 500

This lovely little village in a valley south of Ürgüp could be a late-Ottoman Greek village if it weren't for the kids in Barcelona soccer shirts kicking balls beneath shiny NTT signage. Vegetables and dried flowers line the cobbled streets and tourists are virtually unsighted...for now.

🛏 Sleeping & Eating

Öykü Evi   HOTEL €€€
(☑354 5852; www.oykuevi.net; Ayvalı Koyu 100; d €100-120; 🛜) 'Story House' is a tranquil haven snuggled into the rock, overlooking a secluded gorge where the only sound at night is the frogs. Run by friendly owner (and author) Ayşe, who has stamped her whimsical taste throughout, colourful pottery, pansies and wind-charms abound on the terrace while cosy rooms are a riot of colour and rustic charm.

Gamırasu Hotel   HOTEL €€€
(☑345 5815; www.gamirasu.com; Ayvalı Köyü; d €165-185, ste from €260; 🛜🖥) Occupying a 1000-year-old Byzantine monastery, Gamırasu is an exclusive retreat with a church with frescoes and an ancient winery on the premises. Service is rather wonderful, though for the price, some of the rooms could do with a refurb. A walking trail leads down the valley and horse riding and cycling can be organised.

Aravan Evi Restaurant   ANATOLIAN €€€
(☑354 5838; www.aravan.com; set menu ₺35; ⊙lunch) Simple flavours, quality produce and popular with in-the-know Turks, this restrained, brilliant restaurant on a gorgeous white terrace whips up favourites like *dolmades* and *çorbasi* with delicate surety. You should phone ahead, and you can crash in the family guesthouse if the exquisite desserts make you woozy.

Mustafapaşa
☑0384 / POP 1600
Another beautiful Cappadocian village shifting slowly from yesteryear but remaining well beneath the tourist radar is Mustafapaşa. Still known widely by its pre-WWI Greek name of Sinasos, the stone-carved architecture here is a reminder of its prosperous Hellenic past. The minor rock-cut churches may satisfy your cultural craving, while the gentle pace is appropriate given the remarkable natural scenery. Wise travellers are choosing to stay here as an alternative to the more obvious destinations nearby.

You enter Mustafapaşa at an enlarged intersection, the Sinasos Meydanı, where a signboard indicating the whereabouts of the local rock-cut churches is located. Follow the road downhill and you'll come to Cumhuri-yet Meydanı, the centre of the village, which sports the ubiquitous bust of Atatürk and several teahouses.

There's no tourist office in town, and no ATMs; internet access is available on the main square.

👁 Sights

There are churches in **Monastery Valley**, but they're disappointing compared with others you'll find in Cappadocia. Nonetheless, it's a lovely walk. Also to the west of Mustafapaşa, there are 4km to 8km walks in **Gomeda Valley**, where there is a ruined 11th-century Greek town. Local guide Niyazi, who charges €25 for individuals and groups, can be contacted through Old Greek House.

Ayios Kostantinos-Eleni Kilise   CHURCH
(Church of SS Constantine & Helena; Cumhuriyet Meydanı; admission ₺5; ⊙8.30am-noon & 1-5.30pm) Right on Mustafapaşa main square is the imposing Ayios Kostantinos-Eleni Kilise, erected in 1729 and restored in 1850. A fine stone grapevine runs around the door but the ruined interior with faded 19th-century frescoes is not worth the admission charge. If you are keen to see it, a uniformed council worker should be posted outside; if not, ask for the key at the nearby *belediye*.

Ayios Vasilios Kilise   CHURCH
(St Basil Church; admission ₺5; ⊙9am-6pm) A sign pointing off Sinasos Meydanı leads 1km to the 12th-century Ayios Vasilios Kilise, perched near the top of a ravine. Its interior features unimpressive 20th-century frescoes. There should be someone there with a key; if not, enquire at the *belediye*.

Medrese   MEDRESE
Between Sinasos Meydanı and Cumhuriyet Meydanı is a 19th-century *medrese* (seminary; now utilised as a school) with a fine carved portal. The stone columns on either side of the doorway are supposed to swivel when there's movement in the foundations, thus warning of earthquake damage.

🛏 Sleeping & Eating

Many of Mustafapaşa's accommodation options are closed from November to March.

Most of the hotels and pensions offer meals. Even if you're not staying the night, we highly recommend eating at Old Greek House.

1. Pistachio baklava

This sweet pastry concoction is best sampled in Gazientep: the city is famous for making the best *fıstıklı* baklavas in Turkey.

2. Travertines, Pamukkale (p296)

Pamukkale's glittering travertines are composed of white calcite.

3. Basil II

Basil II (the 'Bulgar Slayer') ruled Turkey under the Byzantine empire.

4. Amasra (p495)

Straddling a peninsula with a rocky island offshore, Amasra is the Black Sea's prettiest port.

3

GOING UNDERGROUND

Thought to have first been carved out by the Hittites, the vast network of underground cities in this region was first mentioned by the ancient Greek historian Xenophon in his *Anabasis* (written in the 4th century BC).

During the 6th and 7th centuries, Byzantine Christians extended and enlarged the cities and used them as a means by which to escape persecution. If Persian or Arab armies were approaching, a series of beacons would be lit in warning – the message could travel from Jerusalem to Constantinople in hours. When it reached Cappadocia, the Christians would gather their belongings and relocate to the underground cities, hiding down in the subterranean vaults for months at a time.

One of the defense mechanisms developed by the cities' inhabitants was to disguise the air shafts as wells. Attackers might throw poison into these 'wells', thinking they were contaminating the water supply. The resulting fires were easy to quench, and the smoke was either absorbed by the soft *tuff* rock or dispersed in the shafts – leaving the attackers none the wiser.

The shafts, which descend almost 100m in some of the cities, also served another purpose. As new rooms were constructed, debris would be excavated into the shafts, which would then be cleared and deepened so work could begin on the next floor. Some of the cities are remarkable in scale – it is thought that Derinkuyu and Kaymaklısome housed about 10,000 and 3000 people respectively.

Around 37 underground cities have already been opened. There are at least 100 more, though the full extent of these subterranean refuges may never be known.

Touring the cities is like tackling an assault course for history buffs. Narrow walkways lead you into the depths of the earth, through stables with handles used to tether animals, churches with altars and baptism pools, walls with air-circulation holes, grainaries with grindstones, and blackened kitchens with ovens. While it's a fascinating experience, be prepared for unpleasantly crowded and sometimes claustrophobic passages. Avoid visiting on weekends, when busloads of domestic tourists descend. Even if you don't normally like having a guide, it's worth having one: they can conjure up the details of life below the ground better than you can on your own.

Kaymaklı underground city (admission ₺15; ☉8am-5pm, last admission 4.30pm) features a maze of tunnels and rooms carved eight levels deep into the earth (only four are open). As this is the most convenient and popular of the underground cities, you should get here early in July and August to beat the tour groups, or from about 12.30pm to 1.30pm when they break for lunch.

To reach **Özlüce underground city** (☉9am-5pm), turn right as you enter Kaymaklı from the north and you'll be heading for the small village of Özlüce, 7km further away. More modest than Kaymaklı or Derinkuyu, this underground city is also less developed and less crowded.

Derinkuyu underground city (Deep Well; admission ₺15; ☉8am-5pm, last admission 4.30pm), 10km south of Kaymaklı, has larger rooms arrayed on seven levels. When you get all the way down, look up the ventilation shaft to see just how far down you are – claustrophobes beware!

Some 18km east of Güzelyurt, just off the road to Derinkuyu, **Gaziemir underground city** (admission ₺3; ☉8am-6pm) opened in 2007. Churches, a winery with wine barrels, food depots, hamams and tandoor fireplaces can be seen. Camel bones and loopholes in the rock for tethering animals suggest that it also served as a subterranean caravanserai.

There are also underground cities at Güzelyurt and Özkonak, near Avanos.

Although you can visit one of the cities on a day tour from Göreme, Avanos or Ürgüp, it's also easy to see them on your own. From Nevşehir, Derinkuyu Koop runs dolmuşes to Derinkuyu (₺3, 45 minutes, service half-hourly between 9am and 6.30pm), which also stop in Kaymaklı (₺2.50, 30 minutes). Dolmuşes leave from the central bus stand on Osmanlı Caddesi. The Göreme–Nevşehir dolmuş can drop you off here.

You'll need a taxi or a hire car to take you to Özlüce from Kaymaklı or to visit Gaziemir.

Old Greek House
HISTORIC HOTEL €€

(☑353 5306; www.oldgreekhouse.com; Şahin Caddesi; s/d ₺100/150-200; 🕾) If it's good enough for the ex-mayor to sleep here, it's good enough for us. These days, the mansion is best known for its Ottoman-flavoured set menus (₺35 to ₺45) starring good versions of the usual suspects: *mantı*, *köfte* (meatballs), lima beans, crispy salads and homemeade baklava. The upstairs dining room with its gorgeous, peeling, painted ceiling and fading frescos makes for wonderfully atmospheric dining. If the Turkish coffee hasn't kicked in, grab a large room in the modern extension, with polished floorboards and a genuine *antik* (antique) vibe.

Ukabeyn Pansiyon
PENSION €€

(☑353 5533; www.ukabeyn.com; Gazi Sokak 62; s/d ₺85/120; 🕾🕾🕾) The double-headed eagle of Hittite mythology sitting above the hotel entrance lends regality and a name to this well-presented, friendly cave hotel. Upstairs light-filled stone-vaulted rooms are simple and modern. Downstairs, backing onto the terrace are some more characterful cave rooms. The Mustafapaşa room is our top pick. The swimming pool on the lower terrace is a big tick, as are the views from the two levels above. The fully equipped apartment (€150) could keep you in town long term.

Perimasali Cave Hotel
HOTEL €€

(☑353 5090; www.perimasalihotel.com; Sehit Aslan Yakar Sokak 6; d €120, ste 200-250; 🕾) Over-the-top sculpture, gilded gold accents and spotlight features; this opulent Cappadocian cave hideaway has rooms that do nothing by half. The attention to detail befits a five-star hotel, though the decor won't be to everyone's taste. Service is charming and the terrace provides killer above-ground views.

Hotel Pacha
PENSION €€

(☑353 5331; www.pachahotel.com; Sinasos Meydanı; s/d ₺75/110; 🕾) This revamped Ottoman-Greek number boasts neat and tidy rooms of various ilks and tasty food in the upstairs restaurant. The sprawling vine-covered courtyard provides sun-seeker bliss on lazy summer afternoons.

❶ Getting There & Away

Dolmuşes leave from the main square for Ürgüp every 30 minutes between 8am and 7pm. A taxi costs ₺20.

Soğanlı

☑0352 / POP 400

Let's get one thing straight: despite the science-fiction setting, no scene in *Star Wars* was ever filmed near Soğanlı, or anywhere else in Turkey. But don't despair, Chewbacca fans, there's still ample reason to travel to this tiny village 36km south of Mustafapaşa, namely a reverential series of rock-cut churches hidden in two dramatic, secluded valleys. An afternoon exploring at the foot of these sheer faces may inspire you to rewrite your own script.

To reach Soğanlı turn off the main road from Mustafapaşa to Yeşilhisar and proceed 4km to the village. Buy your ticket for the churches (adult/child ₺5/free; ☉8am-8.30pm, to 5pm winter) near the Kapadokya Restaurant. In the village square, local women sell the dolls for which Soğanlı is supposedly famous.

◉ Sights

The valleys of **Aşağı Soğanlı** and **Yukarı Soğanlı** were first used by the Romans as necropolises and later by the Byzantines for monastic purposes, with ancient **rock-cut churches**.

Most of the interesting churches are in the right-hand valley (to the north), easily circuited on foot in about two hours. All are signposted, but be careful as many are in a state of disrepair.

Coming from the main road, about 800m before the ticket office, signs point to the **Tokalı Kilise** (Buckle Church), on the right, reached by a steep flight of worn steps; and the **Gök Kilise** (Sky Church), to the left across the valley floor. The Gök has twin naves separated by columns and ending in apses. The double frieze of saints is badly worn.

The first church on the right after the ticket booth, the **Karabaş** (Black Hat), is one of the most interesting. It is covered in paintings showing the life of Christ, with Gabriel and various saints. A pigeon in the fresco reflects the importance of pigeons to the monks, who wooed them with dovecotes cut into the rock.

Furthest up the right-hand valley is the **Yılanlı Kilise** (Church of St George or Snake Church), its frescoes deliberately painted over with black paint, probably to protect them. The hole in the roof of one chamber, surrounded by blackened rock, shows fires were lit there.

Turn left at the Yılanlı Kilise, cross the valley floor and climb the far hillside to find the **Kubbeli** and **Saklı Kilisesi** (Domed and Hidden Churches). The Kubbeli is unusual because of its Eastern-style cupola cut clean out of the rock. Nestling in the hillside, the Hidden Church is indeed hidden from view – until you get close.

In the left-hand valley, accessed from the village, you'll first come across the **Geyikli Kilise** (Deer Church), where the monks' refectory is still clearly visible. The **Tahtalı Kilise** (Church of Santa Barbara), 200m further on, has well-preserved Byzantine and Seljuk decorative patterns.

🛏 Sleeping & Eating

Emek Pansiyon   PENSION €

(☎653 1029; soganli_emekpansion@hotmail.com; dm incl half-board ₺50) Gorgeously rustic and super-friendly, this place is known for its authentic Cappadocian charm. The cave rooms (shared bathroom) sleep up to six on traditional *sedir*-style beds, layered with carpets and cut into the rock. The terrace cafe above, brimming with antiques, family heirlooms and black and white photos, is a relaxing place to while away a few hours after visiting the churches, whether you stay the night or not.

Soğanlı Restaurant   TURKISH €€

(☎653 1016; mains ₺10-15; 🅿) This popular lunch pit stop for Soğanlı day tours rustles up a mean *menemen* as well as decent *çorbas*, *gözleme* and tasty casseroles. The very basic pension rooms (₺35 per person) at the back are small but serviceable.

Kapadokya Restaurant   TURKISH €€

(☎653 1045; mains ₺10-15) Under shady trees, Kapadokya serves stodgy but acceptable omelettes, casseroles and *çorba*. The campsite (₺5) is a patch of grass with a decrepit toilet block.

ⓘ Getting There & Away

It's basically impossible to get to Soğanlı by public transport. Best bet: go to Yeşilhisar from Kayseri (₺2.50, every 30 minutes from 7am to 9pm) then negotiate for a taxi to take you there. It's easier though to rent a car or sign up for a day tour in Ürgüp or Göreme.

Niğde

☎0388 / POP 114,376

Backed by the snowcapped Ala Dağlar range, Niğde, 85km south of Nevşehir, was founded by the Seljuks. It's an agricultural centre with a clutch of historic buildings. You won't want to stay, but may have to if you want to visit the fabulous Eski Gümüşler Monastery, 10km to the northeast. You may also pass through en route to

WORTH A TRIP

ESKİ GÜMÜŞLER MONASTERY

The ancient rock-hewn **Eski Gümüşler Monastery** (admission ₺3; ⊙8.30am-noon & 1-5pm) contains some of Cappadocia's best-preserved and most captivating frescoes.

Only rediscovered in 1963, they are entered via a rock-cut passage, which opens onto a large courtyard with reservoirs for wine and oil, and rock-cut dwellings, crypts, a kitchen and a refectory.

A small hole in the ground acts as a vent for a 9m-deep shaft leading to two levels of subterranean rooms. You can descend through the chambers or climb to an upstairs bedroom.

Even the pillars in the lofty main church are decorated with colourful Byzantine frescoes, painted between the 7th and 11th centuries. The charming Nativity looks as if it is set in a rock-caved structure like this one, and the striking Virgin and Child to the left of the apse has the elongated Mary giving a *Mona Lisa* smile – it's said to be the only smiling Mary in existence.

Eski Gümüşler Monastery sprawls along the base of a cliff about 10km northeast of Niğde. To get there, Gümüşler Belediyesi minibuses (₺1, 15 minutes) depart every hour from the minibus terminal beside Niğde's otogar. As you enter Gümüşler, don't worry when the bus passes a couple of signs pointing to the monastery – it eventually passes right by it. To catch a bus back to Niğde, walk to the roundabout 500m from the monastery entrance and flag down a minibus heading to the left.

the base-camp villages for trekking in the Ala Dağlar National Park.

French is spoken in the helpful **tourist office** (☑232 3393; Belediye Sarayı 38/39; ☺8am-noon & 1-5pm Mon-Fri), located on the 1st floor of the ugly Kültür Merkezi (City Cultural Centre) on Bor Caddesi. There are plenty of internet cafes on the main street, including **Cafe In** (Bor Caddesi; per hr ₺1; ☺9am-midnight), opposite the tourist office. ATMs are dotted along Bankalar/İstiklal/Bor Caddesi.

◎ Sights

Niğde Museum   MUSEUM
(Niğde Müzesi; ☑232 3397; Dışarı Caddesi; admission ₺3; ☺8am-noon & 1-5pm Tue-Sun) Niğde Museum houses a well-presented selection of finds from the Assyrian city of Acemhöyük near Aksaray, through the Hittite and Phrygian ages to sculptures from Tyana (now Kemerhisar), the former Roman centre and Hittite capital 19km southwest of Niğde. Several mummies are exhibited too, including the 11th-century mummy of a blonde nun discovered in the 1960s in the Ihlara Valley.

🛏 Sleeping & Eating

Hotel Şahiner   HOTEL €€
(☑232 2121; www.hotelsahiner.com; Giray Sokak 4; s/d ₺80/120) It's a shame the staff can't be a bit perkier but large, clean rooms with comfortable beds make the Şahiner a solid choice if you need to stay the night in Niğde. It's in an alleyway off Bankalar Caddesi, right in the centre of town.

Sini Lezzet Sofrası   TURKISH €
(İsmail Hakkı Altan Caddesi; mains ₺6-12)   On Niğde's bustling pedestrian strip (one block down from the Atatürk statue) the Sini Lezzet Sofrası *lokanta* dishes up huge plates of pide, spicy *güveç* and sizzling kebaps; all served with mountains of complimentary bread and salad.

❶ Getting There & Away

Bus
Niğde's **otogar** (Adana Yolu) is 4km out of town on the main highway. It has buses to Adana (₺15, 3½ hours, five daily), Aksaray (₺10, 1½ hours, hourly between 7am and 9pm), Ankara (₺25, five hours, five daily), İstanbul (₺50, 11 hours, five daily), Kayseri (₺10, 1½ hours, hourly between 7am and 9pm), Konya (₺20, 3½ hours, 10 daily) and Nevşehir (₺10, one hour, hourly from 7am to 6pm).

Train
Niğde **train station** (İstasyon Caddesi) is on the Ankara–Adana train line. A daily service leaves for Ankara at 11.30pm (₺20, 9½ hours) and for Adana at 3.50am (₺8, four hours).

Ala Dağlar National Park

The Ala Dağlar National Park (Ala Dağlar Milli Parkı) protects the rugged middle range of the Taurus Mountains between Kayseri, Niğde and Adana. It's famous throughout the country for its extraordinary trekking routes, which make their way through craggy limestone ranges dotted with waterfalls. It's best to trek between mid-June and late September; at other times weather conditions can be particularly hazardous, especially since there are few villages along the way and little support other than some mountaineers' huts. Bring warm gear and be sure to prepare for extreme conditions.

The most popular walks start at the small villages of **Çukurbağ** and **Demirkazık**, which lie beneath Demirkazık Dağı (Mt Demirkazık, 3756m), 40km east of Niğde.

You can also reach the mountains via Yahyalı, 80km due south of Kayseri. From here it's another 60km to the impressive **Kapuzbaşı Waterfalls** (best seen between March and May) on the Zamantı River.

Although there are a variety of walks in the mountains, many people opt for the two-day-minimum walk to the beautiful **Yedigöller** (Seven Lakes, 3500m), which starts and finishes at Demirkazık. An easier three- to four-day walk begins at Çukurbağ and leads through the forested Emli Valley before finishing at Demirkazık.

Although solo trekkers do sometimes venture into the mountains, unless you're experienced and prepared you should consider paying for a guide or joining a tour. A guide should cost around €110 per day; horses (to carry luggage) will also need to be added on to the price. If you want to do a full trek in the range, Middle Earth Travel (p452) is a good first port of call in Göreme. The agency offers a five-day program for €340 per person, for a minimum of six people. Guides can also be hired through the campgrounds in Çukurbağ and there are agencies in Niğde: **Demavend Travel** (☑0388-232 7363; www.demavend travel.com; 4th fl, Yıldız Iş Merkezi 10, Sefik Soyer

CAPPADOCIA ALA DAĞLAR NATIONAL PARK

SULTAN MARSHES

An afternoon ploughing the Sultan Marshes in your gumboots might not sound like your cup of birdseed, but there's something undeniably comforting about observing a flock of flamingos at a waterhole, or an eagle swooping to snap the neck of a curious baby squirrel. The giant patch of wetland in between Soğanlı and Ala Dağlar is world-famous among the twitching fraternity who descend here year-round to spot the 300-odd different species on stopover from Africa, Russia and continental Europe. Despite a local myth that bushfires have killed all the ornithology, bird life here is thriving and even a short detour to the flat, open fields can be richly rewarding.

If you decide to stay, the **Sultan Pansiyon** (☑0352-658 5549; www.sultanbirding.com; Sultansazlığı, Ovaçiftliği ; s/d/tr/q €30/50/65/80; P✱@) is pretty much your only option. Luckily it's very comfortable and backs onto the marshes themselves. The affable owners and resident bird freaks can whip you around in their car and help you tick off your newly discovered hit list. It's free and easy to drive yourself, as long as it's not too wet.

Meydanı, Niğde) and **Sobek Travel** (☑0388-232 1507; www.trekkinginturkeys.com; Avanoğlu Apt 70/17, Bor Caddesi, Niğde).

Çukurbağ has basic shops for supplies.

🛌 Sleeping & Eating

Ala Dağlar
Camping   CAMPING GROUND, GUEST HOUSE €
(☑0534 201 8995; www.aladaglarcamping.com; Çukurbağ Köyü Martı Mahallesi; campsites per person €6, cabin without bathroom €22-28, bungalow €35-45, chalet €45-60) Run by climbing couple Zeynep and Recep, this alpine hideaway has an ample camping area with mountain log cabin, bungalows, and chalets for those who don't fancy tenting-it. Shared amenities (including kitchen) are excellent and there's also a cafe. Trekking and climbing guides cost roughly between €130 and €180 per day and a host of activities – from ski touring to birdwatching – can be arranged. The campground is a 2km walk from Çukurbağ junction and village. Transfers from Kayseri or Adana airport are offered.

Şafak Pension
& Camping   PENSION, CAMPING GROUND €
(☑0388-724 7039; www.safaktravel.com; Çurkur bağ Village; campsites per person ₺15, r per person incl half-board ₺60) This place is run by the friendly, English-speaking, walking and climbing guide Hassan. Rooms are simple but clean, with plentiful hot water, heating and comfortable beds. Camp sites have electricity and their own bathroom facilities. The terrace and garden command magnificent views of Mt Demirkazık. The pension is located near the main road,

about 1.5km from a bridge and the signpost marked 'Demirkazık 4, Pinarbaşı 8'.

ℹ️ Getting There & Away

From Niğde, take a Çamardı-bound minibus (₺5, 90 minutes, every hour between 7am and 5.30pm) and ask to be let off at Çukurbağ junction and village (it's 5km before Çamardı).

Ihlara Valley (Ihlara Vadisi)

☑0382

Southeast of Aksaray, Ihlara Valley scythes through the stubbly fields. Once called Peristrema, the valley was a favourite retreat of Byzantine monks, who cut churches into the base of its towering cliffs. This is one of the prettiest strolls in the world. Following the river (Melendiz Suyu), hemmed in by jagged cliffs, as it snakes between painted churches, piles of boulders and a sea of greenery ringing with birdsong and croaking frogs, is an unforgettable experience.

Good times to visit are midweek in May or September when fewer people are about. Midway along the valley, at Belisırma, a swathe of riverside restaurants means you needn't come weighed down with provisions.

There is an ATM in Ihlara village. Internet access is available at **Kappadokya Café** (per hr ₺1; ☺9am-midnight) in Ihlara village, and at **Derren Net** (per hr ₺1.50; ☺8am-10pm) next to the supermarket and the PTT in Selime.

◎ Sights & Activities

There are four entrances along the **Ihlara Valley** (admission ₺8, parking ₺2; ☺8am-

6.30pm). If you only want to walk the short stretch with most of the churches, then enter via the 360 knee-jarring steps leading down from the **Ihlara Vadisi Turistik Tesisleri** (Ihlara Valley Tourist Facility), perched on the rim of the gorge 2km from Ihlara village. Alternatively there are entrances in Ihlara village – signposted after the *belediye* building – at Belısırma and at Selime.

Walking the full route from Ihlara village to Selime (or vice versa) is highly recommended. As most visitors come to Ihlara on tour and only walk the short stretch between the Ihlara Vadisi Turistik Tesisleri and Belısırma, the rest of the path is blissfully serene with farmers tilling their fields and shepherds grazing their flocks the only people you're likely to meet.

It takes about 1½ hours to walk from the Ihlara Vadisi Turistik Tesisleri to Belısırma, and about another two hours to walk from Belısırma to Selime. You'll need around five to six hours if you want to walk the full route stopping in Belısırma for lunch along the way. If you're planning to walk the entire trail, it's best to start early in the day, particularly in summer, when you'll need to take shelter from the fierce sun. The ticket for the valley should also cover Selime Monastery. Along the valley floor, signs mark the different churches. Although they're all worth visiting if you have the time, the following list includes the real must-sees:

Kokar Kilise   CHURCH

(Fragrant Church) This church has some fabulous frescoes – the Nativity and the Crucifixion for starters – and tombs buried in the floors.

Sümbüllü Kilise   CHURCH

(Hyacinth Church) Some frescoes remain, but the church is mostly noteworthy for its well-preserved, simple-but-elegant facade.

Yılanlı Kilise   CHURCH

(Serpent Church) Many of the frescoes are damaged, but it's possible to make out the one outlining the punishments for sinners; especially the three-headed snake with a sinner in each mouth and the nipple-clamped women (ouch) who didn't breastfeed their young.

Kırk Dam Altı Kilise   CHURCH

(St George's Church) It's a scramble to get to, but the views of the valley make all the puffing worthwhile. Although badly graffitied the frescoes are still gloriously vibrant, and above the entrance you can see St George on a white horse, slaying a three-headed snake.

Bahattın'ın Samanlığı Kilise   CHURCH

(Bahattın's Granary) With some of the valley's best-preserved frescoes, the church is named after a local who used to store grain here. Frescoes show scenes from the life of Christ, including the Crucifixion, Massacre of the Innocents and Baptism scenes. Unfortunately the area surrounding the church was roped off when we visited due to safety concerns over rockfalls.

Direkli Kilise   CHURCH

(Columned Church) This cross-shaped church has six columns, hence the name. The large adjoining chamber originally had two storeys, as you can see from what's left of the steps and the holes in the walls from the supporting beams. There are burial chambers

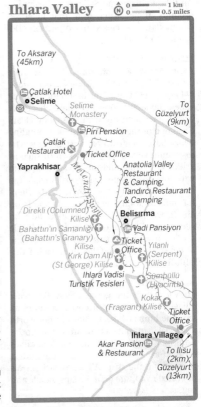

Ihlara Valley

N 0 —————— 1 km
   0 —————— 0.5 miles

To Aksaray
(45km)

Çatlak Hotel
Selime
Selime Monastery   To Güzelyurt
                        (9km)
Piri Pension
Çatlak Restaurant
        Ticket Office
Yaprakhisar
                    Anatolia Valley
                    Restaurant
                    & Camping,
                    Tandırcı Restaurant
                    & Camping
Direkli (Columned) Kilise   Belısırma
Bahattın'ın Samanlığı   Vadi Pansiyon
(Bahattın's Granary) Kilise Ticket
Kırk Dam Altı   Office   Yılanlı
(St George) Kilise   (Serpent)
            Ihlara Vadisi   Kilise
            Turistik Tesisleri   Sümbüllü
                                  (Hyacinth)
                        Kokar
                        (Fragrant) Kilise   Ticket
                                            Office
                        Ihlara Village
                Akar Pansiyon   To Ilısu
                & Restaurant   (2km);
                                            Güzelyurt
                                            (13km)

in the floor. Unfortunately the church was unaccessible when we visited due to safety concerns over rockfalls.

Selime Monastery
MONASTERY

(admission ₺8 ; ☉dawn-dusk) The monastery at Selime is an astonishing rock-cut structure incorporating a vast kitchen with soaring chimney, a church with a gallery around it, stables with rock-carved feed troughs and other evidence of the troglodyte lifestyle. The admission price is included in the Ihlara Valley ticket.

☞ Tours

Travel agencies in Göreme, Avanos and Ürgüp offer full-day tours to Ihlara for about ₺90 per day, including lunch.

🛏 Sleeping & Eating

If you want to walk all of the gorge and don't have your own transport you'll have to stay overnight. There are modest pensions handily placed at both ends of the gorge (in Ihlara village and Selime) and camping grounds in Belisırma. Note that most accommodation is closed out of season (December to March).

IHLARA VILLAGE

Akar Pansion & Restaurant
PENSION ₺

(☎453 7018; www.ihlara-akarmotel.com; s/d/tr ₺40/70/90; 🛜) One of the best options in the valley, the large rooms here have cheerfully bright linen and are kept spotlessly clean. Grab one of the rooms in the new building which have their own private balconies. The restaurant serves tasty dishes (₺10) such as grilled local trout and *saç tava* (cubed lamb with tomatoes, pepper and garlic) while the attached shop sells picnic ingredients. Helpful staff speak English and can fill you in on any Ihlara queries, there's cheap laundry on site (₺6 per load), and they operate a shuttle service for guests to Güzelyurt (₺30), Selime or Belisırma (₺25) and the Ihlara Vadisi Turistik Tesisleri (free).

BELİSIRMA

Midway along the gorge, below Belisırma village, four low-key licensed restaurants feed the hungry hikers. They are not worth a special trip, but benefit from their position right by the river with wonderful tables on platforms above the water – the hottest property on the strip. All serve basic meals of grilled trout, *saç tava*, kebaps, salads and soups.

Tandırcı Restaurant & Camping
CAMPING GROUND ₺

(☎457 3110; lunch ₺15, campsite free) Tour groups often bypass this restaurant, leaving a mellow, shady spot and a chance of scoring a river platform for lunch. Campsites are dotted among vegetable gardens and a small orchard.

Belisırma Restaurant
CAMPING GROUND ₺

(☎457 3057; lunch ₺12, campsite free) The campsite at the rear of the restaurant makes up for its lack of shade with respectable toilets and some hammocks.

Anatolia Valley Restaurant & Camping
CAMPING GROUND ₺

(☎457 3040; lunch ₺12, campsite ₺15) This good site has a couple of vine-covered pergolas for shade, although the toilet block isn't too clean.

Vadi Pansiyon
PENSION ₺

(☎457 3067; d ₺50) In Belisırma village, this spartan pension has rooms with small private bathrooms, and a terrace cafe with views.

SELIME

Çatlak Hotel
HOTEL ₺₺

(☎454 5006; www.catlakturizm.com.tr; s/d ₺45/90; 🛜) Excellent value (despite the gaudy decor), Çatlak has good-sized rooms and smiley staff. Their riverside restaurant (a few steps from the Selime entry to Ihlara Valley) is a great place to have dinner and hang out.

Piri Pension
PENSION ₺

(☎454 5114; s/d ₺30/60) A tranquil, friendly place in a ramshackle yellow house overlooking some fairy chimneys. Owner Mustafa runs guided trips around the valley and neighbouring Selime monastery.

❶ Getting There & Away

On weekdays six dolmuşes per day make the run between Aksaray and Ihlara Village, travelling down the valley via Selime and Belisırma. Dolmuşes leave Aksaray at 7.30am, 10am, noon, 2pm, 4pm and 6pm. They leave Ihlara Village for the return run at 6.45am, 8am, 9am, 11am, 1pm and 3.30pm (₺4, 45 minutes). On the weekend there are fewer services. In Belisırma, dolmuşes stop in the new part of the village, up on the plateau, and you have to hike a few hundred metres down into the valley. To get to Güzelyurt ask the driver to drop you at the Selime T-junction where you can wait for a Güzelyurt dolmuş.

Güzelyurt

📞 0382 / POP 2509 / ELEV 1485M

According to signposts on the deserted roads east of Ihlara Valley, 'a trip without Güzelyurt is not a Cappadocia trip'. It may seem an optimistic slogan, but this hillside tumble of crumbling stone houses, with back alleys presided over by strutting cockerels and the odd stray cow, lead down to a valley studded with the remnants of rock-cut churches. Surrounded by rolling hills, a lakeside monastery, and with the silhouette of Hasan Dağı (Mt Hasan) glowering over the horizon, the gentle-paced rhythm of life here is a refreshing glimpse of rural Cappadocia.

Known as Karballa (Gelveri) in Ottoman times, up till the population exchanges of 1924 the town was inhabited by 1000 Ottoman Greek families and 50 Turkish Muslim families. Afterwards the Greeks of Gelveri went to Nea Karvali in Greece, while Turkish families from Kozan and Kastoria in Greece moved here. The relationship between the two countries is now celebrated in an annual **Turks & Greeks Friendship Festival** held in July.

Güzelyurt has a PTT, a branch of the TC Ziraat Bankası (but no ATM) and several shops. English-speaking staff at the helpful **tourist office** (⊙8.30am-7pm) in the main street can supply information about both the town and the Ihlara Valley, though it is unfortunately often shut.

◎ Sights

Monastery Valley   RUINS

(admission ₺5; ⊙8am-6.30pm) From Güzelyurt's main square, take the signposted right-hand turn and follow the street down about 400m to the ticket booth. Right beside the ticket office is the **underground city**. The restored complex ranges across several levels and includes one hair-raising section where you descend through a hole in the floor. There is also a small, uninteresting satellite of the underground city about 100m back up the road.

Just past the ticket booth is the impressive facade of the **Büyük Kilise Camii** (Mosque of the Great Church). Built as the Church of St Gregory of Nazianzus in AD 385, it was restored in 1835 and turned into a mosque following the population exchange in 1924. St Gregory (AD 330–90) grew up locally and became a theologian, patriarch and one of the four Fathers of the Greek Church. Check out the wooden sermon desk that was reputedly a gift from a Russian tsar. It is quite plain inside but there are plans to uncover the whitewashed frescoes.

Up a set of stairs opposite is the tranquil **Sivişli Kilisesi** with damaged, but still colourful, frescoes decorating the apse and domed ceiling. There are fantastic views over Güzelyurt if you climb up to the ridge from here.

Afterwards you can continue through the 4.5km **Monastery Valley**, a sort of Ihlara in miniature. Panoramic viewpoints abound and just walking through it is pleasant, but there are more rock-cut churches and dwellings to explore. Some 2km after the previous group, the **Kalburlu Kilisesi** (Church with a Screen) has a superb entrance. The almost-adjoining **Kömürlü Kilisesi** (Coal Church) has carvings including an elaborate lintel above the entrance and some Maltese crosses.

Yüksek Kilise & Manastır   MONASTERY

Perched high on a rock overlooking Güzelyurt lake is the Yüksek Kilise and Manastır (High Church and Monastery), some 2km south of a signposted turn-off on the Ihlara road 1km west of Güzelyurt. The road there creeps between huge boulders balancing on other rocks like outsized sculptures in a gallery. The walled compound containing the plain church and monastery is graffitied inside and looks more impressive from afar, but has sweeping views of the lake and mountains.

Kızıl Kilise   CHURCH

(Red Church) Against a backdrop of stark, sweeping fields, the red masonry of the Kızıl Church stands out for miles. One of Cappadocia's oldest churches, it was undergoing thorough restoration work when we visited. It is 8km out of Güzelyurt on the Niğde Road, just past the village of Sivrihisar.

🛏 Sleeping & Eating

There are three *lokantas* on and around the main square, serving cheap beer and rakı and dishes such as kebaps and pide.

Hotel Karballa   HISTORIC HOTEL €€

TOP CHOICE

(📞451 2103; www.karballahotel.com; standard s/d/tr/q €42/58/80/110, deluxe s/d/tr €55/70/95; ❄️🌐♨️) We bet the monks enjoyed living in this 19th-century Greek monastery just to the left of the tea garden in Güzelyurt centre. All the rooms are bright and airy with colourful *suzani* embroidered bedspreads and carpets, but it's really worth splashing out a little extra for a deluxe room in the main building. Named after the holy one-time inhabitants, their cross-shaped windows and stone-vaulted ceilings are seriously atmospheric. The hotel has retained a contemplative atmosphere and you feel like a father breaking his fast in the arched former refectory, now the restaurant (dinner €12). The enthusiastic manager can help with organising hiking in the local area.

Halil Pension PENSION €€
(☑451 2707; Yukarı Mahallesi Amaç Sokak; s/d ₺60/120; ☎) This family home has rooms in a modern extension to the original 140-year-old Greek house. Rooms are simple and small but have loads of natural light and spotlessly clean bathrooms. One has a private balcony and there's a roof terrace with magnificent views over Güzelyurt lake. The food here is a highlight so ask about half-board when you book (₺20 extra) with meals packed with goodies from the garden. As you enter town from the west, it's signposted off to the right, a short walk downhill from the centre.

Kapadokya Ihlara Konakları HOTEL €€
(☑451 2426; www.kapadokyaihlarakonaklari.com; standard s/d ₺90/150, deluxe ₺120/180; ☎) Sprawling across several cobblestone alleyways in the town centre, this jumble of old Greek houses has been restored to finery as a hotel. Rooms abound with local character and individual decoration. Some lead out onto terraces with sumptuous panoramas over the town.

Kadir's Antique Gelveri Houses GUESTHOUSE €€
(☑451 2089; www.cappadociakadirshouses.com; Aksaray Caddesi 37; s/d ₺100/120; ☎) Kadir's occupies a 120-year-old Ottoman house entered through an antique carved wooden door. The six rooms have modern bathrooms, subtle lighting, mezzanines and beds with natural, woollen duvets. Homemade wine is served in the small outdoor bar and dinner costs ₺15. The owner is low-key.

ⓘ Getting There & Away

From Aksaray, dolmuşes leave for Güzelyurt at 7.30am, 9.45am, 11.30am, 1.30pm, 3.30pm, 5.30pm and 6.30pm. Returning dolmuşes travel from Güzelyurt to Aksaray (₺5, one hour) at 6.30am, 7.30am and then every two hours with the last at 5.30pm. On weekends there are fewer services. Going either way, dolmuşes can drop you at the T-junction near Selime from where you can wait for an Ihlara Valley–bound dolmuş.

A taxi to Ihlara village costs ₺35, to Hasan Dağı (Mt Hasan) ₺60, and to Aksaray ₺60.

Aksaray

☑0382 / POP 182,339

Sitting in the shadow of Hasan Dağı (Mt Hasan), Aksaray is symptomatic of Turkey's economic rise; quietly prospering with high consumer confidence. With an ugly modern town centre there's not much to hold your interest, but as a jumping-off point for the Ihlara Valley you may find yourself snared here for a couple of hours. If so, an afternoon among the throng in the attractive town square surrounded by gaudy government buildings is an unequivocally Anatolian experience.

BIG HASAN

If a stroll through Ihlara Valley gets you salivating for more walking, the area around Cappadocia's second-highest mountain, Hasan Dağı (Mt Hasan), is good for trekking. The closest village to the 3268m inactive volcano is **Helvadere**, about 10km southwest of Ihlara village and 20km east of Taşpınar. Helvadere is the site of the ancient city of Nora, the architecturally unique remains of which can be seen 1km east of the village. From the mountain hut, 8km southwest of Helvadere, it takes eight hours to hike to and from the summit, where the basement of what was once Turkey's highest church remains. There are views of the Ala Dağlar and Bolkar ranges and Tuz Gölü, the country's second-largest salt lake. The challenging trek requires some mountaineering experience during the winter. You can get more information in Göreme at Middle Earth Travel (p452), which offers a two-day trip incorporating Kaymaklı and Ihlara Valley from €170 per person.

⊙ Sights

Aksaray Museum   MUSEUM
(Aksaray Müzesi; Konya Caddesi; admission ₺3; ⊙8.30am-noon & 1-5pm Tue-Sun) Well you certainly won't have problems finding this museum, installed in a massive modern building en route from the otogar to Aksaray centre, which has been trussed up to resemble a castle of sorts. The collection covers ethnography and archaeology. Exhibits include neolithic beads, a Hellenic child's sarcophagus, Roman perfume bottles, carpets from the Ulu Cami and, in the hall of mummies, a mummified cat.

Ulu Cami   MOSQUE
(Bankalar Caddesi) The Ulu Cami has decoration characteristic of the post–Seljuk Beylik period. A little of the original yellow stone remains in the grand doorway.

Eğri Minare   MONUMENT
(Crooked Minaret; Nevşehir Caddesi) Built in 1236 and leaning at an angle of 27°, the curious Eğri Minare in the older part of Aksaray is inevitably known to locals as the 'Turkish Tower of Pisa'.

🛏 Sleeping & Eating

The following are within walking distance of the main square.

Otel Vadim   HOTEL €
(Otel Vadi; ☑212 8200; 818 Vadi Sokak 13; s/d/tr ₺55/75/90; 🛜) Located in a quiet side street off Büyük Kergi Caddesi, the southern extension of Bankalar Caddesi, the Vadim is nothing special, but rooms are spacious and clean and the staff try hard to please.

Harman   TURKISH €
(☑212 3311; Bankalar Caddesi 16a; mains ₺7) Aksaray's best restaurant is adorned with photos of visiting celebrities posing with the starstruck waiters. It offers a great selection of *ızgara* (grills), döner kebaps, pide and soups.

❶ Getting There & Away

From Aksaray's **otogar** (Konya Caddesi), buses go to Ankara (₺25, 3½ hours), Göreme (₺10, 1½ hours) via Nevşehir (₺10, one hour), Konya (₺15, two hours) via Sultanhanı (₺5, 45 minutes), and Niğde (₺10, 1½ hours). Minibuses make the regular trundle from the otogar into the centre of town. A taxi to the centre will cost around ₺13.

Dolmuşes run between the **Eski Garaj** (Old Otogar; Atatürk Bulvarı), little more than a group of bus stands next to Migros supermarket in the centre, to Güzelyurt (₺5, one hour) and the Ihlara Valley (₺4, 45 minutes). Most of the dolmuşes begin their run from the small terminal next door to the otogar before heading to the Eski Garaj, so you should be able to pick up a service from there if you don't want to head into the centre.

Around Aksaray

The road between Aksaray and Nevşehir follows one of the oldest trade routes in the world, the Uzun Yol (Long Rd). The route linked Konya, the Seljuk capital, with its other great cities (Kayseri, Sivas and Erzurum) and ultimately with Persia (Iran).

The Long Rd was formerly dotted with *hans* where the traders would stop for accommodation and business. The remains of three caravanserais can be visited from Aksaray, the best preserved being the impressive **Ağzıkara Hanı** (admission ₺3; ⊙7.30am-8pm), 16km northeast of Aksaray, which was built between 1231 and 1239. From Aksaray a taxi will charge about ₺50 for the run there and back. If you'd prefer to go by bus, catch one heading to Nevşehir and jump off at the Ağzıkara Hanı. Day tours from Göreme and Ürgüp also call in on the caravanserai.

Further towards Nevşehir you'll pass the scant remains of the 13th-century **Tepesidelik Hanı**, 23km northeast of Aksaray, and the 12th-century **Alay Hanı**, another 10km on.

Kayseri

☑0352 / POP 1.2 MILLION / ELEV 1067M

Mixing Seljuk tombs, mosques and modern developments, Kayseri is both Turkey's most Islamic city after Konya and one of the economic powerhouses nicknamed the 'Anatolian tigers'. Colourful silk headscarfs are piled in the bazaar, one of the country's biggest, and businesses shut down at noon on Friday, but Kayseri's religious leanings are less prominent than its manufacturing prowess. The city's residents, overlooked and inspired by Erciyes Daği, are confident of its future and proud of its past. With no need to rely on the tourism game for their income, Kayseri's people are often less approachable than folk in Göreme et al, and this can be frustrating and jarring if you arrive fresh from the fairy chimneys. However, if you are passing through this transport hub, it's worth taking a look at a Turkish boom town with a strong sense of its own history.

Kayseri

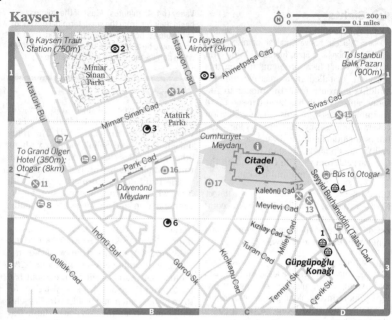

Sights

Citadel
TOP CHOICE

FORTRESS

(Cumhuriyet Meydanı; admission free) The monumental, black volcanic-stone walls of Kayseri citadel (*hisar* or *kale*) were constructed in the early 13th century, during the Seljuk sultan Alaattin Keykubat's reign. Kayseri saw its first castle in the 3rd century, under the Roman emperor Gordian III, and the Byzantine emperor Justinian made alterations 300 years later. Inside the sturdy walls the citadel is now a buzzing bazaar, chock-a-block full of stalls.

Güpgüpoğlu Konağı
TOP CHOICE

MUSEUM

(Ethnography Museum; Tennuri Sokak; admission ₺3; 8am-5pm Tue-Sun) This 18th-century stone Ottoman mansion with beautiful wooden balconies and doorways is home to the Ethnography Museum. Displays are split between an exhibition of Ottoman craft and a mannequin-inhabited section, evoking how life was lived under the multicoloured beams.

Archaeological Museum

MUSEUM

(Hoca Ahmet Yesevi Bulvarı; admission ₺3; 8am-5pm Tue-Sun) Kayseri's small Archaeological Museum (which lies 1.5km south-

east of Kayseri Citadel) is a minor magpie's nest featuring finds from nearby Kültepe (ancient Kaniş, the chief city of the Hatti people and the first Hittite capital). The largest city mound discovered in Anatolia, Kültepe yielded the area's oldest written documents. Many relate to commerce, such as the Assyrian clay tablets and envelopes from 1920 BC to 1840 BC. Other exhibits include a stunning sarcophagus illustrating Hercules' chores, a Bronze Age mother goddess idol, child mummies, Roman and Hellenistic jewellery, hieroglyphic inscriptions relating to King Tuthalia IV and a decapitated but imposing statue of the Hittite monarch.

Mahperi Hunat Hatun Complex

HISTORIC BUILDING

(Seyyid Burhaneddin (Talas) Caddesi) Among Kayseri's distinctive features are several important building complexes that were founded by Seljuk queens and princesses, including the austere-looking Mahperi Hunat Hatun Complex. It comprises the Mahperi Hunat Hatun Camii (1238), built by the wife of Alaattin Keykubat; the Hunat Hatun Medresesi (1237); and a hamam, which is still in use.

Kayseri

Çifte Medrese · MEDRESE
(Twin Seminaries; Mimar Sinan Parkı) These adjoining religious schools were founded at the bequest of the Seljuk sultan Gıyasettin I Keyhüsrev and his sister Gevher Nesibe Sultan (1165–1204). This is the site of one of the world's first medical training schools though the building is unfortunately closed at the moment.

Islamic Buildings · NOTABLE BUILDINGS
The Ottoman-style **Kurşunlu Cami** (Lead-Domed Mosque; Atatürk Parkı), also called the Ahmet Paşa Camii after its founder, was built in the late 16th century, possibly following plans drawn up by the great Sinan (who was born in a nearby village). Another notable mosque is Kayseri's **Ulu Cami** (Great Mosque), begun in the mid-12th century by the Danışmend Turkish *emirs* and finished by the Seljuks in 1205. It features some good examples of early Seljuk style, such as the brick minaret, one of the first built in Anatolia.

Be sure to have a look at the **Sahabiye Medresesi** (Ahmetpaşa Caddesi), an Islamic theological school that now functions as a book bazaar.

Surup Krikor Lusavoriç Kilise · CHURCH
(Church of St Gregory the Illuminator; off Nazım Bey Bulvarı) The 19th-century Surup Krikor Lusavoriç Kilise is one of Anatolia's few remaining Armenian churches. *Asiatic Review* described it as 'tawdry' back in 1937, and the seldom-used building is certainly dilapidated. However, the domed interior is worth a look, mostly for the three gilded altars, containing paintings that replaced the originals last century. The painting on the left, with four fiery columns topped by flaming crosses, depicts the vision of St Gregory, who grew up in Kayseri. Located in a bad part of town, the church is tricky to find, so take a taxi (₺15 return from the tourist office, including waiting time). Ring the bell on the west side of the building to gain entry and leave a tip for the caretaker at the end of your visit.

FREE **Atatürk Evi** · HISTORIC BUILDING
(Tennuri Sokak; ⊙8am-5pm Mon-Fri) This small, originally furnished Ottoman-era house was where Kemal Atatürk stayed when he visited Kayseri.

🛏 Sleeping

Due to Kayseri's cult status among chain-smoking Turkish businessmen, you should book accommodation in advance. Once installed in a room, ensure you reserve it for the duration of your stay or the management may give it to the next claimant.

Hotel Almer · HOTEL €€
(☑320 7970; www.almer.com.tr; Osman Kavuncu Caddesi 1; s/d ₺70/110; ❋⊛) A tribute to the 1980s-style architectural obsession with reflective-glass, the Almer is smoothly professional from the moment you reel through the revolving door. The relaxing reception has a backlit bar, mirrored pillars glint between pink tablecloths in the restaurant, and the comfortable, business-brisk rooms are surprisingly quiet despite the busy road.

SKI ERCİYES DAĞI

If you pluck up the resolve to confront the rugged and handsome Erciyes Dağı, please dispel any notion that you've bagged a Swiss alpine beauty. This is ski season Turkish style, where getting knocked down by an errant snowmobile or devouring a mouthful of yellow snow is considered part of the adventure. For most ski lovers though, this amounts to just a pain in the arse. Luckily it's beautiful as hell up here and the hard-core will still find plenty of empty pistes and not a red flag in sight. Remember when you see a rock, turn.

The popular **Erciyes Dağı Ski Resort** (Erciyes Dağı; 1-day ski pass ₺35) is on the northeast side of the mountain, which is also the best area for mountaineering. In summer, you can camp at sites around Cobaini. The best hotel is **Grand Ergas Erciyes** (☑0352-342 2128; www.granderas.com; Erciyes Dağı; s/d ₺100/150; @🐝), which is new and a bit fancy.

Bent Hotel
HOTEL €€

(☑221 2400; www.benthotel.com; Atatürk Bulvarı 40; s/d/tr ₺70/110/120; 🌸🛜) Its name may not inspire confidence, but the Bent is a solid midrange choice. Unfortunately smoky and small rooms are kept neat and clean and staff try their hardest to please. All rooms have TVs, Efes-stocked minibars and 24-hour room service.

Hotel Çapari
HOTEL €€

(☑222 5278; Donanma Caddesi 12; s/d/tr/ste ₺60/90/110/120; 🌸🛜) With thick red carpets and friendly staff, this three-star hotel on a quiet street is one of the best deals in Kayseri. The well-equipped rooms have satellite TV and massive minibars.

Hotel Sur
HOTEL €

(☑222 4367; Talas Caddesi 12; s/d/tr ₺35/60/75) Beyond the dark reception and institutional corridors, the Sur's rooms are bright and comfortable. The management is friendly and the hotel's withered international flags can almost lean on the ancient city walls for support.

Novotel
HOTEL €€

(☑207 3000; www.novotel.com; Kocasinan Bulvarı; r from €60; 🌸🛜) This is a very good version of the dependable international chain, featuring clean lines, bright colours and five-star service. The hotel is located 3km from the centre of Kayseri, on the way to the airport.

Grand Ülger
HOTEL €€

(☑320 1415; www.grandulgerhotel.com; Osman Kavuncu Caddesi 55; s/d ₺60/80; 🌸🛜) This flashy business hotel is a good choice with comfortable rooms and decent restaurant.

✖ Eating

Kayseri boasts a few special dishes, among them *pastırma* (salted, sun-dried veal coated with *çemen*, a spicy concoction of garlic, red peppers, parsley and water), the original pastrami.

Few restaurants serve alcohol – if you want a tipple with your tucker, try Hotel Almer (p489) or **Kale Rooftop Restaurant** (☑207 5000; Hilton Hotel, Cumhuriyet Meydanı, İstasyon Caddesi 1; mains ₺20-40; ⊙noon-2am) at the Hilton.

The western end of Sivas Caddesi has a strip of pide and kebap joints that still seem to be pumping when everything else in town is quiet.

Elmacıoğlu Merkez
KEBAP €€

(☑222 6965; 1st & 2nd fl, Millet Caddesi 5; mains ₺10-15) Bring on the calories. Whatever you do in Kayseri, you simply have to eat here while in town. Ascend in a lift to the restaurant with its superb views of the citadel and order the İskender kebap (döner kebap on fresh pide and topped with savoury tomato sauce and browned butter) – a traditional house speciality. Your waistline won't thank us but your taste buds will. Recommended.

Tuana
TURKISH €

(☑222 0565; 2nd fl, Sivas Caddesi; mains ₺7) Smart Tuana offers a roll call of classics such as kebaps and Kayseri *mantı*. When it's quiet, the ocean of red tables and chairs adorned with golden ribbons have the air of an out-of-season seaside resort, but it's easy to distract yourself with the views of the citadel and Erciyes Dağı.

İstanbul Balık Pazarı FISH €

(☏231 8973; Sivas Caddesi; mains ₺5-10; ⊙8am-
11pm) Choose between the fish frying at the
door, then head past the glistening catches
in the fishmongers to the small dining room,
with its mishmash of nautical and historical
paintings.

Divan Pastanesi BAKERY €

(☏222 3974; Millet Caddesi; pastries ₺2-9) This
modern pastry shop is a favourite among
Kayseri's sweet tooths.

Anadolu Et Lokantası TURKISH €

(☏320 5209; Osman Kavuncu Caddesi 10; mains
₺5-10) Meaty goodness is the order of the
day at this happening lunchtime hang-out.

🔒 Shopping

Set at the intersection of age-old trade
routes, Kayseri has been an important
commercial centre for millennia and its
kapalı çarşı (vaulted bazaar) was one of
the largest built by the Ottomans. Restored
in the 1870s and again in the 1980s, it remains the heart of the city and is well
worth a wander. The adjoining **bedesten**
(covered market), built in 1497, was first
dedicated to the sale of textiles and is still
a good place to pick up carpets and kilims.
An antique-carpet auction takes place here
on Monday and Thursday.

ℹ Information

English and German are spoken at the helpful **tourist office** (☏222 3903; Cumhuriyet
Meydanı; ⊙8am-5pm Mon-Fri), which gives out
maps and brochures.

You'll find numerous banks with ATMs in the
centre. To collect your email, head to **Soner**

Internet Café (Düvenönü Meydanı; per hr ₺1.50;
⊙8am-midnight).

ℹ Getting There & Away

Air

Kayseri Airport has regular flights to İstanbul
operated by Turkish Airlines (₺99 to ₺229 one
way, 1½ hours, seven daily) and Pegasus Airlines
(₺79 to ₺150 one way, four daily).

A taxi between Kayseri city centre and the
havaalanı (airport) costs ₺15 and a dolmuş is
₺1.25. Airport shuttle buses run between the
airport and villages of central Cappadocia and
must be pre-booked. See p446.

Bus

On an important north–south and east–west
crossroads, Kayseri has plenty of bus services.

The massive **otogar** (☏336 4373; Osman
Kavuncu Bulvarı), 9km west of the centre, has
luggage storage (₺6 for 24 hours), car rental
and a cafe. If there's no *servis* from there to the
merkezi (centre), grab a taxi (₺15) or catch a
local bus (₺1.25).

A few bus companies heading from Kayseri to
Nevşehir will drop off passengers in Göreme on
request. Your best bets are **Süha** (departures
at 7am and 5pm) and **Metro** (departures at 6pm
and 8.30pm).

There is an hourly local bus service between
8am and 7pm to Nevşehir via Avanos and Ürgüp.
You can pick up onward dolmuş connections to
other Cappadocian villages from there.

Train

Kayseri Garı (Kocasinan Bulvarı) is served by
the daily *4 Eylül Mavi* train (between Ankara
and Malatya), the *Doğu Ekspresi* (between
Ankara and Kars) and the *Çukurova Mavi* (between Ankara and Adana). There is also the
daily *Erciyes Ekspresi* which runs between

SERVICES FROM KAYSERI'S OTOGAR

DESTINATION	FARE (₺)	DURATION (HR)	FREQUENCY (PER DAY)
Adana	25	5	3 morning & 4 afternoon/evening
Ankara	25	5	hourly
Erzurum	45	10	2 evening
Gaziantep	45	6	2 evening
Göreme	10	1	1 morning & 3 evening
Kahramanmaraş	20	4	5
Malatya	25	5	2 evening
Nevşehir	12	1½	hourly
Sivas	20	3	2 morning & 4 afternoon/evening
Van	80	13	2 evening

TRAINS FROM KAYSERİ

Trains depart daily unless otherwise stated.

DESTINATION	FARE (₺)	DURATION (HR)	DEPARTURES
Adana	14	6	1.45am & 7.40am
Ankara	13.50	8	12.30am, 2.30am, 3.37am & 9.50am
Kars	29.25	20½	1.30am
Kurtalan	22.75	20	9.14am (Tue, Thu, Fri, Sat & Sun)
Malatya	17.50	9	9.14am & 10.05pm
Tatvan	23.75	24	9.14am (Mon & Wed)

Kayseri and Adana. The *Güney Ekspresi* (Ankara to Kurtalan, five per week) and the *Vangölü Ekspresi* (Ankara to Tatvan, two per week) both also stop at Kayseri. The weekly Trans Asia service to Tehran (Iran) also pulls in here.

To reach the centre from the train station, walk out of the station, cross the big avenue and board any bus heading down Atatürk Bulvarı to Düvenönü Meydanı. Alternatively you could walk along Altan Caddesi, which isn't as busy as Atatürk Bulvarı.

Tram

A state-of-the-art tram system runs in central Kayseri from 6am to 2am daily. It's a very efficient way of getting around and single tickets cost ₺1. The nearest tram station to the otogar is Selimiye, a 10-minute walk away.

Sultan Han

Built in the 1230s, the **Sultan Han** (admission ₺3; ☉dawn-dusk) is a striking old Seljuk caravanserai on the old Kayseri–Sivas highway, 45km northeast of Kayseri. It is a fine, restored example of a Seljuk royal caravan lodging – the largest in Anatolia after the Sultanhanı, near Aksaray.

Locals should unlock the door and issue tickets, but visitors have reported frustrated attempts to gain access. If you are coming from Kayseri, enquire at Kayseri's Archaeological Museum.

Sultan Han is southeast of the Kayseri–Sivas road, near Tuzhisar. To get there from Kayseri, take a Sivas-bound bus (₺5), or a dolmuş (₺2.50) heading to Sarıoğlan or Akkişla from the *doğu* (east) garage.

Black Sea Coast

Best Places to Eat

- » Kalendar (p513)
- » Bordo Mavi (p513)
- » Evvel Zaman (p518)
- » Grand Mıdı Restaurant (p506)
- » Orta Kahve (p508)

Best Places to Stay

- » Sebile Hanım Konaği (p505)
- » Kuşna Butik Pansiyon (p496)
- » Taşbaşı Butik Otel (p506)

Why Go?

While many tourists flock southwest to the Med and Aegean, the Black Sea (Karadeniz) region is equally deserving. After Sinop's seaside-holiday vibe and Trabzon's modern buzz, you can break out the sun cream in little fishing villages or head inland to alpine *yaylalar* (mountain pastures). The craggy and spectacular coastline makes for a scenic route across Turkey to other parts of Anatolia.

This is a historical region, scattered with the legacies of civilisations and empires that have ebbed and flowed like Black Sea waves. Castles, churches and monasteries recall the days of the kings of Pontus, the Genoese and the Ottomans; Queen Hippolyte and her tribe of female Amazon warriors supposedly lived here during the Pontic era; and the chapel at Cape Yason marks the spot where Jason and his Argonauts passed by. More recently, the very existence of modern Turkey owes a massive debt to the passionate local support thrown behind Atatürk's republican revolution.

When to Go

Trabzon

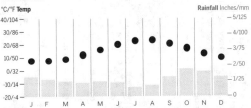

May International Giresun Aksu Festival and spring flowers in the *yaylalar* (mountain pastures).

Jun–Aug Trek in the *yaylalar* and enjoy summer festivals in Trabzon's main square.

Apr & Sep Be one of the few travellers enjoying the lazy-day charm of Amasra and Sinop.

Black Sea Coast Highlights

1 Climb through forests to the **Sumela Monastery** (p515)

2 Slow down and imbibe the easygoing ambience of the fishing harbour at **Sinop**

3 Count the vertigo-inducing curves on the scenic **D010 Hwy**, along the coast from Amasra to Sinop

4 Explore the winding labyrinth of alleys and lanes in Amasra's **castle** (p495)

5 Buy a Trabzonspor soccer top and pound big-city streets in **Trabzon**

6 Discover **mountain plateaus and villages** on day trips from towns such as Giresun and Ordu

7 Hop in a cable car and see where the Turks go for their summer staycations in **Ordu**

8 Have a hilltop brew with a view in **Rize**, Turkey's tea-growing capital

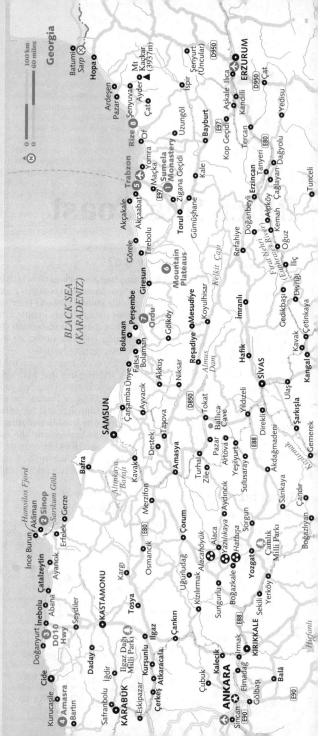

Amasra

☎0378 / POP 7500

It's a six-hour journey from İstanbul to Amasra, but your first glimpse from the hills above will tell you that the trip was worthwhile. Straddling a peninsula with a rocky island offshore, the town is the Black Sea's prettiest port. It's a popular tourist centre, but low-key in comparison with many Aegean and Mediterranean resorts. International visitors are still relatively uncommon, and you will likely receive a warm welcome from locals and Turkish holidaymakers. Summer weekends are hectic; the streets and coves are quieter during the week and throughout the winter.

The Byzantines held Amasra as part of the Pontic kingdom, but rented the port to the Genoese as a trading station from 1270 until 1460, when Mehmet the Conqueror waltzed in without a fight. Under Ottoman rule, Amasra lost its commercial importance to other Black Sea ports, and today it's a laid-back spot to relax and try the classic Turkish combo of rakı (aniseed brandy) and *balık* (fish).

From the intersection by the post office near the entrance to town, head past Hotel Cenova for the Büyük Liman (Large Harbour), and past Amasra Seyahat for the Küçük Liman (Small Harbour) and castle.

◉ Sights & Activities

FREE **Kale** CASTLE

Reached through three massive gateways from Küçük Liman, or up steps from Büyük Liman, Amasra's citadel occupies the promontory fortified by the Byzantines, back when the port was known as Sesamos Amastris.

The citadel is now a residential area, but its impressive original walls and some relics survive, including the restored 9th-century Byzantine **Eski Şapel** (Old Chapel).

Amasra Museum MUSEUM

(Amasra Müzesi; Dereoğlu Sokak 4; admission ₺3; ⊗8.30am-7pm) This excellent museum occupies a 19th-century naval school at the southern end of Küçük Liman. Exhibits from coins to carpets – including Roman, Byzantine, Hellenistic and Ottoman finds – showcase Amasra's many-mastered history.

Boat Trips BOAT TOUR

Amasra's location is best admired from the sea. Operators in Büyük Liman offer boat trips around the harbours and nearby island (about ₺7 for a 45-minute tour, and ₺35 for six hours, including swimming stops and lunch on the island). Boats mostly run on

BLACK SEA HISTORY 101

The thin, meandering coastal strip along the Black Sea has been a hotspot of civilisation, war and conquest for more than a millennium.

Milesians and Arcadians colonised the coast in the 8th century BC, and founded Sinop, Samsun and Trabzon. Later the area became the Kingdom of Pontus. The Pontic king Mithridates VI Eupator waged war against the Romans from 88 to 84 BC. He conquered Cappadocia and other Anatolian kingdoms, but had to settle for peace based on prewar borders. From 74 to 64 BC he was at it again, encouraging his son-in-law, Tigranes I of Armenia, to seize Cappadocia from the Romans. The Roman response was to conquer Pontus; Mithridates fled and later committed suicide. The Romans left a small kingdom of Pontus based in Trebizond (Trabzon).

The coast was subsequently ruled by Byzantium. Alexius Comnenus, son of Emperor Manuel I, proclaimed himself emperor of Pontus when the Crusaders sacked Constantinople in AD 1204. His descendants ruled until 1461, when Mehmet the Conqueror's Ottoman forces captured Pontus. During the Comnenian dynasty's reign, Samsun was under Seljuk rule, with trading privileges granted to the Genoese. But when the Ottomans came, the Genoese burned the city to the ground and sailed away.

After WWI the region's Ottoman Greek citizens attempted to form a new Pontic state with Allied support. Disarmed by the Allied occupation authorities, Turkish inhabitants were persecuted by ethnic Greek guerrillas, who still had weapons. Local Turks thus proved responsive to calls for revolution. Mustafa Kemal (later Atatürk) abandoned the Ottoman military in Allied-occupied Constantinople and landed at Samsun on 19 May 1919, before moving inland to Amasya to organise Turkey's battle for independence.

summer weekends. You can also book trips through **Amasra Turizmcilik** (Küçük Liman), a travel agency next to Amasra Museum.

🛏 Sleeping

Amasra is a good spot for *ev pansiyonu* (pensions in private homes), typically charging ₺30–40 per person (plus ₺10 for breakfast). Look for 'Pansiyon' notices in windows on the seafront and in the *kale*. You can also book through Amasra Turizmcilik.

Rates on busy summer weekends from mid-June to mid-September are up to 50% higher than during other periods, and many places will charge solo travellers the cost of a double room. You'll definitely need to negotiate.

Most pensions close from November to April, and hotels generally only open on weekends during these months.

TOP CHOICE **Kuşna Butik Pansiyon** PENSION €€
(☑315 1033; kusnapansiyon@mynet.com; Kurşuna Sokak 36; s/d ₺50/100; @🖥) The friendly Doğu family has really thought of travellers' requirements at this wonderfully located pension in the *kale*. Eight bright and modern rooms, including a cute attic room in the main house, overlook a verdant garden and rocky cove. The village breakfast features homemade jam and there's an unlimited supply of tea and coffee in the breakfast room-cum-lounge. It's near the Old Chapel, most easily reached up the steps from near the tour boats on Büyük Liman.

Timur Otel HOTEL €€
(☑315 2589; www.timurotel.com; Çekiciler Caddesi 53; s/d ₺100/120; 🞷) This friendly operation has spotless, pretty-in-pink rooms overlooking a quiet square, just off Büyük Liman. Double-glazing ensures a good night's kip despite the nearby mosque.

Pansiyon Evi PENSION €
(☑315 1283; Küçük Liman Caddesi 33; s/d without bathroom ₺40/75; 🞷) Just inside the castle gates on the left, this pink wooden house has tidy rooms, most sharing a bathroom, and a terrace with sweeping views of Küçük Liman. The best room is an ensuite opening onto the terrace. Amasra's postage stamp–sized pub district is nearby.

Çarşı Butik Otel PENSION €€
(☑315 1146; www.carsibutikotel.com; Çekiciler Caddesi 23; s/d ₺60/120; 🞷🖥) Overlooked by the castle walls near the souvenir market,

the friendly Çarşı's wood-trimmed, slightly kitsch rooms have private patios decorated with comfy cushions. Other benefits include *servis* (shuttle buses) to a nearby aquapark.

Hotel Türkili HOTEL €€
(☑315 3750; www.turkilihotel.com.tr; Özdemirhan Sokak 6; s/d from ₺60/120; P🞷🖥) Behind its wrought-iron balconies and dirty pink facade, the popular Türkili's best feature is the fifth-floor bar-restaurant with views over both harbours. There's also a small budget room overlooking an internal shaft.

Sahil Otel HOTEL €€
(☑315 2211; Turgut Işık Caddesi 82; s/d ₺60/120; P🞷@🖥) Opposite the sailing club on the Büyük Liman, the compact but modern Coast Hotel has small balconies. Waterfront eating and drinking is just a stroll away.

Balkaya Pansiyon PENSION €
(☑315 1434; İskele Caddesi 35; s/d without breakfast ₺40/70; 🖥) This is one of Amasra's cheapest formal pensions, offering small, basic rooms on a side street behind Hamam Cafe.

🍴 Eating

Amasra's licensed seafront restaurants serve *canlı balık* (fresh fish) by the portion. Alternatively, grab a takeaway and take your pick of two harbours.

Hamam Cafe CAFE €
(Tarihi Sağır Osmanlar Hamamı; Büyük Liman; gözleme ₺4; 🖥) In an old hamam by the tourist office, this easygoing cafe is perfect for sipping tea and playing backgammon, among colourful lights in marble basins. The *gözleme peynirli* (savoury pancakes with cheese) are moreish.

Canlı Balık SEAFOOD €€
(Küçük Liman Caddesi 8; fish portion ₺12.50-40, meze ₺4) Locals recommend this smart, 70-year-old restaurant, its big windows offering sweeping sea views. The stylish, modern dining room forsakes the usual nautical theme, and the lists of fish and Kavaklıdere wines are satisfyingly long.

Mavi Yeşil SEAFOOD €€
(Büyük Liman Caddesi; fish portion ₺12.50-35) Smart black tables with red overlays populate Mavi Yeşil's first-floor dining room, which rises from Üstü beach near Ziraat Bank. Recommended by locals, it serves calamari and *köfte* (meatballs) as well as the

day's catches. The balcony with views along the coast doubles as the smoking area.

Balıkçının Yeri
SEAFOOD €€

(Büyük Liman Caddesi; fish portion ₺15) This is the standout in a row of cheaper seafood restaurants lining the edge of Büyük Liman. Sea views are limited, but you can buy a takeaway *balık ekmek* (fish kebap, ₺5) and eat elsewhere.

Amasra Sofrası
TURKISH €€

(Hamam Sokak 25; mains ₺8-15;) On a quiet square midway between the two harbours, this grill house and *lokanta* (eatery serving ready-made food) has alfresco tables. Choose between lots of vegetable dishes, pide, kebaps and fish.

Karadeniz Aile Pide Salonu
PIDE €€

(Mithat Ceylan Caddesi 9; mains ₺7-12) This streetside spot just off the Küçük Liman does great pide, including the Amasra Special – a tasty mixed pide with cheese. The alfresco tables are more exciting than the small dining room.

🍷 Drinking

Near Ziraat Bank on the Büyük Liman, **Çekek Cafe** (Büyük Liman) and **Sesamos Cafe** (Büyük Liman) are mellow spots to start the evening with a drink on the beach.

Hayalperest Café & Bistro
BAR, CAFE

(Küçük Liman Caddesi 3) The classy 'Daydreamer' is a winner for Amasra sunsets, with crisply chilled draught beer, meze, a wide range of cocktail-ready spirits and sweeping harbour views.

Ağlayan Ağaç Çay Bahçesi
TEA GARDEN

(Nöbethane Sokak) Head up through the *kale* to this cliff-top kiosk with views of squawking seagulls circling the island; signs point the way. It's a perfect place to spend a few leisurely hours under the umbrellas, getting some perspective on Amasra's location.

Lutfiye
CAFE

(Küçük Liman Caddesi 20a; ⊙11am-6pm) The brick-lined Lutfiye serves cappuccinos, snacks and breakfast to a chilled-out soundtrack. It's also a classy alternative to Amasra's kitsch souvenir market, selling marmalade and delicious nut-studded *lokum* (Turkish delight), among other treats.

Han Kır Çay Bahçesi
TEA GARDEN

(Sefa Park, Küçük Liman) A cosy, log cabin–style cafe with lanterns hanging from creeper-covered beams and pictures of old Amasra on the walls.

Cafe 'N Bistro
PUB

(Küçük Liman Caddesi) This wooden-fronted corner bar is male-dominated inside, but its outside tables are hot property for watching the evening roll in. It's at the end of the souvenir market, with snacks such as *börek* (filled pastry) and fries available.

Arma Cafe
CAFE

(Cumhuriyet Caddesi 1) Just back from Küçük Liman, Rigging Cafe is nautical only in name, with landlubbers enjoying coffees, teas and hot chocolates in its windows. Pastries and Turkish breakfast are also on offer.

Han Bar
BAR

(Küçük Liman Caddesi 17) This is the most popular of Amasra's small cluster of pubs, sandwiched between houses next to the castle gate. There's often live music at night.

ℹ Information

INTERNET ACCESS There are a few internet cafes around the Atatürk statue.

TOURIST INFORMATION **Tourist Office** (Büyük Liman; ⊙Jun-Sep) In a small booth beside Hamam Cafe. Opening hours are often restricted to weekends.

ℹ Getting There & Away

Heading east along the coast, get an early start. Dolmuşes (minibuses) become increasingly scarce later in the day. If you're driving to Sinop, fill up on fuel in Bartın (before Amasra).

Intercity bus companies don't travel to Amasra. Instead, minibuses to Bartın (₺4, 30 minutes) leave every 30 minutes from near the PTT (post office). From Bartın there are buses to Safranbolu (₺17, two hours), Ankara (₺32, five hours) and İstanbul (₺45, seven hours). For Sinop, you will need to change in Karabük (₺17, two hours) and/or Kastamonu (₺27, four hours).

Metro and Kâmil Koç have offices next to the Atatürk statue in Amasra.

Amasra to Sinop

Winding sinuously around rugged hills hugging the Black Sea, the D010 from Amasra to Sinop (312km) is wonderfully scenic, with echoes of California's Hwy 1 or New Zealand's west coast. Expect minimal traffic and stunning views at every turn, with lush, green forested headlands, rugged cliffs and glistening turquoise waters.

The going is extremely slow on these narrow roads, where the surface is often broken, and you will encounter roadworks and even the occasional *heyelan* (landslide). The average driving speed is around 40km/h, which means that it takes more than eight hours to get to Sinop. By public transport, you'll need to use local services between the small towns and villages along the way. Get going at daybreak if you want to complete the journey in a day.

A few villages have camping grounds, including **Çakraz**, just west of **Bozköy Beach**. **Kurucaşile**, 45km east of Amasra, also has modest hotels and pensions, and you can see boats being built here. Other spots within day-trip distance of Amasra are the picturesque two-beach village of **Kapısuyu** and, 10km further east, the tiny harbour at **Gideros**, the idyllic cove of your dreams. There are a couple of restaurants where you can feast on local seafood and watch the sunset.

About 63km east of Amasra, over the hill from Gideros, the road descends to **Kalafat** and a sand-and-pebble beach stretching eight kilometres, past the aptly named **Kumluca** (Sandy). Many dolmuşes terminate in **Cide**, 4km east of Kumluca. Seafront pensions, mostly only open from June to September, and fish restaurants huddle at the western end of town, around 2km from the central otogar (bus station). **Kaptan Aile Pansiyonu** (☑0366-866 3658; per person without breakfast ₺30) is in a friendly elderly couple's home, with the sea at the bottom of the garden.

The road on to İnebolu is particularly bendy and hilly, and you'll likely see more dogs and turtles than cars. Around 12km east of Cide, a signpost on the left points to **Kuscu Köyü**, a small village with access to the **Aydos Canyon**, a steep river ravine. **Doğanyurt**, 31km before İnebolu and about 4½ hours from Amasra, is yet another pleasant harbour town, with a Friday market and a few little cafes and *lokantas*.

About three hours west of Sinop, **İnebolu** is a possible stopping point; onward transport may be hard to find by late afternoon. The **Yakamoz Tatil Köyü** (☑0366-811 3100; www.yakamoztatilkoyu.com.tr; İsmetpaşa Caddesi; bungalow s/d ₺50/75, room s/d ₺60/95, mains ₺15; ❋🞔🛜🏊) is a beachside resort 800m west of the centre, with a cafe and licensed restaurant. Book ahead in summer. In the centre are old Ottoman houses and a relatively lively seafront promenade.

Abana, 24km east of İnebolu, has a decent beach, and about 23km further on, near **Çatalzeytin**, is a long pebble beach surrounded by beautiful scenery. At **Ayancık** the road divides, with the northern route offering the more scenic journey to Sinop (64km). To get on this route, cross the bridge and continue through Ayancık.

Sinop

☑0368 / POP 38,705

Wrapped around a rocky promontory, Sinop is the Black Sea's only southern-facing spot, and its calm waters and vibrant ambience feel more Akdeniz (Mediterranean) than Karadeniz (Black Sea). The Black Sea, as an ancient maritime saying goes, has 'three harbours – July, August and Sinop': the city's naturally sheltered harbour is safe even in the roughest winter weather, when it can be dangerous for ships to enter other Black Sea ports.

Colonised from Miletus in the 8th century BC, Sinop's trade grew, and successive rulers – including the Pontic kings (who made it their capital), Romans and Byzantines – turned it into a busy trading centre. The Seljuks used Sinop as a port after taking it in 1214, but the Ottomans preferred to develop nearby Samsun, which had better land communications. On 30 November 1853, a Russian armada attacked Sinop without any warning, overwhelming the local garrison and killing or wounding about 3000 people. The battle hastened the beginning of the Crimean War, in which the Ottomans allied with the British and French to fight Russian ambitions in the near East.

With a history as a trading port for more than 2500 years (since the date of colonisation), Sinop is today a holiday town with a bustling, cosmopolitan air. Its heritage is reflected in the many shops selling model ships. Tourists start arriving as early as April and peak season runs from mid-June until mid-September, when you should book accommodation in advance.

◉ Sights & Activities

Fortifications   FORTRESS

Open to attack from the sea, Sinop was first fortified by the Hittites around 2000 BC. The existing walls are developments (by the Romans, Byzantines, Seljuks and Ottomans) of those erected in 72 BC by Pontic

Sinop

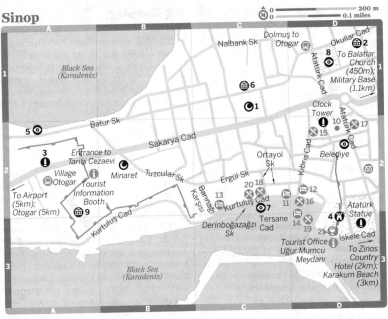

king, Mithridates VI. At one time the walls, some 3m thick, were more than 2km long, with seven gates and 25m-high towers. Walk along the ramparts for sea views.

Pervane Medresesi   HISTORIC BUILDING
(Batur Sokak; ⊙8am-10pm, tourist office 8am-5pm Mon-Sat) The powerful Seljuk grand vizier Muinettin Süleyman Pervane built this seminary in 1262 to commemorate the Seljuk

conquest of Sinop in 1214. It now houses a cafe and shops selling local crafts, including excellent woven linen, for which Sinop is famous.

Tourist information is available in the linen shop.

Tarihi Cezaevi   HISTORIC BUILDING
(Old Gaol; Sarkaya Caddesi; admission ₺5; ⊙9am-7pm) This hulking former prison's empty

yards and corridors are haunting, particularly if you've seen *Midnight Express*, Alan Parker and Oliver Stone's notorious 1978 film about an American trapped in the Turkish penal system. At the base of the tower near the entrance, look out for the brown board with Evliya Çelebi's spine-chilling description of the 17th-century gaolers. Outside the prison entrance, head along Sakarya Caddesi towards the white **Diogenes the Cynic statue** (Sarkaya Caddesi) (the Greek philospoher was born here around 410 BC) and turn right to see the ancient bastion the **Kumkapı** (Sand Gate; Batur Sokak).

Archaeological Museum
MUSEUM

(Okullar Caddesi 2; admission ₺3; ⊙8am-5pm Tue-Sun) The excellent collection here includes poignant Roman stele, Byzantine icons and information on the Greek philosopher Diogenes the Cynic. It's surrounded by pillars, mosaics, turban-topped gravestones and a pleasant fish pond in the garden.

Alaadin Camii
MOSQUE

(Ulu Camii; Sakarya Caddesi) Set in an expansive walled courtyard, this mosque (1267) was constructed for Süleyman Pervane. It has been repaired many times; the local Candaroğlu emir added the marble *mihrab* (niche indicating the direction of Mecca) and wooden *mimber* (pulpit). Following diligent restoration, the austere interior and spacious courtyard are havens from Sinop's energetic buzz.

Martyrs' Monuments
MEMORIAL

Secreted away near the harbour, next to Deniz Sehitleri Hacı Ömer Camii (1903), the poignant **Şehitler Çeşmesi** (Martyrs' Fountain; Kurtuluş Caddesi) commemorates the Turkish soldiers who died in the surprise Russian attack of 1853. It was built using money recovered from the soldiers' pockets. Remembering the same losses, the **Sinop Martyr Monument** (Atatürk Caddesi) contains soldiers' bones.

☞ Tours

Sinope Tours
TOUR

(☑261 7900; www.sinopetours.com; Atatürk Caddesi 2) English- and German-speaking Adem runs group tours (₺50, mid-June to September). Two itineraries cover lakes, waterfalls and bays. Individual tours cost ₺200.

🛏 Sleeping

Otel 57
BUSINESS HOTEL €€

(☑261 5462; www.otel57.com; Kurtuluş Caddesi 29; s/d ₺60/90; P🅟❄🄰) At the friendly 57, spic-and-span leather chairs in reception give way to comfortable rooms. There's plenty in the breakfast buffet and the clientele is a mix of Turkish businessmen and tourists.

Sinop Park Otel
HOTEL €€

(☑261 9660; www.sinoparkotel.com; Kurtuluş Caddesi 9; s/d ₺110/140; ❄🄰) The closest Sinop gets to a designer hotel, the Sinop Park's swish rooms come with LCD TV, Efes-stocked minibar and tiled bathroom.

Zinos Country Hotel
BOUTIQUE HOTEL €€

(☑260 5600; www.zinoshotel.com.tr; Enver Bahadır Yolu 69; s/d ₺100/150; P❄🄰🅢) Around 2km along the peninsula from town near the black-sand Karakum beach, the Zinos fills an old Ottoman house with understated white walls, rug-trimmed wooden floors, and occasional dressers and metal water jugs. Some rooms have a private balcony and suite 303 has sloping attic ceilings. There's a bar-restaurant and sea views throughout, but the new three-star extension may change the atmosphere.

Denizci Otel
HOTEL €€

(☑260 5934; www.denizciotel@hotmail.com; Kurtuluş Caddesi 13; s/d ₺50/80; P❄🄰) A good option with repros decorating the corridors and rooms with big plasma-screen TVs and window alcoves. A renovation was underway when we visited.

Otel Mola
HOTEL €€

(☑261 1814; www.sinopmolaotel.com.tr; Barınağı Karşısı 34; s/d ₺80/140; P❄🄰) Near the harbour, 'Hotel Rest' has sea views over the tea gardens. High marks also go to the friendly staff, smart reception and comfortable rooms.

Martı Camping
CAMPING GROUND €

(☑287 6214; www.marticamping.com; Akliman; campsite per person ₺10, bungalow ₺50-100, breakfast ₺10; ⊙Apr-Oct) This family-run campsite is 10km west of Sinop, past the airport (Akliman harbour and picnic place are nearby). The grassy plots overlook a big sandy beach with views of Sinop, and campers can use the well-equipped kitchen. The basic bungalows have a kitchenette, lounge, two doubles and bathroom with

ADEM TAHTACI: TOUR GUIDE

Top spots around Sinop according to guide Adem Tahtacı of Sinope Tours (p500).

Erfelek It's unique in Turkey, with 28 waterfalls, one after the other; popular for trekking and climbing.

Panoramic view Walk up Derviş Sarabil Caddesi to just below the military base to see Sinop at your feet. On the way look out for Balatlar Church, an Orthodox Byzantine church built in 660.

Hamsilos Fjord It's the only fjord in Turkey and on the way there you pass Akliman, where there's a long beach and picnic place.

İnce Burun The northernmost point of Turkey – the closest to the Ukraine – and there's a lighthouse there.

Sarıkum Gölü (Lake) A very famous and beautiful place mixing forest, desert, lake, sea and beach. Thousands of years ago the sea receded and sand was left there. They planted pine trees to stop the sand blowing into the village. There are water snakes and turtles under the bridge in the village and it's on the migration route of birds.

Turkish toilet. Hourly dolmuşes run here from the village otogar (₺1.50).

Yılmaz Aile Pansiyonu
PENSION €

(☎261 5752; off Tersane Çarşısı; per person without breakfast ₺25, without bathroom ₺20) Tucked away on a lane between Kiyi Cafe & Bar and Dolunay Pastanesi, this friendly, family-run pension a few steps from the waterfront has simple rooms with sea views and blankets on the beds.

✖ Eating

Sinop's waterfront is lined with licensed open-air restaurants. Try Sinop *mantı* (Turkish ravioli), made with lashings of yoghurt. To sweeten a stroll along the nearby harbour, head to **Dolunay Pastaneleri** (Kurtuluş Caddesi 14; desserts from ₺2) for ice cream and baklava.

Diyabakır Sofrası
KEBAP, PIDE €€

(Kıbrıs Caddesi 7; mains ₺12) Diyabakır may resemble a fast-food restaurant, complete with Coke meal deals, but locals swear by the food. Pide, *lahmacun* (Arabic-style pizza), different types of *mantı* and kebabs from Adana to Urfa are offered in clean and friendly surrounds.

Saray Restaurant
SEAFOOD €€

(Tersane Caddesi; fish mains ₺12-20, meze ₺6.50) Excellent salads and continuously sipped rakı make this the preferred spot for local fans of caught-this-morning seafood. Grab a table on the floating pontoon and begin your meal with Saray's excellent mezes.

Mangal
FISH, TURKISH €

(Kurtuluş Caddesi 15; mains ₺7.50-10) Its walls decorated with fishing photos and guns, this homely grill house serves *gözleme*, *mantı* and grilled fish, chicken and *köfte*.

Zeyden Mutfak
CAFE, BREAKFAST €

(Yalı Kahvesi Karşısı; Breakfast ₺10; ⏰7am-4pm; 🛜) This coolly minimalist cafe serves village breakfasts composed of about 10 different elements, including olives, jams and *sahanda yumurta* (fried eggs).

Gaziantep Sofrası
KEBAP, PIDE €

(Atatürk Caddesi; mains ₺6.50-13) Local men, women and families head to Gaziantep's upstairs salon for kepabs, from *patlıcan* (aubergine) to İskender. A welcoming place that's good for female travellers.

Sahil Ocakbaşı
KÖFTE, FISH €

(Ortayol Sokak 12; mains ₺7.50) In this tiny side-street grill house, watch *köfte* being rolled in the kitchen. Grill your own, or leave it to the experts, on the grill which diners sit around. The resulting *köfte* and fish, served with onion, tomato and pepper, is lip-smacking. Solo female travellers may not feel 100% comfortable with the blokey ambience.

Öz Diyarbakır Mangal Sofrası
TURKISH €€

(Kurtuluş Caddesi 18; mains ₺9) Close to the seafront bars and hotels, this simple places serves good *lahmacun*, soup, pide and a range of kebaps. *Paket servis* (takeaway) is available.

BLACK SEA COAST SINOP

SERVICES FROM SİNOP'S OTOGAR

DESTINATION	FARE (₺)	DURATION (HR)	DISTANCE (KM)	FREQUENCY (PER DAY)
Ankara	50	8	443	twice (10.30am, 10.30pm)
İstanbul	60	11	700	twice (10.30am, 7pm)
Karabük (for Safranbolu and Amasra)	35	5	340	twice (10.30am, 7pm)
Kastamonu	25	3	170	once (7pm)
Samsun (for Trabzon)	25	3	168	hourly

 Drinking

Tea gardens line the seafront, offering backgammon and other board games. Stroll along and decide where today's caffeinated fun is.

Burç Café
BAR

(Sinop Kalesi, Tersane Caddesi) In the fortified tower, this atmospheric spot attracts a young crowd for live music (in summer) and ocean views. Bring something warm to wear as it can get chilly.

Kiyi Cafe & Bar
BAR

(Tersane Caddesi) Sit outside under blue lights watching the bobbing boats, with the strains of a troubadour drifting across the walkway from the small bar.

 Information

INTERNET ACCESS Sesli Gövüntülü Chat Oyun (Kaledibi Aralığı Sokağ; per hr ₺1.50; ⊙9am-10pm)

TOURIST INFORMATION The most helpful sources of information (in English) are the 'linen store' at Pervane Medresesi (p499) and Sinope Tours (p500). The **tourist office** (İskele Caddesi; ⊙8am-7pm mid-Jun–mid-Sep, 9am-5pm May–mid-Jun & mid-Sep–Oct) and **booth** (Tarihi Cezaevi) are less helpful.

 Getting There & Away

AIR Sinope Tours (www.sinopetours.com) represents **Turkish Airlines** (www.thy.com), which flies to/from İstanbul only. A taxi to Sinop Airport, 5km west of the centre, costs about ₺20.

BUS Sinop's otogar is 5km southwest of town on the main road to Kastamonu. **Dolmuşes** run there from 100m west of the Archaeological Museum (₺1.50).

Getting Around

Local buses run up Derviş Sarabil Caddesi for views over town. Dolmuşes run to villages such as Akliman from the **village otogar** (Sakarya Caddesi).

Samsun

☑0362 / POP 500.995

Few travellers stop in sprawling Samsun, the Black Sea's biggest port and one of Turkey's booming 'Anatolian Tigers', for more than a change of bus. Even the enterprising Genoese only paused long enough to burn the city to the ground in the 15th century. However, with accommodation and eateries handily located around main square Cumhuriyet Meydanı (Republic Sq), Samsun makes a convenient pit stop. Witnessing the development taking place in the centre gives a sense of Turkey's sheer economic ambition. From Cumhuriyet Meydanı, Cumhuriyet Caddesi runs eastwards, along the south side of Atatürk Park, which is bordered to the north by Atatürk Bulvarı (the coastal highway).

Sights

Archaeology & Ethnography Museum
MUSEUM

(Arkeoloji ve Etnoğrafya Müzesi; Fuar Caddesi; admission ₺3; ⊙8am-7pm Tue-Sun) Most striking in this museum, west of the big pink *valiliği* (provincial government headquarters) building, is the huge Romano-Byzantine mosaic found at nearby Karasamsun (Amisos). It depicts Thetis, Achilles and the Four Seasons alongside sea monsters and nymphs. Other highlights include the elegant gold jewellery thought to date from around 100 BC – the time of the legendary Pontic king Mithridates (VI Eupator) – and a graphic display on ancient skull surgery.

Ghazi Museum MUSEUM
(Gazi Müzesi; Gazi Caddesi; ⊙8am-7pm Tue-Sun)
One block south of Cumhuriyet Meydanı,
this museum commemorates the start of the
War of Independence here on 19 May 1919,
and the Turkish Republic's subsequent foundation. Several of Atatürk's hats feature.

🛏 Sleeping

For budget accommodation, explore the
clothing bazaar (Bedesten) area near Hotel
Necmi.

Yıldızoğlu Hotel BUSINESS HOTEL €€
(☑333 3400; www.yildizogluhotel.com; Talimhane
Caddesi 13; s/d ₺80/160; P🛜) Near the Samsun Park Otel, this stylish option offers
rooms with turquoise trimmings, little black
lampshades, minibar and sizeable shower.
Facilities include a fitness centre, sauna
(₺10) and bar in the blue-lit reception. The
generous breakfast stretches to soup, *börek*
and *dolmas* (vegetables stuffed with rice or
meat).

Otel Necmi HOTEL €
(☑432 7164; www.otelnecmi.com.tr; Bedestan
Sokak 6; s/d/tr without bathroom ₺40/65/90;
P🛜) This homely budget gem at the beginning of the bazaar feels like your eccentric
uncle's house, with pot plants, mirrors and
big old chairs in reception. Rooms are poky
and basic but the staff are helpful, offering
maps and advice.

Samsun Park Otel BUSINESS HOTEL €€
(☑435 0095; www.samsunparkotel.com; Cumhuriyet Caddesi 38; s/d ₺80/110; P🌼@) Book
ahead to bag a compact but comfortable
room at the popular and accommodating
Samsun Park. It's 200m east of Cumhuriyet
Meydanı.

Otel Vidinli HOTEL €€
(☑431 6050; www.otelvildini.com.tr; Kazımpaşa
Caddesi 4; s/d without breakfast ₺80/130, breakfast
₺10; P🌼🛜) In business since 1957, the Vidinli has traditionally been Samsun's best hotel,
although newer options now offer better value. It remains popular among tour groups,
with an old fashioned lift, central location by
Cumhuriyet Meydanı, spacious rooms, barrestaurant and sixth-floor breakfast room.

🍴 Eating & Drinking

The area around Hotel Amisos, 100m east of
Cumhuriyet Meydanı on Cumhuriyet Caddesi, is good for restaurants.

Sıla Restaurant KÖFTE, KEBAP €
(Cumhuriyet Caddesi 36; mains ₺8) Sıla is popular for a meaty lunch – the recommended
chicken *şiş* (roast) kebap comes with
fiery peppers. Split your gaze between the
strange, egg-like sculptures at the southeast
corner of Atatürk Park and the darting waiters – artistes of hustle-bustle even by Turkish standards.

Gaziantep Kebap Salonu KEBAP, TURKISH €
(Osmaniye Caddesi 7; mains ₺4-8) This slice of
southeast Turkey is a relaxed neighbourhood
kebapçı, where couples and male groups
snack on *lahmacun* and tasty Tokat *ayran*
(yoghurt drink). Heading east on Cumhuriyet Caddesi, turn right after Hotel Amisos.

Simit Center CAFE €
(Gazi Caddesi 53; snacks from ₺2; ⊙24hr) Samsun's student population can be found at
this chain cafe in the evening, gossiping
to a Europop soundtrack. Choose between
sausage rolls, baklava, biscuits, cakes,
chocolate desserts and, of course, *simits*
(sesame-encrusted bread rings).

Samsun Balık Restaurant SEAFOOD €€
(Bankalar Caddesi 20; mains ₺15; ⊙11am-10pm)
Samsun's number-one fish eatery occupies
a quaint brick house. A glistening array of
piscine beauties awaits, along with kitschy
hanging shells in the upstairs dining room.

Divan Pastanesi CAFE
(Cumhuriyet Caddesi 6) One block east of Cumhuriyet Meydanı among the bus-company
offices, this stylish patisserie is good for a
morning caffeine and nicotine fix (there's an
outdoor patio). Frothy cappuccinos, baklava
and *börek* are served among baskets of oranges and boxes of chocolates.

ℹ Information

INTERNET ACCESS There are internet cafes
on Hürriyet Sokak, which runs south from Sıla
Restaurant.

TOURIST INFORMATION Tourist Office
(☑431 1228; Atatürk Kültür Merkezi, Atatürk
Bulvarı; ⊙9am-5pm Mon-Fri) Just west of the
Büyük Samsun Otel.

ℹ Getting There & Around

AIR Regular **Havaş** (☑444 0487; www.havas.
net) shuttle buses link the city and Samsun-
Çarşamba Airport (₺8), running to/from the
Atatürk Kültür Merkezi car park, next to the
tourist office. Havaş also connects the airport
and Ordu (₺20) via Ünye and Fatsa (₺15).

SERVICES FROM SAMSUN'S OTOGAR

DESTINATION	FARE (₺)	DURATION (HR)	DISTANCE (KM)	FREQUENCY (PER DAY)
Amasya	15	2½	130	frequent
Ankara	87	7	420	frequent
Giresun	25	3½	220	five
Hopa	40	9½	520	four
İstanbul	79	11	750	several
Kayseri	55	9	530	several
Sinop	25	3	168	hourly
Trabzon	30	6	355	several
Ünye	10	1½	95	half-hourly

Anadolu Jet (www.anadolujet.com) Flies to/from Ankara.

Onur Air (www.onurair.com) Flies to İstanbul.

Pegasus Airlines (www.flypgs.com) Flies to İstanbul and İzmir.

Sun Express (www.sunexpress.com) Flies to Antalya, İstanbul, İzmir and European cities.

Turkish Airlines (www.thy.com) Flies to Ankara, İstanbul, Dusseldorf and Munich (Germany).

BUS Bus companies have offices at the Cumhuriyet Meydanı end of Cumhuriyet Caddesi. *Servises* (shuttle buses) run between there and the otogar, 3km inland. There are also frequent dolmuşes (₺2) from the otogar to Cumhuriyet Meydanı, and left-luggage facilities at the otogar.

CAR & MOTORCYCLE You can hire a car in the city or at Samsun-Çarşamba Airport through Economy Car Rentals (p673).

Ünye

0452 / POP 77,570

Popular with holidaying Turks, this seaside town 95km east of Samsun has one of Anatolia's longest settlement histories. There is evidence of civilisation during the Palaeolithic period – a prehistoric era that lasted from about 2.6 million to 12,000 years ago – and Ünye was an important port at the junction of the Silk Road and the coastal highway during the Ottoman period. Former residents include the 14th-century Turkish mystical poet Yunus Emre, and St Nicholas, before his life morphed into the legend of Santa Claus. Smaller and more conservative than Samsun and Ordu, Ünye is worth a quick stop for its coastal promenade and labyrinth of well-kept winding streets and lanes, which span out from main square Cumhuriyet Meydanı, across the coast road from the seafront.

◉ Sights & Activities

FREE **Ünye Castle** CASTLE, RUIN

(Off D850) About 7km inland of Ünye stands Ünye Castle, a ruined fortress founded by the Pontics and rebuilt by the Byzantines, with an ancient tomb cut into the rock face below. Catch a minibus (₺2) heading to Kaleköy or Akkuş on the D850 road to Niksar and Tokat, and ask to be dropped off at the road to the castle. It's a further 2km trek to the top.

FREE **Tozkoparan Kay Mezarı** TOMB

(Tozkoparan Rock Tomb; off Black Sea Coastal Hwy) This millennia-old cave tomb, one of a few in the area, is off the Black Sea Coastal Hwy, 5km from the centre. Carved bull figures flank the entrance to the tomb, which is thought to date to between 7000 BC and 5000 BC. Eastbound minibuses can drop you by the cement factory at the turn for the tomb (₺1.50).

Çakırtepe PARK

(Çakırtepe Mahallesi; ⊙11am-10pm) Atop the hill north of town, this picnic site with three eateries is a local favourite for summer lunches. Dolmuşes run here from Cumhuriyet Meydanı (₺1.50).

Eski Hamam HAMAM

(Cumhuriyet Meydanı; admission ₺14; ⊙men 5am-midnight Mon, Wed, Thu & Sun, women 11am-5pm Tue, Fri & Sat) The Old Hamam occupies a former church on the southeast corner of the main square.

📠 Sleeping

Camping grounds and beach pensions are spread out along the Black Sea Coastal Highway, west of town (in the direction of Samsun).

There are budget hotels east of Cumhuriyet Meydanı, including **Otel Lider** (☑324 9250; Hükümet Caddesi 32; s/d ₺30/60 without breakfast; 🛜) and **Otel Çinar** (☑323 1148; Hükümet Caddesi 19; s/d ₺30/50 without breakfast; 🛜).

TOP CHOICE Sebile Hanım Konağı BOUTIQUE HOTEL ₺₺
(☑323 7474; www.sebilehanimkonagi.com; Çamurlu Mahallesi, Çubukçu Arif Sokak 10; s/d ₺70/130; P❄🛜) In the former Armenian district, this gloriously restored and romantic hilltop property dating to 1877 has cosy wood-lined rooms with private hamam, fridge and an over-enthusiastic radiator. There's also a characterful restaurant. Follow the signs uphill from the western edge of the old city walls. Book ahead.

Gülen Plaj Camping CAMPING GROUND ₺
(☑324 6686; Devlet Sahil Yolu, Uzunkum; campsites ₺25, bungalow ₺140) Overlooking an idyllic sweep of beach 2.5km west of the centre, Gülen's wooden bungalows with balconies and kitchenettes sleep up to four among the trees.

Hotel Kılıç HOTEL ₺
(☑323 1224; Haciemin Caddesi; s/d ₺30/60 without breakfast) Popular with travelling salesmen, 'Hotel Sword' is slightly better value than the budget hotels east of Cumhuriyet Meydanı, apart from its location right behind the mosque on the square. Rooms are nondescript but clean and there's a dingy lounge.

🍴 Eating & Drinking

There are numerous eateries on and around Cumhuriyet Meydanı.

İskele FISH, TURKISH ₺₺
(Devlet Sahil Yolu 32; meals ₺11-17.50) The most common answer to 'So, what's the best restaurant in Ünye?', 'the Pier' has a waterside location and a reputation for seafood and grilled meats. Ignore the diversions into Italian and Mexican flavours, and stick with fish and Turkish classics. The elegant dining room features interesting black-and-white snapshots of Ünye's past.

Sebile Hanım Konağı FISH, ANATOLIAN ₺₺
(☑323 7474; www.sebilehanimkonagi.com; Çamurlu Mahallesi, Çubukçu Arif Sokak 10; mains ₺10-25) This licensed restaurant, specialising in fresh fish and Black Sea cuisine, is Ünye's most atmospheric eatery, complete with a talking parrot. Book ahead.

Café Vanilya CAFE ₺
(Cumhuriyet Meydanı 3; snacks ₺4.50; ⊘24hr; 🛜) Set in a restored villa-style townhouse on the southwest edge of the main square, 'the Vanilla' is a popular but down-to-earth terrace cafe serving Ünye's bright young things. The courtyard seats are hot property for a game of backgammon in the late afternoon and Turkish pop brings things up to date. Snacks including *tost* (toast) are available.

❶ Information

INTERNET ACCESS **Sohbet Internet** (off Cumhuriyet Meydanı; per hr ₺1; ⊘9am-9pm; 📶) Just east of the Eski Hamam.

TOURIST INFORMATION **Tourist Office** (☑323 4952; Hukumet Binası, Cumhuriyet Meydanı; ⊘8.30am-5.30pm Mon-Fri) In the local government building on the south side of the main square; English spoken.

❶ Getting There & Away

Bus companies have offices on the coast road. Minibuses and midibuses travel to Samsun (₺10, 1½ hours) and Ordu (₺10, 1¼ hours). Go to Fatsa (₺4) to catch a bus along the old coast road to Perşembe (₺5).

Ordu

📞 0452 / POP 145,455

Ordu is 60km east of Ünye, with cafes and a pier dotting its palm tree–lined seafront promenade. Winding narrow lanes give the well-kept centre a village-like ambience.

◉ Sights

Boztepe Picnic Place VIEWPOINT, CABLE CAR
(cable car ₺5; ⊘cable car 10am-10pm) Take a 10-minute *teleferik* (cable car) ride from the seafront up to this hilltop park for breathtaking views (and overpriced restaurants).

Pasha's Palace & Ethnography Museum MUSEUM
(Paşaoğlu Konağı ve Etnoğrafya Müzesi; Taşocak Caddesi; admission ₺3; ⊘9am-noon & 1.30-5pm Tue-Sun) This interesting museum occupies an ornate late-19th-century house, 500m

OLD COAST ROAD

Around 30km east of Ünye, just after Bolaman, the Black Sea Coastal Hwy runs inland and doesn't touch the coast again until just before Ordu. It's a spectacular stretch, traversing one of Turkey's longest road tunnels (3.28km), and the diversion inland has created a lovely alternative route on the old coast road.

A winding few kilometres northeast from Bolaman, a small brown sign points 500m left to rugged **Cape Yason**, where a tiny chapel marks the spot where sailors used to pray at a temple dedicated to Jason and his Argonauts. A couple of cafes serve fish and *köfte* (meatballs). To the east is the surprising **Çaka beach**, a 400m strip of white sand regarded as the Black Sea's best beach.

Further on, 15km west of Ordu, fishing port **Perşembe** is an attractive, slow-paced Black Sea village. Later at night locals fish from the slender pier and fish restaurants prepare the day's catch. Across the main road from the seafront fish restaurants, peaceful **Dede Evi** (📞0452-517 3802; Atatürk Bulvarı; s/d ₺50/100; ❄️🛜) has shipshape rooms with TV and fridge.

This meandering detour is best attempted with your own transport, but there are dolmuşes to Perşembe from Fatsa to the west, and Ordu to the east.

uphill from Cumhuriyet Meydanı past a bazaar; look for signs reading 'Müze – Museum'. The re-created first-floor rooms are telling reminders that upper-class Ottomans enjoyed a sophisticated and cosmopolitan life. There's also a chair where Atatürk supposedly had a rest in 1924. We hope he also enjoyed pide from the stone oven in the peaceful garden.

FREE **Taşbaşı Cultural Centre**   HISTORIC BUILDING
(Taşbaşı Kültür Merkezi; Taşbaşı Mahallesi) Now a cultural centre, this former Greek church (1853) overlooks the seafront from its hillside location about 500m west of the tourist office. The surrounding old Greek quarter is an attractive neighbourhood of tumbledown houses.

🛏️ Sleeping

TOP CHOICE **Taşbaşı Butik Otel**   BOUTIQUE HOTEL €€
(📞223 3530; www.tasbasibutikotel.com; Kesim Evi Sokak 1; s/d ₺70/120; 🅿️❄️🛜) The decor occasionally strays into chintzy territory, but the Black Sea views are terrific at this restored hilltop mansion, behind the Taşbaşı Cultural Centre in Ordu's old Greek neighbourhood. The helpful folk in reception can assist with coastal boat trips and more rugged journeys to the *yaylalar*.

Karlıbel Atlıhan Hotel   HOTEL €€
(📞212 0565; www.karlibelhotel.com; Kazım Karabekir Caddesi 7; s/d ₺70/120; 🅿️❄️🛜) A smooth, relaxing establishment, one block back from

the seafront behind the town hall, with sea and *teleferik* views from the top-floor restaurant. In the creamy rooms, munch a complimentary biscuit and consider repros such as the famous painting of an Ottoman tortoise trainer. The Karlıbel group also runs two nearby boutique hotels, the seafront Atherina and hilltop İkizevler.

Otel Kervansaray   HOTEL €
(📞214 1330; Kazım Karabekir Caddesi 1; s/d ₺40/75; 🅿️❄️🛜) The Kervansaray is a little gloomy, but friendly and good value. The spacious rooms are comfortable despite the bright green bedspreads, and breakfast is pleasant, upstairs in Kervansaray Cafe among bright pink and purple chairs. Ask for a room away from the noisy main street.

🍴 Eating & Drinking

TOP CHOICE **Grand Mıdı Restaurant**   SEAFOOD €€
(İskele Üstü 55; fish ₺10-20, meze ₺5) This licensed pontoon restaurant emanates classy seaside ambience. Watch the *teleferik* climb from the seafront and enjoy a good range of local seafood and fresh meze, including Ordu specialities and aubergine served in numerous ways.

Kervansaray Cafe   TURKISH €
(Şarkiye Mahallesi; mains ₺6-8.50) Adjoining the hotel of the same name, this attractive, modern lunchtime caravanserai serves a good range of kebaps and even a few desserts on place mats bearing pictures of old Ordu. Mouthwatering *hazır yemek* (ready-made food) awaits in the bain-maries.

Jazz Café
CAFE €

(Sımpasa Caddesi 28; snacks ₺4-7; ☺9am-8.30pm Mon-Sat, 11am-8.30pm Sun; 🛜) A sleek and cosmopolitan spot alongside Benetton on Ordu's pedestrian shopping drag, serving cappuccino and sweet treats including hot chocolate and waffles. Savoury palates shouldn't miss the excellent *sigara böreği* (feta cheese and pastry snacks). Sit outside or among pictures of Frank Sinatra and Dizzy Gillespie.

Jazz Pub
BAR, IRISH PUB

(Kazım Karabekir Caddesi) Adjoining the Karlıbel Atlıhan Hotel, this Irish-American-Turkish jazz bar has live music on Wednesday and Saturday nights. With low lighting and English-speaking staff manning the long bar, it's a mellow spot for a glass of Doluca red wine.

ℹ Information

INTERNET ACCESS Ordu Net (Süleyman Felek Caddesi 12B; per hr ₺1.25; ☺11am-midnight) On the inland side of the playground 150m west of the tourist office.

TOURIST INFORMATION Tourist Office (🖉223 1444; www.ordu.gov.tr; Atatürk Bulvarı; ☺8.30am-5.30pm Mon-Sat, 8.30am-1pm Sun) English is spoken at this well-resourced office on the inland side of the coast road, 250m west of the town hall. Recommendations include a trip inland to *yaylalar* such as the Çambaşı Plateau.

ℹ Getting There & Around

Ordu's otogar is 5km east on the coast road. Buses depart regularly to Giresun (₺7, one hour), Ünye (₺10, 1¼ hours) and Perşembe (₺2.25, 20 minutes). You can also usually flag down buses along the coast road.

From Ziraat Bank in the centre, local dolmuşes run uphill to Taşbaşı in one direction, and near the otogar in the other (₺1.75).

Giresun

🖉0454 / POP 101,100

The historic town of Giresun, 46km east of Ordu, was founded around 3000 years ago. The town is credited with introducing cherries to Italy, and from there to the rest of the world. Indeed, its name comes from the Greek for cherry, although the humble hazelnut *(fındık)* now drives Giresun's economy. The area has Turkey's finest plantations and you'll see nut-laden carts on the main street and in the hilltop park. The side streets are slightly grey, but cobbled main drag Gazi Caddesi is attractive for a wander, beneath the green and red flags of Giresun and Turkey.

Giresun's centre is Atapark on the coast road. Don't confuse it with the clock square a few hundred metres to the west. The town hall is on the inland side of Atapark; Gazi Caddesi climbs uphill from there.

Beginning about 40km inland, the alpine **yaylalar** offer opportunities for walking and winter sports at around 2000m. In May Giresun holds the **International Giresun Aksu Festival**.

◉ Sights & Activities

City Museum
MUSEUM

(Şehir Müzesi; Atatürk Bulvarı 62; admission ₺3; ☺8.30am-5.30pm) With an impressive archaeological and ethnographic collection, Giresun's museum occupies the well-preserved 18th-century Gogora church. It's 1.5km around the promontory east of Atapark on the coast road; catch any 'Hastanesi' dolmuş heading east (₺1.25) and ask to be let off at *'müze'*.

Kalepark
PARK

Perched on the steep hillside above the town, this shady park with the remains of a castle has panoramic views, beer gardens and barbecues. Weekends are busy. No public transport serves Kalepark, so you'll need to walk (about 2km) inland and uphill from Atapark on Gazi Caddesi and turn left onto Bekirpaşa Caddesi. Alternatively, a taxi from town costs around ₺5.

🛌 Sleeping & Eating

Kit-Tur Otel
HOTEL €€

(🖉212 0245; www.otelkittur.com; Arifbey Caddesi 2; s/d ₺50/80; 🛜) Overlooking Gazi Caddesi, the friendly Kit-Tur is perfect for relaxing after a long drive, with comfy chairs in the big, marbly reception and low beds in the rooms.

Otel Çarıkçı
HOTEL €€

(🖉216 1026; Osmanağa Caddesi 6; s/d ₺50/85; ❄🛜) At the eastern end of Atapark near the pedestrian bridge, the two-star Çarıkçı's sign features a curly-toed shoe. Staff speak some English and the brown, compact rooms have tiled, modern bathrooms.

Hotel Başar
HOTEL €€

(🖉212 9920; www.hotelbasar.com.tr; Atatürk Bulvarı; s/d ₺100/150; ❄❄🛜) Across the footbridge from Atapark, this eight-storey, blue-

BLACK SEA COAST GIRESUN

and-yellow provincial palace has a licensed penthouse restaurant, surveying the port and sea. Staff speak English and the spacious, Ottoman-style rooms feature beer-stocked minibars and slightly aged bathrooms with hairdryer and phone.

TOP CHOICE Orta Kahve
CAFE €€

(Topal Sokak 1; mains ₺10; ⊙9am-11pm) In this cosy hangout for Giresun's younger, more cosmopolitan crowd, old typewriters provide a backdrop for newspapers, magazines, and different teas and coffees. It's good for breakfast, and healthy eats include salads, crepes and wraps. Turn left about 75m uphill on Gazi Caddesi, after the small green mosque on the right.

Ellez
PIDE, KEBAP €

(Fatih Caddesi 7; pide ₺8-10; ⊙7am-9pm) One block inland from Atapark, behind the Deniz Lokantası restaurant, this friendly, compact *pideci* (pizza place) with a tiny balcony and log-cabin stylings attracts a younger crowd. Pide, kebaps (₺8) and *lahmacun* (₺2) are on offer.

Deniz Lokantası
TURKISH €

(Alpaslan Caddesi 3; mains ₺5-10) Next to the town hall, this modernised cafeteria has been churning out good-value meals since 1953. Expect a short wait at lunchtime, but it's worth it.

❶ Information

Internet cafes are on and around Gazi Caddesi near the post office, a few hundred metres uphill from the town hall.

❶ Getting There & Away

The bus station is 4km west of the centre, but buses usually drop people at Atapark, too. For Trabzon (₺14, two hours) and Ordu (₺7, one hour), it's easiest to pick up midibuses and minibuses from the coast road, either below the mosque overlooking Atapark or by the clock tower opposite the port entrance. Bus company offices are next to the town hall and around Atapark.

Giresun to Trabzon

Heading east to Trabzon from Giresun (150km), the highway does not have the prettiest vistas on the Black Sea coast. Nonetheless, the road passes through several small towns, including attractive **Tirebolu** (after 45km), with a compact harbour and two castles (St Jean Kalesi and Bedrama Kalesi). The Çaykur tea-processing plant signals your arrival in Turkey's çay country.

Görele, 18km from Tirebolu, is famous for big, round loaves of bread. In **Akçakale**, about 50km further on, are the ruins of a 13th-century Byzantine castle on a little peninsula. **Akçaabat**, 10km before Trabzon, is famous for meatballs; to try them, the Korfez and Cemilusta restaurants are conveniently located on the coast road, but small eateries in the centre serve more authentic, handmade Akçaabat *köfte*.

Trabzon

📞0462 / POP 239,700

Trabzon is one of those 'love it or hate it' places, mixing cosmopolitan buzz with, around the harbour, a seedy, port-town character. The Black Sea coast's largest and arguably most sophisticated city (sorry Samsun), Trabzon is too caught up in its own whirl of activity to worry about what's happening in far-off İstanbul or Ankara.

Contrasting with the gracious, medieval church of Aya Sofya, and the Byzantine monastery at nearby Sumela, the modern world shines through on Atatürk Alanı, Trabzon's crazily busy main square in the eastern section of the city centre. Beeping dolmuşes hurtle around like a modern chariot race, events bring live music and dance performances to the square every summer weekend, and local students team headscarves with Converse All Stars. Another popular item of clothing is the Trabzonspor strip; the idolised local soccer team and Bursaspor are the only non-İstanbul teams to have won the Turkish national league.

Trabzon is the eastern Black Sea's busiest port, handling and dispatching goods for Georgia, Armenia, Azerbaijan and Iran. The city certainly makes an impression with its winding bazaar streets and pedestrianised walkways – it's a quintessential Black Sea experience. The buzz is infectious after taking it easy in smaller Anatolian centres.

Trabzon's heart is the area around Atatürk Alanı, also known as Meydan Parkı. The port is east of the square, down a steep hill. There are cafes and restaurants around Atatürk Alanı and west along Uzun Sokak and Kahramanmaraş (Maraş for short) Caddesi. West of the centre, past the bazaar, is Ortahisar, a picturesque old neighbourhood straddling a ravine.

Trabzon – Bazaar Area

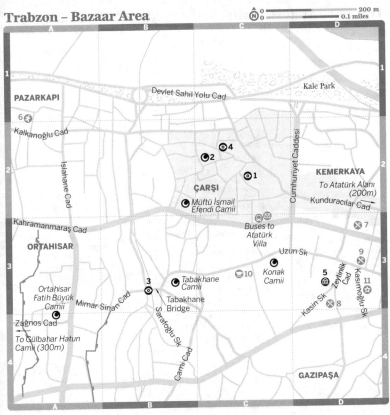

History

Trabzon's recorded history begins around 746 BC, when Miletus colonists came from Sinop and founded a settlement, Trapezus, with an acropolis on the *trápeza* (table) of land above the harbour.

The port town did well for 2000 years, until the Christian soldiers of the Fourth Crusade seized and sacked Constantinople in 1204, forcing its noble families to seek refuge in Anatolia. The Comnenus imperial family established an empire along the Black Sea coast in 1204, with Alexius Comnenus I reigning as the emperor of Trebizond.

The Trapezuntine rulers skilfully balanced alliances with the Seljuks, Mongols and Genoese. Prospering through trade with eastern Anatolia and Persia, the empire peaked under Alexius II (1297–1330), before declining in factional disputes. The empire of Trebizond survived until the Ottoman conquest in 1461, eight years longer than Constantinople.

Trabzon – Bazaar Area

◉ Sights

✚ Activities, Courses & Tours

✖ Eating

🍷 Drinking

✪ Entertainment

Trabzon – Atatürk Alanı

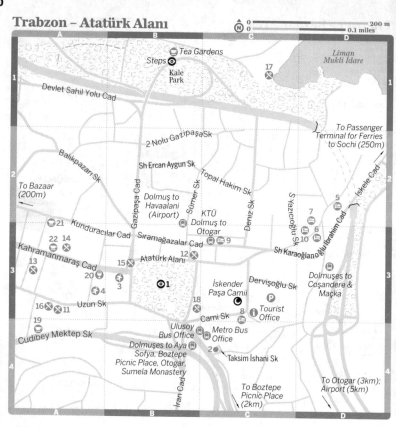

When the Ottoman Empire was defeated after WWI, Trabzon's Greek residents sought to establish a Republic of Trebizond, echoing the old Comneni Empire. The Turks were ultimately victorious, and Atatürk declared Trabzon 'one of the richest, strongest and most sensitive sources of trust for the Turkish Republic'.

Sights & Activities

Trabzon Museum
MUSEUM

(Trabzon Müzesi; Map p509; Zeytinlik Caddesi; admission ₺3; ⊙8.30am-5.30pm Tue-Sun) This Italian-designed mansion, built for a Russian merchant and completed in 1913, briefly hosted Atatürk in 1924. The ornate interiors and original furnishings put most Ottoman re-creations to shame, with high-ceilinged rooms displaying ethnographic and Islamic artefacts, mostly labelled in English. The basement archaeological section also has significant pieces, including a flattened bronze statue of Hermes from local excavations at Tabakhane and some beautiful wooden Byzantine icons.

Bazaar District
MARKET

(Map p509) Pedestrianised Kunduracılar Caddesi leads from Atatürk Alanı to Trabzon's bazaar, located in the *çarşı* (market) quarter. Compared with İstanbul's Grand Bazaar, it's authentic, down to earth and proudly local. Near the restored Çarşı Camii (Market Mosque; Map p509; Bazaar District) (1839), central Trabzon's largest mosque, is the Taş Han (Vakıf Han; Map p509; Bazaar District), a single-domed *han* (caravanserai) constructed around 1647. Trabzon's oldest marketplace, it's full of workshops, stores and cafes – a cool retreat for a çay.

Gülbahar Hatun Camii
MOSQUE

Selim the Grim, the great Ottoman conqueror of Syria and Egypt, built Gülbahar Hatun Camii (Mosque of the Ottomans, 1514)

Trabzon – Atatürk Alanı

in honour of his mother, Gülbahar Hatun. Next to it are a tea garden and reconstructed wooden *serander* (granary). It's a pleasant walk west from the centre over **Tabakhane Bridge** (Map p509), with allotments below. Soon after crossing the next bridge, turn left and head towards the **Atatürk statue** (Map p510).

Atatürk Villa   HISTORIC BUILDING
(Atatürk Köşkü; ☑231 0028; admission ₺2; ⊙8am-7pm) Escape the city at the Atatürk Villa, 5km southwest of Atatürk Alanı. Set above Trabzon in a forested neighbourhood, the three-storey white villa has fine views and lovely gardens. Designed in a Black Sea style popular in the Crimea, it was built between 1890 and 1903 for a wealthy Trabzon banking family, and given to Atatürk when he visited in 1924. It's now a museum of Atatürk memorabilia. Don't miss the simple table in the study with a map of the WWI Dardanelles campaign scratched into the wood.

City **buses** labelled 'Köşk' leave from outside the post office and drop you outside the villa (₺1.25). Don't get out at the stop that says 'Atatürk Köşk 200m'. The actual stop is a steep 1km trek further up the hill.

Boztepe Picnic Place   PARK, HISTORIC SITE
(Boztepe Piknik Alanı) On the hillside 2km southeast of Atatürk Alanı, Boztepe has fine city and sea views, tea gardens and restaurants. In ancient times, it harboured temples to the Persian sun god Mithra. Later, the Byzantines built churches and monasteries here. Today, it's a top place for a sunset beer and there's live music on summer evenings.

Frequent Boztepe dolmuşes run from near the southeastern end of Atatürk Alanı (₺1.50).

Sekiz Direkli Hamamı   HAMAM
(Map p509; Direkli Hamamı Sokak; sauna & massage ₺25; ⊙men 8am-6pm Fri-Wed, women 8am-6pm Thu) Sekiz Direkli means 'Eight Columns' and the rough-hewn pillars date from Seljuk times, although the rest of the building has been modernised. A few of the old-timers working here appear to be only slightly younger than the hamam. They're damn strong though; expect a robust massage.

Meydan Hamamı   HAMAM
(Map p510; www.meydanhamami.com; Kahramanmaraş Caddesi; sauna ₺15, massage ₺6, wash ₺5; ⊙men 6am-11pm, women 8am-8pm) The Public Hamam is clean and efficiently run, although not as atmospheric as the Sekiz Direkli. There are separate areas for men and women; the **women's entrance** (Map p510) is around the corner.

Tours

Eyce Tours   TOUR
(Map p510; ☑326 7174; www.eycetours.com; Taksim İşhanı Sokak 11) Day trips to Sumela (adult/student ₺25/20, 10am to 3pm) and Uzungöl (adult/student ₺35/30, 10am to 5.30pm) daily, and Ayder (₺40, minimum five people) three days a week. Also Batumi, Georgia (₺75, 7am to 9.30pm).

Sleeping

Many of the grimy cheapies downhill towards the harbour double as brothels. At

BLACK SEA COAST TRABZON

AYA SOFYA MUSEUM

Originally called Hagia Sophia (Church of the Divine Wisdom), the **Aya Sofya Museum** (Aya Sofya Müzesi; ☑223 3043; www.trabzonmuzesi.gov.tr; Aya Sofya Sokak; admission ₺5; ☺9am-7pm Jun-Aug, 9am-6pm Apr-May & Sep-Oct, 8am-5pm Nov-Mar) is located 4km west of Trabzon's centre on a terrace that once held a pagan temple. Built in the late Byzantine period, between 1238 and 1263, the church has clearly been influenced by Georgian and Seljuk design, although the wall paintings and mosaic floors follow the prevailing Constantinople style of the time. It was converted to a mosque after the Ottoman conquest in 1461, and later used as an ammunition storage depot and hospital by the Russians, before being fully restored in the 1960s.

The church has a cross-in-square plan, topped by a single dome, showing Georgian influence. A fresco on the southern facade depicts Adam and Eve's expulsion. On the western side of the building, the vaulted narthex has the building's best preserved frescoe, of various biblical themes, and the facade has a relief of an eagle, symbol of the church's founders, the Comnenus family. Unfortunately most of the frescoes within arm's reach have been heavily defaced. Flash photography is prohibited to preserve the remaining painted fragments.

The museum stands in gardens with a square bell tower alongside and tea houses outside. The site is signposted uphill from the coastal highway, reachable by dolmuş (₺1.50) from near the southeastern end of Atatürk Alanı.

the time of writing, the following had the tourist office tick of approval. Many Güzelhisar Caddesi hotels are popular with business travellers, so book ahead and ask for a discount at weekends.

TOP CHOICE Otel Horon HOTEL €€
(Map p510; ☑326 6455; www.hotelhoron.com; Sıramağazalar Caddesi 125; s/d ₺90/140; ❀) In business since 1967, the aubergine-coloured Horon has a good central position and attractively decorated rooms with some of Trabzon's best showers. Efes is among the coldies in the well-stocked minibars and the fifth-floor restaurant has city views.

Novotel LUXURY HOTEL €€€
(☑455 9000; www.novotel.com; Devlet Karayolu Caddesi 17, Yomra; r €125; ❀@) Around 10km east of Trabzon, on the western side of Yomra, at the Novotel you're trading a central location for seafront vistas and four-star luxuries. Facilities include a sauna, a fitness centre, a private beach, landscaped gardens and an air-conditioned bar-restaurant (mains ₺20) with a saxaphone-style Efes tap. Dolmuşes to Trabzon (₺2) pass on the coast road; a taxi costs ₺35 to ₺40. Shuttles run to (but not from) Trabzon airport and the Forum mall.

Hotel Can HOTEL €
(Map p510; ☑326 8281; Güzelhisar Caddesi 2; s/d ₺30/50; ❀) There isn't much difference be-

tween the tall, thin 'Hotel Soul' and some of its more expensive neighbours. The friendly staff make this Trabzon's top budget choice.

Elif Otel BUSINESS HOTEL €€
(Map p510; ☑326 6616; Güzelhisar Caddesi 8; s/d ₺50/80; ❀) Beyond its unimpressive reception, the friendly Elif's rooms are a good deal, with smart bathrooms and lumpy white duvets.

Otel Ural BUSINESS HOTEL €€
(Map p510; ☑321 1414; Güzelhisar Caddesi 1; s/d ₺50/80; ❀@) With warm, chocolate-brown decor, flat-screen TVs and flash bathrooms, the Ural's spacious, spotless rooms raise the bar for Trabzon's hotel alley.

Hotel Nur HOTEL €€
(Map p510; ☑323 0445; www.nurhotel.net; Cami Sokak 15; s/d ₺70/110; ❀) A long-standing travellers' favourite, with a lounge, travel agency, English-speaking staff and cupboard to store bikes. When we visited, the small rooms were more basic than others in its price bracket nearby, but improvements were underway. The nearby mosque doesn't skimp on the 5am call to prayer.

Hotel Nazar HOTEL €€
(Map p510; ☑323 0081; www.nazarotel.com.tr; Güzelhisar Caddesi 5; s/d ₺60/100; ❀) A renovation was underway when we visited the 'Evil Eye', improving the slightly worn rooms with fridges and, in some cases, Black Sea glimpses.

✗ Eating

Trabzon is not the Black Sea's gastronomic high point, but scores of good eateries line Atatürk Alanı and the two streets running west. Got a sweet tooth? Head to Uzun Sokak for ice cream and pastries at **Kılıcoğlu** (Map p509; Uzun Sokak 36; desserts from ₺4); *kuruyemiş* (dried fruit), *lokum* (Turkish delight), *pestil* (sheets of dried fruit), *bal* (honey) and nuts at **Mevlana Kuruyemiş** (Map p510; Uzun Sokak 21); *helva* (sweet made from sesame seeds) at **Beton Helva** (Map p510; Uzun Sokak 15b); and hazelnuts and confectionary at **Cirav Fındık** (Map p510; Ticaret Mektep Sokak 8c).

TOP CHOICE Kalendar   CAFE, TURKISH €
(Map p509; Zeytinlik Caddesi; mains ₺8, salads ₺5; ◷8.30am-9pm) Low tables and mood lighting give this welcoming cafe near Trabzon Museum a cosmopolitan vibe. It's perfect for a post-museum coffee and brunch of *menemen* (scrambled eggs with peppers and tomatoes) or *gözleme* for a break from Turkish breakfasts. The front tables overlook a side street and, on weekdays, you can choose a mixed plate of four of the seven or eight hot and cold daily dishes.

Bordo Mavi   INTERNATIONAL €€
(Map p509; www.bordomavirestaurant.com; off Kahramanmaraş Caddesi, Trabzonspor Sadri Şener Tesisleri; mains ₺15) This cosmopolitan gardencafe adjoins Trabzonspor's clubhouse, and the waiters wear the team strip. You can pick up your own maroon-and-blue top at the merchandise shop nearby. Pizzas, pastas and sandwiches are on the menu alongside breakfast and Turkish meals. A good range of drinks is available, including spirits and wine by the glass, but the female-dominated clientele are far from boozy football fans.

Reis'in Yeri   RESTAURANT, BAR €€
(Map p510; Liman Mukli İdare; meals ₺10-20) Surrounded by traffic around Atatürk Alanı, it's easy to forget Trabzon is a coastal city. Head down Gazipaşa Caddesi and across the bridge to this sprawling fish/chicken/*köfte* grill house, which doubles as a beer garden. It's guaranteed dolmuş-free, and you can even hire rowboats to steer around the tiny cove.

Cemilusta   FISH, KÖFTE €€
(Map p510; Atatürk Alanı; mains ₺10) Trabzon's smart young professionals come to Cemilusta for house specialities fish and *köfte*, and views

of the square from the outside tables and 1st-floor dining room. Various types of *köfte* are available, including Akçaabat, eaten with peppers, rice and salad.

Fevzi Hoca Balık-Köfte   SEAFOOD, KÖFTE €€
(Map p510; İpekyolu İş Merkezi, Kahramanmaraş Caddesi; meals ₺15) There are no menus in this chain fish restaurant. Just choose a *büyük* (big) or *küçük* (small) beastie and it comes in a meal deal with salad, pickles and dessert. The hushed ambience makes it resemble somewhere you'd go with your parents for a birthday dinner. *Köfte* meals are also available, but the dry baklava isn't recommended. It's on the 1st floor of a shopping arcade.

Lezzet Lokantası   TURKISH €€
(Map p510; Gazipaşa Caddesi; mains ₺10) In business since 1935, this *lokanta* serves lunchtime staples, chunky chips, kebaps and commendable *lahmacun*. It all comes with outside seats overlooking the square and a sountrack of the waiters calling to passersby.

Üstad   TURKISH €
(Map p510; Atatürk Alanı 18b; meals ₺8) Locals squeeze into this compact *lokanta*, one of the eateries right on the main square. The lunchtime staples include *biber dolması* (stuffed peppers), which come with a surprisingly robust pinch of chilli, reminding you how far east you've travelled.

♟ Drinking & Entertainment

There are a few top-floor bars along Kahramanmaraş Caddesi. Most of the bars close by midnight.

Koza Caffe   CAFE
(Map p510; 1st floor, cnr Kunduracılar Caddesi & Sanat Sokak; 🛜) Opposite Şekerbank (a bank), studenty 'Cocoon Cafe' has a refreshingly funky interior with a mish-mash of fish tanks and faux medieval stylings. Grab a seat on one of the tiny outdoor balconies and settle in for coffee and snacks with a soundtrack of bouncy Turkish pop.

Stress Cafe   NARGILE CAFE
(Map p509; cnr Cemal & Uzun Sokaks; 🛜) One of Trabzon's best live music and nargile spots, the misnamed Stress is so laid-back it's almost horizontal. The Ottomans-R-Us decor is slightly naff, but this is a relaxing haven. Look for the backgammon-playing mannequins out front. Live music kicks off on the top floor at 8pm most nights.

Paticafe
CAFE, BAR

(Map p510; Kahramanmaraş Caddesi) Atop a shopping arcade, Paticafe serves Efes at outside tables with views uphill of Trabzon's broken Hollywood-style sign.

Edward's Coffee
CAFE

(Map p510; ☑326 8026; www.edwardscoffee.com; Cudibey Mekte Sokak, Canbakkal İş Merkezi) This small Anatolian chain serves cappuccino and other non-Turkish coffees. It has outside seating and a menu featuring sandwiches and salads.

Efes Pub
PUB

(Map p510; Kahramanmaraş Caddesi 5) Two floors of smokey, blokey ambience with draught Efes in 0.5L glasses and 2L 'beer towers'. Climb to the roof terrace for views down Kahramanmaraş Caddesi. Female clients tend to sit in the section at the far end of the roof terrace, although women may prefer to go elsewhere.

Sinema Lara
CINEMA

(Map p509; www.sinemalara.com.tr; Kasımoğlu Sokak; admission ₺10) Hollywood blockbusters show in English, just days after their international release.

🔒 Shopping

Thanks to the influx of cheap goods from former Soviet territories, Trabzon is a good place for cheap clothes. If you're lucky, you might even find a few correctly spelt Western logos on the T-shirts, sweatshirts and sports shoes. Leather shops sell jackets, bags and other garments, with alterations and made-to-measure fittings available. Expect to pay around half as much as in İstanbul's Grand Bazaar.

ℹ️ Information

There are numerous internet cafes and travel agencies around the main square. Banks, ATMs and the PTT are on and around Kahramanmaraş Caddesi.

Ensar Döviz (☑321 8141; Gazipaşa Caddesi; ⏰9am-6pm Mon-Fri) Money changer.

Tourist office (☑326 4760; Cami Sokak; ⏰8am-5pm) This helpful place is used to travellers' needs and English is usually spoken. There's an information screen outside.

ℹ️ Getting There & Away

Air

Anadolu Jet (☑444 2538; www.anadolujet.com) Flies to/from Ankara and İstanbul.

Onur Air (☑325 6292; www.onurair.com.tr) Flies to İstanbul and Northern Cyprus.

Pegasus Airlines (☑0850-250 0737; www.flypgs.com) Flies to Ankara.

SunExpress (☑444 0797; www.sunexpress.com.tr) Flies to Antalya, İstanbul, İzmir and European cities.

Turkish Airlines (0212-444 0849; www.thy.com) Flies to Ankara and İstanbul.

Boat

Timetables for ferries to Sochi, Russia, change regularly. Check the latest situation at the shipping offices by the port entrance or online at www.olympia-line.ru, www.saridenizcilik.com/en, www.seaport-sochi.ru, www.al-port.com and www.ferrylines.com.

Depending on demand, be prepared to wait a few days or longer for a departure. Tickets cost about US$100 to US$200 (prices are lowest in winter).

You usually need to report to the port police several hours before departure time. The journey takes five to 12 hours.

Bus

Bus company offices, serving destinations including Georgia and Azerbaijan, are scattered around Atatürk Alanı. Try the big companies **Metro** and **Ulusoy** first.

For Ayder and the Kaçkar Mountains, catch a Hopa-bound bus and change at Ardeşen or, better, Pazar. If you miss the daily Kars bus, head to Hopa or Erzurum for more services. For Yerevan (Armenia), go to Tbilisi (Georgia).

Car

You can hire a car to pick up, or drop off, in Trabzon or at the airport through **Economy Car Rentals** (www.economycarrentals.com). The following rental agencies also have offices either in town or at the airport: **Avis** (☑322 3740; www.avis.com.tr), **Dollar Rent A Car** (www.dollar.com.tr; Taksim Caddesi), **Europcar** (☑444 1399; www.europcar.com.tr; Cikmaz Sokak 38/1A, off Kunduracılar Caddesi) and **National** (☑325 3252; www.nationalcar.com.tr).

ℹ️ Getting Around

To/From the Airport

Dolmuşes to the *havaalanı* (airport, ₺1.50), 5.5km east of the centre, leave from a side street on the northern side of Atatürk Alanı. They drop you on the opposite side of the coast road from the airport, 500m from the terminal entrance across a pedestrian bridge.

A taxi costs about ₺25. Buses bearing 'Park' or 'Meydan' go to Atatürk Alanı from the airport.

Havaş (☑325 9575; www.havas.net) operates shuttle buses to/from the airport (₺5), but they

SERVICES FROM TRABZON'S OTOGAR

DESTINATION	FARE	DURATION (HR)	DISTANCE (KM)	FREQUENCY (PER DAY)
Ankara	₺45	12	780	several
Artvin	₺30	4½	255	frequent
Baku, Azerbaijan	US$60	30	860km	twice (8am, 9am)
Erzurum	₺25	4	325	several
Hopa	₺20	3½	165	half-hourly
İstanbul	₺60	18	1110	several
Kars	₺40	10	525	once
Kayseri	₺50	12	686	several
Rize	₺7	1	75	half-hourly
Samsun	₺25	6	355	frequent
Sinop	₺50	9	533	once (at 8pm)
Tbilisi, Georgia (via Batumi)	₺50	20	430km	several (8am, 10am, 8pm, 10pm)
Yerevan, Armenia	US$80	25	530km	once (8am) Thu & Sun

are inconvenient as they run along Yavuz Selim Bulvarı south of the centre. More useful are its shuttles to/from Ardeşen and the airport (₺15) via Of, Rize and Pazar.

Bus & Dolmuş

Trabzon's otogar is 3km east of the port, on the landward side of the coastal road. To reach Atatürk Alanı from the otogar, cross the shore road in front of the terminal, turn left, walk to the bus stop and catch any bus with 'Park' or 'Meydan' in its name. The dolmuş for Atatürk Alanı is marked 'Garajlar-Meydan'. A taxi between the otogar and Atatürk Alanı costs around ₺15.

Going to the otogar, catch a dolmuş marked 'Garajlar' from near the southeastern end of Atatürk Alanı, or one marked 'KTÜ' from next to Otel Horon.

Dolmuşes mainly leave from under the flyover near the southeastern end of Atatürk Alanı, although you can flag them down along their routes. Whatever your destination, the fare should be ₺1.50.

Sumela Monastery

The Greek Orthodox **Monastery of the Virgin Mary** (admission ₺8; ⊙9am-7pm) at Sumela (Sumela Monastery), 46km south of Trabzon, is the historical highlight of the Black Sea coast. The monastery was founded in Byzantine times and abandoned in 1923, after the creation of the Turkish Republic quashed local Greek aspirations for a new state.

Sumela clings improbably to a sheer rock wall, high above evergreen forests and a rushing mountain stream. It's a mysterious place, especially when mists swirl in the tree-lined valley below and the call of a hidden mosque drifts ethereally through the forest.

Visit early or late to avoid the hordes of Turkish tourists. Arriving when the site opens will beat the mid-morning flow of tour groups. At the entrance to the **Altındere Vadısı Milli Parkı** (Altındere Valley National Park) there's a ₺15 charge for private vehicles. About 2km further on are a shady riverside park with picnic tables and a restaurant.

The main trail to the monastery begins over the footbridge past the restaurant, and is steep but easy to follow. You'll ascend 250m in about 30 to 45 minutes, the air growing noticeably cooler as you climb through forests and alpine meadows. A second trail begins further up the valley. Follow the concreted road 1km uphill and across two bridges until you come to a wooden footbridge over the stream on the right. This trail cuts straight up through the trees, past the shell of the Ayavarvara chapel. It's usually much quieter than the main route and takes the same amount of time.

You can drive almost to the monastery ticket office; the 3km drive is challenging at busy times, with cars coming from the other way on the narrow mountain road. En route are **waterfalls** and a **lookout point**, from where you can see the monastery suspended on a cliff face high above the forest.

After the ticket office, a steep flight of stairs leads to the monastery complex, sheltered underneath a hefty outcrop. The main chapel, cut into the rock, is the indisputable highlight, covered both inside and outside with colourful frescoes. The earliest examples date from the 9th century, but most of them are 19th-century work. Sadly, bored shepherd boys used the paintings as catapult targets, and later heedless visitors – from Russian tourists to US Air Force grunts (1965 vintage) – scratched their names into them. Even recent visitors have felt the need to commemorate their visit with a marker pen; signs now forbid vandalism.

The monastery has been substantially restored to showcase the various chapels and rooms used by pious types in earlier centuries. Continuing restoration in no way detracts from the experience, although on busy days, the views of the building will likely be more memorable than touring its cramped interiors.

🛏 Sleeping & Eating

From Maçka, the road winds through dense evergreen forests, following a rushing mountain stream past commercial trout pools, fish restaurants, pensions and campsites.

Coşandere Tesisleri
Restaurant & Pansiyon   PENSION €€
(📞0462-531 1190; www.cosandere.com; Sumela Yolu; r ₺100, four-person bungalow ₺170, mains ₺10) Located in Coşandere, a sleepy stream-fed village 5km southeast of Maçka en route to Sumela, this pension has converted, pine-clad *seranders* sleeping up to six, and a huge motel-like building favoured by tour groups. It's a handy way to get out and about in the mountains without your own transport, as various tours, treks and day trips are offered. Anyone for a *yayla* safari or 4WD truck trip? The restaurant makes a pleasant lunch stop for Akçaabat *köfte* or *saç kavurma* (stir-fried cubed meat dishes), with outside tables and waitresses in traditional costume.

ⓘ Getting There & Away

BUS Eyce Tours (p511), Ulusoy and Metro run buses from Trabzon (₺25 return, one hour), leaving at 10am and departing from Sumela at 1pm/2pm in winter/summer.

CAR Driving from Trabzon, take the Erzurum road and turn left at Maçka, 29km south of Trabzon. The monastery is also signposted as Meryemana (Virgin Mary), to whom it was dedicated.

DOLMUŞ Dolmuşes to Maçka (₺3, every 20 minutes) depart Trabzon until 8pm from the minibus ranks downhill from Atatürk Alanı, across the coast road from the port. Dolmuşes sometimes carry on to Coşandere or Sumela. A taxi to Maçka/Sumela costs about ₺90/130; from Maçka to Sumela about ₺45.

Trabzon to Erzurum

Heading south into the mountains, it's a long (325km) but scenic ride to Erzurum. After Maçka (and the Sumela Monastery turning), you can stick to the E97, which runs through the Zigana Tunnel, or turn onto the mountain road, ascending through active landslide zones to the **Zigana Geçidi** (Zigana Pass; 2030m).

The dense, humid coastal air disappears as you rise, becoming light and dry as you reach the southern side of the eastern Black Sea mountains. Snow can normally be seen, except perhaps in July, August and September.

Gümüşhane, about 145km south of Trabzon, is a small town in a mountain valley with a few simple travel services. At the provincial capital of **Bayburt**, 195km from Trabzon, you reach the rolling steppe and low mountains of the high Anatolian plateau. A dry, desolate place, Bayburt has a big medieval fortress.

The road now passes through rolling green farm country with poplar trees and flocks of brown-fleeced sheep. In early summer wild flowers dominate. Exactly 33km past Bayburt is the **Kop Geçidi** (Kop Pass; 2370m), with excellent views. From there, the open road to Erzurum offers fast, easy travelling.

Uzungöl

📞0462 / POP 3000
With its lakeside mosque and Swiss-style forested mountains, Uzungöl is another Turkish scene that's on display in tourist

EASTERN EATS

The eastern Black Sea has a unique culture, and chances are you'll first experience the region's character via your stomach. The local cuisine provides a few taste sensations that you won't find anywhere else.

Black Sea folk have a reverence for cabbage only surpassed by certain Eastern European, and no visit would be complete without sampling *labana sarması* (stuffed cabbage rolls) or *labana lobia* (cabbage and beans). Even if you're not a cabbage fan, you'll find these fibre-rich dishes both healthy and tasty.

Also popular are *muhlama* (or *mıhlama*) and *kuymak*, both types of thick molten cheese served in a metal dish, much like fondue or raclette, but without the fiddly carrot and celery sticks. Scooped up with bread for breakfast, it can sit heavily in your stomach, especially if it's followed by a long bus ride. Try it instead in the Kaçkar Mountains, where it's cooked with egg for a lighter effect. It will set you up for a long day's trekking.

If your taste buds aren't reacting to these savoury treats, there's also *laz böreği*, a delicious flaky pastry layered with custard. Like most Turkish desserts, a few bites can easily become a daily addiction. And when you consider that many Turkish pastry chefs hail from the Black Sea, you know it's going to be good.

A good place to try Black Sea cuisine is Rize's Evvel Zaman.

offices around the country. The idyllic setting still exists, but be prepared for a few tacky hotels and a growing number of visitors from the Gulf States. You'll even see menus in Arabic. It's an inauthentic resort in comparison with much of the Kaçkars, but it makes a good base for day hikes in the Soğanlı Mountains to the lakes around Demirkapı (Holdizen). Summer weekends get very busy, so try to visit during the week.

You can rent **mountain bikes** (per hr ₺5) at the far end of the lake.

In the same area is a clutch of wood-trimmed resorts, motels and pensions, mostly offering wooden bungalows. Uzungöl's accommodation is generally not a good deal; **İnan Kardeşler** (☑656 6222; www.inankardesler.com.tr; s/d ₺70/120; ☎) is one of the best-value options, with one- and two-bedroom bungalows sleeping up to five. On the main road into Uzungöl are cheaper and scruffier pensions.

Minibuses travel to/from Of (₺8), 40km north, and Trabzon (₺12).

Rize

☑0464 / POP 102,145

In the heart of Turkey's tea-plantation area, Rize is a modern city centred on an attractive main square. The hillsides above town are planted with tea, which is dried, blended, and shipped throughout Turkey. Two hilltop tea gardens are good spots for a refreshing cuppa courtesy of the local tea giant Çaykur.

The main square, with an inevitable Atatürk *anıtı* (monument), beautifully reconstructed PTT and the Şeyh Camii, is 200m inland from the *sahil yolu* (coast road). Principal thoroughfares Cumhuriyet and Atatürk Caddesis run east from the square, parallel with the coast.

◉ Sights

Taxis charge ₺6 from the main square up to the tea garden or castle.

Tea Garden　　　　　HILL, PARK

(çay ₺0.50) Rize's fragrant and floral tea garden is next to the Çaykur tea factory; 20 minutes' walk above town via the steep main road leading uphill behind the Şeyh Camii (signposted 'Çaykur Tea and Botany Garden'). Enjoy the superb views with a fresh brew of local leaves – a typical Rizeli experience. A shop sells organic Hemşin çay and the like.

Castle　　　　　CASTLE

(çay ₺1.50; ◷8am-11pm) Built by the Genoese on the steep hill at the back of town, Rize's ancient *kale* contains a tea garden with sweeping coastal views. Head west of the main square to Petrol Ofisi gas station, from where it's signposted.

FREE **Rize Museum**　　　　　MUSEUM

(☑214 0235; ◷9am-noon & 1-4pm Tue-Sun) Uphill behind the tourist office, this fine reconstructed Ottoman house is decorated in traditional style, with a weaving room,

ONE OF THE LAZ

Rize is the last major centre of the Laz, a loose community of around 250,000 people, 150,000 of whom still speak the Caucasian-based Lazuri language. Known for their colourful traditional costumes and *lazeburi* folk music, Laz cultural performances take place at major local festivals in the Rize region.

However, calling someone Laz is not straightforward. The Turkish Laz dispute any categorisation that would lump them in with their Georgian counterparts. Non-Laz locals distinguish themselves as 'Karadenizli' (from the Black Sea), but many Turks use Laz as a catch-all term for anyone living east of Samsun.

The majority population in towns such as Pazar and Ardeşen, the Laz are just as keen to distance themselves from other coastal citizens, and dismiss the demeaning stereotype of the simple, anchovy-munching Laz fisherman. The Laz are having the last laugh: many Turkish shipping lines are owned by wealthy Laz families. They routinely resource their boats with Laz sailors, so don't be surprised if a retired maritime type regales you (in respectable English) with his memories of distant ports.

For more information on the Laz, see p641.

kitchen, antiques, cooking implements and musical instruments. An old record player reminds that the 20th-century Ottomans were part of the modern age. Mannequins model traditional Laz costumes from central Rize and Hemşin costumes from the Ayder region. In the basement is baroque and rococo furniture, and next door are a lovely granary and the Çay Museum, devoted to Rize's Çaykur tea company.

🛏 Sleeping & Eating

Hotels are mostly east of the main square along Cumhuriyet Caddesi.

Hotel Milano HOTEL €
(☎ 213 0028; www.hotelmilanorize.com; Cumhuriyet Caddesi; s/d/tr ₺50/80/120; 🛜) Reached by a lift and corridors with tile floors, rooms have a faint whiff of cigarette smoke but perhaps Rize's strongest shower pressure. Ask for a room at the rear of the building for less noise from the main drag. Staff in the first-floor reception are accommodating.

Otel Kaçkar HOTEL €€
(☎ 213 1490; www.otelkackar.com; Cumhuriyet Caddesi 101; s/d/tr ₺70/100/130; 🌮🛜) Just off the main square, the lower-midrange Kaçkar's mosaic facade conceals neat and simple rooms, with once-smart black furniture, basic bathrooms and a poky lift.

TOP CHOICE Evvel Zaman ANATOLIAN €€
(www.evvelzaman.com.tr; Harem Sokak 2; mains ₺9-10) This lovingly restored Ottoman house – the interior is like a joyously jumbled museum, stretching to a display

case of daggers – is a wonderful place to try traditional Black Sea and Ottoman dishes, such as fondue-like *muhlama* and *etli sarma* (mince-stuffed cabbage or vine leaves). The pictorial menu also features breakfasts packed with goodies such as cheese, cucumbers, tomatoes and honey from local villages, and the restaurant has shaded tables in the garden for hot days. It's at the southeastern (uphill) edge of the main square.

Bekiroğlu KEBAP, PIDE €
(Cumhuriyet Caddesi 161; mains ₺6-10; 🍴) A cut above most *lokantas*, Bekiroğlu has a modern interior and seating on pedestrianised Deniz Caddesi. Dishes on the pictorial menu, delivered by waiters in bow ties and aprons, include top-notch pide.

Dergah Pastaneleri SWEETS €
(Deniz Caddesi; mains ₺4-10; 🛜) Stop for baklava or cake and *dondurma* (ice cream) at this gleaming modern *pastane* (patisserie). You can survey Rize from the roof terrace and there's a branch on Atatürk Caddesi near the main square.

ℹ Information

Park Internet Café (3rd floor, Atatürk Caddesi 336; per hr ₺1.50; ⊙9am-11pm) Overlooking the tea garden next to Garanti Bank.
Tourist Office (☎ 213 0408; ⊙8.30am-7pm)

ℹ Getting There & Away

Bus-company offices and travel agents are around the main square.

Frequent minibuses run to Hopa (₺10, 1½ hours) and Trabzon (₺10, 1½ hours). For the northern Kaçkars, take an east-bound minibus to Ardeşen (₺6) or, better, Pazar (₺5) and change.

The otogar is along the old coast road, 2km northwest of the main square. For Trabzon, Pazar, Ardeşen and Hopa, it's easier to pick up a local minibus from the mini-otogar next to Halkbank, a few blocks northeast of the main square.

Hopa

☑0466 / POP 24,500

Just 30km southwest of the Georgian border, Hopa is an archetypal border town, with cheap hotels, traders' markets and a functional vibe. On the shady streets inland from the seafront highway are shoe shiners, barbers and a town going about its everyday business, seamlessly mixing old and new, headscarves and mobile-phone shops, in classic Turkish fashion. It's not worth overnighting here unless you arrive late en route to/from Georgia. There's a PTT, internet cafes and, near the pedestrian bridge, money changers and banks with ATMs.

🛏 Sleeping

Otel Heyamo   BUSINESS HOTEL ₺₺
(☑351 2315; www.otelheyamo.com in Turkish; Sahil Caddesi 44; s/d ₺60/80; ☀☎) Beyond the grand but surreal lobby, decorated with Dali repros, the bedrooms have flat-screen TV, small desk and dark-wood trimmings.

Otel Huzur   HOTEL ₺
(☑351 4095; Cumhuriyet Caddesi 25; s ₺30-35, d ₺50-60; ☀☀☎) Friendly Huzur's wood-pannelled reception and lounge is good for people-watching border-bound characters. Rooms are reasonably comfortable; the cheaper options have shower and shared toilet.

🍴 Eating & Drinking

Eateries cluster around the hotels. There's a *tekel bayii* (off-licence kiosk) at the pedestrian bridge near Green Garden Kebap.

Green Garden Kebap   PIDE, KEBAP ₺
(Cumhuriyet Caddesi; mains ₺8) A few hundred metres east of the main hotel strip, two terraces and a brick dining room dish up pide and kebaps in a shady park, with a helpful pictorial menu.

ℹ Getting There & Away

Hopa's otogar is on the old coast road around 1km west of town, ₺1 by dolmuş. Ulusoy and Artvin Ekspres buses to Erzurum (₺35, six hours) leave at 6.30am, 9am and 4pm. Artvin Ekspres regularly serves Artvin (₺15, 1½ hours), and Kars (₺40) at 10.30am. Metro has hourly minibuses to Rize (₺10, 1½ hours) and Trabzon (₺20, 3½ hours).

For Georgia, Metro serves Tbilisi (₺35, eight hours) via Batumi (₺10, one hour) at 6am, 6.30am and 7am. From Batumi, you will often save time without adding expense by taking bus 101 to the border, then a waiting minibus to Hopa.

Northeastern Anatolia

Why Go?

If you've a soft spot for far-flung outposts, it's time to discover Turkey's greatest secret. Despite its wealth of attractions, northeastern Anatolia remains largely untouched by even the domestic tourist circuit, and its glorious landscapes are refreshingly coach-party free. Particularly outside the Turkish summer holidays, you may have precipitous gorges and expansive steppe, muscular mountains and highland pastures to yourself. No wonder the region is prime territory for trekking (make a beeline for the Kaçkar Mountains and Mt Ararat), white-water rafting and skiing.

Culturally, the ruins of Ani and Işhak Paşa Palace are famously romantic, and numerous secluded treasures recall once-flourishing ancient civilisations. Palaces, castles, Georgian churches, Armenian monuments and Ottoman humpback bridges all stand in splendid isolation. For urban vibes, Kars is a laidback city with a Russian aesthetic – a staging post in this region of open spaces, mountain solitude and moody skies above the steppe.

Best Places to Eat

» Ocakbaşı Restoran (p540)
» Laşet Tesisleri (p537)
» Erzurum Evleri (p524)
» Simurg (p550)
» Publik Bistro (p529)

Best Places to Stay

» Ekodanitap (p528)
» Otel Doğa (p529)
» Karahan Pension (p533)
» Çamyuva Pension (p533)
» Güngören Otel (p538)

When to Go

Erzurum

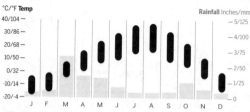

May Vivid hues and scents as the steppe blossoms; Turkish school term continues.

Jun–Sep Hike and raft around the Kaçkar Mountains, scale Mt Ararat, catch festivals.

Dec–Apr Ski at Palandöken and Sarıkamış resorts, cross-country ski in the Kaçkars.

ERZURUM & AROUND

Erzurum

☏ 0442 / POP 382,383 / ELEV 1853M

Lovers of architecture will be in paradise in Erzurum, where fantastic Seljuk, Saltuk and Mongol mosques and *medreses* (seminar-ies) line the main drag. Take it all in from atop the citadel, with mountains and steppe forming a heavenly backdrop to the jumble of billboards and minarets.

Erzurum is not a city resting on its considerable laurels of historical significance; the vibrant life coursing along its shopping-centre-lined streets has earned it a reputation

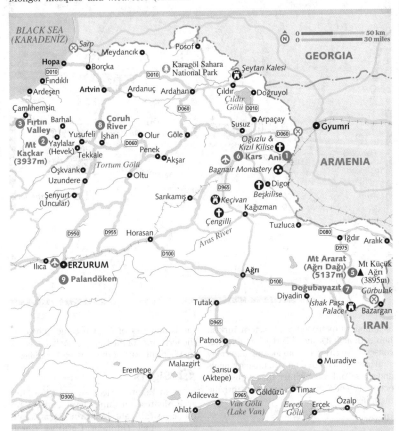

Northeastern Anatolia Highlights

❶ Lose yourself in the past glories of **Ani** (p543), a former Armenian capital strewn across the steppe

❷ Trek over the **Kaçkar Mountains** (p526), or tackle day walks from nearby serene villages like Barhal and Yaylalar

❸ Experience the **Fırtın Valley's** (p529) Hemşin culture (and cuisine)

❹ Cruise the **yaylalar** (mountain pastures) east of Artvin, land of pine forests and emerald slopes

❺ Hit the summit of **Mt Ararat** (5137m; p551), Turkey's highest mountain

❻ Hang out in distinctive **Kars** (p538) and discover Georgian and Armenian ruins nearby

❼ Meet the Kurds in **Doğubayazit** (p548) and explore sights like İshak Paşa Palace (p548)

❽ Test your mettle on a white-water run down the **Çoruh River** (p527)

❾ Rip up some powder at **Palandöken** (p525) ski resort

Erzurum

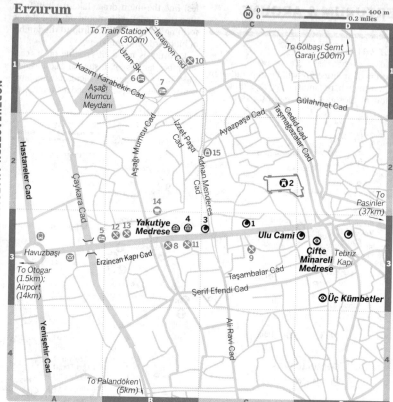

as a modern metropolis and eastern Turkish hub. Although it's one of Turkey's most pious, conservative cities, the hip-looking university students add a relaxed buzz to the pavements and cafes. And come winter, the nearby high-octane Palandöken ski resort has a thriving nightlife.

History

Being in a strategic position at the confluence of roads to Constantinople, Russia and Persia, Erzurum was conquered and lost by armies of Armenians, Persians, Romans, Byzantines, Arabs, Saltuk Turks, Seljuk Turks and Mongols. As for the Ottomans, it was Selim the Grim who conquered the city in 1515. It was captured by Russian troops in 1882 and again in 1916. In July 1919 Atatürk came to Erzurum to attend the congress that provided the rallying cry for the Turkish independence struggle. The Erzurum Congress is most famous for determining the boundaries of what became known as the territories of the National Pact, the lands that became part of the Turkish Republic.

◎ Sights

Between Yakutiye Medrese and Çifte Minareli Medrese on Cumhuriyet Caddesi are the classical **Lala Mustafa Paşa Camii** (1562), small Ottoman **Caferiye Camii** (Caferiye Mosque; Cumhuriyet Caddesi) and restrained but elegant **Ulu Cami** (Great Mosque; Cumhuriyet Caddesi), built by the Saltuk Turkish *emir* of Erzurum in 1179.

Yakutiye Medrese   MUSEUM, MEDRESE

(Yakutiye Seminary; Cumhuriyet Caddesi) Rising above a square slap-bang in the centre, this imposing Mongol theological seminary dates from 1310. The Mongols borrowed the basics of Seljuk architecture and developed their own variations, as seen in the entrance, with its geometric, plant and animal motifs. Of the

Erzurum

two original minarets, only the base of one and the lower part of the other have survived; the one sporting superb mosaic tilework wouldn't look out of place in Central Asia.

Inside is the excellent **Turkish-Islamic Arts & Ethnography Museum** (Türk-İslam Eserleri ve Etnoğrafya Müzesi; admission ₺3; ⊙8am-5pm Tue-Sun), with beautiful exhibits such as Ottoman manuscripts in rooms off the closed courtyard. The striking central dome is lined with faceted stalactite work that catches light from the central opening to make a delightful pattern.

Kale
FORTRESS

(admission ₺3; ⊙8am-5pm) For Erzurum's best views, head up to the citadel, erected by the emperor Theodosius around the 5th century and subsequently damaged and repaired numerous times. Inside, spiral stairs and a step ladder climb to the top of the 12th-century clock tower.

Çifte Minareli Medrese
MEDRESE

(Twin Minaret Seminary; Cumhuriyet Caddesi) Lying east of the centre, the single most definitive image of Erzurum dates from the 1200s when Erzurum was a wealthy Seljuk city, before suffering attack and devastation by the Mongols in 1242. The building is under restoration until 2015. Its facade exemplifies how the Seljuks liked to try out variation even while aiming for symmetry: the panels on either side of the entrance are identical in size and position but different in motif. The panel to the right bears the Seljuk eagle; to the left the motif is unfinished.

The twin brick **minarets** are decorated with eye-catching small blue tiles. The tops of the minarets are gone, having succumbed to the vagaries of Erzurum's violent history (even before the Ottomans claimed the town).

Walk to the back of the building to see the grand, 12-sided domed hall at the far end of the main courtyard from the entrance. It served as the Hatuniye Türbesi, or Tomb of Huand Hatun, the *medrese's* founder.

Üç Kümbetler
TOMBS

(Three Tombs) Walk south between the Çifte Minareli and Ulu Cami until you come to a T-junction. Turn left then immediately right and walk a short block uphill to these three 13th-century mausoleums in a fenced enclosure. Note the near-conical roofs and the elaborately decorated side panels.

🛏 Sleeping

Erzurum has a couple of dependable budget and midrange options, but if you want full-on luxury you'll need to stay at the Palandöken ski resort, 5km south of Erzurum.

Grand Hotel Hitit
HOTEL €€

(233 5001; grandhitit@gmail.com; Kazım Karabekir Caddesi 26; s/d/tr ₺90/150/180; 🌐) On a street with half a dozen budget and lower midrange hotels, the Hitit has Erzurum's pleasantest rooms – with plasma-screen TV, dark wood furnishings, well-sprung mattress, big shower, minibar and safe. It's professionally managed and a good choice for lone women. The bright top-floor breakfast area is the perfect spot to eye up the city.

Esadaş Otel
HOTEL €€

(☑233 5425; www.esadas.com; Cumhuriyet Caddesi 7; s/d ₺70/140; 🗑) Pros: right on the main thoroughfare and close to everything. Cons: right on the main thoroughfare, a bit noisy (traffic ceases around 11pm). That said, it's well maintained and efficiently run and has excellent breakfast too. Bargain down the prices a bit if it's slack.

Otel Polat
HOTEL €€

(☑235 0363; fax 234 4598; Kazım Karabekir Caddesi 4; s/d/tr ₺55/100/120; 🗑) In business since 1967, the two-star Polat has benefitted from a recent renovation. The small rooms have large fridges and sunken beds, plus bath and shower in the en suites. A little English is spoken and the breakfast room has an outside terrace with city views and an Ottoman diorama.

✗ Eating & Drinking

Eateries on Cumhuriyet Caddesi around Yakutiye Medrese serve the students snacks from *çiğ köfte* (raw ground lamb mixed with pounded bulgur, onion, clove, cinnamon, salt and hot black pepper) to *lokum* (Turkish delight). Head to **Arzen** (Cumhuriyet Caddesi; snacks from ₺2) and **Kılıçoğlu** (Cumhuriyet Caddesi; snacks from ₺2) for baklava, ice cream and, in the former, Lavazza coffee.

TOP CHOICE Erzurum Evleri
CAFE €€

(Yüzbaşı Sokak 5; mains ₺10-18) This stunning old wooden house, signposted from Cumhuriyet Caddesi (opposite Caferiye Camii), is filled with Ottoman paraphernalia. Dishes include soup, *börek* (filled pastry) and *tandır kebap* (stew), served in private alcoves with cushions and low tables. Overlooking the courtyard, **Şahane** offers çay, Turkish coffee and, from 7pm, live traditional music. Round the back, **Daşhane** has nargiles (water pipes) and bean-bags.

Gel-Gör Cağ Kebabı
KEBAP €€

(İstasyon Caddesi; mains ₺5-15) This charismatic Erzurum favourite specialises in *cağ kebap* (mutton grilled on a horizontal spit) served with small plates of salad, onions and yoghurt. Eat the tender chunks with a fork, or do as the locals do and chomp from the skewer.

Güzelyurt Restoran
MEZE, INTERNATIONAL €€

(☑234 5001; www.guzelyurtrestaurant.com; Cumhuriyet Caddesi 42; mains ₺9-20) Erzurum's smartest restaurant, in business since 1928, is adorably anachronistic, with shrouded windows, thick carpets and bow-tied waiters creating old-fashioned charm. It's licensed, and a good place to spill money on a great meal. The mezes (₺0.50 to ₺7.50) are the headliner, with about 20 different specialities, but the menu also features a smattering of mains, including 'Bof Straganof' (no typo).

Salon Asya
KEBAP €

(Cumhuriyet Caddesi 27; mains ₺8) Asya does a lively lunchtime trade, keeping diners, who range from students to policemen, happy with Turkish classics including pide (Turkish-style bread), recommended döner kebaps (spit-roasted lamb slices), *çorba* (soup), *lahmacun* (Arabic-style pizza) and tempting desserts.

Yakutiye Park Alışveriş Merkezi
CAFE, LIVE MUSIC

(Yakutiye Meydanı) Step inside this building, its tower aping the Yakutiye Medrese in glass and red lights, and enter Erzurum's student world. Lifts climb between five floors of unlicensed cafes offering *canlı* (live) music and other entertainment. **Şamata Cafe** is a popular hang-out with a snack bar, air hockey, snooker, table tennis, foosball and an outdoor terrace with swing chairs. **Tutku Cafe** has a bowling alley, nargiles and table tennis are on offer in **Xtanbul Cafe**, and board games in **Cafe SS**.

🔒 Shopping

Shops on the eastern and western sides of Çifte Minareli Medrese sell carpets, antiques and souvenirs. On the way there from the main square, there are jewellery shops on the northern side of Cumhuriyet Caddesi before reaching Ulu Cami.

Rüstem Paşa Çarşısı
JEWELLERY

(Adnan Menderes Caddesi) Erzurum is known for the manufacture of jewellery and other items from *oltutaşı,* the local black amber. Buy it in this atmospheric *çarşı* (market; 1550), built by Süleyman the Magnificent's grand vizier.

ℹ Information

INTERNET ACCESS Internet cafes are plentiful in the centre.

MONEY Most banks have branches with ATMs on or around Cumhuriyet Caddesi. In the same area are moneychangers, which keep longer hours.

SERVICES FROM ERZURUM'S OTOGAR

DESTINATION	FARE (₺)	DURATION (HR)	DISTANCE (KM)	FREQUENCY (PER DAY)
Ankara	65	13	925	about 10 buses
Diyarbakır	35	8	485	5 buses
Doğubayazıt	25	4½	285	5 buses
İstanbul	70	19	1275	7 buses
Kars	20	3	205	frequent
Kayseri	50	10	628	several
Trabzon	25	6	325	several
Van	40	6½	410	about 3 buses

❶ Getting There & Away

Air

Travel agents on Cumhuriyet Caddesi between Yakutiye Medrese and the police station sell tickets on behalf of Turkish airlines.

Anadolu Jet (www.anadolujet.com) flies to/from Ankara, **Onur Air** (www.onurair.com.tr) to/from İstanbul, **Sun Express** (www.sunexpress.com.tr) to/from İstanbul and İzmir, and **Turkish Airlines** (www.thy.com) to/from İstanbul and Ankara.

Bus

The otogar (bus station), 2km from the centre along the airport road, handles most of Erzurum's intercity traffic. Many bus companies have offices around Esadaş Otel.

Among other companies, Metro serves all the destinations covered by the table, apart from Diyarbakır and Doğubayazıt, which Hasbingöl serves.

For Iran, take a bus to Doğubayazıt.

The Gölbaşı Semt Garajı, about 1km northeast of Adnan Menderes Caddesi through the back streets (take a cab to get there), handles minibuses to towns to the north and east of Erzurum. Daily departures include Artvin, Hopa, Rize and Yusufeli.

Train

The daily *Doğu Ekspresi* runs to Kars, and to Ankara via Sivas.

❶ Getting Around

A taxi to/from the airport, about 14km northwest of town, costs around ₺40. Buses meet planes and run into central Erzurum for ₺3, with a convenient **bus stop** on Hastaneler Caddesi, just north of the roundabout at the western end of Cumhuriyet Caddesi.

Minibuses and city buses pass the otogar and will take you into town for ₺1; a taxi is about ₺10.

Car-rental operators, including National, Alamo, Europcar and Avis, have branches in Erzurum. **Economy Car Rentals** (www.economycarrentals.com) covers the city and airport.

Palandöken

📞 0442

A mere 5km south of Erzurum, Palandöken is Turkey's best ski resort. Excellent runs for all levels, descending from 3100m, and top-notch infrastructure, including ski lifts, cable cars, snowboard parks and even impressive jumps, are all found here. The resort gained international recognition in 2011, when it hosted the Winter Universiade (World University Games).

The season runs from late November to early April; at weekends, prepare to jostle with other snow lovers for a place in the lift queues and on the slopes. There's also an excellent après-ski scene.

🛏 Sleeping & Eating

The following are open all year. The hotels generally have restaurants, bars, discos, hire outfits, hamams, saunas and fitness centres. The prices quoted here are high-season winter weekend rates (expect discounts of around 30% to 50% in low season). They're usually negotiable, and in winter 'full board plus' packages, including all meals and lift pass, are offered.

Xanadu Snow White HOTEL €€€
(📞230 3030; www.xanaduhotels.com.tr; full board s/d ₺498/664; ❄🖥🏊) The newest and most stylish, with great views of Erzurum.

Ski Lodge Dedeman HOTEL €€€
(📞317 0500; www.dedeman.com; s/d/tr €100/135/180; 🗓Dec-Apr; ❄🖥) Stylish and intimate.

Dedeman
HOTEL €€

(☎316 2414; www.dedeman.com; s/d/tr €100/ 135/180; ☺Dec-Apr; ❋❂❄) Right at the foot of the ski runs, at 2450m.

Polat Renaissance
HOTEL €€€

(☎232 0010; www.renaissancehotels.com; half-/ full board per person €255/280; ❋❂❄) The pyramid-shaped Polat feels like a mini-city.

❶ Getting There & Away

From central Erzurum, a taxi costs about ₺20 to ₺25.

KAÇKAR MOUNTAINS

The Kaçkar Mountains (Kaçkar Dağları) form a rugged range between the Black Sea and the Çoruh River, stretching roughly 30km northeast. Dense forest covers the lower valleys, but above about 2000m grasslands carpet the passes and plateaus, and the jagged ranges are studded with lakes and alpine summer *yaylar* (mountain pastures).

The Kaçkars are renowned for their trekking opportunities. Popular locations include the highest point, Mt Kaçkar (Kaçkar Dağı; 3937m), with a glacier on its northern face, and the northeastern ranges around the peak of Altıparmak (3310m). Try to spend at a few days here to uncover the best of this stunning region.

🏃 Activities

Hiking

The Kaçkars hiking season is short; you can only hike the higher mountain routes between mid-July and mid-August, when the snowline is highest. From May to mid-September there are plenty of walks on the lower slopes. If you are content not to cross the mountains, conditions are more dependably dry and clear in June and September, and the autumn colours in September and October are beautiful.

One of the most popular trips is the **Trans-Kaçkar Trek**: two to three days from Olgunlar to Ayder via the Çaymakçur Pass (approximately 3100m). The hike to the **Kaçkar Summit** by its southern face takes two to three days from Olgunlar, and may require specialist snow equipment. Without a guide, you can tackle the ascent to **Dilber Düzü** campsite beneath Mt Kaçkar (the path is well defined); allow seven to eight hours for this out-and-back walk from Olgunlar.

The three- to four-day **Trans-Altıparmak** route is similar to the Trans-Kaçkar, except that it crosses the Altıparmak range and doesn't climb the summit. From Barhal, you could trek for four to five sweaty hours up to **Karagöl Lake**, camp overnight, and return the next day.

Çamlıhemşin and Yusufeli are easily accessible, and public transport of varying frequency serves Ayder, Şenyuva, Çat, Barhal, Yaylalar and Olgunlar. High in the northwestern Kaçkars around 2000m, there are basic pensions in Yukarı Kavron, Amlakit, Palovit and Elevit. These spots and Avusor, all served by dolmuş in summer, are good spots for day walks around the slopes and lakes. As a general rule, you have to climb above about 1900m to leave the forests and get panoramic views. Culture Routes in Turkey (p661) has marked day walks around Barhal, Yaylalar and Olgunlar. Walks at lower altitudes, with or without a guide, are also stunning, with ancient Georgian churches and Ottoman bridges in the forests.

RESOURCES

The Kaçkar – Trekking in Turkey's Black Sea Mountains The book details different Kaçkar routes over the high passes.

www.trekkinginturkey.com Useful practical information and updates to the above.

www.culturalroutesturkey.com Recommends day walks and longer trails, with practical info.

www.kackar.org In Turkish, but has useful maps and photos.

GUIDES

It's a good idea to hire a local who knows the tracks if you plan to tackle high altitudes or multiday hikes. The walks are mostly unsigned, and misty weather conditions can make orientation difficult. Arranging a guide upon arrival can be difficult – they may be busy in season, and unavailable in winter – so making contact and booking a guide in advance is recommended.

A good tent, mat, sleeping bag and stove are necessary, although with an all-inclusive operator you could get away with a sleeping bag, walking boots and warm clothes. For fully guided tours for two people, including tents, mat, transport and food, expect to pay around US$250 per day from Ayder.

If you don't want to arrange a guide beforehand, many of the pensions we've included can provide guiding services and give pointers. Barhal Pansiyon (p533),

Kaçkar Mountains

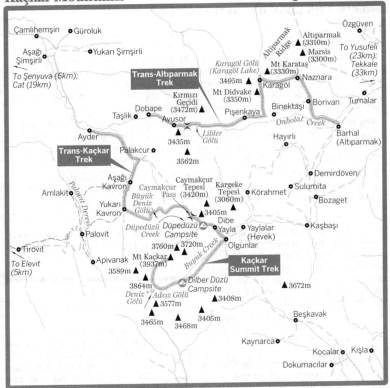

Karahan Pension (p533) and Çamyuva Pension (p533) are especially recommended. Guides can also be arranged through pensions in mountain villages such as Yukarı Kavron, but beware of false guides. Professional operations typically charge about ₺150 to ₺200 per day for a mule and a guide. A mule can carry three people's bags. You can minimise costs by providing your own food and camping equipment.

Turku Tour HIKING
(☑651 7230; www.turkutour.com; İnönü Caddesi 35, Çamlıhemşin) Mehmet Demirci, a friendly local entrepreneur and owner of pensions in Ayder and Çamlıhemşin, offers day walks, longer treks, 4WD safaris, rafting, horse riding, cross-country skiing and photography. He has a mountain house at Kotençur (2300m), one hour's walk from Amlakit, and offers alternative treks following the Silk Road and Xenophon's *Anabasis*.

East Turkey Expeditions HIKING
(☑0543 480 4764; zaferonay@hotmail.com) Zafer Onay (who also covers the Kaçkars) is knowledgeable and English-speaking.

Cumhur Bayrak HIKING
(☑0537 562 4713; cumhurbayrak@hotmail.com; Yusufeli) Knowledgeable about flora and fauna, Cumhur is a recommended guide. Also offers day walks around Yusufeli.

Middle Earth Travel HIKING
(www.middleearthtravel.com) Cappadocia-based nationwide hiking specialists.

White-Water Rafting
YUSUFELİ

The Çoruh River is one of the world's best rafting rivers, with superb rapids and brilliant play holes. The river and its tributaries offer a wide range of rafting options for all skill levels, from 2 to 5, depending on the stretches and the levels of water. Beginners

LOCAL KNOWLEDGE

NECMETTİN COŞKUN: RAFTING GUIDE

Best season The main rafting season begins in June. For beginners, it's best to come in July or August, because the level of water is lower and the rapids less challenging.

Why it's special here The Çoruh and its tributaries are long rivers; you can paddle for hours, even several days if you want. And for serious action, the Çoruh is simply world-class, with thrilling sections complete with rapids, pools and big rocks – they're not called 'King Kong' and 'High Tension' for nothing. The scenery adds to the appeal, with deep gorges, castles and picturesque villages.

Beginners' corner We begin with a practice session and a briefing on a calm section of the river, usually on the İspir River, before tackling more thrilling sections, though there's no obligation to overdo it. There's always a guide on the boat, who gives the instructions to the team, and a minibus follows along the road and picks us up at the end of the ride.

What if the dam project... I think we still have a few more years before the dam becomes reality. Anyway, once it's completed, we'll find other sections on the Çoruh, the İspir or the Barhal Rivers. There are alternatives.

will tackle more forgiving sections on the nearby İspir River (usually from Tekkale to Yusufeli). The Barhal River (18km from Sarıgöl to Yusufeli) is faster and more technical. If you are keen to raft the Çoruh, make sure that is where you are taken, as travellers have been duped and ended up on another river. Beginners can tackle the 21km stretch of the Çoruh between Yusufeli and the petrol station on the Artvin–Erzurum road.

Various local operators run day trips for about ₺100 per person (three or four people ₺70 per person) for around three hours of rafting. Reputable guides:

Necmettin Coşkun (☑0505 541 2522; www .coruhriver.com) In Yusufeli in June/July; speaks good English.

Oktay Alkan (☑811 3620; www.birolrafting .com; Greenpiece Camping & Pansiyon) Former kayak champion; in Yusufeli over the summer.

Sıralı Aydın (☑811 3151, 0533 453 3179; www .coruhoutdoor.com) Office on the far side of Yusufeli suspension footbridge from Hotel Baraka.

ÇAMLIHEMŞİN

White-water rafting is possible in July and August on the rapids around Çamlıhemşin. The rapids are smaller than the more exciting waters near Yusufeli, but the Black Sea region has arguably the more impressive scenery. There are operators on the Ardeşen–Çamlıhemşin road, including **Dağraft** (☑0464-752 4070; www.dagraft.com.tr; per person ₺40-60), which has tours geared towards rafters from amateurs to professionals (grades 1 to 2 and 3 to 4; 3km to 9km). It also offers zip-lining.

Northern Kaçkars

ÇAMLIHEMŞİN & AROUND

☑0464 / POP 3000

At an altitude of 300m, 20km off the coast road, Çamlıhemşin is a climatic transition point. Mist and drizzle indicate that you've left the coastal zone, and once you continue up the valleys past Çamlıhemşin, expect a stronger alpine influence in the climate, terrain and vegetation. The village is a functional, workaday spot, but has an appealing authenticity in comparison with Ayder. The locals are mostly Hemşin. See p641 for more information on this minority group, famous for producing excellent pastry cooks.

Just beyond Çamlıhemşin the road forks. The right fork leads up the Fırtına Valley; the left over the bridge and uphill to Ayder (17km). On the Ayder road, you'll pass several ancient **humpback bridges** across the Fırtına Çayı (Storm Stream), which were restored for the Turkish Republic's 75th anniversary (1998).

Çamlıhemşin has a post office, supermarket, garage, and the only ATM in the northern Kaçkars. Stock up on provisions. Turku Tour (p527) organises excursions in the Kaçkars and sells domestic flight tickets.

There are a couple of camping spots en route from the coast. For more comfortable accommodation, the highly original and wonderful **Ekodanitap** (☑651 7787; www.eko

danitap.com; half-board per person Hemşin house/tree house ₺90/75; 🛜) is hidden up a winding road (just before Çamlıhemşin on the right) and along a forest footpath. Traditional Hemşin houses and tree houses overlook a terrace perched above a river valley with a mountain at the far end. With an organic garden and solar power, sustainability is a priority, but there are modern features such as showers. Eating with gregarious owner Mehmet Demirci and his family is a pleasure, although they are often based at Fora Pansiyon (p530) in Ayder during the trekking season (roughly May to September). Ekodanitap is open year-round.

Çamlıhemşin has basic cafes and the licensed **Publik Bistro** (🛜651 7270; İnönü Caddesi 35; meals ₺10; ⊙8am-5pm winter, to 10pm summer; 🛜), with a riverside terrace and black-and-white Kaçkar scenes overlooking its wooden benches, small library and backgammon sets. The breakfast is kingly, particularly if you incorporate *soğanlı yumurta* (eggs with onion), and dishes include kebaps, pasta and *muhlama* (fondue-like Hemşin dish).

Frequent dolmuş traffic runs to/from Pazar (₺6), with connections to/from Rize (₺10), and Ardeşen (₺6).

FIRTINA VALLEY
📞0464

This beautiful and atmospheric river valley, used as a location in the Turkish film *Bal* (Honey), is a wonderful place to experience traditional Hemşin life. Even the 6km stretch from Çamlıhemşin to Şenyuva is special; winch wires, used for hoisting goods up to remote mountain houses, criss-cross the verdant slopes above the road. Look for the hilltop mansions built in the early 20th century, when locals returned flush with cash after working as chefs and bakers in pre-Revolutionary Russia.

In Şenyuva, about 800m north of Fırtına Pansiyon, is the graceful arch of the **Şenyuva Köprüsü** (Şenyuva Bridge, 1696). The **teahouse** 200m further on has a supreme view of the bridge from its riverside terrace. Don't cross the nearby bridge, but continue along the river and into the hills for 6km to reach the restored **Zil Castle** (Zil Kale). It's a tough but scenic walk. En route, after 2.5km, a sign points to **Pavolit Şelâlesi** – the waterfall is a one-hour walk from here. Lush rhododendron forests surround the spectacularly situated castle, a round stone tower on a stark rock base.

The road disintegrates at the castle, but it's navigable in a normal car. Another 15km takes you to **Çat** (1250m), a riverside hamlet used as a trekking base, and the start of even rougher roads into the mountains. A further 3.5km uphill is **Çat summer village** (1800m), where locals move in the warmer months when the road is passable. It's well worth the walk for the *yaylalar*, overlooked by snowy peaks and swathed in buttercups in spring. Turn left after the humpack stone Ottoman **Çılanç Köprüsü**.

🛏 Sleeping
Booking ahead is recommended in summer. The pensions mostly close from October to April. There's a food shop in Çat.

TOP CHOICE **Otel Doğa** GUEST HOUSE €€
(🛜651 7455; Şenyuva Yolu; half-board per person ₺55; 🛜) About 4.5km from Çamlıhemşin, this friendly old guest house has a spacious sitting room and riverside dining room, where home-cooked food is served. The French- and English-speaking owner, İdris Duman, is a passionate champion of the Kaçkars; he will help you get your bearings at the wall map in the kitchen. Most bedrooms have private bathrooms and balconies; go for a corner room.

Toşi Pansiyon PENSION €€
(🛜654 4002; www.tosipansiyon.com; half-board per person ₺80) The first pension you come to in Çat, Toşi is clean and friendly with a riverside terrace and accommodation in a wooden cabin.

ⓘ Getting There & Away
On summer mornings, a dolmuş heads up the valley from Çamlıhemşin to Çat (₺15) and onto *yaylalar* villages. Turku Tour (p527) runs a minibus on Saturday and Thursday, leaving Çamlıhemşin at 8am and heading up the valley to Amlakit (2000m) via Elevit, Tirovit and Palovit, arriving at 11am and returning at 3pm. At other times, you will likely have to walk or take a taxi from Çamlıhemşin (Şenyuva ₺15, Çat ₺60).

The road currently ends in Amlakit, but improvements to the route between there and Sal will eventually make it possible to drive a one-way loop from Şenyuva, returning to the village along a ridge at 2000m. This will be feasible in summer, by both dolmuş and hire car.

AYDER
📞0464

The tourism hub of the Kaçkars, this high-pasture village revels amid a valley perched at 1300m. Snowy slopes slide towards Ayder's rooftops between woodland in various shades of green, and waterfalls cascade to the river below. Charming alpine-chalet structures dot the steep hillside; new buildings must be in traditional style (ie sheathed in wood). Sadly, aesthetics aren't everything and Ayder's proliferation of pensions has made it more like a ski resort than a village. Çamlıhemşin and the Fırtına Valley have more authenticity and character, but Ayder is worth visiting for an accessible taste of glorious Kaçkars scenery.

Ayder is firmly on the domestic holiday circuit, and becoming increasingly popular with walking groups from Western countries (especially Israel). Consequently, its budget-travel ethos is creeping upmarket, resulting in a better standard of accommodation but also slightly higher prices.

The village is still really only busy during the trekking season (mid-May to mid-September); at other times there may only be a few local families living here. During the **Çamlıhemşin Ayder Festival** (second week of June) accommodation can be almost impossible to secure, and over weekends in July and August, Turkish tourists fill most pensions by mid-afternoon.

The nominal village centre has restaurants, food shops, an internet cafe, dolmuş and taxi stand, and several gift shops. Accommodation and eateries are scattered for about 1km along the road either side of the centre.

About 4.5km below Ayder, you will pass through the entrance gate to the **Kaçkar Dağları Milli Parkı** (Kaçkar Mountains National Park; ₺10 per vehicle).

🏃 Activities

Kaplıca SPA
(Hot Springs; ☑657 2102; www.ayderkaplicalari.com; admission ₺10, private bath ₺25; ⊙7.30am-7pm) Below Ayder Sofrası restaurant, post-trek muscle relief is offered in marble environs at

Ayder's spotless *kaplıca* (spa), where water temperatures reach 56°C.

🛏 Sleeping

Many pensions perch halfway up the hill above the road. Getting up to them can be tricky when the mist rolls in. Often your bags will be dragged up the hill on nifty winch arrangements. Many businesses close from roughly October to April.

TOP CHOICE Kuşpuni Dağ Evi PENSION ₺₺
(☑657 2052; www.ayderkuspuniotel.com; per person ₺55, half-board ₺75; 🖱) This appealing family-run chalet-pension has a stove-heated lounge with decent views, and quaint rooms with traditional cupboard bathrooms and low slanted ceilings. Visitors rave about the food, often served on the pleasant terrace overlooking the valley.

Fora Pansiyon PENSION ₺₺
(☑657 2153; www.forapansiyon.com; half-board per person without bathroom ₺70) This hillside pension provides a cosy sitting room, pine-clad bedrooms with shared bathrooms, balconies and a laundry. Owner Mehmet Demirci also runs Ekodanitap (p528) near Çamlıhemşinin – but he and his welcoming family spend more time here at Fora in season. Dinner on the view-laden terrace with the kids shouldn't be missed.

Zirve Ahşap Pansiyon PENSION ₺
(☑657 2177; mirayzirve@hotmail.com; per person ₺35; 🖱) Above Çağdaş internet cafe at the lower entrance to Ayder, this solid budget option has two floors of spick-and-span rooms, some with bathroom and some without. Views are lacking but the old chairs in reception are great for chatting to friendly owner Sinem.

Otel Haşimoğlu HOTEL ₺₺
(☑657 2037; www.hasimogluotel.com; s/d ₺50 /100; 🖱) The flash pine-clad Haşimoğlu is 100m downhill from the centre. With facilities including a fitness centre and spa,

HEMŞIN CULTURE

If you visit the Ayder area over a summer weekend you may get the chance to see some of the last surviving Hemşin culture. In village meadows, groups of Hemşin holidaymakers often gather to dance the *horon*, a cross between the conga and the hokey-cokey set to the distinctive whining skirl of the *tulum*, a type of goatskin bagpipe. Even if you don't witness one of these parties, you'll see women all around the mountains wearing splendid headdresses, often incongruously matched with cardigans, long skirts and running shoes or woollen boots. Many Hemşin émigrés return from overseas for the Çamlıhemşin Ayder Festival. For more information on Hemşin people, see p641.

you're losing the personal, family touch offered by smaller places, but these are Ayder's most comfortable digs. There's a riverside terrace and rooms have minibar and small terrace.

✖ Eating & Drinking

Most people opt for half-board accommodation at their pensions.

Yılmaz Cafeterya
ANATOLIAN €

(mains ₺10, snacks ₺5) Run by the welcoming Yılmaz family – Kamil shouts choices at you like *çorba* and *pilau*, before whisking you towards a hearty meal whipped up by his wife and daughters – this cafe offers chicken and fish dishes, plus local specialities like *muhlama*. The covered terrace has views down the main drag.

Zümrut Café
CAFE

Sip a çay or Turkish coffee and enjoy the view from the back terrace of romantic cataracts. In season, fish dishes, various kebaps, *muhlama*, and sweet nibbles including *laz böreği* (a creamy custard and pastry treat) are on offer.

❶ Getting There & Away

In summer, there are frequent dolmuşes to/from Pazar and Ardeşen (₺10) via Çamlıhemşin (₺5). Services are scarcer in winter, when passengers are mostly shoppers from the mountain villages, so dolmuşes descend from Ayder in the morning and return in the afternoon. A taxi from Çamlıhemşin to Ayder costs about ₺30.

On summer mornings, dolmuşes run into the mountains. Check with locals for exact schedules, but services generally run to Yukarı Kavron (₺10, one hour) every two hours, returning hourly between 2pm and 5pm; and to Avusor at 9am, returning at 3pm.

Southern Kaçkars

YUSUFELİ
♪ 0466 / POP 7000 / ELEV 560M

This likeable riverside town and part of the nearby valley are, sadly, slated to vanish underwater. The Yusufeli dam project, part of Turkey's national plan to expand its use of hydropower and achieve greater energy independence, is under way, despite local and international resistance. Nobody knows exactly when the flooding is going to happen, which makes matters even more uncertain and painful for residents. They will be relocated higher in the mountains, and Turkish officials have guaranteed that no church will be submerged.

For now, the amicable country town is the gateway to the southern Kaçkars and a good base for the Georgian Valleys. The Çoruh River and its tributaries offer magical white-water experiences for both first-time runners and seasoned enthusiasts.

⌕ Sleeping

The following are all by the Barhal River. To reach Barcelona and Greenpiece, cross either of the bridges, turn right and follow the river for about 700m.

TOP CHOICE Otel Almatur
HOTEL €€

(♪ 811 4056; www.almatur.com.tr; s/d ₺75/125; ☞) This newcomer's rooms have curvy lines, flat-screen TVs, fridges, big beds with white linen, and floor-to-ceiling windows with sweeping views, particularly from the 4th-floor corner suite. The bathrooms, however, are small. The 5th-floor restaurant's tinted windows have more stunning views and dishes include İskender kebap, *köfte* and meze. Next to the road bridge, the hotel also has a sauna.

Otel Barcelona
HOTEL €€

(♪ 811 2627; info@hotelbarcelona.com.tr; Arıklı Mahallesi; s/d €55/75, bungalow s/d €45/65; ℙ✷☞☲) Owned by a Turkish-Spanish (well, Catalan) couple, Barcelona is a restful retreat, with a bar-restaurant, hamam and fitness centre. Renovated in 2012, the smart rooms have black-and-white tiled floors, stylish furniture and flat-screen TVs; the bungalows (well, wooden cabins) are relatively simple affairs. The owners are clued up on the area and English is spoken.

Greenpiece Camping & Pansiyon
PENSION €

(♪ 811 3620; www.birolrafting.com; Arıklı Mahallesi; campsite per person ₺10, s/d ₺35/50; ℙ@☞) Birol Alkan and his twin daughters run this laid-back pension in a peaceful spot. There's a camping area with an ablutions block/bathroom facilities, and there are rooms in three blocks, including a traditional wooden, chalet-style unit. The rooms above the pleasant riverside bar benefit from views of the gurgling Barhal. Rafting trips can be organised here. Breakfast is available for ₺10.

Hotel Baraka
HOTEL €

(♪ 0538 604 1775; s/d/tr ₺30/40/50; ☞) The former Barhal Hotel is a good budget option, with a central location next to the suspension footbridge, and some rooms enjoying river views. Rooms are clean, although paint flakes from the walls. Bathrooms are small and frugal but functional. Get up before the other guests to ensure a hot shower. The annexe across the street is less comfortable. No breakfast.

BETWEEN YUSUFELİ & BARHAL

The following are on the road to Barhal, right by the Barhal River, and easily accessible by minibus from Yusufeli (₺5).

Otel River
GUEST HOUSE €€

(☎824 4345; riverotel@yahoo.com.tr; Sarıgöl Yolu; s/d incl half-board ₺60/100; ❄) Reached over a wooden bridge, this friendly family-run pension is about 12km north of Yusufeli. The pine-clad rooms are small and basic but country-quaint, with TV, well-sprung mattresses, tiled bathrooms and air-con (hence the high prices). Rooms 101 to 105 open onto a riverside terrace. Fresh trout is served on dinky platforms among the greenery.

İhtiyaroğlu
GUEST HOUSE €€

(☎824 4086; www.apartagara.com; Sarıgöl Yolu; campsites per person ₺10, s/d ₺50/100; ☎) About 2km from Otel River en route to Sarıgöl and the mountains, a steep windy dirt road descends 500m to this place of easy bliss. Chalet-like buildings have 20 impeccable, piny rooms and you can camp on the grass. Barbecued trout (₺10) with crispy, seasoned skin can be enjoyed in riverside gazebos.

✖ Eating

Köşk Cafe & Restaurant
TURKISH €

(mains ₺7-10) Clad in more pine than a Swedish sauna, this jolly venture above the tourist office has a good view of Yusufeli boulevardiers sauntering down the main drag. It's good for a simple breakfast, fish and chicken dishes, burgers, tost (toasted sandwich) and rice pudding.

Çardak Döner Restaurant
ANATOLIAN €

(mains ₺7.50; ☺breakfast & lunch) It's a family affair: Ramazan works the döner spit while wife Sevgi and daughters rustle up fresh, organic, traditional daily specials. Choose between goodies such as kahvaltı (breakfast), hazır yemek (ready-made food) and homemade baklava before retiring to the beautiful çardak (balcony). It's next to the suspension footbridge.

Barhal Restaurant
TURKISH €

(mains ₺8) By the suspension footbridge, Barhal is popular for its saç kavurma (stir-fried cubed meat dishes) and riverside bal-

cony. Proprietor Mehmet also dishes up şiş kebaps (roast skewered meat), köfte (meatball) and chicken dishes.

❶ Information

Yusufeli has internet cafes, banks with ATMs, a post office, petrol station and **tourist office** (☺8am-9.30pm May-Oct, 8am-5.30pm Mon-Fri Nov-Apr).

❶ Getting There & Away

Yusufeli's central otogar is near the tourist office.

There are morning buses to Artvin (₺15), Erzurum (₺20, three hours) and the Black Sea coast. You can also take a dolmuş (₺4) or taxi (₺25) to the petrol station on the Artvin–Erzurum road and catch passing buses, including the Kars bus, which passes at about 1pm (₺30).

To/from Barhal (₺15), Yaylalar (₺20) and Olgunlar (₺25), a few dolmuşes descend to Yusufeli between about 5.30am and 7am, returning between 2pm and 5pm. Yaylalar is officially the end of the line, but it should be possible to persuade the driver to continue to Olgunlar. Outside those times, you will likely have to hire a taxi (₺100 between Barhal and Yusufeli or Yaylalar).

Driving into the Kaçkars, the road is surfaced from Yusufeli to Sarıgöl (about 18km). Continuing to Barhal (about 10km), about 60% is surfaced; thereafter, the road is unsurfaced. If it's dry, the winding, narrow road can be braved by confident drivers, in an ordinary car with good clearance (and without sentimental value), all the way up to Olgunlar. Allow plenty of time, seek local advice before setting off, and beware rockfalls and landslides in wet weather and when the snow is melting; springtime is risky. The road is particularly rocky above Yaylalar.

TEKKALE & DÖRTKİLİSE

%0466 / POP 2500

Peaceful Tekkale lies 7km southwest of Yusufeli. On the way there you'll pass a ruined 10th-century Georgian **castle** almost hanging above the road. Turn right in Tekkale and follow the lane 7km northwest to **Dörtkilise** (Four Churches), a ruined 9th-century Georgian monastery complex on a hillside. The building is domeless, with a gabled roof and very few frescoes. Similar to the smaller Barhal church, it's a perfect picturesque ruin, with weeds and vines springing from mossy stones. With a guide, you can walk one hour to a **chapel** where monks from the complex kept guard.

The term 'cheap and cheerful' could have been invented for **Cemil's Pension** (☎811 2908, 0536 988 5829; cemil_pansion@hotmail.com; half-board per person ₺60, students ₺50, campsite per person ₺10). The ageing pension has basic rooms and multiple corners for snoozing on the upstairs balcony, which surveys the fields. Photos of happy travellers decorate the walls and the river gurgles beyond the ramshackle benches, hammock and tree houses. Cemil makes traditional meals using produce from the surrounding fields, vines and river, plus there's rafting, trekking and visits to his mountain house. There's also a kitchen for guest use and a bar.

A few dolmuşes run from Yusufeli to Tekkale (₺3) between 12.30pm and 4pm. Pick services up at Yusufeli otogar or the far side of the road bridge. A taxi to Tekkale costs about ₺25; ₺65 return to Dörtkilise (including waiting time). Work traffic heads towards dams being built beyond Tekkale, so hitching is possible. From Tekkale, you can hike to Dörtkilise; look out for the church high up amid the vegetation on the left of the road. The road is mostly surfaced but narrow and slightly rough from Tekkale; take care driving in wet weather.

BARHAL (ALTIPARMAK)
🖉0466 / POP 1500 / ELEV 1300M

About 27km northwest of Yusufeli, Barhal is an alluring base for forays into the Kaçkars. The *köy* (village) nestles in a verdant valley, with a rippling stream running through its heart, a beautiful mountainscape and inviting pensions, which offer trekking guides and advice on day walks and longer expeditions. Another pull is the well-preserved, 10th-century **Georgian church** next to Karahan Pension. For views over the village and the jagged peaks beyond, you can walk up to two small ruined **chapels** across the valley from the church, from where the upper chapel is visible on a ridge. The walk (unsigned, 90 minutes return) starts over a plank footbridge near the bottom of Karahan Pension's drive.

🛏 Sleeping & Eating

There are food shops for assembling a picnic.

TOP CHOICE **Karahan Pension**   GUEST HOUSE €
(🖉826 2071, 0538 351 5023; www.karahanpen sion.com; Altıparmak Köyü; s/d incl half-board ₺60/110) Run by Mehmet and son Bekir (who speaks some English), cosy Karahan has an adorable hillside setting 1km above the village and a terrace with sofas perfect for unwinding. Rooms are appealing despite bare floorboards; 114 and 115 have views down the valley (a new suite will

have unbeatable vistas). Enjoy homemade honey and authentic cuisine on the covered terrace.

Barhal Pansiyon   GUEST HOUSE €€
(🖉0535 264 6765; per person ₺50, incl half-board ₺70, dm incl half-board ₺30; 🖲) The first place you'll pass on the road through the village, Barhal Pansiyon has 15 modern rooms, including wooden bungalows and, in the main building, simpler budget accommodation with shared facilities. It's good for hikers, with a Kaçkars map for sale, local expertise on hand and a pleasant dining room and garden for planning. No views to speak of, but dinners feature multiple dishes.

Marsis Village House   GUEST HOUSE €
(🖉826 2002; www.marsisotel.com; incl half-board per person ₺50, without bathroom ₺40) Up steps next to Barhal Pansiyon, just back from the river, Marsis feels like a cosy doll's house, with great views from its light-filled dining room and front terrace. Opening off the latter, rooms 106 and 107 are good for solo travellers, featuring the best views (and shared bathrooms). It's a friendly family operation and wholesome dinners get good reviews.

YAYLALAR (HEVEK)
🖉0466 / POP 700

It's a bumpy ride up to Yaylalar, 22km from Barhal, but you'll be rewarded with an uberbucolic setting – expect plenty of traditional farmhouses and scenic *yaylalar* (mountain pastures) all around. Particularly off season, the village is livelier than Olgunlar; you may well agree with the sign proclaiming Yaylalar 'heaven on earth'.

The best place to stay in both Yaylalar and Olgunlar, and the most reliably open year-round, **Çamyuva Pension** (🖉0534 361 6959, 832 2001; www.kackar3937.com; r incl half-board per person ₺80; 🖲) resembles a big Swiss chalet, with comfortable rooms and balconies for watching the village go by. Alongside the well-stocked food shop and bakery (owned by Çamyuva proprietors İsmail and Naim, who also drive the dolmuşes to/from Yusufeli) are wooden cabins with porches and the stream gurgling underneath – soothing in summer, chilly in winter. Dinner and breakfast are hearty affairs, satisfying appetites built up in the mountain air.

OLGUNLAR
🖉0466 / POP 50

About 3km further up from Yaylalar on a scenic white-knuckle road, the quiet hamlet of Olgunlar really feels like the end of the line. Standing in splendid isolation, it's a bucolic spot with bags of natural panache: soaring peaks, soul-stirring vistas, babbling brooks and some of Turkey's purest air.

🛏 Sleeping & Eating

A top choice for walkers, **Kaçkar Pansiyon** (📞0538 306 4564, 832 2047; www.kackar.net; s/d incl half-board €40/60; 🛜) is a haven of peace complete with pine cladding. It features super-clean rooms, a kitchen for guests' use, comfy sitting area and delectable meals. Bag a room overlooking the stream. Friendly owner Ismail speaks some English.

Denizgölü Pansiyon (📞832 2105; r incl half-board per person ₺65) and **Olgunlar Pansiyon** (📞832 2159; r incl half-board per person ₺45) offer more basic accommodation, geared towards hardy trekkers.

There's a small cafe at the end of the hamlet where the walking trail starts, open from roughly June until September/October. It serves dishes like *menemen* (scrambled eggs with tomatoes and peppers) and *muhlama*, and sells basic foodstuffs.

FAR NORTHEAST

Georgian Valleys

The spectacular, mountainous country southeast of Yusufeli is a culturally peculiar area. It was once part of the medieval kingdom of Georgia, with numerous churches and castles to show for it – seldom-visited buildings, mixing characteristics of Armenian, Seljuk and Persian styles. The villages in the mountains and valleys are a delight to explore, and their cherry and apricot orchards bear fruit around mid-June.

Tony Anderson's *Bread and Ashes: A Walk Through the Mountains of Georgia* has a chapter on this corner of Turkey.

Georgian Valleys & Around

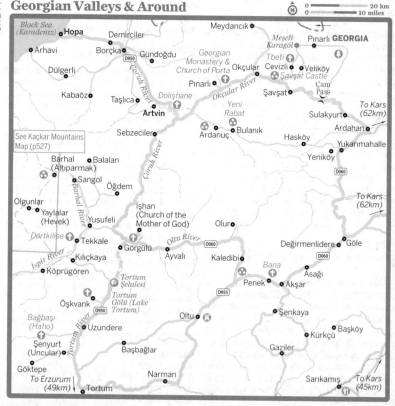

History

The Persians and Byzantines squabbled over this region from the 4th century AD. It was conquered by the Arabs in the 7th century, recovered by the Byzantines, lost again and so on. The region was part of the medieval Georgian kingdom in the 10th century, governed by the Bagratids, from the same lineage as the Armenian Bagratids ruling over the Kars region. The isolation brought about by the rugged terrain, piety and support of Byzantium fostered a flourishing culture that produced the churches.

In 1008, ambitious King Bagrat III looked outside the sheltered valleys and unified Georgia's warring kingdoms. Bagrat shifted the focus of the newly formed kingdom by moving the capital from Tbilisi, nominally under Arab control, to Kutaisi; and by gradually disengaging from the southwest valleys that had been under the sway of the Byzantines since 1001.

The Byzantines and Georgians coexisted relatively harmoniously, but the Seljuk Turks' arrival in 1064 destabilised the area until 1122, when King David IV ('The Builder'; 1089–1125) defeated the Seljuks. David took up where Bagrat had left off, by reunifying Georgia with Tbilisi and the southwest provinces. So began the 'golden age' for Georgian culture, which peaked during Queen Tamar's reign (1184–1213).

Following the Mongol conqueror Tamerlane's arrival in 1386, the Ottoman capture of Constantinople (1453) ended the protection the Georgians had enjoyed under quasi-Byzantine rule. The kingdom went into decline, the Ottomans annexed the Georgian Valleys and, later, imperial Russia took care of the rest. Today, many locals have Georgian heritage.

ⓘ Getting There & Away

Hiring a car in Erzurum is the easiest way to see the valleys. Public transport mostly consists of minibuses that head from the villages to Yusufeli in the morning, returning in the afternoon. It's possible to catch an afternoon minibus to a village such as İşhan, then walk back down to the main road and pick up a passing bus to Yusufeli. if you're catching an Erzurum-bound bus from Yusufeli, you will have to walk/hitch to sights off the main road. Hiring a taxi in Yusufeli costs about ₺85 to İşhan return (including waiting time) or ₺250 for a day.

The following itinerary starts from Yusufeli.

İŞHAN

From Yusufeli, drive to the petrol station on the Artvin–Erzurum road (9km), turn right and follow the brown 'İşhan Kilisesi' signposts for 21km. İşhan upper village is spectacularly situated, 7km up a steep, narrow road carved out of the mountainside. Drive very slowly in wet weather, when the road gets slippery.

Located below İşhan's modern white mosque, the wonderful, 7th-century **Church of the Mother of God** was enlarged in the 12th century. There are traces of blue frescoes (25 years ago whole walls were covered in them) in the near-conical dome, and a superb arcade of horseshoe-shaped arches in the apse, all with different capitals. The four pillars are impressive, as in Öşkvank. Unfortunately, a huge dividing wall was built in the nave; half of the church functioned as a mosque until the replacement mosque was built.

The most detailed of the many fine external reliefs – above the portal of the small neighbouring chapel – ascribes the founding of the church to King Bagrat III. Also worth admiring are the inscriptions above the main building's bricked-up portal and an elaborate fretwork around its windows. The drum also sports some fine blind arcades and elegantly carved colonnades.

TORTUM GÖLÜ & TORTUM ŞELALESİ

Backtrack to the Artvin–Erzurum road and turn left (south). After about 15km, you'll reach the impressive **Tortum Şelalesi** (Tortum Waterfalls), signposted 700m off the main road and overlooked by a tea garden.

Continuing south, Hwy 950 skirts the western shore of **Tortum Gölü** (Lake Tortum), which was formed by landslides about three centuries ago. Various cafes overlook the 8km-long lake. **İskele Et & Balık Lokantası** (✆0535 366 9052; www.tortumgolu .com; fish dishes ₺7.50), about 4km south of the falls, is slightly scruffy but has a great location on a promontory on the lake. Canoes are available (₺10 for 30 minutes) and camping is possible (₺10).

ÖŞKVANK

Continuing 8km south of Tortum Gölü and Tortum Şelalesİ, turn off at the brown 'Öşkvank Kilesesi' sign. Keep on the main road winding up the valley to the village, where the impressive late-10th-century **cathedral** is the grandest of the region's Georgian cathedrals, its three-aisled basilica topped by a dome. Keep an eye out for the blind arcades and the reliefs of archangels.

The interior is jaw-dropping. The central nave has two walled-off aisles on either side. The southwest aisle, like the triple-arched narthex, is still in relatively good shape; note the intricate carvings on the capitals, with elaborate geometric designs, typical of Georgian church decoration. There are other fine relief carvings, both on the massive capitals that supported the equally majestic dome and on the exterior walls. Look for the fine relief of the Three Wise Men, to the right (northeast) of the main entrance.

Much of the roof has fallen in, but there are still well-preserved fragments of frescoes; look in the half-dome on the inside of the main porched portal.

BAĞBAŞI

Continue south along Hwy 950 past Uzundere, where a castle perches dramatically on a rocky outcrop. About 15km south of the Öşkvank turn-off is another turn-off, over a humpbacked bridge, to Bağbaşı village (called Haho by the Georgians). Go about 4km up the asphalted road through orchards and fields to the village, then bear right at the 'Taş Camii Meryem Ani Kilisesi' sign. After 3km, the late-10th-century **monastery** is on the right. Don't miss the conical-topped dome with multicoloured tiles, or the fine reliefs, including stone eagles grasping does in their claws. The alternating light and dark stones add to the building's elegance. It is used as a mosque, so some restoration has taken place.

OLTU

Continuing south from Bağbaşı on Hwy 950, turn onto the Oltu road, which climbs over 2300m. A startling restored **kalesi** (citadel), thought to have been built by Urartus in 1000 BC, dominates the peaceful town. The castle was probably used by Genoese colonies and was of some importance during the Roman and Byzantine periods, before being occupied by the Seljuks and then the Ottomans in the 16th century. At the far end of town is an attractive **church**.

BANA & PENEK

A further 18km northeast of Oltu, along the D955, brings you to a junction with the D060. Turning left, after about 4km you'll see a **castle** on the right at the end of a ridge. It's an eerie sight, in keeping with

the surreal landscape, where craggy gorges alternate with reddish bluffs. About 400m further on you'll see a second crumbling clifftop **castle** on the right, overlooking a poplar-lined river from a rocky outcrop.

Backtrack to the junction with Hwy 955 and turn left onto the D060. A further 14.2km leads you over a bridge crossing the Penek Çayı (signposted). About 100m past the bridge, take the side track on the left. It goes uphill for 2km to **Penek**. Continue through the village and the awesome Armenian **church of Bana** soon comes into view, perching on a hill with the mountains forming a fantastic backdrop. Its most distinctive architectural feature is its rotunda shape. You can approach the church by following a dirt road that branches off to the left about 600m after leaving the village (*don't* brave it in wet weather with an ordinary car).

Artvin

📞 0466 / POP 25,234 / ELEV 600M

Artvin's main claim to fame is its spectacular mountain setting – its vertiginous streets zigzag crazily up a steep hill. Sadly, kilometres of dam and road works have scarred the valley below. The main reasons to pass through are the region's beauteous *yaylalar* and the **Kafkasör Kültür ve Sanat Festivalı** (Caucasus Culture & Arts Festival; ⊙late June/early July). Held in the Kafkasör Yaylası pasture, 7km southwest of town, the festival features *boğa güreşleri* (bloodless bull-wrestling matches). The bulls, classified by the thickness of their necks and matched accordingly, lock horns in Turkey's only bullfighting ring. Weakened bulls are regarded as defeated, and withdrawn from combat.

Tourist information is available in the stilted cabin across the road from the otogar, and at the **tourist office** (Ministry of Culture & Tourism; 📞212 3071; www.artvinkultur turizm.gov.tr; ⊙8am-5pm Mon-Fri), where English is spoken and brochures and maps are available. It's in a 19th-century Russian military building, up the steep steps next to Vakıf Bank.

🛏 Sleeping & Eating

Most hotels are within a block of the *valiliği* (provincial government building). For cheap fare, stroll along İnönü Caddesi and size up the small eateries and pastry shops.

A MAGICAL TRIP IN THE BACKCOUNTRY

In spring and summer, the area northeast of Artvin is simply stunning: a bucolic tapestry of lakes, rivers, canyons, mountains, forests, *yaylalar* and traditional wooden houses, with the added appeal of a Caucasian flavour, courtesy of its proximity to Georgia. Among the off-the-beaten-track villages and towns, several churches and castles stand in delightful settings.

A DIY approach with your own wheels is preferable, as public transport is infrequent. Artvin tourist office gives out maps of the area. Seek local advice before attempting secondary roads, which may be in bad shape.

About 11km east of Artvin on the D010, a signposted turn-off ('Dolişhane Kilisesi 3km') climbs to the beautiful 10th-century **Dolişhane church**, with a few reliefs. Back on the D010, signs 3km further on point right along the scenic Ardanuç road to **Ferhatlı castle** (look up on your right after 3km; it's perched on a rocky outcrop) and, a few kilometres further southeast, to **Gevernik castle** ('Adakale') and **Ardanuç**, set in a dramatic canyon guarded by an impregnable fortress. About 17km past Ardanuç, near Bulanık village, is the harder-to-reach **church of Yeni Rabat**. Seek advice at Ardanuç before driving any further, as some sections of the road may have deteriorated.

Back on the D010, 12.5km northeast of the Ardanuç turn-off, a brown sign on the left points 2km up to the 10th-century **Georgian Monastery & Church of Porta**. About 17km further northeast on the D010, a tarred road leads north to **Meydancık**, a quintessential *yaylalar* settlement near the Georgian border.

About 4km west of Şavşat, the roadside **Saray Motel & Restaurant** (☑0466-517 2947; D010, Köprüyaka Köyü; per person ₺50) has whitewashed rooms with lilac bedspreads above a gloomy restaurant. In the lower section of **Şavşat**, an old Georgian town, a fairytale **castle** stands sentinel. Just past the castle, a brown sign points left 27km to Karagöl Sahara National Park. Cross the bridge, turn right at the T-junction and follow the winding tarred road. After 7km, a brown 'Cevisli Kilesesi' sign on the left points 4km to the ruined 10th-century **Tbeti church**, standing in an idyllic *yaylalar* village. Look for the elaborately carved windows. **Karagöl Sahara National Park** (☑0466-517 1156; www.savsatkaragol. com; car ₺7) encompasses spectacular mountain scenery and the pine-fringed **Meşeli Karagöl**, where you can hire a rowboat (30 minutes ₺15). Overlooking the lake, the modern **Karagöl Pansiyon** (☑0466-531 2137; Meşeli Karagöl, Karagöl Sahara National Park; per person ₺75, incl half-board ₺100) has smart rooms, some with bunk beds.

Back in Şavşat, the D010 leaves the lush, wooded valleys behind and snakes steeply around numerous twists and turns over the Çam Pass (2640m) to **Ardahan**, a typical steppe town. Licensed **Laşet Tesisleri** (☑0466-571 2136; Şavşat-Ardahan Karayolu; mains ₺10), 10km from Şavşat, serves fish and kebaps in a beautiful riverside setting. It also has wooden chalets nearby.

Karahan Otel
HOTEL €€

(☑212 1800; www.artvinkarahan.com; İnönü Caddesi 16; s ₺50-70, d ₺80-100; ❄️🌐) In the town centre, the Karahan is a good deal if you ignore the grotty lift from the main drag (the entrance at the back is more appealing). Fridges, TVs and recently installed bathrooms feature in the comfortable rooms, and the helpful staff speak some English.

Koru Otel
HOTEL €€

(☑212 6565; koru_otel@mynet.com; 19 Mayıs Caddesi; per person ₺50; 🌐) Surveying the valley from its perch above the centre, the Grove Hotel has comfortable rooms with dysfunctional bathrooms. The restaurant is popular for muzak-soundtracked meat dishes, meze and rakı (aniseed brandy).

❶ Getting There & Away

The otogar lies about 500m downhill from the town centre, off a hairpin bend. *Servises* (shuttle buses) run to/from the bus company offices in the centre. Some buses don't go up to the otogar, but drop you by the road at the bottom of the hill.

There are hourly minibuses to local towns including Hopa (1½ hours), Yusufeli (2¼ hours) and Şavşat (1½ hours); all cost about ₺15.

Artvin Express serves Erzurum (₺30, five hours, 6am) and Trabzon (₺30, five hours, 7.30am).

For Ardahan (₺25) and Kars (₺35), catch a minibus to Şavşat and change, or go to the bridge at the D010 and pick up the Artvin Express buses, which pass in the morning.

Companies including Metro serve long-haul destinations.

Kars

📞 0474 / POP 76,928 / ELEV 1768M

With its stately, pastel-coloured stone buildings, dating from the Russian occupation, and its well-organised grid plan, Kars looks like a slice of Russia teleported to northeastern Anatolia. And the city's mix of influences – Azeri, Turkmen, Kurdish, Turkish and Russian – adds to its distinct feel. No wonder it provided the setting for Orhan Pamuk's acclaimed novel *Kar (Snow)*.

Kars is usually regarded as a base for Ani, but it's worth spending a day exploring its sights, soaking up the eclectic vibe, and sampling the delicious local *bal* (honey) and *peynir* (cheese). It also makes a convenient base for exploring remote villages and sights in the surrounding steppe.

History

Dominated by a stark medieval fortress, Kars was once an Armenian stronghold, capital of the Armenian Bagratid kingdom (before Ani) and later a pawn in the imperial land-grabbing tussle played out by Turkey and Russia during the 19th century. The Russians captured Kars in 1878, installed a garrison and held it until 1920 and the Turkish War of Independence, when the republican forces retook it. Many of the sturdier stone buildings along the main streets date back to the Russian occupation.

The locals are said to be descended from the Karsaks, a Turkic tribe that came from the Caucasus in the 2nd century BC and gave their name to the town.

◉ Sights & Activities

FREE **Russian Monuments** HISTORIC BUILDINGS

As you walk around town, you will see a gobsmacking collection of Russian belle époque mansions and Baltic architecture sprinkled around the city centre. Many have been restored and turned into administrative offices. On Ordu Caddesi are the **Health Directorate Building** (1907), with columns and floral motifs; the yellow-and-white **Old Governor's Mansion** (1883), where the

Treaty of Kars was signed in 1921; and the **Gazi Kars Anatolian High School**, occupying a late-19th-century winter mansion. The **Fethiye Camii**, a converted 19th-century Russian Orthodox church, stands majestically south of the centre.

FREE **Kars Museum** MUSEUM

(Kars Müzesi; Cumhuriyet Caddesi; ⊗8am-5pm) Northeast of the centre en route to Ani, the city museum has exhibits from the Old Bronze Age, the Urartian, Roman and Greek periods, and the Seljuk and Ottoman eras. Photographs show excavations at Ani and Kars province's ruined Armenian churches, as well as the Neolithic cave paintings at Camuslu, south of Kars between Keçivan and Çengilli.

FREE **Kars Culture & Art Association** MUSEUM

(Kars Kültür Sanat Derneği; Bakırcılar Cad 39; admission free; ⊗8am-5pm Mon-Sat) Local historian Vedat's paint shop doubles as a small library and a museum about the Molokans ('milk-drinkers' in Russian) order, to which his grandmother belonged. The peaceful Christian group disagreed with the Russian Orthodox Church and came to Kars during the Russian occupation. Last century, rather than fight for the Ottomans, they scattered to the former USSR, USA and Canada.

Balyolu HIKING

(www.balyolu.com) For a sweet, lingering look at the surrounding steppe, hit the 'honey road' with the Kars- and USA-based Balyolu. The operator's one-week honey-tasting walking tours include mountain hikes and visits to remote rural communities.

🛏 Sleeping

TOP CHOICE **Güngören Otel** HOTEL €€

(📞212 6767; www.gungorenhotel.com; Millet Sokak; s/d/tr ₺70/120/150; 🛜) Renovated in 2012, the Güngören is a stalwart on the travelling circuit, with new faces checking in daily and poring over maps in the lobby. A lift climbs to smart, creamy rooms with flat-screen TV, fridge and tiled bathroom. The friendly staff speak some English, the location on a quiet street is convenient, there's a restaurant and the copious breakfast features local cheese and honey.

KARS CASTLE WALK

North of the river in the older part of the city, **Kars Castle** (Kars Kalesi; admission free) is worth the knee-jarring climb, with smashing views over the town and the steppe in fine weather.

On the way to the castle, along the riverbanks huddle assorted reminders of Kars' history, notably the imposing, basalt **Kümbet Camii**. Built between 932 and 937 for the Bagratid King Abas, it was called the Apostles' Church; reliefs representing the 12 Apostles and Maltese Crosses remain on the exterior. It was converted to a mosque in 1064, when the Seljuks conquered Kars, then used as a church again in the late 19th century by the Russians, who added the porches.

Beyond the Kümbet Camii is the 17th-century **Ulu Cami**, Kars' largest Ottoman mosque, and, behind the school, the **Beylerbeyi Sarayı** (Beylerbeyi Palace) nestling beneath the castle.

Records show that Saltuk Turks built a *kale* (fortress) here in 1153. It was demolished by the Mongol conqueror Tamerlane in 1386 and rebuilt several times over the following centuries. The *kale* was the scene of bitter fighting during and after WWI. When the Russian armies withdrew in 1920, control of Kars was left in the hands of the Armenian forces, until the republican armies took the castle. Inside are a Janissary barracks, arsenal, *mescit* and tomb.

One of the more attractive – and intact – structures in the older part of the city is the 16th-century basalt bridge, **Taş Köprü**. Destroyed by a flood and rebuilt by the Ottomans in 1719, the bridge is flanked by the ruined Ottoman **Muradiye Hamam** and **Cuma Hamam**. The basalt, rectangular 18th-century **Mazlum Ağa Hamam** is just before the bridge back to central Kars and leafy riverside tea garden **İstihkam Çay Bahçesi** (Atatürk Caddesi).

Grand Ani Hotel HOTEL €€€
(☎223 7500; www.grandani.com.tr; Ordu Caddesi; s/d/tr/ste €80/100/120/150; ⓟ❄ⓢⓦ) The Grand Ani's impressive facilities include an indoor pool, sauna, hamam, fitness centre, licensed **restaurant** (mains ₺15, meze ₺5), lobby bar, subterranean parking and even a barber. Book ahead to beat the foreign groups and Turkish businessmen to a comfortable room with shiny-clean bathroom, flat-screen TV, huge bed and professional service.

Kar's Otel BOUTIQUE HOTEL €€€
(☎212 1616; www.karsotel.com; Halit Paşa Caddesi; s/d €99/139; ❄ⓦ) With just eight rooms, this boutique hotel – a rarity in northeastern Anatolia – housed in a 19th-century Russian mansion feels like a luxurious cocoon. The rooms are suitably comfortable, though some might find the white colour scheme rather too clinical. With its contemporary furnishings and mood lighting, the licensed Italian restaurant is ideal for romantic meals, and offers some diversity to kebap-jaded palates.

Miraç Otel HOTEL €
(☎212 3768; Cengiz Topel Caddesi 19; s/d/tr ₺30/50/70; ⓦ) At the Ascension, next to Yapı Kredi bank, staircases with worn carpets lead ever upwards to small, simple rooms, which are reasonably clean with old TV and shower. Atop the tall, thin building, a spiral staircase climbs to the breakfast room for views of the hills beyond Kars. A good budget option for women.

Hotel Temel HOTEL €
(☎223 1376; fax 223 1323; Yenipazar Caddesi 9; s/d ₺40/70; ⓦ) Hotel Base offers neat rooms with immaculate sheets and a soothing blue-and-yellow colour scheme, but many of its wood-pannelled interiors are dated and gloomy. The breakfast also gets bad reviews. On the plus side, it's near the minibus terminal and has a lift and satellite TV. Nearby, **Hotel Temel 2's** (☎223 1376; Yenipazar Caddesi; s/d/tr ₺25/40/60; ⓦ) has rooms that are small and old but clean.

Eating

Kars is noted for its excellent honey, sold in several shops along Kazım Paşa Caddesi and Halit Paşa Caddesi towards the minibus terminal. They also sell the local *kaşar peyniri* (a mild yellow cheese), *kuruyemiş* (dried fruits) and other ingredients for a picnic on the steppe.

Kars

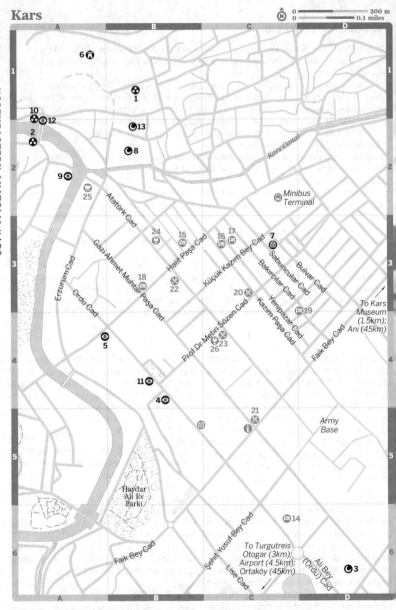

0   200 m
0   0.1 miles

Kars Canal

Minibus Terminal

Atatürk Cad

Erzurum Cad

Gazi Ahmet Muhtar Paşa Cad

Ordu Cad

Halit Paşa Cad

Küçük Kazım Bey Cad

Sabuncular Cad

Bakırcılar Cad

Bulvar Cad

Yenipazar Cad

Kazım Paşa Cad

Prof Dr Metin Sözen Cad

Faik Bey Cad

To Kars Museum (1.5km); Ani (45km)

Army Base

Haydar Ali Ev Parkı

Faik Bey Cad

Şehit Yusuf Bey Cad

Lise Cad

To Turgutreis Otogar (3km); Airport (4.5km); Ortaköy (45km)

Ali Bey (Ordu) Cad

If you want to splurge, the best of the licensed hotel restaurants is at the Grand Ani (p539). It specialises in Turkish classics, prepared to perfection and served in modern surrounds.

TOP CHOICE Ocakbaşı Restoran   TURKISH €€
(☏212 0056; www.kaygisizocakbasi.com; Atatürk Caddesi 276; mains ₺10-15; 🍴) This 40-year-old favourite serves unusual Turkish dishes, such as its house specialities *ali nazik* (aubergine purée with yoghurt and beef

Kars

tenderloin; ask for *et siz* for the vegetarian version) and *ejder kebap* (sesame bread stuffed with meat, cheese, parsley, nuts and eggs). Choose between white table-cloths in the modern dining room and decorative farm implements in the mock-troglodytic affair.

Ani Ocakbaşı   ANATOLIAN, KEBAP €€
(www.aniocakbasi.com; Kazım Paşa Caddesi 128; mains ₺10) This smart restaurant is held in high esteem locally, offering a wide menu, from salads and soups to *köfte* and local dishes. Save room for the *sütlaç* (rice pudding). You can't go wrong with the kebaps and grills, and *yöresel kahvaltı* (local breakfast, ₺15) is also available. The walls are embellished with photos of old Kars.

Döneristan Et Lokantası   TURKISH €
(Atatürk Caddesi 50; mains ₺6-10; 🖉) There's a lot to like about this clean, bright eatery, patronised at lunchtime by locals from office workers to cops. Choose between the *çorba* and *hazır yemek* in the bains-marie. The menu changes according to seasonal produce and whim, but the döner kebap is a perennial favourite.

Antik Cafe & Pastane   CAFE €
(Gazi Ahmet Muhtar Paşa Caddesi; mains ₺8-10) This modern, roomy cafe is a good place to recharge after walking round the centre. All manner of cakes, baklava, *sütlaç* (rice pudding), biscuits, pizza, snacks and a breakfast buffet are offered.

🍷 Drinking

Barış Türkü Cafe Pub   PUB, CAFE
(Atatürk Caddesi) Housed in a historic mansion, this atmosphere-laden cafe-bar-disco attracts students, with a happening buzz and live music most nights. Meze, backgammon and nargiles are available. Upstairs, it's all very relaxed and civilised; down in the groovy basement disco, you might see headscarved women tearing it up on the dance floor.

Soframız   JUICE BAR
(Prof Dr Metin Sözen Caddesi; 📶) Behind Doğuş Pastaneları (also popular for a snack), this white, modern spot has a *meyve suyu* (fruit juice) bar and Segafredo coffee machine. Get a vitamin boost from a *portakal* (orange), *elma* (apple), *havuç* (carrot) or *karışık* (mixed) juice or an Atom smoothie. Eats include *börek*, *tost*, burgers and pizza.

❶ Information

INTERNET ACCESS There are internet cafes around Ocakbaşı Restoran and along Faik Bey Caddesi.

MONEY Banks with ATMs are plentiful in Kars.

TOURIST INFORMATION The **tourist office** (🖉212 1705; cnr Faik Bey and Gazi Ahmet Muhtar Paşa Caddesis; ⊙8am-5pm Mon-Fri) has Kars and Ani maps and brochures.

❶ Getting There & Around

Without your own transport, the best way to see Ani and the countryside around Kars is with **Celil Ersoğlu** (🖉0532 226 3966; celilani@hotmail .com), who acts as a private driver (guiding is

ℹ GETTING TO GEORGIA

Traditionally, the most direct route from Kars to Georgia was a minibus to Ardahan (₺12), where you could hop on the bus from İstanbul to Tbilisi (₺50, 8½ hours, daily at 9am). It stopped in front of the office of the **Özlem Ardahan** (✆0478-211 3568; ozlemardahan.com .tr; Kongre Caddesi) bus company, in the centre, before continuing to the Türkgözü border crossing (2½ hours). **Koç Ardahan** (✆0478-211 3400; eticket.ipektr.com/firms_61/Default .aspx) also ran buses on this route. At the time of writing, however, buses on this route had been indefinitely cancelled. It's worth checking with both companies mentioned above to see if these have been reinstated (both have offices in Ardahan, and Koç Arda-han has an additional office in Kars).

If you get stuck in Ardahan, sleeping options include **Hotel Huzur** (✆0478-211 2838; Kongre Caddesi 119; s/d ₺40/70), with poky but clean rooms across the main road from the *otobüs terminali* (bus station); and across town in the direction of Kars, **Büyük Ardahan Oteli** (✆0478-211 6498; Kars Caddesi 102; s/d ₺50/80), which is slightly dirty but OK for a night.

You can also take a minibus to Posof (₺25), 17km southwest of Türkgözü. You will then have to take the driver to continue to the border or take a taxi (₺35). After crossing the bor-der (no hassles), take a taxi to Vale (7km) and a *marshrutka* (minibus) to Akhaltsikhe, the nearest substantial town, followed by a bus to Borjomi, where you can find accommodation.

A good route to western Georgia is via Hopa on the Black Sea coast. **Metro** runs from here to Tbilisi, via Batumi, early in the morning (see p519).

extra) and speaks good English. Hiring a taxi and a cooperative driver is another option.

Air

A *servis* (₺4) runs from travel agencies to the airport, leaving 1½ hours before departures. In the opposite direction, you'll have to take a taxi (₺15 to ₺18). **Kayadır Turizm** (✆223 7035; Atatürk Cad 122) sells tickets for Turkish airlines.

Anadolu Jet (www.anadolujet.com) Flies daily to/from Ankara.

Sun Express (www.sunexpress.com.tr) İstanbul daily; İzmir thrice weekly.

Turkish Airlines (www.thy.com) Ankara and İstanbul daily

Bus

Kars' **otogar**, for long-distance services, is 2km southeast of the centre. *Servises* ferry pas-sengers to/from the bus companies' city-centre offices, which are mostly on and around Faik Bey Caddesi. Major local companies include **Doğu Kars**, **Iğdırlı Turizm** (✆0476 227 2877; www.igdirliturizm.com.tr), and **Turgutreis** (cnr Faik Bey & Atatürk Caddesis), which ferries pas-sengers to its own otogar. **Metro** (www .metroturizm.com.t) has a daily service to Adana (₺70), Amasya (₺60), Erzurum (₺15), İstanbul (₺70), Kayseri (₺55) and Mersin (₺70).

Minibuses to local towns leave from the **mini-bus terminal** (Küçük Kazım Bey Caddesi). Des-tinations include Ardahan (₺12), Erzurum (₺15), Iğdır (₺15, for Doğubayazıt and Azerbaijan),

Posof (₺25, for Georgia) and Sarıkamış (₺7), most served hourly.

ARTVİN & THE BLACK SEA COAST Iğdırlı Turizm has a daily service to Samsun via Artvin (₺30), Hopa (₺35, for Georgia), Rize (₺40), Of (₺42.50) and Trabzon (₺45). Also leaving at 12.30pm, Aydoğan takes the less scenic route to Trabzon via Bayburt.

DOĞUBAYAZIT Take a minibus to Iğdır and change. Iğdırlı Turizm's daily direct service had been cancelled at the time of writing and was unlikely to restart.

VAN Turgutreis has a daily service at 8.30am (₺50).

YUSUFELİ Take a bus or minibus bound for Artvin or the Black Sea coast and ask to be dropped at the nearest junction, about 10km from Yusufeli on the Artvin–Erzurum road. Dolmuşes run from there to Yusufeli.

Car

Steer clear of the car companies in the centre. They claim they can rent vehicles, but we're told they don't provide proper insurance.

Train

The daily *Doğu Ekspresi* to Ankara (27¾ hours) via Erzurum, Sivas and Kayseri departs at 2.45pm.

North of Kars

Very few tourists even suspect **Çıldır Gölü** exists. It may be less talismanic than Lake

Van, but this loch-like expanse of water, about 60km north of Kars, is well worth a detour for complete peace and quiet. It's also an important breeding ground for various species of bird, best observed at Akçekale Island. Turn right at the petrol station in Doğruyol, the only significant town on the eastern shore, to see the mosque incorporating an ancient **Georgian church**.

A few kilometres past the town of Çıldır, on the northern shore east of Ardahan, a signpost on the right points 1km to Yıldırımtepe village. At the beginning of the village, take the left fork and follow the road around the top of Yıldırımtepe. When it ends, take the right-hand dirt track, park and walk along the hillside for about 700m. You will turn a corner and be rewarded with a spectacular view of **Şeytan Kalesi** (Devil's Castle), standing sentinel on a rocky bluff in the gorge. You can walk to the 6th-century Georgian castle in 45 minutes.

Driving, follow signs for Arpaçay from Kars.

South of Kars

At Ortaköy village, 45km south of Kars, a secondary road climbs 8km through an emerald-green valley, its sides flowing with mountain run-off in spring, to the clifftop village of **Keçivan**. The impressive remains of Keçivan's double-walled 9th-century castle straddle a ridge between two canyons.

About 25km further south of Ortaköy, 1km before the road crosses the Aras River and meets the Iğdır–Erzurum road, a brown sign opposite the petrol station points 24km to **Çengilli** *köyü kilisesi* (village church). Looming over the Kurdish mountain village is a dramatic medieval Georgian monastery, which has some superb carving and recalls the area's Armenian churhes. A few kilometres beyond the village is a *gölü* (lake) and the views over the Aras mountains are unforgettable.

The roads climbing to Çengilli and Keçivan are navigable in a normal car, but care should be taken and local advice sought. They may deteriorate in rainfall and are so steep (both villages are located at about 2000m) that car engines will likely burn out in summer. Hire-car insurance policies are unlikely to cover problems that arise on these minor roads.

Ani

The ruins of **Ani** (admission ₺8; ⊘8.30am-6pm May-Sep, to 3pm Oct-Apr), 45km east of Kars, are an absolute must-see, even if you're not an architecture buff. Your first view is stunning: wrecks of great stone buildings adrift on a sea of undulating grass, landmarks in a ghost city that was once the stately Armenian capital and home to nearly 100,000 people, rivalling Constantinople in power and glory. The poignant ruins, the windswept plateau overlooking the Turkish–Armenian border, and the total lack of crowds make for an eerie ambience that is unforgettable. In the silence broken only by the river gurgling along the border, ponder what went before: the thriving kingdom; the solemn ceremony of the Armenian liturgy; and the travellers, merchants and nobles bustling about their business in this Silk Road entrepôt.

History

On an important east–west trade route and well served by its natural defences, Ani was selected by the Bagratid king Ashot III (r 952–77) as the site of his new capital in 961, when he moved here from Kars. Ashot's successors Smbat II (r 977–89) and Gagik I (r 990–1020) presided over Ani's continued prosperity, but internecine feuds and Byzantine encroachment later weakened the Armenian state.

The Byzantines took over in 1045, then in 1064 came the Great Seljuks from Persia, followed by the Kingdom of Georgia and, for a time, local Kurdish *emirs*. The struggle for the city went on until the Mongols arrived in 1239 and decisively cleared everybody else out. The nomadic Mongols had no use for city life, however, so they cared little when the great earthquake of 1319 toppled much of Ani. The depredations of Tamerlane later that century hastened the decline; trade routes shifted, Ani lost what revenues it had managed to retain, and the city died. The earthquake-damaged hulks of its great buildings have been slowly crumbling away ever since.

◉ Sights

Ani is entered through Arslan Kapısı gate. Follow the path to the left and tour the churches in clockwise order. Not all the site is open to visitors; some parts are off limits. Allow at least 2½ hours here. There are toilets and a small shop at the gate, with a cafe

Ani

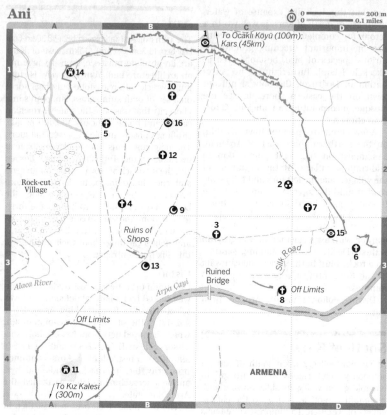

Ani

◉ Sights

1 Arslan Kapısı...C1
2 Bezirhane (Oil Press) C2
3 Cathedral C3
4 Church of St Gregory
   (Abughamrentz) B2
5 Church of St Gregory (Gagik I) B2
6 Church of St Gregory (Tigran
   Honentz) D3
7 Church of the Redeemer D2

8 Convent of the Virgins (Kusanatz) C3
9 Ebul Muhammeran Camii B2
10 Georgian Church (Gürcü Kilisesi) B1
11 İç Kale...A4
12 Kervansaray (Church of the Holy
    Apostles) B2
13 Menüçer Camii...B3
14 Seljuk Palace A1
15 Small Hamam D3
16 Zoroastrian Temple (Fire Temple) B2

possibly opening, but play it safe and bring food and water.

Arslan Kapısı
GATE

Sturdy Arslan Kapısı (or Aslan Kapısı – Lion Gate) was supposedly named after Alp Arslan, the Seljuk sultan who conquered Ani in 1064, but probably also after the *aslan* (lion) relief on the inner wall.

Church of the Redeemer
CHURCH

Just past the remains of an **oil press**, the Church of the Redeemer (Church of St Prkitch, 1034–36) soon comes into view. It's a startling vision: only half of the ruined structure remains, the other half having been destroyed by lightning in 1957. The church was supposedly built to house a portion of the True Cross, brought here from

Constantinople; Armenian inscriptions on the facade relay the history. The facade also sports a superb *khatchkar* (cross stone) designed on an elaborate rectangular background, about 3m above ground around the building from the path. The architecture is typical of the circular-planned, multi-apsed Armenian churches built in this era.

Church of St Gregory (Tigran Honentz) CHURCH

Below the 11th-century **hamam**, down by the walls separating Ani from the gorge of the Arpa Çayı and easy to miss, is the Church of St Gregory the Illuminator (in Turkish, Resimli Kilise – Church with Pictures). Named after the apostle to the Armenians, it was built by a pious nobleman in 1215, and although exposure and vandalism have greatly damaged the interior, it's in better condition than most buildings here. Look for the long Armenian inscription carved on the exterior walls, as well as the colourful and lively frescoes depicting scenes from the Bible and Armenian church history. It also features well-preserved relief work, including animal motifs.

Convent of the Virgins (Kusanatz) CHURCH

Dramatically perched on the edge of the Arpa Çayı gorge, the Convent of the Virgins is off limits. Also built by Tigran Honentz, its distinctive, serrated-domed chapel is enclosed by a defensive wall. It's clearly visible from the Menüçer Camii, but for a closer look, descend the rocky steps leading down the **Silk Road** into the gorge. Scant ruins of a **bridge**, also off limits, stand further on, right below the Menüçer Camii and visible from there.

Cathedral CHURCH

Up on the plateau again, the cathedral, renamed the Fethiye Camii (Victory Mosque) by the Seljuk conquerors, is the largest and most impressive building. It was begun by King Smbat II in 987 and finished under Gagik I in 1010.

Ani was once the seat of the Armenian Orthodox Patriarchate; the three doorways served as separate entrances for the patriarch, the king and the people. As the city's grandest religious edifice, the building was transformed into a mosque whenever Muslims held Ani, but reverted to a church when the Christians took it back again. The spacious dome, once supported by four massive columns, fell down centuries ago.

Seen from a distance, the building looks quite featureless, but a closer inspection reveals eye-catching decorative elements, including several porthole windows, slender windows surrounded by elegant fretwork, several triangular niches, inscriptions in Armenian near the main entrance, and a blind arcade with slim columns running around the structure.

Continuing towards the Menüçer Camii, you'll pass an excavated area, supposed to be a former street lined with shops. Further north are the ruins of a toppled minaret, thought to have belonged to the **Ebul Muhammeran Camii**.

Menüçer Camii MOSQUE

A rectangular building with a tall octagonal, truncated minaret, the Menüçer Camii is said to have been the first mosque built by the Seljuk Turks in Anatolia (1072). Six vaults remain, each of them different, as was the Seljuk style. The odd but interesting blend of Armenian and Seljuk design probably resulted from the Seljuks employing Armenian architects, engineers and stonemasons. The alternating red-and-black stonework is a distinctive feature. Look also for the polychrome stone inlays that adorn the ceilings. The structure next to the mosque may have been a Seljuk *medrese* or palace.

The minaret sports an Arabic inscription: *bismillah* ('in the name of Allah'). Climb, if you dare, the dingy spiral staircase inside for excellent views. There's no parapet at the top, so take care.

Nearby is an excavated area, containing remains of houses, with ovens, a granary and bathrooms.

İç Kale FORTRESS

Across the rolling grass, southwest of the mosque, rises the monumental İç Kale (the Keep), which holds within its extensive ruins half a ruined church. Beyond İç Kale, on a pinnacle of rock above the Arpa Çayı, is the small church called the **Kız Kalesi** (Maiden's Castle). You'll have to look from a distance; both sites are out of bounds.

Church of St Gregory (Abughamrentz) CHURCH

This rotunda-shaped church topped by a conical roof dates from about 994. It was built for the wealthy Pahlavuni family by the same architect as the Church of the Redeemer. On the 12-sided exterior, a series of deep niches are topped by scallop-shell carvings; above them, the windows of the drum

DON'T MISS

ARMENIAN CHURCHES AROUND ANİ

So you loved Ani and want more? No problem, there are other impressive Armenian ruins en route back to Kars. The sites have awesome settings, in the middle of the steppe. Seeking them out is also a great way to see a slice of rural Anatolia: most are in muddy farmyards, surrounded by tractors and sheds and even used as cattle pens.

Kars-based guides and drivers such as Celil Ersoğlu (p541) will add the sites to an Ani visit for an extra fee. The sites can usually be accessed by car, but visiting with a local is a good idea, to facilitate meetings with villagers and handle potential pitfalls, such as ferocious farm dogs. There are no tourist facilities, so stock up on food and water.

Heading back to Kars from Ani, at the end of the second village you come to, Essen, turn left onto the reddy brown track. Head into the hills for 8km, with good views of Ani, and follow the *büyük kilisesi* (big church) signpost on the right. In the Kurdish village of Kozluca is **Bagnair Monastery**, consisting of two Armenian monuments. The larger church, thought to have been constructed in the 10th century, is badly damaged; the minor one, 200m across a small ravine, is in better condition, with a nice 12-sided dome-drum adorned with blind arcades.

Back on the asphalt road, continue 10km towards Kars and turn right at the far end of Subatan village, opposite the memorial, towards Başgedikler. After about 15km, a signpost on the left points to Oğuzlu, 3km along a dirt track. The monumental 10th-century **Oğuzlu Church** rises up from the steppe and dominates the surrounding houses. It's in a bad state: an earthquake in 1936 caused the dome and other structures to collapse.

Backtrack 3km to the asphalt road, turn left at the brown signpost and head 7km past Başgedikler to Yağkesen *köyü kilise* (village church). You'll be overwhelmed by the eerie sight of **Kızıl Kilise** (Karmir Vank) standing on a small mound. The church is the sole towering element in an otherwise flat, treeless grassland. Outstanding features include a conical roof, V-shaped exterior niches, slender windows, an inscription in Armenian above the portal and some handsome carvings. If you're lucky, you'll see Mt Ararat in the distance.

---

are framed by a double set of blind arcades. Having been restored in 1040, the building was undergoing this millennium's restoration at the time of research. From here you can savour the view of a **rock-cut village** beyond the river escarpment.

Kervansaray (Church of the Holy Apostles)   CHURCH
The Church of the Holy Apostles (Arak Elots Kilisesi) dates from 1031, but after the Seljuks took the city in 1064, they added a gateway with a fine dome and used the building as a caravanserai – hence its name.

It's fairly well preserved, with decorative carvings, porthole windows, diagonally intersecting arches in the nave, and ceilings sporting geometric patterns made of polychromatic stone inlays. Look also for the various Armenian inscriptions and *khatchkar* carved on a rectangular background.

Zoroastrian Temple (Fire Temple)   TEMPLE
This ruined temple is thought to have been built between the early 1st century and the

first half of the 4th century AD. It might have been converted into a Christian chapel afterwards. The only remains consist of four circular columns, not exceeding 1.5m in height. They lie between the Kervansaray and the Georgian Church, about 100m north of the former.

Church of St Gregory (Gagik I)   CHURCH
Northwest of the Kervansaray, this gigantic church was begun in 998 to plans by the same architect as Ani's cathedral. Its ambitious dome collapsed shortly after completion, and the rest of the building is now also ruined. You can still see the outer walls and a jumble of columns.

Seljuk Palace   PALACE
Beyond the Church of St Gregory (Gagik I) is a Seljuk palace built into the city's defensive walls – and so painstakingly over-restored that it looks quite out of place.

Georgian Church (Gürcü Kilisesi)   CHURCH
You can't miss the only surviving wall of this Georgian Church, probably erected

in the 13th century. It used to be a large building, but most of the south wall collapsed around 1840. Of the three remaining arcades, two sport bas-reliefs, one representing the Annunciation, the other the Visitation.

❶ Getting There & Away

The easiest option is a taxi minibus to the site (50 minutes), organised by Celil Ersoğlu (p541) or Kars tourist office. One person will pay roughly ₺140, two pay ₺70 each, three pay ₺45 each and four to six pay ₺35 each. If there are other travellers around, you will share the ride and the expense. This includes 2½ hours' waiting time. If you hire a taxi, make sure your driver understands that you want at least 2½ hours (preferably three) at Ani.

Sarıkamış

The town and ski resort of Sarıkamış, 55km southwest of Kars, has deep, dry powder and terrain that pleases both skiers and snowboarders. There are also cross-country options. The vibe is more down to earth and family-oriented than at Palandöken, and the area less windy. The slopes are also more scenic, with vast expanses of Scotch pines. The ski season generally lasts from late November to early April, but Sarıkamış can also be enjoyed in summer, with a good network of hiking trails.

The infrastructure is surprisingly state-of-the-art, with three computerised *telesiej* (chair lifts) climbing to 2650m and nine ski runs (three beginner, three intermediate and three advanced), between 1750m and 3500m long. Rental equipment is available at the hotels (about ₺35 per day).

Leaving town on the old Erzurum road, **Czar Nicholas II's Hunting Lodge** is visible on the hillside on the left as you cross the railway lines. Built during the Russian occupation of Kars, the derelict stone-and-wood building was later used as an Ottoman barracks and a casino. Near Bildik Otel, a mosque occupies a converted **Russian Orthodox church** (c 1880), built for Russian soldiers stationed here.

The following all have copious facilities, including bars, restaurants, discos and hamams, and include lift passes in winter rates. At the resort, 3km from Sarıkamış centre, the best option is the **Çamkar Hotel** (☑0474-413 5259; www.camkar.com; summer per person ₺50, winter full board per person ₺100-190; @⊠); next door is the **Ce-mar Toprak Hotel** (☑0474-413 4111; www.toprakhotels.com; summer s/d/tr/ste ₺135/210/284/420, winter full board from ₺300; @⊠). In town, **Bildik Otel** (☑0474-413 7676; www.bildikotel.com; Gaziler Kolordu Caddesi 34; summer per person ₺70, winter half board per person ₺120, self-catering chalet per person summer/winter ₺85/150) has well-equipped self-catering chalets and plain bedrooms. Its winter rates include transfers to the slopes.

Join Sarıkamış for lunch at **Güleryurt Lokantası** (mains ₺9), where the menu includes soups, salads, *çiğ köfte*, and recommended, build-your-own döner kebabs.

Regular minibuses run to/from Kars (₺7, 45 minutes). From Sarıkamış, take a taxi to the resort (₺10). In winter, shuttles link the resort and Kars airport.

Kars to Doğubayazıt

The quickest route from Kars to Doğubayazıt (about 240km) takes you along the Armenian frontier and past Mt Ararat – via Digor, Tuzluca and Iğdır.

You may have to change bus or minibus in **Iğdır**, where you can get a good lunch about 10km northwest of the centre at **Ağırkaya** (mains ₺8-12). In a garden setting with Ararat views, kebabs, salads and traditional village dishes are served. It's behind the petrol station of the same name, 200m before the sign marking the start of Iğdır.

In Iğdır centre, friendly **Gökçe Restaurant** (Evrenpaşa Caddesi Dörtyol Mevkii; mains ₺10) serves kebabs, recommended pide and *hazır yemek* in modern surrounds.

If you get stuck in Iğdır, accommodation is available next to Gökçe at the two-star **Otel Olimpia** (☑0476-227 1866; Evrenpaşa Caddesi Dörtyol Mevkii 13; s/d/tr ₺60/90/130). It's clean, pleasantly decorated and slightly less decrepit than Iğdır's other hotels, many of which double as brothels.

Bus companies serving numerous destinations have offices on the main drag around Otel Olimpia. The otogar is 1km north of the centre, off the Kars road; from the south, turn left at the roundabout with the bird statues. Pick up regular minibuses to Kars (₺20, three hours) and Doğubayazıt (₺5, 45 minutes) from here or along the main drag in the centre.

Doğubayazıt

📞 0472 / POP 73,505 / ELEV 1950M

Doğubayazıt's setting is superb. On one side, the talismanic Mt Ararat (Ağrı Dağı, 5137m), Turkey's highest mountain, hovers majestically over the horizon. On the other side, İshak Paşa Palace, a breathtakingly beautiful fortress-palace-mosque complex, surveys town from its rocky perch. The town itself doesn't have many obvious attractions, but it's an obvious base for climbing Mt Ararat and exploring a few nearby sights. Nicknamed 'doggy biscuit' by travellers on the hippie trail, it's a friendly place with an appealing sense of border-town wildness. Coming from Erzurum or Kars, you'll quickly notice the distinct atmosphere here. Predominantly Kurdish, Doğubayazıt prides itself on its strong Kurdish heritage, which is celbrated at the **Kültür Sanat ve Turizm Festivalı** (Culture and Arts Festival). Held in June or July, the summer festival allows you to immerse yourself in Kurdish heritage through music, dance and theatre performances. Locals gather to watch outdoor concerts and Doğubayazıt's *çay evis* (teahouses) fill.

◉ Sights

İshak Paşa Palace   PALACE
(İshak Paşa Sarayı; admission ₺5; ⊘8am-7pm) Located 6km uphill southeast of town, İshak Paşa Palace embodies *One Thousand and One Nights* romanticism. Part of its magic derives from its setting, perched on a small plateau abutting stark cliffs and gazing at Mt Ararat across green Anatolian plains. The protective glass roofing means you can tour it on a rainy day.

The palace was begun in 1685 by Çolak Abdi Paşa and completed in 1784 by his son, a Kurdish chieftain named İshak (Isaac). The architecture is a superb amalgam of Seljuk, Ottoman, Georgian, Persian and Armenian styles.

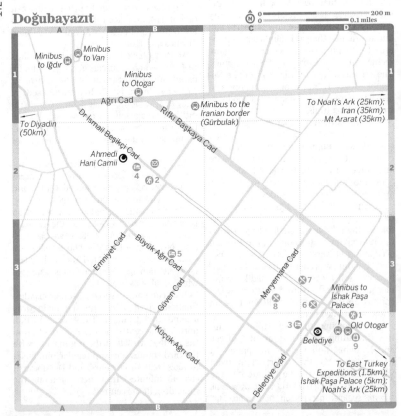

Doğubayazıt

The palace's elaborate main entrance leads into the **first courtyard**, which would have been open to merchants and guests.

Only family and special guests would have been allowed into the **second courtyard**, were you can see the entrance to the *haremlık* (for women), *selamlık* (for men), guards' lodgings and granaries. An elaborate tomb is richly decorated with a mix of Seljuk carvings and Persian relief styles. Steps lead down to the sarcophagi.

From the second courtyard, pass through the marvellously decorated portal of the **haremlık** into the palace living quarters. The highlight here is undoubtedly the beautiful dining room, a melange of styles with walls topped by Seljuk triangular stonework, Armenian floral-relief decoration, ornate column capitals showing Georgian influence, and both black and white stone incorporated. There's a hamam and rooms with stone-carved fireplaces and windows surveying Doğubayazıt.

Returning to the second courtyard, climb a staircase to the **selamlık**. Entry is via the stately hall where guests would have been greeted before being entertained in the ceremonial hall–courtyard to the right. The *selamlık* also has a library, terrace and lovely mosque, which has kept much of its original relief decoration (note the life tree) and ceiling frescoes.

Across the valley from the palace are the ruined foundations of **Eski Beyazıt** (Old Beyazıt), probably founded in Urartian times (c 800 BC). You can also spot a

YENİ HAMAM

To rejuvenate tired and sore muscles after conquering Mt Ararat, Doğubayazıt's **Yeni Hamam** (Şehit Mehmet Özer Caddesi; admission ₺8; ⊙men 6am-midnight, women 7am-6pm), southwest of the centre, comes recommended by trekking guides and locals alike. It's well run and as clean as a whistle. Go for a private massage (₺15); women enjoy the Turkish coffee massage.

mosque, tomb and ruined fortress, which may date from Urartian times (13th to 7th centuries BC). The peaks above the car park here have excellent views of the palace with Doğubayazıt and Mt Ararat beyond.

Minibuses (₺1.50) rattle between the centre and the palace, but there's no fixed schedule – they leave when they are full. Taxis charge about ₺10 to ₺15 one way; ₺20 to ₺25 return, including a one-hour wait at the palace.

Sleeping

Good, reliable accommodation options are scarce. Women are advised to stick to the following. For male backpackers keen to camp, **Lale Zar Camping** (☑0544 269 1960; lalezarcamping@hotmail.com; İshakpaşa Yolu; campsite per person ₺10) and **Murat Camping** (☑0543 635 0494; İshakpaşa Yolu; campsite ₺10, s/d/tr excl breakfast ₺25/50/75) are on the road up to İshak Paşa Palace.

Hotel Tahran　HOTEL €
(☑312 0195; www.hoteltahran.com; Büyük Ağrı Caddesi 124; s/d/tr ₺30/50/70; ☎) The well-managed Tahran exudes mellow vibes. Although small and old, rooms have crisp white sheets, and the top-floor kitchen and dining room have glimpses of Mt Ararat and İshak Paşa Palace. There's a laundry service, book exchange, and reception with inviting chairs and offers of çay. Affable, English-speaking manager Bilal is clued up on subjects such as getting to Iran.

Hotel Ararat　HOTEL €
(☑312 4988; www.hotelararatturkey.com; Belediye Caddesi 16; s/d/tr ₺35/60/85; ☎) Beyond Ararat's grand marbled reception, the comfortable lilac rooms have features including fridge, satellite TV and phone. Some have

balconies with views of the hotel's name-sake, and there's an outdoor terrace for breakfast in summer. Helpful owner Mustafa Arsin, an English-speaking Ararat guide, offers bonuses such as free hot drinks and use of the kitchen.

Hotel Grand Derya
HOTEL €€

(☑312 7531; fax 312 7833; Dr İsmail Beşikçi Caddesi; s/d ₺70/120; ❄🐱🛜) A comfortable retreat after a few days' clambering, the Grand Ocean has Doğubayazit's best rooms; shoot for one with a balcony and Ararat views. Rooms have all mod cons and the reception has seating. It's set back from the main drag, but receives noise in the form of calls to prayer from the nearby mosque. Manager Feyyaz speaks some English.

✗ Eating & Drinking

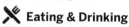

TOP CHOICE Simurg
INTERNATIONAL €

(Meryemana Caddesi 19; mains ₺5-13; 🖊) Doğubayazit's hippest hang-out, its modern interior featuring tiled floors with bright carpets, Klimt and Dali reproductions, and a magazine rack. Dishes include spaghetti, pizza, chicken schnitzel and *köfte*; the mushroom sauté and beefsteak with pepper sauce are recommended.

Doğuş Restaurant
TURKISH €€

(cnr Dr İsmail Beşikçi & Belediye Caddesi; mains ₺10) Doğuş is a winner with views from upstairs of Mt Ararat and the streets below. There's good food, including *hazır yemek* and kebaps (a passable İskender), plus friendly waiters who nurture foreigners' Kurdish skills.

---

❶ GETTING TO AZERBAIJAN

From İğdır, **İğdırlı Turizm** (www .igdirliturizm.com.tr) has direct daily services east to the Azerbaijani enclave of Nakhichevan (₺10, 3½ hours). The company has a few offices in İğdır town centre on the main drag. Note that you need a visa (there's an Azerbaijani consulate in Kars). To get to Baku from Nakhichevan, which is cut off from the rest of Azerbaijan by Armenia, you'll have to fly. İğdırlı Turizm also has connections to/from other Turkish locations including İstanbul.

Öz Urfa Kebap
KEBAP €€

(Dr İsmail Beşikçi Caddesi; mains ₺9) Its attractive, wood-panelled dining room reached up steep stairs, Öz Urfa is popular locally. The lamb kebap and frothy *ayran* are highly recommended.

Türkü Cafe
NARGILE CAFE

(Dr İsmail Beşikçi Caddesi) A popular hang-out, with kids smoking nargiles and playing backgammon on the covered balcony. Alcoholic drinks and snacks such as *tost* are available and there's sometimes live music.

🛍 Shopping

Kurdish Crafts
CARPETS

(http://handmadecarpetskilims.blogspot.com; İshak Paşa Caddesi; ⊘Apr-Oct) Just past the old otogar, you can pick up Kurdish carpets, kilims and saddlebags here. Most items come from nearby villages.

❶ Information

INTERNET ACCESS Internet cafes cluster around the junction of Dr İsmail Beşikçi and Emniyet Caddesis.

MONEY Banks in the centre have ATMs. There are also money-changers, including **Nişantaş Dövız** (Dr İsmail Beşikçi Caddesi; ⊘7am-7pm Mon-Sat, to noon Sun).

TOURIST INFORMATION The travel agencies listed on p552 can organise day trips and help with queries.

❶ Getting There & Away

The otogar is 2km west of town on the D100 to Ağrı. Minibuses to/from the hospital link it with the centre (₺1). For long-distance destinations, you'll often have to travel via Erzurum (₺25, four hours, 285km).

IĞDIR Minibuses leave every 30 minutes (₺7, 45 minutes).

IRAN Minibuses run to the Iranian border (Gürbulak; ₺7, 30 minutes). Get going before 10am, when many people travel to the border; after that you will have to wait longer for vehicles to fill up.

KARS Take a minibus to İğdır and change. **İğdırlı Turizm** (www.igdirliturizm.com.tr) had a direct daily service, which continued to Artvin and the Black Sea coast, but this was cancelled at the time of writing and unlikely to restart.

VAN Minibuses leave at approximately 6.30am, 9am, noon and 2pm daily, with an extra summer service at 4pm (₺15, three hours, 185km).

Around Doğubayazıt

Travel agencies and hotels in Doğubayazıt can help organise an excursion to nearby sights. Half-day tours cost about ₺60 per person; if there are a few of you, a taxi is a cheaper option (about ₺120). Ask your driver to take the scenic back road (less advisable after heavy rains) through the hills from İshak Paşa Palace to **Noah's Ark** (Nu'hun Gemisi). The elongated oval mound on a hillside is one of half a dozen possible ark sites around Mt Ararat. It's also signposted to the south of the D100, 20km from Doğubayazıt en route to the Iranian border.

Turn left (northeast) at the border and follow the signpost to reach the **meteor crater** *(meteor çukuru)*, supposedly dating to 1892. The site is right on the border (the village you can see from here is in Iran), so someone in your vehicle will need to leave their passport or ID at the military check point en route.

Further afield are villages at the base of Mt Ararat and **Diyadin Hot Springs**, west of Doğubayazıt. There are day walks around Mt Ararat and in the hills above Doğubayazıt.

Mt Ararat (Ağrı Dağı)

A highlight of any trip to eastern Turkey, the twin peaks of Mt Ararat have figured in legends since time began, most notably as the supposed resting place of Noah's Ark. The left-hand peak, called Büyük Ağrı (Great Ararat), is 5137m high, while Küçük Ağrı (Little Ararat) rises to about 3895m.

CLIMBING MT ARARAT

For many years permission to climb Ararat was routinely refused because of security concerns, but this fantastic summit is now on the hiking map, albeit with certain restrictions. A permit and guide are mandatory. At the time of research, permits (US$50) were issued in Ağrı and the process took up to two weeks. There were hopes that permits would eventually be issued in Doğubayazıt, shortening the wait to a day or so. Apply in advance through a reputable travel agency such as those listed here, which may include the paperwork in the overall price. Agency **Tamzara Turizm** (0544 555 3582; www.mtararattour.com;

off Dr İsmail Beşikçi Caddesi) gives an idea of the documentation and details required as part of applications on its website (click on Climbing Permit). You need a permit to get past military posts on the approaches to the mountain and for your own safety – to ensure help will be on hand if something goes wrong on the climb. People have died on the mountain; in 2010, Scotsman Donald Mackenzie went missing while searching for Noah's Ark.

If unofficial guides, hotel staff and touts in Doğubayazıt tell you they can get the permit quickly and cut costs, *don't* believe them. There's probably some bribery involved or, even worse, they will let you think they've obtained the permit but in reality will be taking you up Ararat unofficially. This scam has landed hikers in jail. Follow the official procedure, even if you have to endure the slow-turning wheels of bureaucracy, and ask for evidence that the permit has been granted.

Prices vary between agency and package, and drop for larger groups. Shop around, check what's included and consider joining a group if there are just one or two people in your party. Typically, agencies charge about €500 per person to lead a four-person group on a three- to five-day trek from Doğubayazıt, including guides, camping and food. Most reputable agencies recommend four-day treks in order to facilitate acclimatisation before tackling the summit.

Despite the costs involved, climbing Ararat is a fantastic experience. Expect stupendous views and stunning landscapes. The best weather for walking is between mid-June and mid-September; views are best in July and August. You'll need to be comfortable with snow-climbing techniques using crampons past 4800m, even in the height of summer.

A possible route is the southern one, starting from Eliköyü, an abandoned village in the foothills, at about 2200m. There's another route starting from the village of Çevirme (2250m). The first campsite is at 3200m, and the second one at 4200m.

You can also do one- and two-day treks around the mountain, including the Fish Lake walk. Provided you stay under 2500m you won't have to go through as much official hoo-ha, but it's still best to go with a local guide; risks include ferocious shepherd dogs. Expect to pay around €150 per person. Another option is the hills around Doğubayazıt, on sections of the Silk Road between İshak Paşa Palace and Iran.

GUIDES

East Turkey Expeditions (p527) Knowledgeable, English-speaking Zafer Onay also covers the Kaçkars.

Middle Earth Travel (p527) Cappadocia-based nationwide trekking specialists.

Tamzara Turizm (p551) Based next to Hotel Urartu, Tamzara is run by English-speaking Mustafa Arsin. The website is a useful source of information. Also offers walk-and-ski tours.

Mount Ararat Trek (☎0537 502 6683; www.mountararattrek.com) Run by American Amy Beam and a local team. The website is a useful source of information. Also offers walk-and-ski tours.

Southeastern Anatolia

Best Places to Eat

» Yörem Mutfağı (p559)

» Orkide (p560)

» Kamer Cafe Mutfak (p590)

» Meşhur Kahvaltıcı (p586)

Best Places to Stay

» Asude Konak (p558)

» Yuvacali Village Homestay (p569)

» Şahmeran Otanik Pansiyon (p589)

» Kasr-ı Nehroz (p593)

Why Go?

Southeastern Anatolia is a unique part of Turkey, and apart from small Arabic and Christian pockets, this expansive region is predominantly Kurdish and extremely welcoming to visitors. Choose from a menu of historical cities, including Mardin, on a hill dominating Mesopotamia; Şanlıurfa, swathed in historical mystique and featuring the incredible temple of Göbekli Tepe; the old city of Diyarbakır, ensnared in mighty basalt walls; and the endangered honey-coloured riverside town of Hasankeyf. Move on to Nemrut Dağı, topped with colossal ancient statues, or shimmering Lake Van, edged with snowcapped mountains. Wonderfully isolated spots include Darende and the perfect hilltop village of Savur, while Gaziantep is a must-visit destination for its astounding mosaics and superb local food. A few places could be off limits to foreigners when you visit – mainly near the borders with Iraq and Syria – but most of southeastern Anatolia is safe and accessible to independent travellers.

When to Go
Gaziantep

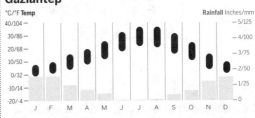

Mar Visit Diyarbakir and celebrate the Kurdish New Year of Nevruz.

May & Sep Temperatures in southeastern Anatolia are less extreme.

Jun Visit the International Kahta Kommagene Festival near Nemrut Dağı.

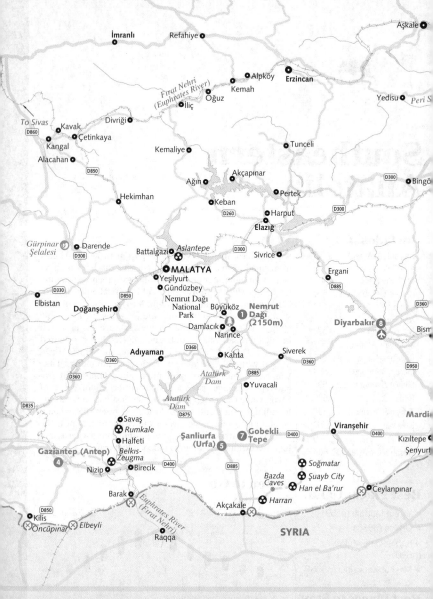

Southeastern Anatolia Highlights

1 Feel elation while watching the sun set (or rise) from **Nemrut Dağı** (p572), the 'thrones of gods'

2 Go heritage-hunting among the historic buildings and honey-coloured stone houses of pretty **Mardin** (p587)

3 Bliss out by a gushing river in the perfect valley-village seclusion of **Savur** (p592)

4 Fall in love with the *Gypsy Girl* and feast on culinary delights in **Gaziantep** (p556)

5 Nourish your soul in the great pilgrimage city of **Şanlıurfa** (p563)

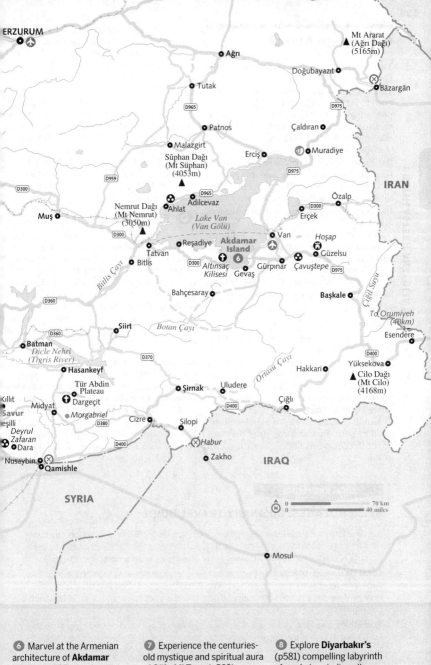

ERZURUM ✈

Mt Ararat
(Ağrı Dağı)
(5165m) ▲

Ağrı

Doğubayazıt

Bäzärgän ⊗

Tutat

D965

Patnos

Çaldıran

Malazgirt

Erciş

Muradiye

Süphan Dağı
(Mt Süphan)
(4053m) ▲

D975

IRAN

D959

Özalp

D965

D300

Adilcevaz

Nemrut Dağı
(Mt Nemrut)
(3050m) ▲

Ahlat

Lake Van
(Van Gölü)

Erçek

Muş ⊗

D300

Reşadiye

**Akdamar
Island** ♿ ⑥

Van ✈

Hoşap

Tatvan

D300

Altınsaç
Kilisesi

Gevaş

Gürpınar

Çavuştepe

Güzelsu

⊗

Bitlis

Bahçesaray

Başkale

D360

Siirt

Botan Çayı

Esendere

D360

D370

Orlasu Çayı

D400

Batman ⊗
Dicle Nehri
(Tigris River)

Hakkari

Yüksekova

Cilo Dağı
(Mt Cilo)
(4168m) ▲

Hasankeyf

Uludere

Çığlı

Tür Abdin
Plateau

Dargeçit

Şırnak

D400

Kıllıt

Midyat

Morgabriel

Cizre

Silopi

eşilli

D380

Deyrul
Zafaran

Dara

D400

⊗ Habur

Nusaybin ⊗
Qamishle

Zakho

IRAQ

SYRIA

0   70 km
0   40 miles

Mosul

⑥ Marvel at the Armenian
architecture of **Akdamar
Kilisesi** (p597) on a boat trip
out to Akdamar Island

⑦ Experience the centuries-
old mystique and spiritual aura
of **Göbekli Tepe** (p563)

⑧ Explore **Diyarbakır's**
(p581) compelling labyrinth
of markets, winding alleys,
restored Armenian houses and
ancient, hushed churches

Gaziantep (Antep)

☑ 0342 / POP 1.35 MILLION

There's one Turkish word you should learn before visiting Gaziantep: *fıstık* (pistachio). This fast-paced and epicurean city is reckoned to harbour more than 180 pastry shops producing the world's best pistachio baklava. Other culinary treats are also on offer for adventurous foodie travellers.

With the biggest city park this side of the Euphrates and a buzzing cafe culture, Gaziantep oozes panache and confidence. It also has one astounding attraction definitely worth travelling across Turkey for – the superb new Gaziantep Zeugma Mosaics Museum.

The older parts of the city are being reinvigorated, and the fortress, bazaars, caravanserai and old stone houses have been lovingly restored. One of southeastern Anatolia's gateways, Gaziantep has rarely been as full of confidence and hope for the future as it is today.

History

By the time the Arabs conquered the town in 638, the Persians, Alexander the Great, the Romans and the Byzantines had all left their imprints on Aintab (as Gaziantep was formerly known). The region remained politically unstable until the the Seljuk Turks arrived from the east around 1070.

Aintab remained a city of Seljuk culture, ruled by petty Turkish lords, until the coming of the Ottomans under Selim the Grim in 1516.

During the Ottoman period, Aintab had a sizeable Christian population, including a large proportion of Armenians. You'll see Armenian churches, community buildings and mansions scattered throughout the city's historical core.

In 1920, as the victorious Allies sought to carve up the Ottoman territories, Aintab was besieged by French forces intent on adding Turkish lands to their holdings in Syria and Lebanon. Aintab's fierce nationalist defenders finally surrendered on 8 February 1921. The epithet 'Gazi' (War Hero) was added to Antep in 1973 to pay homage to their tenacious defence.

◉ Sights & Activities

Ask at the tourist office (p561) for the *Gaziantep Tarih ve Kültür Yolu* (Gaziantep History & Culture Road) brochure, a handy map detailing 40 sights dotted around the city. Gaziantep is also actively promoting itself as a 'museum city', with several new openings planned, including a war museum and a showcase of copper art in the restored Saklı Konak. Ask at the tourist information office for the latest update.

**Gaziantep Zeugma
Mosaic Museum** MUSEUM
(www.gaziantepmuzesi.gov.tr; Sehitkamil Caddesi; admission ₺8; ◷8.30am-5.30pm) Newly opened in 2012, this spectacular modern museum showcases the mosaics unearthed at the Roman site of Belkıs-Zeugma before the Birecik Dam flooded some of the site forever. Highlights include the poignant *Gypsy*

LOCAL KNOWLEDGE

SELIN ROZANES: CULINARY TRAVEL GUIDE

Based in İstanbul, Selin Rozanes regularly leads groups of travellers to explore the culinary heritage of southeastern Anatolia. Back in İstanbul, she introduces visitors to the flavours of Anatolia at cookery classes in her apartment with Turkish Flavours (p97).

Local Gaziantep specialities Don't miss trying an *ali nazik* kebap with a base of smoky aubergine (eggplant) mashed with yoghurt. Gaziantep's odd breakfast habit is *beyran*. Very garlicky and delicious, it's soup, tandoori meat and rice all in one. Try it at Metanet Lokantası (p560).

Something sweeter Try *katmer* (flatbread layered with nuts and clotted cream) and have a box of *kahke*, a wafer-thin biscuit. My favourite is *köylü kahkesi*, peasant-style, made with grape molasses and flavoured with spices and studded with flax seeds and nigella. Not so sweet and really tasty.

Must try A good place to try local dishes is Yörem Mutfağı (p559). For baklava the Güllüoğulu (p557) shop in Elmacı Pazarı is better than their other branches, and you should have coffee in the nearby Tahmis Kahvesi (p557).

Girl and the *Birth of Venus*. Ascend to the 2nd floor for the best views of the virtually complete floor mosaics retrieved from Roman villas. To find the museum, follow the underpass on the left of the railway station, continue under the busy main highway, turn right, and then continue on for another 400m. A taxi from central Gaziantep should be around ₺8.

FREE Kale   FORTRESS
(Citadel; ⊙8.30am-5.30pm) Thought to have been constructed by the Romans, the citadel was restored by Emperor Justinian in the 6th century AD, and rebuilt extensively by the Seljuks in the 12th and 13th centuries. The interior of the castle contains the **Gaziantep Defence & Heroism Panoramic Museum** (admission ₺1; ⊙8.30am-5.30pm), a tribute to the men and women who bravely defended the city against the French in 1920.

Gaziantep Museum   MUSEUM
(İstasyon Caddesi; admission ₺3; ⊙8.30am-noon & 1-5pm Tue-Sun) This museum previously housed the city's astounding collection of mosaics. Following their relocation to the new Gaziantep Mosaic Museum, this location now focuses on Hittite carvings and sculpture, and a wonderful collection of ancient seals.

Bakircilar Çarşisi   MARKET
South of the fortress is Gaziantep's rambling and labyrinthine bazaar area, which includes the **Zincirli Bedesten** (Coppersmiths' Market), now fully restored and full of tap-tap-tap metalworkers and makers of handmade shoes. Keep exploring to find excellent food markets with mini-mountains of multicoloured spices and graceful garlands of dried chillies. South of the Zincirli Bedesten, in the **Elmacı Pazarı** area, you'll find the original **Güllüoğlu** (Elmacı Pazarı) baklava shop.

For a coffee break, seek out **Tahmis Kahvesi** (Buğdaypazarı Sokak; ⊙10am-10pm), possibly the most atmospheric *kahvehane* (coffeehouse) in Gaziantep.

Gaziantep City Museum   MUSEUM
(Gaziantep Kent Müzesi; www.bayazhan.com.tr; Atatürk Bulvarı; admission ₺1; ⊙8.30am-5.30pm) Interactive displays and foreign-language audio guides steer visitors through everything from the story of baklava to Gaziantep's history of shoemaking. You can relax with a tea, coffee or cold beer in the Bayazhan's courtyard cafe, there's occasional live music, and the whole complex is ringed with a halo of compact shops selling interesting and well-priced local crafts.

Emine Göğüş Culinary Museum   MUSEUM
(Köprübaşı Sokak; admission ₺1; ⊙8.30am-5.30pm) Concealed in a narrow lane under the citadel, this interesting museum provides both information and inspiration before you begin exploring Gaziantep's terrific eateries. Excellent English-language translations are key ingredients in the museum's successful recipe of explaining what dishes you should look out for in local restaurants.

Hasan Süzer Ethnography Museum   MUSEUM
(Hanefioğlu Sokak; admission ₺3; ⊙8am-noon & 1-5pm Tue-Sun) This restored 200-year-old stone house features a central *hayat* (courtyard) patterned with light and dark stones. Rooms on the ground floor were for service; those on the 1st floor made up the *selamlık* (quarters for male family members and their visitors); and those on the 2nd floor were the *haremlik* (for female family members and their visitors).

Kurtuluş Camii   MOSQUE
Built on a small hill off the main thoroughfare, this is the most impressive of Gaziantep's many mosques. Initially constructed as a cathedral in 1892, it features alternating black-and-white stone banding.

Another mosque worth admiring is the **Alaüddevle Camii**, near the Coppersmiths' Market. Many other nearby mosques have also been recently restored; details can be found on the *Gaziantep History & Culture Road* map available from the tourist office.

Kendirli Kilisesi   CHURCH
(Atatürk Bulvarı) Wedged between modern buildings and smack in the centre of town, this church was constructed by French priests with the help of Napoleon III in 1860. Seen from a distance, the building looks quite featureless, but a closer inspection reveals eye-catching black-and-white medallions.

FREE Mevlevihane Vakıf Müzesi   MUSEUM
(Tekke Camii Yanı; ⊙9am-5pm Tue-Sun) An interesting museum that focuses on the Mevlevi Sufis (a dervish order). It features various artworks, kilims (woven rugs),

Gaziantep (Antep)

manuscripts, clothing worn by the Mevlevi and other dervish paraphernalia. Panels are in English.

Şıra Hanı
HISTORIC BUILDING

On the southwestern edge of the bazaar, the beautifully restored Şıra Hanı is the location of the stylish Sahan (p560) restaurant.

100 Yıl Atatürk Kültür Parkı
PARK

This park is a lovely space in the middle of the city and provides a green haven for nature lovers, families and courting 20-somethings. There are also a couple of good places for a relaxed sunset beer.

Naib Hamamı
HAMAM

(Kale Arası; spa & massage ₺30; ⊙women 9.30am-5pm, men 6pm-midnight) This elegant restored hamam is immediately north of the citadel.

🛏 Sleeping

Gaziantep is rolling in accommodation, much of it on or near Atatürk Bulvarı and Suburcu, Hürriyet and İstasyon Caddesis. Hotel prices can be high in comparison to other eastern Turkish cities, but the city has some good boutique hotels.

TOP CHOICE **Asude Konak**
BOUTIQUE HOTEL €€

(☑230 4104, 0532 577 8792; www.asudekonak .com; Arkası Millet Sokak 20; s €40-50, d €60-70; ❉@ 🛜) You'll feel like you're staying with friends or family at this lovingly restored courtyard house. Meals are prepared by host Jale Özaslan, and can include gossamer-light *katmer* (flatbread layered with nuts and clotted cream) for breakfast, and the local speciality of *yuvarlama* (soup made with rice, meat, chickpeas and yoghurt) for dinner. Evening meals are often lingering alfresco occasions where conversation comes

Gaziantep (Antep)

naturally after a tipple of rakı (aniseed brandy), beer or wine.

Anadolu Evleri BOUTIQUE HOTEL €€€
(☎220 9525; www.anadoluevleri.com; Köroğlu Sokak; s/d €60/95, 1-/2-person ste €90/120; ❄@🖥) Tastefully restored, this old stone house provides the perfect soft landing into Gaziantep. Local tradition is celebrated with a beguiling courtyard, beamed or painted ceilings, mosaic floors, secret passageways, and antique furniture and artefacts. It's within spitting distance of the bustling bazaar and excellent restaurants, yet still feels quiet and restful behind its historic, storied walls.

Zeynep Hanim Konagi BOUTIQUE HOTEL €€
(☎221 0207; www.zeynephanimkonagi.com; Eski Sinema Sokak; s/d ₺80/150; ❄🖥) Comfortable and spacious rooms look out onto a central courtyard at this lovely boutique hotel. Look forward to sparkling bathrooms and super-comfy beds, and the surrounding Bey neighbourhood is Antep's hippest area for new cafes and restaurants.

Nil Hotel HOTEL €€
(☎220 9452; www.nilhotel.net; Atatürk Bulvarı 53; s/d ₺70/120; ❄🖥) There's nothing overly adventurous in this small 'high-rise' hotel, but it offers everything you'd want from a middle-of-the-road establishment; the bathrooms are spotless and it's high on facilities, with satellite TV, air-con and a central location.

Anit Hotel HOTEL €
(☎220 9656; anithotel@yahoo.com; Atatürk Bulvarı 81; s/d ₺40/70; ❄🖥) Solid budget to mid-range offering with spacious and sunny rooms in a quiet, leafy street. There's a bar on the 1st floor, and Antep's best cafes are just a short stroll away.

Güzel Otel HOTEL €
(☎221 3216; Gaziler Caddesi 7; s/d ₺25/40; ❄🖥) A convenient location near the market and clean, spacious rooms make this one of Gaziantep's best-value hotels.

🍴 Eating

Available at the tourist office, the *Gaziantep Mutfağı* (Gaziantep Cuisine) book describes the city's iconic dishes.

TOP CHOICE Yörem Mutfağı TURKISH €€
(Sokak 15; mains ₺10-12) What began as a simple eatery feeding nearby office workers has morphed into an elegant spot serving some of Gaziantep's best home-style food. Good value lunches are a pick-and-point affair – the dishes change daily – and dinner is more formal with a wider range. Look for the AK

Parti sign on the street skirting the northern edge of the Atatürk Kültür Parkı, and turn right down the street before the sign.

Orkide
BAKERY €

(www.orkidepastanesi.com; Gazimuhtarpaşa Bulvarı 17; cakes ₺4-6) Renowned as the city's finest *pastane* (patisserie), Orkide is also an elegant space to enjoy the best brunch (₺25) in town. Look forward to a mouth-watering spread of local cheeses, jams, honey and salads, all partnered with warm and fluffy flatbread, and including the finest *katmer* we've ever tried. Turn north along Gazimuhtarpaşa Bulvarı 400m west of the tourist information office.

Katmerci Murat
BAKERY €

(Atatürk Bulvarı 11; katmer ₺6) The best entertainment of your day could be watching the graceful actions of Murat's head pastry chef as he transforms a compact ball of dough into a plate of delectable *katmer*, layered with clotted cream and nuts, and topped with a sprinkling of green pistachios.

İmam Çağdaş
TURKISH €€

(Kale Civarı Uzun Çarşı; mains ₺13-18) The Çağdaş family's pistachio baklava is delivered daily to customers throughout Turkey. The secret of their success is fresh, carefully chosen ingredients, and also good are the creamy, chargrilled aubergine flavours of their *ali nazik* kebap. The restaurant is very popular with Turkish tourists.

Çulcuoğlu Et Lokantası
TURKISH €€

(Kalender Sokak; mains ₺8-12) Çulcuoğlu's kebaps are the way to go, but the grilled chicken is also great. Don't be fooled by the unremarkable entrance, as there's a dining area at the back. It's tucked away down a narrow side street across the *otopark* near

the Şıra Hanı, about 20m from a little mosque called Nur Ali.

Metanet Lokantası
TURKISH €

(Kozluca Camii Yanı; mains ₺6-9) Tucked away in a side street near Kozluca Camii, the Metanet has always been a local favourite. The kitchen staff conscientiously mince the succulent lamb in front of a big grill, *ayran* (yoghurt drink) is served in a tin bowl, and the atmosphere is easygoing and convivial. Metanet is also a top place to try *beyran*, a breakfast and lunch dish popular in Gaziantep.

Baro Lokali
RESTAURANT, BAR €€

(Yıl Atatürk Kültür Parkı; mains ₺10-15) It's the setting that's the pull here; an enchanting leaf-dappled outdoor terrace at the western end of the 100 Yıl Atatürk Kültür Parkı (about ₺10 by taxi from the centre) perfect for escaping sticky Gaziantep on a hot summer day. Good choice of mezes and meat dishes, and you can order beer, rakı or wine.

Sahan
TURKISH €€

(Şıra Hanı; meze ₺4-6, mains ₺12-18) Located in the restored Şıra Hanı, Sahan dishes up excellent versions of local specialities. It's licensed, so at the very least pop in for a beer, wine and a few meze in the elegant and spacious courtyard.

Drinking

TOP CHOICE Papirüs Cafeteria
CAFE

(Noter Sokak; ⊙10am-10pm) A student crowd (male *and* female, we promise) gathers here to take advantage of the delightfully authentic setting in a historic Armenian mansion off Atatürk Bulvarı; you'll find them swapping numbers in the leafy court-

---

GAZİANTEP FOR THE SWEET TOOTH

For baklava devotees, Gaziantep is Shangri-la. The city is reckoned to produce the best *fıstıklı* (pistachio) baklavas in Turkey, if not in the world. When they are served ultrafresh, they're impossible to beat. With more than 180 pastry shops scattered around the city, it's hard to determine which is the best, but some baklava shops have reached cult status, such as Güllüoğulu (p557) and the talismanic İmam Çağdaş, established in 1887.

We asked Burhan Çağdaş the owner of the eponymous İmam Çağdaş, a few questions:

What are the qualities of a perfectly crafted baklava? I carefully choose the freshest ingredients imaginable. Everything is organic. I know the best oil and pistachio producers in the Gaziantep area. The nature of the soil here gives a special aroma to pistachios. And we don't go into mass production.

How can one judge whether a baklava is fresh? It's simple: when it's in your mouth, it should make like a *kshhhh* sound.

SERVICES FROM GAZIANTEP'S OTOGAR

DESTINATION	FARE (₺)	DURATION (HR)	DISTANCE (KM)	FREQUENCY (PER DAY)
Adana	20	4	220	frequent
Adıyaman	16	3	162	frequent
Ankara	50	10	705	frequent
Antakya	20	4	200	frequent
Diyarbakır	30	5	330	frequent
İstanbul	70	15	1136	several
Kahramanmaraş	15	1½	80	frequent
Mardin	35	6	330	several
Şanlıurfa	15	2½	145	frequent
Van	55	12	740	several

yard. Don't miss the historic, delicately faded frescoes upstairs.

Adana Şalgamacısı – Gürbüz Usta
JUICE BAR

(Hürriyet Caddesi; juices from ₺2; ⊙8:30am-8pm) See the heaps of grapefruit, banana and orange on the counter at this buzzing hole-in-the-wall? They're just waiting to be squeezed. Try the delicious *atom* (an explosive mixture of milk, honey, banana, hazelnuts and pistachio).

Millet Hanı
TEA GARDEN

(Uzun Çarşı; ⊙10am-8pm) As well as being a top spot for a tea or coffee, this recently restored *han* (caravanserai) is also filled with interesting workshops and studios showcasing traditional crafts. Weaving, mosaics and calligraphy are all represented, and downstairs is a kitchen preparing traditional meals. At the time of writing, folklore nights with music and dancing were also planned.

Cıncık
BAR, RESTAURANT

(Atatürk Kültür Parkı; ⊙noon-11pm) The grills, meze and salads at Cıncık are perfectly fine, but we really like the leafy and relaxed garden bar filled with Antep folk lounging on bean bags, and kicking back with a relaxed combo of draught Efes beer and the occasional nargile (water pipe). It's a shortish stroll through Atatürk Kültür Parkı from the city centre.

Tütün Hanı
TEA GARDEN

(Eski Saray Caddesi Yanı; ⊙8.30am-11pm) Set in the picturesque courtyard of the carefully restored Tütün Hanı, this teahouse is a great place to enjoy a cheap tea and nargile.

Good luck choosing between more than 40 nargile flavours. Turkish tourists love to settle in to the relaxed combo of rugs, low wooden tables and cushions, and there's live Turkish music from 7.30pm to 11pm on Friday and Saturday nights.

ℹ Information

The post office and ATMs are on or around the main square, while internet cafes line up in a lane parallel to Atatürk Bulvarı.

Arsan (☑220 6464; www.arsan.com.tr; Nolu Sokak; ⊙8am-7pm) A reputable travel agency that can arrange various tours (from ₺100 per person), including the 'Magical Triangle' (Birecik, Halfeti/Rumkale, Belkıs-Zeugma). Car rental is also available if you're keen for more flexible exploration.

Tourist Office (☑230 5969; www.gaziantep city.info; 100 Yıl Atatürk Kültür Parkı İçi; ⊙8am-noon & 1-5pm Mon-Fri) In a black and grey building in the city park. The well-informed staff speak English and German, and have good city maps and brochures.

ℹ Getting There & Away

Air

Gaziantep's Oğuzeli airport is 20km from the centre. Ask at a travel agency about the Havas bus to the airport. A taxi is around ₺40.

Onur Air (www.onurair.com.tr) Daily flights to/from İstanbul (from ₺80).

Pegasus (www.flypgs.com) Daily flights to/from İstanbul (from ₺70).

Turkish Airlines (www.turkishairlines.com) Daily flights to/from İstanbul (from ₺92) and to/from Ankara (from ₺64).

ONWARD TRAVEL TO SYRIA

It was previously possible to arrange onward travel to Syria from Gaziantep (through the Öncüpınar border post near Kilis) and Şanlıurfa (through the Akcakale border post). At the time of writing, however, the US, UK and many other governments have recalled their ambassadors from, and advise against all travel in, Syria, urging any of their nationals in the country to leave. When the situation changes – though no one knows when that will be – the country will still present risks to travellers.You are advised to exercise caution and be sure to check the security situation before travelling.

Bus

The otogar (bus station) is 6.5km from the town centre. To get there, catch a bus (₺2.50) or minibus in Hürriyet Caddesi, north of Gaziler Caddesi, or in İstasyon Caddesi, about 400m further north. A taxi costs about ₺20.

Minibuses to Kilis (₺5, 65km) leave every 20 minutes from a separate *garaj* (minibus terminal) on İnönü Caddesi. It's located just past the Petrol Ofisi petrol station.

Car

To see surrounding sights, especially the Yesemek Open-Air Museum, Arsan can arrange car rental. Plan on ₺100 a day.

Train

At the time of writing, trains to Gaziantep from other parts of Turkey had been suspended due to long-term line maintenance.

The train station is 800m north of the centre.

Around Gaziantep

KİLİS
☑ 0348 / POP 84,100

Kilis bristles with lovely ancient buildings scattered around the city centre, including mausoleums, caravanserais, hamams, mosques, fountains and *konaks* (mansions). Many have been recently restored. On or around the main square, look for the superb Adliye, the Mevlevi Hane, the Tekye Camii, the Paşa Hamamı and the Kadı Camii. The Cuneyne Camii and Çalik Camii are a bit more difficult to find (ask around).

There are frequent minibus services to Gaziantep (₺5, 65km, one hour).

BELKIS-ZEUGMA

Once an important city, Belkıs-Zeugma was founded by one of Alexander the Great's generals around 300 BC. It had its golden age with the Romans, and later became a major trading station along the Silk Road.

In modern times, much of the remains of the city disappeared under the waters of the Birecik Dam, and the most interesting mosaics are now on display in Gaziantep. At the original site, a modern hilltop pavillion has recently been erected on the shores of the Euphrates to shelter the labyrinthine remains of the Roman villas of Dionysos and Danae. Kitchens, latrines and spacious rooms are all evident – along with a few more mosaics *in situ* – and a visit to the site is a worthwhile companion activity to viewing the Zeugma mosaics in Gaziantep.

The site is about 50km from Gaziantep and 10km from Nizip, off the main road to Şanlıurfa. (It's signposted from the village of Dutlu). There is no public transport, so you'll need to rent a car or consider a tour with Arsan in Gaziantep.

HALFETI & RUMKALE

This peaceful village lies about 40km north of Birecik, on the bank of the Euphrates. It's the perfect spot to unwind before tackling the busy cities of Şanlıurfa to the east or Gaziantep to the west. The setting couldn't be more appealing, with attractive houses that trickle down the hillside above the river. Sadly, construction of the Birecik Dam meant that half of the city, including several archaeological sites, was inundated and part of the population had to be resettled.

There are several places to soak up the atmosphere along the river. The leafy Siyah Gül Restaurant (mains ₺8-15), overlooking the river, is a sound option and alcohol is served.

From Halfeti, boats to Rumkale can be organised (about ₺80 for the whole boat) – a must-do. Individual travellers should be able to tag along with a group for about ₺30. Boats travel 20 minutes to the base of the rocky bluff on top of which sits a ruined fortress. Accessible by a short but steep path, the fortress features a mosque, church and monastery, all relatively well preserved. Boats continue for 10 minutes until Savaş, another partly inundated village.

On summer weekends, the peaceful surroundings can be ambushed by water sports, and jet skiing, kayaking, water skiing, and wakeboarding can all be undertaken.

Regular dolmuş departures leave from Gaziantep's otogar to Birecik (₺10), and there are also minibuses to Birecik from Urfa (₺12). Halfeti is relatively accessible by public transport on weekdays, but we definitely recommend an early start from Gaziantep or Urfa. Minibuses ply the route between Birecik and Halfeti (₺5), leaving from the Birecik market, around 300m past the Hotel Acar. Make sure you stress you want to go *Eski Halfeti* though, as many of the minibuses stop at Yeni Halfeti, the newer village around 9km from Eski Halfeti. Dolmuş traffic to Eski Halfeti slows to a trickle on weekends, but the site's popularity as a destination for Turkish tourists means that hitching is a viable option.

Şanlıurfa (Urfa)

📋 0414 / POP 515,000 / ELEV 518M

Şanlıurfa (the Prophets' City; also known as Urfa), is a pilgrimage town and spiritual centre. This is where the prophets Job and Abraham left their marks, and your first sight of the Dergah complex of mosques and the holy Gölbaşı area will be a magical moment – especially with the call to prayer as an essential soundtrack.

It's also in Urfa that you begin to feel you've reached the Middle East. Women cloaked in black chadors elbow their way through the odorous crush of the bazaar, and moustached gents in *şalvar* (traditional baggy Arabic pants) swill tea and click-clack backgammon pieces in shady courtyards.

Fuelled by investment in the nearby Southeast Anatolia Project, which combines irrigation projects and community development initiatives, a cosmopolitan sheen is now being added to Urfa's centuries-old heritage. The city's streets hum with an energetic buzz, and the nearby temple of Göbekli Tepe is emerging as one of eastern Turkey's unmissable destinations.

History

The Hittites imposed their rule over the area around 1370 BC. After a period of Assyrian rule, Alexander the Great conquered Urfa and named the town Edessa, after a former capital of Macedonia. It remained the capital of a Seleucid province until 132 BC, when the local Aramaean population set up an independent kingdom and renamed the town Orhai. This, however, turned out to be only temporary, as Orhai finally succumbed to the Romans, as did everywhere hereabouts.

Astride the fault line between the Persian and Roman empires, Edessa was batted back and forth from one to the other. In 533 the two empires signed a Treaty of Endless Peace – that lasted seven years. The Romans and Persians kept at it until the Arabs swept in and cleared them all out in 637. Edessa enjoyed three centuries of peace under the Arabs, after which everything went to blazes again.

Turks, Arabs, Armenians and Byzantines battled for the city from 944 until 1098, when the First Crusade arrived to set up the Latin County of Edessa. This lasted until 1144, when it was conquered by the Seljuk Turkish *emir* Zengi, who was soon after succeeded by Saladin, then by the Mamluks. The Ottomans conquered most of this region in the early 16th century, but Edessa did not become Urfa until 1637, when the Ottomans finally took over.

Urfa became Şanlıurfa (Glorious Urfa) in 1984. Since 1973, when Gaziantep (War Hero Antep) was given its special epithet, the citizens of Urfa had been chafing under a relative loss of dignity. Now that their city is 'Glorious', the inhabitants can look the citizens of 'War Hero' Antep straight in the eye.

⊙ Sights

FREE **Göbekli Tepe**   RUINS
(www.gobeklitepe.info) Catapulted to international fame after a *National Geographic* cover story in June 2011, the fascinating archaeological site of Göbekli Tepe is a must-visit destination from Şanlıurfa. Around 11km northeast of central Urfa, 'Pot Belly Hill' was first unearthed in 1995, and its circular array of Neolithic megaliths is estimated to date back to 9500 BC, around 6500 years before Stonehenge. A carefully constructed wooden walkway circles the site, making it easy to study the centuries-old stone pillars with exquisitely stylised carvings of lions, foxes and vultures.

Previously the site was thought to be a medieval cemetery, but is now thought to be the world's first place of worship, challenging the established view that Neolithic society was only focused on simple subsistence agriculture and the domestication of animals. The carved symbols on the Göbekli Tepe megaliths also predate Sumerian

Şanlıurfa (Urfa)

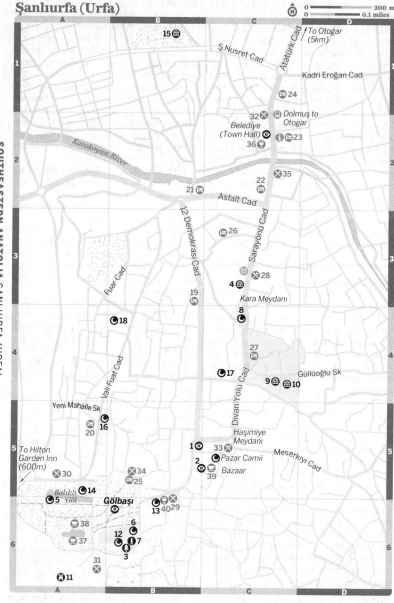

0 — 200 m
0 — 0.1 miles

hieroglyphics – traditionally thought to be the basis of written languages – by around 8000 years.

Geomagnetic surveys and ground-penetrating radar systems have identified another 16 ancient megalithic rings buried nearby, and at present only 5% of the entire site has been excavated.

A return taxi to Göbekli Tepe from Şanlıurfa is around ₺25 to ₺30, and the site can also be visited with Harran-Nemrut Tours (p569), Mustafa Çaycı (p569) and No-

Şanlıurfa (Urfa)

SOUTHEASTERN ANATOLIA ŞANLIURFA (URFA)

mad Tours (p569). Entry was free at the time of writing, but this will no doubt change as the site's popularity inevitably grows.

Gölbaşı HISTORIC AREA
Legend had it that Abraham (İbrahim), a great Islamic prophet, was in old Urfa destroying pagan gods one day when Nimrod, the local Assyrian king, took offence at this rash behaviour. Nimrod had Abraham immolated on a funeral pyre, but God turned the fire into water and the burning coals into fish. Abraham himself was hurled into the air from the hill where the fortress stands, but landed safely in a bed of roses.

The picturesque Gölbaşı area of Urfa is a symbolic re-creation of this story. Two rectangular pools of water (**Balıklı Göl** and **Ayn-i Zeliha**) are filled with supposedly sacred carp, and the area west of the **Hasan Padişah Camii** is a gorgeous rose garden. Local legend has it that anyone catching the carp will go blind. Consequently, these appear to be the most pampered, portly fish in Turkey.

On the northern side of Balıklı Göl is the elegant **Rızvaniye Vakfı Camii & Medresesi**, with a much-photographed arcaded wall, while at the western end is the **Halilur Rahman Camii**. This 13th-century building, replacing an earlier Byzantine church, marks the site where Abraham fell to the ground. The two pools are fed by a spring at the base of Damlacık hill, on which the castle is built.

Bazaar MARKET
(☉Mon-Sat) Spreading east of the **Narıncı Camii**, Urfa's bazaar is a jumble of streets, some covered, some open, selling everything from sheepskins and pigeons to jeans and handmade shoes. It was largely built by Süleyman the Magnificent in the mid-16th century. Women should be on guard for lustful hands.

One of the most interesting areas is the **bedesten** (covered market), an ancient caravanserai where silk goods were sold. Today you'll still find silk scarves here, as well as gaudy modern carpets and the lovely blue and red scarves worn by local women. Right by the *bedesten* is the Gümrük Hanı (p568), with a delightful courtyard that is always full of tea- or coffee-swilling moustached gents playing backgammon.

Also buried in the lanes of the bazaar are several ancient and very cheap hamams, including **Arasa Hamamı**.

Kale
FORTRESS

(Citadel; admission ₺3; ☺8am-8pm) Urfa's fortress on Damlacık hill, from which Abraham was supposedly tossed, has good views of the city, but unfortunately there's really not much to see at the actual site. We've also received reports of women travellers being hassled on the slopes behind the castle, so we recommend visiting only during daylight hours, and sticking to the busy areas.

Multiple conflicting histories claim the fortress was either (a) built in Hellenistic times, (b) built by the Byzantines, (c) built during the Crusades or (d) built by the Turks. On the top, most interesting are the pair of columns that local legend has dubbed the Throne of Nemrut after the supposed founder of Urfa, the biblical King Nimrod.

Dergah
PARK

Southeast of Gölbaşı is the Dergah complex of mosques and parks surrounding the colonnaded courtyard of the **Hazreti İbrahim Halilullah** (Prophet Abraham's Birth Cave; admission ₺1), built and rebuilt over the centuries as a place of pilgrimage. Its western side is marked by the **Mevlid-i Halil Camii**, a large Ottoman-style mosque. At its southern side is the entrance to the cave where Abraham was reputedly born. He lived here in hiding for his first seven years – King Nimrod, responding to a prophecy he'd received in a dream, feared that a newborn would eventually steal his crown, so he had all babies killed. This is still a place of pilgrimage and prayer, with separate entrances for men and women.

To visit these important places of worship you should be modestly dressed.

Ulu Camii
MOSQUE

(Divan Yolu Caddesi) Urfa's Syrian-style Ulu Camii dates from the period 1170–75. Its 13 *eyvans* (vaulted halls) open onto a spacious forecourt with a tall tower topped by a clock with Ottoman numerals.

Hüseyin Paşa Camii
MOSQUE

(Kara Meydanı) At Kara Meydanı, the square midway between the *belediye* (town hall) and Dergah is the Hüseyin Paşa Camii, a late-Ottoman construction built in 1849.

Selahattin Eyubi Camii
MOSQUE

(Vali Fuat Caddesi) On Vali Fuat Caddesi, which leads up from behind Gölbaşı, is this enormous, beautifully restored mosque. It was once St John's church, as evidenced by the altar.

Yeni Fırfırlı Camii
MOSQUE

(Yeni Fırfırlı Camii) North of Selahattin Eyubi Camii you'll notice the Yeni Fırfırlı Camii, a finely restored building, once the Armenian Church of the Twelve Apostles.

Şanlıurfa Museum
MUSEUM

(Şanlıurfa Müzesi; admission ₺3; ☺8am-noon & 1.30-5pm Tue-Sun) The museum's gardens contain various sculptures, as well as several mosaics near the entrance, the most interesting showing wild animals. Inside are Neolithic implements, Assyrian, Babylonian and Hittite relief stones, and other objects from Byzantine, Seljuk and Ottoman times.

Güzel Sanatlar Galerisi
ART GALLERY

(☺8am-5.30pm Mon-Fri, noon-4pm Sat) Delve into Urfa's back streets and you'll find examples of the city's distinctive limestone houses with protruding bays supported on stone corbels. Although many of these houses are falling into decay a few have been restored, most notably the house of Hacı Hafızlar, near the PTT, which has been turned into this art gallery.

Şurkav
HISTORIC BUILDING

(Balıklı Göl Mevkii) If you're keen to admire the local architecture, pop into the Şurkav, a local government building near the entrance to Hotel Edessa, where the courtyard is draped with greenery.

İl Özel İdaresi Kültür ve Sanat Merkezi
HISTORIC BUILDING

North of the market area, in the neighbourhood called Beykapı Mahallesi (take 1001 Sokak), have a look for this splendid house, restored in 2002. It was once a church.

İlköğretim Okulu
HISTORIC BUILDING

This stately building now houses a school.

🛏 Sleeping

Manici Hotel
HISTORIC HOTEL €€€

(☑215 9911; www.manici.com.tr; Balıklı Göl Mevkii; s/d ₺110/180; ❄🅰) The opulent Manici has beautifully restored rooms that will effortlessly fulfil your expectations of a romantic

URFA'S SPECIAL PLACES

Urfa is famed for its atmospheric *konuk evi* – 19th-century stone mansions that have been converted into restaurants and hotels. They usually feature a courtyard with several comfy *şark odası* (Ottoman-style lounges). They are smart places to rest your head and get a typical Urfa experience but can be noisy at weekends when they host *sıra geceleri* (live music evenings) or weddings. Not all rooms have private facilities, and you're definitely paying a premium for the heritage ambience.

Both the Otel Urhay and the Aslan Konuk Evi offer a similar experience for less.

Cevahir Konuk Evi (☏215 4678; www.cevahirkonukevi.com; Yeni Mahalle Sokak; s/d ₺140/220, mains ₺10-15; ❄🛜) Excellent *tebbule* (tabouleh) and faultlessly cooked *tavuk şiş* (roast chicken kebap) is served on the expansive terrace. Accommodation-wise, the rooms are disappointing, with kitsch paintings of Ye Olde Ottoman times and mismatched antique furniture.

Yıldız Sarayı Konukevi (☏215 9494; www.yildizsarayikonukevi.com; Yıldız Meydanı, 944 Sokak; s/d ₺70/130, mains ₺8-12; ❄) This magnificent courtyard residence has a wide array of rooms – sleep on mattresses on the floor or in more traditional bedrooms. There's also an on-site hamam, trimmed with gorgeous turquoise tiles from İznik.

getaway. The luxe furnishings stop just short of being OTT, and there's more of a contemporary vibe than at other heritage accommodation around town. The shared public areas are relaxed and calm-inducing, and there's an excellent licensed restaurant on hand.

Hilton Garden Inn　　HOTEL €€€
(☏318 5000; www.hilton.com; Nisan Fuar Caddesi 11; s/d 150/220; ❄🛜≋) Rooms are exceptionally spacious, and one of Turkey's best breakfast buffets awaits dowstairs (complete with one of Turkey's friendliest chefs). Hotel facilities include an atrium tea garden and an indoor pool and sauna complex, all around a 10-minute stroll from the city's main sights.

Otel Urhay　　HISTORIC HOTEL €€
(☏0544 215 7201, 216 2222; www.otelurhay.com; Sarayönü Caddesi, Beyaz Sokak; s/d ₺50/100; ❄🛜) A cool kilim-decorated lounge/restaurant combines with simple whitewashed rooms that feature both air-con – essential during an Urfa summer – and private bathrooms. The quiet inner courtyard is perfect for a combo of drinking tea and getting your travel diary up-to-date. Note that weddings and parties are sometimes hosted on weekends.

Aslan Konuk Evi　　PENSION €€
(☏0542 761 3065, 215 1575; www.aslankonukevi.com; Demokrasi Caddesi 12; r ₺90-120, dm ₺20-25; ❄@🛜) Simple but spacious high-ceilinged rooms are arranged around a shared central courtyard in a heritage Urfa building.

Efficiently run by local English teacher Özcan Aslan, with good food and cold beer available in the rooftop terrace restaurant. Outside guests are welcome for dinner, but you'll need to make a booking in the morning. Accommodation options range from shared dorm rooms to newer double rooms with private bathrooms. A good-value accommodation deal is ₺120 for two people including breakfast and dinner.

Hotel Uğur　　HOTEL €
(☏0532 685 2942, 313 1340; musma63@yahoo.com; Köprübaşı Caddesi 3; per person without bathroom ₺20; ❄🛜) The Uğur is Urfa's best value option for the pennywise backpacker. Rooms are sparsely decorated and relatively compact, but clean and spotless. There's a great travellers' vibe, enhanced by a few cold beers on the hotel's terrace as you watch Urfa's cinematic buzz unfold before you. Rates exclude breakfast, but there's a good *kahvaltı salonu* (breakfast restaurant) downstairs.

Hotel Güven　　HOTEL €€
(☏215 1700; www.hotelguven.com; Sarayönü Caddesi; s/d ₺85/140; ❄🛜) The Güven's had a sleek, boutique makeover since we last visited, and the marble desk promise of reception doesn't disappoint upstairs, with newly renovated rooms decked out in chocolate-brown and wooden tones. Flash bathrooms and flat-screen TVs also help to transform the Güven into one of central Urfa's best places to stay.

Kilim Otel
HOTEL €€

(☑313 9090; cnr Atatürk Caddesi & 877 Sokak; s/d ₺90/140; ☒) Located down a quiet lane just off the main drag, the Kilim's modern business stylings are equally appealing for mid-range travellers. Rooms are spacious with spotless bathrooms and views across Urfa's sprawl. Breakfast is one of Urfa's best, especially the tasty *menemen* (Turkish omelette).

Hotel Bakay
HOTEL €

(☑215 8975; Asfalt Caddesi; s/d ₺40/70; ☒@🛜) The Bakay is a safe bet that won't hurt the hip pocket, and is remarkably clean, but be prepared to trip over your backpack in the tiny rooms. Some are brighter than others, so check out a few before settling in.

✕ Eating

Local culinary specialities include the Urfa kebap (skewered chunks of lamb served with tomatoes, sliced onions and hot peppers); *çiğ köfte* (minced uncooked mutton), and *şıllık* (crepes filled with walnuts and syrup). Urfa folk like their food spicy, and many dishes come with a hearty addition of *ızot* (dried flaked peppers). You'll see – and smell – mini-mountains of *ızot* in Urfa's market area. Also look out for bottles of pomegranate dressing – used to add a sweet but zingy touch to most salads around town.

It pays to be a bit careful what you eat in Urfa, especially in summer, because the heat makes food poisoning more likely.

Manici Hotel
TURKISH €€

(☑215 9911; Balıklı Göl Mevkii; meze ₺6-8, mains ₺15-20) With excellent meze and traditional Turkish mains, the fully licensed restaurant at the Manici Hotel is an elegant affair framed by paintings of a roll call of Ottoman sultans. If your on-the-road diet has largely been an informal infusion of kebaps and pide, here's your chance to dig out your cleanest dirty shirt for a special night out.

Beyaz Köşk
KEBAP €

(Akarbaşı Göl Cadessi 20; mains ₺6-10) Turkey's best *lahmacun* (Arabic-style pizza) restaurants reputedly huddle in Gölbaşı's labyrinth of lanes, and the 'White House' is a great place to try plate-covering pizza studded with spicy *ızot*. Also served is *ciğer* kebap (grilled skewered liver), a popular breakfast. Grab an upstairs table on the breezy terrace and observe Urfa's gentle mayhem down below as you dig in.

Ikiler Ciğer Salonu
KEBAP €

(Faaliyet Alanı; ₺6-10) Informal streetside *ciğer salonu* (simple eateries serving grilled meats) are easy to find throughout the city, but our favourites are arrayed around a bustling square on the edge of the bazaar. Grab a cornerside table at Ikiler, and tuck into a mini-feast of grilled lamb, chicken or liver, served on tea-towel-sized flatbreads with spice-laden onions and grilled peppers.

Gülhan Restaurant
TURKISH €€

(Atatürk Caddesi; mains ₺8-14) Razor-sharp waiters; well-presented food that impresses rather than threatens; the right mood; slick and salubrious surrounds; a pictorial menu with English translations to help you choose – all good ingredients. For dessert, don't miss the *şıllık*.

Çift Mağara
TURKISH €€

(Çift Kubbe Altı Balıklıgöl; mains ₺10-15) The dining room is directly carved into the rocky bluff that overlooks the Gölbaşı, but the lovely terrace for dining alfresco beats the cavernous interior. Try the *içli köfte* (ground lamb and onion with a bulgur coating).

Zahter Kahvaltı & Kebap Salonu
BREAKFAST €

(Köprübaşı Caddesi; mains ₺5-10) Skip your hotel's breakfast and instead wolf down gooey honey, *pekmez* (grape syrup), jam and cream on flatbread. Wash it all down with a large glass of çay or *ayran* – all for around ₺8.

Baklavacı Badıllı Dedeoğlu
SWEETS €

(Sarayönü Caddesi; pastries ₺2) Death by pistachio baklavas and pistachio *sarması* ('vine leaves').

Çardaklı Köşk
TURKISH €€

(Vali Fuat Caddesi, Tünel Çıkışı; mains ₺10-15) This old house has been so restored it feels almost new. Food is only so-so – the real wow is the regular live music and the view over Gölbaşı from the upstairs terrace.

🍷 Drinking

For a cup of tea in leafy surrounds, head for the various **çay bahçesis** (tea gardens) in the Gölbaşı park. For a cold beer, head to the Altın Kupa pub, or have dinner at the Aslan Guest House or Manici Hotel.

Gümrük Hanı
COFFEEHOUSE

(Customs Depot; Urfa bazaar; coffee ₺3) Here's the ideal spot for the first coffee of the day – a wonderfully restored caravanserai crowded with locals enjoying a caffeine hit. Ask for *kahve mırra*, the super-strong and bitter local variation.

Şampiyon Vitamin
JUICE BAR
(Akarbaşı Göl Cadessi; juices from ₺2) Recharge and replenish your inner traveller at this terrific fresh juice bar on the edge on the Urfa bazaar. It's all good, but we found the zingy *greyfurt suyu* (grapefruit juice) especially refreshing. More substantial is the *atom*, a delicious smoothie combining yoghurt, banana and chopped pistachios.

Altin Kupa
PUB
(Köprübaşı Kişla Caddesi 4) In the middle of an Urfa summer, this centrally located pub and beer garden is a handy hop-fuelled haven from the Anatolian heat. It's probably a tad blokey for single female travellers, but we saw local couples eating and drinking together there on our last visit.

☆ Entertainment

Urfa is an city of contrast: pious during the day, wild in the evening. What makes the city tick are the *sıra geceleri* (live music evenings) that are held in the *konuk evi*, usually at weekends. Guests sit, eat, sing and dance in *şark odası* (Ottoman-style lounges) and, after the meal, a live band plays old favourites that keep revellers rocking and dancing. Foreigners are welcome to join the party. BYO earplugs if you're sleeping upstairs.

ⓘ Information

The post office, internet cafes and ATMs are on Urfa's main drag. In the absence of an official tourist information office, Özcan Aslan at Harran-Nemrut Tours and Mustafa Çaycı at the Hotel Uğur can usually provide good city maps and other English-language information.

Harran-Nemrut Tours (☑0542 761 3065, 215 1575; www.aslankonukevi.com; Demokrasi Caddesi 12) A small travel agency efficiently run by Özcan Aslan, a local teacher who speaks very good English and is a mine of local information. He organises tours to nearby sites, including Göbekli Tepe, Harran, Şuayb City, Soğmatar, Mardin and Nemrut Dağ. Tour prices range from €25 to €50 per person. You'll find Özcan at the Aslan Konuk Evi guesthouse, or see the website for tour details.

Mustafa Çaycı (☑313 1340, 0532 685 2942; musma63@yahoo.com; Köprübaşı Caddesi 3) The friendly Mustafa Çaycı from the Hotel Uğur runs a variety of local tours. Options include short and long tours to Harran (per person ₺30/70), excursions to Göbekli Tepe (per

YUVACALİ VILLAGE HOMESTAY & ABRAHAM'S PATH

Around one hour north of Şanlıurfa, the sleepy Kurdish village of Yuvacali hosts one of the only homestay programs in eastern Turkey. Accommodation is in a simple, but spotless, village house with basic, shared facilities and the attention of a friendly Kurdish family. During summer the best sleeping option is on the roof, under the stars, waking up to the early-morning sounds of the host family's fat-tailed sheep. The same sheep provide milk for the homemade cheese and yoghurt – a perfect accompaniment to freshly made and still-warm flatbread for breakfast. Dinner is a shared affair, with grilled chicken, bulghur wheat and fresh salads. See **Nomad Tours Turkey** (☑0533 747 1850; www.nomadtours turkey.com; per person B&B €30, with full board €35) for more details.

The Yuvacali homestay program supports the local kindergarten and school, and is a friendly and relaxed option to break up the usual southeastern Anatolian routine of cheap pensions and hotels. Transfers from Hilvan – on the main highway from Diyarbakır to Şanlıurfa – to Yuvacali are ₺5.

Run by knowledgeable expat (and Yuvacali resident) Alison Tanik, Nomad also runs full-day tours to Harran (€50), Şanlıurfa (€40), Nemrut Dağı (€100) and Diyarbakır (€60). Longer multiday tours incorporate Mardin, Midyat and Hasankeyf, and trips to Iraqi Kurdistan are also possible. Tours to Şanlıurfa and Harran also include a visit to the temple of Göbekli Tepe.

Nomad Tours have also been influential in establishing the Turkish component of **Abraham's Path** (www.abrahampath.org), a walking trail in the footsteps of the prophet Abraham which traverses Israel, Palestine and the West Bank, Jordan, Syria and Turkey. The southeast Anatolian part of the route incorporates Kurdish village homestays and visits to Şanlıurfa, Harran and Göbekli Tepe. See www.abrahamspathturkey.org.

SOUTHEASTERN ANATOLIA ŞANLIURFA (URFA)

SERVICES FROM ŞANLIURFA'S OTOGAR

DESTINATION	FARE (₺)	DURATION (HR)	DISTANCE (KM)	FREQUENCY (PER DAY)
Adana	30	6	365	several
Ankara	60	13	850	5-6
Diyarbakır	15	3	190	several
Erzurum	55	12	665	1
Gaziantep	15	2½	145	several
İstanbul	75	20	1290	3-4
Kayseri	35	9	515	2
Malatya	40	7	395	1
Mardin	30	3	175	3-4
Van	45	9	585	2

person ₺25), and longer trips to Nemrut Dağı (per person ₺130).

ⓘ Getting There & Away

Air

The airport is 45km from Urfa on the road to Diyarbakır. Ask about the Havas airport bus at **Kalıru Turizm** (☏ 215 3344; www.kaliruturizm .com.tr; Sarayönü Caddesi; ☉ 8.30am-6.30pm).

Pegasus Airlines (www.flypgs.com) Regular flights to/from Ankara (from ₺100), İstanbul (from ₺100) and İzmir (from ₺100).

Turkish Airlines (www.turkishairlines.com) Daily flights to/from Ankara (from ₺84) and İstanbul (₺105).

Bus

Urfa's otogar is 5km north of town off the road to Diyarbakır. Note: some buses will drop passengers at a roundabout around 300m from the otogar. Buses to the otogar can be caught on Atatürk Caddesi (₺1). Taxis usually ask ₺20. Minibuses to Akçakale (₺5), Harran (₺5), Kahta (₺15) and Adıyaman (₺15) leave from the regional minibus terminal underneath the otogar.

Car

For car hire (around ₺80 per day) try Mustafa Çaycı (p569) or Harran-Nemrut Tours (p569).

Harran

☏ 0414 / POP 6900

Harran is reputedly one of the oldest continuously inhabited spots on earth. The Book of Genesis mentions Harran and its most famous resident, Abraham, who stayed for a few years in 1900 BC. Its ruined walls, crumbling fortress and beehive houses are powerful, evocative sights that give the town a feeling of deep antiquity. Traditionally, locals lived by farming and smuggling, but the coming of the Atatürk Dam now sees cotton fields sprouting over what was once arid desert.

On arrival in Harran you'll need to buy a ticket (₺5) from the attendants at the booth near the car park. If anyone else in the castle tries to charge you, insist on being given the official ticket. Good luck dealing with the cheeky local kids who can be slightly annoying. If you really want to understand the history of Harran, an English-speaking guide (around ₺15) is a worthwhile investment.

Note that Turkish tourists are frequent visitors on weekends, and it's worth visiting on a weekday to experience Harran at its sleepy best.

History

Besides being the place of Abraham's sojourn, Harran is famous as a centre of worship of Sin, god of the moon. Worship of the sun, moon and planets was popular in Harran, and at neighbouring Soğmatar, from about 800 BC until AD 830, although Harran's temple to the moon god was destroyed by the Byzantine emperor Theodosius in AD 382. Battles between Arabs and Byzantines occupied the townsfolk until the Crusaders came. The fortress, which some say was built on the ruins of the moon god's temple, was restored when the Crusaders approached. The Crusaders won and maintained it for a while before they, too, moved on.

⊙ Sights

Beehive Houses   HISTORIC AREA

Harran is famous for its beehive houses, the design of which may date back to the 3rd century BC, although the present examples were mostly constructed within the last 200 years. It's thought that the design evolved partly in response to a lack of wood for roofs and partly because the ruins provided a source of reusable bricks. Although the Harran houses are unique in Turkey, similar buildings can be found in northern Syria.

The **Harran Kültür Evi**, within walking distance of the castle, is set up to allow visitors to see inside one of the houses and then sip cold drinks in the walled courtyard afterwards. The **Harran Evi** is similar.

Kale
FORTRESS

On the far (east) side of the hill, the crumbling *kale* stands right by some beehive houses. A castle probably already existed here during Hittite times, but the current construction dates mainly from after 1059, when the Fatimids took over and restored it. Originally, there were four multi-angular corner towers, but only two remain.

City Walls
RUINS

The crumbling stone city walls were once 4km long and studded with 187 towers and four gates. Of these, only the overly restored **Aleppo Gate**, near the new part of town, remains.

Ulu Camii
MOSQUE

Of the ruins inside the village other than the *kale*, the Ulu Camii, built in the 8th century by Marwan II, last of the Umayyad caliphs, is most prominent. You'll recognise it by its tall, square and very un-Turkish minaret. It's said to be the oldest mosque in Anatolia. Near here stood the first Islamic university, and on the hillside above it you'll see the low-level ruins of ancient Harran, dating back some 5000 years.

❶ Getting There & Away

Minibuses (₺4, one hour) leave from Urfa's otogar approximately every hour and will drop you at the new part of Harran near the *belediye* and PTT – it's a 10-minute walk to the old part of town. Minibus traffic back to Urfa diminishes from midafternoon so it's best to ask for details at the Urfa bus station before you leave in the morning.

Around Harran

Although the sites beyond Harran are missable if you're pushed for time, it would be a shame not to see the astonishing transformation wrought on the local scenery by the GAP project – field upon field of cotton and barley where once there was just desert.

To get around the sites without your own transport is virtually impossible unless you have limitless time, so consider a tour by Harran-Nemrut Tours (p569) or Mustafa Çaycı (p569) in Şanlıurfa. You may need to take a picnic lunch, or you might have a village lunch stop. It's useful to have a pocketful of change for tips along the way. The Harran 'long tour' usually incorporates most of the nearby sights listed below.

⦿ Sights

Bazda Caves
RUINS

About 20km east of town, the impressive Bazda Mağaları are supposed to have been used to build the walls of Harran.

Han el Ba'rur
RUINS

Six kilometres east from the Bazda caves are the remains of the Seljuk Han el Ba'rur, a caravanserai built in 1128 to service the local trade caravans.

Şuayb City
RUINS

Twelve kilometres northeast of Han el Ba'rur are the extensive remains of Şuayb City, where hefty stone walls and lintels survive above a network of subterranean rooms. One of these contains a mosque on the site of the supposed home of the prophet Jethro. Bring a torch and to wear sturdy shoes.

Soğmatar
RUINS

About 18km north of Şuayb, the isolated village of Soğmatar is a very atmospheric, eerie place. Sacrifices were made to the sun and moon gods, whose effigies can be seen carved into the side of the ledge. Like Harran, Soğmatar was a centre for the cult worship of Sin, the moon god, from about AD 150 to 200. This open-air altar was the central, main temple. In a cave near the centre of the village you'll find 12 carved statues as well as Assyrian inscriptions.

Standing on the summit of the structure, you can see remains of other temples on the surrounding hills. There were apparently seven in all.

Kahta

🎣 0416 / POP 64,500

Dusty Kahta doesn't exactly scream 'holiday', but it's well set up for visits to Nemrut Dağı, with tours and hotels on tap. Accommodation actually on the mountain, such as the Karadut Pension and Hotel Euphrat, is more inspiring and scenic.

Around 25 June, the three-day **International Kahta Kommagene Festival** has music and folk dancing. It's essential to book accommodation ahead at this time.

🛏 Sleeping

Kommagene Hotel HOTEL €
(☎0532 200 3856, 725 9726; www.kommagene hotel.com; Mustafa Kemal Caddesi 1; s/d ₺45/70; ❇@❂) A recent makeover has transformed the Kommagene from a pretty basic pension into a good budget hotel. The wood-lined rooms are cosy and colourful, and all have private bathrooms. Breakfast is served in a spacious top-floor salon with good views of Kahta's dusty main drag. There's a kitchen and laundry for the use of guests, and free pick-ups from either the Adıyaman or Kahta otogar. During the heat of summer, the hotel can shuttle guests out to the lake formed by the Atatürk Dam. Packages incorporating accommodation and a tour to Nemrut Daği are ₺125 per person. Daily departures are guaranteed from April to November. See www.nemrutguide.com.

Zeus Hotel HOTEL €€
(☎725 5694; www.zeushotel.com.tr; Mustafa Kemal Caddesi; campsites per person ₺20, s/d/ste €60/80/110; ❇❂≋) This solid three-star option gets an A+ for its swimming pool and manicured garden – blissful after a long day's travelling by bus. Angle for the renovated rooms, which feature top-notch bathrooms and flat-screen TVs. Campers can pitch tents on the parking lot, and have access to their own ablutions block.

🍴 Eating

For something different take a taxi (₺15) to the vast lake formed by the Atatürk Dam, about 4km east of Kahta. The lure is the licensed restaurants serving fresh fish, with lovely views over the lake.

Papatya Restaurant TURKISH €
(Mustafa Kemal Caddesi; mains ₺8-10) This snappy place opposite the Zeus Hotel whips up all the usual suspects. There's no menu – just point at what you want.

Akropalian RESTAURANT, BAR €€
(Baraj Yolu; mains ₺8-15) Perched on a hillside, about 1km from the lakeshore. Bag a seat in the verdant *bahçe* and drink in the views with a cold Efes lager.

❶ Getting There & Away

Kahta's small otogar is in the town centre, with the minibus and taxi stands are right beside it. There are regular buses to Adıyaman (₺3, 30 minutes, 32km), Ankara (₺55, 12 hours, 807km), İstanbul (₺80, 20 hours, 1352km), Kayseri (₺40, seven hours, 487km), Malatya (₺20, 3½ hours, 225km), Şanlıurfa (₺17, 2½ hours, 106km), and Diyarbakır (₺25, four hours, 174km). For accurate information about costs and the availability of onward buses be sure to visit the otogar and check for yourself, rather than rely on locals.

Despite what some may say, there are definitely minibuses every couple of hours to Karadut (₺7), but departures drop off in the afternoon, and are less frequent on Saturday and Sunday. We recommend getting a morning start from Kahta. The buses return from Karadut between 7.30am and 8.30am the next day.

Nemrut Daği National Park

The spellbinding peak of **Nemrut Daği** (*ne-hm-root dah-uh*) rises to a height of 2150m in the Anti-Taurus Range between the provincial capital of Malatya to the north and Kahta in Adıyaman province to the south (it's not to be confused with the less-visited Nemrut Daği near Lake Van).

Nobody knew anything about Nemrut Daği until 1881, when a German engineer, employed by the Ottomans to assess transport routes, was astounded to come across the statues covering this remote mountaintop. Archaeological work didn't begin until 1953, when the American School of Oriental Research undertook the project.

The summit was created when a megalomaniac pre-Roman local king cut two ledges in the rock, filled them with colossal statues of himself and the gods (his relatives – or so he thought), then ordered an artificial mountain peak of crushed rock 50m high to be piled between them. The king's tomb and those of three female relatives are reputed to lie beneath those tonnes of rock.

Earthquakes have toppled the heads from most of the statues, and now many of the colossal bodies sit silently in rows, with the 2m-high heads watching from the ground.

Although it's relatively easy to get to the summit with your own vehicle, most people take tours, organised in either Kahta or Malatya, or as a longer day trip from Şanlıurfa or Cappadocia.

Nemrut Dağı Area

Map labels:
- To Büyüköz (8km)
- To Büyüköz (8km)
- Kıran
- Güneş Hotel
- Nemrut Dağı (Mt Nemrut) (2150m)
- Bahçeköy
- *Kahta (Numphaios)*
- Western Terrace
- Eastern Terrace
- Car Park & Café
- Kütüktü
- Cendere Bridge
- Eski Kahta (Kocahisar)
- Eski Kale (Arsameia)
- Gate & Ticket Office
- Çeşme Pansion
- Karadut
- To Gerger (25km)
- Arsemia Kafeterya & Kamping
- Yeni Kale
- Hotel Euphrat
- Karadut Pension
- Seljuk Bridge
- Gate & Ticket Office
- Damlaçık Garden Camping
- Damlaçık
- Sırıkay
- Çıngıl
- Koçtepe
- Narince
- To Diyarbakır
- Tüten Ocak
- Karakuş Tümülüs (Karakuş Burial Mound)
- Köklü
- D360
- Ekinci
- Salkımbağı
- To Kahta (5km)
- Atatürk Gölü (Atatürk Lake)

Plan to visit the **national park** (admission ₺6.50; ☉dawn-dusk) between late May and mid-October, and preferably in July or August; the road to the summit becomes impassable with snow at other times. Even in high summer it will be chilly and windy on top of the mountain. This is especially true at sunrise, the coldest time of the day. Take warm clothing on your trek to the top no matter when you go.

There are three ways of approaching the summit. From the southern side, you pass through **Karadut**, a village some 12km from the top, before embarking upon the last few kilometres to the car park. From the southwestern side, a secondary road goes past **Eski Kale** (Arsameia) and climbs steeply for about 10km until it merges with the Karadut road, some 6km before the car park at the summit. This secondary road is quite rough in parts, and should only be attempted by confident drivers. Travellers staying in Kara-

dut can walk the 12km to the summit. It's a clearly marked road with a steady gradient.

From the northern side, you can travel from Malatya via a recently upgraded 96km road until the Güneş Hotel, near the summit. Note that it is not possible to cross the summit by car from the northern side to the southern side.

It costs T8 to enter Mt Nemrut National Park. Coming from the southwest, the entrance gate is at the turn-off to Eski Kale; from the south, the gate is just past Çeşme Pansion; from the north, the gate is at the Güneş Hotel.

History

From 250 BC onwards, this region straddled the border between the Seleucid Empire and the Parthian Empire.

Under the Seleucid Empire, the governor of Commagene declared his kingdom's independence. In 80 BC, with the Seleucids in disarray and Roman power spreading into Anatolia, a Roman ally named Mithridates I Callinicus proclaimed himself king and set up his capital at Arsameia, near the modern village of Eski Kahta.

Mithridates died in 64 BC and was succeeded by his son Antiochus I Epiphanes (r 64–38 BC), who consolidated his kingdom's security by immediately signing a nonaggression treaty with Rome, turning his kingdom into a Roman buffer against attack from the Parthians. His good relations with both sides allowed him to revel in delusions of grandeur, and it was Antiochus who ordered the building of Nemrut's fabulous temples and funerary mound.

In the 3rd decade of his reign, Antiochus sided with the Parthians in a squabble with Rome, and in 38 BC the Romans deposed him. The great days of Commagene were thus limited to the 26-year reign of Antiochus.

◉ Sights & Activities

Karakuş Tümülüs
RUINS

Highway D360, marked for Nemrut Dağı Milli Parkı, starts in Kahta next to the Hotel Kommagene. After a few kilometres, the road forks left 1.5km to Karakuş Tümülüs, built in 36 BC. A handful of columns ring the mound – there were more, but the limestone blocks were used by the Romans to build the Cendere Bridge. An eagle tops a column at the car park, a lion tops another around the mound, and a third has an inscribed slab explaining that the burial mound holds female relatives of King Mithridates II.

Cendere Bridge
BRIDGE

Some 10km from the Karakuş Tümülüs is a modern bridge over the Cendere River. To the left you'll see a magnificent humpback Roman bridge built in the 2nd century AD. The surviving Latin stelae state that the bridge was built in honour of Emperor Septimius Severus. Of

---

ORGANISED TOURS TO NEMRUT DAĞI (MT NEMRUT)

The main tour centres are Kahta and Malatya, but there are also tours from Karadut, Şanlıurfa and Cappadocia.

From Karadut

Several pensions in Karadut offer return trips to the summit, with one hour at the top, for about ₺50 per vehicle (Karadut Pension; p576) or ₺100 (Hotel Euphrat; p576).

From Kahta

Historically Kahta has had a reputation as a rip-off town, but in recent years we have noticed an improvement in the professionalism and attitudes of local tour operators. Despite this, always check exactly what you will be seeing during the tour, in addition to the heads themselves, and how long you'll be away for.

From Kahta, visitors to the mountain have the option of a 'long tour' or a 'short tour'.

The majority of 'long' tours are timed to capture a dramatic sunrise or sunset. If you opt for the 'sunrise tours', you'll leave Kahta at about 2am via Narince and Karadut, arriving at Nemrut Dağı for sunrise. After an hour or so, you'll go down again following the upgraded direct road to Arsameia. Then you'll stop at Eski Kahta, Yeni Kale, Cendere Bridge and Karakuş Tümülüs. Expect to be back in Kahta at about 10am. If you sign up for the 'sunset tour', you'll do the same loop but in the reverse direction – in other words, you'll leave at 1.30pm and start with the sights around Arsameia, then go up to the summit, before descending via Karadut and Narince. You'll be back in Kahta by 9.30pm. Mt Nemrut Tours (www.nemrutguide.com) at the Kommagene Hotel (p572) offer a 'long tour' package including accommodation for ₺125 per person. Tours are also available at the Zeus Hotel (p572).

A 'short tour' lasts about three hours, and zips you from Kahta to the summit and back again, allowing about an hour for sightseeing. It's less expensive, but much less interesting, as it skips the other sights in the region.

Although Kahta hotels and guesthouses advertise these services as 'tours', you'll quickly catch on that they're only taxi services when your driver proffers comments like, 'That's an old bridge.'

If you're in a group, another option is to hire a taxi at the Kahta otogar. Prices are posted as ₺100 for the 'short tour' and ₺130 for the 'long tour'.

the four original Corinthian columns (two at either end), three are still standing.

Eski Kahta (Kocahisar) & Yeni Kale   RUINS
About 5km from the bridge is a 1km detour to **Eski Kahta**. There was once a palace here, but what's now evident are the ruins of a 13th-century Mamluk castle, **Yeni Kale** (New Fortress). The castle was being renovated at the time of writing and due to reopen any day.

After Yeni Kale, cross the Kahta (Nymphaios) River to see the old road and the graceful **Seljuk Bridge**.

Eski Kale (Arsameia)   RUINS
About 1.5km further, the main road forks left 2km to Eski Kale, the ancient Commagene capital of Arsameia. Nearby is the park entrance for Arsameia and summit access (₺8).

At Eski Kale there is a large **stele** depicting Mithras (or Apollo), the sun god. Further

along are the bases of two stelae depicting Mithridates I Callinicus, with Antiochus I, the taller stele, holding a sceptre. Behind here, a cave entrance leads to an underground chamber built for Mithras-worshipping rites.

Further uphill is a **stone relief** portraying Mithridates I shaking hands with the ancient hero Heracles. Adjacent, another cave temple descends 158m through the rock; the steps into the temple are dangerous. The long Greek inscription above the cave describes the founding of Arsameia; the water trough beside it may have been used for religious ablutions.

On the hilltop are the ruined foundations of Mithridates' capital.

Summit   RUINS
(admission ₺8; ⊙dawn-dusk) The park entrance is 200m up from Çeşme Pansion and 2.5km before the junction with the short cut to Eski Kale.

From Malatya
Malatya offers an alternative way to approach Nemrut Dağı. However, visiting Nemrut from this northern side means you miss out on the other fascinating sights on the southern flanks (reached from Kahta). You can get the best of both worlds by traversing the top by foot and hitching a ride to Kahta; if you're travelling by car you'll have to take the long route via Adıyaman.

Hassle-free minibus tours to Nemrut Dağı are available from early May to the end of September, or to mid-October if the weather is still warm. See Kemal at the Nemrut Dağı Information Booth (p579). Tours leave at noon.

The three-hour drive to the summit traverses a newly sealed road, and after enjoying the sunset for two hours, you overnight at the Güneş Hotel before heading back up to the summit for sunrise. After breakfast at the Güneş, you return to Malatya at around 10am.

The per-person cost of ₺100 (minimum two people) includes transport, dinner, bed and breakfast, but excludes admission to the national park and the site. In theory, the tours run daily, but solo travellers may have to pay more if no one else wants to join you.

From Şanlıurfa
Tours (€50 per person, minimum two) to Nemrut are available from **Harran-Nemrut Tours** (☎0414-215 1575; www.aslankonukevi.com; Demokrasi Caddesi 12, Aslan Konak Evi) in Şanlıurfa. Mustafa Çaycı (p569) at the Hotel Uğur (₺130 per person, minimum two) also offers trips.

Nomad Tours Turkey (p569), based in the Kurdish village of Yuvacali, also runs full-day tours (€100 per person).

From Cappadocia
Many companies in Cappadocia offer minibus tours to Nemrut from mid-April to mid-November, despite the distance of over 500km each way. Two-day tours cost about ₺350 and involve many hours of breakneck driving. If you have enough time, it's better to opt for a three-day tour, which allows the journey to be broken into more manageable chunks. Three-day tours usually also include Harran and Şanlıurfa. Ask for details on night stops and driving times before committing.

Beyond the building, hike 600m (about 20 minutes) over the broken rock of the stone pyramid to the western terrace. Antiochus I Epiphanes ordered the construction of a combined tomb and temple here. The site was to be approached by a ceremonial road and was to incorporate what Antiochus termed 'the thrones of the gods', which would be based 'on a foundation that will never be demolished'.

The first thing you see is the western temple with the conical funerary mound of fist-sized stones behind it. Antiochus and his fellow gods sit in state, although their bodies have partly tumbled down, along with their heads.

From the western terrace it's five minutes' walk to the eastern terrace. Here the bodies are largely intact, except for the fallen heads, which seem more badly weathered than the western heads. On the backs of the eastern statues are inscriptions in Greek. Both terraces have similar plans, with the syncretistic gods, the 'ancestors' of Antiochus, seated. From left to right they are Apollo, the sun god (Mithra to the Persians; Helios or Hermes to the Greeks); Fortuna, or Tyche; Zeus-Ahura Mazda in the centre; then King Antiochus; and on the far right Heracles, also known as Ares or Artagnes.

Low walls at the sides of each temple once held carved reliefs showing processions of ancient Persian and Greek royalty, Antiochus' 'predecessors'. Statues of eagles represent Zeus.

Sleeping & Eating

There are several places to stay along the roads to the summit.

Karadut Pension
PENSION €

(☑0532 566 2857, 0416-737 2169; www.karadut pansiyon.net; campsites per person ₺5, d per person ₺35; ❄@) This pension in Karadut has neat, compact rooms (some with air-con), cleanish bathrooms and a shared kitchen. Meals are available along with wine, beer or rakı in the alfresco terrace bar. Campers can pitch their tent in a partially shaded plot at the back. They'll pick you up from Kahta for ₺18.

Damlacık Garden Camping
CAMPING GROUND €

(☑0539 638 1858, 0416 741 2027; tavsi_campig@ hotmail.com; campsites per person ₺8; @) At Damlacık, about 2km from the junction for the entrance gate, this simple camping ground has a welcoming host family and grassed camping areas. There's also a secure parking lot for campervans, equipped with electricity. Meals are available for ₺10. Transport to Nemrut is ₺120 per vehicle.

Güneş Hotel
HOTEL €

(☑0535 760 5080; kemalmalatya@hotmail .com; r incl half-board per person ₺60) Standing in Gothic isolation about 2.5km from the eastern terrace, this hotel is used by travellers coming from Malatya. The setting is dramatic (bordering on spooky on a cloudy day), amid rocky boulders, the hush is enjoyable and the rooms are ordinary yet clean. See Kemal at the Nemrut Dağı Information Booth (p579) in Malatya about staying here.

Hotel Euphrat
HOTEL €€

(☑0416-737 2175; www.hoteleuphratnemrut.com; s/d/tr incl half-board €45/58/68; ❄≋) The low-rise Euphrat is popular with tour groups in peak season. Recent renovations have made the rooms larger and more comfortable, and the views from the restaurant terrace and new pool are spectacular.

Arsemia Kafeterya & Kamping
CAMPING GOUND €

(☑0533 682 1242, 0416-741 2224; kal_bin_sasi@ hotmail.com; campsites per person ₺8) Pitch your tent or park your campervan on a well laid-out ridge (no grass or shade) and enjoy valley views. Simple meals are available for ₺15. Transport to Nemrut costs ₺1000 per vehicle. It's in Eski Kale, about 1km past the entrance gate.

Çeşme Pansion
PENSION €

(☑0416-737 2032; www.cesmepansion.com; campsites per person ₺5, per person incl half-board ₺40) The closest shut-eye option to the summit (only 6km), the owners will drive you there for ₺40). The rooms (all with private bathrooms) are basic but clean, and campers will enjoy a shaded garden setting.

Getting There & Away

Car

To ascend the southern slopes of Nemrut from Kahta, drive along the D360 via Narince, or take a longer but more scenic route that includes Karakuş, Cendere, Eski Kahta and Eski Kale, then the 15km short cut to the summit. Make sure you have fuel for at least 250km of normal driving. Though the trip to the summit and back is at most 160km, you have to drive some of that in low gear, which uses more fuel. Be prepared for the rough, steep last 3km up to the summit.

You can also approach the summit from Malatya (98km one way) and drive up to the Güneş Hotel. The road has recently been resurfaced. From there, a rough road leads to the eastern terrace, a further 2.5km. It's OK with a normal car in dry weather, but definitely only for confident drivers.

Note there is no road at the summit linking the southern and the northern sides, but a (very!) rough road does skirt the base of the mountain linking the Kahta (southern) side to the Malatya (northern) side. From Kocahisar, a road goes 21km to the village of Büyüköz. The first 7km, up to the village of Kıran, are surfaced. The next 6km, to the hamlet of Taşkale, deteriorates markedly and gradually becomes gravel; the last 8km, up to Büyüköz, is unsurfaced, narrow and very steep (expect nerve-racking twists and turns). Don't brave it in wet weather and seek local advice at Kocahisar (if you're coming from Kahta and going to Malatya) or at Büyüköz (if you're doing Malatya–Kahta) before setting off.

Taxi & Minibus

During the summer season there are minibuses (₺10) around every two hours between Kahta and the Çeşme Pansion, about 6km from the summit. The last minibus usually leaves Kahta around 3pm, but an early start is recommended. They stop at Karadut village (₺5) on the way. Pension owners can also pick you up at Kahta's otogar (agree the price beforehand). Don't believe anyone in Kahta who tells you there are no minibuses to the Çeşme Pansion and Karadut village from Kahta.

All pensions and hotels can run you up to the summit and back, but don't expect anything in the way of guidance. The closer to the summit, the cheaper it will be.

Malatya

📞0422 / POP 420,000 / ELEV 964M

Malatya's architecture wins no prizes and sights are sparse, but the city soon grows on you. The city's rewards include verdant parks, tree-lined boulevards, chaotic bazaars and the smug feeling that you're the only tourist for miles around. For cultural sustenance, there's the nearby historic site of Battalgazi, and many operators also offer tours to Nemrut Dağı (see p574).

Malatya is also Turkey's *kayısı* (apricot) capital, and after the late-June harvest, thousands of tonnes of the luscious fruit are shipped internationally.

History

The Assyrians and Persians alternately conquered the city, and later the kings of Cappadocia and Pontus did the same. In 66 BC Pompey defeated Mithridates and took the town, then known as Melita. The Byzantines, Sassanids, Arabs and Danışmend *emirs* held it until the Seljuks arrived in 1105. Then came the Ottomans (1399), the armies of Tamerlane (1401), the Mamluks, Dülkadır *emirs* and the Ottomans again (1515).

When the Egyptian forces of Mohammed Ali invaded Anatolia in 1839, the Ottomans garrisoned Malatya, leaving much of it in ruins on their departure. Later the residents returned and established a new city on the present site. You can visit the remains of old Malatya (Eski Malatya), now called Battalgazi, nearby.

⊙ Sights

Bazaar   MARKET

(⊙daily) Malatya's vibrant market sprawls north from PTT Caddesi. Especially fascinating is the lively metalworking area. Brush up your Turkish and wind your way to the **Apricot Market** (*kayısı pazarı* or *şire pazarı*). You won't leave Malatya without filling your bags with the fruit.

FREE Malatya Ethnographic Museum   MUSEUM

(Sinema Caddesi; ⊙8am-5pm) Great English-language information brings alive this showcase of jewellery, weaving and a fearsome collection of old weapons. It's all housed near five restored old **Malatyan houses** along Sinema Caddesi.

Museum   MUSEUM

(Fuzuli Caddesi; admission ₺3; ⊙8am-5pm Tue-Sun) About 750m from the town centre, Malatya's museum has interesting finds from the excavations at Aslantepe.

🛏 Sleeping

Grand W Aksaç Hotel   HOTEL €€

(📞324 6565; www.aksachotel.com; Saray Mahallesi, Ömer Efendi Sokak 19; s/d ₺100/140; 🌀🛜) The Grand W Aksaç celebrates a quiet central location with flash services including a hamam, and shiny, spacious bathrooms. Flat-screen TVs, huge beds and chocolate-covered apricots for sale in reception sound like a winning combination if you've been travelling just a little too quickly.

Malatya Palace Hotel   HOTEL €€

(📞326 1114; www.malatyapalacehotel.com; PTT Caddesi 20; s/d ₺70/100; 🌀🛜) This sparkling new opening has quite possibly Malatya's smallest lift – altogether now, breathe in –

Malatya

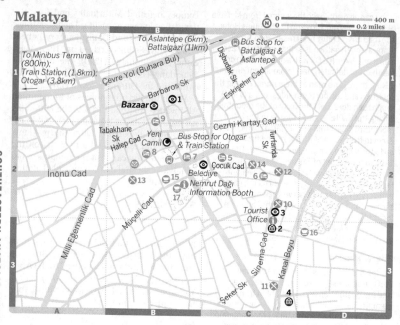

To Aslantepe (6km);
Battalgazi (11km);

Bus Stop for
Battalgazi &
Aslantepe

To Minibus Terminal
(800m);
Train Station (1.8km);
Otogar (3.8km)

Çevre Yol (Buhara Bul)

Barbaros Sk

Bazaar ⊙ ⊙1

Disbudak Sk

Eskişehir Cad

Cezmi Kartay Cad

Tabakhane
Sk
Yeni
Halep Cad Camii
Bus Stop for Otogar
& Train Station

İnönü Cad

Turfanda
Sk

Çocuk Cad
Belediye

Nemrut Dağı
Information Booth

Müçelli Cad

Milli Eğemenlik Cad

Tourist
Office

Sinema Cad

Kanal Boyu

Şeker Sk

---

but the rooms are more spacious, and decked out in modern colours including black, white and chocolate brown. Still-gleaming bathrooms and a diverse breakfast – expect a few local apricots – provide two more big ticks.

Yeni Hotel
HOTEL €€

(☎323 1423; yenihotel@turk.net; Yeni Cami Karşısı Zafer İşhanı; s/d ₺60/90; ☀) This well-run establishment enlivens its rooms with pastel hues, electric blue bedspreads and spotless laminated floors. Keen shoppers should relish the location, right on the edge of the market area.

Grand Sinan Otel
HOTEL €€

(☎325 4747; www.grandsinanotel.com; Atatürk Caddesi 6; s/d €45/85; ☀) The Grand Sinan has relatively compact rooms decked out in designer colours and equipped with spotless bathrooms. The main-drag location is convenient, and double-glazing masks most traffic noise. The crew at reception speak excellent English.

Hotel Pehlivan
HOTEL €

(☎321 2609; Cumhuriyet Caddesi; s/d ₺30/50) Offering good-value digs on the edge of the market, the Pehlivan has clean and spacious rooms decked out in a variety of colours.

✗ Eating

Atatürk Caddesi is awash with inexpensive eateries, and Kanal Boyu's tree-lined boulevard features hip cafes and ice-cream shops. Grab a cone – our favourite is a combo of *limonlu* (lemon) and *fıstıklı* (pistachio) – and promenade slowly with the strolling locals.

Beşkonaklar Malatya Mutfaği
ANATOLIAN €€

(Sinema Caddesi; mains ₺10-15) Housed in the same restored row of houses as the Ethnographic Museum, Beşkonaklar Malatya Mutfaği showcases traditional local food. The interior is crammed with antiques, and if the weather is warm, you can adjourn to the spacious garden to enjoy interesting dishes like *analı kızlı* (soup with marble-sized meatballs and chickpeas).

Evin Gibi Yöresel Yemekler
ANATOLIAN €

(Kanal Boyu; mains ₺7-10) Just metres from the bright lights of Kanal Boyu, this cosy and rustic neighbourhood eatery specialises in *yöresel yemekler* (traditional homestyle Turkish food). Everyday the menu is different, craftily luring a loyal group of regulars for soup, rice dishes and casserole specials. Join them to see what's cooking.

Malatya

Sarı Kurdela   TURKISH €€
(İnönü Caddesi; mains ₺6-14) This super-trendy joint ticks all the boxes, with contemporary decor, efficient wait staff and an eclectic menu, including excellent ready-made meals, vegetarian dishes and a wide choice of sweets. Prices are cheaper in the downstairs cafeteria – and the food is just as good.

Hacıbey Lahmacun   PIDE €
(Kışla Caddesi; mains ₺6-11) Hands down the best joint for a hearty pide or *lahmacun* pizza with a thin, crispy base topped with chopped lamb, onion and tomato, washed down with a refreshing *ayran*.

Sevinç   BAKERY €
(Atatürk Caddesi; pastries from ₺2) This pastry shop features a sleek, modern interior and a batch of mouth-watering desserts, including baklava and cakes.

🍷 Drinking

 Nostalji   CAFE
(Müçelli Caddesi; snacks ₺5-8) This squeaky-boarded, old Malatya mansion is packed with memorabilia. Soak up the cool karma in the light-filled main lounge while listening to mellow music and sipping Turkish coffee. Simple dishes are also available, and it's a good place to meet students of both sexes.

VIP Cafe   TEA GARDEN
(İnönü Caddesi; snacks ₺4-8) Nab a table at VIP Cafe and chow down on *gözleme* (thin savoury crepes cooked with cheese, spinach or potato), or linger over a cuppa. No doubt you'll be approached by the friendly Kemal, who runs the Nemrut Dağı information booth nearby.

Taşkent   CAFE
(Kanal Boyu) One of the busier spots along Kanal Boyu, Taşkent cafe offers a laid-back atmosphere with excellent *mantı* (Turkish ravioli), a menu full of nargile flavours, and the after-dark attention of Malatya's younger populace.

ℹ Information

ATMs and internet cafes are plentiful in the centre of town.

Nemrut Dağı Information Booth (☑0535 760 5080; kemalmalatya@hotmail.com; Atatürk Caddesi; ☺8am-7pm May-Sep) In the tea garden behind the tourist office – ask for Kemal – and managed by the Güneş Hotel (p576) at Nemrut Dağı. Good English is spoken, and Kemal can also supply a good city map.

Tourist Office (☑323 2942; Sinema Caddesi; ☺9am-5pm Mon-Fri) Adjacent to the Malatya Ethnographic Museum; little English is spoken, but they have a few local brochures.

ℹ Getting There & Away

Air

The airport is 35km northwest of the centre. Ask at one of the travel agencies on Atatürk Caddesi about the Havas bus.

Onur Air (www.onurair.com.tr) One flight daily to/from İstanbul (from ₺60).

Pegasus Airlines (www.flypgs.com) To/from İstanbul (from ₺60) and Ankara (from ₺100).

Turkish Airlines (www.thy.com) Two daily flights to/from İstanbul (from ₺63), and a daily flight to/from Ankara (from ₺84).

Bus

Malatya's enormous otogar, MAŞTİ, is around 4km west of town. Most bus companies operate *servises* (shuttle minibuses) to the town centre. Minibuses from the otogar travel along Turgut Özal Bulvarı/Buhara Bulvarı but aren't allowed into the centre. Ask to be let off at the corner of Turan Temelli and Buhara Caddesis, and walk from there. City buses to the otogar leave from near the *vilayet*. A taxi to the otogar costs about ₺30.

SERVICES FROM MALATYA'S OTOGAR

DESTINATION	FARE (₺)	DURATION (HR)	DISTANCE (KM)	FREQUENCY (PER DAY)
Adana	30	8	425	3-4
Adıyaman	15	2½	144	frequent
Ankara	40	11	685	frequent
Diyarbakır	25	4	260	3-4
Elazığ	10	1¾	101	hourly
Gaziantep	18	4	250	3-4
İstanbul	50	18	1130	3-4
Kayseri	30	4	354	several
Sivas	25	5	235	several

Car

Meydan Rent a Car (☑ 325 3434; www.mey danoto.com.tr; İnönü Caddesi, Sıtmapınarı Ziraat Bankası Bitişiği; ☺8am-7pm) is a reliable outlet. Other companies dot the city centre.

Train

Malatya is a major railway hub and is well connected by train to the east (Elazığ, Tatvan, Diyarbakır), the west (Ankara, Sivas, Kayseri) and the south (Adana). A train via here can be a good alternative to tiring bus trips. Note that at the time of writing trains between İstanbul and Ankara were suspended, potentially until 2015. Check www.seat61.com for the latest information.

The *Vangölü Ekspresi* leaves for Ankara via Sivas and Kayseri on Tuesday and Thursday (₺33.25); for Elazığ and Tatvan (₺15) it leaves on Wednesday and Sunday.

The *Güney Ekspresi* leaves for Sivas, Kayseri and Ankara on Monday, Wednesday, Friday and Sunday (₺31.75); for Elazığ and Diyarbakır (₺12), it departs on Tuesday, Thursday, Saturday and Sunday.

The *4 Eylül Ekspresi* leaves daily for Ankara via Sivas and Kayseri (₺28).

Check at the train station for exact departure times of all trains.

Malatya's train station can be reached by minibus (₺1) or by 'İstasyon' city buses from near the *valiliği*. City buses and minibuses marked 'Vilayet' operate between the station and the centre.

Around Malatya

ASLANTEPE

If you have an interest in Anatolian archaeology you'll enjoy the pretty village of Aslantepe, around 6km from Malatya. A recently installed modern pavilion has transformed the **archaeological site** (☺8am-5pm) into an open-air museum, and excellent information in English and Italian brings alive the impact of the site on modern culture and society.

When the Phrygians invaded the Hittite kingdom at Boğazkale, around 1200 BC, many Hittites fled southeast over the Taurus Mountains to resettle and build walled cities. The city of Milidia, now known as Aslantepe, was one of these neo-Hittite city-states. Sporadic excavations since the 1930s have so far uncovered seven layers of remains.

To get to Aslantepe from Malatya, catch a bus marked 'Orduzu' (₺1.50, 15 minutes) from the southern side of Buhara Bulvarı near the junction with Akpınar Caddesi. The site is a pleasant 500m stroll from the bus stop.

BATTALGAZI (OLD MALATYA)

You don't need to be an archaeology buff to be captivated by the remains of old Malatya, the walled city settled alongside Aslantepe, about 11km north of Malatya at Battalgazi.

As you come into the village you'll see the ruins of the old **city walls** with their 95 towers, built during Roman times and completed in the 6th century.

The bus from Malatya terminates in the main square. Just off here, beside the mosque with the smooth-topped minaret, is the **Silahtar Mustafa Paşa Hanı**, an Ottoman caravanserai dating from the 17th century.

From the caravanserai, turn right and follow Osman Ateş Caddesi for about 600m until you see the broken brick minaret of the finely restored 13th-century **Ulu Cami** on the left. This stunning, if fast-fading, Seljuk building dates from the reign of Alaettin

Keykubad I. Also worthy of interest is the **Ak Minare Camii** (White Minaret Mosque), about 50m from the Ulu Cami. This also dates from the 13th century.

Close by is the 13th-century **Halfetih Minaret**, made completely of bricks, and the **Nezir Gazi Tomb**.

Buses to Battalgazi (₺1.50, 15 minutes) leave regularly from Malatya.

Diyarbakır

☑ 0412 / POP 875,000 / ELEV 60M

Full of heart, soul and character, Diyar is finally tapping into its fantastic potential as a destination for travellers. While it's proud of remaining the symbol of Kurdish identity and tenacity, thanks to increasing promotion and restoration programs, Turkish and foreign tourists are streaming back. Behind the grim basalt walls, the old city's twisting alleyways are crammed full of historical buildings and Arab-style mosques.

Speak to Turks from western Turkey and they will recoil in fear if you mention Diyarbakır because, since the 1980s, this animated city has been the centre of the Kurdish resistance movement, and violent street demonstrations still occur from time to time. And yes, nowhere else in eastern Turkey will you hear people priding themselves so much on being Kurdish.

Banned until a few years ago, the Nevruz festival takes place on 21 March and is a great occasion to immerse yourself in Kurdish culture.

Apart from a few slightly annoying street kids, Diyarbakır is as safe as any other city in the region.

History

Mesopotamia, the land between the Tigris and Euphrates Valleys, saw the dawn of the world's first great empires. Diyarbakır's history began with the Hurrian kingdom of Mitanni around 1500 BC and proceeded through domination by the civilisations of Urartu (900 BC), Assyria (1356–612 BC), Persia (600–330 BC) and Alexander the Great and his successors, the Seleucids.

The Romans took over in AD 115, but because of its strategic position the city changed hands numerous times until it was conquered by the Arabs in 639. The Arab tribe of Beni Bakr that settled here named their new home Diyar Bakr, which means the Realm of Bakr.

For the next few centuries the city was occupied by various tribes, until 1497 when the Safavid dynasty founded by Shah İsmail took over Iran, putting an end to more than

---

WORTH A TRIP

DARENDE – THE FORGOTTEN OASIS

About 110km west of Malatya, Darende is a terrific place to kick off your shoes for a day or two in a fabulous setting. There's a splendid canyon right on its doorstep, as well as well-preserved architectural treasures, including the **Somuncu Baba Camii ve Külliyesi** (with a museum), the **Kudret Havuzu**, a purpose-built rock pool set in the **Tohma Canyon**, and the stark **Zengibar Kalesi**, perched high on a rocky outcrop.

Along the riverbank of the canyon are restaurants specialising in fresh trout. **Hasbahçe** (☑ 0422-615 2215; Somuncu Baba Camii Civarı; mains ₺6-12) is a firm favourite, with the scores of local visitors at weekends. In summer, you can dunk yourself in the Kudret Havuzu, and **rafting** (☑ 0422-615 3513, 0555 565 4935; www.tohmarafting.com) is also possible in the Tohma Canyon. Don't expect massive thrills, but look forward to transitting through stunning canyons against the background of a stark cobalt sky.

The brilliant-value **Tiryandafil Otel** (☑ 0422-615 3095; s/d ₺70/100; ✴@) is conveniently located on the outskirts of Darende, about 1km before the canyon and monuments. It has impeccable, spacious rooms, and the on-site restaurant has excellent local specialities – try the şelale sızdırma (meat with melted cheese, mushrooms and butter). Ask for Talha, who speaks excellent English, and can help with any queries.

With your own wheels, you can easily reach the Gürpinar Şelalesi (waterfalls), about 7km from Darende (from the hotel, follow the road to Ankara for 6km; then it's signposted). Don't expect Niagara-like falls, but it's an excellent picnic spot.

Regular minibuses (₺8) link Malatya and Darende. In Malatya, they depart from the minibus terminal kmown as 'Eski Otogar' on Çevre Yol. Buses from Kayseri also run to Darende (₺25), making it a good stop if you're travelling east from Cappadocia.

Diyarbakır

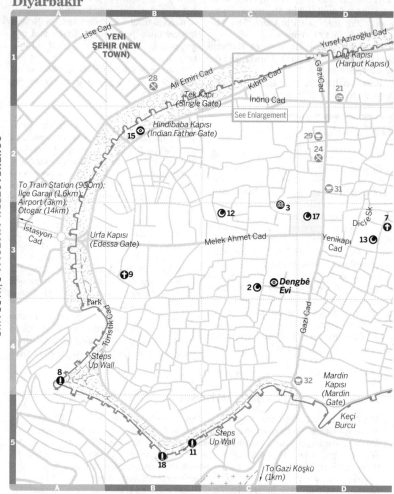

SOUTHEASTERN ANATOLIA DİYARBAKIR

a century of Turkoman rule in this area. The Ottomans came and conquered in 1515, but even then, Diyarbakır was not to know lasting peace. Because it stood right in the way of invading armies originating from Anatolia, Persia and Syria, it suffered many more tribulations.

◉ Sights

When visiting Diyarbakır's mosques, try to time your visit for 20 to 25 minutes after the call to prayer (when the prayers should be finished), as most of them will be locked outside prayer times.

City Walls & Gates   FORTRESS

Diyarbakır's single most conspicuous feature is its great circuit of basalt walls, probably dating from Roman times, although the present walls date from early Byzantine times (AD 330–500). At almost 6km in length, these walls are said to be second in extent only to the Great Wall of China.

Numerous bastions and towers stand sentinel over the massive black walls. There were originally four main gates: **Harput Kapısı** (north), **Mardin Kapısı** (south), **Yenikapı** (east) and **Urfa Kapısı** (west).

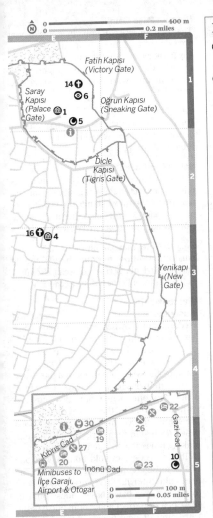

Diyarbakır

◉ Top Sights
Dengbê Evi C3

◎ Sights
1 Archaeology Museum E1
2 Behram Paşa Camii C3
3 Cahit Sıtkı Tarancı Museum C3
4 Esma Ocak Evi E3
5 Hazreti Süleyman Camii E1
6 İç Kale E1
7 Keldani Kilisesi D3
8 Malikşah Burcu A4
9 Meryem Ana Kilisesi B3
10 Nebi Camii F5
11 Nur Burcu B5
12 Safa Camii C3
13 Şeyh Mutahhar Camii D3
14 St George Church E1
15 Sufi Sarcophagi B2
16 Surpağab Kilisesi E3
17 Ulu Camii D3
18 Yedi Kardeş Burcu B5

🛏 Sleeping
19 Aslan Palas E5
20 Balkar Otel E5
   Hotel Evin ....(see 20)
21 Hotel Surkent D1
22 New Tigris Hotel F4
23 SV Business Hotel F5

✖ Eating
24 Çarşı Konağı D2
25 Küçe Başı Et Lokantası........................F4
   Meşhur Kahvaltıcı...................... (see 31)
26 Ocakbaşı Restaurants...........................F5
27 Şafak Kahvaltı & Yemek Salonu E5
28 Selim Amca'nın Sofra Salonu.............. B1

☕ Drinking
29 Dicle Şelale Cafe D2
30 Doğal Vitamin E5
31 Hasan Paşa Hanı................................. D2
32 Otel Büyük Kervansaray D4

Restoration of the city's walls and gates is planned to be completed in 2013.

Fortunately, the most easily accessible stretch of walls is also the most interesting in terms of inscriptions and decoration. Start near the Mardin Kapısı close to the Deliller Han, a stone caravanserai now home to the Otel Büyük Kervansaray. Don't miss **Nur Burcu** (Tower Nur), the **Yedi Kardeş Burcu** (Tower of Seven Brothers) with two Seljuk lion bas-reliefs – only visible from outside the walls – and the bas-reliefs of the **Malikşah Burcu** (Tower of Malik Şah).

Ascend the walls of the **İç Kale** (keep) for fine views of the Tigris. The İç Kale has been undergoing restoration for several years, and includes the beautifully resurrected 3rd-century-AD **St George Church**. Other ongoing restoration projects include a historic prison and a new location for the city's Archaeology Museum.

At various spots inside the walls are brightly painted, open-air **Sufi sarcophagi**, notable for their turbans – their size is a symbol of spiritual authority. There's a cluster a few hundred metres northeast of the Urfa Kapısı.

Be prudent when walking on and along the walls as there have been reports of attempted robberies. Try to go in a group and keep personal items and cameras safe.

Dengbê Evi
CULTURAL CENTRE

(http://turizm.diyarbakir.bel.tr/en/s/Dengbej _House; Kılıççı Sokak, near Behram Paşa Camii; ⊙9am-6pm Tue-Sun) Housed in a cultural centre for Kurdish seniors, the Dengbêj Evi (House of Dengbê) showcases the Kurdish tradition of Dengbjê, storytelling by song. Six days a week, Kurdish elders gather together in informal groups and take turns to sing and chant in an ethereal and mesmerising style. Their associates add bold affirmations to underpin the melancholy, yearning melodies, and it's a compelling way to spend an hour or so in Turkey's most important Kurdish city. The complex also houses a tea garden and a tourist information office.

Ulu Camii
MOSQUE

Diyarbakır's most impressive mosque is the Ulu Camii, built in 1091 by Malik Şah, an early Seljuk sultan. Incorporating elements from an earlier Byzantine church on the site, it was extensively restored in 1155 after a fire. It's rectangular in plan – Arab style, rather than Ottoman. The entrance portal, adorned with two medallions figuring a lion and a bull, leads to a huge courtyard. This is the most elegant section of the building, with two-storey arcades, two cone-shaped *şadırvans* (ritual ablutions fountains), elaborate pillars, and friezes featuring fruits and vegetables. At the time of writing, the Ulu Camii was undergoing additional restoration to resurrect the complex's heritage gravitas and grandeur.

Nebi Camii
MOSQUE

At the main intersection of Gazi and İzzet Paşa/İnönü Caddesis, is Nebi Camii, featuring a detached minaret sporting a stunning combination of black-and-white stone. This alternating black-and-white banding is characteristic of Diyarbakır's mosques, many of which date from the time of the Akkoyunlu dynasty.

Behram Paşa Camii
MOSQUE

The Behram Paşa Camii, in a residential area deep in the maze of narrow streets, is Diyarbakır's largest mosque. More Persian in style, the Safa Camii has a highly decorated minaret with blue tiles incorporated in its design.

Safa Camii
MOSQUE

Persian in style, the Safa Camii has a highly decorated minaret with blue tiles incorporated in its design.

Şeyh Mutahhar Camii
MOSQUE

The Şeyh Mutahhar Camii is famous for its minaret, but its engineering is even more interesting – the tower stands on four slender pillars about 2m high, earning it the name Dört Ayaklı Minare (Four-Legged Minaret).

Hazreti Süleyman Camii
MOSQUE

This 12th-century mosque, beside the İç Kale, is particularly revered because it houses the tombs of heroes of past Islamic wars.

Diyarbakır House Museums
NOTABLE BUILDINGS

Predominantly owned by Armenian families in earlier times, Diyarbakır houses were made of black basalt and decorated with stone stencilling. They were divided into summer and winter quarters, and the centre of the summer part was always the *eyvan*, a vaulted room opening onto the courtyard with a fountain in the centre. In summer, the family moved high wooden platforms called *tahts* into the courtyard for sleeping, making it possible to catch any breeze.

To see inside these old houses, visit one of the museums inside the city walls. The poet Cahit Sıtkı Tarancı (1910–56) was born in a two-storey black basalt house built in 1820, in a side street about 50m north of the Ulu Camii. It now houses the **Cahit Sıtkı Tarancı Museum** (Ziya Gökalp Sokak; ⊙8am-5pm Tue-Sun).

The beautiful grey-and-white-striped **Esma Ocak Evi** was built in 1899 by the Armenian Şakarer family and restored in 1996 by a female writer, Esma Ocak. A live-in caretaker with delightful twin daughters will show you the gracefully furnished living rooms. Admission is by donation (₺3 is expected).

Keldani Kilisesi
CHURCH

(Chaldean Church) The population of Diyarbakır once included many Christians, mainly Armenians and Chaldeans, but most of them were pushed out or perished during the troubles in the early 20th century or, more recently, with the Hezbollah.

Off Yenikapı Caddesi, this plain, brightly lit church is still used by 30 Christian families of the Syrian rite (in communion with the Roman Catholic church). The chaplain from the Meryem Ana Kilisesi holds a service here on the second Sunday of the month. It's fairly easy to find on your own. Walk past the detached minaret of the Nebi Camii, take the first left (Dicle Sokak) then the first right (Şeftali Sokak). The caretaker usually sits outside the Nebi Camii.

Surpağab Kilisesi   CHURCH
This Armenian church has recently been reopened after a wonderful restoration. Press the doorbell and someone will usually appear from within or from the surrounding neighbourhood to provide access. The church is across the lane from the Esma Ocak Evi.

Meryem Ana Kilisesi   CHURCH
(Church of the Virgin Mary) Still used by Orthodox Syrian Christians, this church is beautifully maintained, although only about seven families still attend services. Local kids will show you the way.

Gazi Köşkü   HISTORIC BUILDING
(admission ₺1) About 1km south of the Mardin Kapısı, the Gazi Köşkü is a fine example of the sort of Diyarbakır house to which its wealthier citizens would retire in high summer. The house dates from the time of the 15th-century Akkoyunlu Turkoman dynasty and stands in a well-tended park. The caretaker will expect a tip for showing you around.

To get there, it's a pleasant, if rather isolated, downhill walk. Taxis charge ₺15.

About 1km further south from here is the 11th-century **On Gözlu Köprüsü** (Ten-Eyed Bridge).

Archaeology Museum   MUSEUM
(Arkeoloji Müzesi; İç Kale; admission ₺3) Diyarbakır's original Archaeology Museum was closed at the time of writing, and scheduled to reopen in 2013 in a new location inside the İç Kale. Ask at the Diyarbakır tourist office for an update.

Before the move, the well-presented collection included finds from the neolithic site of Çayönü (7500–6500 BC), 65km north of Diyarbakır. Also showcased was a decent Urartian collection and relics from the Karakoyunlu and Akkoyunlu, powerful tribal dynasties that ruled much of eastern Anatolia and Iran between 1378 and 1502.

🛏 Sleeping

Most accommodation options are conveniently located on Kıbrıs Caddesi and nearby İnönü Caddesi. Kıbrıs Caddesi does suffer from traffic noise, so try and secure a room at the back. In summer it's scorching hot in Diyarbakır, another thing to consider when choosing a room.

New Tigris Hotel   HOTEL €€
(☑224 9696; www.newtigrishotel.com; Kıbrıs Caddesi 3; s/d ₺80/120; ❈ 🛜) In close proximity to good restaurants, the newly opened New Tigris has lifted the game for competing hotels along bustling Kıbrıs Caddesi. Wooden floors, neutral decor, and sparkling and spacious bathrooms make the New Tigris one of the best midrange deals in town. Get in quick before the familar aroma of cigarette smoke takes hold.

SV Business Hotel   BUSINESS HOTEL €€
(☑228 1295; www.svbusinessotel.com; İnönü Caddesi 4; s/d ₺130/170; ❈ 🛜) Diyar's only stab at a modern boutique/business hotel mixes up cool, pastel colours, almost too-trendy furniture, and a relaxed, but professional, English-speaking vibe at reception. Rooms are moderately sized, but show no sartorial '80s hangover from this address' former incarnation as the Büyük Hotel. A compact sauna and fitness centre provide assistance if the city's cuisine is proving too irresistible.

Hotel Evin   HOTEL €€
(☑228 6306; fax 224 9093; Kıbrıs Caddesi 38; s/d ₺60/80; ❈ 🛜) Opened in 2009, the Ekin is a good addition to the Kıbrıs Caddesi hotel scene. Rooms are relatively spacious and sunny, and the views from the rooftop breakfast salon will have you lingering for another glass of tea. The young team at reception are always keen to practise their English language skills.

Hotel Surkent   HOTEL €
(☑228 1014; www.hotelsurkent.com; İzzet Paşa Caddesi; s/d/tr ₺30/45/60; ❈ 🛜) In a quiet centrally located street, the colourful Surkent is a popular choice for overland travellers. Top-floor rooms boast good views – for singles, rooms 501, 502 and 503 are the best. Avoid the downstairs rooms near reception as they can be noisy. Breakfast is an additional ₺5 and there's no lift.

Aslan Palas
HOTEL €

(☑228 9224; Kıbrıs Caddesi; s/d ₺40/70; ❄ 🛜) A worthwhile back-up for cash-strapped (male) travellers, but ageing plumbing is about the worst surprise you'll get. Air-con is in all the rooms. Prices don't include breakfast, but you'll find several *kahvaltı salonu* (eateries specialising in full Turkish breakfasts) on the street. There's no lift and bathrooms are shared.

Balkar Otel
HOTEL €€

(☑228 6306; Kıbrıs Caddesi 38; s/d ₺60/90/120; ❄) This typical middling three-star boasts well-appointed rooms with TV and mini-bar, but very compact bathrooms. Bonuses include a hearty breakfast and a rooftop terrace with sterling views.

✗ Eating

Kıbrıs Caddesi has plenty of good-value, informal eateries. For expertly grilled meat, join the blokey throngs at the various **ocakbaşı restaurants** lining the narrow lanes adjoining Kıbrıs Caddesi.

TOP CHOICE Meşhur Kahvaltıcı
CAFE €€

(Hasan Paşa Hanı; breakfast ₺20) More expensive than the *kahvaltı* spots along Kıbrıs Caddesi, but worth it for the glorious ambience of the restored Hasan Paşa Hanı. Enjoy a leisurely breakfast of multiple small plates on the balcony, and feel very pleased with yourself for adding Diyarbakır to your Turkish itinerary.

TOP CHOICE Selim Amca'nın Sofra Salonu
RESTAURANT €€

(Ali Emiri Caddesi; mains ₺10-15, set menu ₺30) This bright eatery outside the city walls is famous for its *kaburga dolması* (lamb stuffed with rice and almonds). Round it off with a devilish *İrmik helvası* (a gooey dessert). The *saç kavurma* (braised lamb) is also excellent.

Çarşı Konağı
TURKISH €€

(Gazi Caddesi; mains ₺10-15) Escape the main drag's commercial buzz at this lovingly restored 450-year-old house, now concealing a leafy courtyard and poignant reminders of its former Jewish owners. (Look for the carved Star of David in the wooden ceiling). A wide array of kebaps, grills and salads are on offer, and don't be surprised if you're asked to stay for an extended çay session with friendly Diyar locals.

Şafak Kahvaltı & Yemek Salonu
TURKISH €

(Kıbrıs Caddesi; mains ₺8-12; ⊙24 hr) Nosh on freshly prepared meat dishes, hearty casseroles and stuffed vegetables in this brisk Diyarbakır institution. It's a good place to partake in a restorative morning breakfast with still-warm flatbread, luscious *kaymak* (clotted cream) and gooey honey. It also does superb crisp wood-fired pide and is open around the clock if you arrive on a late bus.

Küçe Başı Et Lokantası
TURKISH €

(Kıbrıs Caddesi; mains ₺6-12) This outfit has a wide-ranging menu and original setting (the room at the back is designed like a rustic barn). Try innovative dishes like *tavuk tava* (deep-fried chicken meat in a flat-bottomed pan).

🍷 Drinking & Entertainment

Dicle Şelale Cafe
TEA GARDEN

(Gazi Caddesi, Akıncılar Sokak 3) Concealed in the labyrinth of lanes off busy Gazi Caddesi, this courtyard cafe is worth seeking out for its kilim-bedecked interior, sweet little waterfall, and Anatolian combo of backgammon, çay and nargile. The freshly squeezed juices are good, and the helpful owners are all too happy to pop out and grab you a kebap or sandwich if you're feeling peckish.

Hasan Paşa Hanı
COFFEEHOUSE

(Gazi Caddesi; ⊙8am-10pm) Across from the Ulu Camii, this 16th-century caravanserai is occupied by carpet shops and souvenir sellers. It was extensively restored in 2006 and has some top spots for a leisurely breakfast. Live music is also regularly advertised.

Otel Büyük Kervansaray
TEA GARDEN

(Gazi Caddesi; ⊙11am-10pm) The expansive courtyard is a great place to unwind over a cup of tea and take in the atmosphere. It's also licensed if you feel like a cold beer.

Doğal Vitamin
JUICE BAR

(Kıbrıs Caddesi; juices from ₺2) This handy caravan serves up fresh juices and tasty Turkish snacks.

❶ Information

Old Diyarbakır is encircled by walls, pierced by several main gates. Within the walls the city is a maze of narrow, twisting, mostly unmarked alleys. Most services useful to travellers are in Old Diyarbakır, on or around Gazi Caddesi, including the post office, internet cafes, travel agencies and ATMs.

SERVICES FROM DİYARBAKIR'S OTOGAR

DESTINATION	FARE (₺)	DURATION (HR)	DISTANCE (KM)	FREQUENCY (PER DAY)
Adana	35	8	550	several
Ankara	65	13	945	several
Erzurum	40	8	485	several
Malatya	23	5	260	frequent
Mardin	10	1½	95	hourly
Şanlıurfa	15	3	190	frequent
Sivas	40	10	500	several
Tatvan	25	4	264	several
Van	35	7	410	several

Ali Çalişir (☎0532 283 2367; bbcnews44@
hotmail.com) After a career as a BBC camera-
man throughout the Middle East, Ali Çalişir has
returned home to Diyarbakır to work as a local
guide and fixer. He'll probably seek you out
around Kıbrıs Caddesi, and is a good contact
for walking tours of the old city and for information about visiting Kurdish Iraq.

Municipal Information Bureau (☺9am-noon
& 1-6pm Tue-Sat) Municipal office in the
square off Kıbrıs Caddesi. Ask for the excellent
English-language map.

Tourist Office (☎228 1706; İç Kale; ☺8am-
5pm Mon-Fri) One of Diyarbakır's two tourist
information offices (the other is inside the
Dengbê Evi).

Getting There & Away

Air

Minibuses H1, H2 and H3 run to the airport
(₺1.50) from near Dağ Kapısı. A taxi will cost
about ₺7.

Onur Air (www.onurair.com.tr) Two flights daily
to/from İstanbul (from ₺124).

Pegasus Airlines (www.flypgs.com) Daily flight
to/from İstanbul (from ₺72), and daily flights
to/from Ankara (from ₺120).

Turkish Airlines (www.turkishairlines.com)
Five flights daily to/from İstanbul (from ₺75)
and four flights daily to/from Ankara (from
₺84).

Bus

Many bus companies have ticket offices on
İnönü Caddesi or along Gazi Caddesi near the
Dağ Kapısı. The otogar is about 14km from the
centre, on the road to Urfa (about ₺20 by taxi).

There's a separate minibus terminal (İlçe
Garajı) about 1.5km southwest of the city
walls, with services to Batman (₺10, 1½ hours),
Elazığ (₺10, two hours), Mardin (₺10, 1¼ hours),

Malatya (₺15, five hours), Midyat (₺15) and
Siverek (to get to Kahta without going right
round the lake via Adıyaman). For Hasankeyf,
change in Batman (₺8). To get to the minibus
terminal, catch one of the buses that stops
across the street from the Balkar Otel and ask
for 'İlçe Garajı' (₺2), or take a taxi (₺8).

Car

Avis (☎229 0275, 236 1324; www.avis.com
.tr; Elazığ Caddesi; ☺8am-7pm) Opposite the
belediye and at the airport.

Train

The train station is about 1.5km from the centre, at the western end of İstasyon Caddesi.
The *Güney Ekspresi* leaves for Ankara (₺32)
via Malatya (₺10) and Sivas (₺26) on Monday,
Wednesday, Friday and Sunday. Check times at
the train station.

Mardin

☎0482 / POP 88,000 / ELEV 1325M

Mardin is a highly addictive and unmissable
spot. Minarets emerge from a baked brown
labyrinth of meandering lanes, a castle dominates the old city, and stone houses cascade
down the hillside above the Mesopotamian
plains. As a melting pot of Kurdish, Yezidi,
Christian and Syrian cultures, it also has a
fascinating cultural mix.

Just don't expect to have the whole
place to yourself. With regular flights from
İstanbul, you'll see lots of local visitors in
summer. The Turkish government also has
plans to promote Mardin internationally as
an iconic Turkish destination like Ephesus
and Pamukkale, and have (optimistically)
projected up to five million domestic and
overseas visitors annually within 10 years.

Mardin's honey-coloured collage of old buildings and markets is still definitely worth a look, and for somewhere extra special, take a detour to Dara or Savur.

History

As with Diyarbakır, Mardin's history is one of disputes between rival armies over millennia, though in recent years the only dispute that anyone has really cared about is the one between the PKK (Kurdistan Workers Party) and the government. A castle has stood on this hill from time immemorial. The Turkish army has traditionally occupied the castle to assert authority, but at the time of writing the site was being handed back to the city, and access for visitors was planned.

Assyrian Christians settled here during the 5th century, and the Arabs occupied Mardin between 640 and 1104. After that, it had a succession of Seljuk Turkish, Kurdish, Mongol and Persian overlords, until the Ottomans under Sultan Selim the Grim took it in 1517. In the early 20th century many of the Assyrian Christians were pushed out or perished during the troubles, and in the last few decades many have emigrated. An estimated 600 Christians remain, with 11 churches still in use on a rotational basis.

◉ Sights & Activities

Sakıp Sabancı Mardin City Museum
MUSEUM
(Sakıp Sabancı Mardin Kent Müzesi; www.saban cimuzesimardin.gov.tr; Eski Hükümet Caddesi; admission ₺3; ⊗8am-5pm Tue-Sun) Housed in a carefully restored former army barracks, this superb new museum showcases the fascinating history and culture of Mardin. Excellent English-language translations and effective use of audio and video reinforce how cosmopolitan and multicultural the city's past was. Downstairs is used as an art gallery for a rotating series of exhibitions, often including images by iconic Turkish photographers.

Sultan İsa (Zinciriye) Medresesi
MOSQUE
(Cumhuriyet Caddesi; admission ₺2) Dating from 1385, the complex's highlight is the imposing recessed doorway, but make sure you wander through the pretty courtyards, lovingly tended by the caretaker, and onto the roof to enjoy the cityscape. The tea garden is a top spot to sit and survey Mardin's beauty.

Bazaar
MARKET
Mardin's rambling commercial hub parallels Cumhuriyet Caddesi one block down the hill. Donkeys are still a main form of transport, and look out for saddle repairers resurrecting even the shabbiest examples.

Look for the secluded **Ulu Camii**, a 12th-century Iraqi Seljuk structure that suffered badly during the Kurdish rebellion of 1832. Inside it's fairly plain, but the delicate reliefs adorning the minaret make a visit worthwhile.

Forty Martyrs Church
CHURCH
(Kırklar Kilisesi; Sağlık Sokak) This church dates back to the 4th century, and was renamed in the 15th century to commemorate Cappadocian martyrs, now remembered in the fine carvings above the entrance. Services are held here each Sunday, and there's a wonderful inner courtyard punctuated with delicate birdsong. A caretaker is usually on hand to provide access to the church's compact, but beautiful, interior.

Mardin Museum
MUSEUM
(Mardin Müzesi; Cumhuriyet Caddesi; admission ₺5; ⊗8am-5pm Tue-Sun) This superbly restored late-19th-century mansion sports carved pillars and elegant arcades on the upper floor. Inside, it has a small but well-displayed collection including a finely detailed 7th-century-BC Assyrian vase and finds from Girnavaz, a Bronze Age site 4km north of Nusaybin.

Afterwards, head east along Cumhuriyet Caddesi, keeping your eye out for a fabulous example of the town's domestic architecture on your left – the three-arched facade of an ornately carved **old Mardin house**.

Post Office
HISTORIC BUILDING
(Cumhuriyet Caddesi) Turkey's most impressive former post office is housed in a 17th-century caravanserai covered with carvings, including teardrops in stone dripping down the walls. At the time of writing, the building was being diligently restored and was due to reopen in 2013.

Şehidiye Camii
MOSQUE
(Cumhuriyet Caddesi) Across the street from the post office rises the elegant, slender minaret of this 14th-century mosque. It's superbly carved, with colonnades all around, and three small bulbs superimposed at the summit. The base of the minaret sports a series of pillars.

Also worth visiting is the 14th-century **Latifiye Camii**, behind the Akbank, where a shady courtyard has a *şadırvan* in the middle.

Nearby, in the vicinity of the Artuklu Kervansarayı, the eye-catching **Hatuniye** and **Melik Mahmut Camii** have been fully restored.

Kasımiye Medresesi   MOSQUE

Built in 1469, two domes stand over the tombs of Kasım Paşa and his sister, but the highlights are the sublime courtyard walled with arched colonnades and the magnificent carved doorway. Upstairs, you can see the students' quarters, before ascending the stairs to the rooftop for another great Mardin panorama. It's 800m south of Yeni Yol, and well signposted.

Emir Hamamı   HAMAM

(Cumhuriyet Caddesi; treatments from ₺20; ☺men 6.30am-noon & 6-10pm, women noon-5.30pm) This hamam's history goes back to Roman times. After a sauna and massage combo, take in the great views of the Mesopotamian plains from the hamam's terrace. Unfortunately the heritage ambience of the interior is dulled by the use of fluorescent lighting.

Sleeping

Mardin's popularity means that accommodation is expensive. The city's boutique hotels are undeniably atmospheric, but rooms are often small and lack natural light. Make sure to ask the right questions when you book. Summer weekends are particularly busy,

and you might find it easier to visit Mardin as a day trip from Midyat or Diyarbakır.

TOP CHOICE **Şahmeran**

Otanik Pansiyon   PENSION ₺

(☎213 2300; www.sahmeranpansiyon.com; Cumhuriyet Caddesi, 246 Sokak 10; per person ₺40, without bathroom ₺35; ☎) Old Mardin finally has a good value historic option compared to the more expensive boutique hotels. This lovely recent opening is arrayed around a honey-coloured stone courtyard just a short uphill meander from Mardin's main thoroughfare. Kilims and heritage features punctuate the rustic and simply furnished rooms. Breakfast is an additional ₺5.

Reyhani Kasrı   BOUTIQUE HOTEL ₺₺₺

(☎212 1333; www.reyhanikasri.com.tr; Cumhuriyet Caddesi; s/d ₺150/190; ❄☎) Sleek and modern rooms are concealed within a lovingly restored historic mansion, providing a more contemporary spin on the usual Mardin boutique-hotel experience. Multiple floors cascade down the hillside, making it one of Mardin's more spectacular buildings. Pop in for a drink at the hotel's remarkable 'Sky Terrace' bar. Side orders include the best Mesopotamian views in town.

Antik Tatlıede Butik Hotel   BOUTIQUE HOTEL ₺₺

(☎213 2720; www.tatlidede.com.tr; Medrese Mahallesi; s/d/tr ₺100/150/200; ❄☎) In a quiet location near Mardin's bazaar, a labyrinthine heritage mansion is filled with rooms of varying sizes. Most are fairly spacious, and all are filled with a rustic mix of old kilims

---

ⓘ GETTING TO KURDISH IRAQ

In the not-too-distant past, travelling to Kurdish Iraq from Turkey has involved the tiresome exercise of dealing with the overly zealous and entrepreneurial local taxi mafia in Silopi, 15km northwest of the Turkish–Iraqi border at Habur.

With the recent introduction of direct buses from Diyarbakır to Dohuk (₺50, six hours) or Erbil (₺60, nine hours) in Kurdish Iraq, traversing the border is more straighforward. See the bus companies along Kıbrıs Caddesi in Diyarbakır for the latest information on departure times and prices. You may need to supply your passport details the day before you travel. Note that the bus can be slower to cross the border than a shared taxi, so if time is a consideration, catch a bus from Diyarbakır to Silopi (₺28, 4½ hours), and pick up a more expensive taxi through to the Iraqi border town of Zakho.

Buses to Kurdish Iraq also travel from the Turkish city of Cizre (₺25), around four hours south of Diyarbakır. From Diyarbakır to the border at Habur, it's around four hours, and then it's another 1½ hours to Dohuk, and three hours to Erbil.

For more about travelling in Kurdish Iraq, check out the 'Travel to Kurdistan' Fact Sheet at www.krg.org, the website of the Kurdistan Regional Government.

In Diyarbakır, Ali Çalişir (p587) is a good source of information about travelling to Kurdish Iraq.

Mardin

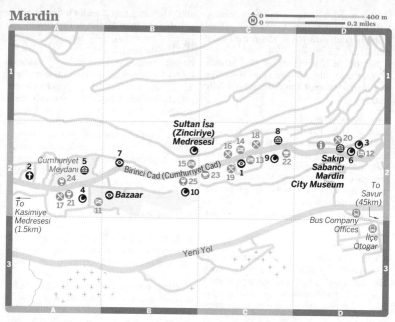

Cumhuriyet Meydanı

Sultan İsa (Zinciriye) Medresesi

Birinci Cad (Cumhuriyet Cad)

Bazaar

Sakıp Sabancı Mardin City Museum

To Savur (45km)

To Kasimiye Medresesi (1.5km)

Yeni Yol

Bus Company Offices

İlçe Otogar

and antique furniture. The expansive lobby flows effortlessly to huge terraces with views across the plains of Mesopotamia.

Zinciriye Butik Hotel   BOUTIQUE HOTEL €€
(☑212 4866; www.zinciriye.com; Sok 243, Medrese Mahallesi; s/d ₺90/140; 🌐 🛜) Tucked away just off the main drag, the Zinciriye features small but quaintly decorated rooms with centuries-old stone walls. Some downstairs rooms lack windows, so try and head upstairs, with the added attraction of a shared terrace with superb views.

Artuklu Kervansarayı   BOUTIQUE HOTEL €€
(☑213 7353; www.artuklu.com; Cumhuriyet Caddesi; s/d ₺120/170/210; 🌐) With dark floorboards and furniture, stone walls and sturdy wooden doors, this place feels like a castle. We're not quite sure how to take the Artuklu, but at least it broke the mould when it conceived the 'medieval' interior of this venture. It sports a wide range of amenities but there are no views to speak of.

Otel Başak   HOTEL €
(☑212 6246; Cumhuriyet Caddesi; s/d ₺30/50; 🛜) Budget old Mardin digs with clean rooms and so-so shared bathrooms. Rooms face onto the main drag, so it can be noisy.

✖ Eating & Drinking

TOP CHOICE Kamer Cafe Mutfak   ANATOLIAN €€
(Cumhuriyet Caddesi; mains ₺10-15) Operated by the Kamer Vakif ('Moon Foundation'), a support organisation for women who are victims of domestic violence, this terrific restaurant serves some of the best local cuisine in Mardin. Different women cook on a rotating basis, dishing up authentic and tasty versions of Kurdish bulgur wheat pilav and *içli köfte*. There's occasional live music amid the rustic and arty ambience.

Cercis Murat Konağı   ANATOLIAN €€€
(☑213 6841; Cumhuriyet Caddesi; mains ₺20-25; ⏰noon-11pm) The Cercis occupies a traditional Syrian Christian home with two finely decorated rooms and a terrace with stunning views. *Mekbuss* (aubergine pickles with walnut), *kitel raha* (Syrian-style meatballs) and *dobo* (lamb with garlic, spices and black pepper) rank among the highlights. Dive into the meze platter (₺35) for a taste of everything that's good. Try and book a couple of days ahead, or drop by at lunchtime and book for dinner. Wine and beer are also served.

Antik Sur   RESTAURANT €€
(Cumhuriyet Caddesi; mains ₺10-15) Ease into the shaded surrounds of this wonderfully

Mardin

restored caravanserai. Turkish tourists love the authentic local flavours and the opportunity to try Assyrian wine. Live music kicks off around 8pm most weekends, and laid-back teahouses fill the upper level if you're ready to bring out your backgammon A-game.

Rido'nun Yeri
KEBAP €€
(Cumhuriyet Caddesi 219; mains ₺10) Keeping it simple for several generations of the same family with perfectly grilled lamb, fluffy flatbreads, and rustic bowls of *ayran*.

Simit Sarayı
CAFE €
(Nolu Cadessi 70; snacks ₺4-6; 🛜) Housed in a beautiful stone mansion, Simit Sarayı is a deliciously cool haven from the Mesopotamian sun and features good coffee, freshly squeezed juices, pastries and muffins. Free wi-fi and a location opposite the Sabancı Museum seal the deal.

Çamli Kösk
TEA HOUSE
(Cumhuriyet Caddesi) Join the moustachioed throngs in Mardin's most authentic tea and coffee house. In between blokey rounds of backgammon, cards and okey, the faded amber patina of the interior also showcases the elaborate and choreographed ritual of *mirra* coffee. Bring along your phrasebook, because conversation with the friendly regulars is virtually mandatory.

Abbabar Bar
BAR
(www.abbabar.com; Cumhuriyet Caddesi) Yes, it is possible to get a cold beer in old Mardin.

Either retire to the expansive terrace for views all the way to Syria, or grab an indoor table downstairs and wait for the live Turkish music to kick off. From Wednesday to Saturday, that's usually from 8pm to 1am.

Vitamin
JUICE BAR
(Cumhuriyet Caddesi; juices from ₺2.50) With bright orange walls adorned with musical instruments, this pea-sized joint is Mardin's kookiest spot. Freshly squeezed juice is served in glasses filled to the brim.

Shiluh
WINE BAR
(www.suryanisarabi.com; Cumhuriyet Caddesi) Viticulture has been practised by Syriac Christian communities throughout the region for more than 5000 years, and up to six different wines are usually available for sampling and purchase here.

Atilla Çay Bahçesi
TEA GARDEN
(Cumhuriyet Caddesi) Tea garden with phenomenal views over old Mardin and the plains of Mesopotamia.

ⓘ Information

The post office, ATMs and internet cafes are all along Cumhuriyet Caddesi, old Mardin's one-way street. Wi-fi is available at the Simit Sarayı cafe.

Tourist Office (Cumhuriyet Caddesi; ⏲8.30am-5.30pm) Just up from the Artuklu Kervansarayı hotel, with free internet and a few worthwhile maps and brochures for sale.

❶ Getting There & Away

Air

Mardin airport is around 20km south of Mardin. There's no airport shuttle, but any minibus to Kızıltepe can drop you at the entrance (₺3). A taxi from the airport to old Mardin is around ₺25.

Turkish Airlines (www.turkishairlines.com) Up to two flights daily to/from İstanbul (from ₺92) and one flight daily to/from Ankara (from ₺64).

Bus

Most buses leave from the **İlçe Otogar** east of the centre. For long-distance destinations, buses stop in front of the **bus company offices** in the old town and in new Mardin. From around 4pm services start to dry up so it's best to make an early start.

Minibuses depart every hour or so for Diyarbakır (₺10, 1¼ hours), and Midyat (₺9, 1¼ hours). There are also relatively frequent minibuses to Savur (₺9, one hour). Other useful regular services for travellers include Şanlıurfa (₺25, three hours), and Cizre (₺18, 2½ hours) for travel to northern Iraq.

Around Mardin

DEYRUL ZAFARAN

The magnificent **Deyrul Zafaran** (Monastery of Mar Hanania; adult/student ₺5/3; ⊗8.30am-noon & 1-5pm) stands about 6km along a good but narrow road in the rocky hills east of Mardin. The monastery was once the seat of the Syrian Orthodox patriarchate but this has now moved to Damascus.

In 495 the first monastery was built on a site previously dedicated to the worship of the sun. Destroyed by the Persians in 607, it was rebuilt, only to be looted by Tamerlane six centuries later.

Shortly after entering the walled enclosure via a portal bearing a Syriac (a dialect of Aramaic) inscription, you'll see the original **sanctuary**, an eerie underground chamber with a ceiling of huge, closely fitted stones. This room was allegedly used by sun worshippers, who viewed their god rising through a window at the eastern end. A niche on the southern wall is said to have been for sacrifices. Nearby is a pair of 300-year-old doors leading to the **tombs** of the patriarchs and metropolitans who have served here.

In the chapel, the **patriarch's throne** to the left of the altar bears the names of all the patriarchs who have served the monastery since 792. Past patriarchs are buried seated and facing east, wearing full robes so they're ready and dressed for God.

To the right of the altar is the **throne of the metropolitan**. The present **stone altar** replaces a wooden one that burnt down about half a century ago. The walls are adorned with wonderful paintings and wall hangings. Services in Aramaic are held here.

In the next rooms you'll see litters used to transport the church dignitaries, and a baptismal font. In a small side room is a 300-year-old **wooden throne**. The floor mosaic is about 1500 years old.

A flight of stairs leads to very simple guest rooms for those coming for worship. The patriarch's small, simple bedroom and parlour are also up here.

There's no public transport here so you must take a taxi or walk around 90 minutes from Mardin. Hopeful drivers wait outside the bus company offices in Mardin and will ask around ₺40 to run you there and back.

Try and visit on a weekday or the monastic hush could be disturbed by busloads of Turkish tourists.

DARA

About 30km southeast of Mardin is a magnificent ancient Roman city forgotten in time. Dating back to the 6th century, Dara is where Mesopotamia's first dam and irrigation canals were built. Ongoing excavation promises to reveal one of southeastern Anatolia's forgotten gems. The highlight is walking down ancient stairways into the towers of Dara's underground aqueducts and cisterns. Natural light ebbs and flows into the expanse to create a remarkable cathedral-like ambience.

Bar a couple of teahouses, there are no facilities in Dara. From Mardin, there are three daily buses (₺6).

SAVUR

Savur is like a miniature Mardin, without the crowds. The atmosphere is laid-back and the setting enchanting, with a weighty citadel surrounded by a honey-coloured crinoline of old houses, lots of greenery and a gushing river running in the valley.

With your own wheels, you can drive to **Kıllıt**, about 7km east of Savur. This Syrian Orthodox village has two restored churches.

🛏 Sleeping & Eating

Hacı Abdullah Bey Konaği　　PENSION €
(☑0535 275 2569; savurkonagi@hotmail.com; r per person incl half-board ₺80) Perched on the hilltop, this gorgeous *konak* has seven rooms cosily outfitted with kilims, brass

beds, and antiques. Another pull is the friendly welcome of the Öztürk family. They don't speak much English, but offer a convivial atmosphere and serve traditional meals prepared from fresh ingredients. The rooftop terrace view will keep you intrigued for hours. Bathrooms are shared.

Uğur Alabalık
Tesisleri Perili Bahçe RESTAURANT **€€**

(☎0482-571 2832; mains ₺8-12; ⊘8am-9pm) For a leisurely alfresco meal, head to this shady garden by the gushing river. Relish fresh trout, salads from local organic vegies, and *içli köfte,* and sluice it all down with a glass of *kıllıt* (local wine) or rakı.

❶ Getting There & Away

From Mardin, around 10 daily minibus services cover the 45km to Savur (₺10, one hour). In winter services are more restricted.

Midyat

☑0482 / POP 58,400

About 65km east of Mardin lies sprawling Midyat, with a drab new section, Estel, linked by 3km of potholed Hükümet Caddesi to the inviting old town.

The centrepiece of the old part of town is a traffic roundabout, but nearby, honey-coloured houses are tucked away behind jewellery shops. Alleyways are lined with houses with demure doorways opening onto huge courtyards surrounded by intricately carved walls, windows and recesses.

Like Mardin, Midyat's Christian population suffered in the early 20th century and during the last few decades, and much of the community has emigrated. There are nine Syrian Orthodox churches in the town, though not all regularly hold services. Although you can see the steeples, it's hard to find the churches in the maze of streets so the best option is to accept the help of one of the local pint-sized guides. They'll expect a small tip.

🛏 Sleeping & Eating

Kasr-ı Nehroz BOUTIQUE HOTEL **€€€**

(☎464 2525; www.hotelnehroz.com; Işıklar Mahallesi Caddesi, Sokak 219; s/d ₺165/210; ❉@🛜) Luxury bathrooms combine with pristine stone walls and colourful kilims, while the spacious inner courtyard demands exploration with staircases and turrets leading to views of Midyat's centuries-old rooftops. Standard rooms are a tad compact, but the glorious shared spaces – including a library and reading room – are where you'll feel right at home.

Shmayaa BOUTIQUE HOTEL **€€€**

(☎464 0696; www.shmayaa.com; Akçakaya Mahallesl Kişla Cadessi 126, Sokak 12; r ₺200-450; ❉🛜) Midyat's second boutique hotel is arguably even more spectacular than the Kasr-ı Nehroz. Parts of Shmayaa's magnificent mansion date back 1600 years, and from 1915 to 1930 the building was used as military garrison. Now the emphasis is on romance, with 15 beautiful rooms dotted throughout the honey-coloured labyrinth. Three honeymoon suites come complete with delicately arched stone ceilings.

Midyat Konuk Evi HISTORIC HOTEL **€**

(Eski Midyat; r ₺75) Also known as the Governor's Guesthouse, here's a cheaper opportunity to bed down amid Midyat's heritage splendour. Rooms are simpy furnished with colourful kilims, and most are surrounded by spacious terraces looking across Midyat's improbable townscape. Breakfast is not provided, but guests have shared use of a kitchen. Note that the building was used in

WORTH A TRIP

HIDDEN GEMS AROUND THE TÜR ABDİN PLATEAU

With your own wheels or by arranging a taxi for the day in Midyat, it's easy to explore the plateau of Tür Abdin, a traditional homeland of the Syrian Orthodox Church. Dotted around the plateau to the east of Midyat (towards Dargeçit), are historic village churches and monasteries, some recently restored. Not-to-be-missed places include **Mor Yakup**, near Barıştepe; **Mor Izozoal**, perched on a knoll in Altıntaş; **Mor Kyriakos** in Bağlarbaşı; **Mor Dimet** in İzbarak; **Meryemana** in Anıtlı; and **Mor Eliyo** in Alagöz (about 3km from Anıtlı).

Roads are asphalted, villages are signposted and villagers will be happy to point you in the right direction. From Midyat, take the road to Hasankeyf (due north). After about 7km you'll reach the turn-off to Mor Yakup, on your right.

the hit Turkish TV series *Sıla*, and is open to visitors during the day (admission ₺1).

Hotel Demirdağ
HOTEL €€

(☑462 2000; www.hoteldemirdag.com; Mardin Caddesi 103; s/d ₺50/80; ❋@⑆) Across in new Midyat, the Demirdağ has well-equipped rooms, colourful as a box of Smarties (but avoid rooms 107 and 109, which are windowless). Its location is handy – the otogar is just one block behind. Recent renovations have brightened up the upper floors.

Saray Lokantası
TURKISH €

(Mardin Caddesi; mains ₺10-12) On the same street as the Hotel Demirdağ, this local haunt delivers good-value kebaps and pide.

ⓘ Getting There & Away

Minibuses regularly ply the bumpy route from outside the Saray Lokantası to old Midyat. Midyat has two otogars, one in new Midyat (one block behind the Hotel Demirdağ) and one in old Midyat, some 200m south of the roundabout along the road to Cizre. There are frequent services for Hasankeyf (₺8, 45 minutes), Batman (₺10, 1½ hours) and Mardin (₺9, 1¼ hours) from the new Midyat otogar. Minibuses for Cizre (₺12, 1½ hours) and Silopi (₺15, two hours), for Iraq, leave from the otogar in old Midyat.

Minibuses from Mardin will pass through the new town, then drop you off at the roundabout in the old town. You could easily base yourself in Midyat and make a day trip to Mardin or Hasankeyf.

Around Midyat

MORGABRIEL

About 18km east of Midyat, **Morgabriel (Deyrul Umur) Monastery** (☉9-11.30am & 1-4.30pm) is surrounded by gently rolling hills dotted with olive groves. Though much restored, the monastery dates back to 397. St Gabriel, the namesake of the monastery, is buried here, and the sand beside his tomb is said to cure illness. You'll see various frescoes as well as the immense ancient dome built by Theodora, wife of Byzantine emperor Justinian.

Morgabriel is home to the archbishop of Tür Abdin (Mountain of the Servants of God), the surrounding plateau. These days he presides over a much-diminished flock of around 70 people, the majority students. Many students have returned from living overseas in Europe and North America, so you may be lucky in getting an English-speaking guide.

The monastery's land continues to be threatened by ongoing legal claims from nearby villages – despite the monastery having been established for more than 1600 years. See the website of the **Syriac Universal Alliance** (www.sua-ngo.org) for more information. (Search for 'Mor Gabriel'.)

Ask about visiting some of the other churches in the region, such as the **Meryem Ana Kilisesi** at Anıttepe.

To get to the monastery from Midyat, take a Cizre minibus (₺7) to the signposted road junction and walk 2.5km uphill to the gate. Start early in the morning as minibuses become less frequent later in the day. A taxi is about ₺60 return, including waiting time.

HASANKEYF
☑0488 / POP 5500

Hasankeyf is a heartbreaker. This gorgeous honey-coloured village clinging to the rocks of a gorge above the Tigris River is a sort of Cappadocia in miniature and a definite must-see, but it's slated to vanish underwater. At the time of writing, this was scheduled for around 2015, and the foundations of Yeni (New) Hasankeyf were already taking shape across the river on higher gound. Meanwhile, don't miss Hasankeyf, which has become a popular tourist destination, especially on weekends with local visitors.

◉ Sights

On the main road towards Batman is the restored **Zeynel Bey Türbesi**, isolated in a riverside field. The conical turquoise-tiled tomb was built in the mid-15th century for Zeynel, son of the Akkoyunlu governor, and is a rare survivor from this period.

A modern bridge now spans the Tigris, but to the right are the broken arches of **Eski Köprü** (Old Bridge). Their size reinforces the importance of Hasankeyf in the period immediately before the arrival of the Ottomans.

Across the bridge is the *kale* (castle) and *mağaras* (caves). The **El-Rizk Camii** (1409) sports a beautiful, slender minaret similar to those in Mardin and is topped with a stork's nest. Just past the mosque, the road forks right down to the river. The left fork cuts through a rocky defile to the ticket office for the **kale** (admission ₺2). This strategic site has been occupied since Byzantine times, but most of the relics you see today were built during the reign of the 14th-century Ayyubids. Dotted throughout the *kale* are caves, which youthful guides will

HASANKEYF UNDER THREAT

The cloud of a giant engineering project hangs menacingly above Hasakeyf. Despite its beauty and history, the town is destined to vanish beneath the waters of the İlisu Dam, part of the GAP irrigation and hydro-electricity project, and scheduled for construction from 2015. The proposed dam will flood a region from Batman to Midyat, drowning this historic site and several other archaeological treasures, and displacing over 37 villages.

Despite the future of the town looking increasingly bleak, opposition supported by the work of the Doğa ('Nature') Foundation (www.dogadernegi.org) continues to be well organised. Stop by their booth in Hasankeyf to sign its petition to save Hasankeyf, or show your support online at http://hasankeyf.dogadernegi.org.

See also http://www.hasankeyfgirisimi.com/en/index.htm, the website of the Save Hasankeyf Initiative. They have an information booth near the tourist shops en route to the castle.

Another source of information is the excellent Hasankeyf Matters blog (www.hasan keyfmatters.com), which includes discussion on all relevant issues, and is a good guide to exploring the site.

describe as shops and houses. At the top of the rock are the ruins of the 14th-century **Küçük Saray** (Small Palace), with pots built into the ceiling and walls for sound insulation.

Nearby is a small **mosque**, once a Byzantine church, and the **Büyük Saray** (Big Palace), with a creepy jail underneath. Adjacent is a former watchtower teetering on the edge of the cliff. The 14th-century **Ulu Cami** was built on the site of a church.

🛏 Sleeping & Eating

Hasankeyf only has a couple of accomodation offerings, and another option is to visit from Midyat or Diyarbakır (via Batman) as a day trip.

You can also kip in one of the *çardaks* (leafy-roofed shelters) along the riverbank. You'll be expected to eat at an adjoining restaurant (around ₺15), but come nightfall you can bed down amid cushions and kilims. Female travellers may wish to err on the side of caution and book a more secure room at Hasbahçe or the motel.

Hasankeyf Hasbahçe   GUEST HOUSE ₺
(📞0530 929 1527, 381 2624; www.hasankeyf hasbahce.com; s/d ₺40/80, campsite ₺20) The best place to stay in town is this quirky combination of simple but colourful guesthouse rooms, fish ponds, organic gardens and fruit trees. Rabbits and the occasional lamb linger across the sprawling complex, and Fırat Argun, the friendly owner, is a wealth of information in good German and rudimentary English. To find Hasbahçe, cross the bridge past the motel and walk

left for around 300m. Excellent trout is often served for dinner.

Hasankeyf Motel   GUEST HOUSE ₺
(📞0542 790 6269, 381 2005; Dicle Sokak; s/d ₺30/60) This modest 'motel' has a good location, right by the Tigris bridge, but rooms are definitely no-frills, carpets are faded, and the simple bathrooms are shared (Turkish toilets). Aim for one of the rooms at the back, with a balcony that overlooks the river. Based at the motel, **Ercan Altue** is a local guide offering walking tours (one/two persons ₺100/150) around the ancient caves dotting the hills above the town

Naman's Place   CAFE ₺
(mains ₺8-10) A riverside location and simple grills, flatbreads and salads add up to a lazy afternoon beside the Tigris. Ask if the friendly Idris is around – he can give you an update of the local situation, all in perfect English. Naman's is right on the river, and is also one of the *çardaks* where you can bed down for the night.

Hasankeyf Elit   TURKISH
(kebap with rice & salad ₺15) This simple *lokanta* with excellent river views stretches the meaning of *elit* (elite) somewhat, but it's still one of the best-value options along Hasankeyf's path to the castle. Trout, lamb kebaps and good pide all feature.

ℹ Getting There & Away

Frequent minibuses run from Batman to Midyat, transitting at Hasankeyf (₺8, 40 minutes). Another option is to visit from Diyarbakır (₺15, two hours), changing buses in Batman.

Bitlis

☏ 0434 / POP 46,300

Bitlis has one of the highest concentrations of restored historic buildings in eastern Anatolia, many of them EU-sponsored projects. A smorgasbord of monuments testifies to rich ancient origins, and the town is spectacularly squeezed into a narrow river canyon.

A **castle** dominates the town, and two ancient bridges span the stream. Make a beeline for the **Ulu Cami** (1126); the newer **Şerefiye Camii** dates from the 16th century. Other must-sees include the splendid **İhlasiye Medrese** (Koranic school), the most significant building in Bitlis, and the **Gökmeydan Camii**.

The **İl Kültür Merkez** (Cumhuriyet Caddesi; ⊙8am-5pm Mon-Fri) has good maps of the city and brochures covering the area. It's housed inside the İhlasiye Medrese.

The **Dideban Hotel** (☏226 2821; didebanotel@hotmail.com; Nur Caddesi; s/d ₺50/80) features spruce rooms and is near local restaurants. It's conveniently located about 100m from the minibus stand for Tatvan and close to most monuments.

Don't leave town without trying the excellent local *bal* (honey). Bitlis is also renowned for its *büryan kebab* (lamb baked in a pit and served with flat bread).

Regular minibuses travel from Tatvan to Bitlis (₺5, 30 minutes).

Tatvan

☏ 0434 / POP 65,100

Tatvan is ideally positioned to visit spectacular Nemrut Dağı (not to be confused with the higher-profile Nemrut Dağı south of Malatya), Ahlat and Bitlis. Several kilometres long and just a few blocks wide, Tatvan is not much to look at, but its setting on the shores of Lake Van (backed by bare mountains streaked with snow) is magnificent. It is also the western port for Lake Van steamers.

🛏 Sleeping & Eating

Otel Dinç   HOTEL ₺₺

(☏827 5960; www.oteldinc.com; Sahil Mahallesi İşletme Caaddesi 9; s/d ₺70/100; ❀🐾) One of Tatvan's newest hotels is also one of its best. Owned by a friendly, eager to please family, the Dinç features brightly coloured, modern, if slightly compact, rooms. It's down a quiet side street on the southern side of town, and

there are excellent lake and mountain views from the breakfast room on the top floor.

Hotel Dilek   HOTEL ₺

(☏827 1516; Yeni Çarşı; s/d ₺35/70) The Dilek gets good marks for colourful rooms with tiled bathrooms. Singles are tiny, so angle for rooms 201, 202, 301 or 302, which are more spacious and get more natural light. It's in a street running parallel to the main drag.

Eyvan Pide Lahmacun
ve Melemen Salonu   PIDE ₺

(1 Sokak; mains ₺6-10) This compact joint is the best place in town for thin-crust pide or a *lahmacun*. After a flavoursome *kaşarli pide* (cheese pide), faultlessly cooked in the *firin* (wood-fired oven) on the ground floor, we reckon it's one of the best pide spots in eastern Turkey. The homemade *ayran* is pretty special, too.

Gökte Ada   PIDE, KEBAB ₺

(Cumhuriyet Caddesi; mains ₺6-11) This snazzy spot atop Tatvan's modern cinema and shopping complex combines tasty renditions of pide and kebaps with expansive views of Lake Van. It's at the northern edge of the town centre.

❶ Getting There & Away

Buses to Van run around the southern shore of the lake (₺15, three hours). The otogar is at the northern edge of town. A ferry crosses the lake twice a day (₺10, about four hours), but its schedule can be very inconsistent.

Minibuses to Ahlat (₺5, 30 minutes) leave about hourly from PTT Caddesi, beside Türk Telekom and the PTT. The minibus stand for Bitlis (₺5, 30 minutes) is a bit further up the street. Direct minibuses to Adilcevaz are infrequent; you'll have to change in Ahlat.

Around Tatvan

NEMRUT DAĞI (MT NEMRUT)

Nemrut Dağı (3050m), rising to the north of Tatvan, is an inactive volcano with several crater lakes – not to be confused with the more famous Nemrut Dağı near Malatya that's topped with the giant heads.

A trip up this Nemrut Dağı is also an unforgettable experience. On the crater rim (13km from the main road), there are sensational views over Lake Van and Tatvan, and over the nearby water-filled craters. From the rim you can hike to the summit (about 45 minutes) – just follow the lip of the crater (the last stretch is a bit of a scramble). Midweek, the only company you're likely to have is the shepherds with their flocks (and dogs) and the hoopoes, nuthatches, skylarks and other birds. Follow the dirt road leading down to the lake from the crater rim and find your own picnic area.

Visits are only possible from around mid-May to the end of October; at other times the summit is under snow.

ⓘ Getting There & Away

A taxi from Tatvan is around ₺150 return. On summer weekends hitching is an option.

With your own transport, leave Tatvan by the road around the lake and then turn left towards Bitlis. About 300m further, turn right following a sign saying 'Nemrut 13km'. The road is rough but passable in an ordinary car except in wet weather. You'll reach the crater rim, from where a dirt road winds down into the crater itself and connects with other dirt roads that snake around the crater.

Guided trips can also be undertaken with Alkan Tours (p602) in Van.

Lake Van (South Shore)

☏ 0432

After the rigours of central Anatolia, this vast expanse of water surrounded by snow-capped mountains sounds deceptively promising for beaches and water sports. Lake Van (Van Gölü) has great potential for activities, but nothing has been really developed yet and infrastructure is lacking. On the positive side, this means it's very scenic and virtually untouched.

The most conspicuous feature on the map of southeastern Turkey, this 3750-sq-km lake was formed when a volcano (Nemrut Dağı) blocked its natural outflow.

Travelling south around the lake between Van and Tatvan offers beautiful scenery, but there's little reason to stop. The exception is 5km west of Gevaş, where the 10th-century Church of the Holy Cross on Akdamar Island is a glorious must-see.

◉ Sights

Gevaş Cemetery   CEMETERY

Like Ahlat on the north shore, Gevaş has a cemetery full of tombstones dating from the 14th to 17th centuries. Notable is the polygonal **Halime Hatun Türbesi**, built in 1358 for a female member of the Karakoyunlu dynasty.

Akdamar Kilisesi   CHURCH

(Church of the Holy Cross; admission ₺3; ⊙8am-6pm) One of the marvels of Armenian architecture is this carefully restored church. It's perched on an island 3km out in the lake; motorboats ferry sightseers back and forth.

In 921 Gagik Artzruni, King of Vaspurkan, built a palace, church and monastery on the island. Little remains of the palace and monastery, but the church walls are in superb condition and the wonderful relief carvings are among the masterworks of Armenian art. If you're familiar with biblical stories, you'll immediately recognise Adam and Eve, Jonah and the whale (with the head of a dog), David and Goliath, Abraham about to sacrifice Isaac, Daniel in the lions' den, Samson etc. There are also some frescoes inside the church.

Altınsaç Kilisesi   CHURCH

Another relatively well-preserved Armenian church, Altınsaç Kilisesi is perched on a mound overlooking the lake. If you have your own transport, be sure to squeeze it into your itinerary.

From Akdamar, drive 12km towards Tatvan until you reach a junction. Turn right onto the road marked for Altınsaç. After 3km the asphalt road ends and becomes a gravel road. The road skirts the shore of the lake for another 14km, until you reach the village of Altınsaç. From the village it's another 2km to the church, which is visible from some distance.

⌕ Sleeping & Eating

FREE **Akdamar**

Restaurant & Camping   CAMPING GROUND

(☏0542 743 1361, 214 3479; www.akdamarrestaurant.net; campsites free; ⊙Apr-Sep) This basic campsite is opposite the ferry departure point for Akdamar Island. The restaurant (mains ₺15) has a terrace with lake views. Another speciality is *kürt tavası* (meat, tomato and peppers cooked in a clay pot). It's licensed so grab a beer (₺6) while you're waiting for a boat to Akdamar to fill up. If you're camping, you'll be expected to eat in the restaurant. When we dropped by, friendly owner İbrahim Alkan was also looking at adding a few bungalows.

ⓘ Getting There & Away

Minibuses run the 44km from Van to Akdamar harbour for ₺7 during high season. At other times, there's an hourly minibus to Gevaş

(₺5). Most drivers will arrange for you to be transferred to another minibus from Gevaş to Akdamar harbour for an additional ₺2. Alternatively, catch a minibus heading to Tatvan and ask to be let off at Akdamar harbour. Make sure you're out on the highway flagging a bus back to Van by 4pm, as soon afterwards the traffic dries up and buses may be full.

Boats to Akdamar Island (₺8) run as and when visitor numbers warrant it (minimum 15 people). From May to September, boats fill up on a regular basis so waiting time is usually minimal. Outside of the summer season, you may need to charter your own boat (around ₺120).

Lake Van (North Shore)

$✏$ 0432

The journey around the north shore of Lake Van from Tatvan to Van is even more beautiful than going around the south shore.

The major bus companies take the shortest route around the south of the lake from Tatvan to Van. To travel around the north shore take a minibus to Ahlat from Tatvan, then hop on another minibus to Adilcevaz, where you can stay overnight. The next morning catch another bus to Van.

AHLAT

A further 42km along the lakeshore from Tatvan is the underrated town of Ahlat, famous for its splendid Seljuk Turkish tombs and graveyard.

Founded during the reign of Caliph Omar (AD 581–644), Ahlat became a Seljuk stronghold in the 1060s. When the Seljuk sultan Alp Arslan rode out to meet the Byzantine emperor Romanus Diogenes in battle on the field of Manzikert, Ahlat was his base.

Just west of Ahlat is an overgrown polygonal 13th-century tomb, **Usta Şağirt Kümbeti** (Ulu Kümbeti), 300m off the highway. It's the largest Seljuk tomb in the area.

Further along the highway on the left is a museum, and behind it a vast **Selçuk Mezarlığı** (Seljuk cemetery), with stele-like headstones of lichen-covered grey or red volcanic *tuff* with intricate web patterns and bands of Kufic lettering.

Over the centuries, earthquakes, wind and water have set the stones at all angles, a striking sight with spectacular Nemrut Dağı as a backdrop. Most stones have a crow as sentinel, and tortoises patrol the ruins.

On the northeastern side of the graveyard is the unusual **Bayındır Kümbeti ve Camii** (Bayındır Tomb and Mosque; 1477), with

a colonnaded porch and its own *mihrab* (niche indicating the direction of Mecca).

The small **museum** (admission ₺3; $⊙$8am-noon & 1-5pm Tue-Sun) has a reasonable collection that includes Urartian bronze belts and needles.

Other sites include the **Çifte Kümbet** (Twin Tombs), about 2km from the museum towards the town centre, and the **Ahlat Sahil Kalesi** (Ahlat Lakeside Fortress), south of the Çifte Kümbet, which was built during the reign of Süleyman the Magnificent.

ℹ Getting There & Away

From Tatvan, minibuses leave for Ahlat (₺4, 30 minutes) from beside Türk Telekom and the PTT. Get let off at the museum on the western outskirts of Ahlat, or you'll have to walk back from the town centre. From Ahlat, there are regular minibuses to Adilcevaz (₺3.50, 20 minutes).

ADILCEVAZ

About 25km east of Ahlat is the town of Adilcevaz, once a Urartian town but now dominated by a great Seljuk Turkish **fortress** (1571).

Snowmelt from the year-round snowfields on Süphan Dağı flows down to Adilcevaz, making its surroundings lush and fertile. On the western edge of town is the **Ulu Camii**, built in the 13th century, and still used for daily prayer.

From the centre of town, take a taxi to the **Kef Kalesi**, another Urartian citadel perched higher up in the valley (about ₺35 return).

The best accommodation in town is the **Cevizlibağ Otel** ($✏$0434-311 3152; www.cevi zlibagotel.com; Recep Tayyip Erdoğan Bulvarı 31/1; s/d ₺50/80; ✲🜚), handily located midway between the otogar and the town centre. The spacious rooms are trimmed in shiny marble with wooden floors and spotless bathrooms. The roof terrace reveals a good restaurant, and it's a short stroll to lakefront tea gardens and eateries.

ℹ Getting There & Away

From Adilcevaz, there are five direct buses to Van (₺15, 2½ hours), but the last one departs around 2pm – make sure you start out early in the day.

Van

$✏$ 0432 / POP 353.500 / ELEV 1727M

More urban, more casual and less rigorous, Van is very different in spirit from the rest of southeastern Anatolia. Young couples walk hand in hand on the main drag, live bands knock out Kurdish tunes in pubs, and a resilient population coping with the impact of recent earthquakes inspires a satisfying urban buzz.

While Van boasts a brilliant location near the eponymous lake, forget about water sports and beaches. Instead, focus on the striking monuments, including Van Kalesi (Van Castle or the Rock of Van), spend a few days journeying around the lake, and explore the nearby historic sites of Çavuştepe and Hoşap.

Hotels, restaurants, internet cafes, ATMs, the post office and bus company offices all lie on or around Cumhuriyet Caddesi.

History

The kingdom of Urartu, the biblical Ararat, flourished from the 13th to the 7th centuries BC. Its capital was on the outskirts of present-day Van. The Urartians borrowed much of their culture (including cuneiform writing) from the neighbouring Assyrians, with whom they were more or less permanently at war. The powerful Assyrians never subdued the Urartians, but when several waves of Cimmerians, Scythians and Medes swept into Urartu and joined in the battle, the kingdom met its downfall.

Later the region was resettled by a people whom the Persians called Armenians. By the 6th century BC the area was governed by Persian and Median satraps (provincial governors).

In the 8th century AD, Arab armies flooded through from the south, forcing the Armenian prince to take refuge on Akdamar Island. Unable to fend off the Arabs, he agreed to pay tribute to the caliph. When the Arabs retreated, the Byzantines and Persians took their place, and overlordship of Armenia seesawed between them as one or the other gained military advantage.

After defeating the Byzantines in 1071 at Manzikert, north of Lake Van, the Seljuk Turks marched on, with a flood of Turkoman nomads in tow, to found the sultanate of Rum, based in Konya. The domination of eastern Anatolia by Turkish *emirs* followed and continued until the coming of the Ottomans in 1468.

During WWI, Armenian guerrilla bands intent on founding an independent Armenian state collaborated with the Russians to defeat the Ottoman armies in Turkey's east. From then on the Armenians, formerly loyal subjects of the sultan, were viewed by the Turks as traitors. Bitter fighting between Turkish and Kurdish forces on the one side and Armenian and Russian forces on the other brought devastation to the entire region and to Van.

The Ottomans destroyed the old city of Van (near Van Castle) before the Russians occupied it in 1915. Ottoman forces counterattacked but were unable to drive the invaders out, and Van remained under Russian occupation until the armistice of 1917. After the founding of the Turkish Republic, a new planned city of Van was built 4km east of the old site.

On October 23 2011, Van was shaken by a 7.1 magnitude earthquake, causing around 100 deaths in the city, and destroying more than 1000 buildings. The town of Erçis on the northern shore of Lake Van also suffered considerable damage and fatalities. A signficant aftershock of magnitude 5.7 struck central Van on 9 November 2011, causing more fatalities and the destruction of several inner-city hotels.

Many apartment blocks were also made unsafe, and tens of thousands of Van residents were made homeless, many escaping the harsh eastern Anatolian winter to the warmer climes of western Turkey. At the time of writing, many Van residents were still living in containers, and the Turkish government was establishing new housing developments on the hills above the city.

◉ Sights

Van Castle (Van Kalesi) & Eski Van   RUINS
About 4km west of the centre, **Van Castle** (Rock of Van; admission ₺3; ⊙9am-dusk) dominates the view of the city. Try to visit at sunset for great views across the lake.

The site is fairly spread out, something to bear in mind when it's scorching hot. Ask to be dropped off at the northwestern corner of the rock, where there's the ticket office and a tea garden.

Just past the ticket office is an old **stone bridge** and some willows. To the left, a stairway leads up the rock. On your way up is a ruined **mosque** with a minaret, as well as an arched-roof building, which used to be a Koranic school.

From the summit, the foundations of **Eski Van** (the old city) reveal themselves on the southern side of the rock. The flat space punctuated by the grass-covered foundations of numerous buildings was the site of

Van

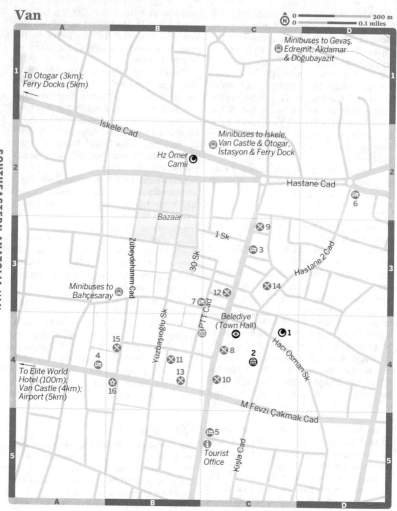

To Otogar (3km);
Ferry Docks (5km)

İskele Cad

Minibuses to Gevaş,
Edremit, Akdamar
& Doğubayazıt

Hz Ömer
Camii

Minibuses to İskele,
Van Castle & Otogar,
İstasyon & Ferry Dock

Hastane Cad

6

Bazaar

1 Sk

9

3

Zübeydehanım Cad

30 Sk

Hastane 2 Cad

14

Minibuses to
Bahçesaray

7

12

Yüzbaşıoğlu Sk

PTT Cad

Belediye
(Town Hall)

1

Hacı Osman Sk

15

4

11

8

2

10

To Elite World
Hotel (100m);
Van Castle (4km);
Airport (5km)

16

13

M Fevzi Çakmak Cad

5

Tourist
Office

Kışla Cad

the old city, destroyed during the upheavals of WWI. A few buildings have survived and are clearly visible from the top: the **Hüsrev Paşa Külliyesi**, dating back to 1567, which has been restored and has a *kümbet* (tomb) attached; the nearby **Kaya Çelebi Camii** (1662), with a similarly striped minaret; the brick minaret of the Seljuk **Ulu Cami**; and the **Kızıl Camii** (Red Mosque).

At the ticket office ask the custodian (he'll expect a tip) to show you the huge cuneiform inscriptions (ask for the *tabela*) as well as the numerous *khachkars* (Armenian crosses) that are carved into the southern

side of the rock. Look out also for the water reservoir, an ancient hamam and a ruined palace (not visible from the top of the rock). The Kızıl Camii and Ulu Cami can also easily be approached, further south. Taking some distance from the rock to get a wider perspective, the custodian may point out various rock-cut **funeral chambers** (not visible from the base of the rock), including that of King Argishti.

On the way back to the ticket office, ask the custodian to show you the **Sardur Burcu** (Sardur Tower; 840–830 BC), in the little willow forest (as there's no sign, it's not easy

Van

to find). It's a large black stone rectangle sporting cuneiform inscriptions in Assyrian praising the Urartian King Sardur I.

To get here take a 'Kale' minibus (₺2) from İskele Caddesi opposite the Hz Ömer Camii.

Van Museum MUSEUM
(Van Müzesi; Kişla Caddesi; admission ₺3; ⊙8am-noon & 1-5pm Tue-Sun) This compact museum was closed at the time of writing following the 2011 earthquakes, and a potential move to near Van Castle was also rumoured. Check at the tourist information office for the latest update.

The museum boasts an outstanding collection of Urartian exhibits, including exquisite gold jewellery, and an array of bronze belts, helmets, horse armour and terracotta figures.

The ethnographic exhibits upstairs include local Kurdish and Turkoman kilims and a carpeted sitting area, such as is found in village houses. The Genocide Section is a piece of one-sided propaganda displaying the contents of graves left from the massacres of Turks and Kurds by Armenians at Çavuşoğlu and Zeve.

🛏 Sleeping

Following the 2011 earthquakes, several central Van hotels were either demolished or had to close because of significant damage. Because of this, accommodation is often in high demand in the city, and rates can be significantly higher than elsewhere in eastern Turkey.

Elite World Hotel HOTEL €€€
(☎0212-444 0883; www.eliteworldhotels.com.tr; Kazım Karabekir Caddesi 54; s/d €85/95; ⊖❄@

⊗) Van's newest hotel – it opened September 2012 – is also its most comfortable with business traveller–friendly features including a bar, nonsmoking rooms, and a spa, sauna and swimming pool. The luxury decor almost strays into OTT territory, but it's easily Van's top place to stay in a city of limited accommodation choices. Posted rates are high, but search online for discounts.

Büyük Asur Oteli HOTEL €€
(☎216 8792; www.buyukasur.com; Cumhuriyet Caddesi, Turizm Sokak; s/d ₺100/150; ❄🛜) Even if you're on a tight budget, consider spending a little more to enjoy the comforts of this reliable midrange venture. The rooms are colourful and come complete with fresh linen, TV and well-scrubbed bathrooms. English is spoken and the hotel can organise tours to Akdamar Island, Hoşap Castle and other local attractions.

Akdamar Otel HOTEL €€
(☎214 9923; www.otelakdamar.com; Kazım Karabekir Caddesi; s/d ₺120/160; ❄🛜) Enjoying increased popularity after a post-earthquake makeover, the Akdamar Otel is centrally located close to good restaurants and pastry shops, and has flat-screen TVs, and newly decorated, spacious bathrooms. The young, English-speaking crew at reception have lots of recommendations for the best of local cafes.

Büyük Urartu Oteli HOTEL €€
(☎212 0660; www.buyukurartuotel.com; Hastane 2 Caddesi; s/d ₺100/140; ❄🛜⊗) This reassuring choice gives off a serious hotel vibe, with professional staff and an impressive lobby. A full array of amenities, including a sauna, pool and rooftop restaurant, is on offer.

A long overdue renovation took place in 2012, so ask about scoring one of the newer, more comfortable rooms.

Cemil Hotel
HOTEL €

(☑215 1520; PTT Caddesi, opposite the Haci Osman Camii; s/d ₺25/30) Budget accommodation is in short supply in Van, and this central spot is good value if you're conserving your travel budget to kick on to Iran. It's actually a simple pension with shared bathrooms, and there are loads of restaurants just metres away. From Van's main drag, walk 100m down the lane between Simit Sarayı and the Adi Güzel gold shop.

Ada Palas
HOTEL €€

(☑216 2716; www.vanadapalas.tr.gg; Cumhuriyet Caddesi; s/d ₺80/120; ❋) The 2nd floor is *yeşil* (green), the 3rd floor canary yellow and the 4th floor electric *mavi* (blue). The owners of the centrally located and well-organised Ada Palas certainly like to add colour to life.

Eating

Tamara Ocakbaşı
STEAKHOUSE €€

(Yüzbaşıoğlu Sokak; mains ₺15-20; ⏱5pm-late) A meal here is dizzying, especially for carnivores. In the Hotel Tamara, the dining room eatery features 40 *ocak* – each table has its own grill. Mood lighting adds a touch of atmosphere in the evening. High-quality meat and fish dishes feature prominently, but the list of meze is equally impressive.

Kervansaray
ANATOLIAN €€

(Cumhuriyet Caddesi; mains ₺12-18) Upstairs from the bustle of Cumhuriyet Caddesi, Kervansaray is Van's go-to spot for a more elegant and refined dining experience. Dive into a few shared plates of excellent meze as you peruse a menu containing more than a few local specialities. Fans of incredibly tender lamb should definitely consider the *kağıt kebap* (paper kebap), wrapped and cooked delicately in paper.

Kebabistan
KEBAP €€

(Sinemalar Sokak; mains ₺8-15) You're within safe boundaries here: the kitchen turns out expertly cooked kebaps (go for the *kuşbaşı*, with little morsels of beef). A second branch, across the street, specialises in pide. Getting there is half the fun: it's in a side street where men can be seen sitting on low chairs, playing backgammon and drinking tea.

Halil İbrahim Sofrası
TURKISH €€

(Cumhuriyet Caddesi; mains ₺8-15) One word describes this downtown hot spot: yum. The eclectic food is well presented and of high quality, with service to match, served in sleek surrounds. Try the rich and tender İskender kebap. Pide buffs should target the generous 'pide special', with a bit of everything.

Safa 3, Çorba 1 Paça Salonu
TURKISH €

(Kazım Karabekir Caddesi; soups ₺5; ⏱24hr) If you're an adventurous foodie, head to this quirky little restaurant. Regulars swear by the *kelle* (mutton's head) – the spicy lentil soup is more approachable.

Akdeniz Tantuni
FAST FOOD €

(Cumhuriyet Caddesi; sandwiches ₺6) This delightful little den on the main drag prepares devilish chicken sandwiches at paupers' prices, in the *tantuni* style from the Akdeniz (Mediterranean) city of Mersin.

Çavuşoğlu
SWEETS €

(Cumhuriyet Caddesi; pastries from ₺2) Luscious ice creams and dangerously good baklavas.

🍷 Drinking & Entertainment

Halay Türkü Bar
LIVE MUSIC, BAR

(Kazım Karabekir Caddesi) Multiple floors add up to multiple ways to enjoy Van's low-key nightlife scene. Kick off with tasty meze and grilled meat before graduating to draught beer, generously poured local spirits and regular live music.

North Shield
PUB

(Yüzbaşıoğlu Sokak, Hotel Tamara) Go on – wanting a cold pint in a dusty Kurdish city is not a hanging offence. Head to the North Shield in the Hotel Tamara for a familiar English pub-type ambience. After a couple of beers make a beeline for the excellent grill restaurant upstairs.

❶ Information

ATMs and internet cafes are easily found on Cumhuriyet Caddesi.

Alkan Tours (☑0530 349 2793, 215 2092; www.easternturkeytour.org; Ordu Caddesi) The friendly Alkan family can advise on everything from train travel to Iran, organised tours throughout Eastern Turkey and into Georgia and Armenia, and the post-earthquake state of play for hotels in Van. Guided day trips (per person €20) taking in Hoşap, Çavuştepe and Akdamar Island are a time-efficient option to get around the region's main sights. More in-depth tours exploring the region's Armenian heritage are available, and excursions to Kars, Doğubeyazit, and Nemrut Dağı near Tatvan can also be arranged.

Tourist Office (☎216 2530; Cumhuriyet Caddesi; ☺8.30am-noon & 1-5.30pm Mon-Fri) English is spoken and there are good maps and brochures.

Getting There & Away

Air

A taxi to the airport costs about ₺30. A municipal bus (₺1.25) leaves frequently from near the Akdamar Hotel.

Pegasus Airlines (www.flypgs.com) Has six weekly flights to/from Ankara (from ₺130) and daily flights to/from İstanbul (from ₺80).

Turkish Airlines (www.turkishairlines.com) Together with Anadolu Jet (www.anadolujet.com) has frequent daily flights to/from İstanbul (from ₺85) and Ankara (from ₺70).

Boat

A ferry crosses Lake Van between Tatvan and Van twice daily. There's no fixed schedule. The trip costs ₺10 per passenger and takes about four hours. 'İskele' dolmuşes ply the route from İskele Caddesi to the harbour (₺2).

Bus

Many bus companies have ticket offices at the intersection of Cumhuriyet and Kazım Karabekir Caddesis. They provide *servises* to shuttle passengers to and from the otogar on the northwestern outskirts.

For Hoşap and Çavuştepe (₺6, 45 minutes), you can take a minibus that leaves from the Yüksekova Garajı or the Başkale Garajı, both on Cumhuriyet Caddesi, a few hundred metres south of the Büyük Asur Oteli. Buses to Hakkari also travel past Hoşap and Çavuştepe. Note that return transport to Van is often hard to find, and

a good-value and straightforward option is to visit with Alkan Tours.

Minibuses to Gevaş and Akdamar (₺7, about 45 minutes) depart from a dusty car park down a side street on the right of the northern extension of Cumhuriyet Caddesi. Transport to Doğubayazıt also leaves from here, an 185km run that's worth taking for the magnificent pastoral scenery along the way, especially if you can pause at the spectacular Muradiye Waterfalls.

There are direct buses to Orumiyeh (in Iran). Ask around at the bus company offices on Cumhuriyet Caddesi.

Car

Consider renting a car to journey around Lake Van. **Avis** (☎214 6375; www.avis.com.tr; Cumhuriyet Caddesi), near the tourist office, rents cars for about ₺100 per day. Other rental agencies line Cumhuriyet Caddesi.

Train

The twice-weekly *Vangölü Ekspresi* from Ankara terminates at Tatvan; from Tatvan, the ferry will bring you to the dock at Van. The weekly *Trans Asya Ekspresi* connects Ankara to Tehran and stops at Van. It leaves for Tabriz (₺15) and Tehran (₺50) on Thursday around 10pm, but this time can be flexible dependent on other connections. A sleeper train also departs Van for Tabriz (₺25, nine hours) in Iran around 8pm on Tuesday. Confirm exact times at the train station or with Alkan Tours. Note it's not possible to book trains running from Van to Ankara once in Turkey, and this leg needs to be booked in Iran.

The main train station is northwest of the centre near the otogar, with another station, İskele İstasyonu, several kilometres to the northwest on the lakeshore. Catch 'İstasyon' minibuses from İskele Caddesi.

BREAKFASTS OF CHAMPIONS

Van is famed for its tasty *kahvaltı* (breakfast). Skip your usually bland hotel breakfast and head straight to Eski Sümerbank Sokak, also called 'Kahvaltı Sokak' (Breakfast St), a pedestrianised side street running parallel to Cumhuriyet Caddesi. Here you'll find a row of eateries specialising in complete Turkish breakfasts, including the buzzing **Sütçü Fevzi** (☎216 6618; Eski Sümerbank Sokak; ☺7am-noon) and **Sütçü Kenan** (☎216 8499; Eski Sümerbank Sokak; ☺7am-noon), which have tables set up outside. The other restaurants on the street are equally good.

On summer mornings the street heaves with punters sampling *otlu peynir* (cheese mixed with a tangy herb, Van's speciality), *beyaz peynir* (a mild yellow cheese), honey from the highlands, olives, *kaymak* (clotted cream), butter, tomatoes, cucumbers and *sucuklu yumurta* (omelette with sausage). Whet your appetite by checking out the photographs at www.vandakahvalti.com (in Turkish). A full breakfast will set you back around ₺12 to ₺15. An essential Van experience.

SERVICES FROM VAN'S OTOGAR

DESTINATION	FARE (₺)	DURATION (HR)	DISTANCE (KM)	FREQUENCY (PER DAY)
Ağrı	30	4	213	frequent
Ankara	90	17	1250	frequent
Diyarbakır	40	7	410	frequent
Erciş	10	1¼	95	several
Erzurum	40	7	410	several
Hakkari	20	4	205	3-4
Malatya	60	12	500	frequent
Şanlıurfa	60	11	585	3-4
Tatvan	15	2	156	frequent
Trabzon	75	15	733	3-4 direct, most via Erzurum

ⓘ Getting Around

For Van Kalesi and the *iskele* (ferry dock), catch a minibus from İskele Caddesi.

Hoşap & Çavuştepe

A day excursion southeast of Van along the road to Başkale and Hakkari takes you to the Urartian site at Çavuştepe (25km from Van) and the spectacular Kurdish castle at Hoşap, 33km further along.

Hoşap Castle perches photogenically on top of a rocky outcrop alongside Güzelsu, a hicksville truck-stop village. Cross one of the two bridges (the one with alternate dark and light stones dates from the 17th century) and follow the signs around the far side of the hill to reach the castle entrance, above which are superb lion reliefs. Looking east there is a row of mud defensive walls that once encircled the village. Built in 1643 by a local Kurdish chieftain, Mahmudi Süleyman, the castle has a very impressive entrance gateway in a round tower. Significant restoration work on the castle was completed in 2010. We've heard reports of female travellers having problems when visiting the castle; if you're concerned, we recommend visiting with Alkan Tours (p602).

The narrow hill on the left side of the highway at Çavuştepe was once crowned by the fortress-palace Sarduri-Hinili, home of the kings of Urartu and built between 764 and 735 BC by King Sardur II, son of Argishti. These are the best-preserved foundations of any Urartian palace.

From the car park, the yukarı kale (upper fortress) is up to the left, and the vast aşağı kale (lower fortress) is to the right.

Climb the rocky hill to the lower fortress temple ruins, marked by a gate of black basalt blocks polished to a gloss; a few blocks on the left-hand side are inscribed in cuneiform. Note other illustrations of Urartian engineering ingenuity, including the cisterns under the pathways, the storage vessels, the kitchen and palace. Down on the plains to the south are canals also created by the Urartians.

ⓘ Getting There & Away

To get to the Hoşap and Çavuştepe sites by public transport catch a minibus from Van heading to Başkale or Yüksekova and get out at Hoşap (₺6). After seeing the castle, flag down a bus back to Çavuştepe, 500m off the highway, and then catch a third bus back to Van. Getting to Hoşap and Çavuştepe from is Van relatively easy, but return transport can be very difficult to secure, and Alkan Tours' day trip also taking in Akdamar Island is a good-value and efficient option.

Understand
Turkey

population per sq km

| TURKEY | USA | UK |

👤 ≈ 30 people

Turkey Today

The very heart of the world during the Ottoman and Byzantine empires, Turkey remains pivotal on the global stage. Its position at the meeting of Europe and Asia informs its political bent: the secular country has a moderate Islamic government and good relations with the West, for which Turkey is a key ally in the Middle East.

Cross-Border Tensions

With eight neighbouring countries including Iran, Iraq and debt-struck Greece, cross-border tensions are a fact of life for the Turkish government. In 2012, its biggest concern was the unrest in Syria. Refugee camps sprung up along the border in southeastern Anatolia, accommodating over 100,000 Syrian refugees. Tensions between the countries stepped up when Syrian air defences gunned down a Turkish warplane, and Turkey's Prime Minister Erdoğan warned Syrian troops to stay well away from the border.

Meanwhile, efforts to normalise Turkish–Armenian diplomatic relations, long strained over the alleged massacre of Ottoman Armenians during WWI, have faltered despite the two countries' increasing cultural and trade ties. The border remains closed, and Turkey was furious when France tabled a law that would have criminalised denying that the events of 1915 were an act of 'genocide'. The law was later annulled, but President Hollande has said he plans to revisit the matter, and a chapter on the claimed genocide is set to be included in French secondary-school textbooks.

EU Ambitions

Turkey's bid to join the European Union (EU) continues; accession talks started in 2005 and discussions relating to 13 of the 35 policy chapters have opened. Key obstacles are Turkey's refusal to recognise EU member Cyprus; the marginalisation of its 15 million Kurds; freedom of speech (YouTube, for example, was banned for two years, for carrying anti-

The army is the heartland of Turkish nationalism. When nine officers were reprimanded for showing *Game of Thrones* in English classes, one reason was that the medieval fantasy series, set in the imaginary Seven Kingdoms of Westeros, 'insulted Turkishness'.

Top Books

» **Birds Without Wings** (Louis de Bernières)

» **Yashim novels** (Jason Goodwin)

» **The Bastard of İstanbul** (Elif Şafak)

» **Portrait of a Turkish Family** (Irfan Orga)

» **Snow** (Orhan Pamuk)

» **Meander: East to West along a Turkish River** (Jeremy Seal)

» **Magic Bus: On the Hippie Trail from Istanbul to India** (Rory MacLean)

» **Turkey: Bright Sun, Strong Tea** (Tom Brosnahan)

Body Language

» 'Yes' is a slight downward nod.

» 'No' is a slight upward nod while making the 'tsk' sound.

» Never point the sole of your foot at anyone.

» The 'OK' sign indicates homosexuality.

ethnic groups
(% of population)

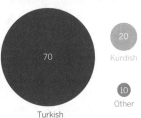

70

Turkish

20
Kurdish

10
Other

if Turkey were
100 people

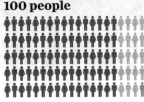

80 would be Muslims
19 would be Alevi Muslims
1 other religions

Atatürk content); and EU discomfort about embracing a 99% Muslim country. In 2012, no chapters had been opened for two years and Turks resented the stalemate, especially given Turkey's economic boom and Eurozone woes. Turkey's economy, driven by the manufacturing prowess of areas such as the Sea of Marmara and the cities known as the Anatolian Tigers, was Europe's fastest growing in 2011.

The Kurdish Question

Domestically, Turkey's most pressing problem is the Kurdish issue, which sparked a near civil war between the military and the Kurdistan Workers Party (PKK), classed internationally as a terrorist group by organisations including the EU and US government, in the 1980s and '90s. The situation has simmered down, but skirmishes continue in southeastern Anatolia, where the PKK has stepped up attacks during the Syrian unrest, and incidents occasionally happen in western Turkey. The creation of an independent Kurdistan is unlikely, as Kurds are dispersed across Turkey, Iran, Iraq and Syria. The Kurds, meanwhile, remain suspicious of promises from nationalistic Turkish politicians, and point to Iraq's semi-autonomous Kurdish region as a way forward.

Political Progress

Despite the misgivings of groups from Kurds to secularist Kemalists, Erdoğan's Justice and Development (AKP) government has ushered in a broadly positive era for Turkey. Decades of military coups have given way to stability and economic growth matching China's. The 2010 referendum on constitutional reform, in which Turkey voted for change, will hopefully lead to greater democracy. In this era of global financial crisis, meeting the positive Turks and witnessing their love for their dynamic, booming nation is refreshing and uplifting.

The AKP is planning 'a crazy and magnificent project', fit for the Turkish Republic's centenary in 2023: a 50km canal through İstanbul, to alleviate Bosphorus tanker traffic. Two new cities by the Bosphorus and a new airport are also planned.

Top Films

» **Vizontele** Black comedy about the first family to get a TV in a small town.

» **Polluting Paradise** A village's heartbreaking struggle to stop a waste site.

» **Once Upon a Time in Anatolia** Steppe murder mystery.

» **Filler ve Çimen** Tells the stories of desperate characters.

» **Hamam** Turkish expat inherits a hamam; addresses gay issues.

» **Bal** Lyrical coming-of-age story set in the Black Sea countryside.

Etiquette

» **Punctuality** Take it seriously.

» **Restaurants** If you are invited, your host pays; if you invite someone, you pay.

» **Meals** Leave nothing on your plate when at someone's house.

» **Wine** Check if your host drinks before taking it as a gift.

History

Straddling the junction of two continents, Turkey is a land bridge, meeting point and battleground that has seen peoples moving between Europe and Asia throughout history.

Archaeologist Ian Hodder's *Çatalhöyük: The Leopard's Tale* is an account of the excavation of the site and vividly portrays life as it was during the city's heyday.

Cultures began arising in Anatolia (the land mass of Turkey within Asia) a very long time ago, with history's first recognised 'city' established at Çatalhöyük over 8000 years ago. Later the Hittites created the first Anatolian empire – they ruled over various peoples while fending off arrivals from Greece. One of the most recognisable of these Greek colonies was Troy (of Homer and the *Iliad* fame); meanwhile a litany of ancient peoples – Lycians, Lydians, Phrygians among others – flitted across the historical stage.

The Persians arrived from the east, prompting Alexander the Great to chase them back again. Alexander's empire didn't last but it sped the Hellenisation of Anatolia and the creation of great wealth through Greek trade networks. The canny Romans arrived in 190 BC to exploit trade and resources, then stuck around to see – and harass – the first Christian communities. Christianity quietly spread until, in the 4th century, the Roman emperor Constantine himself converted and established Constantinople (modern İstanbul). This was to become the capital of the Byzantine Empire, a Greek-speaking, Christian remnant of Rome, which lasted for over 1000 years.

Byzantine control of Anatolia was challenged by the Seljuk Turks, who arrived from Central Asia, via Persia, in the 11th century. The Seljuks were succeeded by the Ottoman Turks, who swallowed up Anatolia and finished the Byzantines off in the 15th century. From then on the Ottomans expanded into southeastern Europe, reaching the very walls of Vienna before being relentlessly pushed back. By 1912 Greek and Serbian armies were advancing on İstanbul, and during and after WWI the European powers sought to dismember Turkey entirely. It was only the inspired leadership of Mustafa Kemal Atatürk that saved the day. In the

TIMELINE	c 6500 BC	c 4000–3000 BC	c 2000 BC
	Founding of Çatalhöyük, the world's first city. Over time 13 layers of houses were built, beehive style, interconnected and linked with ladders. At its peak the city housed around 8000.	Hattian culture develops at Alacahöyük during the early Bronze Age, though settlement has been continuous since the Chalcolithic age. The Hatti develop distinctive jewellery and metalwork and weapons.	The Hittites, an Indo-European people, arrive in Anatolia and conquer the Hatti, claiming their capital at Hattuşa. The Hittites go on to create a kingdom extending to Babylon and Egypt.

struggle for independence, Atatürk and his armies ejected the foreign interlopers, then established the Turkish Republic in 1923. Turkey has since undergone an extensive process of modernisation and democratisation, all the while aiming to re-establish itself on the international stage.

It's been a long story of peoples mixing and mingling, throwing up intriguing events, cultures and individuals to fill many a history book.

Early Cultures, Cities & Clashes

Archaeological finds indicate that Anatolia was inhabited by hunter-gatherers during the Palaeolithic era. By the 7th millennium BC some folk formed settlements; Çatalhöyük arose around 6500 BC. Perhaps the first-ever city, it was a centre of innovation, with locals developing crop irrigation, domesticating pigs and sheep, and creating distinctive pottery. Relics from this settlement can be seen at Ankara's Museum of Anatolian Civilisations (p399).

The Chalcolithic age saw the rise of Hacılar, in Central Anatolia, and communities in the southeast that absorbed Mesopotamian influences, including the use of metal tools. Across Anatolia more and larger communities sprung up and interacted – not always happily; settlements were often fortified.

By 3000 BC advances in metallurgy lead to the creation of various Anatolian kingdoms. One such was at Alacahöyük, in the heart of Anatolia, yet even this place showed Caucasian influence, which was evidence of trade beyond the Anatolian plateau.

Trade was increasing on the western coast too, with Troy trading with the Aegean islands and mainland Greece. Around 2000 BC the Hatti people established a capital at Kanesh (Kültepe, near Kayseri), ruling over a web of trading communities. Here for the first time Anatolian history materialises from the realm of archaeological conjecture and becomes 'real', with clay tablets providing written records of dates, events and names.

No singular Anatolian civilisation had yet emerged, but the tone was set for millennia to come: cultural interaction, trade and war would be recurring themes in Anatolian history.

Ages of Bronze: the Hittites

The Hatti soon declined and the Hittites swallowed their territory. From Alacahöyük, the Hittites shifted their capital to Hattuşa (near present-day Boğazkale) around 1800 BC.

The Hittites' legacy consisted of their great capital, as well as their state archives (cuneiform clay tablets) and distinctive artistic styles. By 1450 BC the kingdom, having endured internal ructions, re-emerged as

Homer
Homer, the Greek author of the *Iliad*, which told the story of the Trojan War, is believed to have been born in Smyrna (present-day İzmir), before 700 BC.

HISTORY

Until the rediscovery of the ruins at Boğazkale in the 19th century, the Hittites were known only through several obscure references in the Old Testament.

c 1200 BC	547 BC	333 BC	205 BC
The destruction of Troy, later immortalised in Homer's *Iliad*. For 10 years the Mycenaeans had besieged the city strategically placed above the Dardanelles and the key to Black Sea trade.	Cyrus of Persia overruns Anatolia, setting the scene for a long Greco-Persian rivalry. Later Darius I and Xerxes further Persian influence in Anatolia and forestall the expansion of Greek colonies.	Alexander the Great rolls the Persians and conquers most of Anatolia. Persian Emperor Darius abandons his wife, children and mother, who is so appalled she disowns him and 'adopts' Alexander.	Lycian League is formed by a group of city-states along the Mediterranean coast including Xanthos, Patara and Olympos. Later Phaselis joined. The leagues persisted after the imposition of Roman rule.

an empire. In creating the first Anatolian empire, the Hittites were war-like but displayed other imperial trappings, ruling over myriad vassal states while also displaying a sense of ethics and an occasional penchant for diplomacy. This didn't prevent them overrunning Ramses II of Egypt in 1298 BC, but did allow them to patch things up by marrying the crest-fallen Ramses to a Hittite princess.

The Hittite empire was harassed in later years by subject principali-ties, including Troy. The final straw was the invasion of the iron-smelting Greeks, generally known as the 'sea peoples'. The landlocked Hittites were disadvantaged during an era of burgeoning sea trade and lacked the latest technology: iron.

Meanwhile a new dynasty at Troy established itself as a regional pow-er. The Trojans in turn were harried by the Greeks, which led to the Tro-jan War in 1250 BC. This allowed the Hittites breathing space but later arrivals hastened their demise. Some pockets of Hittite culture persisted, but the great empire was dead. Later city-states created a neo-Hittite culture, which became the conduit for Mesopotamian religion and art forms to reach Greece.

> Anatolia is so named for the Greek word *anatolē*, meaning 'rising of the sun'. The Turkish *Ana-dolu* translates, very roughly, as 'mother lode'.

Classical Empires: Greece & Persia

Post-Hittite Anatolia was a patchwork of peoples, indigenous Anatolians and recent interlopers. In the east the Urartians, descendants of Anato-lian Hurrians, forged a kingdom near Lake Van. By the 8th century BC the Phrygians arrived in western Anatolia. Under King Gordius, of Gord-ian knot fame, the Phrygians created a capital at Gordion, their power peaking later under King Midas. In 725 BC Gordion was put to the sword by horse-borne Cimmerians, a fate that even King Midas' golden touch couldn't avert.

On the southwest coast, the Lycians established a confederation of city-states extending from modern-day Fethiye to Antalya. Inland, the Lydians dominated western Anatolia from their capital at Sardis and cre-ated the first-ever coinage.

Meanwhile, Greek colonies spread along the Mediterranean coast and Greek influence infiltrated Anatolia. Most of the Anatolian peoples were influenced by the Greeks: Phrygia's King Midas had a Greek wife; the Ly-cians borrowed the legend of the Chimera; and Lydian art was an amal-gam of Greek and Persian art forms. It seems that the admiration was mutual: the Lycians were the only Anatolian people the Greeks didn't deride as 'barbarians', and the Greeks were so impressed by the wealth of the Lydian king Croesus they coined the expression 'as rich as Croesus'.

Heightened Hellenic influence didn't go unnoticed. Cyrus, the emper-or of Persia, would not countenance such temerity in his backyard. He invaded in 547 BC, initially defeating the Lydians, then barrelled on, ex-

133 BC

On his deathbed Per-gamene king Attalus III leaves his state to Rome. The Romans swiftly establish a capital at Ephesus, an already buzzing port, and capitalise on vigorous sea trade.

AD 45–60

St Paul, originally from Antioch (modern Antakya), undertakes his long proselytising treks across Anatolia. St John and the Virgin Mary are thought to have ended up in Ephesus.

» Basilica of St John (p221), near Ephesus

ALEXANDER & THE GORDIAN KNOT

In 333 BC in the former Phrygian capital of Gordion, Alexander encountered the Gordian knot. Tradition stated that whoever untied it would come to rule Asia. Frustrated in his attempts to untie it, Alexander dispatched it with a blow of his sword. He resumed his eastward advance, Asia laying before him. He thundered across Persia to the Indus until all the known world was his dominion. However, the enormous empire Alexander created was to prove short-lived – perhaps he should have been more patient unravelling that pesky twine...

tending control to the Aegean. Under emperors Darius I and Xerxes, the Persians checked the expansion of coastal Greek colonies. They also subdued the interior, ending the era of home-grown Anatolian kingdoms.

Ruling Anatolia through local satraps (provincial governors), the Persians didn't have it all their own way. There was periodic resistance from feisty Anatolians, such as the revolt of the Ionian city of Miletus in 494 BC. Allegedly fomented from Athens, the revolt was abruptly put down. The Persians used the connivance of Athens as a pretext to invade mainland Greece, but were routed at Marathon.

Alexander & After

Persian control continued until 334 BC, when Alexander and his Macedonian adventurers crossed the Dardanelles, intent on relieving Anatolia of the Persian yoke. Sweeping down the coast, they rolled the Persians near Troy then pushed down to Sardis, which willingly surrendered. After later besieging Halicarnassus (modern-day Bodrum), Alexander ricocheted ever-eastwards, disposing of another Persian force on the Cilician plain.

Alexander was more a conqueror than a nation-builder. When he died in Babylon in 323 BC, leaving no successor, his empire was divided in a flurry of civil wars. However, if Alexander's intention was to remove Persian influence and bring Anatolia within the Hellenic sphere, he was entirely successful. In the wake of Alexander's armies, steady Hellenisation occurred, a culmination of a process that had begun centuries earlier. A formidable network of municipal communities – the lifeblood of which was trade – spread across Anatolia. The most notable of these was Pergamum (now Bergama). The Pergamene kings were great warriors and patrons of the arts. Greatest of the Pergamene kings was Eumenes II, who built much of what remains of Pergamum's acropolis. As notable as the building of Hellenic temples and aqueducts in Anatolia was the gradual spread of the Greek language, which eventually extinguished native Anatolian languages.

330	395	412	527–65
Constantine declares his 'New Rome', later Constantinople, as the capital of the eastern Roman Empire (Byzantium). He had earlier converted to Christianity and in 325 hosted the Council of Nicaea.	Under Theodosius the Roman Empire becomes Christian, with paganism forbidden and Greek influence pervasive. Upon his death the empire is split along the line Diocletian had set a century earlier.	Theodosius II builds the land walls of Constantinople to protect the riches of his capital. They prove effective, withstanding multiple sieges, and are only to be breached once: by Mehmet in 1453.	During the reign of Justinian, Byzantium enjoys a golden age. His military conquests include much of North Africa and Spain. He also pursues reform within the empire and embarks on building programs.

The cauldron of Anatolian cultures continued to produce various flavour-of-the-month kingdoms. In 279 BC the Celts romped in, establishing the kingdom of Galatia centred on Ancyra (Ankara). To the northeast Mithridates had carved out the kingdom of Pontus, centred on Amasya, and the Armenians (long established in the Lake Van region) reasserted themselves, having been granted autonomy under Alexander.

Meanwhile, the increasingly powerful Romans, based on the other side of the Aegean, eyed off Anatolia's rich trade networks.

In 1054 the line along which the Roman Empire had split in 395 became the dividing line between Catholicism and Orthodox Christianity; a line that persists to this day.

Roman Rule

Roman legions defeated the Seleucid king at Magnesia (Manisa) in 190 BC. Later Pergamum, the greatest post-Alexandrian city, became the beachhead for the Roman embrace of Anatolia when King Attalus III died in 133 BC, bequeathing the city to Rome. In 129 BC Ephesus was nominated capital of the Roman province of Asia and within 60 years the Romans had overcome all resistance to extend their rule to Armenia, on the Persian border.

Over time, Roman might dissipated. In the late 3rd century AD Diocletian tried to steady the empire by splitting it into eastern and western administrative units, simultaneously attempting to wipe out Christianity. Both endeavours failed. The fledgling religion of Christianity began to spread, albeit clandestinely and subject to intermittent persecution. Tradition states that St John retired to Ephesus to write the fourth Gospel, bringing the Virgin Mary with him. The indefatigable St Paul capitalised on the Roman road system, his sprightly step taking him across Anatolia as he spread the word. Meanwhile, Diocletian's reforms resulted in a civil war, which Constantine won. An earlier convert to Christianity, Constantine was said to have been guided by angels to build a 'New Rome' on the ancient Greek town of Byzantium. The city came to be known as Constantinople (now İstanbul). On his deathbed Constantine was baptised and by the end of the 4th century Christianity was the official religion of the empire.

Julius Caesar made his famous 'Veni, vidi, vici' ('I came, I saw, I conquered') speech about a military victory at Zile, near Tokat, in 47 BC.

Rome Falls, Byzantium Arises

Even with a new capital at Constantinople, the Roman Empire proved unwieldy. Once the steadying hand of Theodosius (379–95) was gone, the empire split. The western – Roman – half of the empire succumbed to decadence and sundry 'barbarians'; the eastern half – Byzantium – prospered, adopting Christianity and the Greek language.

Under Justinian (527–65), Byzantium took up the mantle of imperialism that was previously Rome's. Justinian built the Aya Sofya and codified Roman law, but he also extended the empire's boundaries to envelop southern Spain, North Africa and Italy. It was then that Byzantium came

654–76	867	976–1025	1071
Muslim Arab armies capture Ankara and besiege Constantinople. Arab incursions in the west are temporary but the eastern and southern fringes (Syria and Egypt) of the Byzantine domain are lost forever.	Basil I helps to restore Byzantium's fortunes, catalysing a resurgence in military power and a flourishing of the arts. He was known as the 'Macedonian' but was actually an Armenian from Thrace.	Under Basil II (the Bulgar Slayer), Byzantium reaches its high-tide mark. He overcomes internal crises, pushes the frontiers to Armenia in the east, retakes Italy and defeats the Bulgarians.	New arrivals, the Seljuk Turks take on and defeat a large Byzantine force at Manzikert. The Seljuks don't immediately follow on their success but it is a body blow for the Byzantines.

to be an entity distinct from Rome, although sentimental attachment to the idea of Rome remained: the Greek-speaking Byzantines still called themselves Romans, and later the Turks would refer to them as 'Rum'. However, Justinian's ambition overstretched the empire. Plague and encroaching Avars and Slavic tribes curtailed further expansion.

Later a drawn-out struggle with age-old rivals the Persians further weakened the Byzantines, leaving the eastern provinces of Anatolia easy prey for the Arab armies exploding out of Arabia. The Arabs took Ankara in 654 and by 669 had besieged Constantinople. Here were a new people, bringing a new language, civilisation and religion: Islam.

On the western front, Goths and Lombards advanced, so that by the 8th century Byzantium was pushed back into the Balkans and Anatolia. The empire hunkered down until the emergence of the Macedonian emperors. Basil assumed the throne in 867 and boosted the empire's fortunes, chalking up victories against Islamic Egypt, the Bulgars and Russia. Basil II (976–1025) earned the moniker the 'Bulgar Slayer' after allegedly putting out the eyes of 14,000 Bulgarian prisoners of war. When Basil died, the empire lacked anyone of his calibre – or ferocity, perhaps – and the era of Byzantine expansion comprehensively ended.

Byzantium: The Surprising Life of a Medieval Empire by Judith Herrin takes a thematic approach to life in the Byzantine realm and in doing so reveals the secrets of the little-understood empire.

First Turkic Empire: the Seljuks

From about the 8th century, the nomadic Turks had moved ever westward from Central Asia, encountering the Persians and converting to Islam en route. Vigorous and martial, the Turks swallowed up parts of the Abbasid empire, and built an empire of their own centred on Persia. Tuğrul, of the Turkish Seljuk clan, took the title of sultan in Baghdad, and

BYZANTIUM: THE UNDERRATED EUROPEAN EMPIRE

Byzantium is often relegated to an afterthought in European history. As the Byzantines never accepted the authority of the popes in Rome they were regarded as being outside Latin Christendom, hence barely a part of Europe. Nonetheless, Byzantium acted as a bulwark for Europe, protecting it for centuries against the expanding armies of Islam. On the periphery of Europe, with its combination of Greek learning and language and Orthodox Christianity, Byzantium forged a magnificent cultural and artistic legacy for 11 centuries, yet it is generally – and somewhat dismissively – remembered merely for the complexity and intrigue of its politics.

After the fall of Constantinople in 1453, Europe largely forgot the Greeks. Only in the 19th century did Greece again became flavour of the month when the Romantics, such as Lord Byron and other Hellenophiles, rallied to the cause of Greek liberation. But it was the glories of classical Greece that they aspired to; the Greece of Plato, Aristotle and Sappho, rather than Byzantium.

1080	1204	1207–70	1243
The Armenians, fleeing the Seljuks in Anatolia, establish the kingdom of Cilicia on the Mediterranean coast. The kingdom raises Armenian culture to new heights and lasts almost 300 years.	The rabble of the Fourth Crusade sack Constantinople, an indication of the contempt with which the Western Christians regard the Eastern Orthodox church.	The lifetime of Celaleddin Rumi, known as Mevlâna, founder of the Mevlevi Sufi order of whirling dervishes. A great mystic poet and philosopher, Rumi lived in Konya after fleeing the Mongols.	The Mongols rumble out of Central Asia, taking Erzurum and defeating the Seljuks at Köse Dağ. The Seljuk empire limps on and the Mongols depart, leaving only some minor states.

from there the Seljuks began raiding Byzantine territory. In 1071 Tuğrul's son Alp Arslan faced down the Byzantine army at Manzikert. The nimble Turkish cavalry prevailed, laying Anatolia open to wandering Turkic bands and beginning the final demise of the Byzantine Empire.

Not everything went the Seljuks' way, however. The 12th and 13th centuries saw incursions by Crusaders, who established short-lived statelets at Antioch (modern-day Antakya) and Edessa (now Şanlıurfa). In a sideshow to the Seljuks, an unruly army of Crusaders sacked Constantinople, the capital of the Byzantines, ostensibly the allies of the Crusaders. Meanwhile the Seljuks were riven by power struggles and their vast empire fragmented.

The Seljuk legacy persisted in Anatolia in the Sultanate of Rum, centred on Konya. Celaleddin Rumi, the Sufi mystic who founded the Mevlevi, or whirling dervish, order, was an exemplar of the cultural and artistic heights reached in Konya. Although ethnically Turkish, the Seljuks were purveyors of Persian culture and art. They introduced woollen rugs to Anatolia, as well as remarkable architecture – still visible at Erzurum, Divriği, Amasya and Sivas. These buildings were the first truly Islamic art forms in Anatolia, and were to become the prototypes for Ottoman art.

In the meantime, the Mongol descendants of Genghis Khan rumbled through Anatolia, defeating a Seljuk army at Köse Dağ in 1243. Anatolia fractured into a mosaic of Turkish *beyliks* (principalities), but by 1300 a single Turkish *bey* (tribal leader), Osman, established a dynasty that would eventually end the Byzantine line.

> John Julius Norwich's concise *A Short History of Byzantium* – a distillation of three volumes on the Byzantines – does a fantastic job of cramming 1123 eventful years of history into fewer than 500 pages.

> Painting portraits of the great port cities of Smyrna (modern İzmir), Beirut and Alexandria, *Levant: Splendour and Catastrophe on the Mediterranean* by Philip Mansel tells of the rise and fall of these centres of Ottoman wealth and culture.

Fledgling Ottoman State

Osman's bands flitted around the borderlands between Byzantine and formerly Seljuk territory, but once galvanised they moved with zeal. In an era marked by destruction and dissolution, they provided an ideal that attracted legions of followers and quickly established an administrative and military model that allowed them to expand. From the outset they embraced all the cultures of Anatolia – as many Anatolian civilisations before them had done – and their traditions became an amalgam of Greek and Turkish, Islamic and Christian elements.

Seemingly invincible, the Ottomans forged westward, establishing a first capital at Bursa, then crossing into Europe and taking Adrianople (now Edirne) in 1362. By 1371 they had reached the Adriatic and in 1389 they met and vanquished the Serbs at Kosovo Polje, effectively taking control of the Balkans.

In the Balkans the Ottomans encountered resolute Christian communities and absorbed them neatly into the state with the creation of the *millet* system, by which minority communities were officially recognised

1300

Near Eskişehir on the marches between the moribund Byzantines and the shell-shocked Seljuks, Osman comes to prominence. He takes on the Byzantine army, slowly attracting followers and gaining momentum.

1324

Osman dies while campaigning against the Byzantines at Bursa; he installs his son Orhan as his successor. Bursa becomes the first Ottoman capital, ruling over a rapidly expanding realm.

» Shrine of Osman, Bursa

and allowed to govern their own affairs. However, neither Christian insolence nor military bravado were countenanced: Sultan Beyazıt trounced the armies of the last Crusade at Nicopolis in Bulgaria in 1396. Beyazıt perhaps took military victories for granted thereafter, taunting the Tatar warlord Tamerlane. Beyazıt was captured, his army defeated and the burgeoning Ottoman Empire abruptly halted as Tamerlane lurched through Anatolia.

Ottomans Ascendant: Constantinople & Beyond

It took a decade for the dust to settle after Tamerlane dragged a no-doubt chastened Beyazıt away. Beyazıt's sons wrestled for control until Mehmet I emerged on top and the Ottomans got back to the job at hand: expansion. With renewed momentum they scooped up the rest of Anatolia, rolled through Greece, made a first attempt at Constantinople and beat the Serbs for a second time.

The Ottomans had fully regained their mojo when Mehmet II became sultan in 1451. Constantinople, the last redoubt of the Byzantines, was encircled by Ottoman territory. Mehmet, as an untested sultan, had no choice but to claim it. He built a fortress on the Bosphorus, imposed a naval blockade and amassed his army. The Byzantines appealed forlornly to Europe for help. After seven weeks of siege the city fell on 29 May 1453. Christendom shuddered at the seemingly unstoppable Ottomans, and fawning diplomats declared Mehmet – now known as Mehmet the Conqueror – a worthy successor to the great Roman and Byzantine emperors.

The Ottoman war machine rolled on, alternating campaigns between eastern and western fronts. The janissary system, by which Christian youths were converted and trained for the military, meant that the Ottomans had the only standing army in Europe. They were agile, highly organised and motivated. Successive sultans expanded the realm, with Selim the Grim capturing the Hejaz in 1517, and with it Mecca and Medina, thus claiming for the Ottomans the status as the guardians of Islam's holiest places. It wasn't all mindless militarism, however: Sultan Beyazıt II demonstrated the multicultural nature of the empire when he invited the Jews expelled by the Spanish Inquisition to İstanbul in 1492.

The Ottoman golden age came during the reign of Sultan Süleyman (1520–66). A remarkable figure, Süleyman the Magnificent was noted as much for codifying Ottoman law as for his military prowess. Under Süleyman, the Ottomans enjoyed victories over the Hungarians and absorbed the Mediterranean coast of Algeria and Tunisia; Süleyman's legal code was a visionary amalgam of secular and Islamic law, and his patronage of the arts saw the Ottomans reach their cultural zenith.

HISTORY

Ottomans
Concise, yet covering the vast sweep of Ottoman history, *Osman's Dream* by Caroline Finkel is rich in telling detail and investigates the goings-on of the sultans over six centuries.

Wild Europe: The Balkans in the Gaze of Western Travellers by Božidar Jezernik is a fascinating record of travellers' observations of the Balkans under Ottoman rule.

1349	1396	1402	1453
As allies of the Byzantines, the Ottomans, under Orhan, make their first military foray into Europe. Orhan had earlier consolidated Islam as the religion of the Ottomans.	The Crusade of Nicopolis, a group of Eastern and Western European forces, aims to forestall the Turks marching into Europe with impunity. Ottoman forces abruptly defeat them; Europe is left unguarded.	Beyazıt, victor over the Crusade of Nicopolis, turns his focus to the ultimate prize, Constantinople. Ever cocky, he takes on the forces of Tatar warlord Tamerlane. His army is crushed and he is enslaved.	Mehmet II lays siege to Constantinople, coinciding with a lunar eclipse. The defending Byzantines interpret this as a fatal omen, presaging the doom of Christendom. Sure enough, the Turks are soon victorious.

Süleyman was also notable as the first Ottoman sultan to marry. Where previously sultans had enjoyed the comforts of concubines, Süleyman fell in love and married Roxelana. Sadly, monogamy did not make for domestic bliss: palace intrigues brought about the death of his first two sons and the period after Roxelana's ascension became known as the 'Sultanate of Women'. A wearied Süleyman died campaigning on the Danube in 1566.

Sick Man of Europe

Determining exactly when or why the Ottoman rot set in is tricky, but some historians pinpoint the death of Süleyman. With hindsight it is easy to say that the remarkable line of Ottoman sovereigns – inspirational leaders and generals from Osman to Süleyman – could not continue indefinitely. The Ottoman family tree was bound to throw up some duds eventually. And so it did.

The sultans following Süleyman were not up to the task. Süleyman's son by Roxelana, Selim, known disparagingly as 'the Sot', lasted only briefly as sultan, overseeing the naval catastrophe at Lepanto, which spelled the end of Ottoman naval supremacy. Furthermore, Süleyman was the last sultan to lead his army into the field. Those who came after him were coddled and sequestered in the fineries of the palace, having minimal experience of everyday life and little inclination to administer the empire. This, coupled with the inertia that was inevitable after 250 years of unfettered expansion, meant that Ottoman military might, once famously referred to by Martin Luther as irresistible, was declining.

The siege of Vienna in 1683 was the Ottomans' last tilt at expansion. It failed. Thereafter it was a downward spiral. The empire was vast and powerful, but it was rapidly falling behind the West socially, militarily and scientifically. Napoleon's swashbuckling 1799 Egypt campaign indicated that an emboldened Europe was willing to take the battle up to the Ottomans. Meanwhile, the Habsburgs in central Europe and the Russians were increasingly assertive, and Western Europe had grown rich after centuries of colonising the 'New World'. The Ottomans, for their part, remained inward-looking and unaware of the advances happening elsewhere. An illustration of this was the Ottoman clergy's refusal to allow the use of the printing press until the 18th century – a century and a half after it had been introduced into Europe.

It was nationalism, another idea imported from the West, that sped the Ottoman demise. For centuries manifold ethnic groups had coexisted relatively harmoniously in the empire, but the creation of nation-states in Western Europe sparked a desire among subject peoples to throw off the Ottoman 'yoke' and determine their own destinies. Soon, pieces of the Ottoman jigsaw wriggled free: Greece attained its freedom in 1830.

ROXELANA

Roxelana, the wife of Süleyman, has inspired many artistic works, including paintings, Joseph Haydn's Symphony No 63 and novels in Ukrainian, English and French.

1480–1	1512–16	1520–66	1553
Mehmet II endeavours to establish himself as a true heir to Roman glory by invading Italy. He succeeds in capturing Otranto in Puglia, but he dies before he can march on Rome.	Selim the Grim defeats the Persians at Çaldiran. He proceeds to take Syria and Egypt, assuming the mantle of Caliph, then captures the holy cities of Mecca and Medina.	The reign of Süleyman the Magnificent, the zenith of the Ottoman Empire. Süleyman leads his forces to take Budapest, Belgrade and Rhodes, doubling the size of the empire.	Mustafa, Süleyman's first-born, is strangled upon his father's orders. Allegedly, Roxelana, Süleyman's wife, conspired to have Mustafa killed so her own son could succeed to the throne.

In 1878 Romania, Montenegro, Serbia and Bosnia went their own ways, while at the same time Russia was encroaching on Kars.

As the Ottoman Empire shrank there were attempts at reform, but it was too little, too late. In 1876 Abdülhamid allowed the creation of an Ottoman constitution and the first-ever Ottoman parliament, but he used the events of 1878 as an excuse for doing away with the constitution. His reign henceforth grew increasingly authoritarian.

It wasn't just subject peoples who were restless: educated Turks, too, looked for ways to improve their lot. In Macedonia the Committee for Union and Progress (CUP) was created. Reform-minded and influenced by the West, in 1908 the CUP, who came to be known as the 'Young Turks', forced Abdülhamid to abdicate and reinstate the constitution. Any rejoicing proved short-lived. The First Balkan War saw Bulgaria and Macedonia removed from the Ottoman map, with Bulgarian, Greek and Serbian troops advancing rapidly on İstanbul.

The Ottoman regime, once feared and respected, was now deemed the 'sick man of Europe'. European diplomats plotted how to cherry-pick the empire's choicest parts.

HISTORY

In *Gallipoli*, historian Peter Hart takes a detailed look at the tragic WWI campaign, from its planning stages to the bloody disembarkations at Anzac Cove and the eventual retreat.

WWI & its Aftermath

The military crisis saw a triumvirate of ambitious, nationalistic CUP *paşas* (generals) take de facto control of the ever-shrinking empire. They managed to push back the unlikely alliance of Balkan armies and save İstanbul, but then chose the wrong side in the looming world war. As a consequence the Ottomans had to fend off the Western powers on multiple fronts: Greece in Thrace, Russia in northeast Anatolia, Britain in

GALLIPOLI CAMPAIGN

Engaged on multiple fronts during WWI, the Ottomans held their own only at Gallipoli. This was due partially to the inept British high command but also to the brilliance of Turkish commander Mustafa Kemal. Iron-willed, he inspired his men to hold their lines, while also inflicting shocking casualties on the invading British and Anzac (Australian and New Zealand Army Corps) forces, who had landed on 25 April 1915.

Difficult territory, exposure to the elements on the peninsula and the nature of hand-to-hand trench warfare meant that the campaign was a bloody stalemate; however, there are reports of remarkable civility between invading and defensive forces. The Allies withdrew after eight months.

Unbeknown to anyone at the time, two enduring legends of nationhood were born on the blood-spattered sands of Gallipoli: Australians see that brutal campaign as the birth of their national consciousness, while the Turks regard the successful campaign to defend the Gallipoli shore as the genesis of their independence.

1571	1595–1603	1638	1683
The Ottoman navy is destroyed at Lepanto by resurgent European powers who are in control of Atlantic and Indian Ocean trades, and who are experiencing the advances of the Renaissance.	Stay-at-home sultan, Mehmet, has his 19 brothers strangled to protect his throne. His successor institutes 'the Cage' to keep potential claimants to the throne distracted with concubines and confections.	The Ottomans sign the Treaty of Zohrab with Persia, finally bringing peace between the two Islamic states after nearly 150 years of intermittent war on the eastern fringe of Anatolia.	Sultan Mehmet IV besieges Vienna, ending in the rout of his army. By century's end, the Ottomans have sued for peace for the first time and have lost the Peloponnese, Hungary and Transylvania.

Arabia and a multinational force at Gallipoli. It was during this time of turmoil that the Armenian tragedy unfolded.

By the end of WWI the Turks were in disarray. The French held southeast Anatolia; the Italians controlled the western Mediterranean; the Greeks occupied İzmir; and Armenians, with Russian support, controlled parts of northeast Anatolia. The Treaty of Sèvres in 1920 ensured the dismembering of the empire, with only a sliver of steppe left to the Turks. European haughtiness did not count on a Turkish backlash, but a slowly building Turkish nationalist movement developed, motivated by the humiliation of Sèvres. At the head was Mustafa Kemal, the victorious leader at Gallipoli. He secured the support of the Bektaşi dervishes, began organising Turkish resistance and established a national assembly in Ankara, far from opposing armies and meddling diplomats.

Turchia

European observers referred to Anatolia as 'Turchia' as early as the 12th century. The Turks themselves didn't do this until the 1920s.

In the meantime, a Greek force pushed out from İzmir. The Greeks saw Turkish disorder as an opportunity to realise their *megali idea* (great idea) of re-establishing the Byzantine Empire. They soon took Bursa and Edirne and pushed towards Ankara. This was just the provocation that Mustafa Kemal needed to galvanise Turkish support. After an initial skirmish at İnönü, the Greeks pressed on for Ankara, seeking to crush the Turks. But stubborn Turkish resistance stalled them at the Battle of Sakarya. The two armies faced off again at Dumlupınar. Here the Turks savaged the Greeks, sending them in panicked retreat towards İzmir, where they were expelled from Anatolia amid stricken refugees, pillage and looting.

Mustafa Kemal emerged as the hero of the Turkish people; he realised the dream of the 'Young Turks' of years past: to create a modern Turkish nation-state. The Treaty of Lausanne in 1923 undid the humiliations of Sèvres and saw foreign powers leave Turkey. The borders of the modern Turkish state were set and the Ottoman Empire was no more.

Atatürk & the Republic

The Turks consolidated Ankara as their capital and abolished the sultanate. Mustafa Kemal assumed the newly created presidency of the secular republic (he would later take the name Atatürk – literally, 'Father Turk'). Thereupon the Turks set to work. Mustafa Kemal's energy was apparently limitless; his vision was to see Turkey take its place among the modern, developed countries of Europe.

At the time, the country was devastated after years of war, so a firm hand was needed. The Atatürk era was one of enlightened despotism. Atatürk established the institutions of democracy while never allowing any opposition to impede him. He brooked little dissent yet his ultimate motivation was the betterment of his people. One aspect of the Kemalist vision, however, was to have ongoing consequences: the insistence that

1760–90s	1826	1839	1876
Despite attempts to modernise and military training from France, the Ottomans lose ground to the Russians under Catherine the Great, who anoints herself protector of the Ottomans' Orthodox subjects.	Major attempts at reform under Mahmut II. He centralises the administration and modernises the army, resulting in the 'Auspicious Event' where unruly janissaries are put to the sword.	Reform continues with the Tanzimat, a charter of legal and political rights, the underlying principle of which was the equality of the empire's Muslim and non-Muslim subjects.	Abdülhamid II takes the throne. The National Assembly meets for the first time and a constitution is created but Serbia and Montenegro, emboldened by the pan-Slavic movement, fight for independence.

FATHER OF THE MOTHERLAND

Many Western travellers remark on the Turks' devotion to Atatürk. In response, the Turks simply remark that the Turkish state is a result of his energy and vision, that without him there would be no Turkey. From an era that threw up Stalin, Hitler and Mussolini, Atatürk stands as a beacon of statesmanship and proves that radical reform, deftly handled, can be hugely successful.

The Turks' gratitude to Atatürk manifests itself throughout the country. He appears on stamps, banknotes, statues – often in horse-borne, martial pose – and in town squares across the country. His name is affixed to innumerable bridges, airports and highways. And seemingly every house in which he spent a night, from the southern Aegean to the Black Sea, is now a museum.

Turkish schoolchildren are well versed in Atatürk's life and achievements – they learn them by rote and can dutifully recite them. But it may be that the history-book image of Atatürk is more simplistic than the reality. An avowed champion of Turkish culture, he preferred opera to Turkish music. Though calling himself 'Father Turk', he had no off-spring and a single short and troubled marriage.

Atatürk died relatively young (aged 57) in 1938. No doubt years as a military man, reformer and public figure took their toll. His friend and successor as president, İsmet İnönü, ensured that he was to be lauded by his countrymen. The praise continues. In-deed, any perceived insult to Atatürk is considered highly offensive and is also illegal.

There are several outstanding Atatürk biographies: Patrick Kinross' *Ataturk: Rebirth of a Nation* sticks closely to the official Turkish view; Andrew Mango's *Atatürk* is a de-tached and detailed look at a remarkable life; while *Atatürk: An Intellectual Biography* by Şükrü Hanioğlu examines the intellectual currents that inspired Atatürk's grand vision.

the state be solely Turkish. Encouraging national unity made sense, considering the nationalist separatist movements that had bedevilled the Ottoman Empire, but in doing so a cultural existence was denied the Kurds. Sure enough, within a few years a Kurdish revolt erupted in southeast Anatolia, the first of several to recur throughout the 20th century.

The desire to create homogenous nation-states on the Aegean also prompted population exchanges between Greece and Turkey: Greek-speaking communities from Anatolia were shipped to Greece, while Muslim residents of Greece were transferred to Turkey. These exchanges brought great disruption and the creation of ghost villages, vacated but never reoccupied, such as Kayaköy (Karmylassos) . It was a move aimed at forestalling ethnic violence, but it was a melancholy episode and it hobbled the development of the new state. Turkey found itself without the majority of the educated elites of Ottoman society, many of whom

1908

The Young Turks of the Committee for Union and Progress (CUP), based in Salonika, demand the reintroduction of the constitution. In the ensuing elections the CUP wins a convincing majority.

1912–13

The First and Second Balkan Wars. An alliance of Serbian, Greek and Bulgarian forces take Salonika, previously the second city of the Ottoman Empire, and Edirne. The alliance later turns on itself.

» Engraving of a scene from the Balkan Wars

had not been Turkish speakers; in their stead, Turkey accepted impoverished Muslim peasants from the Balkans.

Atatürk's zeal for modernisation was unwavering, giving the Turkish state a comprehensive makeover. Everything from headgear to language was scrutinised and, where necessary, reformed. Throughout the 1920s and '30s Turkey adopted the Gregorian calendar (as used in the West), reformed its alphabet (adopting the Roman script), standardised the Turkish language, outlawed the fez, instituted universal suffrage and decreed that Turks should take surnames, something they had previously not had. By the time of his death in November 1938, Atatürk had, to a large degree, lived up to his name, having been the pre-eminent figure in the creation of the nation-state and dragging it into the modern era.

Working Towards Democratisation

Though reform proceeded apace, Turkey remained economically and militarily weak, and Atatürk's successor, İsmet İnönü, stepped carefully to avoid involvement in WWII. The war over, Turkey found itself allied to the USA. A bulwark against the Soviets (the Armenian border then marked the edge of the Soviet bloc), Turkey was of strategic importance and received significant US aid. The new friendship was cemented when Turkish troops fought in Korea, and Turkey became a member of NATO.

Meanwhile, democratic reform gained momentum. In 1950 the Democratic Party swept to power. Ruling for a decade, the Democrats failed to live up to their name and became increasingly autocratic; the army intervened in 1960 and removed them. Army rule lasted only briefly, and resulted in the liberalisation of the constitution, but it set the tone for years to come. The military considered themselves the guardians of Atatürk's vision – pro-Western and secular – and felt obliged to step in when necessary to ensure the republic maintained the right trajectory.

The 1960s and '70s saw the creation of political parties of all stripes, but the profusion did not make for a more vibrant democracy. The late 1960s were characterised by left-wing activism and political violence, which prompted a move to the right by centrist parties. The army stepped in again in 1971, before handing power back in 1973.

Political and economic chaos reigned for the rest of the 1970s, so the military seized power again to re-establish order in 1980. This they did through the creation of the highly feared National Security Council, but they allowed elections in 1983. Here, for the first time in decades, was a happy result for Turkey. Turgut Özal, leader of the Motherland Party (ANAP), won a majority and, unhindered by unruly coalition partners,

Population Exchanges

Bruce Clark's *Twice a Stranger* is an investigation of the Greek–Turkish population exchanges of the 1920s. Analysing background events and interviewing those who were transported, Clark shines new light on the two countries' fraught relationship.

1915–18

Turks fight in WWI on the side of the Central Powers. Encroached upon on four fronts, the Turks repel invaders only at Gallipoli. At war's ends, a British fleet is positioned off the coast of İstanbul.

1919–20

The Turkish War of Independence begins. The Treaty of Sèvres (1920) reduces Turkey to a strip of Anatolian territory but the Turks, led by Mustafa Kemal, rise to defend their homeland.

PHILIP GAMERS / GETTY IMAGES ©

» Arıburnu Cemetery (p149), Gallipoli National Historic Park

was able to set Turkey back on course. An astute economist and pro-Islamic, Özal made vital economic and legal reforms that brought Turkey in line with the international community and sowed the seeds of its current vitality.

ARMENIANS OF ANATOLIA

The final years of the Ottoman Empire saw human misery on an epic scale, but nothing has proved as enduringly melancholic and controversial as the fate of Anatolia's Armenians. The tale begins with eyewitness accounts, in the spring of 1915, of Ottoman army units marching Armenian populations towards the Syrian desert. It ends with an Anatolian hinterland virtually devoid of Armenians. What happened in between remains mired in conjecture, obfuscation and propaganda.

Armenians maintain that they were subject to the 20th century's first orchestrated 'genocide', that 1.5 million Armenians were summarily executed or killed on death marches and that Ottoman authorities issued a deportation order intending to remove the Armenian presence from Anatolia. To this day, Armenians demand an acknowledgment of this 'genocide'.

Turkey, though, refutes that any such 'genocide' occurred. It admits that thousands of Armenians died but claim the order had been to 'relocate' Armenians without intending to eradicate them. The deaths, according to Turkish officials, were due to disease and starvation, direct consequences of the chaos of war. Some even claim that it was the Turks who were subjected to 'genocide' by Armenian militias.

Almost a century later the issue is unresolved. The murder of outspoken Turkish-Armenian journalist Hrant Dink in 2007 by Turkish ultranationalists appeared to confirm that the mutual antagonism is insurmountable, but it would seem halting reconciliatory progress is being made: thousands of Turks, bearing placards saying 'We are all Armenians', marched in solidarity with the slain journalist.

The 'football diplomacy' of 2009, when Turkish and Armenian presidents visited each other's countries to watch football matches, saw the re-establishment of diplomatic contact. There is increasing contact between Turkish and Armenian artists, students, academics and civil-society groups. Political obstacles remain, however, with both sides finding it difficult to compromise, particularly as nationalistic voices continue to drown out other opinions. Turkey is concerned that American and French parliaments might officially recognise the 'genocide'. This issue is frequently reignited causing diplomatic arguments and accusations, but as long as the question remains unresolved between Turkish and Armenian governments, such issues will continue to crop up.

Meanwhile, a brisk Turkish–Armenian trade continues, despite their mutual border being closed. Turkish manufacturers send goods to Armenia on a circuitous route through neighbouring Georgia, surely proof that Turks and Armenians have much to gain if they bury their mutual distrust.

1922	1923	1938	1945–50
The Turks push back the Greek expeditionary force, which had advanced into Anatolia, and eject them from Smyrna (İzmir). Turkey reasserts its independence and the European powers accede.	The Treaty of Lausanne, signed by the steadfast İsmet İnönü, undoes the wrongs of Sèvres. The Republic of Turkey is unanimously supported by the members of the National Assembly.	Atatürk dies, at the age of 57, in the Dolmabahçe Palace in İstanbul on 10 November – all the clocks in the palace are stopped at the time that he died: 9.05am.	After WWII, which the Turks avoided, the Truman Doctrine brings aid to Turkey on the condition of democratisation. Democratic elections are held (1950) and the Democratic Party emerges victorious.

Turn of the Millennium

In 1991, Turkey played a supporting role in the allied invasion of Iraq, with Özal supporting sanctions and allowing air strikes from bases in southern Anatolia. In so doing, Turkey, after decades in the wilderness, affirmed its place in the international community and as an important US ally. At the end of the Gulf War millions of Iraqi Kurds fled north into southeastern Anatolia. The exodus caught the attention of the international media, bringing the Kurdish issue into the spotlight, and resulting in the establishment of a Kurdish safe haven in northern Iraq. This, in turn, emboldened the Kurdistan Workers' Party (PKK), who stepped up their terror campaign aimed at creating a Kurdish state in Turkey's southeast. This provoked an iron-fisted response from the Turkish military, such that the southeast effectively endured a civil war.

Meanwhile, Turgut Özal died suddenly in 1993, creating a power vacuum. Various weak coalition governments followed throughout the 1990s, with a cast of figures flitting across the political stage. Tansu Çiller served briefly as Turkey's first female prime minister, but despite high expectations, she did not find a solution to the Kurdish issue or cure the ailing economy.

In December 1995 the religious Refah (Welfare) Party managed to form a government led by veteran politician Necmettin Erbakan. Heady with power, Refah politicians made Islamist statements that raised the ire of the military. In 1997 the National Security Council declared that Refah had flouted the constitutional ban on religion in politics. Faced with what some dubbed a 'postmodern coup', the government resigned and Refah was disbanded.

The capture of PKK leader Abdullah Öcalan in early 1999 may have seemed like a good omen after the torrid '90s. His capture offered an opportunity – still largely unrealised – to settle the Kurdish question. Later that year the disastrous earthquakes centred on İzmit put paid to any premillennial optimism. The government's handling of the crisis was inadequate; however, the global outpouring of aid and sympathy – not least from traditional foes, the Greeks – did much to reassure Turks they were valued members of the world community.

A new political force arose in the new millennium: Recep Tayyip Erdoğan's Justice & Development Party (AKP) heralded an era of societal reforms, capitalising on improved economic conditions. With Islamist roots, the AKP initially sought to pursue Turkey's entry to the EU and to end military intervention in the political scene.

Much of the support for the AKP arose in the burgeoning cities of Anatolia, rather than the traditional power centres of İstanbul and Ankara. The cities of the interior were experiencing an economic boom, proof

Modern Turkey

An appetiser for those wanting to know more, *Turkey: A Short History* by Norman Stone is a succinct and pacey wrap-up of the crucial events and personalities of Turkey's long history.

1971	1980	1983	1985–99
Increasing political strife prompts the military to step in again to restore order. The military chief handed the prime minister a written ultimatum, thus this was known as a 'coup by memorandum'.	The third of Turkey's military coups, this time as the military moves to stop widespread street violence between left- and right-wing groups. The National Security Council is formed.	In elections after the 1980 coup, the Özal era begins. A populist and pragmatic leader, Özal embarks on economic reform, encouraging foreign investment. Turkey opens to the West and the tourism industry takes off.	Abdullah Öcalan establishes the Kurdistan Workers Party (PKK), a terror group calling for a Kurdish state. There is a long, low-intensity war in southeast Anatolia until Öcalan's capture in 1999.

that the modernising and economic development projects begun during the Atatürk era were finally bearing fruit. In fact, the Turkish economy continues to grow strongly, with consistently high annual GDP growth, prompting many Turks to be relieved that their country wasn't absorbed by the EU, thus saving them from the economic perils that have beset Greece.

The AKP pursued a new direction in foreign policy, attempting to restore relations with Turkey's near neighbours, a policy that appeared modestly successful until the outbreak of hostilities in Syria in 2012. On the domestic front, the AKP has worked to curtail military intervention in Turkey's political sphere, while also initiating 'openings' to address long-term dilemmas such as minority rights, the Kurdish issue, acrimonious relations with Armenia and the recognition of Alevi rights. However, thus far these 'openings' have not produced long-term solutions. The AKP has also attracted criticism at home and abroad, particularly for restricting freedom of expression among journalists. Others contend that its Islamic political philosophy is consciously curtailing long-held social freedoms such as drinking alcohol at streetside cafes. Grandiose schemes put forward by Prime Minister Erdoğan – including a proposal to cut a new canal connecting the Black and Marmara seas, and plans to build the world's biggest mosque at Çamlıca in İstanbul – raise a fair few eyebrows, too.

However you look at things, Turkish society and economy are currently extremely dynamic, making for a creative environment where ideas, trends, opportunities (and some problems) continue to bubble up, and the majority of Turks (and Kurds) are along for the ride.

1997	2002	2005	2007–11
The coalition government headed by Necmettin Erbakan's Islamically inspired Refah (Welfare) Party is disbanded, apparently under military pressure, in what has been called a 'post-modern coup'.	Recep Tayyip Erdoğan's Justice and Development Party (AKP) wins a landslide election victory, a reflection of the Turkish public's disgruntlement with the established parties. The economy recovers.	EU-accession talks begin, and economic and legal reforms begin to be implemented. Resistance to Turkish membership by some EU states leads to a decrease in approval by some Turks.	Further resounding election victories for the AKP, which increases it share of the vote, as well as winning two referenda in favour of rewriting the constitution.

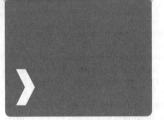

Architecture

Settled over millenia by countless civilisations, Turkey boasts a dizzying array of architectural styles and remnants that display their creators' cultural influences, technical prowess and engineering techniques.

The visually stunning *Constantinople: Istanbul's Historical Heritage,* by Stéphane Yerasimos, provides history and context to many of the city's magnificent buildings.

Ancient

The earliest Anatolian architectural remnants, dated at around 8500 years old, are those of Çatalhöyük, revealing mud-brick constructions that were accessed through their roofs. Dating from 4000 BC, Alacahöyük was characterised by more complex buildings. By the time Troy was established classical temple design was beginning to develop. Elsewhere, the Hittite remains at Hattuşa, including hefty gates, stone walls and earthen ramparts, reveal increasing sophistication in working with the landscape.

In the treeless southeast, distinctive 'beehive' construction techniques developed; these can still be seen at Harran.

Greek & Roman

The architects of ancient Greece displayed a heightened sense of city planning and increasing sophistication in design and construction, incorporating vaults and arches into their buildings. The later-arriving Romans built upon the developments of the Greeks. Elements of classical design such as the amphitheatre, agora and forum can be seen at Side, while Letoön features fine examples of temple-building that characterise Greco-Roman architecture.

The Romans were also accomplished road builders, establishing a comprehensive network linking trading communities and military outposts – portions of Roman road are still visible at Tarsus.

Byzantine

Ecclesiastical construction distinguishes Byzantine architecture from that of the earlier pagan Greeks. The Byzantines developed church and basilica design while working in new media, such as brick and plaster, and displaying a genius for dome construction, such as that of the Aya Sofya.

EPHESUS: CAPITAL OF ROMAN ASIA

Ephesus (Efes) is the pre-eminent example of Roman city construction in Turkey; its flagstoned streets, gymnasium, sewerage system, mosaics, frescoes and theatre form a neat set piece of Roman design and architecture. As a prosperous trading city, Ephesus was endowed with significant buildings. The Temple of Artemis, boasting a forest of mighty columns, was one of the Wonders of the Ancient World, but was later destroyed under orders from a Byzantine archbishop. The Great Theatre, one of the biggest in the Roman world, is evidence of the Roman expertise in theatre design and acoustics, while the nearby Library of Celsus is ingeniously designed to appear larger than it actually is.

Mosaics were a principal Byzantine design feature; fine examples can be seen in the Hatay Archaeology Museum or *in situ* at the nearby the Church of St Peter. Examples of the burgeoning skill of Byzantine engineers include the Basilica Cistern and the Aqueduct of Valens in İstanbul, while the Kariye Museum (Chora Church) is often described as the pinnacle of Byzantine fresco painting.

In the east, skilled Armenian stonemasons, developed their own distinctive architectural style. The 10th-century church at Akdamar is a stunning example, while the site of Ani includes some fascinating ruins and remnants.

For a scholarly investigation of the challenges faced by Byzantine architects see *The Master Builders of Byzantium* by Robert Ousterhout.

Seljuk

The architecture of the Seljuks reveals significant Persian influences, both in design and in its decorative flourishes, including Kufic lettering and intricate stonework. The first Islamic power in Turkey, the Seljuks created cosmopolitan artistic and architectural styles incorporating elements of nomadic Turkic design traditions with Persian know-how and the Mediterranean-influenced architecture of the Anatolian Greeks. The Seljuks left a legacy of magnificent mosques and *medreses* (seminaries), distinguished by their elaborate entrances; you can see the best of them in Konya, Sivas and Divriği. As patrons and beneficiaries of the Silk Road, the Seljuks also built a string of caravanserais through Anatolia, such as at Sultanhanı and in Cappadocia. The Anatolian countryside is also stippled with the grand conical *türbe* (tombs) of the Seljuks, such as those at Hasankeyf, Konya, Battalgazi and on the north and south shores of Lake Van.

In the southeast, contemporaries and competitors to the Seljuks, the Artuklu Turks, created the cityscapes of Mardin and Hasankeyf, featuring distinctive honey-toned stonework and apricot-coloured brick tombs, while also embellishing and adding several towers to the imposing black basalt walls of Diyarbakır.

Ottoman

From the 14th century, as the Ottomans expanded across Anatolia, they became increasingly influenced by Byzantine styles, especially ecclesiastical architecture. This is particularly clear from the Ottoman use of domes as a design feature. Ottoman architects absorbed these Byzantine influences and incorporated them into their existing Persian architectural repertoire to develop a completely new style: the T-shape plan. The Üç Şerefeli Cami in Edirne became the model for other mosques, not only because it was one of the first forays into this T-plan, but because it was the first Ottoman mosque to have a wide dome and a forecourt with an ablutions fountain.

Aside from mosques, the Ottomans also developed a distinctive style of domestic architecture, consisting of multistorey houses with a stone ground floor topped by protruding upper floors balanced on carved brackets. These houses featured separate women's and men's areas (*haremlik* and *selamlık* respectively), and often included intricate woodwork detailing on ceilings and joinery, ornate fireplaces and expansive rooms lined with *sedirs* (low benches along the walls) ideal for the communal interaction that was a feature of Ottoman life. Cities including Amasya, Safranbolu, Muğla and certain neighbourhoods of İstanbul still feature houses of this design.

In later centuries in İstanbul, architects developed the *yalı* (expansively grand seaside mansions generally constructed solely of wood), to which notable families would escape at the height of summer. Prime examples are still visible on the Bosphorus.

Ottoman architectural styles spread beyond the boundaries of modern Turkey. There are still Ottoman constructions (mosques, fortresses, streetscapes, bridges) throughout the Balkans.

Turkish Baroque & Neoclassical

From the mid-18th century, rococo and baroque influences hit Turkey, resulting in a pastiche of hammed-up curves, frills, scrolls, murals and fruity excesses, sometimes described as 'Turkish baroque'. The period's archetype

IMPERIAL MOSQUES

The rippling domes and piercing minarets of mosques are the quintessential image of Turkey for many travellers. The most impressive mosques, in size and grandness, are the imperial mosques commissioned by members of the royal households.

Each imperial mosque had a *külliye*, or collection of charitable institutions, clustered around it. These might include a hospital, asylum, orphanage, *imaret* (soup kitchen), *medrese* (seminary), library, baths and a cemetery in which the mosque's imperial patron, their family and other notables could be buried. Many of these buildings have been demolished or altered, but İstanbul's Süleymaniye mosque complex still has much of its *külliye* intact.

The design, perfected by the Ottoman's most revered architect Mimar Sinan during the reign of Süleyman the Magnificent, proved so durable that it is still being used, with variations, for modern mosques all over Turkey.

is the extravagant Dolmabahçe Palace. Although building mosques was passé, the later Ottomans still adored pavilions where they could enjoy the outdoors; the Küçüksu Kasrı in İstanbul is a good example.

In the 19th and early 20th centuries, foreign or foreign-trained architects began to unfold a neoclassical blend: European architecture mixed in with Turkish baroque and some concessions to classic Ottoman style. Vedat Tek, a Turkish architect educated in Paris, built the capital's central post office, a melange of Ottoman elements and European symmetry. His style is sometimes seen as part of the first nationalist architecture movement, an element of the modernisation project of the early decades of the Turkish republic. This architectural movement sought to draw on Ottoman design elements without reference to Persian or Islamic styles. Notable buildings in this style include the Ethnography Museum in Ankara and Bebek Mosque in İstanbul. Sirkeci Train Station, by the German architect Jachmund, is another example of this eclectic neoclassicism.

Turkey: At the Threshold, edited by Michael Hensel, is a stunning collection of images and articles discussing countless aspects of Turkish design and architecture through the centuries

Modern

There's little worth mentioning as far as modern architecture goes. The rapid growth that Turkey has experienced since the 1940s has seen a profusion of bland, grey apartment blocks and office buildings in Anatolian cities and towns. Yet even these, taken in context of the Turkish landscape, climate and bustle of convivial neighbourhood and streetside interaction, have a distinctive quality all their own.

During the 1940s and '50s a new nationalist architecture movement developed as Turkish-trained architects, working on government building projects, sought to create a home-grown style that reflected the traditions and aspirations of the new republic. This architecture tended to be sturdy and monumental; examples include the Anıt Kabir in Ankara and the Çanakkale Şehitleri Anıtı (Çanakkale Martyrs' Memorial) at Gallipoli.

Since the 1990s and Özal's freeing up of the economy there has been more private-sector investment in architecture, leading to a diversification of building styles. The Levent business district in İstanbul has seen the mushrooming of shimmering office towers, as in other international cities, and other futuristic buildings have arisen, such as the Esenboğa Airport in Ankara.

The most interesting development in recent decades is that Turks have begun to take more notice of their history, particularly the Ottoman era. This has meant reclaiming their architectural heritage, especially those parts of it that can be turned into dollars via the tourism industry. These days, restorations and new buildings built in Sultanahmet and other parts of İstanbul – and even Göreme, in Cappadocia – are most likely to be in classic Ottoman style.

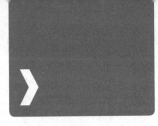

Turkish Table

Food in Turkey is much more than mere belly fuel – it's a celebration of community and life. Meals are joyful, boisterous and almost always communal. Food is used to celebrate milestones, cement friendships and add cohesion to family life. For Turks, the idea of eating in front of a TV or from a freezer is absolute anathema – theirs is a cuisine that is social, slow and seasonal.

Here, kebaps are succulent, *yaprak dolması* (stuffed vine leaves) are filled with subtly spiced rice, and meze dishes such as dips are made daily with the best seasonal ingredients. Freshly caught fish is expertly cooked over coals and served unadorned, accompanied by field-fresh salads and Turkey's famous aniseed-flavoured drink, rakı. Strong çay served in delicate glasses accompanies honey-drenched baklava studded with plump pistachios from Gaziantep.

The basics of Turkish cooking may have evolved on the steppes of Central Asia, but as the Ottoman Empire grew it swallowed the ingredients of Greece, Persia, Arabia and the Balkans, creating a deliciously diverse cuisine. Each region has specialities and signature ingredients, meaning that travelling here will truly tantalise your taste buds.

The Ottomans were masters of the evocative culinary description, inventing such delights as 'Ladies' Thighs', 'The Sultan's Delight', 'Harem Navel' and 'Nightingale Nests'.

Eating Through the Day

Breakfast

The common Turkish *kahvaltı* (breakfast) consists of fresh-from-the-oven white *ekmek* (bread), jam or honey, black olives, slices of cucumber and juicy tomatoes, a hard-boiled egg, a block of *beyaz peynir* (salty white cheese made from ewe's or goat's milk) and innumerable glasses of sweetened black çay. Expect this feast at every hotel. Other breakfast dishes to look out for are *menemen* (eggs scrambled with tomatoes, onions, peppers and white cheese), and bread served with floral-scented honey and rich *kaymak* (clotted cream).

Dalyan, on the Western Mediterranean coast, is home to the only Turkish traditional food listed in the Slow Food Foundation for Biodiversity's Ark of Taste, a register of endangered foods. The *haviar* (dried egg sacks of the grey mullet fish) produced here is one of the most ancient Turkish foods.

Lunch

Many locals eat *öğle yemeği* (lunch) in a *lokanta*. These cheap and cheerful spots serve *hazır yemek* (ready-made food) kept warm in bains-marie. The etiquette is to check out what's in the bain-marie and tell the waiter or cook behind the counter what you would like to eat. You can order one portion *(bir porsiyon)*, a *yarım* (half) *porsiyon* or a plate with a few different choices – you'll be charged by the *porsiyon*.

Dishes to choose from will usually include *çorba* (soup) – the most common are *mercimek* (lentil), *ezo gelin* (red lentil and rice) and *domates* (tomato) – plus a wide range of meat and vegetable dishes, *pilavs* (rice dishes) and *dolmas* (vegetables stuffed with rice or meat).

> ## MARVELLOUS MEZES
>
> You will probably encounter the following dishes while eating your way around the country.
>
> » **Acılı ezme** Spicy tomato and onion paste.
> » **Ançüez** Pickled anchovy.
> » **Beyaz peynir** White ewe's- or goat's-milk cheese.
> » **Cacık** Yoghurt with cucumber and mint.
> » **Fasulye pilaki** White beans cooked with tomato paste and garlic.
> » **Haydari** Yoghurt with roasted aubergine (eggplant) and garlic.
> » **Kalamar tava** Fried calamari, usually served with a *tarator* (breadcrumb, walnut and garlic) sauce.
> » **Lakerda** Strongly flavoured salted kingfish.
> » **Muhammara** Dip of walnuts, bread, tahini and lemon juice; also known as *acuka* or *civizli biber*.
> » **Patlıcan kızartması** Fried aubergine with tomato.
> » **Sigara böreği** Deep-fried cigar-shaped pastries, often stuffed with *peynir* (cheese).
> » **Yaprak sarma/yaprak dolması** Vine leaves stuffed with rice, herbs and pine nuts.
> » **Yeşil fasulye** Green beans.

Dinner

There are plenty of dining options when it comes to *akşam yemeği* (dinner). In a *meyhane* (Turkish tavern) customers usually start with a selection of mezes and then enjoy fish for the main course. A *kebapçı* (kebap restaurant) is where you should go if you're keen on sampling kebaps and a *köfteci* is the equivalent for *köfte* (meatballs) – both usually serve mezes to start the meal. The *ocakbaşı* (fireside) versions of the *kebapçı* are the most fun, with patrons sitting around the sides of a grill and watching their meat being prepared and cooked. Most *restorans* (restaurants) serve mezes, a mixture of kebap and *köfte* dishes, and fish.

What's on the Menu?

Turkey is one of the few countries that can feed itself from its own produce and have leftovers. This means that produce makes its way from ground to table quickly, ensuring freshness and flavour. Here, being a locavore is taken for granted.

Mezes

Mezes aren't just a type of dish, they're a whole eating experience. If you eat in a local household, your host may put out a few lovingly prepared dishes for guests to nibble on before the main course is served. In *meyhanes*, waiters heave around enormous trays full of cold meze dishes that customers can choose from – hot meze dishes are usually ordered from the menu.

Mezes are usually vegetable-based, though seafood dishes can also feature.

Meat

Overall, the Turks are huge meat eaters, which can be a problem if you're a vegetarian. Beef, lamb, mutton, liver and chicken are prepared in a number of ways. The most famous of these is the kebap – *şiş* and döner – but *köfte*, *saç kavurma* (stir-fried cubed meat dishes) and *güveç* (meat and vegetable stews cooked in a terracotta pot) are just as common. In Cappadocia, many restaurants serve *testı kebapı*, kebap in a mushroom and onion sauce that is slow cooked (ideally over coals) in a sealed terra-cotta pot that is then theatrically broken open at the table. The most popular sausage in Turkey is the spicy beef *sucuk,* and garlicky *pastırma* (pressed beef preserved in spices) is regularly used as an accompaniment to egg dishes; it's occasionally served with warm hummus as a meze.

When travelling through central Anatolia, you will often encounter *mantı* (Turkish ravioli stuffed with beef mince and topped with yoghurt, garlic tomato and butter). It's perfect in winter but can be overly rich and heavy in hot weather.

Fish

Fish is wonderful here, but can be pricey. In a *balık restoran* (fish restaurant) you should always try to do as the locals do and choose your own fish from the display. This is important, as the occasional dodgy restaurant may try to serve you old fish. The eyes should be clear and the flesh under the gill slits near the eyes should be bright red, not burgundy. After your fish has been given the all-clear, ask the approximate price. The fish will be weighed, and the price computed at the day's per-kilogram rate.

Popular species include *hamsi* (anchovy), *lüfer* (bluefish), *kalkan* (turbot), *levrek* (sea bass), *lahos* (white grouper), *mezgit* (whiting), *çipura* (gilthead bream) and *palamut* (bonito).

Try to avoid eating *lüfer* when the fish are small (under 24cm in length) – a recent campaign by Slow Food Turkey's İstanbul convivium has highlighted the fact that overfishing is endangering the future of this much-loved local species.

Vegetables & Salads

Turks love vegetables, eating them fresh in summer and pickling them for winter (pickled vegetables are called *turşu*). There are two particularly Turkish ways of preparing vegetables: the first is known as *zeytinyağlı* (sautéed in olive oil) and the second *dolma* (stuffed with rice or meat). *Patlıcan* (aubergine) is the sultan of all vegetables, cooked in every conceivable manner and loved by Turks with a passion.

AUBERGINES

TURKISH TABLE WHAT'S ON THE MENU?

The most famous *patlıcan* (aubergine) dish is *imam bayıldı* (the imam fainted); simply, aubergines slow-cooked in olive oil with tomatoes, onion and garlic. According to legend, an imam fainted with pleasure on first sampling it – and after tasting it you may understand why.

KEBAPS & KÖFTE

The kebap (meat grilled on a skewer) is undoubtedly the national dish, closely followed by *köfte* (meatballs). These meat dishes come in many forms, and are often named after their place of origin. The most popular are the following:

» **Adana kebap** Spicy *köfte* wrapped around a flat skewer and barbecued, then served with onions, sumac, parsley, barbecued tomatoes and pide (bread).

» **Alinazik** Aubergine purée with yoghurt and ground *köfte.*

» **Çiğ köfte** Raw ground lamb mixed with pounded bulgur, onion, clove, cinnamon, salt and hot black pepper.

» **Döner kebap** Compressed meat (usually lamb) cooked on a revolving upright skewer over coals, then thinly sliced.

» **İçli köfte** Ground lamb and onion with a bulgur coating, often served as a hot meze.

» **İskender (Bursa) kebap** Döner lamb served on a bed of crumbled pide and yoghurt, then topped with tomato and burnt butter sauces.

» **Izgara köfte** Grilled meatballs.

» **Şiş kebap** Small pieces of lamb grilled on a skewer and usually served with a side of bulgur and char-grilled peppers. *Çöp şiş* is served rolled in a thin pide with onions and parsley.

» **Tokat kebap** Lamb cubes grilled with potato, tomato, aubergine and garlic.

SEASONAL CALENDAR

In Turkey, as everywhere, it's always best to sample produce when it's in season. Here's a handy guide:

MONTH	FISH	VEGETABLE, NUT & FRUIT
Jan	anchovy, bonito, horse mackerel, bluefish	chestnut, radish, apple, pomegranate, orange
Feb	turbot, white grouper, sea bass, fresh anchovies, bonito, horse mackerel, whiting	chestnut, radish, apple, pomegranate, orange
Mar	turbot, sea bass, white grouper, whiting	radish, lemon
Apr	turbot, sea bass, whiting, shrimp, crab	artichoke, broad bean, lemon
May	sea bass, whiting, shrimp, crab, eel, scorpionfish	artichoke, broad bean, cucumber, green plum, strawberry
Jun	crab, eel, swordfish, scorpionfish, tuna, lobster	artichoke, broad bean, cucumber, green bean, tomato, green plum, strawberry, cherry
Jul	crab, scorpionfish, swordfish, tuna, lobster, gilthead bream, sardine	cucumber, bell pepper, green bean, corn, tomato, cherry, watermelon
Aug	gilthead bream, swordfish, lobster, sardine	walnut, cucumber, bell pepper, green bean, corn, tomato, watermelon, fig
Sep	bonito, sardine, gilthead bream	walnut, cucumber, bell pepper, green bean, corn, tomato, watermelon, fig
Oct	bonito, gilthead bream, bluefish	chestnut, cucumber, green bean, tomato, pomegranate, fig
Nov	anchovy, bonito, horse mackerel, bluefish, gilthead bream	chestnut, tomato, pomegranate, orange
Dec	anchovy, bonito, horse mackerel, bluefish	chestnut, apple, pomegranate, orange

Simplicity is the key to Turkish *salata* (salads), with crunchy fresh ingredients being adorned with a shake of oil and vinegar at the table and eaten with gusto as a meze or as an accompaniment to a meat or fish main course. The most popular summer salad is *çoban salatası* (shepherd's salad), a colourful mix of chopped tomatoes, cucumber, onion and pepper. It's sometimes served as a meze.

Sweets

Turks don't usually finish their meal with a dessert, preferring to serve fruit as a finale. Most of them love a mid-afternoon sugar hit, though, and will often pop into a *muhallebici* (milk pudding shop), *pastane* (cake shop) or *baklavacı* (baklava shop) for a piece of syrup-drenched baklava, a plate of chocolate-crowned profiteroles or a *fırın sütlaç* (rice pudding) tasting of milk, sugar and just a hint of exotic spices. Turkish sweet specialities worth sampling are *fırın sütlaç; dondurma* (the local ice cream); *kadayıf* (dough soaked in syrup and topped with a layer of *kaymak*); and *künefe* (layers of *kadayıf* cemented together with sweet cheese, doused in syrup and served hot with a sprinkling of pistachio).

Fast Food

The nation's favourite fast food is undoubtedly döner kebap – lamb slow-cooked on an upright revolving skewer and then shaved off before being stuffed into bread or pide. Soggy cold French fries and green chillies are sometimes included, at other times garlicky yoghurt, salad and a sprinkling of slightly sour sumac are the accompaniments.

Coming a close second in the popularity stakes is pide, the Turkish version of pizza. It has a canoe-shaped base topped with *peynir* (cheese), *yumurta* (egg) or *kıymalı* (minced meat). A *karaşık* pide has a mixture of toppings. You can sit down to eat these in a *pideci* (Turkish pizza parlour) or ask for your pide *paket* (wrapped to go). *Lahmacun* (Arabic-style pizza) has a thinner crust than pide and is usually topped with chopped lamb, onion and tomato.

Börek (filled pastries) are distinguished by their filling, cooking method and shape, and are sold at small take-away outfits called *börekçi*, usually in the morning only. They come in square, cigar or snail shapes and are filled with *peynir, ispanak* (spinach), *patates* (potatoes) or *kıymalı*. Bun-shaped *poğaca* are glazed with sugar or stuffed with cheese and olives. *Su böreği*, a melt-in-the-mouth lasagne-like layered pastry laced with white cheese and parsley, is the most popular of all *börek* styles – you're sure to be instantly infatuated.

Gözleme (thin savoury crepes cooked with cheese, spinach or potato) are also great quick snacks.

Vegetarians & Vegans

Though it's normal for Turks to eat a vegetarian *(vejeteryen)* meal, the concept of vegetarianism is quite foreign. Say you're a vegan and Turks will either look mystified or assume that you're 'fessing up to some strain of socially aberrant behaviour.

The meze spread is usually dominated by vegetable dishes, and meat-free salads, soups, pastas, omelettes, pides and *böreks,* as well as hearty vegetable dishes, are all readily available. Ask *'etsiz yemek var mı?'* ('is there something to eat that has no meat?') to see what's on offer.

The main source of inadvertent meat eating is *et suyu* (meat stock), which is often used to make otherwise vegetarian *pilav* (a rice dish), soup and vegetable dishes. Your hosts may not even consider *et suyu* to be meat, so they will reassure you that the dish is vegetarian; ask *'et suyu var mı?'* ('is there meat stock in it?') to check.

Eating Etiquette

In rural Turkey locals usually eat two meals a day, the first at around 11am and the second in the early evening. In the cities three meals a day is the norm. In urban areas people sit down to meals at tables and chairs, but in villages it is still usual to sit on the floor around a *tepsi* (low round table or tray) with a cloth spread over one's knees to catch the crumbs. These days people mostly eat from individual plates, although sometimes there will be communal dishes. Most Turks eat with a spoon *(kaşık)* and fork *(çatal)*, rarely with a knife *(bıçak)*.

In restaurants, it's not considered very important that everyone eats the same courses at the same pace, so the kitchen will deliver dishes as they are ready: it's quite normal for all the chicken dishes to arrive and

Forget the Golden Arches – Turkey's favourite fast-food chain is Simit Sarayı, which sells the country's much-loved *simit* (sesame-encrusted bread ring) to tens of thousands of happy customers every day, usually around breakfast time.

The Turks say 'Afiyet olsun' ('May it be good for your health') before starting to eat. After the meal, they say 'Elinize sağlık' ('Health to your hands') to compliment the host or hostess on their cooking.

CONFRONTATIONAL CHOICES

Like most countries, Turkey has some dishes that only a local could love. Top of the confrontational stakes for most visitors is *kokoreç*, seasoned lamb or mutton intestines wrapped around a skewer and grilled over charcoal.

İşkembe (tripe) soup reputedly wards off a hangover; it's even more popular than *kelle paça* (sheep's trotter) soup.

Locals in need of extra reserves of sexual stamina swear by spicy *koç yumurtası* (ram's 'eggs'). When these don't do the trick they often resort to *boza*, a mucous-coloured beverage made from water, sugar and fermented barley.

then, five minutes later, all the lamb. You don't have to wait for everyone's food to arrive to begin eating.

Turkish waiters have a habit of snatching plates away before the diner has finished. Saying '*kalsın*' ('let it stay') may slow them down. When you have finished, put your knife and fork together to indicate that the waiter can take the plate. If this has no effect (or you don't have a knife), say '*biti, alabilirsin*' ('finished, you can take it') to the waiter.

Toothpicking should be done behind your hands, but you don't need to be particularly discreet. Try to avoid blowing your nose in public; sniff or excuse yourself if you need to do this.

Cooking Courses & Tours

Turkish Cookbooks

» *Classical Turkish Cooking* (Ayla Esen Algar)

» *Cooking New Istanbul Style* (Refika Birgül)

» *Turquoise: A Chef's Travels in Turkey* (Greg and Lucy Malouf)

Turkey has a growing number of operators offering foreign-language cookery courses and culinary tours, with several highly regarded cooking schools in İstanbul (see p97); a popular course in Kalkan run by the **Guru's Place** (p339) restaurant; and a residential cooking course at Ula, 135km from Bodrum, run by well-known Turkish cooking writer and broadcaster **Engin Akin** (www.enginakin.com). Selin Rozanes of **Turkish Flavours** (p97) runs culinary tours in İstanbul and around the country that are aimed at serious foodies, as does the **Istanbul Culinary Institute** (Enstitü; Map p84; ☑212-251 2214; www.istanbulculinary.com; Meşrutiyet Caddesi 59, Tepebaşı).

Local Tipples

Alcoholic Drinks

In tourist-heavy destinations along the coast virtually every restaurant serves alcohol. The same applies to more expensive restaurants in the big cities. In smaller towns, there's usually at least one restaurant where alcohol is served, although in religiously conservative places such as Konya you may have to hunt hard to find one. Be warned that although Turks have a fairly relaxed attitude towards alcohol, public drunkenness is frowned upon.

Turkey's most beloved tipple is rakı, a grape spirit infused with aniseed. Similar to Greek ouzo, it's served in long thin glasses and is drunk neat or with water, which turns the clear liquid chalky white; if you want to add ice *(buz)*, do so after adding water, as dropping ice straight into rakı kills its flavour.

TURKISH GRAPE VARIETIES

As well as producing vintages of well-known grape varieties such as chardonnay, fumé blanc, sauvignon blanc, cabernet sauvignon, shiraz and merlot, Turkish winemakers also use local varietals, including the following:

» **Boğazkere** Strong-bodied red wine with distinctive dried-fruits taste and aroma. Black Sea region, eastern Anatolia and southeastern Anatolia.

» **Çalkarası** Sweetish red wine with strong fruit flavours. Western Anatolia.

» **Emir** Light and floral white wine with pleasant acidic finish. Central Anatolia.

» **Kalecik karası** Elegant red wine with aroma of vanilla and cocoa. Aegean coast and central Anatolia.

» **Narince** Fruity yet dry white wine with distinctive golden colour. Black Sea region and eastern Anatolia.

» **Öküzgözü (ox eye)** Dry red wine with fruity flavours. Black Sea region, eastern Anatolia and southeastern Anatolia.

» **Sultaniye** Dry white wine. Aegean coast.

Bira (beer) is also popular. The local drop, Efes, is a perky pilsener that comes in bottles, cans and on tap.

Turkey grows and bottles its own *şarap* (wine), which has greatly improved in quality over the past decade but is quite expensive due to high government taxes. Head to Ürgüp in Cappadocia or to the idyllic Aegean island of Bozcaada to taste-test. If you want red wine ask for *kırmızı şarap;* for white ask for *beyaz şarap.* Labels to look out for include Sarafin (chardonnay, fumé blanc, sauvignon blanc, cabernet sauvignon, shiraz and merlot); Karma (cabernet sauvignon, shiraz and merlot); Kav Tuğra (narince, kalecik karası and öküzgözü) and DLC (most grape varieties). All are produced by the **Doluca Company** (www.doluca.com). Its major competitor, **Kavaklidere** (www.kavaklidere.com), is known for the wines it puts out under the Pendore, Ancyra and Prestige labels (the Pendore boğuazkere is particularly good), as well as its eminently quaffable Çankaya white blend.

Together, Doluca and Kavaklidere dominate the market, but producers such as **Vinkara** (www.vinkara.com) and **Kayra** (www.kayrasaraplari.com) are starting to build a reputation for themselves with wines such as Kayra's excellent buzbağ.

Nonalcoholic Drinks

Drinking çay is the national pastime, and the country's cup of choice is made with leaves from the Black Sea region. Sugar cubes are the only accompaniment and you'll find these are needed to counter the effects of long brewing, although you can always try asking for it *açık* (weaker). In hotels and Western-style cafes it's acceptable to ask for milk *(süt)*, but don't bother trying elsewhere.

The wholly chemical *elma çay* (apple tea) is caffeine-free and only for tourists – locals wouldn't be seen dead drinking the stuff.

Surprisingly, *Türk kahve* (Turkish coffee) isn't widely consumed. A thick and powerful brew, it's drunk in a couple of short sips. If you order a cup, you will be asked how sweet you like it – *çok şekerli* means 'very sweet', *orta şekerli* 'middling', *az şekerli* 'slightly sweet' and *şekersiz or sade* 'not at all'. Your coffee will be accompanied by a glass of water, which is to clear the palate before you sample the delights of the coffee.

Freshly squeezed juice is popular and cheap. *Taze portakal suyu* (fresh orange juice) is everywhere, and delicious *nar suyu* (pomegranate juice) can be ordered in season.

Ayran is a refreshing drink made by whipping yoghurt with water and salt; it's the traditional accompaniment to kebaps.

Sahlep is a hot milky drink that takes off the winter chill. Made from wild orchid bulbs, it's reputed to be an aphrodisiac. You might also want to try *şalgam suyu* – the first gulp is a revolting salty shock, but persevere and you may find yourself developing a fondness for this turnip concoction.

TURKISH COFFEE

TURKISH TABLE LOCAL TIPPLES

Don't drink the grounds when you try *Türk kahve* (Turkish coffee). Instead, go to the Turkish Coffee/ Fortune Telling section of www .mehmetefendi. com, Turkey's most famous coffee purveyor, for a guide to reading your fortune in them.

Arts

Turkey's artistic traditions are rich and diverse, displaying influences of the many cultures and civilisations that have waxed and waned in Anatolia over the centuries. Here, we offer an introduction to some of them.

Carpets

The art form that travellers are most likely to associate with Turkey is the carpet – there are few who do not end up in a carpet shop some time on their travels.

The carpets that travellers know and love are the culmination of an ages-old textile-making tradition. Long ago Turkic nomads wove goat-hair tents and woollen saddle bags and established carpet-making techniques on the steppes of Central Asia. The oldest-known carpet woven in the Turkish double-knotted style dates from over 2000 years ago.

As in many aspects of their culture, the Turks adopted and adapted from other traditions. As well as robust floor coverings they later began making Islamic prayer rugs while incorporating Persian design motifs and Chinese cloud patterns. Moving ever-westward the Turks eventually brought hand-woven carpets to Anatolia in the 12th century.

Within Anatolia, distinctive regional designs evolved. Uşak carpets, with their star and medallion motifs, were the first to attract attention in Europe: Renaissance artist Holbein included copies of them in his paintings. Thereafter, carpet making gradually shifted from cottage industry to big business. During the Ottoman era, textile production and trade contributed significantly to the economy. Village women still weave carpets but usually work to fixed contracts for specific shops. Generally they work to a pattern and are paid for their final effort rather than for each hour of work.

Other carpets are the product of a division of labour, with different individuals responsible for dyeing and weaving. What such pieces lose in individuality is made up for in quality control. Most silk Hereke carpets are mass produced but to standards that make them some of the most sought-after of all Turkish carpets.

Fearing the loss of the old carpet-making methods, the Ministry of Culture has sponsored several projects to revive traditional weaving and dyeing methods in western Turkey. One such scheme is the Natural Dye Research and Development Project (Doğal Boya Arıştırma ve Geliştirme Projesi). Some shops keep stocks of these 'project carpets', which are usually of high quality.

Literature

Only in the last century has Turkey developed a tradition of novel writing, but there is a wealth of writing by Turks and about Turkey that offers insight into the destination and makes fine holiday reading.

Historically, Turkish literature was all about poetry. The literary tradition included warrior epics passed down orally, Sufi mystical verses,

Jon Thompson's beautifully illustrated *Carpets: From the Tents, Cottages and Workshops of Asia* is an excellent introduction that may well tempt you into investing in a carpet.

A magnificent collection of images gathered over decades, *Nomads in Anatolia*, by Harald Böhmer and Josephine Powell looks at the lost nomadic traditions of textile making in Anatolia. Difficult to find but hugely rewarding.

ORHAN PAMUK: NOBEL LAUREATE

The biggest name in Turkish literature is internationally acclaimed author Orhan Pamuk. Long-feted in Turkey, Pamuk has steadily built a worldwide audience since first being translated in the early 1990s. Pamuk is an inventive prose stylist, creating elaborate plots and finely sketched characters while dealing with the weighty issues confronting contemporary Turkey.

His *Black Book* is an İstanbul existential whodunit told through a series of florid newspaper columns; while *My Name is Red* is a 16th-century murder mystery that also delves into Eastern and Western conceptions of art. In his nonfiction *İstanbul: Memories and the City*, Pamuk ruminates on his complex relationship with the beguiling city. *Silent House*, one of his earliest novels, has recently been translated into English for the first time.

The Museum of Innocence, his latest novel, details a love affair between wealthy Kemal and shop girl Füsun and illustrates Pamuk's uncanny ability to evoke the moods and ambience of modern Turkey. In 2012 Pamuk opened a museum in İstanbul based on that in the novel and displaying the ephemera of everyday life.

Pamuk was awarded the Nobel Prize for Literature in 2006. He is the only Turk to have won a Nobel Prize.

including those of Rumi (founder of the Mevlevi order of whirling dervishes), and the legends and elegies of wandering *aşık* (minstrels). Travellers may encounter tales of Nasreddin Hoca, a semi-legendary quasi-holy man noted for his quirky humour and left-of-centre 'wisdom'.

Yaşar Kemal was the first Turkish novelist to win an international audience, writing gritty novels of rural life. His *Memed, My Hawk*, a tale of the desperate plight of Anatolian villagers, won him a nomination for the Nobel Prize for Literature on several occasions.

Recently, the prolific Turkish-American writer and academic Elif Şafak has attracted an international following. Her first novel to be translated into English, *The Flea Palace*, is a wordy story of an elegant İstanbul apartment building fallen on hard times. The later work, *The Bastard of Istanbul*, is a coming-of-age saga bristling with eccentric family members. Şafak's latest novel, *Honour*, delves into family relations and gender issues in deepest Anatolia.

Ayşe Kulin has a huge following in Turkey and her novels have been translated widely. *Last Train to İstanbul* is her novel of a Turkish diplomats' attempts to save Jewish families from the Nazis in Europe, while *Farewell* is a tale set during the difficult era of Allied-occupation after WWI. Another recommended read is *Dear Shameless Death* by Latife Tekin – a heady whirl of Anatolian folklore and magic realism.

Irfan Orga's autobiographical *Portrait of a Turkish Family*, set during the late Ottoman/early Republican era, describes the collapse of his well-to-do İstanbullu family and its struggle to rebuild. In *The Caravan Moves On* Orga offers a glimpse of rural life in the 1950s as he travels with Yörük nomads in the Taurus Mountains.

Jewish-Turkish writer Moris Farhi's pacy and episodic *Young Turk* clearly draws on events from his own life, and includes moments of pathos and comedy, as well as sensual encounters.

One of the giants of Turkish literature was Evliya Çelebi, who travelled the Ottoman realm for 40 years and produced a 10-volume travelogue from 1630. A recent edition, *An Ottoman Traveller* presents a selection of his quirky observations.

Music

Even in the era of MTV and pervasive Western cultural influences, Turkish musical traditions and styles have remained strong and home-grown stars continue to emerge.

A BEGINNERS' GUIDE TO TURKISH MUSIC

These are our picks to start your collection.

» *Turkish Groove* (compilation): must-have introduction to Turkish music, with all the big names.

» *Crossing the Bridge: the Sound of İstanbul* (compilation): soundtrack to a documentary about İstanbul's music scene.

» *Işık Doğdan Yükselir* – Sezen Aksu (contemporary folk): stunning collection drawing on regional folk styles.

» *Nefes* – Mercan Dede (Sufi-electronic-techno fusion): highly danceable synthesis of beats and Sufi mysticism.

» *Keçe Kurdan* – Aynur (Kurdish folk): an impassioned debut album, sung entirely in Kurdish.

» *Duble Oryantal* – Baba Zula (fusion): Baba Zula's classic, 'Belly Double', is mixed by the British dub master Mad Professor.

» *Gipsy Rum* – Burhan Öçal and İstanbul Oriental Ensemble (gypsy): a thigh-slapping introduction to Turkey's gypsy music.

Pop, Rock, Experimental

You'll hear Turkish pop everywhere: in taxis, bars, on long-distance buses. With its skittish rhythms, shimmering sounds and strident vocals, it's not for everyone, but it is undeniably energetic and distinctive.

Sezen Aksu is widely regarded as the queen of Turkish pop music, releasing a string of albums in diverse styles over four decades. However, it is Tarkan, the pretty-boy pop star, who has achieved most international recognition. His 1994 album, *A-acaynpsin,* sold mightily in Turkey and Europe, establishing him as Turkey's biggest-selling pop sensation. 'Şımarık', released in 1999, became his first European number one. He continues to release albums and his metrosexual hip-swivelling ensures he remains a household name in Turkey.

Burhan Öçal is one of the country's finest percussionists. His seminal *New Dream* is a funky take on classical Turkish music, and his Trakya All-Stars albums are a Roma-Balkan investigation of the music of his native Thrace.

Mercan Dede has released a string of albums incorporating traditional instruments and electronic beats. In a similar vein, albeit more given to performance 'events', BaBa ZuLa creates a fusion of dub, *saz* (Turkish lute) and pop – accompanied by live belly dancing!

Attracting an international audience since appearing in Eurovision 2010, maNga creates an intriguing mix of metal, rock and Anatolian folk styles. Their 2012 album *e-akustik* is worth seeking out.

Folk

Turkish folk music includes various subgenres that may not be distinguishable to Western ears. Ensembles consist of *saz* accompanied by various drums and flutes. Arrangements tend to include plaintive vocals and swelling choruses. Names to look out for include female Kurdish singer Aynur Doğan and the ululating Rojin, whose hit 'Hejaye' has an addictive, singalong chorus.

Fasıl is a lightweight version of Ottoman classical. This is the music you hear at *meyhanes* (taverns), usually played by gypsies. This skittish music is played with clarinet, *kanun* (zither), *darbuka* (a drum shaped like an hourglass) and often an *ud* (a six-stringed Arabic lute) and *keman* (violin).

For hard-to-find Turkish music, books and paraphernalia, you can't go past US-based online Turkish shopping emporium, Tulumba (www .tulumba.com), which ships right to your door. You can hear music samples online.

You may spot wandering minstrels playing the *zurna* (pipe) and boom-slapping *davul* (drum). They perform at wedding and circumcision parties, and congregate in bus stations on call-up day to give cadet conscripts a rousing farewell as they leave for compulsory national service.

Arabesk

A favourite of taxi drivers across Turkey is arabesk, an Arabic-influenced blend of crooning backed by string choruses and rippling percussion.

The two biggest names in arabesk are the hugely successful Kurdish singer İbrahim Tatlıses, a burly, moustachioed, former construction worker who survived an assassination attempt in 2011, and Orhan Gencebay, a prolific artist and also an actor.

Cinema

Turkey has long been a favoured location for foreign filmmakers; the latest James Bond pic, *Skyfall* (2012), includes scenes shot in İstanbul and near Adana. The Turkish film industry itself came of age in the 1960s and '70s, when films with a political edge were being made alongside innumerable lightweight Bollywood-style movies, lumped together and labelled *Yeşilçam* movies. During the 1980s the film industry went into decline as TV siphoned off audiences, but the 1990s saw a resurgence in Turkish cinema.

Yılmaz Güney was the first Turkish filmmaker to attract international attention. Joint winner of the best film award at Cannes in 1982, his film *Yol* explored the dilemmas of men on weekend-release from prison, a gripping and tragic tale that Turks were forbidden to watch until 2000. Güney's uncompromising stance lead to confrontations with authorities and several stints in prison. He died in exile in France in 1984. Many Turkish directors continue to make political films: *Güneşe Yolculuk* (Journey to the Sun), by Yeşim Ustaoğlu, is about a Turk who migrates to İstanbul and is mistaken for a Kurd and thereafter endures persistent injustices.

Yılmaz Erdoğan's *Vizontele* is a wry look at the arrival of the first TV in Hakkari, a remote town in the southeast. The follow-up, *Vizontele Tuuba,* is similarly quirky and entertaining. Ferzan Özpetek received international acclaim for *Hamam* (Turkish Bath), which follows a Turk living in Italy who reluctantly travels to İstanbul after he inherits a hamam. His *Harem Suare* (Soireé in the Harem) was set in the Ottoman harem.

Fatih Akin captured the spotlight after winning the Golden Bear award at the 2004 Berlin Film Festival with *Duvara Karsi* (Head On), a gripping telling of Turkish immigrant life in Germany. He followed this with *Edge of Heaven,* again pondering the Turkish experience in Germany. In 2010 Semih Kaplanoğlu won the Golden Bear award with *Bal* (Honey), a coming-of-age tale in the Black Sea region; while Reha Erdem has won acclaim as an up-and-coming director.

The most expensive Turkish movie ever made, and a box-office smash, is *Fetih 1453* (the Conquest 1453) an epic and melodramatic retelling of the capture of Constantinople/ İstanbul, released in 2012. Visually spectacular, but not offering any great historical insights.

The biggest cinema event in the Turkish calendar, the Antalya Golden Orange Film Festival (www .altinportakal. org.tr/en) brings together film industry figures, glitterati and a range of Turkish and international films every October.

ARTS

A CINEMA AUTEUR IN ANATOLIA

Internationally, Nuri Bilge Ceylan has become the most widely recognised Turkish director. Since emerging in 2002 with *Uzak* (Distant), a bleak meditation on the lives of migrants in Turkey, he has been a consistent favourite at international film festivals. *Uzak* won the Grand Prix at Cannes in 2003; he also won best director at Cannes in 2008 for *Üç Maymun* (Three Monkeys).

Ceylan's second film, *İklimler* (Climates), which he also starred in, examines relationships between men and women in Turkey, and featured long landscape shots, brooding silences and minimal dialogue. His latest, *Once Upon a Time in Anatolia*, with a similar ambience, is an intriguing all-night search for a corpse in the Turkish backwoods.

Visual Arts

Turkey does not have a long tradition of painting or portraiture. Turks channelled their artistic talents into textiles and carpet making, as well as *ebru* (paper marbling), calligraphy and ceramics. İznik became a centre for tile production from the 16th century. The exuberant tiles that adorn the interior of İstanbul's Blue Mosque and many other Ottoman-era mosques hail from İznik. You'll find examples of *ebru,* calligraphy and ceramics in bazaars across Turkey.

By the late 19th century, educated Ottomans were being influenced by European-style painting. In the Republican era, Atatürk encouraged this artistic expression, and the government opened official painting and sculpture academies, promoting this 'modern' secular art in place of the religious art of the past. Various artistic 'schools' developed thereafter. İstanbul is the best place to see what modern Turkish artists are up to. İstanbul Modern and Santralİstanbul are the country's best modern art galleries, but the small private art galleries along İstiklal Caddesi are worth seeing as well.

Ara Güler is one of Turkey's most respected photographers. For over 50 years he has documented countless facets of Turkish life; his *Ara Güler's İstanbul* is a poignant photographic record of the great city.

Panoramic Photographs of Turkey, by noted film director Nuri Bilge Ceylan, is a cloth-bound, limited-edition album of stunningly beautiful images of Turkish landscapes and cityscapes.

Dance

If you thought that Turks, being Muslims, would be staid on the dance floor, think again. Turkey boasts a range of folk dances, ranging from the frenetic to the ponderous and hypnotic, and Turks tend to be enthusiastic and unself-conscious dancers, swivelling their hips and shaking their shoulders in ways that are entirely different from Western dance styles.

Folk dance can be divided into several broad categories. Although originally a dance of central, southern and southeastern Anatolia, the *halay,* led by a dancer waving a handkerchief, can be seen all over the country, especially at weddings and in *meyhanes* in İstanbul, when everyone has downed their fill of rakı (aniseed-flavoured brandy). The *horon,* from the Black Sea region, is most eye catching – it involves all manner of dramatic kicking, Cossack-style.

The *sema* (dervish ceremony) of the whirling dervishes is not unique to Turkey, but it's here that you are most likely to see it performed.

Belly dancing may not have originated in Turkey, but Turkish women have mastered the art, reputedly dancing with the least inhibition and the most revealing costumes. Although belly dancers are frequently seen at weddings, your best chance of seeing a decent belly dancer is at a folk show in İstanbul.

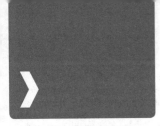

People

Turkey has a population of almost 80 million, the great majority of whom are Muslim and Turkish. Kurds form the largest minority, but there is an assortment of other groups – both Muslim and non-Muslim – leading some to say Turkey is comprised of 40 nations.

Since the 1950s there has been a steady movement of people away from the countryside and into urban areas, so that today 70% of the population lives in cities. This process has been a result of people seeking economic opportunity, but also fleeing the disruption that plagued the southeast during the 1990s. Cities such as İstanbul have turned into pervasive sprawls, their historic hearts encircled by rings of largely unplanned new neighbourhoods.

Nonetheless, whether urban or rural, Muslim or Christian, Turkish, Kurdish or otherwise, all the peoples of Turkey tend to be family-focused, easygoing, hospitable, gregarious and welcoming. Many travellers return from a holiday in Turkey remarking on the friendliness of the locals.

> Various (not exactly academically rigorous) theories state that the Turks are descendants of Japheth, the grandson of Noah. The Ottomans themselves claimed that Osman could trace his genealogy back through 52 generations to Noah.

Turks

The first definitive mentions of the Turks appear in medieval Chinese sources, which record them as the Tujue in 6th-century Mongolia and Siberia. The modern Turks are the descendants of Central Asian tribal groups that began moving westward through Eurasia over 1000 years ago. As such the Turks retain cultural and linguistic links with various peoples through southern Russia, Azerbaijan, Iran, the nations of Central Asia and western China.

As they moved westward the predecessors of the modern Turks encountered the Persians and converted to Islam. The Seljuks established the Middle East's first Turkic empire. The Seljuks' defeat of the Byzantines in battle in 1071 opened up Anatolia to wandering Turkish groups,

---

IN THE FAMILY WAY

Perhaps exhibiting vestiges of their tribal origins, Turks retain a strong sense of family and community. One endearing Turkish habit is to use familial titles to embrace friends, acquaintances and even strangers. A teacher may address his student as *'çocuğum'* (my child); passers-by address old men in the street as *'dede'* (literally, 'grandfather'); and old women on buses are comfortable being called her *'teyze'* (auntie) by strangers.

It is also common for children to call family friends *'amca'* (uncle) and for males of all ages to address slightly older men as *'ağabey'* (pronounced 'abi', and roughly equivalent to the English 'guv'nor'). You will also hear small children referring to their teenage sisters as *'abla'*, equivalent to 'big sister', which is rather charming in its simplicity.

These terms are a sign of respect but also of affection and inclusiveness. Perhaps this intimacy explains how the rural village sense of community persists amid the tower blocks of sprawling cities, where most Turks now live.

ISLAM IN TURKEY

For many travellers, Turkey is their first experience of Islam. While it may seem 'foreign', Islam in fact has much in common with Christianity and Judaism. Like Christians, Muslims believe that Allah (God) created the world and everything in it, pretty much according to the biblical account. They also revere Adam, Noah, Abraham, Moses and Jesus as prophets, although they don't believe that Jesus was divine. Muslims call Jews and Christians 'People of the Book', meaning those with a revealed religion (in the Torah and Bible) that preceded Islam.

Where Islam differs from Christianity and Judaism is in the belief that Islam is the 'perfection' of these earlier traditions. Although Moses and Jesus were prophets, Mohammed was the greatest and last to whom Allah communicated his final revelation.

Islam has diversified into many 'versions' since the time of Mohammed; however, the five basic 'pillars' of Islam – the profession of faith, daily prayers, alms giving, the fasting month of Ramazan, pilgrimage to Mecca – are shared by the entire Muslim community (or *umma*).

Islam is the most widely held belief in Turkey, however many Turks take a relaxed approach to religious duties and practices. Fasting during Ramazan is widespread and Islam's holy days and festivals are observed, but for many Turks Islamic holidays are the only times they'll visit a mosque. You can also tell by the many bars that Turks like a drink or two. Turkish Muslims have also absorbed and adapted other traditions over the years, so it's not uncommon to see Muslims praying at Greek Orthodox shrines or monasteries, while the Alevis, a heterodox Muslim minority, have developed a tradition combining elements of Anatolian folklore, Sufism and Shia Islam.

speeding up the westward drift the Turks. Over the following centuries, Anatolia became the heartland of the Ottoman Empire and the core of the modern Turkish Republic. During the Ottoman centuries, Turkish rule extended into southeast Europe so that today there are people of Turkish ancestry in Cyprus, Iraq, Macedonia, Greece, Bulgaria and Ukraine.

The ancestry that Turks share with peoples in Central Asia and the Balkans means that Turks can merrily chat to locals all the way from Novi Pazar in Serbia to Kashgar in China. Turkish is one of the Turkic languages, a family of – largely mutually intelligible – languages spoken by over 150 million people across Eurasia.

A Modern History of the Kurds by David McDowall investigates the plight of Kurds in Turkey, Iraq and Iran, examining how they have fared over the last two centuries as modern states have arisen in the Middle East.

Kurds

Turkey has a significant Kurdish minority estimated at over 15 million people. Sparsely populated southeastern Anatolia is home to perhaps eight million Kurds, while seven million more live elsewhere in the country, largely integrated into mainstream Turkish society. Kurds have lived for millennia in the mountains where the modern borders of Turkey, Iran, Iraq and Syria meet.

Despite having lived side by side with Turks for centuries, the Kurds retain a distinct culture and folklore and speak a language related to Persian (and, distantly, to the Indo-European tongues of Europe). The majority of Turkish Kurds are Sunni Muslims. The Kurds have their own foundation myth which is associated with Nevruz, the Persian New Year (celebrated on 21 March); some Kurds claim descent from the Medes of ancient Persia.

The struggle between Kurds and Turks has been very well documented. Kurds and Turks fought together during the battle for independence in the 1920s, but unlike the Greeks, Jews and Armenians, the Kurds were not guaranteed rights as a minority group under the 1923 Treaty of Lausanne. The Turkish state was decreed to be unitary, or inhabited solely by Turks, hence the Kurds were denied a cultural existence. After the fragmentation along ethnic lines of the former domains of the Ottoman Empire, such an approach may have seemed prudent, but as the Kurds were so numerous problems swiftly arose.

Until relatively recently the Turkish government refused to recognise the existence of the Kurds, insisting they were 'Mountain Turks'. Even today the census form and identity cards do not allow anyone to identify as Kurdish. However, this lack of recognition is gradually being overcome, with vigorous debate ensuing on how a Kurdish identity can be accommodated in Turkey, and the recent decision to allow Kurdish language courses at government schools.

Muslim Minorities

Turkey is home to a range of other Muslim minorities, both indigenous and more recent arrivals, most of whom are regarded as Turks, but who nonetheless retain aspects of their culture and their native tongue.

Laz & Hemşin

The Black Sea region is home to the Laz and the Hemşin peoples, two of the largest Muslim minorities after the Kurds.

The Laz mainly inhabit the valleys between Trabzon and Rize. East of Trabzon you can't miss the women in their vivid maroon-striped shawls. Laz men are less conspicuous, although they were once among the most feared of Turkish warriors. Once Christian but now Muslim, the Laz are a Caucasian people speaking a language related to Georgian. They are renowned for their sense of humour and business acumen.

Speaking a language related to Armenian, the Hemşin, like the Laz, were originally Christian. They mainly come from the far-eastern end of the Black Sea coast, although perhaps no more than 15,000 still live there; most have migrated to the cities where they earn a living as bread and pastry cooks. In and around Ayder, Hemşin women are easily identified by their leopard-print scarves (more eye-catching than those worn by Laz women) coiled into elaborate headdresses.

PEOPLE

Small numbers of Turkish Kurds profess the Yazidi faith, a complex mix of indigenous beliefs and Sufi tradition, in which *Tavus Melek* – a peacock angel – is seen as an earthly guardian appointed by God.

SEPARATISM OR THE 'BROTHERHOOD' OF PEOPLES?

In 1984 Abdullah Öcalan formed the Kurdistan Workers Party (PKK), which became the most enduring – and violent – Kurdish organisation that Turkey had seen. The PKK remains outlawed. Many Kurds, while not necessarily supporting the demands of the PKK for a separate Kurdish state, wanted to be able to read newspapers in their own language, have their children taught in their own language and watch Kurdish TV. The Turkish government reacted to the PKK's violent tactics and territorial demands by branding calls for Kurdish rights as 'separatism'. Strife escalated until much of southeastern Anatolia was in a permanent state of emergency. After 15 years of fighting, suffering and the deaths of over 30,000 people, Öcalan was captured in Kenya in 1999.

There has since been progress made in solving the 'Kurdish question', but a definitive solution remains elusive. Following Öcalan's arrest, an increasingly reasoned approach by both the military and government bore some fruit. In 2002 the Turkish government approved broadcasts in Kurdish and gave the go-ahead for Kurdish to be taught in language schools, and emergency rule was lifted in the southeast. The government's 2009 'Kurdish opening' was an attempt to address the social and political roots of the issue. The creation of TRT6, a government-funded Kurdish-language TV channel, was hailed as a positive initiative. It appears that in not relying solely on military solutions, recent initiatives will be more likely to resolve the Kurdish issue.

Others

The last link to the wandering Turkic groups who arrived in Anatolia in the 11th century, the Yörük maintain a nomadic lifestyle around the Taurus Mountains. Named from the verb *yürük* (to walk), the Yörük move herds of sheep between summer and winter pastures.

In Turkey's far southeast, particularly around the Syrian border, there are various communities of Arabic speakers. There are also various Muslim groups that arrived from the Caucasus and the Balkans during the latter years of the Ottoman Empire. These include Circassians, Abkhazians, Crimean Tatars, Bosnians and Turkic Uighurs from China.

The Turkic Speaking Peoples, edited by Ergün Çağatay and Doğan Kuban, is a monumental doorstop of a volume investigating, in full colour, the traditions and cultures of Turkic groups across Eurasia.

Non-Muslim Groups

The Ottoman Empire was notable for its large Christian and Jewish populations. These have diminished considerably in the modern republic, nonetheless some remain.

There has been a Jewish presence in Anatolia for over 2000 years. A large influx of Jews arrived in the 16th century fleeing the Spanish Inquisition. Today most of Turkey's Jews live in İstanbul, and some still speak Ladino, a Judaeo-Spanish language.

Originally from the Caucasian highlands, Armenians have lived in Anatolia for a very long time; a distinct Armenian people existed by the 4th century, at which point they became the first nation to collectively convert to Christianity. The Armenians created their own alphabet and went on to establish various kingdoms in the borderlands between Byzantine, Persian and Ottoman empires. Until 1915 there were significant communities throughout Anatolia. The controversy surrounding the Armenians in the final years of the Ottoman Empire means that relations between Turks and Armenians remain predominantly sour. About 70,000 Armenians still live in Turkey, mainly in İstanbul, and in isolated pockets in Anatolia. Turkish–Armenian relations are tense, but happily there are signs of rapprochement. In 2007 the Arme-nian church on Akdamar Island was refurbished by the Turkish Culture Ministry and reopened amid hopes that relations would improve. Since 2010 a service has been held annually (in September) in the church attracting worshippers from across the border.

The International Turkish Language Olympiad, run annually since 2003, attracts students from over 130 countries to compete in poetry recitations, theatrical productions and essay-writing competitions – all in Turkish.

Turkey's other significant Christian minority is the Greeks. Large Greek populations once lived throughout the Ottoman realm, but after the population exchanges of the early Republican era and acrimonious events in the 1950s, the Greeks were reduced to a small community in İstanbul. Recent years, however, have seen a warming of relations between Greece and Turkey and the return of some young Greek professionals and students to İstanbul.

Rugged southeastern Anatolia is also home to ancient Christian communities. These include adherents of the Syriac Orthodox Church, centred on Midyat, who speak Aramaic and maintain the monastery of Deyrul Zafran. There's also the Chaldean Catholic Church, some of whom remain in Diyarbakır.

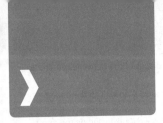

Environment

The Land

Turkey has one foot in Europe and another in Asia, its two parts separated by İstanbul's famous Bosphorus, the Sea of Marmara and the Dardanelles. Eastern Thrace (European Turkey) makes up a mere 3% of Turkey's 769,632-sq-km land area. The remaining 97% is Anatolia (Asian Turkey).

Boasting 7200km of coastline, snowcapped mountains, rolling steppe, vast lakes and broad rivers, the country is stupendously diverse.

The Aegean coast is lined with coves and beaches and the Aegean islands, most belonging to Greece and within a few kilometres of mainland Turkey. Inland, western Anatolia has the vast Lake District and Uludağ (Great Mountain; 2543m), one of over 50 Turkish peaks above 2000m.

The Mediterranean coast is backed by the jagged Taurus Mountains. East of Antalya, it opens up into a fertile plain, before the mountains close in again after Alanya.

Central Anatolia consists of a vast high plateau of rolling steppe, broken by mountain ranges and Cappadocia's fantastical valleys of fairy chimneys (rock formations).

Like the Mediterranean, the Black Sea is often hemmed in by mountains, and the coastline is frequently rugged and vertiginous. At the eastern end, Mt Kaçkar (Kaçkar Dağı; 3937m) is the highest point in the

The action of wind and water on *tuff* (rock composed of compressed volcanic ash, thrown for miles around by prehistoric eruptions) created Cappadocia's fairy chimneys.

EARTHQUAKE DANGER

Turkey lies on at least three active earthquake fault lines: the North Anatolian, the East Anatolian and the Aegean. Most of Turkey lies south of the North Anatolian fault line, which runs roughly parallel with the Black Sea coast. As the Arabian and African plates to the south push northward, the Anatolian plate is shoved into the Eurasian plate and squeezed west towards Greece.

More than 25 major earthquakes, measuring up to 7.8 on the Richter scale, have been recorded since 1939. A 7.6-magnitude quake in 1999 hit İzmit (Kocaeli) and Adapazarı (Sakarya) in northwestern Anatolia, killing more than 18,000. A 7.1-magnitude earthquake shook the Van area in 2011, killing more than 600, injuring over 4000 and causing massive structural damage, with some 60,000 locals left homeless.

If a major quake struck İstanbul, much of the city would be devastated, due to the prevalence of unlicensed, jerry-built construction. When a 4.4-magnitude earthquake hit in 2010, no deaths or damage were caused, but it highlighted how ill-prepared the city was, with many locals hitting the phone and social-networking sites rather than evacuating their houses.

In 2012, the Environment and Urbanisation Ministry said that 6.5 million of Turkey's 20 million residential dwellings were potentially dangerous and could be demolished in the next 20 years.

TOP BIRD-WATCHING SPOTS

Birecik (p562) One of the world's last known nesting places of the *Geronticus eremita* (eastern bald ibis). Between Gaziantep and Şanlıurfa.

Çıldır Gölü (Lake Çıldır, p542) Important breeding ground. Also well off the beaten track, north of Kars in northeastern Anatolia.

Göksu Delta (p380) Over 330 species have been recorded here, including the rare purple gallinule. Near Silifke.

Pamucak (p228) Home to flamingos during February and March. Also more readily accessible than the eastern sites.

beauteous Kaçkar range, where peaks and glaciers ring mountain lakes and *yaylalar* (highland pastures).

Mountainous and somewhat forbidding, the rest of northeastern Anatolia is also wildly beautiful, from Yusufeli's valleys and white-water rapids via the steppe around Kars to snowcapped Mt Ararat (Ağrı Dağı; 5137m), dominating the area bordering Iran, Armenia and Azerbaijan. Southeastern Anatolia offers windswept rolling steppe, jagged outcrops of rock, and the extraordinary alkaline, mountain-ringed Lake Van (Van Gölü).

Wildlife

Animals

In theory, you could see bears, deer, jackals, caracal, wild boars and wolves, although you're unlikely to spot any wild animals unless you're trekking.

Kangal dogs were originally bred to protect sheep from wolves and bears on mountain pastures. These huge, yellow-coated, black-headed animals are most often seen in eastern Turkey. Their mongrel descendants live on Turkey's streets.

Birds

Some 400 species of bird are found in Turkey, with about 250 of these passing through on migration from Africa to Europe. Spring and autumn are particularly good times to see the feathered commuters. It's particularly easy to spot eagles, storks, (beige) hoopoes, (blue) rollers and (green) bee-eaters. There are several *kuş cennetler* (bird sanctuaries) dotted about the country, but they are often popular with noisy, picnicking locals who frighten the birds away.

Endangered Species

Anatolia's lions, beavers and Caspian tigers are extinct, and its lynx, striped hyena and Anatolian leopard have all but disappeared. The last official sighting of the distinctive leopard was in 1974, when one was shot for mauling a village woman outside Beypazarı. Another feline, the beautiful, pure-white Van cat, often with one blue and one amber eye, has also become endangered in its native Turkey.

Rare loggerhead turtles still nest on various beaches, including Anamur, Patara, İztuzu Beach at Dalyan, and the Göksu Delta. A few rare Mediterranean monk seals live around Foça, but you would be very lucky to see them. Greenpeace has criticised Turkey for not following international fishing quotas relating to Mediterranean bluefin tuna, which is facing extinction.

Plants

Turkey is one of the world's most biodiverse temperate-zone countries. Not only does its fertile soil produce an incredible range of fruit and vegetables, it is blessed with an exceptionally rich flora: over 9000 species, 1200 of them endemic, with a new species of flora reportedly discovered every week (on average).

Common trees and plants are pine, cypress, myrtle, laurel, rosemary, lavender, thyme, and on the coast, purple bougainvillea, introduced from South America. Isparta is one of the world's leading producers of attar of roses, a valuable oil extracted from rose petals and used in perfumes and cosmetics.

National Parks & Reserves

In the last few years, thanks to EU aspirations, Turkey has stepped up its environmental protection practices. It has 13 Ramsar sites (wetlands of international importance) and is a member of Cites, which covers international trade of endangered species. The growing number of protected areas includes 33 *milli parkis* (national parks), 16 nature parks and 35 nature reserves. In the parks and reserves the environment is supposedly protected, and hunting controlled. Sometimes the regulations are carefully enforced, but in other cases problems such as litter-dropping picnickers persist.

Tourism is not well developed in the national parks, which are rarely well set up with facilities. It is not the norm for footpaths to be clearly marked, and camping spots are often unavailable. Most of the well-frequented national parks are as popular for their historic monuments as they are for the surrounding natural environment.

Environmental Issues

Turkey faces the unenviable challenge of balancing environmental management with rapid economic growth and urbanisation, and to date it's done a sloppy job. Inadequate enforcement of environmental laws, lack of finances and poor education have placed the environment a long way down the country's list of priorities. But there are glimmers of improvement, largely due to the country's desire to join the EU.

Nuclear Energy

One of the biggest challenges facing Turkey's environmentalists is the government's plan to build three nuclear power plants. One plant is slated to be built at Akkuyu, on the eastern Mediterranean coast, a controversial site located 25km from a seismic fault line. Previous plans to build a plant there were scrapped in 2000. Another proposed location is the

> Turkey's 58 'nature monuments' are mostly protected trees, including 1500- to 2000-year-old cedars in Finike, southwest of Antalya; a 1000-year-old plane tree in İstanbul; and a 700-year-old juniper at 2100m near Gümüşhane, south of Trabzon.

POPULAR PARKS

The following are among the most popular with foreign visitors to Turkey. Visit the Turkish **Ministry of Culture and Tourism** (www.turizm.gov.tr) for more information.

Gallipoli National Historic Park (p148) Historic battlefield sites on a gloriously unspoilt peninsula surrounded by coves.

Göreme National Park (p449) An extraordinary landscape of gorges and fairy chimneys.

Küre Dağları National Park (Kaçkar Mountain National Park; p418) Stunning high mountain ranges popular with trekkers.

Köprülü Kanyon National Park (Bridge Canyon National Park; p364) Dramatic canyon with spectacular scenery and white-water rafting facilities.

Nemrut Dağı National Park (Mt Nemrut National Park; p572) Pre-Roman stone heads surmounting a man-made mound with wonderful views.

Saklıkent National Park (p332) Famous for its 18km-long gorge.

TAKE ONLY PHOTOS, LEAVE ONLY FOOTPRINTS

Tourism is not the only thing that has had a damaging impact on the Turkish environment, but it is certainly one of them. So what can you do to help?

» Don't buy coral or seashells, no matter how lovely they look in a necklace.

» Avoid using plastic bags, although in Turkey these are occasionally made from recycled material.

» Tourists are not the worst offenders when it comes to abandoned rubbish; nonetheless, never drop litter anywhere.

» Complain to the captain if you think your excursion boat is discharging sewage into the sea or dropping anchor in an environmentally sensitive area. Even better, complain to **Greenpeace Mediterranean** (0212-292 7619; www.greenpeace.org/mediterranean).

» Try to stay in accommodation that has been designed with some thought for its surroundings.

» Refrain from purchasing water in plastic bottles wherever possible. Water in glass bottles is served in many Turkish restaurants, and you can buy filtration systems from home before your departure. At the very least, buy the 5L bottles of water, which you can keep in your hotel room and use to fill a reusable smaller bottle for carrying with you.

Black Sea town of Sinop, with a vocal opponent in the community-run **Sinop is Ours** (www.sinopbizim.org). The country's seismic vulnerabilities increase the risk posed by nuclear reactors.

The government says the three plants will aid economic growth and and reduce dependency on natural-gas supplies from Russia and Iran. Demand for electricity is growing by about 8% a year in Turkey, which only has significant domestic supplies of coal. Construction is set to begin at Akkuyu in 2013, with the first of four reactors operational by 2018.

Experts also claim that sharing a border with Iran (which has a nuclear-power program) has pushed Turkey to develop some nuclear capacity. In 2010 Turkey and Brazil tried to help Iran avoid further international sanctions by negotiating a deal in which Iran would outsource its uranium enrichment to Turkey.

Privatisation of the Turkish energy sector picked up pace in 2008 following legislation to encourage investment, with incentives offered to companies bringing facilities online by 2012.

Lauded German-Turkish director Fatih Akin's *Polluting Paradise* tells the heartbreaking story of his father's village, which was wrecked by a waste landfill site.

The Bosphorus

One of the biggest environmental challenges facing Turkey is the threat from maritime traffic along the Bosphorus. The 1936 Montreux Convention decreed that, although Turkey has sovereignty over the strait, it must permit the free passage of shipping through it. At that time, perhaps a few thousand ships a year passed through, but this has risen to over 45,000 vessels annually; around 10% are tankers, which carry over 100 million tons of hazardous substances through the strait every year.

There have already been serious accidents, such as the 1979 *Independenta* collision with another vessel, which killed 43 people and spilt and burnt some 95,000 tonnes of oil (around 2½ times the amount spilt by the famous *Exxon Valdez*). Following the Gulf of Mexico disaster, the Turkish government renewed its efforts to find alternative routes for oil transportation. Its ambitious plans include a US$12 billion canal to divert tankers, which would see the creation of two new cities by the Bosphorus. There is already an 1800km-long pipeline between Baku,

Azerbaijan and the Turkish eastern Mediterranean port of Ceyhan, and another pipeline is planned between Samsun and Ceyhan.

Construction & Dams

Building development is taking a terrible toll on the environment, especially along the Aegean and Mediterranean coasts. Spots such as Kuşadası and Marmaris, once pleasant fishing villages, have been near swamped by urban sprawl and are in danger of losing all appeal. Worse still, much of the development is only used during the warmer months, placing intensive strains on the infrastructure. The number of secluded bays glimpsed on the blue voyage cruises has plummeted, and the development continues to spread: new marinas have appeared in İzmir and Sığacık, in the north Aegean, in recent years.

Short of water and electricity, Turkey is one of the world's major builders of dams. There are already more than 600 dams and many more on the way, with controversy surrounding proposed developments. The gigantic Southeast Anatolia Project, known as GAP, is one of Turkey's major construction efforts. Harnessing the headwaters of the Tigris and Euphrates Rivers, it's creating a potential political time bomb, causing friction with the arid countries downstream that also depend on this water. Georgia recently added to Iraq and Syria's protests, and a UN report said the building is in danger of violating human rights.

In 2008, Hasankeyf featured on the World Monuments Watch list of the planet's 100 most endangered sites, thanks to the İlisu Dam Project's plans to drown the historic southeastern town. This is now slated for 2015 and work has begun on a replacement for the town, which was a Silk Road commercial centre on the border of Anatolia and Mesopotamia. Organised opposition is ongoing, but the ruins look set to vanish, along with their atmospheric setting on the Tigris River and dozens of villages. Up to 70,000 people will be displaced, many of them Kurds and minority groups.

The ruins of the world's oldest-known spa settlement, Allianoi, disappeared beneath the waters of the Yortanlı Dam in 2011. A last-ditch

Despite its many environmental shortcomings, Turkey is doing well at beach cleanliness, with 352 beaches and 19 marinas qualifying for Blue Flag status. Visit www.blueflag.org for the complete list.

EU ACCESSION

Turkey's intended accession to the EU is thankfully forcing it to lift its environmental standards. The country has started improving its environmental practices and laws, and even ratified the Kyoto Protocol in 2009.

The government aims to harmonise all environmental legislation with the EU, for example adopting the 'polluter pays' policy. The ambitious project could cost some €70 billion, although the European Commission believes Turkey will eventually recoup €120 billion from the investment. In 2009, Turkey received the first-ever loan given by the World Bank's Clean Technology Fund, amounting to US$250 million.

Prime Minister Erdoğan has displayed an ambivalent attitude towards environmentalists, and myriad challenges face his Ministries of Environment and Urbanisation, and Forest and Water Affairs. Priorities include waste-water disposal and building water treatment facilities. Food safety has been a major stumbling block, although EU accession talks covering this area began in 2010, following the opening of the environment chapter the previous year. Other key issues include soil erosion, deforestation and degradation of biodiversity.

In 2011, the European Commission reported that Turkey had made good progress on waste management, but limited progress in areas including air and water quality, industrial pollution control and risk management, and climate change. It reported no progress on nature protection.

appeal from the tenor Plácido Domingo, president of the European cultural heritage federation Europa Nostra, failed to save the 2nd-century Roman spa near Bergama.

Other Issues

Blue recycling bins are an increasingly common sight on the streets of İstanbul, but the government still has a long way to go in terms of educating its citizens and businesses. The head of a parliamentary environmental commission said in 2010 that Turkish municipalities were improperly disposing of more than 60% of urban waste.

Many feel the government often shuts the gate after the horse has bolted. In early 2006, fines for dumping toxic waste increased from a maximum of €4500 to €1.5 million – legislative changes that were announced only after barrels of toxic waste were discovered in empty lots around İstanbul. One of the worst-hit places was Dilovası, with deaths from cancer nearly three times the world average, and a report saying it should be evacuated and labelled a medical disaster area. Neither happened, and the over-industrialised area on the Sea of Marmara remains a reminder of the country's environmental shortcomings.

Southwest Turkey, especially around Köyceğiz, is one of the last remaining sources of *Liquidambar orientalis* (frankincense trees). Their resin, once used by the Egyptians in embalming, is exported for use in perfume and incense.

Survival Guide

Directory A–Z

Accommodation

Turkey has accommodation options to suit all budgets, with concentrations of good, value-for-money hotels, pensions and hostels in places most visited by independent travellers, such as İstanbul and Cappadocia.

Rooms are discounted by about 20% during the low season (October to April), but not during the Christmas and Easter periods and major Islamic holidays. Places within easy reach of İstanbul and Ankara may hike up their prices during summer weekends.

If you plan to stay a week or more in a coastal resort, check package-holiday deals. British, German and French tour companies in particular often offer money-saving flight-and-accommodation packages to the South Aegean and Mediterranean.

Accommodation options in more Westernised spots such as İstanbul often quote tariffs in euros as well as (or instead of) lira. Accommodation in less-touristy locations generally quote in lira. Many places will accept euro (or even US dollars in İstanbul). We've used the currency quoted by the business being reviewed.

Sleeping options generally have a website where reservations can be made.

Many pensions operate in informal chains, referring travellers from one to another. If you've enjoyed staying in a place, you will probably enjoy its owner's recommendations, but stay firm and try not to sign up to anything sight unseen.

Price Ranges

Ranges are based on the cost of a double room. The rates quoted in this book are for high season (June to August, apart from İstanbul, where high season is April, May, September and October). Unless otherwise mentioned, they include tax (KDV), an en suite and breakfast. Listings are ordered by preference.

İstanbul

€   less than €70
€€   €70 to €180
€€€   more than €180

Rest of Turkey

€   less than ₺80
€€   ₺80 to ₺170
€€€   more than ₺170

Apartments

» Good value for money, especially for families and small groups.

» Outside İstanbul and a few Aegean and Mediterranean locations, apartments for holiday rentals are often thin on the ground.

» In coastal spots such as Kaş, Antalya and the Bodrum Peninsula, *emlakçı* (real-estate agents) hold lists of available holiday rentals.

» *Emlakçı* are used to dealing with foreigners.

WEBSITES

» www.holidaylettings.co.uk
» www.ownersdirect.co.uk
» www.perfectplaces.com
» www.turkeyrenting.com
» www.vrbo.com

Camping

» Most camping facilities are along the coasts.

» Usually privately run.

» Camping facilities fairly rare inland, with the exception of Cappadocia and Nemrut Dağı National Park.

» Best facilities inland are often on Orman Dinlenme Yeri (Forestry Department land); you usually need your own transport to reach these.

» Pensions and hostels often let you camp on their grounds and use their facilities for a fee.

» Camping outside official sites is often more hassle than it's worth:

• The police may drop by to check you out and possibly move you on.

BOOK YOUR STAY ONLINE

For more accommodation reviews by Lonely Planet authors, check out http://hotels.lonelyplanet.com. You'll find independent reviews, as well as recommendations on the best places to stay. Best of all, you can book online.

- Out east, there are wolves in the wild; be wary, and don't leave food and rubbish outside your tent.
- Also look out for Kangal dogs.
- Female travellers should stick to official sites and camp where there are plenty of people, especially out east.

Hostels

» There are plenty of hostels with dormitories in popular destinations.

» Dorm beds usually about ₺20 to ₺45 per night.

» Hostelling International members in İstanbul, Cappadocia and the Aegean and Turquoise Coast areas.

Hotels

BUDGET

» Good, inexpensive beds are readily available in most cities and resort towns.

» Difficult places to find good cheap rooms include İstanbul, Ankara, İzmir and package-holiday resort towns such as Alanya and Çeşme.

» The cheapest hotels typically charge from around ₺35/40 for a single room without/with bathroom, including breakfast.

» The cheapest hotels are mostly used by working-class Turkish men; not suitable for solo women.

MIDRANGE

» One- and two-star hotels are less oppressively masculine in atmosphere, even when clientele is mainly male.

» Such hotels charge around ₺80 to ₺125 for an en-suite double, including breakfast.

» Three-star hotels generally used to catering for female travellers.

» Hotels in more traditional towns normally offer only Turkish TV, Turkish breakfast and none of the 'extras' commonplace in pensions.

» In many midrange hotels, a maid will not make your bed and tidy your room unless you ask in reception or hang the sign on the handle.

» Prices should be displayed in reception.

» You should never pay more than the prices on display, and will often be charged less.

» Often you will be able to haggle.

» Unmarried foreign couples don't usually have problems sharing rooms.

» Out east, couples are often given a twin room even if they ask for a double.

» Some establishments refuse to accept an unmarried couple when one of the parties is Turkish.

» The cheaper the hotel, and the more remote the location, the more conservative its management tends to be.

BOUTIQUE HOTELS

» Old Ottoman mansions, caravanserais and other historic buildings refurbished, or completely rebuilt, as hotels.

» Equipped with all mod-cons and bags of character.

» Most in the midrange and top-end price brackets.

» Many reviewed at **Small Hotels** (www.boutiquesmall hotels.com).

Pensions

In destinations popular with travellers you'll find *pansiyons* (pensions): simple, family-run guest houses, where you can get a good, clean single/double from around ₺40/70. Many also have triple and quadruple rooms. Be sure to remove your shoes when you enter.

In touristy areas in particular, the advantages of staying in a pension, as opposed to a cheap hotel, include:

» a choice of simple meals

» book exchange

» laundry service

» international TV channels

» staff who speak at least one foreign language.

EV PANSIYONU

In a few places, old-fashioned *ev pansiyonu* (pension in a private home) survive. These are simply rooms in a family house that are let to visitors at busy times of the year. They do not normally advertise their existence in a formal way; ask locals where to find them and look out for *kiralık oda* (room for rent) signs. English is rarely spoken by the proprietors, so some knowledge of Turkish would be helpful.

TREE HOUSES

Olympos, on the Teke peninsula, is famous for its 'tree houses': rough-and-ready shelters in forested settings near the beach. The success of these backpacker hangouts has spawned imitators elsewhere in the western Mediterranean, for example in nearby Çıralı and Saklıkent Gorge.

Touts

In smaller tourist towns such as Selçuk, touts may approach you as you step from a bus and offer you accommodation. Some may string you a line about the pension you're looking for, in the hope

---

NO VACANCY

Along the Aegean, Mediterranean and Black Sea coasts, and in parts of Cappadocia, the majority of hotels, pensions and camping grounds close roughly from mid-October to late April. Before travelling to those regions in the low season, check if there is accommodation available.

of reeling you in and getting a commission from another pension. Taxi drivers also play this game.

It's generally best to politely decline these offers, but if you're on a budget, touts sometimes work for newly opened establishments offering cheap rates. Before they take you to the pension, establish that you're only looking and are under no obligation to stay.

Business Hours

Most museums close on Monday; from April to October, they shut 1½ to two hours later than usual. The following also experience seasonal variation: a bar is likely to stay open later in summer than in winter; and tourist offices in popular locations open for longer hours and at weekends during summer.

The working day shortens during the holy month of Ramazan, which currently falls during summer. More Islamic cities such as Konya and Kayseri virtually shut down during noon prayers on Friday (the Muslim sabbath); apart from that, Friday is a normal working day.

Information 8.30am to noon and 1.30pm to 5pm Monday to Friday

Eating breakfast 7.30am to 10am, lunch noon to 2.30pm, dinner 7.30pm to 10pm

Drinking 4pm to late

Nightclubs 11pm to late

Shopping 9am to 6pm Monday to Friday (longer in tourist areas and big cities – including weekend opening)

Government departments, offices and banks 8.30am to noon and 1.30pm to 5pm Monday to Friday

Customs Regulations

Turkish Ministry of Customs & Trade (www.gumruk.gov.tr) has more information.

Imports

Items valued over €1500 will be liable for import duty. Jewellery valued over US$15,000 should be declared, to ensure you can take it out when you leave. Goods including the following can be imported duty-free:

» 600 cigarettes
» 200g of tobacco
» 2kg of coffee, tea, chocolate or sugar products
» 1L of spirits (over 22%)
» 2L of wine and beer (under 22%)
» 600mL of different types of perfume
» one camera with five films
» one video camera with 10 tapes
» one laptop
» one GSM mobile phone
» one GPS
» unlimited currency
» souvenirs/gifts worth up to €430 (€150 if aged under 15).

Exports

» Buying and exporting genuine antiquities is illegal.
» Carpet shops should be able to provide a form certifying that your purchase is not an antiquity.
» Ask for advice from vendors you buy from.
» Keep receipts and paperwork.

Discount Cards

The Museum Pass İstanbul (p54) offers a possible ₺36 saving on entry to the city's major sights, and allows holders to skip admission

PRACTICALITIES

» Turkey uses the metric system for weights and measures.
» Electrical current is 230V AC, 50Hz.
» You can buy plug adaptors at most electrical shops.
» Take a surge protector.
» A universal AC adaptor is also a good investment.
» *Today's Zaman* (www.todayszaman.com) is an English-language newspaper. *Hürriyet Daily News* (www.hurriyetdailynews.com) and *Sabah* (www.sabahenglish.com) have English editions.
» *Journal of Turkish Weekly* (www.turkishweekly.net), published by the Ankara-based International Strategic Research Organization, carries news and commentary in English.
» *Turkishpress.com* (http://turkishpress.com) is an American site covering Turkish news.
» *Cornucopia* (www.cornucopia.net) is a glossy magazine in English about Turkey.
» Turkish Airlines' in-flight monthly, *Skylife* (www.thy.com), is worth a read.
» TRT broadcasts news daily, in languages including English, on radio and at www.trt-world.com.
» Digiturk offers numerous Turkish and international TV channels.

queues. Rechargeable travel card the İstanbulkart (p129) offers savings on the city's public transport.

The following are available in Turkey but easier to get in your home country:

International Student Identity Card (ISIC; www .isic.org) Discounts on accommodation, eating, entertainment, shopping and transport. Applicants need documents including a matriculation card or letter from your college or university confirming they are a student.

These cards offer similar benefits to ISIC, but far fewer businesses accept them:

International Youth Travel Card (IYTC; http://tinyurl .com/25tlbv7) Applicants need a passport or similar showing they are aged under 26.

International Teacher Identity Card (ITIC; http:// tinyurl.com/25tlbv7) Applicants need documents including a letter from an educational establishment stating that they work there for a minimum of 18 hours per week and one academic year.

Embassies & Consulates

» Most embassies and consulates in Turkey open from 8am or 9am to noon Monday to Friday, then after lunch until 5pm or 6pm for people to pick up visas.

» Embassies of some Muslim countries may open Sunday to Thursday.

» To ask the way to an embassy, say: '[Country] *başkonsolosluğu nerede?*'

» For details on getting visas to neighbouring countries, see Transport.

» Visit Turkey's **Ministry of Foreign Affairs** (www.mfa .gov.tr) website for details of other countries' missions.

» Embassies are generally in Ankara.

» There are consulates in other Turkish cities (check the websites listed in the table on p654 for their locations and contact details).

Electricity

230V/50Hz

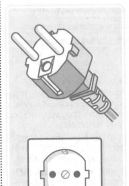

230V/50Hz

Food

This book uses the following price ranges, based on the cost of a main course.

İstanbul

€	less than ₺15
€€	₺15 to ₺25
€€€	more than ₺25

Rest of Turkey

€	less than ₺9
€€	₺9 to ₺17.50
€€€	more than ₺17.50

Gay & Lesbian Travellers

Homosexuality is legal in Turkey and attitudes are changing, but prejudice remains strong and there are sporadic reports of violence towards gay people – the message is discretion.

İstanbul has a flourishing gay scene, as does Ankara. In other cities there may be a gay bar or two.

Kaos GL (www.kaosgl.com) Based in Ankara, the LGBT rights organisation publishes a gay-and-lesbian magazine and its website has news and information in English.

Lambda (☎212-245 7068; www.lambdaistanbul.org; 2nd fl, Tel Sokak; ◔3-8pm Sat & Sun) Lambda is the Turkish branch of the International Lesbian, Gay, Bisexual, Trans and Intersexual Association.

My Gay Web (www.mygay web.com) Travel section with Turkey recommendations.

Pride Travel Agency (www .turkey-gay-travel.com) Gay-friendly travel agent, with useful links on the website.

Insurance

» A policy covering theft, loss and medical expenses is recommended.

» Huge variety of policies available; check small print.

» Some policies exclude 'dangerous activities', which can include scuba diving, motorcycling and even hiking.

» Some policies may not cover you if you travel to regions of the country where your government warns against travel.

EMBASSIES IN ANKARA

EMBASSY	CONTACT DETAILS	ADDRESS
Armenia	Contact Russian embassy; www.mfa.am/en	
Australia	0312-459 9500; www.turkey.embassy.gov.au	7th fl, Uğur Mumcu Caddesi 88, Gaziosmanpaşa
Azerbaijan	0312-491 1681; www.azembassy.org.tr	Diplomatik Site, Bakü Sokak 1, Oran
Bulgaria	0312-467 2071; www.bulgaria.bg/en/	Atatürk Bulvarı 124, Kavaklıdere
Canada	0312-409 2700; www.canadainternational.gc.ca	Cinnah Caddesi 58, Çankaya
France	0312-455 4545; www.ambafrance-tr.org	Paris Caddesi 70, Kavaklıdere
Georgia	0312-491 8030; www.turkey.mfa.gov.ge	Diplomatik Site, Kılıç Ali Sokak 12, Oran
Germany	0312-455 5100; www.ankara.diplo.de	Atatürk Bulvarı 114, Kavaklıdere
Greece	0312-448 0873; www.mfa.gr/ankara	Zia Ur Rahman Caddesi 9-11, Gaziosmanpaşa
Iran	0312-468 2821; www.mfa.gov.ir	Tehran Caddesi 10, Kavaklıdere
Iraq	0312-468 7421; http://iraqmissions.hostinguk.com	Turan Emeksiz Sokak 11, Gaziosmanpaşa
Ireland	0312-459 1000; www.embassyofireland.org.tr	3rd fl, MNG Building, Uğur Mumcu Caddesi 88, Gaziosmanpaşa
Netherlands	0312-409 1800; http://turkije.nlambassade.org	Hollanda Caddesi 5, Yıldız
New Zealand	0312-446 3333; www.nzembassy.com/turkey	Kizkulesi Sokak 11, Gaziosmanpaşa
Russia	0312-439 2122; www.turkey.mid.ru	Karyağdı Sokak 5, Çankaya
Syria	0312-440 9657; http://tinyurl.com/6ywt8a	Sedat Simavi Sokak 40, Çankaya
UK	0312-455 3344; http://ukinturkey.fco.gov.uk	Şehit Ersan Caddesi 46a, Çankaya
USA	0312-455 5555; http://turkey.usembassy.gov	Atatürk Bulvarı 110, Kavaklıdere

» If you cancel your trip on the advice of an official warning against travel, your insurer may not cover you.

» Look into whether your regular health insurance and motor insurance will cover you in Turkey (see p678 and p673).

» Worldwide travel insurance is available at www.lonelyplanet.com/bookings/insurance.do. You can buy, extend and claim online anytime, even if you're already on the road.

Internet Access

» Throughout Turkey, the majority of accommodation options of all standards offer wi-fi.

» Wi-fi networks are also found at locations from travel agencies and carpet shops to otogars (bus stations) and ferry terminals.

» In this book, the wi-fi access icon (🛜) indicates that a business offers a network.

» Internet access icon (@) indicates that an establishment provides a computer with internet access for guest use.

Internet Cafes

» Internet cafes are widespread, although declining with the proliferation of wi-fi and hand-held devices.

» Typically open roughly from 9am until midnight, and charge around ₺1.50 an hour (İstanbul ₺3).

» Connection speeds vary, but generally fast.

» Viruses rife.

» The best cafes have English keyboards.

» Some cafes have Turkish keyboards, on which 'ı' occupies the position held by 'i' on English keyboards.

» On Turkish keyboards, create the '@' symbol by holding down the 'q' and ALT keys at the same time.

Language Courses

İstanbul is the most popular place to learn Turkish, though there are also courses in Ankara, İzmir and a few other spots across the country. Try to sit in on a class before you commit, as the quality of your experience definitely depends on the teacher and your classmates.

Private tuition is more expensive, but tutors often advertise at http://istanbul .en.craigslist.com.tr and in the classifieds section of the expat website www.mymerh aba.com.

Many books are available. *Teach Yourself Turkish* by David and Asuman Çelen Pollard is recommended; *Teach Yourself Complete Turkish* is a more recent book by the same authors.

Schools include the following. Tömer and Dilmer are the most popular, but both have their detractors as well as fans.

Dilmer (www.dilmer.com) Located near İstanbul's Taksim Meydanı, its courses last from one to 12 weeks, catering to seven levels of proficiency (€50 to €384).

EFINST Turkish Centre (www.turkishlesson.com) The school in Levent, İstanbul, offers options including part-time 7½- to 12-week courses (€578), private lessons (from €42) and packages combining study with excursions.

Spoken Turkish (www.spo kenenglishtr.com) Conveniently located on İstanbul's İstiklal Caddesi (as well as other parts of the city), but relatively untested, it offers part-time courses lasting four hours a week.

Tömer (www.tomer.com.tr) Affiliated with Ankara University, and with branches throughout the country, Tömer offers four- and eight-week courses (₺420 and ₺504).

Legal Matters

Technically, you should carry your passport at all times. There have been cases of police stopping foreigners and holding them until someone brings their passport. In practice, you may prefer to carry a photocopy.

There are laws against lese-majesty (p657), buying and smuggling antiquities, and illegal drugs. Turkish jails are not places where you want to spend any time.

Maps

Maps are widely available at tourist offices and bookshops, although quality maps are hard to find. In İstanbul try on İstiklal Caddesi; online, check Amazon.com and Tulumba.com.

Mep Medya's city and regional maps are recommended, as are its touring maps including the following:

» Türkiye Karayolları Haritası (1:1,200,000), a sheet map of the whole country.

» Adım Adım Türkiye Yol Atlası (Step by Step Turkey Road Atlas; 1:400,000).

Money

Turkey's currency is the Türk Lirası (Turkish lira; ₺). The lira comes in notes of five, 10, 20, 50, 100 and 200, and coins of one, five, 10, 25 and 50 kuruş and one lira.

After decades of rampant inflation, the lira is now stable. The Yeni Türk Lirası (new Turkish lira; Y₺) was used between 2005 and 2008 as an anti-inflationary measure; watch out for people dumping their old-currency kuruş coins on you. Yeni Türk Lirası is no longer valid, but if you have some notes and coins left over from a previous visit to Turkey, branches of Ziraat bank will exchange your 'new' lira for the same value of today's lira.

Because hyperinflation led to Turkish lira having strings of zeros (six noughts were dropped from the notes in the transition to new lira in 2005), many people, confusingly, still work in thousands and millions. Don't be alarmed if you're buying items worth, say, ₺6 and the shopkeeper asks you for ₺6,000,000.

Lack of change is a constant problem; try to keep a supply of coins and small notes for minor payments. Post offices have Western Union counters.

ATMs

ATMs dispense Turkish lira, and occasionally euros and US dollars, to Visa, MasterCard, Cirrus and Maestro card holders. Look for these logos on machines, which are found in most towns. Machines generally offer instructions in foreign languages including English.

It's possible to get around Turkey using only ATMs if you draw out money in the towns to tide you through the villages that don't have them. Also keep some cash in reserve for the inevitable day when the machine throws a wobbly. If your card is swallowed by a stand-alone ATM booth, it may be tricky to get it back. The booths are often run by franchisees rather than by the banks themselves.

Credit Cards

Visa and MasterCard are widely accepted by hotels, shops and restaurants, although often not by pensions and local restaurants outside the main tourist areas. You can also get cash advances on these cards. Amex is less commonly accepted outside top-end establishments. Inform your credit-card provider of your travel plans; otherwise, transactions may be stopped, as credit-card fraud does happen in Turkey.

Foreign Currencies

Euros and US dollars are the most readily accepted foreign currencies. Foreign currencies are accepted in shops, hotels and restaurants in many tourist areas, and taxi drivers will take them for big journeys.

Moneychangers

The Turkish lira is weak against Western currencies,

THE ART OF BARGAINING

Traditionally, when customers enter a Turkish shop to make a significant purchase, they're offered a comfortable seat and a drink (çay, coffee or a soft drink). There is some general chitchat, then discussion of the shop's goods in general, then of the customer's tastes, preferences and requirements. Finally, a number of items are displayed for the customer's inspection.

The customer asks the price; the shop owner gives it; the customer looks doubtful and makes a counter-offer 25% to 50% lower. This procedure goes back and forth several times before a price acceptable to both parties is arrived at. It's considered bad form to haggle over a price, come to an agreement, and then change your mind.

If you can't agree on a price, it's perfectly acceptable to say goodbye and walk out of the shop. In fact, walking out is one of the best ways to test the authenticity of the last offer. If shopkeepers know you can find the item elsewhere for less, they'll probably call after you and drop their price. Even if they don't stop you, there's nothing to prevent you from returning later and buying the item for what they quoted.

To bargain effectively you must be prepared to take your time, and you must know something about the items in question, not to mention their market price. The best way to do this is to look at similar goods in several shops, asking prices but not making counter-offers. Always stay good-humoured and polite when you are bargaining – if you do this the shopkeeper will too. When bargaining you can often get a discount by offering to buy several items at once, by paying in a strong major currency, or by paying in cash.

If you don't have sufficient time to shop around, follow the age-old rule: find something you like at a price you're willing to pay, buy it, enjoy it, and don't worry about whether or not you received the world's lowest price.

In general, you shouldn't bargain in food shops or over transport costs. Outside tourist areas, hotels may expect to 'negotiate' the room price with you. In tourist areas pension owners are usually fairly clear about their prices, although if you're travelling in winter or staying a long time it's worth asking about *indirim* (discounts).

and you will probably get a better exchange rate in Turkey than elsewhere. The lira is virtually worthless outside Turkey, so make sure you spend it all before leaving.

US dollars and euros are the easiest currencies to change, although many exchange offices and banks will change other major currencies such as UK pounds and Japanese yen.

You'll get better rates at exchange offices, which often don't charge commission, than at banks. Exchange offices operate in tourist and market areas, with better rates often found in the latter, and some post offices (PTTs), shops and hotels. They generally keep longer hours than banks.

Banks are more likely to change minor currencies, although they tend to make heavy weather of it. Turkey has no black market.

Tipping

Turkey is fairly European in its approach to tipping and you won't be pestered with demands for baksheesh as elsewhere in the Middle East.

Some more expensive restaurants automatically add the *servis ücreti* (service charge) to your bill, although there's no guarantee this goes to the staff.

For more on tipping, see p19.

Travellers Cheques

Banks, shops and hotels usually see it as a burden to have to change travellers cheques, and will either try to persuade you to go elsewhere or charge you a premium for the service. If you must use travellers cheques and you do have to change them, try one of the major banks.

Photography

People in Turkey are generally receptive to having their photo taken. The major exception is when they are praying or performing other religious activities. As in most countries, do not take photos of military sites, airfields, police stations and so on, as it could arouse the authorities' suspicions.

Post

Turkish *postanes* (post offices) are indicated by black-on-yellow 'PTT' signs. Most post offices follow the hours we've listed (p652), but a few offices in major cities have extended opening hours.

Letters take between one and several weeks to get to/from Turkey. Postcards sent abroad cost about ₺2.

When posting letters, the *yurtdışı* slot is for mail to foreign countries, *yurtiçi* for mail to other Turkish cities, and *şehiriçi* for local mail. Visit www.ptt.gov.tr for more information.

Parcels

If you are shipping something from Turkey, don't close your parcel before it has been inspected by a customs official. Take packing and wrapping materials with you to the post office.

Airmail tariffs are typically about ₺40 for the first kilogram, with an additional charge for every extra kilogram (typically ₺5 to Europe).

Parcels take months to arrive.

International couriers including DHL also operate in Turkey.

Public Holidays

New Year's Day (Yılbaşı; 1 January)

National Sovereignty & Children's Day (Ulusal Egemenlik ve Çocuk Günü; 23 April) Commemorates the first meeting of the Turkish Grand National Assembly in 1920.

International Workers' Day (May Day; 1 May) Reinstated in 2010, the holiday features marches through İstanbul. Thousands gather around Taksim Meydanı, where a massacre occured on 1 May 1977 during a period of political violence.

Youth & Sports Day (Gençlik ve Spor Günü; 19 May) Dedicated to Atatürk and the youth of the republic.

Şeker Bayramı (Sweets Holiday; see table) Also known as Ramazan Bayramı, it celebrates the end of Ramazan.

Victory Day (Zafer Bayramı; 30 August) Commemorates the republican army's victory over the invading Greek army at Dumlupınar during the War of Independence.

Kurban Bayramı (Festival of the Sacrifice; see table) The most important holiday of the year, it marks İbrahim's near-sacrifice of İsmael on Mt Moriah (Koran, Sura 37; Genesis 22). Transport and accommodation fill up fast.

Republic Day (Cumhuriyet Bayramı; 28 to 29 October) Commemorates the proclamation of the republic by Atatürk in 1923.

Safe Travel

Although Turkey is by no means a dangerous country to visit, it's always wise to be a little cautious, especially if you're travelling alone.

Turkey is not a safety-conscious country: holes in pavements go unmended; precipitous drops go unguarded; safety belts are not always worn; lifeguards on beaches are rare; dolmuş (minibus) drivers negotiate bends while counting out change.

The two areas to be most cautious are İstanbul, where various scams operate, and southeastern Anatolia, where the PKK (Kurdistan Workers' Party) stepped up its terrorist activities in 2010.

The Kurdish issue occasionally also leads to violence in western Turkey; in 2010, the PKK's commander vowed to attack cities and resorts in the west of the country, and a suicide bomber injured 32 people on Taksim Meydanı, İstanbul.

Sexual assaults have occurred against travellers of both sexes in hotels in central and eastern Anatolia. Make enquiries, check forums and do a little research in advance if you are travelling alone or heading off the beaten track.

See p17 for emergency numbers.

Flies & Mosquitoes

In high summer, mosquitoes are troublesome even in İstanbul; they can make a stay along the coast a nightmare. Some hotel rooms come equipped with nets and/or plug-in bugbusters, but it's a good idea to bring some insect repellent and mosquito coils.

Lese-Majesty

The laws against insulting, defaming or making light of Atatürk, the Turkish flag, the Turkish people, the Turkish Republic and so on are taken very seriously. Even if derogatory remarks were never made, Turks have been

MAJOR ISLAMIC HOLIDAYS

The rhythms of Islamic practice are tied to the lunar calendar, which is slightly shorter than its Gregorian equivalent, so the Muslim calendar begins around 11 days earlier each year. The following dates are approximate.

ISLAMIC YEAR	NEW YEAR	PROPHET'S BIRTHDAY	RAMAZAN	ŞEKER BAYRAMI	KURBAN BAYRAMI
1434	16 Nov 2012	25 Jan 2013	10 July 2013	8 Aug 2013	15 Oct 2013
1435	5 Nov 2013	14 Jan 2014	29 Jun 2014	28 Jul 2014	4 Oct 2014
1436	25 Oct 2014	3 Jan 2015	18 Jun 2015	17 Jul 2015	23 Sep 2015

known to claim they were in the heat of a quarrel, which is enough to get the foreigner carted off to jail.

Scams & Druggings

In a notorious İstanbul scam, normally targeted at single men, a pleasant local guy befriends you in the street and takes you to a bar. After a few drinks, and possibly the attention of some ladies, to whom you offer drinks, the bill arrives. The prices are astronomical and the proprietors can produce a menu showing the same prices. If you don't have enough cash, you'll be frogmarched to the nearest ATM. If this happens to you, report it to the tourist police; some travellers have taken the police back to the bar and received a refund.

A less common variation on this trick involves the traveller having their drink spiked and waking up in an unexpected place with their belongings, right down to their shoes, missing – or worse.

Single men should not accept invitations from unknown folk in large cities without sizing the situation up carefully. You could invite your new-found friends to a bar of *your* choice; if they're not keen to go, chances are they are shady characters.

The spiking scam has also been reported on overnight trains, with passengers getting robbed. Turks are often genuinely sociable and generous travelling companions, but be cautious about accepting food and drinks from people you are not 100% sure about.

ANTIQUITIES
Do not buy coins or other artefacts offered to you by touts at ancient sites such as Ephesus and Perge. It is a serious crime here, punishable by long prison terms, and the touts are likely in cahoots with the local policemen.

SHOE CLEANERS
In Sultanahmet, İstanbul, if a shoe cleaner walking in front of you drops his brush, don't pick it up. He will insist on giving you a 'free' clean in return, before demanding an extortionate fee.

VAT
Various VAT (value-added tax) scams operate. When buying a precious item such as a carpet, do not pay on the understanding that you will receive a VAT refund at the airport, even if you are asked to sign an official-looking Turkish document. The document may be a statement that you have received your refund, leaving you out of pocket when you reach the airport.

Some shops have signs indicating that they offer tax-free shopping. In most cases, the best policy is to assume you will not receive a refund and pay a price that you are happy with. Do not sign any paperwork unless you can understand it and, if you suspect a vendor of underhand dealings, take your business elsewhere.

Smoking

Turks love smoking and there's even a joke about the country's propensity for puffing: Who smokes more than a Turk? Two Turks.

Note that smoking in enclosed public spaces is banned, and punishable by a fine. Hotels, restaurants and bars are generally smoke-free, although bars sometimes relax the rules as the evening wears on. Off the tourist trail in budget and midrange hotels, the ban is enforced in public areas but more leniently in rooms, which often have ashtrays. Public transport is meant to be smoke-free, although taxi and bus drivers sometimes smoke at the wheel.

Traffic

As a pedestrian, note that Turks are aggressive, dangerous drivers; 'right of way'

doesn't compute with many motorists, despite the little green man on traffic lights. Give way to vehicles in all situations, even if you have to jump out of the way.

Telephone

Türk Telekom (www.turktelekom.com.tr) has a monopoly on phone services, and service is efficient if costly. Within Turkey, numbers starting with 444 don't require area codes and, wherever you call from, are charged at the local rate.

See p17 for important phone codes and numbers.

Kontörlü Telefon

If you only want to make one quick call, it's easiest to look for a booth with a sign saying *kontörlü telefon* (metered telephone). You make your call and the owner reads the meter and charges you accordingly. In touristy areas you can get rates as low as ₺0.50 per minute to Europe, the UK, the US and Australia.

Mobile Phones

» Turks adore mobile (*cep*, pocket) phones.

» Reception is excellent across most of Turkey.

» Mobile phone numbers start with a four-figure number beginning with 05.

» Major networks are **Turkcell** (www.turkcell.com.tr), the most comprehensive, **Vodafone** (www.vodafone.com.tr) and **Avea** (www.avea.com.tr).

» Service is often better in the smaller networks' stores, but Turkcell coverage is considerably better out east.

» A pay-as-you-go Turkcell SIM costs ₺30 (including ₺5 credit) or ₺40 (with ₺20 credit).

» Ask about Turkcell's tourist package (tinyurl.com/ckynd6j).

» An Avea SIM costs ₺29 (with ₺1 credit).

» You need to show your passport, and ensure the seller phones through or inputs your details to activate your account.

» SIM cards and *kontör* (credit) are widely available – at streetside booths and shops as well as mobile phone outlets.

» You can buy a local SIM and use it in your mobile from home, but the network detects and bars foreign phones within about two weeks to a month.

» To avoid barring, register your phone when you buy your Turkish SIM (or soon afterwards). At a certified cell phone shop, show your passport and fill out a short form declaring your phone is in Turkey. The process costs about ₺5. You can only declare one phone. The registered phone cannot be used with another Turkish SIM card for two years.

» You can pick up a second-hand mobile phone for about ₺50.

» Turkcell credit comes in cards with units of ₺5, ₺10, ₺15, ₺20 (*standart*), ₺30 (*avantaj*), ₺50 (*süper*), ₺95 (*süper* plus) and ₺180 (*mega*).

» The bigger the card, the better the rates you receive.

» The networks offer SMS bundles (for Turkey or abroad).

» Dial ☑*123# to check credit.

» For assistance in English, call ☑8090/9333 on Turk-cell/Avea.

» On Turkcell, reverse charges by dialling ☑*135*53, followed by the number, followed by #.

» On Turkcell, text NERE-DEYIM to ☑7777 or 2222 to receive a text with your approximate address, location in degrees longitude and latitude, and details of nearest emergency services.

Payphones & Phonecards

» Türk Telekom payphones can be found in most major public buildings and facilities,

TIME DIFFERENCES IN SUMMER

COUNTRY	CAPITAL CITY	DIFFERENCE FROM TURKEY (HR)
Australia	Canberra	+7
Canada	Ottawa	-7
France	Paris	-1
Germany	Berlin	-1
Japan	Tokyo	+6
Netherlands	Amsterdam	-1
New Zealand	Wellington	+9
UK	London	-2
USA	Washington DC	-7

public squares and transport terminals.

» International calls can be made from payphones.

» All payphones require cards that can be bought at telephone centres or, for a small mark-up, at some shops. Some payphones accept credit cards.

» Two types of card are in use: floppy cards with a magnetic strip, and Smart cards, embedded with a chip.

» The cards come in units of 50 (₺3.75), 100 (₺7.50), 200 (₺15) and 350 (₺19).

» Fifty units are sufficient for local calls and short intercity calls; 100 units are suitable for intercity or short international conversations.

INTERNATIONAL PHONECARDS

» Phonecards are the cheapest way to make international calls.

» Cards can be used on landlines, payphones and mobiles.

» As in other countries, you call the access number, key in the PIN on the card and dial away.

» Stick to reputable phone-cards such as IPC.

» With a ₺20 IPC card you can speak for about 200 minutes to Europe and beyond.

» Cards are widely available in the tourist areas of major cities, but can be difficult to find elsewhere.

Time

» Standard Turkish time is two hours ahead of GMT/UTC.

» During daylight saving (summer time), the clocks go forward one hour, and Turkey is three hours ahead of GMT/UTC.

» Daylight saving runs from the last Sunday in March until the last Sunday in October.

» Turkish bus timetables and so on use the 24-hour clock, but Turks rarely use it when speaking.

» Visit www.timeanddate.com for more on time differences.

Toilets

Most hotels have sit-down toilets, but hole-in-the-ground models – with a conventional flush, or a tap and jug – are common. Toilet paper is often unavailable, so keep some with you. Many taps are unmarked and reversed (cold on the left, hot on the right).

In most bathrooms you can flush paper down the

toilet, but in some places this may flood the premises. This is the case in much of İstanbul's old city. If you're not sure, play it safe and dispose of the paper in the bin provided. Signs often advise patrons to use the bin. This may seem slightly gross to the uninitiated, but many Turks (as well as people from other Middle Eastern and Asian countries) use a jet spray of water to clean themselves after defecating, applying paper to pat dry. The used paper is thus just damp, rather than soiled.

Public toilets can usually be found at major attractions and transport hubs; most require a payment of around 50 kuruş. In an emergency it's worth remembering that mosques have basic toilets (for both men and women).

Tourist Information

Every Turkish town of any size has an official tourist office run by the **Ministry of Culture and Tourism** (www.goturkey.com). Staff are often enthusiastic and helpful, particularly when it comes to supplying brochures, but may have sketchy knowledge of the area, and English speakers are rare. Tour operators, pension owners and so on are often better sources of information.

Visit the Ministry of Culture and Tourism website for details of Turkish tourist offices overseas.

Travellers with Disabilities

Turkey is a challenging destination for disabled (*engelli* or *özürlü*) travellers. Ramps, wide doorways and properly equipped toilets are rare, as are Braille and audio information at sights. Crossing most streets is particularly challenging, as everyone does so at their peril.

Airlines and the top hotels and resorts have some provision for wheelchair access, and ramps are beginning to appear elsewhere. Dropped kerb edges are being introduced to cities, especially in western Turkey – in places such as Edirne, Bursa and İzmir they seem to have been sensibly designed. Selçuk, Bodrum and Fethiye have been identified as relatively user-friendly towns for people with mobility problems because their pavements and roads are fairly level. In İstanbul, the tram and the metro are the most wheelchair-accessible forms of public transport.

Turkish Airlines offers 25% discounts on domestic flights to travellers with minimum 40% disability and their companions. Some Turkish trains have disabled-accessible lifts, toilets and other facilities.

Organisations

Businesses and resources serving travellers with disabilities include the following:

Access-Able (www.access-able.com) Includes disabled travellers' reports and a small list of tour and transport operators in Turkey.

Apparleyzed (www.apparelyzed.com) Features a report on facilities in İstanbul under 'Accessible Holidays'.

Hotel Rolli (www.hotel-rolli.de) Specially designed for wheelchair users.

Mephisto Voyage (www.mephistovoyage.com) Special tours for mobility-impaired people, utilising the Joëlette wheelchair system.

Physically Disabled Support Association (www.bedd.org.tr) Based in İstanbul.

SATH (www.sath.org) Society for Accessible Travel and Hospitality.

Visas

» Nationals of countries including Denmark, Finland, France, Germany, Israel, Italy, Japan, New Zealand, Sweden and Switzerland don't need a visa to visit Turkey for up to 90 days.

» Nationals of countries including Australia, Austria, Belgium, Canada, Ireland, the Netherlands, Norway, Portugal, Spain, the UK and USA need a visa, but it is just a sticker bought on arrival at the airport or border post.

» The above nationals are given a 90-day multiple-entry visa. In many cases it stipulates 'per period 180 days'. This means you can spend three months in Turkey within a six-month period; when you leave after three months, you can't re-enter for three months.

» Nationals of countries including Slovakia and South Africa are given a one-month multiple-entry visa on arrival.

» Check the **Ministry of Foreign Affairs** (www.mfa.gov.tr) for the latest information.

» The cost of the visa varies. At the time of writing, Americans paid US$20 (or €15), Australians and Canadians US$60 (or €45) and British citizens UK£10 (or €15 or US$20).

» At major entry points such as İstanbul Atatürk International Airport, it is possible to pay with Visa and MasterCard. Many land border crossings are less equipped, with no ATMs or money changing facilities. In all cases it is worth having the fee ready in one of the above currencies, in hard-currency cash. Try to have the correct amount as you may not receive change.

» No photos required.

Residency Permits

» There are various types of *ikamet tezkeresi* (residence permit).

» Apply at a *yabalcılar şube* (foreigners police/aliens department) soon after arrival.

» Plug http://yabancilar.iem.gov.tr (the foreign depart-

GOVERNMENT TRAVEL ADVICE

For the latest travel information log on to the following websites:

www.auswaertiges-amt.de German Federal Foreign Office

www.fco.gov.uk/travel UK Foreign and Commonwealth Office

www.minbuza.nl Dutch Ministry of Foreign Affairs

www.mofa.go.jp Japanese Ministry of Foreign Affairs

www.safetravel.govt.nz New Zealand Ministry of Foreign Affairs and Trade

www.smartraveller.gov.au Australian Department of Foreign Affairs and Trade

www.travel.state.gov US Department of State's Bureau of Consular Affairs

www.voyage.gc.ca Canadian Foreign Affairs and International Trade

ment of İstanbul's *emniyet müdürlüğü* – security police) into a website translator for more information.

» If you don't have a Turkish employer or spouse to support your application, you can get a permit for touristic purposes.

» Touristic permits are typically available for up to six months, costing from a few hundred lira including administrative charges. Different lengths are available to residents of different countries.

» To apply for a residence permit in İstanbul, make an appointment with the *emniyet müdürlüğü* in Fatih; visit http://tinyurl.com/28ck5vo. The process can be demoralising and assistance hard to come by; those working behind the desks in cities such as İzmir (www.izmir polis.gov.tr) are reputedly more helpful.

» Little English is spoken, so take a Turkish-speaking friend with you if possible.

» If your application is successful, you will be given a 'blue book', which is like a mini-passport.

» There are more details in Pat Yale's *A Handbook for Living in Turkey*, a comprehensive source of information for people planning to settle in Turkey.

» Websites mentioned under Work (p663) are also sources of (anecdotal) information and advice.

Working Visas

» Visit www.konsolosluk.gov. tr for information on obtaining a *çalışma izni* (work permit).

» Your Turkish employer should help you get the visa.

» If it's an employer such as a school or international company, they should be well versed in the process and can handle the majority of the paperwork.

» The visa can be obtained in Turkey or from a Turkish embassy or consulate.

Volunteering

Opportunities include everything from teaching to working on an organic farm.

Alternative Camp (www .ayder.org.tr) A volunteer-based organisation running camps for disabled people around the country.

Culture Routes in Turkey (tinyurl.com/d6fld8l) Opportunities to help waymark and repair its hiking trails such as the Lycian Way. A project on the Evliya Çelebi Way in Western Anatolia is coming up in 2013.

Gençlik Servisleri Merkezi (Youth Services Centre; www .gsm-youth.org) GSM runs voluntary work camps in Turkey.

Gençtur (http://genctur.com .tr) Organises voluntourism including farmstays, with offices in İstanbul and Berlin.

European Voluntary Service (http://tinyurl.com /8632hbt) Opportunities across Turkey for Europeans aged 18 to 30.

GoAbroad.com (www.volun teerabroad.com) A US-based company listing volunteering opportunities through international organisations in Turkey.

Ta Tu Ta (www.tatuta.org) Turkey's branch of WWOOF (Worldwide Opportunities on Organic Farms) organises work on dozens of organic farms around the country, where you can stay for free or for a small donation to cover costs. Readers have recommended Yüksel Demirer Farm (between Sivas and Giresun).

Women Travellers

Travelling in Turkey is straightforward for women, provided you follow some simple guidelines.

Accommodation

The cheapest hotels, as well as often being fleapits, are generally not suitable for lone women. Stick with family-oriented midrange hotels.

If conversation in the lobby grinds to a halt as you enter, the hotel is not likely to be a great place for a woman.

If there is a knock on your hotel door late at night, don't open it; in the morning, complain to the manager.

VISAS FOR NEIGHBOURING COUNTRIES

Visa regulations change, particularly for some of Turkey's Middle Eastern and Central Asian neighbours, so check www.lonelyplanet.com/thorntree and the following websites and publications for updates.

Armenia

At the time of writing, the Turkey–Armenia border was closed. Visas available at entry points. See Lonely Planet's *Georgia, Armenia & Azaerbaijan* guide, www.lonelyplanet .com/armenia and www.mfa.am/en.

Azerbaijan

Visas must be obtained in advance at Azerbaijani missions. Applying in your home country is a better option than in Turkey. See www.azerbaijan24.com, Lonely Planet's *Georgia, Armenia & Azerbaijan* guide, www.lonelyplanet.com/azerbaijan and www.mfa.gov.az.

Bulgaria

Citizens of nations including Australia, Canada, Israel, Japan, New Zealand, the US and EU countries can enter for up to 90 days without a visa. Bulgaria is set to join the Schengen Area in the coming years. See Lonely Planet's *Bulgaria* guide, www.lonelyplanet .com/bulgaria and www.mfa.bg.

Georgia

Most people (including those from Canada, Israel, Japan, EU countries, the US, Australia and New Zealand) can enter for up to 360 days without a visa. See Lonely Planet's *Georgia, Armenia & Azerbaijan* guide, www.lonelyplanet.com/georgia and www.mfa.gov.ge.

Greece

Greece is in the Schengen Area. See Lonely Planet's *Greece* or *Discover Greece* guide, www.lonelyplanet.com/greece and www.mfa.gr.

Iran

Most people need to apply in advance. Apply in your home country if possible. In Turkey, the Trabzon consulate is reportedly the most helpful, followed by the embassy in Ankara; the Erzurum and İstanbul consulates are not as helpful. See www.iranianvisa.com, Lonely Planet's *Iran* guide, www.lonelyplanet.com/iran and www.mfa.gov.ir.

Iraq

The Kurdish Regional Government issues its own tourist visa at the point of entry, good for travelling within Kurdish Iraq only. See Lonely Planet's *Middle East* guide, www.lonely planet.com/iraq and www.mofa.gov.iq.

Northern Cyprus

Citizens of countries including the USA, Canada, Australia, New Zealand and EU nations do not require a visa to enter the Turkish Republic of Northern Cyprus (TRNC) for up to three months. See Lonely Planet's *Cyprus* guide, www.lonelyplanet.com/cyprus, www .mfa.gov.cy and www.mfa.gov.tr.

Syria

At the time of writing, Westerners were not allowed into Syria. Visas were unavailable at the border and from Syrian missions. Westerners may be permitted entry once again if the situation in Syria improves. If this happens, visas will likely be obtainable through Syrian missions and not at the border. See Lonely Planet's *Syria & Lebanon* guide, www .lonelyplanet.com/syria and www.mofa.gov.sy.

We recommend female travellers stick to official campsites and camp where there are plenty of people around – especially out east. If you do otherwise, you will be taking a risk.

Clothing

Tailor your behaviour and your clothing to your surrounds. Look at what local women are wearing. On the streets of Beyoğlu in İstanbul you'll see skimpy tops and tight jeans, but cleavage and short skirts without leggings are a no-no everywhere except nightclubs in İstanbul and heavily touristed destinations along the coast.

Bring a shawl to cover your head when visiting mosques.

On the street, you don't need to don a headscarf, but in eastern Anatolia long sleeves and baggy long pants should attract the least attention.

Eating & Drinking

Restaurants and tea gardens aiming to attract women and children usually set aside a special room (or part of one) for families. Look for the term *aile salonu* (family dining room), or just *aile*.

Holiday Romances

It is not unheard of, particularly in romantic spots such as Cappadocia, for women to have holiday romances with local men. As well as fuelling the common Middle Eastern misconception that Western women are more 'available', this has led to occasional cases of men exploiting such relationships. Some men, for example, develop close friendships with visiting women, then invent sob stories, such as their mother has fallen ill, and ask them to help out financially.

Regional Differences

Having a banter with men in restaurants and shops in western Turkey can be fun, and many men won't necessarily think much of it.

Particularly out east, however, passing through some towns, you can count the number of women you see on one hand, and those you do see will be headscarved and wearing long coats. Life here for women is largely restricted to the home. Eastern Anatolia is not the place to practise your Turkish (or Kurdish) and expect men not to get the wrong idea; even just smiling at a man or catching his eye is considered an invitation. Keep your dealings with men formal and polite, not friendly.

Transport

When travelling by taxi and dolmuş, avoid getting into the seat beside the driver.

On the bus, lone women are often assigned seats at the front near the driver. There have been cases of male passengers or conductors on night buses harassing female travellers. If this happens to you, complain loudly, making sure that others on the bus hear, and repeat your complaint on arrival at your destination; you have a right to be treated with respect.

Work

Outside professional fields such as academia and the corporate sector, bagging a job in Turkey is tough. Most people teach English or nanny.

Check whether potential employers will help you get a work permit. Many employers, notably language schools, are happy to employ foreigners on an informal basis, but unwilling to organise work permits due to the time and money involved in the bureaucratic process. This necessitates working illegally on a tourist visa/residence permit. The '90 days within 180 days' regulation stipulated by tourist visas rules out the option of cross-border 'visa runs' to pick up a new visa on re-entry to Turkey (see p660).

Following the worldwide economic crash, locals also occasionally report illegal workers, and there have even been cases of English teachers being deported.

INTERNET RESOURCES

Job hunters may have luck with the following expat and advertising websites:

» http://istanbul.craigslist.org
» www.expatinturkey.com
» www.mymerhaba.com
» www.sahibinden.com
» www.sublimeportal.com

Nannying

One of the most lucrative nonspecialist jobs open to foreigners is nannying for the wealthy city elite, or looking after their teenage children and helping them develop their language skills.

There are opportunities for English, French and German speakers, and a few openings for young men as well as women.

You must be prepared for long hours, demanding employers and spoilt children.

Accommodation is normally included, and the digs will likely be luxurious. However, living with the family means you are always on call, and you may be based in the suburbs.

Teaching English

You can earn a decent living, mostly in İstanbul and the other major cities, as an English teacher at a university or a school. Good jobs require a university degree and TEFL (Teaching English as a Foreign Language) certificate or similar.

As well as the job-hunting resources listed in the introduction to this section, log onto www.eslcafe.com, which has a Turkey forum, and www.tefl.com.

If you want to proactively contact potential employers, Wikipedia has lists of educational institutions in Turkey.

DERSHANE

There are lots of jobs at *dershane* (private schools), which pay good wages and offer attractions such as accommodation (although it may be on or near the school campus in the suburbs) and work permits. Some even pay for your flight to Turkey and/or flights home.

Jobs are available at all levels, from kindergarten to high school. Teachers who can't speak Turkish often find very young children challenging; many are spoilt and misbehave around foreign teachers.

The best preschools pair a foreign teacher with a Turkish colleague.

You will often be required to commit to an unpaid trial period, lasting a week or two.

Unless a teacher has dropped out before the end of their contract, these jobs are mostly advertised around May and June, when employers are recruiting in preparation for the beginning of the academic year in September. Teachers are contracted until the end of the academic year in June.

The typical monthly salary is ₺2000 to ₺3500.

LANGUAGE SCHOOLS

Teaching at a language school is not recommended. The majority are exploitative institutions untroubled by professional ethics; for example making false promises in job interviews. Schools with a bad reputation are often 'blacklisted' on Craigslist.

At some you teach in a central classroom, but at business English schools you often have to schlep around the city between the clients' workplaces.

Schools often promise you a certain number of hours a week, but classes are then cancelled, normally at the last minute, making this a frustrating and difficult way to make a living in Turkey.

The typical hourly rate is ₺19 to ₺25, rising to ₺35 at business English schools where you travel to clients' offices and give one-to-one tuition.

PRIVATE TUITION

The advantage of this is you don't need a TEFL certificate or even a university degree. You can advertise your services on http://istanbul.craigslist.org and www.sahibinden.com.

The disadvantage is that, unless you are willing to travel to clients' offices and homes (which is time-consuming, and potentially risky for women), they tend to cancel when they get busy and learning English suddenly becomes a low priority. As with business English schools, most teaching takes place on weekends and evenings, when the students have spare time.

Hourly rates range from ₺35 to ₺60.

UNIVERSITIES

University jobs command the best wages, with work permits and, often, flights thrown in. Universities also generally operate more professionally than many establishments in other sectors.

The teacher's job is often to prepare freshman students for courses that will largely be taught in English.

As with *dershane,* jobs are advertised around May and June, and run roughly from September until June.

Tourism

Travellers sometimes work illegally for room and board in pensions, bars and other businesses in tourist areas. These jobs are generally badly paid and only last a few weeks, but they are a fun way to stay in a place and get to know the locals.

Given that you will be in direct competition with unskilled locals for such employment, and working in the public eye, there is a danger of being 'shopped' (reported to authorities) and deported.

Transport

GETTING THERE & AWAY

Flights, cars and tours can be booked online at lonelyplanet.com.

Entering the Country

The main idiosyncrasy to be aware of is that most visitors need a 'visa' – really just a sticker in their passport, issued at the point of entry. You must buy the visa before joining the queue for immigration. Bring enough cash to pay for your visa (see p660).

Security at the borders of countries to the east and southeast (Georgia, Azerbaijan, Iran, Iraq and Syria) is generally tight, and customs officers may want to see what you are bringing in. If you're travelling by train or bus, expect to be held up at the border for two to three hours – or even longer if your fellow passengers don't have their paperwork in order.

Travellers arriving from a yellow fever infected country (and people who have been in such a country recently) need to show proof of vaccination before entry.

Passport

Make sure your passport will still have at least six months' validity after you enter Turkey.

Air

It's a good idea to book flights months in advance if you plan to arrive in Turkey any time from April until late August. If you plan to visit a resort, check with travel agents for flight and accommodation deals. Sometimes you can find cheap flights with Turkish carriers and less-usual airlines.

Airports

The main international airports are in western Turkey:

Ankara International Airport (www.esenboga airport.com)

Antalya International Airport (www.aytport.com)

Bodrum International Airport (www.bodrum-air port.com)

Dalaman International Airport (www.atmairport.aero)

İstanbul Atatürk (www.atatur kairport.com) Turkey's principal international airport.

İstanbul Sabiha Gökçen (www.sgairport.com) Served by many European budget carriers.

İzmir International Airport (www.adnanmenderes airport.com)

Airlines

Turkish Airlines (📞0850-333 0849; www.thy.com), the national carrier, has extensive international and domestic networks, including budget subsidiaries **Sun Express** (www.sunexpress.com) and **Anadolu Jet** (📞444 2538; www.anadolujet.com). Turkish Airlines has had nine crashes since 1974; most recently, nine people died when one of its planes crashed at Amsterdam's Schiphol airport in 2009.

Other airlines serving Turkey are listed below by region.

AUSTRALIA & NEW ZEALAND

You can fly from the main cities in Australia and New Zealand to İstanbul, normally via Dubai, Kuala Lumpur or Singapore.

You can often get cheaper flights with European airlines, if you're prepared to change flights again in Europe.

CONTINENTAL EUROPE

There's not much variation in fares from one European airport to another; with the exception of Germany, which has the biggest Turkish community outside Turkey, enabling some great deals.

Most European national carriers fly directly to İstanbul. Cheaper indirect flights can be found, for example changing in Frankfurt en route from Amsterdam to İstanbul.

Charter airlines fly between several German cities and the major western Turkish airports.

Condor (www.condor.com)

Corendon Airlines (www.corendon-airlines.com)

Germanwings (www.german wings.com)

Pegasus Airlines (www.pegasusairlines.com)

MIDDLE EAST & ASIA

From Central Asia and the Middle East, you can usually pick up flights with Turkish Airlines or the country's national carrier.

One of the cheapest ways to fly further afield is from İstanbul via Dubai.

Armavia Airlines (www.armavia.aero)

Atlasjet (www.atlasjet.com)

Azerbaijan Airlines (www.azal.az)

Onur Air (www.onurair.com.tr)

Pegasus Airlines (www.pegasusairlines.com)

UK & IRELAND

In addition to the airlines listed, flights are available with European carriers via continental Europe. With major airlines such as British Airways and Turkish Airlines, by far the cheapest flights are in and out of London airports.

Charter flights are a good option, particularly at the beginning and end of the peak summer holiday season. Try the online charter and discounted flight agents:

Atlasjet (www.atlasjet.com)

EasyJet (www.easyjet.com)

Just the Flight (www.justtheflight.co.uk).

Thomson (www.thomsonfly.com)

USA & CANADA

Most flights connect with İstanbul-bound flights in the UK or continental Europe, so it's worth looking at European and British airlines in addition to North American airlines.

Another option is to cross the Atlantic to, say, London or Paris, and continue on a separate ticket with a budget carrier.

Land

Crossing borders by bus and train is fairly straightforward, but expect one- to three-hour delays. You'll usually have to disembark and endure paperwork and baggage checks for all travellers – on both sides of the border. The process is elongated by a trainload of passengers or the long lines of trucks and cars that build up at some borders.

Turkey's relationships with most of its neighbours tend to be tense, which can affect the availability of visas and when and where you can cross. Check for the most up-to-date information before leaving home - the Turkish embassy in your country and Lonely Planet's Thorn Tree forum are two sources of information.

Crossing the border into Turkey with your own vehicle should be fairly straightforward, providing your paperwork is in order (see p672).

Armenia

At the time of writing, the Turkey–Armenia border was closed.

BUS

Buses run from İstanbul and Trabzon to Tbilisi (Georgia), with connections to Armenia.

Azerbaijan

The remote Borualan–Sadarak crossing, east of Iğdır (Turkey), leads to the Azerbaijani enclave of Nakhichevan, from where you need to fly across Armenian-occupied Nagorno-Karabakh to reach capital Baku and the rest of Azerbaijan.

BUS

Buses run from İstanbul and Trabzon to Tbilisi (Georgia), with connections to Baku. Daily buses run from Trabzon to Baku, and from Iğdır to Nakhichevan.

Öz Nuhoğlu (www.oznuhogluseyahat.com) Daily buses from İstanbul to Baku.

Bulgaria & Eastern Europe

Bulgarian border guards only occasionally allow pedestrians to cross the frontier; take a bus or hitch a lift with a cooperative motorist. There are three border crossings:

Kapitan Andreevo–Kapıkule This 24-hour post is the main crossing – and the world's busiest land border crossing. Located 18km northwest of Edirne (Turkey) on the E80 and 9km from Svilengrad (Bulgaria).

Lesovo–Hamzabeyli Some 25km northeast of Edirne, this is favoured by big trucks and lorries and should be avoided.

Malko Tărnovo–Aziziye Some 70km northeast of Edirne via Kırklareli and 92km south of Bulgaria, this is only useful for heading to Bulgaria's Black Sea resorts.

CLIMATE CHANGE & TRAVEL

Every form of transport that relies on carbon-based fuel generates CO_2, the main cause of human-induced climate change. Modern travel is dependent on aeroplanes, which might use less fuel per kilometre per person than most cars but travel much greater distances. The altitude at which aircraft emit gases (including CO_2) and particles also contributes to their climate change impact. Many websites offer 'carbon calculators' that allow people to estimate the carbon emissions generated by their journey and, for those who wish to do so, to offset the impact of the greenhouse gases emitted with contributions to portfolios of climate-friendly initiatives throughout the world. Lonely Planet offsets the carbon footprint of all staff and author travel.

BUS

Half-a-dozen companies have daily departures from İstanbul to eastern European destinations including Sofia, Varna and Burgas (Bulgaria); Skopje, Tetovo and Gostivar (Macedonia); Constanta (Romania), Albania and Kosovo:

Ulusoy (☎444 1888; www .ulusoy.com.tr; İnönü Caddesi 59)

Metro Turizm (☎444 3455; www.metroturizm.com.tr)

Varan Turizm (☎444 8999; www.varan.com.tr)

Drina Trans (www.drinatrans .com)

TRAIN

The daily *Bosfor/Balkan Ekspresi* runs from İstanbul to Bucharest (Romania), Sofia (Bulgaria) and Belgrade (Serbia), with onward connections. Until the end of 2013, a rail replacement bus is covering the section of the route between İstanbul and the Bulgarian border.

You'll need to take your own food and drinks as there are no restaurant cars on these trains. Note also that the Turkey–Bulgaria border crossing is in the early hours of the morning and you need to leave the train to get your passport stamped. We've heard stories of harassment, especially of women, at the border, so lone women may be best taking an alternative route. Travelling in the sleeper cars is the safest and most comfortable option, although many trains on this line offer less-recommended couchette cars with six-bunk compartments. For more information, see **Turkish State Railways** (www.tcdd. gov.tr) and **The Man in Seat Sixty-One** (www.seat61.com).

Georgia

Sarp The main, 24-hour crossing, on the Black Sea coast between Hopa (Turkey) and Batumi (Georgia).

Türkgözü Near Posof (Turkey), north of Kars and southwest of Ahalcihe (Georgia). The border should open from 8am to 8pm, but in winter you might want to double-check it's open at all.

BUS

Several bus companies depart from İstanbul, Ankara, Trabzon and other cities to Batumi, Kutaisi and Tbilisi.

Mahmudoğlu (☎0212-658 0505; www.otogaristanbul.com; Office 3, Big İstanbul Bus Station, Esenler, İstanbul) Direct İstanbul to Tbilisi buses.

Öz Nuhoğlu (www. oznuhogluseyahat.com) İstanbul to Batumi and Tbilisi daily.

Özlem Ardahan (www.ozlem ardahan.com.tr) İstanbul to Tbilisi via Ardahan, Posof and Akhalkalaki (Georgia) daily.

TRAIN

A 98km line between Kars and Akhalkalaki (with an onward line to Tbilisi) is set to open in 2013.

Greece & Western Europe

Greek and Turkish border guards allow you to cross the frontier on foot. The following are open 24 hours.

Kastanies–Pazarkule 9km southwest of Edirne.

Kipi–İpsala 29km northeast of Alexandroupolis (Greece) and 35km west of Keşan (Turkey).

BUS

Germany, Austria and Greece have most direct buses to İstanbul, so if you're travelling from other European countries, you'll likely have to catch a connecting bus. Several companies have daily departures for Greece and beyond.

Metro Turizm (☎444 3455; www.metroturizm.com.tr) Destinations including Athens (Greece).

Ulusoy (☎444 1888; www.ulu soy.com.tr; İnönü Caddesi 59) Weekly departures to/from Germany (about €200). One line runs through Slovenia and eastern Europe, and the other through Italy and Greece with a sea crossing.

Varan Turizm (☎444 8999; www.varan.com.tr) Destinations including Budapest (Hungary) and Vienna (Austria).

Gürel Metro (☎0284-714 1051) Four daily minibuses from Keşan to Greek destinations including Thessaloniki and Athens.

CAR & MOTORCYCLE

The E80 highway makes its way through the Balkans to Edirne and İstanbul, then on to Ankara. Using the car-ferries from Italy and Greece can shorten driving times from Western Europe, but at a price.

From Alexandroupolis, the main road leads to Kipi–İpsala, then to Keşan and east to İstanbul or south to Gallipoli, Çanakkale and the Aegean.

TRAIN

From Western Europe (apart from Greece) you will come via Eastern Europe. A suggested route from London to İstanbul is the three-night journey via Paris, Munich, Budapest and Bucharest; see www.seat61.com/turkey.htm for more information and other routes.

At the time of writing, the overnight *Dostluk–Filia Express* service between İstanbul and Thessaloniki (Greece), run by Turkish State Railways and Hellenic Railways Organisation, had been cancelled due to Greece's economic crisis. See www.seat61.com/turkey .htm for updates.

Iran

Gürbulak–Bazargan This busy post, 35km southeast of Doğubayazıt (Turkey), is open 24 hours.

Esendere–Sero Southeast of Van. This crossing should be open from 8am until midnight, but double-check in winter. Travellers are increasingly using this crossing, which takes you through the breathtaking scenery of far southeastern Anatolia.

BUS

There are regular buses from İstanbul and Ankara to Tabriz and Tehran. Try **Thor Travel Agency** (www.thortourism .com), who offer nightly buses from İstanbul, and three a week from Ankara, to Tabriz and Tehran.

From Doğubayazıt Catch a dolmuş to Gürbulak, then walk or catch a shared taxi (₺1) across the border. It's Iran's busiest border crossing, and Turkey's second busiest. The crossing might take up to an hour, although tourists are normally waved through without much fuss. Change any unused Turkish lira in Bazargan, as it's harder to do so in Tabriz and Tehran. From Bazargan there are onward buses to Tabriz.

From Van There are daily dolmuşes to Yüksekova (Iran), west of Esendere-Sero, and buses to Orumiyeh (Iran).

TRAIN

For information on train travel in Iran visit www .seat61.com/iran.htm or the websites of **Turkish State Railways** (www.tcdd.gov .tr) and **RAJA Passenger Trains Co** (www.raja.ir).

Trans-Asya Ekspresi

Leaves Ankara every Wednesday morning and arrives in Tehran on Friday evening, travelling via Van and Tabriz. The journey involves a six-hour ferry crossing of Lake Van.

Van–Tabriz (nine hours) Leaves Tuesday evening.

Iraq

Between Silopi (Turkey) and Zahko (Kurdish Iraq), there's no town or village at the Habur–Ibrahim al-Khalil crossing and you can't walk across it.

BUS

There are direct buses from Diyarbakır to Dohuk (₺50, six hours) or Erbil (₺60, nine hours) in Kurdish Iraq, and from Cizre.

TAXI

More hassle than the bus, a taxi from Silopi to Zakho costs between US$50 and US$70. Your driver will manoeuvre through a maze of checkpoints and handle the paperwork. On the return journey, watch out for taxi drivers slipping contraband into your bag.

Syria

At the time of writing, most foreigners were not allowed to enter Syria (see p562). Should the security situation change, the below border crossings were previously available:

Reyhanlı–Bab al-Hawa The most convenient, and busiest; easily accessible.

Yayladağı Close to Antakya.

Öncüpınar Outside Kilis, 65km south of Gaziantep.

Akçakale 54km south of Şanlıurfa.

Nusaybin–Qamishle 75km southeast of Mardin.

It was previously possible to travel by bus from İstanbul and Ankara to the Syrian cities of Aleppo (Halab) and Damascus (Şam), often with a change in Antakya. Buses, minibuses and taxis also used to run from Antakya, Gaziantep, Şanlıurfa and Mardin in southeastern Anatolia to the Syrian border crossings and various cities in Syria.

The İstanbul–Aleppo *Toros Ekspresi* has been indefinitely suspended. See www.seat61.com/syria.htm and **Turkish State Railways** (www.tcdd.gov.tr) for updates on this service and those connecting southeastern Anatolia and Tehran (Iran) with Syria.

Sea

Departure times change between seasons, with fewer ferries generally running in winter. The routes available also change from year to year. A good starting point for information is **Ferrylines** (www.ferrylines.com).

Day trips on ferries to Greece are popular. Remember to take your passport, and check you have a multiple-entry Turkish visa so you can get back into the country at the end of the day. (Tourist visas issued on arrival in Turkey normally allow multiple entries.)

Tours

International tour companies offering trips to Turkey include the following:

Backroads (www.backroads .com; USA) Offers a combined bike and sailing tour on the Mediterranean and Aegean.

Cultural Folk Tours (www .culturalfolktours.com; USA) Group and private cultural and history tours.

EWP (www.ewpnet.com; UK) Mountaineering and trekking specialist covering the Kaçkars, Ararat, Lycian Way, Cappadocia and elsewhere.

Exodus (www.exodus.co.uk; UK) Adventure company offering a range of tours covering walking, biking, kayaking and history.

Green Island Holidays (www.greenislandholidays.com; UK) Packages covering Turkey and Northern Cyprus, including boutique hotels in İstanbul and Alaçatı, North Aegean.

Pacha Tours (www.pacha tours.com; USA, Turkey, Portugal & Brazil) Long-running Turkey specialist offering general tours plus special-interest packages and itineraries incorporating Greece.

GETTING AROUND

Air

Airlines

Turkey is well connected by air throughout the country, although note that many flights go via the major hubs of İstanbul or Ankara. Internal flights are a good option in such a large country, and competition between the following airlines keeps tickets affordable.

Anadolu Jet (☑444 2538; www.anadolujet.com) The Turkish Airlines subsidiary serves some 30 airports in its parent company's network.

Atlasjet (☑0850-222 0000; www.atlasjet.com) A limited network including Adana, Antalya, Bodrum, Dalaman, İstanbul, İzmir, and Lefkoşa (Nicosia) in Northern Cyprus.

Onur Air (☑0850-210 6687; www.onurair.com.tr) Onur Air flies from İstanbul to Adana, Antalya, Bodrum, Dalaman, Diyarbakır, Erzurum, Gaziantep, İzmir, Malatya, Samsun and Trabzon.

Pegasus Airlines (☑0850-250 0737; www.pegasus airlines.com) Has a useful network of some 20 airports, including most of the locations mentioned in the above listings plus less-usual spots such as Kayseri and Van.

Sun Express (☑444 0797; www.sunexpress.com.tr) The Turkish Airlines subsidiary has a useful network of about 15 airports, with most flights from Antalya, İstanbul and İzmir.

Turkish Airlines (☑0850-333 0849; www.thy.com) State-owned Turkish Airlines provides the main domestic network in the country, covering airports from Çanakkale to Kars.

Bicycle

Turkish cycling highlights include spectacular scenery, easy access to archaeological sites, which you may have all to yourself in some obscure corners, and the curiosity and hospitality of locals, especially out east.

Bicycles and parts Good-quality spare parts are generally only available in İstanbul and Ankara. **Bisan** (www.bisantr.com) is the main bike manufacturer in Turkey, but you can buy international brands in shops such as **Delta Bisiklet** (www.delta bisiklet.com), which has branches in İstanbul, Ankara, İzmir and Antalya. Delta services bicycles and can send parts throughout the country.

Hazards These include Turkey's notorious road-hog drivers, rotten road edges and, out east, stone-throwing children, wolves and ferocious Kangal dogs. Avoid main roads between cities; secondary roads are safer and more scenic.

Hire You can hire bikes for short periods in tourist towns along the coast and in Cappadocia.

Maps The best map for touring by bike is the Köy Köy Türkiye Yol Atlası, available in bookshops in İstanbul.

Transport You can often transport your bike by bus, train or ferry free of charge, although some buses will charge for the space it takes.

Boat

İstanbul Deniz Otobüsleri (İDO; ☑212-444 4436; www.ido .com.tr) operates passenger and car ferries across the Sea of Marmara, with routes including:

» İstanbul Kabataş to Çınarcık (west of Yalova) and the Princes' Islands.

» İstanbul Yenikapı to Bandırma, Bursa and Yalova.

Bus

Turkey's intercity bus system is as good as any you'll find, with modern, comfortable coaches crossing the country at all hours and for very reasonable prices. Virtually every first-time visitor to the country comments on the excellence of its bus system. On the journey, you'll be treated to hot drinks and snacks, plus liberal sprinklings of the Turks' beloved *kolonya* (lemon cologne).

Companies

These are some of the best companies, with extensive route networks:

Kamil Koç (☑444 0562; www.kamilkoc.com.tr) Serves most major cities throughout western and central Turkey.

Metro Turizm (☑444 3455; www.metroturizm. com.tr) Serves most major cities and towns throughout Turkey. Readers have complained about lost luggage and unhelpful staff, but it generally has a good reputation.

Ulusoy (☑444 1888; www .ulusoy.com.tr; İnönü Caddesi 59) Serves most major cities and towns, particularly in western and central Turkey, going as far east as Erzurum.

Varan Turizm (☑444 8999; www.varan.com.tr) Mostly focuses on western Turkey, going as far east as Ankara, Samsun and Trabzon.

Costs

Bus fares are subject to fierce competition between companies, and bargains such as student discounts may be offered. Prices reflect what the market will bear, so the fare from a big city to a village is likely to be different to the fare in the opposite direction.

ISIC Some companies are nominally part of the scheme, but it doesn't guarantee you a saving.

FERRY ROUTES FROM TURKEY

ROUTE	FREQUENCY	DURATION
Ayvalık–Lesvos, Greece	Mon-Sat May-Sep; 3 weekly Oct-Apr	1½hr
Alanya–Girne (Kyrenia), Northern Cyprus	2 weekly in summer	3½hr
Bodrum–Kos, Greece	daily	1hr
Bodrum–Rhodes, Greece	2 weekly Jun-Sep	2¼hr
Çeşme–Chios, Greece	daily mid-May–mid-Sep; 2 weekly mid-Sep–mid-May	1½hr
Datça–Rhodes, Greece	Sat May-Sep	45min
Datça–Simi, Greece	hydrofoil Sat May-Sep, *gület* 2 weekly	hydrofoil 15min, *gület* 70min
İstanbul–Illyichevsk (Odessa), Ukraine	2 weekly	28½hr
Kaş–Meis (Kastellorizo), Greece	daily	20min
Kuşadası– Samos, Greece	daily Apr-Oct	1¼hr
Marmaris–Rhodes, Greece	daily Apr-Oct	50min
Taşucu–Girne (Kyrenia), Northern Cyprus	daily	from 2hr
Trabzon–Sochi, Russia	weekly	5-12hr
Turgutreis–Kos, Greece	daily 25 May-31 Oct	30min

Tickets

Although you can usually walk into an otogar (bus station) and buy a ticket for the next bus, it's wise to plan ahead on public holidays, at weekends and during the school holidays from mid-June to early September. You can reserve seats online with some of the companies listed.

At the otogar When you enter bigger otogars prepare for a few touts offering buses to the destination of your choice. It's usually a good idea to stick to the reputable big-name companies. You may pay a bit more, but you can be more confident the bus is well maintained, will run on time, and will have a relief driver on really long hauls. For shorter trips, some companies have big regional networks.

Men and women Unmarried men and women are not supposed to sit together, but the bus companies rarely enforce this in the case of foreigners. You may be asked if you are married, without having to produce any proof of your wedlock, or both travellers may find their tickets marked with *bay* (man).

Refunds Getting a refund can be difficult; exchanging it for another ticket with the same company is easier.

Seats All seats can be reserved, and your ticket will bear a specific seat number. The ticket agent will have a chart of the seats with those already sold crossed off. They will often assign you a seat, but if you ask to look at the chart and choose a place, you can avoid sitting in the following blackspots:

» **At the front** On night buses you may want to avoid the front row of seats behind the driver, which have little leg room, plus you may have to inhale his cigarette smoke and listen to him chatting to his conductor into the early hours.

» **Above the wheels** Can get bumpy.

» **In front of the middle door** Seats don't recline.

» **Behind the middle door** Seats have little leg room.

» **At the back** Can get stuffy, and may have 'back of the cinema' connotations if you are a lone woman.

Otogar

Most Turkish cities and towns have a bus station, called the otogar, *garaj* or *terminal,* generally located on the outskirts. Besides intercity buses, otogars often handle dolmuşes (minibuses that follow prescribed routes) to outlying districts or villages. Most bus stations have an *emanetçi* (left luggage) room, which you can use for a nominal fee.

FARE (ONE WAY/RETURN)	COMPANY
₺60/70, car ₺120/130	Jale Tour (www.jaletour.com)
₺77/127	Fergün Denizcilik (www.fergun.net)
single or same-day return €32; open return €60	Bodrum Ferryboat Association (www.bodrumferryboat.com); Bodrum Express Lines (www.bodrumexpresslines.com)
single or same-day return €60; open return €120	Bodrum Ferryboat Association (www.bodrumferryboat.com)
₺65/100, car ₺150/260	Ertürk (www.erturk.com.tr)
₺90/180	Knidos Yachting (www.knidosyachting.com)
hydrofoil ₺L60/120, gület ₺140	Knidos Yachting (www.knidosyachting.com)
one way US$150, car US$325	Sea Lines (www.sea-lines.net)
single or same-day return €20	Meis Express (www.meisexpress.com)
€35/55	Meander Travel (www.meandertravel.com)
from €45/65, car from €110/190	Yeşil Marmaris Travel & Yachting (www.yesilmarmaris.com)
₺69/114	Akgünler Denizcilik (www.akgunler.com.tr)
one way US$100 to US$200	Olympia Line (www.olympia-line.ru), Öz Star Denizcilik (Princess Victoria), Sarı Denizcilik (www.saridenizcilik.com/en); see also www.seaport-sochi.ru and www.al-port.com
€12/20	Bodrum Ferryboat Association (www.bodrumferryboat.com)

Particularly in eastern Anatolia, don't believe taxi drivers at otogars who tell you there is no bus or dolmuş to your destination; they may be trying to trick you into taking their taxi. Check with the bus and dolmuş operators.

Servis

Because most bus stations are some distance from the town or city centre, the bus companies provide free *servis* shuttle minibuses. These take you to the bus company's office or another central location, possibly with stops en route to drop off other passengers. Ask '*Servis var mı?*' ('Is there a *servis*?'). Rare cities without such a service include Ankara and Konya.

Leaving town Ask about the *servis* when you buy your ticket at the bus company's central office; they will likely instruct you to arrive at the office an hour before the official departure time.

Drawbacks This service saves you a taxi or local bus fare to the otogar, but involves a lot of hanging around. If you only have limited time in a location, a taxi fare may be a good investment.

Scams Pension owners may try to convince you the private minibus to their pension is a bus company *servis*. Taxi drivers may say the *servis* has left or isn't operating in the hope of convincing you that their cab is the only option. If you do miss a *servis*, inquire at the bus company office – they normally run regularly.

Car & Motorcycle

Driving around Turkey gives you unparalleled freedom to enjoy the marvellous countryside and coastline. You can stop at roadside stalls selling local specialities, explore back roads leading to hidden villages and obscure ruins, and picnic at every opportunity, just like the locals.

Bear in mind that Turkey is a huge country and spending time in the car travelling long distances will eat up your time and money. Consider planes, trains and buses for covering long journeys, and cars for localised travel.

Public transport is a much easier and less stressful way of getting around the traffic-clogged cities.

Automobile Associations

Turkey's main motoring organisation is the **Türkiye Turing ve Otomobil Kurumu** (TTOK, Turkish Touring & Automobile Club; ☎212-513 3660; www.turing .org.tr; Soğukçeşme Sokağı, Sultanahmet).

Motorcyclist website **Horizons Unlimited** (www.horizonsunlimited.com/country/turkey) also has Turkey-related information and contacts.

Motorcyclists may want to check out **One More Mile Riders Turkey** (www.ommriders.com), a community resource for riding in Turkey.

Bring Your Own Vehicle

You can bring your vehicle into Turkey for six months without charge. Ensure you have your car's registration papers, tax number and insurance policy with you.

The fact that you brought a vehicle to Turkey will be marked in your passport to ensure you take it back out again. Don't plan on selling it there, and be prepared to be pay a hefty charge for any time over the six months – possibly a customs duty equal to the full retail value of the car.

If you want to leave your car in Turkey and return to collect it later, the vehicle must be put under a customs seal, which is a tedious process.

Checkpoints

Roadblocks are increasingly common in Turkey, with police checking vehicles and paperwork are in order. As well their licence and vehicle papers, foreign drivers occasionally need to show their passport. In southeastern Anatolia, you may encounter military roadblocks – part of operations against the PKK (Kurdistan Workers Party). They will likely check your ID and vehicle papers before waving you on, although roads in the region are sometimes closed completely if there is trouble ahead.

Driving Licences

Drivers must have a valid driving licence. Your own national licence should be sufficient, but an international driving permit (IDP) may be useful if your licence is from a country likely to seem obscure to a Turkish police officer

Fines

You may be stopped by blue-uniformed *trafik polis*, who can fine you on the spot for speeding. If you know you have done nothing wrong and the police appear to be asking for money, play dumb. You'll probably have to pay up if they persist, but insisting on proof of payment may dissuade them from extracting a fine destined only for their pocket. If the police don't ask for on-the-spot payment, contact your car-rental company (or mention the incident when you return the vehicle), as it can pay the fine and take the money from your card. Do the same in the case of fines for other offences, such as not paying a motorway toll. Note that you get a discount for early payment.

Fuel & Spare Parts

Turkey has the world's second-highest petrol prices (Norway tops the list). Petrol/diesel cost about ₺4/4.70 per litre. There are petrol stations everywhere, at least in western Turkey, and many are mega enterprises. In the vast empty spaces of central and eastern Anatolia, it's a good idea to have a full tank when you start out in the morning.

Yedek parçaları (spare parts) are readily available in the major cities, especially for European models such as Renaults, Fiats and Mercedes-Benz. Elsewhere, you may have to wait a day or two for parts to be ordered and delivered. Ingenious Turkish mechanics can contrive to keep some US models in service. The *sanayi bölgesi* (industrial zone) on the outskirts of every town generally has a repair shop, usually closed on Sunday, and repairs are usually quick and cheap. Roadside repair shops can often provide excellent, virtually immediate service,

although they (or you) may have to go somewhere else to get the parts. It's always wise to get an estimate of the repair cost in advance. For tyre repairs find an *oto lastikçi* (tyre repairer).

Spare motorcycle parts may be hard to come by everywhere except the major cities, so bring what you might need, or rely on the boundless ingenuity of Turkish mechanics to find, adapt or make you a part. If you do get stuck for a part you could also ring an İstanbul or Ankara repair centre and get it delivered.

Hire

You need to be at least 21 years old, with a year's driving experience, to hire a car in Turkey. Most car hire companies require a credit card. Most hire cars have standard (manual) transmission; you'll pay more for automatic. The majority of the big-name companies charge hefty one-way fees, starting at around ₺150 (eg pick up in İstanbul and drop off in İzmir) and climbing to hundreds of euros (eg pick up in Erzurum and drop off in İstanbul).

The big international companies – including Avis, Budget, Europcar, Hertz, National and Sixt – operate in the main cities, towns and most airports. Particularly in eastern Anatolia, stick to the major companies, as the local agencies often do not have insurance. Even some of the major operations are actually franchises in the east, so you should always check the contract carefully; particularly the section relating to insurance. Ask for a copy in English.

If your car incurs any accident damage, or if you cause any, do not move the car before finding a police officer and obtaining a *kaza raporu* (accident report). The officer may ask you to take an alcohol breath-test. Contact your car-rental company as soon as possible. In the case of an accident, your hire-car insurance may be void if it can be shown you were operating under the influence of alcohol or drugs, were speeding, or if you did not submit the required accident report within 48 hours to the rental company.

Because of high local fuel prices, agencies generally deliver cars with virtually no fuel, unless you specifically request otherwise.

Car Rental Turkey (www.carrentalturkey.info) İstanbul-based car hire.

CarHireExpress.co.uk (www.carhireexpress.co.uk/turkey) A booking engine.

Economy Car Rentals (www.economycarrentals.com) Gets excellent rates with other companies, including Budget and National; recommended.

Green Car (☎0232-446 9060; www.greenautorent.com; Mithatpaşa Caddesi 57, Karataş, İzmir) This local company is one of the largest in the Aegean region.

Insurance

You must have international insurance, covering third-party damage, if you are bringing your own car into the country (further information is available from the Turkish Touring & Automobile Association, www.turing.org.tr/eng/green_card.asp). Buying it at the border is a straightforward process (one month €80).

When hiring a car, 100%, no-excess insurance is increasingly the only option on offer. If this is not the only option, the basic, mandatory insurance package should cover damage to the vehicle and theft protection – with an excess, which you can reduce or waive for an extra payment. You may be offered personal accident insurance; your travel insurance should cover any personal accident costs in the case of a crash.

As in other countries, insurance generally does not cover windows and tyres. You will likely be offered cover for an extra few euros a day.

Parking

Parking is easy to find in most towns and smaller settlements, and you can generally park next to accommodation and sights outside Turkey's main centres. Space is at a premium in cities and some towns, but there are normally plenty of car parks where you can park cheaply for an hour or so, or safely leave your car overnight. You will often have to leave your keys with car park attendants.

Accommodation Top-end and a handful of midrange hotels offer undercover parking for guests, and most midrange and budget options have a roadside parking place or two that is nominally theirs to use. If they don't, parking will be close by in an empty block overseen by a caretaker, or on the road; in both cases you have to pay a fee. Your best bet is to set it up in advance when you book your room.

Clamping This is a fact of life in Turkey. Park in the wrong place and you risk having your car towed away, with the ensuing costs and hassle.

Road Conditions

Road surfaces and signage are generally good – on the main roads, at least. The most popular route with travellers, along the Aegean and Mediterranean coasts, offers excellent driving conditions. There are good *otoyols* (motorways) from the Bulgarian border near Edirne to İstanbul and Ankara, and from İzmir around the coast to Antalya.

Elsewhere, roads are being steadily upgraded, although they still tend to be worst in the east, where severe winters play havoc with the surfaces. In northeastern Anatolia, road conditions change from year to year; seek local advice before setting off on secondary roads. There are frequent roadworks in the northeast; even on main roads traffic can crawl along at 30km/hr. The new dams near Artvin and Yusufeli will flood some roads, and the construction causes waits of up to half an hour. Ask locally about the timing of your journey; on roads such as the D010 between Artvin and Şavşat, traffic flows according to a regular timetable, posted at the roadside.

In winter, be careful of icy roads. In bad winters, you will need chains on your wheels almost everywhere except along the Aegean and Mediterranean coasts. The police may stop you in more-remote areas to check you're properly prepared for emergencies. In mountainous areas such as northeastern Anatolia, landslides and rockfalls are a danger, caused by wet weather and snow-melt in spring. Between İstanbul and Ankara, be aware of the fog belt around Bolu that can seriously reduce visibility, even in summer.

Road Rules

In theory, Turks drive on the right and yield to traffic approaching from the right. In practice, they often drive in the middle and yield to no one. Maximum speed limits, unless otherwise posted, are 50km/h in towns, 90km/h on highways and 120km/h on *otoyols*.

Safety

Turkey has one of the world's highest motor-vehicle accident rates. Turkish drivers are impatient and incautious; rarely use their indicators and pay little attention to anyone else's; drive too fast both on the open road and through towns; and have an irrepressible urge to overtake – including on blind corners.

To survive on Turkey's roads:

» Drive cautiously and defensively.

» Do not expect your fellow motorists to obey road signs or behave in a manner you would generally expect at home.

» As there are only a few divided highways and many two-lane roads are serpentine, reconcile yourself to spending hours crawling along behind slow, overladen trucks.

» Avoid driving at night, when you won't be able to see potholes, animals, or even vehicles driving without lights, with lights missing, or stopped in the middle of the road. Drivers sometimes flash their lights to announce their approach.

» Rather than trying to tackle secondary, gravel roads when visiting remote sights such as northeastern Anatolia's churches, hire a taxi for the day. It's an extra expense, but the driver should know the terrain and the peace of mind is invaluable.

» The US embassy in Ankara has a page of safety tips for drivers at http://turkey .usembassy.gov/driver_safe ty_briefing.html.

Tolls

You must pay a toll to use the major *otoyols*. You can buy green-and-orange toll cards and place *kontör* (credit) on them at the offices near motorway toll gates. The offices are not open 24 hours; most close on Sunday. There is a ₺100 fine for non-payment, which takes about two weeks to come through.

Dolmuşes & Midibuses

As well as providing transport within cities and towns, dolmuşes (minibuses) run between places; you'll usually use them to travel between small towns and villages. Ask, '[Your destination] *dolmuş var mı?*' (Is there a dolmuş to [your destination]?). Some dolmuşes depart at set times, but they often wait until every seat is taken before leaving. To let the driver know that you want to hop out, say '*inecek var*' (someone wants to get out).

Midibuses generally operate on routes that are too long for dolmuşes, but not popular enough for full-size buses. They usually have narrow seats with rigid upright backs, which can be uncomfortable on long stretches.

Hitching

Although we don't recommend it, if you must *otostop* (hitch), offer to pay something towards the petrol, although most drivers pick up foreign hitchers for their curiosity value. You could be in for a long wait on some roads in central and eastern Anatolia; ask locals about the viability of your intended hitch before setting out. As the country is large and vehicles scarce in some areas, short hitches are quite normal. If you need to get from the highway to an archaeological site, hitch a ride with whatever comes along, be it a tractor, lorry or private car.

Instead of sticking out your thumb for a lift, you should face the traffic, hold your arm out towards the road, and wave it up and down as if bouncing a basketball.

Local Transport

Bus

For most city buses you must buy your *bilet* (ticket) in advance at a special ticket kiosk. Kiosks are found at major bus terminals and transfer points, and sometimes attached to shops near bus stops. The fare is normally around ₺2.

Private buses sometimes operate on the same routes as municipal buses; they are usually older, and accept either cash or tickets.

Local Dolmuş

Dolmuşes are minibuses or, occasionally, *taksi dolmuşes* (shared taxis) that operate on set routes within a city. They're usually faster, more

comfortable and only slightly more expensive than the bus. In larger cities, dolmuş stops are marked by signs; look for a 'D' and text reading '*Dolmuş İndirme Bindirme Yeri*' (Dolmuş Boarding and Alighting Place). Stops are usually conveniently located near major squares, terminals and intersections.

Metro

Several cities now have underground or partially underground metros, including İstanbul, İzmir, Bursa and Ankara. These are usually quick and simple to use, although you may have to go through the ticket barriers to find a route map. Most metros require you to buy a *jeton* (transport token; around ₺2) and insert it into the ticket barrier.

Taxi

Turkish taxis are fitted with digital meters. If your driver doesn't start his meter, mention it right away by saying '*saatiniz*' (your meter). Check your driver is running the right rate, which varies from city to city. The *gece* (night) rate is 50% more than the *gündüz* (daytime) rate, but some places, including İstanbul, do not have a night rate.

Some taxi drivers – particularly in İstanbul – try to demand a flat payment from foreigners. In this situation, drivers sometimes offer a decent fare; for example to take you to an airport, where they can pick up a good fare on the return journey. It is more often the case that they demand an exorbitant amount, give you grief, and refuse to run the meter. If this happens find another cab and, if convenient, complain to the police. Generally, only when you are using a taxi for a private tour involving waiting time (eg to an archaeological site) should you agree on a set fare, which should work out cheaper than using the meter. Taxi companies normally have set fees for longer journeys written in a ledger at the rank – they can be haggled down a little. Always confirm such fares in advance to avoid argument later.

Tram

Several cities have *tramvays* (trams), which are a quick and efficient way of getting around, and normally cost around ₺2 to use.

Tours

Every year we receive complaints from travellers who feel they have been fleeced by local travel agents, especially some of those operating in Sultanahmet, İstanbul. However, there are plenty of good agents alongside the sharks. Figure out a ballpark figure for doing the same trip yourself using the prices in this book, and shop around before committing.

Operators

Amber Travel (www.amber travel.com) British-run adventure travel company specialising in hiking, biking and sea kayaking.

Bougainville Travel (Map p342; ☑0242-836 3737; www.bougainville-turkey.com; İbrahim Serin Sokak 10, Kaş) Long-established English-Turkish tour operator offering a range of Mediterranean activities plus tailor-made nationwide tours.

Crowded House Tours (☑0286-814 1565; www.crowd edhousegallipoli.com; Eceabat) Tours to the Gallipoli Peninsula and other areas including Cappadocia and Ephesus.

Dragoman (www.dragoman .com; UK) Overland itineraries starting in İstanbul and heading through Turkey and the Middle East to various far-flung African destinations.

Eastern Turkey Tours (☑0432-215 2092, 0530 349 2793; www.easternturkeytour. org; Ordu Caddesi) Also known as Alkan Tours, this recommended Van-based outfit specialises in eastern Anatolia, Georgia and Armenia.

Fez Travel (www.feztravel .com) Tours around Turkey, including the Gallipoli Peninsula and 'Fez Bus' backpacker tours.

Hassle Free Travel Agency (☑213 5969; www .anzachouse.com; Çanakkale) Tours to the Gallipoli Peninsula plus itineraries including other parts of western and central Turkey.

Imaginative Traveller (www.imaginative-traveller.com; UK) Various overland adventures through Turkey and into Georgia.

Intrepid Travel (www.intre pidtravel.com.au) Offers a variety of small-group tours, covering Turkey and the Middle East, for travellers who like the philosophy of independent travel but prefer to travel with others.

Kirkit Voyage (www.kirkit .com) Cappadocia specialists offering customised tours around Turkey, including İstanbul and Ephesus. French spoken too.

Train

Train travel through Turkey is becoming increasingly popular as improvements are made, with high-speed lines such as Ankara–Konya appearing.

If you're on a budget, an overnight train journey is a great way to save accommodation costs. Many fans also appreciate no-rush travel experiences such as the stunning scenery rolling by and immersion with fellow passengers. Occasional unannounced hold-ups and public toilets gone feral by the end of the long journey are all part of the adventure.

Classes

Turkish trains typically have several seating and sleeping options. Most have comfortable reclining Pullman seat carriages. Some have 1st- and 2nd-class compartments, with six and eight seats respectively; some-

times bookable, sometimes 'first come, best seated'.

A *küşet* (couchette) wagon has shared four- or six-person compartments with seats that fold down into shelf-like beds. Bedding is not provided unless it's an *örtülü küşetli* ('covered' couchette). A *yataklı* wagon has one- and two-bed compartments, with washbasin and bedding provided; the best option for women travelling alone on overnight trips.

Costs

Train tickets are usually about half the price of bus tickets. A return ticket is 20% cheaper than two singles. Students (though you may need a Turkish student card) and seniors (60 years plus; proof of age required) get a 20% discount. Children under eight travel free.

InterRail, Balkan Flexipass and Eurodomino passes are valid on the Turkish railway network, but Eurail passes aren't. Train Tour Cards allow unlimited travel on Turkish trains for a month.

Long-Distance Trips

The following trains depart from Ankara (see p409):

» Adana via Kayseri
» Diyarbakır via Kayseri, Sivas and Malatya
» İzmir via Eskişehir
» Kars via Kayseri, Sivas and Erzurum
» Kurtalan (near Hasankeyf) via Kayseri, Sivas, Malatya and Diyarbakır
» Tatvan (Lake Van) via Kayseri, Sivas and Malatya

Network

The **Turkish State Railways** (www.tcdd.gov.tr) network covers the country fairly well, with the notable exception of the coastlines. For the Aegean and Mediterranean coasts you can travel by train to either İzmir or Konya, and take the bus from there.

While the line running into Anatolia from İstanbul's Haydarpaşa station is being upgraded, trains running

MARK SMITH, THE MAN IN SEAT 61

According to an old Turkish joke, the Germans were paid by the kilometre to build most of Turkey's railways, and they never used a straight line where a dozen curves would do! You'll certainly come to believe this as your train snakes its way across Turkey, round deep valleys and arid mountains, with occasional glimpses of forts on distant hilltops. Turkish train travel is incredibly cheap, but the best trains are air-conditioned and as good as many in Western Europe. The scenery is often better! Chilling out over a meal and a beer in the restaurant car of an express train is a great experience, and night trains can be a romantic and time-effective way to go. Some trains are slow and old, but just put your feet up, open a bottle of wine, and let the scenery come to you!

Mark Smith, aka the Man in Seat Sixty-One, is a global rail travel authority and founder of the website www.seat61.com. If you're interested in travelling by train, check it out.

southeast from the city have been cancelled until 2014 or 2015. In the meantime, to access Turkish State Railways' Anatolian network from İstanbul, you must take a bus to Arifiye, 150km east of the city (near Adapazari), or catch a ferry across the Sea of Marmara to Bandırma. Trains to eastern Anatolia now depart from Ankara, easily reached from İstanbul by bus.

Useful routes include:
» Ankara–Konya
» İstanbul–İzmir (including ferry to/from Bandırma)
» İzmir–Selcuk

Reservations

Most seats and all sleepers on the best trains must be booked in advance. For the *yataklı* wagons, reserve as far in advance as possible, especially if a religious or public holiday is looming. Weekend trains tend to be busiest.

You can buy tickets at stations, through an agency, or with a credit card at www.tcdd.gov.tr as much as 14 days before departure; www.seat61.com/Turkey2.htm gives step-by-step instructions for navigating the transaction.

Timetables

You can double-check train departure times, which do change, at www.tcdd.gov.tr.

Timetables usually indicate stations rather than cities; most refer to Haydarpaşa and Sirkeci rather than İstanbul, and to Basmane and Alsancak in İzmir.

Health

Before You Go

Recommended Vaccinations

Vaccinations for the following are recommended as routine for all travellers, regardless of the region they are visiting. The consequences of these diseases can be severe, and outbreaks do occur in the Middle East.

» tetanus
» diphtheria
» pertussis (whooping cough)
» varicella (chicken pox)
» measles
» mumps
» rubella
» polio

Vaccinations for the following are also recommended for travellers to Turkey:

» typhoid
» hepatitis A and B

Rabies is endemic in Turkey, so if you will be travelling off the beaten track consider an antirabies vaccination.

Malaria is found in a few areas near the Syrian border.

Many vaccines don't ensure immunity until two weeks after they are given, so visit a doctor four to eight weeks before departure.

Ask your doctor for an International Certificate of Vaccination or Prophylaxis (ICVP or 'the yellow card'), listing all the vaccinations you've received.

Medical Checklist

Consider packing the following in your medical kit:

» acetaminophen/paracetamol (Tylenol) or aspirin
» adhesive or paper tape
» antibacterial ointment (eg Bactroban) for cuts and abrasions
» antibiotics (if travelling off the beaten track)
» antidiarrhoeal drugs (eg loperamide)
» antihistamines (for hay fever and allergic reactions)
» anti-inflammatory drugs (eg ibuprofen)
» bandages, gauze and gauze rolls
» insect repellent for the skin that contains DEET
» insect spray for clothing, tents and bed nets
» iodine tablets (for water purification)
» oral rehydration salts (eg Dioralyte)
» pocket knife
» scissors, safety pins and tweezers
» steroid cream or cortisone (for allergic rashes)
» sunblock (it's expensive in Turkey)
» syringes and sterile needles (if travelling to remote areas)
» thermometer

Websites

It's a good idea to consult your government's travel health website before departure, if one is available.

Lonely Planet (www.lonelyplanet.com/turkey) Has a Health & Safety section under Practical Information.
Australia (www.smartraveller.gov.au)
Canada (www.phac-aspc.gc.ca)
International Association for Medical Assistance to Travellers (IAMAT; www.iamat.org)
MD Travel Health (www.mdtravelhealth.com)
UK (www.fitfortravel.nhs.uk; tinyurl.com/6jx4yw)
US (www.cdc.gov/travel)
World Health Organization (www.who.int)

Further Reading

The following are recommended references:

» *Travellers' Health* by Dr Richard Dawood
» *International Travel Health Guide* by Stuart R Rose MD
» *The Travellers' Good Health Guide* by Ted Lankester (useful for volunteers and long-term expats)
» *Travel With Children* published by Lonely Planet

In Turkey

Prevention is the key to staying healthy while travelling in Turkey. Infectious diseases can and do occur here, but they are usually associated with poor living conditions and poverty, and can be avoided with a few precautions. Most injuries to travellers occur because of car accidents.

Availability & Cost of Health Care

GETTING TREATED
If you need basic care for problems such as cuts, bruises and jabs, you could ask for the local *sağlık ocağı* (health centre), but don't expect anyone to speak anything but Turkish.

The travel assistance provided by your insurance may be able to locate the nearest source of medical help – otherwise, ask at your hotel. In an emergency, contact your embassy or consulate.

To receive details of your nearest medical services using a mobile with a Turkcell SIM card, text NEREDEYIM HASTANE/ECZANE (hospital/pharmacy) to ☏7777 or 2222.

STANDARDS
The standard of Turkish healthcare varies. Although the best private hospitals in İstanbul and Ankara offer world-class service, they are expensive. Elsewhere, even private hospitals don't always have high standards of care and their state-run equivalents even less so.

Hospitals & clinics Medicine, and even sterile dressings or intravenous fluids, may need to be bought from a local pharmacy. Nursing care is often limited or rudimentary, the assumption being that family and friends will look after the patient.

Dentists Standards vary and there is a risk of hepatitis B and HIV transmission via poorly sterilised equipment, so watch the tools in use carefully. Travel insurance will not usually cover you for anything other than emergency dental treatment.

Pharmacists For minor illnesses, such as diarrhoea, pharmacists can often provide advice and sell over-the-counter medication, including drugs that would require a prescription in your home country. They can also advise when more specialised help is needed.

Infectious Diseases

DIPHTHERIA
Spread through Close respiratory contact.

Symptoms & effects A high temperature and severe sore throat. Sometimes a membrane forms across the throat, requiring a tracheotomy to prevent suffocation.

Prevention The vaccine is given as an injection, alone or with tetanus; recommended for those likely to be in close contact with the local population in infected areas.

HEPATITIS A
Spread through Contaminated food (particularly shellfish) and water.

Symptoms & effects Jaundice, dark urine, a yellow colour to the whites of the eyes, fever and abdominal pain. Although rarely fatal, it

can cause prolonged lethargy and delayed recovery.

Prevention Vaccine (Avaxim, VAQTA, Havrix) is given as an injection, with a booster extending the protection offered. Hepatitis A and typhoid vaccines can also be given as a combined single-dose vaccine (hepatyrix or viatim).

HEPATITIS B
Spread through Infected blood, contaminated needles and sexual intercourse.

Symptoms & effects Jaundice and liver problems (occasionally failure).

Prevention The vaccination is worth considering for Turkey, where the disease is endemic. Many countries give hepatitis B vaccination as part of routine childhood vaccinations. It is given singly, or at the same time as hepatitis A.

LEISHMANIASIS
Spread through The bite of an infected sandfly or dog.

Symptoms & effects A slowly growing skin lump or ulcer. It may develop into a serious, life-threatening fever, usually accompanied by anaemia and weight loss.

LEPTOSPIROSIS
Spread through The excreta of infected rodents, especially rats. It is unusual for travellers to be affected unless living in poor sanitary conditions.

Symptoms & effects Fever, jaundice, and hepatitis and

INSURANCE

Turkish doctors generally expect payment in cash. Find out in advance if your insurance plan will make payments directly to providers or reimburse you later for overseas health expenditures. If you are required to pay upfront, make sure you keep all documentation. Some policies ask you to call a centre in your home country (reverse charges) for an immediate assessment of your problem. It's also worth ensuring your travel insurance will cover ambulances and transport – either home or to better medical facilities elsewhere. Not all insurance covers emergency medical evacuation home by plane or to a hospital in a major city, which may be the only way to get medical attention in a serious emergency.

TRAVELLER'S DIARRHOEA

To prevent diarrhoea, avoid tap water unless it has been boiled, filtered or chemically disinfected (with iodine or purification tablets). Eat fresh fruit or vegetables only if they're cooked or you have peeled them yourself, and avoid dairy products that might contain unpasteurised milk. Buffet meals are risky since food may not be kept hot enough; meals freshly cooked in front of you in a busy restaurant are more likely to be safe.

If you develop diarrhoea, drink plenty of fluids, and preferably an oral rehydration solution containing salt and sugar. A few loose stools don't require treatment, but if you start having more than four or five motions a day, you should start taking an antidiarrhoeal agent (such as loperamide) – or if that's not available, an antibiotic (usually a quinolone drug). If diarrhoea is bloody, persists for more than 72 hours or is accompanied by fever, shaking chills or severe abdominal pain, you should seek medical attention.

renal failure that may be fatal.

MALARIA
Spread through Mosquito bites. You stand the greatest chance of contracting malaria if you travel in southeastern Turkey. The risk is minimal in most cities, but check with your doctor if you are considering travelling to rural areas.

Symptoms & effects Malaria almost always starts with marked shivering, fever and sweating. Muscle pain, headache and vomiting are common. Symptoms may occur anywhere from a few days to three weeks after a bite by an infected mosquito. The illness can start while you are taking preventative tablets, if they are not fully effective, or after you have finished taking your tablets.

Prevention Taking antimalarial tablets is inconvenient, but malaria can kill. You must take them if the risk is significant.

RABIES
Spread through Bites or licks on broken skin from an infected animal.

Symptoms & effects Initially, pain or tingling at the site of the bite, with fever, loss of appetite and headache. With 'furious' rabies, there is a growing sense of anxiety, jumpiness, disorientation, neck stiffness,

sometimes seizures or convulsions, and hydrophobia (fear of water). 'Dumb' rabies (less common) affects the spinal cord, causing muscle paralysis then heart and lung failure. If untreated, both forms are fatal.

Prevention People travelling to remote areas, where a reliable source of post-bite vaccine is not available within 24 hours, should be vaccinated. Any bite, scratch or lick from a warm-blooded, furry animal should immediately be thoroughly cleaned. If you have not been vaccinated and you get bitten, you will need a course of injections starting as soon as possible after the injury. Vaccination does not provide immunity, it merely buys you more time to seek medical help.

TUBERCULOSIS
Spread through Close respiratory contact and, occasionally, infected milk or milk products.

Symptoms & effects Can be asymptomatic, although symptoms can include a cough, weight loss or fever months or even years after exposure. An X-ray is the best way to confirm if you have tuberculosis.

Prevention BCG vaccine is recommended for those likely to be mixing closely with the local population – visiting family, planning a long stay, or working as a

teacher or healthcare worker. As it's a live vaccine, it should not be given to pregnant women or immunocompromised individuals.

TYPHOID
Spread through Food or water that has been contaminated by infected human faeces.

Symptoms & effects Initially, usually fever or a pink rash on the abdomen. Septicaemia (blood poisoning) may also occur.

Prevention Typhim Vi or Typherix vaccine. In some countries, the oral vaccine Vivotif is also available.

Environmental Hazards
HEAT ILLNESS
Causes Sweating heavily, fluid loss and inadequate replacement of fluids and salt. Particularly common when you exercise outside in a hot climate.

Symptoms & effects Headache, dizziness and tiredness.

Prevention Drink sufficient water (you should produce pale, diluted urine). By the time you are thirsty you are already dehydrated.

Treatment Replace fluids by drinking water, fruit juice or both, and cool down with cold water and fans. Treat salt loss by consuming salty fluids, such as soup or broth,

TAP WATER

It's not wise to drink tap water if you're only in Turkey on a short visit. Stick to bottled water, boil tap water for 10 minutes or use purification tablets or a filter.

Do not drink river or lake water, which may contain bacteria or viruses that can cause diarrhoea or vomiting.

and adding a little more table salt to foods.

HEATSTROKE

Causes Extreme heat; high humidity; dehydration; drug or alcohol use or physical exertion in the sun. Occurs when the body's heat-regulating mechanism breaks down.

Symptoms & effects An excessive rise in body temperature, sweating stops, irrational and hyperactive behaviour, and eventually loss of consciousness and death.

Treatment Rapidly cool down by spraying the body with water and using a fan. Emergency fluids and replacing electrolytes by intravenous drip is usually also required.

INSECT BITES & STINGS

Causes Mosquitoes, sand-flies (located around the Mediterranean beaches), scorpions (frequently found in arid or dry climates), bees and wasps (in the Aegean and Mediterranean coastal areas, particularly around Marmaris).

Symptoms & effects Even if mosquitoes do not carry malaria, they can cause irritation and infected bites. Mosquitoes also spread dengue fever (although there isn't an ongoing transmission risk in Turkey). Sandflies have a nasty, itchy bite, and can carry the rare skin disorder leishmaniasis.

Turkey's small white scorpions can give a painful sting that will bother you for up to 24 hours.

Prevention DEET-based insect repellents. If you have a severe allergy (anaphylaxis) to bee or wasp stings, carry an adrenalin injection or similar.

SNAKE BITES

Prevention Do not walk barefoot or stick your hands into holes or cracks when exploring nature or even touring overgrown ruins and little-visited historic sites.

Treatment If bitten, do not panic. Half of those bitten by venomous snakes are not actually injected with poison (envenomed). Immobilise the bitten limb with a splint (eg a stick) and bandage the site with firm pressure, similar to applying a bandage over a sprain. Do not apply a tourniquet, or cut or suck the bite. Get the victim medical help as soon as possible so that antivenene can be given if necessary.

Language

WANT MORE?

For in-depth language information and handy phrases, check out Lonely Planet's *Turkish Phrasebook*. You'll find it at **shop .lonelyplanet.com**, or you can buy Lonely Planet's iPhone phrasebooks at the Apple App Store.

Turkish belongs to the Ural-Altaic language family. It's the official language of Turkey and northern Cyprus, and has approximately 70 million speakers worldwide.

Pronouncing Turkish is pretty simple for English speakers as most Turkish sounds are also found in English. If you read our coloured pronunciation guides as if they were English, you should be understood just fine. Note that the symbol ew represents the sound 'ee' pronounced with rounded lips (as in 'few'), and that the symbol uh is pronounced like the 'a' in 'ago'. The Turkish r is always rolled and v is pronounced a little softer than in English.

Word stress is quite light in Turkish – in our pronunciation guides the stressed syllables are in italics.

BASICS

Hello.
Merhaba.   mer·ha·ba

Goodbye.
Hoşçakal.   hosh·cha·kal
(said by person leaving)

Güle güle.   gew·le gew·le
(said by person staying)

Yes.
Evet.   e·vet

No.
Hayır.   ha·yuhr

Excuse me.
Bakar mısınız.   ba·kar muh·suh·nuhz

Sorry.
Özür dilerim.   er·zewr dee·le·reem

Please.
Lütfen.   lewt·fen

Thank you.
Teşekkür ederim.   te·shek·kewr e·de·reem

You're welcome.
Birşey değil.   beer·shay de·eel

How are you?
Nasılsınız?   na·suhl·suh·nuhz

Fine, and you?
İyiyim, ya siz?   ee·yee·yeem ya seez

What's your name?
Adınız nedir?   a·duh·nuhz ne·deer

My name is ...
Benim adım ...   be·neem a·duhm ...

Do you speak English?
İngilizce   een·gee·leez·je
konuşuyor   ko·noo·shoo·yor
musunuz?   moo·soo·nooz

I understand.
Anlıyorum.   an·luh·yo·room

I don't understand.
Anlamıyorum.   an·la·muh·yo·room

ACCOMMODATION

Where can I find a ...?	Nerede ... bulabilirim?	ne·re·de ... boo·la·bee·lee·reem
campsite	kamp yeri	kamp ye·ree
guesthouse	misafirhane	mee·sa·feer·ha·ne
hotel	otel	o·tel
pension	pansiyon	pan·see·yon
youth hostel	gençlik hosteli	gench·leek hos·te·lee

How much is it per night/person?
Geceliği/Kişi   ge·je·lee·ee/kee·shee
başına ne kadar?   ba·shuh·na ne ka·dar

Is breakfast included?
Kahvaltı dahil mi?   kah·val·tuh da·heel mee

Do you have a ...?	... odanız var mı?	... o·da·nuz var muh
single room	Tek kişilik	tek kee·shee·leek
double room	İki kişilik	ee·kee kee·shee·leek

air conditioning	klima	klee·ma
bathroom	banyo	ban·yo
window	pencere	pen·je·re

DIRECTIONS

Where is ...?
... nerede?   ... ne·re·de

What's the address?
Adresi nedir?   ad·re·see ne·deer

Could you write it down, please?
Lütfen yazar   lewt·fen ya·zar
mısınız?   muh·suh·nuhz

Can you show me (on the map)?
Bana (haritada)   ba·na (ha·ree·ta·da)
gösterebilir   gers·te·re·bee·leer
misiniz?   mee·seen·neez

It's straight ahead.
Tam karşıda.   tam kar·shuh·da

at the traffic lights
trafik   tra·feek
ışıklarından   uh·shuhk·la·ruhn·dan

at the corner	köşeden	ker·she·den
behind	arkasında	ar·ka·suhn·da
far (from)	uzak	oo·zak
in front of	önünde	er·newn·de
near (to)	yakınında	ya·kuh·nuhn·da
opposite	karşısında	kar·shuh·suhn·da
Turn left.	Sola dön.	so·la dern
Turn right.	Sağa dön.	sa·a dern

EATING & DRINKING

What would you recommend?
Ne tavsiye   ne tav·see·ye
edersiniz?   e·der·see·neez

What's in that dish?
Bu yemekte neler var?   boo ye·mek·te ne·ler var

I don't eat ...
... yemiyorum.   ... ye·mee·yo·room

Cheers!
Şerefe!   she·re·fe

KEY PATTERNS

To get by in Turkish, mix and match these simple patterns with words of your choice:

When's (the next bus)?
(Sonraki otobüs)   (son·ra·kee o·to·bews)
ne zaman?   ne za·man

Where's (the market)?
(Pazar yeri) nerede?   (pa·zar ye·ree) ne·re·de

Where can I (buy a ticket)?
Nereden (bilet   ne·re·den (bee·let
alabilirim)?   a·la·bee·lee·reem)

I have (a reservation).
(Rezervasyonum)   (re·zer·vas·yo·noom)
var.   var

Do you have (a map)?
(Haritanız)   (ha·ree·ta·nuhz)
var mı?   var muh

Is there (a toilet)?
(Tuvalet) var mı?   (too·va·let) var muh

I'd like (the menu).
(Menüyü)   (me·new·yew)
istiyorum.   ees·tee·yo·room

I want to (make a call).
(Bir görüşme   (beer ger·rewsh·me
yapmak)   yap·mak)
istiyorum.   ees·tee·yo·room

Do I have to (declare this)?
(Bunu beyan   (boo·noo be·yan
etmem) gerekli mi?   et·mem) ge·rek·lee mee

I need (assistance).
(Yardıma)   (yar·duh·ma)
ihtiyacım var.   eeh·tee·ya·juhm var

That was delicious!
Nefisti!   ne·fees·tee

The bill/check, please.
Hesap lütfen.   he·sap lewt·fen

I'd like a table for ...	... bir masa ayırtmak istiyorum.	... beer ma·sa a·yuhrt·mak ees·tee·yo·room
(eight) o'clock	Saat (sekiz) için	sa·at (se·keez) ee·cheen
(two) people	(İki) kişilik	(ee·kee) kee·shee·leek

Key Words

appetisers	mezeler	me·ze·ler
bottle	şişe	shee·she
bowl	kase	ka·se
breakfast	kahvaltı	kah·val·tuh
(too) cold	(çok) soğuk	(chok) so·ook

cup	*fincan*	feen·*jan*
delicatessen	*şarküteri*	shar·*kew*·te·ree
dinner	*akşam yemeği*	ak·*sham* ye·me·ee
dish	*yemek*	ye·*mek*
food	*yiyecek*	yee·ye·*jek*
fork	*çatal*	cha·*tal*
glass	*bardak*	bar·*dak*
grocery	*bakkal*	bak·*kal*
halal	*helal*	he·*lal*
highchair	*mama sandalyesi*	ma·*ma* san·dal·ye·see
hot (warm)	*sıcak*	suh·*jak*
knife	*bıçak*	buh·*chak*
kosher	*koşer*	ko·*sher*
lunch	*öğle yemeği*	er·le ye·me·ee
main courses	*ana yemekler*	a·na ye·mek·ler
market	*pazar*	pa·*zar*
menu	*yemek listesi*	ye·mek lees·te·see
plate	*tabak*	ta·*bak*
restaurant	*restoran*	res·to·*ran*
spicy	*acı*	a·*juh*
spoon	*kaşık*	ka·*shuhk*
vegetarian	*vejeteryan*	ve·zhe·ter·*yan*

olive	*zeytin*	zay·*teen*
onion	*soğan*	so·*an*
orange	*portakal*	por·ta·*kal*
peach	*şeftali*	shef·ta·*lee*
potato	*patates*	pa·ta·*tes*
spinach	*ıspanak*	uhs·pa·*nak*
tomato	*domates*	do·ma·*tes*
watermelon	*karpuz*	kar·*pooz*

Other

bread	*ekmek*	ek·*mek*
cheese	*peynir*	pay·*neer*
egg	*yumurta*	yoo·moor·*ta*
honey	*bal*	bal
ice	*buz*	booz
pepper	*kara biber*	ka·ra bee·ber
rice	*pirinç/ pilav*	pee·reench/ pee·lav
salt	*tuz*	tooz
soup	*çorba*	chor·*ba*
sugar	*şeker*	she·ker
Turkish delight	*lokum*	lo·*koom*

Meat & Fish

anchovy	*hamsi*	ham·*see*
beef	*sığır eti*	suh·*uhr* e·tee
calamari	*kalamares*	ka·la·ma·res
chicken	*piliç/ tavuk*	pee·*leech*/ ta·*vook*
fish	*balık*	ba·*luhk*
lamb	*kuzu*	koo·*zoo*
liver	*ciğer*	jee·*er*
mussels	*midye*	meed·*ye*
pork	*domuz eti*	do·*mooz* e·tee
veal	*dana eti*	da·*na* e·tee

Drinks

beer	*bira*	bee·*ra*
coffee	*kahve*	kah·*ve*
(orange) juice	*(portakal) suyu*	(por·ta·*kal* soo·yoo)
milk	*süt*	sewt
mineral water	*maden suyu*	ma·den soo·yoo
soft drink	*alkolsüz içecek*	al·kol·*sewz* ee·che·jek
tea	*çay*	chai
water	*su*	soo
wine	*şarap*	sha·*rap*
yoghurt	*yoğurt*	yo·*oort*

Fruit & Vegetables

apple	*elma*	el·*ma*
apricot	*kayısı*	ka·yuh·*suh*
banana	*muz*	mooz
capsicum	*biber*	bee·*ber*
carrot	*havuç*	ha·*vooch*
cucumber	*salatalık*	sa·la·ta·*luhk*
fruit	*meyve*	may·*ve*
grape	*üzüm*	ew·*zewm*
melon	*kavun*	ka·*voon*

Signs

Açık	Open
Bay	Male
Bayan	Female
Çıkışı	Exit
Giriş	Entrance
Kapalı	Closed
Sigara İçilmez	No Smoking
Tuvaletler	Toilets
Yasak	Prohibited

EMERGENCIES

Help!
İmdat!   eem·dat

I'm lost.
Kayboldum.   kai·bol·doom

Leave me alone!
Git başımdan!   geet ba·shuhm·dan

There's been an accident.
Bir kaza oldu.   beer ka·za ol·doo

Can I use your phone?
Telefonunuzu   te·le·fo·noo·noo·zoo
kullanabilir miyim?   kool·la·na·bee·leer mee·yeem

Call a doctor!
Doktor çağırın!   dok·tor cha·uh·ruhn

Call the police!
Polis çağırın!   po·lees cha·uh·ruhn

I'm ill.
Hastayım.   has·ta·yuhm

It hurts here.
Burası ağrıyor.   boo·ra·suh a·ruh·yor

I'm allergic to (nuts).
(Çerezlere)   (che·rez·le·re)
alerjim var.   a·ler·zheem var

SHOPPING & SERVICES

I'd like to buy ...
... almak istiyorum.   ... al·mak ees·tee·yo·room

I'm just looking.
Sadece bakıyorum.   sa·de·je ba·kuh·yo·room

May I look at it?
Bakabilir miyim?   ba·ka·bee·leer mee·yeem

The quality isn't good.
Kalitesi iyi değil.   ka·lee·te·see ee·yee de·eel

How much is it?
Ne kadar?   ne ka·dar

It's too expensive.
Bu çok pahalı.   boo chok pa·ha·luh

Do you have something cheaper?
Daha ucuz birşey   da·ha oo·jooz beer·shay
var mı?   var muh

There's a mistake in the bill.
Hesapta bir   he·sap·ta beer
yanlışlık var.   yan·luhsh·luhk var

Question Words

How?	*Nasıl?*	na·seel
What?	*Ne?*	ne
When?	*Ne zaman?*	ne za·man
Where?	*Nerede?*	ne·re·de
Which?	*Hangi?*	han·gee
Who?	*Kim?*	keem
Why?	*Neden?*	ne·den

ATM	*bankamatik*	ban·ka·ma·teek
credit card	*kredi kartı*	kre·dee kar·tuh
post office	*postane*	pos·ta·ne
signature	*imza*	eem·za
tourist office	*turizm*	too·reezm
	bürosu	bew·ro·soo

TIME & DATES

What time is it?	*Saat kaç?*	sa·at kach
It's (10) o'clock.	*Saat (on).*	sa·at (on)
Half past (10).	*(On) buçuk.*	(on) boo·chook

in the morning	*öğleden evvel*	er·le·den ev·vel
in the afternoon	*öğleden sonra*	er·le·den son·ra
in the evening	*akşam*	ak·sham
yesterday	*dün*	dewn
today	*bugün*	boo·gewn
tomorrow	*yarın*	ya·ruhn

Monday	*Pazartesi*	pa·zar·te·see
Tuesday	*Salı*	sa·luh
Wednesday	*Çarşamba*	char·sham·ba
Thursday	*Perşembe*	per·shem·be
Friday	*Cuma*	joo·ma
Saturday	*Cumartesi*	joo·mar·te·see
Sunday	*Pazar*	pa·zar

January	*Ocak*	o·jak
February	*Şubat*	shoo·bat
March	*Mart*	mart
April	*Nisan*	nee·san
May	*Mayıs*	ma·yuhs
June	*Haziran*	ha·zee·ran
July	*Temmuz*	tem·mooz
August	*Ağustos*	a·oos·tos
September	*Eylül*	ay·lewl
October	*Ekim*	e·keem
November	*Kasım*	ka·suhm
December	*Aralık*	a·ra·luhk

TRANSPORT

Public Transport

At what time	*... ne zaman*	*... ne za·man*
does the ...	*kalkacak/*	kal·ka·jak/
leave/arrive?	*varır?*	va·ruhr
boat	*Vapur*	va·poor
bus	*Otobüs*	o·to·bews
plane	*Uçak*	oo·chak
train	*Tren*	tren

Numbers

1	bir	beer
2	iki	ee·kee
3	üç	ewch
4	dört	dert
5	beş	besh
6	altı	al·tuh
7	yedi	ye·dee
8	sekiz	se·keez
9	dokuz	do·kooz
10	on	on
20	yirmi	yeer·mee
30	otuz	o·tooz
40	kırk	kuhrk
50	elli	el·lee
60	altmış	alt·muhsh
70	yetmiş	et·meesh
80	seksen	sek·sen
90	doksan	dok·san
100	yüz	yewz
1000	bin	been

Does it stop at (Maltepe)?
(Maltepe'de) | (mal·te·pe·de)
durur mu? | doo·roor moo

What's the next stop?
Sonraki durak | son·ra·kee doo·rak
hangisi? | han·gee·see

Please tell me when we get to (Beşiktaş).
(Beşiktaş'a) | (be·sheek·ta·sha)
vardığımızda | var·duh·uh·muhz·da
lütfen bana | lewt·fen ba·na
söyleyin. | say·le·yeen

I'd like to get off at (Kadıköy).
(Kadıköy'de) inmek | (ka·duh·kay·de) een·mek
istiyorum. | ees·tee·yo·room

I'd like a ... | (Bostancı'ya) | (bos·tan·juh·ya)
ticket to | ... bir bilet | ... beer bee·let
(Bostancı). | lütfen. | lewt·fen

1st-class | Birinci mevki | bee·reen·jee mev·kee
2nd-class | İkinci mevki | ee·keen·jee mev·kee
one-way | Gidiş | gee·deesh
return | Gidiş-dönüş | gee·deesh·der·newsh

first | ilk | eelk
last | son | son
next | geleçek | ge·le·jek

I'd like | ... bir yer | ... beer yer
a/an ... seat. | istiyorum. | ees·tee·yo·room
aisle | Koridor tarafında | ko·ree·dor ta·ra·fuhn·da
window | Cam kenarı | jam ke·na·ruh

cancelled | iptal edildi | eep·tal e·deel·dee
delayed | ertelendi | er·te·len·dee
platform | peron | pe·ron
ticket office | bilet gişesi | bee·let gee·she·see
timetable | tarife | ta·ree·fe
train station | istasyon | ees·tas·yon

Driving & Cycling

I'd like to | Bir ... | beer ...
hire a ... | kiralamak istiyorum. | kee·ra·la·mak ees·tee·yo·room
4WD | dört çeker | dert che·ker
bicycle | bisiklet | bee·seek·let
car | araba | a·ra·ba
motorcycle | motosiklet | mo·to·seek·let

bike shop | bisikletçi | bee·seek·let·chee
child seat | çocuk koltuğu | cho·jook kol·too·oo
diesel | dizel | dee·zel
helmet | kask | kask
mechanic | araba tamircisi | a·ra·ba ta·meer·jee·see
petrol/gas | benzin | ben·zeen
service station | benzin istasyonu | ben·zeen ees·tas·yo·noo

Is this the road to (Taksim)?
(Taksim'e) giden | (tak·see·me) gee·den
yol bu mu? | yol boo moo

(How long) Can I park here?
Buraya (ne kadar | boo·ra·ya (ne ka·dar
süre) park | sew·re) park
edebilirim? | e·de·bee·lee·reem

The car/motorbike has broken down (at Osmanbey).
Arabam/ | a·ra·bam/
Motosikletim | mo·to·seek·le·teem
(Osmanbey'de) | (os·man·bay·de)
bozuldu. | bo·zool·doo

I have a flat tyre.
Lastiğim patladı. | las·tee·eem pat·la·duh

I've run out of petrol.
Benzinim bitti. | ben·zee·neem beet·tee

GLOSSARY

acropolis – hilltop citadel and temples of a classical Hellenic city

ada(sı) – island

agora – open space for commerce and politics in a Greco-Roman city

Anatolia – the Asian part of Turkey; also called *Asia Minor*

arabesk – Arabic-style Turkish music

arasta – row of shops near a mosque, the rent from which supports the mosque

Asia Minor – see *Anatolia*

bahçe(si) – garden

bedesten – vaulted, fireproof market enclosure where valuable goods are kept

belediye (sarayı) – municipal council, town hall

bey – polite form of address for a man; follows the name

bilet – ticket

bouleuterion – place of assembly, council meeting place in a classical Hellenic city

bulvar(ı) – boulevard or avenue; often abbreviated to 'bul'

cadde(si) – street; often abbreviated to 'cad'

cami(i) – mosque

caravanserai – large fortified way-station for (trade) caravans

çarşı(sı) – market, bazaar; sometimes town centre

çay bahçesi – tea garden

çayı – stream

çeşme – spring, fountain

Cilician Gates – a pass in the Taurus Mountains in southern Turkey

dağ(ı) – mountain

deniz – sea

dervish – member of Mevlevi Muslim brotherhood

dolmuş – shared taxi; can be a minibus or sedan

döviz (bürosu) – currency exchange (office)

emir – Turkish tribal chieftain

eski – old (thing, not person)

ev pansiyonu – pension in a private home

eyvan – vaulted hall opening into a central court in a *medrese* or mosque; balcony

fasıl – Ottoman classical music, usually played by gypsies

GAP – Southeastern Anatolia Project, a mammoth hydroelectric and irrigation project

geçit, geçidi – (mountain) pass

gişe – ticket kiosk

göl(ü) – lake

gület – traditional Turkish wooden yacht

hamam(ı) – Turkish bathhouse

han(ı) – see *caravanserai*

hanım – polite form of address for a woman

haremlik – family/women's quarters of a residence; see also *selamlık*

heykel – statue

hisar(ı) – fortress or citadel

Hittites – nation of people inhabiting Anatolia during 2nd millennium BC

hükümet konağı – government house, provincial government headquarters

imam – prayer leader, Muslim cleric

imaret(i) – soup kitchen for the poor, usually attached to a *medrese*

indirim – discount

iskele(si) – jetty, quay

jeton – transport token

kale(si) – fortress, citadel

kapı(sı) – door, gate

kaplıca – thermal spring or baths

Karagöz – shadow-puppet theatre

kaya – cave

KDV – katma değer vergisi, Turkey's value-added tax

kebapçı – place selling kebaps

kervansaray(ı) – Turkish for *caravanserai*

keyif – relaxation (refined to a fine art in Turkey)

kilim – flat-weave rug

kilise(si) – church

köfte – meatballs

köfteci – *köfte* maker or seller

konak, konağı – mansion, government headquarters

köprü(sü) – bridge

köşk(ü) – pavilion, villa

köy(ü) – village

kule(si) – tower

külliye(si) – mosque complex including seminary, hospital and soup kitchen

kümbet – vault, cupola, dome; tomb topped by this

liman(ı) – harbour

lokanta – eatery serving ready-made food

mağara(sı) – cave

mahalle(si) – neighbourhood, district of a city

medrese(si) – Islamic theological seminary or school attached to a mosque

mescit, mescidi – prayer room, small mosque

Mevlâna – also known as Celaleddin Rumi, a great mystic and poet (1207–73), founder of the Mevlevi whirling *dervish* order

meydan(ı) – public square, open place

meyhane – tavern, wine shop

mihrab – niche in a mosque indicating the direction of Mecca

milli parkı – national park

mimber – pulpit in a mosque

minare(si) – minaret, tower from which Muslims are called to prayer

müze(si) – museum

nargile – traditional water pipe (for smoking); hookah

necropolis – city of the dead, cemetery

oda(sı) – room
otobüs – bus
otogar – bus station
Ottoman – of or pertaining to the Ottoman Empire which lasted from the end of the 13th century to the end of WWI

pansiyon – pension, B&B, guesthouse
paşa – general, governor
pastane – pastry shop (patisserie); also *pastahane*
pazar(ı) – weekly market, bazaar
peribacalar – fairy chimneys
pideci – pide maker or seller
plaj – beach
PTT – Posta, Telefon, Telegraf; post, telephone and telegraph office

Ramazan – Islamic holy month of fasting

saat kulesi – clock tower

şadırvan – fountain where Muslims perform ritual ablutions
saray(ı) – palace
sedir – bench seating that doubled as a bed in Ottoman houses
şehir – city; municipality
şehir merkezi – city centre
selamlık – public/men's quarters of a residence; see also *haremlik*
Seljuk – of or pertaining to the Seljuk Turks, the first Turkish state to rule Anatolia from the 11th to 13th centuries
sema – *dervish* ceremony
semahane – hall where whirling *dervish* ceremonies are held
serander – granary
servis – shuttle minibus service to and from the *otogar*
sinema – cinema
sokak, sokağı – street or lane; often abbreviated to 'sk'

Sufi – Muslim mystic, member of a mystic (*dervish*) brotherhood

TCDD – Turkish State Railways
tekke(si) – *dervish* lodge
tersane – shipyard
tramvay – tram
TRT – Türkiye Radyo ve Televizyon, Turkish broadcasting corporation
tuff, tufa – soft stone laid down as volcanic ash
türbe(si) – tomb, grave, mausoleum

valide sultan – mother of the reigning sultan
vezir – vizier (minister) in the Ottoman government
vilayet, valilik, valiliği – provincial government headquarters

yalı – grand waterside residence
yayla – highland pastures
yeni – new
yol(u) – road, way

Behind the Scenes

SEND US YOUR FEEDBACK

We love to hear from travellers – your comments keep us on our toes and help make our books better. Our well-travelled team reads every word on what you loved or loathed about this book. Although we cannot reply individually to postal submissions, we always guarantee that your feedback goes straight to the appropriate authors, in time for the next edition. Each person who sends us information is thanked in the next edition – the most useful submissions are rewarded with a selection of digital PDF chapters.

Visit **lonelyplanet.com/contact** to submit your updates and suggestions or to ask for help. Our award-winning website also features inspirational travel stories, news and discussions.

Note: We may edit, reproduce and incorporate your comments in Lonely Planet products such as guidebooks, websites and digital products, so let us know if you don't want your comments reproduced or your name acknowledged. For a copy of our privacy policy visit lonelyplanet.com/privacy.

OUR READERS

Many thanks to the travellers who used the last edition and wrote to us with helpful hints, useful advice and interesting anecdotes:

Kerem Akartunali, Sain Alizada, Bruce Allardice, Gerlinde Aringer, Lütfiye Aydınoğlu, Grant Berg, Kate Boerlage, Simon Bond, Chris Brien, Tanja Brodtrager, Lorenzo Bucci, Ivan Bukovnik, Ceyda Bulat, Christian Cantos, Elisa Carnielli, Mary Carryer, Rowan Castle, Omer Cavusoglu, Ersun Çeviker, Helen Cole, Tamsin Cox, Val Cunningham, Mario Difiore, Ernest Djan, John Donald, Will Dong, Brendon Douglas, Anton Dudnikov, Tessa Dugmore, Nesma Ellethey, Mehmet Emin, Sheryl Entwisle, Teresa Ferreri, Ken Fields, Linda Garai-Pasztor, Ayhan Gedikoğlu, Freek Geldof, Suzanne Geoghegan, Emmelie Gerrits, Alberto Giordano, Arthur Clement de Givry, Kim Goldsmith, Philip Golobish, Anthea Mason Gokyilmaz, Bulent Guzelkan, Fiona Harrison, Chris Harvey, Liz Harwood, Kelvin Hayes, Louise Hewitt, E Hillsman, Steven Houben, Lea Hupke, Wendy Hutchinson, Ingo Ibelshäuser, Avril Ingram, Adam Jaques, Steve Juniper, Abdullah Kalkan, Anna Karmann, Nick Keal, Chloe Kenward, Laura Korthauer, Unsal Koslu, Tom Kyffin, Julien Lagarde, Tim Laslavic, Cecily Lavery, Noah Levin, Janet Martin, Veronica Martin, Felix Mayer, John C Miller, Tim Nelson, James Newton, Woody Newton, Jon Okami, Jenny Orhan, Julie Osborne, Angelika Pagel, Katarına Panıkova, Aurélie Payrastre, Florencia Peña, Edith Peters, Paola Pinna, Barbara Pizziconi, Renai Platts, Karen Pringle, Judith Ransom, Ole Rapson, Liesbeth Rijpma, Ohnmar Ruault, Pascale Ruffat, Seham Hassan Salem, Alice Samson, Tuna Sarikaya, Omid Sarwari, Frank Schleif, Faye Scott, Ketan Shah, Brenda Sherwood, Julian Simidjiyski, Barney Smith, Hannie Spel, Rob Stoeckart, Kevin Sundstrom, Mikhal Szabo, Sunil Thakar, Nihat Tokdil, Marianne Toll, Meg Troughear-Jones, Gerard Tuin, Serhat Uzunel, Trudy Van Schie, Moniek Vandenberghe, Umberto Visconti, Ksenija Vukovic, Ben Walker, Julia Ward, Kate Warren, Philipp Wendel, Sarah Whitham, Teresa Wong, Patricia Wood, Tahir Yasin, Gong-Chu Yu, Penny Yiannakidou, Huseyin Yilmaz, Dimitris Zafeiriadis, Ariana Znaor

AUTHOR THANKS

James Bainbridge

A heartfelt *çok teşekkürler* to everyone who helped me find my way around the Anatolian steppe on my hire-car odyssey from Erzurum to İstanbul. In particular, thanks to Celil in Kars; Zafer and Cumhur in Yusufeli; Mehmet and İdris in the Kaçkars; Bilal, Ibrahim, Mustafa and Amy in Doğubayazıt; Yahya in Trabzon; Adem in Sinop; Necmettin and the Akçaabat constabulary. *Baie dankie* to my wife L-R for enduring travel widowhood so soon after tying the knot, and cheers to my coauthors for your help and dedication.

Brett Atkinson

Huge thanks to Sabahattin and family in Van for the assistance and friendship. In Gaziantep thanks to Jale and Filiz for the trip's definite culinary highlights, and to Baran and friends in Adana for the company and conversation. In Yuvacali, it's always a pleasure to see the Tanik and Salva families. At Lonely Planet, cheers to my fellow scribes and all the hardworking editors and cartos, and final thanks to Carol for holding the fort (again...) back home in Yeni Zelanda.

Chris Deliso

There are too many remarkable locals who provided assistance, advice and camaraderie to identify on what was, even by the usual standards, quite the adventure. My deepest appreciation goes out to Şahin, Arda, Ibrahim and Muslum; Yekta, Murat and Canlis; Mehmet and Oktay; Jeff, Atilla and Co; Gungor and Mutalip from the organisation; and most of all to the English tourist who (literally) saved my life. Thanks also go out to Team Lonely Planet: Cliff, Brigitte, James, David, the cartos, production and my fellow scribes.

Steve Fallon

A very special çok teşekkürler to the oracle, the font of all knowledge, Jayne Pearson in Kaş. My partner, Michael Rothschild, was a helpful travelling companion. Others who provided assistance, ideas and/or hospitality along the way included İlknur and Münir İdrisoğlu, Mehmet Celal Yahyabeyoğlu and June Haimoff in Dalyan; Omer Yapis in Fethiye; Kazım and Ayşe Akay in Patara; Saffet Tezcan in Kaleköy; Mete Engin Özel and Aynur Kurt in Çıralı; and Nermin Sümer and Aziz Tankut in Antalya.

Will Gourlay

Thanks are due to Clifton Wilkinson for getting me on board the Turkey team again (even though he got to visit Mardin first!). Thanks also to the authors and the in house editorial team at Lonely Planet. In Turkey, Pat Yale has again been a great source of information. Finally, thanks to Claire, Bridget and Tommy, still my all-time favourite Turkey travel companions. Let's do it all again, soon. Hayde gideliz!

Jessica Lee

A huge çok teşekkürler to Yakup Bastem in Safranbolu; Deniz Aşık and Murat Bektaş in Boğazkale; the Turkcell office in Amasya who solved a minor USB modem crisis; Kate Drummond, Beşir Acibuca and Mehmet in Sivas; and Jodie Redding, Yılmaz and Angela Şisman, Ruth Lockwood, Pat Yale, Danny Elle North and Mehmet Güngör in Cappadocia. And at Lonely Planet, big thanks to Cliff for putting me on the book in the first place.

Virginia Maxwell

Many thanks to Pat Yale, Faruk Boyacı, Tahir Karabaş, Eveline Zoutendijk, George Grundy, Saffet Tonguç, Demet Sabancı Çetindoğan, Ercan Tanrıvermiş, Ann Nevans, Tina Nevans, Jennifer Gaudet, Özlem Tuna, Shellie Corman, Mehmet Umur, Emel Güntaş, Tuna Mersinli, Halûk Dursun, İnci Döndaş, İlber Ortaylı, Selin Rozanes, Ansel Mullins, Megan Clark, Atilla Tuna, Elif Aytekin and the many locals who shared their knowledge and love of the city with me.

Tom Spurling

Thanks to Redmint in London for the advice. In Alacati, to the artist lady. In Bergama, to the gods (the lot of 'em). In Assos, to Athena and the fish. To Gallipoli Houses – tremendous on every level. Special thanks to Tom and Marthe, you're (road)trippin'! To my boy Oliver for loving my girl Poppy. And Mum, thanks for taking care of them both. Lastly, kisses to my beautiful wife Lucy for tagging along again – Turkey is ours, baby!

ACKNOWLEDGMENTS

Climate map data adapted from Peel MC, Finlayson BL & McMahon TA (2007) 'Updated World Map of the Köppen-Geiger Climate Classification', Hydrology and Earth System Sciences, 11, 163344.

Illustrations pp58-9, pp70-1, pp216-17 by Javier Zarracina.

Cover photograph: Whirling dervishes, Konya; Bruno Morandi/4Corners ©.

THIS BOOK

This 13th edition of Lonely Planet's *Turkey* guidebook was researched and written by James Bainbridge, Brett Atkinson, Chris Deliso, Steve Fallon, Will Gourlay, Jessica Lee, Virginia Maxwell and Tom Spurling. This guidebook was commissioned in Lonely Planet's London office, and produced by the following:

Commissioning Editor Clifton Wilkinson

Coordinating Editor Bella Li

Coordinating Cartographer Alex Leung

Coordinating Layout Designer Adrian Blackburn

Managing Editors Brigitte Ellemor, Bruce Evans

Managing Cartographer Adrian Persoglia

Managing Layout Designer Jane Hart

Assisting Editors Elin Berglund, Janice Bird, Carolyn Boicos, Samantha Forge, Evan Jones, Kate Kiely, Helen Koehne, Sally O'Brien, Luna Soo, Sam Trafford, Fionn Twomey, Amanda Williamson

Assisting Cartographers Mick Garrett, Jeff Cameron

Assisting Layout Designer Wendy Wright

Cover Research Naomi Parker

Internal Image Research Claire Gibson, Aude Vauconsant

Language Content Branislava Vladisavljevic

Thanks to Dan Austin, Laura Crawford, Ryan Evans, Larissa Frost, Jouve India, Asha Ioculari, Carol Jackson, Kate McDonell, Andrea McGinniss, Lucy Monie, Darren O'Connell, Trent Paton, Lieu Thi Pham, Raphael Richards, Averil Robertson, Silvia Rosas, Dianne Schallmeiner, Fiona Siseman, Gerard Walker, Danny Williams

NOTES

index

how to use this book

These symbols will help you find the listings you want:

- 👁 Sights
- 🐟 Beaches
- 🏃 Activities
- 🍲 Courses
- 👉 Tours
- 🎉 Festivals & Events
- 🛏 Sleeping
- 🍴 Eating
- 🍷 Drinking
- ☆ Entertainment
- 🛍 Shopping
- ❶ Information/ Transport

These symbols give you the vital information for each listing:

- 📋 Telephone Numbers
- 🕐 Opening Hours
- P Parking
- ⊜ Nonsmoking
- ❄ Air-Conditioning
- @ Internet Access
- 📶 Wi-Fi Access
- 🏊 Swimming Pool
- 🥗 Vegetarian Selection
- 📖 English-Language Menu
- 👪 Family-Friendly
- 🐾 Pet-Friendly
- 🚍 Bus
- ⛴ Ferry
- Ⓜ Metro
- Ⓢ Subway
- 🚊 Tram
- 🚆 Train

Reviews are organised by author preference.

Map Legend

Sights
- 🏖 Beach
- 🛕 Buddhist
- 🏰 Castle
- ✝ Christian
- 🕉 Hindu
- ☪ Islamic
- ✡ Jewish
- ❶ Monument
- 🏛 Museum/Gallery
- 🏚 Ruin
- 🍇 Winery/Vineyard
- 🐾 Zoo
- 👁 Other Sight

Activities, Courses & Tours
- Diving/Snorkelling
- Canoeing/Kayaking
- Skiing
- Surfing
- Swimming/Pool
- Walking
- Windsurfing
- Other Activity/ Course/Tour

Sleeping
- 🛏 Sleeping
- ⛺ Camping

Eating
- 🍴 Eating

Drinking
- ☕ Drinking
- ☕ Cafe

Entertainment
- ☆ Entertainment

Shopping
- 🛍 Shopping

Information
- ✉ Post Office
- ❶ Tourist Information

Transport
- ✈ Airport
- ⊗ Border Crossing
- 🚍 Bus
- Cable Car/ Funicular
- Cycling
- Ferry
- Monorail
- P Parking
- Ⓢ S-Bahn
- Taxi
- Train/Railway
- Tram
- Ⓤ U-Bahn
- Ⓜ Underground Train Station
- • Other Transport

Routes
- Tollway
- Freeway
- Primary
- Secondary
- Tertiary
- Lane
- Unsealed Road
- Plaza/Mall
- Steps
- Tunnel
- Pedestrian Overpass
- Walking Tour
- Walking Tour Detour
- Path

Boundaries
- International
- State/Province
- Disputed
- Regional/Suburb
- Marine Park
- Cliff
- Wall

Population
- ❂ Capital (National)
- ◉ Capital (State/Province)
- ● City/Large Town
- ○ Town/Village

Geographic
- 🏠 Hut/Shelter
- 🗼 Lighthouse
- 🔭 Lookout
- ▲ Mountain/Volcano
- 🌴 Oasis
- 🌳 Park
-)(Pass
- 🧺 Picnic Area
- 💧 Waterfall

Hydrography
- River/Creek
- Intermittent River
- Swamp/Mangrove
- Reef
- Canal
- Water
- Dry/Salt/ Intermittent Lake
- Glacier

Areas
- Beach/Desert
- + + + Cemetery (Christian)
- × × × Cemetery (Other)
- Park/Forest
- Sportsground
- Sight (Building)
- Top Sight (Building)

Steve Fallon
Antalya & the Turquoise Coast With a house in Kalkan, Steve treats Turkey like a second home. And this assignment kept him pretty much in his own backyard (Lycia) from the riverine turtle town of Dalyan to pulsating Antalya, capital of Turkey's Mediterranean coast. OK, OK...*Türkçe'yi hala mağara adamí gibi konuşuyor* (he still speaks Turkish like a caveman), but no Turk has called him Tarzan – yet.

Will Gourlay
History, Architecture, Arts, People A serial visitor to Turkey, Will has been leaving his home base of Melbourne on regular Turkish forays for more than 20 years. As a backpacker, English teacher and writer he has explored all corners of Anatolia, the more remote the better. His most recent trips have been with his wife and children in tow, although they usually stay on the beach while he rummages around in the backwoods or takes the train into Iran. He is currently researching a PhD on Turkish politics and society.

Jessica Lee
Ankara & Central Anatolia, Cappadocia Jessica spent four years traversing the breadth of Turkey as a tour leader. In late 2011 she returned here to live and this edition saw her researching the Seljuk splendour and Hittite ruins of central Anatolia and the surreal scenery of Cappadocia. Jessica has authored several guidebooks to Middle Eastern destinations and her travel writing has appeared in publications including the *Independent*, the *Daily Telegraph* and *Wanderlust*.

Virginia Maxwell
İstanbul, Turkish Table Although based in Australia, Virginia spends much of her year researching guidebooks in the Mediterranean countries. Of these, Turkey is unquestionably her favourite. As well as working on the previous four editions of this country guide, she is also the author of Lonely Planet's *İstanbul* city and pocket guides and writes about the city for a host of international magazines and websites. Virginia usually travels with partner Peter and son Max, who have grown to love Turkey as much as she does.

Read more about Virginia at:
lonelyplanet.com/members/virginiamaxwell

Tom Spurling
Thrace & Marmara, İzmir & the North Aegean Tom Spurling lives in Perth with his wife Lucy and their two children, Oliver and Poppy. He has worked in five continents for Lonely Planet and this is his 3rd edition of *Turkey*. When not travelling he teaches high-school English and is currently completing a Masters in International Education Policy. Advice for first-time travellers to Turkey? Çay, hamam, çay. Repeat daily.

OUR STORY

A beat-up old car, a few dollars in the pocket and a sense of adventure. In 1972 that's all Tony and Maureen Wheeler needed for the trip of a lifetime – across Europe and Asia overland to Australia. It took several months, and at the end – broke but inspired – they sat at their kitchen table writing and stapling together their first travel guide, *Across Asia on the Cheap*. Within a week they'd sold 1500 copies. Lonely Planet was born.

Today, Lonely Planet has offices in Melbourne, London and Oakland, with more than 600 staff and writers. We share Tony's belief that 'a great guidebook should do three things: inform, educate and amuse'.

OUR WRITERS

James Bainbridge

Coordinating Author, Black Sea Coast, Northeastern Anatolia, Turkey Today, Plan, Survival Guide Coordinating this guide for the third time, media assignments and extracurricular wanderings have taken James to most of Turkey's far-flung regions. He lived in İstanbul (Cihangir to be exact) while coordinating the previous edition of this book, and learnt to love suffixes while studying a Turkish-language course. For this edition, discovering northeastern Anatolia's mountains and steppe, ruins and Caucasian ambience showed him yet another side of this multifaceted and endlessly intriguing country. When he's not venturing to Kaçkar *yaylalar* (high-altitude pastures) or tucking into Black Sea cuisine, he lives in Cape Town, South Africa. Visit James' website at www.jamesbainbridge.net.

Read more about James at:
lonelyplanet.com/members/james_bains

Brett Atkinson

Eastern Mediterranean, Southeastern Anatolia Since first visiting Turkey in 1985, Brett has returned regularly to one of his favourite countries. For his third Lonely Planet trip to Turkey, he explored the Kurdish heartland of southeastern Anatolia and reignited an interest in archaeology while travelling along the stunning Mediterranean coast. Brett is based in Auckland, New Zealand, and has covered more than 40 countries as a guidebook author and travel and food writer. See www.brett-atkinson.net for what he's been eating recently and where he's travelling to next.

Chris Deliso

Ephesus, Bodrum & the South Aegean, Western Anatolia Chris first experienced İstanbul's total sensory overload in 1999, during an Oxford MPhil dedicated to Turkey's Byzantine incarnation. Since then he's travelled widely throughout Turkey, from the Iran–Iraq border area and the lush Black Sea coast to semi-tropical Aegean beaches in the west. Having developed a deep affection for this ever-surprising country, Chris was delighted to return to western Anatolia and the South Aegean for this book. He also writes about nearby Greece, Bulgaria, Romania and Macedonia for Lonely Planet.

Read more about Chris at:
lonelyplanet.com/members/chrisdeliso

OVER PAGE MORE WRITERS

Published by Lonely Planet Publications Pty Ltd
ABN 36 005 607 983
13th edition – April 2013
ISBN 978 1 74220 039 2
© Lonely Planet 2013   Photographs © as indicated 2013
10 9 8 7 6 5 4 3 2 1
Printed in China